SOURCEBOOK ON LAND LAW

Second Edition

Cavendish Publishing Limited

London • Sydney

SOURCEBOOK ON LAND LAW

Second Edition

SH Goo, LLB, LLM
Lecturer in Law, University of Hong Kong
Former Lecturer in Law, University of Exeter

Cavendish Publishing Limited

London • Sydney

First published in Great Britain 1994 by Cavendish Publishing Limited,
The Glass House, Wharton Street, London WC1X 9PX.
Telephone: 0171-278 8000 Facsimile: 0171-278 8080
E-mail: info@cavendishpublishing.com
Visit our Home Page on http://www.cavendishpublishing.com

First edition 1994

Goo, S H
Sourcebook on Land Law – 2nd ed
1. Land tenure – Law and legislation – England
2. Land tenure – Law and legislation – Wales
I Title
346.4'2'043

ISBN 1 85941 185 1
Printed and bound in Great Britain

To Mum and Dad

PREFACE TO THE FIRST EDITION

Land law has long been regarded as a difficult subject for many students. It is worsened by the fact that students are often swamped with a large amount of cases, statutes, and other materials. With thorough reading, some are fortunate (or I should say intelligent) enough to be able to understand the subject and to see the wood for the trees at the end of their course. For them, land law is, so far as law can be, a coherent and logical subject; it is like a jigsaw puzzle, where, in the end, every little piece fits. For others, land law is always too complicated and remains a mystery. They need not fear if they get to grips with the fundamental principles and try to understand them in a practical context. A useful textbook will go a long way towards achieving this aim. As one begins to grasp the basic rules and principles, a good selection of reading will help achieve a better understanding of the subject.

While students of land law are fortunate to be surrounded with excellent textbooks such as Megarry and Wade's *The Law of Real Property*, Cheshire and Burn's *Modern Law of Real Property*, and Gray's *Elements of Land Law*, to name a few, in the nature of things, they may be a little too 'heavy' for some students. Yet there is no substitute for reading the original sources of law. On the other hand, other excellent casebooks which contain extracts of cases and materials, such as Maudsley and Burns' *Cases and Materials on Land Law*, are not intended to be a substitute for a textbook. For students, it means reading and referring constantly to at least two books or more: a textbook, a casebook, and a statutebook.

This book cannot possibly compete with, let alone be a substitute for, those classic works of eminent authors which are authoritative in their field. This book attempts, however, to guide students through the subject by providing a clear and comprehensive guide to the elements of land law within the law syllabus. It is hoped that the book will have the flow and coherence of a textbook in explaining the fundamental principles and will present extracts of original materials from a diversity of sources which supplement and complement other texts.

Another problem which the majority of students often come up against is a lack of personal experience in matters relating to land. Consequently they find it difficult to relate to this complicated subject. I have attempted to explain the fundamental principles of land law in its practical and conveyancing context as much as possible where appropriate. I have also devoted a chapter (Chapter 4) to explaining, in some detail, the process of transferring land by way of sale which often raises the many issues discussed throughout this book. The book also makes a modest attempt to provide students with a sense of future direction of the development of land law by reproducing substantial parts of the law reform proposals, particularly those of the Law Commission. Ideally, I would like to include in this book the detailed treatment by the Law Commission in its many reports on the problems of the present law. However, as the reports are often bulky and priority should be given to the sources of law in a book of this kind, with a few exceptions, I have only reproduced the summary of the Law Commission's recommendations. It is hoped that with these features this book will be an essential and useful tool for all students studying land law, and more particularly those who have limited resources or have no ready access to the law library, in their preparation for tutorials or seminars and examinations.

This book is longer than was originally intended. But I hope the length is justified by my careful selection of the cases, statutes and relevant materials which cannot, in my view, be ignored if the quality of reading is not to be compromised. The steady stream of the Law Commission's recommendations, the numerous recent cases of great significance and the publisher's insistence on generous spacing for the students' more comfortable reading, have all contributed to the length.

Many colleagues and friends have contributed to the completion of this book by way of constant encouragement or practical advice and help. I must particularly thank Laura Chapman who so patiently read all the drafts from a student's point of view, my colleagues John Coombes for reading some of the early drafts, Lesley Austen for reading Chapter 4, and Honor Lowless for reading Chapter 9. Any mistakes and failings which no doubt can be found in this book remain entirely mine and I must be held wholly responsible. I can only hope that any suggestions for improvement will be made to me by readers which will no doubt be acted upon, should there be sufficient support for the publication, in a second edition. I must also thank my students who helped, too many of them to name. I am likewise grateful to the University for its research grant which made it possible for me to acquire secretarial support and research assistance in the preparation of this book. Finally, I should record my indebtedness to the authors and publishers for permission to reproduce copyright materials which are more particularly acknowledged on the acknowledgment page; and Jo Reddy, Sonny Leong, Kate Nicol and the production team at Cavendish Publishing Ltd for their help and efficiency in the publication of this book.

I have attempted to state the law as at 15 August 1994 based on materials available to me.

SH Goo
Exeter
August 1994

PREFACE TO THE SECOND EDITION

In this second edition, I have followed the same approach which underlay the first: I have tried to explain the fundamental principles of land law, with a practical approach where appropriate, with selected extracts from a wide range of sources, carefully knitted together to help students to see the bigger picture. Apparently, from the publisher's questionnaire, received from many lecturers who took the trouble to return it, for which I am most grateful, this approach has been very well received.

In a short period of three years since the appearance of the first edition, there have been many changes in land law. The Trusts of Land and Appointment of Trustees Act 1996, arguably the most significant legislation since 1925, which came into force on 1 January 1997, has necessitated rewriting Chapter 12. The Landlord and Tenant (Covenants) Act 1995 relating to the enforcement of leasehold covenants and the Law of Property (Miscellaneous Provisions) Act 1994 relating to implied covenants for title also required major revision of the relevant parts of the text and materials. Some extracts from the Law Commission's reports which led to the enactment of these new legislation have also been taken out. The Law Society has also produced a new edition of the Standard Conditions of Sale to reflect some of these changes. On the case law front, there have been no less than 100 reported cases, most of which have been referred to in this edition. Some of these cases, such as the post-*O'Brien* cases including *Midland Bank plc v Massey*, *Banco Exterior International SA v Thomas*, and *Credit Lyonnais Bank Nederland NV v Burch*; *Brunei Airlines Sdn Bhd v Tan* on knowing assistance in breach of trust; *Midland Bank plc v Cooke* on quantification of beneficial interest; *Ivin v Blake* on constructive trust; *Sledmore v Dalby* and *Wayling v Jones* on proprietary estoppel; *Friends' Providence Life Office v British Railways Board* on tenants' continuing liability; *Cornillie v Saha and Bradford & Bindley Building Society* on waiver; *Costello v Costello* and *Dent v Dent* on strict settlement; *Crawley Borough Council v Ure* on notice to quit a periodic tenancy by a joint tenant; *Wheeler v JJ Saunders Ltd* on the rule in *Wheeldon v Burrows*; *Cheltenham and Gloucester Building Society v Norgan* on mortgagor's ability to repay within 'reasonable period'; *Mortgage Corpn v Nationwide Credit Corpn Ltd* on priority between minor interests, to name just a few, have raised interesting questions and furthered our understanding of land law. In view of the length of this book, and in anticipation of future development of the law, with a few exceptions, I have resisted the temptation of producing yet more extracts from these recent cases.

Although there are new materials included in this edition, the length of this book has been reduced to a reasonable size. As always I am grateful to friends and colleagues and the publisher who have helped in various ways in the publication of this edition.

This edition is up to date as at 30 July 1997.

SH Goo
Hong Kong
1 August 1997

ACKNOWLEDGMENTS

The author and publisher wish to thank the following for permission to reproduce material from the sources indicated:

Butterworths and the author

Gray, *Elements of Land Law* (2nd edn, 1994)

Butterworths

The All England Law Reports

Woodstead Finance Ltd v Petrou [1986] *New Law Journal* 188

Crown Copyright

Various statutory materials

Specimen Register and filed plan

Goo, SH and the journal

'Priority of Substituted Mortgagees' (1993) *Northern Ireland Legal Quarterly* 51

Her Majesty's Stationery Office

Various Law Commission's Reports and Command Papers

Oyez Publishing Ltd

Marjorie Burnett v Barclay (1981) 125 *Solicitors Journal* 199

Stevens & Sons Ltd and the authors

Megarry and Wade, *The Law of Real Property* (5th edn, 1984)

Pollock (1903) 19 *The Law Quarterly Review* 359

Sweet & Maxwell and the authors

Goo, SH, 'Satisfying Proprietary Estoppel' (1993) *The Conveyancer and Property Lawyer* 173

Sweet & Maxwell

Property, Planning and Compensation Reports

The Estates Gazette Ltd

Cases reported in the *Estates Gazette*

The Incorporated Council of Law Reporting for England & Wales

The Law Reports

Weekly Law Reports

The Law Society

Law Society Council Statement and National Conveyancing Protocol (3rd edn, 1994)

Standard Conditions of Sale (3rd edn, 1995)

Butterworth & Co, Publishers

The English Reports

CONTENTS

TABLE OF CASES

TABLE OF STATUTES

TABLE OF ABBREVIATIONS

Books

Barnsley	Barnsley, DG, Barnsley's *Conveyancing Law and Practice*, 3rd edn, 1988, London, Edinburgh: Butterworths
Bl Comm	Sir William Blackstone, *Commentaries on the Laws of England*, 15th edn (by Christian, E), 1809
Cheshire and Burn	Cheshire, GC, Cheshire and Burn's *Modern Law of Real Property* (Burn, EH, ed) 15th edn, 1994, London: Butterworths
Co Litt	Coke upon Littleton, 19th edn (by Hargrave, F and Butler, C), 1832
Gray	Gray, KJ, *Elements of Land Law*, 2nd edn, 1993, London: Butterworths
HEL	Searle, Sir William, *Holdsworth, A History of English Law*, various editions, London: Methuen and Sweet & Maxwell
Litt	Littleton's Tenures
Maitland, *Equity*	FW Maitland, *Equity*, 2nd edn, revised by Brunyate, JW, 1936, Cambridge: University Press
Maudsley and Burn	Maudsley and Burn's *Land Law: Cases and Materials* (Burn, EH ed), 6th edn, 1992, London: Butterworths
Megarry and Wade	Megarry, Sir Robert Edgar, and Wade, HWR, *The Law of Real Property*, 5th edn, 1984, London: Stevens & Sons
Megarry's *Manual*	Megarry, Sir Robert Edgar, *Megarry's Manual of the Law of Real Property* (Megarry, Sir Robert and Thompson, MP, eds) 7th edn, 1993, London: Sweet & Maxwell
Ruoff & Roper	Ruoff, TBF and Roper, *The Law and Practice of Registered Conveyancing* (looseleaf edn), 1991, London: Sweet & Maxwell

Statutes and Rules

AEA	Administration of Estates Act
LCA	Land Charges Act
LP (MP) Act	Law of Property (Miscellaneous Provisions) Act 1989
LPA	Law of Property Act
LRA	Land Registration Act
LRR	Land Registration Rules
SLA	Settled Land Act
TLATA	Trusts of Land and Appointment of Trustees Act 1996

CHAPTER 1

TENURES AND ESTATES

1 DOCTRINE OF TENURE

Since William the Conqueror invaded England in 1066, all land has been held of the King. The theory was that all land in England 'must be held of the King of England, otherwise he would not be the King of all England'.[1] Soon after the conquest, the King rewarded others who followed him with the use of land in return for certain services such as the provision of knights to form the King's army. The ownership of land was never transferred. Those who held land direct of the King were called the 'tenants in chief'. They in turn could grant the land they held to other inferior tenants, who themselves granted the land to tenants of their own. This process was known as subinfeudation and it repeated itself down the scale endlessly. The result of this process was a feudal pyramid of land holding with the King at its apex. Under this feudal system, the King was the supreme feudal lord. All occupiers of land were 'tenants' and rendered services of some kind in return for their grants, either to the King himself or their immediate overlord who in turn rendered certain services to the King.

One of the problems of subinfeudation was the inevitably cumbersome nature of a long feudal ladder. By the Statute *Quia Emptores* 1290, subinfeudation was prohibited, and the process of alienating land by 'substitution', already common then, was favoured. Every conveyance henceforth substituted the grantee into the shoes of the grantor in his tenurial position. It is this which explains the conveyance of land in fee simple today: the purchaser is simply put into the shoes of the vendor of the fee simple. And today, in the absence of contrary evidence, all tenants in fee simple are presumed to hold directly of the Crown as tenant in chief.[2]

There were many different types of land holding, known as tenures, each indicating the type of feudal services required of the tenants. Thus, the doctrine of tenures defined the terms upon which the land was held of a superior lord.

Types of tenure[3]

The various types of tenure that existed before 1925 are today of historical interest only. Those tenures which formed part of the feudal ladder were called

1 Pollock, Sir Frederick, and Maitland, FW, *The History of English Law*, 2nd edn, 1968, London: Cambridge UP, Vol 2, p 3.

2 Williams, J, *Principles of the Law of Real Property*, 23rd edn (by Williams, TC), 1920, p 58; Challis, HW, *The Law of Real Property*, 3rd edn (by Sweet, C), 1911, London: Butterworths, p 33; *Re Lowe's WT* [1973] 1 WLR 882.

3 See Megarry, Sir Robert Edgar, and Wade, HWR, *The Law of Real Property*, 5th edn, 1984, London: Stevens & Sons, pp 14–28.

'free tenures'. The holders of the tenures were deemed to have seisin[4] at common law. These were people who provided knight's service (the tenure of knight's service), or carried high office at the King's court (the tenure of grant sergeanty) or sacred office (spiritual tenures of divine service[5] and frankalmoign[6]), or rendered agricultural service to their lord (the tenure of socage). The tenures of knight's service and grand sergeanty were also known as tenures in chivalry. These tenures also carried with them privileges enjoyed by the lord (known as incidents).[7]

The villein tenants, who were common labourers, had no place in the feudal pyramid. They occupied land only on behalf and at the will of their lord. Their lord could at any time evict them.[8] Their tenures were known as villeinage and were of an unfree nature. By the end of the 15th century the common law court came to recognise the villein tenants' rights in accordance with the custom of the manor.[9] Thus, the tenants held at the will of the lord according to the custom of the manor and any tenant ejected by his lord otherwise than in accordance with the custom would have an action of ejectment.[10] Tenure in villeinage became known as copyhold tenure.

In time, the feudal system of land holding in return for services fell into decay. This brought about a major change under the Tenures Abolition Act 1660, which, in effect, converted all free tenures into free and common socage. The unfree copyhold tenure was, on the other hand, retained until the Law of Property Act 1922 which converted copyhold automatically into free and common socage tenure or freehold tenure. Therefore, today common socage is the only one surviving feudal tenure. Although it is still theoretically true to say that no one owns land except the Crown, the doctrine of tenure is practically obsolete.

Owners of leasehold estates, on the other hand, were never on the feudal ladder. They did not enjoy the same protection given to the freehold owners until as late as 1499, when leasehold was recognised as a legal estate.[11] Thus,

4 Possession of land of freehold tenure by a person who has a freehold estate in the land. Seisin was important because (i) it was the person seised of the land who had to offer feudal services (ii) an action for the specific recovery of land could only be brought against the person seised and (iii) only the person seised could convey the freehold land by delivering the seisin in a solemn ceremony to the grantee who entered the land. Someone must always be seised or otherwise the feudal system could not work. Seisin was, however, a fact, not a right. A person seised of the land may lose his seisin by being disseised by another person. The person having disseised the other and being in actual possession of the land now had seisin until the land was recovered from him.

5 Tenant's obligations were definite spiritual services, such as singing mass every Friday or giving a certain sum of money to the poor. See Megarry and Wade, p 21.

6 Tenant's sole obligation was to pray for the repose of the grantor's soul. See Megarry and Wade, p 21.

7 The number of incidents of various tenures was reduced over the years. The only incidents that exist today relate to common socage: see Riddall, *Introduction to Land Law*, 5th edn, 1993, Butterworths, pp 12–19; Megarry and Wade, pp 33–36.

8 Pollock and Maitland, *History of English Law before the time of Edward I*, 2nd edn, 1968, London: Cambridge UP, Vol 2, p 3.

9 See Megarry and Wade, p 25.

10 *Brown's* case (1581) 4 Co Rep 21a. For action of ejectment see Megarry and Wade, p 1156.

11 HEL, Vol iii, p 216; Megarry and Wade, p 1157.

while freehold estates are real property or realty,[12] leasehold estates have traditionally been treated as personal property, or personalty,[13] to be passed on intestacy with chattels.[14] When leasehold estate became a new type of estate, it also became a new type of tenure because every tenant had to hold by tenure of some sort if he was to hold an estate at all. This is still the case today, and the tenure is between the landlord and tenant. As it grew outside the feudal ladder, this non-feudal tenure is not touched by the Statute *Quia Emptores* 1290 and therefore the grant of sub-lease is possible. Leasehold tenure is today the only tenure which has some practical importance. A rent is almost always payable, and the landlord enjoys his tenurial remedy of distress and power to determine the lease for the tenant's breach of obligations.

The Law Commission has made proposals for the introduction of a new form of tenure known as commonhold. This will be discussed in Chapter 17.

2 DOCTRINE OF ESTATES

As the King owned the land, what the tenants owned were estates, ie specific rights and powers to use the land granted for a duration.

> The Land itself is one thing, and the estate in the land is another thing, for an estate in the land is a time in the land, or land for a time, and there are diversities of estates, which are no more then diversities of times.[15]

As will be seen, an estate could be granted in fee simple, in tail, for life, or for a term of years. Each estate varied in temporal extent. The largest estate that a tenant could own was an estate in fee simple. As an estate denoted the duration of a grant, no one could grant another an estate greater than that he had himself. Since what a tenant owned was only the rights and powers to use the land for the duration of his term, it was possible for different estates in land to be granted to different tenants, for example, to A for life with remainder to B in tail with remainder to C in fee simple. A, B and C each had specific rights and powers to use the land for a different duration, each of the set of rights and powers having a present existence, despite the fact that B and C would not be entitled to take possession of the land until some future date. As a result of the doctrine of estates, it is possible to create successive estates in land.

There are two types of estates, the freehold estate and the leasehold estate (or the term of years). The freehold estate is an estate held by freehold tenure. As mentioned above, they are freehold because they were recognised by the feudal order and the King's Court would give the owner of such an estate

---

12 'Real property' is property right which can be enforced by an order of specific recovery to restore the property itself to the dispossessed owner, eg land and any interest in land.

13 'Personal property' is property right which may be enforced by an order for compensation for the loss in a personal action. The property itself may not be specifically recoverable, eg chattels, shares, etc.

14 Before 1926, where a person died intestate (without a will), all his realty passed to his heir and his personalty to his next-of-kin. After 1925, all his realty and personalty pass on intestacy to persons ascertained according to the Administration of Estates Act 1925 (as amended). Leaseholds, however, remain personalty in law.

15 *Walsingham's* case (1573) 75 ER 805 at 816f.

certain remedies including specific recovery. The fee simple, fee tail and life estate are all freehold estates. Leaseholds were initially treated as mere contractual rights to occupy land, but by the end of the 15th century they were recognised as legal estates.

Fee simple estate

'Fee' indicates an inheritable estate, and 'simple' indicates that the fee is an ordinary fee as opposed to fee tail. A fee simple estate was an estate which could last for as long as the original grantee or his heirs survived. It was therefore capable of being succeeded by the grantee's heirs. By the 13th century it became settled that while the original grantee was still alive, the heirs only had a *spes successionis*, a mere chance of succeeding to the fee. The words 'and his heirs' in a conveyance became words of limitation rather than words of purchase. Thus, the original grantee could alienate the estate *inter vivos* so as to defeat the heirs' claims. By about the beginning of the 14th century, the courts held that the estate could last for as long as there was an heir of the owner for the time being and did not depend on the existence of the heirs of the original grantee.[16] A fee simple now became potentially eternal.

Any land not disposed of *inter vivos*, however, must descend to the heir and so it could not be disposed of by will. By the 14th century it became possible to devise[17] land by use (later known as trust).[18] The Statute of Uses 1535 executed uses[19] and this brought about a public outcry since people thought that they could no longer devise land. The Statute of Wills 1540 was enacted to make it possible for up to two-thirds of land held by tenure of knight service and all socage tenure in fee simple to be devised. With the conversion of all land held by knight service into socage tenure, under the Tenures Abolition Act 1660, it was possible for all land in fee simple to be disposed of by will.

If the estate was not disposed of *inter vivos* or by will, when the original grantee died, his heir would inherit it. Prior to 1926, there were detailed rules for ascertaining the heir.[20] These rules still apply to property limited after 1925, whether *inter vivos* or by will, to the heir of a deceased person, for example 'to A's heirs in fee simple' and A being dead at the time of the conveyancing.[21] After 1925, under the Administration of Estates Act 1925, if the present tenant dies intestate, his estate will not pass to his heir but to persons determined under the Act, for example, to the deceased's surviving spouse who could never be heir under the old rules.[22]

---

16 YB 33–35 Edw 1 (RS) 362 (1306); HEL, Vol iii, 106–07; Megarry and Wade, p 60.

17 That is to dispose of real property by will.

18 Common law only recognised legal rights. The right of a beneficiary (B) for whose benefit the land was conveyed to the legal owner (A) was not recognised at law. B's beneficial right was, however, recognised by equity and this right was known as use. Thus, where property was conveyed to A to the use of B, A was the legal owner and B was the beneficiary. See Chapter 2, pp 37–40.

19 That is converted the rights of a beneficiary to legal rights.

20 See Megarry and Wade, pp 540–42.

21 Section 132 of the LPA 1925; s 51(1) of the AEA 1925.

22 Sections 45 and 46 of the AEA 1925.

Therefore, today, a fee simple is the largest possible estate anyone can have under the feudal system which still survives in theory. Thus, although the owner of a fee simple estate is a tenant in chief of the Crown, because the land is granted in perpetuity, in that it is inheritable and is capable of being transferred *inter vivos* or by will, the estate is tantamount to absolute ownership.

Fee tail estate

A fee tail estate (or entailed interest) is an estate which lasts for as long as the original grantee or his lineal descendants survive. It could be limited to male or female lineal descendants. It was designed to keep the land within the family. It was created by the Statute *De Donis Conditionalibus* 1285, which provided that where the grant was made to the grantee and 'the heirs of his body', the will of the grantor, according to the form in the deed of gift manifestly expressed, should be observed and that notwithstanding any alienation by the grantee, the land should descend to his issue on his death. The Act further provided that if the grantee died without issue, the land would revert to the grantor or, if by then the grantor was dead, his heir. The effect of the Act was that although it was possible for the grantee to alienate the land outside the family, the estate he created could be defeated when he died; the alienation could only create a life interest. When the grantee died, the estate descended to his issues and when all his issues died, it reverted to the grantor. Thus, an entailed interest was for a duration shorter than a fee simple. As the grantor did not exhaust his interest, an entailed interest was always followed either by a 'reversion' (eg 'to A in tail') or a 'remainder' (eg 'to A in tail with remainder to B in fee simple').

The Statute *De Donis Conditionalibus* thus made it possible for the nobility to tie the property within the family. As the tenant in tail could not in effect grant more than a life estate which was not very valuable, he lacked the resources, incentive and real powers of management to maintain the property. By the 15th century the courts began to recognise devices by which the Statute could be circumvented. This process was known as barring the entail and involved the abuse of an action at law and taking advantage of the binding effect of a judgment of the court.

Prior to the Fines and Recoveries Act 1833, in a grant 'to A for life, to B in tail, to C in fee simple', there were two ways in which the intention of the grantor of an entailed interest could be defeated by B. An example of an unbarrable entail was the Blenheim Estate granted in 1705 to the first Duke of Marlborough by Queen Anne in fee simple which was subsequently settled in 1706 by an Act of Parliament (5 Anne, c. 3) upon the successive Dukes for an estate in tail which under s 5 of the Act could not be barred. Other examples were the Willoughby de Broke estate (settled by the private Act of 27 Hen 8, c. xvi), the Abergavenny estate (2 and 3 Ph & M, c. xxiii), the Shrewsbury estate (6 Geo 1, c. xxix). Such settlements were exempt from the Fines and Recoveries Act 1833 (s 18). However, s 58 of the Settled Land Act 1882 (now s 20 of the SLA 1925) has given the tenant for life of an entailed estate the powers of sale and management. In exercising his powers, he may effect any transaction including resettling the estate for future generations with the approval of the court (see, for example, *Hambro v The Duke of Marlborough* [1994] 3 WLR 341. The first was the common recovery, which was recognised in 1472 in *Taltarum's* case.[23] In a collusive arrangement, the tenant in tail (B) offered no defence and admitted readily in an action brought by a stranger (X) for bad title. Because actions for land had to be brought against the person seised, the disentailing tenant (B) must be in possession. If he was not in possession, the person seised (A) must consent to the collusive action. The judgment for bad title, however, only bound the tenant in tail (and his issue) and the stranger. Thus, it was only effective to bar the entail interest (ie the tenant in tail's issue), but not any remaindermen or reversioners (C). Another artificial device was needed. The tenant in tail (B) then asked a collaborator (Y) (normally the common crier of the court for a small fee) to admit, falsely, that the collaborator had granted him with warranty of good title, and so judgment for the collaborator to recompensate him land with good title (ie fee simple) was entered. The fictitious element was that the court allowed the judgment on warranty to be entered without further investigation. By the process of common recovery, the stranger (X) now became owner in fee simple and all that remained to be done was for the stranger to reconvey the land in fee simple to the tenant in tail (or to pay the purchase money if the stranger was himself to buy it).

The second way of barring the fee tail was by levying a fine. This was made possible by the Statutes of Fines 1489 and 1540. The tenant in tail or his issue could levy a fine in favour of a third party. A fine was a final compromise whereby an agreement to convey the land was entered in the court records. No consent of the person seised was needed. A fine only created a base fee which continued so long as the disentailing tenant and his issue lived. It was not capable of barring the remaindermen or reversioners.

In the course of time, the old methods of recoveries and fines became complicated and expensive. The Fines and Recoveries Act 1833 was designed to achieve exactly the same result using simpler methods. Under the Act, which is still in force, the disentailing tenant may bar the entail by giving a disentailing assurance (ie any conveyance or transfer) by which a fee simple could be disposed of. A mere declaration that the entailed was barred is not enough. The disentailing assurance must be made or evidenced by a deed. If the disentailing tenant wants to retain the land himself, he conveys it to some trustee for him. If he wants to dispose of it to X, he makes the disentailing assurance in favour of X. The disentailing assurance must be enrolled within six months of execution in the Central Office of the Supreme Court. A disentailing assurance can only transfer a fee simple absolute if it was executed by a tenant in tail in possession, or by a tenant in tail in remainder with the consent of the 'protector of the settlement'. If a special protector is not appointed, the tenant for life in possession is usually the protector. A disentailing assurance executed without the consent of the protector only creates a base fee. Thus, by a disentailing assurance properly executed and enrolled, the estate barred is enlarged into a fee simple. However, the disentailment cannot expand the property in which the entail existed. Thus, the disentailment of an estate originally 'to A for life, to

23 YB 12 Edw 4, Mich, fo 14b, pl 16, fo 19a, pl 25; 13 Edw 4 , Mich, fo 1a, pl 1. See also Kiralfy, AKR, *A Source Book of English Law*, 1957, London: Sweet & Maxwell, pp 86–99.

B in tail' is limited to a base fee. But an estate originally 'to A in tail with remainder to B in fee simple' can be barred by A to create a fee simple. Before 1926, it was impossible to bar the entail by will. Under s 176 of the Law of Property Act 1925, a tenant in tail of full age can bar his entail by will provided he is in possession. A tenant in tail in remainder cannot bar an entail by will even if the protector consents. As from 1 January 1996, now new entail can be created.[24]

Life estate

A life estate was an estate that lasted for as long as the original grantee was alive. The estate came to an end on the death of the grantee. His estate was not inheritable. If the grantee alienated the land *inter vivos*, the alienee could not get more than the alienor himself had. The alienee's estate would come to an end when the alienor died. The alienee had a life estate, but the life was that of the alienor. This type of estate was known as a life estate *pur autre vie* (for the life of another).

Leasehold estate

A leasehold estate was an estate for a fixed term of years. This represents a very important form of estate today and is dealt with in more detail in Chapters 8 and 9 below.

3 WORDS OF LIMITATION

It was always necessary to use appropriate words to create or limit the estate to be granted. These are called 'words of limitation'. At common law, it was always necessary to use the word 'heirs' to create a fee *inter vivos*. No other words possess the magic which 'heirs' had. Thus, 'issue', 'relatives', 'for ever', 'in fee simple', 'in tail' etc would only create a life estate. On the other hand, where the grant was made in a will, no words of limitation were required and only words of intention were needed. This was because the Court of Chancery looked to intent rather than form and would interpret wills liberally. As wills were mostly home made and would not operate until the testator was dead it was impossible to put right any mistakes.

Words of limitation for a fee simple

(a) Inter vivos

To create a fee simple *inter vivos* in favour of a natural person it was necessary to use the words 'and his heirs' following the grantee's name, eg 'to A and his heirs'. Any other expressions would not be sufficient. Thus, the words 'and his heirs' were words of limitation. They gave no estate in the land to the heirs. They were not words of purchase. The words of purchase in the example above are 'to A' which gave A the estate and 'and his heirs' limited that estate to a fee

24 See s 2, Sched 1, para 5 of the TLATA 1996.

simple estate. If A had a son at the time of the grant, the son would not acquire any estate in the land but would only have a chance of succeeding to the fee simple granted to A if A did not dispose of it before his death.[25] This was because of the legal maxim *nemo est heres viventis*: a living person has no heir. A living person may have an heir apparent or an heir presumptive but until he is dead, his heir cannot be ascertained.[26] On the other hand, in a grant 'to A's heir and his heirs', 'heir' is a word of purchase and 'heirs' is a word of limitation. Thus, if such a grant was made after A's death, A's heir at the time of the grant would be entitled to a fee simple. However, if the grant was made before A's death, the whole grant would fail because A's heir was still not ascertainable at the time of the grant. Under the rule in *Shelley's* case (1581) 1 Co Rep 886, a grant 'to A for life with remainder to his heirs' would give A a fee simple and his heirs nothing. This rule was abolished in 1925.[27]

Section 51 of the Conveyancing Act 1881 provided additional words of limitation for a fee simple. It provided that the words 'in fee simple' in a deed executed after 1881 would be sufficient to create a fee simple without the words 'and his heirs'. However, the expression 'and his heirs' was still effective to create a fee simple.

Section 60(1) of the Law of Property Act 1925 abolished the need for words of limitation to be used to create a fee simple in a deed executed after 1925. The grantee takes the fee simple if the grantor has a fee simple, unless a contrary intention appears in the conveyance.

Law of Property Act 1925

60. Abolition of technicalities in regard to conveyances and deeds

(1) A conveyance of freehold land to any person without words of limitation, or any equivalent expression, shall pass to the grantee the fee simple or other the whole interest which the grantor had power to convey in such land, unless a contrary intention appears in the conveyance.

Quite different rules applied to corporations. There are two types of corporation: a corporation aggregate and a corporation sole. A corporation aggregate is a corporation which is made up of two or more persons acting under a corporate name. No special words of limitation are required to convey a fee simple to it by its corporate name.[28] A corporation sole, on the other hand, is an individual holding an office which has a perpetual succession. The only few corporations sole known to the law are the Crown, a bishop, a parson, the Treasury Solicitor, Public Trustee and the Secretaries of State. To create a fee simple in favour of a corporation sole which could pass with the office, the words 'and his successors' were required, otherwise only a life estate to the

25 *Re Parsons* (1890) 45 Ch D 51 at 55.

26 *Re Parsons, supra*, p 63.

27 Section 131 of the LPA 1925. For a detailed account of the rule in *Shelley's* case, see Megarry and Wade, pp 1161–63.

28 *Re Woking UDC (Basingstoke Canal) Act 1911*; [1914] 1 Ch 300 at 312.

incumbent was created.[29] But the words 'to the Bishop of Barchester and his heirs' would give the Bishop a fee simple in his private capacity, because while proper words of limitation for a fee simple to a corporation sole were not used, words of limitation for a fee simple in favour of a person were used and the person of the grantee was described.[30]

The 1881 Act did not extend to corporations sole. Thus, it was still necessary to use the words 'and his successors' after 1881 to grant a corporation sole a fee simple. However, as the words 'in fee simple' were intended as an alternative to the words 'and his heirs' for a grant of a fee simple to a natural person as opposed to a corporation sole, a grant after 1881 'to the Bishop of Barchester in fee simple' would presumably give the Bishop a fee simple in his personal capacity.[31]

After 1925, no words of limitation are required to create a fee simple to a corporation sole under s 60(2).

Law of Property Act 1925

60. Abolition of technicalities in regard to conveyances and deeds

(2) A conveyance of freehold land to a corporation sole by his corporate designation without the word "successors" shall pass to the corporation the fee simple or other the whole interest which the grantor had power to convey in such land, unless a contrary intention appears in the conveyance.

Even though it is no longer necessary to use words of limitation to create a fee simple in the case of either natural persons or corporations sole, in practice the words 'in fee simple' are often used to rule out any contrary intention.

(b) By will

Before 1838, no words of limitation were needed. Only words of intention were required. Thus, 'to A for ever' or 'to A and his heirs' were sufficient to pass a fee simple, but not 'to A', which would only pass a life estate.

By ss 28 and 34 of the Wills Act 1837, no words of limitation or intention are needed today. Thus, a devise by a fee simple owner 'to A' passes the fee simple unless a contrary intention is shown.

Wills Act 1837

28. A devise of real estate without any words of limitation shall pass the fee, etc

... where any real estate shall be devised to any person without any words of limitation, such devise shall be construed to pass the fee simple, or other the whole estate or interest which the testator had power to dispose of by will in such real estate, unless a contrary intention shall appear by the will.

---

29 *Ex p Vicar of Castle Bytham* [1895] 1 Ch 348 at 354.

30 Megarry and Wade, p 52.

31 Megarry and Wade, p 53.

34. Act not to extend to wills made before 1838, or to estates *pur autre vie* of persons who die before 1838

... this Act shall not extend to any will made before the first day of January one thousand eight hundred and thirty-eight; and every will re-executed or republished, or revived by any codicil, shall for the purposes of this Act be deemed to have been made at the time at which the same shall be so re-executed, republished or revived; and this Act shall not extend to any estate *pur autre vie* of any person who shall die before the first day of January one thousand eight hundred and thirty-eight.

Words of limitation for a fee tail

(a) Inter vivos

Rules similar to those applied in the case of a fee simple applied to the creation of a fee tail. The word 'heirs' was needed but it must be qualified by some words of procreation which confined 'heirs' to lineal descendants of the grantee. Thus, words such as 'to A and the heirs of his body', 'to A and the heirs of his flesh' were required. An entail could further be limited by appropriate words to a particular class of descendants. Thus, 'to A and the heirs male of his body' or 'to A and the heirs female of his body' would pass the entail only to A's male or female descendants. A grant 'to A and the heirs of his body begotten upon Mary' would pass an entail to the lineal descendant of A and Mary.

As with a fee simple, the words following A's name were words of limitation and not words of purchase. They gave A's heir apparent or heir presumptive no estate. On the other hand, a grant 'to the heirs of the body of A' made at the time when A was dead would give A's heir a fee tail. Similarly, under the rule in *Shelley's* case [1851] 1 Co Rep 886, a grant 'to A for life with remainder to the heirs of his body' gave A a fee tail but nothing to his heirs.

After 1881, additional words of limitation were introduced by s 51 of the Conveyancing Act 1881. The words 'to A in tail', 'to A in tail male' were sufficient. These rules were preserved by s 60(4) of the Law of Property Act 1925 until they were abolished by the Trusts of Land and Appointment of Trustees Act 1996 as new entails are prohibited.[32]

(b) By will

Before 1926, no words of limitation were needed as long as there were words showing an intention to create an entail. Thus 'to A and his seed,' 'to A and his heirs male', 'to A and his descendants', 'to A and his issue', were all sufficient. After 1925, the rules which apply to the creation of an entail in a deed before 1926 are extended to the creation of an entail by will. Thus, in both deeds and wills, either the word 'heirs' followed by words of procreation discussed above or the word 'in tail' must be used.[33] Entails by will are now prohibited under the Trusts of Land and Appointment of Trustees Act 1996.[34]

32 Section 25(2), Sched 4; Sched 1, para 5 of the TLATA 1996.

33 Section 130(1) of the LPA 1925 (now repealed by s 25(2), Sched 4 of the TLATA 1996).

34 Section 2, Sched 1, para 5 of the TLATA 1996.

Words of limitation for a life estate

(a) Inter vivos

At common law, any expression which showed an intention to create a life estate or which was insufficient to create a fee simple or fee tail were enough, for example 'to A for life', 'to A', or 'to A for ever'. After 1925, as a fee simple or the whole of the interest the grantor owns passes unless a contrary intention is shown, in order to create a life interest, words used before 1925, eg 'to A for life', showing such an intention, must be used.

(b) By will

Before the Wills Act 1837, no particular words were needed to create a life estate. Any expressions insufficient to create a fee simple or a fee tail were sufficient. Today, under s 28 of the 1837 Act, it is necessary to use the words 'to A for life'.

4 ESTATES AND INTERESTS BEFORE 1926

The English law of real property is based on a fundamental distinction between 'legal' and 'equitable' rights. The reason for this is historical. Before the Judicature Acts 1873 and 1875, there were two separate systems of the administration of justice: the common law court and the Court of Chancery. The judges in the common law courts were concerned only with rights which could be enforced by using the appropriate writs. Although new writs were frequently invented, many cases were left without remedy because there were no existing writs suitable to cover the case. Those rights recognised and enforced at common law were therefore termed as legal. Those who were denied legal remedy then petitioned to the King who heard the petitions with his Council, of which the Chancellor in the Court of Chancery was an important member. Later, petitions were addressed to the Chancellor who acted independently of the King's Council to make decrees and administer a system of justice called equity. The Court of Chancery would give the claimant the appropriate remedy and deny the other his strict legal rights if he was guilty of unconscionable conduct. The rights recognised by the Court of Chancery were therefore termed equitable rights. The Court of Chancery became a court of equity or conscience.

The decrees of the Chancellor frequently conflicted with those of the common law judges. After the *Earl of Oxford's* case[35] it became settled that where there was a conflict between the rules of law and those of equity, the rules of equity should prevail. This was preserved by s 25(1) of the Judicature Act 1873 and now s 49(1) of the Supreme Court Act 1981.

Insofar as the law of real property was concerned, before 1926, fee simple, fee tail, and life estate were all legal estates recognised by the King's Court at common law, whether they were granted 'in possession', 'in remainder' or 'in

35 (1615) 1 Ch Rep 1.

reversion'. So was the leasehold estate. Other important interests in or over another's land recognised at common law included easements, mortgages, rentcharges and rights of re-entry.

Trusts were, however, not recognised by common law. Thus, if land was conveyed to A in fee simple on trust for B in fee simple, A would be regarded by the common law courts as the absolute owner and B would not be regarded as having any right in the land. But the Chancellor would enforce trusts, as he regarded it as against A's conscience for him to deny B's true ownership. Thus A is the legal owner while B is the equitable owner. A is required to hold the legal estate on trust for B, who enjoys the beneficial interest in the land. It was therefore possible also, before 1926, to leave fee simple, fee tail, life estate, or term of years, or any of the interests recognised at law on trust for certain beneficiaries. These interests which existed behind a trust were therefore equitable. Thus, a grant 'to A on trust for B for life with remainder to C in fee simple' would make A the trustee who owned the legal estate, but would give B an equitable life estate in possession and C an equitable fee simple in remainder.

There were also three new interests created in equity which had no common law equivalents: estate contracts,[36] restrictive covenants[37] and the mortgagor's equity of redemption.[38] These were treated as proprietary rights[39] by equity. Other equitable interests are equitable charge, equitable lien and licence by estoppel. It should be noted that equity also enforced certain rights which fell short of an equitable proprietary interest in land. These are sometimes termed as 'mere equities'. Examples of mere equities are the right of a party to a deed to have the deed set aside on grounds of fraud,[40] misrepresentation,[41] or undue influence[42] and the right to have a document rectified for mutual mistake.[43]

Thus, legal and equitable rights were basically rights enforced by separate courts. To put an end to multiplicity of proceedings, particularly where both legal and equitable rights arose in the same case, the courts of law and equity were fused into one Supreme Court, divided into a High Court and Court of Appeal, under the Judicature Act 1873. All parts of the Supreme Court were given full power to administer both common law and equitable rights and remedies. However, rules of law and equity remain distinct and the distinction between them remains significant.

5 ESTATES AND INTERESTS AFTER 1925

After 1925, in an attempt to simplify the conveyancing process, the number of estates capable of being legal are reduced to two: the fee simple absolute in

36 See Chapter 6, p 204 below.

37 See Chapter 14 below.

38 See Chapter 16, pp 750–51.

39 Rights that endure against the successors of the obligee.

40 *Bowen v Evans* (1844) 1 Jo and Lat 178 at 263, 264.

41 *Barclays Bank Plc v O'Brien* [1993] 4 All ER 417.

42 *Bainbrigge v Browne* (1881) 18 Ch D 188.

43 *Garrard v Frankel* (1862) 30 Beav 445.

possession and the term of years absolute under s 1(1) of the Law of Property Act 1925. Interests that are capable of being legal are also limited to the five categories listed in s 1(2). All other estates, interests or charges in or over land become equitable under s 1(3). It should be noted here that estates, interests or charges corresponding to those listed in s 1(1) and (2) are only potentially legal (are capable of being legal). Whether they are actually legal when created must also depend on whether the proper formalities have been followed. In the vast majority of cases, to convey a legal estate, interest or charge, the conveyance must be by deed.[44]

Law of Property Act 1925

1. Legal estates and equitable interests

(1) The only estates in land which are capable of subsisting or of being conveyed or created at law are:

(a) An estate in fee simple absolute in possession;

(b) A term of years absolute.

(2) The only interests or charges in or over land which are capable of subsisting or of being conveyed or created at law are:

(a) An easement, right, or privilege in or over land for an interest equivalent to an estate in fee simple absolute in possession or a term of years absolute;

(b) A rentcharge in possession issuing out of or charged on land being either perpetual or for a term of years absolute;

(c) A charge by way of legal mortgage;

(d) ... and any other similar charge on land which is not created by an instrument;

(e) Rights of entry exercisable over or in respect of a legal term of years absolute, or annexed, for any purpose, to a legal rentcharge.

(3) All other estates, interests, and charges in or over land take effect as equitable interests.

Legal estates

(a) Fee simple absolute in possession

It is clear from s 1(1) of the Law of Property Act 1925 that to be a legal estate, the fee simple must be absolute and in possession. Prior to 1926, a fee simple in remainder or in reversion or a modified fee could be a legal estate. This is no longer the case.

44 Section 52(1) of the LPA 1925. The exceptions are listed in ss 52(2) and 54(2).

(i) Absolute

A fee simple may be absolute or modified. An absolute fee is an estate which is perpetual and not determinable or capable of being cut short by the occurrence of a certain specified event. As will be seen, this does not mean that any fee simple subject to a condition can never be regarded as absolute. A modified fee on the other hand is an estate which is less than an absolute fee. It is either a determinable or a conditional fee simple.

A determinable fee is a fee simple which will automatically come to an end on the occurrence of some event, specified in the grant, which may never occur. The determining event sets the limit of the estate first granted. If the event specified is bound to happen at some point, it cannot be a fee because an essential characteristic of every fee is that it may last for ever. But if the occurrence of the specified event has become impossible, the fee becomes absolute.

A conditional fee is a grant of a fee simple at the outset but the grant may be cut short by the occurrence of the condition subsequent specified in the grant. The condition subsequent is an independent clause which operates to defeat the fee simple absolute.

Whether or not a grant is a determinable fee or a conditional fee is a matter of construction, and is thus reduced to a matter of words.[45] Words such as 'while', 'during', 'until', 'as long as' and so on have been regarded as capable of creating a determinable fee whereas words such as 'provided that', 'on condition that', 'but if', 'if it happens that' will create a conditional fee.[46] Thus, a grant 'to A in fee simple until he qualifies as a solicitor' will confer on A a determinable fee. A grant 'to A on the condition that he does not qualify as a solicitor' will create a conditional fee. Descriptive words in a grant 'to A and his heirs tenants of the manor of Dale' would also create a determinable fee for as long as A and his heirs remain tenants of the manor of Dale. 'The question is whether the words limit the utmost time of continuance of the estate, or whether they mark an event which, if it takes place in the course of that time, will defeat an estate already granted; in the first case the words take effect as a limitation, in the second as a condition. A limitation marks the bounds or compass of the estate, a condition defeats the estate before it attains its boundary.'[47] The distinction has been described as 'little short of disgrace of the English jurisprudence'.[48] They are similar, but yet different, and the line between the two must be drawn somewhere as there are important consequences in the distinction.

First, a determinable fee comes to an end and the land reverts back to the grantor (if he is dead, to the person entitled under his will or intestacy) automatically on the occurrence of the event specified, whereas a conditional fee

45 Maudsley and Burn, p 25.

46 *Mary Portington's* case (1613) 10 Co Rep 35b at 41b, 42a.

47 Megarry and Wade, p 70.

48 *Re King's Trusts* (1892) 29 LR Ir 401, at 410, *per* Porter MR.

continues even after the occurrence of the condition subsequent until the grantor exercises the right of re-entry.[49]

Second, where an event in a determinable fee is held void for uncertainty or against public policy, the determinable fee will also be destroyed. This is because the event forms an integral part of the duration of the estate granted. An offending condition in a conditional fee, on the other hand, does not render the whole grant void; the condition will be struck out and the fee becomes an absolute one. This is because the condition is an independent clause added to cut down the otherwise absolute estate granted.[50]

Third, because an event when held void would destroy a determinable fee but a void condition would make a conditional fee absolute, the court is reluctant to hold an event void for uncertainty or in restraint of marriage or alienation in a determinable fee, but is more willing to do so in a conditional fee. Thus, the conditions requiring a donee to 'continue to reside in Canada',[51] or not to marry a person 'not of Jewish parentage and of the Jewish faith',[52] have been held not sufficiently certain, whereas a determining event that the donee should 'be or become a Roman Catholic' has been upheld as sufficiently certain.[53] Similarly, a condition which totally restrains marriage, such as 'to E in fee simple on condition that he never marries', is void unless the intention is not to restrain marriage, but simply to make provision for the donee until marriage.[54] Partial restraints are, on the other hand, acceptable. Thus, conditions restraining marriage with a particular person,[55] or a Scotsman,[56] or a Roman Catholic,[57] or a domestic servant[58] were all valid. In the case of a determinable fee, the court is more tolerant to restraint of marriage whether partial or total. Thus, a grant in fee simple until the grantee marries is valid.[59] Again, total restraints by way of condition on alienation, such as alienation during a person's life,[60] alienation to anyone except X,[61] mortgage,[62] or disposition by will,[63] have all been held invalid. Partial restraints, for example a condition requiring the grantee not to sell outside the family, may be upheld.[64]

49 *Matthew Manning's* case (1609) 8 Co Rep 94b at 95b.

50 *Morley v Rennoldson* (1843) 2 Hare 570 at 579f.

51 *Clavering v Ellison* (1859) 7 HL Cas 707; *Sifton v Sifton* [1938] AC 320.

52 *Clayton v Ramsden* [1943] AC 320.

53 *Blathwayt v Baron Cawley* [1976] AC 397.

54 *Jones v Jones* (1876) 1 QBD 279.

55 *Re Hanlon* [1933] Ch 254.

56 *Perrin v Lyon* (1807) 9 East 170.

57 *Duggan v Kelly* (1848) 10 1 Eq R 295.

58 *Jenner v Turner* (1880) 16 Ch D 188.

59 *Morley v Rennoldson* (1843) 2 Hare 570.

60 *Re Rosher* (1884) 26 Ch D 801.

61 *Re Cockerill* [1929] 2 Ch 131; *Re Brown* [1954] Ch 39.

62 *Ware v Cann* (1830) 10 B and C 433.

63 *Re Jones* [1898] 1 Ch 438.

64 *Re Macleay* (1875) LR 20 Eq 186.

But in the case of a determinable fee, partial or total restraints will be generally upheld.[65]

On the other hand, where a condition is against public policy, it will be void whether it is in a determinable or conditional fee. Thus, a condition in a grant of a fee simple to the wife who is separated from her husband 'on condition that she never returns to her husband' or 'until she returns to her husband' is void.[66] A condition in restraint of religion is, however, not against public policy so long as there is no uncertainty in the faith prescribed for to do so would reduce freedom of testamentary disposition which is firmly rooted in our law.[67]

Fourth, after 1925, while all modified fees are equitable and must exist behind a trust under s 1(3) of the Law of Property Act 1925, a conditional fee which is not followed by a gift over (ie where the grantor reserves a right of re-entry) is treated as 'absolute' for the purposes of the Law of Property Act 1925 under s 7(1) of the Act (as amended by the Schedule to the Law of Property (Amendment) Act 1926). A conditional fee with a right of re-entry may therefore be a legal estate if it is granted 'in possession'. The reason for the amendment to s 7(1) is well explained in Megarry and Wade, *The Law of Real Property*, 5th edn, 1984, London, pp 127–28).

In some parts of the country, particularly Manchester and the north, it has been a common practice to sell a fee simple not for a capital sum, but for an income in the form of a perpetual rentcharge (an annual sum charged on the land). Rentcharges of this kind are commonly called 'fee farm rents'. A scheme for their commutation and extinguishment was enacted in 1977, but this will not be completed until 2037.

Now the remedies for non-payment of a rentcharge include a right to enter on the land temporarily to collect the rents and profits; further, in a number of cases an express right of re-entry is reserved by the conveyance, entitling the grantor to enter and determine the fee simple and thus regain his old estate if any payment is a specified number of days in arrears. The reservation of a right of re-entry clearly made the fee simple less than absolute, and it was thought by some that even a temporary right of entry might have this effect. This meant that those who had purchased land in this way before 1926 and had obtained legal estates suddenly found that their estates might no longer be legal and that it was doubtful who had the legal estate. Further, the complicated provisions of the Settled Land Act 1925 probably applied.

To remedy these difficulties the Schedule to the Law of Property (Amendment) Act 1926 added a clause to s 7(1) of the Law of Property Act 1925, providing that 'a fee simple subject to a legal or equitable right of entry or re-entry is for the purposes of this Act a fee simple absolute.' This amendment thus allows a fee simple to remain a legal estate even though it is subject to a right of entry, and rules out any possible complication with the Settled Land Act 1925, where land is subject to a legal rentcharge such as a fee farm rent. But the exception is so widely drawn that it affects all conditional fees; for the effect of a condition subsequent annexed to the fee simple is to give rise to a right of re-entry exercisable on breach of the condition, and until this right of re-entry is exercised, the fee simple continues. Consequently, by virtue of the Amendment Act any

65 *Hood v Oglander* (1865) 34 Beav 513, at 322.

66 *Wilkinson v Wilkinson* (1871) LR 12 Eq 604; *Re Johnson's WT* [1967] Ch 387.

67 *Blathwayt v Baron Cowley* [1976] AC 397.

fee simple defeasible by condition subsequent appears able to rank as a legal estate if limited to take effect as such, even though it is far from being 'absolute' in the ordinary sense of the word.

Thus, a grant 'to A in fee simple on the condition that he does not qualify as a solicitor' will create a legal estate to him because when the condition is fulfilled the grantor has a right of re-entry and A's conditional fee is in possession. Whereas a grant 'to A in fee simple provided that if he qualifies as a solicitor then to B in fee simple' will not give A a legal estate as the grantor in this case does not reserve a right of re-entry; there is a gift over to B in fee simple.

(ii) In possession

A fee simple 'in possession' confers its owner a present right of present enjoyment.[68] The owner is entitled to have immediate occupation and enjoyment of the land. His right is not in remainder or reversion. In a grant 'to A in fee simple' A is in possession, whereas a grant 'to A for life, to B in fee simple' gives B a fee simple in remainder. Where the grantor does not exhaust his entire estate, he retains the reversion. Thus, in a grant 'to A for life' the grantor retains the fee simple in reversion. Possession is defined in the Law of Property Act, s 205(1)(xix) as including 'receipt of rents and profits or the right to receive the same, if any'. Thus, the grant of a lease by the owner of a fee simple absolute does not render his estate no longer 'in possession' as the landlord is in receipt of rents and profits.

An interest 'in remainder' gives the grantee a present right to future enjoyment. His interest may be vested at the time of the grant even though he cannot take possession (ie have occupation and enjoyment) immediately. His possession is postponed until the estate in possession comes to an end. Thus, in our earlier example, 'to A for life, to B in fee simple', B's fee simple is vested at the time the grant is created, but he can only take possession when A's estate comes to an end on A's death. A is the person who is currently in possession, and B's fee simple is in remainder.

A vested remainder interest must not be confused with a contingent remainder interest which is a future interest and is governed by the rule against perpetuities.[69] A contingent remainder is an interest which may become vested in the future but not at the time of the grant. The vesting in interest is dependent on certain conditions which may or may not occur in the future. Before the interest is vested, the grantee only has a chance of getting the interest granted. An example is 'to A for life with remainder to B in fee simple if he attains the age of 21 years'. At the time of the grant, A has a life estate in possession, B has a contingent remainder – a chance of getting a remainder for he may die before he attains the age of 21. B's remainder is only vested when he attains the age of 21 and vests in possession when A dies. A remainder is vested where the person entitled to it is ascertained and the interest is ready to take

68 *Pearson v IRC* [1981] AC 753 at 772 A–D, *per* Viscount Dilhorne.

69 For the rule against perpetuities, see Megarry and Wade, Chapter 7.

effect in possession forthwith, but is prevented from doing so only by the existence of some prior interest.[70]

An interest 'in reversion' is the interest not disposed of but retained by the grantor. Thus, if the tenant in fee simple grants a life estate, he retains the fee simple in reversion. This must not be confused with the right of the grantor of a conditional or determinable fee. The grantor in those cases has a possibility of reverter which is neither a reversion nor a remainder because the grantor has granted away the entire fee simple even though the fee simple granted is determinable or can be defeated by a condition. As a reversion is the interest which is still with the grantor, it is always vested. It may also be noted that when the landlord of a fee simple grants a lease, although it is common to say that he retains a reversion, his 'reversion' is not a reversion because he has never given away his seisin. Furthermore, as pointed out above, under s 205(1)(xix) the landlord is regarded as 'in possession' as he has the right to receive rents and profits. What he has is a freehold in possession subject to the term of years.

Remainders and reversions are today equitable and must exist behind a trust. They tended to exist behind a strict settlement under the Settled Land Act 1925 and the legal estate would be vested in the tenant for life or the statutory owner.[71] As from 1 January 1996, such an interest will exist behind a trust of land and be governed by the Trusts of Land and Appointment of Trustees Act 1996.

(b) Term of years absolute

This is essentially an estate granted for a fixed duration. A 'term of years' is defined as including a term for less than a year, or for a year or years and a fraction of a year or from year to year.[72] It seems, therefore, that any term for any fixed and certain duration is a 'term of years', for example a term of 99 years, or a yearly or monthly tenancy which has a minimum duration of a year or a month respectively.

'Absolute' means that the term of years is not subject to the dropping of a life, or the determination of a determinable life interest.[73] However, if it is liable to determination by notice, re-entry, operation of law, or by a provision for cesser on redemption, or in any other event (other than the dropping of a life, or the determination of a determinable life interest), it is still regarded as 'absolute'.[74] Thus, a lease for 99 years containing a clause which enables either party to give notice to quit or which enables the landlord to recover the land if the tenant fails to pay rent would still be 'absolute'.

This type of estate originally grew outside the feudal system and was not recognised as a legal estate until 1499. It still does not give the owner seisin and

70 Megarry and Wade, p 232; Cheshire and Burn, p 279.

71 See Chapter 11.

72 Section 205(1)(xxvii) of the LPA 1925. See Chapter 8, p 337.

73 *Ibid*, pp 337, 346.

74 *Ibid.*

is treated as personalty. However, it is today one of the only two legal estates and its significance in practice can scarcely be ignored. It will therefore be treated in detail in Chapters 8 and 9.

Legal interests

(a) Easements, rights and privileges (s 1(2)(a))

This subsection covers the rights to use someone else's land in some form, for example, the right of way over the neighbouring land, a right to take natural produce of the stranger's land, etc. In order for it to be a legal interest, apart from the fact that the right must be created by deed, statute or prescription,[75] it must also be created for a period equivalent to an estate in fee simple absolute in possession or a term of years absolute. Thus, if A is granted (by deed) an easement in perpetuity or for a fixed term, his easement is legal. On the other hand, if he is granted an easement for as long as he is alive, then his easement must necessarily be equitable because it is not granted for a period of time equivalent to an estate in fee simple (which is perpetual) or a term of years (which is a fixed term). The fact that the easement for life is granted by deed does not alter its equitable nature.

(b) Rentcharges (s 1(2)(b))

These are annuities secured on land other than a rent paid by the tenant to the landlord and interests paid by the mortgagor to the mortgagee. The owner of the rentcharge is entitled to a periodical sum of money. The land charged is used as a security and if payment is in arrears he has a right of entry on the land to receive the income. No new rentcharges can be created as from 22 July 1977 and existing ones will come to an end 60 years after 22 July 1977 or the date on which the rentcharge in question first became payable, whichever is the later.[76] Again, to be a legal rentcharge, it must be granted in perpetuity or for a fixed term of years. Furthermore, under s 1(2)(b) of the Law of Property Act 1925 the rentcharge must also be 'in possession'. However, s 2 of the Law of Property (Entailed Interests) Act 1932 provides:

Law of Property (Entailed Interest) Act 1932

2. Definition of rent charge

For removing doubt it is hereby declared that a rentcharge (not being a rentcharge limited to take effect in remainder after or expectant on the failure or determination of some other interest) is a rentcharge in possession within the meaning of paragraph (b) of sub-s (2) of s 1 of the Law of Property Act 1925, notwithstanding that the payments in respect thereof are limited to commence or accrue at some time subsequent to its creation.

75 See Chapter 15, pp 706–42.

76 Sections 2(1) and 3(1) of the Rentcharges Act 1977.

Thus, if A conveys land to B in consideration of a perpetual rentcharge payable one year after the conveyance,[77] B's rentcharge is legal. Whereas if the rentcharge is granted to B for life with remainder to C absolutely, B's rentcharge is equitable because it is not perpetual and C's is equally equitable because it is not 'in possession'.

(c) Charge by way of legal mortgage (s 1(2)(c))

This is one of the ways in which a legal mortgage can be created after 1925.[78] A mortgage is a form of security granted by the owner of land in favour of the mortgagee (usually one of the lending institutions) in return for a loan advanced by the mortgagee. It is a security for the loan in that if the mortgagor is not able to repay the loan, the mortgagee can take possession and receive any income from the land or sell the land to satisfy the debts. This form of security is legal if it is also granted by deed.

(d) Statutory charges (s 1(2)(d))

This is a group of charges imposed by statutes which is of very little practical significance.

(e) Rights of entry (s 1(2)(e))

This deals with the right of the original grantor to terminate a lease or an estate which is subject to a legal rentcharge on default by the grantee. The right of re-entry is a proprietary interest distinct from the legal estate over which the right is exercisable or to which it is annexed.

It is common for a lease to provide that the landlord may re-enter the land if the tenant is in breach of his obligation. If the right is contained in a legal lease, it is a legal interest. But if it is contained in an equitable lease,[79] then it is equitable.

It was also common in some parts of the country to convey a fee simple subject to a rentcharge. The right of re-entry annexed to a rentcharge gives the original grantor the right to forfeit the fee simple if the grantee fails to fulfil his obligation to pay the rentcharge. As we have seen earlier, the grantee's conditional fee simple was regarded as 'absolute' for the purposes of the Law of Property Act 1925 by the 1926 amendments, the fee simple could be a legal estate if it is granted in possession. The rentcharge would also be legal if it is granted in perpetuity or for a fixed term. The right of re-entry annexed to the legal rentcharge is also a legal interest. On the other hand, if the right of re-entry is annexed to an equitable rentcharge, it is necessarily equitable under s 1(3) of the Law of Property Act.

---

77 This practice was common in some parts of the country, particularly in Manchester, Bristol and Bath.

78 Sections 85(1) and 86(1) of the LPA 1925. See Chapter 16, pp 907–09, 911–12.

79 An equitable lease is a specifically enforceable contract to create a legal lease. See Chapter 8, p 341.

Equitable interests

Under s 1(3) of the Law of Property Act 1925, any interest which does not fall within the categories in s 1(1) and s 1(2) is, by exclusion, equitable. This represents a large category of interest today. Examples of some of them are determinable fees, conditional fees where the grantor has no right of re-entry, fees simple in reversion or in remainder, life interests, existing entailed interests, easements or rentcharges for life, mortgages of equitable interest, equitable charges, rights of re-entry in an equitable lease or annexed to an equitable rentcharge, interests behind a trust, restrictive covenants, estate contracts, mortgagor's right of redemptions, equitable liens and licences by estoppel.[80]

6 DIFFERENCE BETWEEN LEGAL AND EQUITABLE INTERESTS

As mentioned above, the distinction between legal and equitable is fundamental in English land law. Where there is a subsequent transfer of land, whether the rights or interests in land should bind a subsequent purchaser becomes an important issue. The extent to which a right or interest in land is enforceable upon a transfer against a purchaser depends on whether the right or interest in question is legal or equitable. This is particularly so where the title to the land is unregistered. In the case of registered land, priority is to be settled by reference to estates and interests which appear on the register and those which do not. Since all land in the whole of England and Wales is today[81] in compulsory registration areas and is thus subject to the land registration regime, the significance of the distinction between legal and equitable interest is on the decline. However, many lands are still unregistered and it will take quite a while to complete the whole registration process in England and Wales. Furthermore, the question of priority in registered land occasionally turns on the question of whether the interest is legal or equitable.[82]

The cardinal principles are stated in the maxim: *Legal rights are good against all the world; equitable rights are good against all persons except a bona fide purchaser of a legal estate for value without notice, and those claiming under such a purchaser.*[83]

Legal rights bind the world

This means that a legal right in or over land binds whoever subsequently acquires an interest in the land. Thus, if A has a legal lease in the land owned by B, C who later acquires the land from B will be bound by A's legal lease whether C was aware of A's lease at the time he acquired the land or not. This same principle applies to other legal estates or interests. Therefore, if A has a

80 For licences by estoppel, see Chapter 10.

81 Since 1 December 1990 (Land Registration, England and Wales: The Registration of Title Order 1989 (SI 1989/1347)).

82 See, for examples, *Barclays Bank Ltd v Taylor* [1974] Ch 137; *Peffer v Rigg* [1977] 1 WLR 285; *Lyus v Prowsa Developments Ltd* [1982] 1 WLR 1044.

83 Maitland, FW, *Equity*, 2nd edn, revised by JW Brunyate, 1936, Cambridge: Cambridge UP, pp 114, 115.

right to walk over B's garden (a legal easement), C who subsequently buys the house from B will be bound by A's right of way because being a legal right it binds the whole world including C.

Equitable rights bind all persons except the 'Equity's Darling'

According to the cardinal principles stated above, equitable rights bind all persons other than a *bona fide* purchaser of a legal estate for value without notice of the equitable rights (sometimes called the 'Equity's Darling'). This is also known as the equitable doctrine of notice. As will be seen, this doctrine of notice is, after 1925, modified by the system of registration of land charges in unregistered land. It is also superseded by the statutory mechanisms provided by the Settled Land Act 1925 and the Law of Property Act 1925 for overreaching[84] equitable interests behind a strict settlement, trust for sale and now trust of land respectively. Nevertheless, it still plays a residual role in providing the solution to the problems of priority of certain equitable interests not covered by the land charges registration system and the overreaching principle. It is therefore fundamentally important to understand the doctrine of notice.

Under the doctrine of notice, a person who can show that he is a *bona fide* purchaser of a legal estate for value without notice of the equitable interest can take the legal estate free of the equitable interest. James LJ put it most succinctly, in *Pilcher v Rawlins* (1872) 7 LR Ch App 259 at 268:

> I propose simply to apply myself to the case of a purchaser for valuable consideration, without notice, obtaining, upon the occasion of his purchase, and by means of his purchase deed, some legal estate, some legal right, some legal advantage; and, according to my view of the established law of this Court, such a purchaser's plea of a purchase for valuable consideration without notice is an absolute, unqualified, unanswerable defence, and an unanswerable plea to the jurisdiction of this Court. Such a purchaser, when he has once put in that plea, may be interrogated and tested to any extent as to the valuable consideration which he has given in order to shew the *bona fides* or *mala fides* of his purchase, and also the presence or the absence of notice; but when once he has gone through that ordeal, and has satisfied the terms of the plea of purchase for valuable consideration without notice, then, according to my judgment, this Court has no jurisdiction whatever to do anything more than to let him depart in possession of that legal estate, that legal right, that legal advantage which he has obtained, whatever it may be. In such a case a purchaser is entitled to hold that which, without breach of duty, he has had conveyed to him.
>
> My view of the principle is, that when once you have arrived at the conclusion that the purchaser is a purchaser for valuable consideration without notice, the

84 The process by which beneficial interests in land are converted on sale of the land into the proceeds of sale. A conveyance made by a tenant for life under the SLA 1925, or trustees of land can overreach the beneficial interests behind the strict settlement or trust of land provided the statutory requirements respecting the payment of capital money are complied with. Similarly, a conveyance by a mortgagee or personal representative can overreach certain beneficial interests if the capital money arising therefrom is paid to them respectively. See Chapter 6, pp 214–15, 259–62.

> Court has no right to ask him, and has no right to put him to contest the question, how he is going to defend himself, or what he is going to rely on. He may say, honestly and justly, 'I am not going to tell you. I have got the deeds; I defend them, and you will never be able to make me produce them, and you will never be able to produce secondary evidence of them. I am not obliged to produce them at all; probably before you get half way through your action of ejectment you will find a *jus tertii* which you will not dispose of; the estate is in the hands of a legal tenant to whom I have let it, and no one can determine that tenancy without notice, and no one can give that notice but myself; I will not give that notice, and no Court has any power to compel me to give it. I have a right to rely, as every person defending his position has, on the weakness of the title of the person who is seeking to displace me.'
>
> I am therefore of opinion that whatever may be the accident by which a purchaser has obtained a good legal title, and in respect of which he has paid his money and is in possession of the property, he is entitled to the benefit of that accident, just as a purchaser would be entitled to avail himself of the possession so acquired, without any reference to the rights of the persons who may be otherwise interested ...

(a) Bona fide

The requirement of *bona fide* or good faith is a separate test which may have to be passed even though absence of notice is proved. The purchaser must show that his absence of notice is genuine and honest.[85] There is, however, no clear example of the application of good faith in the absence of notice.

(b) Purchaser

In its technical sense a 'purchaser' is a person who takes property by grant (eg donee of a gift or buyer) and not by mere operation of law (eg person entitled under the intestacy rule or a squatter who derives title from effluxion of time). Thus, while a squatter can never be a purchaser, a donee ranks as a purchaser.

(c) Of a legal estate

The purchaser must have the legal estate vested in him (ie the purchaser must take either a fee simple absolute in possession or a term of years absolute) before he has notice. By s 87(1) of the Law of Property Act 1925, a mortgagee who takes a charge by way of legal mortgage is also regarded as a purchaser of a legal estate.

If the purchaser merely acquires an equitable interest, then the rule is 'where equities are equal the first in time prevails'.[86] This means that an earlier equitable interest will take priority over a subsequent equitable interest. Thus, in the case of a sale of a legal estate, if the purchaser has notice, before the legal

85 *Midland Bank Trust Co Ltd v Green* [1981] AC 513, at 528, *per* Lord Wilberforce.

86 Snell, EHT, *Equity*, 29th edn (by Baker, PV, and Lanyon, P St J), 1990, London: Sweet & Maxwell, p 46. *Cave v Cave* (1880) 15 Ch D 639.

estate is vested in him on completion, of an equitable interest which exists before his contract of purchase, he is bound by the equitable interest.[87] This is because at the time he has notice of the earlier equitable interest, he is a purchaser of an equitable interest and so his equitable interest must defer priority to the earlier one. And at the time the legal estate is conveyed to him he cannot claim to have no notice of the prior equitable interest. A different view was however taken in *Bailey v Barnes*[88] where it was held that a purchaser of an equitable interest who at the time of the purchase had no notice of a prior equitable interest took free if he later acquired the legal estate, even with notice, so long as it was not conveyed to him in breach of trust. However, if the purchaser took the equitable interest with notice of the prior equitable interest his subsequent acquisition of the legal estate would not help him to get priority.[89]

It has been suggested that the rule in *Wigg v Wigg*[90] does not apply if the competing equitable interest only arises between the date of contract and the date of completion. Here the purchaser will take free of the competing equitable interest because his equitable interest created under the contract exists before the competing equitable interest arises, and the conveyance merely carries out the contract.[91] This view first appears to sit uncomfortably with the rule that a purchaser of a legal estate with notice of an equitable interest is bound by it. Furthermore, as will be seen below, if a purchaser is required to give value before he has notice of an equitable interest in order to take free of the equitable interest,[92] then why should the purchaser not be required to have no notice of the equitable interest before his legal estate is conveyed to him? The purchaser who discovers the existence of the subsequent competing equitable interest can always rescind the contract and possibly sue for damages against the vendor. If he insists on buying the property he should be required to take it subject to the subsequent competing equitable interest of which he has notice. On the other hand, if the purchaser in *Bailey v Barns* who took an equitable interest without notice of a prior equitable interest was given priority when he later acquired the legal estate, the same principle should perhaps apply here. When such a principle is applied, the purchaser of an equitable interest who is followed by a subsequent equitable interest will also get priority over the subsequent equitable interest when he later acquires the legal estate.

A purchaser of an equitable interest who has no notice of a prior 'mere equity' is not bound by it. This is because it is only where the equities are equal that the first in time prevails. A 'mere equity' has the weakness of not being a full proprietary interest and depends more on the discretion of the court. Thus, where a prior mere equity is competing with a subsequent equitable interest,

87 *Wigg v Wigg* (1739) 1 Atk 382 at 384. But see *Bailey v Barnes* [1894] 1 Ch 25 at 36.

88 [1894] 1 Ch 25 at 36.

89 *McCarthy & Stone Ltd v Julian S Hodge & Co Ltd* [1971] 1 WLR 1547.

90 (1739) 1 Atk 382.

91 Megarry and Wade, p 144 and fn 23; Gray, p 78, fn 2.

92 *Story v Windsor* (1743) 2 Atk 630.

the purchaser of the subsequent equitable interest may take free of the equity if he has no notice of it.[93]

(d) For value

The purchaser must also have given value before he has notice of the equitable interest. 'Value' includes any consideration in money, money's worth and marriage consideration. Value does not have to be of full value; the adequacy of consideration is not called into question.[94] Only future marriage consideration (an ante-nuptial agreement) provided by the purchaser is sufficient value.[95] A past marriage (a post-nuptial agreement)[96] or natural love and affection[97] is not sufficient value. If the conveyance to the purchaser is for money consideration, he does not become a purchaser for value until he actually pays all the money. Thus, if he has notice before the purchase money is paid he will be bound by the equitable interest even if he has had the legal estate vested in him in advance of payment.[98]

Because a purchaser must take the legal estate for value, although the technical meaning of a 'purchaser' includes those who derive title by operation of law (eg a donee), they cannot take free of an earlier equitable interest even if they have no notice of it.

(e) Without notice

Only a purchaser who takes a legal estate for value without notice of the earlier equitable interest can claim that his conscience is unaffected by the equitable interest. 'Notice' means not only actual notice but also constructive and imputed notice.

(i) Actual notice

If a purchaser has actual knowledge or notice of the equitable interest, he is bound by it no matter how he acquired that knowledge.[99] On the other hand, he is not to attend to vague rumours.[100] As will be seen, where the title of the land is unregistered, registration of certain registrable land charges is deemed to constitute actual notice.[101]

93 *Phillips v Phillips* (1862) (1861) 4 De GF & J 208.

94 *Basset v Nosworthy* (1673) Rep t Finch 102.

95 *AG v Jacobs Smith* [1895] 2 QB 341.

96 White and Tudor's *Leading Cases in Equity*, 9th edn, 1928, Vol ii, p 791.

97 *Goodright d Humphreys v Moses* (1774) 2 Wm Bl 1019.

98 *Story v Windsor* (1743) 2 Atk 630.

99 *Lloyd v Banks* (1868) 3 Ch App 488.

100 *Barnhart v Greenshields* (1853) 9 Moo PCC 18 at 36.

101 Section 198(1) of the LPA 1925.

(ii) Constructive notice

The doctrine of constructive notice is preserved by s 199(1)(ii)(a) of the Law of Property Act 1925.

Law of Property Act 1925

199. Restrictions on constructive notice

(1) A purchaser shall not be prejudicially affected by notice of:

(ii) any other instrument or matter or any fact or thing unless:

(a) it is within his own knowledge, or would have come to his knowledge if such inquiries and inspections had been made as ought reasonably to have been made by him.

If a purchaser has actual notice of a defect in title or incumbrance, and any proper inquiry would have revealed the true nature of the defect, he will be fixed with constructive notice of such defect or incumbrance. Similarly, if the purchaser deliberately abstained from inquiry in order to avoid notice of the incumbrance, or omitted to make an inquiry which a purchaser acting on skilled legal advice would have inquired and revealed the incumbrance, he will be fixed with constructive notice of such incumbrance.[102] In the case of a purchase of land, particularly from a sole owner,[103] to avoid being fixed with constructive notice of any prior equitable interests in the land, the reasonable steps a purchaser is expected to take are sufficient inspection of land and investigation of title. In inspecting the land, the purchaser must make inquiry as to anything which appears inconsistent with the title offered by the vendor. If anyone except the vendor is in occupation the purchaser must make inquiry of the occupier personally.[104] Anyone who shares occupation with the vendor must be asked about his or her possible rights.[105] This is sometimes known as the rule in *Hunt v Luck*.

Hunt v Luck [1902] 1 Ch 428, CA

Vaughan Williams LJ: If a purchaser or a mortgagee has notice that the vendor or mortgagor is not in possession of the property, he must make inquiries of the person in possession – of the tenant who is in possession – and find out from him what his rights are, and, if he does not choose to do that, then whatever title he acquires as purchaser or mortgagee will be subject to the title or right of the tenant in possession.

However, if the person in occupation of the land deliberately withholds information about his interest, the purchaser will not be fixed with constructive notice of that person's equitable interest. He may also be estopped from relying

---

102 *Jones v Smith* (1841) 1 Hare 43 at 55.

103 This is because there is a danger that the vendor may be holding the legal estate on trust. (See Chapter 13.)

104 *Hodgson v Marks* [1971] Ch 892 at 932, *per* Russell LJ.

105 *Williams & Glyn's Bank v Boland* [1980] 2 All ER 408, a registered land case, but the principle applies to unregistered land; see too *Kingsnorth Finance v Tizard* [1986] 2 All ER 54, a case of unregistered land.

on constructive notice as a defence to the purchaser's claim of unincumbered title.[106]

In *Midland Bank Ltd v Farmpride Hatcheries Ltd*,[107] the company granted a mortgage on its property to the bank for a loan. The loan was negotiated by the company's director, Mr Willey, who had been granted a licence for himself and his family by the company under a service agreement to occupy the property rent free for 20 years. The licence was never disclosed by the director to the bank although the bank's negotiator, Mr Timbers was aware of the family's presence in the property. Later, when the bank sought possession on the company's default in payment, the director argued that his licence was binding on the bank because it had constructive notice of the licence.

Midland Bank Ltd v Farmpride Hatcheries Ltd (1980) 260 EG 493, CA

Shaw LJ: In my judgment Mr Willey set up a smoke-screen designed to hide even the possible existence of some interest in himself which could derogate from the interest of the company ostensibly conferred by the mortgage. To change the metaphor, he deliberately put Mr Timbers off the scent and the bank accepted the mortgage as a consequence. They would not have done so but for Mr Willey's subtle but positive indication that he had communicated all that had to be told which could be relevant to the bank's consideration of the company's application.

This being so, I am of the opinion that Mr Willey is estopped from setting up any facts which would go to show that he held an interest which overrides or stands in priority to their interest as mortgagees from the company.

Oliver LJ: Now of course, an agent who negotiates a sale or mortgage on his principal's behalf does not thereby make any representation that his principal has an indefeasible title to the property offered for sale or as security. As to that the purchaser or mortgagee must satisfy himself by making the usual enquiries before he completes. But in negotiating on his principal's behalf he does, in my judgment, at least represent that he has his principal's authority to offer the property free from any undisclosed adverse interest of his own. I would therefore be prepared to hold that the purchaser or mortgagee dealing with such an agent can reasonably assume that if the agent with whom he is dealing has himself an interest adverse to the title which he offers on his principal's behalf, he will disclose it. It was in my judgment reasonable for Mr Timbers not to make enquiry about an adverse interest of the negotiating agent which that agent's own reticence entitled him to assume did not exist and he did not, therefore, have constructive notice of it.

A purchaser has constructive notice of all rights which he would have discovered had he investigated the vendor's good root of title which is at least 15 years old.[108] A good root of title is a conveyance which deals with the whole of the legal estate and equitable interest. A purchaser who asks for a relevant

---

106 *Midland Bank Ltd v Farmpride Hatcheries Ltd* (1980) 260 EG 493.

107 (1980) 260 EG 493.

108 Section 23 of the LPA 1969.

title deed and is met with a reasonable excuse for its non-production is free from notice of its contents.[109]

A mortgagee like any prudent purchaser is also expected to inspect the land and investigate the title. Where a wife gives security for her husband's debts, the mortgagee may also be expected, in a separate meeting, to explain the nature of the security transaction to her and advise her to get an independent legal advice.[110] This latter view was taken by the House of Lords recently in *Barclays Bank Plc v O'Brien*.[111] Here, Mrs O'Brien signed a legal charge over the co-owned family home as a security for her husband's debts to the bank. The bank did not explain the contents to her and did not tell her to obtain independent legal advice. Neither did Mrs O'Brien read the documents before signing them. She subsequently argued that the security was not enforceable against her because she signed the documents under undue influence by her husband and that he had misrepresented to her the effect of the charge. The Court of Appeal held that Mr O'Brien's influence on his wife was not undue and by leaving it to Mr O'Brien to procure his wife to agree to enter into the security transaction, the bank did not appoint the husband as an agent of the bank. However, the bank was aware of the nature of their relationship, and that Mr O'Brien was likely to have some influence on her and that she was likely to place reliance on him and his business judgment, but failed to take reasonable steps to ensure that she had an adequate comprehension of the effect of the charge. The bank, by leaving it to Mr O'Brien to explain the transaction to her, it was held, had to take the consequences of his conduct. Thus, as Mr O'Brien misrepresented to her that the charge was limited to £60,000, her security was enforceable only to that extent. The bank appealed to the House of Lords. The claim based on undue influence was not pursued. The case rested solely on Mr O'Brien's misrepresentation. It was common ground that Mrs O'Brien had an equity to set aside the transaction against her husband. The key question was whether the bank was bound by the equity. Dismissing the appeal, the House of Lords held that as the bank knew that Mr and Mrs O'Brien were man and wife and Mrs O'Brien was induced to act as surety for the debts of her husband's company in which she had no direct pecuniary interest, and the bank had not taken reasonable steps to explain the nature of the transaction to her and recommended her to take independent legal advice, the bank had constructive notice of Mrs O'Brien's equity in setting aside the transaction against her husband and is therefore bound by it.

Barclays Bank plc v O'Brien [1993] 4 All ER 417, HL

Lord Browne-Wilkinson: A wife who has been induced to stand as a surety for her husband's debts by his undue influence, misrepresentation or some other legal wrong has an equity as against him to set aside that transaction. Under the ordinary principles of equity, her right to set aside that transaction will be enforceable against third parties

109 *Peto v Hammond* (1861) 30 Beav 495.

110 *Barclays Bank plc v O'Brien* [1993] 4 All ER 417. See further pp 788–94.

111 [1993] 4 All ER 417. See (1994) 57 MLR 467 (B Fehlberg); (1994) LQR 167 (Lehane, JRF); [1994] Conv 140 (Thompson, MP); [1994] Fam Law 78 (Cretney, S); (1995) 15 *Oxford Journal of Legal Studies* 119 (Goo, SH).

(eg against a creditor) if either the husband was acting as the third party's agent or the third party had actual or constructive notice of the facts giving rise to her equity. Although there may be cases where, without artificiality, it can properly be held that the husband was acting as the agent of the creditor in procuring the wife to stand as surety, such cases will be of very rare occurrence. The key to the problem is to identify the circumstances in which the creditor will be taken to have had notice of the wife's equity to set aside the transaction.

The doctrine of notice lies at the heart of equity. Given that there are two innocent parties, each enjoying rights, the earlier right prevails against the later right if the acquirer of the later right knows of the earlier right (actual notice) or would have discovered it had he taken proper steps (constructive notice). In particular, if the party asserting that he takes free of the earlier rights of another knows of certain facts which put him on inquiry as to the possible existence of the rights of that other and he fails to make such inquiry or take such other steps as are reasonable to verify whether such earlier right does not exist, he will have constructive notice of the earlier right and take subject to it. Therefore, where a wife has agreed to stand surety for her husband's debts as a result of undue influence or misrepresentation, the creditor will take subject to the wife's equity to set aside the transaction if the circumstances are such as to put the creditor on inquiry as to the circumstances in which she agreed to stand surety.

Therefore in my judgment a creditor is put on inquiry when a wife offers to stand surety for her husband's debts by the combination of two factors:

(a) the transaction is on its face not to the financial advantage of the wife; and

(b) there is a substantial risk in transactions of that kind that, in procuring the wife to act as surety, the husband has committed a legal or equitable wrong that entitles the wife to set aside the transaction.

It follows that unless the creditor who is put on inquiry takes reasonable steps to satisfy himself that the wife's agreement to stand surety has been properly obtained, the creditor will have constructive notice of the wife's rights.

What, then are the reasonable steps which the creditor should take to ensure that it does not have constructive notice of the wife's rights, if any? Normally, the reasonable steps necessary to avoid being fixed with constructive notice consist of making inquiry of the person who may have the earlier right (ie the wife) to see whether such right is asserted. It is plainly impossible to require of banks and other financial institutions that they should inquire of one spouse whether he or she has been unduly influenced or misled by the other. But in my judgment the creditor, in order to avoid being fixed with constructive notice, can reasonably be expected to take steps to bring home to the wife the risk she is running by standing as surety and to advise her to take independent advice. As to past transactions, it will depend on the facts of each case whether the steps taken by the creditor satisfy this test. However, for the future in my judgment a creditor will have satisfied these requirements if it insists that the wife attend a private meeting (in the absence of the husband) with a representative of the creditor at which she is told of the extent of her liability as surety, warned of the risk she is running and urged to take independent legal advice. If these steps are taken, in my judgment, the creditor will have taken such reasonable steps as are necessary to preclude a subsequent claim that it had constructive notice of the wife's rights. I should make it clear that I have been considering the ordinary case where the creditor knows only that the wife is to stand surety for her husband's debts. I would not exclude exceptional cases where a creditor has knowledge of further facts which render the presence of undue influence not only possible but probable. In such cases, the creditor to be safe will have to insist that the wife is separately advised.

I have hitherto dealt only with the position where a wife stands surety for her husband's debts. But in my judgment the same principles are applicable to all other cases where there is an emotional relationship between cohabitees. The 'tenderness' shown by the law to married women is not based on the marriage ceremony but reflects the underlying risk of one cohabitee exploiting the emotional involvement and trust of the other. Now that unmarried cohabitation, whether heterosexual or homosexual, is widespread in our society, the law should recognise this. Legal wives are not the only group which are now exposed to the emotional pressure of cohabitation. Therefore if, but only if, the creditor is aware that the surety is cohabiting with the principal debtor, in my judgment the same principles should apply to them as apply to husband and wife.

In addition to the cases of cohabitees, the decision of the Court of Appeal in *Avon Finance Co Ltd v Bridger* [1985] 2 All ER 281 shows (rightly in my view) that other relationships can give rise to a similar result. In that case a son, by means of misrepresentation, persuaded his elderly parents to stand surety for his debts. The surety obligation was held to be unenforceable by the creditor, inter alia, because to the bank's knowledge the parents trusted the son in their financial dealings. In my judgment that case was rightly decided: in a case where the creditor is aware that the surety reposes trust and confidence in the principal debtor in relation to his financial affairs, the creditor is put on inquiry in just the same way as it is in relation to husband and wife.

(iii) Imputed notice

Notice, actual or constructive, received by the purchaser's agent acting as such and in the same transaction is imputed to the purchaser.

Law of Property Act 1925

199. Restrictions on constructive notice

(1) A purchaser shall not be prejudicially affected by notice of:

(ii) any other instrument or matter or any fact or thing unless:

(b) in the same transaction with respect to which a question of notice to the purchaser arises, it has come to the knowledge of his counsel, as such, or of his solicitor or other agent, as such, or would have come to the knowledge of his solicitor or other agent, as such, if such inquiries and inspections had been made as ought reasonably to have been made by the solicitor or other agent.

Once the legal estate is passed to the purchaser of it for value without notice, the equitable interests are destroyed. Anyone who claims through that purchaser can take free of the equitable interests even if he has notice of them.[112] This is subject to the principle that a man cannot take advantage of his own wrong. Thus, if a trustee disposes of trust property to a purchaser without notice, and later acquires the property, he will hold it subject to the trusts.[113]

112 *Wilkes v Spooner* [1911] 2 KB 473.

113 *Re Stapleford Colliery* (1880) 14 Ch D 432.

CHAPTER 2

TRUST

> Of all the exploits of Equity the largest and the most important is the invention and development of the Trust. It is an 'institution' of great elasticity and generality; as elastic, as general as contract. This perhaps forms the most distinctive achievement of English lawyers. It seems to us almost essential to civilisation, and yet there is nothing quite like it in foreign law.[1]

The concept of trust has, indeed, ever since its invention, influenced the development of the English law of real property. The importance of some basic knowledge of trust cannot therefore be over-emphasised. It is relevant to determining the beneficial interests in property held on trust. It would also help understand the 1925 legislation in general and the protection of fragmented family interests (such as life estate, fee tail and fee simple in remainder, etc), strict settlements, trusts for sale, trust of land and the acquisition of property by joint owners in particular.

1 WHAT IS A TRUST?

A trust is an arrangement whereby property, legal or equitable, real or personal, is vested in a person, called the trustee, who has to hold, or exercise the right in the property for and on behalf of the true owner, called the beneficiary. Equity requires the trustee to apply the property faithfully in accordance with the confidence placed in him. The essence of the concept of trust is the separation of title and real (or beneficial) ownership. The legal title is vested in the trustee whereas the real ownership is in the beneficiary.

Although the trustees have the legal estate vested in them, they cannot take the property for their own benefit. They can never profit from their position as trustees without proper authorisation.[2] However, the trustees have the powers of management and disposition. They must exercise the powers with due diligence. They must manage the trust property in a productive manner to produce income and apply the income according to certain rules for the benefit of the beneficiary. If they dispose of the trust property, the proceeds of sale must still be held on trust and often must be reinvested in another form to produce income for the beneficiary.[3]

2 THE ORIGIN OF TRUSTS

Trust developed from 'use'. It all started with the problem that it was not possible to leave property by will before the Statute of Wills 1540. As Maitland pointed out[4]:

---

1 Maitland, *Equity*, 2nd edn, 1936, p 23.

2 *Keech v Sandford* (1726) 2 Eq Cas Abr 741.

3 For rules on trusteeships see Hanbury and Martin, *Modern Equity* (Martin, JE, ed) 14th edn, 1993, London: Sweet & Maxwell, Chapters 16–22.

4 *The Collected Papers of Frederic William Maitland* (Fisher, HAL, ed) 1911, Cambridge, Vol III, p 335.

> ... the Englishman would like to leave his land by will. He would like to provide for the weal of his sinful soul, and he would like to provide for his daughters and younger sons. That is the root of the matter ... the law is hard upon him at the hour of death, more especially if he is one of the great.

To overcome this problem, by the 14th century, it became common for a landowner to convey his land *inter vivos* to his close friends, in whom he reposed his confidence, who were instructed to hold the land to his 'use'. The landowner was known as the 'feoffor', the close friends to whom the land was conveyed were known as the 'feoffees' and the beneficiary the *cestui que* use. The feoffees could also be instructed to hold the land to the use of other members of the deceased's family.

Although the common law only recognised the feoffee as the legal owner, the Court of Chancery would recognise and enforce the use. Thus, by the 14th century, it became possible to devise land by will.

However, the institution of use had wider implications.[5] It was used to avoid some of the feudal incidents. For example, the lord was entitled to a payment when the land was succeeded by the deceased tenant's heir, and the land reverted to him when the tenant died without heirs. All these burdens could be avoided by conveying the land to feoffees to uses. The feoffees were not minors and were unlikely to die at the same time or without heirs. Those who died could be replaced. This device represented a loss in revenues to the Crown who was lord of all and tenant of none. Henry VIII found this unacceptable and abolished the use by the Statute of Uses 1535. The effect of the Statute was to convert the rights of the *cestui que* use to legal rights. Thus, the feoffees disappeared from the picture and the *cestui que* use had the legal estate.

The execution of uses, however, brought about a public outcry as people believed that it was no longer possible to devise land. The Statute of Wills was passed in 1540 to make it possible for a testator to devise land held by him in socage and two-thirds of his land in knight's service. Thus, land became generally devisable at law.

However, the Statute of Uses did not execute a use upon a use because it was resolved, before 1535, that a use upon a use, for example, a conveyance 'to A to the use of B to the use of C' was void.[6] A use upon a use was later to become what is today known as 'trust'. In the next century after the Statute of Uses was passed, the Chancellor began to recognise the second uses.[7] Thus, uses were brought back to life and land could be granted 'to A to the use of B in trust for C'. B would get the legal estate because of the execution of use by the Statute of Uses 1535 but would have to hold it on trust for C because the second use, which was now called a trust, was not executed by the Statute and was now

---

5 See Megarry and Wade, p 1165.

6 Bro Abr Feff al Uses, 40 (1532); Sanders, Uses, i, 42, 43. For cases decided after 1535, see *Dillam v Frain* (1595) 1 And 309 at 313; *Corbet's* case (1600) 2 And 134 at 136; *Daw v Newborough* (1716) 1 Com 242 at 243; *Tyrrel's* case (1557) 2 Dy 155a.

7 The precise date when this was done is uncertain but it was certainly well settled by 1700 in *Symson v Turner* (1700) 1 Eq Cas Abr 383: see Simpson, AWB, *A History of the Land Law*, 2nd edn, 1986. Oxford: Clarendon Press, pp 202–03; (1966) 82 LQR 215 (Barton, JL); (1977) 93 LQR 33 (Baker, JH).

recognised by the Court of Chancery. The new expression denoting C's interest was 'trust' rather than 'use'. They were synonymous in law but in practice 'trust' was used for C's equitable interest while 'use' was reserved to uses executed by the Statute. An alternative formula was 'unto and to the use of B in trust for C'. Here, the legal estate was conveyed to B to his own use in trust for C. As the Statute did not apply where a person was seised to his own use,[8] B's first use was not executed and he was the owner at common law. But the trust in favour of C was not executed either as it was a second use.[9] B, therefore, would be required to hold the legal estate on trust for C. Thus, uses, now in the name of trusts, could be created as easily as uses had been before 1535. What was required was to use the formula 'unto and to the use of [the trustee] in trust for [the beneficiary]', or simply 'to the use of [the trustee] in trust for [the beneficiary]'.

Thus, the ancient use was reborn in the modern name of trust. The Statute of Uses 1535 was eventually repealed in 1925. Today, it is no longer necessary to use the expression 'unto and to the use of X in trust for'. The land could be simply conveyed 'to X in trust for'.

3 THE BINDING EFFECT OF A TRUST

Trust is the invention of equity in its jurisdiction of conscience. The trustee is directly bound by the trust to act faithfully in accordance with the term of the trust for the benefit of the beneficiary. Having agreed with the author of the trust to follow his instruction faithfully and to observe the conditions upon which the trust property was conveyed to him, it would be against the trustee's conscience to apply the property otherwise than for the benefit of the beneficiary.

However, the long arm of equity does not stop there. The trustee's personal representative who succeeds to the trust property[10] is also bound by the trust for he is regarded as simply filling the place of the trustee.[11] Similarly, the trustee's creditors may not take the trust property to satisfy the trustee's personal debts for the trustee does not hold the trust property for his own benefit.[12]

Where the trustee transfers the trust property in breach of trust to an innocent third party without consideration, the maxim 'equity will not assist a volunteer' (ie a person who has not given consideration) applies. The donee is

---

8 *Sammes's* case (1609) 13 Co Rep 54 at 56; *Peacock v Eastland* (1870) LR 10 Eq 17; *Orme's* case (1872) LR 8 CP 281.

9 *Doe d Lloyd v Passingham* (1827) 6 B & C 305.

10 Prior to 1898, the personal representatives did not take the deceased's realty; the heir or devisee took directly. Under s 1(1) of the Land Transfer Act 1897 in the case of deaths after 1897, all property, real or personal, was vested in the personal representatives. This was substantially repeated by s 1(1) of the AEA 1925 which is still in force today. See Megarry and Wade, pp 559–62.

11 Personal representatives are regarded as 'sustaining wholly or partially the persona of the original trustee and being bound by his obligations as regards the proprietary rights to which they have succeeded': Maitland, *Equity*, p 112.

12 *Worrall v Harford* (1802) 8 Ves 4, p 8; ss 283(1)(a), (3)(a), 306 of the Insolvency Act 1986.

required to take the legal estate subject to the claim of the beneficiary. This is because equity regards it as against the donee's conscience for him to take the trust property after he has later come to know that it was conveyed to him in breach of trust.

As equity acts in conscience, it is not surprising that if the trust property is conveyed to a purchaser with notice, actual or constructive, the beneficiary's initial rights against the trustee are now enforceable against the purchaser. The purchaser will be required to hold the property on trust for the beneficiary. However, if the purchaser has acquired the property for valuable consideration without notice, actual or constructive, of the trust, he has an absolute, unqualified and unanswerable defence to the beneficiary's claim.[13] Equity cannot touch him because his conscience is unaffected by the trust.[14]

The binding effect of a trust has thus been formulated in either of two ways by Maitland:

Formulation A

The *cestui que* trust may enforce his rights against:

(i) the trustee; and

(ii) all who claim through the trustee as volunteers (personal representatives, devisees,[15] donees); and

(iii) all those who acquire the trust property with actual or constructive notice of the trust.

Formulation B

The *cestui que* trust may enforce his rights against all persons (taking the property) except a *bona fide* purchaser of a legal title for valuable consideration without notice of the trust (whether actual or constructive).

Of the two formulations, Maitland himself preferred the first 'because it puts us at what is historically the right point of view'.[16] However, formulation B is now the more common way of stating the principle and constitutes what is known as the equitable doctrine of notice.[17]

4 ASCERTAINING THE BENEFICIAL OWNERSHIP

It is trite law that a transfer of the legal title *prima facie* carries with it the absolute beneficial interest in the property conveyed.[18] Thus, a transferee is *prima facie* the legal, as well as the beneficial, owner unless some other person can establish a beneficial interest in the property conveyed in opposition to the absolute ownership of the legal owner. A person may establish his beneficial

13 *Pilcher v Rawlins* (1872) 7 Ch App 259 at 268f, *per* James LJ; see pp 26–27 above.

14 Maitland, *Equity*, p 115.

15 The beneficiaries of a gift of real property by will.

16 Maitland, *Equity*, p 115.

17 See Chapter 1, pp 26–35 above.

18 *Pettitt v Pettitt* [1970] AC 777 at 813H–814A, *per* Lord Upjohn; *Gissing v Gissing* [1971] AC 886 at 902A, *per* Lord Pearson.

entitlement to the property by showing that the property was expressly conveyed to the legal owner on trust for him: that the property is held on an *express trust* for the claimant. This is perhaps the most common way in which the true beneficial interest is ascertained. The transfer documents often contain details of beneficial ownership and such declarations are generally conclusive.[19] However, on occasions, the transfer documents may be silent on the beneficial entitlement and dispute may arise in future as to who owns the beneficial interest. The claimant may show that his beneficial ownership arises as a result of what the law infers as having been the parties' intention at the time of the transfer: that the property is held on a *resulting (or implied) trust* for the claimant; or he may show that it was their common intention, at the time or after the transfer, that the claimant should have some beneficial interest in the property and he has acted on that common intention to his detriment; or in any event it is unconscionable for the legal owner to deny the claimant a beneficial interest in the property: that the property is held on a *constructive trust* for the claimant. Disputes between married couples on the beneficial entitlement to the family home on divorce or death are quite often also resolved by certain statutory provisions.[20] Disputes between unmarried cohabitees are still solved by recourse to the rules of equity.[21]

As already mentioned, there are three ways in which a claimant can establish his beneficial entitlement, *viz*, under an express, resulting or constructive trust. Before we examine each of them in detail, it is important to say a few words on the use of terminology. Classifying trusts into express, implied, resulting or constructive trusts has been largely judicial.[22] It is widely agreed, however, that the use of terminology in judgments as regards constructive, implied or resulting trusts has been inconsistent and at times confusing.[23] There is a clear distinction between resulting trust on the one hand and constructive trust on the other hand.[24] The grey area between is variously called implied or constructive trusts and their development is continuous.[25] It is convenient to describe all trusts not expressly created as implied trusts and divide implied trusts into resulting and constructive trusts. On the other hand, as constructive trusts can be imposed by equity in circumstances where the intention of the parties are not relevant at all so long as justice demands its imposition, it seems more appropriate to treat the term implied trusts as including resulting trusts. Thus, for the present purposes, as has been adopted above, we shall treat resulting and implied trusts as one category and constructive trusts as the other.

---

19 *Pettitt v Pettitt* [1970] AC 777 at 813E, *per* Lord Upjohn. But see *City of London Building Society v Flegg* [1988] AC 54 where the express declaration of trust for sale was held not conclusive and was rebutted by evidence of contributions.

20 See ss 23–25 of the Matrimonial Causes Act 1973; ss 1–3 of the Inheritance (Provision for Family and Dependants) Act 1975; s 37 of the Matrimonial Proceedings and Property Act 1970.

21 *Grant v Edwards* [1986] Ch 638 at 651G, *per* Mustill LJ.

22 Section 53(2) of the LPA 1925 does however refer to resulting, implied or constructive trusts.

23 See Megarry and Wade, p 466; Gray, p 372.

24 (1973) 37 Con 65; (1973) 4 CLJ 41; (1973) 89 LQR 2; Oakley, AJ, *Constructive Trusts*, 2nd edn 1987, London: Sweet & Maxwell, Chapters 1–2.

25 For example, *Gissing v Gissing* [1971] AC 886 at 906.

Express trusts – creation

(a) Formality

Express trusts are declared by the grantor or settlor. To create a trust expressly, where the subject matter of the trust is any land or interest in land, under s 53(1)(b) of the Law of Property Act 1925 the declaration of trust must be manifested and proved by some writing signed by some person who is able to declare such trust, or by his will.[26]

Law of Property Act 1925

53. Instruments required to be in writing

(1) Subject to the provisions hereinafter contained with respect to the creation of interests in land by parol:

(b) a declaration of trust respecting any land or any interest therein must be manifested and proved by some writing signed by some person who is able to declare such trust, or by his will;

This does not mean that the declaration must be itself in writing. It means that the existence of the trust must be capable of being proved by some writing signed by the grantor or by his will. If the declaration of trust is parol[27] and cannot be proved by any written evidence, the trust will take effect at will only. It is valid but unenforceable.[28]

Law of Property Act 1925

54. Creation of interests in land by parol

(1) All interests in land created by parol and not put in writing and signed by the persons so creating the same, or by their agents thereunto lawfully authorised in writing, have, notwithstanding any consideration having been given for the same, the force and effect of interests at will only.

It should, however, be noted that the purpose of s 53(1)(b) is to prevent fraud which might otherwise arise against the trustee. On the other hand, the trustee may be tempted to plead the lack of formality to deny the beneficiary's interest under the trust. It is to prevent fraud perpetrated by the trustee that 'equity will not permit a statute to be used as an instrument of fraud'.[29] In *Rochefoucauld v Boustead*, Lindley LJ expressed the view that:

... it is a fraud on the part of a person to whom land is conveyed as a trustee, and who knows it was so conveyed, to deny the trust and claim the land himself. Consequently,

---

26 This derives from s 7 of the the Statute of Frauds 1677. For the background of this section see Youdan [1984] CLJ 306 at 307ff.

27 Word of mouth.

28 *Gardner v Rowe* (1828) 5 Russ 258 at 262; *Gissing v Gissing* [1971] AC 886 at 910E–F, *per* Lord Diplock; *Cowcher v Cowcher* [1972] 1 WLR 425 at 430H–431A; *Midland Bank plc v Dobson* [1986] 1 FLR 171 at 175C–D; *Wratten v Hunter* [1978] 2 NSWLR 367 at 371B.

29 *Rochefoucauld v Boustead* [1897] 1 Ch 196.

notwithstanding the statute, it is competent for a person claiming land conveyed to another to prove by parol evidence that it was so conveyed upon trust for the claimant, and that the grantee, knowing the facts, is denying the trust and relying upon the form of the conveyance and the statute, in order to keep the land himself.[30]

Thus, if A acquires the property on an oral undertaking that he will hold the property on trust for B from the moment of acquisition, then A cannot claim that the trust is void under s 53(1)(b) for want of written evidence.

Section 53(1)(b) only applies to declaration of trust of land or any interest in land. Declaration of trust of other forms of property can be made orally without written evidence.[31]

(b) Certainty

To create a trust expressly, the intention to create a trust, the subject matter of the trust and the objects of the trust must all be certain.

The intention to create a trust must be shown by imperative, not precatory words.[32] Words such as 'in the full confidence', 'recommending', 'my dying request' would not be enough today. If the grantor fails to express an intention to create a trust, the grantee (the intending trustee) holds the property beneficially free of any trust.[33]

The trust property must be described with certainty. If the property to be conveyed to the trustee is insufficiently defined, the whole transaction is void.[34] The grantor retains the property. If the extent of the beneficial interest is insufficiently defined, the trustee will hold the property on a resulting trust for the grantor.[35]

The beneficiaries of the trust must be defined with sufficient certainty.[36] Where the object of the trust is for a purpose, the purpose must be defined with certainty,[37] unless the trust is for charitable purposes in which case the objects need not be certain as long as the purpose is not so vague and uncertain that the court is unable to control the application of the trust property.[38] Where the trust

30 *Ibid* at 206.

31 *Re Kayford Ltd* [1975] 1 WLR 279.

32 *Re Adams and the Kensington Vestry* (1884) 27 Ch D 394 at 419.

33 *McCormick v Grogan* (1869) LR 4 HL 82.

34 *Palmer v Simmonds* (1854) 2 Drew 221.

35 *Boyce v Boyce* (1849) 16 Sim 476.

36 *Re Vandervell's Trusts (No 2)* [1974] Ch 269 at 319, *per* Lord Denning. In the case of a fixed trust, each and every beneficiary must be ascertainable. In the case of a discretionary trust (ie a trust under which the trustees have discretion to decide who within a class chosen by the settlor should benefit from the trust and how much) the test is: can it be said with certainty that any individual is or is not a member of the class? *McPhail v Doulton* [1971] AC 424.

37 *Morie v Bishop of Durham* (1804) 9 Ves Jr 399 ('such objects of benevolence and liberality as the Bishop of Durham in his own discretion shall most approve of'. Trust held void because 'benevolence' and 'liberality' wider than charity and uncertain).

38 *Re Koeppler's W T* [1986] Ch 423.

is void for uncertainty of objects, the trustee must hold the property on resulting trust for the grantor.[39]

Resulting (or implied) and constructive trusts – creation

(a) Formality

The hallmark of implied, resulting or constructive trusts is their informality because s 53(1)(b) does not apply to their creation or operation.[40]

(b) Resulting (or implied) trust

(i) Failure to dispose beneficial interest

Where a grantor conveys his property on trust but does not effectively dispose of the beneficial interest in the property, there is a resulting trust in favour of the grantor.[41] An example of this is where a property is held on trust for A for life and then equally among his children, but A dies childless. The beneficial interest will result back to the grantor automatically on A's death or, if the grantor is now dead, to his residuary legatees, or the persons entitled under the intestacy rules.[42]

(ii) Where a trust fails

Where an express trust fails for any reason, for example, if there is no beneficiary under the trust, or if the purpose of the trust is void, or if the trust is void for uncertainty, then a resulting trust arises in favour of the grantor. For example, in *Re Diplock*,[43] a large sum of money was left on trust for purposes thought to be charitable. The trust was later found void because the purpose was non-charitable. The money resulted to the deceased settlor's next-of-kin.

(iii) Purchase in the name of another

It was held in *Dyer v Dyer* that a resulting trust would arise when A, the person who provided money for the purchase of the property asked for the property to be conveyed to someone, B, other than himself.[44] This is because equity presumes that it was A's intention that B, to whom the legal title is conveyed,

39 *Kendall v Granger* (1842) 5 Beav 300; *Re Carville* [1937] 4 All ER 464.

40 Section 53(2) of the LPA 1925.

41 Called 'automatic resulting trusts' by Megarry J in *Re Vandervell's Trusts (No 2)* [1974] Ch 269 at 294.

42 An example is *Vandervell v IRC* [1967] 2 AC 291 where an option to repurchase shares from the college to which the shares were originally granted was held by trustees on trust not hitherto defined, thus option resulted back to the settlor.

43 [1941] Ch 253; [1944] AC 341.

44 (1788) 2 Cox Eq Cas 92 at 93.

should hold it on trust for A. But this is only a presumption and it can be rebutted. Thus, if there is evidence that the property was intended as a gift to B, no resulting trust would arise.[45]

The presumption in *Dyer v Dyer* may be rebutted by another equitable presumption. That is, where A is regarded by equity as being under an obligation to provide for B, the presumption is that a gift to B was intended. This is called the presumption of advancement. Therefore, if a man buys property and has it conveyed to his wife or fiancee, there is a presumption of advancement.[46] There is no presumption of advancement in favour of a man's mistress.[47] Similarly, there is no such presumption where a wife conveys property into the name of her husband.[48]

There is a presumption of advancement where any person who stands in *loco parentis* to a child, that is, assumes the responsibility of a father in providing for the child, buys property and has it conveyed into the name of the child.[49] A father is always presumed to be in *loco parentis*,[50] but not a mother unless she has herself assumed a father's responsibility for the child.[51]

It must be noted that these are only presumptions and can be rebutted easily by comparatively slight evidence showing the purchaser's real intention, for example, it was only the person to whom the property was conveyed who would have been accepted as a mortgagor of the property or it had been proposed that the beneficial interest should be shared at certain proportions.[52]

The principles of presumption of advancement have, however, been questioned in connection with ownership of the matrimonial home. With the increasing financial independence of women, the presumption of advancement laid down in *Re Eykyn's Trusts* is diminished in modern times in the context of the matrimonial home, and its application has been reclassified as a judicial instrument of last resort (see *McGrath v Wallis* [1995] 2 FLR 114 at 115, *per* Nourse LJ). In *Falconer v Falconer*, Lord Denning thought that the presumption of advancement 'found its place in Victorian days when a wife was utterly subordinate to her husband. It has no place, or at any rate, very little place, in our law today'.[53] Lord Diplock in *Pettitt v Pettitt* has said that:

> ... it would in my view be an abuse of the legal technique for ascertaining or imputing intention to apply to transactions between the post-war generation of married couples 'presumptions' which are based upon inferences of fact which an earlier generation of

45 *Cowcher v Cowcher* [1872] 1 WLR 425 at 431C; *Winkworth v Edward Baron development Co Ltd* [1986] 1 WLR 1512 at 1516D.

46 *Re Eykyn's Trusts* (1877) 6 Ch D 115 at 118.

47 *Diwell v Farnes* [1959] 1 WLR 624.

48 *Mercier v Mercier* [1903] 2 Ch 98.

49 *Shephard v Cartwright* [1855] AC 431 at 445. The presumption also applies to an illegitimate child (*Beckford v Beckford* (1774) 98 ER 763 at 764), an adopted child (*Standing v Bowring* (1886) 31 Ch D 282 at 287) and a stepson (*In Re Paradise Motor Co Ltd* [1968] 1 WLR 1125 at 1140A).

50 *Dyer v Dyer* (1788) 2 Cox Eq Cas 92 at 93f.

51 *Bannet v Bannet* (1879) 10 Ch D 474.

52 *McGrath v Wallis* [1995] 2 FLR 114.

53 [1970] 1 WLR 1333 at 1335H–36A.

judges drew as the most likely intentions of earlier generations of spouses belonging to the propertied classes of a different social era.[54]

So if H and W contributed money for the purchase of their home and the house is conveyed into the name of W alone, the presumption of advancement is much weakened. The result is likely to be that W holds the property on trust for herself and H.[55]

But if the property is conveyed into H's name, then it is clear that H holds it on trust for himself and W, because W's contribution is not presumed to be a gift to H.[56] The presumed intention is that W, by contribution, is to get a share in the property. This kind of resulting trust can also arise where the contribution is towards the mortgage repayments.[57] Whether indirect financial contribution to the purchase of the house, eg contribution to household expenses, is enough is more complicated. It seems that there must be an agreement or common intention *at the time of the acquisition* that W should have a beneficial interest. Any indirect financial contribution which may be made at the time of, or after, the acquisition will raise the presumption of resulting trust so long as the contribution is referable to the acquisition of the property (or referable to the agreement or common intention)[58] If there is no agreement or common intention, only direct financial contribution will raise a resulting trust[59]; indirect financial contribution will not suffice to give rise to an inference of a common intention.[60] The basis of the present law was laid down in *Pettit v Pettit* and *Gissing v Gissing.*

Gissing v Gissing [1971] AC 886, HL

Viscount Dilhorne: ... I agree with my noble and learned friend Lord Diplock that a claim to a beneficial interest in land made by a person in whom the legal estate is not

54 [1970] AC 777 at 824C.

55 *Falconer v Falconer* [1970] 3 All ER 449, CA.

56 *Re Curtis* (1885) 52 LT 244; *Rich v Cockell* (1802) 9 Ves 369; *Mercier v Mercier* [1903] 2 Ch 98, CA; *Pearson v Pearson* (1965) *The Times*, 30 November; *Heseltine v Heseltine* [1971] 1 All ER 952, CA (Lord Denning called this 'a resulting trust which resulted from all the circumstances of the case' (at 955h) but it has been suggested that the context and the language is consistent rather with a constructive trust (see Pettit, *Equity and the Law of Trusts*, 7th edn, p 178). The Law Commission cited *Heseltine v Heseltine* as a case of resulting trust (Law Commission, Family Law: Matrimonial Property, Law Com No 125, para 2.6).

57 *Cowcher v Cowcher* [1972] 1 WLR 425; *Walker v Hall* [1984] 127 Sol Jo 550. *Cf Pearson v Pearson* (1965) *The Times*, 30 November (wife who not only provided initial payments but also all mortgage instalments was held to be solely entitled).

58 In *Grant v Edwards*, the man's excuse for not putting the woman's name onto the title showed that there was at the time of the acquisition a common intention that she should have a beneficial interest and her contribution, though indirect, was referable to the acquisition.

59 In *Lloyds Bank v Rosset*, Lord Bridge said that where there is no agreement or common intention it is extremely doubtful whether anything less than direct financial contribution will be enough to raise a constructive trust. It is submitted that the use of the term 'constructive trust' is unfortunate, confusing, misleading and most unhelpful.

60 For example, in *Burns v Burns*, the woman made various forms of indirect contribution but failed to obtain any beneficial interest because there was no express agreement to her beneficial entitlement. See Pettit, *Equity and the Law of Trust*, 6th edn, pp 132, 133–35.

vested and whether made by a stranger, a spouse or a former spouse must depend for its success on establishing that it is held on a trust to give effect to the beneficial interest of the claimant as a *cestui que* trust.

Where there was a common intention at the time of the acquisition of the house that the beneficial interest in it should be shared, it would be a breach of faith by the spouse in whose name the legal estate was vested to fail to give effect to that intention and the other spouse will be held entitled to a share in the beneficial interest ...

In a great many cases, perhaps in the vast majority, no consideration will have been given by the parties to the marriage to the question of beneficial ownership of the matrimonial home at the time that it is being acquired. If, on the evidence, that appears to have been the case, then a claim based upon the existence of such an intention at the time must fail.

It may be that one spouse will say that if he or she had thought about it, he or she would have agreed to sharing the beneficial interest with the other, but that in my view will not justify or entitle the court to hold that they share the beneficial interest. As I read the opinions of the majority in *Pettitt v Pettitt* [1970] AC 777 that was their conclusion. One cannot counteract the absence of any common intention at the time of acquisition by conclusions as to what the parties would have done if they had thought about the matter. If such a common intention is absent, in my opinion the law does not permit the courts to ascribe to the parties an intention they never had and to hold that property is subject to a trust on the ground that that would be fair in all the circumstances.

My Lords, in determining whether or not there was such a common intention, regard can of course be had to the conduct of the parties. If the wife provided part of the purchase price of the house, either initially or subsequently by paying or sharing in the mortgage payments, the inference may well arise that it was the common intention that she should have an interest in the house.

To establish this intention there must be some evidence which points to its existence. It would not, for instance, suffice if the wife just made a mortgage payment while her husband was abroad. Payment for a lawn and provision of some furniture and equipment for the house does not of itself point to the conclusion that there was such an intention ...

My Lords, I do not think that any useful purpose will be served by my expressing any views on what will suffice to justify the drawing of such an inference. In one case the evidence may just fall short of doing so; in another it may just suffice. But what is important is that it should be borne in mind that proof of expenditure for the benefit of the family by one spouse will not of itself suffice to show any such common intention as to the ownership of the matrimonial home ...

Lord Diplock: ... A resulting, implied or constructive trust – and it is unnecessary for present purposes to distinguish between these three classes of trust – is created by a transaction between the trustee and the *cestui que* trust in connection with the acquisition by the trustee of a legal estate in land, whenever the trustee has so conducted himself that it would be inequitable to allow him to deny to the *cestui que* trust a beneficial interest in the land acquired. And he will be held so to have conducted himself if by his words or conduct he has induced the *cestui que* trust to act to his own detriment in the reasonable belief that by so acting he was acquiring a beneficial interest in the land.

This is why it has been repeatedly said in the context of disputes between spouses as to their respective beneficial interests in the matrimonial home, that if at the time of its acquisition and transfer of the legal estate into the name of one or other of them an express agreement has been made between them as to the way in which the beneficial interest shall be held, the court will give effect to it – notwithstanding the absence of any written declaration of trust. Strictly speaking this states the principle too widely, for if the agreement did not provide for anything to be done by the spouse in whom the legal estate was not to be vested, it would be a merely voluntary declaration of trust and unenforceable for want of writing. But in the express oral agreements contemplated by these dicta it has been assumed *sub silentio* that they provide for the spouse in whom the legal estate in the matrimonial home is not vested to do something to facilitate its acquisition, by contributing to the purchase price or to the deposit or the mortgage instalments when it is purchased upon mortgage or to make some other material sacrifice by way of contribution to or economy in the general family expenditure. What the court gives effect to is the trust resulting or implied from the common intention expressed in the oral agreement between the spouses that if each acts in the manner provided for in the agreement the beneficial interests in the matrimonial home shall be held as they have agreed ...

But parties to a transaction in connection with the acquisition of land may well have formed a common intention that the beneficial interest in the land shall be vested in them jointly without having used express words to communicate this intention to one another; or their recollections of the words used may be imperfect or conflicting by the time any dispute arises. In such a case – a common one where the parties are spouses whose marriage has broken down – it may be possible to infer their common intention from their conduct ...

In drawing such an inference, what spouses said and did which led up to the acquisition of a matrimonial home and what they said and did while the acquisition was being carried through is on a different footing from what they said and did after the acquisition was completed. Unless it is alleged that there was some subsequent fresh agreement, acted upon by the parties, to vary the original beneficial interests created when the matrimonial home was acquired, what they said and did after the acquisition was completed is relevant if it is explicable only upon the basis of their having manifested to one another at the time of the acquisition some particular common intention as to how the beneficial interests should be held. But it would in my view be unreasonably legalistic to treat the relevant transaction involved in the acquisition of a matrimonial home as restricted to the actual conveyance of the fee simple into the name of one or other spouse. Their common intention is more likely to have been concerned with the economic realities of the transaction than with the unfamiliar technicalities of the English law of legal and equitable interests in land. The economic reality which lies behind the conveyance of the fee simple to a purchaser in return for a purchase price the greater part of which is advanced to the purchaser upon a mortgage repayable by instalments over a number of years, is that the new freeholder is purchasing the matrimonial home upon credit and that the purchase price is represented by the instalments by which the mortgage is repaid in addition to the initial payment in cash. The conduct of the spouses in relation to the payment of the mortgage instalments may be no less relevant to their common intention as to the beneficial interests in a matrimonial home acquired in this way than their conduct in relation to the payment of the cash deposit.

It is this feature of the transaction by means of which most matrimonial homes have been acquired in recent years that makes difficult the task of the court in inferring from the conduct of the spouses a common intention as to how the beneficial interest in it should be held. Each case must depend upon its own facts but there are a number of factual situations which often recur in the cases.

Where a matrimonial home has been purchased outright without the aid of an advance on mortgage it is not difficult to ascertain what part, if any, of the purchase price has been provided by each spouse. If the land is conveyed into the name of a spouse who has not provided the whole of the purchase price, the sum contributed by the other spouse may be explicable as having been intended by both of them either as a gift or as a loan of money to the spouse to whom the land is conveyed or as consideration for a share in the beneficial interest in the land. In a dispute between living spouses the evidence will probably point to one of these explanations as being more probable than the others, but if the rest of the evidence is neutral the *prima facie* inference is that their common intention was that the contributing spouse should acquire a share in the beneficial interest in the land in the same proportion as the sum contributed bore to the total purchase price. This *prima facie* inference is more easily rebutted in favour of a gift where the land is conveyed into the name of the wife: but as I understand the speeches in *Pettitt v Pettitt* four of the members of your Lordships' House who were parties to that decision took the view that even if the 'presumption of advancement' as between husband and wife still survived today, it could seldom have any decisive part to play in disputes between living spouses in which some evidence would be available in addition to the mere fact that the husband had provided part of the purchase price of property conveyed into the name of the wife.

Similarly, when a matrimonial home is not purchased outright but partly out of moneys advanced on a mortgage repayable by instalments, and the land is conveyed into the name of the husband alone, the fact that the wife made a cash contribution to the deposit and legal charges not borrowed on a mortgage gives rise, in the absence of evidence which makes some other explanation more probable, to the inference that their common intention was that she should share in the beneficial interest in the land conveyed. But it would not be reasonable to infer a common intention as to what her share should be without taking account also of the sources from which the mortgage instalments were provided. If the wife also makes a substantial direct contribution to the mortgage instalments out of her own earnings or unearned income this would be *prima facie* inconsistent with a common intention that her share in the beneficial interest should be determined by the proportion which her original cash contribution bore either to the total amount of the deposit and legal charges or to the full purchase price. The more likely inference is that her contributions to the mortgage instalments were intended by the spouses to have some effect upon her share.

Where there has been an initial contribution by the wife to the cash deposit and legal charges which point to a common intention at the time of the conveyance that she should have a beneficial interest in the land conveyed to her husband, it would be unrealistic to regard the wife's subsequent contributions to the mortgage instalments as without significance unless she pays them directly herself. It may be no more than a matter of convenience which spouse pays particular household accounts, particularly when both are earning, and if the wife goes out to work and devotes part of her earnings or uses her private income to meet joint expenses of the household which would otherwise be met by the husband, so as to enable him to pay the mortgage instalments out of his moneys this would be consistent with and might be corroborative of an original common intention that she should share in the beneficial interest in the matrimonial home and that her payments of other household expenses were intended by both spouses to be treated as including a contribution by the wife to the purchase price of the matrimonial home.

Even where there has been no initial contribution by the wife to the cash deposit and legal charges but she makes a regular and substantial direct contribution to the mortgage instalments it may be reasonable to infer a common intention of the spouses from the outset that she should share in the beneficial interest or to infer a fresh agreement reached after the original conveyance that she should acquire a share. But it is unlikely that the mere fact that the wife made direct contributions to the mortgage instalments would be the only evidence available to assist the court in ascertaining the common intention of the spouses ...

Where the wife has made no initial contribution to the cash deposit and legal charges and no direct contribution to the mortgage instalments nor any adjustment to her contribution to other expenses of the household which it can be inferred was referable to the acquisition of the house, there is in the absence of evidence of an express agreement between the parties no material to justify the court in inferring that it was the common intention of the parties that she should have any beneficial interest in a matrimonial home conveyed into the sole name of the husband, merely because she continued to contribute out of her own earnings or private income to other expenses of the household. For such conduct is no less consistent with a common intention to share the day-to-day expenses of the household, while each spouse retains a separate interest in capital assets acquired with their own moneys or obtained by inheritance or gift. There is nothing here to rebut the *prima facie* inference that a purchase of land who pays the purchase price and takes a conveyance and grants a mortgage in his own name intends to acquire the sole beneficial interest as well as the legal estate.

Lord Pearson: ... If the respondent's claim is to be valid, I think it must be on the basis that by virtue of contributions made by her towards the purchase of the house there was and is a resulting trust in her favour. If she did make contributions of substantial amounts towards the purchase of the house, there would *prima facie* be a resulting trust in her favour. That would be the presumption as to the intention of the parties at the time or times when she made and he accepted the contributions ...

Contributions are not limited to those made directly in part payment of the price of the property or to those made at the time when the property is conveyed into the name of one of the spouses. For instance, there can be a contribution if by arrangement between the spouses one of them by payment of the household expenses enables the other to pay the mortgage instalments.

On the facts of the present case the learned judge, Buckley J, decided in effect that the respondent had not made, either directly or indirectly, any substantial contribution to the purchase of the house, and therefore there was no resulting trust in her favour. I agree with him and would therefore allow the appeal.

Appeal allowed.

Lords Reid and Morris of Borth-y-Gest also concurred.

In *Burns v Burns*,[61] W's housework, decorating and the purchase of chattels for the home over a period of 17 years gave her no share.[62]

Burns v Burns [1984] Ch 317, CA

Fox LJ: The house with which we are concerned in this case was purchased in the name of the defendant and the freehold was conveyed to him absolutely. That was in 1963. If, therefore, the plaintiff is to establish that she has a beneficial interest in the property she must establish that the defendant holds the legal estate upon trust to give effect to that interest. That follows from *Gissing v Gissing* [1971] AC 886. For present purposes I think that such a trust could only arise (a) by express declaration or agreement *or* (b) by way of a resulting trust where the claimant has directly provided part of the purchase price *or* (c) from the common intention of the parties.

In the present case (a) and (b) can be ruled out. There was no express trust of an interest in the property for the benefit of the plaintiff; and there was no express agreement to create such an interest. And the plaintiff made no direct contribution to the purchase price. Her case, therefore, must depend upon showing a common intention that she should have a beneficial interest in the property. Whether the trust which would arise in such circumstances is described as implied, constructive or resulting does not greatly matter. If the intention is inferred from the fact that some indirect contribution is made to the purchase price, the term 'resulting trust' is probably not inappropriate. Be that as it may, the basis of such a claim, in any case, is that it would be inequitable for the holder of the legal estate to deny the claimant's right to a beneficial interest ...

Looking at the position at the time of the acquisition of the house in 1963, I see nothing at all to indicate any intention by the parties that the plaintiff should have an interest in it ... The plaintiff made no financial contribution; she had nothing to contribute ...

I come then to the position in the year after the house was purchased. I will deal with them under three heads, namely financial contributions, work on the house and finally housekeeping. There is some overlapping in these categories.

So far as financial contributions are concerned, the plaintiff's position really did not change during the 1960's. She had no money of her own and could not contribute financially to the household ...

The judge's findings as to expenditure by the plaintiff were as follows. (i) She made gifts of clothing and other things to the defendant and the children. (ii) She paid for the housekeeping. The defendant allowed her, latterly, £60 per week for housekeeping. It seems to be accepted that the defendant was generous with money and the plaintiff was not kept short as regards housekeeping money. (iii) She paid the rates. The housekeeping payments made by the defendant were, however, fixed at an amount which took account of this. (iv) She paid the telephone bills. That was a matter of agreement between her and the defendant because she spent a lot of time on the telephone talking to her friends. (v) She bought a number of chattels for domestic use: a dishwasher, a washing machine, a

61 [1984] Ch 317.

62 Professor Pettit suggests that in *Grant v Edwards* [1986] Ch 638 a differently constituted Court of Appeal treated *Burns v Burns* as a case of constructive trust (Pettit, PH, *Equity and the Law of Trusts*, 6th edn, 1989, London: Butterworths, p 133).

tumble dryer and either a drawing room suite or three armchairs and a bed for her separate room. The bed, the dishwasher and the chairs she took with her when she left in 1980. (vi) She provided some doorknobs and door furnishings of no great value.

None of this expenditure, in my opinion, indicates the existence of the common intention which the plaintiff has to prove. What is needed, I think, is evidence of a payment or payments by the plaintiff which it can be inferred was referable to the acquisition of the house. Lord Denning MR in *Hazell v Hazell* [1972] 1 WLR 301 at 304 thought that expression, which appears in the speech of Lord Diplock in *Gissing v Gissing* [1971] AC 886 at 909, was being over-used. He said quoting from *Falconer v Falconer* [1970] 1 WLR 1333 at 1336, that if there was a substantial financial contribution towards the family expenses that would raise an inference of a trust. I do not think that formulation alters the essence of the matter for present purposes. If there is a substantial contribution by the woman to family expenses, and the house was purchased on a mortgage, her contribution is, indirectly, referable to the acquisition of the house since, in one way or another, it enables the family to pay the mortgage instalments. Thus, a payment could be said to be referable to the acquisition of the house if, for example, the payer either (a) pays part of the purchase price or (b) contributes regularly to the mortgage instalments or (c) pays off part of the mortgage or (d) makes a substantial financial contribution to the family expenses so as to enable the mortgage instalments to be paid.

But if a payment cannot be said to be, in a real sense, referable to the acquisition of the house it is difficult to see how, in such a case as the present, it can base a claim for an interest in the house. Looking at the items which I have listed above, and leaving aside, for the present, the housekeeping which I will deal with separately, none of the items can be said to be referable to the acquisition of the house. The making of ordinary gifts between members of a family certainly is not. Nor, in the circumstances as found by the judge, are the payments of rates or of the telephone bills. The provision of the doorknobs etc is of very small consequence. As regards the purchase of chattels for domestic use, the plaintiff must, I think, have regarded at any rate some of these as her own property since she took them away with her when she left. But quite apart from that I do not think that the provision of chattels, by itself, is evidence of any common intention that the plaintiff should have a beneficial interest in the house ...

As regards work on the house, in 1971 a fairly substantial improvement was made to the house; the attic was converted into a bedroom with a bathroom en suite. That was paid for wholly by the defendant.

In 1977 or 1978, the plaintiff decorated the house throughout internally because she wished the house to be wallpapered and not painted. I do not think that carries her case any further. Thus in *Pettitt v Pettitt* [1970] AC 777 at 826, Lord Diplock said:

> If the husband likes to occupy his leisure by laying a new lawn in the garden or building a fitted wardrobe in the bedroom while the wife does the shopping, cooks the family dinner and bathes the children, I, for my part, find it quite impossible to impute to them as reasonable husband and wife any common intention that these domestic activities or any of them are to have any effect upon the existing proprietary rights in the family home ...

Accordingly, I think that the decoration undertaken by the plaintiff gives no indication of any such common intention as she must assert.

There remains the question of housekeeping and domestic duties. So far as housekeeping expenses are concerned, I do not doubt that (the house being bought in the man's name) if the woman goes out to work in order to provide money for the family expenses, as a result of which she spends her earnings on the housekeeping and the man is thus able to pay the mortgage instalments and other expenses out of his earnings, it can be inferred that there was a common intention that the woman should have no interest in the house – since she will have made an indirect financial contribution to the mortgage instalments. But that is not this case.

During the greater part of the period when the plaintiff and the defendant were living together she was not in employment or, if she was, she was not earning amounts of any consequence and provided no money towards the family expenses. Nor is it suggested that the defendant ever asked her to. He provided, and was always ready to provide, all the money that she wanted for housekeeping. The house was not bought in the contemplation that the plaintiff would, at some time, contribute to the cost of its acquisition. She worked to suit herself. And if towards the very end of the relationship she had money to spare she spent it entirely as she chose. It was in no sense 'joint' money. It was her own; she was not expected and was not asked to spend it on the household.

I think it would be quite unreal to say that, overall, she made a substantial financial contribution towards the family expenses. That is not in any way a criticism of her; it is simply the factual position.

But, one asks, can the fact that the plaintiff performed domestic duties in the house and looked after the children be taken into account? I think it is necessary to keep in mind the nature of the right which is being asserted. The court has no jurisdiction to make such order as it might think fair; the powers conferred by the Matrimonial Causes Act 1973 in relation to the property of married persons do not apply to unmarried couples. The house was bought by the defendant in his own name and, *prima facie*, he is the absolute beneficial owner. If the plaintiff, or anybody else, claims to take it from him, it must be proved the claimant has, by some process of law, acquired an interest in the house. What is asserted here is the creation of a trust arising by common intention of the parties. That common intention may be inferred where there has been a financial contribution, direct or indirect, to the acquisition of the house. But the mere fact that parties live together and do the ordinary domestic tasks is, in my view, no indication at all that they thereby intended to alter the existing property rights of either of them ...

Appeal dismissed.

May LJ: ... For present purposes I will assume that it is the man, although the same approach will be followed if it is taken in the name of the woman. Where a matrimonial or family home is bought in the man's name alone on mortgage by the mechanism of deposit and instalments, then if the woman pays or contributes to the initial deposit this points to a common intention that she should have some beneficial interest in the house. If thereafter she makes direct contributions to the instalments, then the case is a fortiori and her rightful share is likely to be greater. If the woman, having contributed to the deposit, but although not making direct contributions to the instalments, nevertheless uses her own money for other joint household expenses so as to enable the man the more easily to pay the mortgage instalments out of his money, then her position is the same. Where a woman has made no contribution to the initial deposit, but makes regular and substantial contributions to the mortgage instalments, it may still be reasonable to infer a common intention that she should share the beneficial interest from the outset or a fresh agreement after the original conveyance that she should acquire such a share. It is only when there is no evidence upon which a court can reasonably draw an inference about the extent of the share of the contributing woman, that it should fall back on the maxim 'equality is equity'. Finally, when the house is taken in the man's name alone, if the woman makes no 'real' or 'substantial' financial contribution towards either the purchase price, deposit or mortgage instalments by the means of which the family home was acquired, then she is not entitled to any share in the beneficial interest in that home even though over a very substantial number of years she may have worked just as hard as the man in maintaining the family in the sense of keeping the house, giving birth to and looking after and helping to bring up the children of the union.

On the facts of the instant case, which Waller LJ has outlined, I think that it is clear that the plaintiff falls into the last of the categories to which I have just referred and accordingly I too would dismiss this appeal.'

Waller LJ concurred.

In *Grant v Edwards*,[63] W made substantial indirect contributions to the mortgage by applying her earnings to the joint household expenses in addition to keeping house and bringing up the children. She was given a half share because her contributions were made in reliance on a common intention that she was to have an interest in the house and were referable to the acquisition of the property.

Grant v Edwards [1986] 1 Ch 638, CA

Sir Nicholas Browne-Wilkinson VC: I agree. In my judgment, there has been a tendency over the years to distort the principles as laid down in the speech of Lord Diplock in *Gissing v Gissing* [1971] AC 886 by concentrating on only part of his reasoning. For present purposes, his speech can be treated as falling into three sections: the first deals with the nature of the substantive right; the second with the proof of the existence of that right; the third with the quantification of that right.

1.The nature of the substantive right: [1971] AC 886, 905B–G

If the legal estate in the joint home is vested in only one of the parties ('the legal owner') the other party ('the claimant'), in order to establish a beneficial interest, has to establish a constructive trust by showing that it would be inequitable for the legal owner to claim sole beneficial ownership. This requires two matters to be demonstrated: (a) that there was a common intention that both should have a beneficial interest; (b) that the claimant has acted to his or her detriment on the basis of that common intention.

2.The proof of the common intention

(a) Direct evidence (p 905H). It is clear that mere agreement between the parties that both are to have beneficial interests is sufficient to prove the necessary common intention.

63 [1986] Ch 638. Lord Bridge seems to treat *Grant v Edwards* as a case of constructive trust when he cited it as an example where a constructive trust was imposed to give effect of the parties' common intention. Looking at the result of the case as decided by the Court of Appeal that the wife was to have a half share by reason of her substantial contribution and the payment of insurance money into a joint account which evidenced an intention of equal share, it may be argued indeed that it is a case of constructive trust. This is because had it been a case of resulting trust, the share will have to be quantified by reference to the contribution alone. (But see *Midland Bank plc v Cooke* [1995] 4 All ER 562.) However, it may be said that there is always a presumption of resulting trust when money is paid to joint account (see *Re Figgis* [1969] Ch 123). The Law Commission, on the other hand, cited *Grant v Edwards* as an example of proprietary estoppel (Law Commission, Family Law: Matrimonial Property, Law Com No 175, para 2.2(iv)).

Other passages in the speech point to the admissibility and relevance of other possible forms of direct evidence of such intention: see pp 907C and 908C.

(b) Inferred common intention (pp 906A–08D). Lord Diplock points out that, even where parties have not used express words to communicate their intention (and therefore there is no direct evidence), the court can infer from their actions an intention that they shall both have an interest in the house. This part of his speech concentrates on the types of evidence from which the courts are most often asked to infer such intention viz contributions (direct and indirect) to the deposit, the mortgage instalments or general housekeeping expenses. In this section of the speech, he analyses what types of expenditure are capable of constituting evidence of such common intention: he does not say that if the intention is proved in some other way such contributions are essential to establish the trust.

3.The quantification of the right (pp 908D–09)

Once it has been established that the parties had a common intention that both should have a beneficial interest and that the claimant has acted to his detriment, the question may still remain 'what is the extent of the claimant's beneficial interest?' This last section of Lord Diplock's speech shows that here again the direct and indirect contributions made by the parties to the cost of acquisition may be crucially important.

If this analysis is correct, contributions made by the claimant may be relevant for four different purposes, *viz*: (1) in the absence of direct evidence of intention, as evidence from which the parties' intentions can be inferred; (2) as corroboration of direct evidence of intention; (3) to show that the claimant has acted to his or her detriment in reliance on the common intention: Lord Diplock's speech does not deal directly with the nature of the detriment to be shown; (4) to quantify the extent of the beneficial interest.

I have sought to analyse Lord Diplock's speech for two reasons. First, it is clear that the necessary common intention can be proved otherwise than by reference to contributions by the claimant to the cost of acquisition. Secondly, the remarks of Lord Diplock as to the contributions made by the claimant must be read in their context.

In cases of this kind the first question must always be whether there is sufficient direct evidence of a common intention that both parties are to have a beneficial interest. Such direct evidence need have nothing to do with the contributions made to the cost of acquisition. Thus, in *Eves v Eves* [1975] 1 WLR 1338, the common intention was proved by the fact that the claimant was told that her name would have been on the title deeds but for her being under age. Again, in *Midland Bank plc v Dobson* (unreported), 12 July 1985; Court of Appeal (Civil Division) Transcript No 381 of 1985 this court held that the trial judge was entitled to find the necessary common intention from evidence which he accepted that the parties treated the house as 'our house' and had a 'principle of sharing everything.' Although, as was said in the latter case, the trial judge has to approach such direct evidence with caution, if he does accept such evidence the necessary common intention is proved. One would expect that in a number of cases the court would be able to decide on the direct evidence before it whether there was such a common intention. It is only necessary to have recourse to inferences from other circumstances (such as the way in which the parties contributed, directly or indirectly, to the cost of acquisition) in cases such as *Gissing v Gissing* [1971] AC 886 and *Burns v Burns* [1984] Ch 317 where there is no direct evidence of intention.

Applying those principles to the present case, the representation made by the defendant to the plaintiff that the house would have been in the joint names but for the plaintiff's matrimonial disputes is clear, direct evidence of a common intention that she was to have an interest in the house: *Eves v Eves* [1975] 1 WLR 1338. Such evidence was in my judgment sufficient by itself to establish the common intention: but in any event it is wholly consistent with the contributions made by the plaintiff to the joint household expenses and the fact that the surplus fire insurance moneys were put into a joint account.

But as Lord Diplock's speech in *Gissing v Gissing* [1971] AC 886, 905D and the decision in *Midland Bank plc v Dobson* (unreported) make clear, mere common intention by itself is not enough: the claimant has also to prove that she has acted to her detriment in the reasonable belief by so acting she was acquiring a beneficial interest.

There is little guidance in the authorities on constructive trusts as to what is necessary to prove that the claimant so acted to her detriment. What 'link' has to be shown between the common intention and the actions relied on? Does there have to be positive evidence that the claimant did the acts in conscious reliance on the common intention? Does the court have to be satisfied that she would not have done the acts relied on but for the common intention, eg would not the claimant have contributed to household expenses out of affection for the legal owner and as part of their joint life together even if she had no interest in the house? Do the acts relied on as a detriment have to be inherently referable to the house, eg contribution to the purchase or physical labour on the house?

I do not think it is necessary to express any concluded view on these questions in order to decide this case. *Eves v Eves* [1975] 1 WLR 1338 indicates that there has to be some 'link' between the common intention and the acts relied on as a detriment. In that case the acts relied on did inherently relate to the house (*viz* the work the claimant did to the house) and from this the Court of Appeal felt able to infer that the acts were done in reliance on the common intention. So, in this case, as the analysis of Nourse LJ makes clear, the plaintiff's contributions to the household expenses were essentially linked to the payment of the mortgage instalments by the defendant: without the plaintiff's contributions, the defendant's means were insufficient to keep up the mortgage payments. In my judgment where the claimant has made payments which, whether directly or indirectly, have been used to discharge the mortgage instalments, this is a sufficient link between the detriment suffered by the claimant and the common intention. The court can infer that she would not have made such payments were it not for her belief that she had an interest in the house. On this ground therefore I find that the plaintiff has acted to her detriment in reliance on the common intention that she had a beneficial interest in the house and accordingly that she has established such beneficial interest.

I suggest that in other cases of this kind, useful guidance may in the future be obtained from the principles underlying the law of proprietary estoppel which in my judgment are closely akin to those laid down in *Gissing v Gissing* [1971] AC 886. In both, the claimant must to the knowledge of the legal owner have acted in the belief that the claimant has or will obtain an interest in the property. In both, the claimant must have acted to his or her detriment in reliance on such belief. In both, equity acts on the conscience of the legal owner to prevent him from acting in an unconscionable manner by defeating the common intention. The two principles have been developed separately without cross-fertilisation between them: but they rest on the same foundation and have on all other matters reached the same conclusions.

In many cases of the present sort, it is impossible to say whether or not the claimant would have done the acts relied on as a detriment even if she thought she had no interest in the house. Setting up house together, having a baby, making payments to general housekeeping expenses (not strictly necessary to enable the mortgage to be paid) may all be referable to the mutual love and affection of the parties and not specifically referable to the claimant's belief that she has an interest in the house. As at present advised, once it has been shown that there was a common intention that the claimant should have an interest in the house, any act done by her to her detriment relating to the joint lives of the parties is, in my judgment, sufficient detriment to qualify. The acts do not have to be inherently referable to the house: see *Jones (AE) v Jones (FW)* [1977] 1 WLR 438 and *Pascoe v Turner* [1979] 1 WLR 431. The holding out to the claimant that she had a beneficial interest in the house is an act of such a nature as to be part of the inducement to her to do the acts relied on. Accordingly, in the absence of evidence to the contrary, the right inference is that the claimant acted in reliance on such holding out and the burden lies on the legal owner to show that she did not do so: see *Greasley v Cooke* [1980] 1 WLR 1306 ...

Appeal allowed.

Nourse LJ and Mustill LJ delivered concurring judgments.

It seems, therefore, that where the contributions are indirect, there must be an agreement or common intention that W is to have a beneficial interest, and the contributions are substantial and referable to the costs of acquisition, to give rise to a resulting trust in favour of the contributor.

Other indirect contributions may be in the form of physical work done for the improvement of the property. This is today very unlikely to found a resulting trust in the absence of an agreement or common intention formed at the time of the acquisition. In *Pettitt v Pettitt*,[64] W used her own money to purchase a cottage in her own name. H improved the garden and made some internal decorations. The House of Lords held that H had acquired no beneficial interest in the property.

Similarly, in *Lloyds Bank v Rosset*,[65] H purchased a semi-derelict farmhouse in his own name. W made no financial contributions to the purchase of it. She, however, carried out restoration work on the property relying on the alleged common intention that the property should be jointly owned. The House of Lords held that she had acquired no beneficial interest in the property because there was no express agreement that she should acquire a share in it. Since there was no contribution, no presumed resulting trust could arise. Restoration work was not sufficient to raise an inference of a common intention that the property should be jointly held. And since there was no common intention upon which W had allegedly acted to her detriment, no constructive trust could arise. This aspect of constructive trust will be discussed again later (see p 67 below).

---

64 [1970] AC 777.

65 [1991] 1 AC 107.

The position of married couples, however, is improved by s 37 of the Matrimonial Proceedings and Property Act 1970. Recognising the need to protect a spouse who makes indirect contribution, s 37 provides that where a spouse contributes in money (direct financial contribution) or money's worth (such as work done on the property) to the improvement of real or personal property in which either or both of them has or have a beneficial interest, the spouse so contributing shall, if the contribution is substantial, subject to express or implied agreement to the contrary, be entitled to a share in the beneficial interest. While the principles of resulting trust discussed above also apply to unmarried couples, s 37 only applies to married couples.

(iv) Voluntary conveyance

Before 1535 where land was conveyed in a voluntary conveyance[66] to the grantee without express use, there was a presumption of a resulting use to the grantor of the whole estate granted.[67] Thus, if A conveyed land 'to B and his heirs' without express use in a voluntary conveyance, B would hold the land on a resulting use for A. However, as mentioned above, the Statute of Uses 1535 executed uses including resulting uses. This meant that in the above example after 1535, the conveyance would be totally ineffective to give B any legal estate as there was no express use to B (such as 'unto and to the use of B'). A held the same estate as before.[68] However, the Statute of Uses 1535 did not execute a use upon a use which was later known as a trust. Thus, the express use in a voluntary conveyance, 'unto and to the use of B', would be executed so that B would have the legal estate. However, B would have to hold the legal estate on a resulting trust for A if the circumstances showed that B was not intended to take beneficially,[69] but in the absence of such evidence B would take for his own benefit.[70] The Statute of Uses 1535 was repealed in 1925 and uses can no longer be executed. It is unnecessary in a voluntary conveyance to use the expression 'unto and to the use of B' to convey the legal estate to him. It is sufficient simply to convey the legal estate 'to B'. Under the old equitable principle, a resulting trust would have arisen in favour of A. However, the Law of Property Act 1925, having repealed the Statute of Uses, went on to provide, under s 60(3), that a resulting use or trust should not be implied automatically simply because there is no express use for the grantee (B).

Law of Property Act 1925

60. Abolition of technicalities in regard to conveyances and deeds

(3) In a voluntary conveyance a resulting trust for the grantor shall not be implied merely by reason that the property is not expressed to be conveyed for the use or benefit of the grantee.

---

66 A transfer made otherwise than for valuable consideration or for good consideration where the transferee was a near relation of the transferor.

67 *Beckwith's* case (1589) 2 Co Rep 56b at 58a; *Armstrong d Neve v Wolsey* (1755) 2 Wils KB 19.

68 *Beckwith's* case; *Armstrong d Neve v Wolsey, ibid; Godbold v Freestone* (1694) 3 Lev 406 at 487.

69 *Duke of Norfolk v Browne* (1697) Prec Ch 80; *R v Williams* (1735) Bunb 342.

70 *Lloyd v Spillet* (1740) 2 Atk 148; *Young v Peachey* (1741) 2 Atk 254.

Thus, 'to B' in a voluntary conveyance would today *prima facie* convey the whole of the legal estate as well as the beneficial interest in the property to B. However, where there is evidence that B is not to take the property beneficially but to hold it as a trustee, there will still be a resulting trust in favour of A.[71]

Section 60(3) refers to 'property' and s 205(1)(xx) defines 'property' as including, unless the context otherwise requires, 'any thing in action, and any interest in real or personal property'. However, it would appear that in the context of s 60 'property' is confined to land. Thus, in the case of a voluntary transfer of a form of property other than land, there seems to be a presumption of resulting trust.[72]

(c) Constructive trusts

Cardozo J put it most elegantly that the constructive trust is:

> ... the formula through which the conscience of equity finds expression. When property has been acquired in such circumstances that the holder of the legal title may not in good conscience retain the beneficial interest, equity converts him into a trustee.[73]

There are many situations in which a constructive trust may be imposed. They could be broadly grouped into three categories.

(i) Breach of trust, knowing receipt, dealing and assistance

A trustee or a fiduciary (ie a person who holds a position of trust and confidence)[74] must not act in breach of trust, or his fiduciary duties.[75] Where the fiduciary acts in breach of his fiduciary duties, a constructive trust can be imposed on him so that he will be liable as a constructive trustee.[76] Any benefit

---

71 See, for example, *Hodgson v Marks* [1971] Ch 892.

72 Nathan, JA and Marshall, Sir Oshley Roy: *Cases and Commentary on the Law of Trusts*, 9th edn (by Hayton, DJ), 1991, London: Sweet & Maxwell, p 434; *Fowkes v Pascoe* (1875) 10 Ch App 343 at 348; *Re Howes* (1905) 21 TLR 501; *Vandervell v IRC* [1967] 2 AC 291, 312.

73 *Beatty v Guggenheim Exploration Co* (1919) 225 NY 380 at 386.

74 England cases do not offer a clear test as to how a person can be made a fiduciary. There exists, however, a core of well-established fiduciary relationships, eg company director-company, principal-agent, partner-co-partner, solicitor-client, employer-employee-with-confidential-information. The fiduciary duties owed in each type of fiduciary relationship may not be exactly the same depending on the bases for the relationship. Outside this core of relationships, the position is rather uncertain. Wilson J in the Supreme Court of Canada has in *Frame v Smith* (1987) 42 DLR (4th) 81 adopted a three-fold test in determining whether a fiduciary relationship exists: (1) the fiduciary has scope for the exercise of some discretion of power; (2) the fiduciary can unilaterally exercise that power or discretion so as to effect the beneficiary's legal or practical interest; and (3) the beneficiary is peculiarly vulnerable to or at the mercy of the fiduciary holding the discretion or power. This test has subsequently been approved by Canadian court in *LAC Minerals Ltd v International Corona Resources Ltd* (1989) 61 DLR (4th) 14; *Canson Enterprises Ltd v Boughton & Co* (1991) 85 DLR (4th) 129; and *Norberg v Wynrib* (1992) 92 DLR (4th) 449; and by the New Zealand Court of Appeal in *DHL International (NZ) Ltd v Richmond Ltd* [1993] 3 NZLR 10.

75 For example, he must not benefit from his position as a trustee: *Keech v Sanford* (1726) Sel Ca t King 61.

76 For example, a company director who receives unauthorised payment of remuneration will be held a constructive trustee of the payment received: *Guiness plc v Saunders* [1990] 2 AC 663, HL.

the trustee or fiduciary receives by reason of his position as a trustee or fiduciary must be held on trust for the beneficiary. The trustee or fiduciary may also be held personally liable for the loss suffered by the beneficiary as a result of the breach of trust or fiduciary duties.

Where the trustee or fiduciary transfers the legal estate in the trust property to a purchaser in breach of trust, the purchaser may have to hold the legal estate on constructive trust for the beneficiary, if he is not a purchaser of the legal estate for value without notice.[77] The beneficiary can trace the trust property against the purchaser. If the purchaser has dissipated the trust property so that the trust property is not now traceable, the beneficiary may of course hold the trustee or fiduciary personally liable for the beneficiary's loss. However, whether the purchaser can be made personally liable as a constructive trustee for once receiving the trust property does not depend on the old doctrine of notice. For the purchaser to be personally liable as constructive trustee, it is necessary to show that he had actual knowledge of the breach of trust or knowledge he would have had had he not wilfully shut his eyes to the obvious or failed to make inquiries.[78] The position was summarised by Sir Robert Megarry VC in *Re Montagu's Settlement Trusts*.[79]

Re Montagu's Settlement [1987] 2 WLR 1192

Sir Robert Megarry VC: ... I shall attempt to summarise my conclusions. In doing this, I make no attempt to reconcile all the authorities and *dicta*, for such a task is beyond me; and in this I suspect I am not alone. Some of the difficulty seems to arise from judgments that have been given without all the relevant authorities having been put before the judges. All I need do is to find a path through the wood that will suffice for the determination of the case before me, and to assist those who have to read this judgment.

(1) The equitable doctrine of tracing and the imposition of a constructive trust by reason of the knowing receipt of trust property are governed by different rules and must be kept distinct. Tracing is primarily a means of determining the rights of property, whereas the imposition of a constructive trust creates personal obligations that go beyond mere property rights.

(2) In considering whether a constructive trust has arisen in a case of the knowing receipt of trust property, the basic question is whether the conscience of the recipient is sufficiently affected to justify the imposition of such a trust.

(3) Whether a constructive trust arises in such a case primarily depends on the knowledge of the recipient, and not on notice to him; and for clarity it is desirable to use the word 'knowledge' and avoid the word 'notice' in such cases.

(4) For this purpose, knowledge is not confined to actual knowledge, but includes at least knowledge of types (ii) and (iii) in the *Baden* case,[80] ie actual knowledge

77 *Boursot v Savage* (1866) LR 2 Eq 134.

78 *Re Montagu's Settlement Trusts* [1987] 2 WLR 1192; *Polly Peck International plc v Nadir (No 2)* [1993] BCLC 187 at 209b.

79 *Re Montagu's Settlement Trusts* [1987] 2 WLR 1192 at 1204.

80 [1983] BCLC 325 at 407. (i) actual knowledge; (ii) wilfully shutting one's eyes to the obvious; (iii) wilfully and recklessly failing to make such inquiries as an honest and reasonable man would make; (iv) knowledge of circumstances which would indicate the facts to an honest and reasonable man; and (v) knowledge of circumstances which would put an honest and reasonable man on inquiry.

that would have been acquired but for shutting one's eyes to the obvious, or wilfully and recklessly failing to make such inquiries as a reasonable and honest man would make; for in such cases there is a want of probity which justifies imposing a constructive trust.

(5) Whether knowledge of the *Baden* types (iv) and (v) suffices for this purpose is at best doubtful; in my view, it does not, for I cannot see that the carelessness involved will normally amount to a want of probity.

(6) For these purposes, a person is not to be taken to have knowledge of a fact that he once knew but has genuinely forgotten; the test (or a test) is whether the knowledge continues to operate on that person's mind at the time in question.

(7) (a) It is at least doubtful whether there is a general doctrine of 'imputed knowledge' that corresponds to 'imputed notice.' (b) Even if there is such a doctrine, for the purposes of creating a constructive trust of the 'knowing receipt' type the doctrine will not apply so as to fix a donee or beneficiary with all the knowledge that his solicitor has, at all events if the donee or beneficiary has not employed the solicitor to investigate his right to the bounty, and has done nothing else that can be treated as accepting that the solicitor's knowledge should be treated as his own. (c) Any such doctrine should be distinguished from the process whereby, under the name 'imputed knowledge', a company is treated as having the knowledge that its directors and secretary have.

(8) Where an alleged constructive trust is based not on 'knowing receipt' but on 'knowing assistance', some at least of these considerations probably apply; but I need not decide anything on that, and I do not do so ...

The third party who is not an original trustee or fiduciary but who holds the trust property on behalf of the trustee may be liable as a constructive trustee if he deals with or assists the trustee or fiduciary in dealing with the property inconsistently with, or in breach of, the trust or fiduciary duties.[81] Even if the third party does not receive or hold the trust property, he may still be personally liable as a constructive trustee if he nevertheless knowingly and fraudulently[82] assists in the breach of trust or fiduciary duties.[83] For such a liability to arise, 'the stranger to the trust must be proved subjectively to know of the fraudulent[84] scheme of the trustee when rendering assistance, or to shut his eyes to the obvious, or to have wilfully and recklessly failed to make such enquiries as a reasonable and honest man would make'.[85] However, as Lord Nicholls points out recently in *Royal Brunei Airlines Sdn Bhd v Tan*,[86] it is not necessary to show that the breach of trust or fiduciary duties was fraudulent on the part of the trustee or fiduciary; it is sufficient to show that the third party was dishonest or fraudulent in assisting the breach. Here, Royal Brunei Airlines appointed Borneo Leisure Travel as its agent to sell passenger and cargo

81 *Soar v Ashwell* [1893] 2 QB 390.

82 *Royal Brunei Airlines Sdn Bhd v Tan* [1995] 3 All ER 97, PC.

83 *Karak Rubber Co Ltd v Burden* [1972] 1 All ER 1210; *Lipkin Gorman v Karpnale Ltd* [1987] 1 WLR 987.

84 'Fraudulent' must now be replaced in view of *Royal Brunei Airlines Sdn Bhd v Tan* [1995] 3 All ER 97, PC.

85 *Lipkin Gorman v Karpnale Ltd* [1987] 1 WLR 987 at 1006B, *per* Alliott J.

86 [1995] 2 AC 378; [1995] 3 All ER 97, PC.

transportation. BLT was required under the agreement to hold the moneys received from such sales on trust for the airline and to pay them to it within 30 days. BLT paid all such moneys into its current account for the conduct of its business. When BLT was insolvent later, the airline brought an action against BLT's managing director and principal shareholder, Tan Kok Ming, for unpaid money alleging that he was liable as a constructive trustee because he had knowingly assisted in a fraudulent and dishonest breach by BLT. The High Court of Brunei upheld the claim, but the Court of Appeal of Brunei allowed the appeal. The airline successfully appealed to the Privy Council.

Brunei Airlines Sdn Bhd v Tan [1995] 3 All ER 97, PC

Lord Nicholls of Birkenhead: The proper role of equity in commercial transactions is a topical question. Increasingly, plaintiffs have recourse to equity for an effective remedy when the person in default, typically a company, is insolvent. Plaintiffs seek to obtain relief from others who were involved in the transaction, such as directors of the company or its bankers or its legal or other advisers. They seek to fasten fiduciary obligations directly onto the company's officers or agents or advisers, or to have them held personally liable for assisting the company in breaches of trust or fiduciary obligations.

This is such a case. An insolvent travel agent company owed money to an airline. The airline seeks a remedy against the travel agent's principal director and shareholder. Its claim is based on the much-quoted *dictum* of Lord Selborne LC, sitting in the Court of Appeal in Chancery, in *Barnes v Addy* [1874] LR 9 Ch App 244 at 251–52:

> That responsibility [of a trustee] may no doubt be extended in equity to others who are not properly trustees, if they are found ... actually participating in any fraudulent conduct of the trustee to the injury of the *cestui que* trust. But ... strangers are not to be made constructive trustees merely because they act as the agents of trustees in transactions within their legal powers, transactions, perhaps of which a Court of Equity may disapprove, unless those agents receive and become chargeable with some part of the trust property, or unless they assist with knowledge in a dishonest and fraudulent design on the part of the trustees.

In the conventional shorthand, the first of these two circumstances in which third parties (non-trustees) may become liable to account in equity is 'knowing receipt', as distinct from the second where liability arises from 'knowing assistance'. Stated even more shortly, the first limb of Lord Selborne LC's formulation is concerned with the liability of a person as a *recipient* of trust property or its traceable proceeds. The second limb is concerned with what, for want of a better compendious description, can be called the liability of an *accessory* to a trustee's breach of trust. Liability as an accessory is not dependent upon receipt of trust property. It arises even though no trust property has reached the hands of the accessory. It is a form of secondary liability in the sense that it only arises where there has been a breach of trust. In the present case the plaintiff relies on the accessory limb. The particular point in issue arises from the expression 'a dishonest and fraudulent design on the part of the trustees.

[His Lordship read the facts, referred to the decisions of the trial judge and the Court of Appeal of Brunei and continued:]

Delivering the judgment of the [Court of Appeal of Brunei] Fuad P stated:

> As long-standing and high authority shows, conduct which may amount to a breach of trust, however morally reprehensible, will not render a person who has

knowingly assisted in the breach of trust liable as a constructive trustee, if that conduct falls short of dishonesty.

This view of the state of the law has the support of the English Court of Appeal. In *Selangor United Rubber Estates Ltd v Cradock (a bankrupt) (No 3)* [1968] 2 All ER 1073 at 1105; [1968] 1 WLR 1555 at 1591, Ungoed-Thomas J held that the expression 'dishonest and fraudulent design' was to be understood according to the principles of a court of equity. That approach was emphatically rejected by the Court of Appeal in *Belmont Finance Corp Ltd v Williams Furniture Ltd* [1979] 1 All ER 118 at 130; [1979] Ch 250 at 267, Buckley LJ observed that the rule as formulated by Lord Selborne LC had stood for more than 100 years, and that to depart from it would introduce an undesirable degree of uncertainty to the law over what degree of unethical conduct would suffice if dishonesty was not to be the criterion. Goff LJ agreed that it would be dangerous and wrong to depart from 'the safe path of the principle as stated by Lord Selborne' to the 'uncharted sea of something not innocent ... but still short of dishonesty' (see [1979] 1 All ER 118 at 135; [1979] Ch 250 at 274).

In short, the issue on this appeal is whether the breach of trust which is a prerequisite to accessory liability must itself be a dishonest and fraudulent breach of trust by the trustee.

The honest trustee and the dishonest third party

It must be noted at once that there is a difficulty with the approach adopted on this point in the *Belmont* case. Take the simple example of an honest trustee and a dishonest third party. Take a case where a dishonest solicitor persuades a trustee to apply trust property in a way the trustee honestly believes is permissible but which the solicitor knows full well is a clear breach of trust. The solicitor deliberately conceals this from the trustee. In consequence, the beneficiaries suffer a substantial loss. It cannot be right that in such a case the accessory liability principle would be inapplicable because of the innocence of the trustee. In ordinary parlance, the beneficiaries have been defrauded by the solicitor. If there is to be an accessory liability principle at all, whereby in appropriate circumstances beneficiaries may have direct recourse against a third party, the principle must surely be applicable in such a case, just as much as in a case where both the trustee and the third party have been dishonest. Indeed, if anything, the case for liability of the dishonest third party seems stronger where the trustee is innocent, because in such a case the third party alone was dishonest and that was the cause of the subsequent misapplication of the trust property.

The position would be the same if, instead of *procuring* the breach, the third party dishonestly *assisted* in the breach. Change the facts slightly. A trustee is proposing to make a payment out of the trust fund to a particular person. He honestly believes he is authorised to do so by the terms of the trust deed. He asks a solicitor to carry through the transaction. The solicitor well knows that the proposed payment would be a plain breach of trust. He also well knows that the trustee mistakenly believes otherwise. Dishonestly he leaves the trustee under his misapprehension and prepares the necessary documentation. Again, if the accessory principle is not to be artificially constricted, it ought to be applicable in such a case.

These examples suggest that what matters is the state of mind of the third party sought to be made liable, not the state of mind of the trustee. The trustee will be liable in any event for the breach of trust, even if he acted innocently, unless excused by an exemption clause in the trust instrument or relieved by the court. But *his* state of mind is essentially irrelevant to the question whether the *third party* should be made liable to the beneficiaries for the breach of trust. If the liability of the third party is fault-based, what matters is the nature of his fault, not that of the trustee. In this regard dishonesty on the part of the third party would seem to be a sufficient basis for his liability, irrespective of the state of mind of the trustee who is in breach of trust. It is difficult to see why, if the third party dishonestly assisted in a breach, there should be a further prerequisite to his liability, namely that the trustee also must have been acting dishonestly. The alternative view would mean that a dishonest third party is liable if the trustee is dishonest, but if the trustee did not act dishonestly that of itself would excuse a dishonest third party from liability. That would make no sense.

[His Lordship referred to earlier authorities, discussed the questions whether a third party should never be made liable for assisting a breach of trust or should be strictly liable, or whether his liability should be fault-based and concluded in favour of the third option and said that the predominant view was that it should be based on 'dishonesty', and continued:]

Dishonesty

Before considering this issue further it will be helpful to define the terms being used by looking more closely at what dishonesty means in this context. Whatever may be the position in some criminal or other contexts (see, for instance, *R v Ghosh*) [1982] 2 All ER 689; [1982] QB 1053, in the context of the accessory liability principle acting dishonestly, or with a lack of probity, which is synonymous, means simply not acting as an honest person would in the circumstances. This is an objective standard. At first sight this may seem surprising. Honesty has a connotation of subjectivity, as distinct from the objectivity of negligence. Honesty, indeed, does have a strong subjective element in that it is a description of a type of conduct assessed in the light of what a person actually knew at the time, as distinct from what a reasonable person would have known or appreciated. Further, honesty and its counterpart dishonesty are mostly concerned with advertent conduct, not inadvertent conduct. Carelessness is not dishonesty. Thus for the most part dishonesty is to be equated with conscious impropriety.

However, these subjective characteristics of honesty do not mean that individuals are free to set their own standards of honesty in particular circumstances. The standard of what constitutes honest conduct is not subjective Honesty is not an optional scale, with higher or lower values according to the moral standards of each individual. If a person knowingly appropriates another's property, he will not escape a finding of dishonesty simply because he sees nothing wrong in such behaviour.

In most situations there is little difficulty in identifying how an honest person would behave. Honest people do not intentionally deceive others to their detriment. Honest people do not knowingly take others' property. Unless there is a very good and compelling reason, an honest person does not participate in a transaction if he knows it involves a misapplication of trust assets to the detriment of the beneficiaries. Nor does an honest person in such a case deliberately close his eyes and ears, or deliberately not ask questions, lest he learn something he would rather not know, and then proceed regardless. However, in the situations now under consideration the position is not always so straightforward. This can best be illustrated by considering one particular area: the taking of risks.

Taking risks

All investment involves risk. Imprudence is not dishonesty, although imprudence may be carried recklessly to lengths which call into question the honesty of the person making the decision. This is especially so if the transaction serves another purpose in which that person has an interest of his own.

This type of risk is to be sharply distinguished from the case where a trustee, with or without the benefit of advice, is aware that a particular investment or application of trust property is outside his powers, but nevertheless he decides to proceed in the belief or hope that this will be beneficial to the beneficiaries or, at least, not prejudicial to them. He takes a risk that a clearly unauthorised transaction will not cause loss. A risk of this nature is for the account of those who take it. If the risk materialises and causes loss, those who knowingly took the risk will be accountable accordingly. This is the type of risk being addressed by Peter Gibson in *Baden's* case [1992] 4 All ER 161 at 234; [1993] 1 WLR 509 at 574, when he accepted that fraud includes taking 'a risk to the prejudice of another's rights, which risk is known to be one which there is no right to take' (quoting from the Court of Appeal judgment in *R v Sinclair* [1968] 2 All ER 246; [1968] 1 WLR 1246 at 1249).

This situation, in turn, is to be distinguished from the case where there is genuine doubt about whether a transaction is authorised or not. This may be because the trust instrument is worded obscurely, or because there are competing claims as in *Carl-Zeiss-Stiftung v Herbert Smith & Co (a firm) (No 2)* [1969] 2 All ER 367; [1969] 2 Ch 276, or for other reasons. The difficulty here is that frequently the situation is neither clearly white nor clearly black. The dividing edge between what is within the trustee's powers and what is not is often not clear cut. Instead there is a gradually darkening spectrum which can be described with labels such as clearly authorised, probably authorised, possibly authorised, wholly unclear, probably unauthorised and, finally, clearly unauthorised.

The difficulty here is that the differences are of degree rather than of kind. So far as the trustee himself is concerned the legal analysis is straightforward. Honesty or lack of honesty is not the test for his liability. He is obliged to comply with the terms of the trust. His liability is strict. If he departs from the trust terms he is liable unless excused by a provision in the trust instrument or relieved by the court. The analysis of the position of the accessory, such as the solicitor who carries through the transaction for him, does not lead to such a simple, clear cut answer in every case. He is required to act honestly, but what is required of an honest person in these circumstances? An honest person knows there is doubt. What does honesty require him to do?

The only answer to these questions lies in keeping in mind that honesty is an objective standard. The individual is expected to attain the standard which would be observed by an honest person placed in those circumstances. It is impossible to be more specific. Knox J captured the flavour of this, in a case with a commercial setting, when he referred to a person who is 'guilty of commercially unacceptable conduct in the particular context involved': see *Cowan de Groot Properties Ltd v Eagle Trust plc* [1992] 4 All ER 700 at 761. Acting in reckless disregard of others' rights or possible rights can be a tell-tale sign of dishonesty. An honest person would have regard to the circumstances known to him, including the nature and importance of the proposed transaction, the nature and importance of his role, the ordinary course of business, the degree of doubt, the practicability of the trustee or the third party proceeding otherwise and the seriousness of the adverse consequences to the beneficiaries. The circumstances will dictate which one or more of the possible courses should be taken by an honest person. He might, for instance, flatly decline to become involved. He might ask further questions. He might seek advice, or insist on further advice being obtained. He might advise the trustee of the risks but then proceed with his role in the transaction. He might do many things. Ultimately, in most cases, an honest person should have little difficulty in knowing whether a proposed transaction, or his participation in it, would offend the normally accepted standards of honest conduct.

Likewise, when called upon to decide whether a person was acting honestly, a court will look at all the circumstances known to the third party at the time. The court will also have regard to personal attributes of the third party such as his experience and intelligence, and the reason why he acted as he did.

Before leaving cases where there is real doubt, one further point should be noted. To inquire, in such cases, whether a person dishonestly assisted in what is later held to be a breach of trust is to ask a meaningful question, which is capable of being given a meaningful answer. This is not always so if the question is posed in terms of 'knowingly' assisted. Framing the question in the latter form all too often leads one into tortuous convolutions about the 'sort' of knowledge required, when the truth is that 'knowingly' is inapt as a criterion when applied to the gradually darkening spectrum where the differences are of degree and not kind.

[His Lordship thought that as a general proposition, beneficiaries cannot reasonably expect that all the world dealing with their trustees should owe them a duty to take care lest the trustees are behaving dishonestly. He also rejected 'unconscionable conduct' as the basis for liability in assisting a breach of trust.]

The accessory liability principle

Drawing the threads together, their Lordships' overall conclusion is that dishonesty is a necessary ingredient of accessory liability. It is also a sufficient ingredient. A liability in equity to make good resulting loss attaches to a person who dishonestly procures or assists in a breach of trust or fiduciary obligation. It is not necessary that, in addition, the trustee or fiduciary was acting dishonestly although this will usually be so where the third party who is assisting him is acting dishonestly. 'Knowingly' is better avoided as a defining ingredient of the principle, and in the context of this principle the *Baden* scale of knowledge is best forgotten...'

The decision of the Privy Council has been welcomed by academics.[87] It is interesting to note, however, that Lord Nicholls has suggested that '"Knowingly" is best avoided as a defining ingredient of the principle, and in the context of this principle the *Baden* scale of knowledge is best forgotten'. With respect, it appears that knowledge is still a necessary ingredient under the 'dishonesty' principle; while it is no longer necessary to show knowledge of a dishonest design on the part of the trustee, it is still necessary to show that the stranger assists dishonestly with knowledge of the breach (whether dishonest or innocent) of trust. Indeed, in explaining what amounts to 'dishonesty' in this

87 See (1995) Conv 339 (Halliwell, M); [1995] (111) LQR 545 (Harpum, C).

context, Lord Nicolls himself said that 'unless there is a very good and compelling reason, an honest person does not participate in a transaction if he knows it involves a misapplication of trust assets to the detriment of the beneficiaries. Nor does an honest person in such a case deliberately close his eyes and ears, or deliberately not ask questions, lest he learn something he would rather not know, and then proceed regardless'.[88] This seems to suggests knowledge of *Baden* types (i)–(iii) would still be relevant in determining whether the stranger is dishonest in assisting a breach of trust. Secondly, Lord Nicholls suggests that dishonesty is an objective standard.[89] It is submitted that, as Lord Nicholls's subsequent explanation makes it clear, the test is in fact a quasi-subject-objective test. It is not a subjective standard because individuals are not free to set their own standards of honesty; 'honesty is not an optional scale, with higher or lower values according to the moral standards of each individual. If a person knowingly appropriates another's property, he will not escape a finding of dishonesty simply because he sees nothing wrong in such behaviour'.[90] Instead, 'the individual is expected to attain the standard which would be observed by an honest person placed in those circumstances';[91] thus, in this respect the test is objective. On the other hand, the test is not entirely objective because 'when called upon to decide whether a person was acting honestly, a court will look at all the circumstances known to the third party at the time. The court will also have regard to personal attributes of the third party such as his experience and intelligence, and the reason why he acted as he did'.[92]

(ii) Vendor as qualified constructive trustee

It is well settled that a vendor, after the exchange of contracts but before the completion,[93] is in a position akin to that of a constructive trustee towards the purchaser.[94] The vendor is often called a qualified constructive trustee. This means the vendor has to exercise a duty of care in managing and maintaining the property prior to completion and he must not convey the property in breach of contract to a third party. In *Lake v Bayliss*,[95] V contracted to sell land to P in

88 *Royal Brunei Airlines Sdn Bhd v Tan* [1995] 3 All ER 97 at 106d.

89 *Ibid* at 105j.

90 *Ibid* at 106b–c.

91 *Ibid* at 107c.

92 *Ibid* at 107g.

93 See Chapter 4 below. What is required is a specifically enforceable contract between the vendor and the purchaser for the sale of the property to give rise to this type of qualified constructive trust. This means that the contract must, if made prior to 27 September 1989, satisfy the requirement of s 40 of the LPA 1925 (ie the contract is evidenced by writing or sufficient act of part performance). If the contract is made on or after 27 September 1989, it must be in writing containing all the terms of the agreement and signed by both parties under s 2 of the LP(MP) Act 1989.

94 *Lysaght v Edwards* (1876) 2 Ch D 499 at 506.

95 [1974] 2 All ER 1114.

consideration of a withdrawal of writs. In breach of the contract V subsequently conveyed the land to P2. P's contract was capable of registration as a Class C(iv) land charge which would bind any subsequent transferee from V.[96] As P did not register his contract, P2 took free of his interest. It was held that V was accountable as a constructive trustee to P for the net proceeds of sale he received from P2 subject to P's fulfilling his obligations under the contract.

(iii) Fraudulent, unconscionable or inequitable conduct

This is perhaps the most important class for land law students seeking to find out the beneficial interest in the property conveyed. Disputes relating to the beneficial entitlement in matrimonial property normally arise where the property is transferred to the sole name of a partner (A) and later the other partner (B) who has not contributed financially to the purchase seeks to claim a beneficial interest in the property. As mentioned above, it is a common practice to stipulate in clear terms the beneficial interests in the conveyance and such a stipulation is normally conclusive. There are, however, circumstances where this has not been done. If B is unable to show any contribution sufficient to justify a resulting trust under the principles discussed above, B's claim will depend on the principles of constructive trusts. Where A seeks to benefit from his fraudulent, unconscionable or inequitable conduct or transaction against B, he may be required to hold the property on a constructive trust for B.

The underlying principle could be seen in the much cited classic statement of Lord Diplock in *Gissing v Gissing*.

> A resulting, implied or constructive trust – and it is unnecessary for present purposes to distinguish between these three classes of trust – is created by a transaction between the trustee and the *cestui que* trust in connection with the acquisition by the trustee of a legal estate in the land, *whenever the trustee has so conducted himself that it would be inequitable to allow him to deny to the* cestui que *trust a beneficial interest in the land acquired. And he will be held so to have conducted himself if by his words or conduct he has induced the* cestui que *trust to act to his own detriment in the reasonable belief that by so acting he was acquiring a beneficial interest in the land.*[97]

Although Lord Diplock was clearly speaking of implied trusts generally, the statement has come to be applied more often in the area of constructive trusts. From the statement, it appears that the imposition of a constructive trust depends on three fundamental elements: (1) words or conduct giving rise to a common belief that B is to have a beneficial interest; (2) reliance by B to his own detriment; and (3) it would be inequitable for A to deny B a beneficial interest. It would also appear that the elements of a constructive trust thus stated are remarkably similar to those of proprietary estoppel.[98] Indeed, Browne-Wilkinson VC (as he then was) has said that 'The two principles have been developed separately without cross-fertilization between them: but they

96 See Chapter 6, p 224.

97 [1971] AC 886 at 905B–C (italics added).

98 See Chapter 3, below.

rest on the same foundation and have on all other matters reached the same conclusions'.[99]

(1) Agreement or common intention

The common intention that B is to have a beneficial interest in the property conveyed to A must be proved by some express agreement or be inferred from the conduct of the parties.

Lloyds Bank plc v Rosset [1991] 1 AC 107, HL

Lord Bridge of Harwich: It is clear from these passages in the judgment that the judge based his inference of a common intention that Mrs Rosset should have a beneficial interest in the property under a constructive trust essentially on what Mrs Rosset did in and about assisting in the renovation of the property between the beginning of November 1982 and the date of completion on 17 December 1982. Yet by itself this activity, it seems to me, could not possibly justify any such inference. It was common ground that Mrs Rosset was extremely anxious that the new matrimonial home should be ready for occupation before Christmas if possible. In these circumstances, it would seem the most natural thing in the world for any wife, in the absence of her husband abroad, to spend all the time she could spare and to employ any skills she might have, such as the ability to decorate a room, in doing all she could to accelerate progress of the work quite irrespective of any expectation she might have of enjoying a beneficial interest in the property. The judge's view that some of this was work 'upon which she could not reasonably have been expected to embark unless she was to have an interest in the house' seems to me, with respect, quite untenable. The impression that the judge may have thought that the share of the equity to which he held Mrs Rosset to be entitled had been 'earned' by her work in connection with the renovation is emphasised by his reference in the concluding sentence of his judgment to the extent to which her 'qualifying contribution' reduced the cost of the renovation.

On any view the monetary value of Mrs Rosset's work expressed as a contribution to a property acquired at a cost exceeding £70,000 must have been so trifling as to be almost *de minimis*. I should myself have had considerable doubt whether Mrs Rosset's contribution to the work of renovation was sufficient to support a claim to a constructive trust in the absence of writing to satisfy the requirements of s 51 of the Law of Property Act 1925 even if her husband's intention to make a gift to her of half or any other share in the equity of the property had been clearly established or if he had clearly represented to her that that was what he intended. But here the conversations with her husband on which Mrs Rosset relied, all of which took place before November 1982, were incapable of lending support to the conclusion of a constructive trust in the light of the judge's finding that by that date there had been no decision that she was to have any interest in the property. The finding that the discussions 'did not exclude the possibility' that she should have an interest does not seem to me to add anything of significance.

These considerations lead me to the conclusion that the judge's finding that Mr Rosset held the property as constructive trustee for himself and his wife cannot be supported and it is on this short ground that I would allow the appeal. In the course of the argument your Lordships had the benefit of elaborate submissions as to the test to be

99 *Grant v Edwards* [1986] Ch 638 at 656H.

applied to determine the circumstances in which the sole legal proprietor of a dwelling house can properly be held to have become a constructive trustee of a share in the beneficial interest in the house for the benefit of the partner with whom he or she has cohabited in the house as their shared home. Having in this case reached a conclusion on the facts which, although at variance with the views of the courts below, does not seem to depend on any nice legal distinction and with which, I understand, all your Lordships agree, I cannot help doubting whether it would contribute anything to the illumination of the law if I were to attempt an elaborate and exhaustive analysis of the relevant law to add to the many already to be found in the authorities to which our attention was directed in the course of the argument. I do, however, draw attention to one critical distinction which any judge required to resolve a dispute between former partners as to the beneficial interest in the home they formerly shared should always have in the forefront of his mind.

The first and fundamental question which must always be resolved is whether, independently of any inference to be drawn from the conduct of the parties in the course of sharing the house as their home and managing their joint affairs, there has at any time prior to acquisition, or exceptionally at some later date, been any agreement, arrangement or understanding reached between them that the property is to be shared beneficially. The finding of an agreement or arrangement to share in this sense can only, I think, be based on evidence of express discussions between the partners, however imperfectly remembered and however imprecise their terms may have been. Once a finding to this effect is made, it will only be necessary for the partner asserting a claim to a beneficial interest against the partner entitled to the legal estate to show that he or she has acted to his or her detriment or significantly altered his or her position in reliance on the agreement in order to give rise to a constructive trust or a proprietary estoppel.

In sharp contrast with this situation is the very different one where there is no evidence to support a finding of an agreement or arrangement to share, however reasonable it might have been for the parties to reach such an arrangement if they had applied their minds to the question, and where the court must rely entirely on the conduct of the parties both as the basis from which to infer a common intention to share the property beneficially and as the conduct relied on to give rise to a constructive trust. In this situation direct contributions to the purchase price by the partner who is not the legal owner, whether initially or by payment of mortgage instalments, will readily justify the inference necessary to the creation of a constructive trust. But, as I read the authorities, it is at least extremely doubtful whether anything less will do.

The leading cases in your Lordships' House are *Pettitt v Pettitt* [1970] AC 777 and *Gissing v Gissing* [1971] AC 886. Both demonstrate situations in the second category to which I have referred and their Lordships discuss at great length the difficulties to which these situations give rise. The effect of these two decisions is very helpfully analysed in the judgment of Lord MacDermott LCJ in *McFarlane v McFarlane* [1972] NI 59.

Outstanding examples, on the other hand, of cases giving rise to situations in the first category are *Eves v Eves* [1975] 1 WLR 1338 and *Grant v Edwards* [1986] Ch 638. In both these cases, where the parties who had cohabited were unmarried, the female partner had been clearly led by the male partner to believe, when they set up home together, that the property would belong to them jointly. In *Eves v Eves*, the male partner had told the female partner that the only reason why the property was to be acquired in his name alone was because she was under 21 and that, but for her age, he would have had the house put into their joint names. He admitted in evidence that this was simply an 'excuse'. Similarly, in *Grant v Edwards* the female partner was told by the male partner that the only reason for not acquiring the property in joint names was because she was involved in divorce proceedings and that, if the property were acquired jointly, this might operate to her prejudice in those proceedings. As Nourse LJ put it, at 649:

> Just as in *Eves v Eves* [1975] 1 WLR 1338, these facts appear to me to raise a clear inference that there was an understanding between the plaintiff and the defendant, or a common intention, that the plaintiff was to have some sort of proprietary interest in the house; otherwise no excuse for not putting her name on to the title would have been needed.

The subsequent conduct of the female partner in each of these cases, which the court rightly held sufficient to give rise to a constructive trust or proprietary estoppel supporting her claim to an interest in the property, fell far short of such conduct as would by itself have supported the claim in the absence of an express representation by the male partner that she was to have such an interest. It is significant to note that the share to which the female partners in *Eves v Eves* and *Grant v Edwards* were held entitled were one quarter and one half respectively. In no sense could these shares have been regarded as proportionate to what the judge in the instant case described as a 'qualifying contribution' in terms of the indirect contributions to the acquisition or enhancement of the value of the houses made by the female partners.

I cannot help thinking that the judge in the instant case would not have fallen into error if he had kept clearly in mind the distinction between the effect of evidence on the one hand which was capable of establishing an express agreement or an express representation that Mrs Rosset was to have an interest in the property and evidence on the other hand of conduct alone as a basis for an inference of the necessary common intention.

Appeal allowed.

Lords Griffiths, Ackner, Oliver of Aylmerton and Jauncey of Tullichettle all concurred.

As we have seen from Lord Bridge's statement quoted above, the finding of an agreement or an arrangement to share can only be based on evidence of express discussion between the partners, however imperfectly remembered and however imprecise the terms may have been.[100] Excuses by a man in both *Eves v Eves*[101] (that the woman was under 21) and *Grant v Edwards*[102] (that the matrimonial proceedings between her and her husband would be prejudiced if her name was on the title) were thought sufficient to raise an inference of a common understanding that the claimant should have a proprietary interest. It should be noted, however, that the agreement or common intention may be formed *either at the time of the acquisition or after it* so long as it has been acted upon to the claimant's detriment. This is perhaps the root of the confusion in the

100 From Lord Bridge's judgment, it also appears that the agreement need not be a specifically enforceable one. It does not have to comply with the requirement of writing under s 40 of the LPA 1925 or s 2 of the LP(MP) Act 1989.

101 [1975] 1 WLR 1338. Lord Denning expressly called this a case of constructive trust when he decided it. But he was later in *Hall v Hall* [1982] 3 FLR 379, CA to refer to it as a case of resulting trust.

102 [1986] Ch 638.

use of terminology. Where the agreement is formed at the time of the acquisition, as stated above, it is more common to describe the trust as a resulting trust, particularly where the contribution is also made at the time of the acquisition. But as a constructive trust is imposed whenever the trustee has by his words or conduct induced the beneficiary to act to his detriment, it matters not whether such words or conduct took place at the time of or after the acquisition. It would therefore seem plausible to describe a trust based on an agreement or common intention formed at the time of acquisition as a constructive trust. Some of the cases confusingly referred to either as resulting trusts or constructive trusts are *Grant v Edwards*[103] *Burns v Burns*,[104] and *Cooke v Head*.[105]

Where, however, the agreement was formed after the acquisition of the trust property, only a constructive trust may arise; a resulting trust can arise only if the presumed intention had been present at the date of the acquisition.

Where there is no agreement or common intention, Lord Bridge thought that only direct contribution to the purchase price will readily justify the inference necessary to the creation of a constructive trust.[106] An interesting example of this approach may be the case of *Hussey v Palmer*,[107] where Lord Denning said that a constructive trust is a trust imposed by law whenever justice and good conscience require it. Thus, an elderly widow who had spent money in building an extension to a house already owned by A was allowed an interest proportionate to the value of her contributions in the extension under a constructive trust.[108] It would also seem that, as *Gissing v Gissing* shows, mere detrimental conduct by one party which is not referable to the acquisition of property will not be enough to give rise to an inference of a common intention upon which a constructive trust can be found (neither could such conduct in itself be enough to find a resulting trust as discussed above). Thus, for example, in *Ivin v Blake*,[109] where a daughter had by her own work in a public house run by her mother contributed to the profits derived from the business which was used in buying a house, her claim for a beneficial interest failed. On the facts,

103 [1986] Ch 638. In *Lloyds Bank v Rosset* [1991] 1 AC 107 Lord Bridge thought this case was an example where a constructive trust was imposed to give effect of the parties' common intention.

104 See Pettit, *Equity and the Law of Trust*, 6th edn, p 133 where he suggests that in *Grant v Edwards, Burns v Burns* was treated as a constructive trust.

105 [1972] 2 All ER 38, CA (it was not made clear by the Court of Appeal whether this was a resulting trust or constructive trust). In *Re Densham* [1975] 3 All ER 726, Goff J seemed to treat it as a resulting trust for he said that this decision laid down the principle to be applied in assessing the share in cases of indirect contribution. In *Hall v Hall* [1982] 3 FLR 379, CA, Lord Denning also referred to it as a resulting trust. But Glass JA in *Allen v Snyder* [1977] 2 NSWLR 685 in another jurisdiction treated it as a constructive trust.

106 Lord Bridge seems to have confused constructive trust with resulting trust because where there is direct contribution there will normally be a resulting trust.

107 [1972] 1 WLR 1286. See (1973) 37 Conv 65 (D J Hayton); (1973) 89 LQR 2; (1973) 32 CLJ 41 (P B Fairest); (1973) 36 MLR 426 (T C Ridley); (1973) 26 CLP 17 (A J Oakley).

108 Phillimore LJ however thought that it was a case of resulting trust (at 1291G).

109 [1995] 1 FLR 70; [1996] Conv 462 (Anna Lawson).

the judge found that her contribution was not substantial. The Court of Appeal held that even if it had been substantial, it was indirect financial contribution and in the absence of an express agreement for a beneficial interest would not be sufficient.[110]

An agreement between A and B that B should retain a beneficial interest in the land to be conveyed to A if acted upon by B to his detriment can also give rise to a constructive trust in B's favour. A good example is the case of *Bannister v Bannister*[111] where two cottages were conveyed by an elderly lady to the plaintiff on the oral agreement that she could continue to live in one of them rent-free for as long as she wished. A constructive trust was imposed on the plaintiff even though the agreement was oral and was not contained in the conveyance. The plaintiff could not use the statute as an instrument of fraud.

The principle in *Bannister v Bannister* can be applied even in cases where the agreement that B should retain a beneficial interest in the property to be conveyed was not made between A and B but between A and X who held the legal estate. A can further be prevented from relying on B's failure to protect his interest under the provisions of the Land Registration Act 1925. Thus, in *Lyus v Prowsa Developments Ltd,*[112] a case which will be discussed again in the context of registered land, a constructive trust was imposed where the agreement between the vendor and the purchaser was that a third party should retain an estate contract in the property even after the transfer of it to the purchaser, ie where the purchaser agreed with the vendor to take the property subject to an estate contract in favour of the third party.

A may also be held a constructive trustee even if he has not himself agreed to give B a beneficial interest, if at the date of the conveyance, A had either actual or deemed knowledge of a trust, because it will be unconscionable for him to deny the existence of the trust. In *Peffer v Rigg*[113] a house with registered title was held on trust by X for himself and B in equal shares. B did not protect his beneficial half-share by the entry of a minor interest on the register of X's title. X later purported to transfer the property to his ex-wife A who was fully aware of the existence of the trust. The court held that A took the title on a constructive trust for B. This case appears inconsistent with ss 20 and 59 of the Land Registration Act 1925 because, as Lord Wilberforce put it, 'the law as to notice as it might affect purchasers of unregistered land, whether in decided cases or in a statute, has no application, even by analogy, to registered land'.[114] Perhaps *Peffer v Rigg* was not just an application of the doctrine of notice. It was rather a case of constructive trust against unconscionable conduct. Equity would not allow a statute (in this case ss 20 and 59) to be used as an instrument of fraud.

110 [1995] 1 FLR 70 at 83F.

111 [1948] 2 All ER 133.

112 [1982] 1 WLR 1044.

113 [1977] 1 WLR 285.

114 *Williams & Glyn's Bank v Boland* [1981] AC 487 at 504. *Peffer v Rigg* [1977] 1 WLR 285 was, however, not cited.

(2) Detrimental reliance

This can take the form of financial contributions. Normally, payments made by B contemporaneously with A's acquisition give rise to a resulting trust. However, if there is an agreement at the outset that the beneficial ownership should be in proportion different from the share of financial contribution, or if the financial contributions are made as a result of an agreement subsequent to the purchase, a constructive trust may arise.

Detriment can also take the form of payments or personal labour for the improvement of the trust property. In *Eves v Eves* and *Grant v Edwards,* the woman's extensive decorative work and heavy gardening were held to be sufficiently detrimental.

The detriment must, however, be referable to the agreement or common intention. That is, there must be a detrimental reliance. In *Gissing v Gissing,* the wife's indirect financial contributions toward general household expenditure were also insufficient for a constructive trust to arise because she could not show that these contributions were made in reliance on a common intention that she should be rewarded with a beneficial share in the home.

In *Grant v Edwards,* the Court of Appeal took a more liberal stand on the question of referability. It was sufficient that without the woman's contributions, the man's means would have been insufficient to keep up the mortgage payments. The court could infer that the woman would not have made such contributions were it not for her belief that she had an interest in the house.

Where the agreement was made after the acquisition of the property, although Lord Denning has allowed a constructive trust to be imposed in the case of *Hussey v Palmer,* it is often more difficult to show that the detrimental reliance is referable to the acquisition of the property, because the property had already been bought and paid for in full. The detrimental reliance cannot in itself raise a common intention that B is to have a beneficial interest. In this situation, there has to be a clear express agreement that B will be given a beneficial interest if he makes some contribution and B did so in reliance on such agreement.[115]

Winkworth v Edward Baron Development Co Ltd [1986] 1 WLR 1512, HL

Lord Templeman: ... It is now contended on behalf of Mrs Wing that the payment of £8,600.91 into the company's bank account in November 1980 obtained for Mrs Wing an equitable interest in Hayes Lane in the proportion that £8,600.91 bears to £70,000, and that her equitable interest takes priority over the claims of the company's creditors, secured and unsecured. This bold and astonishing proposition would enable Mrs Wing to continue in occupation of Hayes Lane, without any contribution to its expenses, until a court, on the application by the company under s 30 of the Law of Property Act 1925, [(repealed), now see s 14 of the Trusts of Land and Appointment of Trustees Act 1996]

115 *Winkworth v Edward Baron Development* [1986] 1 WLR 1512, HL.

thought fit to order Hayes Lane to be sold with vacant possession for the benefit of the company and Mrs Wing as tenants in common in equity ...

The argument on behalf of Mrs Wing exploits the equitable doctrine that a legal owner holds in trust for the persons who contribute to the purchase price of the property or make contributions referable to the acquisition of the property. The doctrine was discussed in *Burns v Burns* [1984] Ch 317, and other authorities mentioned in the judgment of Nourse LJ in the present case. The sum of £8,600.91, paid into the company's bank account from the proceeds of sale of The Drive belonging to Mr and Mrs Wing, reduced the company's overdraft which was secured by the solicitors' undertaking to hold the title deeds of Hayes Lane to the order of the bank. Therefore, it is said, the payment of £8,600.91 was referable to the acquisition of Hayes Lane by the company, and equity requires the company to hold Hayes Lane in trust for the company and Mr and Mrs Wing or one of them. The simple answer to this tortuous argument is that the payment of £8,600.91 was not referable to the acquisition of Hayes Lane which had already been bought and paid for in full. There was no connection between the payment for Hayes Lane and the incurring of the overdraft. There was no connection between the acquisition of Hayes Lane and the payment of £8,600.91. The proper inference to be drawn from the admitted facts is that Hayes Lane, acquired by the company, and the sum of £8,600.91 paid into the company's bank account, became assets of the company, managed by Mr Wing for the benefit of himself and Mrs Wing, as sole and equal shareholders and not as owners of equitable interests ...

Appeal allowed.

Lords Keith of Kinkel, Griffiths, Mackay of Clashfern and Ackner all concurred.

(3) Inequity

Having established a common intention and detrimental reliance, B must also show that it is inequitable for A to deny him a beneficial interest in the property. The court must be satisfied that the conscience of A is affected. A must have 'so conducted himself that it would be inequitable to allow him to deny to the *cestui que* trust a beneficial interest in the land acquired'.[116] However, once an agreement or common intention can be shown and has been relied on to B's detriment, it will often be inequitable for A to deny B a beneficial interest in the property. The inequity or unconscionability lies in A's denial or attempted denial of B's beneficial interest.

Quantification of beneficial interest

Once a claimant has established a beneficial interest, it is necessary to ascertain the size of that interest. Where the interest is acquired under an express trust, the trust instrument will normally have stipulated the size of the shares. However, with the beneficial interest acquired under a resulting or constructive trust, it is more problematic. The size of the interest under a resulting trust depends normally on the size of the contribution, in the absence of a contrary intention. However, it has been held by the Court of Appeal in *Midland Bank plc v Cooke*,[117] that the court is not bound to deal with the matter on the strict basis

116 *Gissing v Gissing* [1971] AC 886 at 905C, *per* Lord Diplock.

117 [1995] 4 All ER 562; [1997] Conv 66 (Martin Dixon).

of the trust resulting from the contribution to the purchase price, and is free to attribute to the parties an intention to share the beneficial interest in some different proportions. In assessing the size of their shares, the court is entitled to undertake a survey of the whole course of dealing between the parties relevant to their ownership and occupation of the property and their sharing of its burdens and advantages, could take into account all conduct which shed light on the question of what shares were intended. The fact that the parties had neither discussed nor intended any agreement as to the proportions of their beneficial interest did not preclude the court from inferring one on general equitable principles.

Midland Bank plc v Cooke [1995] 4 All ER 562

Waite LJ: Guidance out of this difficulty is to be found, fortunately, in the passage in the speech of Lord Diplock in *Gissing v Gissing* [1970] 2 All ER 780 at 792–93, [1971] AC 886 at 908–09, where he is dealing with the approach to be adopted by the court when evaluating the proportionate shares of the parties, once it has been duly established through the direct contributions of the party without legal tide, that some beneficial interest was intended for both. He said:

> Where in any of the circumstances described above contributions, direct or indirect, have been made to the mortgage instalments by the spouse into whose name the matrimonial home has not been conveyed, and the court can infer from their conduct a common intention that the contributing spouse should be entitled to some beneficial interest in the matrimonial home, what effect is to be given to that intention if there is no evidence that they in fact reached any express agreement as to what the respective share of each spouse should bet I take it to be clear that if the court is satisfied that it was the common intention of both spouses that the contributing wife should have a share in the beneficial interest and that her contributions were made on this understanding, the court in the exercise of its equitable jurisdiction would not permit the husband in whom the legal estate was vested and who had accepted the benefit of the contributions to take the whole beneficial interest merely because at the time the wife made her contributions there had been no express agreement as to how her share in it was to be quantified. In such a case, the court must first do its best to discover from the conduct of the spouses whether any inference can reasonably be drawn as to the probable common understanding about the amount of the share of the contributing spouse on which each must have acted in doing what each did, even though that understanding was never expressly stated by one spouse to the other or even consciously formulated in words by either of them independently. It is only if no such inference can be drawn that the court is driven to apply as a rule of law, and not as an inference of fact, the maxim 'equality is equity', and to hold that the beneficial interest belongs to the spouses in equal shares. The same result however may often be reached as an inference of fact. The instalments of a mortgage to a building society are generally repayable over a period of many years. During that period, as both must be aware, the ability of each spouse to contribute to the instalments out of their separate earnings is likely to alter, particularly in the case of the wife if any children are born of the marriage. If the contribution of the wife in the early part of the period of repayment is substantial but is not an identifiable and uniform proportion of each instalment, because her contributions are indirect or, if direct, are made irregularly, it may well be a reasonable inference that their common intention at the time of acquisition of the

> matrimonial home was that the beneficial interest should be held by them in equal shares and that each should contribute to the cost of its acquisition whatever amounts each could afford in the varying exigencies of family life to be expected during the period of repayment. In the social conditions of today, this would be a natural enough common intention of a young couple who were both earning when the house was acquired but who contemplated having children whose birth and rearing in their infancy would necessarily affect the future earning capacity of the wife. The relative size of their respective contributions to the instalments in the early part of the period of repayment, or later if a subsequent reduction in the wife's contribution is not to be accounted for by a reduction in her earnings due to motherhood or some other cause from which the husband benefits as well, may make it a more probable inference that the wife's share in the beneficial interest was intended to be in some proportion other than one-half. And there is nothing inherently improbable in their acting on the understanding that the wife should be entitled to a share which was not to be quantified immediately on the acquisition of the home but should be left to be determined when the mortgage was repaid or the property disposed of, on the basis of what would be fair having regard to the total contributions, direct or indirect, which each spouse had made by that date. Where this was the most likely inference from their conduct it would be for the court to give effect to that common intention of the parties by determining what in all the circumstances was a fair share. Difficult as they are to solve, however, these problems as to the amount of the share of a spouse in the beneficial interest in a matrimonial home where the legal estate is vested solely in the other spouse, only arise in cases where the court is satisfied by the words or conduct of the parties that it was their common intention that the beneficial interest was not to belong solely to the spouse in whom the legal estate was vested but was to be shared between them in some proportion or other.

The decision of this court in *Grant v Edwards* [1986] 2 All ER 426; [1986] Ch 638 also affords helpful guidance. The context was different, in that the court was there dealing with a legal owner who has made representations to the occupier on which the latter has relied to her detriment so as to introduce equities in the nature of estoppel. Once a beneficial interest had been established by that route, however, the court then proceeded – as I read the judgments – to fix the proportions of the beneficial interests on general grounds which were regarded as applying in all cases. That appears from the judgments of Nourse LJ ([1986] 2 All ER 426 at 434; [1986] Ch 638 at 650) and of Browne-Wilkinson VC, where (after citing the passage I have quoted from Lord Diplock in *Gissing v Gissing*) he says:

> Where, as in this case, the existence of some beneficial interest in the claimant has been shown, *prima facie*, the interest of the claimant will be that which the parties intended: see *Gissing v Gissing* [1970] 2 All ER 780 at 792; [1971] AC 886 at 908. In *Eves v Eves* [1975] 3 All ER 768 at 775; [1975] 1 WLR 1338 at 1345, Brightman LJ plainly felt that a common intention that there should be a joint interest pointed to the beneficial interests being equal. However, he felt able to find a lesser beneficial interest in that case without explaining the legal basis on which he did so. With diffidence, I suggest that the law of proprietary estoppel may again provide useful guidance. If proprietary estoppel is established, the court gives effect to it by giving effect to the common intention so far as may fairly be done between the parties. For that purpose, equity is displayed at its most flexible: see *Crabb v Arun DC* [1975] 3 All ER 865; [1976] Ch 179. Identifiable contributions to the purchase of the house will of course be an important factor in many cases.

> But in other cases, contributions by way of the labour or other unquantifiable actions of the claimant will also be relevant. Taking into account the fact that the house was intended to be the joint property, the contributions to the common expenditure and the payment of the fire insurance moneys into the joint account, I agree that the plaintiff is entitled to a half interest in the house. (See [1986] 2 All ER 426 at 439440, [1986] Ch 638 at 657–58.)

The general principle to be derived from *Gissing v Gissing* and *Grant v Edwards* can in my judgment be summarised in this way. When the court is proceeding, in cases like the present where the partner without legal title has successfully asserted an equitable interest through direct contribution, to determine (in the absence of express evidence of intention) what proportions the parties must be assumed to have intended for their beneficial ownership, the duty of the judge is to undertake a survey of the whole course of dealing between the parties relevant to their ownership and occupation of the property and their sharing of its burdens and advantages. That scrutiny will not confine itself to the limited range of acts of direct contribution of the sort that are needed to found a beneficial interest in the first place. It will take into consideration all conduct which throws light on the question what shares were intended. Only if that search proves inconclusive does the court fall back on the maxim that 'equality is equity'.

My answer to question B would therefore be No. The court is not bound to deal with the matter on the strict basis of the trust resulting from the cash contribution to the purchase price, and is free to attribute to the parties an intention to share the beneficial interest in some different proportions.

Mr Bergin submits, however, that in the particular circumstances of this case, that is an approach which the court is precluded from following by the evidence of actual intention given by the spouses themselves. That brings me to his last submission.

(C) Can an agreement be attributed by inference of law to parties who have expressly stated that they reached no agreement?

Mr Bergin begins by pointing out (rightly) that this is an area of the law in which there is no scope for discretion. The entire jurisdiction rests upon the very limited exception provided by Parliament to the general requirement in s 53 of the Law of Property Act 1925 that trusts must be evidenced in writing. It is an exception in favour of trusts that are 'resulting, implied or constructive'. Mr Bergin then submits that the resulting trust is that which results from a contribution to the purchase price, and *prima facie* that fixes the proportion of the beneficial interest. Any implied or constructive trust relied on to alter or enlarge that *prima facie* entitlement must rest upon an imputed agreement inferred from conduct by equity. If the parties themselves testify on oath that they made no agreement, there is no scope for equity to make one for them.

That is a submission which, if it fell to be considered without assistance from a authority, I would reject instinctively on the ground that it runs counter to the very system of law-equity-on which it seeks to rely. Equity has traditionally been a system which matches established principle to the demands of social change. The mass diffusion of home ownership has been one of the most striking social changes of our own time. The present case is typical of hundreds, perhaps even thousands, of others. When people, especially young people, agree to share their lives in joint homes they do so on a basis of mutual trust and in the expectation that their relationship will endure. Despite the efforts that have been made by many responsible bodies to counsel prospective cohabitants as to the risks of taking shared interests in property without legal advice, it is unrealistic to expect that advice to be followed on a universal scale. For a couple embarking on a serious relationship, discussion of the terms to apply at parting is almost a contradiction of the shared hopes that have brought them together. There will inevitably be numerous couples, married or unmarried, who have no discussion about ownership and who, perhaps advisedly, make no agreement about it. It would be anomalous, against that background, to create a range of home-buyers who were beyond the pale of equity's assistance in formulating a fair presumed basis for the sharing of beneficial title, simply because they had been honest enough to admit that they never gave ownership a thought or reached any agreement about it.

Mr Bergin submits, however, that his proposition is supported by authority. He relies upon the passage already quoted from the judgment of Dillon LJ in *Springette v Defoe* [1992] 2 FLR 388 at 393. He also relies on the judgment in the same case of Steyn LJ, who quoted the finding of the trial judge in that case that 'It is my judgment that there is sufficient evidence on the facts of inference of common intention or arrangement between the parties that the property should be owned in equal shares', and then commented as follows (at 395):

> But these factors could not support such an inference because the assistant recorder had already found as a matter of fact that no such common intention was communicated between the parties. The simple answer to the man's case is that there was no communicated common intention. Given that no actual intention to share the property in equal beneficial shares was established, one is driven back to the equitable principle that the shares are presumed to be in proportion to the contributions.

These observations of Dillon and Steyn LJJ (with which Sir Christopher Slade agreed) are of course entitled to the highest respect, and if they formed part of the ratio of the decision would be binding on us. But they are observations-which need to be read in the context of a decision relating to the part-pooling of resources by a middle-aged couple already established in life whose house purchasing arrangements were clearly regarded by the court as having the same formality as if they had been the subject of a joint venture or commercial partnership. I cannot for my part believe that it was intended in that case to lay down a principle, applicable to all instances, that absence of express agreement precludes inference of presumed agreement. This impression is confirmed by the subsequent participation of Dillon LJ in the decision in the *McHardy* case [1994] 2 FLR 338.

I would, therefore, hold that positive evidence that the parties neither discussed nor intended any agreement as to the proportions of their beneficial interest does not preclude the court, on general equitable principles, from inferring one.

Where the claim is established under constructive trust, the size of that interest depends on the common intention or agreement.[118] Where, however, it is not possible to ascertain the size of the interest from the common intention or agreement, the conduct of the parties and the circumstances of the case, such as all payments made and acts done, will be relevant.[119] Only as the last resort, will the maxim 'equality is equity' be applied.[120]

---

118 *Gissing v Gissing* [1971] AC 886 at 908F, *per* Lord Diplock; *Grant v Edwards* [1986] Ch 638 at 657F–G, *per* Browne-Wilkinson VC.

119 *Stokes v Anderson* [1991] 1 FLR 391 at 400B.

120 *Gissing v Gissing* [1971] AC 886 at 908G.

5 CONVEYANCING CLASSIFICATION

The classification of trusts into express, implied, resulting or constructive trusts is primarily about how a trust is created. The principles of trust law discussed above are not only relevant to the determination of beneficial interest in property held on trust. They are also relevant to the study of land law in its conveyancing context; after all conveyancing is land law in practice. The conveyancers are often interested in the question of how the beneficial interests behind a trust are enjoyed and how they can be protected when the trust property is subsequently conveyed to a purchaser and likewise the question of whether the purchaser is able to take free of the beneficial interests. All the various trusts we have seen hitherto created before 1 January 1997 could be classified, from the point of view of a conveyancer, into strict settlements, trusts for sale and bare trusts. This type of classification was indeed also adopted by the 1925 legislation.[121] As from 1 January 1997, all newly created trusts are known as trusts of land and are governed by the Trusts of Land and Appointment of Trustees Act 1996. Existing strict settlements are retained but trusts for sale and bare trusts are brought within the new system.

Strict settlements[122]

These are trusts under which successive beneficial interests were created in favour of a number of beneficiaries provided the land was not held under an immediate binding trust for sale.[123] They, if created before the Trusts of Land and Appointment of Trustees Act 1996 came into force, would continue to exist and operate under the Settled Land Act 1925. Under s 1(1) of the Settled Land Act 1925 a strict settlement arose where a property was held on trust for any persons by way of succession (including fee tail, fee simple or term of years subject to a gift over, base fee or determinable fee) or for a person who was an infant. In a strict settlement the legal estate was vested in the tenant for life who had the right to enjoy the property for the time being,[124] or statutory owner[125] where there was no tenant for life[126] or where the tenant for life was a minor.[127] The tenant for life or statutory owner was given wide powers of disposition of the trust property, including power to sell,[128] to lease,[129] to grant various options[130] and to mortgage.[131] There were also trustees of the settlement to

121 See eg s 2(1) of the LPA 1925.

122 See Chapter 11

123 Section 1(7) of the SLA.

124 Sections 19 and 20 of the SLA 1925.

125 Section 117(1)(xxvi) of the SLA 1925.

126 Sections 23, 30(3), 34 of the SLA 1925.

127 Section 26 of the SLA 1925.

128 Section 38 of the SLA 1925.

129 Section 41 of the SLA 1925.

130 Section 51 of the SLA 1925.

131 Section 71 of the SLA 1925.

safeguard the interest of the beneficiaries under the settlement. Where there was a sale of the settled land, the trustees were there to receive the capital money and to make appropriate investment. The income would normally be paid to the tenant for life subject to apportionment.[132] The remaindermen would be entitled to the capital in future. As long as the purchaser paid to all the trustees of the settlement, who must be at least two in number, or a trust corporation, he could take the trust property free of all the beneficial interests under the settlement.[133] The beneficial interests were 'overreached', ie converted into the proceeds of sale.

Trusts for sale[134]

These are trusts under which the trustees were imposed with an immediate duty to sell the property and to hold the proceeds upon the trusts as directed by the settlor. The duty to sell could be coupled with a power to postpone sale. This type of trust was often expressly created by the conveyance. In a number of situations the Law of Property Act imposed a trust for sale or statutory trust. These trusts imposed by statute were sometimes called implied trusts for sale.[135] Legal estates were vested in a trustee or trustees for sale, and they were given all the powers of a tenant for life and the trustees of the settlement.[136] Where there was a disposition of the legal estate, so long as the purchaser paid to at least two trustees for sale or a trust corporation, he could take free of the beneficial interests behind the trust for sale.[137] Most co-owned properties were held under a trust for sale and it was by far the most important type of trust affecting land. This type of trust, however, is today converted into the new trust of land under the Trusts of Land and Appointment of Trustees Act 1996.

Bare trusts

These are trusts whereby the trustee's duty was simply to hold or manage the trust property for the sole benefit of one beneficiary who was of full age and sound mind. Otherwise the trustee had no duties to perform.[138] Thus, where B had provided money for the purchase of the property and had it conveyed to A, the resulting trust upon which A was required to hold the property for B's benefit was a bare trust.[139] Where a property was conveyed 'to A in fee simple on trust for B in fee simple', the express trust here was also a bare trust. In such a case, the trustee must deal with the property in accordance with B's

132 For detail on the rule on apportionment see Hanbury and Martin, *Modern Equity*, 14th edn, 1993, pp 526–39.

133 Section 2(1)(i) of the LPA 1925, and s 18(1)(b),(c), s 72(2),(3) of the SLA 1925.

134 See Chapter 12

135 Sections 36(1), 34(2) of the LPA 1925.

136 Section 28(1) of the LPA 1925, (now repealed).

137 Sections 2(1)(ii) and 27 of the LPA 1925 (as they were before the amendments by s 5, Sched 2, paras 4(2), (8) of the TLATA 1996).

138 *Re Cunningham and Frayling* [1891] 2 Ch 567 at 572.

139 *Dyer v Dyer* (1788) 2 Cox Eq 92 at 93.

instructions and must permit B to occupy the land or receive the rents and profits.[140] Under the rule in *Saunders v Vautier*[141] B might also require A to convey the legal estate to him, thereby putting an end to the trust. The legal estate held on a bare trust which existed before 1926 had on 1 January 1926 been automatically vested in the beneficiary without further formality.[142] But there was nothing to prevent a bare trust from being created after 1925. However, as from 1 January 1997, bare trusts are also brought within the new system of trusts of land.

140 Lewin on *Trusts*, 16th edn (by Mowbray, WJ), 1964, p 6; Williams, J, *Principles of the Law of Real Property*, 23rd edn (by Williams, TC), 1920, p 191; *Christie v Ovington* (1875) 1 Ch D 279 at 281.

141 (1841) 4 Beav 115.

142 Schedule 1, Part II, paras 3 and 6(d) of the LPA 1925.

CHAPTER 3

PROPRIETARY ESTOPPEL[1]

1 INTRODUCTION

The doctrine of proprietary estoppel, developed over a century by different judges in slightly different terms, has, in recent times, played a significant role in the acquisition of interest in land. The doctrine is founded on the wider principle of equity against unconscionability. Under the doctrine, a person is prevented from enforcing his strict legal rights 'when it would be inequitable for him to do so having regard to the dealings which have taken place between the parties'.[2] Furthermore, unlike the doctrine of promissory estoppel, proprietary estoppel may be used as a cause of action by the aggrieved party. Many proprietary interests have been acquired under this doctrine, for example, easement[3] or licence by estoppel,[4] and in appropriate circumstances even the transfer of legal estate.[5] Thus, a good knowledge of the operation of the doctrine is essential.

2 ELEMENTS OF PROPRIETARY ESTOPPEL

The doctrine of proprietary estoppel emerges from three classes of cases. First, where a gift is intended by X to Y, but the gift is incomplete because the appropriate formality is not complied with, and Y has nevertheless acted on X's intention by incurring expenses on the subject matter of the intended gift. In *Dillwyn v Llewelyn*,[6] a father allowed his son to have possession of his land and signed an informal memorandum to the effect that the land should be given to the son as a gift for the purpose of providing him with a house. On the strength of the promise and with the father's knowledge, the son incurred substantial expenditure to build a house on the land. Although there was no formal deed for the gift, and as a general rule equity will not perfect an imperfect gift, Lord Westbury LC held that as the son had incurred expenditure in reliance on the father's promise, he had acquired a right to call on the father to perform that contract and complete the imperfect donation which was made.

The second class of cases from which the doctrine of proprietary estoppel emerges is where there is no clear express promise of a gift as such from X, but X and Y have nevertheless consistently dealt with each other in such a way as to reasonably cause Y to believe that he would acquire some rights in X's land. In *Ramsden v Dyson*,[7] Lord Kingsdown said that:

1 For an excellent account of the modern law of proprietary estoppel see Gray, Chapter 11.

2 *Crabb v Arun DC* [1976] Ch 179 at 187H–88A.

3 *ER Ives Investment Ltd v High* [1967] 2 QB 379.

4 *Inwards v Baker* [1965] 1 All ER 446.

5 *Pascoe v Turner* [1979] 1 WLR 431; *Dillwyn v Llewelyn* (1862) 4 De GF & J 517; 45 ER 1285.

6 (1862) 4 De GF & J 517; 45 ER 1285. See also *Pascoe v Turner* [1979] 1 WLR 431.

7 (1866) LR 1 HL 129 at 170.

> If a man, under a verbal agreement with a landlord for a certain interest in land, or, what amounts to the same thing, under an expectation, created or encouraged by the landlord, that he shall have a certain interest, takes possession of such land, with the consent of the landlord, and upon the faith of such promise or expectation, with the knowledge of the landlord, and without objection by him, lays out money upon the land, a court of equity will compel the landlord to give effect to such promise or expectation.

Thus stated, this form of estoppel closely resembles the first class of cases mentioned above, except there there is a clear promise of gift whereas here there is an expectation by Y encouraged by X. In *Inwards v Baker*,[8] a father allowed his son to build a bungalow at his expense and labour on the father's land. The son then moved into occupation of the bungalow in the belief, encouraged by the father, that he could live there for life. The son's expectation was upheld by the court when later the father's executors sought possession of the bungalow.

The third class of cases is where Y has made a unilateral mistake about his rights, and has acted on such a mistaken belief to his detriment, but X has wilfully stood by and allowed Y to suffer such 'detriment'. In *Ramsden v Dyson*, Lord Cranworth LC said that:

> If a stranger begins to build on my land supposing it to be his own, and I, perceiving his mistake, abstain from setting him right, and leave him to persevere in his error, a court of equity will not allow me afterwards to assert my title to the land on which he had expended money on the supposition that the land was his own. It considers that, when I saw the mistake into which he had fallen, it was my duty to be active and to state my adverse title; and that it would be dishonest of me to remain wilfully passive on such an occasion, in order afterwards to profit by the mistake which I might have prevented.

Fry J was later to lay down, in *Willmott v Barber*,[9] more restrictive requirements for this type of estoppel,

> A man is not to be deprived of his legal rights unless he has acted in such a way as would make it fraudulent for him to set up those rights. What, then, are the elements or requisites necessary to constitute fraud of that description? In the first place, the plaintiff must have made a mistake as to his legal rights. Secondly, the plaintiff must have expended some money or must have done some act (not necessarily upon the defendant's land) on the faith of his mistaken belief. Thirdly, the defendant, the possessor of the legal rights, must know of the existence of his own right which is inconsistent with the right claimed by the plaintiff. If he does not know of it he is in the same position as the plaintiff, and the doctrine of acquiescence is founded upon conduct with a knowledge of your legal rights. Fourthly, the defendant, the possessor of the legal right, must know of the plaintiff's mistaken belief of his rights. If he does not, there is nothing which calls upon him to assert his own rights. Lastly, the defendant, the possessor of the legal right, must have encouraged the plaintiff in his expenditure of money or in the other acts which he has done, either directly or by abstaining from asserting his legal right. Where all these elements exist, there is fraud of such a nature as

---

8 [1965] 2 QB 29. See (1965) 81 LQR 183 (Maudsley, RH). A similar approach was taken in *ER Ives Investment Ltd v High* [1967] 2 QB 379 and *Crabb v Arun DC* [1976] Ch 179.

9 (1880) 15 Ch D 96 at 105.

> will entitle the court to restrain the possessor of the legal right from exercising it, but, in my judgment, nothing short of this will do.

The three classes of estoppel have laid the foundation upon which the more modern and wider approach of proprietary estoppel is based. Oliver J in *Taylors Fashions Ltd v Liverpool Victoria Trustees Co Ltd*,[10] expressed it in much broader terms. He took the view that the test was whether or not the assertion of strict legal rights would be unconscionable, and that the five requirements, sometimes known as 'the five probanda', were not intended to be applied universally.[11]

Taylors Fashions Ltd v Liverpool Victoria Trustees Co Ltd [1982] QB 133 (Note)

Oliver J: The starting point of both Mr Scott's and Mr Essayan's arguments on estoppel is the same and was expressed by Mr Essayan in the following proposition: if A under an expectation created or encouraged by B that A shall have a certain interest in land, thereafter, on the faith of such expectation and with the knowledge of B and without objection by him, acts to his detriment in connection with such land, a court of equity will compel B to give effect to such expectation. This is a formulation which Mr Millett accepts but subject to one important qualification, namely that at the time when he created and encouraged the expectation and (I think that he would also say) at the time when he permitted the detriment to be incurred (if those two points of time are different) B not only knows of A's expectation but must be aware of his true rights and that he was under no existing obligation to grant the interest.

This is the principal point upon which the parties divide. Mr Scott and Mr Essayan contend that what the court has to look at in relation to the party alleged to be estopped is only his conduct and its result, and not – or, at any rate, not necessarily – his state of mind. It then has to ask whether what that party is now seeking to do is unconscionable. Mr Millett contends that it is an essential feature of this particular equitable doctrine that the party alleged to be estopped must, before the assertion of his strict rights can be considered unconscionable, be aware both of what his strict rights were and of the fact that the other party is acting in the belief that they will not be enforced against him.

The point is a critical one in the instant case and it is one upon which the authorities appear at first sight to be divided. The starting point is *Ramsden v Dyson* (1866) LR 1 HL 129 where a tenant under a tenancy at will had built upon the land in the belief that he would be entitled to demand a long lease. The majority in the House of Lords held that he would not, but Lord Kingsdown dissented on the facts. There was no – or certainly no overt – disagreement between their Lordships as to the applicable principle, but it was stated differently by Lord Cranworth LC and Lord Kingsdown and the real question is how far Lord Cranworth was purporting to make an exhaustive exposition of principle and how far what he stated as the appropriate conditions for its application are to be treated, as it were, as being subsumed *sub silentio* in the speech of Lord Kingsdown. Lord Cranworth expressed it thus, at pp 140–41:

---

10 [1982] QB 133 (Note). See (1981) 97 LQR 513 (Thompson, JM); [1982] Conv 450 (Jackson, P).

11 But see *Matharu v Matharu* (1994) *The Times*, 13 May, CA; [1994] 2 FLR 597, where Roch LJ in a majority judgment applied the 'five probanda' in accordance with *Willmott v Barber* (1880) 15 Ch D 96.

> [See Lord Cranworth's statement cited above] But it will be observed that to raise such an equity two things are required, first, that the person expending the money supposes himself to be building on his own land; and, secondly, that the real owner at the time of the expenditure knows that the land belongs to him and not to the person expending the money in the belief that he is the owner. For if a stranger builds on my land knowing it to be mine, there is no principle of equity which would prevent my claiming the land with the benefit of all the expenditure made on it. There would be nothing in my conduct, active or passive, making it inequitable in me to assert my legal rights.

So here, clearly stated, is the criterion upon which Mr Millett relies. Lord Kingsdown stated the matter differently and rather more broadly although in the narrower context of landlord and tenant. He says, at p 170:

[His Lordship read the passage of Lord Kingsdown's judgment quoted at p 80 above]

So here, there is no specific requirement, at any rate in terms, that the landlord should know or intend that the expectation which he has created or encouraged is one to which he is under no obligation to give effect.

Mr Millett does not – nor could he in the light of the authorities – dispute the principle. What he contends is that even if (which he contests) this is a case where the defendants could be said to have encouraged the plaintiffs' expectations – and that it is not necessarily the same as having encouraged or acquiesced in the expenditure – the principle has no application to a case where, at the time when the expectation was encouraged, both parties were acting under a mistake of law as to their rights.

There is, he submits, a clear distinction between cases of proprietary estoppel or estoppel by acquiescence on the one hand and promissory estoppel or estoppel by representation (whether express or by conduct) on the other. In the latter case, the court looks at the knowledge of the party who has acted and the effect upon him of his having acted. The state of mind of the promissor or representor (except to the extent of knowing, either actually or inferentially, that his promise or representation is likely to be acted upon) is largely irrelevant. In the former case, however, it is essential, Mr Millett submits, to show that the party alleged to have encouraged or acquiesced in the other party's belief himself knew the true position, for if he did not there can be nothing unconscionable in his subsequently seeking to rely upon it. Mr Millett concedes that there may be cases which straddle this convenient dichotomy – cases which can be put either as cases of encouragement or proprietary estoppel on Lord Kingsdown's principle or as estoppel by representation, express or implied. But, he submits, the party alleging the estoppel must, whichever way he elects to put his case or even if he runs them as alternatives, demonstrate the presence of all the essential ingredients of whatever type of estoppel he relies on. He cannot manufacture a third and new hybrid type of estoppel by an eclectic application of some of the ingredients of each. So, if he wishes to put his case as one of estoppel by representation, he must, for instance, show an unequivocal representation of existing fact. Equally, if he wants to rely upon the circumstances of the case as raising a proprietary estoppel arising from acquiescence in his having acted upon an erroneous supposition of his legal rights, then he must accept the burden of showing that the error was known to the other party.

So far as proprietary estoppel or estoppel by acquiescence is concerned, he supports his submission by reference to the frequently cited judgment of Fry J in *Willmott v Barber* (1880) 15 Ch D 96 which contains what are described as the five 'probanda'. The actual case was one where what was alleged was a waiver by acquiescence. A lease contained a covenant against assigning, subletting or parting with possession without the lessor's consent and the lessee had let a sublessee into possession of part of the land under an agreement with him which entitled him to occupy that part for the whole term and conferred an option to purchase the remaining land for the balance of the term outstanding when the option was exercised. The sublessee built on the land and the head landlord was aware that he was in possession and was expending money. It was, however, proved that he did not then know that his consent was required to a sub-letting or assignment. The question arose between the sublessee and the head landlord when the sublessee tried to exercise his option over the remaining land and found himself met with the response that the head landlord refused consent to the assignment. The case was, on Fry J's finding of fact, one simply of acquiescence by standing by and what was being argued was that the landlord was estopped by his knowledge of the plaintiff's expenditure on the part of the land of which the plaintiff was in possession from withholding his consent to an assignment of that part of which he was not. It having been found as a fact that the landlord did not, at the time of the plaintiff's expenditure, know about the covenant against assignment and that there was nothing in what had passed between them to suggest either that the landlord was aware that the plaintiff was labouring under the belief that no consent was necessary or to encourage that belief, Fry J dismissed the plaintiff's claim. It has to be borne in mind, however, in reading the judgment, that this was a pure acquiescence case where what was relied on was a waiver of the landlord's rights by standing by without protest. It was a case of mere silence where what had to be established by the plaintiff was some duty in the landlord to speak. The passage from the judgment in *Willmott v Barber* (1880) 15 Ch D 96 most frequently cited is where Fry J says, at pp 105–06:

[His Lordship read the passage of Fry J's judgment quoted at p 81 above.]

Mr Millett's submission is that when one applies these five probanda to the facts of the instant case it will readily be seen that they are not all complied with. In particular, Mr Millett submits, the fourth probandum involves two essential elements, *viz*, (i) knowledge by the possessor of the legal right of the other party's belief; and (ii) knowledge that that belief is mistaken. In the instant case, the defendants were not aware of their inconsistent right to treat the option as void and equally they could not, thus, have been aware that the plaintiffs' belief in the validity of the option was a mistaken belief. The alternative approach via estoppel by representation is not, he submits, open to the plaintiffs in this case because so far as Taylors were concerned the defendants made no representation to them at all and so far as Olds were concerned the representation of the continuing validity of the option, if there was one at all, was a representation of law.

Now, convenient and attractive as I find Mr Millett's submissions as a matter of argument, I am not at all sure that so orderly and tidy a theory is really deducible from the authorities – certainly from the more recent authorities, which seem to me to support a much wider equitable jurisdiction to interfere in cases where the assertion of strict legal rights is found by the court to be unconscionable. It may well be (although I think that this must now be considered open to doubt) that the strict *Willmott v Barber* (1880) 15 Ch D 96 probanda are applicable as necessary requirements in those cases where all that has happened is that the party alleged to be estopped has stood by without protest while his rights have been infringed. It is suggested in Spencer Bower and Turner, *Estoppel by Representation*, 3rd edn, 1977, para 290 that acquiescence, in its strict sense, is merely an instance of estoppel by representation and this derives some support from the judgment of the Court of Appeal in *De Bussche v Alt* (1878) 8 Ch D 286 at 314. If that is a correct analysis then, in a case of mere passivity, it is readily intelligible that there must be shown a duty to speak, protest or interfere which cannot normally arise in the absence of knowledge or at least a suspicion of the true position. Thus, for a landowner to stand by while a neighbour lays drains in land which the landowner does not believe that he owns (*Armstrong v Sheppard & Short Ltd* [1959] 2 QB 384) or for a remainderman not to protest at a lease by a tenant for life which he believes he has no right to challenge (*Svenson v Payne* (1945) 71 CLR 531) does not create an estoppel. Again, where what is relied on is a waiver by acquiescence, as in *Willmott v Barber* itself, the five probanda are no doubt appropriate. There is, however, no doubt that there are judicial pronouncements of high authority which appear to support as essential the application of all the five probanda over the broader field covering all cases generally classified as estoppel by 'encouragement' or 'acquiescence': see, for instance, the speech of Lord Diplock in *Kammins Ballrooms Co Ltd v Zenith Investments (Torquay) Ltd* [1971] AC 850, 884.

Mr Scott submits, however, that it is historically wrong to treat these probanda as holy writ and to restrict equitable interference only to those cases which can be confined within the strait-jacket of some fixed rule governing the circumstances in which, and in which alone, the court will find that a party is behaving unconscionably. Whilst accepting that the five probanda may form an appropriate test in cases of silent acquiescence, he submits that the authorities do not support the absolute necessity for compliance with all five probanda, and, in particular, the requirement of knowledge on the part of the party estopped that the other party's belief is a mistaken belief, in cases where the conduct relied on has gone beyond mere silence and amounts to active encouragement. In Lord Kingsdown's example in *Ramsden v Dyson*, (1866) LR 1 HL 129, for instance, there is no room for the literal application of the probanda, for the circumstances there postulated do not presuppose a 'mistake' on anybody's part, but merely the fostering of an expectation in the minds of both parties at the time but from which, once it has been acted upon, it would be unconscionable to permit the landlord to depart. As Scarman LJ pointed out in *Crabb v Arun District Council* [1976] Ch 179, the 'fraud' in these cases is not to be found in the transaction itself but in the subsequent attempt to go back upon the basic assumptions which underlay it.

[His Lordship referred to *Stiles v Cowper* (1748) 3 Atk 692; *Jackson v Cator* (1800) 5 Ves 688; *Gregory v Mighell* (1811) 18 Ves 328; *Plimmer v Wellington Corpn* (1884) 9 App Cas 699; *Sarat Chunder Dey v Gopal Chunder Laha* (1892) 19 LR Ind App 203; *Craine v Colonial Mutual Fire Insurance Co Ltd* (1920) 28 CLR 305; *Re Eaves* [1940] Ch 109; *Hopgood v Brown* [1955] 1 WLR 213; *Electrolux Ltd v Electric Ltd* (1953) 71 RPC 23 and continued:]

Furthermore, the more recent cases indicate, in my judgment, that the application of the *Ramsden v Dyson* (1966) LR 1 HL 129 principle – whether you call it proprietary estoppel, estoppel by acquiescence or estoppel by encouragement is really immaterial – requires a very much broader approach which is directed rather at ascertaining whether, in particular individual circumstances, it would be unconscionable for a party to be permitted to deny that which, knowingly, or unknowingly, he has allowed or encouraged another to assume to his detriment than to inquiring whether the circumstances can be fitted within the confines of some preconceived formula serving as a universal yardstick for every form of unconscionable behaviour.

So regarded, knowledge of the true position by the party alleged to be estopped, becomes merely one of the relevant factors – it may even be a determining factor in certain cases – in the overall inquiry. This approach, so it seems to me, appears very clearly from the authorities to which I am about to refer. In *Inwards v Baker* [1965] 2 QB 29, there was no mistaken belief on either side. Each knew the state of the title, but the defendant had been led to expect that he would get an interest in the land on which he had built and, indeed, the overwhelming probability is that that was indeed the father's intention at the time. But it was not mere promissory estoppel, which could merely be used as a defence, for, as Lord Denning MR said, at p 37, 'it is for the court to say in what way the equity can be satisfied'. The principle was expressed very broadly both by Lord Denning MR and by Danckwerts LJ. Lord Denning said at p 37:

> But it seems to me, from *Plimmer's* case (1884) 9 App Cas 699, 713–14 in particular, that the equity arising from the expenditure on land need not fail 'merely on the ground that the interest to be secured has not been expressly indicated ... the court must look at the circumstances in each case to decide in what way the equity can be satisfied'.

And a little further down he said:

> All that is necessary is that the licensee should, at the request or with the encouragement of the landlord, have spent the money in the expectation of being allowed to stay there. If so, the court will not allow that expectation to be defeated where it would be inequitable so to do.

And Danckwerts LJ said, at p 38:

> It seems to me that this is one of the cases of an equity created by estoppel, or equitable estoppel, as it is sometimes called, by which the person who has made the expenditure is induced by the expectation of obtaining protection, and equity protects him so that an injustice may not be perpetrated.

An even more striking example is *ER Ives Investment Ltd v High* [1967] 2 QB 379. Here again, there does not appear to have been any question of the persons who had acquiesced in the defendant's expenditure having known that his belief that he had an enforceable right of way was mistaken. Indeed, at the stage when the expenditure took place, both sides seem to have shared the belief that the agreement between them created effective rights. Nevertheless, the successor in title to the acquiescing party was held to be estopped. Lord Denning MR said, at pp 394–95:

> The right arises out of the expense incurred by Mr High in building his garage, as it is now, with access only over the yard: and the Wrights standing by and acquiescing in it, knowing that he believed he had a right of way over the yard. By so doing the Wrights created in Mr High's mind a reasonable expectation that his access over the yard would not be disturbed. That gives rise to an 'equity arising out of acquiescence'. It is available not only against the Wrights but also their successors in title. The court will not allow that expectation to be defeated when it would be inequitable so to do. It is for the court in each case to decide in what way the equity can be satisfied ...

It should be mentioned that the Wrights themselves clearly also believed that Mr High had a right of way, because when they came to sell, they sold expressly subject to it. So, once again, there is an example of the doctrine of estoppel by acquiescence being applied without regard to the question of whether the acquiescing party knew that the belief of the other party in his supposed rights was erroneous.

Mr Scott and Mr Essayan have also drawn my attention to the Privy Council decision in *Bank Negara Indonesia v Hoalim* [1973] MLJ 3 where again, it seems that the misconception of the legal position which gave rise to the assurance creating the estoppel seems to have been shared by both parties. This is, however, rather a case of promissory estoppel than of the application of the *Ramsden v Dyson* principle. More nearly in point is *Crabb v Arun District Council* [1976] Ch 179 where the plaintiff had altered his legal position in the expectation, encouraged by the defendants, that he would have a certain access to a road. Now there was no mistake here. Each party knew that the road was vested in the defendants and each knew that no formal grant had been made. Indeed, I cannot see why, in considering whether the defendants were behaving unconscionably, it should have made the slightest difference to the result if, at the time when the plaintiff was encouraged to open his access to the road, the defendants had thought that they were bound to grant it. The fact was that he had been encouraged to alter his position irrevocably to his detriment on the faith of a belief, which was known to and encouraged by the defendants, that he was going to be given a particular right of access, a belief which, for all that appears, the defendants probably shared at that time.

The particularly interesting features of the case in the context of the present dispute are, first, the virtual equation of promissory estoppel and proprietary estoppel or estoppel by acquiescence as mere facets of the same principle and secondly the very broad approach of both Lord Denning MR and Scarman LJ, both of whom emphasised the flexibility of the equitable doctrine. It is, however, worth noting that Scarman LJ adopted and applied the five probanda in *Willmott v Barber* (1880) 15 Ch D 96 which he described as 'a valuable guide'. He considered that those probanda were satisfied and it is particularly relevant here to note again the fourth one – namely that the defendant, the possessor of the legal right, must know of the plaintiff's mistaken belief. If Scarman LJ had interpreted this as meaning – as Mr Millett submits that it does mean – that the defendant must know not only of the plaintiff's belief but also that it was mistaken, then he could not, I think, have come to the conclusion that this probandum was satisfied, for it seems clear from Lord Denning's recital of the facts that, up to the critical moment when the plaintiff acted, both parties thought that there was a firm assurance of access. The defendants had, indeed, even erected a gate at their own expense to give effect to it. What gave rise to the necessity for the court to intervene was the defendants' attempt to go back on this subsequently when they fell out with the plaintiff. I infer therefore that Scarman LJ must have construed this probandum in the sense which Mr Scott and Mr Essayan urge upon me, namely that the defendant must know merely of the plaintiff's belief which, in the event, turns out to be mistaken.

Finally, there ought to be mentioned the most recent reference to the five probanda which is to be found in *Shaw v Applegate* [1977] 1 WLR 970. That was a case where the plea of estoppel by acquiescence failed on appeal, but it is significant that two members of the court expressed serious doubt whether it was necessary in every case of acquiescence to satisfy the five probanda. Buckley LJ said, at 977–78:

> 'As I understand that passage' and there he is referring to the passage from the judgment of Fry J in *Willmott v Barber* to which I have already referred, 'what the judge there is saying is that where a man has got a legal right – as the plaintiffs have in the present case, being legal assignees of the benefit of the covenant binding the defendant – acquiescence on their part will not deprive them of that legal right unless it is of such a nature and in such circumstances that it would really be dishonest or unconscionable of the plaintiffs to set up that right after what has occurred. Whether in order to reach that stage of affairs it is really necessary to comply strictly with all five tests there set out by Fry J may, I think,

> still be open to doubt, although no doubt if all those five tests were satisfied there would be shown to be a state of affairs in which it would be dishonest or unconscionable for the owner of the right to insist upon it. In *Electrolux Ltd v Electrix Ltd* (1953) 71 RPC 23 Sir Raymond Evershed MR said, at 33: "I confess that I have found some difficulty – or should find some difficulty if it were necessary to make up my mind and express a view whether all five requisites which Fry J stated in *Willmott v Barber* (1880) 15 Ch D 96 must be present in every case in which it is said that the plaintiff will be deprived of his right to succeed in an action on the ground of acquiescence. All cases (and this is a trite but useful observation to repeat) must be read in the light of the facts of the particular case." So I do not, as at present advised, think it is clear that it is essential to find all the five tests set out by Fry J literally applicable and satisfied in any particular case. The real test, I think, must be whether upon the facts of the particular case the situation has become such that it would be dishonest or unconscionable for the plaintiff, or the person having the right sought to be enforced, to continue to seek to enforce it.'

And Goff LJ referred again to the judgment in *Willmott v Barber*, 15 Ch D 96 and said, at p 980:

> But for my part, I share the doubt entertained by Sir Raymond Evershed MR in the *Electrolux* case, whether it is necessary in all cases to establish the five tests which are laid down by Fry J, and I agree that the test is whether, in the circumstances, it has become unconscionable for the plaintiff to rely upon his legal right.

So here, once again, is the Court of Appeal asserting the broad test of whether in the circumstances the conduct complained of is unconscionable without the necessity of forcing those incumbrances into a Procrustean bed constructed from some unalterable criteria.

The matter was expressed by Lord Denning MR in *Moorgate Mercantile Co Ltd v Twitchings* [1976] QB 225 at 241 as follows:

> Estoppel is not a rule of evidence. It is not a cause of action. It is a principle of justice and of equity. It comes to this: when a man, by his words or conduct, has led another to believe in a particular state of affairs, he will not be allowed to go back on it when it would be unjust or inequitable for him to do so. Dixon J put it in these words: 'The principle upon which estoppel in pais is founded is that the law should not permit an unjust departure by a party from an assumption of fact which he has caused another party to adopt or accept for the purpose of their legal relations.' Sir Owen said so in 1937 in *Grundt v Great Boulder Proprietary Gold Mines Ltd* (1937) 59 CLR 641 at 674. In 1947 after the *High Trees* case (*Central London Property Trust Ltd v High Trees House Ltd* [1947] KB 130), I had some correspondence with Sir Owen about it: and I think I may say that he would not limit the principle to an assumption of fact, but would extend it, as I would, to include an assumption of fact or law, present or future. At any rate, it applies to an assumption of ownership or absence of ownership. This gives rise to what may be called proprietary estoppel. There are many cases where the true owner of goods or of land had led another to believe that he is not the owner, or, at any rate, is not claiming an interest therein, or that there is no objection to what the other is doing. In such cases it has been held repeatedly that the owner is not to be allowed to go back on what he has led the other to believe. So much so that his own title to the property, be it land or goods, has been held to be limited or extinguished, and new rights and interests have been created therein. And this operates by reason of his conduct – what he has led the other to believe – even though he never intended it.

The inquiry which I have to make therefore, as it seems to me, is simply whether, in all the circumstances of this case, it was unconscionable for the defendants to seek to take advantage of the mistake which, at the material time, everybody shared ...

Thus, it seems clear that there are three elements of proprietary estoppel:

Assurance

It is necessary for the claimant to show that there has been some kind of assurance, made by the person against whom estoppel is sought, which led the claimant to reasonably believe that he had or would acquire rights over the land in question.[12] Relevant assurances may range from a direct and positive promise, to a mere abstention from asserting one's rights. Where a clear promise or representation is made, the promise or representation does not have to amount to a binding contract.[13] The assurance may derive from an agreement which is void for uncertainty.[14]

What is more problematic is whether silent assurance is sufficient. As Professor Gray points out:

> This troubled frontier represents one of the potential growth-points of the modern law of estoppel. At present in English law no proprietary estoppel can properly be founded on a mere legitimate expectation of rights, however reasonable the expectation, if the owner of the relevant land has failed to 'encourage or allow a belief or expectation' that the claimant would acquire rights.[15] Detrimental reliance upon a self-induced expectation cannot give rise to a valid claim of estoppel.[16]

It is clear, however, that the owner does not have to act unconscionably in making the assurance; unconscionability lies in the owner's attempt to go back on the assumption or belief that the claimant was led to make to his detriment.[17] Although the owner must have intended that the claimant should act in reliance on his assurance, and the owner has knowledge of the reliance, it is not necessary to show that the owner has knowledge of the precise nature of the disadvantage incurred by the claimant.[18] Where the assurance takes the form of a positive promise, it is not necessary to show that the owner was fully aware of his own legal rights.[19] But if the assurance takes the form of passive

12 *JT Developments Ltd v Quinn* (1991) 62 P & CR 33 at 50.

13 See eg *Inwards v Baker* [1965] 2 QB 29 (the son was not contractually bound to build a bungalow on the father's land).

14 *Lim Teng Huan v Ang Swee Chuan* [1992] 1 WLR 113 at 116F, 118B–C. See [1993] Conv 173 (Goo, SH).

15 See *AG of Hong Kong v Humphrey's Estate (Queen's Gardens) Ltd* [1987] AC 114 at 124F–125A, where the Privy Council declined to uphold an estoppel in favour of a party who had 'acted in the confident and not unreasonable hope' that an agreement in principle would subsequently be formalised.

16 Gray, p 330. See also *AG of Hong Kong v Humphrey's Estate (Queen's Gardens) Ltd* [1987] AC 114.

17 *Taylors Fashions Ltd v Liverpool Victoria Trustees Co Ltd* [1982] QB 133.

18 *Crabb v Arun DC* [1976] Ch 179 at 198A–G.

19 *Taylors Fashions Ltd v Liverpool Victoria Trustee Co Ltd* [1982] QB 133.

acquiescence or sheer silence, it is necessary to show that the owner was aware of his own rights, otherwise he is 'in the same position as the plaintiff, and the doctrine of acquiescence is founded upon conduct with a knowledge of your legal rights.'[20] It is equally unnecessary to establish that the owner knows that the claimant is acting under a mistake to his detriment, although in some cases it may be a decisive factor.[21]

Detrimental reliance

The withdrawal of assurance by the land owner will only be unconscionable if the claimant has acted to his detriment in reliance on the assurance. When the owner makes a representation intending that the claimant should act on it, said Lord Denning in *Brikom Investments Ltd v Carr*:

> It is no answer for the man to say: 'You would have gone on with the transaction anyway.' That must be mere speculation. No one can be sure what he would, or would not, have done in a hypothetical state of affairs which never took place ... Once it is shown that a representation was calculated to influence the judgment of a reasonable man, the presumption is that he was so influenced.[22]

Lord Denning repeated himself in *Greasley v Cooke*.[23] Here, C was employed as a maid servant in G's house. C began to form a relationship with G's son, Kenneth. When G died, C continued to live in the house and perform the duties of housekeeper and looked after G's mentally ill daughter, Clarice, but without pay. Kenneth and his brother, Hedley, both inherited their father's house and assured C that she could live in the house rent free for as long as she liked. Lord Denning, having referred to his statement in *Brikom Investments Ltd v Carr* quoted above, continued:

> So here. These statements to Miss Cooke were calculated to influence her – so as to put her mind at rest – so that she should not worry about being turned out. No one can say what she would have done if Kenneth and Hedley had not made those statements. It is quite possible that she would have said to herself, 'I am not married to Kenneth. I am on my own. What will happen to me if anything happens to him? I had better look out for another job now: rather than stay here where I have no security.'
>
> So, instead of looking for another job, she stayed on in the house looking after Kenneth and Clarice. There is a presumption that she did so relying on the assurances given to her by Kenneth and Hedley. The burden is not on her, but on them, to prove that she did not rely on their assurances. They did not prove it, nor did their representatives. So she is presumed to have relied on them. So on the burden of proof it seems to me that the judge was in error.

What is necessary therefore is a change of position by the claimant. This often takes the form of expenditure on improvements to the land in question by the

20 *Willmott v Barber* (1880) 15 Ch D 96 at 105.

21 *Taylors Fashions Ltd v Liverpool Victoria Trustee Co Ltd* [1982] QB 133, at 152A.

22 [1979] QB 467 at 482–83.

23 [1980] 1 WLR 1306. See [1981] Conv 154 (Annand, RE); 44 MLR 461 (Woodman, G); 125 NLJ 539 (Thompson, MP).

claimant.[24] It may, however, take the form of other disadvantages not related to the land, such as a failure to reserve a right of way over the land sold.[25] Housekeeping in the family home,[26] or abandoning an existing job and home in order to live near the owner,[27] may also be sufficient. Indeed, Browne-Wilkinson VC said, in *Grant v Edwards*,[28] that, if there was a common intention that the claimant should have an interest in the land in question:

> ... any act done by her to her detriment relating to the joint lives of the parties is ... sufficient detriment to qualify [such as], setting up house together, having a baby, making payments to general housekeeping expenses [even though these might be more accurately referable], to the mutual love and affection of the parties and not specifically referable to the claimant's belief that she has an interest in the house.

The promise relied on does not have to be the sole inducement for the conduct by the claimant. Although it is necessary for the claimant to establish reliance,[29] where his conduct is of such a nature that reliance can be inferred, the burden of proof shifts to the legal owner to establish that the claimant has not relied on the promise.[30]

Unconscionability

As seen, the claimant must show 'as a fact that the defendant, by setting up his right, is taking advantage of him in a way which is unconscionable, inequitable or unjust'.[31] Unconscionability often lies in the defendant's attempt to go back on his promise or to withdraw his assurance by setting up his strict legal right. However, the claimant must not be guilty of unconscionable conduct himself. He must come with 'clean hands'.[32] Likewise, a claim of proprietary estoppel will be defeated by the claimant's unreasonable delay in pursuing it. In rare cases, where it is no longer inequitable to deny the claimant the equity through change of circumstances, a remedy may be refused. In *Sledmore v Dalby*,[33] Mr and Mrs Sledmore allowed Dalby, who had married their daughter to move into their house. The Sledmores accepted rent from them for a while until their daughter became ill and Dalby became unemployed. The Dalbys carried out improvements to the house and were led to believe that Mr Sledmore would give the house to them. But later, Mr Sledmore conveyed his share of the freehold of the house to his wife, who left the house by will to their daughter to

24 See eg *Inwards v Baker* [1965] 2 QB 29; *Dillwyn v Llewelyn* (1862) 4 De G F & J 517; 45 ER 1285.

25 *Crabb v Arun DC* [1976] Ch 179.

26 *Greasley v Cooke* [1980] 1 WLR 1306.

27 *Jones (AE) v Jones (FW)* [1977] 1 WLR 438.

28 [1986] Ch 638 at 657A–B. See [1986] CLJ 394 (D J Hayton); [1986] Conv 291 (J Warburton).

29 *AG of Hong Kong v Humphrey's Estate (Queen's Gardens) Ltd* [1987] AC 114.

30 *Wayling v Jones* [1995] 2 FLR 1029; [1995] Conv 409 (Christine J Davis).

31 *Crabb v Arun DC* [1976] Ch 179 at 195B–C.

32 *Chalmers v Pardoe* [1963] 1 WLR 677 (conduct relied on was a breach of statutes).

33 (1996) 72 P & CR 196.

the exclusion of Dalby. After the deaths of Mr Sledmore and Dalby's wife, Dalby continued to stay in the house rent-free. Much later, he was in employment again and spent only a few nights a week in the house, spending the rest of the week in his new partner's house. Mrs Sledmore was herself in financial difficulties now, and needed to repair her own house. She was living on income support and relying on the Department of Social Security to pay her mortgage interest. She sought possession against Dalby who claimed to have a freehold interest or at least a life interest in the house. The Court of Appeal allowed possession holding that the extent of equity was to satisfy the expectations of Dalby, which the Sledmores had encouraged, but the present needs and situations of Mrs Sledmore should be taken into account and balanced against the present use of the house made by Dalby and his need for it. In the circumstances, it was no longer inequitable for Dalby's expectation to be defeated by permitting Mrs Sledmore to enforce her legal rights as the owner of the house.

3 SATISFYING PROPRIETARY ESTOPPEL

Once the claimant can establish his case, the court must look at the circumstances in each case to decide in what way the equity in favour of the claimant can be satisfied.[34] This principle is easy to state but difficult to apply. The way in which the equity is satisfied varies according to the length of the Chancellor's foot. Here 'equity is displayed at its most flexible'.[35]

The possible remedies include the following.

Transfer of estate or interest in land

In some cases, an 'equity' of estoppel can only be satisfied by a court order directing the transfer of the fee simple to the claimant. Such an order was made in *Dillwyn v Llewelyn*[36] and *Pascoe v Turner*.[37] An order was also made for the grant of a right of access and way without payment in *Crabb v Arun DC*.[38]

Dillwyn v Llewelyn (1862) 4 De G F & J 517; 45 ER 1285

Lord Westbury LC: About the rules of the Court there can be no controversy. A voluntary agreement will not be completed or assisted by a Court of Equity, in cases of mere gift. If anything be wanting to complete the title of the donee, a Court of Equity will not assist him in obtaining it; for a mere donee can have no right to claim more than he has received. But the subsequent acts of the donor may give the donee that right or ground of claim which he did not acquire from the original gift. Thus, if A gives a house to B, but makes no formal conveyance, and the house is afterwards, on the marriage of B, included, with the knowledge of A, in the marriage settlement of B, A would be bound

34 *Plimmer v Wellington Corporation* [1884] 9 App Cas 699 at 713.

35 *Crabb v Arun DC* [1976] Ch 179 at 189F.

36 (1862) 4 De GF & J 517; 45 ER 1285.

37 [1979] 1 WLR 431.

38 [1976] Ch 179.

to complete the title of the parties claiming under that settlement. So if A puts B in possession of a piece of land, and tells him, 'I give it to you that you may build a house on it,' and B on the strength of that promise, with the knowledge of A, expends a large sum of money in building a house accordingly, I cannot doubt that the donee acquires a right from the subsequent transaction to call on the donor to perform that contract and complete the imperfect donation which was made. The case is somewhat analogous to that of verbal agreement not binding originally for the want of the memorandum in writing, signed by the party to be charged, but which becomes binding by virtue of the subsequent part performance. The early case of *Foxcroft v Lester* (2 Vern 456), decided by the House of Lords, is an example nearly approaching to the terms of the present case.

The Master of the Rolls, however, seems to have thought that a question might still remain as to the extent of the estate taken by the donee, and that in this particular case the extent of the donee's interest depended on the terms of the memorandum. I am not of that opinion. The equity of the donee and the estate to be claimed by virtue of it depend on the transaction, that is, on the acts done, and not on the language of the memorandum, except as that shows the purpose and intent of the gift. The estate was given as the site of a dwelling house to be erected by the son. The ownership of the dwelling house and the ownership of the estate must be considered as intended to be co-extensive and co-equal. No one builds a house for his own life only, and it is absurd to suppose that it was intended by either party that the house, at the death of the son, should become the property of the father. If, therefore, I am right in the conclusion of law that the subsequent expenditure by the son, with the approbation of the father, supplied a valuable consideration originally wanting, the memorandum signed by the father and son must be thenceforth regarded as an agreement for the soil extending to the fee-simple of the land. In a contract for sale of an estate no words of limitation are necessary to include the fee-simple; but, further, upon the construction of the memorandum itself, taken apart from the subsequent acts, I should be of opinion that it was the plain intention of the testator to vest in the son the absolute ownership of the estate. The only inquiry therefore is, whether the son's expenditure of the faith of the memorandum supplied a valuable consideration and created a binding obligation. On this I have no doubt; and it therefore follows that the intention to give the fee-simple must be performed, and that the decree ought to declare the son the absolute owner of the estate comprised in the memorandum.

I propose, therefore, to vary the decree of the Master of the Rolls, and to declare, by virtue of the original gift made by the testator and of the subsequent expenditure by the Plaintiff with the approbation of the testator, and of the right and obligation resulting therefrom, the Plaintiff is entitled to have a conveyance from the trustees of the testator's will and other parties interested under the same of all their estate and interest under the testator's will in the estate of Hendrefoilan in the pleadings mentioned, and with this declaration refer it to the Judge in Chambers to settle such conveyance accordingly.

Pascoe v Turner [1979] 1 WLR 431, CA

Cumming-Bruce LJ: The judge found that the plaintiff had made a gift to her of the contents of the house. I have no doubt that he was right about that. She was already in possession of them as a bailee when he declared the gift. Counsel for the plaintiff submitted that there was no gift because it was uncertain what he was giving her. He pointed to a safe and to the defendant's evidence that she had sent round an orange bedroom suite to the plaintiff so that he should have a bed to sleep on. The answer is that he gave her everything in the house, but later, recognising his need, she gave back some bits and pieces to him. So much for the contents.

Her rights in the realty are not quite so simply disposed of because of s 53 and s 54 of the Law of Property Act 1925. There was nothing in writing. The judge considered the plaintiff's declarations, and decided that they were not enough to found an express trust. We agree. But he went on to hold that the beneficial interest in the house had passed under a constructive trust inferred from words and conduct of the parties. He relied on the passage in Snell's *Principles of Equity*, 27th edn, 1973, p 185, in which the editors suggest a possible definition of a constructive trust. But there are difficulties in the way. The long and short of events in 1973 is that the plaintiff made an imperfect gift of the house. There is nothing, in the facts from which an inference of a constructive trust can be drawn. If it had not been for s 53 of the Law of Property Act 1925 the gift of the house would have been a perfect gift, just as the gift of the contents was a perfect gift. In the event it remained an imperfect gift and, as Turner LJ said in *Milroy v Lord* (1862) 4 De GF & J 264, 274, 'there is no equity in this court to perfect an imperfect gift'. So matters stood in 1973, and if the facts had stopped there the defendant would have remained a licensee at will of the plaintiff.

But the facts did not stop there. On the judge's findings the defendant, having been told that the house was hers, set about improving it within and without. Outside she did not do much: a little work on the roof and an improvement which covered the way from the outside toilet to the rest of the house, putting in a new door there, and Snowcem to protect the toilet. Inside she did a good deal more. She installed gas in the kitchen with a cooker, improved the plumbing in the kitchen and put in a new sink. She got new gas fires, putting a gas fire in the lounge. She redecorated four rooms. The fitted carpets she put in the bedrooms, the stair carpeting, and the curtains and the furniture that she bought are not part of the realty, and it is not clear how much she spent on those items. But they are part of the whole circumstances. There she was, on her own after he left her in 1973. She had £1,000 left of her capital, and a pension of some kind. Having, as she thought, been given the house, she set about it as described. On the repairs and improvement to the realty and its fixtures she spent about £230. She had £300 of her capital left by the date of the trial, but she did not establish in evidence how much had been expended on refurbishing the house with carpets, curtains and furniture. We would describe the work done in and about the house as substantial in the sense that that adjective is used in the context of estoppel. All the while the plaintiff not only stood by and watched but encouraged and advised, without a word to suggest that she was putting her money and her personal labour into his house. What is the effect in equity?

The cases relied upon by the plaintiff are relevant for the purpose of showing that the judge fell into error in deciding that on the facts a constructive trust could be inferred. They are the cases which deal with the intention of the parties when a house is acquired. But of those cases only *Inwards v Baker* [1965] 2 QB 29 is in point here. For this is a case of estoppel arising from the encouragement and acquiescence of the plaintiff between 1973 and 1976 when, in reliance upon his declaration that he was giving and, later, that he had given the house to her, she spent a substantial part of her small capital upon repairs and improvements to the house. The relevant principle is expounded in Snell's *Principles of Equity*, 27th edn, p 565 in the passage under the heading 'Proprietary Estoppel' and is elaborated in Spencer, Bower and Turner, *Estoppel by Representation*, 3rd edn, 1977, Chapter 12 entitled 'Encouragement and Acquiescence'.

The cases in point illustrating that principle in relation to real property are *Dillwyn v Llewelyn* (1862) 4 De GF & J 517; *Ramsden v Dyson* (1866) LR 1 HL 129 and *Plimmer v Wellington Corporation* (1884) 9 App Cas 699. One distinction between this class of case and the doctrine which has come to be known as 'promissory estoppel' is that where estoppel by encouragement or acquiescence is found on the facts, those facts give rise to a cause of action. They may be relied upon as a sword, not merely as a shield. In *Ramsden v Dyson,* the plaintiff failed on the facts, and the dissent of Lord Kingsdown was upon the inferences to be drawn from the facts. On the principle, however, the House was agreed, and it is stated by Lord Cranworth LC and by Lord Wensleydale as well as by Lord Kingsdown. Likewise in *Plimmer's* case the plaintiff was granted a declaration that he had a perpetual right of occupation.

The final question that arises is: to what relief is the defendant entitled upon her counterclaim? In *Dillwyn v Llewelyn* (1862) 4 De GF & J 517 there was an imperfect gift of land by a father who encouraged his son to build a house on it for £14,000.

[His Lordship referred to the first paragraph of Lord Westbury LC's judgment cited at p 93 above and continued.]

In *Plimmer's* case (1884) 9 App Cas 699 the Privy Council pose the question, how should the equity be satisfied? (see pp 713 at 714). And the Board declare that on the facts a licence revocable at will became irrevocable as a consequence of the subsequent transactions. So in *Thomas v Thomas* [1956] NZLR 785 the Supreme Court of New Zealand ordered the defendant to execute a proper transfer of the property.

In *Crabb v Arun District Council* [1976] Ch 179, this court had to consider the principles upon which the court should give effect to the equity: see Lord Denning MR at p 189. Lawton and Scarman LJJ agreed with the remedy proposed by Lord Denning MR. On the facts of that case Scarman LJ expressed himself thus at pp 198–99:

> I turn now to the other two questions – the extent of the equity and the relief needed to satisfy it. There being no grant, no enforceable contract, no licence, I would analyse the minimum equity to do justice to the plaintiff as a right either to an easement or to a licence upon terms to be agreed. I do not think it is necessary to go further than that. Of course, going that far would support the equitable remedy of injunction which is sought in this action. If there is no agreement as to terms, if agreement fails to be obtained, the court can, in my judgment, and must, determine in these proceedings upon what terms the plaintiff should be put to enable him to have the benefit of the equitable right which he is held to have. It is interesting that there has been some doubt amongst distinguished lawyers in the past as to whether the court can so proceed. Lord Kingsdown refers in fact to those doubts in a passage, which I need not quote, in *Ramsden v Dyson* (1866) LR 1 HL 129 at 171. Lord Thurlow clearly thought that the court did have this power. Other lawyers of that time did not. But there can be no doubt that since *Ramsden v Dyson* the courts have acted upon the basis that they have to determine not only the extent of the equity, but also the conditions necessary to satisfy it, and they have done so in a great number and variety of cases. I need refer only to the interesting collection of cases enumerated in Snell's *Principles of Equity*, 27th edn, pp 567–68, para 2(b). In the present case the court does have to consider what is necessary now in order to satisfy the plaintiff's equity.

So the principle to be applied is that the court should consider all the circumstances, and the counterclaimant having at law no perfected gift or licence other than a licence revocable at will, the court must decide what is the minimum equity to do justice to her having regard to the way in which she changed her position for the worse by reason of the acquiescence and encouragement of the legal owner. The defendant submits that the only appropriate way in which the equity can here be satisfied is by perfecting the imperfect gift as was done in *Dillwyn v Llewelyn*.

Counsel for the plaintiff on instruction has throughout submitted that the plaintiff is entitled to possession. The only concession that he made was that the period of notice given in the letter of 9 April 1976, was too short. He made no submission upon the way the equity, if there was an equity, should be satisfied save to submit that the court should not in any view grant a remedy more beneficial to the defendant than a licence to occupy the house for her lifetime.

We are satisfied that the problem of remedy on the facts resolves itself into a choice between two alternatives: should the equity be satisfied by a licence to the defendant to occupy the house for her lifetime, or should there be a transfer to her of the fee simple?

The main consideration pointing to a licence for her lifetime is that she did not by her case at the hearing seek to establish that she had spent more money or done more work on the house than she would have done had she believed that she had only a licence to live there for her lifetime. But the court must be cautious about drawing any inference from what she did not give in evidence as the hypothesis put is one that manifestly never occurred to her. Then it may reasonably be held that her expenditure and effort can hardly be regarded as comparable to the change of position of those who have constructed buildings on land over which they had no legal rights.

This court appreciates that the moneys laid out by the defendant were much less than in some of the cases in the books. But the court has to look at all the circumstances. When the plaintiff left her she was, we were told, a widow in her middle fifties. During the period that she lived with the plaintiff her capital was reduced from £4,500 to £1,000. Save for her invalidity pension that was all that she had in the world. In reliance upon the plaintiff's declaration of gift, encouragement and acquiescence she arranged her affairs on the basis that the house and contents belonged to her. So relying, she devoted a quarter of her remaining capital and her personal effort upon the house and its fixtures. In addition, she bought carpets, curtains and furniture for it, with the result that by the date of the trial she had only £300 left. Compared to her, on the evidence the plaintiff is a rich man. He might not regard an expenditure of a few hundred pounds as a very grave loss. But the court has to regard her change of position over the years 1973–76.

We take the view that the equity cannot here be satisfied without granting a remedy which assures to the defendant security of tenure, quiet enjoyment, and freedom of action in respect of repairs and improvements without interference from the plaintiff. The history of the conduct of the plaintiff since 9 April 1976, in relation to these proceedings leads to an irresistible inference that he is determined to pursue his purpose of evicting her from the house by any legal means at his disposal with a ruthless disregard of the obligations binding upon conscience. The court must grant a remedy effective to protect her against the future manifestations of his ruthlessness. It was conceded that if she is granted a licence, such a licence cannot be registered as a land charge, so that she may find herself ousted by a purchaser for value without notice. If she has in the future to do further and more expensive repairs she may only be able to finance them by a loan, but as a licensee she cannot charge the house. The plaintiff as legal owner may well find excuses for entry in order to do what he may plausibly represent as necessary works and so contrive to derogate from her enjoyment of the licence in ways that make it difficult or impossible for the court to give her effective protection.

Weighing such considerations this court concludes that the equity to which the facts in this case give rise can only be satisfied by compelling the plaintiff to give effect to his promise and her expectations. He has so acted that he must now perfect the gift.

Crabb v Arun DC [1976] Ch 179, CA

Lord Denning MR: This case cannot be properly understood without a map: but I will try to explain it as best I can.

[His Lordship stated the facts and continued.]

In June 1971, the plaintiff brought this action claiming a right of access at point B and a right of way along the estate road. He had no such right by any deed or conveyance or written agreement. So, in strict law, on the conveyance, the defendants were entitled to their land, subject only to an easement at point A, but none at point B. To overcome this strict law, the plaintiff claimed a right of access at B on the ground of equitable estoppel, promissory or proprietary. The judge held that he could not avail himself of any estoppel. He said, 'In the absence of a definite assurance by the representative of the council, no question of estoppel can arise, and that really concludes the action.' The plaintiff appeals to this court.

When Mr Millett, for the plaintiff, said that he put his case on an estoppel, it shook me a little because it is commonly supposed that estoppel is not itself a cause of action. But that is because there are estoppels and estoppels. Some do give rise to a cause of action. Some do not. In the species of estoppel called proprietary estoppel, it does give rise to a cause of action. We had occasion to consider it a month ago in *Moorgate Mercantile Co Ltd v Twitchings* [1976] QB 225 where I said, at 242, that the effect of estoppel on the true owner may be that:

> ... his own title to the property, be it land or goods, has been held to be limited or extinguished, and new rights and interests have been created therein. And this operates by reason of his conduct – what he has led the other to believe – even though he never intended it.

The new rights and interests, so created by estoppel, in or over land, will be protected by the courts and in this way give rise to a cause of action. This was pointed out in Spencer, Bower and Turner, *Estoppel by Representation*, 2nd edn, 1966, pp 279–82.

The basis of this proprietary estoppel – as indeed of promissory estoppel – is the interposition of equity. Equity comes in, true to form, to mitigate the rigours of strict law. The early cases did not speak of it as 'estoppel'. They spoke of it as 'raising an equity'. If I may expand what Lord Cairns LC said in *Hughes v Metropolitan Railway Co* (1877) 2 App Cas 439 at 448, 'it is the first principle upon which all courts of equity proceed', that it will prevent a person from insisting on his strict legal rights – whether arising under a contract, or on his title deeds, or by statute – when it would be inequitable for him to do so having regard to the dealings which have taken place between the parties.

What then are the dealings which will preclude him from insisting on his strict legal rights? If he makes a binding contract that he will not insist on the strict legal position, a court of equity will hold him to his contract. Short of a binding contract, if he makes a promise that he will not insist upon his strict legal rights – then, even though that promise may be unenforceable in point of law for want of consideration or want of writing – then, if he makes the promise knowing or intending that the other will act upon it, and he does act upon it, then again a court of equity will not allow him to go back on that promise: see *Central London Property Trust Ltd v High Trees House Ltd* [1947] KB 130 and *Charles Rickards Ltd v Oppenhaim* [1950] 1 KB 616 at 623. Short of an actual promise, if he, by his words or conduct, so behaves as to lead another to believe that he will not insist on his strict legal rights – knowing or intending that the other will act on that belief – and he does so act, that again will raise an equity in favour of the other; and it is for a court of equity to say in what way the equity may be satisfied. The cases show that this equity does not depend on agreement but on words or conduct. In *Ramsden v Dyson* (1866) LR 1 HL 129 at 170 Lord Kingsdown spoke of a verbal agreement 'or what amounts to the same thing, an expectation, created or encouraged'. In *Birmingham and District Land Co v London and North Western Railway Co* (1888) 40 Ch D 268 at 277, Cotton LJ said that '... what passed did not make a new agreement, but ... what took place ... raised an equity against him'. And it was the Privy Council in *Plimmer v Wellington Corporation* (1884) 9 App Cas 699 at 713–14 who said that '... the court must look at the circumstances in each case to decide in what way the equity can be satisfied' giving instances.

Recent cases afford illustrations of the principle. In *Inwards v Baker* [1965] 2 QB 29, it was held that, despite the legal title being in the plaintiffs, the son had an equity to remain in the bungalow 'as long as he desired to use it as his home'. Danckwerts LJ said, at p 38: 'equity protects him so that an injustice may not be perpetrated'. In *ER Ives Investment Ltd v High* [1967] 2 QB 379, it was held that Mr High and his successors had an equity which could only be satisfied by allowing him to have a right of access over the yard, 'so long as the block of flats has its foundations on his land'. In *Siew Soon Wah v Yong Tong Hong* [1973] AC 836 the Privy Council held that there was an 'equity or equitable estoppel protecting the defendant in his occupation for 30 years'. In *Bank Negara Indonesia v Hoalim* [1973] 2 MLJ 3, the Privy Council held that, despite the fact that the defendant had no protection under the Rent Acts, he had an equity to remain 'so long as he continued to practise his profession'.

The question then is: were the circumstances here such as to raise an equity in favour of the plaintiff? True the defendants on the deeds had the title to their land, free of any access at point B. But they led the plaintiff to believe that he had or would be granted a right of access at point B. At the meeting of 26 July 1967, Mr Alford and the plaintiff told the defendants' representative that the plaintiff intended to split the two acres into two portions and wanted to have an access at point B for the back portion; and the defendants' representative agreed that he should have this access. I do not think the defendants can avoid responsibility by saying that their representative had no authority to agree this. They entrusted him with the task of setting out the line of the fence and the gates, and they must be answerable for his conduct in the course of it: see *Attorney-General to the Prince of Wales v Collom* [1916] 2 KB 193 at 207; and *Moorgate Mercantile Co Ltd v Twitchings* [1976] QB 225 at 243.

The judge found that there was 'no definite assurance' by the defendants' representative, and 'no firm commitment' but only an 'agreement in principle' meaning I suppose that, as Mr Alford said, there were 'some further processes' to be gone through before it would become binding. But if there were any such processes in the mind of the parties, the subsequent conduct of the defendants was such as to dispense with them.

The defendants actually put up the gates at point B at considerable expense. That certainly led the plaintiff to believe that they agreed that he should have the right of access through point B without more ado.

The judge also said that, to establish this equity or estoppel, the defendants must have known that the plaintiff was selling the front portion without reserving a right of access for the back portion. I do not think this was necessary. The defendants knew that the plaintiff intended to sell the two portions separately and that he would need an access at point B as well as point A. Seeing that they knew of his intention – and they did nothing to disabuse him but rather confirmed it by erecting gates at point B – it was their conduct which led him to act as he did: and this raises an equity in his favour against them.

In the circumstances, it seems to me inequitable that the council should insist on their strict title as they did; and to take the high-handed action of pulling down the gates without a word of warning: and to demand of the plaintiff £3,000 as the price for the easement. If he had moved at once for an injunction in aid of his equity – to prevent them removing the gates – I think he should have been granted it. But he did not do so. He tried to negotiate terms, but these failing, the action has come for trial. And we have the question: in what way now should the equity be satisfied?

Here equity is displayed at its most flexible, see Snell's *Principles of Equity*, 27th edn, 1973, p 568, and the illustrations there given. If the matter had been finally settled in 1967, I should have thought that, although nothing was said at the meeting in July 1967, nevertheless it would be quite reasonable for the defendants to ask the plaintiff to pay something for the access at point B, perhaps – and I am guessing – some hundreds of pounds. But, as Mr Millett pointed out in the course of the argument, because of the defendants' conduct, the back land has been landlocked. It has been sterile and rendered useless for five or six years: and the plaintiff has been unable to deal with it during that time. This loss to him can be taken into account. And at the present time, it seems to me that, in order to satisfy the equity, the plaintiff should have the right of access at point B without paying anything for it.

I would, therefore, hold that the plaintiff, as the owner of the back portion, has a right of access at point B over the verge on to Mill Park Road and a right of way along that road to Hook Lane without paying compensation. I would allow the appeal and declare that he has an easement, accordingly.

Grant of an irrevocable licence or a long lease

It is more common to find that the equity is satisfied by granting the claimant an irrevocable licence rent-free for life or for a short period. Examples are *Inwards v Baker*,[39] and *Greasley v Cooke*.[40] As will be seen,[41] this can raise difficulties in that arguably when the claimant is granted a 'life interest' by reason of the estoppel claim, the Settled Land Act 1925 is brought into play and the land suddenly becomes settled land. Russell LJ in *Dodsworth v Dodsworth* (1973) 228 EG 1115 said that this was a point which appeared to have been overlooked in *Inwards v*

39 [1965] 2 QB 29. See also *Matharu v Matharu* (1994) *The Times*, 13 May CA; [1994] 2 FLR 597 where a licence for life or such shorter period as the claimant might decide was ordered.

40 [1980] 1 WLR 1306.

41 See Chapter 11.

Baker [1965] 2 QB 29. The court has therefore sometimes tried to satisfy the equity by making other types of order, such as an order to grant a long lease at a nominal rent, as in *Griffiths v Williams*,[42] or an award of monetary compensation for the claimant's detriment.[43]

Inwards v Baker [1965] 2 QB 29, CA

Lord Denning MR: The trustees say that at the most Jack Baker had a licence to be in the bungalow but that it had been revoked and he had no right to stay. The judge has held in their favour. He was referred to *Errington v Errington and Woods* [1952] 1 KB 290; (1952) 1 TLR 231; [1952] 1 All ER 149, CA, but the judge held that that decision only protected a contractual licensee. He thought that, in order to be protected, the licensee must have a contract or promise by which he is entitled to be there. The judge said, 'I can find no promise made by the father to the son that he should remain in the property at all – no contractual arrangement between them. True, the father said that the son could live in the property, expressly or impliedly, but there is no evidence that this was arrived at as the result of a contract or promise – merely an arrangement made casually because of the relationship which existed and knowledge that the son wished to erect a bungalow for residence.' Thereupon, the judge, with much reluctance, thought the case was not within *Errington's* case, and said the son must go. The son appeals to this court. We have had the advantage of cases which were not cited to the county court judge – cases in the last century, notably *Dillwyn v Llewelyn* (1862) 4 De GF & J 517 and *Plimmer v Wellington Corporation* (1884) 9 App Cas 699, PC. This latter was a decision of the Privy Council which expressly affirmed and approved the statement of the law made by Lord Kingsdown in *Ramsden v Dyson* (1866) LR 1 129 at 170, HL. It is quite plain from those authorities that if the owner of land requests another, or indeed allows another, to expend money on the land under an expectation created or encouraged by the landlord that he will be able to remain there, that raises an equity in the licensee such as to entitle him to stay. He has a licence coupled with an equity. Mr Goodhart urged before us that the licensee could not stay indefinitely. The principle only applied, he said, when there was an expectation of some precise legal term. But it seems to me, from *Plimmer's* case in particular, that the equity arising from the expenditure on land need not fail 'merely on the ground that the interest to be secured has not been expressly indicated ... the court must look at the circumstances in each case to decide in what way the equity can be satisfied'.[44]

So, in this case, even though there is no binding contract to grant any particular interest to the licensee, nevertheless, the court can look at the circumstances and see whether there is an equity arising out of the expenditure of money. All that is necessary is that the licensee should, at the request or with the encouragement of the landlord, have spent the money in the expectation of being allowed to stay there. If so, the court will not allow that expectation to be defeated where it would be inequitable so to do. In this case, it is quite plain that the father allowed an expectation to be created in the son's mind that this bungalow was to be his home. It was to be his home for his life or, at all events, his home as long as he wished it to remain his home. It seems to me, in the light

42 (1977) 248 Estates Gazette 947.

43 See eg *Dodsworth v Dodsworth* (1973) 228 Estates Gazette 1115.

44 (1884) 9 App Cas 699, 713–14, PC

of that equity, that the father could not in 1932 have turned to his son and said, 'You are to go. It is my land and my house.' Nor could he at any time thereafter so long as the son wanted it as his home.

Mr Goodhart put the case of a purchaser. He suggested that the father could sell the land to a purchaser who could get the son out. But I think that any purchaser who took with notice would clearly be bound by the equity. So here, too, the present plaintiffs, the successors in title of the father, are clearly themselves bound by this equity. It is an equity well recognised in law. It arises from the expenditure of money by a person in actual occupation of land when he is led to believe that, as the result of that expenditure, he will be allowed to remain there. It is for the court to say in what way the equity can be satisfied. I am quite clear in this case it can be satisfied by holding that the defendant can remain there as long as he desires to as his home.

I would allow the appeal accordingly and enter judgment for the defendant.

Greasley v Cooke [1980] 1 WLR 1306, CA

Lord Denning MR:

[Having found that Dorris Cooke had relied on the assurance given to her by Kenneth and Hedley, his Lordship continued.]

The second point is about the need for some expenditure of money – some detriment – before a person can acquire any interest in a house or any right to stay in it as long as he wishes. It so happens that in many of these cases of proprietary estoppel there has been expenditure of money. But that is not a necessary element. I see that in Snell's *Principles of Equity*, 27th edn, 1973, p 565, it is said, 'A must have incurred expenditure or otherwise have prejudiced himself.' But I do not think that that is necessary. It is sufficient if the party, to whom the assurance is given, acts on the faith of it – in such circumstances that it would be unjust and inequitable for the party making the assurance to go back on it: see *Moorgate Mercantile Co Ltd v Twitchings* [1976] QB 225 and *Crabb v Arun District Council* [1976] Ch 179 at 188. Applying those principles here it can be seen that the assurances given by Kenneth and Hedley to Doris Cooke – leading her to believe that she would be allowed to stay in the house as long as she wished – raised an equity in her favour. There was no need for her to prove that she acted on the faith of those assurances. It is to be presumed that she did so. There is no need for her to prove that she acted to her detriment or to her prejudice. Suffice it to say that she stayed on the house – looking after Kenneth and Clarice – when otherwise she might have left and got a job elsewhere. The equity having thus been raised in her favour, it is for the courts of equity to decide in what way that equity should be satisfied. In this case, it should be by allowing her to stay on in the house as long as she wishes.

I would therefore allow the appeal and grant a declaration on the counterclaim that Miss Cooke is entitled to occupy 32 George Street, Riddings, rent-free so long as she wishes to stay there.

Griffiths v Williams (1977) 248 EG 947, CA

Goff LJ: I direct my mind to the first question: Was there an equity? ... Mrs Williams' evidence, which the learned judge preferred to that of Mrs Griffiths, was as follows: 'Whenever the question arose in any discussion Mrs Williams had always been assured that the house was her home for life. That was always what was said and she never expected more than a life interest.' That does not read as if it was the lady giving evidence, but the notes of the evidence appear throughout in that form, and this was obviously a record which the learned judge was making of the evidence which had been given before him. Then Mr Hedley Williams, whose evidence the learned judge also accepted, said – or the effect of his evidence is recorded – as follows, 'He had always understood that the house was his mother's for life, and this had been said to, or in front of, him over many years by both his grandmother and his mother'; and, again, 'As to the improvements, etc there was no objection by the grandmother and he had never heard any mention (prior to his grandmother's death) of his mother leaving, or being asked to leave.' So when the learned judge speaks of what Mrs Williams would have thought had it occurred to her, it is clear that it would have occurred to her but for the fact that Mrs Cole, the testatrix, was throughout repeatedly assuring Mrs Williams that she could live in the house for the rest of her life. It seems to me, on this evidence, clear that Mrs Williams expended her money on the faith of those repeated assurances, and it is, I think, an irresistible inference that Mrs Cole knew that Mrs Williams was relying on the assurances which she herself was repeatedly making to her daughter. In my judgment, therefore, there is no doubt at all in this case but that an equity is made out.

I therefore pass to the second question, and that is: What is the equity? That must be an equity to have made good, so far as may fairly be done between the parties, the representation that Mrs Williams should be entitled to live in the house rent-free for the rest of her life.

So I come to the third question, which is really the one which gives rise to such difficulties as there are in this case [namely, what constitutes the settlement within s 1(1) of the Settled Land Act 1925] ...

Happily, by the good sense of the parties in accepting a solution of the problem which I propounded for their consideration, it is unnecessary for this court to resolve those problems. In *Dodsworth v Dodsworth*, having decided that a right of occupation for the whole life of the claimant would be a wrong way of giving effect to the equity because it would create a settlement under the Settled Land Act and give the claimant too much, the court then adopted an alternative suggestion of compensation by recouping the claimant his expenditure (I think with interest) and giving him possession until payment. They recognised that that really went too far the other way; and certainly it would not be appropriate in this case – if for no other reason, because of the difficulty of quantification. But it seems to me that *Dodsworth v Dodsworth* proceeded upon the basis which I have spelt out of *Crabb's* case – that the third problem is one of discretion: the court ought to see, having regard to all the circumstances, what is the best and fairest way to secure protection for the person who has been misled by the representations made to him and subsequently repudiated.

In the present case, it seemed to me, and I suggested to the parties, that the fairest way of dealing with the matter would be to direct the plaintiffs to grant Mrs Williams a long lease, determinable upon her death, at a nominal rent, since that would give her the right of occupation for her whole life and could not in any event give her the statutory powers under the Settled Land Act. The nominal rent would be an obligation not contemplated when the representations were made to her, but perfect equity is seldom possible.

There appeared to be only two objections to this course. One was that she might assign the lease; but that can be dealt with by including in the lease an absolute covenant not to assign, and by her giving an undertaking to this court, which I understand she is prepared to do, not to assign. The other difficulty was that, if she were to marry again, her husband might be able to claim a protected tenancy under the Rent Acts. I know that to Mrs Williams that appears a flight of fantasy; but we have to take precautions to see that what we propose is something which will not go wrong in an event which is not impossible and could happen. Counsel have made inquiries and they assured us that the husband would not be entitled to protection under the Rent Acts if the rent did not exceed two-thirds of the rateable value at the relevant date; and they have ascertained that that rateable value is £46 per annum. Therefore, if we direct the lease to be at a rent of £30 per annum, we will have served the two ends of keeping it below two-thirds of the rateable value and making it nominal; and that is what I would propose. I took the precaution of making it clear to counsel, and they have made it clear to the parties, that, while we might order that as a term after deciding whether or not a life interest would be a 'settlement' within the meaning of the Act, if we were to decide that it was not a settlement within the Act Mrs Williams would be entitled to claim a full life interest without reservation of any rent, and therefore we could only adopt this course of a long lease at this stage if the parties consented to it, otherwise we must first determine the problem which I have mentioned and then consider what it would be right to order in the light of that determination. Counsel, having withdrawn and consulted with their clients and taken instructions, say that they are content that we should adopt the solution proposed by me.

I would therefore allow the appeal, discharge the order of the learned deputy circuit judge, and direct the plaintiffs to grant to Mrs Williams the lease which I have indicated.

Award of monetary compensation

This remedy is particularly appropriate where the claimant has incurred expenditure in making improvements to the disputed land, but the transfer of an estate or interest in land, or the grant of a life interest is otherwise inappropriate. An example is *Dodsworth v Dodsworth*[45] where to avoid the Settled Land Act 1925, the court awarded monetary compensation to the claimant for the money and labour invested in making improvements to the land.

Dodsworth v Dodsworth (1973) 228 EG 1115, CA

Russell LJ: In this case the plaintiff, aged over 70, owned, in 1967, a bungalow near Boston, Lincolnshire, and lived there alone. Her younger brother and his wife – the two defendants – returned to England from Australia and were looking for a house to acquire as their home. The plaintiff persuaded them to join her in her bungalow. The judge held on the evidence that the defendants spent a sum of over £700 on improvements to the plaintiff's bungalow in the expectation, encouraged and induced by the plaintiff, that the defendants and the survivor of them would be able to remain in the bungalow as their home – sharing of course with the plaintiff while she lived – for as long as they wished to do so, in circumstances that raised an equity in favour of the defendants on the footing of principles exemplified in a passage from Lord Kingsdown's speech in *Ramsden v Dyson* (1866) LR 1 HL 129, and in other cases since then. The judge, however, held on the evidence that the parties did not intend to create a legal relationship. Not many months after the defendants moved into the bungalow, the plaintiff repented of her invitation for

45 (1973) 228 *Estates Gazette* 1115.

reasons, or alleged reasons, which need not be rehearsed. She started proceedings for possession: the defendants counterclaimed to assert an equity. The plaintiff did not appear at the hearing, and her claim for possession was non-suited. The question on the counterclaim was whether the proper way in which the equity should be satisfied would be to make some order which would assure the defendants in their occupation of the bungalow as their home for as long as they wished, or, on the other hand, to declare in effect that possession could only be obtained against them by the plaintiff if they were repaid their outlay on improvements to the bungalow.

The judge decided upon the latter as the appropriate course. His main ground was this. The plaintiff was anxious to sell the bungalow and buy a smaller and less expensive one for herself. She could not do this, having no other capital asset, if the defendants were entitled to stay rent free. She would therefore have to continue sharing her home for the rest of her life with the defendants, with whom she was, or thought she was, at loggerheads. Against this the defendants would, on leaving, recover, and have available towards another home, the expenditure which they laid out in the expectation, albeit encouraged by the plaintiff, of ability to stay there as their home. We think that the judge in balancing these considerations was entitled, and right, to come to that decision. We do not accept that the judge was wrong on the ground submitted to us that where the extent of the expectations was derived, though without intention to create a legal relationship, between the parties, compensation for outlay could not be an appropriate satisfaction of the equity. On the appeal, the plaintiff having died intestate after notice of appeal, leave was given to the respondents, who are her administrators under a grant of letters of administration, to be joined as parties to the appeal. They do not contend that there was not an equity. They support the view, in the changed circumstances, of the judge that it was proper to satisfy the defendants' equity by protecting their occupation unless and until their expenditure was reimbursed.

Now it is clear that the ground upon which the judge mainly decided upon the appropriate remedy has, by the plaintiff's death, disappeared. But what is the situation now? Apart from the equity, the situation is this. The estate vested in the legal personal representatives consists only of the bungalow. This is subject to a standing mortgage of some £200 to £300. Its value free of any occupation rights in the defendants might be £5,000. Under the Administration of Estates Act 1925, the administrators hold the bungalow on trust for sale and to pay out of the proceeds of sale debts, duties, if any, and administration expenses (which must include their costs of this appeal), and then to divide among 10 stirps of beneficiaries, the first defendant in fact being one stirps. The immediate problem seems to be this. If immediate and direct effect is given to the expectations of the defendants, to take effect in priority to the respondents' entitlement and statutory duties, we cannot see but that it will lead, by virtue of the provisions of the Settled Land Act, to a greater and more extensive interest than was ever contemplated by the plaintiff and the defendants. The defendants would necessarily become joint tenants for life. As such they could sell the property, or quit and let it. In the one case, they would be entitled to the income of the invested proceeds of sale for life and the life of the survivor: in the other, they would be entitled to the net rents. None of these possibilities could conceivably have been embodied in the expectations giving rise to the equity in question, and we do not think that it can be right to satisfy such an equity by conferring upon the defendants a greater interest in the property than was envisaged by the parties. This, we should say, is a point which appears to have been overlooked in *Inwards v Baker* [1965] 2 QB 29; [1965] 1 All ER 446.

Is it possible in the present case to give effect to the expectation without falling foul of the impact of the Settled Land Act? ... Yes it was. In short therefore we do not see how we can sensibly, and without awarding to the defendants a greater interest in law than was within the induced expectation, satisfy this equity save by securing their occupation until this expenditure has been reimbursed, which was the effect of the judge's order or declaration.

Other remedies

In some cases, the land owner may be ordered to transfer his land to the claimant, but that the claimant should, however, pay the land owner compensation for the loss of his land. The recent Privy Council decision in *Lim Teng Huan v Ang Swee Chuan*[46] is just such an example.

Lim Teng Huan v Ang Swee Chuan [1992] 1 WLR 113, PC

Lord Browne-Wilkinson: ... the trial judge held that no proprietary estoppel had been established, apparently on the grounds that the plaintiff had not been guilty of any conduct which would render it unconscionable for him to rely on his strict legal rights. He therefore gave the plaintiff leave to withdraw his claim but dismissed the counterclaim.

On appeal, the Court of Appeal held that the judge had erred in law. The decision in *Taylors Fashions Ltd v Liverpool Victoria Trustees Co Ltd* (Note) [1982] QB 133 showed that, in order to found a proprietary estoppel, it is not essential that the representor should have been guilty of unconscionable conduct in permitting the representee to assume that he could act as he did: it is enough if, in all the circumstances, it is unconscionable for the representor to go back on the assumption which he permitted the representee to make. The Court of Appeal, therefore, held that, upon payment of compensation, the defendant was entitled to a declaration of ownership of the plaintiff's share and to the injunction which he sought on the counterclaim.

Before the Court of Appeal the defendant accepted throughout that he was bound to compensate the plaintiff for the value of the one half share in the land. The only evidence of the value of the land before the Court of Appeal was an agreed valuation of the land alone at $760,000 and of the building (being the house) at $1.54m, making a total for the whole of $2.4m. The land element in this valuation had been valued on the basis that the preparatory works carried out in 1982 had been carried out at the defendant's sole expense. On the basis of evidence given by the defendant that those preparatory works had cost between $300,000 and $350,000, the Court of Appeal took the median figure of $325,000 and deducted this from the agreed valuation of the land at $760,000, giving an unimproved value for the whole of the land (ignoring the preparatory works) of $435,000 one half of which is $217,500. They therefore made the declaration that the defendant owned the plaintiff's share and granted the injunction sought by the counterclaim but also ordered that such declaration and order were conditional upon the defendant paying to the plaintiff the sum of $217,500. Although Mr Chan (for the defendant) asked the court to direct that the plaintiff transfer his interest in the land to the defendant, no such direction was included in the Court of Appeal order.

46 [1992] 1 WLR 113. See [1993] Conv 173 (Goo, SH).

Before their Lordships' Board, two main points were in issue. First, were the Court of Appeal right in holding that the plaintiff was perpetually estopped from claiming title to his one half share of the land? Second, were the Court of Appeal justified in assessing the compensation payable by the defendant in the way that they did?

As to the first question, their Lordships have no hesitation in agreeing with the conclusions and reasoning of the Court of Appeal. Sir Michael Ogden (for the plaintiff), accepted that the Court of Appeal were right in applying the law as laid down in *Taylors Fashions Ltd v Liverpool Victoria Trustees Co Ltd* (Note) [1982] QB 133 and that recitals (3) and (4) to the agreement could provide evidence as to the parties' intentions, even if the agreement was legally unenforceable for uncertainty. However, he submitted that there was no evidence that the defendant had relied on the agreement or the recitals in it when he proceeded with the construction of the house. As a result, one of the necessary ingredients for an estoppel was missing. Their Lordships reject this submission. Although the defendant did not give direct evidence of such reliance, the sole purpose of the agreement was to regularise the position so that the defendant's house would be built on land to which he was solely entitled: the inference that thereafter the defendant proceeded in reliance on that agreed arrangement is inevitable and was the inference rightly drawn by the trial judge in the passage to which their Lordships have referred.

Next Sir Michael Ogden submitted that in any event the right way to give effect to the estoppel was not to vest the whole of the land in the defendant absolutely but to confer on him a status of irremovability, ie the defendant should be entitled to live free in the house so long as he wished but if the house and land were sold in the future the plaintiff should be entitled to his half share. Sir Michael Ogden was not able to elucidate how long this status of irremovability was to endure: for example, on the defendant's death would those succeeding his estate also be irremovable? Moreover, such an estoppel would not give effect to the manifest common intention of the parties, *viz* that the land should belong outright to the defendant and that the plaintiff should be entitled to compensation for giving up his half share. Their Lordships agree with the decision of the Court of Appeal.

As to the second point, there is no disagreement on the general principle: the plaintiff should receive, by way of compensation, the value of the land as a site excluding such part of its value as is attributable to the preparatory works carried out in 1982. Whilst their Lordships are sympathetic to the desire of the Court of Appeal to produce finality in the matter, they are unable to accept that there was sufficient evidence to justify the Court of Appeal in assessing such value in the way that they did. Quite apart from there being serious doubts whether the cost of the preparatory works exactly represents the increase in the value of the land attributable to such works, the evidence as to the amount of such cost was inadequate. At the trial, the valuation was agreed. At a late stage, Mr Chan (for the defendant) sought to call a contractor to prove the actual cost of preparatory works. For some reason, the judge did not permit this, but he did permit the defendant to be recalled to deal with the point. The defendant was asked approximately how much he had spent in 1982 to prepare the site: the note of his reply is 'Need to check records. Between $300,000 to $350,000.'

In their Lordships' view in the absence of acceptance by the parties that the court should act on such vague evidence, it was not legitimate for the Court of Appeal to determine the unimproved value of the land on such evidence, which on its face is merely an unverified approximation on a matter capable of exact computation and proof.

There was some discussion before the Board as to whether the parties had agreed to the Court of Appeal taking the course that they did. That involved an investigation of what exactly had transpired before the Court of Appeal, the suggestion being that the parties had agreed to the Court of Appeal taking the course which they did. The skeleton argument submitted by Mr Chan to the Court of Appeal included a submission that there was sufficient evidence to decide the value of the land: alternatively, it submitted that there should be an inquiry before the registrar. It is common ground that Mr Angking (counsel for the plaintiff before the Court of Appeal) did not invite the court to make an order for an inquiry. In their Lordships' view this falls short of an agreement by the plaintiff to accept a rough and ready assessment of the amount of compensation by the Court of Appeal. An inquiry must therefore now be directed.

It was agreed by the parties before the Board that, if an inquiry was necessary, the appropriate direction should be that the registrar should determine the unimproved value of the land ie the value of the land as at the date of the inquiry on the assumption that none of the works carried out on the land since 1981 had in fact been carried out.

As to the cross-appeal, Sir Michael Ogden accepted that, if the main point argued by him on the appeal failed, it would be right to order the plaintiff to transfer his share to the defendant, provided that the requirements of s 23 of the Land Code (Laws of Brunei, Land Code (c 40), revised edn (1984)) (which renders void any transfer which has not received prior written approval from His Majesty the Sultan in Council) are not infringed.

Their Lordships are therefore of the opinion that the order of the Court of Appeal should be varied so as to provide as follows: (1) an immediate declaration that the defendant is the beneficial owner of the share of the land formerly belonging to the plaintiff, conditional upon payment of the compensation mentioned at para (4) below; (2) an immediate injunction restraining the plaintiff from entering upon or dealing with the land or any interest therein; (3) an order for an inquiry as to the present value of the land on the footing that no works have been carried out thereon since 1981; (4) an order that on payment by the defendant to the plaintiff of a sum equal to one half of that found by the inquiry, the plaintiff transfer his one half share of the land to the defendant or any person nominated by him and approved by His Majesty in Council under s 23 of the Land Code.

The order as to costs in the Court of Appeal will stand but the plaintiff must pay nine-tenths of the defendant's costs before their Lordships' Board.

Their Lordships will advise His Majesty the Sultan and Yang de-Pertuan that the order of the Court of Appeal should be varied accordingly.

S H Goo (1993) Conv 173 at 175

It is submitted, however, that the decision of the Privy Council does not fully give effect to the parties' common intention. The 1985 agreement manifested a common intention that the plaintiff should receive unspecified land in exchange for his half share in the co-owned land. The value of the unspecified land was uncertain and it was clear that the plaintiff did not intend it to be precise compensation for the loss of his half share. The value of the unspecified land could well have been much higher than the value of the plaintiff's half share. It was intended to be a bargain, though it was void for uncertainty.

The Privy Council's decision was, however, perhaps inevitable in the circumstances. As the agreement was void for uncertainty, the doctrine of part performance could not apply. There was no contract that could be partly performed by building the house. The doctrine of proprietary estoppel mitigates the harshness this caused to the defendant. Its operation is, however, much more uncertain than a simple case of enforcing an otherwise void contract. Equity is at its most innovative and flexible in cases of this kind and the void agreement is only to be taken into account in deciding how to satisfy the equity. In the circumstances, financial compensation to the defendant for the preparatory and building works while allowing the plaintiff to share the whole property is clearly impracticable and could create further disputes. To order an immediate sale of the whole property and to divide the balance of the proceeds of sale between them after deducting the increase in value attributable to the defendant's works is equally not equitable. This is because the purpose of the original arrangement evidenced by the 1985 agreement was that the defendant should be allowed to build his house on the land and to reside in it. The defendant's interest is not just in the proceeds of sale but in the enjoyment of the property itself. On the other hand, the plaintiff was clearly expecting compensation in the form of a piece of land to be allotted in the future by the Brunei Government. Whilst this consideration was wholly uncertain in all respects, the court chose to compensate the plaintiff financially for transfer of his interest in the disputed land. The decision that the plaintiff should convey his half share to the defendant on condition that the defendant pay the plaintiff compensation for the value of the land as a site excluding the increase in value attributable to the preparatory work seems justifiable in the circumstances.

CHAPTER 4

SALE OF LAND

Land may be disposed of *inter vivos* by sale or as a gift or as part of a family settlement.[1] It may also be passed on to a person by will or, if the owner dies intestate, to those persons entitled under the intestacy rules. This chapter only deals with the disposition of land by sale, as it is by far the most common and significant form of disposition in practice. It is beyond the scope of this book to examine the details of land transfer, and reference to specialist conveyancing books should be made.[2] Some basic knowledge of disposition by sale is however essential for a better understanding of the remaining chapters, particularly those on the protection of legal estates and fragmented equitable interests in both unregistered and registered systems.[3]

The process of land transfer by sale involves, invariably, two main transactions: the contract and the completion (ie the conveyance).[4] There are, however, various things a buyer and a seller, or more usually their solicitors, have to do before the contract, after the contract, before the completion, and after the completion. There are therefore five stages in the conveyancing of land by sale.

1 STAGE ONE: PRE-CONTRACT

Subject to contract

At pre-contract stage, the buyer and the seller are simply negotiating. They may, however, 'agree' on the sale 'subject to contract'; and until a contract is signed and exchanged in the usual way, they are not contractually bound.[5] There has been abuse of the 'subject to contract' proviso. However, in 1975 the Law Commission recommended that no legal status should be given to the 'subject to contract' proviso[6] and in 1987 recommended that a pre-contract deposit of 0.5% of the purchase price should be made by both the prospective seller and buyer as soon as they agree on the sale 'subject to contract'. They must then exchange the contract within four weeks and any party who withdraws otherwise than for good cause within that period will lose the deposit.[7]

1 For settlement see Chapters 11 and 12.

2 Storey, IR, *Conveyancing*, 4th edn, 1993, London: Butterworths; Barnsley; Emmet, LE *Emmet on Title*, 19th edn (by Farrand, JT), 1986, Looseleaf, London: Longman; Ruoff & Roper.

3 See Chapters 6 and 7.

4 Other forms of transfer, eg as a gift or by will, etc are not normally preceded by a contract.

5 *Spottiswoode, Ballantyne & Co Ltd v Doreen Appliances Ltd* [1942] 2 KB 32 at 35; *Keppel v Wheeler* [1927] 1 KB 577 at 584.

6 Law Commission, 'Report on 'Subject to Contract' Agreements' (Law Com 65, January 1975), para 4.

7 Law Commission, 'Pre-Contract Deposits: A Practice Recommendation by the Conveyancing Standing Committee' (1987), paras 5 and 7.

Searches, inquiries and inspections[8]

As in many other contracts, the basic rule in a contract for the sale of land is *caveat emptor* (let the buyer beware). It is therefore important and common for the buyer's solicitors to carry out searches, enquiries and inspections to find out more about the property to be transferred. The seller is, of course, under a duty to disclose any latent defects in his title. Latent defects are incumbrances and any other adverse interests which a prospective buyer cannot discover for himself by a reasonable inspection of the property and cover estate contracts, restrictive covenants, certain easements such as underground pipelines, leases where the tenant is not in possession etc. When questions are asked about the property, the answers the seller gives must be accurate to the best of his knowledge. If the buyer exchanges the contracts as a result of certain misrepresentation on the part of the seller, he may rescind the contract and/or sue for damages.[9] But otherwise the seller does not have to volunteer any information. Thus the buyer has to make standard enquiries such as any existing disputes over the property, the ownership of boundary walls, hedges and fences, rights of way, ownership and maintenance of drive way, planning matters etc. This exercise represents the biggest hazard for prospective buyers who have to incur considerable time and effort to gather information which may have already been possessed by the seller. An attempt to solve this problem has been made by the Law Society in 1990 by introducing a 'National Conveyancing Protocol' as a result of the recommendations by the Law Commission's Conveyancing Standing Committee in 1989.[10] The Protocol is intended to be used in all domestic conveyancing transactions. Under the third edition (1994) of the Protocol,[11] a seller is required to provide certain standard information including a series of questionnaires contained in the 'Property Information Form' and a Fixtures, Fittings and Contents Form'. It should be noted that the Protocol is only a time saving device and does not change the caveat emptor rule: it is still the buyer's responsibility to find out any other information not covered by the Protocol. Furthermore, the Protocol is only voluntary rather than compulsory. A copy of the Protocol is provided at the end of this chapter.

(a) Local searches

Unliked the previous edition of the Protocol, under the third edition, the buyer himself has to make local searches. There are two separate local searches: the local land charges search, maintained under the Local Land Charges Act 1975, and additional enquiries of the local authority. The Local Land Charges Register may be searched personally or by an application for an official search (using Form LLC1). The advantage of an official search is that the buyer can get compensation for existing charges not revealed by the official search

8 See Silverman, F, *Searches and Enquiries: A Conveyancer's Guide*, 2nd edn, 1992, London: Butterworths.

9 Section 2(1) of the Misrepresentation Act 1967.

10 'Let the buyer be well informed' (Reports of Conveyancing Standing Committee, December 1989), para 33. For an examination of the 1st edition of the National Protocol see [1990] Conv 137 (Wilkinson, HW).

11 With effect from 1 May 1994.

certificate.[12] The certificate does not give any priority period and becomes out of date soon after it is issued. The search will reveal matters such as compulsory purchase order, planning matters, buildings listed as being of historical interest, tree preservation orders, financial charges etc. Additional enquiries of the local authority can be made (by using Form CON 29) of the same authority as the search, and in practice the two forms are submitted together. These additional enquiries cover matters such as liability to maintain the roadway abutting the property; whether what used to be a private roadway has been adopted by the local authority to be maintained at the public expense; whether the property drains into a public sewer; whether there are any plans for new roads, subways, flyovers within 200 metres of the property, planning permission and related matters; whether the property is in a smoke controlled area and whether it is in the Register of Contaminated Land, etc.

(b) Central land charges searches[13]

Where the title the buyer is buying is unregistered, under the Standard Conditions of Sale[14] the seller promises to sell the property free of entries made in Land Register or Land Charges register and if the seller does not intend to do so, he must disclose it in the contract to be approved by the buyer. Thus land charges rank as latent defects in title and should be brought to the buyer's attention by the seller. The position is the same where the Standard Conditions of Sale are not used if the seller gives full title guarantee.[15] Furthermore, s 24 of the Law of Property Act 1969 provides that the question whether a buyer has knowledge of a registered land charge prior to contract is to be determined by reference to his *actual* knowledge, without regard to s 198 which provides that a buyer is *deemed* to have notice of registered land charges. Therefore, the buyer is not required by law to make pre-contract land charges searches. However, as a matter of good practice, it is advisable for the buyer to make the search to avoid entering into a troublesome contract. Where the Protocol is used, the seller is required to provide the buyer with a full search of land charges.

(c) Company Registrar searches

If the seller is a company registered under the Companies Acts, it is necessary to undertake a company register search.

This is to discover any fixed charge or floating charge over the land. A fixed charge on unregistered land created before 1 January 1970 may be registered either under the Land Charges Act or at Companies House under the Companies Act 1985. Likewise, floating charges created at any time may be, and often are, registered at Companies House. Fixed charges created after 1 January 1970 must be registered both under the Land Charges Act 1972 and the Companies Act 1985. Thus, although the buyer may rely on the Land Charges Register for fixed charges created after 1 January 1970, it is necessary to search

12 Section 10 of the Local Land Charges Act 1975.

13 See Chapter 6, pp 197–285.

14 Condition 3.1.1.

15 See s 3(1) of the Law of Property (Miscellaneous Provisions) Act 1995.

at Companies House to reveal any pre-1970 charges and floating charges at any time.

(d) Other searches

Other searches include searches at the Register of Common Land and Town or Village Greens where the property to be bought is in an area likely to be affected by a right of common, now registered under the Commons Registration Act 1965, which may restrict future development. Under the second edition of the Protocol, the seller would do the search for the buyer. Under the third edition, the buyer would have to do the search himself.

Where the title of the property to be bought is unregistered, the buyer should also make the public index map search at the district land registry. This is to verify that the seller's title is unregistered and ensure that there are no interests registered at the Land Registry adverse to the seller's title. Under the Protocol, the seller's solicitor will make the search.

(e) Inspections of property

The buyer should also inspect the property carefully to find out if anyone other than the seller is in occupation and if so whether they have an interest in the property. Inquiry must be made of the persons in occupation themselves and not just the seller.[16] The buyer should also look out for any patent defects in title, such as a neighbour's right to walk over the garden, etc. The seller is not obliged to disclose these patent defects to the buyer. Inspections of property are normally done by the buyer himself with perhaps some advice from his solicitors on the matters to look out for.

Survey

It is also advisable for the buyer to commission a structural survey of the property to be bought. In practice, many house purchases are financed by lending institutions which will instruct a surveyor to assess whether the security offered is sound. This will have to be paid for by the buyer and the buyer will normally be reluctant to commission his own additional survey. If the surveyor is negligent in his assessment and report made to the lending institution which helps financing the purchase, and the buyer suffers loss subsequently, the surveyor can be liable to the buyer.[17]

Drafting and approving of contract and checking evidence of title

Having made all the relevant searches, enquiries and inspections, if the buyer is happy with the property on offer and agrees to purchase, the seller's solicitors

16 *Hodgson v Marks* [1971] Ch 892 at 932, *per* Russell LJ.

17 *Yianni v Edwin Evans & Sons* [1982] QB 438; *Smith v Eric Bush* [1990] 1 AC 831.

will prepare two copies of a draft contract for the buyer's approval. Usually, documentary evidence of title will also be included. But the time-honoured practice is to do this after the contract. It is a common practice for the parties to adopt the Standard Conditions of Sale (see pp 151–63)[18] perhaps with some modifications. As will be seen, the contract must comply with certain formalities. The buyer's solicitors will check the draft contract and may make further enquiries concerning the draft contract or make suggestions for any amendment. They may also raise questions about the evidence of title provided. The seller's solicitors will then reply to the enquiries and submit two copies of the amended draft contract. If the buyer is now happy with the seller's replies and the amended draft contract, and pre-contract searches, enquiries and inspections, his solicitors will return a copy of the draft contract to the seller's solicitors. The parties may then fix a date for the exchange of contracts which will create a legally binding relation.

2 STAGE TWO: CONTRACT

At this stage, the buyer and the seller each have a copy of the approved draft contract. They must then sign their copies and exchange them. This is known as the exchange of contracts. On the exchange of contracts, the buyer is normally required to pay 10% deposit of the purchase price. The deposit will be forfeited where the purchaser is in default[19] unless the court otherwise orders, for example, where the vendor was in default, or where although the purchaser was in default the justice of the case nevertheless requires the return of deposit.[20] The fact that the purchaser was only minutes late in completing does not normally justify departure from this rule. Once the contracts are exchanged, the parties are bound irrevocably and must be ready to proceed to the completion of contract whereby the legal estates will be conveyed or transferred. Under the Standard Conditions of Sale,[21] the completion will normally take place within 20 working days of the exchange of contracts. If the seller later changes his mind, the buyer may seek an order of specific performance compelling the seller to carry out the sale. An order of specific performance is often made almost as a matter of course[22] (because, land being unique, monetary compensation will not be an adequate remedy) provided that the buyer can establish that there is an enforceable contract for the sale of land and he has given consideration.[23] This is because specific performance is an equitable remedy and equity will not assist a volunteer. Usually, before the buyer seeks an order of specific performance, he may, on or after the completion

18 Standard Conditions of Sale, 3rd edn, 1995. It is also the 23rd edition of the National Conditions of Sale and the Law Society's Conditions of Sale 1995. For an analysis of the 1st edition of the Standard Conditions of Sale see Adams, JE [1990] Conv 179.

19 See eg *Union Eagle v Golden Achievement* [1997] 2 WLR 341, PC.

20 Section 49(2) of the LPA 1925; *Country and Metropolitan Homes Surety Ltd v Topclaim Ltd* [1997] 1 All ER 254.

21 Standard Conditions of Sale, 3rd edn, 1995, Condition 6.1.1.

22 *Patel v Ali* [1984] Ch 283 at 286G; *Graham v Pitkin* [1992] 1 WLR 403 at 406D.

23 *Hall v Warren* (1804) 9 Ves 605; 32 ER 738.

date, give the seller a notice to complete within 10 working days making time of completion of the essence of the contract.[24] Alternatively, he may choose to simply sue for damages or, if time of completion is of the essence, rescind the contract on or after due completion date. Likewise, if the buyer later refuses to proceed with the sale, the seller may keep the deposit and sue him for breach of contract.

For a contract for the sale of land to be enforceable by legal action, certain formalities must be complied with. The precise formality requirements depend on the date the contract is created.

Contracts made before 27 September 1989

(a) Formality

Before 27 September 1989, a contract for the sale of land could be made orally. It could be made in the same way as any other contract. However, under s 40(1) of the Law of Property Act 1925, a contract for the sale of land had to be in writing or evidenced by a memorandum in writing or sufficient act of part performance otherwise it was unenforceable by action.[25] Thus, although a purely oral contract was as valid as a written one, it would be unenforceable.

Law of Property Act 1925

40. Contracts for sale, etc of land to be in writing

(1) No action may be brought upon any contract for the sale or other disposition of land or any interest in land, unless the agreement upon which such action is brought, or some memorandum or note thereof, is in writing, and signed by the party to be charged or by some other person thereunto by him lawfully authorised.

(2) This section applies to contracts whether made before or after the commencement of this Act and does not affect the law relating to part performance, or sales by the court.

(b) Effect of s 40 on oral contract

Section 40 did not render the contract void altogether but simply precluded the bringing of an action to enforce it.[26] The contract is binding but yet unenforceable.[27] The contract could still be enforced in any way except by action. Therefore, if the buyer paid a deposit under an oral contract, the seller

24 Standard Conditions of Sale, 3rd edn, 1995, Condition 6.8. Notice which fails to allow 10 working days for completion is ineffective: *Country and Metropolitan Homes Surrey Ltd v Topclaim Ltd* [1997] 1 All ER 254.

25 The origin of this statutory requirement as to written evidence was s 4 of the Statute of Frauds 1677. The purpose was to prevent fraud and perjury by false allegations of contracts.

26 *Crosby v Wadsworth* (1805) 6 East 602 at 611, *per* Lord Ellenborough CJ; *Maddison v Alderson* (1883) 8 App Cas 467 at 474, *per* Lord Selbourne LC; *Bristol, Cardiff & Swansea Aereated Bread Co v Maggs* (1890) 44 Ch D 616 at 622; *Leroux v Brown* (1852) 12 CB 801; *Britain v Rossiter* (1879) 11 QBD 123.

27 This is described as 'indefensibly confusing', Law Commission, 'Transfer of Land: Formalities for Contracts for Sale, etc of Land' (Law Com 164, 29 June 1987), para 4.2.

could keep the deposit if the buyer defaulted as it was normally an implied term in the contract that deposit was paid as a guarantee against breach of contract and could be forfeited on breach.[28] If s 40 had rendered an oral contract void, the deposit would have to be returned, for there would be no ground upon which the seller could rely to retain the deposit.[29] If there was no contract at all, the buyer would be able to recover the deposit on the ground of total failure of consideration under the law of restitution.[30]

(c) Contracts governed by s 40

Section 40 applied to any contract for the sale or other disposition of land or any interest in land. 'Disposition' is defined as including 'a conveyance and also a devise, bequest, or an appointment of property contained in a will'.[31] 'Conveyance' is defined as including 'a mortgage, charge, lease, assent,[32] vesting declaration,[33] vesting instrument,[34] disclaimer,[35] release[36] and every other assurance[37] of property or of an interest therein by any instrument, except a will'.[38] Thus, a contract for the sale of freehold land, for the grant of a lease, for the assignment of a lease, for the grant of a mortgage, easement or restrictive covenant etc is caught by the section. A contract for the grant of a licence such as lodgings[39] is not caught by the section because it does not create an interest in land.

---

28 *Thomas v Brown* (1876) 1 QBD 714; *Monnickendam v Leanse* (1923) 39 TLR 445.

29 *Chillingworth v Esche* [1924] 1 Ch 97 at 112.

30 Used to be called quasi-contract. See Goff, RG and Jones, GH, *The Law of Restitution*, 3rd edn, 1986, London: Sweet & Maxwell.

31 Section 205(1)(ii) of the LPA 1925.

32 This is a document by which personal representatives transfer property to the beneficiaries under the will or according to the intestacy rules. The assent must be in writing signed by the personal representatives but need not be by deed: s 36(1), (2), (4) of the AEA 1925.

33 This is a declaration made in a deed of appointment of new trustees that the trust property should be vested in them jointly with any existing trustees: s 40(1)(a) of the Trustees Act 1925.

34 Including vesting deed and vesting assent. Where a settlement is created *inter vivos*, it is effected by a trust instrument and a vesting deed. A vesting deed is the document by which the legal estate in the settled land is transferred from the settlor to the tenant for life or statutory owner. Where the settlement is created by will, the will is regarded as the trust instrument and legal estate having devolved (passed) to the testator's personal representatives has to be vested in the immediate beneficiary by a vesting assent. Similarly, a vesting assent is used to transfer the legal estate of settled land from the personal representatives of a deceased tenant for life or statutory owner to the immediate beneficiaries (see Chapter 11).

35 The termination, refusal or renunciation of a right, claim, or property, eg a tenant may disclaim a lease.

36 A document by which a person discharges his claim of a proprietary interest in or over the other's land, eg release of an easement, profit *à prendre* and rentcharge.

37 A disposition or transfer.

38 Section 205(1)(ii) of the LPA 1925.

39 *Wright v Stavert* (1860) 2 E & E 721.

(d) Form of memorandum

There was no statutory form of memorandum. Any written document which showed that there was a contract and what that contract was was enough.[40] A letter to the writer's own solicitor or agent or to a third party,[41] a note in a rent book,[42] a receipt,[43] etc are all examples of a sufficient written memorandum. But a written memorandum which referred to an agreement 'subject to contract' could not be a sufficient memorandum, as there was yet no contract to be evidenced by the memorandum.[44] The memorandum must be created simultaneously with or after the contract was concluded.[45] In practice, most agreements for the sale of land were made 'subject to contract' so that any correspondence relating to the agreements 'subject to contract' before the exchange of contracts could not be used as a sufficient memorandum. The actual contract was made by the exchange of the formal contracts prepared by the seller's solicitors which were themselves in written form. Thus, in practice where the contract was made by the exchange of contracts, s 40 was satisfied by the formal contracts. However, if the contract was for some reason made before the formal exchange of contracts, the formal contract would serve as a sufficient memorandum.[46]

(e) Content of memorandum

The memorandum should state all the important terms of the contract: the names or descriptions of the contracting parties,[47] a description of the property,[48] the consideration,[49] any agreed special terms,[50] the signature of the party to be charged or his lawfully authorised agent.[51] The memorandum must also contain some indication that the party to be charged recognised that a contract existed.[52] Where the memorandum did not include all the terms, it

40 *Thirkell v Cambi* [1919] 2 KB 590 at 597.

41 *Gibson v Holland* (1865) LR 1 CP 1; *Moore v Hart* (1682) 1 Vern 110 at 201.

42 *Hill v Hill* [1947] Ch 231.

43 *Evans v Prothero* (1852) 1 De GM & G 572.

44 *Tiverton Estates Ltd v Wearwell Ltd* [1975] Ch 146. Contrast *Griffiths v Young* [1970] Ch 675 ('subject to contract' agreement held to have been waived orally by a subsequent telephone conversation) and *Law v Jones* [1974] Ch 112 (correspondence relating to 'subject to contract' agreement held to be sufficient memorandum).

45 Exceptionally, a prior memorandum might be accepted where a written offer (a prior memorandum) was accepted orally or in writing: *Reuss v Picksley* (1866) LR 1 Ex 342; *Parker v Clark* [1960] 1 WLR 286.

46 *Cf Wanchford v Fotherley* (1694) 2 Free Ch 201 at 202; *Gray v Smith* (1889) 43 Ch D 20 (rough draft of an agreement).

47 *Potter v Duffield* (1874) LR 18 Eq 4.

48 *Ogilvie v Foljambe* (1817) 3 Mer 53 ('Mr Ogilvie's House' was accepted with parol evidence).

49 Or the means of ascertaining it: *Smith v Jones* [1952] 2 All ER 907 ('the controlled price fixed by the government' held sufficient).

50 *North v Loomes* [1919] 1 Ch 378 (one party to pay legal fees of the other); *Tweddell v Henderson* [1975] 2 All ER 1096 (payment by instalments); *Hawkins v Price* [1947] Ch 645 (agreed date of vacant possession).

51 Section 40(1) of the LPA 1925.

52 *Tiverton Estates Ltd v Wearwell Ltd* [1975] Ch 146; *cf Law v Jones* [1974] Ch 112.

would not be sufficient unless the term could be waived by the plaintiff.[53] In the case of a contract to grant a lease, the memorandum must also contain the following terms: the duration of the lease and the date of commencement.[54] If the parties have not agreed on the duration or the commencement date, there is simply no concluded contract.[55] Where it was agreed that the commencement of the lease was subject to a condition precedent which was likely to occur but the precise date of occurrence was uncertain, the commencement could be made certain by the occurrence of the event specified in the condition,[56] the memorandum must therefore also contain the condition precedent.

(f) Joinder of documents

Where all the terms of the agreement were not in a single document but in several written documents, they might all together constitute a sufficient memorandum under the doctrine of joinder of documents. For the doctrine to operate, as Jenkins LJ put it:

> ... there should be a document signed by the party to be charged which while not containing in itself all the necessary ingredients of the required memorandum, does contain some reference, express or implied, to some other document or transaction. Where any such reference can be spelt out of a document so signed, then parol evidence may be given to identify the other document referred to, or as the case may be, to explain the other transaction, and to identify any document relating to it.[57]

It is clear from Jenkins LJ's statement above that the starting point is the document signed by the defendant. It is this document which must make reference to other documents before other documents could be read together with the document signed by the defendant to form a complete memorandum.

(g) Part performance

Where there was no sufficient memorandum, the party seeking to enforce an oral contract had to show that he had nevertheless partly performed the contract.[58] As Lord Simon once said:

> Where ... a party to a contract unenforceable under the Statute of Frauds stood by while the other party acted to his detriment in performance of his own contractual obligations, the first party would be precluded by the Court of Chancery from claiming exoneration, on the ground that the contract was unenforceable, from performance of his reciprocal obligations; and the court

53 If the term omitted from the memorandum is exclusively to the detriment or for the benefit of one of the parties, the plaintiff may perform it or waive the benefit of it as the case may be. See *North v Loomes* [1919] 1 Ch 378 at 385–86 (if the memorandum failed to contain the term requiring the buyer to pay the seller's legal fees, the seller could still use the memorandum if he was prepared to waive the benefit of the term).

54 *Dolling v Evans* (1867) 36 LJ Ch 474.

55 *Cartwright v Miller* (1877) 36 LT 398; *Edwards v Jones* (1921) 124 LT 740.

56 *Brilliant v Michaels* [1945] 1 All ER 121.

57 *Timmins v Moreland Street Property Co Ltd* [1958] Ch 110 at 130.

58 Section 40(2) of the LPA 1925 expressly preserved the operation of the doctrine of part performance.

> would, if required, decree specific performance of the contract. Equity would not, as it was put, allow the Statute of Frauds 'to be used as an engine of fraud'. This became known as the doctrine of part performance – the 'part' performance being that of the party who had, to the knowledge of the other party, acted to his detriment in carrying out irremediably his own obligations (or some significant part of them) under the otherwise unenforceable contract.[59]

It is important to note that the doctrine did not create an otherwise non-existent or incomplete contract. For equity to intervene there must be an already concluded but unenforceable contract.[60] But the act of part performance must be sufficient to prove the existence of a contract. As Lord Reid stated in *Steadman v Steadman*:

> You must not first look at the oral contract and then see whether the alleged acts of part performance are consistent with it. You must first look at the alleged acts of part performance and see whether they prove that there must have been a contract and it is only if they do so prove that you can bring in the oral contract.[61]

Taking possession of the seller's property with his consent[62] and making alterations to the property[63] are classic examples of sufficient acts of part performance. Payment of money alone was generally not regarded as sufficient[64] since it could be a gift, a loan, or the discharge of some obligation and did not necessarily point to a contract let alone a contract relating to land.[65] But payment of money together with other acts such as forbearances in relation to the matrimonial proceedings and the sending of the transfer document for execution could amount to sufficient acts of part performance.[66] Acts done in contemplation of the making of a contract could not on the other hand be sufficient part performance. Some examples were: conducting a survey, instructing a solicitor to draft a formal contract, making a mortgage application, etc.[67]

Despite the House of Lords' decision in *Steadman v Steadman* that the plaintiff's unilateral act in forwarding a transfer for execution was a sufficient act of part performance,[68] it seemed that the act of part performance must be carried out with the defendant's knowledge and consent. In *Steadman v Steadman*, the defendant's knowledge of the plaintiff's forwarding of a

59 *Steadman v Steadman* [1976] AC 536 at 558, HL.

60 *Lockett v Norman-Wright* [1925] Ch 56.

61 [1976] AC 536 at 541.

62 *Smallwood v Sheppards* [1895] 2 QB 627; see also *Wu Koon Tai v Wu Yan Loi* [1996] 3 WLR 778, PC.

63 *Farrall v Davenport* (1861) 3 Griff 363.

64 *Lacon v Mertins* (1743) 3 Atk 1; *Chaproniere v Lambert* [1917] 2 Ch 356; *Hughes v Morris* (1852) 2 De GM & G 349 at 356.

65 See Barnsley, p 126; *cf* Megarry and Wade, p 594.

66 *Steadman v Steadman*, [1976] AC 536.

67 For more examples, see *Barnsley*, pp 123 and 126.

68 [1976] AC 536. See (1974) 38 Conv (NS) 388; (1974) 90 LQR 433; [1979] Conv 402 (MP Thompson); Law Com No 164, para 1.9 (the doctrine is in a most uncertain state after the decision).

document for execution after the making of the contract was probably implied because what the plaintiff did was a common conveyancing practice.[69] It also appeared that the act relied upon must point to the existence of a contract in respect of land and not just any contract.[70]

Once sufficient acts of part performance could be established, it opens the door to parol evidence of the whole agreement.[71] The entire contract with all its terms including those omitted from any written memorandum could be proved by parol evidence. Once the contract could be proved, equity might decree specific performance. The court had a discretion to award damages in lieu of specific performance under s 50 of the Supreme Court Act 1981. The grant of specific performance or discretionary damages was governed by the equitable principles and if these equitable discretionary remedies were rejected, the plaintiff could not claim damages at common law.[72] This was because part performance did not make an oral contract enforceable at law, it only made the contract enforceable in equity. On the other hand, if the plaintiff could show sufficient memorandum, the contract would be enforceable at law, and he would be entitled to common law damages as of right and in a proper case would also be entitled to an order of specific performance.

Contracts made on or after 27 September 1989

(a) Formality

Section 40 of the Law of Property Act 1925 has now been superseded by s 2 of the Law of Property (Miscellaneous Provisions) Act 1989 as regards contracts made on or after 27 September 1989 as a result of the Law Commission's recommendations.[73]

Law of Property (Miscellaneous Provisions) Act 1989

2. Contracts for sale etc of land to be made by signed writing

(1) A contract for the sale or other disposition of an interest in land can only be made in writing and only by incorporating all the terms which the parties have expressly agreed in one document or, where contracts are exchanged, in each.

(2) The terms may be incorporated in a document either by being set out in it or by reference to some other document.

69 [1976] AC 536 at 540, *per* Lord Reid; at 554, *per* Viscount Dilhorne.

70 In *Re Gonin, Decd* [1979] Ch 16 at 31B–D. See [1979] Conv 402 (MP Thompson). The House of Lords was divided on this point in *Steadman v Steadman, supra*: Lord Reid (at 541) and Viscount Dilhorne (at 554–55) thought that acts pointed to any contract were sufficient while Lord Morris (at 547) and Lord Salmon (at 567–70) seemed to favour the view that the acts must refer to a contract relating to land. Lord Simon did not think it necessary to consider this point.

71 *Brough v Nettleton* [1921] 2 Ch 25 at 28, *per* Lawrence J.

72 *H & A Productions Ltd v Taylor* (1955) 105 L Jo 681, CA.

73 See Law Commission, 'Transfer of Land: Formalities for Contracts for Sale etc of Land' (Law Com 164, 29 June 1987), paras 4.10–11. For an analysis of s 2 of the 1989 Act, see Pettit, PH [1989] Conv 431; (1989) 105 LQR 553 (Annand, RE).

(3) The document incorporating the terms or, where contracts are exchanged, one of the documents incorporating them (but not necessarily the same one) must be signed by or on behalf of each party to the contract.

(4) Where a contract for the sale or other disposition of an interest in land satisfies the conditions of this section by reason only of the rectification of one or more documents in pursuance of an order of a court, the contract shall come into being, or be deemed to have come into being, at such time as may be specified in the order.

(5) This section does not apply in relation to:

(a) a contract to grant such a lease as is mentioned in s 54(2) of the Law of Property Act 1926 (short leases);

(b) a contract made in the course of a public auction; or

(c) a contract regulated under the Financial Services Act 1986;

and nothing in this section affects the creation or operation of resulting, implied or constructive trusts.

(6) In this section:

'disposition' has the same meaning as in the Law of Property Act 1925; 'interest in land' means any estate, interest or charge in or over land.

(7) Nothing in this section shall apply in relation to contracts made before this section comes into force.

(8) Section 40 of the Law of Property Act 1925 (which is superseded by this section) shall cease to have effect.

The contract for the sale of land must itself be in writing containing all the terms of the agreement and signed by both parties. Note that the contract must be signed by both parties,[74] and not just by the party to be charged.[75] Where a letter purporting to constitute a contract for the sale of land contains a reference to the plan enclosed with it, the letter is a separate document from the plan itself and it is the letter which makes reference to the plan which is required to be signed, so that signatures on the plan itself are insufficient.[76] Where contracts are exchanged, both copies must be signed – one by the seller and the other by the buyer. Written offer and acceptance, which are not reduced into one document signed by both parties or two documents which are to be exchanged between them, are not sufficient to give rise to a written contract.[77] If the contract does not satisfy the requirements of s 2, there is simply no contract. The contract is not only unenforceable but utterly void. The doctrine of part performance cannot now help to establish an otherwise non-existing contract;

74 'Signs' means to write one's name with one's own hand: *Goodman v J Eban Ltd* [1954] 1 All ER 763 at 765 (at 768, *per* Denning LJ); *Firstpost Homes Ltd v Johnson* [1995] 4 All ER 355.

75 Section 2(3) of the LP(MP) Act 1989.

76 *Firstpost Homes Ltd v Johnson* [1995] 4 All ER 355.

77 *Commission for New Towns v Cooper (GB) Ltd* [1995] 2 All ER 929, CA; *Hooper v Sherman* [1994] NPC 153 not followed.

there is simply no contract for the plaintiff to partly perform.[78] This is envisaged by the Law Commission[79] and is an inevitable result of the written requirements of s 2. However, the role previously played by the doctrine of part performance can now be replaced by other equitable principles in particular by the doctrine of proprietary estoppel.[80] One such example is the case of *Lim Teng Huan v Ang Swee Chuan*.[81] Here, the plaintiff and the defendant jointly purchased a piece of land in the names of their fathers. Later, the defendant decided to build a house on the land for himself. Extensive preparatory works on the land were carried out and construction started at his own expense. In 1985, the parties entered into a badly worded agreement whereby the plaintiff acknowledged that he consented to the construction on condition that he received other unspecified land expected to be allotted to the defendant by the government in exchange for his undivided half share in the co-owned land in question. The house was completed in November 1985 and the defendant went into occupation, fencing in virtually the whole of the land. The plaintiff did not complain about the construction of the house or the defendant's use of it as his residence until 1986 when they fell out.

Applying the principles of proprietary estoppel, the Privy Council held that in the circumstances, it was unconscionable for the plaintiff to go back on the assumption which he permitted the defendant to make. Although the 1985 agreement was void for uncertainty it provided good evidence of that assumption. This is interesting because it shows that an agreement which does not satisfy the requirements of s 2 of the Law of Property (Miscellaneous Provisions) Act 1989 can nevertheless be enforced in some way under the doctrine of proprietary estoppel. Although s 2 of the 1989 Act has expressly superseded s 40(2) of the Law of Property Act 1925, proprietary estoppel seems to be capable of taking the place of the doctrine of part performance in this regard.

The doctrine of joinder of documents is preserved.[82] The requirements of writing under s 2 do not apply to a contract to grant a lease taking effect in possession for a term not exceeding three years at the best rent reasonably obtainable without taking a fine.[83] This removes one of the anomalies under the old s 40 that a contract for such a lease must be in writing or evidenced by written memorandum or part performance while the grant of such a lease can be oral under s 54(2) of the Law of Property Act 1925. The section does not apply to any contract made before 27 September 1989 and those contracts are still governed by the old law which has been discussed above. It should be noted that the 1989 Act was designed, as its preamble indicates, to make new

78 Section s 2(8) of the LP(MP) Act 1989; *Firstpost Homes Ltd v Johnson* [1995] 4 All ER 355 at 358e, *per* Gibson LJ; but see *Singh v Beggs* (1996) 71 P & CR 120 at 122, *per* Neill LJ ('it may be that in certain circumstances the doctrine could be relied upon').

79 Law Com 164, para 4.13

80 Law Com 164, paras 5.1f, 5.4, 5.6. For proprietary estoppel, see Chapter 3.

81 [1992] 1 WLR 113. See [1993] Conv 173 (Goo, SH).

82 Section 2(2) of the LP(MP) Act 1989.

83 Section 54(2) of the LP(MP) Act 1989, s 2(5)(a) and LPA 1925.

provision which was intended to make radical changes to contracts for the sale or other disposition of interest in land and to simplify the law and to avoid dispute. Thus, cases on the old law may not be authority for the construction of the wording of the new provision; it is not right 'to encumber the new Act with so much ancient baggage'.[84]

(b) Contracts governed by s 2

Section 2 applies to all contracts for the sale or other disposition of an interest in land. 'Disposition' has the same meaning as in s 205(1)(ii) of the Law of Property Act. An '"interest in land" means any estate, interest or charge in or over land'.[85] Thus, all transactions previously covered by the old s 40 are governed by s 2. The scope of s 2 is, however, limited by the judiciary in a number of cases. In *Spiro v Glencrown Properties Ltd*,[86] it was held that although the agreement for an option to purchase land had to comply with s 2,[87] the exercise of the option did not. It has also been held that s 2 does not apply to a collateral contract, not of itself a sale of contract, which stands side by side with the main sale of land contract.[88] In *Record v Bell*,[89] it was held that an oral warranty as to the seller's title was part of a collateral contract and therefore was binding on the seller and did not render the main contract void. A 'lock-out' agreement by which the vendor agrees with a prospective purchaser not to negotiate with anyone else for a duration is a collateral contract, and not a contract for the sale of an interest in land, so outside the scope of s 2 (*Pitt v PHH Asset Management Ltd* (1994) 68 P & CR 269). Similarly, in *Tootal Clothing Ltd v Guinea Properties Ltd*,[90] it was held that any executed agreement supplemental to a contract was not affected by s 2. However, the variation of a sale of land contract has to comply with s 2.[91]

Spiro v Glencrown Properties Ltd and Another [1991] Ch 537

Hoffmann J: This is an action for damages for breach of a contract to buy land. On 14 November 1989, the plaintiff granted an option to the first defendant ('the purchaser') to buy a property in Finchley for £745,000. The option was exercisable by notice in writing delivered to the vendor or his solicitors by 5 pm on the same day. The purchaser gave a notice exercising the option within the stipulated time. He failed to complete and the vendor, after serving a notice to complete and issuing a writ for specific performance,

84 *Firstpost Homes Ltd v Johnson* [1995] 4 All ER 355 at 362h, *per* Gibson LJ (old cases on the meaning of 'signature', eg *Evans v Hoare* [1892] 1 QB 593, and *Leeman v Stocks* [1951] 1 All ER 1043 were not followed).

85 Section 2(6) of the LP(MP) Act 1989 (as amended by the s 25(2), Sched 4 of the TLATA 1996).

86 [1991] Ch 537. See [1991] CLJ 236 (Oakley, AJ); [1990] Conv 9 (Adams, JE); [1991] Conv 140 (Smith, PF).

87 See *Commission for the New Towns v Cooper (GB) Ltd* [1995] 2 All ER 929, CA.

88 *Record v Bell* [1991] 1 WLR 853.

89 *Ibid*, see [1991] Conv 471 (Harwood, M).

90 (1992) 64 P & CR 452, see [1993] Conv 89 (Luther, P).

91 *McCausland v Duncan Lawrie Ltd* [1996] 4 All ER 995.

rescinded the contract. The second defendant, Mr Berry, is guarantor of the purchaser's obligations. On 1 May 1990 the vendor obtained judgment in default of defence against the purchaser for damages to be assessed. There are now before me a summons by the vendor for judgment under RSC, Ord 14 against Mr Berry as guarantor and a summons by the purchaser to set aside the judgment against it. Since both summonses raise the same short point of law and there are no other issues in the case, the parties have agreed to treat this hearing as the trial of the action.

The only question for decision is whether the contract on which the vendor relies complied with the provisions of s 2 of the Law of Property (Miscellaneous Provisions) Act 1989, which came into force on 27 September 1989, some seven weeks before the grant and exercise of the option. It is a question which has produced a lively debate in conveyancing journals.

[His Lordship read s 2 of the 1989 Act and continued.]

If the 'contract for the sale ... of an interest in land' was for the purposes of s 2(1) the agreement by which the option was *granted*, there is no difficulty. The agreement was executed in two exchanged parts, each of which incorporated all the terms which had been agreed and had been signed by or on behalf of the vendor and purchaser respectively. But the letter which *exercised* the option was of course signed only on behalf of the purchaser. If the contract was made by this document, it did not comply with s 2.

Apart from authority, it seems to me plain enough that s 2 was intended to apply to the agreement which created the option and not to the notice by which it was exercised. Section 2, which replaced s 40 of the Law of Property Act 1925, was intended to prevent disputes over whether the parties had entered into a binding agreement or over what terms they had agreed. It prescribes the formalities for recording their mutual consent. But only the grant of the option depends upon consent. The exercise of the option is a unilateral act. It would destroy the very purpose of the option if the purchaser had to obtain the vendor's countersignature to the notice by which it was exercised. The only way in which the concept of an option to buy land could survive s 2 would be if the purchaser ensured that the vendor not only signed the agreement by which the option was granted but also at the same time provided him with a countersigned form to use if he decided to exercise it. There seems no conceivable reason why the legislature should have required this additional formality.

The language of s 2 places no obstacle in the way of construing the grant of the option as the relevant contract. An option to buy land can properly be described as a contract for the sale of that land conditional on the exercise of the option. A number of eminent judges have so described it. In *Helby v Matthews* [1895] AC 471 at 482, which concerned the sale of a piano on hire-purchase, Lord MacNaughten said:

> The contract, as it seems to me, on the part of the dealer was a contract of hiring coupled with a conditional contract or undertaking to sell. On the part of the customer it was a contract of hiring only until the time came for making the last payment.

In *Griffith v Pelton* [1958] Ch 205, which raised the question of whether the benefit of an option was assignable, Jenkins LJ said, at 225:

> An option in gross for the purchase of land is a conditional contract for such purchase by the grantee of the option from the grantor, which the grantee is entitled to convert into a concluded contract of purchase, and to have carried to completion by the grantor, upon giving the prescribed notice and otherwise

> complying with the conditions upon which the option is made exercisable in any particular case.

In the context of s 2, it makes obvious sense to characterise it in this way. So far, therefore, the case seems to me to be clear.

The purchaser, however, submits that I am constrained by authority to characterise an option as an irrevocable offer which does not become a contract for the sale of land until it has been accepted by the notice which exercises the option. It follows that the 'contract for the sale ... of an interest in land' within the meaning of s 2 can only have been made by the letter.

[His Lordship referred to *Helby v Matthews* [1895] AC 471 but distinguished it.]

But the concept of an offer is of course normally used as part of the technique for ascertaining whether the parties have reached that mutual consent which is a necessary element in the formation of a contract. In this primary sense, it is of the essence of an offer that by itself it gives rise to no legal obligations. It was for this reason that Diplock LJ said in *Varty v British South Africa Co* [1965] Ch 508 at 523:

> To speak of an enforceable option as an 'irrevocable offer' is juristically a contradiction in terms, for the adjective 'irrevocable' connotes the existence of an obligation on the part of the offeror, while the noun 'offer' connotes the absence of any obligation until the offer has been accepted.

This does not mean that in Lord Diplock's opinion, Lord Herschell LC and Lord Watson in *Helby v Matthews* [1895] AC 471 were speaking nonsense. They were not using 'offer' in its primary sense but, as often happens in legal reasoning, by way of metaphor or analogy. Such metaphors can be vivid and illuminating but prove a trap for the unwary if pressed beyond their original context. As I said recently in another connection in In *Re K (Enduring Powers of Attorney)* [1988] Ch 310 at 314:

> ... there are dangers in reasoning from the metaphor as if it expressed a literal truth rather than from the underlying principle which the metaphor encapsulates.

Here the underlying principles are clear enough. The granting of the option imposes no obligation on the purchaser and an obligation on the vendor which is contingent on the exercise of the option. When the option is exercised, vendor and purchaser come under obligations to perform as if they had concluded an ordinary contract of sale. And the analogy of an irrevocable offer is, as I have said, a useful way of describing the position of the purchaser between the grant and exercise of the option. Thus, in *J Sainsbury plc v O'Connor* [1990] STC 516, Millett J used it to explain why the grantee of an option to buy shares did not become the beneficial owner until he had exercised the option.

But the irrevocable offer metaphor has much less explanatory power in relation to the position of the vendor. The effect of the 'offer' which the vendor has made is, from his point of view, so different from that of an offer in its primary sense that the metaphor is of little assistance. Thus, in the famous passage in *London and South Western Railway Co v Gomm* (1882) 20 Ch D 562 at 581, Sir George Jessel MR had no use for it in explaining why the grant of an option to buy land confers an interest in the land upon the grantee:

> The right to call for a conveyance of the land is an equitable interest or an equitable estate. In the ordinary case of a contract for purchase there is no doubt about this, and an option for repurchase is not different in its nature. A person exercising the option has to do two things, he has to give notice of his intention to purchase, and to pay the purchase money; but as far as the man who is liable

> to convey is concerned, his estate or interest is taken away from him without his consent, and the right to take it away being vested in another, the covenant giving the option must give that other an interest in the land.

The fact that the option binds the vendor contingently to convey was the reason why an option agreement was held to fall within s 40 of the Law of Property Act 1925: see *Richards v Creighton Griffiths (Investments) Ltd* (1972) 225 EG 2104, where Plowman J rejected a submission that it was merely a contract not to withdraw an offer. Similarly, in *Weeding v Weeding* (1861) 1 J & H 424, Page-Wood VC held that the grant of an option to buy land was sufficient to deem that land converted into personalty for the purposes of the grantor's will, even though the option had not yet been exercised when he died. The Vice-Chancellor said, at pp 430–31:

> I cannot agree with the argument that there is no contract. It is as much a conditional contract as if it depended on any other contingency than the exercise of an option by a third person, such as, for example, the failure of issue of a particular person.

Thus, in explaining the vendor's position, the analogy to which the courts usually appeal is that of a conditional contract. This analogy might also be said to be imperfect, because one generally thinks of a conditional contract as one in which the contingency does not lie within the sole power of one of the parties to the contract. But this difference from the standard case of a conditional contract does not destroy the value of the analogy in explaining the *vendor's* position. So far as he is concerned, it makes no difference whether or not the contingency is within the sole power of the purchaser. The important point is that 'his estate or interest is taken away from him without his consent'.

[His Lordship was referred to *Griffith v Pelton* [1958] Ch 205 but did not find it helpful.]

The purchaser's argument requires me to say that 'irrevocable offer' and 'conditional contract' are mutually inconsistent concepts and that I must range myself under one or other banner and declare the other to be heretical. I hope that I have demonstrated this to be a misconception about the nature of legal reasoning. An option is not strictly speaking either an offer or a conditional contract. It does not have all the incidents of the standard form of either of these concepts. To that extent it is a relationship *sui generis*. But there are ways in which it resembles each of them. Each analogy is in the proper context a valid way of characterising the situation created by an option. The question in this case is not whether one analogy is true and the other false, but which is appropriate to be used in the construction of s 2 of the Law of Property (Miscellaneous Provisions) Act 1989.

[His Lordship referred to *Beesly v Hallwood Estates Ltd* [1960] 1 WLR 549 at 556; *London and South Western Railway Co v Gomm*; (1881–82) 20 Ch D 562 at 581; and *United Scientific Holdings Ltd v Burnley Borough Council* [1978] AC 904 and continued.]

Perhaps the most helpful case for present purposes is In *Re Mulholland's Will Trusts* [1949] 1 All ER 460. A testator had let premises to the Westminster Bank on a lease which included an option to purchase. He appointed the bank his executor and trustee and after his death the bank exercised the option. It was argued for his widow and children that the bank was precluded from exercising the option by the rule that a trustee cannot contract with himself. Wynn-Parry J was pressed with the irrevocable offer metaphor, which, it was said, led inexorably to the conclusion that when the bank exercised the option, it was indeed entering into a contract with itself. But Wynn-Parry J held that if one considered the purpose of the self-dealing rule, which was to prevent a trustee from being subjected to a conflict of interest and duty, the only relevant contract was the grant of the option. The rule could only sensibly be applied to a consensual transaction. While for some purposes it might be true to say that the exercise of the option brought the contract into existence, there could be no rational ground for applying the self-dealing rule to the unilateral exercise of a right granted before the trusteeship came into existence. Wynn-Parry J quoted, at p 464, from Sir George Jessel MR in *Gomm's* case (1881–82) 20 Ch D 562 at 582, and said:

> As I understand that passage, it amounts to this, that, as regards this option, there was between the parties only one contract, namely, the contract constituted by the provisions in the lease which I have read creating the option. The notice exercising the option did not lead, in my opinion, to the creation of any fresh contractual relationship between the parties, making them for the first time vendors and purchasers, nor did it bring into existence any right in addition to the right conferred by the option.

The contrast between this passage and my citation from Lord Simon of Glaisdale in *United Scientific Holdings* [1978] AC 904 at 945, is a striking illustration of how in different contexts the law can accommodate analogies which appear to lead to diametrically opposing conclusions.

In my judgment, there is nothing in the authorities which prevents me from giving s 2 of the Act of 1989 the meaning which I consider to have been the clear intention of the legislature. On the contrary, the purposive approach taken in cases like *Mulholland* [1949] 1 All ER 460 encourages me to adopt a similar approach to s 2. And the plain purpose of s 2 was, as I have said, to prescribe the formalities for recording the consent of the parties. It follows that in my view the grant of the option was the only 'contract for the sale or other disposition of an interest in land' within the meaning of the section and the contract duly complied with the statutory requirements. There must be judgment for the plaintiff against both defendants with costs.

Record v Bell [1991] 1 WLR 853

Judge Paul Baker QC: The other ground for giving leave to defend is that the contract for the sale of the house does not comply with the terms of s 2 of the Law of Property (Miscellaneous Provisions) Act 1989. It is a point of some general importance, arising under a new statute which has made very substantial changes in the law relating to contracts for the sale of land. The particular area I am concerned with is where a contract in two parts has been duly signed by the respective parties and is awaiting exchange and then some term is orally agreed immediately prior to exchange and confirmed by the exchange of letters. Is the statute satisfied? As I see it, that is a very common situation, especially where there is some pressure to get contracts exchanged, as there frequently is, and when not all the loose ends are tidied up and some last minute adjustment is necessary which takes the form of side letters. I am most indebted to both counsel for interesting arguments on s 2 of the Act.

Those provisions are more stringent than were contained in s 40 of the Law of Property Act 1925 which the Act of 1989 supersedes. In particular, a contract for the sale of land has to be in writing; it is not sufficient that it be evidenced in writing. Secondly, the contract must contain *all* the terms expressly agreed. Thirdly, the terms must be either set out in the contract or incorporated in it by reference to some other document. Fourthly, the document incorporating the terms must be signed by or on behalf of each party. Lastly, where the documents are being exchanged, all the terms must be incorporated in each document, but the parties of course can sign separately.

In his submissions to me on this, Mr Halpern for the purchaser said, first, that s 2 does not cater for side letters of the sort involved in the present case unless they are incorporated into the main agreement; secondly, that the letters were not incorporated as required by the section; and thirdly, that in any event they had to be in identical terms when there were two parts to the contract, and these letters were not in identical terms. He also said, indeed, that these letters were not more than memoranda of a pre-existing oral contract between the solicitors, a situation which it was the purpose of the Act to outlaw.

In reply to that, Mr Ritchie for the vendor submitted, first, that side letters may amount to a collateral contract outside the Act. Mr Halpern conceded that there was a possibility of side letters being a collateral contract and that unless they were themselves a contract for the sale of land the Act would not bite. Secondly, Mr Ritchie said that if that was wrong, these letters were incorporated; thirdly, meeting Mr Halpern's point about identity, that these letters were sufficiently identical; and lastly, that if all those failed, this was a clear case for rectification or estoppel on which summary judgment could be given.

I start with Mr Halpern's first two points, that is to say, if there are to be side letters, they have to be incorporated into the main agreement, and that these side letters were not incorporated. If there has to be a last minute addition to the contract after the document has been prepared and is awaiting exchange, it could be written into the draft contract before exchange, or some reference to it could be added to the contract so long as all that was done with the authority of the parties who signed it. I would see no difficulty in adjusting the contract before the exchange in that way. But, in my judgment, it could not be done simply by a document which itself refers to the contract, and I reject Mr Ritchie's submission on this.

Section 2(1) states that a contract for the sale or other disposition 'can only be made in writing and only by incorporating all the terms which the parties have expressly agreed in one document.' The 'document' in that subsection must be the document which contains the contract for sale. Subsection (2) says 'the terms may be incorporated in a document either by being set out in it or by reference to some other document'. The former document was a direct reference to the document referred to in sub-s (1), and the purpose of sub-s (2) is to expand what is meant in sub-s (1) by incorporating the terms. There are two ways they could be incorporated. They could be set out at length in the contract for sale, or the contract for sale could refer to some other document in which these terms were to be found. The document referred to need not itself be signed, but it has to be identified in the document which is signed.

A letter of variation or a letter of additional terms, not itself a contract for sale, which is signed by both parties may be a variation of the original contract after it has been exchanged as, indeed, we have in this very case relating to the completion date. But it could not, as I see it, be part of the original contract without there being some reference to it contained in the contract for sale. The terms agreed before exchange have to be incorporated. I do not have to deal with the case of physical attachment of a paper containing an additional term without verbal reference to it in the main contract. On the facts before me, there was no reference in the contracts for sale to the supplementary term. It is true that Mr Offenbach's letter had been physically attached to the purchaser's part of the contract, but there was no similar attachment of the other party's letter to the other part of the contract. Under the Act of 1989 the terms have to be expressly incorporated in each of the contracts where there is more than one.

I return to Mr Ritchie's point that what happened here amounted to a collateral contract, that is, an independent contract collateral to the main contract. In such a case, it is not caught by s 2 unless it is itself a contract for sale.

[His Lordship referred to *De Lassalle v Guildford* [1901] 2 KB 215; and *City and Westminster Properties Ltd v Mudd* [1959] Ch 129 and continued.]

The terms of the two solicitors' letters in this case are not precisely identical. I look first at Mr Offenbach's letter to Mr Berns to see whether there was indeed a collateral contract between them or whether I would have to say the matter was unclear and give leave to defend. Just looking at it with that in mind, Mr Halpern says the status of the letter is uncertain. It was attached to the contract for sale and was intended to be part of the contract between the parties. It was strongly urged on me that that showed that it was sought to amend the contract and not to conclude a collateral contract. But that would not be fatal: as A L Smith MR said in *De Lassalle v Guildford* [1901] 2 KB 215 at 221:

> It must be a collateral undertaking forming part of the contract by agreement of the parties express or implied, and must be given during the course of the dealing which leads to the bargain, and should then enter into the bargain as part of it.

Further, I note that one of the points that AL Smith MR made was that one has to see whether it was intended that what the vendor assumed to assert was a fact or an opinion. Here we have statements of fact within the vendor's exclusive knowledge. The statement was that the office copy entries on the register did contain entries which had been vouched for. Further, Mr Offenbach's letter is not inconsistent with the contract, and in particular it is not inconsistent with special condition H.

Turning to Mr Berns' letter, I observed it to be stated that the contracts were exchanged conditionally on the following basis: that the office copies would reveal the vendor and that there were no other entries on the register other than financial charges. I do not find in the terms of these letters any difference between what Mr Offenbach has put forward and what Mr Berns has put forward as to what the vendor is purporting to guarantee. Mr Berns' letter, as one might expect, explains the reasons why it is necessary to put that forward; that he had failed to obtain up to date copies of the Land Registry entries up to the point of exchange. He describes it that contracts 'were exchanged conditional upon the following basis', but myself I would not regard that as fatal to this being a warranty of the sort described in *De Lassalle v Guildford* [1901] 2 KB 215 and indeed my conclusion on this is unhesitating. This was, in my judgment, an offer of a warranty by Mr Berns to Mr Offenbach as to the state of the title, and it was done to induce him to exchange. That offer was accepted by exchanging contracts. It would be unfortunate if common transactions of this nature should nevertheless cause the contracts to be avoided. It may, of course, lead to a greater use of the concept of collateral warranties than has hitherto been necessary.

In those circumstances, I do not find it necessary to deal with the questions which have been argued relating to the degree of identity of documents necessary for the purposes of the Act of 1989 where the contract is in two parts, or those relating to rectification or estoppel.

Tootal Clothing Ltd v Guinea Properties Ltd (1992) 64 P & CR 452, CA

Scott LJ: This is an appeal from the judgment of Douglas Brown J given on 12 July 1991, on a preliminary issue of law. The facts which give rise to the preliminary issue are not in dispute and can be shortly stated.

Guinea Properties Management Ltd, the respondent, and Tootal Clothing Ltd, the appellant, were in the summer of 1990 negotiating about the terms of a lease of commercial premises, 16/18 High Street Brecon, proposed to be granted by Guinea Properties as Landlord, to Tootal as tenant. The terms that were under negotiation and that were in the end agreed between the parties included the following:

(i) Tootal were to carry out shop-fitting works to the premises;

(ii) Tootal was to have a rent-free period of three months, within which it was expected to carry out the shop-fitting works; and

(iii) On the satisfactory completion of the shop-fitting works Guinea Properties would pay Tootal £30,000 towards the cost of the works.

Formal agreements were prepared embodying the terms that had been agreed between the parties. The formal agreements were signed by each of the parties. They were dated 10 August 1990 and exchanged on that date. There were two agreements that were signed, dated and exchanged. One was an agreement for a lease whereby it was agreed (i) that Guinea Properties would grant and Tootal would accept the grant of a 25-year lease in the form of the draft lease annexed thereto; (ii) that the grant of the lease would be completed on 17 August 1990; (iii) that Tootal would within 12 weeks from the date of the agreement (or a later date in the event of certain delays occurring) carry out the shop-fitting works at its own expense; (iv) that rent under the lease would commence to be payable three months from the date of the grant thereof; and (v) that 'this Agreement sets out the entire agreement of the parties ...'.

This agreement, which I will hereafter call 'the lease agreement,' contained no reference to the other agreement, also dated 10 August 1990, and exchanged on that date.

The other agreement (which I will call the 'supplemental agreement') contained a recital that:

> ... the parties have agreed that this Agreement is supplemental to the [Lease] Agreement and have agreed terms whereby the Landlord will contribute towards the cost of the Tenant's Works referred to in Clause 3 of the [Lease] Agreements.

There was also a recital of the lease agreement. This supplemental agreement, after the two recitals to which I have referred, then set out the terms on which the £30,000 would be payable by Guinea Properties to Tootal. I have said before, and I repeat, that both agreements were signed by each of the parties thereto.

The lease agreement was duly completed on 31 August 1990. A lease bearing that date in the form of the draft lease annexed to the lease agreement was granted by Guinea Properties to Tootal. Tootal thereupon set about carrying out the necessary shop-fitting works. Having completed the shop-fitting works, I assume satisfactorily, because the contrary has not been suggested, Tootal applied to Guinea Properties for payment of the £30,000. Guinea Properties declined to pay, contending that s 2 of the Law of Property (Miscellaneous Provisions) Act 1989 barred recovery by Tootal of the £30,000. Tootal, not surprisingly, commenced proceedings. The only defence pleaded by Guinea Properties to the claim by Tootal for the £30,000 was the s 2 point. It was pleaded in Guinea Properties' defence that:

> 7. The terms embodied in the Document [ie the supplemental agreement] were not incorporated into the Agreement [ie the lease agreement] or the Lease and are void and/or unenforceable by virtue of s 2 of the Law of Property (Miscellaneous Provisions) Act 1989.

[His Lordship read s 2(1), (2), (3), (4), (8) and continued.]

The preliminary issue brought before Douglas Brown J for decision was whether the supplemental agreement was one to which s 2 of the 1989 Act applied.

The argument put forward by Mr Ritchie, on behalf of Guinea Properties, before the judge as before us, is a simple one. Section 2 requires all the terms of a contract for the sale or other disposition of an interest in land, ie a land contract, to be incorporated in one document. The document must be signed by each of the parties. The term regarding the £30,000 was an intrinsic part of the bargain which had been agreed between the parties. It was part of the consideration passing from Guinea Properties to Tootal in exchange for which Tootal was to accept the lease and was to carry out the shop-fitting works. The bargain was a land contract. Accordingly, s 2 required the terms regarding the £30,000 to be in the same document as the other contractual terms of the land contract.

The learned judge, although, as he put it, 'without any enthusiasm at all', concluded that this argument was sound. He accordingly made a declaration that the supplemental agreement was one to which s 2 of the 1989 Act applied.

In my opinion, the reliance in Guinea Properties' defence on s 2 of the 1989 Act misses the point about the purpose and effect of s 2.

Section 2, superseding and replacing s 40 of the Law of Property Act 1925, is dealing with the circumstances in which a valid and enforceable contract for the sale or other disposition of an interest in land can come into existence. As Hoffman J put it in *Spiro v Glencrown Properties Ltd*:[92]

> Section 2 was intended to prevent disputes over whether the parties had entered into a binding agreement or over what terms they had agreed.

However, s 2 is of relevance only to executory contracts. It has no relevance to contracts which have been completed. If parties choose to complete an oral land contract or a land contract that does not in some respect or other comply with s 2, they are at liberty to do so. Once they have done so, it becomes irrelevant that the contract they have completed may not have been in accordance with s 2.

In the present case, the parties have agreed all the terms under which the new 25-year lease would be granted, including those relating to the shop-fitting works and the contribution by Guinea Properties of £30,000 towards the cost incurred by Tootal in carrying out the shop-fitting works, chose to incorporate the terms in two documents instead of one, namely the lease agreement and the supplemental agreement. They then completed the lease agreement. The lease agreement thereupon ceased to be an executory contract. The question whether s 2 of the 1989 Act would, because not all the terms of the contractual bargain had been incorporated into the lease agreement, have rendered the lease agreement unenforceable became irrelevant. All that was left was the

92 [1991] 2 WLR 931 at 933; 62 P & CR 402 at 404.

supplemental agreement. The supplemental agreement was not and is not by itself a land contract, or, at least, if it is, by incorporation therein of the terms of the lease agreement, a land contract, then there is no issue in the case that need detain the court. But on the footing that the supplemental agreement by itself is not a land contract, which is the contention of Mr Ritchie for Guinea Properties, there was no longer, after the completion of the lease agreement, any executory land contract in existence to which s 2 of the 1989 Act could apply. There was simply a contract recorded in writing, signed by each party, for the payment of £30,000 in a certain event by one party to the other.

I am of the opinion, speaking for myself, that even before completion of the lease agreement on 31 August 1990, s 2 would not have prevented the enforcement of the lease agreement. If parties choose to hive off part of the terms of their composite bargain into a separate contract distinct from the written land contract that incorporates the rest of the terms, I can see nothing in s 2 that provides an answer to an action for enforcement of the land contract, on the one hand, or of the separate contract on the other hand. Each has become, by the contractual choice of the parties, a separate contract.

But it is not necessary for us on the present appeal to decide that point. It suffices, in my judgment, to say that once the lease agreement had been executed by completion, s 2 had no relevance to the contractual enforceability of the supplemental agreement, whether or not that supplemental agreement was negotiated as part of one bargain that included the terms of the lease agreement.

I would therefore allow this appeal. Guinea Properties has, in my opinion no defence to the action.

Boreham J. I agree. For the reasons given by my Lord I, too, would allow this appeal.

Parker LJ. I also agree. The order under appeal provides as follows:

> The contract specified in paragraph 2 of the Statement of Claim [which is the supplemental agreement] is one to which s 2 of the Law of Property (Miscellaneous Provisions) Act 1989 applies.

If one looks only at the supplemental agreement it does not appear on its face to be a contract for the sale or other disposition of land at all. The declaration which is made therefore appears to be defective. It can only be made a contract to which s 2 of the Act applies if, by reason of its reference to the agreement for the lease and the terms thereof, the two must be read together. If one reaches the conclusion therefore that the supplemental agreement is a contract for the sale or other disposition of land or purported so to be, it follows that all the terms of s 2 must have been complied with, because all the terms must be in that document. Accordingly, it appears to me that either the matter of the supplemental agreement falls wholly outside s 2, or, if it does fall within s 2, it does not avail the landlords because s 2 would then have been fully complied with. I agree that the appeal should be allowed and that there is no defence.

Appeal allowed with costs here and below. Application for leave to appeal to the House of Lords refused.

Implied covenants for title

Before 1 July 1995, it was a common practice for the seller to state the capacity in which he was selling the property, for example, as beneficial owner. This was important for the relevant covenants for title to be implied into the contract under s 76 of the Law of Property Act 1925 (now repealed). Since 1 July 1995, when Part I of the Law of Property (Miscellaneous Provisions) Act 1994 came into force,[93] it is no longer necessary to do this. Instead, it is necessary now for the seller to state in the contract whether he is offering a full, or a limited, guarantee of title, and certain covenants for title will then apply.[94] Where the Standard Conditions of Sale are used, the buyer will get a full title guarantee.[95] Whether the contract is made with full title guarantee or with limited title guarantee, the covenants to be implied are that the seller has the right (with the concurrence of any other person conveying the property) to dispose of the property as he purports to, and that he will at his own cost do all that he can reasonably do to give the buyer the title he purports to give.[96] Furthermore, if the contract is made with full title guarantee, there is an implied covenant that the seller is disposing of the property free from all charges and incumbrances (whether monetary or not) and from all other rights exercisable by third parties, other than any charges, incumbrances or rights which he does not or could not reasonably be expected to know about.[97] If the contract is made with limited title guarantee there is an implied covenant that the person making the contract has not since the last disposition for value charged or incumbered the property or granted third party rights over the property or suffered the property to be so charged or incumbered, and that he is not aware that anyone else has done so since the last disposition for value.[98]

3 STAGE THREE: BETWEEN CONTRACT AND COMPLETION

The buyer's interest once the contract is concluded

(a) Estate contract

Once a legally enforceable contract has been concluded, 'equity looks on that as done which ought to be done'. The buyer is regarded by equity as enjoying a certain proprietary interest. His legally enforceable contract is an estate contract. Occasionally, some unscrupulous seller may, having contracted to sell the land to the buyer, convey it to a third party. In order for the buyer's estate contract to take priority over any subsequent third party he should protect it as a Class C (iv) land charge if the title to the property he is buying is unregistered.[99] If the title is registered, the estate contract should be protected as a minor interest.[100]

93 Law of Property (Miscellaneous Provisions) Act 1994 (Commencement No 2) Order 1995 (SI 1995/1317).

94 Section 1 of the Law of Property (Miscellaneous Provisions) Act 1994.

95 Standard Conditions of Sale, 3rd edn, 1995, Condition 4.5.2.

96 Section 2(1) of the Law of property (Miscellaneous Provisions) Act 1994.

97 *Ibid*, s 3(1).

98 *Ibid*, s 3(3).

99 Section 2(4)(iv) of the LCA 1972. See Chapter 6, p 204.

100 Sections 49(1)(c), 59(2), 54, 58(1) of the LRA 1925.

In practice, as most of the contracts are completed within a relatively short period, they are not protected unless the completion is to be delayed considerably or there is now a dispute between the parties.[101]

(b) Seller as qualified constructive trustee

Jessel MR once put it in *Lysaght v Edwards*, 'the moment you have a valid contract for sale the vendor becomes in equity a trustee for the purchaser of the estate sold.'[102] This statement should be treated with caution. First, it is inapt to say that the fiduciary relationship arises when a valid contract is made. Rather, there should be an enforceable contract before such a relationship could arise.[103] The existence of this relationship depends on whether the contract is specifically enforceable, ie whether the contract is one which the court will decree specific performance.[104] Thus, if the contract is valid but unenforceable (where s 40 is not satisfied) or if for some reason the court will not decree specific performance, then the seller will not be regarded as a trustee.

Secondly, the fiduciary relationship here is a qualified one. The seller is still entitled to retain possession and to receive the rents and profits until completion.[105] He also has a lien over the property until the purchase money is paid in full.[106] He still enjoys a paramount right to protect his own interest as seller of the property.[107] What it means is that the seller has to exercise a duty of care in managing and maintaining the property from the exchange of contracts till completion.[108] If the property is damaged during the interim period due to the seller's negligence, he will be liable to the buyer for the loss.[109] If he conveys the property in breach of the contract to a third party for consideration, he is required to hold the proceeds of sale on trust for the buyer subject to buyer satisfying his own obligations under the contract.[110]

(c) Passing of risk

On the exchange of contract, the risk passes to the buyer.[111] It is, therefore, the buyer's responsibility to insure the property. Under the Standard Conditions of

101 See Barnsley at 214.

102 (1876) 2 Ch D 499 at 506. The Law Commission favoured the retention of this peculiar type of trust relationship: Law Commission, 'Transfer of Land: Risk of Damage after Contract for Sale' (Law Com 191, 23 April 1990), paras 2.7–2.8.

103 See Barnsley at 226 note 8.

104 *Howard v Miller* [1915] AC 318 at 326, PC, *per* Lord Parker.

105 *Gedye v Montrose* (1858) 26 Beav 45; *Cuddon v Tite* (1858) 1 Giff 395.

106 *Re Birmingham, Savage v Stannard* [1959] Ch 523.

107 *Shaw v Foster* (1872) LR 5 HL 321 at 338.

108 *Clarke v Ramuz* [1891] 2 QB 456, CA.

109 *Royal Bristol Permanent Building Society v Bomash* (1887) 35 Ch D 390; *Ware v Verderber* (1978) 247 EG 1081; *Lucie-Smith v Gorman* [1981] CLY 2866.

110 *Lake v Bayliss* [1974] 2 All ER 1114. See Chapter 2, p 62.

111 *Lysaght v Edwards*, (1876) 2 Ch D 499 at 507. The Law Commission has criticised this rule as 'fundamentally unsatisfactory and unfair' because it imposes on the buyer a responsibility to protect his property at a time when he has no physical control over it: Law Com 191, para 2.9. The Law Commission has recommended that the risk of physical damage should only pass to the buyer on completion and this is in line with the Standard Conditions of Sale. See also [1984] Conv 43 (Thompson, MP).

Sale, the seller is to transfer the property in the same physical state as it was at the date of the contract (except for fair wear and tear), and he retains the risk until completion.[112] But the seller is not under any obligation to insure the property.[113]

Investigating the title

The modern practice is to inspect the documents of title before the contract. Under the National Protocol, the documents of title are given to the buyer before the contract. But the time-honoured procedure is to do this after the contract. This is the position under the Standard Conditions of Sale.[114]

With unregistered title, the contract normally specifies a particular document as the good root of title which is a document that covers the transfer of the whole of the legal and equitable interests in the property, which describes the property adequately and which does not cast doubt on the seller's power to sell. Under s 23 of the Law of Property Act 1969 the seller is required to produce a good root of title which is at least 15 years old. Thus, immediately after the exchange of contracts and before the completion, the seller's solicitors must provide the buyer's solicitors (if they have not already done so) with a list of documents of title starting from the good root, usually accompanied by photocopies of the documents (known as an epitome) or a document in the form of legal shorthand which summarises the main contents of title deeds starting from the good root (known as an abstract of title). The usual process of raising any queries regarding the evidence of title and the replies thereto will then follow. Much of the study of the substantive law relating to the sale by trustees for sale or a tenant for life of settled land will be relevant here to help inspecting the devolution of title where these dispositions form part of the title.

Where the title is registered, the evidence of title is the register.[115] There is no root of title and usually there is no need to look at all the documents of title. Occasionally, earlier deeds which contain covenants or easements referred to in the register may need to be examined because the register does not always set these out in full. Section 110(1) of the Land Registration Act 1925 requires the sellers to produce copies of the entries on the register and of the filed plan (see end of chapter). Under the Standard Conditions of Sale, the evidence of title given must be office copies of the register.[116] The buyer may also today search the entries on the Land Register himself and consent of the seller is not needed.[117] If he gets an official search certificate, he will have a priority period of 30 working days. The register is divided into three separate registers (the property register, the proprietorship register, and the charges register) and each has to be checked carefully. Under s 110(2) of the Land Registration Act 1925,

112 Condition 5.1.1.

113 Condition 5.1.3.

114 Condition 4.1.1.

115 For details on registered land see Chapter 7.

116 Condition 4.2.1.

117 Section 112(1) of the LRA 1925, as substituted by s 1(1) of the LRA 1988. See also Land Registration (Open Register) Rules 1991 (SI 1992/122), rr 2–4.

the seller must also provide evidence in respect of any appurtenant rights and interests as to which the register is not conclusive, such as rights claimed to exist by prescription. Where the registered title is possessory or qualified, earlier deeds will have to be investigated and the seller has to provide copies of them under s 110(2).

Drafting of purchase deed

Once the buyer is satisfied that the seller can pass a good title to him, the buyer's solicitors will prepare two copies of the draft purchase deed. Under s 52(1) of the Law of Property Act 1925 '[a]ll conveyances of land or any interest therein are void for the purpose of conveying or creating a legal estate unless made by deed'. One notable exception to this requirement, apart from those stated in s 52(2), is that under s 54(2) of the Act, a lease by parol, taking effect in possession for a term not exceeding three years at the best rent reasonably obtainable without taking a fine, does not have to be granted by deed. Thus sale of freehold land or leasehold for more than three years must be perfected by a deed. The purchase deeds, when drafted, are then sent to the seller's solicitors for approval. The seller's solicitors check the draft purchase deeds and, when approved, return a copy to the buyer's solicitor. The buyer's solicitors will then prepare the actual deed in its final form (known as engrossing the purchase deed) and obtain the buyer's signature to it. It will then be sent to the seller's solicitor for the seller's signature.

(a) Formality

(i) Prior to 31 July 1990

Prior to 31 July 1990 all deeds must be signed, sealed and delivered.[118] It had always been a crucial requirement for a deed to be sealed before it was effective.[119] The requirement of signature was added by s 73(1) of the Law of Property Act 1925. Any words or conduct by the grantor which signifies that he adopts the deed irrevocably as his own was sufficient to deliver the deed.[120] Attestation (or witnessing) was not a legal requirement but was exceedingly common in practice.

(ii) From 31 July 1990

Since 31 July 1990,[121] the formalities of due execution of a deed have been changed.[122] Section 1 of the Law of Property (Miscellaneous Provisions) Act 1989 provides as follows:

118 Norton, RF, *A Treatise on Deeds*, 2nd edn (by Morrison, JA and Gooldens HJ), 1928, Holmes Beach: Gaunt, p 3.

119 Sheepard's *Touchstone of Common Assurances*, 8th edn, 1826, p 56.

120 *Xenos v Wickham* (1867) LR 2 HL 296 at 312; Co Litt, at 36a; [1990] Conv 85 (D N Clarke).

121 Law of Property (Miscellaneous Provisions) Act 1989 (Commencement) Order 1990 (SI 1990/1175), para 2.

122 As recommended by the Law Commission, Deeds and Escrows (Law Com 163, 1987) para 2.4.

Law of Property (Miscellaneous Provisions) Act 1989

1. Deeds and their execution

(1) Any rule of law which:

(a) the substances on which a deed may be written;

(b) requires a seal for the valid execution of an instrument as a deed by an individual; or

(c) requires authority by one person to another to deliver an instrument as a deed on his behalf to be given by deed,

is abolished.

(2) An instrument shall not be a deed unless:

(a) it makes it clear on its face that it is intended to be a deed by the person making it or, as the case may be, by the parties to it (whether by describing itself as a deed or expressing itself to be executed or signed as a deed or otherwise); and

(b) it is validly executed as a deed by that person or, as the case may be, one or more of those parties.

(3) An instrument is validly executed as a deed by an individual if, and only if:

(a) it is signed:

(i) by him in the presence of a witness who attests the signature; or

(ii) at his discretion and in his presence and the presence of two witnesses who each attest the signature; and

(b) it is delivered as a deed by him or a person authorised to do so on his behalf.

(4) In sub-s (2) and (3) above 'sign', in relation to an instrument, includes making one's mark on the instrument and 'signature' is to be construed accordingly.

(5) Where a solicitor or licensed conveyancer, or an agent or employee of a solicitor or licensed conveyancer, in the course of or in connection with a transaction involving the disposition or creation of an interest in land, purports to deliver an instrument as a deed on behalf of a party to the instrument, it shall be conclusively presumed in favour of a purchaser that he is authorised so to deliver the instrument.

(6) In sub-s (5) above:

'disposition' and 'purchaser' have the same meanings as in the Law of Property Act 1925; and

'interest in land' means any estate, interest or charge in or over land.

Thus, the requirement of sealing a deed is now abolished.[123] An instrument will only be a deed if it is made clear on its face that it is intended to be a deed, and it is signed by the grantor (or one of them if there are more than one) in the presence of a witness who attests the signature and it is delivered as a deed by him or a person authorised to do so on his behalf.[124] The grantor may direct

123 Section 1(1) of the LP(MP) Act 1989.

124 Section 1(2), (3) of the LP(MP) Act 1989.

someone to sign the deed for him in his presence and the presence of two witnesses who each attest the signature.[125]

The intention that an instrument is a deed is often made clear by words such as 'IN WITNESS WHEREOF the vendor (or the parties hereto) have signed this document as a deed the day and year first above written'.

Attestation which was already a common practice before 1989 has now become a formal legal requirement. In registered conveyancing, attestation has also been made part of the formal requirements in Transfer Form 19.[126]

LAND REGISTRATION (EXECUTION OF DEEDS) RULES 1990

FORM 19 – Transfer of Freehold Land (Whole) (Rule 98)

H M LAND REGISTRY

Land Registration Acts 1925 to 1986

[County and District or London Borough] ....

Title No ....

Property ....

Date ....

In consideration of pounds (£) receipt of which is acknowledged [1] AB of &c., transfer[s] to CD of &c., the land comprised in the title above referred to.

where the transfer is to be executed personally by an individual add

[Signed as a deed *or* Signed and delivered] } (*Signature of AB*)
by AB in the presence of: }

(Signature, name and address of witness)

where the transfer is to be executed by an individual directing another to sign on his behalf add

[Signed as a deed *or* Signed and delivered] }
by XY at the direction and on behalf of }
AB in [his *or* her] }
presence and in the presence of: } (Signature of AB by XY)

(Signatures, names and addresses of two witnesses)

where the transfer is to be executed by a company registered under the Companies Acts, using its common seal, add

125 Section 1(3)(a)(ii) of the LP (MP) Act 1989.

126 Rule 98 and Schedule of the LRR 1925.

The common seal of AB was affixed in the } (Common seal of AB)
presence of: }

Director ....

Secretary ....

where the transfer is to be executed by a company registered under the Companies Act, without using a common seal, add

[Signed as a deed *or* Signed and delivered] by AB } .... Director
acting by [a director and its secretary *or* two directors } .... [Secretary *or* Director]

Precedent of a conveyance[127]

THIS CONVEYANCE is made the 1st day of June, 1984,

BETWEEN Victor Vendor of No 1 Smith Street Dorking in the County of Surrey Clerk (hereinafter called 'the vendor') of the one part and Percy Purchaser of No 2 Brown Street Lewes in the County of Sussex Auctioneer (hereinafter called 'the purchaser') of the other part

WHEREAS –

(1) The vendor is the estate owner in respect of the fee simple of the property hereby assured for his own use and benefit absolutely free from incumbrances

(2) The vendor has agreed with the purchaser to sell to him the said property free from incumbrances for the price of £50,000

NOW THIS CONVEYANCE WITNESSETH that in consideration of the sum of £50,000 now paid by the purchaser to the vendor (the receipt whereof the vendor hereby acknowledges) the vendor hereby conveys to the purchaser with [full/limited] title guarantee.

ALL THAT messuage or dwelling house with the yard gardens offices and outbuildings thereto belonging known as No 703 Robinson Street Ashford in the County of Kent which premises are more particularly delineated and coloured pink on the plan annexed to these presents

TO HOLD the same unto the purchaser in fee simple

IN WITNESS WHEREOF the parties to these presents have signed this document as a deed the day and year first above written

Signed and }
delivered by the }
vendor in the presence }
of Charles } VICTOR VENDOR
Brown clerk to }
Benham and Gambling }
solicitors }

127 Reproduced with kind permission from Megarry and Wade, pp 156–57.

Searches, enquiries and inspections between contract and completion

It is important from the buyer's point of view to do the usual searches, enquiries and inspections all over again within the priority period before the completion. These include searches at the Central Land Charges Registry[128] in the case of unregistered title and the District Land Registry[129] in the case of registered title, and inspecting the property itself. The purpose of these searches, enquiries and inspections is to ascertain whether the seller can actually sell the property as he has contracted to do free of third parties incumbrances other than those already disclosed in the contract.

(a) Searches

Where the title is unregistered, the buyer needs to search the land charges register. Although the seller would, under the National Protocol, have supplied the buyer with a copy of the official search certificate of the land charges register, priority is for only 15 working days and it will probably be out of date by now. Any searches the buyer did himself earlier on before the contract are, likewise, likely to be out of date. Another search is therefore necessary. This is because if the search reveals any registered land charge entered after the contract (the existence of which was not disclosed by the seller before the contract), the buyer can refuse to proceed to completion and rescind the contract immediately. An official search which reveals no registered land charges will also give the buyer a new priority period of 15 working days. The buyer who completes within this priority period will not be bound by any land charges registered within the priority period.[130] Furthermore, s 24 of the Law of Property Act 1969 does not apply to entries made after the contract and the buyer will be deemed to have actual notice of any land charges registered after the contract. Where the title is registered, as mentioned above, at some point after the contract, the buyer needs to make an official search (usually using form 94A) and to obtain an official search certificate. The certificate is essentially the same as the office copy he was provided with by the seller before the contract but it is more up to date and gives him a priority period of 30 working days.

(b) Inspections of property

Although this should normally have been done before the contract, it should be done again before the completion. The purpose is the same, that is to find out any third party's interests which cannot be registered at the Land Charges Register or noted on the Land Register in order that the buyer will not be fixed with constructive notice of the interests or be bound by any overriding interest.

---

128 Priority period is 15 working days (s 11(5), (6)(a) of the LCA 1925).

129 Priority period is 30 working days (Land Registration (Official Searches) Rules 1981 (SI 1981/1135).

130 Section 11(5), (6)(a) of the LCA 1972.

Pre-completion registration of land charge

With unregistered title, one problem the seller who sells part of his property may face is the protection of the restrictive covenants the buyer will make in the purchase deed on completion which are in favour of the seller. The restrictive covenants will no doubt be binding on the buyer when the deed is executed on completion. But the seller needs to protect the restrictive covenants as a Class D(ii) land charges before any future purchaser acquires any legal estate or interest from the buyer, in order that the covenants will bind the purchaser. The buyer might resell the property before the seller has had a chance to register his restrictive covenants. Although it is very unlikely that the buyer of a residential property will resell it before the seller could effect a land charge registration, it is common for the buyer to buy with a mortgage which finances the purchase. A mortgagee is a purchaser for the purposes of the Land Charges Act 1972, s 4(6)[131] and when he finances the purchase of a legal estate in the property, a legal mortgage is often granted. Thus, a mortgagee will be a purchaser for money or money's worth of a legal estate and take free of the restrictive covenants under s 4(6) of the 1972 Act. And if the mortgagee later has to exercise his power of sale, any purchaser who buys from the mortgagee would likewise take free of the unregistered restrictive covenants.[132] The restrictive covenants cannot be registered before the completion because they do not exist until the deed of purchase is executed on completion.

To solve the problem, the Land Charges Act 1972, s 11(1) and sub-s (6)(a) provides that the owner of a registrable incumbrance may give a priority notice of at least 15 working days to the registrar before the incumbrance is created (ie in this case before the date of completion) and, as long as he then registers within 30 working days of entering the priority notice,[133] the restrictive covenants will bind any subsequent purchaser (including the mortgagee) from the buyer. Any purchaser who carries out a usual search, as any prudent purchaser would do, would be warned of the new land charge which is about to be created.

4 STAGE FOUR: COMPLETION[134]

At this stage, the seller signs the purchase deed, has it witnessed and delivers it through his solicitors to the buyer's solicitors. In practice, transfer of the balance of the purchase price always precedes delivery of purchase deed. In unregistered title, the deed will convey the legal estate to the buyer and today as all land in England and Wales is in compulsory registration areas since 1 December 1990[135] the buyer has to register his title within two months of the

131 Section 17(1) of the LCA 197.

132 *Wilkes v Spooner* [1911] 2 KB 473.

133 Section 11(3), (6)(b) of the LCA 1972.

134 See [1991] Conv 15, at 81 and at 185 (Barnsley, DG).

135 Land Registration, England and Wales: The Registration of Title Order 1989 (SI 1989/1347).

date of conveyance.[136] In registered title, the process of transferring land is by a deed called a transfer (Form 19)[137] instead of the deed of conveyance and the process is only completed by the buyer's registration of his title in the Land Registry.

On completion the parties' legal obligations alter. Their contractual obligations covered directly or indirectly by the purchase deed are now generally superseded. No action can normally be brought on the contract. The buyer's remedy, if any, must now lie in the express covenants made in the deed or the implied covenants for title. There are, however, matters which will not be superseded by the purchase deed. These are obligations which the parties did not intend to be extinguished by the conveyance, and agreements for vacant possession,[138] for compensation for misdescription,[139] for completion of the building of a house in a proper manner.[140] Likewise, the buyer's remedies for any misrepresentation under the Misrepresentation Act 1967 survive the completion.

5 STAGE FIVE: POST-COMPLETION

Where the title bought is unregistered, it is now due for first registration and, as mentioned above, it must be registered within two months of the unregistered conveyance. Any registrable land charges, such as a D(ii) land charge to be created in pursuance of a priority notice discussed above, must, however, be registered before the freehold title is substantively registered under the Land Registration Acts.

If the title to the property bought is already registered, as mentioned above, no legal estate passes until the buyer is registered as the new proprietor of it. The buyer must now apply for registration within 30 working days from the date of the search certificate which he obtained before the completion. The mortgagee who finances the purchase must also register his mortgage.

6 CASES WHERE A CONTRACT MAY NOT BE NECESSARY

Our discussion so far has been centred round the various stages of a sale of land where a formal contract is fundamentally important. A formal contract is also necessary where a lease at a ground rent is assigned in consideration of a capital payment. A mortgage is also usually preceded by a contract.[141] In other types of transaction, where there is no payment of a capital sum, it is not usually

136 Section 123 of the LRA 1925,.

137 As prescribed under rules 98 and 115 of the LRR 1925.

138 *Hisset v Reading Roofing Co Ltd* [1970] 1 All ER 122.

139 *Palmer v Johnson* (1884) 13 QBD 351, CA.

140 *Lawrence v Cassel* [1930] 2 KB 83, CA.

141 See Storey, *Conveyancing*, 4th edn, 1993, p 212. But see Megarry's *Manual*, p 123. See n 2 above.

necessary to have a formal contract. The grant will be made after the necessary searches and enquiries have been made. Thus the grant or assignment of a lease at a rack rent is not normally preceded with a contract.

On the other hand, as we have seen, short leases (ie leases for three years or less) taking effect in possession at a rent are normally granted in an 'agreement'[142] as they are not required to be granted by deed under s 54(2) of the Law of Property Act 1925. They may of course be granted orally. The document of transfer is called an 'agreement' even though it is not an agreement to grant a lease but an actual grant itself.

Where the short leases only take effect in a future date, then it seems that a deed is required for the grant. The agreement to grant a short lease which will not take effect in possession when it is granted must still satisfy the requirement of s 2.

142 For example, an assured shorthold tenancy.

STANDARD CONDITIONS OF SALE (3rd EDITION)

(National Conditions of Sale, 23rd Edition. Law Society's Conditions of Sale 1995)

1 *General*

1.1 Definitions

1.1.1 In these conditions:

(a) 'accrued interest' means:

(i) if money has been placed on deposit or in a building society share account, the interest actually earned

(ii) otherwise, the interest which might reasonably have been earned by depositing the money at interest on seven days' notice of withdrawal with a clearing bank less, in either case, any proper charges for handling the money

(b) 'agreement' means the contractual document which incorporates these conditions, with or without amendment

(c) 'banker's draft' means a draft drawn by and on a clearing bank

(d) 'clearing bank' means a bank which is a member of CHAPS Limited

(e) 'completion date', unless defined in the agreement, has the meaning given in condition 6.1.1

(f) 'contract' means the bargain between the seller and the buyer of which these conditions, with or without amendment, form part

(g) 'contract rate', unless defined in the agreement, is the Law Society's interest rate from time to time in force

(h) 'lease' includes sub-lease, tenancy and agreement for a lease or sub-lease

(i) 'notice to complete' means a notice requiring completion of the contract in accordance with condition 6

(j) 'public requirement' means any notice, order or proposal given or made (whether before or after the date of the contract) by a body acting on statutory authority

(k) 'requisition' includes objection

(l) 'solicitor' includes barrister, duly certificated notary public, recognised licensed conveyancer and recognised body under ss 9 or 32 of the Administration of Justice Act 1985

(m) 'transfer' includes conveyance and assignment

(n) 'working day' means any day from Monday to Friday (inclusive) which is not Christmas Day, Good Friday or a statutory Bank Holiday.

1.1.2 When used in these conditions the terms 'absolute title' and 'office copies' have the special meanings given to them by the Land Registration Act 1925.

1.2 Joint parties

If there is more than one seller or more than one buyer, the obligations which they undertake can be enforced against them all jointly or against each individually.

1.3 Notices and documents

1.3.1 A notice required or authorised by the contract must be in writing.

1.3.2 Giving a notice or delivering a document to a party's solicitor has the same effect as giving or delivering it to that party.

1.3.3 Transmission by fax is a valid means of giving a notice or delivering a document where delivery of the original document is not essential.

1.3.4 Subject to conditions 1.3.5 to 1.3.7, a notice is given and a document delivered when it is received.

1.3.5 If a notice or document is received after 4.00 pm on a working day, or on a day which is not a working day, it is to be treated as having been received on the next working day.

1.3.6 Unless the actual time of receipt is proved, a notice or document sent by the following means is to be treated as having been received before 4.00 pm on the day shown below:

(a) by first-class post: two working days after posting

(b) by second-class post: three working days after posting

(c) through a document exchange: on the first working day after the day on which it would normally be available for collection by the addressee.

1.3.7 Where a notice or document is sent through a document exchange, then for the purposes of condition 1.3.6 the actual time of receipt is:

(a) the time when the addressee collects it from the document exchange or, if earlier

(b) 8.00 am on the first working day on which it is available for collection at that time.

1.4 VAT

1.4.1 An obligation to pay money includes an obligation to pay any value added tax chargeable in respect of that payment.

1.4.2 All sums made payable by the contract are exclusive of value added tax.

2 *Formation*

2.1 Date

2.1.1 If the parties intend to make a contract by exchanging duplicate copies by post or through a document exchange, the contract is made when the last copy is posted or deposited at the document exchange.

2.1.2 If the parties' solicitors agree to treat exchange as taking place before duplicate copies are actually exchanged, the contract is made as so agreed.

2.2 Deposit

2.2.1 The buyer is to pay or send a deposit of 10 per cent of the purchase price no later than the date of the contract. Except on a sale by auction, payment is to be made by banker's draft or by a cheque drawn on a solicitors' clearing bank account.

2.2.2 If before completion date the seller agrees to buy another property in England and Wales for his residence, he may use all or any part of the deposit as a deposit in that transaction to be held on terms to the same effect as this condition and condition 2.2.3.

2.2.3 Any deposit or part of a deposit not being used in accordance with condition 2.2.2 is to be held by the seller's solicitor as stakeholder on terms that on completion it is paid to the seller with accrued interest.

2.2.4 If a cheque tendered in payment of all or part of the deposit is dishonoured when first presented, the seller may, within seven working days of being notified that the cheque has been dishonoured, give notice to the buyer that the contract is discharged by the buyer's breach.

2.3 Auctions

2.3.1 On a sale by auction the following conditions apply to the property and, if it is sold in lots, to each lot.

2.3.2 The sale is subject to a reserve price.

2.3.3 The seller, or a person on his behalf, may bid up to the reserve price.

2.3.4 The auctioneer may refuse any bid.

2.3.5 If there is a dispute about a bid, the auctioneer may resolve the dispute or restart the auction at the last undisputed bid.

3 Matters affecting the property

3.1 Freedom from incumbrances

3.1.1 The seller is selling the property free from incumbrances, other than those mentioned in condition 3.1.2.

3.1.2 The incumbrances subject to which the property is sold are:

(a) those mentioned in the agreement

(b) those discoverable by inspection of the property before the contract

(c) those the seller does not and could not know about

(d) entries made before the date of the contract in any public register except those maintained by H M Land Registry or its Land Charges Department or by Companies House

(e) public requirements.

3.1.3 The buyer accepts the property in the physical state it is in at the date of the contract, unless the seller is building or converting it.

3.1.3 After the contract is made, the seller is to give the buyer written details without delay of any new public requirement and of anything in writing which he learns about concerning any incumbrances subject to which the property is sold.

3.1.4 The buyer is to bear the cost of complying with any outstanding public requirement and is to indemnify the seller against any liability resulting from a public requirement.

3.2 Physical state

3.2.1 The buyer accepts the property in the physical state it is in at the date of the contract unless the seller is building or converting it.

3.2.2 A leasehold property is sold subject to any subsisting breach of a condition or tenant's obligation relating to the physical state of the property which renders the lease liable to forfeiture.

3.2.3 A sub-lease is granted subject to any subsisting breach of a condition or tenant's obligation relating to the physical state of the property which renders the seller's own lease liable to forfeiture.

3.3 Leases affecting the property.

3.3.1 The following provisions apply if the agreement states that any part of the property is sold subject to a lease.

3.3.2 (a) The seller having provided the buyer with full details of each lease or copies of the documents embodying the lease terms, the buyer is treated as entering into the contract knowing and fully accepting those terms

(b) The seller is to inform the buyer without delay if the lease ends or if the seller learns of any application by the tenant in connection with the lease; the seller is then to act as the buyer reasonably directs, and the buyer is to indemnify him against all consequent loss and expense

(c) The seller is not to agree to any proposal to change the lease terms without the consent of the buyer and is to inform the buyer without delay of any change which may be proposed or agreed

(d) The buyer is to indemnify the seller against all claims arising from the lease after actual completion; this includes claims which are unenforceable against a buyer for want of registration

(e) The seller takes no responsibility for what rent is lawfully recoverable, nor for whether or how any legislation affects the lease

(f) If the let land is not wholly within the property, the seller may apportion the rent.

3.4 Retained land

3.4.1 The following provisions apply where after the transfer the seller will be retaining land near the property.

3.4.2 The buyer will have no right of light or air over the retained land, but otherwise the seller and the buyer will each have the rights over the land of the other which they would have had if they were two separate buyers to whom the seller had made simultaneous transfers of the property and the retained land.

3.4.3 Either party may require that the transfer contain appropriate express terms.

4 *Title and transfer*

4.1 Timetable

4.1.1 The following are the steps for deducing and investigating the title to the property to be taken within the following time limits:

Step	*Time limit*
1. The seller is to send the buyer evidence of title in accordance with condition 4.2	Immediately after making the contract
2. The buyer may raise written requisitions	Six working days after either the date of the contract or the date of delivery of the seller's evidence of title on which the requisitions are raised whichever is the later
3. The seller is to reply in writing to any requisitions raised	Four working days after receiving the requisitions

4. The buyer may make written observations on the seller's replies	Three working days after receiving the replies

The time limit on the buyer's right to raise requisitions applies even where the seller supplies incomplete evidence of his title, but the buyer may, within six working days from delivery of any further evidence, raise further requisitions resulting from that evidence. On the expiry of the relevant time limit the buyer loses his right to raise requisitions or make observations.

4.1.2 The parties are to take the following steps to prepare and agree the transfer of the property within the following time limits:

Step	*Time Limit*
A. The buyer is to send the seller a draft transfer	At least twelve working days before completion date
B. The seller is to approve or revise that draft and either return it or retain it for use as the actual transfer	Four working days after delivery of the draft transfer
C. If the draft is returned the buyer is to send an engrossment to the seller	At least five working days before completion date

4.1.3 Periods of time under conditions 4.1.1 and 4.1.2 may run concurrently.

4.1.4 If the period between the date of the contract and completion date is less than 15 working days, the time limits in conditions 4.1.1 and 4.1.2 are to be reduced by the same proportion as that period bears to the period of 15 working days. Fractions of a working day are to be rounded down except that the time limit to perform any step is not to be less than one working day.

4.2 Proof of title

4.2.1 The evidence of registered title is office copies of the items required to be furnished by s 110(l) of the Land Registration Act 1925 and the copies, abstracts and evidence referred to in s 110(2).

4.2.2 The evidence of unregistered title is an abstract of the title, or an epitome of title with photocopies of the relevant documents.

4.2.3 Where the title to the property is unregistered, the seller is to produce to the buyer (without cost to the buyer):

(a) the original of every relevant document; or

(b) an abstract, epitome or copy with an original marking by a solicitor of examination, either against the original or against an examined abstract or against an examined copy.

4.3 Defining the property

4.3.1 The seller need not:

(a) prove the exact boundaries of the property

(b) prove who owns fences, ditches, hedges or walls

(c) separately identify parts of the property with different titles further than he may be able to do from information in his possession.

4.3.2 The buyer may, if it is reasonable, require the seller to make or obtain, pay for and hand over a statutory declaration about facts relevant to the matters mentioned in condition 4.3.1. The form of the declaration is to be agreed by the buyer, who must not unreasonably withhold his agreement.

4.4 Rents and rentcharges

The fact that a rent or rentcharge, whether payable or receivable by the owner of the property, has been or will on completion be, informally apportioned is not to be regarded as a defect in title.

4.5 Transfer

4.5.1 The buyer does not prejudice his right to raise requisitions, or to require replies to any raised, by taking any steps in relation to the preparation or agreement of the transfer.

4.5.2 If the agreement makes no provision as to title guarantee, then subject to condition 4.5.3 the seller is to transfer the property with full title guarantee.

4.5.3 The transfer is to have effect as if the disposition is expressly made subject to all matters to which the property is sold subject under the terms of the contract.

4.5.4 If after completion the seller will remain bound by any obligation affecting the property, but the law does not imply any covenant by the buyer to indemnify the seller against liability for future breaches of it:

(a) the buyer is to covenant in the transfer to indemnify the seller against liability for any future breach of the obligation and to perform it from then on, and

(b) if required by the seller, the buyer is to execute and deliver to the seller on completion a duplicate transfer prepared by the buyer.

4.5.5 The seller is to arrange at his expense that, in relation to every document of title which the buyer does not receive on completion, the buyer is to have the benefit of:

(a) a written acknowledgement of his right to its production, and

(b) a written undertaking for its safe custody (except while it is held by a mortgagee or by someone in a fiduciary capacity).

5 Pending completion

5.1 Responsibility for property

5.1.1 The seller will transfer the property in the same physical state as it was at the date of the contract (except for fair wear and tear), which means that the seller retains the risk until completion.

5.1.2 If at any time before completion the physical state of the property makes it unusable for its purpose at the date of the contract:

(a) the buyer may rescind the contract

(b) the seller may rescind the contract where the property has become unusable for that purpose as a result of damage against which the seller could not reasonably have insured, or which it is not legally possible for the seller to make good.

5.1.3 The seller is under no obligation to the buyer to insure the property.

5.1.4 Section 47 of the Law of Property Act 1925 does not apply.

5.2 Occupation by buyer

5.2.1 If the buyer is not already lawfully in the property, and the seller agrees to let him into occupation, the buyer occupies on the following terms.

5.2.2 The buyer is a licensee and not a tenant. The terms of the licence are that the buyer:

(a) cannot transfer it

(b) may permit members of his household to occupy the property

(c) is to pay or indemnify the seller against all outgoings and other expenses in respect of the property

(d) is to pay the seller a fee calculated at the contract rate on the purchase price (less any deposit paid) for the period of the licence

(e) is entitled to any rents and profits from any part of the property which he does not occupy

(f) is to keep the property in as good a state of repair as it was in when he went into occupation (except for fair wear and tear) and is not to alter it

(g) is to insure the property in a sum which is not less than the purchase price against all risks in respect of which comparable premises are normally insured

(h) is to quit the property when the licence ends.

5.2.3 On the creation of the buyer's licence, condition 5.1. ceases to apply, which means that the buyer then assumes the risk until completion.

5.2.4 The buyer is not in occupation for the purposes of this condition if he merely exercises rights of access given solely to do work agreed by the seller.

5.2.5 The buyer's licence ends on the earliest of: completion date, rescission of the contract or when five working days' notice given by one party to the other takes effect.

5.2.6 If the buyer is in occupation of the property after his licence has come to an end and the contract is subsequently completed he is to pay the seller compensation for his continued occupation calculated at the same rate as the fee mentioned in condition 5.2.2(d).

5.2.7 The buyer's right to raise requisitions is unaffected.

6 Completion

6.1 Date

6.1.1 Completion date is twenty working days after the date of the contract but time is not of the essence of the contract unless a notice to complete has been served.

6.1.2 If the money due on completion is received after 2.00 pm, completion is to be treated, for the purposes only of conditions 6.3 and 7.3, as taking place on the next working day.

6.1.3 Condition 6.1.2 does not apply where the sale is with vacant possession of the property or any part and the seller has not vacated the property or that part by 2.00 pm on the date of actual completion.

6.2 Place

Completion is to take place in England and Wales, either at the seller's solicitor's office or at some other place which the seller reasonably specifies.

6.3 Apportionments

6.3.1 Income and outgoings of the property are to be apportioned between the parties so far as the change of ownership on completion will affect entitlement to receive or liability to pay them.

6.3.2 If the whole property is sold with vacant possession or the seller exercises his option in condition 7.3.4, apportionment is to be made with effect from the date of actual completion; otherwise, it is to be made from completion date.

6.3.3 In apportioning any sum, it is to be assumed that the seller owns the property until the end of the day from which apportionment is made and that the sum accrues from day to day at the rate at which it is payable on that day.

6.3.4 For the purpose of apportioning income and outgoings, it is to be assumed that they accrue at an equal daily rate throughout the year.

6.3.5 When a sum to be apportioned is not known or easily ascertainable at completion, a provisional apportionment is to be made according to the best estimate available. As soon as the amount is known, a final apportionment is to be made and notified to the other party. Any resulting balance is to be paid no more than ten working days later, and if not then paid the balance is to bear interest at the contract rate from then until payment.

6.3.6 Compensation payable under condition 5.2.6 is not to be apportioned.

6.4 Amount payable

The amount payable by the buyer on completion is the purchase price (less any deposit already paid to the seller or his agent) adjusted to take account of:

(a) apportionments made under condition 6.3

(b) any compensation to be paid or allowed under condition 7.3.

6.5 Title deeds

6.5.1 The seller is not to retain the documents of title after the buyer has tendered the amount payable under condition 6.4.

6.5.2 Condition 6.5.1 does not apply to any documents of title relating to land being retained by the seller after completion.

6.6 Rent receipts

The buyer is to assume that whoever gave any receipt for a payment of rent or service charge which the seller produces was the person or the agent of the person then entitled to that rent or service charge.

6.7 Means of payment

The buyer is to pay the money due on completion in one or more of the following ways:

(a) legal tender

(b) a banker's draft

(c) a direct credit to a bank account nominated by the seller's solicitor

(d) an unconditional release of a deposit held by a stakeholder.

6.8 Notice to complete

6.8.1 At any time on or after completion date, a party who is ready able and willing to complete may give the other a notice to complete.

6.8.2 A party is ready able and willing:

(a) if he could be, but for the default of the other party, and

(b) in the case of the seller, even though a mortgage remains secured on the property, if the amount to be paid on completion enables the property to be transferred freed of all mortgages (except those to which the sale is expressly subject).

6.8.3 The parties are to complete the contract within ten working days of giving a notice to complete, excluding the day on which the notice is given. For this purpose, time is of the essence of the contract.

6.8.4 On receipt of a notice to complete:

(a) if the buyer paid no deposit, he is forthwith to pay a deposit of 10 per cent

(b) if the buyer paid a deposit of less than 10 per cent, he is forthwith to pay a further deposit equal to the balance of that 10 per cent.

7 Remedies

7.1 Errors and omissions

7.1.1 If any plan or statement in the contract, or in the negotiations leading to it, is or was misleading or inaccurate due to an error or omission, the remedies available are as follows.

7.1.2 When there is a material difference between the description or value of the property as represented and as it is, the injured party is entitled to damages.

7.1.3 An error or omission only entitles the injured party to rescind the contract:

(a) where it results from fraud or recklessness, or

(b) where he would be obliged, to his prejudice, to transfer or accept property differing substantially (in quantity, quality or tenure) from what the error or omission had led him to expect.

7.2 Rescission

If either party rescinds the contract:

(a) unless the rescission is a result of the buyer's breach of contract the deposit is to be repaid to the buyer with accrued interest

(b) the buyer is to return any documents he received from the seller and is to cancel any registration of the contract.

7.3 Late completion

7.3.1 If there is a default by either or both of the parties in performing their obligations under the contract and completion is delayed, the party whose total period of default is the greater is to pay compensation to the other party.

7.3.2 Compensation is calculated at the contract rate on the purchase price, or (where the buyer is the paying party) the purchase price less any deposit paid, for the period by which the paying party's default exceeds that of the receiving party, or, if shorter, the period between completion date and actual completion.

7.3.3 Any claim for loss resulting from delayed completion is to be reduced by any compensation paid under this contract.

7.3.4 Where the buyer holds the property as tenant of the seller and completion is delayed, the seller may give notice to the buyer, before the date of actual completion, that he intends to take the net income from the property until completion. If he does so, he cannot claim compensation under condition 7.3.1 as well.

7.4 After completion

Completion does not cancel liability to perform any outstanding obligation under this contract.

7.5 Buyer's failure to comply with notice to complete

7.5.1 If the buyer fails to complete in accordance with a notice to complete, the following terms apply.

7.5.2 The seller may rescind the contract, and if he does so:

(a) he may

(i) forfeit and keep any deposit and accrued interest

(ii) resell the property

(iii) claim damages

(b) the buyer is to return any documents he received from the seller and is to cancel any registration of the contract.

7.5.3 The seller retains his other rights and remedies.

7.6 Seller's failure to comply with notice to complete

7.6.1 If the seller fails to complete in accordance with a notice to complete, the following terms apply.

7.6.2 The buyer may rescind the contract, and if he does so:

(a) the deposit is to be repaid to the buyer with accrued interest

(b) the buyer is to return any documents he received from the seller and is, at the seller's expense, to cancel any registration of the contract.

7.6.3 The buyer retains his other rights and remedies.

8 *Leasehold property*

8.1 Existing leases

8.1.1 The following provisions apply to a sale of leasehold land.

8.1.2 The seller having provided the buyer with copies of the documents embodying the lease terms, the buyer is treated as entering into the contract knowing and fully accepting those terms.

8.1.3 The seller is to comply with any lease obligations requiring the tenant to insure the property.

8.2 New leases

8.2.1 The following provisions apply to a grant of a new lease.

8.2.2 The conditions apply so that:

'seller' means the proposed landlord

'buyer' means the proposed tenant

'purchase price' means the premium to be paid on the grant of a lease.

8.2.3 The lease is to be in the form of the draft attached to the agreement.

8.2.4 If the term of the new lease will exceed 21 years, the seller is to deduce a title which will enable the buyer to register the lease at H M Land Registry with an absolute title.

8.2.5 The buyer is not entitled to transfer the benefit of the contract.

8.2.6 The seller is to engross the lease and a counterpart of it and is to send the counterpart to the buyer at least five working days before completion date.

8.2.7 The buyer is to execute the counterpart and deliver it to the seller on completion.

8.3 Landlord's consent

8.3.1 The following provisions apply if a consent to assign or sub-let is required to complete the contract.

8.3.2 (a) The seller is to apply for the consent at his expense, and to use all reasonable efforts to obtain it

(b) The buyer is to provide all information and references reasonably required.

8.3.3 The buyer is not entitled to transfer the benefit of the contract.

8.3.4 Unless he is in breach of his obligation under condition 8.3.2, either party may rescind the contract by notice to the other party if three working days before completion date:

(a) the consent has not been given or

(b) the consent has been given subject to a condition to which the buyer reasonably objects.

In that case, neither party is to be treated as in breach of contract and condition 7.2 applies.

9 Chattels

9.1 The following provisions apply to any chattels which are to be sold.

9.2 Whether or not a separate price is to be paid for the chattels, the contract takes effect as a contract for sale of goods.

9.3 Ownership of the chattels passes to the buyer on actual completion.

Law Society Council Statement and the National Conveyancing Protocol

COUNCIL STATEMENT

1. The Council recommend that solicitors follow the procedures set out in the Protocol in all domestic conveyancing transactions.
2. The procedures set out in the Protocol include the use of standardised documentation. This will simplify the checking of variables and will enable departures from the recommended format to be readily identified. The Protocol does not preclude the use of printed or typed contracts produced by firms themselves, although it may be thought desirable that the full text of the Conditions of Sale are reproduced rather than merely included by reference.
3. The introduction of a National Protocol is designed to streamline conveyancing procedures. Experience has shown that where local protocols have been implemented, these have speeded up the completion of pre-contract formalities and have improved communications between solicitors and their clients.

4. The Protocol is a form of 'preferred practice' and its requirements should not be construed as undertakings. Nor are they intended to widen a solicitor's duty save as set out in the next paragraph. The Protocol must always be considered in the context of a solicitor's overriding duty to his or her own client's interests and where compliance with the Protocol would conflict with that duty, the client's wishes must always be paramount.
5. A solicitor acting in domestic conveyancing transactions should inform the solicitor acting for the other party at the outset of a transaction, whether or not he or she is proposing to act in accordance with the Protocol in full or in part. If the solicitor is using the Protocol he or she should give notice to the solicitor acting for the other party if during the course of the transaction it becomes necessary to depart from Protocol procedures.
6. A solicitor is, as a matter of professional conduct, under a duty to keep confidential client's business. The confidentiality continues until the client permits disclosure or waives the confidentiality (Principle 16.03 of *The Guide to Professional Conduct of Solicitors* (1993)). With reference to paragraphs 4.5 and 5.3 of the National Protocol, the disclosure of information about a client's position is strictly subject to obtaining that client's authority to disclose. In the absence of such authority, a solicitor is not deemed to be departing from the terms of the Protocol and, as such, is not required to give notice as set out in paragraph 5 of this Statement.

THE NATIONAL CONVEYANCING PROTOCOL (THIRD EDITION)

ACTING FOR THE SELLER

1. The first step

The seller should inform the solicitor as soon as it is intended to place the property on the market so that delay may be reduced after a prospective buyer is found.

2. Preparing the Package: assembling the information

On receipt of instructions, the solicitor shall then immediately take the following steps, at the seller's expense:

2.1 Locate the title deeds and, if not in the solicitor's custody, obtain them.

2.2 Obtain a copy of the O.S. Map, if necessary, where deeds do not have a suitable plan.

Preparing the Package: information from the seller

2.3 Obtain from the seller details to complete the Seller's Property Information Form.

2.4 Obtain such original guarantees with the accompanying specification, planning decisions and building regulation approvals as are in the seller's possession and copies of any other planning consents that are with the title deeds or details of any highway and sewerage agreements and bonds.

2.5 Give the seller the Fixtures, Fittings and Contents Form, with a copy to retain, to complete and return prior to the submission of the draft contract.

2.6 Obtain details of all mortgages and other financial charges of which the seller's solicitor has notice including where applicable improvement grants and discounts repayable to a local authority. Redemption figures should be obtained at this stage in respect of all mortgages on the property so that cases of negative equity can be identified at an early stage.

2.7 Ascertain the identity of all the people aged 18 or over living in the dwelling and ask about any financial contribution they or anyone else may have made towards its purchase or subsequent improvement. All persons identified in this way should be asked to confirm their consent to the sale proceeding.

2.8 In leasehold cases, ask the seller to produce, if possible:

(1) A receipt or evidence from the landlord of the last payment of rent.

(2) The maintenance charge accounts for the last three years, where appropriate, and evidence of payment.

(3) Details of the buildings insurance policy.

If any of these are lacking, and are necessary for the transaction, the solicitor should obtain them from the landlord. At the same time investigate whether a licence to assign is required and if so enquire of the landlord what references are necessary and, in the case of some retirement schemes, if a charge is payable to the management company on change of ownership.

3. Preparing the Package: the draft documents

As soon as the title deeds are available, the solicitor shall:

3.1 If the title is unregistered:

(1) Make a Land Charges Search against the seller and any other appropriate names.

(2) Make an Index Map Search in the Land Registry in order to verify that the seller's title is unregistered and ensure that there are no interests registered at the Land Registry adverse to the seller's title.

(3) Prepare an epitome of title. Mark copies or abstracts of all deeds which will not be passed to the buyer as examined against the original.

(4) Prepare and mark as examined against the originals copies of all deeds, or their abstracts, prior to the root of title containing covenants, casements etc., affecting the property.

(5) Check that all plans on copied documents are correctly coloured.

3.2 If the title is registered, obtain office copy entries of the register and copy documents incorporated into the land certificate.

3.3 Prepare the draft contract and Seller's Property Information Form Part II using the standard forms.

4. A Buyer's offer is accepted

When made aware that a buyer has been found the solicitor shall

4.1 Inform the buyer's solicitor in accordance with paragraph 5 of the Council Statement that the Protocol will be used.

4.2 Ascertain the buyer's position on any related sale and in the light of that reply, ask the seller for a completion date.

4.3 Send to the buyer's solicitor as soon as possible as many of the following items as are available:

(1) Draft contract.

(2) Office copy entries, or a photocopy of the land or charge certificate if they are not available, or the epitome of title (including details of any prior matters referred to but not disclosed by the documents themselves). The Index Map Search. A photocopy of the land or charge certificate should have marked on it the date that the certificate was last examined by the Land Registry.

(3) The Seller's Property Information Form with copies of all relevant planning decisions, guarantees etc.

(4) The completed Fixtures, Fittings and Contents Form. Where this is provided it will form part of the contract.

(5) In leasehold cases, a copy of the lease with all the information about maintenance charges and insurance which has so far been obtained and about the procedure (including references required) for obtaining the Landlord's consent to the sale.

(6) The seller's target date for completion.

The remaining items should be forwarded to the buyer's solicitor as soon as they are available.

4.4 Ask the buyer's solicitor if a 10% deposit will be paid and, if not, what arrangements are proposed.

4.5 If and to the extent that the seller consents to the disclosure, supply information about the position on the seller's own purchase and of any other transactions in the chain above, and thereafter, of any change in circumstances.

ACTING FOR THE BUYER

5. The Buyer's Response

On receipt of instructions, the buyer's solicitor shall promptly:

5.1 Confirm to the seller's solicitor in accordance with paragraph 5 of the Council Statement that the Protocol will be used.

5.2 Ascertain the buyer's position on any related sale, mortgage arrangements and whether a 10% deposit will be provided.

5.3 If and to the extent that the buyer consents to the disclosure, inform the seller's solicitor about the position on the buyer's own sale, if any, and of any connected transactions, the general nature of the mortgage application, the amount of the deposit available and if the seller's target date for completion can be met, and thereafter, of any change in circumstances.

5.4 Make Local Search with the usual Part I Enquiries and any additional enquiries relevant to the property.

5.5 Make Commons Registration Search if appropriate.

5.6 Make Mining Enquiries if appropriate and any other relevant searches.

On receipt of draft documents:

5.7 Confirm approval of the draft contract and return it approved as soon as possible, having inserted the buyer's full names and address, subject to any outstanding matters.

5.8 At the same time ask only those specific additional enquiries which are required to clarify some point arising out of the documents submitted or which are relevant to the particular nature or location of the property or which the buyer has expressly requested omitting any enquiry, including those about the state and condition of the building, which is capable of being ascertained by the buyer's own enquiries or survey or personal inspection. Additional duplicated standard forms should not be submitted; if they are, the seller is under no obligation to deal with them nor need answer any enquiry seeking opinions rather than facts.

5.9 Ensure that buildings insurance arrangements are in place.

6. Exchange of Contracts

On exchange, the buyer's solicitor shall send or deliver to the seller's solicitor:

6.1 The signed contract with all names, dates and financial information completed.

6.2 The deposit provided in the manner prescribed in the contract. Under the Law Society's Formula C the deposit may have to be sent to another solicitor nominated by the seller's solicitor.

6.3 If contracts are exchanged by telephone, the procedures laid down by the Law Society's Formulae A, B or C must be used and both solicitors must ensure (unless otherwise agreed) that the undertakings to send documents and pay the deposit on that day are strictly observed.

6.4 If contracts are exchanged in the post the seller's solicitor shall, once the buyer's signed contract and deposit are held unconditionally, having ensured that details of each contract are fully completed and identical send the seller's signed contract on the day of exchange.

7. Between exchange and the day of completion

As soon as possible after exchange and in any case within the time limits contained in the Standard Conditions of Sale:

7.1 The buyer's solicitor shall send to the seller's solicitor, in duplicate:

(1) Completion Information and Requisitions on Title Form.

(2) A draft conveyance, transfer or assignment.

(3) Other documents eg draft receipt for fixtures, fittings and contents.

7.2 As soon as possible after receipt of these documents, the seller's solicitor shall send to the buyer's solicitor:

(1) Replies to Completion Information and Requisitions on Title Form.

(2) Draft conveyance, transfer or assignment approved.

(3) If appropriate, completion statement supported by photocopy receipts or evidence of payment of apportionments claimed.

(4) Copy of licence to assign obtained from the landlord if appropriate.

7.3 The buyer's solicitor shall then:

(1) Engross the approved draft conveyance, transfer or assignment, obtain the buyer's signature to it (if necessary) and sent it to the seller's solicitor in time to enable the seller to sign it before completion without suffering inconvenience.

(2) Take any steps necessary to ensure that the amount payable on completion will be available in time for completion.

(3) Dispatch the Land Registry and Land Charges Searches and, if appropriate, a company search.

7.4 The seller's solicitor shall request redemption figures for all financial charges on the property revealed by the deeds/office copy entries.

8. Completion: the day of payment and removals

8.1 If completion is to be by post, the Law Society's Code for Completion shall be used, unless otherwise agreed.

8.2 As soon as practicable and not later than the morning of completion, the buyer's solicitor shall advise the seller's solicitor of the manner of transmission of the purchase money and of the steps taken to dispatch it.

8.3 On being satisfied as to the receipt of the balance of the purchase money, the seller's solicitor shall authorise release of the keys and notify the buyer's solicitor of release.

8.4 The seller's solicitor shall check that the seller is aware of the need to notify the local and water authorities of the change in ownership.

8.5 After completion, where appropriate, the buyer's solicitor shall give notice of assignment to the lessor.

9. Relationship with Estate Agents

Where the seller has instructed estate agents, the seller's solicitor shall take the following steps:

9.1 Inform them when draft contracts are submitted.

9.2 Inform them of any unexpected delays or difficulties likely to delay exchange of contracts.

9.3 Inform them when exchange has taken place and the date of completion.

9.4 On receipt of their commission account send a copy to the seller and obtain instructions as to arrangements for payment.

9.5 Inform them of completion and, if so instructed, pay the commission.

CHAPTER 5

LIMITATION ACT AND ADVERSE POSSESSION[1]

So far we have seen how ownership of an estate or interest in land can be acquired by formal act of conveyance, or transfer and registration. There is another way in which an estate in land can be acquired, and that is by adverse possession. Acquisition by adverse possession is the upshot of two principles. First, as will be seen,[2] 'property' is a relative concept, and 'possession' is the evidence of ownership of property. Possession of land is *prima facie* evidence of seisin which 'gives ownership good against everyone except a person who has a better, because older, title'.[3] Thus, where the paper owner is dispossessed by an adverse possessor who is now in possession, no one can seek possession against the adverse possessor except the paper owner who can prove a better title against him. If the adversor is himself dispossessed by a second subsequent adverse possessor, as the first adverse possessor can prove his earlier possession against the second adverse possessor, he can repossess against the second adverse possessor. The second adverse possessor cannot use the first adverse possessor's lack of proper title as a defence. The second principle, upon which ownership by adverse possession is based, is that a person who has a better claim to an estate in land should assert his claim within an acceptable period of time from the date when his right accrued. The limitation period is prescribed by the Limitation Act 1980. 'There shall be an end of litigation', and 'those who go to sleep upon their claims should not be assisted by the courts in recovering their property'.[4] For otherwise, not only the evidence might have been lost, 'every transfer of real property would be jeopardised by the encroachment of ancient or increasingly stale claims in derogation of the transferor's rights'.[5] 'Every grantor of land would be required to trace his title back to the Garden of Eden; and every "landowner" would live under the perpetual shadow of apprehended repossession at the behest of some earlier and more meritorious claimant of title.'[6] Thus, under the two principles, an adverse possessor can acquire a good title against the whole world if the paper owner fails to claim possession within the prescribed period. After the prescribed period, the paper owner's claim will be time-barred or statute-barred. And no one else can assert a title better than that of the adverse possessor. The adverse possessor's title becomes unchallengeable. The law of adverse possession, therefore, validates the rights of adverse possessor who has no formal ownership. 'Land claims, however unmeritorious, come in time to enjoy a certain self-righting quality', as Professor Gray put it.[7]

1 See [1985] Conv 272 (Dockray, M); [1988] Conv 357 (JEM).

2 See Chapter 17.

3 *Newington v Windeyer* (1985) 3 NSWLR 555 at 563E–F, *per* McHugh, JA.

4 RB Policies at *Lloyd's v Butler* [1950] 1 KB 76 at 81.

5 Gray, p 282.

6 Gray, p 282.

7 Gray, p 283.

It is common to think of adverse possession in terms of aggressive squatter's rights, whose wrongful possession is eventually validated by the passage of time. However, the use of adverse possession today is more diverse than that. The rule of adverse possession can, for instance, be invoked to resolve the problem of imperfect title due to failure to execute formal conveyance or transfer. For example, in *Bridges v Mees*,[8] in 1936, the plaintiff orally agreed to purchase certain registered land from the vendor company. He went into possession and paid the full purchase price. The fee simple was never transferred to him and he never protected his right by notice or caution. In 1955, the vendor company conveyed the fee simple to the defendant who was duly registered as the proprietor. The defendant sought possession from the plaintiff. The plaintiff brought an action claiming a declaration that he was the owner by adverse possession and for rectification of the register on the ground that his ownership was an overriding interest under s 70(1)(f) and (g) of the Land Registration Act 1925. Harman J held that the plaintiff had acquired the fee simple by adverse possession and that it was overriding under s 70(1)(f) and (g).[9] Adverse possession may also be used to correct the problem caused by defective conveyancing or a defectively drawn ground plan which erroneously includes a small portion of a neighbour's land.

It should be noted that the law of adverse possession is in some way similar to the law of prescription in easements and profits *à prendre*, in that the adverse possessor and prescriptive user are also to acquire certain interest in land through long user. However, the significant distinction between them is that prescription operates positively as a presumed grant – the prescriptive user thus derives a right from the owner of land, whereas adverse possession operates negatively, so as to extinguish a prior, better competing title.[10] Thus, since an adverse possessor does not derive his title from the owner, but merely extinguishes the owner's better title, he may not be able to bar the claim of a different person who may also have a better title against him. For example, as will be seen, if a tenant is dispossessed, whose claim is now statute-barred, the landlord may not be barred.

1 EFFECT OF LIMITATION ACT ON PRESENT INTERESTS

Limitation period

As seen, the adverse possessor acquires his title because the person who can show a better title fails to vindicate his claim within the statutorily prescribed period. Actions for recovery of land by any person are statute-barred after 12 years from the date the right of action accrued. The limitation period for actions for recovery of land by the Crown is 30 years, and the period for actions for recovery of foreshore is 60 years.

8 [1957] Ch 475.

9 For Harman J's judgment see Chapter 7, at 272–73.

10 *Buckinghamshire CC v Moran* [1990] Ch 623 at 644B–C.

Limitation Act 1980

15. Time limit for actions to recover land

(1) No action shall be brought by any person to recover any land after the expiration of 12 years from the date on which the right of action accrued to him or, if it first accrued to some person through whom he claims, to that person.

Schedule 1

Modifications of Section 15 where Crown or certain Corporations Sole are involved

10. Subject to paragraph 11 below, s 15(1) of this Act shall apply to the bringing of an action to recover any land by the Crown or by any spiritual or eleemosynary corporation sole with the substitution for the reference to 12 years of a reference to 30 years.

11. (1) An action to recover foreshore may be brought by the Crown at any time before the expiration of 60 years from the date mentioned in s 15(1) of this Act.

Accrual of right of action

Where the right of action accrues, time begins to run for the purposes of the limitation period. So when does the right of action accrue? When does time begin to run? Time begins to run (i) when the owner is dispossessed by an adverse possessor,[11] or (ii) when the owner discontinues his possession and possession is taken by an adverse possessor.[12]

Limitation Act 1980

Schedule 1

ACCRUAL OF RIGHTS OF ACTION TO RECOVER LAND

ACCRUAL OF RIGHTS OF ACTION IN CASE OF PRESENT INTERESTS IN LAND

1. Where the person bringing an action to recover land, or some person through whom he claims, has been in possession of the land, and has while entitled to the land been dispossessed or discontinued his possession, the right of action shall be treated as having accrued on the date of the dispossession or discontinuance.

Right of action not to accrue or continue unless there is adverse possession

8. (1) No right of action to recover land shall be treated as accruing unless the land is in the possession of some person in whose favour the period of limitation can run (referred to below in this paragraph as 'adverse possession'); and where under the preceding provisions of this Schedule any such right of action is treated as accruing on a certain date and no person is in adverse possession on that date, the right of action shall not be treated as accruing unless and until adverse possession is taken of the land.

   (2) Where a right of action to recover land has accrued and after its accrual, before the right is barred, the land ceases to be in adverse possession, the right of action shall no longer be treated as having accrued and no fresh right of action shall be treated as accruing unless and until the land is again taken into adverse possession.

---

11 Schedule 1, para 1 of the Limitation Act 1980.

12 Schedule 1, para 8(1) of the Limitation Act 1980.

Section 15(1) expressly provides that the limitation period may be established by adding together a series of adverse possessions. For example, if O, the paper owner, is dispossessed by A1, the first adverse possessor who is in turn dispossessed by A2, the second adverse possessor, A2 may claim the period of A1's adverse possession against O to make up the 12 year period. A2, of course, cannot claim the period of A1's adverse possession as a defence to A1's action for recovery.[13] He has to establish his own independent 12 years of adverse possession against A1. However, it is clear from Schedule 1, para 8(2) that the series of adverse possessions must be continuous. If A1 abandons his adverse possession sometime before A2 takes adverse possession, A2 cannot add to his own the period of adverse possession established earlier by A1.

Dispossession or discontinuance of possession

Dispossession occurs where the owner is literally driven out of possession by the adverse possessor who claims adverse possession.[14] Dispossession may also occur even if the owner knows nothing of it.[15] Cases of dispossession are today rare. Adverse possession is more likely to occur where there is a discontinuance of possession by the owner.

Discontinuance of possession is the abandonment of possession by the owner.[16] However, non-user will not necessarily be abandonment.[17] Discontinuance must be followed by an adverse possession. 'Without the element of a new "possession" asserted by an intruder there would of course be no right of action in the paper owner to be statute-barred through the effluxion of time.'[18] Where the owner allows his land to lie dormant for the time being but intends to use it for some specific purpose in the future, it used to be thought that the possession of the owner was wholly undisturbed by the act of the adverse possessor which did not interfere with the intended future use of the land.[19] The Court of Appeal in *Buckinghamshire County Council v Moran* has rejected this idea. Slade LJ said that it was too broad a proposition 'to suggest that an owner who retains a piece of land with a view to its utilisation for a specific purpose in the future can never be treated as dispossessed, however firm and obvious the intention to dispossess, and however drastic the acts of dispossession of the person seeking to dispossess him may be'.[20] It was held that to establish adverse possession, the claimant must show a sufficient degree of possession, and that he has the necessary *animus possidendi*. And where the claimant was aware of the owner's intended future use of the land, very clear evidence of possession and *animus possidendi* is required.

13 *Mount Carmel Investments Ltd v Peter Thurlow Ltd* [1988] 1 WLR 1078 at 1086. See [1988] Conv 359 (JEM).

14 *Rains v Buxton* (1880) 14 Ch D 537 at 539.

15 *Powell v McFarlane* (1977) 38 P & CR 452 at 480.

16 *Rimington v Cannon* (1853) 12 CB 18 at 33.

17 *Tecbild Ltd v Chamberlain* (1969) 20 P & CR 633.

18 Gray, p 294.

19 *Leigh v Jack* (1879) 5 Ex D 264.

20 [1990] Ch 623 at 639A.

(a) Possession

Whether the claimant has sufficient possession is a matter of fact. He must show a degree of physical control of the land.[21] In *Buckinghamshire County Council v Moran*,[22] in 1955, the plaintiffs bought a piece of land (the disputed land) adjacent to the defendant's house. Since 1967, the defendant's predecessors in title had always maintained the disputed land, and used it for their own purposes. The house was later conveyed to the defendant in 1971 together with 'all such rights estate title and interests as the vendors may have in or over' the disputed land. The defendant later successfully claimed that he had acquired title to the disputed land by adverse possession.

Buckinghamshire County Council v Moran [1990] Ch 623, CA

Slade LJ: First, as at 28 October 1973 did the defendant have factual possession of the plot? I venture to repeat what I said in *Powell v McFarlane:*[23]

> Factual possession signifies an appropriate degree of physical control. It must be a single and [exclusive] possession ... Thus an owner of land and a person intruding on that land without his consent cannot both be in possession of the land at the same time. The question what acts constitute a sufficient degree of exclusive physical control must depend on the circumstances, in particular the nature of the land and the manner in which land of that nature is commonly used or enjoyed.

On the evidence it would appear clear that by 28 October 1973 the defendant had acquired complete and exclusive physical control of the plot. He had secured a complete enclosure of the plot and its annexation to Dolphin Place. Any intruder could have gained access to the plot only by way of Dolphin Place, unless he was prepared to climb the locked gate fronting the highway or to scramble through one or other of the hedges bordering the plot. The defendant had put a new lock and chain on the gate and had fastened it. He and his mother had been dealing with the plot as any occupying owners might have been expected to deal with it. They had incorporated it into the garden of Dolphin Place. They had planted bulbs and daffodils in the grass. They had maintained it as part of that garden and had trimmed the hedges. I cannot accept Mr Douglas's submission that the defendant's acts of possession were trivial. It is hard to see what more he could have done to acquire complete physical control of the plot by October 1983. In my judgment, he had plainly acquired factual possession of the plot by that time.

What can amount to sufficient physical control must depend on the circumstances of the case, and the nature of the land. 'Enclosure is the strongest possible evidence of adverse possession, but it is not indispensable'.[24] Where the land is suitable for grazing or shooting, these acts will be sufficient.[25] But trivial

21 *Buckinghamshire CC v Moran* [1990] Ch 623.

22 [1990] Ch 623. See [1990] CLJ 23 (Harpum, C); [1989] Conv 211 (McCormack, G).

23 (1977) 38 P & CR 452 at 470–471.

24 *Seddon v Smith* (1877) 36 LT 168 at 169.

25 *Red House Farms (Thorndon) Ltd v Catchpole* [1977] EGD 798; *Treloar v Nute* [1976] 1 WLR 1295.

or equivocal acts, such as the claimant's use of the land for his children to play on,[26] cannot be sufficient.

Possession must be 'peaceable and open'.[27] It is not entirely clear what 'peaceable' means. It seems that it cannot mean that the possession of the adverse possessor must not be with force, for one of the more ancient ways of dispossession was to drive the owner out of possession. Possession must not be with permission, consent or licence from the owner.[28] Prior to the enactment of Schedule 1, para 8(4) as added by s 4 of the Limitation Amendment Act 1980, it was held in *Wallis's Cayton Bay Holiday Camp Ltd v Shell-Mex and BP Ltd*[29] that where the owner had left his land unoccupied, any user by an intruder was to be regarded as an act with an implied 'licence or permission of the true owner'.

Limitation Act 1980

Schedule 1

8. (4) For the purpose of determining whether a person occupying any land is in adverse possession of the land it shall not be assumed by implication of law that his occupation is by permission of the person entitled to the land merely by virtue of the fact that his occupation is not inconsistent with the latter's present or future enjoyment of the land.

This provision shall not be taken as prejudicing a finding to the effect that a person's occupation of any land is by implied permission of the person entitled to the land in any case where such a finding is justified on the actual facts of the case.

Possession must be open and unconcealed, and not secret.[30] It must be visible to the owner so that he has every opportunity to challenge the intruder's possession within the limitation period.

Possession can be of only part of the owner's land, leaving the owner with effective possession of the remainder of his land.[31] In some circumstances, possession of parts of the land may constitute 'evidence of possession of the whole' and 'whether or not acts of possession done on parts of an area establish title to the whole area must, however, be a matter of degree' depending on the nature of the land.[32] In *Pavledes v Ryesbridge Properties Ltd*,[33] a claimant's use of a small part of land as a car park was held insufficient to constitute possession of the whole of the land.

26 *Tecbild Ltd v Chamberlain* (1969) 20 P & CR 633.

27 *Browne v Perry* [1991] 1 WLR 1297 at 1302A.

28 *Bladder v Phillips* [1991] EGCS 109.

29 [1975] QB 94. See also *Treloar v Nute* [1976] 1 WLR 1295; *Leigh v Jack* (1879) 5 Ex D 264; *Williams Brothers Direct Supply Ltd v Raftery* [1958] 1 QB 159.

30 *Lord Advocate v Lord Lovat* (1880) 5 App Cas 273 at 291.

31 *Rains v Buxton* (1880) 14 Ch D 537.

32 *Powell v McFarlane* (1977) 38 P & CR 452 at 471.

33 (1989) 58 P & CR 459.

(b) *Animus possidendi*

The claimant must also show that he has an *animus possidendi*, ie an intention to possess the land to the exclusion of all other persons including the owner.[34] Such an intention to dispossess must be made sufficiently clear to the owner.[35] It is not necessary to show that he intended to own or acquire ownership of the land.[36]

Buckinghamshire County Council v Moran [1990] Ch 623, CA

Slade LJ: However, as the judge said, the more difficult question is whether the defendant had the necessary *animus possidendi*. As to this, Mr Douglas accepted the correctness of the following statement (so far as it went) which I made in *Powell v McFarlane*:[37]

> the *animus possidendi* involves the intention, in one's own name and on one's own behalf, to exclude the world at large, including the owner with the paper title if he be not himself the possessor, so far as is reasonably practicable and so far as the process of the law will allow.

At least at first sight the following observations of Lord Halsbury LC in *Marshall v Taylor*,[38] which were referred to by Hoffmann J in his judgment, are very pertinent to the present case:

> The true nature of this particular strip of land is that it is enclosed. It cannot be denied that the person who now says he owns it could not get to it in any ordinary way. I do not deny that he could have crept through the hedge, or, if it had been a brick wall, that he could have climbed over the wall; but that was not the ordinary and usual mode of access. That is the exclusion – the dispossession – which seems to me to be so important in this case.

As a number of authorities indicate, enclosure by itself *prima facie* indicates the requisite *animus possidendi*. As Cockburn CJ said in *Seddon v Smith*:[39] 'Enclosure is the strongest possible evidence of adverse possession'. Russell LJ in *George Wimpey & Co Ltd v Sohn*,[40] similarly observed, 'Ordinarily, of course, enclosure is the most cogent evidence of adverse possession and of dispossession of the true owner.' While Mr Douglas pointed out that the plot was always accessible from the north where no boundary demarcation existed, it was only accessible from the defendant's own property, Dolphin Place. In my judgment, therefore, he must be treated as having enclosed it.

Mr Douglas, however, submitted that even if enclosure had occurred, the defendant's intention must be assessed in the light of the particular circumstances of this case. The defendant knew that the council had acquired and retained the plot with the specific intention of building a road across it at some future time. The council had no use for the land in the interim. It was for all practical purposes waste land. None of the

34 *Buckinghamshire CC v Moran* [1990] Ch 623.

35 *Powell v McFarlane* (1977) 38 P & CR 452 at 480.

36 *Buckinghamshire CC v Moran* [1990] Ch 623 at 641B; *Lodge v Wakefield Metropolitan City Council* [1995] 2 EGLR 124.

37 (1977) 38 P & CR 452 at 471–72.

38 [1895] 1 Ch 641 at 645.

39 (1877) 36 LT 168 at 169

40 [1967] Ch 487 at 511A.

defendant's acts, he submitted, were inconsistent with the council's known future intentions. He invoked, *inter alia*, the words of Cockburn CJ in *Leigh v Jack*,[41] which, he submitted, applied in the present case:

> I do not think that any of the defendant's acts were done with the view of defeating the purpose of the parties to the conveyances; his acts were those of a man who did not intend to be a trespasser, or to infringe upon another's right. The defendant simply used the land until the time should come for carrying out the object originally contemplated.

If the defendant had stopped short of placing a new lock and chain on the gate, I might perhaps have felt able to accept these submissions. Mr Douglas submitted that this act did not unequivocally show an intention to exclude the council as well as other people. (It is well established that it is no use for an alleged adverse possessor to rely on acts which are merely equivocal as regards the intention to exclude the true owner: see for example *Tecbild Ltd v Chamberlain*,[42] *per* Sachs LJ). In my judgment, however, the placing of the new lock and chain and gate did amount to a final unequivocal demonstration of the defendant's intention to possess the land. I agree with the judge in his saying:[43]

> ... I do not think that if the council, on making an inspection, had found the gate newly padlocked, they could have come to any conclusion other than that [the defendant] was intending to exclude everyone, including themselves, from the land.

The other main point which Mr Douglas has argued in support of this appeal has caused me slightly more difficulty. In his submission there can be no sufficient *animus possidendi* to constitute adverse possession for the purpose of the Act of 1980 unless there exists the intention to exclude the owner with the paper title in all future circumstances. The defendant's oral statements to Mr Harris in the conversation of 10 November 1975, as recorded in the attendance note, do appear to have constituted an implicit acknowledgment by the defendant that he would be obliged to leave the plot if in the future the council required it for the purpose of constructing the proposed new road. The letter of 18 December 1975, which I have concluded should be admitted in evidence, contains an express acknowledgment of this nature. If the intention to exclude the owner with the paper title in all future circumstances is a necessary constituent of the animus possidendi, the attendance note and the letter of 18 December 1975 show that this constituent was absent in the present case.

There are some *dicta* in the authorities which might be read as suggesting that an intention to *own* the land is required. Sir Nathaniel Lindley MR, for example, in *Littledale v Liverpool College*,[44] referred to the acts of ownership relied upon by the plaintiffs. Russell LJ in *George Wimpey & Co Ltd v Sohn*,[45] said:

> ... I am not satisfied that the actions of the predecessors in bricking up the doorway and maintaining a lock on the gate to the roadway were necessarily referable to an intention to occupy the [land] as their own absolute property.

41 (1879) 5 Ex D 264 at 271.

42 (1969) 20 P & CR 633 at 642.

43 (1988) 86 LGR 472 at 479.

44 [1900] 1 Ch 19 at 23.

45 [1967] Ch 487 at 510.

At one point in my judgment in *Powell v McFarlane*,[46] I suggested:

> ... any objective, informed observer might probably have inferred that the plaintiff was using the land simply for the benefit of his family's cow or cows, during such periods as the absent owner took no steps to stop him, without any intention to appropriate the land as his own.

Nevertheless, I agree with the judge that 'what is required for this purpose is not an intention to own or even an intention to acquire ownership but an intention to possess', that is to say, an intention for the time being to possess the land to the exclusion of all other persons, including the owner with the paper title. No authorities cited to us establish the contrary proposition. The conversation with Mr Harris, as recorded in the attendance note and the letter of 18 December 1975, to my mind demonstrate the intention of the defendant for the time being to continue in possession of the plot to the exclusion of the council unless and until the proposed by-pass is built. The form of the conveyance to the defendant and of the contemporaneous statutory declaration which he obtained from Mr and Mrs Wall, are, of course, entirely consistent with the existence of an intention on his part to take and keep adverse possession of the plot, at least unless and until that event occurred.

In the light of the line of authorities to which we have been referred, beginning with *Leigh v Jack*,[47] I have already accepted that the court should be slow to make a finding of adverse possession in a case such as the present. However, as the judge pointed out, in none of those earlier cases, where the owner with the paper title successfully defended his title, was there present the significant feature of complete enclosure of the land in question by the trespasser. On the evidence in the present case he was, in my judgment, right in concluding that the defendant had acquired adverse possession of the plot by 28 October 1973 and had remained in adverse possession of it ever since. There is no evidence that any representative of the council has even set foot on the plot since that date.

This appeal, which has been well argued on both sides, should in my judgment be dismissed.

Adverse possessor's title and rights[48]

Limitation Act 1980

17. Extinction of title to land after expiration of time limit

Subject to:

(a) section 18 of this Act; and

(b) section 75 of the Land Registration Act 1925;

at the expiration of the period prescribed by this Act for any person to bring an action to recover land (including a redemption action) the title of that person to the land shall be extinguished.

46 (1977) 38 P & CR 452 478.

47 (1879) 5 Ex D 264.

48 See (1973) 37 Conv 85 (Omotola, JA); [1956] CLJ 177 (Wade, HWR).

As Lord Radcliffe summed up, in *St Marylebone Property Co Ltd v Fairweather*,[49] the effect of the Limitation Act 1980 is to extinguish an existing better title. The Act does not operate as a parliamentary conveyance of the owner's title to the adverse possessor.[50] However, if the paper owner was a fee simple owner, as no one else can show a better title against the adverse possessor, the adverse possessor acquires a new title in fee simple which is unimpeachable.

St Marylebone Property Co Ltd v Fairweather [1963] AC 510, HL

Lord Radcliffe: It is necessary to start, I think, by recalling the principle that defines a squatter's rights. He is not at any stage of his possession a successor to the title of the man he has dispossessed. He comes in and remains in always by right of possession, which in due course becomes incapable of disturbance as time exhausts the one or more periods allowed by statute for successful intervention. His title, therefore, is never derived through but arises always in spite of – the dispossessed owner. At one time during the 19th century it was thought that s 34 of the Act of 1833 had done more than this and effected a statutory transfer of title from dispossessed to dispossessor at the expiration of the limitation period. There were eminent authorities who spoke of the law in just these terms. But the decision of the Court of Appeal in 1892 in *Tichborne v Weir* put an end to this line of reasoning by holding that a squatter who dispossessed a lessee and 'extinguished' his title by the requisite period of occupation did not become liable in covenant to the lessee's landlord by virtue of any privity of estate. The point was fully considered by the members of the court and they unanimously rejected the idea that the effect of the limitation statute was to make a 'Parliamentary conveyance' of the dispossessed lessee's title or estate to the dispossessing squatter.

In my opinion, this principle has been settled law since the date of that decision. It formed the basis of the later decision of the Divisional Court in *Taylor v Twinberrow* in which it was most clearly explained by Scrutton LJ that it was a misunderstanding of the legal effect of 12 years' adverse possession under the Limitation Acts to treat it as if it gave a title whereas its effect is 'merely negative' and, where the possession had been against a tenant, its only operation was to bar his right to claim against the man in possession. I think that this statement needs only one qualification: a squatter does in the end get a title by his possession and the indirect operation of the Act and he can convey a fee simple.

In unregistered land, although the adverse possessor has acquired a new title, his title is not free from prior incumbrances which were binding on the paper owner. This is because the adverse possessor, often known as squatter, is not a 'purchaser'. He has not purchased the land but has acquired the title to it by operation of law.[51] Even an unregistered land charge is binding on the squatter.[52]

49 [1963] AC 510

50 *Tichborne v Weir* (1892) 67 LT 735 at 736.

51 *Re Nisbet and Potts' Contract* [1906] 1 Ch 386 at 402.

52 See Chapters 1 and 6, pp 23, 223.

Nisbet and Potts' Contract [1906] 1 Ch 386, CA

Romer LJ: I think that with regard to a subsequent squatter, dealing in the first place with the time before that squatter has acquired any statutory right by lapse of time, inasmuch as he could not say he was a purchaser of a legal estate without notice, he would be bound by the covenant during his squatting, and accordingly the covenant, if he sought to break it, could be enforced against him at the instance and on behalf of the covenantee.

Now that being, in my opinion, the position of the squatter before he has acquired a statutory right under the Statute of Limitations, let me consider what would be the position of a squatter after a 12 years' occupation under the statute. By that occupation he has no doubt acquired a statutory title as against the covenantor or the heirs or assigns of the land of the covenantor who during those 12 years has, or have been, so remiss as not to eject him; but he does not thereby of necessity become entitled to hold the land free from the obligation of the negative covenant. That obligation is one existing against the title of the true owner of the land. The right of the true owner to the land has, no doubt, gone as against the successful squatter, who had acquired a title against him under the statute, but the original equitable right of the covenantee still exists. It was not a right that could be barred by the operation of the Statute of Limitations in favour of the statutory squatting owner. The covenantee was not an assign of the land, or of any part of the land, or of any estate in the land, which was capable of being barred by the operation of the Statute of Limitations; nor was the covenantor a trustee, in any sense, of the land for the covenantee, or of any part of it, or of any estate in it. The covenantee could not, directly or indirectly, by any person representing him and his right, in respect of that right under the restrictive covenant, take proceedings to recover possession against the squatter during the 12 years; and, in the case I am considering, the covenantee would, in my opinion, be no more barred by the operation of the Statute of Limitations by not taking proceedings against the squatter during the 12 years than he would have been barred by not taking proceedings against the true owner, had that true owner remained in possession during that period.

In registered land, while the paper owner remains the registered proprietor, he still has the legal estate in the land now possessed by the adverse possessor. However, s 75(1) of the Land Registration Act 1925 provides that the paper owner is to hold the legal estate on trust for the adverse possessor. Furthermore, the adverse possessor can apply to be registered as the new proprietor of the land, and meanwhile his rights are overriding interests under s 70(1)(f) of the Land Registration Act 1925.[53]

Land Registration Act 1925

75. Acquisition of title by possession

(1) The Limitation Acts shall apply to registered land in the same manner and to the same extent as those Acts apply to land not registered, except that where, if the land were not registered, the estate of the person registered as proprietor would be extinguished, such estate shall not be extinguished but shall be deemed to be held by the proprietor

53 See Chapter 7, p 272.

> for the time being in trust for the person who, by virtue of the said Acts, has acquired title against any proprietor, but without prejudice to the estates and interests of any other person interested in the land whose estate or interest is not extinguished by those Acts.
>
> (2) Any person claiming to have acquired a title under the Limitation Acts to a registered estate in the land may apply to be registered as proprietor thereof.

It should be noted that even before the adverse possessor acquires successfully his new title under the Limitation Act 1980, he has acquired a title, by virtue of his possession, as against the whole world except those who can claim a better title than him.[54] He can assign this title, even within the limitation period, or dispose of it by will or under the intestacy rule.[55] The assignee, or those who succeed to the adverse possession under his will or the intestacy rule, can count the period of his possession towards the period of their adverse possession.[56]

Asher v Whitlock (1865) LR 1 QB 1

Cockburn CJ: ... assuming the defendant's possession to have been adverse, we have then to consider how far it operated to destroy the right of the devisee and her heir-at-law. Mr Merewether was obliged to contend that possession acquired, as this was, against a rightful owner, would not be sufficient to keep out every other person but the rightful owner. But I take it as clearly established, that possession is good against all the world except the person who can shew a good title; and it would be mischievous to change this established doctrine. In *Doe d Hughes v Dyeball*,[57] one year's possession by the plaintiff was held good against a person who came and turned him out; and there are other authorities to the same effect. Suppose the person who originally inclosed the land had been expelled by the defendant, or the defendant had obtained possession without force, by simply walking in at the open door in the absence of the then possessor, and were to say to him, 'You have no more title than I have, my possession is as good as yours', surely ejectment could have been maintained by the original possessor against the defendant. All the old law on the doctrine of disseisin was founded on the principle that the disseisor's title was good against all but the disseisee. It is too clear to admit of doubt, that if the devisor had been turned out of possession he could have maintained ejectment. What is the position of the devisee? There can be no doubt that a man has a right to devise that estate, which the law gives him against all the world but the true owner. Here the widow was a prior devisee, but *durante viduitate* only, and as soon as the testator died, the estate became vested in the widow; and immediately on the widow's marriage the daughter had a right to possession; the defendant, however, anticipates her, and with the widow takes possession. But just as he had no right to interfere with the testator, so he had no right against the daughter, and had she lived she could have brought ejectment; although she died without asserting her right, the same right belongs to her heir. Therefore I think the action can be maintained, in as much as the defendant had not acquired any title by length of possession. The devisor might have brought

54 *Asher v Whitlock* (1865) LR 1 QB 1 at 5.

55 *Asher v Whitlock* (1865) LR 1 QB 1 at 6.

56 *Asher v Whitlock* (1865) LR 1 QB 1 at 6.

57 (1829) Mood & M 346.

ejectment, his right of possession being passed by will to his daughter, she could have maintained ejectment, and so therefore can her heir, the female plaintiff. We know to what extent encroachments on waste lands have taken place; and if the lord has acquiesced and does not interfere, can it be at the mere will of any stranger to disturb the person in possession? I do not know what equity may say to the rights of different claimants who have come in at different times without title; but at law, I think the right of the original possessor is clear. On the simple ground that possession is good title against all but the true owner, I think the plaintiffs entitled to succeed, and that the rule should be discharged.

If the person dispossessed was a tenant, the adverse possessor acquires only a tenancy, since, during the tenancy, the landlord who either owns a headlease or a fee simple, has a better claim against the adverse possessor. However, the landlord cannot enforce the leasehold covenants against the adverse possessor for he is not an assignee or sub-tenant.[58] The landlord may, on the other hand, forfeit the lease against the adverse possessor for non-performance of the leasehold covenants.[59] It also seems that the dispossessed tenant may surrender his tenancy, thereby putting an end to the adverse possessor's title to the tenancy.[60]

St Marylebone Property v Fairweather [1963] AC 510, HL

Lord Denning: My Lords, at the back of a leasehold house in Hempstead there is a shed. In the year 1920 the next-door neighbour, Mr Millwood, saw it was unused and out of repair. He went in and repaired it and has treated it as his own ever since. Mr Millwood has actually sublet it as part of his own house. Now a property company has bought the freehold of the property on which the shed stands and wants to recover possession of the shed. Can it do so or is it barred by the Statutes of Limitation? There are three important persons to consider:

(1) The *freeholder* who, in 1893, let the premises on which the shed stands on a lease for 99 years at a ground rent with a repairing covenant and a proviso for re-entry. The 99 years will not expire till 1992.

(2) The *leaseholder* who has taken no steps for more than 12 years to recover possession of the shed which stands on part of his leasehold premises. His right of action first accrued in 1920. So the 12 years for him to sue expired in 1932.

(3) The *squatter*, who has been in possession of the shed since 1920, by himself or his sub-tenants.

And there is one important event to consider: The *surrender* in 1959 by the *leaseholder* to the *freeholder* of the rest of the term of 99 years. Whereupon the freeholder claims that he is entitled to possession of the shed. But the *squatter* says he is entitled to stay in it until 1992.

It is quite clear from the Statutes of Limitation that in the year 1932 the 'title' of the leaseholder to the land was 'extinguished'. What does this mean? There are four suggestions to consider.

58 *Tichborne v Weir* (1892) 67 LT 735 at 737; *St Marylebone Property Co Ltd v Fairweather* [1963] AC 510 at 535.

59 *Tickner v Buzzacott* [1965] Ch 426 at 434E–G.

60 *St Marylebone Property Co Ltd v Fairweather* [1963] AC 510. See, however, Lord Morris's dissenting speech that the tenant could not surrender the lease which he no longer had.

The first suggestion is that the title of the leaseholder to the shed is extinguished completely, not only against the squatter, but also against the freeholder. So that the leasehold interest disappears altogether, and the freeholder becomes entitled to the land. I reject this suggestion completely. It would mean in this case that the freeholder would have become entitled to possession of the shed in the year 1932 and time would have begun to run against him from 1932. So that 12 years later the title of the freeholder to the shed would have been extinguished, that is, in 1944. That cannot be right, and it was not seriously suggested. In 99 cases out of 100, the freeholder has no knowledge that the squatter is on the premises at all. It would be utterly wrong if the title of the freeholder could be eroded away during the lease without his knowledge. The correct view is that the freehold is an estate in reversion within s 6(1) of the Act of 1939, and time does not run against the freeholder until the determination of the lease: see *Doe d Davy v Oxenham*.[61]

The second suggestion is that the title of the leaseholder to the shed is extinguished so far as the leaseholder is concerned – so that he is no longer entitled to the shed – but that the leasehold interest itself persists and is vested in the squatter. In other words, the squatter acquired a title which is 'commensurate' with the leasehold interest which has been extinguished. This suggestion was made in 1867 in the first edition of Darby and Bosanquet's book [*Statutes of Limitation*] at p 390, and it was accepted in 1889 as correct by the court in Ireland in *Rankin v M'Murtry*.[62] But it has since been disapproved. If it were correct, it would mean that the squatter would be in the position of a statutory assignee of the shed, and he would by reason of privity of estate, be liable on the covenants and subject to the conditions of the lease. I reject this suggestion also: for the simple reason that the operation of the Statutes of Limitation is merely negative. It destroys the leaseholder's title to the land but does not vest it in the squatter. The squatter is not liable on the repairing covenants: see *Tichborne v Weir*.[63] Nor, when the leasehold is a tenancy from year to year, does he step into the shoes of the tenant so as to be himself entitled to six months' notice to quit: see *Taylor v Twinberrow*.[64]

The third suggestion is that the *title* of the leaseholder is extinguished but that his *estate* in the land is not. This is too fine a distinction for me. And so it was for Parliament. For Parliament itself uses the two words as if they meant the same: see s 16 of the Limitation Act 1939, and s 75 of the Land Registration Act 1925.

The fourth suggestion is that the title of the leaseholder to the shed is extinguished *as against the squatter*, but remains good as against the freeholder. This seems to me the only acceptable suggestion. If it is adopted, it means that time does not run against the freeholder until the lease is determined – which is only just. It also means that until that time the freeholder has his remedy against the leaseholder on the covenants, as he should have; and can also re-enter for forfeiture, as he should be able to do: see *Humphry v Damion*,[65] and can give notice to determine on a 'break' clause or notice to quit, as the case may be. Further, it means that if the leaseholder should be able to induce the squatter to leave the shed – or if the squatter quits and the leaseholder resumes

61 (1840) 7 M & W 131.

62 (1889) 24 LR Ir 290.

63 (1892) 67 LT 735.

64 [1930] 2 KB 16.

65 (1612) 3 Cro Jac 300.

possession – the leaseholder is at once in the same position as he was originally, being entitled to the benefits and subject to the burdens of the lease in regard to the shed. All this seems to me eminently reasonable but it can only be achieved if, despite the presence of the squatter, the title of the leaseholder remains good as against the freeholder.

On this footing it is quite apparent that at the date of the surrender, the leaseholder had something to surrender. He still had his title to the shed as against the freeholder and was in a position to surrender it to him. The maxim *nemo dat quod non habet* has no application to the case at all.

But there still remains the question: What was the effect of the surrender? There are here two alternatives open:

(1) On the one hand, it may be said that the surrender operated to *determine* the term, just as a forfeiture does. If this is correct, it would mean that the freeholder would be entitled to possession at once as soon as the leaseholder surrendered the house. He could evict the squatter by virtue of his freehold estate against which the squatter could say nothing. And time would begin to run against the freeholder as soon as the surrender took place. This view is based on *Ecclesiastical Commissioners of England and Wales v Rowe*,[66] and s 6(1) of the Limitation Act 1939.

(2) On the other hand, it may be said that the surrender operated as an assignment by the leaseholder to the freeholder of the rest of the 99 years. If this is correct, it would mean that the freeholder could not evict the squatter because the freeholder would be 'claiming through' the leaseholder and would be barred for the rest of the 99 years, just as the leaseholder would be: see s 4(3) of the Limitation Act. Time would not begin to run against the freeholder until the 99 years expired. This view is based on *Walter v Yalden*.[67]

My Lords, I have come to the clear conclusion that a surrender operates as a determination of the term. It is not an assignment of it. I am aware that no less an authority than Lindley LJ once said that 'the surrender of the term only operated as an assignment of the surrenderor's interest in it': see *David v Sabin*.[68] But if that be true, it is not by any rule of the common law, only by force of statute: and then only in the case of underleases, not in the case of trespasser or squatter.

At common law, if a leaseholder made an underlease and afterwards surrendered his term to the freeholder, then the freeholder could not evict the underlessee during the term of the underlease: see *Pleasant (Lessee of Hayton) v Benson*.[69] But this was not because there was any assignment from surrenderor to surrenderee. It is clear that, upon the surrender, the head term was determined altogether. It was extinguished completely, so much so that the freeholder could not sue the underlessee on the covenants or enforce the proviso for re-entry: see *Webb v Russell*.[70] The underlessee could enjoy the property without payment of rent and without performance of the covenant and conditions until the end of the term of the underlease: see *Ecclesiastical Commissioners for England v Treemer*.[71] This was remedied by the statutes of 1740 and 1845, which have been

66 (1880) 5 App Cas 736.

67 [1902] 2 KB 304.

68 [1893] 1 Ch 523, 533; 9 TLR 240, CA.

69 (1811) 14 East 234.

70 (1789) 3 Term Rep 393.

71 [1893] 1 Ch 166, 174; 9 TLR 78.

re-enacted in ss 139 and 150 of the Law of Property Act 1925. Under those statutes, on a surrender of the head lease, an underlessee becomes a direct tenant of the freeholder on the terms of his underlease. So that the surrender does operate as if it were an assignment of the surrenderor's interest. But those statutes have no application to trespassers or squatters.

The question may be asked: why did the common law on a surrender protect the underlessee from eviction? The answer is to be found in Coke upon Littleton II, p 338b, where it is said that:

> ... having regard to the parties to the surrender, the estate is absolutely drowned ... But having regard to strangers, who were not parties or privies thereunto, lest by a voluntary surrender they may receive prejudice touching any right or interest they had before the surrender, the estate surrendered hath in consideration of law a continuance.

This passage applies in favour of an underlessee so as to protect him from eviction during the term of his underlease: but it does not apply in favour of a trespasser. The reason for the difference is because the underlessee comes in under a grant from the lessee; and the lessee cannot, by a surrender, derogate from his own grant: see *Davenport's* case[72] and *Mellor v Watkins*,[73] by Blackburn J. But a trespasser comes in by wrong and not by grant of the lessee. If the lessee surrenders his term, the freeholder is at once entitled to evict the trespasser for the simple reason that, on the surrender, the lease is determined, and there is no bar whatever to the freeholder recovering possession: see *Ecclesiastical Commissioners of England and Wales v Rowe*.[74] And I see no reason why the same reasoning should not apply even though, at the date of the surrender, the trespasser is a squatter who has been there more than 12 years. For, as against the freeholder, he is still a trespasser. The freeholder's right to possession does not arise until the lease is determined by the surrender. It then comes into being and time begins to run against him under s 6(1) of the Limitation Act 1939.

The only reason, it seems to me, which can be urged against this conclusion is that it means that a squatter's title can be destroyed by the leaseholder and freeholder putting their heads together. It is said that they can by a surrender – or by a surrender and regrant – destroy the squatter's title completely and get rid of him. So be it. There is no way of preventing it. But I would point out that, if we were to deny the two of them this right, they could achieve the same result in another way. They could easily do it by the leaseholder submitting to a forfeiture. If the leaseholder chooses not to pay the rent, the freeholder can determine the lease under the proviso for re-entry. The squatter cannot stop him. He cannot pay the rent without the authority of the leaseholder. He cannot apply for relief against forfeiture. The squatter's title can thus be defeated by a forfeiture – or by a forfeiture and regrant – just as it can by a surrender – or by a surrender and regrant. So there is nothing in the point.

My Lords, so far as these questions under the Limitation Acts are concerned, I must say that I see no difference between a surrender or merger or a forfeiture. On each of those events, the lease is determined and the freeholder is entitled to evict the squatter, even though the squatter has been on the land during the lease for more than 12 years:

72 (1608) 8 Co Rep 144b.

73 (1874) LR 9 QB 400 at 405.

74 (1880) 5 App Cas 736.

and on the determination of the lease, time then begins to run against the freeholder. It follows that, in my opinion, *Walter v Yalden* was wrongly decided and *Taylor v Twinberrow* was rightly decided.

One word about s 75(1) of the Land Registration Act 1925. That point was not raised in the county court and its availability depends on facts which were not proved. I do not think it is open to the appellant here. But in any case I doubt if that puts registered land on a very different footing from unregistered land. It is machinery so as to apply the Limitation Acts to registered land but it does not alter the substantive position very materially. The registered leaseholder clearly remains liable on the covenants and subject to the conditions of the lease, including the proviso for re-entry: and I do not see why, on a surrender, the freeholder should not recover possession from a squatter, just as he can on a forfeiture. The freeholder has no notice of the trust in favour of the squatter and his interests are not to be prejudiced by the fact that the leasehold is registered. I say no more because the point is not available here. Suffice it to say that for the reasons I have given, I would dismiss this appeal.

But the decision in *St Marylebone Property Co Ltd v Fairweather* was not followed by Browne-Wilkinson J in a registered land case of *Spectrum Investment v Holmes*.[75]

Spectrum Investment v Holmes [1981] 1 WLR 221

Browne-Wilkinson J: I can now shortly state the contentions of the plaintiff. The plaintiff submits that the Land Registration Act 1925 introduces mere machinery for proving title to and transferring land and does not affect the substantive rights which parties enjoy under the general law. Accordingly, it is said that the rights of the plaintiff (as established by *St Marylebone Property Co v Fairweather* [1963] AC 510) must be reflected in the provisions of the Act of 1925 and are preserved by the words in s 11 which expressly provide that registration with possessory title 'shall not affect or prejudice the enforcement of any estate, right, or interest (whether in respect of the lessor's title or otherwise) adverse to or in derogation of' the proprietor with possessory title. So, it is said, having obtained a surrender of the lease from Mrs David, the plaintiff's right to possession as against the defendant is preserved.

There is in my judgment a short answer to the claim by the plaintiff. Accepting for the moment the broad proposition that the Act of 1925 was not intended to alter substantive rights, it undoubtedly was intended to alter the manner in which such rights were to be established and transferred. The surrender by Mrs David to the plaintiff is the linchpin of the plaintiff's claim. But in my judgment that surrender has not been effected by the only means authorised by the Land Registration Act 1925 for the disposal of a registered leasehold interest by act of the parties. At the date of the alleged surrender the lease was registered under title no NGL 65073 in the name of the defendant. Mrs David was not registered as proprietor, her title no LN 66166 having been taken off the register. By virtue of s 69(1) the effect of the registration of the defendant as proprietor of the lease was, as against Mrs David, to vest the term or deem it to be vested in the defendant.

75 [1981] 1 WLR 221. See (1981) 32 NILQ 254 (Wallace, H); [1981] Conv 157 (Sydenham, C); [1982] Conv 201 (Kenny, PH); (1981) 131 NLJ 718 (Smith, PF); (1981) 131 NLJ 774 (Nugee, EG).

Section 69(4) provides: 'The estate for the time being vested in the proprietor shall only be capable of being disposed of or dealt with by him in a manner authorised by this Act.'

In my judgment, the effect of these provisions is that, so long as the defendant is registered as proprietor of the lease, only she can dispose of it. Moreover, by virtue of ss 21 and 22, even the defendant can only do so by a registered disposition. Accordingly, in my judgment there has, as yet, been no valid surrender of the lease and the plaintiff's claim fails in limine.

Mr Tager for the plaintiff sought to avoid this result by saying that a surrender was not a registrable disposition and referred me to s 46 of the Act. This argument does not meet the point that Mrs David was not registered as proprietor when she purported to surrender the lease. But even if she had been, in my judgment the surrender would have had to be effected by a registered disposition. Section 69(4) makes it clear that even a registered proprietor only has power to deal with any estate vested in him in the manner authorised by the Act. The only powers of disposition are those conferred by s 21 of the Act which authorises the transfer of the registered estate. In my judgment the word 'transfer' in this section must include surrendering the term, otherwise the Act does not authorise a surrender. Any disposition under s 21 has to be completed by registration: s 22. Section 46, on which Mr Tager relied, merely directs the registrar to note on the register the determination of the lease, however that occurs, which will include determination by effluxion of time or operation of law. Section 46 does not purport to lay down the ways in which the determination can be effected by disposition of one of the parties.

Mr Tager submitted further that there ought to have been two registered titles to the lease, of which Mrs David was the proprietor of one and the defendant was the proprietor of the other. This suggestion seems to have no warrant in any provision of the Act and in my judgment runs contrary to the whole scheme of the Act, which is intended to ensure that there shall be one title for any interest in registered land and anyone dealing with that land can treat the registered proprietor of that interest as the owner of that interest.

For these reasons, in my judgment, there has, as yet, been no surrender of the term by Mrs David to the plaintiff. Therefore, the plaintiff's claim fails since, so long as the term exists, it has no immediate right to possession. However, in order to determine the real issue between the parties, I gave leave for Mrs David to be joined as co-plaintiff. If she is entitled to rectification of the register, she may thereafter be able to execute the necessary registered surrender and, if she can, the plaintiff's claim to possession would be unanswerable.

Mr Charles's submissions for the defendant were very far-reaching. He submitted that the whole scheme of the Land Registration Act 1925 shows that the position of the squatter on registered land is totally different from that of a squatter on unregistered land as laid down by the House of Lords in *St Marylebone Property Co Ltd v Fairweather* [1963] AC 510. He submits that s 75(2) makes it clear that the squatter who has obtained title against the documentary lessee is entitled to apply to be registered as proprietor of the documentary lessee's registered estate in the land, ie as proprietor of the lease itself. Section 75(3) then requires the registrar, if satisfied of the facts, to effect such registration. Accordingly, it is said that what was done in the present case was quite correct: the defendant is rightly registered as proprietor of the lease itself. As a result, it is said, the legal term of years is vested in the defendant by a parliamentary conveyance contained in s 69 of the Act. By virtue of ss 9 and 11 of the Act the defendant as registered proprietor is deemed to have vested in her the possession of the leasehold interest, subject to the express and implied obligations in the lease and subject to any rights of the freeholder adverse to her interest. Therefore, Mr Charles submits, the scheme of the Land Registration Act 1925 is to produce exactly the result which the House of Lords held was not the result in relation to unregistered land, namely to make the squatter the successor in title to the documentary lessee by parliamentary conveyance, the squatter taking subject to and with the benefit of the covenants in the lease.

This is a formidable and far-reaching submission. But, on the other side I was strongly pressed with authority suggesting that squatter's rights were the same over both registered and unregistered land. In *St Marylebone Property Co Ltd v Fairweather* [1963] AC 510 it emerged at a late stage in the proceedings that the land there in question was registered land. The squatter was not registered as proprietor of the lease, but contended that the provisions of s 75(1) of the Act (which makes the documentary lessee as registered proprietor a trustee for the squatter) prevented the documentary lessee from surrendering the term to the freeholder. It was not proved at what date the documentary lessee was registered, and on that ground it was held that s 75 had no application. But Lord Radcliffe said at 542–43:

> I do not think, therefore, that the appellant can succeed on this point. I only wish to add that at present I am not at all satisfied that s 75(1) does create a trust interest in the squatter of the kind that one would expect from the words used. So to hold would raise difficulties which I do not now explore; and the trust of the dispossessed owner's title under sub-s (1) must somehow be reconciled with the provision under sub-s (2) for the squatter to apply to register his own title, which would presumably be his independent possessory title acquired by the adverse possession.

See also *per* Lord Denning at 548.

To similar effect are the remarks of Sir John Pennycuick in *Jessamine Investment Co v Schwartz* [1978] QB 264 at 275:

> I should be very reluctant to introduce a substantive distinction in the application of a provision of the Limitation Act to registered land and unregistered land respectively, based upon what is plainly a conveyancing device designed to adapt that provision to the former class of land.

Although these are *obiter dicta*, they are obviously of some weight in supporting the contention that the position of a squatter does not vary according to whether the land is registered or unregistered.

Finally, the words of s 75(1) itself state that the Limitation Acts shall apply to registered land 'in the same manner and to the same extent' as it applies to unregistered land, and then goes on to state exceptions.

On the other hand, I take into account the recent decision of the House of Lords in *Williams & Glyn's Bank Ltd v Boland* (decided since the conclusion of the argument in this case) [1980] 3 WLR 138 which shows that, if the words of the Land Registration Act 1925 are clear, they are to be given their natural meaning and not distorted so as to seek to produce uniformity in the substantive law as between registered and unregistered land. I therefore approach this question on the basis that one would expect that substantive legal rights would be the same whether the land is registered or unregistered but that clear words in the Act of 1925 must be given their natural meaning even if this leads to a divergence.

I do not find it necessary to reach any conclusion on the far-reaching propositions which Mr Charles put forward, since I think that I can decide this case on quite a narrow ground, leaving it to others to resolve the more fundamental questions. In my judgment, if Mrs David is to succeed in any claim to have the defendant deleted from the register as proprietor of the lease, she (Mrs David) must show at least that the registration of the defendant was not a mandatory requirement of the provisions of the Land Registration Act 1925. It is clear from the references in s 75(3) that s 75 applies to a leasehold interest. Under s 75(3) the registrar is under a mandatory duty to register the squatter on the application made by the squatter under s 75(2) if the registrar is satisfied as to the squatter's title. For what does the squatter make application? I will read s 75(2) again: 'Any person claiming to have acquired a title under the Limitation Acts to a registered estate in the land may apply to be registered as proprietor thereof.'

To my mind, the words are clear and unequivocal: the squatter claims to have acquired a title to 'a registered estate in the land' (ie the leasehold interest) and applies to be registered as a proprietor '*thereof*' (my emphasis). Therefore, under s 75(2), references to the squatter having acquired title to a registered estate must include the rights which under the Limitation Act 1939 the squatter acquires in relation to leasehold interests. Section 75(2) then refers to the squatter applying to be registered as proprietor 'thereof.' This word can, in my judgment, only refer back to the registered estate in the land against which the squatter has acquired title under the Act of 1939, ie the leasehold interest. The clear words of the Act therefore seem to require that, once the 12 years have run, the squatter is entitled to be registered as proprietor of the lease itself, and is bound to be so registered if he applies for registration. It follows that in my judgment the defendant (as the squatter) is correctly registered as proprietor of the lease itself in accordance with the clear requirements of s 75. If that is right, Mrs David cannot be entitled to rectification of the register as against the defendant, and she can therefore never get into a position in which she is competent to surrender the lease to the plaintiff.

I am conscious that in so deciding I am reaching a conclusion which produces at least a limited divergence between squatter's rights over registered and unregistered land. Once the squatter is rightly registered as proprietor under s 75(3) the documentary lessee and the freeholder can no longer defeat the squatter's rights by a surrender. But I am not deciding anything as to the position during the period between the date when the squatter obtains his title by adverse possession and the date on which he obtains registration of it. This is the period covered by s 75(1) which is the subsection on which Lord Radcliffe in *St Marylebone Property Co Ltd v Fairweather* [1963] AC 510 at 542, and Sir John Pennycuick in *Jessamine Investment Co v Schwartz* [1978] QB 264 at 275, were commenting. It may well be, as their *dicta* suggest, that during the period preceding any registration of the squatter's rights, the documentary lessee (as registered proprietor of the lease) and the freeholder can deal with the legal estate without reference to a person whose rights are not recorded on the register. But once the Act provides for registration of the squatter's title, it must in my judgment follow that the squatter's rights (once registered) cannot be overriden. The difference between registered and unregistered land in this respect is an inevitable consequence of the fact that the Land Registration Act 1925 provides for registration of the squatter as proprietor and that registered proprietors have rights.

I can summarise my conclusions as follows:

(a) The plaintiff cannot, under s 11 of the Act, have any estate right or interest adverse to or in derogation of the title of the defendant (as registered proprietor of the lease with possessory title) unless and until the lease has come to an end.

(b) The lease has not come to an end by virtue of the purported surrender of 7 May 1975, since at that date the leasehold interest was registered land and the surrender was not made in accordance with the provisions of the Act.

(c) Mrs David is not entitled to rectification of the register reinstating her as registered proprietor of the lease, since the defendant is registered in accordance with the mandatory requirements of s 75 of the Act.

Therefore (d) Mrs David can never surrender the term so as to merge it in the freehold, and accordingly the plaintiff cannot become entitled to possession by reason of such a surrender.

In these circumstances, it is not necessary for me to consider the argument that in exercising my discretion whether or not to rectify the register, I should not in any event order rectification against the defendant, the registered proprietor in possession, at the suit of those whose disregard of their own property interest has led to the defendant's registration.

I therefore dismiss the claim by the plaintiff.

As mentioned earlier, where an adverse possessor has acquired a possessory title against a lessee, when the lease expires, the lessor is entitled to oust the squatter. Thus, if the original lease contained no option for the lessee to renew, and the lessor grants a new lease either to the original dispossessed lessee or to another person, the lessee under the new lease acquires new title from the landlord and can eject the squatter. But if the original lease contains an option to renew for a further term, the lessee has an existing property right to renew, the adverse possession for the prescribed period would bar the lessee from asserting all his rights including those resulting from the renewed lease against the squatter.[76]

2 EFFECT OF LIMITATION ACT ON FUTURE INTERESTS

A person who is entitled to an interest in reversion or in remainder, when adverse possession is taken, cannot bring an action after 12 years from adverse possession being taken, or six years from the falling of his interest into possession, whichever is the longer.[77]

76 *Chung Ping Kwan v Lam Island Co Ltd* [1996] 3 WLR 448, PC.

77 Section 15(2), Sched 1, para 4 of the Limitation Act 1980.

Limitation Act 1980

15. Time limit for actions to recover land

(2) Subject to the following provisions of this section, where:

(a) the estate or interest claimed was an estate or interest in reversion or remainder or any other future estate or interest and the right of action to recover the land accrued on the date on which the estate or interest fell into possession by the determination of the preceding estate or interest; and

(b) the person entitled to the preceding estate or interest (not being a term of years absolute) was not in possession of the land on that date;

no action shall be brought by the person entitled to the succeeding estate or interest after the expiration of 12 years from the date on which the right of action accrued to the person entitled to the preceding estate or interest or six years from the date on which the right of action accrued to the person entitled to the succeeding estate or interest, whichever period last expires.

Schedule 1

Accrual of right of action in case of future interests

4. The right of action to recover any land shall, in a case where:

(a) the estate or interest claimed was an estate or interest in reversion or remainder or any other future estate or interest; and

(b) no person has taken possession of the land by virtue of the estate or interest claimed;

be treated as having accrued on the date on which the estate or interest fell into possession by the determination of the preceding estate or interest.

Thus, suppose there is a grant 'to A for life with remainder to B in fee simple', and A is dispossessed 10 years before his death. Under the 12 years rule, on the death of A, B has two years to bring an action against the adverse possessor, whereas under the six years rule, he has six years to bring the action. Thus, under s 15(2), B has six years from A's death in which to sue. But if A is dispossessed two years before his death, under the 12 years rule, on A's death, B has 10 years to bring an action for recovery of land, whereas under the six years rule he has six years to bring the action. Thus, under s 15(2), B has 12 years from the dispossession of A or 10 years from A's death to bring the action.

Different rules apply where A has an entail interest.[78] In this case, B, the remainderman 'claim through' A, the tenant in tail, so that if time has started to run against A on his dispossession, it continues to run against B, and does not start afresh on the determination of the entail.

78 Section 15(3) of the Limitation Act 1980.

Limitation Act 1980

15. Time limit for actions to recover land

(3) Sub-s (2) above shall not apply to any estate or interest which falls into possession on the determination of an entailed interest and which might have been barred by the person entitled to the entailed interest.

3 EFFECT OF LIMITATION ACT ON LEASEHOLD INTERESTS

As is provided by Schedule 1, para 4, where a tenant is dispossessed, the limitation period does not begin to run, as against the landlord, until the tenancy expires. This is because the landlord's right to resume possession only accrues on the expiry of the tenancy.[79] Where the tenancy is periodic and not in writing,[80] the tenancy is treated as being terminated at the expiration of the first year or other period.[81] Where rent is received, time runs from the last receipt of rent.[82] In the case of a tenancy at will, time does not begin to run until the landlord has terminated the tenancy by demanding possession or some other act of ownership which is inconsistent with the tenancy.[83] Similarly, time does not run in favour of a licensee until the licence is terminated, because during the term of the licence, the licensee occupies the land with the owner's consent.[84] In the case of a tenancy at sufferance, time begins to run at the start of the 'tenancy', because it arises where the tenant holds over without the landlord's consent or dissent after the expiry of an initially valid tenancy.[85] A tenant at sufferance has no tenancy at all but is in adverse possession.[86]

A tenant cannot claim adverse possession during the term of the tenancy because his possession cannot be regarded as adverse: he occupies the land with the landlord's permission and in accordance with the tenancy.[87] If the tenant encroaches on adjoining land owned by the landlord, the presumption is that he has done so as an extension of his lease for the benefit of the landlord.[88]

79 *Tichborne v Weir* (1892) 67 LT 735 at 737; *St Marylebone Property Co Ltd v Fairweather* [1963] AC 510 at 537, 544, 548, 553.

80 A written document is not a 'lease in writing' for the purposes of para 5(1) of Sched 1 to the Limitation Act 1980 if the writing does not create a leasehold estate at law, but merely evidences the existence of a lease, whatever its terms and however comprehensively it sets out the terms of the lease: *Long Tower Hamlets London Borough Council* [1996] 2 All ER 683.

81 Schedule 1, para 5(1) of the Limitation Act 1980); *Jessamine Investment Co v Schwartz* [1978] QB 264; *Palfrey v Palfrey* (1974) 229 EG 1593 at 1595.

82 Schedule 1, para 5(2) of the Limitation Act 1980.

83 Section 3(1) of the Limitation Act 1980.

84 *Hughes v Griffin* [1969] 1 WLR 23.

85 Co Litt 57b.

86 See Megarry and Wade, p 1039.

87 *Smirk v Lyndale Developments Ltd* [1975] 1 Ch 317; *Hayward v Chaloner* [1968] 1 QB 107 at 122C–D.

88 *Smirk v Lyndale Developments Ltd* [1975] 1 Ch 317.

Smirk v Lyndale Developments Ltd [1975] 1 Ch 317, CA

Pennycuick VC: I turn now to the law applicable where a tenant takes possession of adjoining land – a tenant, during the currency of his tenancy, who takes possession of adjoining land belonging to his landlord. The law on this point, if I may respectfully say so, has got into something of a tangle.

I will refer first to *Kingsmill v Millard* (1855) 11 Exch 313. The headnote is as follows:

> Where a tenant incloses land, whether adjacent to, or distant from, the demised premises, and whether the land be part of a waste, or belong to the landlord or a third person, it is a presumption of fact, that the enclosure is part of the holding, unless the tenant, during the term, does some act disclaiming his landlord's title ...

In the course of argument, Alderson B, made this comment at 316:

> It seems to me, that the acts of the tenant to rebut the presumption should be such acts as in a manner set the landlord at defiance; for instance, if the tenant gave the landlord notice of a conveyance, and he did not interfere: but if the landlord has no knowledge of it, what is there to undeceive him in supposing that the tenant occupies the waste as part of the holding?

Then Parke B gave judgment in these terms, at p 318:

> It is laid down in all the cases – whether the inclosed land is part of the waste, or belongs to the landlord or a third person – that the presumption is, that the tenant has inclosed it for the benefit of his landlord, unless he has done some act disclaiming the landlord's title. I am disposed to discard the definition, that the encroachment is made 'for the benefit of the landlord', and to adopt that of Lord Campbell, *viz* that the encroachment must be considered as annexed to the holding, unless it clearly appears that the tenant made it for his own benefit. It is not necessary that the land inclosed should be adjacent to the demised premises; the same rule prevails when the encroachment is at a distance. That is now the law; and I must add, that even though at the time of making the encroachment there is nothing to rebut the presumption that the tenant intended to hold it as a portion of his farm, yet circumstances may afterwards occur by which it may be severed from the farm: for instance, if the tenant conveys it to another person, and the conveyance is communicated to the landlord, then it can no longer be considered as part of the holding. But if the landlord is allowed to remain under the belief that the encroachment is part of the farm, the tenant is estopped from denying it, and must render it up at the end of the term as a portion of the holding.

Then both Alderson B and Platt B agreed.

It will be observed that in his judgment Parke B in terms states that the presumption that the tenant has inclosed for the benefit of the landlord applies, irrespective of whether the inclosed land is part of the waste or belongs to the landlord; and indeed he uses the word 'encroachment' as appropriate in either case. He then goes on to state in terms, following and agreeing what Alderson B said in the course of the argument, that in order to displace the presumption there must be communication to the landlord. That decision of high authority seems to me to be in accordance with justice and common sense, and unless I were compelled to do otherwise by subsequent authority, I would certainly adopt it. I should add, as is perhaps obvious, as appears in some of the later cases, that the presumption may be rebutted by any form of express or implied agreement or, in some cases, as Parke B says, by estoppel ...

Having been through the authorities I propose, as I have said earlier, to adopt and apply the principle laid down in *Kingsmill v Millard*, 11 Exch 313.

To return to the present case, there is nothing on the facts which could in any way rebut the presumption, which it seems to me is applicable here, namely that the tenant, the plaintiff, was occupying the plots by way of an addition to land comprised with his tenancy, and not otherwise adversely to the landlord.

Where the tenant fails to pay rent, under s 19 of the Act, '[n]o action shall be brought, or distress made, to recover arrears of rent, or damages in respect of arrears of rent, after the expiration of six years from the date on which the arrears become due'.[89] Failure to pay rent has no effect on the landlord's title to the land.

Adverse possession may take the form of an adverse possession of the rent from a tenancy to which the landlord is entitled provided the rent paid is at least £10 per annum. Thus, if a person has wrongfully received rent of at least £10 per annum from the tenant for 12 years, and no rent is paid to the landlord, he can claim the landlord's reversion.[90] The landlord's right to the reversion is barred.

Where there is a forfeiture clause for breach of covenants, Limitation Act 1980, Schedule 1, para 7(1) provides that '[s]ubject to sub-paragraph (2) below, a right of action to recover land by virtue of a forfeiture or breach of condition shall be treated as having accrued on the date on which the forfeiture was incurred or the condition broken'. Thus, time runs as soon as there is a breach, and as a right of re-entry under a forfeiture clause is a right to recover land,[91] the limitation period is 12 years. Furthermore, a fresh right of entry arises every time there is a breach. Schedule 1, para 7(2) provides that '[i]f any such right has accrued to a person entitled to an estate or interest in reversion or remainder and the land was not recovered by virtue of that right, the right of action to recover the land shall not be treated as having accrued to that person until his estate and interest fell into possession, as if no such forfeiture or breach of condition had occurred'. This means that failure to re-enter under a forfeiture clause under para 7(1) does not affect the landlord's title to the reversion because he will have a fresh right of action when the lease expires.

4 EFFECT OF LIMITATION ACT ON LAND HELD ON TRUST

Where land is held on trust, and it may be a trust of land, or a strict settlement, and adverse possession is taken by a stranger, the trustee's title to the legal estate is not affected until all the beneficiaries have been barred.[92]

89 This section applies not only to actions against the lessee but also to actions against the guarantor of the lessee's undertaking to pay rent: *Romain v Scuba TV Ltd* [1996] 2 All ER 377.

90 Schedule 1, para 6 of the Limitation Act 1980.

91 Section 38(7) of the Limitation Act 1980.

92 Section 18(2) of the Limitation Act 1980.

Limitation Act 1980

18. Settled land and land held on trust

(2) Where the period prescribed by this Act has expired for the bringing of an action to recover land by a tenant for life or a statutory owner of settled land:

(a) his legal estate shall not be extinguished if and so long as the right of action to recover the land of any person entitled to a beneficial interest in the land either has not accrued or has not been barred by this Act; and

(b) the legal estate shall accordingly remain vested in the tenant for life or statutory owner and shall devolve in accordance with the Settled Land Act 1925;

but if and when every such right of action has been barred by this Act, his legal estate shall be extinguished.

(3) Where any land is held upon trust and the period prescribed by this Act has expired for the bringing of an action to recover the land by the trustees, the estate of the trustees shall not be extinguished if and so long as the right of action to recover the land of any person entitled to a beneficial interest in the land either has not accrued or has not been barred by this Act; but if and when every such right of action has been so barred the estate of the trustees shall be extinguished.

Thus, if land is held on trust for A for life, with remainder to B, 12 years' adverse possession by a stranger bars only A's beneficial interest. As will be seen, A, being the tenant for life under a strict settlement,[93] has the legal estate and holds it as a trustee. A's beneficial interest (life interest) is barred but his legal estate is not affected by the adverse possession, because B's beneficial interest (remainder interest) is not barred yet. Time will not run against B until A's death. In the meantime, A will hold the legal estate, once his beneficial interest is barred after 12 years' adverse possession by a stranger, on trust for the stranger for A's life, with remainder to B.

A trustee cannot claim the title to the land for himself by adverse possession against the beneficiaries because no limitation period applies to an action brought by a beneficiary in respect of any fraud or fraudulent breach of trust by the trustee, or to recover trust property converted to his use.[94]

Limitation Act 1980

21. Time limit for actions in respect of trust property

(1) No period of limitation prescribed by this Act shall apply to an action by a beneficiary under a trust, being an action:

(a) in respect of any fraud or fraudulent breach of trust to which the trustee was a party or privy; or

(b) to recover from the trustee trust property or the proceeds of trust property in the possession of the trustee, or previously received by the trustee and converted to his use.

93 See Chapter 11.

94 Section 21(1) of the Limitation Act 1980.

Thus, where land is held by X and Y as legal joint tenants on trust for themselves as beneficial tenants in common, X cannot bar Y's beneficial claim no matter how long he has excluded Y from the land or its rents and profits.[95]

Where the beneficiaries' claims are not covered by s 21(1)(a) and (b), for example, claims for trust property already in a third party's hands, or any other breach of trust such as an unauthorised investment, there is a limitation period and they should sue within six years.[96]

Limitation Act 1980

21. Time limit for actions in respect of trust property

(3) Subject to the preceding provisions of this section, an action by a beneficiary to recover trust property or in respect of any breach of trust, not being an action for which a period of limitation is prescribed by any other provision of this Act, shall not be brought after the expiration of six years from the date on which the right of action accrued.

For the purposes of this subsection, the right of action shall not be treated as having accrued to any beneficiary entitled to a future interest in the trust property until the interest fell into possession.

Section 21(1)(b) and sub-s (3) are, however, subject to s 21(2).

Limitation Act 1980

21. Time limit for actions in respect of trust property

(2) Where a trustee who is also a beneficiary under the trust receives or retains trust property or its proceeds as his share on a distribution of trust property under the trust, his liability in any action brought by virtue of sub-s (1)(b) above to recover that property or its proceeds after the expiration of the period of limitation prescribed by this Act for bringing an action to recover trust property shall be limited to the excess over his proper share.

This subsection only applies if the trustee acted honestly and reasonably in making the distribution.

Thus, if A holds the land on trust for himself, B, C and D, in distributing the proceeds of sale when the land is sold, if A takes one-third of it for himself in the honest and reasonable belief that it is to be divided equally between himself and B and C, after the expiration of six years, his liability to D is limited to the excess over his proper share only. But if D claims his share within six years of distribution, he is entitled to his full share.

Where the beneficiary, who is not solely and absolutely entitled, is in possession of the trust land, his possession cannot be adverse possession against the trustee (including a statutory owner), and other beneficiaries (including a tenant for life).[97] Time does not run against these persons.

95 *Re Landi* [1939] Ch 828. See (1941) 57 LQR 26 (REM); (1971) 35 Conv (NS) 6 (Battersby, G).

96 Section 21(3) of the Limitation Act 1980.

97 Schedule 1, para 9 of the Limitation Act 1980.

Limitation Act 1980

Schedule 1

Possession of beneficiary not adverse to others interested in settled land or land subject to a trust of land.

9. Where any settled land or any land subject to a trust of land is in the possession of a person entitled to a beneficial interest in the land (not being a person solely or absolutely entitled to the land), no right of action to recover the land shall be treated for the purposes of this Act as accruing during that possession to any person in whom the land is vested as tenant for life, statutory owner or trustee, or to any other person entitled to a beneficial interest in the land.

5 CLAIMS THROUGH CROWN

As has been seen, the Crown has 30 years to bring an action for recovery of land. Where time has started to run against the Crown and the Crown then conveys the land to a private individual, the latter is barred 30 years after the original dispossession or 12 years after the conveyance to him, whichever is the shorter.[98]

Limitation Act 1980

Schedule 1

12. Notwithstanding s 15(1) of this Act, where in the case of any action brought by a person other than the Crown or a spiritual or eleemosynary corporation sole the right of action first accrued to the Crown or any such corporation sole through whom the person in question claims, the action may be brought at any time before the expiration of:

(a) the period during which the action could have been brought by the Crown or the corporation sole; or

(b) twelve years from the date on which the right of action accrued to some person other than the Crown or the corporation sole;

whichever period first expires.

It should be noted, however, that if in the converse case, where a person against whom time has started to run conveys his land to the Crown, the limitation period from the dispossession is extended from 12 years to 30 years in favour of the Crown.

6 POSTPONEMENT OF LIMITATION PERIOD

The limitation period mentioned above may be postponed on grounds of disability, fraud, concealment and mistake.

98 Schedule 1, para 12 of the Limitation Act 1980.

Disability

Where the owner of an interest in land is suffering from disability when the right of action accrues, he has 12 years from the dispossession or six years from the time when he ceases to be under a disability, whichever is the longer, to bring an action for the recovery of his interest in land.[99] This is, however, subject to a maximum period of 30 years.

Limitation Act 1980

28. Extension of limitation period in case of disability

(1) Subject to the following provisions of this section, if on the date when any right of action accrued for which a period of limitation is prescribed by this Act, the person to whom it accrued was under a disability, the action may be brought at any time before the expiration of six years from the date when he ceased to be under a disability or died (whichever first occurred) notwithstanding that the period of limitation has expired.

(2) This section shall not affect any case where the right of action first accrued to some person (not under a disability) through whom the person under a disability claims.

(3) When a right of action which has accrued to a person under a disability accrues, on the death of that person while still under a disability, to another person under a disability, no further extension of time shall be allowed by reason of the disability of the second person.

(4) No action to recover land or money charged on land shall be brought by virtue of this section by any person after the expiration of 30 years from the date on which the right of action accrued to that person or some person through whom he claims.

For s 28 to operate, a disability must exist at the time when the cause of action accrued. If the owner of an interest in land suffers from disability after he is dispossessed, s 28 does not apply.

In the case of successive disabilities, ie a person who is suffering from one disability, then suffers from another disability before the first disability ceases, his six years' extended period starts to run only after both disabilities cease, subject to the maximum period of 30 years.[100] But if one disability ceases before another disability begins, time runs from the date when the first disability ceases.[101] Similarly, if the person under disability is succeeded by another person under disability, the six years run from the date when the first person ceases to suffer from disability.[102]

Section 38(2) of the Limitation Act 1980 provides that '[f]or the purposes of this Act a person shall be treated as under a disability while he is an infant, or of unsound mind'.

99 Section 28 of the Limitation Act 1980.

100 Section 28(1) of the Limitation Act 1980.

101 Section 28(3) of the Limitation Act 1980.

102 Section 28(3) of the Limitation Act 1980.

Subsection (3) provides that '[f]or the purposes of s (2) above a person is of unsound mind if he is a person who, by reason of mental disorder within the meaning of the Mental Health Act 1983, is incapable of managing and administering his property and affairs'.

Fraud, concealment and mistake

Limitation Act 1980

32. Postponement of limitation period in case of fraud, concealment or mistake

(1) Subject to sub-ss (3) and (4A) below, where in the case of any action for which a period of limitation is prescribed by this Act, either:

(a) the action is based upon the fraud of the defendant; or

(b) any fact relevant to the plaintiff's right of action has been deliberately concealed from him by the defendant; or

(c) the action is for relief from the consequences of a mistake;

the period of limitation shall not begin to run until the plaintiff has discovered the fraud, concealment or mistake (as the case may be) or could with reasonable diligence have discovered it.

References in this subsection to the defendant include references to the defendant's agent and to any person through whom the defendant claims and his agent.

(2) For the purposes of sub-s (1) above, deliberate commission of a breach of duty in circumstances in which it is unlikely to be discovered for some time amounts to deliberate concealment of the facts involved in that breach of duty.

(3) Nothing in this section shall enable any action:

(a) to recover, or recover the value of, any property; or

(b) to enforce any charge against, or set aside any transaction affecting, any property;

to be brought against the purchaser of the property or any person claiming through him in any case where the property has been purchased for valuable consideration by an innocent third party since the fraud or concealment or (as the case may be) the transaction in which the mistake was made took place.

(4) A purchaser is an innocent third party for the purposes of this section:

(a) in the case of fraud or concealment of any fact relevant to the plaintiff's right of action, if he was not a party to the fraud or (as the case may be) to the concealment of that fact and did not at the time of the purchase know or have reason to believe that the fraud or concealment had taken place; and

(b) in the case of mistake, if he did not at the time of the purchase know or have reason to believe that the mistake had been made.

It should be noted that the rule as to mistake under s 32(1)(c) applies only where the mistake is an essential ingredient of the cause of action, for example, where the action is for money paid under a mistake of fact.[103]

7 PREVENTING TIME FROM RUNNING/STARTING TIME RUNNING AFRESH

Time may be prevented from running, and it will have to start running afresh by another adverse possession, where there is (i) an effective assertion by the owner of his rights; (ii) a signed written acknowledgment of the owner's title; or (iii) part payment of principal or interest by the adverse possessor or his agent. An assertion of right by the owner occurs when he takes legal proceedings against the adverse possessor or makes an effective entry on the land. Acknowledgement of the owner's right, or part payment where the right is to payment of money, has no effect if it is given after the limitation period has run its full course.[104]

Limitation Act 1980

29. Fresh accrual of action on acknowledgment or part payment

(1) Subs-ss (2) and (3) below apply where any right of action (including a foreclosure action) to recover land or an advowson or any right of a mortgagee of personal property to bring a foreclosure action in respect of the property has accrued.

(2) If the person in possession of the land, benefice or personal property in question acknowledges the title of the person to whom the right of action has accrued:

(a) the right shall be treated as having accrued on and not before the date of the acknowledgment; and

(b) in the case of a right of action to recover land which has accrued to a person entitled to an estate or interest taking effect on the determination of an entailed interest against whom time is running under s 27 of this Act, s 27 shall thereupon cease to apply to the land.

(3) In the case of a foreclosure or other action by a mortgagee, if the person in possession of the land, benefice or personal property in question or the person liable for the mortgage debt makes any payment in respect of the debt (whether of principal or interest) the right shall be treated as having accrued on and not before the date of the payment.

(4) Where a mortgagee is by virtue of the mortgage in possession of any mortgaged land and either:

(a) receives any sum in respect of the principal or interest of the mortgage debtor; or

(b) acknowledges the title of the mortgagor, or his equity of redemption;an action to redeem the land in his possession may be brought at any time before the expiration of 12 years from the date of the payment or acknowledgment.

103 *Phillips-Higgins v Harper* [1954] 1 QB 411.

104 *Sanders v Sanders* (1881) 19 Ch D 373.

(5) Subject to sub-s (6) below, where any right of action has accrued to recover:

(a) any debt or other liquidated pecuniary claim; or

(b) any claim to the personal estate of a deceased person or to any share or interest in any such estate; and the person liable or accountable for the claim acknowledges the claim or makes any payment in respect of it the right shall be treated as having accrued on and not before the date of the acknowledgment or payment.

(6) A payment of a part of the rent or interest due at any time shall not extend the period for claiming the remainder then due, but any payment of interest shall be treated as a payment in respect of the principal debt.

(7) Subject to sub-s (6) above, a current period of limitation may be repeatedly extended under this section by further acknowledgments or payments, but a right of action, once barred by this Act, shall not be revived by any subsequent acknowledgment or payment.

30. Formal provisions as to acknowledgments and part payments

(1) To be effective for the purposes of s 29 of this Act, an acknowledgment must be in writing and signed by the person making it.

(2) For the purposes of s 29, any acknowledgment or payment –

(a) may be made by the agent of the person by whom it is required to be made under that section; and

(b) shall be made to the person, or to an agent of the person, whose title or claim is being acknowledged or, as the case may be, in respect of whose claim the payment is being made.

31. Effect of acknowledgment or part payment on persons other than the maker or recipient

(1) An acknowledgment of the title to any land, benefice, or mortgaged personalty by any person in possession of it shall bind all other persons in possession during the ensuing period of limitation.

(2) A payment in respect of a mortgage debt by the mortgagor or any other person liable for the debt, or by any person in possession of the mortgaged property, shall, so far as any right of the mortgagee to foreclose or otherwise to recover the property is concerned, bind all other persons in possession of the mortgaged property during the ensuing period of limitation.

(3) Where two or more mortgagees are by virtue of the mortgage in possession of the mortgaged land, an acknowledgment of the mortgagor's title or of his equity of redemption by one of the mortgagees shall only bind him and his successors and shall not bind any other mortgagee or his successors.

(4) Where in a case within sub-s (3) above the mortgagee by whom the acknowledgment is given is entitled to a part of the mortgaged land and not to any ascertained part of the mortgage debt the mortgagor shall be entitled to redeem that part of the land on payment, with interest, of the part of the mortgage debt which bears the same proportion to the whole of the debt as the value of the part of the land bears to the whole of the mortgaged land.

(5) Where there are two or more mortgagors, and the title or equity of redemption of one of the mortgagors is acknowledged as mentioned above in this section, the acknowledgment shall be treated as having been made to all the mortgagors.

(6) An acknowledgment of any debt or other liquidated pecuniary claim shall bind the acknowledgor and his successors but not any other person.

(7) A payment made in respect of any debt or other liquidated pecuniary claim shall bind all persons liable in respect of the debt or claim.

(8) An acknowledgment by one of several personal representatives of any claim to the personal estate of a deceased person or to any share or interest in any such estate, or a payment by one of several personal representatives in respect of any such claim, shall bind the estate of the deceased person.

(9) In this section, 'successor', in relation to any mortgagee or person liable in respect of any debt or claim, means his personal representatives and any other person on whom the rights under the mortgage or, as the case may be, the liability in respect of the debt or claim devolve (whether on death or bankruptcy or the disposition of property or the determination of a limited estate or interest in settled property or otherwise).

8 REMEDIES

The dispossessed owner is entitled to recover possession of the land by injunction or possession order against the adverse possessor, and is also entitled to mesne profits for the wrongful use of the land.[105] The court has no discretion to allow total dispossession by means of an award of damages *in lieu* of an injunction or possession order; the adverse possessor cannot in effect buy adverse title through an award of damages.[106] Where adverse possession takes the form of encroaching building works the owner can either accept the building as an accretion on his land (keep them or demolish them or deal with them out of court in whatever way he chooses), or insists on a possession order of the encroached land or an order for demolition of the encroaching building works.[107]

105 *Inverngie Investments Ltd v Hackett* [1996] 1 EGLR 149, PC.

106 *Harrow London Borough Council v Donoghue* [1995] 1 EGLR 257.

107 *Ibid* at 259E-G.

CHAPTER 6

UNREGISTERED LAND AND PRIORITY

1 INTRODUCTION

The distinctions between legal and equitable interests, and how they can be acquired by sale, under the doctrine of proprietary estoppel and adverse possession, have been seen. It is now essential to examine how these legal and equitable interests are accommodated and protected under the English law of real property.

Legal and equitable interests in land are today protected under two distinct systems of conveyancing: unregistered system, ie the system which applies to the title of land which is unregistered, and registered system, ie the system which applies to the title of land which is registered. These two systems, as existing today, are the result of the 1925 legislation. Before the details of the two systems are examined, it is essential to look at the background and the policy of the 1925 legislation.

Sir Robert Megarry and Professor Wade sum it up so well:

> It was plain enough in the latter 19th century that the law of real property and conveyancing was antiquated and unnecessarily complex, despite the considerable reforms of the years from 1832–45. But no root-and-branch amendment was attempted ... But it was out of the desire for registration of title that the proposals for a general reform of the law grew. It tends to be forgotten today that the object of those who first put forward the new ideas was to pave the way for the universal registration of title.
>
> It became obvious that the practice of private conveyancing was wasteful and laborious, for the same title had to be fully investigated *de novo* upon every transaction. 'Registration of title was invented, from the necessity of the case, when stocks and shares became an important form of property; it is a scientific system of conveyancing, based on common sense and modern requirements. The problem is how we are to engraft this system on our law of real property, which has been frequently described, by practical conveyancers, as a disgrace to a civilised community.'[1] The Royal Commission on the Land Transfer Acts, which had to consider the defects of the Act of 1897, reported in 1911 that registration of title was greatly impeded by the state of the law, and by the differences between the rules for real and personal property. It became the accepted truth that 'to legislate for the registration of titles without, as a preliminary step, simplifying the titles to be registered is to begin at the wrong end.'[2] A sound system of registration requires titles to be properly proved to the registrar in the first instance, and this enormous task must obviously be lightened in every way possible. Hence arose the cry for the simplification of conveyancing.
>
> When the legislation came, its sponsors did not commit themselves to universal registration, in order to placate the opposition in the profession. They proposed an experimental period of 10 years in which the merits of registered and

1 (1912) 28 LQR 6 at 10 (Sweet, C).

2 Underhill, A, 'The Line of Least Resistance' appendix to Cmnd 424 (1919) at 34, citing the Report of the Select Committee on Land Titles and Transfer of 1828.

unregistered conveyancing might again be compared. There were two main schools of thought: 'Some think that the present system of private conveyancing, which has been patched and repatched until the original material is hardly recognisable, only wants a little more patching to make it perfect. Others think that registration of title is inevitable, and resign themselves to their fate, without reflecting that there are good and bad systems of registration.'[3] The Bills of 1922–25 were designed to win the support of both sides.

The foundation on which the legislation was built was the reduction in the number of legal estates. This had been advocated by Wolstenholme as early as 1862, and his scheme for effecting it (and other improvements adopted in 1925) may be seen in his draft Conveyancing Bill of 1898. Assimilation to personalty was the guiding policy ...

After the Royal Commission had reported in 1911, work on a general overhaul of the law was put in hand by Lord Haldane LC, and Bills were produced in 1913, 1914 and 1915. After the war the work was resumed, first under the Minister of Reconstruction and then under Lord Birkenhead LC by a Committee over which Sir Leslie Scott presided. The fourth report of the Scott Committee was the immediate cause of the Law of Property Act 1922, drafted by Sir Benjamin Cherry. As Solicitor General, Sir Leslie Scott presented it as 'the biggest Bill ever introduced into Parliament' though before it came into force it was amended and sub-divided into the Acts of 1925.[4] Credit for much of the earlier work belongs to The Law Society, which commissioned the Wolstenholme Bill and other projects. But the immediate authors of the Acts of 1925 were Sir Benjamin Cherry, its principal draftsman, Sir Leslie Scott, and Lord Birkenhead LC, whose powers secured not only the passage of the Acts through the House of Lords but also the overwhelming support of the legal profession and of the public.

Sir Leslie Scott's speech on the second reading of the Law of Property Bill 1922 gives a good general account of the intended legislation. 'It is not revolution' he said, 'it is evolution ... It is the slow and gradual product of half a century's work by legal reformers, building on existing foundations.' He stated that expert opinion was still sharply divided as to the merits of registration of title, and for that reason the ten-year trial period was proposed. Now that more than half a century has passed, it may be added that the advantages of registered title are clearly appreciated, and that registration is at last proceeding as fast as the Land Registry can undertake it with the facilities and funds allowed. The initial work required by each extension of the system is heavy, but the speed of progress has nevertheless increased.

Apart from many incidental reforms, the principal changes effected by the legislation of 1925 may be grouped under three heads of policy: (a) The assimilation of the law of real property to that of personal property (b) The simplification of conveyancing (c) The abolition of anachronisms.[5]

Speaking highly of the 1925 legislation, Sir Robert Megarry and Professor Wade said:

[The reforms] were without doubt the greatest single monument of legal wisdom, industry and ingenuity which the statute-book can display. Perhaps the best tribute to the workmanship of their authors is the fact that in nearly 60 years the

3 (1912) 28 LQR 24 (Sweet, C).

4 Serious mistakes were made in the subdivisions.

5 Megarry and Wade, pp 1144–47.

Acts have been litigated and amended so little. When introducing the Law of Property Bill 1922, Sir Leslie Scott claimed that it deserved the encomium (of a kind which falls but rarely from the bench) which Lord MacNaghten once bestowed upon another statute: 'Drawn with consummate skill it avoids all technical expressions, and yet there is not a single word misused or out of place, nor any expression which it would be easy to improve.' Persons familiar with the weaker points of the final legislation of 1925 may feel that this praise is rather too high. Nevertheless the Acts as a whole have stood the test of time, and the benefits which they have conferred were not exaggerated by their sponsors. They are many and great.[6]

2 OUTLINE OF UNREGISTERED AND REGISTERED SYSTEM

Unregistered system

Where the title of land is unregistered, except interests which are to be registered as land charges on the Land Charges Register, the details of ownership do not appear on any central record of register. As has been seen,[7] the purchaser has to make full inquiries and investigation of his vendor's title in order to find out the details of ownership and incumbrances binding on the land.

Registered system

The idea is that virtually all details of ownership of land should be recorded definitively on a central register maintained by the Land Registry. The Land Register is kept permanently up-to-date and any prospective purchaser can search the Register to discover all the relevant details about the land he proposes to buy.

3 THE SCHEME OF 1925 LEGISLATION

The English law of unregistered land is profoundly shaped by two conflicting considerations of facilitating free alienability of land, and fragmentation of benefit from land and the security of fragmented benefit. As Sir Robert Megarry and Professor Wade put it:

> The central dilemma of land law is how to reconcile security of title with ease of transfer. The law permits a wide variety of incumbrances and charges such as leases, easements, restrictive covenants, estate contracts and mortgages ... The owners of these interests are concerned that the land should not be transferred in any manner which might defeat them. A purchaser of land, on the other hand, is concerned that he should not be bound by an interest not fully known to him in advance.[8]

6 Megarry and Wade, p 1144.

7 See Chapter 4, pp 108–10, 132–33, 137.

8 Megarry and Wade, p 141.

And as Professor Gray points out:

> The twin objectives of alienability of title and fragmentation of benefit are, in the first analysis, set against each other in irreconcilable opposition. If the legal title in land is to be freely alienable, how can rights to various forms of fragmented benefit in that land be other than transient and defeasible rights which perish when the legal title passes into the hands of a purchaser? The interest of the alienee in taking title utterly free of conflicting rights militates directly against the objective of fragmentation of benefit. The free transferability of title seems to be in conflict with the durable creation – whether for family or commercial reasons – of lesser rights in the land which are capable of surviving subsequent dealings with the legal title.[9]

Despite the fact that the twin objectives were seemingly self-conflicting, one of the greatest achievements of the 1925 reformers was to accommodate just these objectives. The objective of simplifying the process of transferring land is achieved by the reduction of legal estates to fee simple absolute in possession and term of years absolute, and the reduction of the number of legal owners to four. To achieve the objectives of protecting fragmented benefits, the cardinal principles that legal estate or interest binds the whole world including a subsequent purchaser, whereas equitable interest binds the whole world except a *bona fide* purchaser for value of a legal estate without notice of the equitable interest, is modified. The equitable interests were divided by the 1925 reformers into two main categories: those family interests which exist behind a strict settlement or a trust for sale,[10] and those commercial interests which are to be registered in the land charges register. The cardinal principle is modified, in the case of family interests by the extension of 'overreaching' principle. In the case of commercial interests, it is modified by the extension of registration in the land charges register. As will be seen, there is, however, perhaps unforeseen by the 1925 reformers, a group of equitable interests not affected by the 'overreaching' principle and the land charges registration. This group of interests is still governed by the cardinal principle. At the same time, provision was made for the progressive replacement of the unregistered system by the registered system which will be examined in Chapter 7.

Reduction of number of legal estates

As has been seen,[11] prior to 1926, many kinds of limited interests could exist as legal estates. From the purchaser's point of view, this was extremely inconvenient and could hardly promote the objective of free alienability. This was because in order to obtain a good legal title, he had to require all owners of legal estates to join in the conveyance to convey to him all the legal estates in land. To simplify this aspect of the conveyancing, the number of legal estates

9 Gray, p 98.

10 As from 1 January 1997 a trust for sale is converted into a trust of land under the TLATA 1996 and the overreaching principle applicable to a trust for sale is extended to a trust of land.

11 See Chapter 1, pp 3–7, 11–12.

was reduced to two: the fee simple absolute in possession, and the term of years absolute. The purchaser is thereby able to acquire a legal estate in land by taking a conveyance only from the fee simple owner or leasehold owner, and will not have to request other limited owners to join in the conveyance. The purchaser's position is also rendered stronger *vis-à-vis* limited owners, as Sir Robert Megarry and Professor Wade point out:

> ... a purchaser who buys without notice of some adverse right is bound by that right if it is legal and takes free from it if it is equitable. Consequently, the fewer legal estates and interests which can exist in land, the less precarious is the position of a purchaser.[12]

However, the reduction of the number of legal estates naturally leads to the corresponding increase in the number of equitable interests. As is pointed out:

> But conversely, the more equitable interests which can exist in land the more precarious are rights in real property generally, for all such equitable interests lie open to the risk that the legal estate may be bought without notice.[13]

If the objective of fragmentation of benefit in the form of limited beneficial ownerships is to be promoted, these equitable interests must obviously be protected too. This is achieved by extending the overreaching principle.

Extension of 'overreaching'

As will be seen,[14] where the land owner intended to keep certain land within the family, it was common to create a strict settlement. If the intention was to sell the land whenever desirable, a trust for sale was the obvious choice. By the conveyancing practice before 1926, the legal estate was normally vested in the trustees for certain beneficiaries. By the terms of the trust for sale, from the moment of sale of the land held on trust to a purchaser, these beneficial interests attached not to the land but to the purchase money. The beneficial interests were shifted from the land to the proceeds of sale, a process known as 'overreaching'. Thus, the purchaser who paid the proceeds of sale was not concerned with the beneficial interests, whether he had notice of them or not. This machinery proved to be very convenient. Thus, it was extended to the strict settlement by s 20 of the Settled Land Act 1882. Thus, so long as the purchaser paid to at least two trustees or into court, the beneficial interests would be shifted to the proceeds of sale. This was so whether the legal estate was vested in the trustees or split up between the beneficiaries. A tenant for life was able to convey the entire legal estate, something which he did not have, to the purchaser.

The practice of 'overreaching' was adopted and further extended by the 1925 legislation to protect the now equitable limited interests. It was enacted that, in the case of equitable limited interests, if the purchaser pays to all the trustees of the settlement, these beneficial interests will be overreached. If the purchaser does not pay according to the Act, the conveyance of the legal estate

12 Megarry and Wade, p 123.

13 Megarry and Wade, p 123.

14 Chapter 11.

by the tenant for life will be rendered ineffective.[15] The purchaser will only acquire the tenant for life's limited interest. In the case of a trust for sale, as long as the purchaser paid to at least two trustees, the equitable limited interests would be overreached, otherwise the purchaser took the legal estate subject to them if he had notice of them. Under the Trusts of Land and Appointment of Trustees Act 1996, whereby all trusts for sale are converted into trusts of land and all beneficial interests in land will exist behind a simple trust of land, the overreaching principle is extended to a trust of land.

So the twin objectives of alienability and fragmentation are achieved. The purchaser only has to pay according to the Settled Land Act 1925 or the Law of Property Act 1925 as the case may be, and does not have to be concerned with limited interests which have become equitable since 1925. He takes the legal estate free of any equitable interests, as long as he pays in the prescribed manner, whether he has notice of the equitable interests or not. The fragmented beneficial interests which were legal, but which have since 1925 become equitable, are protected in that their interests are now shifted to the proceeds of land safe in the hands of the trustees, who are under a duty to make proper investment for their benefit. Although the beneficiaries lose the prospect of enjoying the land after sale, they are not defrauded because they have corresponding interests in the proceeds of sale. Their interests are now protected in the form of proceeds of sale.

Reduction of number of trustees and legal owners

However, as in the case of a trust of land the legal estate is vested in the trustees, the purchaser has to require all of them to join in the conveyance. Although he no longer has to ask the limited owners to join in the conveyance, if the number of trustees is not limited, the object of avoiding a cumbersome, costly and time-consuming conveyance will be frustrated. Thus, the number of trustees permitted is reduced to four. As will be seen,[16] it is further required that the trustees hold the legal estate as joint tenants. Similarly, in the case of a strict settlement, the legal estate cannot be vested in more than four persons.

Registration of land charges and other matters

In unregistered land, a group of equitable interests under the Land Charges Act 1925, now under the Land Charges Act 1972, are required to be registered in the land charges register. This must not be confused with the registration of legal interests and entry of equitable interests in the land register where the title of land is registered. The Land Charges Acts in effect codify the doctrine of notice by providing that registration of registrable equitable interests 'shall be deemed to constitute actual notice', thereby binding on the whole world.[17] Non-registration renders the registrable interest void against certain types of purchaser, whether he has notice or not.[18] This mechanism creates certainty and

15 Section 18 of the SLA 1925.

16 See Chapter 13, p 547–48.

17 Section 198(1) of the LPA 1925.

18 Section 4(5), (6) of the LCA 1972; *Midland Bank Trust Co Ltd v Green* [1981] AC 513.

protects both the prospective purchaser and the owner of a registrable interest. It protects the purchaser in that he can find out the existence of equitable interests which affect the land he is buying by a simple search of the Land Charges Register. The owners of registrable interests can protect themselves by a simple act of registration.

Introduction of registered system

A formal system of registration of title, intended to cover all land in England and Wales gradually, was introduced under the Land Registration Act 1925 to simplify the conveyancing process and to give greater protection to the prospective purchaser and the owners of legal and equitable interests.

Under the registered system, the same kinds of legal and equitable interests exist. However, the distinction between legal and equitable interests is less significant. All interests in land, whether legal or equitable, are to be entered in the land register, with the exception of 'overriding interests'. The purchaser, or rather the 'transferee' or 'grantee', who is registered as the proprietor of a legal estate takes the legal estate subject only to those interests appearing on the register and overriding interests, but otherwise free of all other incumbrances, whether he has notice or not.[19] Furthermore, the overreaching principle also applies to registered land, so that the purchaser who pays in the prescribed manner can take free of beneficial interests even though they are entered on the land register. Thus, apart from overriding interests, the purchaser who searches at the Land Registry knows if the land he is buying is subject to any incumbrances, and he is able to take free of incumbrances not already entered on the land register. As will be seen, the existence of overriding interests represents a potential problem for a prospective purchaser of a registered land. Likewise, the owners of estates or interests can protect their interests by a simple act of protective entry.

Having set the scene of the scheme of 1925 legislation, it is now necessary to examine the protection of the three categories of equitable interests *vis-à-vis* a subsequent purchaser in unregistered land in greater detail. A good understanding of this aspect is crucially important for it is the fundamental basis upon which modern English land law is founded.

As mentioned above, in unregistered land, legal estates and interests bind the whole world regardless of whether the purchaser has notice or not. Equitable interests are, however, divided into three groups with different protective mechanisms. These are interests which are registrable, overreachable, and those that are not registrable nor overreachable but governed by the equitable doctrine of notice.

4 LAND CHARGES REGISTRATION

The cardinal principle that equitable interest binds the whole world except a *bona fide* purchaser of a legal estate for value without notice has the

19 Sections 20(1), 59(6) of the LRA 1925.

disadvantage of uncertainty. The purchaser of a legal estate could not know for certain if he had taken the legal estates free of equitable interests of which he might later be found to have constructive notice. Likewise, the position of the owners of equitable interests were insecure, as a subsequent purchaser of the legal estate who had no notice might destroy their interests. The inherent insecurity of many equitable interests, largely commercial in nature, were removed by the Land Charges Act 1925, now consolidated in the Land Charges Act 1972.[20]

The mechanism of land charges registration is relatively simple. It is based on two fundamental principles. First, registration is deemed actual notice to all persons for all purposes of the interests registered. Thus, a registrable interest once registered binds the whole world. Secondly, non-registration of a registrable interest renders the interest void as against certain types of purchaser. A purchaser, for the purposes of the Land Charges Act 1972, is 'any person (including a mortgagee or lessee) who, for valuable consideration, takes any interest in land or in a charge on land'.[21] However, as will be seen, if a third party does not qualify for the protection conferred on those certain types of purchaser, the cardinal equitable principles will apply to determine the question of priority between the owner of an unregistered registrable interest and the third party.

Registrable interests

The types of interests registrable under the Land Charges Act 1972 are pending actions, writs and orders affecting land, deeds of arrangement, and land charges. Land charges are further divided into different classes under s 2 of the Act.

(a) Pending actions

Land Charges Act 1972

5. The register of pending actions

(1) There may be registered in the register of pending actions:

(a) a pending land action;

(b) a petition in bankruptcy filed on or after 1 January 1926.

(7) A pending land action shall not bind a purchaser without express notice of it unless it is for the time being registered under this section.

(8) A petition in bankruptcy shall not bind a purchaser of a legal estate in good faith, for money or money's worth ... unless it is for the time being registered under this section.

(10) The court, if it thinks fit, may upon the determination of the proceedings, or during the pendency of the proceedings if satisfied that they are not prosecuted in good faith,

20 Other matters, actions and documents relating to land are also registrable.

21 Section 17(1) of the LCA 1972.

make an order vacating a registration under this section, and direct the party on whose behalf it was made to pay all or any of the costs and expenses occasioned by the registration and by its vacation.

(11) The county court has jurisdiction under sub-s (10) of this section where the action was brought or the petition in bankruptcy was filed in that court.

The register of pending actions is used to register pending land actions and bankruptcy petitions filed on or after 1 January 1926.[22] A pending land action 'means' any action or proceeding pending in court relating to land or any interest in or charge on land.[23] Thus, any claims affecting the title to land or any claims of proprietary interest in land can be registered in the register of pending actions. These include a spouse's claim to a house on divorce,[24] a claim to easement,[25] and claims of rights of occupation by beneficiaries under a trust for sale, or those based on proprietary estoppel.[26]

Registration of pending actions lasts for five years in the first instance and can be renewed for another five years if the action has not then been decided.[27] Registration is deemed to be actual notice.[28] Non-registration renders a pending land action void against 'a purchaser without express notice of it.'[29] Similarly, non-registration renders a bankruptcy petition void against 'a purchaser of a legal estate in good faith, for money or money's worth.'[30]

(b) Writs and orders affecting land

Land Charges Act 1972

6. The register of writs and orders affecting land

(1) There may be registered in the register of writs and orders affecting land:

(a) any writ or order affecting land issued or made by any court for the purpose of enforcing a judgment or recognisance;

(b) any order appointing a receiver or sequestrator of land;

(c) any bankruptcy order, whether or not the bankrupt's estate is known to include land.

(1A) No writ or order affecting an interest under a trust of land may be registered under sub-s (1) above.

(4) Except as provided by sub-s (5) below and by s 37(5) of the Supreme Court Act 1981 and s 107(3) of the County Courts Act 1984 (which make special provision as to receiv-

22 Section 5(1) of the LCA 1972.

23 Section 17(1) of the LCA 1972.

24 *Whittingham v Whittingham* [1979] Fam 9 at 13E. But contrast *Sowerby v Sowerby* (1982) 44 P & CR 192 at 195.

25 *Greenhi Builders Ltd v Allen* [1979] 1 WLR 156 at 159G.

26 *Haslemere Estates Ltd v Baker* [1982] WLR 1109 at 1119H–20A.

27 Section 8 of the LCA 1972.

28 Section 198(1) of the LPA 1925.

29 Section 5(7) of the LCA 1972.

30 Section 5(8) of the LCA 1972.

ing orders in respect of land of judgment debtors) every such writ and order as is mentioned in sub-s (1) above, and every delivery in execution or other proceeding taken pursuant to any such writ or order, or in obedience to any such writ or order, shall be void as against a purchaser of the land unless the writ or order is for the time being registered under this section.

(5) Subject to sub-s (6) below, the title of a trustee in bankruptcy shall be void as against a purchaser of a legal estate in good faith for money or money's worth unless the bankruptcy order is for the time being registered under this section.

(6) Where a petition in bankruptcy has been registered under s 5 above, the title of the trustee in bankruptcy shall be void as against a purchaser of a legal estate in good faith for money or money's worth ... claiming under a conveyance made after the date of registration, unless at the date of the conveyance either the registration of the petition is in force or a receiving order on the petition is registered under this section.

Any writ or order issued by the court for the enforcement of a judgment or order, receivership or sequestration order,[31] bankruptcy order, and access order under the Access to Neighbouring Land Act 1992,[32] are registrable in the register of writs and orders affecting land.[33] When registered, they bind all persons for all purposes.[34] If they are not registered, they are void as against 'a purchaser of the land'.[35] Registration lasts for five years and is renewable for another five years.[36]

(c) Annuities

Annuities created between 1855 and 1926 were registrable in a register of annuities. This was closed in 1925. Modern annuities are registrable either under Class C(iii) or Class E.

(d) Deeds of arrangement

Land Charges Act 1972

7. The register of deeds of arrangement affecting land

(1) The deed of arrangement affecting land may be registered in the register of deeds of arrangement affecting land, in the name of the debtor, on the application of a trustee of the deed or a creditor assenting to or taking the benefit of the deed.

(2) Every deed of arrangement shall be void as against a purchaser of any land comprised in it or affected by it unless it is for the time being registered under this section.

---

31 A sequestration order is a writ appointing usually four commissioners, often known as sequestrators, ordering them to seize a person's property. It may be made against a person who is in contempt of court by failing to comply with the court order, and the property will be retained until the order is complied with.

32 See Chapter 15, pp 744–45.

33 Section 6(1) of the LCA 1972.

34 Section 198(1) of the LPA 1925.

35 Section 6(4) of the LCA 1972.

36 Section 8 of the LCA 1972.

Deeds of arrangement are defined in the Deeds of Arrangement Act 1914.[37] They are written agreements between a debtor and his creditors, where no bankruptcy order has been made, arranging for the control over his property to be given for the benefit of his creditors generally or, when he is insolvent, for the benefit of at least three of his creditors.

(e) Land charges

Land Charges Act 1972

2. The register of land charges

(1) If a charge on or obligation affecting land falls into one of the classes described in this section, it may be registered in the register of land charges as a land charge of that class.

(2) A Class A land charge is:

(a) a rent or annuity or principal money payable by instalments or otherwise, with or without interest, which is not a charge created by deed but is a charge upon land (other than a rate) created pursuant to the application of some person under the provisions of any Act of Parliament, for securing to any person either the money spent by him or the costs, charges and expenses incurred by him under such Act, or the money advanced by him for repaying the money spent or the costs, charges and expenses incurred by another person under the authority of an Act of Parliament; or

(b) a rent or annuity or principal money payable as mentioned in paragraph (a) above which is not a charge created by deed but is a charge upon land (other than a rate) created pursuant to the application of some person under any of the enactments mentioned in Schedule 2 to this Act.

(3) A Class B land charge is a charge on land (not being a local land charge ...) of any of the kinds described in paragraph (a) of sub-s (2) above, created otherwise than pursuant to the application of any person.

(4) A Class C land charge is any of the following (not being a local land charge), namely:

(i) a puisne mortgage;

(ii) a limited owner's charge;

(iii) a general equitable charge;

(iv) an estate contract;

and for this purpose:

(i) a puisne mortgage is a legal mortgage which is not protected by a deposit of documents relating to the legal estate affected;

(ii) a limited owner's charge is an equitable charge acquired by a tenant for life or statutory owner under the Inheritance Tax Act 1984 or under any other statute by reason of the

37 Section 17(1) of the LCA 1972.

discharge by him of any capital transfer tax or other liabilities and to which special priority is given by the statute;

(iii) a general equitable charge is any equitable charge which:

- (a) is not secured by a deposit of documents relating to the legal estate affected; and
- (b) does not arise or affect an interest arising under a trust of land or a settlement; and
- (c) is not a charge given by way of indemnity against rents equitably apportioned or charged exclusively on land in exoneration of other land and against the breach or non- observance of covenants or conditions; and
- (d) is not included in any other class of land charge;

(iv) an estate contract is a contract by an estate owner or by a person entitled at the date of the contract to have a legal estate conveyed to him to convey or create a legal estate, including a contract conferring either expressly or by statutory implication a valid option to purchase, a right of pre-emption or any other like right.

(5) A Class D land charge is any of the following (not being a local land charge), namely –

(i) an Inland Revenue Charge;

(ii) a restrictive covenant;

(iii) an equitable easement; and for this purpose:

- (i) an Inland Revenue charge is a charge on land, being a charge acquired by the Board under the Inheritance Tax Act 1984;
- (ii) a restrictive covenant is a covenant or agreement (other than a covenant or agreement between a lessor and a lessee) restrictive of the user of land and entered into on or after 1 January 1926;
- (iii) an equitable easement is an easement, right or privilege over or affecting land created or arising on or after 1 January 1926, and being merely an equitable interest.

(6) A Class E land charge is an annuity created before 1 January 1926 and not registered in the register of annuities.

(7) A Class F land charge is a charge affecting any land by virtue of the Matrimonial Homes Act 1983.

(8) A charge or obligation created before 1 January 1926 can only be registered as a Class B land charge or a Class C land charge if it is acquired under a conveyance made on or after that date.

Land charges are the most important type of registrable interests. There are six classes of land charge of which the most important are Classes C(i), (iv), D(ii), (iii), and F.

(i) Class A

This type of land charge is imposed by statute but only comes into existence when some person makes an application. It comprises a rent or sum of money charged upon land for money spent on the land, pursuant to the application of some person under statute. Thus, if the landlord has to pay compensation to an outgoing agricultural tenant, but is able to apply under the statute for a charge on the land for the amount of compensation paid, once he has applied for and obtained such a charge, the charge can be registered as a Class A land charge. If it is not registered, it is 'void as against a purchaser of the land charged with it or of any interest in such land, unless the land charge is registered in the register of land charges before the completion of the purchase.[38]

(ii) Class B

Class B charges are similar to those in Class A except that they are created automatically by virtue of statute, and not pursuant to the application of any person.[39] An example is the Law Society's charge on land recovered or preserved for a legally aided litigant in respect of unpaid contributions to the legal aid fund.[40]

(iii) Class C

There are four types of Class C land charge.

C(i): Puisne Mortgage

'A puisne mortgage is a legal mortgage which is not protected by a deposit of documents relating to the legal estate affected'.[41] This, in practice, comprises a second legal mortgage as the documents of title are often already retained by the first mortgagee. It should be noted, however, that this does not mean that a first legal mortgage which is not protected by title deeds cannot be protected as a puisne mortgage.

C(ii): Limited owner's charge

This is an equitable charge acquired by a tenant for life or statutory owner[42] for the money he has incurred, to discharge any statutory liability,[43] out of his own pocket, to which he is entitled to have reimbursement from the settled estate. Such a charge arises automatically.[44] But, as will be seen, to bind a purchaser of a legal estate for valuable consideration without notice, it should be registered.[45]

C(iii): General equitable charge

This is a residuary class which covers any equitable charges not registrable in any other class of land charge. In particular, as is envisaged by s 2(4)(iii) of the Land Charges Act 1972, it covers an equitable charge not protected by the deposit of title deeds. It also includes equitable annuities created after 1925 and

38 Section 4(2) of the LCA 1972.

39 Section 2(3) of the LCA 1972.

40 Section 16(6) of the Legal Aid Act 1988.

41 Section 2(4)(i) of the LCA 1972.

42 For the meaning of tenant for life and statutory owner, see ss 19, 20 of the SLA 1925. See also Chapter 11 below.

43 Such as inheritance tax under the Inheritance Tax Act 1984.

44 *Lord Advocate v Countess of Moray* [1905] AC 531 at 539.

45 Section 4(5) of the LCA 1972.

possibly an unpaid vendor's equitable lien.[46] It does not include an equitable mortgage or charge which affects a trust of land or strict settlement.[47] Those charges will be overreached on a conveyance to a purchaser who complies with the requirement of overreaching machinery.[48] What is less clear is whether Class C(iii) includes an equitable mortgage of a legal estate.[49]

C(iv): Estate contract

This is a contract by an estate owner to convey or create a legal estate, interest or charge in or over land.[50] Thus, a contract by a freehold owner to sell his freehold, to grant a mortgage or an easement over his freehold, or to grant a leasehold of his freehold, is an estate contract. It is to protect the purchaser's proprietary right to have the legal estate conveyed to him after the contract is concluded. This is because otherwise the vendor may, during the interim period between the exchange of contracts and the completion, convey the legal estate, in breach of the contract, to a third party who has no notice of the purchaser's right. However, it is not the normal practice to register estate contracts. They are only registered in cases of suspicion or delayed completion.

The estate owner need not own a legal estate at the time of the contract so long as he is entitled to have a legal estate conveyed to him at the date of the contract.[51] However, an estate contract can only be a contract to convey a legal estate, interest or charge. Thus, it does not include a boundary agreement, unless it clearly involves the transfer of land.[52] Nor does it include a contract to convey an equitable interest, such as an interest under a trust for sale or a trust of land,[53] or a contract to create an equitable charge.

Under s 2(4)(iv) of the Land Charges Act 1972, an estate contract includes a contract which confers either expressly or by statutory implication a valid option to purchase, a right of pre-emption or any other like right. An option gives the grantee of the option the right to demand the grantor of the option to transfer to him the agreed estate or interest at any time the grantee chooses. The grantee of the option does not have to exercise the right to demand a transfer of the agreed estate or interest, but he has the option to do it whenever he wants to.[54] When the option to purchase has been granted for valuable consideration,

---

46 Wolstenholme, EP, *Wolstenholme and Cherry's Conveyancing Statute*, 13th edn (by Farrand, JT), 1972, London: Oyez, Vol ii, p 18.

47 Section 2(4)(iii) of the LCA 1972.

48 Sections 2(1) and 2(1A) of the LPA 1925 (as added by s 5, Sched 2, para 4 of the TLATA 1996, s 72(2) of the SLA 1925. Under s 72(2) of the SLA 1925, an annuities, a limited owner's charge and a general equitable charge are also overreached even if duly registered.

49 Megarry and Wade suggest that an equitable mortgage of a legal estate may be registrable as a C(iii) land charge (at 175), but they leave open the possibility that it may be an estate contract registrable as a C(iv) land charge (p 176, fn 81, and p 998).

50 Section 17(1) of the LCA 1972, s 205(1)(x) of the LPA 1925.

51 Section 2(4)(iv) of the LCA 1972.

52 *Neilson v Poole* (1969) 20 P & CR 909.

53 *Re Rayleigh Weir Stadium* [1954] 1 WLR 786.

54 An option is often subject to a time limit, that is it must be exercised, if at all, within a specified period. If it is not so limited, a perpetuity period of 21 years is imposed on it: s 9(2) of the Perpetuities and Accumulations Act 1964.

it is binding on the grantor as a matter of contract.[55] The grantor cannot revoke the option. When the option to purchase is exercised, the grantor is bound to transfer the agreed estate or interest to the grantee. An option thus confers on the grantee a proprietary interest in land.[56] It can bind a third party when the grantor of the option transfers his legal estate to the third party, if the grantee of the option has registered the option as a Class C(iv) land charge.[57] Examples of an option to purchase registrable as a Class C(iv) land charge are an option to purchase a fee simple or a legal lease,[58] a tenant's option to renew his lease,[59] or the option to purchase the leasehold reversion.[60] The exercise of a registered option to purchase does not have to be registered.[61]

Armstrong & Holmes Ltd v Holmes [1994] 1 All ER 826

Judge Paul Baker QC: Mr Burroughs for the second defendant started by observing that, if an estate contract is to prevail against a subsequent purchaser, the only thing that matters is that it should be registered. If it is not, the purchaser takes free of it, even if he had express notice of it, nay more, that he expressly took subject to it. Mr Burroughs is on firm ground here, supported by high authority: *Midland Bank Trust Co Ltd v Green* [1981] 1 All ER 153; [1981] AC 513. He went on to argue that an option is an irrevocable offer to enter into a contract for the sale of land, binding on the grantor, but the option holder is under no obligation. It is thus not an estate contract in the normal meaning of that expression. However, the expression is given an extended meaning in the Land Charges Act 1972 to include options as estate contracts and hence require that they be registered. When the option is exercised, a true contract comes into existence; the grantor becomes discharged under the option agreement and assumes the rights and liabilities of a vendor. The option holder as purchaser for the first time assumes a liability to the vendor. This new relationship is registrable as an estate contract, whether or not the option had been registered as an earlier and different estate contract. Mr Burroughs read and adopted a passage from Barnsley's *Land Options*, 2nd edn, 1992, p 99:

> The initial registration of the option does not extend to the subsequent contract for sale; the equitable interest created by the option differs from and is superseded by that existing under the contract. If after the holder has exercised the option but before completion of the contract the grantor conveys the land to a purchaser, he will take free from the option holder's rights under the unprotected contract.

Mr Michell for the plaintiffs urged me to adopt a purposive approach to the construction of the Land Charges Act 1972. The purpose of the provision requiring registration is to protect the holders of options and others dealing with the land. It is sufficient for their protection that the option should be registrable. The additional requirement that the

55 *Mountford v Scott* [1975] 1 All ER 198.

56 *London and South Western Railway Co v Gomm* (1882) 20 Ch D 562 at 580.

57 *Midland Bank Trust Co Ltd v Green* [1981] AC 513.

58 *Phillips v Mobil Oil Co Ltd* [1989] 1 WLR 888 at 890H–891B.

59 *Beesly v Hallwood Estates Ltd* [1960] 1 WLR 549 at 558.

60 See eg s 5(5) of the Leasehold Reform Act 1967; *Phillips v Mobil Oil Co Ltd* [1989] 1 WLR 888 at 891C.

61 *Armstrong & Holmes Ltd v Holmes* [1994] 1 All ER 826.

contract arising from the exercise of the option should also be registrable adds nothing to that protection, especially as in the normal course completion will quickly follow the exercise. Further, he argues that an option is not sufficiently or exclusively to be defined as an irrecoverable offer to enter into a contract. In the context of the Land Charges Act 1972, the appropriate analysis is that of a conditional contract. What the Act is concerned with is the obligation imposed on the land rather than the precise rights held by or obligations imposed on the parties.

Both counsel referred to authority. Mr Burroughs pressed me with cases in which an option is analysed in terms of an offer; no contract for sale comes into existence until it is exercised. He referred particularly to *Mountford v Scott* [1975] 1 All ER 198, [1975] Ch 258. The plaintiffs in that case were seeking to enforce specifically a contract resulting from the exercise of an option granted for a token payment. In the judgment of Brightman J at first instance we learn that the plaintiffs' counsel conceded 'that an option on a proper analysis is no more than an ordinary offer coupled with a promise not to withdraw the offer during the period of the option'. In the Court of Appeal Russell LJ said ([1975] 1 All ER 198 at 201; [1975] Ch 258 at 264):

> As I have said, a valid option to purchase constitutes an irrevocable offer to sell during the period stated, and a purported withdrawal of the offer is ineffective. When, therefore, the offer is accepted by the exercise of the option, a contract for sale and purchase is thereupon constituted, just as if there were then constituted a perfectly ordinary contract for sale and purchase without a prior option agreement.

Another case relied on by Mr Burroughs as supporting his analysis of an option is the decision at first instance of Buckley J in *Beesly v Hallwood Estates Ltd* [1960] 2 All ER 314; [1960] 1 WLR 549. The question was whether an option to renew contained in a lease was registrable as an estate contract. Buckley J said ([1960] 2 All ER 314 at 320; [1960] 1 WLR 549 at 555):

> An option to purchase a legal estate in land may have the appearance of a conditional contract on the part of the grantor to convey or create that estate, but this is not, I think, the true nature of such an option.

From this Buckley J went on to reason that an option before its exercise was not an estate contract as defined in the first limb of the definition in the Land Charges Act but was only brought in by the second limb. This part of the judgment was later disapproved by the Court of Appeal in *Greene v Church Comrs for England* [1974] 3 All ER 609 at 613, 614; [1974] Ch 467 at 476, 478.

Mr Michell referred to two cases of great significance in this context. The first was *Re Mulholland's Will Trusts, Bryan v Westminster Bank Ltd* [1949] 1 All ER 460. A testator had leased land to a bank, the lease containing an option to purchase the freehold at a fixed price. He thereafter appointed the bank as the executor of his will. After his death, the bank proved the will, and exercised the option, paying the proceeds of sale into the estate. The beneficiaries sought to set aside the transaction contending that as trustees they were not allowed to place themselves in a position where their interest and duty conflicted. Wynn-Parry J dismissed the action, holding that the bank had a pre-existing contractual right which could not be annulled by their appointment as executor. After citing a well-known passage from the judgment of Jessel MR in *London and South Western Rly Co v Gomm* (1882) 20 Ch D 562 at 582 on the nature of an option to purchase land, Wynn-Parry J said ([1949] 1 All ER 460 at 464):

> 'As I understand that passage, it amounts to this, that, as regards this option, there was between the parties only one contract, namely, the contract constituted by the provisions of the lease which I have read creating the option. The notice exercising the option did not lead, in my opinion, to the creation of any fresh contractual relationship between the parties, making them for the first time vendors and purchasers, nor did it bring into existence any right in addition to the right conferred by the option.'

Mr Burroughs invited me to regard this case as wrongly decided and to follow the reasoning of Buckley J. I am quite unable to do that. In the first place, that reasoning has been criticised, as we have seen. Further, and more importantly, *Re Mulholland's Will Trusts, Bryan v Westminster Bank Ltd* [1948] 1 All ER 460 has never been criticised and is manifestly just. The position of a trustee is sufficiently onerous without his having to surrender rights which he has acquired prior to his taking up his office.

The other case to which Mr Michell referred me is of even greater significance. It contains an analysis of the nature of an option by Hoffmann J which I have found most helpful. In *Spiro v Glencrown Properties Ltd* [1991] 1 All ER 600; [1991] Ch 537 the question was whether an agreement creating an option to purchase land was a contract for the sale of land within s 2 of the Law of Property (Miscellaneous Provisions) Act 1989 or whether no contract for sale came into existence until the exercise of the option. If the former, the requirements of the Act were satisfied; if the latter, they were not. Hoffmann J pointed out that in calling an option an irrevocable offer, or a conditional contract, one is using metaphors or analogies which should not be pressed too far. The following passages show the reasoning ([1991] 1 All ER 600 at 604–06; [1991] Ch 537 at 543–44):

> [His Lordship read passages of Hoffmann J's judgment cited in Chapter 4 at pp 130-132 above starting 'The granting of the option ...' and ending with '... used in the construction of s 2 of the Law of Property (Miscellaneous Provisions) Act 1989'.]

I gratefully adopt that reasoning. The question for me is which analogy is appropriate to be used in construing the Land Charges Act 1972. Here, too, I am greatly assisted by the comments of Hoffmann J. Immediately following the passage last cited he says (see [1991] 1 All ER 600 at 606; [1991] Ch 537 at 544–45):

> There is only one case in which, as it seems to me, the adoption of the irrevocable offer metaphor was allowed to dictate the result without regard to the context. This was *Beesly v Hallwood Estates Ltd* [1960] 2 All ER 314; [1960] 1 WLR 549 in which Buckley J decided that an option was not 'a contract ... to convey or create a legal estate' within the meaning of that part of the definition of an estate contract in s 10(1) of the Land Charges Act 1925. He arrived at this conclusion on the ground that the option was not a contract to convey but only an irrevocable offer. It seems to me, with respect to Buckley J, that this was a misuse of the irrevocable offer metaphor. The purpose of including estate contracts in the Land Charges Act 1925 was to enable a purchaser to obtain notice of contracts which created interests binding upon the land. For this purpose, as Jessel MR pointed out in *Gomm's Case* (1882) 20 Ch D 562 at 581, there is no difference between an option and an ordinary contract of sale. In both cases the land is bound by an agreement which entitles a third party, either conditionally or unconditionally, to demand a conveyance. A purposive construction of s 10(1) therefore requires that one characterise the option from the point of view of its effect on the land in the hands of the grantor. For this purpose, it is more appropriate to regard it as a conditional contract than an irrevocable offer.

In the light of these observations I accept the submissions of Mr Michell rather than those of Mr Burroughs. The purpose of the Land Charges Act 1972 is to give notice of contracts creating interests in land. The original option created an equitable interest in land; pace Professor Barnsley, I do not see that interest being altered or superseded by some other and different interest on the exercise of the option, although no doubt the respective rights and obligations of the grantor and option-holder change. If we look at the matter more practically, the exercise of the option does not add to the burden on the land. Indeed, it may diminish it, as the option-holder may exercise the option well within the option period but subsequently fail to complete, so that rescission follows. In other words, a later potential purchaser from the grantor is sufficiently warned by the registration of the option and does not require the further registration of the contract of sale envisaged by the option.

A right of pre-emption is different from an option to purchase. Unlike an option to purchase, a right of pre-emption does not give the grantee the right to demand for the transfer of the agreed estate or interest at any time of his choosing. The grantor is not bound to transfer his estate to the grantee or any person at any time if he does not want to. But when he decides to sell his estate, he must first offer it to the grantee of the right of pre-emption. The grantee thus has the right of first refusal. The grantor cannot transfer his estate to a third party without first offering it to the grantee of the right of pre-emption. So, the grantor has absolute control on the timing of the sale, but when he wants to sell he must first offer the estate to the grantee of the right of pre-emption. Only when the grantee has rejected the offer can the grantor offer it to a third party on the same terms as those in the offer first made to the grantee.

A right of pre-emption is only exercisable when the grantor decides to sell. Before the grantor decides to sell, it is a mere contractual right to have an offer made to him by the grantor, when the grantor chooses to sell, in preference to other potential purchasers. It is when the grantor has decided to sell that the grantee's contractual right is transformed into a proprietary interest to buy the grantor's estate. Thus, it has been held in *Pritchard v Briggs*[62] that a right of pre-emption, despite the clear statutory definition in s 2(4)(iv) of the Land Charges Act 1972, is registrable as a C(iv) land charge only when it has become exercisable.[63] This means that if the vendor sells to a third party who is a purchaser of the legal estate for money or money's worth, without first offering it to the grantee of the right of pre-emption, the third party can never be bound by the pre-emptive right, for it was a pure contractual right.[64] The grantee's sole remedy will be to sue the grantor for breach of contract.

62 [1980] Ch 338.

63 [1980] Ch 338. See [1980] CLJ 35 (Harpum, C); (1980) 96 LQR 488 (Wade, HR).

64 As soon as the vendor decides to sell to a third party who is a purchaser of the legal estate for money or money's worth, the pre-emptive right becomes exercisable. Once it becomes exercisable, it is a proprietary interest which can bind a third party, but is now to be registered as a C(iv) land charge. Because it is not registered at the time of the sale to the third party, it is void against him.

Pritchard v Briggs [1980] Ch 338, CA

Goff LJ: I start with the famous analysis made by Sir George Jessel MR in *London and South Western Railway Co v Gomm* (1881) 20 Ch D 562, 581, which is in these terms:

> The right to call for a conveyance of the land is an equitable interest or equitable estate. In the ordinary case of a contract for purchase there is no doubt about this, and an option for repurchase is not different in its nature. A person exercising the option has to do two things, he has to give notice of his intention to purchase, and to pay the purchase money; but as far as the man who is liable to convey is concerned, his estate or interest is taken away from him without his consent, and the right to take it away being vested in another, the covenant giving the option must give that other an interest in the land.

In my judgment, a right of pre-emption, and particularly that in the present case which is in purely negative form, does not satisfy this test. Mr Francis argued that it does because it fetters one of the important rights inherent in ownership, that of freedom of alienation. I cannot accept that, however, because a right of pre-emption gives no present right, even contingent, to call for a conveyance of the legal estate. So far as the parties are concerned, whatever economic or other pressures may come to affect the grantor, he is still absolutely free to sell or not. The grantee cannot require him to do so, or demand that an offer be made to him. Moreover, even if the grantor decides to sell and makes an offer it seems to me that so long as he does not sell to anyone else he can withdraw that offer at any time before acceptance.

The judge said, *ante*, 361H–62D:

> ... there would appear to be no essential difference, from the point of view of creating an interest in land, between an option on the one hand and a right of pre-emption on the other. In the well-known option case, *London and South Western Railway Co v Gomm*, 20 Ch D 562, at 573, Kay J in the court of first instance put it happily thus, '... a present right to an interest in property which may arise at a period beyond the legal limit is void ...' and thus the option in that case was in any event void as infringing the rule against perpetuities. But the point of his remark is that it is, so far as I can see, equally applicable to a right of pre-emption: it is a present right to an interest in property which may arise in the future ... It is, however, difficult to see why in theory the fact that the condition is one which may be controllable by the owner of the land should make any difference.

With respect I find myself unable to accept this reasoning. The condition being one which leaves the grantee's interest subject to the volition of the grantor is different in kind from other conditions; does prevent a present interest from arising; and takes the case out of the principle enunciated by Sir George Jessel MR in *Gomm's* case, 20 Ch D 562.

Templeman LJ: Rights of option and rights of pre-emption share one feature in common; each prescribes circumstances in which the relationship between the owner of the property which is the subject of the right and the holder of the right will become the relationship of vendor and purchaser. In the case of an option, the evolution of the relationship of vendor and purchaser may depend on the fulfilment of certain specified conditions and will depend on the volition of the option holder. If the option applies to land, the grant of the option creates a contingent equitable interest which, if registered as an estate contract, is binding on successors in title of the grantor and takes priority from the date of its registration. In the case of a right of pre-emption, the evolution of the relationship of vendor and purchaser depends on the grantor, of his own volition, choosing to fulfil certain specified conditions and thus converting the pre-emption into an option. The grant of the right of pre-emption creates a mere spes which the grantor of the right may either frustrate by choosing not to fulfil the necessary conditions or may convert into an option and thus into equitable interest by fulfilling the conditions. An equitable interest thus created is protected by prior registration of the right of pre-emption as an estate contract but takes its priority from the date when the right of pre-emption becomes exercisable and the right is converted into an option and the equitable interest is then created. The holder of a right of pre-emption is in much the same position as a beneficiary under a will of a testator who is still alive, save that the holder of the right of pre-emption must hope for some future positive action by the grantor which will elevate his hope into an interest. It does not seem to me that the property legislation of 1925 was intended to create, or operated to create an equitable interest in land where none existed.

(iv) Class D

There are three types of Class D land charge.

D(i): Inland Revenue charge

This is a charge on land acquired by the Inland Revenue for tax payable on death.

D(ii): Restrictive covenant

This covers restrictive covenants entered into, on, or after 1 January 1926. It does not cover restrictive covenants entered into before 1 January 1926, which, as will be seen, are still governed by the old doctrine of notice. Similarly, it does not cover restrictive covenants made in a lease. These are never registrable and are governed by the old doctrine of notice.

The details of the law relating to restrictive covenant affecting freehold and leasehold land will be examined in Chapters 14 and 9 respectively. Suffice it to say, for the present purposes, that a restrictive covenant is an agreement made in a deed restricting the use of the land owned by one party in a particular manner for the benefit of the land owned by the other party. A common example of a restrictive covenant is a covenant by the covenantee not to use his land for trade or business purposes.

A restrictive covenant is enforceable as between the original covenantor and the original covenantee as a matter of contract. However, as will be seen, when the land for the benefit of which the restrictive covenant was made and the land upon which the burden of the restrictive covenant has been imposed change hands, the question of whether the restrictive covenant is still enforceable as between the successor of the original covenantor and the successor of the original covenantee arises. This depends on whether the benefit of the restrictive covenant has passed to the successor of the original covenantee and whether the corresponding burden has likewise passed to the successor of the original covenantor (see Fig 1).

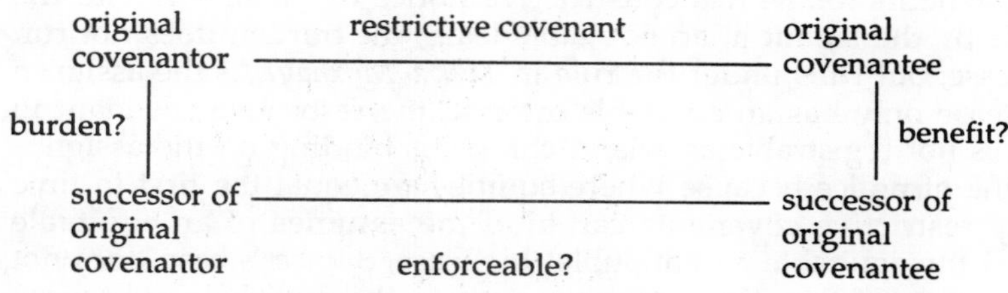

Fig 1.

In the case of covenants affecting freehold land, at common law, the burden of a covenant does not run.[65] But equity allows the burden of a restrictive or negative covenant to run with the land to the successor in title of the original covenantor provided the covenant 'touches and concerns' the land.[66] However, as the burden of the covenant can only run in equity, under the cardinal principle, it does not bind a *bona fide* purchaser of a legal estate for value without notice of the restrictive covenant. It is here that registration of the restrictive covenant created, on or after 1 January 1926, as a Class D(ii) land charge, comes into play. Registration of the restrictive covenant is deemed actual notice to all person for all purposes.[67] Restrictive covenants created before 1 January 1926 are still governed by the cardinal doctrine of notice.

The rules relating to the covenants in a lease are in some respects different. For leases created before 1 January 1996, the burden of a covenant made by the landlord in a legal or equitable lease can pass to his assignee under s 142 of the Law of Property Act 1925 if the covenant has 'reference to the subject matter of the lease'.[68] This applies to both positive and restrictive covenants. The burden of a covenant, which touches and concerns the lease, made by the tenant in a legal lease can likewise pass to his assignee under the rule in *Spencer's* case.[69] Under *Spencer's* case, the burden of a covenant, positive or negative, runs with the lease if it 'touches and concerns' the lease. But if the tenant sublet, instead of assigning, the lease, the rule in *Spencer's* case does not apply. The subtenant is only bound by the covenant if the rule in *Tulk v Moxhay* is satisfied. Thus, only negative covenants can bind the subtenant. Furthermore, a subtenant who has no notice of the restrictive covenant will not be bound. As restrictive covenants in a lease are not registrable under Class D(ii), the position is governed by the doctrine of notice. However, as the subtenant has the right to call for the superior title of the head lease which contains the restrictive covenants,[70] he is

65 *Austerberry v Oldham Corpn* (1885) 29 Ch D 750.

66 *Tulk v Moxhay* (1848) 2 Ph 774; *Haywood v Brunswick Permanent Benefit Building Society* (1881) 8 QBD 403.

67 Section 198(1) of the LPA 1925.

68 'Reference to the subject matter of the lease' means that the covenant must 'touch and concern' the lease.

69 (1583) 5 Co Rep 16a.

70 *Gosling v Woolf* [1893] 1 QB 39 at 40; (1893) 68 LT 89 at 90.

bound by the covenants for he has constructive notice of them.[71] Where the covenant is made by the tenant in an equitable lease, the burden does not run under *Spencer's* case, but runs under the rule in *Tulk v Moxhay*. As the assignee of an equitable lease only has an equitable interest, the restrictive covenant in the lease, which is not registrable as a land charge, is binding on the assignee under the doctrine of notice because where equities are equal the first in time prevails. So only restrictive covenants can bind the assignee of an equitable lease. Likewise, if the equitable tenant sublet his lease, *Spencer's* case does not apply, but the burden of negative covenant runs to the equitable subtenant under the rule in *Tulk v Moxhay*. For leases created on or after 1 January 1996, the position is greatly simplified. The benefit and burden of all covenants in a lease run with an assignment of the lease whether the covenants touch and concern the land or not provided they are not personal to the covenantee.[72]

D(iii): Equitable easement

This class covers equitable easement which is defined as 'an easement, right or privilege over or affecting land created or arising on, or after, 1 January 1926, and being merely an equitable interest'.[73] A legal easement being a legal interest, binds the whole world and therefore need not be registered. It is equitable easement which is vulnerable and needs to be protected as a land charge. An easement is equitable either because the grant of a legal easement is not by deed or because the easement granted is not for a period equivalent to a fee simple absolute in possession or a term of years absolute. Thus an easement for life is an equitable easement.

However, only easements which are created on or after 1 January 1926 need to be registered as Class D(iii) land charges. Easements created before 1 January 1926 are therefore governed by the old doctrine of notice. Furthermore, Lord Denning had taken the view in *E R Ives Investment Ltd v High*,[74] that Class D(iii) embraces only those equitable easements which were legal prior to the 1925 legislation but which became equitable as a result of the legislation. It does not cover an easement which arises out of acquiescence and the doctrine of mutual benefit and burden which has always been equitable even before the 1925 legislation. These equitable easements are therefore not registrable as land charges but are governed by the old doctrine of notice.

(v) Class E

This class covers annuities created before 1 January 1926 but not registered as such in the register of annuities. They are to be registered, after 1925, under Class E.

71 *Teape v Douse* (1905) 92 LT 319 at 320.

72 For further details see pp 396–401.

73 Section 27(5)(iii) of the LCA 1972.

74 [1967] 2 QB 379.

(vi) Class F

This class of land charge is a charge affecting any land by virtue of the Matrimonial Homes Act 1983. Under s 1(1) of the 1983 Act, where one spouse has a beneficial interest in the matrimonial home and the other does not, the non-owner spouse has statutory 'rights of occupation'. Similarly, if a spouse owns the legal estate in the matrimonial home and the other does not, the spouse who does not own the legal estate has statutory 'rights of occupation' even if he or she has a beneficial interest in the home.[75] The 'rights of occupation' are, if in occupation, a right not be evicted or excluded from the home by the other spouse, and if not in occupation, a right with the leave of the court to enter into and occupy the home.[76] The 'rights of occupation' continue so long as the marriage subsists and the other spouse owns the beneficial interest or legal estate in the house.[77] These rights come to an end on the death of the owner spouse, or on the termination of the marriage.[78]

Matrimonial Homes Act 1983

1. Rights concerning matrimonial home where one spouse has no estate, etc

(1) Where one spouse is entitled to occupy a dwelling house by virtue of a beneficial estate or interest or contract or by virtue of any enactment giving him or her the right to remain in occupation, and the other spouse is not so entitled, then, subject to the provisions of this Act, the spouse not so entitled shall have the following rights (in this Act referred to as 'rights of occupation') –

(a) if in occupation, a right not to be evicted or excluded from the dwelling house or any part thereof by the other spouse except with the leave of the court given by an order under this section;

(b) if not in occupation, a right with the leave of the court so given to enter into and occupy the dwelling house.

(10) This Act shall not apply to a dwelling house which has at no time been a matrimonial home of the spouses in question; and a spouse's rights of occupation shall continue only so long as the marriage subsists and the other spouse is entitled as mentioned in sub-s (1) above to occupy the dwelling house, except where provision is made by s 2 of this Act for those rights to be a charge on an estate or interest in the dwelling house.

(11) It is hereby declared that a spouse who has an equitable interest in a dwelling house or in the proceeds of sale thereof, not being a spouse in whom is vested (whether solely or as a joint tenant) a legal estate in fee simple or a legal term of years absolute in the dwelling house, is to be treated for the purpose only of determining whether he or she has rights of occupation under this section as not being entitled to occupy the dwelling house by virtue of that interest.

75 Section 1(11) of the Matrimonial Homes Act 1983.

76 Section 1(1)(a), (b) of the Matrimonial Homes Act 1983.

77 Section 1(10) of the Matrimonial Homes Act 1983.

78 Section 2(4)(a), (b) of the Matrimonial Homes Act 1983.

A spouse's statutory 'rights of occupation' are only personal rights which bind on the owner-spouse. However, the Land Charges Act 1972 makes it possible for these rights to be registered as a Class F charge so as to bind the whole world. It should be noted, however, that where the owner-spouse has become bankrupt, the non-owner spouse's statutory 'rights of occupation', if duly registered, can bind the bankrupt spouse's trustee in bankruptcy, but the trustee in bankruptcy may apply for a sale of the house with vacant possession under s 14 of the Trusts of Land and Appointment of Trustees Act 1996.[79] The spouse who registered the 'rights of occupation' against the owner-spouse may, however, 'release' his rights in writing, or 'agree in writing that any other charge on, or interest in, that estate or interest shall rank in priority to the charge to which that spouse is so entitled'.

Registration

Under s 3(1) of the Land Charges Act 1972, 'A land charge shall be registered in the name of the estate owner whose estate is intended to be affected.'[80] It is not uncommon to find estate owners with different versions for different purposes. For the system of registration to work, it is necessary to have 'some fixed point of reference, equally available to both parties which is ... conclusive as to the name to be used.'[81] Thus, in *Standard Property Investment plc v British Plastics Federation*,[82] Walton J held that the name against which registration and the subsequent search should be made is the name of the estate owner 'as disclosed by the conveyance to him or her'.

The system of registration against the name of the estate owner as disclosed in the conveyance to him or her has unfortunately two problems. First, any system of registration against a name as opposed to a number presents the problem that the incumbrancer may be unaware of the correct version of the name of the estate owner as disclosed in his or her conveyance. For example, in *Diligent Finance Co v Alleyne*,[83] the estate owner, as recorded on his title deeds, was Erskine Owen Alleyne. His wife registered a Class F land charge against the name of Erskine Alleyne. The plaintiff mortgagee made a search against Erskine Owen Alleyne and obtained a clear certificate. Foster J held that the wife's Class F land charge was void against the mortgagee whose certificate was conclusive in its favour.

Secondly, an incumbrancer who is unaware that he is dealing with a sub-vendor will not know that it is necessary to register his incumbrance against the name of the current estate owner, and not the name of the sub-vendor. His registration against the sub-vendor will be void. For example, if A has exchanged contracts for the sale of his freehold with B, before completion, B exchanges contracts with C for the sale of the same freehold by

79 Section 336(2), (4) and (5) of the Insolvency Act 1986. See Chapter 12, pp 524–35.

80 A land charge created before the death of the estate owner is nevertheless registrable against his name despite his death: s 3(4A) of the LCA 1972 as added by s 15(3) of the LP(MP) Act 1995.

81 *Standard Property plc v British Plastics Federation* (1985) 53 P & CR 25, at 28.

82 (1985) 53 P & CR 25 at 28.

83 (1972) 23 P & CR 346.

way of sub-sale. Two registrable estates contracts arise here. The first is that between A and B which should be registered by B against A's name who is the current estate owner. The second is that between B and C which should be registered against A's name which is at all material times the estate owner. C who is unaware that he is dealing with a sub-vendor B will have registered his estate contract against B's name which is a nullity.

Effect of registration

Law of Property Act 1925

198. Registration under the Land Charges Act 1925, to be notice

(1) The registration of any instrument or matter in any register kept under the Land Charges Act 1972 or any local land charges register, shall be deemed to constitute actual notice of such instrument or matter, and of the fact of such registration, to all persons and for all purposes connected with the land affected, as from the date of registration or other prescribed date and so long as the registration continues in force.

Section 198(1) sets out, in very clear terms, that registration is deemed actual notice to all person for all purposes. Thus, once registered the land charge is binding on the whole world. This has been held to be the case *vis-à-vis* a tenant where there has been a registration against the landlord. Under s 44 of the Law of Property Act 1925, a lessee or an assignee of a term of years is not entitled to call for the title to the freehold or to a leasehold reversion. To protect the lessee or assignee from undisclosed matters contained in the title to such freehold or leasehold reversion, s 44(5) of the Act provides that he shall not be deemed to be affected with notice of any such matter or thing of which, if he had contract that such title should be furnished, he might have had notice. However, it was held in *White v Bijou Mansions Ltd*,[84] that a land charge registered by an incumbrancer against the superior title of a lessor is binding under s 198(1) on a lessee or sublessee even though the latter has no right to investigate the lessor's title.

Effect of non-registration

Non-registration, on the other hand, of a registrable interest renders such interest void against certain types of purchaser depending on the nature of the interest in question.

(a) Classes A, B, C(i), (ii) and (iii), and F

Where a land charge of Classes A, B, C (i), (ii) and (iii), and F, is not registered, it is 'void as against a *purchaser* of the land charged with it, or of any interest' in such land.[85] A 'purchaser' is defined in s 17(1) of the Land Charges Act 1972 as 'any person (including a mortgagee or lessee) who, for valuable consideration, takes any interest in land or in a charge on land'. It should be noted that the

84 [1937] Ch 610 at 619.

85 Section 4(2), (5), (8) of the LCA 1972.

definition of a 'purchaser' for the purposes of the Land Charges Act 1972 is therefore different from that under s 205(1)(xxi) of the Law of Property Act 1925, which is 'a purchaser in *good faith* for valuable consideration' and includes a lessee, mortgagee or other person who for valuable consideration acquires an interest in property.[86] Thus, for the purposes of the Land Charges Act a purchaser does not have to act in good faith.[87]

'Valuable consideration' is not defined in the Land Charges Act. It is defined in s 205(1)(xxi) of the Law of Property Act 1925 and s 3(xxxi) of the Land Registration Act 1925 as including marriage, but not a nominal consideration in money. Lord Wilberforce said in *Midland Bank Trust Co Ltd v Green*[88] that the definition in s 205(1)(xxi) of the Law of Property Act 1925 and s 3(xxxi) of the Land Registration Act does not apply to s 4(5) (and presumably also s 4(2) and (8)) of the Land Charges Act 1972. He said that for s 4(5), the adequacy of consideration must not be questioned. So a person who has provided any consideration, including a nominal consideration in money, is a purchaser for the purposes of s 4(5).

(b) Classes C(iv) and D

Under s 4(6) of the Land Charges Act 1972, an unregistered Class C(iv) or Class D land charge is 'void as against a purchaser for money or money's worth of a legal estate in the land charged with it'. 'Purchaser', as mentioned above, is 'any person (including a mortgagee or lessee) who, for valuable consideration, takes any interest in land or in a charge on land' unless the context otherwise requires.[89] In the context of s 4(6), however, the requirement of money or money's worth means that a person who gives consideration of marriage is not regarded as a purchaser for money or money's worth. But the adequacy of the money consideration is not to be questioned.[90]

Thus, it is clear that non-registration of Classes A, B, C(i), (ii) and (iii), and F renders these interests void against a purchaser of any interest in land who gives any consideration, whether he has acted in good faith or not. An unregistered Class C(iv) or Class D land charge is void against a purchaser of a legal estate who provides money or money's worth. Furthermore, under s 199(1)(i) of the Law of Property Act, such a purchaser 'shall not be prejudicially affected by notice of any instrument or matter capable of registration under the provisions of the Land Charges Act 1972, or any enactment which it replaces, which is void or not enforceable as against him under that Act or enactment, by reason of the non-registration thereof.'

Might it not be argued that as 'purchaser' in s 199(1)(i) has a meaning different from that in s 17(1) of the Land Charges Act 1972, a purchaser who acts

86 Except that in Part I of the LPA 1925 and elsewhere where so expressly provided 'purchaser' only means a person who acquires an interest in or charge on property for money or money's worth: see s 205(1)(xxi) of the LPA 1925.

87 *Midland Bank Trust Co Ltd v Green* [1981] AC 513.

88 [1981] AC 513.

89 Section 17(1) of the LCA 1972.

90 *Midland Bank Trust Co Ltd v Green* [1988] AC 513.

in bad faith or who provides only a nominal consideration cannot be protected by s 199(1)(i), and is therefore implicitly affected by notice of an unregistered land charge? Such a question arose in *Hollington Bros Ltd v Rhodes*.[91] Here the defendant lessees contracted to grant a sublease to the plaintiffs. The contract was an estate contract to be registered as a Class C(iv) land charge, but the plaintiffs failed to do so. Later the defendants assigned their lessee to an assignee expressly 'subject to and with the benefit of such tenancies as may affect the premises'. The assignee gave the plaintiffs notice to quit unless they paid a premium and higher rent. The plaintiffs brought proceedings against the defendants for the extra cost as damages for breach of contract to grant a sublease. The question was whether the contract had bound the assignee, because if it had, the plaintiffs would have suffered no loss. Harman J held that the plaintiffs' estate contract was void against the assignee for want of registration. He added that 'I do not see how that which is void and which is not to prejudice the purchaser can be validated by some equitable doctrine.'[92]

Hollington Bros v Rhodes [1951] 2 All ER 578n

Harman J: After 1925 by virtue of s 10(1) of the Land Charges Act, 1925, this contract came within Class C(iv) as a 'charge or obligation affecting land', and, therefore, might be registered as a land charge in the register of land charges. Accordingly, by virtue of s 13(2), this being a land charge of Class C, it is void:

> ... against a purchaser of the land charged therewith, or of any interest in such land, unless the land charge is registered in the appropriate register before the completion of the purchase ...

Moreover, by s 199(1)(i) of the Law of Property Act, 1925, a purchaser is not to be prejudicially affected by notice of any instrument or matter capable of registration under the Land Charges Act, 1925, which is void against him by reason of non-registration. This land charge was not registered, and, accordingly, it is said that it was void against Daymar Estates Ltd, notwithstanding their notice or knowledge, and, moreover, that there was no duty lying on the plaintiffs to register the contract to prevent this result. This has been held to be so by Wynn-Parry, J, in *Wright v Dean*, where he said ([1948] 2 All ER 418) that it could not be urged that there was any such duty on the plaintiff. I propose to follow the decision of Wynn-Parry, J, although I may observe in passing that in s 200 (4) of the Law of Property Act 1925, there is a reference to:

> ... the obligation to register a land charge in respect of ... (b) any estate contract.

The defendants' answer to this point was that Daymar Estates Ltd, did not contract to obtain, and did not by the assignment get, any estate in the land expressed to override the plaintiffs' rights, and that, consequently, they took subject to those rights, which are expressly mentioned, and that the land which they purchased was, in fact, only an interest in the land subject to the rights of the plaintiffs in it. This argument seemed to me attractive because it appears at first glance wrong that a purchaser, who knows perfectly well of rights and is expressed to take subject to them, should be able to ignore

91 [1951] 2 All ER 578n.

92 580A; *Markfaith Investment Ltd v Chiap Hua Flashlights Ltd* [1991] 2 AC 43 at 60D. See [1956] CLJ 216 at 217 (Wade, HWR). See however, *Lyus v Prowsa Developments Ltd* [1982] 1 WLR 1044; *Peffer v Rigg* [1977] 1 WLR 285 both of registered land where the doctrine of notice was supposed to be irrelevant.

them. It was, moreover, pointed out that *Wright v Dean* was distinguishable in this respect because there the option which was overridden by the conveyance was not mentioned in it, nor did the purchaser take expressly subject to it. It seems to me, however, that this argument cannot prevail having regard to the words in s 13(2) of the Land Charges Act 1925, coupled with the definition of 'land' in s 20(6) of the Act. The fact is that it was the policy of the framers of the legislation of 1925 to get rid of equitable rights of this kind unless registered. [His Lordship referred by way of comparison to *Re Monolithic Building Co*, and, in particular, to the judgment of Lord Cozens-Hardy, MR ([1915] 1 Ch 665), and continued.] Finally, as under s 13(2) of the Land Charges Act 1925, an unregistered estate contract is void as against a purchaser of the land, and under s 199(1) of the Law of Property Act 1925, the purchaser is not to be prejudicially affected by it, I do not see how that which is void and which is not to prejudice the purchaser can be validated by some equitable doctrine. There is, after all, no great hardship in this. The plaintiffs could, at any time until the completion of the assignment to Daymar Estates Ltd, have preserved their rights by registration, just as the defendants could have protected their obligations by completing the underlease, of which Daymar Estates Ltd, could not have complained as they knew all about it.

It is further affirmed by the House of Lords in *Midland Bank Trust Co Ltd v Green*[93] that the purchaser's notice of the unregistered incumbrances is irrelevant. Here a father granted his son an option to purchase his fee simple for £22,500. The son failed to register the option as an estate contract under Class C(iv). Later, as a result of a family dispute, the father, who discovered that his son had failed to register his option to purchase, quietly and speedily conveyed the fee simple to his wife for £500, with the intention of defeating the son's unprotected option to purchase. The mother refused to sell the fee simple to her son when he sought to exercise the option. The son brought proceedings against his father and the executors of his mother's estate (his mother had died by then) for a declaration that his mother's estate is bound by his option, and an order of specific performance of the option. The son then died and the plaintiff bank continued the action as his executor.

Midland Bank Trust v Green [1981] AC 513, HL

Lord Wilberforce: This option was, in legal terms, an estate contract and so a legal charge, Class C, within the meaning of the Land Charges Act 1925. The correct and statutory method for protection of such an option is by means of entering it in the Register of Land Charges maintained under the Act. If so registered, the option would have been enforceable, not only (contractually) against Walter, but against any purchaser of the farm.

The option was not registered, a failure which inevitably called in question the responsibility of Geoffrey's solicitor. To anticipate, Geoffrey in fact brought proceedings against his solicitor which have been settled for a considerable sum, payable if the present appeal succeeds.

[His Lordship read the facts and ss 13(2) and 20(8) of the Land Charges Act 1925 and continued.]

93 [1981] AC 513.

Thus the case appears to be a plain one. The 'estate contract', which by definition (s 11) includes an option of purchase, was entered into after 1 January 1926; Evelyne took an interest (in fee simple) in the land 'for valuable consideration' – so was a 'purchaser': she was a purchaser for money – namely £500: the option was not registered before the completion of the purchase. It is therefore void as against her.

In my opinion, this appearance is also the reality. The case is plain: the Act is clear and definite. Intended as it was to provide a simple and understandable system for the protection of title to land, it should not be read down or glossed: to do so would destroy the usefulness of the Act. Any temptation to remould the Act to meet the facts of the present case, on the supposition that it is a hard one and that justice requires it, is, for me at least, removed by the consideration that the Act itself provides a simple and effective protection for persons in Geoffrey's position – *viz* – by registration.

The respondents submitted two arguments as to the interpretation of s 13(2): the one sought to introduce into it a requirement that the purchaser should be 'in good faith'; the other related to the words 'in money or money's worth'.

The argument as to good faith fell into three parts: first, that 'good faith' was something required of a 'purchaser' before 1926; secondly, that this requirement was preserved by the 1925 legislation and in particular by s 13(2) of the Land Charges Act 1925. If these points could be made good, it would then have to be decided whether the purchaser (Evelyne) was in 'good faith' on the facts of the case.

My Lords, the character in the law known as the *bona fide* (good faith) purchaser for value without notice was the creation of equity. In order to affect a purchaser for value of a legal estate with some equity or equitable interest, equity fastened upon his conscience and the composite expression was used to epitomise the circumstances in which equity would or rather would not do so. I think that it would generally be true to say that the words 'in good faith' related to the existence of notice. Equity, in other words, required not only absence of notice, but genuine and honest absence of notice. As the law developed, this requirement became crystallised in the doctrine of constructive notice which assumed a statutory form in the s 3 of the Conveyancing Act 1882. But, and so far I would be willing to accompany the respondents, it would be a mistake to suppose that the requirement of good faith extended only to the matter of notice, or that when notice came to be regulated by statute, the requirement of good faith became obsolete. Equity still retained its interest in and power over the purchaser's conscience. The classic judgment of James LJ in *Pilcher v Rawlins* (1872) LR 7 Ch App 259 at 269 is clear authority that it did: good faith there is stated as a separate test which may have to be passed even though absence of notice is proved. And there are references in cases subsequent to 1882 which confirm the proposition that honesty or *bona fides* remained something which might be inquired into (see *Berwick & Co v Price* [1905] 1 Ch 632 at 639; *Taylor v London and County Banking Co* [1901] 2 Ch 231 at 256; *Oliver v Hinton* [1899] 2 Ch 264 at 273).

But did this requirement, or test, pass into the property legislation of 1925?

My Lords, I do not think it safe to seek the answer to this question by means of a general assertion that the property legislation of 1922–25 was not intended to alter the law, or not intended to alter it in a particular field, such as that relating to purchases of legal estates. All the Acts of 1925, and their precursors, were drafted with the utmost care, and their wording, certainly where this is apparently clear, has to be accorded firm respect. As was pointed out in *Grey v Inland Revenue Commissioners* [1960] AC 1, the Acts of 1922–24 effected massive changes in the law affecting property and the House, in consequence, was persuaded to give to a plain word ('disposition') its plain meaning, and not to narrow it by reference to its antecedents. Certainly, that case should firmly discourage us from muddying clear waters. I accept that there is merit in looking at the corpus as a whole in order to produce if possible a consistent scheme. But there are limits to the possibilities of this process: for example it cannot eliminate the difference between registered and unregistered land, or the respective charges on them.

As to the requirement of 'good faith' we are faced with a situation of some perplexity. The expression 'good faith', appears in the Law of Property Act 1925 definition of 'purchaser' ('a purchaser in good faith for valuable consideration'), s 205(1)(xxi); in the Settled Land Act 1925, s 117(1)(xxi) (ditto); in the Administration of Estates Act 1925, s 55 (1)(xviii) ('Purchaser' means a lessee, mortgagee or other person who in good faith acquires an interest in property for valuable consideration) and in the Land Registration Act 1925, s 3(xxi) which does not, however, as the other Acts do, include a reference to nominal consideration. So there is certainly some indication of an intention to carry the concept of 'good faith' into much of the 1925 code. What then do we find in the Land Charges Act 1925? We were taken along a scholarly peregrination through the numerous Acts antecedent to the final codification and consolidation in 1925 – the Land Charges Registration and Searches Act 1888, the Law of Property Act 1922, particularly Sched 7, the Law of Property (Amendment) Act 1924 as well as the Yorkshire and Middlesex Deeds Registration Acts. But I think, with genuine respect for an interesting argument, that such solution as there is of the problem under consideration must be sought in the terms of the various Acts of 1925 themselves. So far as concerns the Land Charges Act 1925, the definition of 'purchaser' quoted above does not mention 'good faith' at all. 'Good faith' did not appear in the original Act of 1888, nor in the extension made to that Act by the Act of 1922, Sched 7, nor in the Act of 1924, Sched 6. It should be a secure assumption that the definition of 'purchaser for value' which is found in s 4 of the Act of 1888 ('person who for valuable consideration takes any interest in land') together with the limitation which is now the proviso to s 13(2) of the Act of 1925, introduced in 1922, was intended to be carried forward into the Act of 1925. The expression 'good faith' appears nowhere in the antecedents. To write the word in, from the examples of contemporaneous Acts, would be bold. It becomes impossible when it is seen that the words appear in s 3(1) and in s 7(1), in each case in a proviso very similar, in structure, to the relevant proviso in s 13(2). If canons of constructions have any validity at all, they must lead to the conclusion that the omission in s 13(2) was deliberate.

My Lords, I recognise that the inquiring mind may put the question: why should there be an omission of the requirement of good faith in this particular context? I do not think there should be much doubt about the answer. Addition of a requirement that the purchaser should be in good faith would bring with it the necessity of inquiring into the purchaser's motives and state of mind. The present case is a good example of the difficulties which would exist. If the position was simply that the purchaser had notice of the option, and decided nevertheless to buy the land, relying on the absence of notification, nobody could contend that she would be lacking in good faith. She would merely be taking advantage of a situation, which the law has provided, and the addition of a profit motive could not create an absence of good faith. But suppose, and this is the respondents' argument, the purchaser's motive is to defeat the option, does this make any difference? Any advantage to oneself seems necessarily to involve a disadvantage for another: to make the validity of the purchase depend upon which aspect of the transaction was prevalent in the purchaser's mind seems to create distinctions equally difficult to analyse in law as to establish in fact: avarice and malice may be distinct sins, but in human conduct they are liable to be intertwined. The problem becomes even more acute if one supposes a mixture of motives. Suppose – and this may not be far from the truth – that the purchaser's motives were in part to take the farm from Geoffrey, and in part to distribute it between Geoffrey and his brothers and sisters, but not at all to obtain any benefit for herself, is this acting in 'good faith' or not? Should family feeling be denied a protection afforded to simple greed? To eliminate the necessity for inquiries of this kind may well have been part of the legislative intention. Certainly there is here no argument for departing – violently – from the wording of the Act.

Before leaving this part of the case, I must comment on *In Re Monolithic Building Co* [1915] 1 Ch 643, which was discussed in the Court of Appeal. That was a case arising under s 93 of the Companies (Consolidation) Act 1908 which made an unregistered mortgage void against any creditor of the company. The defendant Jenkins was a managing director of the company, and clearly had notice of the first unregistered mortgage: he himself subsequently took and registered a mortgage debenture and claimed priority over the unregistered mortgage. It was held by the Court of Appeal, first that this was not a case of fraud: 'it is not fraud to take advantage of legal rights, the existence of which may be taken to be known to both parties' (*per* Lord Cozens-Hardy MR, at 663), secondly that s 93 of the Act was clear in its terms, should be applied according to its plain meaning, and should not be weakened by infusion of equitable doctrines applied by the courts during the nineteenth century. The judgment of Lord Cozens-Hardy MR contains a valuable critique of the well known cases of *Le Neve v Le Neve* (1748) 3 Atk 646 and *Greaves v Tofield* (1880) 14 Ch D 563 which, arising under the Middlesex Registry Act 1708 and other enactments, had led the judges to import equitable doctrines into cases of priority arising under those Acts, and establishes that the principles of those cases should not be applied to modern Acts of Parliament.

My Lords, I fail to see how this authority can be invoked in support of the respondents' argument, or of the judgments of the majority of the Court of Appeal. So far from supporting them, it is strongly the other way. It disposes, for the future, of the old arguments based, ultimately, upon *Le Neve v Le Neve* (1748) 3 Atk 643 for reading equitable doctrines (as to notice, etc) into modern Acts of Parliament: it makes it clear that it is not 'fraud' to rely on legal rights conferred by Acts of Parliament: it confirms the validity of interpreting clear enactments as to registration and priority according to their tenor.

The judgment of Phillimore LJ in *In Re Monolithic Building Co* [1915] 1 Ch 643 at 669, 670 does indeed contain a passage which appears to favour application of the principle of *Le Neve v Le Neve* (1748) 3 Atk 646 and to make a distinction between a transaction designed to obtain an advantage, and one designed to defeat a prior (unregistered) interest. But, as I have explained, this distinction is unreal and unworkable: this whole passage is impossible to reconcile with the views of the other members of the Court of Appeal in the case, and I respectfully consider that it is not good law.

My Lords, I can deal more shortly with the respondents' second argument. It relates to the consideration for the purchase. The argument is that the protection of s 13(2) of the Land Charges Act 1925 does not extend to a purchaser who has provided only a nominal consideration and that £500 is nominal. A variation of this was the argument accepted by the Court of Appeal that the consideration must be 'adequate' – an expression of transparent difficulty. The answer to both contentions lies in the language of the subsection. The word 'purchaser' by definition (s 20(8)), means one who provides valuable consideration – a term of art which precludes any inquiry as to adequacy. This definition is, of course, subject to the context. Section 13(2), proviso, requires money or money's worth to be provided: the purpose of this being to exclude the consideration of marriage. There is nothing here which suggests, or admits of, the introduction of a further requirement that the money must not be nominal.

The argument for this requirement is based upon the Law of Property Act 1925 which, in s 205(1)(xxi) defining 'purchaser' provides that 'valuable consideration' includes marriage but does not include a 'nominal consideration in money'. The Land Charges Act 1925 contains no definition of 'valuable consideration', so it is said to be necessary to have resort to the Law of Property Act definition: thus 'nominal consideration in money' is excluded. An indication that this is intended is said to be provided by s 199(1)(i). I cannot accept this. The fallacy lies in supposing that the Acts – either of them – set out to define 'valuable consideration'; they do not: they define 'purchaser,' and they define the word differently (see the first part of the argument). 'Valuable consideration' requires no definition: it is an expression denoting an advantage conferred or detriment suffered. What each Act does is, for its own purposes, to exclude some things from this general expression: the Law of Property Act includes marriage but not a nominal sum in money; the Land Charges Act excludes marriage but allows 'money or money's worth'. There is no coincidence between these two – no link by reference or necessary logic between them. Section 199(1)(i) by referring to the Land Charges Act 1925, necessarily incorporates – for the purposes of this provision – the definition of 'purchaser' in the latter Act, for it is only against such a 'purchaser' that an instrument is void under that Act. It cannot be read as incorporating the Law of Property Act definition into the Land Charges Act. As I have pointed out the land charges legislation has contained its own definition since 1888, carried through, with the addition of the reference to 'money or money's worth' into 1925. To exclude a nominal sum of money from s 13(2) of the Land Charges Act would be to rewrite the section.

This conclusion makes it unnecessary to determine whether £500 is a nominal sum of money or not. But I must say that for my part I should have great difficulty in so holding. 'Nominal consideration' and a 'nominal sum' in the law appear to me, as terms of art, to refer to a sum or consideration which can be mentioned as consideration but is not necessarily paid. To equate 'nominal' with 'inadequate' or even 'grossly inadequate' would embark the law upon inquiries which I cannot think were contemplated by Parliament.

I would allow the appeal.

Unlike the position of an incumbrancer in registered land, whose unprotected minor interest can be overriding by virtue of his actual occupation of the land under s 70(1)(g) of the Land Registration Act 1925, an unprotected incumbrancer of an unregistered land loses his interest against a purchaser, even if he is 'in possession or in actual occupation'. Section 14 of the Law of Property Act 1925 which provides that 'This part of this Act shall not prejudicially affect the interest of any person in possession or in actual occupation of land to which he may be entitled in right of such possession or occupation' was held not to be applicable.[94] This was because the application of s 14 is expressly restricted to Part I of the Law of Property Act 1925, and the effect of non-registration is spelt out in the Land Charges Act. It is interesting to note that the provisions in s 14 were originally contained in s 33 of the Law of Property Act 1922 which clearly covered s 3(5) of Part I of the 1922 Act which laid down the effect of non-registration. The Law of Property Act 1922 was later consolidated in the 1925 legislation and divided into several separate Acts. Sections 3(5) and 33 of the 1922 Act were consequently separated and contained in the Land Charges Act and the Law of Property Act respectively in the form of s 4 and s 14 respectively. By, presumably, a legislative accident, the reference to 'this part of this Act' in s 14 of the Law of Property Act 1925, which should have been amended to read 'Part I of the Land Charges Act', was unintentionally left unamended. This legislative accident has enabled the court to take the view that s 14 does not apply to s 4 of the Land Charges Act 1972.

It should, however, be noted that non-registration is only void against certain types of purchaser. An unregistered Class A, B, C (other than C(iv)), and F is only void as against a purchaser of any interest in land for valuable consideration. If the third party is not 'a purchaser of any interest in land for valuable consideration' (eg a donee or a squatter), the position is governed by the doctrine of notice. A donee, although technically a purchaser, is a person who has not given valuable consideration. As he cannot claim to be a purchaser for value, he is bound by the unregistered land charge under the doctrine of notice. Likewise, the unprotected land charge is binding on a squatter who is not a 'purchaser' at all.

An unregistered Class C(iv) or Class D land charge is only void as against a purchaser for money or money's worth of a legal estate charged with the land charge. It is not necessarily void against other persons. The position is again governed by the doctrine of notice. A donee is again bound by an unprotected land charge under the doctrine of notice because he has not given any valuable consideration. But a purchaser who takes a legal estate for marriage consideration, though not for money or money's worth, takes the legal estate free of the unregistered land charge if he has no notice of it. If the purchaser only takes an equitable interest then he will be bound by the unregistered land charge whether he has notice of it or not because where equities are equal the first in time prevails.[95] Likewise, a squatter is bound by the unregistered land charge because he is not a 'purchaser'.

It should also be noted that a restrictive covenant or an equitable easement created before 1 January 1926 is never registrable as a Class D(ii) or (iii) land charge.[96] It is governed by the doctrine of notice and is therefore binding on the

94 *City of London Building Society v Flegg* [1988] AC 54 at 80C–F; *Lloyds Bank plc v Carrick* [1996] 4 All ER 630 at 642 f–j.

95 *McCarthy and Stone Ltd v Julian S Hodge & Co Ltd* [1971] 2 All ER 973 (option to purchase not registered still binds a subsequent equitable mortgagee; where equities are equal the first in time prevails).

96 Section 2(5)(ii) and (iii) of the LCA 1972.

whole world except a *bona fide* purchaser of a legal estate for value without notice.

Search of the land charges register

As has been seen in Chapter 4, although the seller is under a duty to disclose entries on the Land Charges Register at the time of the contract, he is not under such a duty after the exchange of contracts. Furthermore, s 24 of the Law of Property Act 1969 does not apply to entries made after the contract and the buyer will be deemed to have actual notice of land charges registered after the contract.[97] To avoid being bound by registered land charges, as soon as the contracts are exchanged, the purchaser must make an official search of the land charge register and complete within the priority period.

Suppose A has contracted to buy from B a fee simple in 1994. Suppose B has obtained the fee simple from C in 1990, who in his turn obtained the fee simple from D in 1980, who obtained the fee simple from E in 1965, who obtained the fee simple in 1950 from F, who obtained the fee simple in 1935 from G and so on as follows:

G conveyed to F in 1935
F conveyed to E in 1950
E conveyed to D in 1965
D conveyed to C in 1980
C conveyed to B in 1990
A is buying from B in 1994

To carry out the search as required by law, A has to inspect all the vendor's deeds until he uncovers a valid document which relates to the disposition of the whole legal and equitable interest and which is at least 15 years old.[98] He then has to see all subsequent documents which trace the dealing with the property. He would then uncover the names of various previous estates owners comprised within those documents of title against whom land charges may have been registered. This means that he has to ask for the conveyance in 1990 which is only four years old, the 1980 conveyance which is 14 years old, and the 1965 conveyance which is 31 years old. The 1965 conveyance is the root of title here because it is at least 15 years old. The 1980 conveyance is not the root because it is not at least 15 years old. However, all three conveyances must be examined, because they all form the chain of documents of title. The 1950 conveyance need not be examined as it exists behind the root of title.

Where the land A is buying was originally part of a larger estate, (for example, E conveyed only part of the land to D in 1965, and A is now buying

97 Section 24 of the LPA 1969 provides that the question whether a buyer has knowledge of a registered land charge is to be determined by reference to his actual knowledge without regard to s 198 which provides that a buyer is deemed to have actual notice of a registered land charge.

98 Section 23 of the LPA 1969.

that part from B in 1994), the 1965 conveyance is not a good root even though it is more than 15 years old because it does not cover the whole of the original legal estate. The 1950 conveyance needs to be investigated.[99]

Once A uncovers the names of B, C, D, and E, he can then search the Land Charges Register against those names. Search may be personal,[100] but he may apply for an official search with the payment of a small fee. The advantage of an official search is that the result of the search is guaranteed. An official search certificate will be issued indicating whether there is any land charge registered against the names of the previous estates owners. The certificate is conclusive in favour of the purchaser.[101] A duly registered land charge erroneously omitted in a certificate will become void against the purchaser. The owner of the now destroyed land charge may sue the Land Charges Registry for negligence.[102]

Land Charges Act 1972

10. Official searches

(1) Where any person requires search to be made at the registry for entries of any matters or documents, entries of which are required or allowed to be made in the registry by this Act, he may make a requisition in that behalf to the registrar, which may be either:

(a) a written requisition delivered at or sent by post to the registry; or

(b) a requisition communicated by teleprinter, telephone or other means in such manner as may be prescribed in relation to the means in question, in which case it shall be treated as made to the registrar if, but only if, he accepts it;

and the registrar shall not accept a requisition made in accordance with paragraph (b) above unless it is made by a person maintaining a credit account at the registry, and may at his discretion refuse to accept it notwithstanding that it is made by such a person.

(2) The prescribed fee shall be payable in respect of every requisition made under this section; and that fee:

(a) in the case of a requisition made in accordance with sub-s (1)(a) above, shall be paid in such manner as may be prescribed for the purposes of this paragraph unless the requisition is made by a person maintaining a credit account at the registry and the fee is debited to that account;

(b) in the case of a requisition made in accordance with sub-s (1)(b) above, shall be debited to the credit account of the person by whom the requisition is made.

---

99 The 1950 conveyance is, however, still in the hands of E and was not given to D so that B does not possess it. E's 1950 conveyance would have been endorsed with a memorandum of the 1965 sale of part of the land. D would also have ensured that E as seller had given an acknowledgment for the production and safe-keeping of the 1950 conveyance.

100 Section 2(1) of the LCA 1972.

101 Section 10(4) of the LCA 1972.

102 *Ministry of Housing and Local Government v Sharp* [1970] 1 All ER 1009.

(3) Where a requisition is made under sub-s (1) above and the fee payable in respect of it is paid or debited in accordance with sub-s (2) above, the registrar shall thereupon make the search required and:

(a) shall issue a certificate setting out the result of the search; and

(b) without prejudice to paragraph (a) above, may take such other steps as he considers appropriate to communicate that result to the person by whom the requisition was made.

(4) In favour of a purchaser or an intending purchaser, as against persons interested under or in respect of matters or documents entries of which are required or allowed as aforesaid, the certificate, according to its tenor, shall be conclusive, affirmatively or negatively, as the case may be.

The certificate also protects the purchaser against incumbrances registered in the 15 working days' interval between search and completion; the purchaser is said to have a priority period of 15 working days, from the date of the search certificate, within which to complete the conveyance.[103]

Land Charges Act 1972

11. Date of effective registration and priority notices

(5) Where a purchaser has obtained a certificate under s 10 above, any entry which is made in the register after the date of the certificate and before the completion of the purchase, and is not made pursuant to a priority notice entered on the register on or before the date of the certificate, shall not affect the purchaser if the purchase is completed before the expiration of the relevant number of days after the date of the certificate.

(6) The relevant number of days is:

(a) for the purposes of sub-ss (1) and (5) above, 15;

(b) for the purposes of sub-s (3) above, 30;

or such other number as may be prescribed; but in reckoning the relevant number of days for any of the purposes of this section any days when the registry is not open to the public shall be excluded.

However, to get a valid certificate, the purchaser must search against the full name of the estate owner as recorded on his deeds of title, and not any other names. In *Diligent Finance Co v Alleyne*,[104] the estate owner, was recorded on his title deeds as Erskine Owen Alleyne. His wife registered a Class F land charge against the name of Erskine Alleyne. The plaintiff mortgagee made a search against Erskine Owen Alleyne and not surprisingly obtained a clear certificate. Foster J held that the wife's Class F land charge was void against the mortgagee whose certificate was conclusive in its favour. Similarly, a purchaser who has

103 Section 11(5) of the LCA 1972.

104 (1972) 23 P & CR 346.

made an official search against an incorrect name will lose priority to an incumbrancer who has registered a land charge against the correct name of the estate owner as it appears on the title deeds.[105]

Diligent Finance Co Ltd v Alleyne and Another (1972) 23 P & CR 346

Foster J: ... in the absence of evidence to the contrary that the proper name of a person is that in which the conveyancing documents have been taken. It is unfortunate, to say the least, that the Class F registration was not made against the proper name Erskine Owen Alleyne but only against Erskine Alleyne, but that is a mistake which I for my part cannot unfortunately rectify.

Standard Property Investment plc v British Plastics Federation (1985) 53 P & CR 25

Walton J: On 1 May 1980 three things happened. First, the freehold property known as 22 Holts Green, Great Brickhill, Buckinghamshire was conveyed by the then owners to two persons jointly, named in the conveyance to them as 'Roger Caudrelier' and 'Hilary Caudrelier'. This property was not, of course, registered land. The second event was that the new owners of this property executed a mortgage thereof to the Abbey National Building Society. In that mortgage the purchasers were described as 'Roger Denis (with one 'n') Caudrelier' and 'Hilary Claire Caudrelier'. Obviously, the building society obtained the title deeds, and there can be no question as to their position at all times being that of first mortgagee.

The third event was that the purchasers executed a legal charge of the property to the plaintiff. In that legal charge they were described simply as 'Roger Caudrelier' and 'Hilary Caudrelier'.

In order to preserve its priority, it was obviously necessary to register that legal charge pursuant to the provisions of the Land Charges Act 1972, and such registration was effected by the plaintiff's solicitors, the second defendant, on its behalf on 11 July 1980 against the names 'Roger Caudrelier' and 'Hilary Caudrelier'.

Some time later, the Caudreliers sought to obtain a further advance on the security of the same property from the first defendant, who either actually was or had been the employer of Roger Caudrelier. Before effecting this transaction, the first defendant duly caused a search to be made, of course in respect of the correct land, against the names of 'Roger Denis (with one 'n') Caudrelier' and 'Hilary Claire Caudrelier'. This search was, for present purposes, entirely negative; that is to say it did not reveal the registration effected on behalf of the plaintiff on 11 July 1980. Naturally, the first defendant went ahead and granted the Caudreliers an advance on the security of the property, effected by a legal charge dated 24 April 1981. In that legal charge the Caudreliers were described as 'Roger Denis (with one 'n') Caudrelier' and 'Hilary Claire Caudrelier'.

The Caudreliers in fact were not satisfied with effecting these three mortgages on the property to which I have referred: They effected a number of other mortgages with other parties. As, in the view I have formed, these are wholly immaterial to anything I have to decide, I do not notice them further.

105 *Standard Property Investment plc v British Plastics Federation* (1985) 53 P & CR 25.

What has now happened is that the first defendant, in exercise of the statutory power conferred by s 101(l)(i) of the Law of Property Act 1925 has now sold the mortgaged property. There being no conceivable doubt about the position of the Abbey National Building Society as first mortgagee, the first defendant has paid off that mortgage: indeed, otherwise it would not have been able to acquire the deeds to hand over to the purchaser. But the crunch comes in relation to the mortgage to the plaintiff. It relies upon the provisions of s 105 of the Law of property Act 1925, which, in effect, provides that the proceeds of sale must be applied by the vendor mortgagee in discharge of prior incumbrances to which the sale is not made subject. It is common ground that the sale was not made subject to the plaintiff's mortgage; but the first defendant denies that the plaintiff's mortgage ranks in priority to its own mortgage. Hence, these proceedings in which the plaintiff claims as against the first defendant a declaration as to the priority of its mortgage over that of the first defendant, and consequential relief based upon that declaration, or, if that claim should fail, as against the second defendant damages for negligence in not ensuring that its mortgage was registered in such a manner as to obtain priority against that of any subsequent incumbrances, in effect, against that of the first defendant.

[His Lordship read s 198 and s 199(1) of the Law of Property Act 1925.]

Turning next to the Land Charges Act 1972, which has replaced the Land Charges Act 1925 so far as material for present purposes, the crucial provision is to be found in s 3(1) which reads, 'A land charge shall be registered in the name of the estate owner whose estate is intended to be affected.' And the other important provision is to be found in s 10(4) which reads as follows:

[His Lordship read s 10(4) of the Land Charges Act 1972.]

The certificate referred to is a certificate of the result of an official search.

I do not think that much assistance is to be obtained from the Land Charges Rules 1974.[106] The relevant form provided for registration of a land charge is Form K.l. in Schedule 2 and it simply says 'name' or 'forenames' and 'surname' except in relation to 'full names of the parties to the instrument creating the charge'. I take the reference here to 'full' names as simply meaning that any christian names which are given in the document must be set out in full and not abbreviated, as one perhaps normally would in reference to such a document. I certainly cannot deduce that the 'forms and contents of applications for registration' and so on and so forth as mentioned in s 16 of the 1972 Act as the subject matter of general rules were in any manner intended to affect the true interpretation of s 3(1).

There is just one other thing that I would add at this stage, and it is simply this. Quite obviously, the proper names for registration and for search must coincide. Therefore, one would expect to find in the legislation expressly or by implication, some fixed point of reference equally available to both the party registering the charge and to the person effecting the search. It cannot possibly be right that if either of such parties has some special inside information as to the true full and proper names of the estate owner he may either, as registrant, register in a name against which the searcher cannot possibly effectively search; or, as searcher, can effectively search against a name which the person making the registration did not in fact know and had no means of knowing was the full

106 SI 1974/1286.

and proper name of the estate owner. Or, that the situation might possibly arise where neither of them had sufficient knowledge of the name of the estate owner either to effect a proper registration or to make a proper search.

This suggests, and suggests very strongly, that what is required is some fixed point of reference, equally available to both parties, which is, for this purpose, conclusive as to the name to be used. It cannot possibly be the birth certificate; what use is the birth certificate of 'Winston Spencer Churchill' if he has changed his name, as he is entitled to do, to 'Winston Spencer Attlee?' It will, however, be seen from the examination of this problem subsequently effected in this judgment that there is, indeed, such a fixed point which effectively and conclusively settles the matter for all such purposes.

The crucial question therefore is, what is meant by the words 'name of the estate owner' in s (3)(1) of the Land Charges Act 1972, I think that this can only be approached by making some general observations in the first place, all of which in my judgment, point unerringly in one, and only one, direction. The first consideration is that, quite apart from all other considerations, no name, and especially not that of a surname, is immune from change ...

This being the case, suppose that registration under the 1972 Act is effected against a person whose name at the time of registration is 'John William Smith'. Afterwards, he changes his surname, so that his name becomes indisputably 'John William Brown'. Perhaps even less surprisingly, 'Jane Mary Foster' may have become 'Jane Mary Brown'. When a person comes to make a search, against what name should he effect the search? It would be ludicrously stupid to search against a subsequent name in either case, for in neither case would there be any possibility of the search revealing what on any footing was perfectly properly registered at the time when it was registered. I need not multiply examples; they readily suggest themselves. Accordingly, one is driven back to the fact that the search, to be effective, must be against the name actually borne by the estate owner at the time when he, or she, acquired the estate. So on this consideration alone, we are already some distance away from being safe if the search is conducted in the true and actual name or, as Mr Baker for the first defendant would have it, the 'full name' which the person against whom the search is made bears.

Now what is the name which was borne by such person at the time when he or she acquired the estate? The first and most obvious answer to that is, the name in which he or she took the conveyance. But Mr Barker would have none of this. He insisted upon the fact that the registration and the search must be in the 'full' name of the estate owner, however much, or little, that differed from the name in which he took the conveyance of the estate. I may say that in so doing he shot himself, or rather his client, in the foot; for the search which his client made was in the name of 'Roger Denis (with one 'n') Caudrelier', whilst that gentleman's birth certificate clearly shows that his christian name is spelt with two 'nn'; and in case anybody should think that this is, in the nature of matters, a mere quibble, it should be pointed out that it has been established for the purposes of this case that whereas a search against 'Roger Denis (with one 'n') Caudrelier' does indeed produce entries which have been entered against that name, a search against 'Roger Dennis (with two 'nn') Caudrelier' does not. Which led Mr Barker on to submit that the original registration by the plaintiffs was a nullity; a point I shall have to consider later.

Now there is no limit to the number of christian names which a man or woman may have, so that there is no obvious and easy way in which a person wishing to register a land charge will have of finding out what the full name of the estate owner in the sense indicated by Mr Barker, is ...

However, one may suppose that the 'birth certificate' possibility is one which, so far as borrowers are concerned, could conceivably be adopted. But one is entitled, in my view, to assume that the system was meant to work, as far as possible, fairly and sensibly in all cases; and that, if Mr Barker is correct, it could not possibly do. The reason is simple. When a purchaser who has contracted to purchase an estate is verifying the title, part of his solicitor's duty is to search in the land charges registry against all the estate owners from time to time since the root of title to see whether any of them have incumbered the land in some way or not. In such a case, all that the purchaser's solicitor has to work upon is the examined abstract of title. So the only names against which he can search are those which are therein shown as being the names of the estate owners from time to time. It would be a wholly impossible task to find out whether those names were the 'full' names of the various estate owners over the years. Once again, if this had been part of the duty of solicitors in such a situation, it is inconceivable that some hint of such a duty, however vague, would not have surfaced in some text book or even in a judgment. Nothing of the kind.

I have the impression that the bar is much less concerned with conveyancing now than it was when I was still a junior; but I must have told solicitors on many hundreds of occasions to search against the names of the estate owners as disclosed by the documents of title, and so, I venture to think, must all of my contemporaries of those days. The taking of any alternative course is wholly unrealistic.

So, by the simple process of considering how the system must be made to work, it appears to me quite inevitable that one ends up with the position that 'the name of the estate owner' is the name as disclosed by the conveyance of that estate to him or her. This is in fact the assumption which to my knowledge has always been made by those who had to do with registration ever since I first came to the bar: and it is correct ...

And so I come to the simple, practical and hardly surprising conclusion that the name against which registrations should be effected, and equally against which search should subsequently be made, are the names of the estate owner as disclosed by the conveyance to him or her. I am only too well aware that this simple solution, whilst being in full accord with ordinary conveyancing practice, and providing a simple, just and easily worked pattern for most ordinary transactions, including sales and mortgages (for in each case the other party to the transaction has full access either to the title deeds or a fully examined abstract thereof) does not solve the difficulty in all cases, notably in the case of an estate contract, where this is usually not the situation. But as regards such matters, the system is in any event fatally flawed; and the solution I have certainly does nothing to make it any worse ...

The conclusion is simple. The second defendant properly registered the plaintiff's mortgage in the only proper way in which it should have been registered; the first defendant did not search against the proper names; and the plaintiff's mortgage therefore has priority against that of the first defendant.

In the rare event where an incumbrancer has registered against an incorrect name, but the purchaser has likewise made an official search against an incorrect name, then it would seem that the registration is of no effect since the land charge is not registered in the name of the estate owner and the purchaser takes free.

However, in *Oak Co-operative Building Society v Blackburn*,[107] Russell LJ gave some effect to registration in a wrong 'version' of a name. He said that 'if there be registration in what may be fairly described as a version of the full names of the vendor, albeit not a version which is bound to be discovered on a search in the correct full names, we would not hold it a nullity against someone who does not search at all, or who searches in the wrong name'. In *Oak Co-operative Building Society v Blackburn*, the estate owner was Francis David Blackburn. He entered into an agreement to sell his property to D. D registered her estate contract against the name of Frank David Blackburn. The plaintiff mortgagee's solicitor made an official search against the name of Francis Davis Blackburn. The Court of Appeal held in favour of D.

Oak Co-operation Building Society v Blackburn [1968] 2 All ER 117, CA

Russell LJ: The real problem is, what is meant by the name or the names of the estate owner in this legislation?

As a matter of theoretical approach it is obvious that it is intended or hoped by the legislation that every registered land charge will be safeguarded by registration because due diligence in search will reveal it: and correspondingly that every duly diligent search will reveal every registered land charge affecting the land to be purchased. It is realised that if an official search certificate is issued there may be a blunder for which some innocent person must suffer, and s 17(3) provides, for example, that if a nil certificate is given the owner of the land charge suffers, however valid his registration. It would be supposed, however, that it would be intended to reduce error to a minimum, what then is meant by the requirement that the name – surname and Christian names – of the estate owner be given when requisitioning a search? People use different names at different times and for different purposes; but the matter now under consideration relates to two things: first, the investigation into the soundness of the paper title of a proposed vendor by a proposed purchaser: second, the attempt to prevent by registration the disposal by the owner of that paper title of the legal estate in a manner which will override the interest of the owner of the land charge.

In the case of a request for an official search, which of course takes place before completion after title examined, we can only think that the name or names referred to in the request should be that or those appearing on the title. A nil certificate here as to Francis Davis Blackburn would not have served to override the purchaser's land charge had it been registered in the name Francis David Blackburn, though it could have been issued.

In most cases of contracts to purchase land nowadays many of the formalities precede exchange of contracts, and indeed those acting for the vendor would have used in the contract the name of the proposed vendor as appearing on the title. There are other cases, however, such as the present, where the contract is much less formally arrived at, and the purchaser has no ready means of ascertaining the 'title' names of the vendor. It would seem to be a great hardship on a purchaser registering in the name by which the vendor ordinarily passed that his registration should be entirely without operation, which is of course the submission of the mortgagee in this case. We have said earlier that

107 [1968] 2 All ER 117 at 122.

if in this case the search had been against 'Francis David Blackburn' and the certificate had referred to the fact that an estate contract was registered against 'Frank David Blackburn' in respect of this property, the proposed mortgage transaction would have been blown sky-high. If, however, the mortgagee's contention is correct the registration would be no registration at all, and by force of s 199 of the Law of Property Act 1925, and s 13(2) of the Land Charges Act 1925, the mortgagee could have carried through the mortgage ignoring the estate contract though in fact aware of its existence. Indeed, if the mortgagee had contracted to grant a mortgage loan subject to getting good title, he would have been in breach of his contract by refusing to grant it.

We have come to the conclusion that the registration on this occasion ought not to be regarded as a nullity simply because the formal name of Blackburn was Francis and not Frank, and notwithstanding that Frank as a name is not merely an abbreviation or version of Francis, but also a name in its own right, as are also for example Harry and Willie. We are not led to this conclusion by the fact that initials would seem to suffice for registration of a *lis pendens* (see *Dunn v Chapman*),[108] at least under the then legislation and rules: for presumably a request for search under a full name having the same initials should throw up all entries under those initials. We take a broader view that so far as possible the system should be made to work in favour of those who seek to make use of it in a sensible and practical way. If a proposing purchaser here had requested a search in the correct full names he would have got a clean certificate and a clear title under s 17(3) of the Land Charges Act 1925, and would have suffered no harm from the fact that the registration was not in such names: and a person registering who is not in a position to satisfy himself what are the correct full names runs that risk. If, however, there be registration in what may be fairly described as a version of the full names of the vendor, albeit not a version which is bound to be discovered on a search in the correct full names, we would not hold it a nullity against someone who does not search at all, or who (as here) searches in the wrong name.

There is one objection to this approach, and that is that provision is made for personal as distinct from official search: a personal searcher in the full correct name in the present case would, it seems, not have encountered the registration in the present case: he would not have had the benefit of an official certificate under s 17(3) and on the contrary would have been affected by a deemed actual notice of the estate contract under s 198 of the Law of Property Act 1925. We think, however, that anyone who nowadays is foolish enough to search personally deserves what he gets: and if the aim of the statute is to arrive at a sensible working system that aim is better furthered by upholding a registration such as this than by protecting a personal searcher from his folly.

We do not feel we need shed any tears for the respondent mortgagee, which could easily have protected itself by a proper official search but which owing to the error of its solicitor it never made. It could indeed have taken the precaution of investigating the discrepancy between the proposed mortgage and the application which the mortgagor filled in for it, to which we have already drawn attention; or it could without great trouble have caused somebody to visit the property in question, when they would have found the purchaser living there. We allow the appeal.

108 [1920] 2 Ch 474.

Priority notice

In many cases, a registrable equitable interest is created almost simultaneously with a subsequent conveyance (often the creation of a mortgage) before there is time to register the equitable interest. For example, a seller who sells part of his land may require the buyer to create certain restrictive covenants limiting the use of that part of land sold. The restrictive covenants are only created at the completion and will no doubt bind the buyer. But the buyer may finance his purchase with a mortgage which is almost inevitably granted at the same time as the completion of the purchase which includes the creation of the restrictive covenants. To bind the mortgagee, the seller has to register his restrictive covenants. There will be no time for the seller to do so. To protect the seller's incumbrance, he can give a priority notice to the registrar at least 15 working days before the incumbrance is to be created,[109] and he must then register his charge within 30 working days of the entry of the priority notice in the register.[110] The registration then dates back to the moment of the creation of the incumbrance. Any prudent purchaser (including the mortgagee) who carries out a usual search will be warned of the new land charge to be created.

Land Charges Act 1972

11. Date of effective registration and priority notices

(1) Any person intending to make an application for the registration of any contemplated charge, instrument or other matter in pursuance of this Act or any rule made under this Act may give a priority notice in the prescribed form at least the relevant number of days before the registration is to take effect.

(2) Where a notice is given under sub-s (1) above, it shall be entered in the register to which the intended application when made will relate.

(3) If the application is presented within the relevant number of days thereafter and refers in the prescribed manner to the notice, the registration shall take effect as if the registration has been made at the time when the charge, instrument or matter was created, entered into, made or arose, and the date at which the registration so takes effect shall be deemed to be the date of registration.

(4) Where:

(a) any two charges, instruments or matters are contemporaneous; and

(b) one of them (whether or not protected by a priority notice) is subject to or dependent on the other; and

(c) the latter is protected by a priority notice,

the subsequent or dependent charge, instrument or matter shall be deemed to have been created, entered into or made, or to have arisen, after the registration of the other.

109 Section 11(1) and (6)(a) of the LCA 1972.

110 Section 11(3) and (6)(b) of the LCA 1972.

The flaw of land charges system and its solution

As a purchaser is only statutorily required to investigate a good root of title which is at least 15 years old, there may be a registered land charge hidden behind the root of title. Thus, in the example given above, if there has been a land charge registered against F's name in 1948, A who searches against the root of title as required by law will not discover F's name and will therefore not discover the land charge concealed behind the root of title. In such a case the purchaser is still bound by the registered land charge under s 198 of the Law of Property Act 1925, as registration is deemed actual notice to all persons for all purposes. However, s 25(1) of the Law of Property Act 1969 enables the purchaser who takes the conveyance on or after 1 January 1970 to receive compensation from the Chief Land Registrar provided the purchaser has no actual knowledge of the charge at the date of the purchase and the land charge is truly concealed behind the root of title.

Law of Property Act 1969

25. Compensation in certain cases for loss due to undisclosed land charges

(1) Where a purchaser of any estate or interest in land under a disposition to which this section applies has suffered loss by reason that the estate or interest is affected by a registered land charge, then if:

(a) the date of completion was after the commencement of this Act; and

(b) on that date the purchaser had no actual knowledge of the charge; and

(c) the charge was registered against the name of an owner of an estate in the land who was not as owner of any such estate a party to any transaction, or concerned in any event, comprised in the relevant title;

the purchaser shall be entitled to compensation for the loss.

(2) For the purposes of sub-s (1)(b) above, the question whether any person had actual knowledge of a charge shall be determined without regard to the provisions of s 198 of the Law of Property Act 1925 (under which registration under the Land Charges Act 1925 or any enactment replaced by it is deemed to constitute actual notice).

(9) This section applies to the following dispositions, that is to say:

(a) any sale or exchange and, subject to the following provisions of this subsection, any mortgage of an estate or interest in land;

(b) any grant of a lease for a term of years derived out of a leasehold interest;

(c) any compulsory purchase, by whatever procedure, of land; and

(d) any conveyance of a fee simple in land under Part I of the Leasehold Reform Act 1967;

but does not apply to the grant of a term of years derived out of the freehold or the mortgage of such a term by the lessee; and references in this section to a purchaser shall be construed accordingly.

(11) For the purposes of this section any knowledge acquired in the course of a transaction by a person who is acting therein as counsel, or as solicitor or other agent, for another shall be treated as the knowledge of that other.

5 OVERREACHABLE INTERESTS

Law of Property Act 1925

2. Conveyances overreaching certain equitable interests and powers

(1) A conveyance to a purchaser of a legal estate in land shall overreach any equitable interest or power affecting that estate, whether or not he has notice thereof, if:

(i) the conveyance is made under the powers conferred by the Settled Land Act 1925 or any additional powers conferred by a settlement, and the equitable interest or power is capable of being overreached thereby, and the statutory requirements respecting the payment of capital money arising under the settlement are complied with;

(ii) the conveyance is made by trustees of land and the equitable interest or power is at the date of the conveyance capable of being overreached by such trustees under the provisions of sub-s (2) of this section or independently of that subsection, and the requirements of s 27 of this Act respecting the payment of capital money arising on such a conveyance are complied with;

(iii) the conveyance is made by a mortgagee or personal representative in the exercise of his paramount powers, and the equitable interest or power is capable of being overreached by such conveyance, and any capital money arising from the transaction is paid to the mortgagee or personal representative;

(iv) the conveyance is made under an order of the court and the equitable interest or power is bound by such order, and any capital money arising from the transaction is paid into, or in accordance with the order of, the court.

(1A) An equitable interest in land subject to a trust of land which remains in, or is to revert to, the settlor shall (subject to any contrary intention) be overreached by the conveyance if it would be so overreached were it an interest under the trust.

Under s 2(1) of the Law of Property Act 1925, a number of conveyances by various persons can overreach overreachable interests. First, a conveyance to a purchaser of a legal estate made under the powers conferred by the Settled Land Act 1925, can overreach overreachable interest if the capital money has been paid to or by the direction of the trustees of the settlement or into court, and it shall not, except where the trustee is a trust corporation, be paid to or by the direction of fewer persons than two as trustees of the settlement.[111] Secondly, a conveyance by trustees of land can overreach certain overreachable equitable interests provided the proceeds of sale are not paid to or applied by the direction of fewer than two persons as trustees, except where the trustee is a trust corporation.[112] Thirdly, a conveyance by a mortgagee or personal

111 Section 2(1)(i) of the LPA 1925; s 18(1)(b), (c) of the SLA 1925.

112 Sections 2(1)(ii), 27(2) of the LPA 1925, as amended by s 25(1), Sched 3, para 4(2), (8) of the TLATA 1996.

representative in the exercise of his paramount powers can overreach certain overreachable equitable interest provided the capital money is paid to the mortgagee or personal representative.[113] Fourthly, a conveyance under an order of the court also has overreaching effect if the capital money is paid into, or in accordance with the court order.[114]

In the case of conveyance made under the powers conferred by the Settled Land Act, where the requirement respecting the payment of the proceeds of sale are not complied with, the conveyance shall not take effect.[115] In the case of a conveyance by the trustees of land, if the proceeds are not paid to at least two trustees, or a trust corporation, the transaction is effective to pass the legal estate in land, but will have no overreaching effect. In such a case, there is nothing in the Act to displace the principle that a *bona fide* purchaser of the legal estate for value without notice of the trust will take free from it.[116]

It is noticeable that only overreachable interests can be overreached. What interests are overreachable? Where a deed of conveyance is executed by the tenant for life or statutory owner under the power of the Settled Land Act 1925, s 72 of the Settled Land Act 1925 provides a list of interests capable of being overreached.

Settled Land Act 1925

72. Completion of transactions by conveyance

(2) Such a deed [by the tenant for life or statutory owner under the power of the Settled Land Act 1925], to the extent and in the manner to and in which it is expressed or intended to operate and can operate under this Act, is effectual to pass the land conveyed, or the easements, rights, privileges or other interests created, discharged from all the limitations, powers, and provisions of the settlement, and from all estates, interests, and charges subsisting or to arise thereunder, but subject to and with the exception of:

(i) all legal estates and charges by way of legal mortgage having priority to the settlement; and

(ii) all legal estates and charges by way of legal mortgage which have been conveyed or created for securing money actually raised at the date of the deed; and

(iii) all leases and grants at fee-farm rents or otherwise, and all grants of easements, rights of common, or other rights or privileges which:

(a) were before the date of the deed granted or made for value in money or money's worth, or agreed so to be, by the tenant for life or statutory owner, or by any of his predecessors in title, or any trustees for them, under the settlement, or under any statutory power, or are at that date otherwise binding on the successors in title of the tenant for life or statutory owner; and

113 Section 21(1)(iii) of the LPA 1925.

114 Section 2(1)(iv) of the LPA 1925.

115 Section 18(1)(b) of the SLA 1925.

116 See eg *Caunce v Caunce* [1969] 1 All ER 722 (beneficial interests under a statutory trust for sale defeated by a legal mortgagee without notice).

(b) are at the date of the deed protected by registration under the Land Charges Act 1925, if capable of registration thereunder.

(3) Notwithstanding registration under the Land Charges Act 1925, of:

(a) an annuity within the meaning of Part 11 of that Act;

(b) a limited owner's charge or a general equitable charge within the meaning of that Act;

a disposition under this Act operates to overreach such annuity or charge which shall, according to its priority, take effect as if limited by the settlement.

Thus, a number of legal estates, interests and charges are not overreachable. Commercial interests such as an equitable mortgage protected by title deed,[117] puisne mortgage, estate contract, restrictive covenant and equitable easement are not overreachable, and a Class F land charge is equally not overreachable.[118] Beneficial interests which exist under a strict settlement are, however, overreachable. A land charge of Class C(ii) or C(iii) is also overreachable, even if duly registered.[119] Where the conveyance is executed by the trustees of land, there seems no provisions which explain what is overreachable, although it seems clear that beneficial interests behind the trust are overreachable.

Once the equitable interests are overreached, the purchaser takes the legal estate free of them. The equitable interests behind the trust are now swept off the land and converted into the proceeds of sale. The trustees of the settlement or the trustees of land now hold the proceeds of sale for the beneficial owners. So after the sale the purchaser takes a clean and unfettered title to the land while the beneficial interests are now preserved in the form of the proceeds of sale which will be invested by the trustees.

Note that for the purposes of s 2(1) and s 27(2) of the Law of Property Act 1925, 'purchaser' means 'a person who acquires an interest in or charge on property for money or money's worth.'[120] Thus marriage consideration is not good enough. Under s 2(1A), an equitable interest in land subject to a trust of land, which remains in, or is to revert to, the settlor, shall (subject to any contrary intention) be overreached by the conveyance if it would be so overreached were it an interest under the trust.

6 INTERESTS GOVERNED BY EQUITABLE PRINCIPLES

As mentioned, there is a residual group of equitable interests which are neither registrable nor overreachable. This small category of anomalous equitable rights are still governed by the old doctrine of notice. Some examples are a conveyance by a sole trustee of land,[121] an equitable right arising by

117 Section 72(2)(iii)(a) of the SLA 1925.

118 Section 72(2)(iii)(b) of the SLA 1925.

119 Section 72(3) of the SLA 1925.

120 Section 205(1)(xxi) of the LPA 1925.

121 *Cf Caunce v Caunce* [1969] 1 All ER 722.

acquiescence or estoppel,[122] an equitable right of entry,[123] and a Class D(ii) or (iii) land charge created before 1926.[124] A conveyance by a bare trustee was governed by the doctrine of notice,[125] but a bare trust exists today as a trust of land. In addition, as has been seen, an unregistered Class C(iv), or Class D land charge may bind a purchaser of an equitable interest, or a purchaser of a legal estate who does not give consideration in money or money's worth under the doctrine of notice.

Under the old doctrine of notice an equitable interest binds the whole world except a *bona fide* purchaser for value of a legal estate without notice. The operation of the doctrine has been considered in detail in Chapter 1.

Shiloh Spinners Ltd v Harding [1973] AC 691, HL

Lord Wilberforce: The right of entry, it is said, is unenforceable against the respondent, although he took with actual notice of it, because it was not registered as a charge under the Land Charges Act 1925. There is no doubt that if it was capable of registration under that Act, it is unenforceable if not registered: the appellants deny that it was so capable either (i) because it was a legal right, not an equitable right, or (ii) because, if equitable, it does not fall within any of the classes or descriptions of charges registration of which is required. I consider first whether the right of entry is legal in character or equitable, using these adjectives in the technical sense in which they are used in the 1925 property legislation.

[His Lordship read ss 1 and 205(1)(x) of the Law of Property Act 1925.]

The right of entry in this case is not contained in a lease, so as to be annexed to a reversion, nor is it exercisable for a term of years, or (comparably with a fee simple) indefinitely. Its duration is limited by a perpetuity period. Whether it can be said to be 'exercisable over or in respect of a legal term of years absolute' appears obscure. It is not exercisable for a legal term of years (whether that granted by the lease or any other term): it is not so exercisable as to determine a legal term of years. To say that a right of entry is exercisable in respect of a legal term of years appears to me, with respect, to be without discernible meaning. The effect of this right of entry is to cause a legal term of years to be divested from one person to another upon an event which may occur over a perpetuity period. It would, I think, be contrary to the whole scheme of the Act, which requires the limiting and vesting of legal estates and interests to be by reference to a fee simple or a term of years absolute, to allow this to rank as a legal interest. In my opinion it is clearly equitable.

So I pass, as did the Court of Appeal, to the Land Charges Act 1925. The original contention of the respondents was that the equitable right of entry was capable of registration under Class D(iii) of the Act. In the Court of Appeal an alternative contention was raised, apparently at the court's suggestion, that it might come within Class C(iv). In my opinion this is unmaintainable. Class C(iv) embraces:

---

122 *Ives v High* [1967] 1 All ER 504.

123 *Shiloh Spinners v Harding* [1973] AC 691.

124 Section 2(5)(ii) and (iii) of the LCA 1972.

125 *Hodgson v Marks* [1971] 2 All ER 684.

> Any contract by an estate owner or by a person entitled at the date of the contract to have a legal estate conveyed to him to convey or create a legal estate, including a contract conferring either expressly or by statutory implication a valid option of purchase, a right of pre-emption or any other like right (in this Act referred to as 'an estate contract').

The only words capable of including a right of entry are 'any other like right,' but, in my opinion, no relevant likeness can be found. An option or right of pre-emption eventuates in a contract for sale at a price; this is inherent in 'purchase' and 'pre-emption'; the right of entry is penal in character and involves the revesting of the lease, in the event of default, in a previous owner. There is no similarity in law or fact between these situations.

Class D(iii) reads:

> A charge or obligation affecting land of any of the following kinds, namely: ... (iii) Any easement right or privilege over or affecting land created or arising after the commencement of this Act, and being merely an equitable interest (in this Act referred to as an 'equitable easement').

The argument for inclusion in this class falls into two parts. First, it is said that a right of entry falls fairly within the description, or at least that, if the words do not appear to include it, they are sufficiently open in meaning to admit it. Secondly, it is said that the provisions of the Law of Property Act as to "overreaching" compel the conclusion that a right of entry must fall under some class or sub-class of the Land Charges Act, and since this is the only one whose words can admit it, they should be so interpreted as to do so. Thus, the argument depends for its success upon a combination of ambiguity, or openness of Class D(iii) with compelling consideration brought about in the overreaching provisions. In my opinion it fails under both limbs: Class D(iii) cannot be interpreted so as to admit equitable rights of entry, and no conclusive, compelling, or even clear conclusions can be drawn from the overreaching provisions which can influence the interpretation of Class D(iii).

Dealing with Class D(iii), I reject at once the suggestion that any help (by way of enlarging the content of this class) can be derived either from the introductory words, for they limit themselves to the 'following kinds', or from the words 'and being merely an equitable interest', for these are limiting, not enlarging, words. I leave out of account the label at the end – though I should think it surprising if so expert a draftsman had attached that particular label if the class included a right of entry. To include a right of entry in the description of 'equitable easement' offends a sense both of elegance and accuracy. That leaves 'easement right or privilege over or affecting land.' If this were the only place where the expression occurred in this legislation, I should find it difficult to attribute to 'right' a meaning so different in quality from easement and privilege as to include a right of entry. The difference between a right to use or draw profit from another man's land, and a right to take his land altogether away, is one of quality, not of degree. But the words are plentifully used both in the Law of Property Act and elsewhere in the 1925 legislation, so are the words 'rights of entry,' and I find it impossible to believe that in this one context the one includes the other. The two expressions are even used by way of what seems deliberate contrast in two contexts: first in s 1 of the Law of Property Act, where sub-s (2)(a) mentions 'An easement, right, or privilege in or over land' and paragraph (e) of the same subsection 'Rights of entry': secondly, in s 162(1)(d) which mentions both. An argument, unattractive but perhaps just palatable, can be devised why it might have been necessary in s 1 of the Law of Property

Act to mention both easements, rights or privileges and the particular rights of entry described in sub-s (2)(e), but no explanation can be given why, if the latter are capable of being included in the former, they should be mentioned with such a degree of separation. I do not further elaborate this point because a reading of their judgments leaves little doubt that the Lords Justices would themselves have read Class D(iii) as I can only read it but for the influence of the overreaching argument.

So I turn to the latter. This, in my opinion, only becomes compelling if one first accepts the conclusion that all equitable claims relating to land are either registrable under the Land Charges Act, or capable of being overreached under s 2 of the Law of Property Act; ie, are capable by use of the appropriate mechanism of being transferred to the proceeds of sale of the land they affect. If this dilemma could be made good, then there could be an argument for forcing, within the limits of the possible, an equitable right of entry into one of the registrable classes, since it is obviously not suitable for overreaching. But the dilemma cannot be made good. What may be overreached is 'any equitable interest or power affecting that estate': yet 'equitable interest' (for powers do not enter into the debate) is a word of most uncertain content. The searcher after a definition has to be satisfied with s 1(8) 'Estates, interests, and charges in or over land which are not legal estates are in this Act referred to as "equitable interests"'– a tautology rather than a definition. There is certainly nothing exhaustive about the expression 'equitable interests' – just as certainly it has no clear boundaries. The debate whether such rights as equity, over the centuries, has conferred against the holder of the legal estate are truly proprietary in character, or merely rights in personam, or a hybrid between the two, may have lost some of its vitality in the statutory context but the question inevitably rises to mind whether the 'curtain' or 'overreaching' provisions of the 1925 legislation extend to what are still conveniently called 'equities' or 'mere equities' such as rights to rectification, or to set aside a conveyance. There is good authority, which I do not presume to doubt, for a sharp distinction between the two – I instance Lord Upjohn in *National Provincial Bank Ltd v Hastings Car Mart Ltd* [1965] AC 1175 at 1238 and Snell's *Principles of Equity*, 25th edn, 1960, p 38. I am impressed by the decision in *E R Ives Investment Ltd v High* [1967] 2 QB 379 in which the Court of Appeal held that a right by estoppel – producing an effect similar to an easement – was not registrable under Class D(iii). Lord Denning MR referred to the right as subsisting only in equity. Danckwerts LJ thought it was an equity created by estoppel or a proprietary estoppel: plainly this was not an equitable interest capable of being overreached, yet no member of the court considered that the right – so like an easement – could be brought within Class D(iii). The conclusion followed, and the court accepted it, that whether it was binding on a purchaser depended on notice. All this seems to show that there may well be rights, of an equitable character, outside the provisions as to registration and which are incapable of being overreached.

That equitable rights of entry should be among them is not in principle unacceptable. First, rights of entry, before 1925, were not considered to confer an interest in the land. They were described as bare possibilities (Challis, HW, *Law of Real Property*: chiefly in relation to conveyancing, 3rd edn (by Sweet, C), 1911, London: Butterworth, p 76) so that it is not anomalous that equitable rights of entry should not be treated as equitable interests. Secondly, it is important that s 10 of the Land Charges Act 1925 should be given a plain and ordinary interpretation. It is a section which involves day to day operation by solicitors doing conveyancing work: they should be able to take decisions and advise their clients upon a straightforward interpretation of the registration classes, not upon one depending upon a sophisticated, not to say disputable, analysis of other statutes. Thirdly, the consequence of equitable rights of entry not being registrable is that they are subject to the doctrine of notice, preserved by s 199 of the Law of Property Act. This may not give complete protection, but neither is it demonstrable that it is likely to be less effective than the present system of registration against names. I am therefore of opinion that Class D(iii) should be given its plain *prima facie* meaning and that so read it does not comprise equitable rights of entry. It follows that non-registration does not make the appellants' right unenforceable in this case.

Where, however, the claimant has a registrable estate contract which is not registered and therefore void against a purchaser of a legal estate for money or money's worth, he cannot avoid the consequence of non-registration by means of a bare trust or proprietary estoppel of which the purchaser has notice;[126] the claimant cannot defeat the purchaser's priority and obtain by means of estoppel that which s 4(6) of the Land Charges Act 1972 prevents him from obtaining directly under a void contract.

7 DEALINGS OF EQUITABLE INTEREST

So far we have seen issues concerning priority in unregistered land where the legal estate is conveyed to a third party; ie how the various legal or equitable interests bind a third party. Where it is the equitable interest which is disposed of, for example, where there is a dealing of the beneficial interests under a strict settlement or trust by way of an assignment of the beneficial interest or an equitable mortgage of it, and it is followed by a subsequent dealing of the legal estate, the rules mentioned earlier would apply to determine whether the subsequent legal owner is bound by the prior equitable assignment or mortgage. But if the prior equitable dealing is followed by a further dealing in the equitable interests, for example, a prior mortgage of the beneficial interests is followed by another mortgage of the same beneficial interest, priority between them depends on the order in which notice by the equitable mortgagee is received by the trustees of the settlement or the trustees of land under s 137 of the Law of Property Act 1925 which incorporates the rule in *Dearle v Hall*.[127]

126 *Lloyds Bank plc v Carrick* [1996] 4 All ER 630; *Western Fish Products Ltd v Penwith District Council* [1981] 2 All ER 204.

127 (1828) 3 Russ 1.

CHAPTER 7

REGISTERED LAND AND PRIORITY

1 INTRODUCTION

Registration of title is not a recent invention of the 1925 legislation; it has quite a long history.[1] The first British territory to adopt a system of registration of title was South Australia. The system there, commonly known as the 'Torrens system', was introduced by Sir Robert Torrens in 1858.[2] The 'Torrens system' has been followed in many other countries, but the system of registration finally adopted in England is very different from this system.[3]

The English system of registration started as a voluntary registration of title under the Land Registry Act 1862 and the Land Transfer Acts 1875. The first compulsory registration of title was introduced by the Land Transfer Act 1897 to dealing with land in the county of London. The first major compulsory registration was introduced in 1925 to other populous parts of the country by the Land Registration Act 1925. The 1925 Act is further amended by a series of subsequent Acts.[4] These Acts are supplemented by the Land Registration Rules 1925 as amended. Since 1 December 1990, the system of registration of title has been extended to the whole of England and Wales.[5] Thus all conveyances on sale taking effect on or after such date must now be registered.

The 1925 registration system provides for the registration of all legal estates or interests in land, and the protection of other equitable interests in or over land. The idea is that the process of investigation of title needs only to be done once and done by the Chief Land Registrar. All interests in land will then be recorded on a central register, the Land Register. Only certain types of incumbrances which are readily discoverable on inspection of property can be left off the register. Any prospective purchaser will be able to verify from the Register, by a simple search, the vendor's power to sell and any incumbrances binding on the land. The system therefore provides a State guaranteed single title. This is a wholly new system of conveyancing which is designed to replace the 'self-perpetuating, repetitive, protracted and costly',[6] old fashion unregistered system of conveyancing, the 'wearisome and intricate task of examining title'.[7]

As mentioned in Chapter 6, registration of title was invented to enable owners 'to deal with land in as simple and easy a manner, as far as the title is

---

1 For the history of land registration see Ruoff and Roper, Chapter 1; Simpson, SR, *Land Law and Registration* 1976, Cambridge: Cambridge UP, p 40; (1939) 55 LQR 547 (Walker, RRA); (1983) 127 Sol J 3 (E J Pryer).

2 Simpson, SR, *Land Law and Registration* 1976, Cambridge: Cambridge UP, p 68.

3 For a comparison of them, see Ruoff & Roper, paras 2.03-2.06; Simpson, SR, *Land Law and Registration*, 1976, Cambridge: Cambridge UP, p 76.

4 See LRA 1936, LRA 1966, Land Registration and Land Charges Act 1971, LRA 1986, and LRA 1988.

5 Land Registration, England and Wales: The Registration of Title Order 1989 (SI 1989/1347).

6 Gray, p 167.

7 *Williams & Glyn's Bank Ltd v Boland* [1981] AC 487 at 511D, *per* Lord Scarman.

concerned, and the difference in the nature of the subject matter may allow, as they can now deal with moveable chattels or stock'.[8] 'The problem is how we are to engraft this system on our law of real property.'[9] Three fundamental principles shape the system of registration which was ultimately adopted, as Professor Gray explained:

> It has been said that the fundamental features of any scheme for registration of title, whether in the form of Torrens legislation or in the form of the Land Registration Act 1925, are three in number.[10] First, the register of title is intended to operate as a 'mirror', reflecting accurately and incontrovertibly the totality of estates and interests which at any time affect the registered land (the 'mirror principle'). Second, trusts relating to the registered land are kept off the title, with the result that third parties may transact with the registered proprietor safe in the assurance that the interests behind any trust will be overreached (the 'curtain principle'). Third, the State itself guarantees the accuracy of the registered title, in that an indemnity is payable from public funds if a registered proprietor is deprived of his title or is otherwise prejudiced by the operation of the registration scheme (the 'insurance principle').[11]

The doctrine of notice, as is applied in unregistered conveyancing, was not intended to play a part in the system. However, in cases where the Act fails to provide an answer, there have been attempts to bring back something akin to the equitable doctrine.[12] As will be seen, the three fundamental principles mentioned above have not always been realised. The Law Commission has made proposals for reform to deal with the problems in the system. But first, it is necessary to examine the operation of the registration of title in detail.

2 THE REGISTER

The Land Register is centrally controlled by the Chief Land Registrar in London, with 19 regional district land registries.[13] Each title is registered by reference to a title number, and not against the name of the current estate owner. The Registrar has a limited quasi-judicial power to hear and determine any matters which arise in the day-to-day operation of the register, and to make such order as he shall think just.[14] Any person aggrieved by an order or decision of the Registrar may appeal to the court.[15]

The register of a title is divided into three 'registers'. The three divisions are correlated on one index card. The current registered proprietor is issued with a copy of this card which is known as the 'land certificate'. Under s 63(1) of the Land Registration Act 1925:

8 Report of the Commissioners on the Registration of Title with reference to the Sale and Transfer of Land (CP 2215, 1857 – Session 2), para XL.

9 (1912) 28 LQR 6 at 11 (Sweet, C).

10 See Ruoff, TBF, *An Englishman Looks at the Torrens System*, 1957, Sydney: Law Book Co of Australasia, p 8.

11 Gray, p 169.

12 See eg *Peffer v Rigg* [1977] 1 WLR 285; *Lyus v Prowsa Developments Ltd* [1982] 1 WLR 1044.

13 Land Registration (District Registries) Order 1991 (SI 1991/2634), Schedule.

14 LRR 1925, r 298(1).

15 LRR 1925, r 299.

> On the first registration of a freehold or leasehold interest in land, and on the registration of a charge, a land certificate, or charge certificate, as the case may be, shall be prepared in the prescribed form; it shall state whether the title is absolute, good leasehold, qualified or possessory, and it shall be either delivered to the proprietor or deposited in the registry as the proprietor may prefer.

The land certificate is the registered land equivalent of the title deeds in unregistered conveyancing. A copy of a land certificate is to be found at the end of this chapter.

The three divisions of the Land Register are the 'Property Register', the 'Proprietorship Register', and the 'Charges Register'.

The 'Property Register'

As the land certificate at the end of this chapter shows, this register contains 'a description of the land and estate comprised in the title, with a reference to the General Map or to the filed plan of the land.'[16] It also contains 'notes relating to the ownership of the mines and minerals, to the exemption from any of the overriding interests mentioned in s 70 of the Land Registration Act 1925, and to easements, rights, privileges, conditions and covenants for the benefit of the land, and other like matters.'[17] Rule 5(1) of the Land Registration Rules 1925 provides that:

> In the case of leasehold land there shall be entered in the Property Register a reference to the registered lease, and such particulars of the lease, and of the exceptions or reservations therefrom (if any) as the applicant may desire, and the registrar approve; and a reference to the lessor's title, if registered.

The 'Proprietorship Register'

Rule 6 of the 1925 Rules provides that:

The Proprietorship Register shall state the nature of the title, and shall contain the name, address, and description of the proprietor of the land, and cautions, inhibitions, and restrictions affecting his right of disposing thereof.

Thus, whether the title enjoyed by the proprietor is 'absolute', 'good leasehold', 'qualified', or 'possessory', is indicated in this register.

The 'Charges Register'

Rule 7 of the 1925 Rules provides:

The Charges Register shall contain:

(a) incumbrances subsisting at the date of first registration;

(b) subsequent charges, and other incumbrances (including notices of leases and other notices of adverse interests or claims permitted by the Act);

16 LRR 1925, r 3(1).

17 LRR 1925, r 3(2).

(c) such notes as have to be entered relating to covenants, conditions, and other rights adversely affecting the land;

(d) all such dealings with registered charges and incumbrances as are capable of registration.

The Land Register has since 3 December 1990 been, subject to the payment of a fee, open to inspection by the public.[18] As a seller is under a duty to disclose any latent defect in title (under the open contract rule or the Standard Conditions of Sale), any entries on the Land Register at the time of the contract would have been disclosed by the seller. The buyer does not have to make searches at this stage (although to avoid buying a law suit, a prudent buyer often makes searches). But, after the contract and before completion, the buyer must make an official search to take advantage of the priority period and should complete sale within the priority period. A full official search with priority of a register gives the searcher a priority period of 30 working days.[19] As long as the buyer completes his transaction within the priority period, he will not be affected by any supervening entry made during the period.[20]

It should be noted that any unrevealed entry made prior to the official search will bind the buyer even though he is entirely blameless.[21] The buyer may, however, claim a statutory indemnity against the Land Registry for the loss suffered.[22] This is entirely different from the position in unregistered land where an unrevealed land charge is void against a purchaser who obtains a clear official search certificate which is conclusive. It is for the owner of the destroyed land charge to sue the Land Charges Registry for negligence.[23]

3 THE CLASSIFICATION OF INTERESTS IN REGISTERED CONVEYANCE

All estates and interests are to be registered or entered on the register, except those which are readily discoverable on inspection of property, so that the register can 'mirror' the totality of estates and interests which at any time affect the registered land. Those not required to be entered on the register and which can still bind any subsequent registered proprietor are known as 'overriding interests'. Those which are required to be registered or entered are divided into two categories: 'registrable interests' and 'minor interests'. 'Registrable interests' represent the ownership of land upon which many incumbrances may be binding. These are registered under an individual title number. 'Minor interests', on the other hand, are those incumbrances which affect the registered land. These are not registered under a separate number in their own right, but

18 Section 112(1) of the LRA 1925,, as substituted by s 1(1) of the LRA 1988, brought into effect by Land Registration Act 1988 (Commencement) Order 1990 (SI 1990/1359). See also Land Registration (Open Register) Rules 1991 (SI 1992/122), rr 1(1), 2–4.

19 Land Registration (Official Searches) Rules 1990, r 6.

20 Land Registration (Official Searches) Rules 1990, r 5.

21 *Parkash v Irani Finance Ltd* [1970] Ch 101, at 110H–111A.

22 Section 83(1) of the LRA 1925.

23 See Chapter 6, p 225.

are simply 'entered' on the Proprietorship Register or Charges Register, as the case may be, of a particular title number of a registered interest, upon which they bind.

4 REGISTRABLE INTERESTS

Registrable interests

Section 2(1) of the Land Registration Act 1925 provides that:

After the commencement of this Act, estates capable of subsisting as legal estates shall be the only interests in land in respect of which a proprietor can be registered and all other interests in registered land (except overriding interests and interests entered on the register at or before such commencement) shall take effect in equity, as minor interests ...

Thus, only *legal estates* are registrable. Under s 3(xi) of the Land Registration Act 1925:

> 'legal estates' means the estates interests and charges in or over land subsisting or created at law which are by the Law of Property Act 1925, authorised to subsist or to be created at law.

As has been seen in Chapter 1, under s 1(1) of the Law of Property Act 1925, the only estates in land which are capable of subsisting or of being conveyed or created at law are an estate in fee simple absolute in possession, and a term of years absolute. Thus a fee simple and a term of years, except a lease which is overriding under s 70(1)(k) of the Land Registration Act 1925, are registrable interests.

Under s 1(2), the only interests or charges in or over land capable of subsisting or being created at law are a legal easement right or privilege, legal rentcharge, legal mortgage, statutory charges, and a legal right of entry. Thus, legal interests under s 1(2) of the Law of Property Act 1925 also appear to be registrable.

(a) Legal easements, rights or privileges

A legal easement, right, or privilege cannot be registered separately from the dominant land.[24] A legal easement, right or privilege forms part of the ownership of the dominant land in that its use benefits the dominant land and it is therefore normally registered on the Property Register of the dominant title. However, even if the right is not registered on the title of the dominant land, it can still be claimed by successive proprietors of the dominant land as long as it actually benefits the property.[25] The right is, on the other hand, a burden on the servient land which should be noted on the Charges Register of the servient title. However, if, when the title of the servient land is first registered, the easement is for some reason not so registered, it is protected as an overriding interest, under s 70(1)(a) of the Land Registration Act 1925, and therefore is

24 LRR 1925, r 257.

25 Section 72 of the LRA 1925; LRR 1925, r 251.

binding on any subsequent registered proprietor.[26] The practice of the Chief Land Registrar is to enter, on first registration, automatically on the register any appurtenant legal rights disclosed in the evidence of title.[27] Similarly, on the registration of a transfer of part of the land, appropriate entries of legal easement granted or reserved will be made automatically on the dominant and servient titles.[28] But if the legal easement is separately granted, this will be a disposition of registered land which will have to be completed by an entry of the right as appurtenant to the dominant title and as a burden on the servient title.[29] On the other hand, even if it is not completed by registration and cannot be legal, it is equitable and may still be overriding under s 70(1)(a) of the Land Registration Act.[30]

(b) Legal rentcharges

When a rentcharge is created, there must be a substantive registration of the title to the rentcharge, and the entry of notice of the rentcharge as an incumbrance against the title of the landowner. If these processes have not been completed, the rentcharge takes effect only in equity.[31] In practice it is the purchaser of the land charged with the rentcharge who makes two applications for registration: one for the rentcharge to be registered in favour of the vendor, the rent owner, the other for himself to be registered as the new proprietor. The vendor will be registered as the proprietor of the rentcharge under a separate title, and be given a rentcharge certificate, and the rentcharge is noted in the Charges Register of the purchaser's title as an incumbrance.[32]

(c) Legal mortgages or charges

A legal mortgage or charge over a registered title is only completed with registration of the mortgage or charge. The title of the mortgagee or chargee cannot be registered independently of the estate which is charged so long as a right of redemption subsists.[33] Thus, the title of a legal mortgagee or chargee of an unregistered land cannot be registered without the title of the estate owner of the unregistered land, ie the mortgagor, also being registered. But when the title of the mortgagor is registered the interest of the mortgagee or chargee may also be protected by substantive registration, whether the mortgage or charge was created before or after the date of first registration.[34]

---

26 Where the servient land remains unregistered, the unregistered land principles discussed in Chapter 6 apply: a legal easement binds the whole world and an equitable easement created on or after 1 January 1926 must be registered as a D(iii) land charge.

27 See Ruoff and Roper, at paras 9–13, 12–34.

28 See Ruoff and Roper, at paras 9–13, 17–46.

29 See Ruoff and Roper, at paras 9–13, 17–47.

30 LRR 1925, r 258; *Celsteel Ltd v Alton House Holdings Ltd* [1985] 1 WLR 204.

31 Section 19(2) of the LRA 1925.

32 LRR 1925, r 108; Ruoff and Roper, at para 26–17.

33 Section 8(1)(a) of the LRA 1925.

34 LRR 1925, r 160.

When a mortgage or charge is registered, the mortgagee or chargee is registered as the proprietor of the mortgage or charge. The mortgagee or chargee needs to produce the mortgagor's land certificate which will be retained at the Land Registry. The details of the mortgage will be noted on the Charges Register of the mortgagor's title and the mortgagee will be issued a charge certificate.

(d) Legal rights of entry

A legal right of entry or re-entry is normally exercisable over a term of years or is annexed to a legal rentcharge. It is registered as appurtenant to the lessor's reversion or the rentcharge. It cannot be registered independently of the lessor's estate or the rentcharge. It is, however, not necessary even to register the legal right of entry together with the lessor's estate or the rentcharge, because the registration of the latter automatically vests in the registered proprietor of the latter all appurtenant rights.[35] Such appurtenant rights can also pass automatically to a subsequent registered transferee of the lessor's estate or the rentcharge.[36]

First registration

As mentioned above, two legal estates, a fee simple absolute in possession and a term of years absolute, are substantively registrable. This does not mean that where an area is designated a compulsory registration area, land within that area has to be registered immediately. Under s 123(1) of the Land Registration Act 1925:

> In any area in which an Order in Council declaring that registration of title to land within that area is to be compulsory on sale is for the time being in force, every conveyance on sale of freehold land and every grant of a term of years absolute of more than 21 years from the date of the delivery of the grant, and every assignment on sale of leasehold land held for a term of years absolute having more than 21 years to run from the date of delivery of the assignment, shall (save as hereinafter provided), on the expiration of two months from the date thereof or of any authorised extension of that period, become void so far as regards the grant or conveyance, grant, or assignment, or so much of such land as is situated within the area affected, unless the grantee (that is to say, the person who is entitled to be registered as proprietor of the freehold or leasehold land) or his successor in title or assign has in the meantime applied to be registered as proprietor of such land ...

Thus, it is only when there is a conveyance on sale of freehold, or a grant of a lease of more than 21 years, or an assignment of a lease having more than 21 years to run, that first registration is required. Once the freehold or leasehold is registered, any subsequent disposition of it is governed by the Land Registration Acts and must equally be registered.

35 Sections 5, 9 of the LRA 1925; LRR 1925, r 251.

36 Sections 20(1) 23(1) of the LRA 1925; LRR 1925, r 258.

All lands in England and Wales are, since 1 December 1990, compulsorily registrable. Thus, any land which remains unregistered must be registered when there is a conveyance on sale of freehold, or grant of a leasehold of more than 21 years, or an assignment of a lease with more than 21 years to run. The unregistered land is by this process gradually converted into a registered system of conveyancing.

First registration must be made within two months of the relevant conveyance. After two months, non-registration renders the conveyance of the legal estate void.[37] This means that while the title remains unregistered, the legal estate is conferred on the purchaser by the deed of conveyance. The purchaser has two months, subject to extension being granted, to register his legal estate. If he does not register it within two months of the conveyance or any extension, the legal estate will be revested in the vendor who holds it as a trustee for the purchaser. As the vendor is only a trustee, under the rule in *Saunders v Vautier*,[38] the purchaser can put an end to this trust by calling for the legal estate to be vested in him. Such a reacquisition of the legal estate is again caught by s 123(1).

In practice, however, the remedy for failure of first registration to register within two months is 'simple, effective and cheap'.[39] The Chief Land Registrar and the court may, under the proviso to s 123(1):

> ... on the application of any persons interested in any particular case in which the registrar or the court is satisfied that the application for first registration cannot be made within the said period, or can only be made within that period by incurring unreasonable expense, or that the application has not been made within the said period by reason of some accident or other sufficient cause, make an order extending the said period ...

'The Chief Land Registrar is always willing to make an order whenever some quite ordinary but reasonable excuse for the delay is put forward by the applicant.'[40] Once the Chief Land Registrar registers the purchaser as proprietor, the legal estate will be divested automatically to him.[41]

Once registered, the registered proprietor is vested with the legal estate, without any conveyance.[42] Section 69(1) of the Land Registration Act 1925 provides that:

> The proprietor of land (whether he was registered before or after the commencement of this Act) shall be deemed to have vested in him without any conveyance, where the registered land is freehold, the legal estate in fee simple in possession, and where the registered land is leasehold the legal term created by the registered lease, but subject to the overriding interests, if any, including any

37 Section 123 of the LRA 1925.

38 (1841) 4 Beav 115, 49 ER 282.

39 Ruoff and Roper, at paras 11–13.

40 Ruoff and Roper, at paras 11–13.

41 Section 69(1) of the LRA 1925.

42 Section 69 of the LRA 1925.

mortgage term or charge by way of legal mortgage created by or under the Law of Property Act 1925, or this Act or otherwise which has priority to the registered estate.

Registration takes effect as of the date of the delivery of the application to register,[43] and if s 123(1) is satisfied, any dealings, which take place between the date of the conveyance and the date of the application to register, take effect as if they had taken place after the date of the application. Before the conveyance of the legal estate and the commencement of the application for first registration, the land remains unregistered, and a contracting purchaser should protect his estate contract by a Class C(iv) land charge, or by a caution against first registration. Where the purchaser who has to effect first registration of his estate fails to do so, if his estate is charged with a mortgage or a charge, the mortgagee or chargee may apply for first registration on his behalf.[44]

(e) Freehold

Any estate owner holding an estate in fee simple, or any other person who is entitled to be vested with a legal estate in fee simple may apply to be registered as the proprietor.[45] Where a person is registered with an absolute title, he is vested with an estate in fee simple in possession with all rights, etc subject to the incumbrances appearing on the register, and overriding interests.[46] Where the registered proprietor holds the property not for his own benefit, he is also bound by any minor interests of such persons of which he has notice, even if they are not protected by entries on the register.[47]

Land Registration Act 1925

4. Application for registration of freehold land

Where the title to be registered is a title to a freehold estate in land:

(a) any estate owner holding an estate in fee simple (including a tenant for life, statutory owner, personal representative, or trustee of land) whether subject or not to incumbrances; or

(b) any other person (not being a mortgagee where there is a subsisting right of redemption or a person who has merely contracted to buy land) who is entitled to require a legal estate in fee simple whether subject or not to incumbrances, to be vested in him;

may apply to the registrar to be registered in respect of such estate, or, in the case of a person not in a fiduciary position, to have registered in his stead any nominee, as proprietor with an absolute title or with a possessory title:

43 LRR 1925, r 42.

44 LRR 1925, r 73(2).

45 Section 4 of the LRA 1925.

46 Section 5 of the LRA 1925.

47 Section 5 of the LRA 1925.

Provided that:

(i) Where an absolute title is required the applicant or his nominee shall not be registered as proprietor until and unless the title is approved by the registrar;

(ii) Where a possessory title is required, the applicant or his nominee may be registered as proprietor on giving such evidence of title and serving such notices, if any, as may for the time being be prescribed;

(iii) If, on an application for registration with possessory title, the registrar is satisfied as to the title to the freehold estate, he may register it as absolute, whether the applicant consents to such registration or not, but in that case no higher fee shall be charged than would have been charged for registration with possessory title.

Land Registration Act 1925

5. Effect of first registration with absolute title

Where the registered land is a freehold estate, the registration of any person as first proprietor thereof with an absolute title shall vest in the person so registered an estate in fee simple in possession in the land, together with rights, privileges, and appurtenances belonging or appurtenant thereto, subject to the following rights and interests, that is to say:

(a) Subject to the incumbrances, and other entries, if any, appearing on the register; and

(b) Unless the contrary is expressed on the register, subject to such overriding interests, if any, as affect the registered land; and

(c) Where the first proprietor is not entitled for his own benefit to the registered land subject, as between himself and the persons entitled to minor interests, to any minor interests of such persons of which he has notice,

but free from all other estates and interests whatsoever, including estates and interests of His Majesty.

6. Effect of first registration with possessory title

Where the registered land is a freehold estate, the registration of any person as first proprietor thereof with a possessory title only shall not affect or prejudice the enforcement of any estate, right or interest adverse to or in derogation of the title of the first proprietor, and subsisting or capable of arising at the time of registration of that proprietor; but save as aforesaid, shall have the same effect as registration of a person with an absolute title.

7. Qualified title

(1) Where an absolute title is required, and on the examination of the title it appears to the registrar that the title can be established only for a limited period, or only subject to certain reservations, the registrar may, on the application of the party applying to be registered, by an entry made in the register, except from the effect of registration any estate, right, or interest:

(a) arising before a specified date; or

(b) arising under a specified instrument or otherwise particularly described in the register, and a title registered subject to such excepted estate, right, or interest shall be called a qualified title.

(2) Where the registered land is a freehold estate, the registration of a person as first proprietor thereof with a qualified title shall have the same effect as the registration of such person with an absolute title, save that registration with a qualified title shall not affect or prejudice the enforcement of any estate, right or interest appearing by the register to be excepted.

(f) Leasehold

When a lease is registered, there will be two registrations of title affecting one piece of land, that of the fee simple, and that of the lease itself. A separate land certificate is issued in respect of the lease and the lease is noted on the Charges Register of the superior title.

Not all leases are registrable. Registration is prohibited if the lease is granted for a term of 21 years or less or if the lease is a mortgage term still subject to a right of redemption.[48]

Land Registration Act 1925

19. Registration of disposition of freeholds

(2) All interests transferred or created by dispositions by the proprietor, other than a transfer of the registered estate in the land, or part thereof, shall, subject to the provisions relating to mortgages, be completed by registration in the same manner and with the same effect as provided by this Act with respect to transfers of registered estates and notice thereof shall also be noted on the register:

Provided that nothing in this subsection:

(a) shall authorise the registration of a lease granted for a term not exceeding 21 years, or require the entry of a notice of such a lease ... ; or

(b) shall authorise the registration of a mortgage term where there is a subsisting right of redemption; or

(c) shall render necessary the registration of any easement, right, or privilege except as appurtenant to registered land, or the entry of notice thereof except as against the registered title of the servient land.

Every such disposition shall, when registered, take effect as a registered disposition, and a lease made by the registered proprietor under the last foregoing section which is not required to be registered or noted on the register shall nevertheless take effect as if it were a registered disposition immediately on being granted.

22. Registration of disposition of leaseholds

(2) All interests transferred or created by dispositions by the registered proprietor other than the transfer of his registered estate in the land or in part thereof shall (subject to the provisions relating to mortgages) be completed by registration in the same manner

48 Sections 19(2), 22(2) of the LRA 1925.

and with the same effect as provided by this Act with respect to transfers of the registered estate, and notice thereof shall also be noted on the register in accordance with this Act:

Provided that nothing in this subsection:

(a) shall authorise the registration of an underlease originally granted for a term not exceeding 21 years, or require the entry of a notice of such an underlease ... ; or

(b) shall authorise the registration of a mortgage term where there is a subsisting right of redemption; or

(c) shall render necessary the registration of any easement, right, or privilege except as appurtenant to registered land, or the entry of notice thereof except as against the registered title of the servient land.

Every such disposition shall, when registered, take effect as a registered disposition, and an underlease made by the registered proprietor which is not required to be registered or noted on the register shall nevertheless take effect as if it were a registered disposition immediately on being granted.

If the lease contains an absolute prohibition against assignment, no registration will be allowed until provision preventing any dealing in contravention of the prohibition or restriction is entered on the register.[49] Leases granted on or after 1 January 1987 for more than 21 years are now registrable.[50] This is so even if at the time the application for registration is made the lease has only 21 years or less to run.[51]

A lease registered with an absolute title gives the proprietor the leasehold interest with all implied or expressed rights etc subject to all implied and expressed covenants, obligations, and liabilities, and the incumbrances appearing on the register, and overriding interests.[52] Where the proprietor does not hold the leasehold interest for his own benefit, he is also bound by any minor interests of such persons of which he has notice.[53]

Land Registration Act 1925

8. Application for registration of leasehold land

(1) Where the title to be registered is a title to a leasehold interest in land:

(a) any estate owner (including a tenant for life, statutory owner, personal representative, or trustee of land, but not including a mortgagee where there is a subsisting right of redemption), holding under a lease for a term of years absolute of which more than 21 are unexpired, whether subject or not to incumbrances; or

49 Section 8(2) of the LRA 1925 as amended by s 3(1) of the LRA 1986,which also applies to leases granted before 1 January 1987.

50 Section 123(1) of the LRA 1925 as substituted bys 2(1) of the LRA 1986.

51 Section 8(1A) of the LRA 1925 as amended by s 2(2) LRA 1986.

52 Section 9 of the LRA 1925.

53 Section 9 of the LRA 1925.

(b) any other person (not being a mortgagee as aforesaid and not being a person who has merely contracted to buy the leasehold interest) who is entitled to require a legal leasehold estate held under such a lease as aforesaid (whether subject or not to incumbrances) to be vested in him,

may apply to the registrar to be registered in respect of such estate, or in the case of a person not being in a fiduciary position to have registered in his stead any nominee, as proprietor with an absolute title, with a good leasehold title or with a possessory title:

Provided that:

(i) Where an absolute title is required, the applicant or his nominee shall not be registered as proprietor until and unless the title both to the leasehold and to the freehold, and to any intermediate leasehold that may exist, is approved by the registrar;

(ii) Where a good leasehold title is required, the applicant or his nominee shall not be registered as proprietor until and unless the title to the leasehold interest is approved by the registrar;

(iii) Where a possessory title is required, the applicant or his nominee may be registered as proprietor on giving such evidence of title and serving such notices, if any, as may for the time being be prescribed;

(iv) If on an application for registration with a possessory title the registrar is satisfied as to the title to the leasehold interest, he may register it as good leasehold, whether the applicant consents to such registration or not, but in that case no higher fee shall be charged than would have been charged for registration with possessory title.

(1A) An application for registration in respect of leasehold land held under a lease in relation to the grant or assignment of which s 123(1) of this Act applies (whether by virtue of this Act or any later enactment) may be made within the period allowed by s 123(1), or any authorised extension of that period, notwithstanding that the lease was granted for a term of not more than 21 years or that the unexpired term of the lease is not more than 21 years.

(2) Leasehold land held under a lease containing a prohibition or restriction on dealings therewith *inter vivos* shall not be registered under this Act unless and until provision is made in the prescribed manner for preventing any dealing therewith in contravention of the prohibition or restriction by an entry on the register to that effect, or otherwise.

(3) Where on an application to register a mortgage term, wherein no right of redemption is subsisting, it appears that the applicant is entitled in equity to the superior term, if any, out of which it was created, the registrar shall register him as proprietor of the superior term without any entry to the effect that the legal interest in that term is outstanding, and on such registration the superior term shall vest in the proprietor and the mortgage term shall merge therein.

Provided that this subsection shall not apply where the mortgage term does not comprise the whole of the land included in the superior term, unless in that case the rent, if any, payable in respect of the superior term has been apportioned, or the rent is of no money value or no rent is reserved, and unless the covenants, if any, entered into for the benefit of the reversion have been apportioned (either expressly or by implication) as respects the land comprised in the mortgage term.

9. Effect of first registration with absolute title

Where the registered land is a leasehold interest, the registration under this Act of any person as first proprietor thereof with an absolute title shall be deemed to vest in such person the possession of the leasehold interest described, with all implied or expressed rights, privileges, and appurtenances attached to such interest, subject to the following obligations, rights, and interests, that is to say:

(a) Subject to all implied and express covenants, obligations, and liabilities incident to the registered land; and

(b) Subject to the incumbrances and other entries (if any) appearing on the register; and

(c) Unless the contrary is expressed on the register, subject to such overriding interests, if any, as affect the registered land; and

(d) Where such first proprietor is not entitled for his own benefit to the registered land subject, as between himself and the persons entitled to minor interests, to any minor interests of such persons of which he has notice,

but free from all other estates and interests whatsoever, including estates and interests of His Majesty.

10. Effect of first registration with good leasehold title

Where the registered land is a leasehold interest, the registration of a person as first proprietor thereof with a good leasehold title shall not affect or prejudice the enforcement of any estate, right or interest affecting or in derogation of the title of the lessor to grant the lease, but, save as aforesaid, shall have the same effect as registration with an absolute title.

11. Effect of first registration with possessory title

Where the registered land is a leasehold interest, the registration of a person as first proprietor thereof with a possessory title shall not affect or prejudice the enforcement of any estate, right, or interest (whether in respect of the lessor's title or otherwise) adverse to or in derogation of the title of such first registered proprietor, and subsisting or capable of arising at the time of the registration of such proprietor; but save as aforesaid, shall have the same effect as registration with an absolute title.

12. Qualified title

(1) Where on examination it appears to the registrar that the title, either of the lessor to the reversion or of the lessee to the leasehold interest, can be established only for a limited period, or subject to certain reservations, the registrar may, upon the request in writing of the person applying to be registered, by an entry made in the register, except from the effect of registration any estate, right or interest:

(a) arising before a specified date; or

(b) arising under a specified instrument, or otherwise particularly described in the register,

and a title registered subject to any such exception shall be called a qualified title.

(2) Where the registered land is a leasehold interest, the registration of a person as first proprietor thereof with a qualified title shall not affect or prejudice the enforcement of

any estate, right, or interest appearing by the register to be excepted, but, save as aforesaid, shall have the same effect as registration with a good leasehold title or an absolute title, as the case may be.

Subsequent dealing with registered freehold

Any subsequent transfer of the registered freehold estate must also be registered. The transfer is only completed by entering on the register the transferee as the new proprietor. Until such entry is made the transferor remains the proprietor.[54]

Land Registration Act 1925

19. Registration of disposition of freeholds

(1) The transfer of the registered estate in the land or part thereof shall be completed by the registrar entering on the register the transferee as the proprietor of the estate transferred, but until such entry is made the transferor shall be deemed to remain proprietor of the registered estate; and, where part only of the land is transferred, notice thereof shall also be noted on the register.

Subsequent dealing with registered leasehold

Any subsequent disposition of registered leasehold must also be registered. The effect of registration is set out in s 23 in respect of absolute title, good leasehold title, qualified, or possessory title.

Land Registration Act 1925

22. Registration of dispositions of leaseholds

(1) A transfer of the registered estate in the land or part thereof shall be completed by the registrar entering on the register the transferee as proprietor of the estate transferred, but until such entry is made the transferor shall be deemed to remain the proprietor of the registered estate; and where part only of the land is transferred, notice thereof shall also be noted on the register.

23. Effect of registration of dispositions of leaseholds

(1) In the case of a leasehold estate registered with an absolute title, a disposition (including a subdemise thereof) for valuable consideration shall, when registered, be deemed to vest in the transferee or underlessee the estate transferred or created to the extent of the registered estate, or for the term created by the subdemise, as the case may require, with all implied or expressed rights, privileges, and appurtenances attached to the estate transferred or created, including (subject to any entry to the contrary on the register) the appropriate rights and interests which would under the Law of Property Act 1925, have been transferred if the land had not been registered, but subject as follows:

(a) To all implied and express covenants, obligations, and liabilities incident to the estate transferred or created; and

(b) To the incumbrances and other entries (if any) appearing on the register and any charge for capital transfer for subject to which the disposition takes effect under s 73 of this Act; and

54 Section 19(1) of the LRA 1925.

(c) Unless the contrary is expressed on the register, to the overriding interests, if any, affecting the estate transferred or created,

but free from all other estates and interests whatsoever, including estates and interests of His Majesty; and the transfer or subdemise shall operate in like manner as if the registered transferor or sublessor were (subject to any entry to the contrary on the register) absolutely entitled to the registered lease for his own benefit.

(2) In the case of a leasehold estate registered with a good leasehold title, a disposition (including a subdemise thereof) for valuable consideration shall, when registered, have the same effect as it would have had if the land had been registered with an absolute title, save that it shall not affect or prejudice the enforcement of any right or interest affecting or in derogation of the lessor to grant the lease.

(3) In the case of a leasehold estate registered with a qualified title, a disposition (including a subdemise thereof) for valuable consideration shall, when registered, have the same effect as it would have had if the land had been registered with an absolute title, save that such disposition shall not affect or prejudice the enforcement of any right or interest (whether in respect of the lessor's title or otherwise) appearing by the register to be excepted.

(4) In the case of a leasehold estate registered with a possessory title, a disposition (including a subdemise thereof) for valuable consideration shall not affect or prejudice the enforcement of any right or interest (whether in respect of the lessor's title or otherwise) adverse to or in derogation of the title of the first registered proprietor, and subsisting or capable of arising at the time of the registration of such proprietor, but save as aforesaid shall, when registered, have the same effect as it would have had if the land had been registered with an absolute title.

(5) Where any such disposition is made without valuable consideration it shall, so far as the transferee or underlessee is concerned, be subject to any minor interests subject to which the transferor or sublessor held the same; but, save as aforesaid, shall, when registered, in all respects, and in particular as respects any registered dealings on the part of the transferee or underlessee, have the same effect as if the disposition had been made for valuable consideration.

It is clear from s 22(1) of the Land Registration Act 1925 that the transfer is not effective to transfer any legal estate until the transfer is registered, and until then the transferor remains the legal owner. However, in *Brown & Root Technology Ltd v Sun Alliance and London Assurance Co Ltd*,[55] the court held that once an assignment of a lease had been fully completed by a tenant (ie executed, whether or not registered), the tenant was unable to give a notice to quit under the tenancy. This was because 'the tenant/assignor gives up the property on that date; he has no control over the stamping of the transfer, or its submission to the Land Registry. He becomes a bare trustee for the assignee as regards the legal title'.[56] The court treated the act of registration as purely administrative in nature which merely perfected a title which had already been effected and completed as between the parties. This view does seem to be inconsistent with

55 [1995] 3 WLR 558.

56 *Ibid* at 571.

the principle that it is the act of registration which confers title (not the conveyance) as is evidenced by s 69(1) of the Land Registration Act 1925. Furthermore, the same argument can be made by anyone who fails to register their interests. It is therefore doubtful if this line of reasoning should be followed by subsequent cases.

5 MINOR INTERESTS

All interests in land other than legal estates and overriding interests shall take effect in equity as minor interests.[57] Minor interests are defined as interests which are not registrable and not overriding.[58]

Land Registration Act 1925

3. Interpretation

In this Act unless the context otherwise requires, the following expressions have the meanings hereby assigned to them respectively, that is to say:

(xv)'Minor interests' mean the interests not capable of being disposed of or created by registered dispositions and capable of being overridden (whether or not a purchaser has notice thereof) by the proprietors unless protected as provided by this Act, and all rights and interests which are not registered or protected on the register and are not overriding interests, and include:

(a) in the case of land subject to a trust of land, all interests and powers which are under the Law of Property Act 1925, capable of being overridden by the trustees, whether or not such interests and powers are so protected; and

(b) in the case of settled land, all interests and powers which are under the Settled Land Act 1925, and the Law of Property Act 1925, or either of them, capable of being overridden by the tenant for life or statutory owner, whether or not such interests and powers are so protected as aforesaid.

Therefore minor interests include beneficial interests under a trust of land or strict settlement, those interests in unregistered land registrable as land charges under the Land Charges Act 1972, and the rights, until registration, of those who are entitled to be registered as proprietor of registrable interests. Minor interests may be protected by entries on the register by way of restriction, notice, caution, or inhibition.[59]

Restriction

A restriction is an entry on the Proprietorship Register, which prevents dealings in registered land until certain conditions and requirements have been complied with.[60] A restriction cannot be entered if the land certificate is not lodged with

57 Section 2 of the LRA 1925.

58 Section 3(xv) of the LRA 1925.

59 Section 101(3) of the LRA 1925.

60 Section 58(1) of the LRA 1925.

the registrar.[61] A restriction is particularly appropriate to protect beneficial interests under a trust of land or strict settlement.[62] Such a restriction will normally impose the condition that the capital money be paid to at least two trustees or a trust corporation. This ensures that the purchaser cannot be registered as the new proprietor without overreaching the beneficiaries.

Notice

A notice is entered on the Charges Register. This is normally appropriate for those interests which are, in unregistered land, protected as land charges. Before a notice can be entered, however, the land certificate must be lodged with the Registry,[63] with the exception of an entry of notice to protect a spouse's statutory rights of occupation where the production of land certificate is not necessary.[64] Section 49(2) provides that interests behind a trust of land or a strict settlement which are protected by a restriction cannot be protected by a notice. Notice of any liability, right, or interest which appears to the Registrar to be of a trivial or obvious character cannot be entered.[65]

If a notice has been entered, any disposition of the land affected takes effect subject to the estate or interest protected by the notice so far as it is valid and is not overriden by the disposition.[66] Thus, an entry of notice gives the owner of the minor interest priority over any subsequent registered proprietor. It does not, however, give the owner priority over any prior unprotected minor interest. In *The Mortgage Corpn Ltd v Nationwide Credit Corpn Ltd*,[67] the Court of Appeal affirmed the Deputy judge, David Neuberger QC's decision[68] said that priority between minor interests depends on the order of creation.

The Mortgage Corporation Ltd v Nationwide Credit Corporation Ltd [1994] Ch 49, CA

Dillon LJ: This appeal, from a decision of Mr David Neuberger QC, sitting as a deputy High Court judge in the Chancery Division, raises a question of priority as between two charges on registered land. The judge held that a charge on the land in favour of the plaintiffs, Mortgage Corporation Ltd, made on 10 July 1989, had priority to a charge on the same land in favour of the defendants, Nationwide Credit Corporation Ltd, made on 31 July 1989, notwithstanding that the defendants' charge was, and the plaintiffs' was not, protected by a notice in the charges register of the title to the land under s 49 of the Land Registration Act 1925 ...

There is no difficulty as to the priorities of registered charges since s 29 of the Act of 1925 provides in clear terms that, subject to any entry to the contrary on the register,

61 Section 64(1)(c) of the LRA 1925.

62 For example, interest of a minor under a trust or will.

63 Section 64(1)(c) of the LRA 192.

64 Section 64(5) of the LRA 192 as inserted by s 4(1) of the Matrimonial Homes and Property Act 1981.

65 LRR 1925, r 199.

66 Section 52(1) of the LRA 1925.

67 [1994] Ch 49. See also *Barclays Bank Ltd v Taylor* [1974] Ch 137.

68 (1992) *The Times*, 27 July.

registered charges on the same land shall as between themselves rank according to the order in which they are entered on the register, and not according to the order in which they are created.

As regards charges, however, which for the time being are not registered charges, the first provision to be considered is s 106 of the Act, as substituted by s 26 of the Administration of Justice Act 1977. Section 106(1) to (3) provides:

> (1) The proprietor of any registered land may, subject to any entry to the contrary on the register, mortgage, by deed or otherwise, the land or any part of it in any manner which would have been permissible if the land had not been registered and, subject to this section, with the like effect. (2) Unless and until the mortgage becomes a registered charge – (a) it shall take effect only in equity, and (b) it shall be capable of being overridden as a minor interest unless it is protected as provided by sub-s (3) below. (3) A mortgage which is not a registered charge may be protected on the register by – (a) a notice under s 49 of this Act, (b) any such other notice as may be prescribed, or (c) a caution under s 54 of this Act.

The effect of that, as I understand it, is that although a charge which is protected by a notice under s 49 will no longer be capable of being overridden as a minor interest, it will still only take effect in equity unless and until it becomes a registered charge.

Subject to the effect of the registration of a notice under s 49 in respect of an equitable charge, the general rule as to the priority of equitable charges is *qui prior est tempore potior est jure*: see, for example, *Cory v Eyre* (1863) I De G J & S 149, 167, *per* Turner LJ This has been applied by this court in relation to competing equitable interests in registered land in *Barclays Bank Ltd v Taylor* [1974] Ch 137.

There is no doubt that the main purpose of protecting an equitable charge by a notice under s 49 is to affect every subsequent purchaser or encumbrancer with notice of the charge: see In *re White Rose Cottage* [1965] Ch 940, 949G, 955D–E, *per* Lord Denning MR, Harman LJ; and see also the judgment of Wilberforce J [1964] Ch 483, 491. in that case at first instance. But the actual protection accorded by the Act is apparently expressed in wider terms in certain sections. Thus s 20 of the Act, which is concerned with the effect of registration of dispositions of freeholds, provides that a disposition of the registered land for valuable consideration shall, when registered, confer on the transferee or grantee an estate in fee simple with the appropriate rights 'subject ... to the incumbrances and other entries, if any, appearing on the register'. This would include all matters protected by notices in the charges register, and *prima facie* the effect would be that if the plaintiffs had sold the land without having effected any registration or notice in the register in respect of their charge, their purchaser would have taken the land subject to the defendants' charge protected by the notice registered on 14 August 1989.

The protection of a notice appears to go even further as against the proprietor of a registered charge. Section 27 of the Act provides that a registered charge shall take effect as a charge by way of legal mortgage or may contain an express demise or sub-demise. It is then provided by sub-s (3) that:

> Any such demise or sub-demise or charge by way of legal mortgage shall take effect from the date of delivery of the deed containing the same, but subject to the estate or interest of any person (other than the proprietor of the land) whose estate or interest (whenever created) is registered or noted on the register before the date of registration of the charge.

This, standing alone, would mean that if the plaintiffs' charge in the present case had been registered as a registered charge before the sale to the purchaser, the plaintiffs' charge would have ranked subject to the defendants' charge and the moneys thereby secured, because the defendants' charge was a charge, whenever created, noted on the register before the date of (assumed) registration of the plaintiffs' charge. For the purposes of s 27(3) the dates of registration are crucial, and not the dates of the original execution of documents subsequently registered .

Mr Hodge has submitted, for the plaintiffs, that little weight can be attached to s 27(3), since s 27 was described by Lord Evershed MR in *Crace Rymer Investments Ltd v Waite* [1958] Ch 831, 849, as a section directed to procedure and form. But while that may apply to sub-ss (1) and (2) of s 27, sub-s (3) is, in my judgment, clearly directed to the effect of the charge, demise or sub-demise.

One of the oddities in the present case is that it is not clear whether the plaintiffs' charge was in fact registered as a registered charge before the sale of the property to the purchasers took place. On the one hand, there is a letter from the Land Registry of 19 March 1991, which says that the plaintiffs' charge had been substantively registered under s 26 of the Act and this is apparently echoed in a further letter from another representative of the Land Registry. On the other hand, in the only affidavit sworn in the proceedings, it is said by the plaintiffs' solicitor in relation to the plaintiffs' charge that it was lodged in the registry for registration against the title in June 1990 but the registration was still pending at the date of the affidavit, 10 June 1991, which was after completion of the sale to the purchaser.

In these circumstances, we must, I apprehend, conclude that it is not shown, on the balance of probabilities, that the plaintiffs' charge was substantially registered as a registered charge. Consequently the defendants do not bring the case within s 27(3) of the Act.

It is anyhow necessary, however, to turn to s 52 of the Act, which is concerned with the effect of notices under s 49. It provides:

> (1) A disposition by the proprietor shall take effect subject to all estates, rights, and claims which are protected by way of notice on the register at the date of the registration or entry of notice of the disposition, but only if and so far as such estates, rights, and claims may be valid and are not (independently of this Act) overridden by the disposition. (2) Where notice of a claim is entered on the register, such entry shall operate by way of notice only, and shall not operate to render the claim valid whether made adversely to or for the benefit of the registered land or charge.

The judge construed s 52(1) as applying only where the document which gave rise to the estate, right or claim protected by the notice on the register had been entered into at a date which was earlier than the date on which the disposition whose registration was in question had been made – ie, as he put it, the effect of a notice is limited to giving priority to a person who has registered the notice only in relation to interests granted subsequently to his interest.

As I read s 52(1), the opening part applies generally irrespective of the date of the execution of the document which gave rise to the estate, right or claim protected by the notice on the register or the date of the making of the rival disposition which is to be registered or to be the subject of the entry of a later notice. So far as the opening part is concerned, the only relevant date is the date of registration or entry of notice. But the general effect of the opening part is then cut down by the final proviso: 'but only if and so far as such estates, rights and claims may be valid and are not (independently of this Act) overridden by the disposition.'

In the present case, there is no difficulty over the first half of that proviso 'so far as such estates, rights and claims may be valid' since the defendants' charge is unquestionably valid. It is therefore necessary to consider the second half of the proviso 'and are not (independently of this Act) overridden by the disposition.' As I see it, independently of the Act, the defendants' charge is necessarily overridden by the plaintiffs' charge. If, by virtue of s 106, neither charge having been registered, both are regarded as taking effect only in equity, then the equitable rule as to the priorities that *qui prior est tempore potior est jure* applies; if they are considered independently even of s 106 of the Act, then they are both charges by way of legal mortgage, and the later, in time, the defendants' charge, can only take effect as a charge on the equity of redemption in the property subject to the plaintiffs' charge.

I therefore agree with the judge's conclusion, though I am not sure that I have followed quite the same course of reasoning as he did.

In my judgment s 52 is enacted to prescribe the effect of a notice entered on the register. That may not necessarily be the same as the effect of a caution since the effect of a caution is prescribed by ss 54 and 55. The effect of a notice, as determined under s 52, will cut down any apparently wider effect that the general wording in other ss such as s 20 and s 27(3) would otherwise have had. The particular qualifications imposed by the proviso to s 52(1) are, first of all, that the interest protected by the notice must be valid apart from the notice and, secondly, that the interest protected by the notice would not independently of the Act be overridden by the rival disposition. Notice is indeed notice, but it does not give validity, if validity is not otherwise there, and it does not give priority which would not, apart from the Act, have been there. Therefore, the plaintiffs' charge has priority to the defendants' charge.

Caution

A caution can be entered on the Proprietorship Register.[69] It is appropriate for almost all types of minor interest, particularly where the registered proprietor, whose land is charged with the minor interest, refuses to co-operate by withholding his land certificate. No land certificate is needed to lodge a caution.[70]

There are two types of caution: caution against dealings and caution against first registration. Caution against dealings is appropriate where the title of the incumbered land is already registered. Once a caution against dealings is lodged, no future dealing with the land can be registered until the proprietor has served notice on the cautioner about his intended registration and the cautioner makes no objection to the dealing within a prescribed period of 14 days.[71] The cautioner is therefore given an opportunity to substantiate his claim within 14 days. If he succeeds, his interest which was previously protected by way of caution can now be given a superior and permanent form of protection

69 Section 54 of the LRA 1925.

70 Section 64(1)(c) of the LRA 1925.

71 Section 55 of the LRA 1925.

such as by way of notice or restriction. If he fails to substantiate his claim, the new proprietor will take free from his interest.

Where the land is not already registered, caution against first registration is more appropriate. Any person having or claiming an interest in it may lodge a caution with the registrar to the effect that first registration shall not be made until notice has been served on the cautioner and the latter makes no objection within 14 days.[72]

The registration of a caution merely gives the cautioner a right to be given notice of any proposed dealings. It does not give him priority over a subsequent registered charge.[73] If the subsequent charge is registered by the Land Registry without giving notice to the cautioner, the cautioner's remedy will be to sue the Chief Land Registrar for indemnity under s 83 of the Land Registration Act 1925.[74]

Inhibition

This form of entry which is entered on the proprietorship register has the effect of precluding any dealing with the title until the occurrence of certain specified events or until further court order. It is, however, rarely used. It is used in cases where the registered proprietor's land certificate has been lost or stolen, or where there has been a fraudulent dealing with the title. It is also commonly used in cases of bankruptcy to prevent the bankrupt from disposing of his land.

Effect of failure to protect a minor interest by an appropriate entry

Land Registration Act 1925

20. Effect of registration and dispositions of freeholds

(1) In the case of a freehold estate registered with an absolute title, a disposition of the registered land or of a legal estate therein, including a lease thereof, for valuable consideration shall, when registered, confer on the transferee or grantee an estate in fee simple or the term of years absolute or other legal estate expressed to be created in the land dealt with, together with all rights, privileges, and appurtenances belonging or appurtenant thereto, including (subject to any entry to the contrary in the register) the appropriate rights and interests which would, under the Law of Property Act 1925, have been transferred if the land had not been registered, subject:

(a) to the incumbrances and other entries, if any, appearing on the register and any charge for capital transfer tax subject to which the disposition takes effect under s 73 of this Act; and

(b) unless the contrary is expressed on the register, to the overriding interests, if any, affecting the estate transferred or created,but free from all other estates and interests whatsoever, including estates and interests of His Majesty, and the disposition shall

72 Section 53 of the LRA 1925.

73 *Chancery plc v Ketteringham* (1995) 69 P & CR 426.

74 *Clark v Chief Land Registrar* (1994) *The Times*, 10 May; [1994] 4 All ER 96, CA

operate in like manner as if the registered transferor or grantor were (subject to any entry to the contrary in the register) entitled to the registered land in fee simple in possession for his own benefit.

59. Writs, orders, deeds of arrangement, pending actions, etc

(6) Subject to the provisions of this Act relating to fraud and to the title of a trustee in bankruptcy, a purchaser acquiring title under a registered disposition, shall not be concerned with any pending action, writ, order, deed of arrangement, or other document, matter, or claim (not being an overriding interest or a charge for capital transfer tax subject to which the disposition takes effect under s 73 of this Act) which is not protected by a caution or other entry on the register, whether he has or has not notice thereof, express, implied, or constructive.

Thus, where a minor interest is not protected, it is void against a transferee or grantee, or a purchaser for valuable consideration. It is not void against a volunteer.[75] Neither s 20 nor s 59(6) makes any reference to the transferee or purchaser's 'notice' or knowledge of the unprotected minor interest. Cross J made it clear in *Strand Securities Ltd v Caswell* that it is 'vital to the working of the land registration system that notice of something which is not on the register should not affect a transferee unless it is an overriding interest'.[76] As Lord Wilberforce declared in *Williams & Glyn's Bank v Boland*, 'the law as to notice as it might affect purchasers of unregistered land, whether in decided cases or in a statute, has no application, even by analogy, to registered land'.[77]

However, it is clear that where there is fraud or bad faith on the part of the purchaser, an unprotected minor interest may still affect him.[78] It had always been understood that notice was not equivalent to fraud, until the decision of Graham J in *Peffer v Rigg*.[79]

Peffer v Rigg [1977] 1 WLR 285

Graham J: The purported transfer, however, of the whole of the beneficial interest in the property by the first defendant to the second defendant on the occasion of the divorce agreement in the light of their knowledge of the true facts as I have found them, seems to me to be in a very different position. It was argued by Mr Banks, for the second defendant, that the property was transferred to her for valuable consideration as part of the divorce agreement and that, therefore, the combined effect of ss 20 and 59 of the Land Registration Act 1925 protected the second defendant against any claim or interest of the plaintiff because there is no entry on the register in his favour prior to the transfer

75 Section 20(4) of the LRA 1925.

76 [1965] Ch 373, at 390A–B.

77 [1981] AC 487, at 504B

78 *De Lusignan v Johnson* (1973) 230 *Estates Gazette* 499. See [1985] CLJ 280 (Thompson, MP).

79 [1977] 1 WLR 285. See (1977) 41 Conv (NS) 207 (Crane, FR); (1977) 93 LQR 341 (Smith, RJ); [1977] CLJ 227 (Hayton, DJ); [1978] Conv 52 (Martin, J). Even in the context of unregistered land, Lord Wilberforce had said in *Midland Bank Trust Co Ltd v Green* [1981] 1 All ER 153 that notice of an unregistered land charge was not relevant. Despite the fact that under s 4(5) or 4(6) of the LCA a purchaser must act in good faith, notice was not treated as equivalent to bad faith. On the contrary, Lord Wilberforce thought that taking a legal advantage was not fraud or bad faith.

to the second defendant. This argument would be convincing if it were not for my finding that the second defendant at the time knew perfectly well that the first defendant could not transfer to her more than a half share of the property. It is this knowledge which seems to me to cause great difficulty to her and prevents her argument succeeding for a number of different reasons put forward by Mr Poulton for the plaintiff at the second hearing. He argues first that the purported transfer from the first defendant to the second defendant of the beneficial interest of the whole of the property of 103, Leighton Road was expressed to be for the consideration of £1. This is a nominal consideration and not valuable consideration and it follows that the second defendant is not protected by s 20 of the Land Registration Act 1925. In accordance with the provisions of s 20(4) she can only take subject to any minor interests subject to which the first defendant held the same. He was party to the trust deed of 30 May 1968, and clearly had notice of the plaintiff's half interest in the property. The second defendant can therefore only take subject to the minor interest of the plaintiff in the property subject to which the first defendant held it.

The argument to the contrary is that the transfer was only part of the whole agreement entered into by the first and second defendants on the occasion of the divorce and it is not therefore right to limit the consideration for the transfer to the £1 expressed to be therefor. The consideration, there, was a great deal more and included all the obligations undertaken by the second defendant. Such consideration was therefore not nominal but valuable within s 20 and the second defendant received the protection of the section. I do not see why, when the parties have chosen to express a transfer as being for a nominal consideration, the court should seek to hold that the consideration was in fact otherwise than as agreed and stated. If, however, the proper view is that there was valuable consideration for the transfer here, then it is argued as follows. There is a contrast between ss 20 and 59 of the Act. Section 20(1) protects any 'transferee' for valuable consideration. By s 18(5) 'transfer' and 'transferee' in relation to freehold land have very wide meanings but are not specifically defined in s 3. It is to be noted, however, that s 20, though it mentions valuable consideration, does not mention 'good faith' as being necessary on the part of the transferee, nor does it mention notice. It can be argued therefore that the section seems to be saying that a transferee whether he has good faith or not, and whether he has notice or not, takes free of all interests (other than overriding interests) provided he has given valuable consideration.

This at first sight seems a remarkable proposition and though undoubtedly the property legislation of 1925 was intended to simplify such matters of title as far as possible, I find it difficult to think that s 20 of this Act can have been intended to be as broad in scope as this. Similar doubt is expressed in Brickdale and Stewart-Wallace's *Land Registration Act 1925*, 4th edn, 1939, p 107, note (1). The provisions for rectification in s 82 as against a proprietor in possession who has been a party to a fraud, mistake or an omission in consequence of which rectification of the register is sought also seems to me to show that s 20 must be read with some limitations: see also Ruoff, TBF and Roper, *Law and Practice of Registered Conveyancing*, 3rd edn, 1972, London: Stevens, p 417. Section 59(6) on the other hand speaks of a "purchaser" not being affected by matters which are not protected by a caution or other entry on the register. By definition, however (see s 3(xxi)), 'purchaser' means a purchaser in good faith for valuable consideration. It seems clear therefore that as a matter of construction a purchaser who is not in fact one 'in good faith' *will* be concerned with matters not protected by a caution or other entry on the register, at any rate, as I hold, if he has notice thereof. If these ss 20 and 59 are read together in the context of the Act they can be reconciled by holding that if the 'transferee' spoken of in s 20 is in fact a 'purchaser' he will only be protected if he has given valuable consideration and is in good faith. He cannot in my judgment be in good faith if he has in fact notice of something which affects his title as in the present case. Of course, if he and, *a fortiori*, if a purchaser from him has given valuable consideration and in fact has no notice he is under no obligation to go behind the register, and will in such a case be fully protected. This view of the matter seems to me to enable the two sections to be construed consistently together without producing the unreasonable result of permitting a transferee purchaser to take advantage of the Act, and divest himself of knowledge of defects in his own title, and secure to himself a flawless title which he ought not in justice to be allowed to obtain. This view of the Act produces a result which is also produced by applying the principles applicable in the case of a constructive trust, which I will now consider.

On the evidence in this case, I have found that the second defendant knew quite well that the first defendant held the property on trust for himself and the plaintiff in equal shares. The second defendant knew this was so and that the property was trust property when the transfer was made to her, and therefore she took the property on a constructive trust in accordance with general equitable principles: see Snell's *Principles of Equity*, 27th edn, 1973, pp 98-99. This is a new trust imposed by equity and is distinct from the trust which bound the first defendant. Even if, therefore, I am wrong as to the proper construction of ss 20 and 59, when read together, and even if s 20 strikes off the shackles of the express trust which bound the first defendant, this cannot invalidate the new trust imposed on the second defendant.

On this assumption it seems to me that the ground is properly laid for granting rectification of the register under s 82. The second defendant, even though in possession, comes within the exceptions of sub-s (3) and this would in my judgment be a case where rectification could properly be ordered against her. Mr Reid, for the first defendant, supported the propositions of Mr Poulton and adopted his argument. In addition he referred to *Jones v Lipman* [1962] 1 WLR 832, which, he submitted, could only have been decided on the basis that the company in that case could not escape from, or divest itself of, its knowledge by reason of ss 20 and 59. It seems that this must be so, and Russell J mentions and rejects the argument at 837 ...

It follows that in my judgment the second defendant holds the property in question in trust for herself and the plaintiff and that the latter is entitled to appropriate relief. I will hear the parties' submission as to the form this relief should take.

Where appropriate, the court may also impose a constructive trust on the legal owner in favour of a claimant whose interest has not been properly protected as a minor interest. In *Lyus v Prowsa Developments Ltd*,[80] a developer having mortgaged his registered land plot 29, contracted to build a house on it and sell it to the plaintiffs. The developer went insolvent and the mortgagee sold the land, in 1979, to the first defendants 'subject to and with the benefit of the plaintiffs' contract, even though the mortgagee was not bound by the contract. The first defendants in turn sold the land to the second defendants in similar

80 [1982] 1 WLR 1044.

terms. Dillon J held that the defendants were bound by the plaintiffs' contract even though the contract was not protected as a minor interest because they have agreed to take subject to it and the Land Registration Act 1925 could not be used as an instrument of fraud.

Lyus v Prowsa Developments Ltd [1982] 1 WLR 1044

Dillon J: [Having applied *Bannister v Bannister* [1948] 2 All ER 133 and a *dictum* of Lord Denning MR in *Binions v Evans* [1972] Ch 359 at 368; [1972] 2 All ER 70 at 76, continued:]

This does not, however, conclude the matter since I also have to consider the effect of the provisions of the Land Registration Act 1925, Plot 29 having at all material times, as I have mentioned, been registered land. In the course of the argument, emphasis was laid on the effect of s 34(4) of the Land Registration Act 1925, which is concerned with the effect on subsequent interests of a transfer of registered land by a mortgagee. Section 34 has, however, to be read with s 20, which is concerned with the effect of the registration of a transfer of registered land by the registered proprietor. The protection conferred by s 34 on a transfer by a mortgagee is thus additional to the protection which is conferred by s 20 on registration of a transfer by a registered proprietor.

It has been pointed out by Lord Wilberforce in *Midland Bank Trust Co Ltd v Green* [1981] AC 513 at 531; [1981] 1 All ER 153 at 159, that it is not fraud to rely on legal rights conferred by Act of Parliament. Under s 20, the effect of the registration of the transferee of a freehold title is to confer an absolute title subject to entries on the register and overriding interests, but, 'free from all other estates and interests whatsoever, including estates and interests of His Majesty ...' In *Miles v Bull (No 2)* [1969] 3 All ER 1585, Bridge J expressed the view that the words which I have quoted embraced, *prima facie*, not only all kinds of legal interests, but all kinds of equitable interests: see p 1589. He therefore held at 1590, as I read his judgment, that actual or constructive notice on the part of a purchaser of an unregistered interest would not have the effect of imposing a constructive trust on him. The interest in *Miles v Bull (No 2)* was the interest in the matrimonial home of a deserted wife who had failed to protect her interest by registration under the Matrimonial Homes Act 1967 [(now the Matrimonial Homes Act 1983)]. The contract for sale between the husband, who was the registered proprietor, and the purchaser provided that the house concerned was sold subject to such rights of occupation as might subsist in favour of the wife, with a proviso that this was not to imply that the wife had, or would after completion have any such rights as against the purchaser. Plainly, therefore, the clause was only included in the contract for the protection of the husband who was the vendor. The wife was to get no fresh rights, and it was not in *Miles v Bull (No 2)* a stipulation of the bargain between the vendor and the purchaser that the purchaser should give effect to the rights as against the vendor of the deserted wife. *Miles v Bull (No 2)* is thus distinguishable from the facts of the present case as I interpret those facts.

It seems to me that the fraud on the part of the defendants in the present case lies not just in relying on the legal rights conferred by an Act of Parliament, but in the first defendant relying on a positive stipulation in favour of the plaintiffs in the bargain under which the first defendant acquired the land. That makes, as it seems to me, all the difference. It has long since been held, for instance, in *Rochefoucauld v Boustead* [1897] 1 Ch 196, that the provisions of the Statute of Frauds 1677 now incorporated in certain sections of the Law of Property Act 1925, cannot be used as an instrument of fraud, and that it is fraud for a person to whom land is agreed to be conveyed as trustee for another to deny the trust and relying on the terms of the statute to claim the land for himself. *Rochefoucauld v Boustead* was one of the authorities on which the judgment in *Bannister v Bannister* [1948] 2 All ER 133 was founded.

It seems to me that the same considerations are applicable in relation to the Land Registration Act 1925. If, for instance, the agreement of 18 October 1979, between the bank and the first defendant had expressly stated that the first defendant would hold Plot 29 upon trust to give effect for the benefit of the plaintiffs to the plaintiffs' agreement with the vendor company, it would be difficult to say that that express trust was over-reached and rendered nugatory by the Land Registration Act 1925. The Land Registration Act 1925 does not, therefore, affect the conclusion which I would otherwise have reached in reliance on *Bannister v Bannister* and the judgment of Lord Denning MR in *Binions v Evans* [1972] Ch 359; [1972] 2 All ER 70 had Plot 29 been unregistered land.

The plaintiffs are, therefore, entitled to succeed in this action. The appropriate relief in that event is that specific performance should be ordered as against the second defendants of the sale to the plaintiffs of Plot 29, with the completed house thereon, on the terms of the agreement of 30 January 1978, made between the plaintiffs and the vendor company.

In *Lyus*, the purchasers clearly agreed to take subject to a third party's rights for the benefit of the third party as the mortgagee intended the third party's contract be honoured. However, in most other cases, in agreeing to take subject to a third party's rights, the purchaser is simply promising to the seller not to raise any objections if it transpires that the third party's rights exist and he is bound by them. In such a case, the Court of Appeal held in *Ashburn Anstalt v Arnold* that a mere agreement to take subject to a third party would not be enough to give rise to a constructive trust, unless the purchaser's conscience was affected. Where the purchaser is able to negotiate a lower price by agreeing to take subject to the third party's rights, as in *Binions v Evans*, a constructive trust may be imposed.

6 OVERRIDING INTERESTS

This is a group of interests which are not recorded on the register but are nevertheless binding on the transferee. They are supposed to be interests which are readily discoverable by any person who bothered to go and look at the property.[81] The transferor is normally bound to disclose any overriding interest he knew (both under open contract rule and the standard conditions of sale). But the transferee still has to find out, by inspection and enquiries, those which the seller did not know. Section 3(xvi) defines overriding interests as:

> all the incumbrances, interests, rights, and powers not entered on the register but subject to which registered dispositions are by this Act to take effect ...

The effect of an overriding interest is that it binds any subsequent registered dispositions. This is so even if the holder of an overriding interest has signed a consent form to postpone his rights to those of the subsequent transferee, unless

81 *Lloyds Bank plc v Rosset* [1989] Ch 350 at 394G, 402B.

a provision to that effect is 'expressed on the register'.[82] Overriding interests are listed under s 70(1) of the Land Registration Act 1925. If an overriding interest does appear on the register, then, by definition, it ceases to be an overriding interest and takes effect as a minor interest. Beneficial interests under a strict settlement take effect as minor interests and not otherwise; they cannot be overriding interests.[83] Likewise, a spouse's statutory right of occupation cannot be an overriding interest.[84] There are other statutory restrictions. Thus, any notice served by a qualifying tenant for the exercise of the right to buy the landlord's freehold or a long leasehold, or a public housing sector secure tenant's right to buy a freehold or long leasehold cannot be overriding interests.

Land Registration Act 1925

70. Liability of registered land to overriding interests

(1) All registered land shall, unless under the provisions of this Act the contrary is expressed on the register, be deemed to be subject to such of the following overriding interests as may be for the time being subsisting in reference thereto, and such interests shall not be treated as incumbrances within the meaning of this Act, (that is to say):

(a) Rights of common, drainage rights, customary rights (until extinguished), public rights, profits *à prendre*, rights of sheepwalk, rights of way, watercourses, rights of water, and other easements not being equitable easements required to be protected by notice on the register;

(b) Liability to repair highways by reason of tenure, quit-rents, crown rents, heriots, and other rents and charges (until extinguished) having their origin in tenure;

(c) Liability to repair the chancel of any church;

(d) Liability in respect of embankments, and sea and river walls;

(e) ... payments in lieu of tithe, and charges or annuities payable for the redemption of tithe rentcharges;

(f) Subject to the provisions of this Act, rights acquired or in course of being acquired under the Limitation Acts;

(g) The rights of every person in actual occupation of the land or in receipt of the rents and profits thereof, save where enquiry is made of such person and the rights are not disclosed;

(h) In the case of a possessory, qualified, or good leasehold title, all estates, rights, interests, and powers excepted from the effect of registration;

(i) Rights under local land charges unless and until registered or protected on the register in the prescribed manner;

(j) Rights of fishing and sporting, seignorial and manorial rights of all descriptions (until extinguished), and franchises;

82 *Woolwich Building Society v Dickman* [1996] 3 All ER 204.

83 Section 86(2) of the LRA 1925.

84 Section 2(8)(b) of the Matrimonial Homes Act 1983.

(k) Leases granted for a term not exceeding 21 years;

(l) In respect of land registered before the commencement of this Act, rights to mines and minerals, and rights of entry, search, and user, and other rights and reservations incidental to or required for the purpose of giving full effect to the enjoyment of rights to mines and minerals or of property in mines or minerals, being rights which, where the title was first registered before the first day of January, eighteen hundred and ninety-eight, were created before that date, and where the title was first registered after the thirty-first day of December, eighteen hundred and ninety-seven, were created before the date of first registration:

Provided that, where it is proved to the satisfaction of the registrar that any land registered or about to be registered is exempt from land tax, or tithe rentcharge or payments in lieu of tithe, or from charges or annuities payable for the redemption of tithe rentcharge, the registrar may notify the fact on the register in the prescribed manner.

Some categories of overriding interests need to be mentioned:

Section 70(1)(a)

This covers many types of rights and privileges, including legal easements, legal or equitable profit *à prendre*. On the face of it, it seems that s 70(1)(a) does not cover equitable easements. But r 258 of the Land Registration Rules 1925, which is given the same statutory force as if enacted in the Land Registration Act 1925 by s 144(2) of the Act, provides that:

> Rights, privileges, and appurtenances appertaining or reputed to appertain to land or demised, occupied, or enjoyed therewith or reputed or known as part or parcel of or appurtenant thereto, which adversely affect registered land, are overriding interests within s 70 of the Act, and shall not be deemed incumbrances for the purposes of the Act.

Scott J was therefore of the view, in *Celsteel Ltd v Alton House Holdings Ltd*,[85] that a right of way 'openly enjoyed and exercised' and adversely affecting registered land is categorised as an overriding interest and does not need to be protected by an entry of notice on the register. Because it is not an easement which needs to be protected by an entry of notice on the register, it is an overriding interest under s 70(1)(a). Although the equitable easement in *Celsteel* was openly enjoyed, this is not a requirement of r 258. This could subject a purchaser to a variety of undiscoverable rights.

'Public rights', for the purposes of s 70(1)(a), are rights exercisable by anyone, whether he owns land or not, merely by virtue of the general law. An agreement which purports to confer rights for the benefit of the public which are, however, not exercisable at the time of the agreement cannot be regarded as 'public rights', so that rights under such an agreement cannot be overriding but must be protected by caution or notice.[86]

---

85 [1985] 1 WLR 204. See [1986] Conv 31 (Thompson, MP). For an extract of Scott J's judgment, see Chapter 15, pp 702–03 below.

86 *Overseas Investment Services Ltd v Simcobuild Construction Ltd and Swansea City Council* (1995) 70 P & CR 322.

Section 70(1)(f)

This covers the 'rights acquired or in the course of being acquired under the Limitation Acts'. In *Bridges v Mees*,[87] the purchaser contracted to buy from the vendor his registered freehold, paid the purchase price and moved into possession for nearly 20 years. The vendor never transferred his registered title to the purchaser and the purchaser never protected his estate contract. Later the vendor transferred his registered title to the defendant who was registered as the new proprietor. Harman J held that the defendant was bound by the purchaser's overriding interest under s 70(1)(f).

Bridges v Mees [1957] Ch 475

Harman J having stated the facts, read the following judgment: The result of the transactions which I have described is, admittedly, that the defendant is seised of the property for an estate in fee simple in possession. This is so even if the plaintiff has acquired by possession a right to the property under the Limitation Act 1939; for, this being registered land, the defendant gets the title which the register gives him, even though the title of the transferor would, in the case of unregistered land, have been extinguished by virtue of s 16 of the Limitation Act 1939. It is provided by s 75 of the Land Registration Act 1925, that the registered proprietor's title shall not be extinguished after time has run, but shall be held on trust for the person who, if the land were unregistered, would have acquired a title by adverse possession. It follows (and s 69 of the Land Registration Act so enacts) that the defendant, as proprietor, is seised for an estate in fee simple in possession, subject, however, to what is called any 'overriding interest'.

[His Lordship read s 70(1)(f) and (g).]

It is the plaintiff's claim that he is entitled to an overriding interest under one or both of the subsections I have read. As to the former, his claim is that when he entered into possession in 1936 under the contract to buy made in that year, that, no doubt, was by the permission of the vendor, who retained a lien on the property for the purchase money. By 1937, however, the plaintiff had paid off by instalments all the purchase money and the lien disappeared and he became, he says, the sole beneficial owner. The vendor retained the legal estate which entitled him *prima facie* to resume possession, but as he did not exercise that right for 12 years, the plaintiff says it was extinguished and at the end of that time he became a trustee of the legal estate for the purchaser (that is to say, the plaintiff) as above described. If that be right, the defendant is in no better position; but his answer is that the plaintiff's possession did not ripen into ownership, because it was not 'adverse', on the ground that possession can only be adverse if it be not referable to a lawful right. For this proposition, the defendant referred me to *Thomas v Thomas*,[88] as approved by *Corea v Appuhamy*.[89]

As to this, I am of opinion that so far the plaintiff's claim is right. No doubt possession, when originally taken, may be referred to the vendor's leave and licence, but this

87 [1957] Ch 475.

88 (1855) 2 K & J 79.

89 [1912] AC 230.

position is altered when the vendor's lien disappeared. The defendant, however, further points out that by s 10 of the Limitation Act, 1939, this is enacted: 'No right of action to recover land shall be deemed to accrue unless the land is in the possession of some person in whose favour the period of limitation can run (hereafter in this section referred to as 'adverse possession').' Can it therefore be said that the plaintiff is a person in whose favour the period of limitation 'can run'? For the answer to this, reference must be made to s 7(3) of the Limitation Act.

[His Lordship read s 7(3) of the Limitation Act, 1939 (now s 18(3) of the Limitation Act 1980, see p 182 above), and continued.]

In this case the vendor became a trustee of the legal estate in 1936, and from 1937 a bare trustee, and no beneficiary had any right of action to recover. It seems to me to follow that from that date the period of limitation could and therefore did run in favour of the beneficial owner and that thus (but for the provisions as to registered land) the trustee's title would have been extinguished in 1949.

[His Lordship also concluded that the plaintiff was entitled to an overriding interest under s 70(1)(g) by virtue of the 1936 contract coupled with his actual occupation.]

Section 70(1)(g)

This is perhaps the most important type of overriding interest. Its purpose is to protect the interest of anyone who is in actual occupation or who is in receipt of rents and profits. A purchaser can only take free of such persons' rights if he has made inquiry of them and the rights are not disclosed. If, at the time when the purchaser inspects the property, the occupiers are not present so that the purchaser cannot make inquiry of them, he is still bound by their overriding interest. This is stricter than the case in unregistered land, where the purchaser only has to make reasonable inspection of the property, and inquiry of any persons in the premises, unless there is other evidence to suggest that there may be other persons who have an interest in the property but who are currently absent from it.[90]

As a registered proprietor takes subject to the overriding interests which exist at the time of registration,[91] it seems clear that an overriding interest crystallises at the date of registration.[92] The application of this rule to s 70(1)(g) would, however, have created a conveyancing absurdity, because the registration is bound to be some time after the purchase has been completed, there was a danger that any overriding interest may arise between the date of the completion of a transaction and the date of registration of it. This danger

90 An example is *Kingsnorth Finance v Tizard* [1986] 2 All ER 54, where the bank was bound by the wife's interest because, although it inspected the house while the wife was absent from the premises, and all evidence of her occupation had been eliminated, two children were present at the premises, and this was contrary to the husband's declaration in the loan application which described him as being 'single'. Had the children not been there, the bank might have discharged their duty to make inquiry.

91 That is the date of the delivery at the Land Registry of the application for registration: LRR 1925, rr 42 and 83(2).

92 [1991] 1 AC 56 at 87C.

was particularly acute with regard to the position of a mortgagee. When the mortgage is created, it has to be registered and it is bound to be registered at a date later than the date of completion of the mortgage. The registration gap would have allowed a person who has an interest in the mortgaged property to claim an overriding interest against the mortgagee if he moves into actual occupation during the gap. There is no way the mortgagee can prevent this. Neither could he have discovered his existence before the mortgage was granted. This danger is now removed by the House of Lords in *Abbey National Building Society v Cann*.[93] It was held that although an overriding interest takes effect at the date of registration of a registrable interest, the actual occupation of the person who claims an adverse interest must exist at the date of the completion and must still subsist at the later date of registration.[94]

Abbey National Building Society v Cann [1991] 1 AC 56, HL

Lord Bridge: The most important and most difficult question which arises for decision concerns the date at which to determine, in relation to the transfer or creation of a legal estate in registered land, what are the subsisting overriding interests in the land to which the estate transferred or created will be subject. One might be forgiven for starting from the a priori assumption that on its true construction the Land Registration Act 1925 must be capable of yielding a single answer to that question in the sense either that the transferee or chargee takes subject to overriding interests subsisting at the date of transfer or creation of the estate and free of overriding interests created between that date and the date of registration or that he takes subject to all overriding interests subsisting at the date of registration. But neither of these single answers will do. As my noble and learned friends cogently demonstrate, to adopt either answer and apply it to all overriding interests across the board would produce at least one conveyancing absurdity. Thus, it would be a conveyancing absurdity that the purchaser of a legal estate should take subject to the rights under s 70(l)(g) of any person who was not in occupation at the date of purchase so that the purchaser could know nothing of his existence. But it would equally be a conveyancing absurdity that the purchaser should not be subject, pursuant to s 70(1)(i), to rights under local land charges arising between the date of his purchase and the date of registration which, by virtue of the statutes creating them, bind all interests for the time being subsisting in the land.

I am entirely satisfied that it must be right to avoid both these conveyancing absurdities. But I confess that I have difficulty in finding any wholly convincing and consistent construction of the statute which achieves this result. it seems to me that it makes better sense of the scheme of the Act in relation to overriding interests if one can regard the rule to be applied to an overriding interest under para (g) of s 70(1), ie that it will only affect the legal estate if it was subsisting as such at the date when the estate was transferred or created, as an example of the general rule, and the contrary rule to be applied under para (i) as the exception. This avoids other conveyancing absurdities which would arise if the transferor of the legal estate could, between the date of transfer and the date of registration, create new overriding interests, such as profits *à prendre* or easements under para (a), rights of fishing or sporting under para (j) or leases under para

93 [1991] 1 AC 56. See [1990] CLJ 397 (Oakley, AJ); (1990) 106 LQR 545 (Smith, RJ).

94 [1991] 1 AC 56 at 88C–H.

(k), which would affect the estate in the hands of the transferee. One does not, of course, expect conveyancing absurdities from the pens of the skilled parliamentary draftsmen who implemented Lord Birkenhead's great scheme for the reform of English real property law embodied in the 1925 legislation, but even they may have occasionally expressed their complex interlocking concepts in forms of words which do not precisely fit every case. If the choice is between accepting a conveyancing absurdity on the one hand and straining or even modifying the draftsman's language to avoid it on the other hand, I have no doubt that the latter alternative is to be preferred. For the present, however, I need do no more than express my concurrence in the opinion that a person not in actual occupation of land at the date when a legal estate in the land is transferred or created cannot substantiate a claim to an overriding interest in the land under s 70(1)(g) against the transferee or chargee.

Lord Oliver of Aylemerton: My Lords, this appeal raises yet again what has become a familiar hazard for banks and building societies advancing money on the security of real property. The respondent society is the proprietor of a registered charge on property at 7 Hillview, South Lodge Avenue, Mitcham, Greater London, securing a sum of £25,000 together with interest. The property is leasehold and the title is registered at H M Land Registry under the provisions of the Land Registration Acts 1925 to 1986. The registered proprietor and the chargor under the society's charge is the son of the first appellant and the charge was given by him on the completion of his purchase of the property on 13 August 1984 in order to enable him to complete the purchase. The chargor was registered as proprietor of the property on 13 September 1984 simultaneously with the registration of the society as proprietors of the charge. The chargor having defaulted in payment of principal and interest, the society sought to enforce their security and on 5 August 1987 commenced proceedings for possession of the property against the chargor in the Croydon County Court. In fact the chargor had never lived in the property, which had been purchased by him for the occupation of the first appellant, his mother, and the second appellant, the gentleman whom she subsequently married. At all material times since the completion of the purchase they had occupied the property as their home and it was therefore necessary to join them as defendants to the proceedings. Their defence was that they had an equitable interest in the property which took priority over the interest of the society and was binding on the society as an overriding interest by virtue of their occupation of the property having regard to the provisions of ss 23(1) and 70(1)(g) of the Land Registration Act 1925 ...

In the Court of Appeal, Mrs Cann's claim failed because, in the view of all members of the court, she was aware that the balance of the purchase price of 7 Hillview, over and above the net amount to be produced by the sale of 30 Island Road, was going to be raised by George Cann by mortgage of the premises. Having thus impliedly authorised him to raise this amount on mortgage she must necessarily have authorised him to that extent to create a charge to the society having priority to her interest and could not, as against the society, complain that George had exceeded a limitation on his authority of which the society was unaware. Dillon LJ, however, took the view that the events which took place between 11.45 am and 12.20 pm on 13 August did constitute actual occupation of the property by Mrs Cann sufficient to enable her to claim an overriding interest, a proposition which was doubted by Ralph Gibson and Woolf LJJ.

If, of course, the ground on which the Court of Appeal rejected Mr and Mrs Cann's claim to resist an order for possession in the society's favour is correct, it is strictly unnecessary to determine any of the other points which arise, but since they have been fully argued and having regard to the pending appeal in *Lloyds Bank plc v Rosset*, which immediately follows this appeal, it is desirable that then, should be decided.

First in logical order is the question of the appropriate date for ascertaining the existence of overriding interests under the Land Registration Acts. Curiously enough the point appears never to have arisen directly for decision in any reported case prior to *Rosset's case*, save in one case in 1985 in the Bristol County Court which was decided on appeal on a different point (see *Paddington Building Society v Mendelsohn* (1985) 50 P & CR 244). In *Re Boyle's Claim* [1961] 1 All ER 620 at 623–24; [1961] 1 WLR 339 at 344, Wilberforce J expressed the view that the relevant date was the date of acquisition of the registered title, but the issue in that case was quite a different one and the point does not appear to have been argued. That case has, however, been used as the basis for statements in a number of leading conveyancing textbooks that that is the date at which occupation for the purposes of s 70(1)(g) has to be ascertained (see, for example, Wolstenholme and Cherry's *Conveyancing Statutes*, 13th edn, 1972, vol 6, p 65 and Emmet on *Title*, 19th edn, 1986, para 5.197). The question arose directly in *Rosset's* case, in which the Court of Appeal decided unanimously that the relevant date was the date of completion of the purchase and not that of registration. Your Lordships are now invited to overrule that decision.

My Lords, the conclusion at which the Court of Appeal arrived makes good conveyancing sense and, speaking for myself, I should be extremely reluctant to overrule it unless compulsively driven to do so, the more so because it produces a result which is just, convenient and certain, as opposed to one which is capable of leading to manifest injustice and absurdity. It has, I think, to be acknowledged that the interrelation between the provisions of ss 3(xvi), 20 and 23, 37, 69 and 70(1) is not altogether easy to understand, particularly in relation to the position of a chargee whose charge is created by a purchaser of land who is not yet himself the registered proprietor. The solution propounded by the trial judge and by counsel for the bank in *Rosset's* case depends on the words 'affecting the estate transferred or created' in ss 20(1)(b) and 23(1)(c) and construes them as if there were added the words 'at the time at which it was transferred or created', thus excluding from the category of interests affecting the estate the rights of a person entering into occupation after the transfer or creation of the estate effected by completion of the transaction. It will be convenient to refer to this as 'the judge's construction'.

This is an attractive solution because it is, as Nicholls LJ observed in the course of his judgment in *Rosset's* case [1988] 3 All ER 915 at 922, [1989] Ch 350 at 373, a conveyancing absurdity that, for instance, a mortgagee should, after completion and after having made all possible inquiries and parted with his money, be bound by the interest asserted by a newly-arrived occupant coming in between completion and the registration of his charge. So far as registered interests are concerned the chargee can protect himself by an official search which will preserve his priority over any further registered entries during a priority period well sufficient to enable him to have his charge stamped and lodged for registration: see rr 3 and 5 of the Land Registration (Official Searches) Rules 1981, SI 1981/1135. There is, however, no similar protection against overriding interests which are not recorded on the register and whose existence can be ascertained only by inquiry and there is, accordingly, good sense in so construing ss 20(1) and 23(1) as to preserve the priority of the purchaser or chargee as from the date of completion, when both are irrevocably committed to the transaction, which only awaits the formal step of registration in order to vest the legal estate.

In *Rosset's* case, however, the Court of Appeal found some difficulty in accepting that the solution could be found simply in construing s 20(l) and 23(1) in the manner suggested. Nicholls LJ pointed out that it was common ground that para (a) of s 20(1) (para (b) of s 23(1)), which subjects the land transferred to entries appearing on the register, undoubtedly refers to entries so appearing at the date of registration (see [1988] 3 All ER 915 at 921; [1989] Ch 350 at 371). This appears to me to be beyond doubt. One would, therefore, expect that the paragraph subjecting the land to overriding interests would be related to the same date. Nicholls LJ reached, in relation to overriding interests within s 70(l)(g), the same result as that produced by the judge's construction but by reference to the words 'for the time being subsisting' in s 70(1) and by holding that, in relation to para (g) specifically, an interest was not a subsisting interest except in a case in which the claimant was in occupation of the land prior to and at the date of completion of the purchase.

I share the difficulty that Nicholls LJ felt in accepting the attractive solution of the judge's construction and I agree with him that the key to the problem lies in the words of s 70(1) rather than in the reference to the interests affecting the estate transferred or created in ss 20(1) and 23(1). The 1925 Act displays a degree of circularity in its general definition of what an overriding interest is. Section 3(xvi) defines it as an unregistered incumbrance 'subject to which registered dispositions ... take effect', but when one turns to inquire to what unregistered incumbrances a disposition is subject, ss 20(1) and 23(1) merely specify that they are 'overriding interests, if any, affecting the estate transferred or created'. As a definition, therefore, this is a little less than satisfactory, for it simply means 'overriding interests' are 'overriding interests'. It does, however, involve this consequence, that if the judge's construction is correct no interest which does not affect the estate or interest at the time when a relevant disposition is effected by transfer, grant or charge can be an overriding interest. That, of course, does not demonstrate that the judge's construction is erroneous, but it might be thought to be a surprising result when consideration is given to the remaining words in ss 20 and 23 and to the terms of ss 69 and 70.

I turn to those sections, because the circularity of the definition so far compels a reference to other provisions of the 1925 Act in order to ascertain the nature of the interests which are to override. They are, to begin with, not 'minor interests' (s 3(xv)), that is to say interests not capable of being disposed of or created by registered dispositions and interests created by unregistered dealings and subsisting only in equity. Unless protected by notice, caution, inhibition or restriction entered on the register, these will be overriden by registered dispositions for valuable consideration. Specifying what overriding interests are not does not, however, assist in determining what they are and, moreover, it is clear from *Williams & Glyn's Bank Ltd v Boland* [1980] 2 All ER 408; [1981] AC 487 that a minor interest may become an overriding interest if the claimant is in actual occupation. Section 69 is of some assistance in that it demonstrates that the list of miscellaneous overriding interests contained in s 70(1) is not exhaustive, since the legal estate is vested in the registered proprietor under this section subject to:

> the overriding interests ... including any ... charge by way of legal mortgage created ... under ... this Act or otherwise which has priority to the registered estate.

(See s 69(1).) Section 70(1) contains no reference to a mortgage or charge as an overriding interest, but s 69(1) necessarily implies that it is one so long as it has priority to the registered estate.

When regard is had to the list of overriding interests in s 70(1) it is apparent that all of them are interests which can come into being at any time, and some of them may arise without any volition on the part of the registered proprietor or anyone else seised of an estate in the land. A right of way or a profit *à prendre* may be acquired by a neighbouring landowner by prescription. A third party may acquire title to the land by adverse possession. A local land charge may be imposed on the land at any time under a variety of different statutes. A lease at a rent for a term not exceeding 21 years may be granted at any time. Yet, on the judge's construction, a purchaser would, on registration, take free from any such interests arising after completion of his purchase (in the sense of payment of the price against delivery of the executed transfer) even though, if the land were unregistered land, he would clearly be subjected to them. This necessarily follows, if the judge's construction is right, from the words which immediately follow para (b) of s 20(1) (para (c) of s 23(1)): 'but free from all other estates and interests whatsoever ...'. It also involves, I think, a conflict between ss 20(1) and 23(1) on the one hand and ss 69(1) and 70(1) on the other. Section 69, as it seems to me, is looking at the continuous position of the registered proprietor and providing that the legal estate is deemed to be vested in him subject to such overriding interests as shall from time to time subsist during his proprietorship, whereas, if the judge's construction is correct, it is indeed subject to all such interests but with the exception of those which come into being between the date when he took his transfer and the date when he became registered. Moreover it would also follow that the effect of registration of the transferee would be to free him even from overriding interests which he himself had created in the interval between completion and registration.

That cannot, I think, have been the intention of the legislature and the difficulty can be illustrated by a number of examples. Section 70(1)(i) specifies as overriding interests 'Rights under local land charges unless and until registered ...' etc. This was cited by Nicholls LJ in the course of his judgment and it is a useful example. I pause to remark that the reference to 'registration' here is clearly a reference to registration under the 1925 Act, a necessary step before realisation of the charge. Under the Land Charges Act 1925, and until the Local Land Charges Act 1975, local land charges required to be registered in the register of local land charges if they were not to be void against a purchaser for money or money's worth of the legal estate pursuant to s 15 of that Act. That applied equally whether the land affected by the charge was registered or unregistered. Now, if we suppose a simple purchase of the freehold without the added complication of an advance on mortgage, the purchaser would take free from any local land charge which had arisen but had not been registered under the Land Charges Act prior to his acquisition of the legal estate, and that would be the case whether the land was registered or unregistered. Assuming a local land charge arising prior to that date but not then registered, there is nothing in s 70(1)(i) which would or could have the effect of reviving the charge against the land if it were subsequently to be registered in the register of land charges, for there could be no 'right under' the charge once it had been avoided. But suppose that the charge did not even arise until the day after the completion of the purchase by delivery of the transfer or conveyance and that it was then immediately registered under the Land Charges Act 1925. In the case of unregistered land there is no difficulty. The charge attached to the land in the hands of the purchaser as the estate owner for the time being pursuant to the statute imposing it. I can see no reason why the purchaser of registered land should be in any different position simply because his transfer had not yet been registered. Thus, for instance, the local authority was enabled under s 144 of the Highways Act 1959 to take steps to alleviate a danger on land adjoining the highway and to recover the expenses of so doing from the owner of the land for the time being. Under s 264(1) such expenses were a charge on the premises 'as from the date of the completion of the works' and such charges were registrable under s 15(1) of the Land Charges Act 1925. Let it be assumed for the purposes of the example that the work of the appropriate character had been undertaken by the authority on land which was the subject matter of a pending sale and that it was completed after completion of the sale but before the purchaser was registered as proprietor. Let it also be assumed that the local authority's charge was duly registered immediately under the Land Charges Act 1925. In the case of unregistered land there would be no question but that the charge attached to the land in the hands of the purchaser as the owner for the time being and I cannot accept that the legislature could have intended that the purchaser of registered land should take free from it as a result of the accidental circumstance that the work came to be completed and the charge arose on a date between completion of the purchase and that of registration of the purchaser as proprietor.

It is not difficult to think of other examples of local land charges coming into being after the date of completion but before registration of the purchaser as proprietor, for instance the designation of the property purchased as a listed building under s 54(1) of the Town and Country Planning Act 1971. That section requires the list to be deposited with the appropriate borough or district council and registered as a local land charge under the Land Charges Act 1925. Again, I cannot accept that the effect of s 20(1) was that the purchaser, prior to the Local Land Charges Act 1975, held free from the restriction which is the consequence of listing because of the circumstance that the list was deposited on a date falling between completion of the purchase and registration. Another example would be, for instance, the issue of a certificate by the Secretary of State under s 19 of the Leasehold Reform Act 1967 which happened to occur between completion of a purchase of the freehold reversion and the registration of the purchaser as its proprietor.

Now, I do not think that this difficulty can be overcome by reference to the fact that local land charges, being imposed by statute, are, as it were, free-standing and attach to the land by virtue of their own statutory force, so that ss 20(1) and 23(1) fall to be construed as if the words 'free from all other estates and interests' were followed by the words 'other than interests conferred by local land charges'. There appear to me to be insuperable difficulties about this as a matter of construction.

I conclude, therefore, like Nicholls LJ, that the relevant date for determining the existence of overriding interests which will 'affect the estate transferred or created' is the date of registration. This does, of course, give rise to the theoretical difficulty that, since a transferor remains the registered proprietor until registration of the transfer, it would be possible for him in breach of trust, to create overriding interests, for instance by grant of an easement or of a lease, which would be binding on the transferee and against which the transferee would not be protected by an official search. That would, of course, equally be the case in a purchase of unregistered land where the purchaser pays the price in advance of receiving a conveyance. I cannot, however, find in the theoretical possibility of so improbable event a context for preferring the judge's construction.

The question remains, however, whether the date of registration is also the relevant date for determining whether a claimant to a right is in actual occupation. It is to be noted that it is not the actual occupation which gives rise to the right or determines its existence. Actual occupation merely operates as the trigger, as it were, for the treatment of the right, whatever it may be, as an overriding interest. Nor does the additional quality of the right as an overriding interest alter the nature or quality of the right itself. If it is an equitable right it remains an equitable right. As was observed in *Williams & Glyn's Bank Ltd v Boland* [1980] 2 All ER 408 at 412; [1981] AC 487 at 504, the purpose of s 70(1)(g) was to make applicable to registered land the same rule for the protection of persons in actual occupation as had been applied in the case of unregistered land in, for instance, *Hunt v Luck* [1902] 1 Ch 428; [1900–3] All ER Rep 295. In relation to legal rights it does nothing, for it is not easy to conceive of a legal right in the land which would not already be an overriding interest under some other head, as, for instance, para (a) or (k). Again, as regards equitable rights in an occupier which arise before completion and are supported by occupation at that date there is no difficulty. A chargee who advances money and so acquires an equitable charge prior to the creation of the occupier's right does not lose his priority because the occupier's right becomes an overriding interest. That interest remains what it always was, an interest subject to the prior equity of the chargee which, on registration, is fortified by the legal estate. Equally, a chargee advancing his money after the creation of the occupier's equitable right is, as one would expect, subject to such right.

The case which does give rise to difficulty if the date of registration is the relevant date for determining whether there is a claimant in actual occupation is one in which the sequence of events is that the right, unaccompanied by occupation, is created before completion and before the chargee has advanced his money and then subsequently, the claimant enters into actual occupation after completion and remains in occupation up to the date when the registration of the charge is effected. The chargee in that event would have no possibility of discovering the existence of the claimant's interest before advancing his money and taking his charge, but would nevertheless be subject, on registration, to the claimant's prior equitable interest which, ex hypothesis would not have been subject to the charge at its creation.

This does indeed produce a conveyancing absurdity and there is, as Nicholls LJ observed, an internal context for supposing that the legislature, in enacting para (g), must have been contemplating an occupation which preceded and existed at completion of a transfer or disposition. Not only was the paragraph clearly intended to reflect the rule discussed in *Hunt v Luck* with regard to unregistered conveyancing, but the reference to inquiry and failure to disclose cannot make any sense unless it is related to a period in which such inquiry could be other than otiose. That absurdity can, I think, be avoided only by the route which the Court of Appeal adopted and by referring the 'actual occupation' in para (g) to the date of completion of the transaction by transfer and payment of the purchase money. Section 70(1) refers to such interests 'as may be for the time being subsisting' and in order to affect 'the estate transferred or created' on registration such interests would no doubt require to be subsisting on that date. But I see no insuperable difficulty in holding that the actual occupation required to support such an interest as a subsisting interest must exist at the date of completion of the transaction giving rise to the right to be registered, for that is the only date at which the inquiry referred to in para (g) could, in practice, be made and be relevant. I agree, therefore, with the conclusion of the Court of Appeal in *Rosset's* case that it is at that moment that it falls to be determined whether there is an actual occupation for the purposes of para (g). I do not think that I can improve on Nicholls LJ's analysis when he said, in the course of his judgment in *Rosset's* case [1988] 3 All ER 915 at 923; [1989] Ch 350 at 374:

> If this is right, the pieces of the jigsaw fit together reasonably well. A purchaser or mortgagee inspects and inquires before completion, in the established fashion. Or he fails to do so, at his own risk. He then completes the transaction, taking an executed transfer or mortgage. Whether or not an overriding interest under para (g) subsists so far as his freehold or mortgage is concerned falls to be determined at that moment. If an overriding interest does subsist, then his estate when registered takes subject to that interest. If it does not, then subsequent entry of a person into occupation before the transfer or mortgage has been registered (and 'completed' for the purposes of s 19) does not have the consequence of creating an overriding interest under para (g) in relation to that freehold or mortgage ...

Section 70(1)(g) also protects the rights of a person who is in receipt of rents and profits. It seems that such a person must actually receive rents and profits and not simply have a right to receive them. Thus, if a landlord grants a licence of rent-free accommodation, the landlord's reversion cannot be overriding under s 70(1)(g) as he is not in actual receipt of the rents and profits, neither is the licensee's licence overriding because, as will be seen, a licence is not a right which is capable of overriding.[95]

Strand Securities v Caswell [1965] Ch 958, CA

Lord Denning: Section 70(1)(g) is an important provision. Fundamentally its object is to protect a person in actual occupation of land from having his rights lost in the welter of registration. He can stay there and do nothing. Yet he will be protected. No one can buy the land over his head and thereby take away or diminish his rights. It is up to every purchaser before he buys to make inquiry on the premises. If he fails to do so, it is at his own risk. He must take subject to whatever rights the occupier may have. Such is the doctrine of *Hunt v Luck*,[96] for unregistered land. Section 70(1)(g) carries the same doctrine forward into registered land but with this difference. Not only is the actual occupier protected, but also the person from whom he holds. It is up to the purchaser to inquire of the occupier, not only about the occupier's own rights, but also about the rights of his immediate superior. The purchaser must ask the occupier: 'To whom do you pay your rent?' And the purchaser must inquire what the rights of that person are. If he fails to do so, it is at his own risk for he takes subject to 'the rights of every person in actual occupation of the land or in receipt of the rents and profits thereof'.

In this case, it is clear that the second defendant was in actual occupation of the flat. The plaintiffs, therefore, took subject to her rights, whatever they were; see *National Provincial Bank Ltd v Hastings Car Mart Ltd*.[97] She was not a tenant but only a licensee; see *Foster v Robinson*;[98] *Cobb v Lane*.[99] She had no contractual right to stay there. Her licence could be determined at any time and she would have to go in a reasonable time thereafter; see *Minister of Health v Bellotti*.[100] So the plaintiffs could get her out, provided always that they could get rid of the first defendant's sublease.

95 *Strand Securities Ltd v Caswell* [1965] Ch 958.

96 [1901] 1 Ch 45.

97 [1964] Ch 665; [1964] 3 WLR 463; [1964] 3 All ER 93, CA.

98 [1951] 1 KB 149; 66 TLR (Pt 2) 120; [1950] 2 All ER 342, CA.

99 [1952] 1 TLR 1037; [1952] 1 All ER 1199, CA.

100 [1944] KB 298; 60 TLR 228; [1944] 1 All ER 238, CA.

But although the second defendant was in actual occupation, it is said that the first defendant was also in actual occupation. We have had several cases lately in which we have held that 'possession in law is, of course, single and exclusive but occupation may be shared with others or had on behalf of others;' see *Hills (Patents) Ltd v University College Hospital Board of Governors*,[101] and *Willis v Association of Universities of the British Commonwealth*.[102] In this case, it is said that the first defendant did share the actual occupation of the flat with the second defendant.

I would like to hold that the first defendant was sharing the occupation of the flat with the second defendant. But I cannot bring myself to this conclusion. The truth is that he allowed her to be in actual occupation, and that is all there is to it. She was a licensee rent free and I fear that it does not give him protection. It seems to be a very rare case – a case which the legislature did not think of. For it is quite clear that if the second defendant had paid a token sum as rent, or for use and occupation, to the first defendant, he would be 'in receipt of the rents and profits' and his rights would be protected under s 70(1)(g). Again if the first defendant put his servant or caretaker into the flat, rent free, he would be protected because his agent would have actual occupation on his behalf. It is odd that the first defendant is not protected simply because he let his stepdaughter in rent free. Odd as it is, however, I fear the words of the statute do not cover this case and the first defendant does not succeed on this point.

Russell LJ read the following judgment, which stated the facts and continued:

The first defendant claims to have had at 24 April 1962, an overriding interest in the land as being then a person in actual occupation thereof within the scope of that phrase in s 70(1)(g). If this be correct, lack of registration cannot harm him on the facts, for admittedly the plaintiffs had full knowledge of his rights as sublessee at all times ...

... does the first defendant succeed in establishing an overriding interest subject to which the registration of the plaintiffs as at 24 April 1962, must have taken effect? At that date and for some time past he had allowed the second defendant, his stepdaughter, and her children to live there rent and rate free, her husband having left her, as a matter of compassion and family obligation ...

It is to be remarked that if instead of making his application on 5 April 1962, for registration he had moved up to London and occupied the son's bedroom until after 24 April or received from or demanded of his stepdaughter during the same period a penny a week for the privilege of remaining there, he would have had an unanswerable claim to his sublease being an overriding interest under s 70(1)(g) as he would be in the one case a person in actual occupation and in the other in receipt of the rents and profits. Of course he did neither of these things. Their possibility, however, serves to show how rare it must be that an actual sublessee entitled to possession is not a person either in actual occupation or in receipt of the rents and profits ...

On the facts, was the first defendant, at 24 April 1962, a person in actual occupation, though he was not in any ordinary sense residing there or treating it as his home, and the second defendant and her family were allowed by him to reside there? As a matter of the ordinary use of language, I would not consider the first defendant to be such. For him it was argued that the phrase 'in actual occupation' derives from cases in which 'actual

101 [1956] 1 QB 90, 99; [1955] 3 WLR 523; [1955] 3 All ER 365, CA.

102 [1965] 1 QB 140; [1964] 2 WLR 946.

occupation' and 'actual possession' are used indifferently to describe a condition of enjoyment of the land itself, and that the phrase 'actual occupation' here involves that form of the legal concept of possession as distinct from the other or notional forms of that concept consisting of the receipt of money payments derived from land, or of the right to possession though the land be vacant. And it was argued that 'actual possession' was avoided by the draftsman as a phrase because of the difficulty which would flow from the definition of 'possession' in s 3(xviii) of the Land Registration Act 1925. Reference was made to a number of authorities, including cases in the fields of rating, poor law, and landlord and tenant, with a view to showing that possession, and therefore occupation, may be had through the medium of another. Suppose, it was said, that the first defendant employed a resident caretaker to look after the flat in question, would the first defendant not be a person in actual occupation? I think that is correct. Then, it was argued, that is because the caretaker would be his licensee, bound to go at his will, and that was the position of the second defendant. But I think that here is the distinction between occupation by the caretaker as a matter of duty on behalf of the first defendant and the occupation of the second defendant on her own behalf; both were licensees, but the former, by her occupation for which she was employed, was the representative of the first defendant and her occupation may therefore be regarded as his. The proposition that in each case the first defendant was in actual occupation because neither the caretaker nor the second defendant had a right to occupy independently of him seems to me too broadly stated and to ignore that distinction. I do not say that a contract of employment or agency with the person residing there is essential to actual occupation by the other person. I think that it might well be that if a house was used as a residence by a wife, separated from the tenant, her husband (whether or not in desertion), he could also be regarded as in actual occupation through her; the question whether the husband was also a person in actual occupation did not, of course, arise in *National Provincial Bank Ltd v Hastings Car Mart Ltd*. But this conception, even if valid, could not extend to the relationship in the present case.

Nor, it seems to me, can the presence on the premises of some of the first defendant's furniture, nor the previously mentioned use by him and others of the family of the flat, nor the fact, which I am prepared to assume though it was not proved, that he had a key, nor a combination of those matters, constitute actual occupation by him.

(a) 'Rights' capable of overriding

Section 70(1)(g) gives protection to the 'rights' enjoyed by the person in actual occupation or in receipt of rents and profits. The actual occupation alone (or receipt of rents and profits) would not render an otherwise non-existing right an overriding interest. A good example is *Strand Securities v Caswell* where the actual occupation by the licensee, who did not have any 'rights', except a licence which is not a 'right' capable of overriding, did not give her any overriding interest. There has to be a 'right' which is capable of overriding, whatever that 'right' may be. Actual occupation simply triggers off the operation of s 70(1)(g) so as to protect the 'rights' which are not protected on the register.

So what 'rights' have the quality to be overriding if supported by evidence of actual occupation? In *National Provincial Bank Ltd v Ainsworth*,[103] Lord

103 [1965] AC 1175, at 1261B.

Wilberforce said that in order to ascertain what 'rights' can be overriding under s 70(1)(g):[104]

> ... one must look outside the Land Registration Act and see what rights affect purchasers under the general law. To suppose that the subsection makes any right, of howsoever a personal character, which a person in occupation may have, an overriding interest by which a purchaser is bound, would involve two consequences: first that this Act is, in this respect, bringing about a substantive change in real property law by making personal rights bind purchasers; second, that there is a difference as to the nature of the right by which a purchaser may be bound between registered and unregistered land; for purely personal rights cannot affect purchasers of unregistered land even with notice. One may have to accept that there is a difference between unregistered and registered land as regards what kind of notice binds a purchaser, or what kind of inquiries a purchaser has to make. But there is no warrant in the terms of this paragraph or elsewhere in the Act for supposing that the nature of the rights which are to bind a purchaser is to be different, excluding personal rights in one case, including them in another.

Thus, it is clear that s 70(1)(g) only protects proprietary interests and not personal rights. Examples of rights accepted as capable of overriding are an option to purchase,[105] a legal tenancy which is not substantively registered, an equitable lease, the right to an unpaid vendor's lien,[106] the beneficial interests under a trust,[107] and the right to have the register rectified on the ground of mistake.[108] Similarly, the rights of the transferee who has gone into possession before his transfer has been registered, the rights of a tenant at will, and those of a protected or statutory tenant under the Rent Acts are all capable of overriding under s 70(1)(g). A contractual or a bare licence, on the other hand, cannot be overriding, because it creates no proprietary interest in land.[109] In *National Provincial Bank Ltd v Hastings Car Mart Ltd*,[110] Lord Denning was of the view that the rights of an estoppel licensee can be overriding under s 70(1)(g). This must today be reconsidered in the light of the Court of Appeal's view in *Ashburn Anstalt v Arnold*[111] that a contractual licence does not create a proprietary interest.

Just as the actual occupation must exist at the date of the completion of the transfer of a registrable interest, so must the 'rights' have existed and been

---

104 [1965] AC 1175 at 1261B–E.

105 *Webb v Pollmount Ltd* [1966] Ch 584; *Kling v Keston Properties Ltd* (1983) 49 P & CR 212.

106 *London and Cheshire Insurance Co Ltd v Laplagrene Property Co Ltd* [1971] Ch 499 at 502H.

107 *Hodgson v Marks* [1971] Ch 892 at 934F–G (a bare trust). *Williams & Glyn's Bank Ltd v Boland* [1981] AC 487 at 508A–B (a trust for sale).

108 *Blacklocks v JB Developments (Godalming) Ltd* [1982] Ch 183 at 196D–E.

109 *Cf Ashburn Anstalt v Arnold* [1989] Ch 1 at 24D. Contrast *National Provincial Bank Ltd v Hastings Car Mart Ltd* [1964] Ch 665 at 688.

110 [1964] Ch 665 at 689.

111 [1988] Ch 1.

enforceable at that time. If the 'rights' have been otherwise destroyed or their priority postponed, they cannot be overriding under s 70(1)(g). Thus, in *City of London Building Society v Flegg*,[112] where the mortgagee had paid the mortgage loan to two trustees for sale, the claimant's beneficial interest under the trust for sale was held to have been overreached. As such, the right could not be an overriding interest binding on the mortgagee even though the claimant was at the date of the mortgage in actual occupation. In *Paddington Building Society v Mendelsohn*,[113] where the mortgage and the purchase, which was partly financed by the mortgage, were simultaneous, the beneficial owner, who knew that the mortgage was necessary to finance the purchase, was taken to have deferred her priority to that of the mortgagee. The court thought that the only possible intention to impute to the parties was an intention that the beneficial owner's rights were subject to the rights of the mortgagee. As such, the beneficial owner could not claim that her rights were overriding *vis-à-vis* the mortgagee under s 70(1)(g).

(b) Actual occupation

'Actual occupation' is not defined anywhere in the Land Registration Acts. It is clear, however, that it requires evidence of physical occupation of the land transferred or charged, discoverable on inspection by a purchaser.[114] '"Actual occupation" is a matter of fact, not matter of law'.[115] It was first considered by Russell LJ in *Hodgson v Marks*.[116]

Hodgson v Marks [1971] Ch 892, CA

Russell LJ: I turn first to the question whether at the relevant time the plaintiff was in 'actual occupation' of the house. For years it had been her property and her home. Mr Evans was taken in by her as a lodger. I now quote from the findings of the judge at p 912c:

> So I will now come to the facts which bear on whether Mrs Hodgson was, independently of the context of s 70(1)(g) of the Land Registration Act 1925, in actual occupation in this case. Before Mrs Hodgson's transfer of the house to Mr Evans and its registration in his name, it is undisputed and indisputable that Mrs Hodgson was in actual occupation of it. After the registration, she continued to live there to all appearances and as a physical fact in exactly the same way as before; and so did Mr Evans. They lived and ate and slept in the house exactly as before. The financial arrangements of payment by Mr Evans to Mrs Hodgson for board and lodging and by Mrs Hodgson to Mr Evans for investment for her and for the payment of bills continued unchanged. Mrs Hodgson continued too as the rateable occupier. There was no change in the physical appearance of occupation nor was there any other change at all, except that Mrs Hodgson

112 [1988] AC 54 at 88A–B. See also *State Bank of India v Sood* [1997] 1 All ER 169.

113 (1985) 50 P & CR 244. See also *Bristol and West Building Society v Henning* [1985] 1 WLR 778.

114 *Hodgson v Marks* [1971] Ch 892, at 932C–D; *Lloyds Bank plc v Rosset* [1989] Ch 350 at 394G, 397A–B, CA.

115 *Williams & Glyn's Bank Ltd v Boland* [1979] Ch 312 at 332E, CA.

116 [1971] Ch 892. See (1971) 35 Conv (NS) 225 (Leeming, I); (1972) 88 LQR 14 (Barton, JL); (1973) 36 MLR 25 (Maudsley, RH).

transferred the house to Mr Evans upon oral trust for herself and that Mr Evans was registered as proprietor. Except that Mr Evans held the legal estate on trust for Mrs Hodgson, the transfer and registration made no difference as between Mrs Hodgson and Mr Evans. She was absolutely beneficially entitled and could at any time call for a transfer of the legal estate and then be registered as proprietor. Mr Evans as bare trustee of the legal estate for Mrs Hodgson was not entitled to occupy the house, but she as absolute beneficial owner was so entitled. After, as before Mr Evans' registration, Mr Evans' presence in the house was exclusively as lodger and Mrs Hodgson's presence was in virtue of being absolute owner, legally and beneficially before the registration, and beneficially afterwards. She could terminate Mr Evans' presence in the house after the registration just as she could before. As between Mrs Hodgson and Mr Evans, her occupation and her dominion over the house was the same after the registration as before.

So at all material times, Mrs Hodgson was in fact in physical occupation of the premises and, more, had the right to occupy them. It seems to me that in general (if this matter can be considered at all independently of context) such physical occupation, even apart from such right to occupy, would constitute what would be meant by actual occupation generally.

With those findings I entirely agree.

But the judge then proceeded to attach a different and special meaning to the words 'in actual occupation' in s 70(1)(g). He took as a starting point to justify departure from the ordinary meaning of the words first the fact that every person in actual occupation could not include the vendor himself; but that only puts a gloss on the words 'every person' and, indeed, assumes the ordinary meaning of 'actual occupation'; moreover, it is not in the context a special construction of 'every person' to exclude the vendor who ex hypothesi has transferred his rights to the purchaser. Secondly, the judge relied upon the correct conclusion that 'the land' included part of the land. I cannot see that this can properly be used as a justification for departure from the ordinary meaning of the words 'in actual occupation'. Having by this means freed himself from the fetters of the golden rule, he then, after considering the circumstances in which in the case of unregistered land a purchaser would be fixed with constructive notice of the rights of persons in occupation of the land sold, concluded that 'actual' should be construed in the sense of 'actual and apparent'. I do not see that this adds to or detracts from the words in the section. In connection with the word 'apparent' I remark on the phrase of the judge that, after the registration of the transfer to Mr Evans, 'to all appearances' the plaintiff continued in actual occupation. I am prepared, for the purposes of this case, to assume (without necessarily accepting) that s 70(1)(g) of the Land Registration Act 1925 is designed only to apply to a case in which the occupation is such, in point of fact, as would in the case of unregistered land affect a purchaser with constructive notice of the rights of the occupier; and it is be observed that the words 'actual occupation' are used in s 14 of the Law of Property Act 1925 and were used in *Barnhart v Greenshields* (1853) 9 Moo PCC 18 at 34. But, nevertheless, how can it be said that the plaintiff was not in actual occupation of the house? The judge said that in all fairness a purchaser of this house (if unregistered) should not be fixed with notice of the plaintiff's rights. But why not? It is a principle of law (and of the Land Registration Act 1925) that a person in occupation is protected in his rights by that occupation, unless, of course, the rights are such that they require registration if they are to be protected. A purchaser must pay heed to anyone in occupation if he is to be sure of getting a good title. It was argued, on the basis of a quotation from the judgment of Vaughan Williams LJ in *Hunt v Luck* [1902] 1 Ch 428 at 432 that this does not apply when the vendor is in occupation, and that (as is the fact) there is no reported case of unregistered land where a purchaser was fixed with constructive notice of the rights of any other occupier when the vendor was in occupation, and that any other view would lead to an impossible burden of inquiry on a purchaser and more particularly on a lender of money on mortgage such as the building society. As to the defendant building society it is plain that it made no inquiries on the spot save as to repairs; it relied on Mr Marks, who lied to it; and I waste no tears on it. I do not think this is a real problem. Conveyancing is conducted generally upon a basis of good faith, with something of a long stop in the shape of covenants for title. Moreover, I do not consider that it is correct in law to say that any rights of a person who is in occupation will be overridden whenever the vendor is, or appears to be, also in occupation.

I do not think it desirable to attempt to lay down a code or catalogue of situations in which a person other than the vendor should be held to be in occupation of unregistered land for the purpose of constructive notice of his rights, or in actual occupation of registered land for the purposes of s 70(1)(g). It must depend on the circumstances, and a wise purchaser or lender will take no risks. Indeed, however wise he may be he may have no ready opportunity of finding out; but, nevertheless, the law will protect the occupier. Reliance upon the untrue ipse dixit of the vendor will not suffice. Take the present case – though the test of occupation must be objective. Mr Evans was only a lodger, and whether in law he was in occupation at all is at least doubtful. But the plaintiff was there for Mr Marks to see and he saw her on two occasions. He did not introduce himself to her as an intending purchaser. He made no inquiry of her. He assumed her to be Mr Evans' wife who knew all about the proposed purchase. This assumption may well have stemmed from a lie told by Mr Evans, though neither Mr Marks nor Mrs Marks actually said so. Nonetheless, there was the plaintiff de facto living in the house as her house, and, if the judge's gloss were to be accepted, I should say just as much in apparent actual occupation of it as before the transfer to Mr Evans: and, indeed, if Mr Evans had stopped lodging there before the registration in Mr Marks' name she would unquestionably have been in actual occupation. In short, unless it can be established in law that a person is not to be regarded as in actual occupation for the purposes of s 70(1)(g) merely because the vendor appears also to be occupying the property, it seems to me that the judge's decision on this point cannot be supported. (I observe that it was necessary for the defendants' argument on actual occupation to contend that if the plaintiff had said in conversation to Mr Marks that it was her house and Mr Evans her lodger, and Mr Marks had believed Mr Evans when he said, 'The old lady has a bee in her bonnet and is talking rubbish', her interest would not have been enforceable against Mr Marks because she was not in actual occupation and, accordingly, without an overriding interest.) I do not accept that proposition of law. Accordingly, I would hold that the plaintiff was at all material times a person in actual occupation of the property.'

In *Williams & Glyn's Bank Ltd v Boland*,[117] Lord Wilberforce said that what is required is 'physical presence' at the property. More recently the issue of what

117 [1981] AC 487.

constitutes actual occupation for the purposes of s 70(1)(g) has once again been considered by the House of Lords in *Abbey National Building Society v Cann*.[118]

Abbey National Building Society v Cann [1991] 1 AC 56, HL

Lord Oliver of Aylmerton: I have, up to this point, been content to assume that the facts of the instant case justify the proposition which found favour with Dillon LJ, that she was in actual occupation of the property at the material time. This is, of course, essentially a question of fact, but there is the serious question of what, in law, can amount to 'actual occupation' for the purposes of s 70(1)(g). In *Williams & Glyn's Bank Ltd v Boland* [1980] 2 All ER 408 at 412; [1981] AC 487 at 504, Lord Wilberforce observed that these words should be interpreted for what they are, that is to say ordinary words of plain English. But even plain English may contain a variety of shades of meaning. At the date of completion, Mrs Cann was not personally even in England, leave alone in personal occupation of the property, and the trial judge held that the acts done by Mr Abraham Cann and Mr George Cann amounted to:

> ... no more than the taking of preparatory steps leading to the assumption of actual residential occupation on or after completion, whatever the moment of the day when completion took place ...

For my part, I am content to accept this as a finding of fact which was amply justified by the evidence before him, and I share the reservations expressed by Ralph Gibson and Woolf LJJ in the Court of Appeal. It is, perhaps, dangerous to suggest any test for what is essentially a question of fact, for 'occupation' is a concept which may have different connotations according to the nature and purpose of the property which is claimed to be occupied. It does not necessarily, I think, involve the personal presence of the person claiming to occupy. A caretaker or the representative of a company can occupy, I should have thought, on behalf of his employer. On the other hand, it does, in my judgment, involve some degree of permanence and continuity which would rule out mere fleeting presence. A prospective tenant or purchaser who is allowed, as a matter of indulgence, to go into property in order to plan decorations or measure for furnishings would not, in ordinary parlance, be said to be occupying it, even though he might be there for hours at a time. Of course, in the instant case, there was, no doubt, on the part of the persons involved in moving Mrs Cann's belongings, an intention that they would remain there and would render the premises suitable for her ultimate use as a residential occupier. Like the trial judge, however, I am unable to accept that acts of this preparatory character carried out by courtesy of the vendor prior to completion can constitute 'actual occupation' for the purposes of s 70(1)(g). Accordingly, all other considerations apart, Mrs Cann fails, in my judgment, to establish the necessary condition for the assertion of an overriding interest.

Actual occupation must have a sufficient degree of continuity, and not be merely intermittent. However, it does not require an uninterrupted physical presence on the land by the claimant. A claimant who is temporarily absent from the land may succeed if he can show that there is sufficient evidence of continued residence (*corpus possessionis*) together with an intention to return to the property (*animus*

118 [1991] 1 AC 56.

revertendi). In *Chhokar v Chhokar*,[119] a husband who held the legal estate in the matrimonial home on trust for sale for himself and his wife, sold it secretly to a purchaser who conspired with the husband to complete the transfer while the wife was having a baby in the hospital. When the wife later returned from the hospital she was denied access to her home. Ewbank J was able to find that the wife's furniture in the home was sufficient evidence of her continuing occupation, and, coupled with her intention to resume residence, constituted actual occupation. Thus, her beneficial interest in her home was overriding under s 70(1)(g) and binding on the purchaser.

(c) Enquiry under s 70(1)(g)

If a claimant can establish proprietory rights and evidence of actual occupation at the time a purchaser completes his purchase, and as long as the actual occupation subsists until the date of registration, the purchaser will be bound by the claimant's rights by way of overriding interests when he is registered as the new proprietor. However, s 70(1)(g) expressly provides an exception, that is that if the purchaser has made inquiry of the claimant and the rights are not disclosed, the purchaser will be free of the claimant's rights. The claimant's rights will not become overriding interests. It is for this reason that a minor, who may have rights in land within the meaning of s 70(1)(g) and reside on the premises, cannot claim the benefit of s 70(1)(g). The minor is taken to be incapable of any adequate or intelligible response to the purchaser's inquiries.[120]

Any inquiry by the purchaser must be made of the person whose rights might otherwise be overriding interests. It is not enough to make enquiry of the registered proprietor if the property is held on trust. Thus, in *Hodgson v Marks*,[121] where the registered proprietor held the land on trust for an elderly lady, the purchaser, who only made inquiry of the registered proprietor, was bound by the lady's beneficial interest by way of an overriding interest. The purchaser should have made inquiry of the lady herself; 'reliance on the untrue ipse dixit of the vendor will not suffice'.[122]

(d) Overlap between minor and overriding interests

There is an obvious overlap between minor interests and overriding interests. Many proprietary rights are to be protected as minor interests, and yet the same types of rights are capable of being overriding interests under s 70(1)(g) if the owners of such rights are in actual occupation at the relevant time. On the other hand, once the rights are protected as minor interests on the register they cease to be an overriding interest. Thus, the owners of proprietary rights who are in

119 [1984] FLR 313.

120 *Bird v Syme-Thomson* [1979] 1 WLR 440 at 444D. See [1979] CLJ 23 (Prichard, MJ); [1979] Conv 72 (Crane, FR).

121 [1971] Ch 892.

122 [1971] Ch 892 at 932D.

actual occupation are given dual protection by appropriate entries on the register, or failing that, under s 70(1)(g).

Section 70(1)(i)

This covers local land charges. It is therefore necessary for the purchaser of registered land to make a local land charges search with the local authority before exchanging contracts in much the same way as is necessary for the purchaser of unregistered land.

Section 70(1)(k)

As has been seen, only leases which are granted for more than 21 years, or assignments of leases with more than 21 years to run, can be substantively registered with a separate title number. To avoid the register being cluttered by short terms leases granted for not more than 21 years, they are not registrable. These leases become overriding interests instead under s 70(1)(k). However, it should be noted that only legal leases can be overriding under s 70(1)(k). This means that the lease must be granted by deed unless it is granted for a term not exceeding three years taking effect in possession at the best rent reasonably obtainable without taking a fine.[123] Thus, a mere agreement to grant a lease for less than 21 years, which is an equitable lease, cannot be an overriding interest under s 70(1)(k).[124] Of course, there is nothing to prevent such an equitable lease from being an overriding interest under s 70(1)(g) if the owner of it is in actual possession at the relevant time.

City Permanent Building Society v Miller [1952] Ch 840, CA

Jenkins LJ: Mr Marsh founded himself on the contention that the agreement between the mortgagor and the tenant, evidenced by the memorandum of 16 October 1950, created an 'overriding interest' within s 70(1)(k) of the Land Registration Act 1925.

[His Lordship read s 70(1)(k) and continued.]

In support of this contention Mr Marsh advanced two arguments. First, he submitted that the agreement evidenced by the memorandum signed by the mortgagor was apt to create a legal term in the tenant, and would have done so but for the fact that at the time it was entered into the mortgagor himself had not got the requisite estate to support the term. But (the argument proceeds) when the mortgagor completed his purchase and the property was transferred to him, then, although the transfer was immediately followed by the legal charge to the building society, and although the registration of his interest as proprietor and the building society's interest as chargees were effected contemporaneously, nevertheless there must have been a scintilla of time when the mortgagor was the unincumbered owner of the property, and in that instant of time (so proceeds the argument) the tenant's interest as lessee was perfected by estoppel, and she thus became entitled to a lease which was an overriding interest within s 70(1)(k), being a lease for a term not exceeding 21 years granted at a rent without taking a fine.

---

123 Sections 52(1), 54(2) of the LPA 192.

124 *City Permanent Building Society v Miller* [1952] Ch 840.

To that argument I cannot accede. I have no wish to traverse again unnecessarily the ground covered by my Lord's judgment, but (putting the point as shortly as I can) the fatal flaw in the argument appears to me to be this, that by the combined effect of ss 52(1) and (2)(d), 53 (1)(a) and 54(2) of the Law of Property Act, 1925, this agreement, evidenced by the memorandum signed by the mortgagor, was not apt to create a legal term in the premises, inasmuch as the agreement, being for a term of three years from 16 October 1950, and thereafter on a weekly basis at a rental of 30s per week, was an agreement for a term necessarily exceeding the three years by a period of at least one week, and accordingly related to a term which could only be created by deed. It follows, in my view, that the interest of the tenant under this agreement was, at highest, that of a person who had a contract for the grant of a lease and a right to obtain specific performance of that contract.

Mr Marsh, however, contended that this did not conclude the matter, and he submitted as his second argument that, even if there is no actual lease here, nevertheless the tenant is entitled to succeed on the ground that the description of 'overriding interest' mentioned in s 70(1)(k) of the Land Registration Act, 1925, extends to agreements for leases. Now conceding all else in the tenant's favour, conceding that the agreement is a sufficiently complete and definite agreement to make it capable of specific performance, and conceding that, for a moment of time during the completion of the transaction consisting of the transfer to the mortgagor and the charge by the mortgagor to the building society, the mortgagor had a sufficient interest in the property to constitute this a specifically enforceable contract, nevertheless in my judgment this second argument must also fail. I take that view because, in my judgment, the description of "overriding interest" mentioned in s 70(1)(k) of the Land Registration Act, 1925, is not apt to include a mere agreement for a lease.

Mr Marsh relied on the definition of 'lease' contained in s 3(x) of the Land Registration Act, 1925, which is in these terms: 'Lease' includes an underlease and any tenancy or agreement for a lease, underlease or tenancy. He argued that the word 'leases' in s 70(1)(k) of the same Act must accordingly be construed as including agreements for leases; but, as my Lord has pointed out, the definitions in s 3 are prefaced by the familiar form of words 'In this Act, unless the context otherwise requires, the following expressions have the meanings hereby assigned to them respectively, that is to say.' In my view, the context afforded in s 70(1)(k) does 'otherwise require'. It refers to 'Leases for any term or interest not exceeding 21 years, granted at a rent without taking a fine'. In my judgment, the use there of the word 'granted' clearly imports the actual creation of a term of years, whether it is done by deed or by an agreement under hand only, in that class of case in which a legal term can be created by a document not under seal, or indeed by parol in any case in which an actual tenancy taking effect at law may be created without writing. But in my judgment, the word 'granted' necessarily imports the actual creation of a term, and that excludes, by force of the context, the case of a mere agreement for a lease, having no more than a contractual effect. To include such a case, in my judgment, s 70(1)(k) should have read 'granted or agreed to be granted'.

7 RECTIFICATION AND INDEMNITY

Rectification

The register may be rectified to correct mistakes and the registered proprietor against whom rectification is made may get indemnity from the Land Registry. The jurisdiction to rectify is plainly discretionary.[125] But the exercise of the discretion is guided by the eight grounds on which rectification may be sought under s 82(1) of the Land Registration Act 1925.

Land Registration Act 1925

82. Rectification of the register

(1) The register may be rectified pursuant to an order of the court or by the registrar, subject to an appeal to the court, in any of the following cases, but subject to the provisions of this section:

(a) Subject to any express provisions of this Act to the contrary, where a court of competent jurisdiction has decided that any person is entitled to any estate right or interest in or to any registered land or charge, and as a consequence of such decision such court is of opinion that a rectification of the register is required, and makes an order to that effect;

(b) Subject to any express provision of this Act to the contrary, where the court, on the application in the prescribed manner of any person who is aggrieved by any entry made in, or by the omission of any entry from, the register, or by any default being made, or unnecessary delay taking place, in the making of any entry in the register, makes an order for the rectification of the register;

(c) In any case and at any time with the consent of all persons interested;

(d) Where the court or the registrar is satisfied that any entry in the register has been obtained by fraud;

(e) Where two or more persons are, by mistake, registered as proprietors of the same registered estate or of the same charge;

(f) Where a mortgagee has been registered as proprietor of the land instead of as proprietor of a charge and a right of redemption is subsisting;

(g) Where a legal estate has been registered in the name of a person who if the land had not been registered would not have been the estate owner; and

(h) In any other case where, by reason of any error or omission in the register, or by reason of any entry made under a mistake, it may be deemed just to rectify the register.

It should be noted that only the court has jurisdiction to order rectification on the grounds set out in s 82(1)(a), and (b), whereas s 82(1)(c) to (h) allow rectification by the court or the registrar. The application of s 82(1) has recently been considered

125 *Norwich and Peterborough Building Society v Steed* [1992] 3 WLR 669 at 683B–C.

by the Court of Appeal in *Norwich and Peterborough Building Society v Steed*.[126] In particular, it was held that the court's power to order rectification was limited to the grounds specified in s 82(1)(a) to (h) and the court had no general discretion to grant rectification merely because it might be thought just to do so.

Norwich and Peterborough Building Society v Steed [1992] 3 WLR 669, CA

Scott LJ: *Rectification of the register*

The transfer of 4 September 1979 was induced by the fraud of Mr and Mrs Hammond. It was voidable but not void. The building society advanced £15,000 to the Hammonds on the security of the charge which they executed and which was subsequently registered. The question is whether the court has power under s 82 of the Land Registration Act 1925 to order the register to be rectified by deletion of the entry of the building society's registered charge in the charges register. The question is primarily one of construction of the statutory language used in s 82. Section 82, as amended by ss 24 and 32 of, and Schedule 5 to, the Administration of Justice Act 1977, provides:

[His Lordship read s 82(1)(a)–(h), (2), (3) and (5) and s 83(1)–(6) and continued.]

If an order of rectification is to be made the case must be brought within at least one of paragraphs (a) to (h) of s 82(1). The dispute in the present case is as to the breadth of the power conferred by paragraphs (a) and (b) and, to a lesser extent, (d) and (h). There is no doubt but that, if Mrs Steed's signature had been forged or if the non est factum plea had been made good, the case would have fallen squarely within paragraph (g). In neither case, if the land had been unregistered, would the Hammonds or the building society have obtained a legal estate. I cannot see any reasonable basis on which an order of rectification could have been withheld. If, however, as is the case, the transfer is only voidable, paragraph (g) does not apply. It is plain that, if title to the property had been unregistered, Mr Steed would have had no remedy against the building society. He would have recovered the property from the Hammonds but the property would have remained subject to the charge. It is submitted, however, that paragraphs (a), (b), (d) or (h) can, since title is registered, be prayed in aid. This submission is made on the footing that, under one or more of these paragraphs, the court is given a general discretion to order rectification in any case in which it may be thought just to do so. If the submission is right, then s 82, or its statutory predecessors, achieved a remarkable and unnoticed change in the substantive law. If the discretion can be exercised where there has been a fraudulent misrepresentation, as in the present case, it must be exercisable also where a merely innocent misrepresentation has been made. It would, as Mr Lloyd conceded, be exercisable also in a case where no misrepresentation inducing the transaction could be pointed to but where a registered proprietor had entered into a transaction under a misapprehension for which the other party to the transaction was not responsible, a misapprehension as to the value of the property, for example. Mr Lloyd said that in such a case the discretion to order rectification against a *bona fide* purchaser, such as the building society in the present case, would be very unlikely ever to be exercised. But the proposition that the discretionary power contended for can be spelled out of the statutory language is, to me, so startling as to require the premise of the proposition to be very carefully examined.

126 [1992] 3 WLR 669.

There is a sense in which the power to rectify under s 82 is undoubtedly discretionary. The words in sub-s (1) are 'may be rectified'. Section 83(2) shows that rectification is not automatic. The power to rectify may, in a particular case, be present but, nonetheless, there is a general discretion to refuse rectification. It does not follow, however, that there is, in every case, a general discretion to grant rectification. The power to grant rectification is limited in sub-s (1) to 'any of the following cases'. The power to order rectification must, therefore, be found within one or other of the sub-s (1) paragraphs and cannot be spelled out of the words 'may be rectified'.

Paragraphs (a) and (b) provide a power to rectify that can only be exercised by the court. The power conferred by the other paragraphs can be exercised either by the registrar or by the court. Paragraph (a) enables an order of rectification to be made where the court 'has decided that any person is entitled to any estate right or interest in or to any registered land or charge ...'. This, in my judgment, is a clear reference to an entitlement under the substantive law. An example would be a case, such as Mr Steed's case against the Hammonds, for the setting aside of a transaction on the ground of misrepresentation or some other sufficient cause. Another example would be the successful assertion of a possessory title. A third example might be the assertion of a right by a beneficiary under a trust who had become absolutely entitled to the land. In each of these cases, once the entitlement had been established the court would have power under para (a) to order the register to be rectified so as to reflect the entitlement. But para (a) does not, in my judgment, give any substantive cause of action where none before existed. It does not enable a voidable transaction to be set aside as against a *bona fide* purchaser who has acquired by registration a legal estate. And if no entitlement as against such a purchaser can be established, para (a) does not, in my judgment, enable the register to be rectified as against such a purchaser. Paragraph (a) does not assist Mr Steed in his rectification claim against the building society.

Paragraph (b) is the paragraph on which Mr Lloyd pinned his main hopes. It applies, he submitted, whenever any person is 'aggrieved' by an entry on the register. Paragraph (b) is something of a puzzle, not least because the form of the 'application' is not 'prescribed' by any rules made under the Act. The same language was used in s 96 of the Act of 1875, but there, too, no form of application was 'prescribed.' The legislative intention underlying para (b) and its statutory predecessor is difficult to identify with clarity. The reference to 'the application in the prescribed manner' makes me believe that it was contemplated that some form of summary process would be prescribed in order to enable speedy relief to be given in clear cases. Be that as it may, the real question at issue is whether the provision was intended simply to provide a remedy in respect of proprietary rights that either entitled the proprietor to have some entry made on the register or entitled the proprietor to have some entry removed from the register or whether the provision should be construed as creating a new cause of action entitling the court to make rectification orders as it might in its discretion think fit in favour of persons who would not under substantive law, apart from para (b), have any proprietary rights which they could assert against the registered proprietor or chargee. In my judgment, the question has only to be put for the answer to be apparent. Parliament could not have intended para (b) to produce new substantive rights in respect of registered land, enabling registered dispositions to be set aside and removed from the register in circumstances where, if the land had not been registered, no cause of action would have existed. In my judgment, para (b), like para (a), provides a remedy but does not create any new substantive rights or causes of action.

The scope of para (c) is self-evident and not relevant in the present case.

Paragraph (d) too was relied on by Mr Lloyd. He contended that since the transfer had been induced by the Hammonds' fraud, both the registration of the Hammonds as proprietors and the registration of the building society's legal charge could be described as having been 'obtained by fraud'. In my judgment, this is a misreading of the paragraph. The paragraph is directed, in my opinion, to fraud practised upon the Land Registry in order to obtain the entry in question. No fraud was used to obtain the entry on the charges register of the building society's legal charge.

This construction of para (d) derives support from the language used in s 174(1)(c) of the Law of Property Act 1922, the statutory predecessor of para (d). Section 174(l)(c) enabled the register to be rectified:

> Where the court or the registrar is satisfied that the registration of ... a charge, mortgage, or other entry in the register ... has been obtained by fraud, by annulling the registration, notice or other entry ...

This provision was reduced to its present succinct form in the Law of Property (Amendment) Act 1924: see s 8 and Sched 8, para 16. It is the registration that must be obtained by fraud.

The registration of a forged transfer could, in my opinion, at least if the application for registration had been made by the forger, be annulled under para (d). The entry would have been obtained by fraud in the presenting of a forged transfer for registration. But if a voidable disposition were registered before being avoided, I would doubt whether the register could be rectified under para (d), even if the disposition were voidable on account of fraud. In such a case the entry on the register would not, it seems to me, have been obtained by fraud. Rectification could, of course, in such a case be obtained under para (a) or para (b). Whether or not that is right, and it need not be decided in this case, a registered disposition made by the fraudster to a *bona fide* purchaser cannot in my judgment be removed from the register under para (d). The registration would not have been obtained by fraud. So para (d) cannot in my judgment assist Mr Steed as against the building society.

Paragraphs (e) and (f) are self-explanatory and are of no relevance to this case.

Paragraph (g) does not, in the event that the transfer is voidable, assist Mr. Steed as against the building society. It is, however, an important paragraph so far as an understanding of the scheme of s 82(1) is concerned.

In my opinion, the scheme is reasonably clear. Paragraphs (a) and (b) give power to the court to make orders of rectification in order to give effect to property rights which have been established in an action or which are clear. Paragraph (c) enables orders to be made by consent. The remaining paras, (d) to (h), are intended to enable errors to be corrected. Paragraph (d), para (e), para (f) and para (g) each deals with an error of a particular character. But, since these paragraphs might not cover comprehensively all errors, paragraph (h) was added as a catch-all provision to cover any other errors. The breadth of the catch-all provision was, I imagine, the reason why it was thought appropriate to make the power exercisable [where ... it may be deemed just to rectify the register]. There are no comparable words in any of the other paragraphs.

Paragraph (h) is relied on by Mr Lloyd. But in order for the paragraph to be applicable some 'error or omission in the register' or some 'entry made under a mistake' must be shown. The entry in the charges register of the building society's legal charge was not an error and was not made under a mistake. The legal charge was executed by the Hammonds, who were at the time transferees under a transfer executed by Mrs Steed as attorney for the registered proprietor. The voidable transfer had not been set aside. The registration of the Hammonds as proprietors took place at the same time as the registration of the legal charge. Neither registration was an error. Neither entry was made under a mistake. So the case for rectification cannot be brought under para (h).

As a matter of principle, if, as I think, the appellant's case for rectification as against the building society cannot be brought under any of the paragraphs of s 82(1), I would conclude that that must be an end to the rectification claim. Mr Lloyd, however, has relied strongly on passages in the judgment of Slade LJ in *Argyle Building Society v Hammond.*

[His Lordship referred to *Chowood Ltd v Lyall (No 2)* [1930] 2 Ch 156; [1930] All ER Rep 402; *Calgary and Edmonton Land Co Ltd v Discount Bank (Overseas) Ltd* [1971] 1 All ER 551; [1971] 1 WLR 81 and continued]

In *Re Leighton's Conveyance* [1936] 1 All ER 667 a *non est factum* case was raised. The plaintiff sought rectification, first, against her daughter, who had fraudulently induced the plaintiff to sign a transfer leading to the daughter's registration as proprietor, and secondly, against chargees who, without any notice of the daughter's fraud, had advanced money to the daughter on the security of registered charges. The case was, therefore, very similar to the present case. Luxmoore J ordered rectification as against the daughter but, having concluded that the *non est factum* plea failed, he dismissed the rectification claim against the chargees. He said (at 673):

> I am satisfied that there are no grounds on which I can say that these charges are bad, but with regard to the equity of redemption I am satisfied on the evidence that what Mrs Wardman did was at the request of and in reliance on her daughter, and under her influence ... It follows that the conveyance to Mrs Bergin can have no effect as against Mrs Wardman, and she is still entitled to the equity of redemption in the property ... With regard to the charges register, there is no ground for interfering with it and directing a rectification. They are good charges and remain enforceable against the property.

It was not stated in the judgment which paragraph or paragraphs of s 82(1) Luxmoore J regarded as applicable, but the report of the argument of counsel and an editorial note suggest that the judge was invited to act under para (d) (at 667). It appears also from the report of argument that rectification as against the daughter was conceded and that the only issue in the case against the chargees was the *non est factum* issue. In my opinion, para (a), rather than para (d), provided the power to rectify as against the daughter. If the *non est factum* case had succeeded, para (g) also would have been in point, both against the daughter and against the chargees. And there is nothing in the judgment of Luxmoore J to indicate that, having rejected the *non est factum* plea, he thought that he had any discretionary power to order rectification of the charges register.

I now come to the judgment of Slade LJ in *Argyle Building Society v Hammond*. For the purposes of his judgment, Slade LJ assumed that the allegation of forgery would succeed. He assumed nothing else. References to the 'assumed facts' are references to the facts regarding the forgery. Having set out the text of s 82(1), he said (at 157):

> First, registers of title made pursuant to the 1925 Act consist of three parts, namely the property register, the proprietorship register and the charges register. The jurisdiction to rectify under the subsection plainly extends to all or any of

these parts. Secondly, on the assumed facts in the present case, the court would, in our judgment, have clear jurisdiction to rectify the proprietorship register of the house by substituting the name of the appellant for that of Mr and Mrs Hammond, since the case would fall within all or any of sub-paras (a), (b), (d), (g) and (h) of s 82(1). The present argument relates to the possibility or otherwise of rectification of the charges register.'

... Slade LJ then referred to *Re Leighton's Conveyance*, cited the passage from the judgment of Luxmoore J that I have cited and continued (at 160):

> Reverting to the decision at first instance in the *Leighton* case, the report of the argument shows that the provisions of s 82(1) and (2) of the 1925 Act were drawn to the attention of Luxmoore J. We feel no doubt that he would have appreciated that, even in the absence of a successful plea of forgery or *non est factum*, the section would in terms have conferred a discretion on the court to rectify the charges register, even as against the innocent chargees. Nevertheless, it is readily intelligible that Luxmoore J should have considered that, when the discretion fell to be exercised, the equities were all on one side – that is to say in favour of the chargees, who had acted on the faith of a document of transfer which the mother had herself executed after having failed to make inquiries which would have revealed that the document related to the property. If the title to the land had not been registered, the title of the daughter would, at worst, have been voidable, not void; and under general principles of equity, mortgagees from the daughter in good faith and for value, without notice of the facts giving rise to the voidability, would have acquired a good title to their mortgages. We can see no reason why the court in the *Leighton* case should have regarded the equities as being any different, as between the mother and the chargees, merely because the land happened to be registered land.

In my respectful opinion, this analysis of *Re Leighton's Conveyance* is not justified by Luxmoore J's judgment. There is nothing in the judgment or in the report of counsel's argument to suggest that the possibility of rectification against the chargees, in the absence of a successful plea of forgery or *non est factum* was ever considered. Slade LJ commented (at 162):

> ... in a case where one or more of the conditions of s 82(1) are fulfilled, the court has at least theoretical discretion to rectify any part of the register, even as against innocent third parties ...

I would respectfully agree with this comment, based as it is on the premise that the case can be brought within one or other of the paragraphs of s 82(1). But Slade LJ then went on to distinguish the case of a party 'deprived of his title as a result of a forged document which he did not execute' from the case where the party 'has been deprived as a result of a document which he himself executed, albeit under a mistake induced by fraud' and commented that 'when the court comes to exercise its discretion, different considerations may well apply'. The paragraph of s 82(1) under which the latter case could be brought was not identified. On the true construction of s 82(1) there is not, in my opinion, any paragraph under which the latter case could be brought.

Mr Lloyd's argument that the court has a general discretionary power to order rectification of the register was based on the passages from Slade LJ's judgment to which I have referred. The passages were not part of the *ratio* of the decision, by which we are bound and with which I respectfully agree. A voidable transfer was not part of the 'assumed facts' on which the *ratio* was based. In my judgment, the *obiter* passages, regarding voidable transfers and innocent third parties claiming thereunder, were based on an innocent construction of s 82(1) and should not be followed.

In my opinion, if the appellant's *non est factum* case is rejected, the court has no power under s 82(1) to order rectification as against the building society.

Restrictions on rectification

Land Registration Act 1925

82. Rectification of the register

(3) The register shall not be rectified, except for the purpose of giving effect to an overriding interest or an order of the court, so as to affect the title of the proprietor who is in possession:

(a) unless the proprietor has caused or substantially contributed to the error or omission by fraud or lack of proper care; or

(b) ...

(c) unless for any other reason, in any particular case, it is considered that it would be unjust not to rectify the register against him.

The register, however, cannot be rectified, on any of the grounds set out in s 82(1), so as to affect the title of the proprietor who is in 'possession'.[127] 'Possession' is defined in s 3(xviii) of the Land Registration Act 1925 as including receipt of rents and profits or the right to receive the same *unless the context otherwise requires*. In this context, it seems that 'possession' means physical occupation, otherwise every registered proprietor will be in 'possession' and the eight grounds of rectification will be redundant. This protection for the proprietor in possession is subject to four exceptions under s 82(3), under which the register may be rectified against a registered proprietor in possession:

(a) to give effect to an overriding interest;

(b) pursuant to an order of the court;

(c) if the registered proprietor has caused or substantially contributed to the error or omission by fraud or lack of proper care;

(d) where it would be unjust not to rectify the register.

Under s 82(2) of the Land Registration Act 1925, 'the register may be rectified notwithstanding that the rectification may affect any estates, rights, charges, or interests acquired or protected by registration, or by any entry on the register, or otherwise'. On the face of it, this subsection seems not only to authorise rectification against the registered proprietor against whom rectification was sought and ordered on one of the grounds under s 82(1), but also rectification which can adversely affect the interests of innocent third parties whose rights are already registered. This would have been the case where an innocent third party had been registered as a chargee who has advanced on the charge to a registered proprietor against whom rectification was sought under s 82(1). This

127 Section 82(3) of the LRA 1925.

was the view taken by the Court of Appeal in *Argyle Building Society v Hammond*.[128] On the assumption that there had been a forgery, it was held that the original proprietor was entitled to rectification not only against the defendants' fraudulently acquired title, but also against a duly protected chargee who took the charge in good faith.

As has been seen from Scott LJ's judgment above, the Court of Appeal in *Norwich and Peterborough Building Society v Steed*,[129] however, has questioned the view taken in *Argyle Building Society v Hammond*. Scott LJ's view seems to be right. It is arguable, as a commentator puts it, that:

> ... s 82(2) does not clearly authorise rectification so as to affect persons other than the person against whom the ground for rectification is established; it can equally be read as simply making it clear that if a ground for rectification has been established it is irrelevant that the person against whom the ground has been established has acquired his interest from a registered proprietor and duly protected it by registration. Section 82 should be strictly construed because it derogates from the idea of a guaranteed title. Moreover, it seems only right that effectively a separately claim for rectification should have to be brought against each person to be affected.[130]

Where the jurisdiction to rectify is established, it remains for the court or the registrar to decide whether to exercise the discretion to allow rectification.[131]

Indemnity

Land Registration Act 1925

83. Right to indemnity in certain cases

(1) Subject to the provisions of this Act to the contrary, any person suffering loss by reason of any rectification of the register under this Act shall be entitled to be indemnified.

(2) Where an error or omission has occurred in the register, but the register is not rectified, any person suffering loss by reason of such error or omission, shall, subject to the provisions of this Act, be entitled to be indemnified.

(3) Where any person suffers loss by reason of the loss or destruction of any document lodged at the registry for inspection or safe custody or by reason of an error in any official search, he shall be entitled to be indemnified under this Act.

(4) Subject as hereinafter provided, a proprietor of any registered land or charge claiming in good faith under a forged disposition shall, where the register is rectified, be deemed to have suffered loss by reason of such rectification and shall be entitled to be indemnified under this Act.

128 (1985) 49 P & CR 148. See [1985] Conv 135 (Sydenham, A).

129 [1992] 3 WLR 669 (an appeal of a new trial of the previous case of *Argyle Building Society v Hammond* (1985) 49 P & CR 148). See [1992] Conv 293 (Davis, C).

130 [1992] Conv 293 at 295 (Davis, C).

131 *Argyle Building Society v Hammond* (1984) 49 P & CR 148.

(5) No indemnity shall be payable under this Act in any of the following cases –

(a) Where the applicant or a person from whom he derives title (otherwise than under a disposition for valuable consideration which is registered or protected on the register) has caused or substantially contributed to the loss by fraud or lack of proper care.

Thus, any person who suffers loss by reason of any rectification of the register is entitled to be indemnified.[132] Rectification which gives effect to an overriding interest does not cause any loss but merely gives effect to a loss previously suffered; indemnity is therefore not available.[133] Where the title of a proprietor who claimed in good faith under a forged disposition is rectified, he is deemed to have suffered loss by reason of the rectification.[134]

Where a person suffers loss by reason of an error or omission in the register which is not rectified, he is entitled to be indemnified.[135] Any person who suffers loss, by reason of the loss or destruction of any document lodged at the registry for inspection or safe custody, or by reason of an error in any official search, is entitled to be indemnified.[136]

The right to indemnity is withheld if the applicant or his predecessor in title (except under a disposition for value protected on the register) has caused or substantially contributed to the loss by fraud or lack of proper care.[137]

8 DEALINGS OF EQUITABLE INTEREST

So far, we have seen issues concerning priority in registered land where the legal estate is transferred to a third party; ie how the various legal or equitable interests bind a third party. As we have seen, the beneficial interests, under a strict settlement or trust are protected as minor interests. Any dealing of them, such as an assignment or a mortgage of the beneficial interests is not protected by any entry.[138] It is protected by giving notice to the trustees, so the priority between two equitable dealings depends on the order in which notice is received by the trustees.[139]

9 REFORM

The Law Commission has in its Third and Fourth Reports on Land Registration[140] examined the current problems of the registered system of conveyancing. It

132 Section 83(1) of the LRA 1925.

133 *Re Chowood's Registered Land* [1933] Ch 574 at 581.

134 Section 83(4) of the LRA 1925.

135 Section 83(2) of the LRA 1925.

136 Section 83(3) of the LRA 1925.

137 Section 83(5)(a) of the LRA 1925, s 83(5)(a).

138 It used to be protected by an entry in the Minor Interests Index which was abolished in 1986.

139 Section 5 of the LRA 1986.

140 Law Commission, Property Law: Third Report on Land Registration (Law Com No 158, 31 March 1987); Property Law: Fourth Report on Land Registration (Law Com No 173, 8 November 1988).

identifies two new guiding principles for future reform.[141] First, 'in the interest of certainty and of simplifying conveyancing, the class of right which may bind a purchaser otherwise than as the result of an entry in the register should be as narrow as possible'. Secondly, 'interest should be overriding where protection against purchasers is needed, yet it is either not reasonable to expect or not sensible to require any entry on the register'. The proposals for reform are summarised as follows:

Law Commission, Property Law: Third Report on Land Registration (Law Com No 158), 31 March 1987

SUMMARY OF PART II

2.105 Our positive recommendations in this Part are that only the following should be overriding interests:

(1) legal easements and profits *à prendre;*[142]

(2) rights acquired by adverse possession;[143]

(3) leases for 21 years or less;[144]

(4) rights of persons in actual occupation of the land;[145]

(5) customary rights.[146]

2.106 Also recommended are the following three amendments to apply to all these five categories of overriding interests:

(i) that they should be expressly subject to a general provision regarding fraud or estoppel;[147]

(ii) that their relevant date should be, not registration, but completion of a disposition[148] thus removing the problem of the 'registration gap';[149]

(iii) that indemnity should become available.[150]

---

141 Law Com No 158, para 2.6.

142 See paras 2.25–2.35; note the exclusion of easements and profits expressly created by a registered proprietor which remain equitable until completed by registration.

143 See paras 2.36 and 2.37; note that such rights in the course of acquisition call for a separate provision.

144 See paras 2.38–2.53; in detail this head would cover rights having reference to the subject-matter of a lease granted (not a contract) for a continuous term not exceeding 21 years taking effect in possession either immediately or within one month (see paras 2.49 and 2.52).

145 See paras 2.54–2.70; note the inclusion of part occupation (para 2.55) and of rights under strict settlements (para 2.69) but the exclusion of receipt of rents and profits (para 2.70).

146 See para 2.73.

147 See para 2.75.

148 See para 2.77.

149 This problem has now been removed judicially: see *Abbey National Building Society v Cann* [1990] 1 All ER 1085.

150 See paras 2.10–2.14; also Part III, para 3.29.

2.107 In addition, the recognition of general burdens as a class of rights over registered land is recommended.[151] These rights would bind registered proprietors, as do overriding interests, but the matters mentioned in the preceding paragraph would not apply. Certain existing overriding interests should, we recommend, become such burdens, namely public rights,[152] chancel repairs liability,[153] local land charges,[154] mineral rights[155] and franchises.[156]

2.108 Negatively, the recommendation follows that any other existing overriding interests should cease to be such and become minor interests.[157] No transitional period is recommended.[158]

SUMMARY OF PART IV

4.117 (i) Minor interest should embrace a wide variety of property interests and rights. [Paragraphs 4.4–4.13]

(ii) These rights and interests should be protected by entry in the register in order to prevail against a registered proprietor being a purchaser for value and in good faith. [Paragraphs 4.14–4.18]

(iii) Entry of a notice should be available to protect an interest in a registered charge as well as to protect an interest in land. [Paragraph 4.38 at (iii)]

(iv) The machinery for protection should distinguish between rights and interests which are acknowledged by the registered proprietor and those which are not. [Paragraph 4.38 at (iv)]

(v) Generally the notice should be used for acknowledged rights and interests and the caution for unacknowledged rights and interests. [Paragraph 4.38 at (iv)]

(vi) In accordance with this, whenever entry of a notice is requested, the land or charge certificate should be produced or, if either of these is already on deposit, the written consent of the registered proprietor of the land or charge to the entry. [Paragraph 4.38 at (v)]

(vii) A minor interest holder should have the right to require production of the land or charge certificate where the minor interest has been created by agreement under the hand or seal of the registered proprietor of the land or charge. [Paragraph 4.113]

(viii) It should be possible to apply to change the name and address of a person in whose favour a caution is lodged without the need to withdraw and relodge the caution itself. [Paragraph 4.47]

(ix) The only exception to the para (v) policy is the protection of charging orders which should continue to be by notice only subject to para (xiii) below. [Paragraph 4.42]

---

151 See para 2.15.

152 See paras 2.79 and 2.80.

153 See para 2.81.

154 See para 2.94.

155 See paras 2.101 and 2.102; note that this recommendation applies to the right and title of the National Coal Board only.

156 See para 2.100.

157 See Part IV of this report for methods of protection on the register; also Part III as to the possibilities of rectification and/or indemnity.

158 See paras 2.16–2.18.

(x) The inhibition should not be abolished as it is a useful procedural device; s 57 should be amended to allow the inhibition to be resorted to by those seeking Mareva or other injunctions extending to land. [Paragraph 4.59]

(xi) The restriction should be the only entry used to protect the interest of a beneficiary under a trust of land, be it a trust for sale, settled land or other trust. To this end the Registrar should have power to enter a restriction of his own motion wherever it is apprehended that a registered proprietor holds the land on trust for sale. [Paragraphs 4.38 at (vi), 4.50–4.53, 4.55]

(xii) Equally for mortgages of an interest under a trust, the restriction should be the only method of protection. [Paragraph 4.83]

(xiii) Consistently with the preceding paragraphs, a charging order obtained against the beneficial interest under a trust of a debtor in any registered land should be capable of protection by restriction only. [Paragraph 4.43]

(xiv) It should not be necessary to require production of the land or charge certificate on the entry of a restriction. [Paragraphs 4.38 at (vii), 4.53–4.54]

(xv) The restriction should continue to be available for a particular interest or claim which the parties expressly agree should be protected by restriction. [Paragraph 4.49]

(xvi) The existing methods of creating charges of registered land should all continue. [Paragraph 4.63]

(xvii) Protection of a charge by substantive registration should be extended to include equitable mortgages created by deed, not being mortgages of an equitable interest. [Paragraphs 4.76–4.78]

(xviii) The notice of deposit should no longer be available as a method of protection. [Paragraph 4.81]

(xix) Except for the 'negative pledge clause' which should be capable of protection by restriction only, floating charges should not be capable of protection on the register until they have crystallised. Once crystallised they are no different from any other equitable charge. [Paragraph 4.92]

(xx) Priority of minor interests *inter se* should be governed by their order of protection on the register subject to any agreement or statutory provision to the contrary. [Paragraph 4.98(iii)]

(xxi) Any revision in the chronological order of priorities by agreement should be the subject of an entry in the register. [Paragraph 4.98(iv)]

(xxii) There should be no charge to the occasions when production of certificates to the Land Registry is required for dispositions except that registration of a lease at a rent without a fine should also entail production. [Paragraph 4.110]

(xxiii) Otherwise the certificate need not be produced on the entry of a caution, a notice of a charging order or a restriction (whether applied for by the beneficiary or entered of his own motion by the Registrar) to protect a beneficial interest. Nor need it be produced where protection of a second charge by notice is desired and the certificate is with the first chargee whose compliance cannot be obtained. [Paragraph 4.112 at (ii), (iii), (iv) and (vii)]

(xxiv) Where a notice is applied for but the application is technically defective, protection by caution should be obtainable without loss of priority. [Paragraph 4.116]

BIRKENHEAD

HALDANE

HALSBURY

CAIRNS

SELBORNE

WESTBURY

HM Land Registry

This is to certify

that the land described within and shown on the official plan is registered at HM Land Registry with the title number and class of title stated in the register.

There are contained in this certificate office copies of the entries in the register and of the official plan and, where so indicated in the register, of documents filed in the Land Registry.

Under section 68 of the Land Registration Act, 1925 and rule 264 of the Land Registration Rules, 1925 this certificate shall be admissible as evidence of the matters contained herein and must be produced to the Chief Land Registrar in the circumstances set out in section 64 of the said Act.

WARNING

All persons are cautioned against altering, adding to or otherwise tampering with either this certificate or any document annexed to it.

Specimen Register

HM Land Registry

TITLE NUMBER: CS72510

Edition date: 31 August 1990

Entry No.	**A. PROPERTY REGISTER** containing the description of the registered land and the estate comprised in the Title
	COUNTY: CORNSHIRE — DISTRICT: MARADON
1.	(19 December 1989) The Freehold land shown edged with red on the plan of the above Title filed at the Registry and being 13 Augustine Way, Kerwick.
2.	(19 December 1989) The land has the benefit of a right of way on foot only over the passageway at the rear leading into Monks Mead.

Entry No.	**B. PROPRIETORSHIP REGISTER** stating nature of the Title, name, address and description of the proprietor of the land and any entries affecting the right of disposing thereof **TITLE ABSOLUTE**
1.	(31 August 1990) Proprietor(s): PAUL JOHN DAWKINS and ANGELA MARY DAWKINS both of 13 Augustine Way, Kerwick, Maradon, Cornshire.
2.	(31 August 1990) RESTRICTION: Except under an order of the registrar no disposition by the proprietor(s) of the land is to be registered without the consent of the proprietor(s) of the Charge dated 29 July 1990 in favour of Weyford Building Society referred to in the Charges Register.

Entry No.	**C. CHARGES REGISTER** containing charges, incumbrances etc. adversely affecting the land and registered dealings therewith
1.	(31 August 1990) A Transfer of the land in this title dated 29 July 1990 made between (1) JOHN EDWARD CHARLES BROWN and (2) PAUL JOHN DAWKINS and ANGELA MARY DAWKINS contains restrictive covenants. *NOTE:– Copy in Certificate*
2.	(31 August 1990) REGISTERED CHARGE dated 29 July 1990 to secure the moneys including the further advances therein mentioned.
3.	(31 August 1990) Proprietor(s): WEYFORD BUILDING SOCIETY of Society House, The Avenue, Weymouth, Cornshire

***** END OF REGISTER *****

NOTE A: A date at the beginning of an entry is the date on which the entry was made in the Register.

NOTE B: This certificate was officially examined with the register on **31 August 1990**.

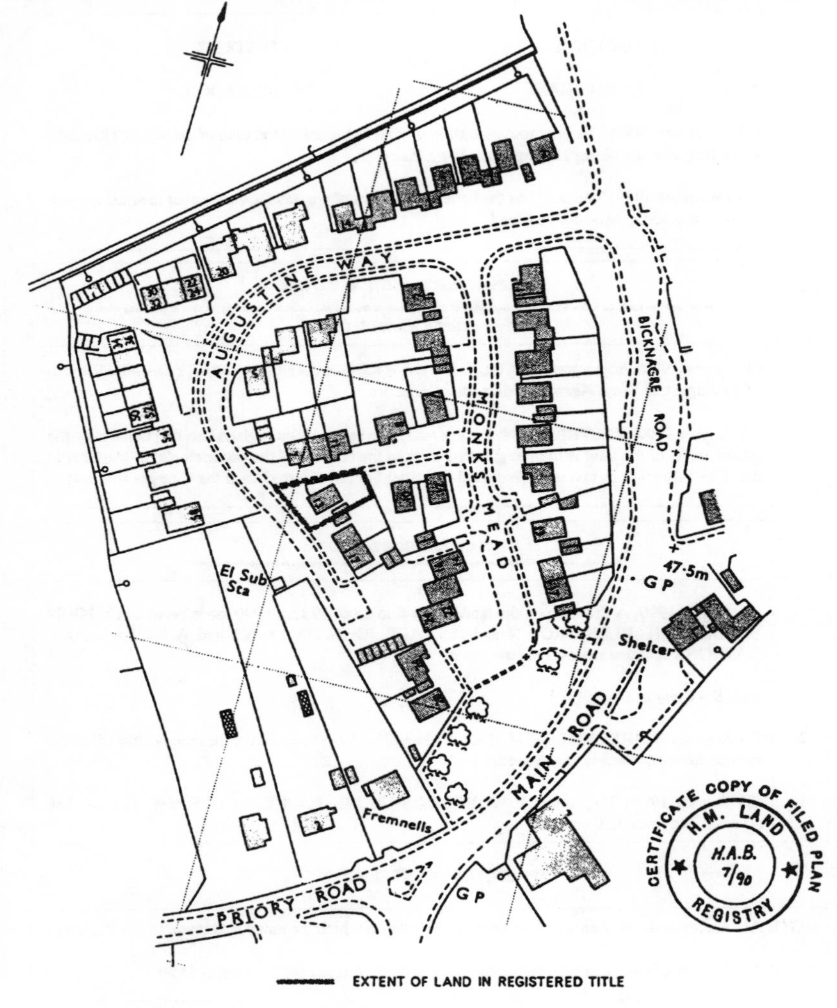
TITLE NUMBER
H.M. LAND REGISTRY
CS72510
ORDNANCE SURVEY PLAN REFERENCE
TL 7802
SECTION U
Scale
1/1250 Enlarged from 1/2500
COUNTY CORNSHIRE
DISTRICT MARADON
© Crown copyright 1977
AUGUSTINE WAY
MONKS MEAD
BICKNAGRE ROAD
El Sub Sta
47·5m
G P
Shelter
MAIN ROAD
Fremnells
PRIORY ROAD
G P
CERTIFICATE COPY OF FILED PLAN
H.M. LAND REGISTRY
H.A.B.
7/90
EXTENT OF LAND IN REGISTERED TITLE

CHAPTER 8

LEASES[1]

1 DEFINITION

A lease is a legal estate under s 1(1)(b) of the Law of Property Act 1925. It is called a 'term of years absolute' and is defined in s 205(1)(xxvii) of the Act.

Law of Property Act 1925

205. General definitions

(1) In this Act unless the context otherwise requires, the following expressions have the meanings hereby assigned to them respectively, that is to say:

(xxvii) 'Term of years absolute' means a term of years (taking effect either in possession or in reversion whether or not at a rent) with or without impeachment for waste, subject or not to another legal estate, and either certain or liable to determination by notice, re-entry, operation of law, or by a provision for cesser on redemption, or in any other event (other than the dropping of a life, or the determination of a determinable life interest); but does not include any term of years determinable with life or lives or with the cesser of a determinable life interest, nor, if created after the commencement of this Act, a term of years which is not expressed to take effect in possession within 21 years after the creation thereof where required by this Act to take effect within that period; and in this definition the expression 'term of years' includes a term for less than a year, or for a year or years and a fraction of a year or from year to year.

Term

To be a lease, what is granted must be for a definite period, rather than for an indefinite one, fixed in advance at the commencement date. As Blackstone once put it, a leasehold is a term 'because its duration or continuance is bounded, limited and determined: for every such estate must have a certain beginning, and certain end.'[2] Thus, the commencement date of the lease must be certain, or can be made certain before the commencement of the term.[3] Similarly, the maximum duration of the lease must be certain at the date of commencement.[4] In *Lace v Chantler*,[5] a lease granted 'for the duration of the war' was held void.[6]

---

1 See Evans, DL and Smith, PF *The Law of Landlord and Tenant*, 4th edn, 1993, London: Butterworths; Gray, Chapter 17.

2 Bl Comm, Vol II, p 143.

3 *Say v Smith* (1563) 1 Plowd 269 at 272, 75 ER 410 at 415; *Brilliant v Michaels* [1945] 1 All ER 121 at 126. For certainty of terms, see (1993) 13 *Legal Studies* 38 (Bright, S).

4 *Prudential Assurance Co Ltd v London Residuary Body* [1992] 2 AC 386 at 392B. The Court of Appeal's view, in *Ashburn Anstalt v Arnold* [1989] Ch 1, that a lease was valid so long as the maximum duration could be made certain restrospectively at the date of the determination, which was within the parties' control, was rejected by the House of Lords.

5 [1944] KB 368.

6 *Lace v Chantler* [1944] KB 368. Such 'leases' were retrospectively turned into determinable leases of 10 years by s 1(1) of the Validation of Wartime Leases Act 1944.

So is a lease for 'so long as the company is trading'.[7] An agreement purporting to 'continue until the land is required by the council for road widening' did not create a lease.[8]

Lace v Chantler [1944] KB 368, CA

Lord Greene MR: Normally there could be no question that this was an ordinary weekly tenancy, duly determinable by a week's notice, but the parties in the rent-book agreed to a term which appears there expressed by the words 'furnished for duration', which must mean the duration of the war. The question immediately arises whether a tenancy for the duration of the war creates a good leasehold interest. In my opinion, it does not. A term created by a leasehold tenancy agreement must be expressed either with certainty and specifically or by reference to something which can, at the time when the lease takes effect, be looked to as a certain ascertainment of what the term is meant to be. In the present case, when this tenancy agreement took effect, the term was completely uncertain. It was impossible to say how long the tenancy would last. Mr Sturge in his argument has maintained that such a lease would be valid, and that, even if the term is uncertain at its beginning when the lease takes effect, the fact that at some future time it will be rendered certain is sufficient to make it a good lease. In my opinion, that argument is not to be sustained.

I do not propose to go into the authorities on the matter, but in Foa's *Landlord and Tenant*, 6th edn, p 115, the law is stated in this way, and, in my view, correctly: 'The *habendum* in a lease must point out the period during which the enjoyment of the premises is to be had; so that the duration, as well as the commencement of the term, must be stated. The certainty of a lease as to its continuance must be ascertainable either by the express limitation of the parties at the time the lease is made, or by reference to some collateral act which may, with equal certainty, measure the continuance of it, otherwise it is void. If the term be fixed by reference to some collateral matter, such matter must either be itself certain (eg a demise to hold for 'as many years as A has in the manor of B') or capable before the lease takes effect of being rendered so, (eg for 'as many years as C shall name'.) The important words to observe in that last phrase are the words 'before the lease takes effect'. Then it goes on: 'Consequently, a lease to endure for "as many years as A shall live", or "as the coverture between B and C shall continue", would not be good as a lease for years, although the same results may be achieved in another way by making the demise for a fixed number (99 for instance) of years determinable upon A's death, or the dissolution of the coverture between B and C'. In the present case, in my opinion, this agreement cannot take effect as a good tenancy for the duration of the war.

The principle in *Lace v Chantler* was said to have reaffirmed 500 years of judicial acceptance of the requirement that a term must be certain, and applied to all leases and tenancy agreements.[9] This principle of certainty has more recently been endorsed by the House of Lords in *Prudential Assurance Co Ltd v London Residuary Body*.[10]

7 *Birrell v Carey* (1989) 58 P & CR 184 at 186. See [1990] Conv 288 (Martin, JE).

8 *Prudential Assurance Co Ltd v London Residuary Body* [1992] 2 AC 386, HL.

9 *Prudential Assurance Co Ltd v London Residuary Body* [1992] 2 AC 386 at 394E–H.

10 [1992] 2 AC 386.

Prudential Assurance Co Ltd v London Residuary Body [1992] 2 AC 386, HL

Lord Templeman: A demise for years is a contract for the exclusive possession and profit of land for some determinate period. Such an estate is called a 'term'. Thus Co Litt, 19th edn, 1832, vol 1, para 45b said that:

> ['Terminus'] in the understanding of the law does not only signify the limits and limitation of time, but also the estate and interest that passes for that time.

Blackstone's *Commentaries on the Laws of England*, 2nd edn, 1766, vol II said, at p 143:

> Every estate which must expire at a period certain and prefixed, by whatever words created, is an estate for years. And therefore this estate is frequently called a term, terminus, because its duration or continuance is bounded, limited and determined: for every such estate must have a certain beginning, and certain end.

In *Say v Smith* (1563) Plowd 269 a lease for a certain term purported to add a term which was uncertain; the lease was held valid only as to the certain term. Anthony Brown J is reported to have said, at 272:

> ... every contract sufficient to make a lease for years ought to have certainty in three limitations, *viz* in the commencement of the term, in the continuance of it, and in the end of it; so that all these ought to be known at the commencement of the lease, and words in a lease, which don't make this appear, are but babble ... And these three are in effect but one matter, showing the certainty of the time for which the lessee shall have the land, and if any of these fail, it is not a good lease, for then there wants certainty.

[His Lordship read ss 1(1) and 205(1)(xxvii) of the Law of Property Act 1925 and continued.]

The term expressed to be granted by the agreement in the present case does not fall within this definition.

Ancient authority, recognised by the Act of 1925, was applied in *Lace v Chantler* [1944] KB 368.

The legislature concluded that it was inconvenient for leases for the duration of the war to be void and therefore by the Validation of Wartime Leases Act 1944 Parliament provided, by s 1(1), that any agreement entered into before or after the passing of the Act which purported to grant a tenancy for the duration of the war:

> ... shall have effect as if it granted or provided for the grant of a tenancy for a term of 10 years, subject to a right exercisable either by the landlord or the tenant to determine the tenancy, if the war ends before the expiration of that term, by at least one month's notice in writing given after the end of the war ...

Parliament granted the fixed and certain term which the agreements between the parties lacked in the case of tenancies for the duration of the war and which the present agreement lacks.

When the agreement in the present case was made, it failed to grant an estate in the land. The tenant, however, entered into possession and paid the yearly rent of £30 reserved by the agreement. The tenant entering under a void lease became by virtue of possession and the payment of a yearly rent, a yearly tenant holding on the terms of the agreement so far as those terms were consistent with the yearly tenancy. A yearly tenancy is determinable by the landlord or the tenant at the end of the first or any subsequent year of the tenancy by six months' notice unless the agreement between the parties provides otherwise. Thus, in *Doe d Rigge v Bell* (1793) 5 Durn & E 471, a parol agreement for a seven-year lease did not comply with the Statute of Frauds 1677 (29 Car 2, c 3) but the tenant entered and paid a yearly rent and it was held that he was tenant from year to year on the terms of the agreement ...

Now it is said that when in the present case the tenant entered pursuant to the agreement and paid a yearly rent he became a tenant from year to year on the terms of the agreement including clause 6 which prevents the landlord from giving notice to quit until the land is required for road widening. This submission would make a nonsense of the rule that a grant for an uncertain term does not create a lease and would make nonsense of the concept of a tenancy from year to year because it is of the essence of a tenancy from year to year that both the landlord and the tenant shall be entitled to give notice determining the tenancy.

[His Lordship referred to *Doe d Warner v Browne* (1807) 8 East 165; *Cheshire Lines Committee v Lewis & Co* (1880) 50 LJ QB 121 and continued.]

These authorities indicate plainly enough that the agreement in the present case did not create a lease and that the tenancy from year to year enjoyed by the tenant as a result of entering into possession and paying a yearly rent can be determined by six months' notice by either landlord or tenant. The landlord has admittedly served such a notice. The Court of Appeal have however concluded that the notice was ineffective and that the landlord cannot give a valid notice until the land is required 'for the purposes of the widening of Walworth Road' in conformity with clause 6 of the agreement.

The notion of a tenancy from year to year, the landlord binding himself not to give notice to quit, which was exploded long before 1807 according to Lawrence J in *Doe d Warner v Browne* (1807) 8 East 165, 167, was however revived and applied by the Court of Appeal in In *Re Midland Railway Co's Agreement* [1971] Ch 725. In that case, a lease for a period of six months from 10 June 1920 was expressed to continue from half year to half year until determined. The agreement provided for the determination of the agreement by three months' written notice given by either party to the other subject to a proviso that the landlords should not exercise that right unless they required the premises for their undertaking. The successors to the landlords served a six months' written notice to quit under s 25 of the Landlord and Tenant Act 1954 although they did not require the premises for their undertaking. The Court of Appeal, upholding Foster J, declared that the notice to quit was invalid and of no effect because the landlords did not require the premises for their undertaking. The Court of Appeal held that the decision in *Lace v Chantler* [1944] KB 368 did not apply to a periodic tenancy and declined to follow *Doe d Warner v Browne* (1807) 8 East 165 or *Cheshire Lines Committee v Lewis & Co* (1880) 50 LJQB 121. Russell LJ delivering the judgment of the court held that the decision in *Lace v Chantler* [1944] KB 368 did not apply to a tenancy from year to year and said [1971] Ch 725, 733:

> ... we are persuaded that, there being no authority to prevent us, it is preferable as a matter of justice to hold parties to their clearly expressed bargain rather than to introduce for the first time in 1971 an extension of a doctrine of land law so as to deny the efficacy of that bargain.

My Lords, I consider that the principle in *Lace v Chantler* [1944] KB 368 reaffirming 500 years of judicial acceptance of the requirement that a term must be certain applies to all leases and tenancy agreements. A tenancy from year to year is saved from being uncertain because each party has power by notice to determine at the end of any year.

The term continues until determined as if both parties made a new agreement at the end of each year for a new term for the ensuing year. A power for nobody to determine or for one party only to be able to determine is inconsistent with the concept of a term from year to year: see *Doe d Warner v Browne*, 8 East 165 and *Cheshire Lines Committee v Lewis & Co*, 50 LJQB 121. In *In Re Midland Railway Co's Agreement* [1971] Ch 725 there was no 'clearly expressed bargain' that the term should continue until the crack of doom if the demised land was not required for the landlord's undertaking or if the undertaking ceased to exist. In the present case, there was no 'clearly expressed bargain' that the tenant shall be entitled to enjoy his 'temporary structures' in perpetuity if Walworth Road is never widened. In any event, principle and precedent dictate that it is beyond the power of the landlord and the tenant to create a term which is uncertain.

A lease can be made for five years subject to the tenant's right to determine if the war ends before the expiry of five years. A lease can be made from year to year subject to a fetter on the right of the landlord to determine the lease before the expiry of five years unless the war ends. Both leases are valid because they create a determinable certain term of five years. A lease might purport to be made for the duration of the war subject to the tenant's right to determine before the end of the war. A lease might be made from year to year subject to a fetter on the right of the landlord to determine the lease before the war ends. Both leases would be invalid because each purported to create an uncertain term. A term must either be certain or uncertain. It cannot be partly certain because the tenant can determine it at any time and partly uncertain because the landlord cannot determine it for an uncertain period. If the landlord does not grant and the tenant does not take a certain term the grant does not create a lease.

The decision of the Court of Appeal in *In Re Midland Railway Co's Agreement* [1971] Ch 725 was taken a little further in *Ashburn Anstalt v Arnold* [1989] Ch 1. That case, if it was correct, would make it unnecessary for a lease to be of a certain duration. In an agreement for the sale of land the vendor reserved the right to remain at the property after completion as licensee and to trade therefrom without payment of rent:

> ... save that it can be required by Matlodge [the purchaser] to give possession on not less than one quarter's notice in writing upon Matlodge certifying that it is ready at the expiration of such notice forthwith to proceed with the development of the property and the neighbouring property involving, *inter alia*, the demolition of the property.

The Court of Appeal held that this reservation created a tenancy. The tenancy was not from year to year but for a term which would continue until Matlodge certified that it was ready to proceed with the development of the property. The Court of Appeal held that the term was not uncertain because the vendor could either give a quarter's notice or vacate the property without giving notice. But of course the same could be said of the situation in *Lace v Chantler* [1944] KB 368. The cumulative result of the two Court of Appeal authorities In *Re Midland Railway Co's Agreement* [1971] Ch 725 and *Ashburn's Case* [1989] Ch 1, would therefore destroy the need for any term to be certain.

In the present case, the Court of Appeal were bound by the decisions in *In Re Midland Railway Co's Agreement* and *Ashburn's* case. In my opinion, both these cases were wrongly decided. A grant for an uncertain term does not create a lease. A grant for an uncertain term which takes the form of a yearly tenancy which cannot be determined by the landlord does not create a lease. I would allow the appeal.

The principle that the commencement of a lease must be certain does not mean that it has to take effect immediately at the date of the grant. It can start in the future so long as this does not happen more than 21 years after the date of the grant.[11] Such a lease is known as a 'reversionary lease'. A contract to grant a lease which, when granted, will take effect more than 21 years from the date of the grant is also void. But a contract to grant a lease in the future which, when granted, will take effect immediately is not caught by s 149(3) of the Law of property Act 1925. Such a practice is commonly adopted by landlord to give the tenant an option of renewal.

The requirement of certainty of term in relation to leases determinable on death, leases for life or until marriage, perpetually renewable leases, and periodic tenancies must be examined in greater detail.

(a) Leases determinable on death

Under s 205, a fixed term which is liable to determination on the dropping of a life is not a term of years. Thus, a lease 'to A for 50 years if he shall live so long' is not a legal term of years. It is an equitable lease for 50 years determinable on A's death.[12]

(b) Leases for life or until marriage

A lease for life or until marriage[13] does not have a certain ending and is therefore not a legal or equitable term of years. Such leases are generally void.[14] But if granted at a rent or a fine, they are converted into a fixed term of 90 years determinable on the tenant's death, or marriage. The term does not terminate automatically, but on one month's notice by either party expiring on a quarter day.

As mentioned, a fixed term determinable on death is equitable. But if it is granted at a rent or a fine, it is caught by s 149(6). Thus, a lease 'to A for 50 years if he shall live so long' at a rent or a fine is converted into a fixed term of 90 years determinable on A's death by notice.[15] However, it does not apply to any term of years determinable by notice after the tenant's earlier death.[16]

Law of Property Act 1925

149. Abolition of *interesse termini*, and as to reversionary leases and leases for lives

(6) Any lease or underlease, at a rent, or in consideration of a fine, for life or lives or for any term of years determinable with life or lives, or on the marriage of the lessee, or

11 Section 149(3) of the LPA 1925.

12 As will be seen, such a lease, if granted at a rent or a fine, is converted into a fixed term of 90 years determinable on A's death by notice under s 149(6) of the LPA 1925.

13 A fixed term of years determinable on marriage is valid as a legal estate and not covered by s 149(6) of the LPA 1925 because it has a fixed and certain term and s 205 of the Act covers a lease which is determinable 'in any other event'.

14 Bl Comm, Vol II, at 143.

15 *Bass Holdings Ltd v Lewis* [1986] 2 EGLR 40.

16 *Ibid*.

any contract therefor, made before or after the commencement of this Act, or created by virtue of Part V of the Law of Property Act 1922, shall take effect as a lease, underlease or contract therefor, for a term of ninety years determinable after the death or marriage (as the case may be) of the original lessee, or of the survivor of the original lessees, by at least one month's notice in writing given to determine the same on one of the quarter days applicable to the tenancy, either by the lessor or the persons deriving title under him, to the person entitled to the leasehold interest, or if no such person is in existence by affixing the same to the premises, or by the lessee or other persons in whom the leasehold interest is vested to the lessor or the persons deriving title under him:

Provided that:

(a) this subsection shall not apply to any term taking effect in equity under a settlement or created out of an equitable interest under a settlement for mortgage, indemnity, or other like purposes;

(b) the person in whom the leasehold interest is vested by virtue of Part V of the Law of Property Act 1922 shall, for the purposes of this subsection, be deemed an original lessee;

(c) if the lease, underlease, or contract therefor is made determinable on the dropping of the lives of persons other than or besides the lessees, then the notice shall be capable of being served after the death of any person or of the survivor of any persons (whether or not including the lessees) on the cesser of whose life or lives the lease, underlease, or contract is made determinable, instead of after the death of the original lessee or of the survivor of the original lessees;

(d) if there are no quarter days specially applicable to the tenancy, notice may be given to determine the tenancy on one of the usual quarter days.

(c) Perpetually renewable lease

A lease which gave the tenant a right to renew the lease at the end of the term 'on identical terms and conditions'[17] or to renew at the same rent and with the like covenants 'including the present covenant for renewal',[18] was held to be perpetually renewable. Such a lease is converted by s 145 of the Law of Property Act 1922[19] into a term of 2,000 years determinable only by the lessee.

Today, however, the court is less willing to hold that a perpetually renewable lease is intended in the absence of express words to that effect. Thus a renewal covenant in a seven year lease which provided that a renewed lease must also contain a renewal covenant for a further seven years on expiry of the renewed term was held not to create a perpetually renewable lease. The tenant was only entitled to a double renewal.[20]

Marjorie Burnett Ltd v Barclay (1980) 125 Sol Jo 199

Nourse J said that in *Parkus v Greenwood* [1950] Ch 33, Harman J, in a case where the landlord had agreed to grant a tenancy 'for a further term of three years from the

17 *Northchurch Estates v Daniels* [1947] Ch 117.

18 *Parkus v Greenwood* [1950] Ch 644.

19 Schedule 15, para 1.

20 *Marjorie Burnett Ltd v Barclay* (1980) 125 Sol Jo 199. See (1981) 131 NLJ 683 (Wilkinson, HW).

expiration of the [existing] term at the same rent and containing the like agreements and provisions as are herein contained, including the present covenant for renewal', had commented that a careful conveyancer, if he wished to avoid trouble and did not wish to have it said that there might be a perpetual right, would use the opposite words, ie 'excluding this present covenant', but nevertheless Harman J went on to hold that one had to find expressly in the lease a covenant or obligation for perpetual renewal which he did not find in that case. Harman J's decision was reversed by the Court of Appeal, see [1950] Ch 644, but that reversal was on the basis that the relevant words in that case did in fact contain such an obligation for perpetual renewal. *Caerphilly Concrete Products Ltd v Owen* [1972] 1 WLR 372, showed that the court should see what the second lease would contain when the requirements of the renewal covenant in the first lease had been duly observed. Here, the second lease would contain a covenant for a further seven years and a rent to be agreed, but the final words, requiring yet another covenant for renewal, could not possibly be included, because they were not part of the covenant for renewal. A point of equal force appeared to be that the notion of a 2,000 year term was completely inimical to a lease containing a rent review every seven years. Declaration granted.

(d) Periodic tenancy

The House of Lords in *Prudential Assurance Co Ltd v London Residuary Body*[21] held that the rule in *Lace v Chantler*[22] applies also to periodic tenancies. Russell LJ's view, in *Re Midland Railway Co's Agreement*,[23] that the requirement of certainty of term did not apply to periodic tenancies, was rejected by the House of Lords.

Periodic tenancies are, however, 'saved from being uncertain because each party has power by notice to determine at the end of any [period]. The term continues until determined as if both parties made a new agreement at the end of each [period] for a new term for the ensuing [period]'.[24]

Of years

Section 205(1)(xxvii) of the Law of Property Act 1925 provides that a 'term of years' includes 'a term for less than a year, or for a year or years and a fraction of a year or from year to year'. So a lease can be for any fixed duration. It may be granted for a week. It may be granted for a very long term, such as 3,000 years,[25] or 999 years or 99 years.[26] The period of letting needs not be continuous. It can be for a period of three successive bank holidays.[27] This is reaffirmed by the phenomenon of 'holiday timesharing' which is now regulated by the Timeshare Act 1992.[28]

21 [1992] AC 386.

22 [1944] KB 368.

23 [1971] Ch 725 at 732F. See [1971] CLJ 198 (MacIntyre, D).

24 [1992] AC 386 at 394E–F.

25 As in the case of a lease granted to secure a loan: see Chapter 16, pp 735–54.

26 As is often the case for leasehold flats.

27 *Smallwood v Sheppards* [1895] 2 QB 627 at 630.

28 See [1992] Conv 301 (Wilkinson, HW).

Absolute

As mentioned earlier, this means that the tenancy must not be subject to the dropping of a life, or the determination of a determinable life interest.[29] Such a lease will only be equitable.

2 BASIC REQUIREMENTS FOR A LEASE AND DISTINCTION BETWEEN LEASES AND LICENCES

The distinction between a lease and a licence is important because of the different legal consequences they entail. A lease confers an interest in land to the tenant, but a licence does not.[30] As a tenant has an interest in land, he can assign it to a stranger, but a licensee can never do this. Furthermore, only a lease is capable of binding the successor in title of the landlord. A licence is traditionally regarded as incapable of binding a third party[31] and only a tenant[32] can sue a third party for nuisance or trespass, but not a licensee.[33] In the past 20 years or so, the distinction is amplified by various protective legislation notably the full protection given by the Rent Act 1977. These statutory protections are given to tenants but not licensees.

Before the interest granted can qualify as a lease, apart from, and in addition to, the requirement of certainty of terms mentioned above, it must possess the characteristics to be discussed below. The essential criterion which marks off the boundary between a lease and a licence is, however, the test of exclusive possession.

Exclusive possession

There can be no lease without exclusive possession.[34] An occupant who does not enjoy exclusive possession is merely a licensee. It is the right to use the premises to the exclusion of all others, including the grantor himself, albeit temporarily and with some restrictions,[35] which gives the grantee a leasehold

---

29 Section 205(1)(xxvii) of the LPA 1925. See Chapter 1, p 18.

30 See Chapter 10.

31 See Chapter 10. Lord Denning's view in *Errington v Errington and Woods* [1952] 1 KB 290, that a contractual licence can bind a third party who takes with notice in unregistered land, and can be overriding under s 70(1)(g) of the Land Registration Act 1925 in registered land, has been rejected by the Court of Appeal in *Ashburn Anstalt v Arnold* [1989] Ch 1. In view of this, it seems that his view in *E R Ives Investment v High* [1967] 2 QB 379, that a licence by estoppel can bind the successor of the licensor with notice in unregistered land, is perhaps also open to doubt now.

32 *Harper v Charlesworth* (1825) 4 B & C 574 at 585; 107 ER 1174 at 1178; *Street v Mountford* [1985] AC 809 at 816B–C.

33 *Hill v Tupper* (1863) 2 H & C 121 at 127; 159 ER 51 at 53; *AG Securities v Vaughan* [1990] 1 AC 417 at 454A–B. See, however, *Khorasandjian v Bush* [1993] NLJ 329 (licensee allowed injunction against harassment by persistent phonecalls).

34 *Street v Mountford* [1985] AC 809 at 816C, 818E.

35 For example, the lease may reserve the right for the landlord to enter the premises on certain occasions, such as to inspect or to repair the property: *Street v Mountford* [1985] AC 809 at 816B–C.

interest. Thus, if the landlord has a right to introduce other licensees to share the premises with the occupant at a later date, there is no exclusive possession.[36] A term which entitles the owner at his convenience to move the occupier from one room to another within the same house negatives any claim for exclusive possession which the occupier might otherwise have in respect of the room originally allocated to him.[37] In *Westminster City Council v Clarke*,[38] where the occupant of a council-run hostel for homeless persons was not entitled to any particular room, could be asked to share a room with others, was not allowed to see visitors without permission from hostel staff, had to comply with the directions of the warden and other conditions, it was held that no tenancy was created.

An occupier who enjoys exclusive possession is not a tenant if it is not granted for a fixed or a periodic term. But normally the enjoyment of exclusive possession for a term in consideration of periodical payments creates a tenancy, save in exceptional circumstances.[39]

Exclusive possession should be distinguished from exclusive occupation. The former is an attribute of a tenancy, whilst the latter simply gives the occupant a right of sole occupation. Exclusive occupation, whilst giving the occupant the exclusive physical occupation of the premises, does not give him the overall control over the use of, and access to, the premises. Thus, students in university halls of residence, lodgers in hotels or boardinghouses[40] or a furnished home,[41] and residents in nursing homes[42] may all enjoy exclusive occupation, but they do not have exclusive possession.

While it is necessary to show exclusive possession for a lease, it does not follow that whenever exclusive possession is established, a tenancy exists. There are many cases where the occupant has enjoyed exclusive possession of land, but no tenancy has been created. There may be circumstances which negative the existence of a tenancy. Thus, where a residential accommodation is offered and accepted with 'exclusive possession' for a term at a rent, the occupier may be a lodger or a tenant. The occupant is a lodger if the landlord provides attendance or services which require the landlord or his servants to exercise unrestricted access to and use of the premises.[43] Where the occupancy does not require attendance or services, the grant is likely to be a tenancy.[44] But if there is contractual requirement of attendance or service, the fact that it is never actually

36 *Somma v Hazelhurst* [1978] 2 All ER 1011. However, the House of Lords in *Street v Mountford* [1985] AC 809 thought that the agreement in *Somma* was a sham.

37 *Crancour v Da Silvaesa* [1986] 1 EGLR 80.

38 [1992] 2 AC 288. See [1992] JSWFL 334 (J Baxter); [1992] Conv 113 (JE Martin); [1992] Conv 285 (DS Cowan). See also *Oxford Overseas Student Housing Association v Mukherjee*, unreported, Court of Appeal, 21 November 1989.

39 *Street v Mountford* [1985] AC 809.

40 *Appah v Parncliffe* [1964] 1 WLR 1064.

41 *Marchant v Charters* [1977] 1 WLR 1181 at 1185G–H.

42 *Abbeyfield (Harpenden) Society Ltd v Woods* [1968] 1 WLR 374 at 376F–H, approved by the House of Lords in *Street v Mountford* [1985] AC 809 at 824B.

43 *Street v Mountford* [1985] AC 809 at 818A; *Antoniades v Villiers* [1990] 1 AC 417 at 459 F–G.

44 *Street v Mountford* [1985] AC 809 at 818C.

provided does not convert a licence into a tenancy.[45] It is not the services or attendance which negatives the tenancy; it is the occupant's inability to resist intrusion by the owner who requires access to supply the services or attendance which is fatal.[46] Circumstances such as a family arrangement,[47] an act of friendship or generosity, or such like may also negative any intention to create a tenancy.[48] It should be noted that occupancy granted by circumstances of friendship or generosity does not inevitably lead to a mere licence.[49] Neither would the fact of family relationship prevent a lease from being granted.[50] If the occupant is an object of charity[51] or a service occupant,[52] there is no tenancy even if he enjoys exclusive occupation because his possession should be treated in law as the possession of someone else or that there is no intention to create any contractual relationship at all.[53] If the service occupancy is simply incidental to, and not contingent on the employment, the position may be different.[54] Exclusive occupation provided in return for performance of cooking and other domestic services and payment of certain household bills was closely akin to those produced by family arrangements to share a house and therefore is a mere personal licence to occupy.[55] If the employee is required to occupy his employer's premises for better performance of his duties, it would be a mere licence.[56] Accommodation provided under gentleman's agreement to an occupier in the role of a caretaker or a friend looking after the place and who pays minimal payments as to fall far short of an economic rent does not create tenancy.[57]

Duration of occupancy and provision of furniture are irrelevant factors in determining whether a particular occupancy is a lease or a licence.[58] It is

45 *Crancour Ltd v Da Silvaesa* (1986) 52 P & CR 204 at 212, 230.

46 *Antoniades v Villiers* [1990] 1 AC 417 at 459F–G, 467A–B.

47 *Booker v Palmer* [1942] 2 All ER 674 at 677C; *Cobb v Lane* [1952] 1 All ER 1199 at 1201A; *Errington v Errington and Woods* [1952] 1 KB 290 at 298.

48 *Facchini v Bryson* [1952] 1 TLR 1386 at 1389 affirmed by *Street v Mountford* [1985] AC 809 at 821F–22A; *Marcroft Wagons Ltd v Smith* [1951] 2 KB 496. See also (1969) 32 MLR 92 (Harris, JW).

49 *Sopwith v Stutchbury* (1983) 17 HLR 50 at 55.

50 *Nunn v Dalrymple* (1990) 59 P & CR 231 at 239f.

51 *Street v Mountford* [1985] AC 809 at 818E. See also *Brent People's Housing Association Ltd v Winsmore*, unreported, County Court, 20 November 1985; *Westminster City Council v Clarke* [1992] 2 AC 288.

52 *Street v Mountford* [1985] AC 809 at 818E–G, 827A; *Wrotham Park Settled Estates v Naylor* (1991) 62 P & CR 233 at 237; *Norris v Checksfield* [1991] 1 WLR 1241 at 1246A; *Smith v Seghill Overseers* (1875) LR 10 QB 422 at 428.

53 *Facchini v Bryson* [1952] TLR 1386 at 1389 affirmed by the House of Lords in *Street v Mountford* [1985] AC 809, at 818F-G, 819C, 820D, 821H–822A. See also *AG Securities v Vaughan* [1990] AC 417 at 426H–427A.

54 *Facchini v Bryson* [1952] 1 TLR 1386 at 1389; *Royal Philanthropic Society v County* (1985) 276 *Estates Gazette* 1068 at 1072 ([1986] Conv 215 (Smith, PF)).

55 *Barnes v Barratt* [1970] 2 QB 657 at 670A.

56 *Street v Mountford* [1985] AC 809.

57 *Barnes v Barratt* [1970] 2 QB 657 at 670A; *David v London Borough of Lewisham* (1977) 34 P & CR 112 at 115f; *Heslop v Burns* [1974] 1 WLR 1241 at 1244C, 1252G; *Garland v Johnson*, unreported, CA, 24 February 1982.

58 *Marchant v Charters* [1977] 3 All ER 918 at 922g.

irrelevant that the parties call the payment for the occupancy 'rent' or even use a 'rent book'.[59] Equally, the potential application of the Rent Acts should not be taken into account.[60] The 'label' used by the parties referring to the occupancy agreement as 'tenancy or lease' or 'licence' is not conclusive.[61] In Lord Templeman's words, '[i]f the agreement satisfied all the requirements of a tenancy, then the agreement produced a tenancy and the parties cannot alter the effect of the agreement by insisting that they only created a licence. The manufacturer of a five-pronged implement for manual digging results in a fork even if the manufacturer, unfamiliar with the English language, insists that he intended to make and has made a spade'.[62] The agreement has to be construed carefully in the light of the surrounding circumstances to see if a right of exclusive possession has been genuinely denied or granted.[63] The courts must 'be astute to detect and frustrate sham devices and artificial transactions whose only object is to disguise the grant of a tenancy and to evade the Rent Acts'.[64] Any sham or pretence witnessed by inconsistent or unrealistic terms will be dismissed and the residue of rights and obligations which had been concealed behind the 'smokescreen' or 'window-dressing' of the supposed 'licences' will be given effect. A good example of a sham arrangement detected by the court is the case of *Antoniades v Villiers*.[65] Here, an unmarried couple entered into identical 'licence' agreements with the owner of a small attic flat. The owner reserved a right at any time to use the premises in common with the licensee 'and such other licensees or invitees as the licensor may permit from time to time to use the said rooms'. The House of Lords thought that no realistic significance could be attached to the owner's reservation of a right to share, or authorise a stranger to share, the flat which had been 'specifically adapted for the occupation by a couple living together'.[66]

The House of Lords in *Street v Mountford*[67] disapproved of the test of professed intention of the parties laid down in *Somma v Hazelhurst and Savelli*.[68] Their Lordships thought that the task of differentiation between a contractual tenancy and a contractual licence would be impossible if it was done by reference to the test. 'The only intention which is relevant is the intention demonstrated by the agreement to grant exclusive possession for a term at a rent.'[69]

59 *Street v Mountford* (1984) 49 P & CR 324 at 328, CA.

60 *Street v Mountford* [1985] AC 809 at 819G-H; *Antoniades v Villiers* [1990] AC 417 at 445E–F.

61 *Antoniades v Villiers* [1990] 1 AC 417 at 466G-H; *Aslan v Murphy* [1990] 1 WLR 766 at 770D.

62 [1985] AC 809 at 819E–F.

63 [1985] AC 809 at 817G–H; *Hadjiloucas v Crean* [1988] 1 WLR 1006 at 1022E–G.

64 [1985] AC 809 at 825H.

65 [1990] 1 AC 417. See [1989] CLJ 19 (Harpum, C); [1989] Conv 128 (Smith, PF); (1989) 52 MLR 408 (Hill, J); (1989) 105 LQR 165 (Baker, PV).

66 [1990] 1 AC 417 at 468A.

67 [1985] AC 809.

68 [1978] 1 WLR 1014. See [1979] CLJ 38 (Gray, KJ).

69 *Street v Mountford* [1985] AC 809 at 826G.

Street v Mountford [1985] AC 809, HL

Lord Templeman: My Lords, by an agreement dated 7 March 1983, the respondent Mr Street granted the appellant Mrs Mountford the right to occupy the furnished rooms numbers 5 and 6 at 5, St Clements Gardens, Boscombe, from 7 March 1983 for £37 per week, subject to termination by 14 days' written notice and subject to the conditions set forth in the agreement. The question raised by this appeal is whether the agreement created a tenancy or a licence.

A tenancy is a term of years absolute. This expression, by s 205(l)(xxvii) of the Law of Property Act 1925, reproducing the common law, includes a term from week to week in possession at a rent and liable to determination by notice or re-entry. Originally a term of years was not an estate in land, the lessee having merely a personal action against his lessor. But a legal estate in leaseholds was created by the Statute of Gloucester 1278 and the Act of 1529 21 Hen VIII, c 15. Now by s 1 of the Law of Property Act 1925 a term of years absolute is an estate in land capable of subsisting as a legal estate. In the present case if the agreement dated 7 March 1983 created a tenancy, Mrs Mountford having entered into possession and made weekly payments acquired a legal estate in land. If the agreement is a tenancy, the occupation of Mrs Mountford is protected by the Rent Acts.

A licence in connection with land while entitling the licensee to use the land for the purposes authorised by the licence does not create an estate in the land. If the agreement dated 7 March 1983 created a licence for Mrs Mountford to occupy the premises, she did not acquire any estate in the land. If the agreement is a licence then Mrs Mountford's right of occupation is not protected by the Rent Acts. Hence the practical importance of distinguishing between a tenancy and a licence ...

My Lords, there is no doubt that the traditional distinction between a tenancy and a licence of land lay in the grant of land for a term at a rent with exclusive possession. In some cases it was not clear at first sight whether exclusive possession was in fact granted. For example, an owner of land could grant a licence to cut and remove standing timber. Alternatively, the owner could grant a tenancy of the land with the right to cut and remove standing timber during the term of the tenancy. The grant of rights relating to standing timber therefore required careful consideration in order to decide whether the grant conferred exclusive possession of the land for a term at a rent and was therefore a tenancy or whether it merely conferred a bare licence to remove the timber.

In *Glenwood Lumber Co Ltd v Phillips* [1904] AC 405, the Crown in exercise of statutory powers 'licensed' the respondents to hold an area of land for the purpose of cutting and removing timber for the term of 21 years at an annual rent. Delivering the advice of the Judicial Committee of the Privy Council, Lord Davey said, at 408–09:

> The appellants contended that this instrument conferred only a licence to cut timber and carry it away, and did not give the respondent any right of occupation or interest in the land itself. Having regard to the provisions of the Act under the powers of which it was executed and to the language of the document itself, their Lordships cannot adopt this view of the construction or effect of it. In the so-called licence itself it is called indifferently a licence and a demise, but in the Act it is spoken of as a lease, and the holder of it is described as the lessee. It is not, however, a question of words but of substance. If the effect of the instrument is to give the holder an exclusive right of occupation of the land, though subject to certain reservations or to a restriction of the purposes for which it may be used, it is in law a demise of the land itself. By [the Act] it is enacted that the lease shall vest in the lessee the right to take and keep exclusive

possession of the lands described therein subject to the conditions in the Act provided or referred to, and the lessee is empowered (amongst other things) to bring any actions or suits against any party unlawfully in possession of any land so leased, and to prosecute all trespassers thereon. The operative part and habendum in the licence is framed in apt language to carry out the intention so expressed in the Act. And their Lordships have no doubt that the effect of the so-called licence was to confer a title to the land itself on the respondent.

This was a case in which the court after careful consideration of the purposes of the grant, the terms of the grant and the surrounding circumstances, came to the conclusion that the grant conferred exclusive possession and was therefore a tenancy.

A contrary conclusion was reached in *Taylor v Caldwell* (1863) 3 B & S 826 in which the defendant agreed to let the plaintiff have the use of the Surrey Gardens and Music Hall on four specified days giving a series of four concerts and day and night fetes at the gardens and hall on those days, and the plaintiff agreed to take the gardens and the hall and to pay £100 for each day. Blackburn J said, at 832:

> The parties inaccurately call this a 'letting,' and the money to be paid a 'rent,' but the whole agreement is such as to show that the defendants were to retain the possession of the hall and gardens so that there was to be no demise of them, and that the contract was merely to give the plaintiffs the use of them on those days.

That was a case where the court after considering the purpose of the grant, the terms of the grant and the surrounding circumstances came to the conclusion that the grantee was not entitled to exclusive possession but only to use the land for limited purposes and was therefore a licensee.

In the case of residential accommodation there is no difficulty in deciding whether the grant confers exclusive possession. An occupier of residential accommodation at a rent for a term is either a lodger or a tenant. The occupier is a lodger if the landlord provides attendance or services which require the landlord or his servants to exercise unrestricted access to and use of the premises. A lodger is entitled to live in the premises but cannot call the place his own. In *Allan v Liverpool Overseers* (1874) LR 9 QB 180, 191–92 Blackburn J said:

> A lodger in a house, although he has the exclusive use of rooms in the house, in the sense that nobody else is to be there, and though his goods are stowed there, yet he is not in exclusive occupation in that sense, because the landlord is there for the purpose of being able, as landlords commonly do in the case of lodgings, to have his own servants to look after the house and the furniture, and has retained to himself the occupation, though he has agreed to give the exclusive enjoyment of the occupation to the lodger.

If, on the other hand, residential accommodation is granted for a term at a rent with exclusive possession, the landlord providing neither attendance nor services, the grant is a tenancy; any express reservation to the landlord of limited rights to enter and view the state of the premises and to repair and maintain the premises only serves to emphasise the fact that the grantee is entitled to exclusive possession and is a tenant. In the present case it is conceded that Mrs Mountford is entitled to exclusive possession and is not a lodger. Mr Street, provided neither attendance nor services and only reserved the limited rights of inspection and maintenance and the like set forth in clause 3 of the agreement. On the traditional view of the matter, Mrs Mountford not being a lodger must be a tenant.

There can be no tenancy unless the occupier enjoys exclusive possession; but an occupier who enjoys exclusive possession is not necessarily a tenant. He may be owner in fee simple, a trespasser, a mortgagee in possession, an object of charity or a service occupier. To constitute a tenancy the occupier must be granted exclusive possession for a fixed or periodic term certain in consideration of a premium or periodical payments. The grant may be express, or may be inferred where the owner accepts weekly or other periodical payments from the occupier.

Occupation by service occupier may be eliminated. A service occupier is a servant who occupies his master's premises in order to perform his duties as a servant. In those circumstances the possession and occupation of the servant is treated as the possession and occupation of the master and the relationship of landlord and tenant is not created; see *Mayhew v Suttle* (1854) 4 El & Bl 347. The test is whether the servant requires the premises he occupies in order the better to perform his duties as a servant:

> Where the occupation is necessary for the performance of services, and the occupier is required to reside in the house in order to perform those services, the occupation being strictly ancillary to the performance of the duties which the occupier has to perform, the occupation is that of a servant; *per* Mellor J in *Smith v Seghill Overseers* (1875) LR 10 QB 422, 428.

The cases on which Mr Goodhart relies begin with *Booker v Palmer* [1942] 2 All ER 674. The owner of a cottage agreed to allow a friend to install an evacuee in the cottage rent free for the duration of the war. The Court of Appeal held that there was no intention on the part of the owner to enter into legal relationships with the evacuee. Lord Greene MR, said, at 677:

> To suggest there is an intention there to create a relationship of landlord and tenant appears to me to be quite impossible. There is one golden rule which is of very general application, namely, that the law does not impute intention to enter into legal relationships where the circumstances and the conduct of the parties negative any intention of the kind. It seems to me that this is a clear example of the application of that rule.

The observations of Lord Greene MR were not directed to the distinction between a contractual tenancy and a contractual licence. The conduct of the parties (not their professed intentions) indicated that they did not intend to contract at all.

In the present case, the agreement dated 7 March 1983 professed an intention by both parties to create a licence and their belief that they had in fact created a licence. It was submitted on behalf of Mr Street that the court cannot in these circumstances decide that the agreement created a tenancy without interfering with the freedom of contract enjoyed by both parties. My Lords, Mr Street enjoyed freedom to offer Mrs Mountford the right to occupy the rooms comprised in the agreement on such lawful terms as Mr Street pleased. Mrs Mountford enjoyed freedom to negotiate with Mr Street to obtain different terms. Both parties enjoyed freedom to contract or not to contract and both parties exercised that freedom by contracting on the terms set forth in the written agreement and on no other terms. But the consequences in law of the agreement, once concluded, can only be determined by consideration of the effect of the agreement. If the agreement satisfied all the requirements of a tenancy, then the agreement produced a tenancy and the parties cannot alter the effect of the agreement by insisting that they only created a licence. The manufacture of a five-pronged implement for manual digging results in a fork even if the manufacturer, unfamiliar with the English language, insists that he intended to make and has made a spade.

It was also submitted that in deciding whether the agreement created a tenancy or a licence, the court should ignore the Rent Acts. If Mr Street has succeeded, where owners have failed these past 70 years, in driving a coach and horses through the Rent Acts, he must be left to enjoy the benefit of his ingenuity unless and until Parliament intervenes. I accept that the Rent Acts are irrelevant to the problem of determining the legal effect of the rights granted by the agreement. Like the professed intention of the parties, the Rent Acts cannot alter the effect of the agreement.

In *Marcroft Wagons Ltd v Smith* [1951] 2 KB 496 the daughter of a deceased tenant who lived with her mother claimed to be a statutory tenant by succession and the landlords asserted that the daughter had no rights under the Rent Acts and was a trespasser. The landlords expressly refused to accept the daughter's claims but accepted rent from her while they were considering the position. If the landlords had decided not to apply to the court for possession but to accept the daughter as a tenant, the moneys paid by the daughter would have been treated as rent. If the landlords decided, as they did decide, to apply for possession and to prove, as they did prove, that the daughter was not a statutory tenant, the moneys paid by the daughter were treated as mesne profits. The Court of Appeal held with some hesitation that the landlords never accepted the daughter as tenant and never intended to contract with her although the landlords delayed for some six months before applying to the court for possession. Roxburgh J said, at 507:

> Generally speaking, when a person, having a sufficient estate in land, lets another into exclusive possession, a tenancy results, and there is no question of a licence. But the inference of a tenancy is not necessarily to be drawn where a person succeeds on a death to occupation of rent-controlled premises and a landlord accepts some rent while he or the occupant, or both of them, is or are considering his or their position. If this is all that happened in this case, then no tenancy would result.

In that case, as in *Booker v Palmer*, the court deduced from the conduct of the parties that they did not intend to contract at all.

Errington v Errington and Woods [1952] 1 KB 290 concerned a contract by a father to allow his son to buy the father's house on payment of the instalments of the father's building society loan. Denning LJ referred, at p 297, to the judgment of Lord Greene MR in *Booker v Palmer* [1942] 2 All ER 674 at 677 where, however, the circumstances and the conduct of the parties negatived any intention to enter into legal relationships. Denning LJ continued, at 297–98:

> We have had many instances lately of occupiers in exclusive possession who have been held to be not tenants, but only licensees. When a requisitioning authority allowed people into possession at a weekly rent: ... when a landlord told a tenant on his retirement that he could live in a cottage rent free for the rest of his days: ... when a landlord, on the death of the widow of a statutory tenant, allowed her daughter to remain in possession, paying rent for six months: *Marcroft Wagons Ltd v Smith* [1951] 2 KB 496; when the owner of a shop allowed the manager to live in a flat above the shop, but did not require him to do so, and the value of the flat was taken into account at £1 a week in fixing his wages: ... in each of those cases the occupier was held to be a licensee and not a tenant ... The result of all these cases is that, although a person who is let into exclusive possession is *prima facie* to be considered a tenant, nevertheless he will not be held to be so if the circumstances negative any intention to create a tenancy. Words alone may not suffice. Parties cannot turn a tenancy into a licence merely

> by calling it one. But if the circumstances and the conduct of the parties show that all that was intended was that the occupier should be granted a personal privilege, with no interest in the land, he will be held to be a licensee only.

In *Errington v Errington and Woods* [1952] 1 KB 290 and in the cases cited by Denning LJ at 297 there were exceptional circumstances which negatived the *prima facie* intention to create a tenancy, notwithstanding that the occupier enjoyed exclusive occupation. The intention to create a tenancy was negatived if the parties did not intend to enter into legal relationships at all, or where the relationship between the parties was that of vendor and purchaser, master and service occupier, or where the owner, a requisitioning authority, had no power to grant a tenancy. These exceptional circumstances are not to be found in the present case where there has been the lawful, independent and voluntary grant of exclusive possession for a term at a rent.

If the observations of Denning LJ are applied to the facts of the present case it may fairly be said that the circumstances negative any intention to create a mere licence. Words alone do not suffice. Parties cannot turn a tenancy into a licence merely by calling it one. The circumstances and the conduct of the parties show that what was intended was that the occupier should be granted exclusive possession at a rent for a term with a corresponding interest in the land which created a tenancy.

In *Cobb v Lane* [1952] 1 TLR 1037, an owner allowed her brother to occupy a house rent free. The county court judge, who was upheld by the Court of Appeal, held that there was no intention to create any legal relationship and that a tenancy at will was not to be implied. This is another example of conduct which negatives any intention of entering into a contract, and does not assist in distinguishing a contractual tenancy from a contractual licence.

In *Facchini v Bryson* [1952] 1 TLR 1386, an employer and his assistant entered into an agreement which, *inter alia*, allowed the assistant to occupy a house for a weekly payment on terms which conferred exclusive possession. The assistant did not occupy the house for the better performance of his duty and was not therefore a service occupier. The agreement stipulated that 'nothing in this agreement shall be construed to create a tenancy between the employer and the assistant'. Somervell LJ said, at 1389:

> If, looking at the operative clauses in the agreement, one comes to the conclusion that the rights of the occupier, to use a neutral word, are those of a lessee, the parties cannot turn it into a licence by saying at the end 'this is deemed to be a licence;' nor can they, if the operative paragraphs show that it is merely a licence, say that it should be deemed to be a lease.

Denning LJ referred to several cases including *Errington v Errington and Woods* and *Cobb v Lane* and said, at 1389–90:

> In all the cases where an occupier has been held to be a licensee there has been something in the circumstances, such as a family arrangement, an act of friendship or generosity, or such like, to negative any intention to create a tenancy ... In the present case, however, there are no special circumstances. It is a simple case where the employer let a man into occupation of a house in consequence of his employment at a weekly sum payable by him. The occupation has all the features of a service tenancy, and the parties cannot by the mere words of their contract turn it into something else. Their relationship is determined by the law and not by the label which they choose to put on it ...
>
> The decision, which was thereafter binding on the Court of Appeal and on all lower courts, referred to the special circumstances which are capable of

> negativing an intention to create a tenancy and reaffirmed the principle that the professed intentions of the parties are irrelevant. The decision also indicated that in a simple case a grant of exclusive possession of residential accommodation for a weekly sum creates a tenancy.

In *Murray Bull & Co Ltd v Murray* [1953] 1 QB 211, a contractual tenant held over, paying rent quarterly. McNair J found, at 217:

> ... both parties intended that the relationship should be that of licensee and no more ... The primary consideration on both sides was that the defendant, as occupant of the flat, should not be a controlled tenant.

In my opinion, this case was wrongly decided. McNair J citing the observations of Denning LJ in *Errington v Errington and Woods* [1952] 1 KB 290 at 297 and *Marcroft Wagons Ltd v Smith* [1951] 2 KB 496 failed to distinguish between first, conduct which negatives an intention to create legal relationships, secondly, special circumstances which prevent exclusive occupation from creating a tenancy and thirdly, the professed intention of the parties. In *Murray Bull & Co Ltd v Murray*, the conduct of the parties showed an intention to contract and there were no relevant special circumstances. The tenant holding over continued by agreement to enjoy exclusive possession and to pay a rent for a term certain. In those circumstances, he continued to be a tenant notwithstanding the professed intention of the parties to create a licence and their desire to avoid a controlled tenancy.

In *Addiscombe Garden Estates Ltd v Crabbe* [1958] 1 QB 513, the Court of Appeal considered an agreement relating to a tennis club carried on in the grounds of a hotel. The agreement was:

> ... described by the parties as a licence ... the draftsman has studiously and successfully avoided the use either of the word 'landlord' or the word 'tenant' throughout the document *per* Jenkins LJ at 522.

On analysis of the whole of the agreement the Court of Appeal came to the conclusion that the agreement conferred exclusive possession and thus created a tenancy. Jenkins LJ said, at 522:

> The whole of the document must be looked at; and if, after it has been examined, the right conclusion appears to be that, whatever label may have been attached to it, it in fact conferred and imposed on the grantee in substance the rights and obligations of a tenant, and on the grantor in substance the rights and obligations of a landlord, then it must be given the appropriate effect, that is to say, it must be treated as a tenancy agreement as distinct from a mere licence.

In the agreement in the *Addiscombe* case it was by no means clear until the whole of the document had been narrowly examined that exclusive possession was granted by the agreement. In the present case, it is clear that exclusive possession was granted and so much is conceded. In these circumstances, it is unnecessary to analyse minutely the detailed rights and obligations contained in the agreement.

In the *Addiscombe* case Jenkins LJ referred, at 528, to the observations of Denning LJ in Errington and Errington and Woods to the effect that 'The test of exclusive possession is by no means decisive' Jenkins LJ continued:

> I think that wide statement must be treated as qualified by his observations in *Facchini v Bryson* [1952] 1 TLR 1386, 1389; and it seems to me that, save in exceptional cases of the kind mentioned by Denning LJ in that case, the law remains that the fact of exclusive possession, if not decisive against the view that

> there is a mere licence, as distinct from a tenancy, is at all events a consideration of the first importance.

Exclusive possession is of first importance in considering whether an occupier is a tenant; exclusive possession is not decisive because an occupier who enjoys exclusive possession is not necessarily a tenant. The occupier may be a lodger or service occupier or fall within the other exceptional categories mentioned by Denning LJ in *Errington v Errington and Woods* [1952] 1 KB 290.

In *Isaac v Hotel de Paris Ltd* [1960] 1 WLR 239, an employee who managed a night bar in a hotel for his employer company which held a lease of the hotel negotiated 'subject to contract' to complete the purchase of shares in the company and to be allowed to run the nightclub for his own benefit if he paid the head rent payable by the company for the hotel. In the expectation that the negotiations 'subject to contract' would ripen into a binding agreement, the employee was allowed to run the nightclub and he paid the company's rent. When negotiations broke down the employee claimed unsuccessfully to be a tenant of the hotel company. The circumstances in which the employee was allowed to occupy the premises showed that the hotel company never intended to accept him as a tenant and that he was fully aware of that fact. This was a case, consistent with the authorities cited by Lord Denning in giving the advice of the Judicial Committee of the Privy Council, in which the parties did not intend to enter into contractual relationships unless and until the negotiations 'subject to contract' were replaced by a binding contract.

In *Abbeyfield (Harpenden) Society Ltd v Woods* [1968] 1 WLR 374, the occupier of a room in an old people's home was held to be a licensee and not a tenant. Lord Denning MR said, at 376:

> The modern cases show that a man may be a licensee even though he has exclusive possession, even though the word 'rent' is used, and even though the word 'tenancy' is used. The court must look at the agreement as a whole and see whether a tenancy really was intended. In this case, there is, besides the one room, the provision of services, meals, a resident housekeeper, and such like. The whole arrangement was so personal in nature that the proper inference is that he was a licensee.

As I understand the decision in the *Abbeyfield* case, the court came to the conclusion that the occupier was a lodger and was therefore a licensee, not a tenant.

In *Shell-Mex and BP Ltd v Manchester Garages Ltd* [1971] 1 WLR 612, the Court of Appeal after carefully examining an agreement whereby the defendant was allowed to use a petrol company's filling station for the purposes of selling petrol, came to the conclusion that the agreement did not grant exclusive possession to the defendant who was therefore a licensee. At 615 Lord Denning MR in considering whether the transaction was a licence or a tenancy said:

> Broadly speaking, we have to see whether it is a personal privilege given to a person (in which case it is a licence), or whether it grants an interest in land (in which case it is a tenancy). At one time it used to be thought that exclusive possession was a decisive factor. But that is not so. It depends on broader considerations altogether. Primarily on whether it is personal in its nature or not: see *Errington v Errington and Woods* [1952] 1 KB 290.

In my opinion, the agreement was only 'personal in its nature' and created 'a personal privilege' if the agreement did not confer the right to exclusive possession of the filling station. No other test for distinguishing between a contractual tenancy and a contractual licence appears to be understandable or workable.

Heslop v Burns [1974] 1 WLR 1241 was another case in which the owner of a cottage allowed a family to live in the cottage rent free and it was held that no tenancy at will had been created on the ground that the parties did not intend any legal relationship. Scarman LJ cited with approval, at 1252, the statement by Denning LJ in *Facchini v Bryson* [1952] 1 TLR 1386 at 1389:

> In all the cases where an occupier has been held to be a licensee there has been something in the circumstances, such as a family arrangement, an act of friendship or generosity, or such like, to negative any intention to create a tenancy.

In *Merchant v Charters* [1977] 1 WLR 1181, a bedsitting room was occupied on terms that the landlord cleaned the rooms daily and provided clean linen each week. It was held by the Court of Appeal that the occupier was a licensee and not a tenant. The decision in the case is sustainable on the grounds that the occupier was a lodger and did not enjoy exclusive possession. But Lord Denning MR said, at 1185:

> What is the test to see whether the occupier of one room in a house is a tenant or a licensee? It does not depend on whether he or she has exclusive possession or not. It does not depend on whether the room is furnished or not. It does not depend on whether the occupation is permanent or temporary. It does not depend on the label which the parties put upon it. All these are factors which may influence the decision but none of them is conclusive. All the circumstances have to be worked out. Eventually, the answer depends on the nature and quality of the occupancy. Was it intended that the occupier should have a stake in the room or did he have only permission for himself personally to occupy the room, whether under a contract or not? In which case he is a licensee.

But in my opinion, in order to ascertain the nature and quality of the occupancy and to see whether the occupier has or has not a stake in the room or only permission for himself personally to occupy, the court must decide whether upon its true construction the agreement confers on the occupier exclusive possession. If exclusive possession at a rent for a term does not constitute a tenancy then the distinction between a contractual tenancy and a contractual licence of land becomes wholly unidentifiable.

In *Somma v Hazelhurst* [1978] 1 WLR 1014, a young unmarried couple H and S occupied a double bedsitting room for which they paid a weekly rent. The landlord did not provide services or attendance and the couple were not lodgers but tenants enjoying exclusive possession. But the Court of Appeal did not ask themselves whether H and S were lodgers or tenants and did not draw the correct conclusion from the fact that H and S enjoyed exclusive possession. The Court of Appeal were diverted from the correct inquiries by the fact that the landlord obliged H and S to enter into separate agreements and reserved power to determine each agreement separately. The landlord also insisted that the room should not in form be let to either H or S or to both H and S but that each should sign an agreement to share the room in common with such other persons as the landlord might from time to time nominate. The sham nature of this obligation would have been only slightly more obvious if H and S had been married or if the room had been furnished with a double bed instead of two single beds. If the landlord had served notice on H to leave and had required S to share the room with a strange man, the notice would only have been a disguised notice to quit on both H and S. The room was let and taken as residential accommodation with exclusive possession in order that H and S might live together in undisturbed quasi-connubial bliss making weekly payments. The agreements signed by H and S constituted the grant to H and S jointly of exclusive possession at a rent for a term for the purposes for which the room was taken and the agreement therefore created a tenancy. Although the Rent Acts must not be allowed to alter or influence the construction of an agreement, the court should, in my opinion, be astute to detect and frustrate sham devices and artificial transactions whose only object is to disguise the grant of a tenancy and to evade the Rent Acts. I would disapprove of the decision in this case that H and S were only licensees and for the same reason would disapprove of the decision in *Aldrington Garages Ltd v Fielder* (1978) 37 P & CR 461 and *Sturolson & Co v Weniz* (1984) 272 EG 326.

In the present case, the Court of Appeal, 49 P & CR 324 held that the agreement dated 7 March 1983 only created a licence. Slade LJ, at 329 accepted that the agreement and in particular clause 3 of the agreement 'shows that the right to occupy the premises conferred on the defendant was intended as an exclusive right of occupation, in that it was thought necessary to give a special and express power to the plaintiff to enter ...'. Before your Lordships it was conceded that the agreement conferred the right of exclusive possession on Mrs Mountford. Even without clause 3, the result would have been the same. By the agreement Mrs Mountford was granted the right to occupy residential accommodation. The landlord did not provide any services or attendance. It was plain that Mrs Mountford was not a lodger. Slade LJ proceeded to analyse all the provisions of the agreement, not for the purpose of deciding whether his finding of exclusive possession was correct, but for the purpose of assigning some of the provisions of the agreement to the category of terms which he thought are usually to be found in a tenancy agreement and of assigning other provisions to the category of terms which he thought are usually to be found in a licence. Slade LJ may or may not have been right that in a letting of a furnished room it was almost unusual to find a provision in a tenancy agreement obliging the tenant to keep his rooms in a 'tidy condition' (at 329). If Slade LJ was right about this and other provisions there is still no logical method of evaluating the results of his survey. Slade LJ reached the conclusion that 'the agreement bears all the hallmarks of a licence rather than a tenancy save for the one important feature of exclusive occupation': at 329. But in addition to the hallmark of exclusive occupation of residential accommodation there were the hallmarks of weekly payments for a periodical term. Unless these three hallmarks are decisive, it really becomes impossible to distinguish a contractual tenancy from a contractual licence save by reference to the professed intention of the parties or by the judge awarding marks for drafting. Slade LJ was finally impressed by the statement at the foot of the agreement by Mrs. Mountford 'I understand and accept that a licence in the above form does not and is not intended to give me a tenancy protected under the Rent Acts.' Slade LJ said, at p 330:

> ... it seems to me that, if the defendant is to displace the express statement of intention embodied in the declaration, she must show that the declaration was either a deliberate sham or at least an inaccurate statement of what was the true substance of the real transaction agreed between the parties ...

My Lords, the only intention which is relevant is the intention demonstrated by the agreement to grant exclusive possession for a term at a rent. Sometimes, it may be difficult to discover whether, on the true construction of an agreement, exclusive possession is conferred. Sometimes it may appear from the surrounding circumstances that there was no intention to create legal relationships. Sometimes, it may appear from the surrounding circumstances that the right to exclusive possession is referable to a legal relationship other than a tenancy. Legal relationships to which the grant of exclusive possession might be referable and which would or might negative the grant of an estate or interest in the land include occupancy under a contract for the sale of the land, occupancy pursuant to a contract of employment or occupancy referable to the holding of an office. But where as in the present case the only circumstances are that residential accommodation is offered and accepted with exclusive possession for a term at a rent, the result is a tenancy.

The position was well summarised by Windeyer J sitting in the High Court of Australia in *Radaich v Smith* (1959) 101 CLR 209, 222 at where he said:

> What then is the fundamental right which a tenant has that distinguishes his position from that of a licensee? It is an interest in land as distinct from a personal permission to enter the land and use it for some stipulated purpose or purposes. And how is it to be ascertained whether such an interest in land has been given? By seeing whether the grantee was given a legal right of exclusive possession of the land for a term or from year to year or for a life or lives. If he was, he is a tenant. And he cannot be other than a tenant, because a legal right of exclusive possession is a tenancy and the creation of such a right is a demise. To say that a man who has, by agreement with a landlord, a right of exclusive possession of land for a term is not a tenant is simply to contradict the first proposition by the second. A right of exclusive possession is secured by the right of a lessee to maintain ejectment and, after his entry, trespass. A reservation to the landlord, either by contract or statute, of a limited right of entry, as for example to view or repair, is, of course, not inconsistent with the grant of exclusive possession. Subject to such reservations, a tenant for a term or from year to year or for a life or lives can exclude his landlord as well as strangers from the demised premises. All this is long established law: see Cole on *Ejectment*, 1857 pp 72, 73, 287, 458.

My Lords, I gratefully adopt the logic and the language of Windeyer J. Henceforth the courts which deal with these problems will, save in exceptional circumstances, only be concerned to inquire whether as a result of an agreement relating to residential accommodation the occupier is a lodger or a tenant. In the present case I am satisfied that Mrs. Mountford is a tenant, that the appeal should be allowed, that the order of the Court of Appeal should be set aside and that the respondent should be ordered to pay the costs of the appellant here and below.

(a) The application of Street v Mountford

The test laid down in *Street v Mountford* applies to both commercial letting and residential tenancy. On the other hand, in commercial or business occupancy, the court tended to invoke the criterion of overall control as the determining factor.[70] The formula, that an occupier of residential accommodation at a rent for a term is either a lodger or a tenant, is not very useful in commercial context.[71]

In shared residential accommodation, in considering one or more documents for the purpose of deciding whether a tenancy has been created, the

70 *Shell-Mex and BP Ltd v Manchester Garages Ltd* [1971] 1 WLR 612.

71 *University of Reading v Johnson Houghton* [1985] 2 EGLR 113.

court must consider the surrounding circumstances including any relationship between the prospective occupiers, the course of negotiations and the nature and extent of the accommodation and the intended and actual mode of occupation of the accommodation.[72] Where the agreements were entered into at a different time (no unity of time) and the remaining occupiers could not collectively exclude a new occupier nominated by the owner, then there would be no exclusive possession and no joint tenancy had been created.[73]

Where the owner's power to go into possession of the premises at any time jointly with the occupiers, or authorise someone to do so, cannot be realistically intended to be exercised, it is a mere pretence, and cannot deprive of the occupiers their exclusive possession otherwise enjoyed by them.[74]

AG Securities v Vaughan [1990] 1 AC 417, HL

Lord Oliver of Aylmerton: My Lords, since lettings of residential property of an appropriate rateable value attract the consequences of controlled rent and security of tenure provided by the Rent Acts, it is not, perhaps, altogether surprising that those who derive their income from residential property are constantly seeking to attain the not always reconcilable objectives on the one hand of keeping their property gainfully occupied and, on the other, of framing their contractual arrangements with the occupants in such a way as to avoid, if they can, the application of the Acts. Since it is only a letting which attracts the operation of the Acts, such endeavours normally take the form of entering into contractual arrangements designed, on their face, to ensure that no estate is created in the occupant for the time being and that his occupation of the land derives merely from a personal and revocable permission granted by way of licence. The critical question, however, in every case is not simply how the arrangement is presented to the outside world in the relevant documentation, but what is the true nature of the arrangement. The decision of this House in *Street v Mountford* [1985] AC 809 established quite clearly that if the true legal effect of the arrangement entered into is that the occupier of residential property has exclusive possession of the property for an ascertainable period in return for periodical money payments, a tenancy is created, whatever the label the parties may have chosen to attach to it. Where, as in that case, the circumstances show that the occupant is the only occupier realistically contemplated and the premises are inherently suitable only for single occupation, there is, generally, very little difficulty. Such an occupier normally has exclusive possession, as indeed she did in *Street v Mountford*, where such possession was conceded, unless the owner retains control and unrestricted access for the purpose of providing attendance and services. As my noble and learned friend, Lord Templeman, observed in that case, the occupier in those circumstances is either a lodger or a tenant. Where, however, the premises are such as, by their nature, to lend themselves to multiple occupation and they are in fact occupied in common by a number of persons under different individual agreements with the owner, more difficult problems arise. These two appeals, at different ends of the scale, are illustrations of such problems ...

72 *AG Securities v Vaughan and Antoniades v Villiers* [1990] 1 AC 417.

73 *AG Securities v Vaughan* [1990] 1 AC 417.

74 *Antoniades v Villiers* [1990] 1 AC 417 approving *Hadjiloucas v Crean* [1987] 3 All ER 1008 (owner's right to require one of the ladies to share flat with stranger was a pretence).

Antoniades v Villiers and Another

The appellants in this appeal are a young couple who at all material times were living together as man and wife. In about November 1984 they learned from a letting agency that a flat was available in a house at 6, Whiteley Road, London SE19, owned by the respondent, Mr Antoniades. They inspected the flat together and were told that the rent would be £174 per month. They were given the choice of having the bedroom furnished with a double bed or two single beds and they chose a double bed. So, right from the inception, there was never any question but that the appellants were seeking to establish a joint home and they have, at all material times, been the sole occupants of the flat. There is equally no question but that the premises are not suitable for occupation by more than one couple, save on a very temporary basis. The small living-room contains a sofa capable of being converted into a double bed and also a bed-table capable of being opened out to form a narrow single bed. The appellants did in fact have a friend to stay with them for a time in what the trial judge found to be cramped conditions, but the size of the accommodation and the facilities available clearly do not make the flat suitable for multiple occupation. When it came to drawing up the contractual arrangements under which the appellants were to be let into possession, each was asked to and did sign a separate licence agreement in the terms set out in the speech of my noble and learned friend, Lord Templeman, under which each assumed an individual, but not a joint, responsibility for payment of one half of the sum of £174 previously quoted as the rent.

There is an air of total unreality about these documents read as separate and individual licences in the light of the circumstance that the appellants were together seeking a flat as a quasi-matrimonial home. A separate licensee does not realistically assume responsibility for all repairs and all outgoings. Nor in the circumstances can any realistic significance be given to clauses 16 and 17 of the document. It cannot realistically have been contemplated that the respondent would either himself use or occupy any part of the flat or put some other person in to share accommodation specifically adapted for the occupation by a couple living together. These clauses cannot be considered as seriously intended to have any practical operation or to serve any purpose apart from the purely technical one of seeking to avoid the ordinary legal consequences attendant upon letting the appellants into possession at a monthly rent. The unreality is enhanced by the reservation of the right of eviction without court order, which cannot seriously have been thought to be effective, and by the accompanying agreement not to get married, which can only have been designed to prevent a situation arising in which it would be quite impossible to argue that the 'licensees' were enjoying separate rights of occupation.

The conclusion seems to me irresistible that these two so-called licences, executed contemporaneously and entered into in the circumstances already outlined, have to be read together as constituting in reality one single transaction under which the appellants became joint occupiers. That of course does not conclude the case because the question still remains, what is the effect?

The document is clearly based upon the form of document which was upheld by the Court of Appeal as an effective licence in *Somma v Hazelhurst* [1978] 1 WLR 1014. That case, which rested on what was said to be the impossibility of the two licensees having between them exclusive possession, was overruled in *Street v Mountford* [1985] AC 809. It was, however, a case which related to a single room and it is suggested that a similar agreement relating to premises containing space which could, albeit uncomfortably, accommodate another person is not necessarily governed by the same principle. On the other hand, the trial judge found that apart from the few visits by the respondent (who, on all but one occasion, sought admission by knocking on the door) no one shared with the appellants and that they had exclusive possession. He held that the licences were 'artificial transactions designed to evade the Rent Acts,' that a tenancy was created and that the appellants occupied as joint tenants.

His decision was reversed by the Court of Appeal, *ante*, at 438E, on, broadly, the grounds that he had erred in treating the subsequent conduct of the parties as admissible as an aid to construction of the agreements and that in so far as the holding above referred to constituted a finding that the licences were a sham, that was unsupported by the evidence inasmuch as the appellants' intention that they should enjoy exclusive possession was not shared by the respondent. The licences could not, therefore, be said to mask the real intention of the parties and fell to be construed by reference to what they said in terms.

If the documents fall to be taken seriously at their face value and to be construed according to their terms, I see, for my part, no escape from the conclusion at which the Court of Appeal arrived. If it is once accepted that the respondent enjoyed the right – whether he exercised it or not – to share the accommodation with the appellants, either himself or by introducing one or more other persons to use the flat with them, it is, as it seems to me, incontestable that the appellants cannot claim to have had exclusive possession. The appellants' case therefore rests, as Mr Colyer frankly admits, upon upholding the judge's approach that the true transaction contemplated was that the appellants should jointly enjoy exclusive possession and that the licences were mere sham or window-dressing to indicate legal incidents which were never seriously intended in fact, but which would be inconsistent with the application to that transaction of the Rent Acts. Now to begin with, I do not, for my part, read the notes of the judge's judgment as showing that he construed the agreement in the light of what the parties subsequently did. I agree entirely with the Court of Appeal that if he did that he was in error. But though subsequent conduct is irrelevant as an aid to construction, it is certainly admissible as evidence on the question of whether the documents were or were not genuine documents giving effect to the parties' true intentions. Broadly what is said by Mr Colyer is that nobody acquainted with the circumstances in which the parties had come together and with the physical lay-out and size of the premises could seriously have imagined that the clauses in the licence which, on the face of them, contemplate the respondent and an apparently limitless number of other persons moving in to share the whole of the available accommodation, including the bedroom, with what, to all intents and purposes, was a married couple committed to paying £174 a month in advance, were anything other than a smoke-screen; and the fact that the respondent, who might be assumed to want to make the maximum profit out of the premises, never sought to introduce anyone else is at least some indication that that is exactly what it was. Adopting the definition of a sham formulated by Purchas LJ in *Hadjiloucas v Crean* [1988] 1 WLR 1006 at 1013, Mr Colyer submits that the licences clearly incorporate clauses by which neither party intended to be bound and which were obviously a smoke-screen to cover the real intentions of both contracting parties. In the Court of Appeal, *ante*, pp 446H–47A, Bingham LJ tested the matter by asking two questions, *viz*: (1) on what grounds, if one party had left the premises, could the remaining party have been made liable for anything more than the £87 which he or she had agreed to pay, and (2) on what ground could they have resisted a demand by the respondent to introduce a further person into the premises? For my part, however, I do not see how this helps. The assumed negative answers prove nothing, for they rest upon the assumption that the licences are not sham documents, which is the very question in issue.

If the real transaction was, as the judge found, one under which the appellants became joint tenants with exclusive possession, on the footing that the two agreements are to be construed together, then it would follow that they were together jointly and severally responsible for the whole rent. It would equally follow that they could effectively exclude the respondent and his nominees.

Although the facts are not precisely on all fours with *Somma v Hazelhurst* [1978] 1 WLR 1014, they are strikingly similar and the judge was, in my judgment, entitled to conclude that the appellants had exclusive possession of the premises. I read his finding that, 'the licences are artificial transactions designed to evade the Rent Acts' as a finding that they were sham documents designed to conceal the true nature of the transaction. There was, in my judgment, material on which he could properly reach this conclusion and I, too, would allow the appeal.

AG Securities v Vaughan and Others

The facts in this appeal are startlingly different from those in the case of *Antoniades*. To begin with the appeal concerns a substantial flat in a mansion block consisting of four bedrooms, a lounge, a sitting-room and usual offices. The trial judge found, as a fact, that the premises could without difficulty provide residential accommodation for four persons. There is no question but that the agreements with which the appeal is concerned reflect the true bargain between the parties. It is the purpose and intention of both parties to each agreement that it should confer an individual right on the licensee named, that he should be liable only for the payment which he had undertaken, and that his agreement should be capable of termination without reference to the agreements with other persons occupying the flat. The judge found that the agreements were not shams and that each of the four occupants had arrived independently of one another and not as a group. His finding was that there was never a group of persons coming to the flat all together. That has been challenged because, it is said, the evidence established that initially in 1977 and 1978 there was one occupant who was joined by three others who, although they came independently and not as a trio, moved in at about the same time. Central heating was then installed, so that the weekly payments fell to be increased and new agreements were signed by the four occupants contemporaneously. Speaking for myself, I cannot see how this can make any difference to the terms upon which the individuals were in occupation. If they were in as licensees in the first instance, the mere replacement of their agreements by new agreements in similar form cannot convert them into tenants, and the case has, in my judgment, to be approached on the footing that agreements with the occupiers were entered into separately and individually. The only questions are those of the effect of each agreement *vis-à-vis* the individual licensee and whether the agreements collectively had the effect of creating a joint tenancy among the occupants of the premises for the time being by virtue of their having between them exclusive possession of the premises.

Taking first, by way of example, the position of the first occupier to be let into the premises on the terms of one of these agreements, it is, in my judgment, quite unarguable, once any question of sham is out of the way, that he has an estate in the premises which entitles him to exclusive possession. His right, which is, by definition, a right to share use and occupation with such other persons not exceeding three in number as the licensor shall introduce from time to time, is clearly inconsistent with any exclusive possession in him alone even though he may be the only person in physical occupation at a particular time. He has no legal title which will permit him to exclude other persons to whom the licensor may choose to grant the privilege of entry. That must equally apply to the additional licensees who join him. None of them has individually nor have they collectively the right or power lawfully to exclude a further nominee of the licensor within the prescribed maximum.

I pause to note that it has never been contended that any individual occupier has a tenancy of a particular room in the flat with a right to use the remainder of the flat in common with the tenants of other rooms. I can envisage that as a possibility in cases of arrangements of this kind if the facts support the marking out with the landlord's concurrence of a particular room as the exclusive domain of a particular individual. But to support that there would, I think, have to be proved the grant of an identifiable part of the flat and that simply does not fit with the system described in the evidence of the instant case.

The real question – and it is this upon which the respondents rely – is what is the position when the flat is occupied concurrently by all four licensees? What is said then is that since the licensor has now exhausted, for the time being, his right of nomination, the four occupants collectively have exclusive possession of the premises because they can collectively exclude the licensor himself. Because, it is argued, (1) they have thus exclusive possession and, (2) there is an ascertainable term during which all have the right to use and occupy, and (3) they are occupying in consideration of the payment of periodic sums of money, *Street v Mountford* [1985] AC 809 shows that they are collectively tenants of the premises. They are not lodgers. Therefore, they must be tenants. And because each is not individually a tenant, they must together be joint tenants.

My Lords, there appear to me to be a number of fallacies here. In the first place, the assertion of an exclusive possession rests, as it seems to me, upon assuming what it is sought to prove. If, of course, each licence agreement creates a tenancy, each tenant will be sharing with other persons whose rights to be there rest upon their own estates which, once they have been granted, they enjoy in their own right independently of the landlord. Collectively they have the right to exclude everyone other than those who have concurrent estates. But if the licence agreement is what it purports to be, that is to say, merely an agreement for permissive enjoyment as the invitee of the landlord, then each shares the use of the premises with other invitees of the same landlord. The landlord is not excluded for he continues to enjoy the premises through his invitees, even though he may for the time being have precluded himself by contract with each from withdrawing the invitation. Secondly, the fact that under each agreement an individual has the privilege of user and occupation for a term which overlaps the term of user and occupation of other persons in the premises, does not create a single indivisible term of occupation for all four consisting of an amalgam of the individual overlapping periods. Thirdly, there is no single sum of money payable in respect of use and occupation. Each person is individually liable for the amount which he has agreed, which may differ in practice from the amounts paid by all or some of the others.

The respondents are compelled to support their claims by a strange and unnatural theory that, as each occupant terminates his agreement, there is an implied surrender by the other three and an implied grant of a new joint tenancy to them together with the new incumbent when he enters under his individual agreement. With great respect to the majority in the Court of Appeal, this appears to me to be entirely unreal. For my part, I agree with the dissenting judgment of Sir George Waller in finding no unity of interest, no unity of title, certainly no unity of time and, as I think, no unity of possession. I find it impossible to say that the agreements entered into with the respondents created either individually or collectively a single tenancy either of the entire flat or of any part of it. I agree that the appeal should be allowed.

It is interesting to note that in *AG Securities v Vaughan*,[75] no single occupier claimed to be a tenant of a bedroom. Would such a claim have succeeded? Lord Oliver in *AG Securities v Vaughan* said that it was possible if the facts supported the marking out with the landlord's concurrence of a particular room as the exclusive domain of a particular individual, and the grant of an identifiable part of the flat had to be proved.[76]

In *Antoniades v Villiers*,[77] each occupier was required to pay rent separately under a separate but identical agreement. Lord Templeman said that a tenancy remained a tenancy even though the landlord might choose to require each of two joint tenants to agree expressly to pay one half of the rent. On the other hand, in *Mikeover Ltd v Brady*,[78] the issue was similar to that in *Antoniades v Villiers*.[79] An unmarried couple took a flat, signing separate agreements in identical terms. The Court of Appeal held that they were not joint tenants because they were not jointly liable for the rent. Slade LJ said that unity of interest imported the existence of joint rights and joint obligations. The provisions for payment contained in these two agreements were genuinely intended to impose and did impose on each party an obligation to pay no more than the sums reserved to the plaintiffs by his or her separate agreement. These provisions were incapable in law of creating a joint tenancy, because the monetary obligations of the two parties were not joint obligations and there was accordingly no complete unity of interest.

A term shorter than that of the grantor

The term granted by the grantor must be shorter than his own estate. Thus, a lease granted by a fee simple owner must be less than a fee simple. If the grantor only has a leasehold interest, he may grant a sublease which must be shorter than the grantor's leasehold interest. If the grantor grants a term longer than that he has, the grant would not create a sublease, but an assignment of his lease.[80]

---

75 [1990] 1 AC 417.

76 However, if the room is not let as a separate dwelling, the tenant is not protected by the Rent Acts: *Curl v Angelo* [1948] 2 All ER 189. Where a tenant with exclusive possession of the room shares some other essential living premises such as a kitchen with his landlord or other persons, the room is not let as a separate dwelling within s 1 of the Rent Act 1977: *AG Securities and Antoniades* [1990] 1 AC 417 at 459E, *per* Lord Templeman, approving *Neale v Del Soto* [1945] KB 144 (see ss 21 and 22 of the Rent Act 1977).

77 [1990] 1 AC 417.

78 [1989] 3 All ER 618.

79 [1990] 1 AC 417.

80 *Hallen v Spaeth* [1923] AC 684.

Payment of rent

Payment of rent or performance of rent-service used to be an integral part of the landlord and tenant relationship.[81] The obligation to pay rent was absolute and unqualified.[82] The modern view, however, is that rent is an usual obligation, but not an essential characteristic of a lease.[83] It may serve, nevertheless, as a positive pointer towards the existence of a tenancy.[84]

Rent often takes the form of monetary compensation for the use of the demised premises. But it may be in the form of services in kind,[85] chattles[86] or a peppercorn. The amount of rent payable and the time of payment must be certain at the commencement of the lease,[87] or the amount payable must be ascertainable at the due date for payment.[88] Rent may, however, fluctuate during the course of the lease as long as it can be ascertained.[89] It may also change in accordance with an express rent review clause.[90] However, if the amount of rent payable is uncertain and cannot be ascertained with certainty at the due date for payment, as where the rent is to be agreed from time to time,[91] the lease is void for uncertainty.[92] Where a lease contains an option for renewal 'at a rent to be agreed', the option may be valid if it requires that the new rent should not exceed the existing rent.[93]

Concurrent leases

Once the landlord has granted a lease, he retains the reversion. As will be seen, he may assign his reversion and cease to be the landlord. But it is possible, although perhaps not common, for the landlord to grant another lease of his reversion to another tenant, thereby creating two concurrent leases. The lease of the reversion can be for a period longer or shorter than the initial lease. It does not give the tenant a right to occupy the land during the subsistence of the initial lease, but passes to the him the landlord's right to receive rent and other rights and obligations. But if the lease of the reversion is longer than the initial

---

81 HEL, Vol VII, at 262; *Street v Mountford* [1985] AC 809 at 818E, 826E.

82 *Paradine v Jane* (1647) Aleyn 26 at 27; 82 ER 897 at 898.

83 *Ashburn Anstalt v Arnold* [1989] Ch 1 at 9F–10C; *AG Securities v Vaughan* [1990] 1 AC 417 at 430C–G.

84 *Ashburn Anstalt v Arnold* [1989] Ch 1 at 10C.

85 Co Litt at 96a; *Doe d Tucker v Morse* (1830) 1 B & Ad 365 at 369; 109 ER 822 at 824.

86 Co Litt at 142a.

87 *Parker v Harris* (1692) 1 Salk 262; 91 ER 230.

88 *Greater London Council v Connolly* [1970] 2 QB 100 at 109A.

89 Co Litt, at 96a; *Kendall v Baker* (1852) 11 CB 842 at 850; 138 ER 706 at 710; *Blumenthal v Gallery Five Ltd* (1971) 220 *Estates Gazette* 31 at 33.

90 *Greater London Council v Connolly* [1970] 2 QB 100.

91 *King's Motors (Oxford) Ltd v Lax* [1970] 1 WLR 426; *King v King* (1980) 41 P & CR 311.

92 But see *Beer v Bowden* (Note) [1981] 1 WLR 522, where a lease for 10 years, which fixed the rent for the first five years, but stipulated that the rent for the second five years was to be agreed, was upheld.

93 *Corson v Rhuddlan BC* (1990) 59 P & CR 185 at 194. See [1990] Conv 290 (Martin, JE).

lease, or if the initial lease is brought to a premature end, the tenant of the lease of the reversion will become entitled to occupy the land.

Under the Landlord and Tenant (Covenants) Act 1995, a landlord is required to grant a lease of the reversion (known as an 'overriding lease' under the Act) to a former tenant or guarantor who has had to pay for the breach of a covenant by a defaulting subsequent tenant.[94] This puts the former tenant or guarantor into the position of the landlord in relation to the defaulting tenant thereby enabling him to pursue remedies directly or to take possession against the defaulting tenant.

3 TYPES OF LEASE

There are various types of lease or tenancy.

Fixed term leases

A lease can be granted for a fixed term of years. The period granted can be long or short. It is extremely common for a lease of 99 years to be purchased. The tenant pays a premium or an initial lump sum and a periodic nominal ground rent in accordance with the lease.

A fixed term lease is terminated automatically when the term expires. It may be terminated on notice if the lease so stipulates.

Periodic tenancies

This may arise either from an express grant or by implication of law. Where the tenancy is expressly granted, the grant will indicate the type of periodic tenancy being granted, for example yearly, monthly, weekly etc. Where no express period is indicated, it is determined by reference to the period for which rent is due or calculated.[95] A periodic tenancy arises by implication of law where the tenant is in possession and is paying rent which is calculated on a periodic basis.[96] The nature of the tenancy depends on the way in which the rent is calculated, not on the way in which it is actually paid.[97] However, where the tenant moves into possession while negotiating for a long fixed term lease, it is less likely that the court will find a periodic tenancy on the basis of periodic payment only.[98] The periodic payment is only one, albeit an important one, factor to be taken into account in determining the nature of the tenancy.[99]

Periodic tenancies continue automatically from period to period until they are determined at the end of any period by a notice to quit given by one party to

94 Section 19 of the Landlord and Tenant (Covenants) Act 1995.

95 *Cole v Kelly* [1920] 2 KB 106 at 132.

96 *Doe d Lord v Crago* (1848) 6 CB 90 at 98; 136 ER 1185 at 1188; *Cole v Kelly* [1920] 2 KB 106 at 132.

97 *Ladies' Hosiery & Underwear Ltd v Parker* [1930] 1 Ch 304 at 328; *E O N Motors Ltd v Secretary of State for the Environment* (1981) 258 Estates Gazette 1300.

98 *Javad v Mohammed Aqil* [1991] 1 WLR 1007 at 1012E. See [1991] CLJ 232 (Bridge, S).

99 [1991] WLR 1007 at 1012F–G.

the other. In the case of a yearly tenancy, a notice to quit must be expressed to expire at the end of any year of the tenancy and a six month's notice is required. But periodic tenancies for less than a year are terminable on one full period's notice at common law and therefore would not normally be terminable at the end of the first period. Thus, a monthly tenancy requires a month's notice to quit, and a weekly tenancy requires a week's notice. But it should be noted that s 5(1) of the Protection from Eviction Act 1977 provides that no notice to quit any premises let as a dwelling is valid unless it is given not less than four weeks before the date on which it is to take effect.

Any provision in a periodic tenancy which is repugnant to its nature will be void and unenforceable. As mentioned, a periodic tenancy continues indefinitely until it is terminated by an appropriate notice. Thus, a condition precluding the landlord from serving a notice to quit as long as the tenant complies with the covenants,[100] or a condition allowing only the tenant to serve a notice to quit,[101] is repugnant to the nature of a periodic tenancy. On the other hand, an agreement by the landlord not to serve a notice to quit during the first three years of the tenancy unless he requires the premises for his own occupation is not repugnant.[102] Nor is an agreement precluding the landlord from terminating the tenancy at any time unless he requires it for the purposes of his own undertaking, even though it is unlikely that the landlord will ever wish to terminate for that reason.[103] This is because the landlord's right to give notice to quit is not permanently taken away.

Tenancies at will

A tenancy at will arises where a person occupies land or premises with the consent of the owner under a tenancy of uncertain duration and either party may at any time terminate the arrangement at will.[104] It can also arise where the tenant of a tenancy holds over with the landlord's consent at the expiry of tenancy.[105] It is terminable at any time without notice to quit.[106] Section 5 of the Protection from Eviction Act 1977 is inapplicable to a tenancy at will.[107] Such a tenancy is not a legal estate because it is not a 'term of years absolute'. Like a licence, the tenant at will has no estate in land. However, a tenancy at will is different from a licence in that the tenant at will is in 'possession' of the land,[108] and may bring an action in trespass against a stranger.[109]

---

100 *Doe d Warner v Browne* (1807) 8 East 165.

101 *Centaploy Ltd v Matlodge Ltd* [1973] 2 All ER 720.

102 *Breams Property Investment v Strougler* [1948] 1 All ER 758.

103 *Re Midland Railways Co's Agreement* [1971] 1 All ER 1007.

104 *Errington v Errington and Woods* [1952] 1 KB 290 at 296; *Doe d Groves v Groves* (1847) 10 QB 486 at 491, 116 ER; 185 at 187; *Buck v Howarth* [1947] 1 All ER 342 at 343G; *Javad v Mohammed Agil* [1991] 1 WLR 1007 (noted [1991] CLJ 232).

105 See, eg *Dean and Church of Christ Canterbury v Whitbread* (1996) 72 P & CR 9.

106 *Crane v Morris* [1965] 1 WLR 1104 at 1108B–C.

107 *Crane v Morris* [1965] 3 All ER 77.

108 *Lynes v Snaith* [1899] 1 QB 486 at 488.

109 *Heslop v Burns* [1974] 1 WLR 1241 at 1253C.

Rent may be payable. But if the rent is calculated by reference to a period, paid and accepted, then a periodic tenancy is created.[110]

Tenancies at sufferance

A tenancy at sufferance arises where a tenant wrongfully holds over on termination of a previous tenancy without the landlord's consent or dissent.[111] The absence of the landlord's consent distinguishes a tenancy at sufferance from a tenancy at will.[112]

Tenancies by estoppel

A tenant cannot deny the title of his landlord to grant a lease and the landlord cannot deny the tenant's right to occupation under it.[113] If a person with no legal estate in land purports to grant a lease to a tenant, it is enforceable between the parties and their assigns.[114] This type of tenancy is known as a tenancy by estoppel. When the landlord subsequently acquires the legal estate out of which the purported lease could have been granted, the tenancy by estoppel is fed.[115] Prior to the House of Lords' decision in *Abbey National Building Society v Cann*,[116] where the landlord having purported to grant a lease before he acquired the legal estate, subsequently acquired the legal estate with the help of a legal mortgage or a legal charge, which took effect when the landlord acquired the legal estate, it was thought that as the feeding of estoppel notionally preceded in point of time the execution of the legal mortgage or charge, the tenant would have priority over the legal mortgagee or chargee.[117] The House of Lords in *Cann* held that where the acquisition of the legal estate is wholly or partly funded by a legal mortgage or a legal charge, the acquisition and the creation of the mortgage or charge is simultaneous. There is no *scintilla temporis* between the acquisition and the creation of mortgage. The landlord never acquires more than an equity of redemption and the interest which feeds the estoppel is therefore subject to the mortgage. The decision in *Cann* does not apply to mortgages created in a separate transaction after the acquisition which feeds the estoppel.

---

110 *Doe d Bree v Lees* (1777) 2 W Bl 1171 at 1173; 96 ER 691 at 691; *Richardson v Langridge* (1811) 4 Taunt 128 at 132; 128 ER 277 at 278; *Doe d Hull v Wood* (1845) 14 M & W 682 at 687; 153 ER 649 at 651.

111 Co Litt at 57b; *Reman v City of London Real Property Co Ltd* [1921] 1 KB 49 at 58.

112 *Wheeler v Mercer* [1957] AC 416 at 426.

113 *Tadman v Henman* [1893] 2 QB 168.

114 *Webb v Austin* (1844) 7 Man & G 701.

115 *Universal Permanent Building Society v Cooke* [1951] 2 All ER 893.

116 [1990] 1 All ER 1085.

117 *Church of England Building Society v Piskor* [1954] 2 All ER 85.

4 CREATION OF LEGAL LEASES

Grant of a legal lease

The landlord may grant a lease to the tenant in various ways. A grant of a legal lease for a fixed term of more than three years must be made by deed.[118] Furthermore, if the lease is for more than 21 years it must itself be substantively registered.[119] Leases created expressly by parol taking effect in possession for a term not exceeding three years at the best rent reasonably obtainable without taking a fine is not affected by s 52(1) of the Law of Property Act 1925.[120] It may be created by writing or even orally.[121] Indeed, as a result of s 54(2), certain periodic tenancies may be created orally.[122] or may arise by implication where a person is in possession with the owner's consent and rent is paid and accepted.[123] Similarly, where a lease not exceeding three years contains an option for renewal, the lease is still covered by s 54(2).[124] Provided the renewed lease does not exceed three years, no formality is required for the renewal. The option for renewal, when exercised, merely creates a new lease, and does not extend the initial lease beyond three years.[125] Conversely, where a determinable lease is granted for more than three years, it must be granted by deed, even though it may be determined within the first three years.[126] However, a determinable 90 year lease, into which leases for life are converted under s 149(6) of the Law of Property Act 1925, does not have to be created by deed because the term of 90 years takes effect by operation of law.[127]

An individual cannot grant to himself an effective lease of property of which he is the owner.[128] Likewise, a nominee cannot grant an effective lease to his principal because such a contract involves the creation of mutual rights and obligations which can only be given any meaning if the contract is made between two independent parties.[129] Such a purported lease is a pure fiction to which the law cannot give effect.

118 Section 52(1) of the LPA 1925.

119 Sections 123(1), 19 and 22 of the LRA 1925.

120 Section 54(2) of the LPA 1925.

121 *Kushner v Law Society* [1952] 1 KB 264 at 272; *Crago v Julian* [1992] 1 WLR 372 at 376D–E.

122 *Kushner v Law Society* [1952] 1 KB 264 at 274.

123 *Doe d Lord v Crago* (1848) 6 CB 90 at 98; 136 ER 1185 at 1188; *Cole v Kelly* [1920] 2 KB 106 at 132.

124 *Hall v Hall* (1877) 2 Ex D 355 at 358; *Markfaith Investment Ltd v Chiap Hua Flashlights Ltd* [1991] 2 AC 43, at 58E.

125 *Rider v Ford* [1923] 1 Ch 541 at 547.

126 *Kushner v Law Society* [1952] 1 KB 264 at 274.

127 Section 52(2)(g) of the LPA 1925.

128 *Rye v Rye* [1962] 1 All ER 146.

129 *Ingram v IRC* [1995] 4 All ER 334.

Contract to create a legal lease

The landlord may have agreed to grant a legal lease. The grant of the legal lease may be preceded by the exchange of contracts to create the leasehold estate. Such is a common feature for a long lease, for example, a leasehold flat for 99 years.

Prior to 27 September 1989, a contract to grant a lease must satisfy s 40 of the Law of Property Act 1925.[130] From 27 September 1989, a contract to grant a lease for more than three years must satisfy s 2(1) of the Law of Property (Miscellaneous Provisions) Act 1989.[131] However, a contract to grant a lease for not more than three years need not satisfy s 2(1) of the 1989 Act.

Implied periodic tenancy

Where the tenant moves into possession with the landlord's consent before a valid formal legal lease for a fixed term is conferred on him, as has been seen, the tenant is a tenant at will.[132] But once the tenant pays a periodic rent and the payment is accepted by the landlord, the tenancy at will is converted by implication of law into a periodic tenancy.[133] There is a presumption that a yearly tenancy is created.[134] But more recently, Nicholls LJ in *Javad v Mohammed Aqil* has expressed the view that, where the tenant moves into possession on payment of a weekly or monthly rent, 'failing more the inference sensibly and reasonably to be drawn is that the parties intended that there should be a weekly or monthly tenancy'.[135] It should, however, be noted that the duration of the periodic tenancy created in this situation is limited to the term originally contemplated in the contract for the lease, or in the ineffective legal demise. If the periodic tenancy is not terminated by an appropriate notice during its term, it will simply come to an end, without further notice to quit, on the expiry of the term originally contemplated.[136]

The terms of the lease contained in the contract or defective demise are incorporated into the implied periodic tenancy insofar as they are compatible with the implied periodic tenancy.[137] Thus, restrictive covenants in the contract or defective demise, or covenants reserving the landlord's right of entry will form part of the periodic tenancy. On the other hand, in *Martin v Smith*,[138] a

130 See Chapter 4.

131 Section 2(5)(a) of the LP (MP) Act 1989.

132 *Braythwayte v Hitchcock* (1842) 10 M & W 494 at 497; 152 ER 565 at 567.

133 *Doe d Bree v Lees* (1777) 2 W Bl 1171 at 1173; 96 ER 691 at 691; *Richardson v Langridge* (1811) 4 Taunt 128 at 132; 128 ER 277 at 278; *Doe d Hull v Wood* (1845) 14 M & W 682 at 687; 153 ER 649 at 651.

134 *Doe d Martin and Jones v Watts* (1797) 7 TR 83 at 85; 101 ER 866 at 868; *Low v Adams* [1901] 2 Ch 598 at 601; Bl Comm, Vol II, at 147; HEL, Vol VII at 244.

135 [1991] 1 WLR 1007 at 1012E–G.

136 *Doe d Davenish v Moffatt* (1850) 15 QB 257 at 265; 117 ER 455 at 458.

137 *Martin v Smith* (1874) LR 9 Ex 50 at 52; *Prudential Assurance Co Ltd v London Residuary Body* [1992] 2 AC 386 at 392B–C.

138 (1874) LR 9 Ex 50 at 52.

term requiring the tenant to redecorate the premises at the end of the seventh year could not form part of the periodic tenancy because the periodic tenancy could be no more than a yearly one and may be terminated before the seventh year expires.

As already mentioned, this type of periodic tenancy does not have to be by deed or even in writing. It arises by implication of law and continues until an appropriate notice to quit is given or until the originally contemplated term expires.

Informal and equitable leases

As mentioned, a legal lease for more than three years must be granted by deed. Any purported conveyance of a lease for more than three years not by deed is declared 'void for the purpose of conveying or creating a legal estate.'[139] If the purported conveyance nevertheless satisfies the requirement of s 40 of the Law of Property Act 1925, or s 2 of the Law of Property (Miscellaneous Provisions) Act 1989, and the tenant has given valuable consideration, it will be regarded as a specifically enforceable contract for the grant of a legal lease. Equity will enforce such a specifically enforceable contract to grant a legal lease. The purported grant is therefore effective to create an equitable lease. As equity looks on that as done which ought to be done, equity regards the parties as governed by the covenants originally stipulated in the contract or defective demise for the period as stipulated in such contract or demise, as if a legal lease for the term agreed has been granted. This is known as the doctrine in *Walsh v Lonsdale*.[140]

Conflict between implied periodic tenancy and equitable lease

It should now be apparent that where a tenant, having exchanged contracts for the grant of a legal lease, say for seven years, moves into possession with the landlord's consent and starts to pay rent periodically, say monthly, the tenant has an implied legal monthly tenancy and an equitable lease for a fixed term of seven years. Similarly, if the tenant moves into possession after the landlord has purported to grant him a legal lease for seven years, but the grant is not by deed but in writing, and the tenant starts to pay rent monthly, the tenant acquires an implied monthly tenancy, and an equitable lease for a term of seven years. As mentioned earlier, the terms of the contract or defective demise will be incorporated into the implied legal periodic tenancy, insofar as they are consistent with the periodic tenancy. But there may be cases where the terms of the contract or the defective demise cannot be incorporated into the periodic tenancy because they are inconsistent with it. In such a case, the rights and obligations of the parties under the implied periodic tenancy will be inconsistent with those of the equitable lease. The question is: How is this conflict resolved?

139 Section 52(1) of the LPA 1925. See, eg *Rochester Poster Services Ltd v Dartford BC* (1991) 63 P & CR 88 at 93.

140 (1882) 21 Ch D 9.

This problem arose in the case of *Walsh v Lonsdale*[141] for the first time. Here the defendant granted the plaintiff a lease for seven years in writing. One of the terms required rent to be paid one year in advance. The plaintiff entered into possession but paid rent in arrears. Later, the defendant demanded that the plaintiff should pay rent in advance in accordance with the term in the written lease granted. The plaintiff refused to pay rent in advance. The defendant proceeded to distrain for the rent by seizing the plaintiff's goods. The plaintiff sought damages for trespass and a decree of specific performance of the written lease. Under the periodic tenancy, as a matter of law, rent was payable in arrears. But under the equitable lease, the rent was payable in advance. The defendant's liability in trespass therefore depended on whether the parties' obligations were governed by the periodic tenancy or the equitable lease. The Court of Appeal held that as a result of the Judicature Acts 1873–1875, where there was a conflict between common law rules and equitable principles, the rules of equity prevailed.[142] Thus, the defendant's action in distraining upon the plaintiff's goods was perfectly lawful in accordance with the term of the equitable lease.

Walsh v Lonsdale (1882) 21 Ch D 9, CA

Jessel MR: There is an agreement for a lease under which possession has been given. Now since the Judicature Act the possession is held under the agreement. There are not two estates as there were formerly, one estate at common law by reason of the payment of the rent from year to year, and an estate in equity under the agreement. There is only one Court, and the equity rules prevail in it. The tenant holds under an agreement for a lease. He holds, therefore, under the same terms in equity as if a lease had been granted, it being a case in which both parties admit that relief is capable of being given by specific performance. That being so, he cannot complain of the exercise by the landlord of the same rights as the landlord would have had if a lease had been granted. On the other hand, he is protected in the same way as if a lease had been granted; he cannot be turned out by six months' notice as a tenant from year to year. He has a right to say, 'I have a lease in equity, and you can only re-enter if I have committed such a breach of covenant as would if a lease had been granted have entitled you to re-enter according to the terms of a proper proviso for re-entry.' That being so, it appears to me that being a lessee in equity he cannot complain of the exercise of the right of distress merely because the actual parchment has not been signed and sealed.

Thus, it is clear that a tenant who enters into possession under a specifically enforceable contract for a lease, and pays rent periodically, holds not a legal periodic tenancy, but an equitable tenancy.[143] But if the contract is not specifically enforceable, for example, if the contract does not satisfy s 40 of the Law of Property Act 1925 or s 2 of the Law of Property (Miscellaneous Provisions) Act 1989, or where the tenant has not given valuable consideration, then the tenant will have an implied legal periodic tenancy.[144]

141 (1882) 21 Ch D 9.

142 See now s 49(1) of the Supreme Court Act 1981.

143 *Swain v Ayres* (1888) 21 QBD 289 at 293.

144 *Coatsworth v Johnson* (1886) 55 LJQB 220 at 222.

From the tenant's point of view, with the exception of the circumstances in *Walsh v Lonsdale* where the terms in the equitable lease were least favourable to the tenant, the equitable lease gives him more protection *vis-à-vis* the landlord. This is because a periodic tenancy can be terminated by an appropriate notice by the landlord, whereas the landlord is bound by the equitable lease for the full term. On the other hand, the tenant's position *vis-à-vis* the landlord's successors in title is less certain. Where he has a legal periodic tenancy, it binds the world including the landlord's successors in title in unregistered land, and in registered land if he is in actual occupation. But as mentioned, the landlord's successors in title may give an appropriate notice to terminate the tenancy. On the other hand, if the tenant has an equitable lease, it has to be protected as a Class C(iv) land charge in unregistered land, or as a minor interest in registered land, to bind the landlord's successors in title. If the tenant fails to protect his equitable lease, the successors in title of the landlord who take the legal reversion for money or money's worth (in unregistered land), or who register as the new proprietors (in registered land), will not be bound by the equitable lease. But once the equitable lease is protected, it binds the landlord's successors in title for the full term.

In *Walsh v Lonsdale*,[145] the tenant cannot rely on his implied tenancy as against the landlord. What is not clear, however, is whether a tenant can rely on an implied periodic tenancy to gain priority against a third party. Where a tenant who enters into possession under a specifically enforceable contract for a lease, and pays rent periodically, has failed to protect his equitable lease, and the landlord has now assigned the reversion to a purchaser for money consideration, the purchaser will take free of the equitable lease. Whereas, on the other hand, if the tenant can claim a legal periodic tenancy, the tenancy will bind the purchaser. Even though the purchaser may then give the tenant an appropriate notice to quit, the tenant can at least remain in possession until the notice expires. What is not clear is whether the tenant can choose to rely on his rights under the implied periodic tenancy? Likewise, as will be seen, if there is a prior competing unregistered land charge, the land charge will have priority over the equitable lease, but not over the implied periodic tenancy. Can the tenant choose to rely on the implied periodic tenancy to take free of the prior unprotected land charge?

An equitable lease is not as good as a legal lease

As we have seen, where the tenant has a specifically enforceable contract for the grant of a legal lease, equity regards the contract for a lease, or the defective demise as sufficient to confer the rights on the tenant on the terms of the parties' original agreement. Thus, even before the tenant obtains a decree of specific performance, the parties' rights and obligations are governed by the contract or defective demise, as if a legal lease has been granted. Furthermore, all usual covenants are only implied in a contract for a lease and not in a lease. However, in some cases, an equitable lease is still not as good as a legal lease:

145 (1882) 21 Ch D 9.

(a) The enforcement of an equitable lease is discretionary. It depends on the availability of a decree of specific performance.

(b) An equitable lease is vulnerable against the landlord's successors in title. In unregistered land, it requires registration as a Class C(iv) land charge. If it is not so registered, it is void against a purchaser of a legal estate for money or money's worth.[146] In registered land, it depends on an entry as a minor interest or actual occupation by the tenant to be overriding under s 70(1)(g) of the Land Registration Act 1925. If it is not so protected it is void against a subsequent registered proprietor of a registrable interest.

(c) A conveyance of legal estate carries with it automatically certain rights and easements enjoyed in connection with the land conveyed under s 62 of the Law of Property Act 1925. But an equitable lease, which is an estate contract, is not a 'conveyance' for the purposes of s 62.[147]

(d) For leases created before 1 January 1996, the covenants in a legal lease are binding on the successors in title of both the landlord and tenant. But the covenants in an equitable lease are not binding on the tenant's successors. Only the benefit may be assigned to them but not the burden. So an assignee of an equitable lease may obtain the benefit of the covenants in the lease by assignment, but he will not take the burden of them. The successor of the landlord will, however, as will be seen, have the benefit and burden of an equitable lease under ss 141 and 142 of the Law of Property Act 1925.[148] So, from the point of view of the landlord, an equitable lease is not as good as a legal lease. However, under the Landlord and Tenant (Covenants) Act 1995 all covenants by the landlord and tenant will bind their successors in respect of leases granted on or after 1 January 1996,[149] as the Act treats legal and equitable leases and assignments in the same way.[150]

(e) Where there is a prior competing unprotected Class C(iv) or Class D land charge, the equitable lessee cannot claim priority over the prior competing land charge. Under s 4(6) of the Land Charges Act 1972, the prior unprotected land charge is only void as against a purchaser of a legal estate for money or money's worth. The unregistered land charge is not void against the tenant of an equitable lease, and will indeed take priority over the equitable tenant because where equities are equal the first in time prevails. Likewise, any prior competing unregistrable and non-overreachable equitable interest, for example, a restrictive covenant created before 1926,[151] or an equitable right of entry,[152] will have priority over the equitable tenant because priority in these cases is

146 Section 4(b) of the LCA 1972.

147 *Borman v Griffith* [1930] 1 Ch 493 at 497.

148 These two sections do not apply to new tenancies created on or after 1 January 1996: s 30(4) of the Landlord and Tenant (Covenants) Act 1995.

149 Section 3 of the Landlord and Tenant (Covenants) Act 1995.

150 Section 28(1) of the Landlord and Tenant (Covenants) Act 1995. See, however, Mackenzie, J-A and Phillips, M, *A Practical Approach to Land Law*, 6th edn, 1996, London: Blackstone Press, suggesting that the Act may only apply to legal leases (at 105) citing *City Permanent Building Society v Miller* [1952] Ch 840.

151 Section 2(5)(ii) of the LCA 1972.

152 *Shiloh Spinners Ltd v Harding* [1973] AC 691.

governed by the equitable doctrine of notice, under which, where equities are equal the first in time prevails.

In registered land, the equitable lease is a minor interest. Any prior competing equitable interest is also a minor interest. As between the two competing minor interests, the first in time prevails.[153] This is so even if the equitable tenant has protected his minor interest by an appropriate entry.[154] Priority will not be affected by the order of entry.

5 TITLE TO THE FREEHOLD

Law of Property Act 1925

44. Statutory commencements of title

(2) Under a contract to grant or assign a term of years, whether derived or to be derived out of freehold or leasehold land, the intended lessee or assign shall not be entitled to call for the title to the freehold.

(3) Under a contract to sell and assign a term of years derived out of a leasehold interest in land, the intended assign shall not have the right to call for the title to the leasehold reversion.

(4) On a contract to grant a lease for a term of years to be derived out of a leasehold interest, with a leasehold reversion, the intended lessee shall not have the right to call for the title to that reversion.

(5) Where by reason of any of the three last preceding subsections, an intending lessee or assign is not entitled to call for the title to the freehold or to a leasehold reversion, as the case may be, he shall not, where the contract is made after the commencement of this Act, be deemed to be affected with notice of any matter or thing of which, if he had contracted that such title should be furnished, he might have had notice.

(11) This section applies only if and so far as a contrary intention is not expressed in the contract.

In *Shears v Wells*,[155] the first defendant was the landlord who owned the freehold, and the second defendant was the tenant. The plaintiff brought an action for injunction to restrain the breach of a restrictive covenant contained in the first defendant's freehold conveyance. On the question of the second defendant's liability, Luxmore J said that:

I think that [the second defendant] is not liable under the covenant at all. He took the tenancy of the garage in 1929 after the passing of the Law of Property Act 1925.

[His Lordship read s 44(2), (4), (5) and continued.]

It follows that the onus of proving that the [second defendant] had notice when he took the tenancy is on the plaintiff. There is no evidence here that he had notice and the onus

153 *Barclays Bank Ltd v Taylor* [1973] Ch 63.

154 *Mortgage Corpn Ltd v Nationwide Credit Corpn Ltd* [1992] *The Times*, 27 July.

155 [1936] 1 All ER 832.

is not discharged. The [second defendant] is therefore not subject to the covenants in the deed.

However, the person entitled to the benefit of the covenant can prove that the tenant has notice of the covenant by registering it as a land charge, as registration is deemed actual notice under s 198(1) of the Law of Property Act 1925. In *White v Bijou Mansions*,[156] Simonds J suggested that 's 198 ... appears, notwithstanding the unqualified language of s 44(5), to affect a lessee with notice of all those charges which are registered under the Land Charges Act 1925'. This is unsatisfactory, because, as has been seen, registration of land charges is made against the names of the previous estate owners, and not against the land concerned. A tenant who has no right to see the title deeds will not know under whose name to search.

On the other hand, covenants created before 1926, and covenants originally entered into between landlord and tenant are not registrable and therefore the tenant may be safe under s 44(5) of the Law of Property Act 1925.

In registered land, the tenant is deemed to have notice of restrictive covenants entered on the landlord's freehold title under s 50(2) of the Land Registration Act 1925, even though the tenant has no right to see the landlord's title.[157]

6 ASSIGNMENT AND SUBLETTING

(a) By the landlord

Where the landlord has a freehold reversion, he can dispose of his freehold by a simple conveyance subject to the lease. In registered land, the landlord can simply transfer his freehold reversion subject to the lease and the transferee can register himself as the new proprietor of the freehold reversion. The transferee of the freehold reversion may likewise dispose of the reversion by a further conveyance or transfer. As mentioned earlier, the landlord may also grant another lease of his reversion so that there are two concurrent leases.

Where the landlord has a leasehold reversion (ie he himself is a tenant), he may create a sub-lease for a term shorter than his own. He may, however, assign his entire leasehold reversion. The assignment of a legal lease must be by deed under s 52(1) of the Law of Property Act 1925. If the assignment is not by deed, it will take effect as an equitable assignment provided it is in writing signed by the assignor.[158] Assignment may also arise by operation of law. This happens when the the landlord-tenant purports to sublet for a term equivalent to or greater than his own leasehold.[159]

156 [1937] Ch 610 at 619.

157 *White v Bijou Mansions Ltd* [1937] Ch 610.

158 Section 53(1)(a) of the LPA 1925.

159 *Beardman v Wilson* (1868) LR 4 CP 57.

(b) By the tenant

The tenant may also assign or sublet. His right to assign or sublet is unqualified in the absence of a contractual limitation.[160] Even if the tenant assigns or sublets in clear breach of a covenant prohibiting assignment or subletting, the assignment or subletting can confer a good title on the assignee or sublessee unless and until the landlord forfeits the headlease on the ground of breach of covenant.[161]

The tenant may be prohibited absolutely from assigning or subletting. But more frequently, he is only prohibited from assigning or subletting without the landlord's consent. The landlord may not withhold consent unreasonably.[162] It used to be that the tenant had to show that the landlord was unreasonable in withholding consent. But the burden shifted to the landlord under the Landlord and Tenant Act 1988.[163] However, under the Landlord and Tenant (Covenants) Act 1995, a new balance has been struck which applies only to new tenancies created on or after 1 January 1996, whereby the landlord and tenant can enter into an agreement specifying the terms or conditions on which the landlord can grant or withhold consent to an assignment of the tenancy by the tenant. Where there is such an agreement, if the landlord refuses consent on the ground that the conditions have not been met, or if he gives consent subject to such condition, he cannot be taken to have withheld consent unreasonably, or to have given consent subject to unreasonable condition.[164]

7 DETERMINING A LEASE

There are many ways in which a lease or tenancy can be terminated.

Effluxion of time

A fixed term lease ends automatically when the term expires. If the fixed term lease is subject to termination on the occurrence of a specified event, the lease terminates automatically when the event occurs. As will be seen, where the determining event is breach of covenant, the landlord must serve a notice under s 146(1) of the LPA 1925. It should be noted that when a fixed term lease expires, under which the premises are let as a dwelling, and the occupier continues to reside in the premises, the landlord can only take possession by

---

160 *Williams v Earle* (1868) LR 3 QB 739 at 750.

161 *Williams v Earle* (1868) LR 3 QB 739 at 750; *Governors of the Peabody Donation Fund v Higgins* [1983] 1 WLR 1091 at 1095E–G.

162 Section 19(1)(a) of the Landlord and Tenant Act 1927. This does not apply to an assured tenancy under the Housing Act 1988, in the absence of contrary agreement. For cases on reasonableness of refusal of consent, see *Houlder Bros v Gibbs* [1925] 1 Ch 575; *Tredegar v Harwood* [1929] AC 72; *Bickel v Duke of Westminster* [1977] QB 517; *Parker v Boggon* [1947] KB 346; *Pimms Ltd v Tallow Chandlers Co* [1964] 2 QB 547.

163 Section 1(6) of the Landlord and Tenant Act 1988.

164 Section 22 of the Landlord and Tenant (Covenants) Act 1995.

proceedings in court.[165] And as will be seen, in many cases, the tenant has a right to request for a new lease[166] or may become a protected tenant.[167]

Notice to quit

In the case of a fixed term lease, the parties may agree to confer on either, or both, parties a right to give a notice to quit before the fixed term expires. This clause is often known as a 'break clause'. A break clause cannot be exercised by a single joint tenant unilaterally.[168] The right under the break clause can only be exercised by serving a notice which complies with it. If the notice clearly and specifically purports to determine a fixed term lease on a date not authorised by the lease, even by one day, the notice would be invalid.[169]

A periodic tenancy may be terminated by either party by a notice to quit. As has been seen, any restriction on either party's right to give notice to quit is likely to be void.[170] And an appropriate notice to quit served by a single joint tenant unilaterally, unlike a break clause, can be effective.[171] This is so even if there is an order restraining the joint tenant against whom the order is directed from serving a notice to quit.[172] Where a single joint tenant purports to give a notice to quit unilaterally which does not satisfy the period of notice required,[173] the notice will not be effective.[174] Where the periodic tenancy contains an express agreement on the length of notice required,[175] the agreement will be regarded as a break clause and a notice given pursuant to it can only be given by all the joint tenants.[176] A notice to terminate a periodic tenancy can be given to take effect either on the last day of the term or the anniversary of its commencement date, in either case the tenancy would terminate on the last day of the term.[177]

Where the premises are let as a dwelling, the Protection from Eviction Act 1977 requires that notice to quit by the landlord or the tenant must be in writing.[178] The notice must be in a statutory form drawing to the attention of

165 Section 3(1) of the Protection from Eviction Act 1977.

166 Part II of the Landlord Tenant Act 1954.

167 Section 1(1) of the Rent Act 1977.

168 *Hammersmith and Fulham LBC v Monk* [1992] 1 AC 478 at 490G; *Hounslow LBC v Pilling* (1993) 25 HLR 305; [1994] 1 All ER 432.

169 *Mannai Investment Co Ltd v Eagle Star Life Assurance Co Ltd* [1996] 1 All ER 55.

170 *Doe d Warner v Browne* (1807) 8 East 165; *Centaploy Ltd v Matlodge Ltd* [1973] 2 All ER 720; *Prudential Assurance Co Ltd v London Residuary Body* [1992] 2 AC 386 at 394F, 395G.

171 *Hammersmith and Fulham LBC v Monk* [1992] 1 AC 478.

172 *Harrow London Borough Council v Johnstone* [1997] 1 All ER 929, HL.

173 Now at least four weeks: see s 5(1)(b) of the Protection from Eviction Act 1977.

174 *Hounslow London Borough Council v Pilling* (1993) 25 HLR 305; [1994] 1 All ER 432.

175 Subject to the requirement of four weeks' notice under s 5(1)(b) of the Protection from Eviction Act 1977.

176 *Hounslow London Borough Council v Pilling* (1993) 25 HLR 305; [1994] 1 All ER 432.

177 *Sidebotham v Holland* [1895] 1 QB 378; *Crate v Miller* [1947] 2 All ER 45 at 46; *Mannai Investment Co Ltd v Eagle Star Life Assurance Co Ltd* [1996] 1 All ER 55 at 60.

178 Section 5(1) of the Protection from Eviction Act 1977.

the tenant the fact that he may be entitled to security of tenure. Notice to quit premises let as a dwelling must be given not less than four weeks before the date on which it is to take effect.[179] Subject to this rule, where a fixed term lease contains a break clause, the correct notice period is that specified in the clause.

In the case of a yearly tenancy, if the rent is payable at quarter days, two quarters' notice is required,[180] otherwise a half year's notice is needed. Notice should expire at the end of a year of the tenancy.

Other periodic tenancies are terminated by a full period's notice[181] subject to the minimum requirement of the Protection from Eviction Act 1977 in the case of a letting as a dwelling. A notice to quit given either by the landlord or the tenant, which terminates a headlease, would also bring to an end the sublease which is carved out of the headlease.[182]

Surrender

A surrender requires the agreement of the landlord. It releases the tenant from any future liability but not accrued liability.[183] A surrender by a single joint tenant is ineffective.[184] A surrender of the headlease will not end the sublease. The subtenant becomes tenant of the original landlord on the terms and conditions of the sublease.[185] An express surrender of a lease exceeding three years has to be made by deed under s 52(1) of the Law of Property Act 1925. However, where surrender occurs by operation of law, no deed is required.[186] A surrender arises by operation of law where the tenant, with the landlord's concurrence or acquiescence, does some act to signify his intention to give up possession of the land,[187] for example, where the landlord accepts back possession of the property and agrees that the tenant will be free of further liability. Where a deed of variation of lease has affected the legal estate by either increasing the extent of the premises demised or the term for which they were held, it would constitute a surrender by operation of law, and a re-grant of a new term in accordance with the variation.[188] Similarly, where a tenant holding under a lease accepts a new lease of the same land from his landlord, he is taken to have surrendered his original lease immediately before he accepts the new one.[189]

---

179 Section 5(1)(b) of the Protection from Eviction Act 1977; *Hounslow London Borough Council v Pilling* (1993) 25 HLR 305; [1994] 1 All ER 432.

180 *Morgan v Davies* (1878) 3 CPD 260.

181 *Javad v Mohammed Aqil* [1991] 1 WLR 1007 at 1009B.

182 *Pennell v Paynes* [1995] 2 All ER 592, CA.

183 *Torminster Properties Ltd v Green* [1983] 1 WLR 676.

184 *Leek and Moorlands Building Society v Clark* [1952] 2 QB 788 at 795.

185 *Pleasant (lessee of Hayton) v Benson* (1811) 14 East 234; 104 ER 590. *Cf David v Sabin* [1893] 1 Ch 523.

186 Section 52(2)(c) of the LPA 1925.

187 *Fredco Estates Ltd v Bryant* [1961] 1 All ER 34.

188 *Friends' Provident Life Office v British Railways Board* [1996] 1 All ER 336, CA.

189 *Jenkin R Lewis & Son Ltd v Kerman* [1971] Ch 477 at 496, *per* Russell LJ. But an agreement to surrender a lease does not give rise to a new lease in the absence of a clear intention for a new lease: *Take Harvest Ltd v Liu* (1994) 67 P & CR 150, PC.

Forfeiture

Where there is a forfeiture clause enforceable on breach of certain covenants, the landlord may forfeit on certain conditions and bring an end to the lease.

Disclaimer

A tenant may deny his landlord's title by setting up a rival claim to the ownership or by asserting a claim of ownership in himself.[190] Such conduct operates as a disclaimer which automatically entitles the landlord to forfeit the lease on the ground that the disclaimer is a breach of an implied covenant that the tenant shall not do anything which may prejudice the landlord's position.[191] However, the landlord is entitled to ignore the disclaimer and treat the lease as still subsisting.[192]

Where the tenant becomes bankrupt, the lease vests in his trustees in bankruptcy by operation of law. The trustee in bankruptcy is entitled to disclaim a subsisting lease under s 315 of the Insolvency Act 1986.[193]

Insolvency Act 1986

315. Disclaimer (general power)

(1) Subject as follows, the trustee may, by the giving of the prescribed notice, disclaim any onerous property and may do so notwithstanding that he has taken possession of it, endeavoured to sell it or otherwise exercised rights of ownership in relation to it.

(2) The following is onerous property for the purposes of this section, that is to say:

(a) any unprofitable contract; and

(b) any other property comprised in the bankrupt's estate which is unsaleable or not readily saleable, or is such that it may give rise to a liability to pay money or perform any other onerous act.

(3) A disclaimer under this section:

(a) operates so as to determine, as from the date of the disclaimer, the rights, interests and liabilities of the bankrupt and his estate in or in respect of the property disclaimed; and

(b) discharges the trustee from all personal liability in respect of that property as from the commencement of his trusteeship, but does not, except so far as is necessary for the purpose of releasing the bankrupt, the bankrupt's estate and the trustee from any liability, affect the rights or liabilities of any other person.

(4) A notice of disclaimer shall not be given under this section in respect of any property that has been claimed for the estate under s 307 (after-acquired property) or 308 (per-

190 *Warner v Sampson* [1959] 1 QB 297 at 318, 324.

191 *W G Clark (Properties) Ltd v Dupre Properties Ltd* [1992] Ch 297 at 308D.

192 *W G Clark (Properties) Ltd v Dupre Properties Ltd* [1992] Ch 297 at 303B.

193 For example, *MEPC plc v Scottish Amicable Life Assurance Society* (1994) 67 P & CR 314.

sonal property of bankrupt exceeding reasonable replacement value) or 308A, except with the leave of the court.

(5) Any person sustaining loss or damage in consequence of the operation of a disclaimer under this section is deemed to be a creditor of the bankrupt to the extent of the loss damage and accordingly may prove for the loss or damage as a bankruptcy debt.

Merger

A lease comes to an end where the tenant acquires the landlord's reversion or where a third party acquires both the landlord's reversion and the tenant's lease.

Frustration

In *National Carriers Ltd v Panalpina (Northern) Ltd*,[194] the House of Lords confirmed that a lease may come to an end under the doctrine of frustration if the supervening event has rendered the performance of the parties' obligation under the lease so fundamentally different from what they originally contemplated. Cases in which the doctrine may apply are, however, likely to be exceedingly rare.[195]

Enlargement

A long lease of at least 300 years with at least 200 years to run, and where no rent of money value is payable, may be enlarged into a fee simple thereby ending the lease.[196] Once enlarged, all the covenants in the now extinguished lease will be incorporated into the enlarged fee simple.[197]

8 STATUTORY CONTROL ON PRIVATE SECTOR HOUSING

Many statutes have altered or restricted the contractual rights and obligations of the parties to a tenancy or to a licence to occupy land. Two particular aspects regulated by statutes are rent control and security of tenure. The main piece of legislation aimed at providing greater protection to tenants in private sector housing is the Rent Act 1977. The Rent Act 1977 has been very unpopular with private sector landlords and many have tried to avoid the Act by purporting to grant a licence rather than a lease. The scope of the Act has been narrowed by successive legislations, and the Housing Act 1988 marks the watershed by proving that no new Rent Act tenancies can be granted on or after 15 January 1989, and by providing a much curtailed version of protection to private residential tenants.[198]

194 [1981] AC 675. See [1981] Conv 227 (Hodhinson, K); (1981) 32 NILQ 162 (Dickson, B); [1981] CLJ 217 (Tromans, S).

195 [1981] AC 675 at 692B–D, 697A.

196 Section 153(1) of the LPA 1925.

197 Section 153(8) of the LPA 1925.

198 Section 34(1) of the Housing Act 1988.

Rent Act 1977: protected tenancies

A protected tenancy is a tenancy where a dwelling house is let as a separate dwelling and the tenancy is granted before 15 January 1989.[199] A licence is not covered by s 1 of the Rent Act 1977. The Housing Act 1988, however, allows certain tenancies granted on or after 15 January 1989 to be protected tenancy, for example, a tenancy granted pursuant to a contract made before 15 January 1989,[200] a tenancy granted by the landlord to a person who immediately before the grant was a protected or statutory tenant,[201] or a protected tenancy granted as a suitable alternative accommodation to a previous protected tenancy pursuant to a court order.[202]

Further, the rateable value of the dwelling house must not exceed the statutory limits,[203] and the tenancy must not be excluded by ss 5–16 of the Rent Act 1977. Where the tenancy is granted on or after 1 April 1990 in pursuant to a contract made before 1 April 1990 the annual rent must not exceed £25,000.[204]

The Rent Act 1977 provides that certain types of tenancies cannot be protected tenancies:

(a) Tenancies at a low rent.[205] These may qualify as long residential tenancies under the Landlord and Tenant Act 1954 (see below).

(b) Dwelling-houses let with other land.[206]

(c) Tenancies with payments for board.[207] These may qualify as restricted contracts.

(d) Letting to students.[208]

(e) Holiday letting.[209]

(f) Tenancies of agricultural holdings.[210]

(g) Tenancies of licensed premises.[211]

(h) Tenancies granted by a residential landlord.[212] These may qualify as restricted contracts.

---

199 Section 1 of the Rent Act 1977; s 34(1) of the Housing Act 1988.

200 Section 34(1)(a) of the Housing Act 1988.

201 Section 34(1)(b) of the Housing Act 1988.

202 Section 34(1)(c) of the Housing Act 1988.

203 From 1 April 1973 to 31 March 1990, £1,500 in Greater London and £750 elsewhere. From 22 March 1973 to 31 March 1973, £600 in Greater London and £300 elsewhere. Before 22 March 1973, £400 in Greater London and £200 elsewhere: see s 4 of the Rent Act 1977.

204 Section 4(4) of the Rent Act 1977 as inserted by the References to Rating (Housing) Regulations 1990, SI 1990 No 434, Reg 2.

205 Section 5 of the Rent Act 1977.

206 Sections 6 and 26 of the Rent Act 1977.

207 Section 7 of the Rent Act 1977.

208 Section 8 of the Rent Act 1977.

209 Section 9 of the Rent Act 1977.

210 Section 10 of the Rent Act 1977.

211 Section 11 of the Rent Act 1977.

212 Section 12 of the Rent Act 1977.

(i) Crown tenancies.[213]

(j) Tenancies granted by exempt landlords such as local authorities.[214]

(k) Business tenancies.[215]

Where a tenancy is a protected tenancy under s 1 of the Rent Act 1977, either the landlord or the tenant may at any time apply to the Rent Officer to have a fair rent registered for the dwelling house.[216]

When a protected tenancy comes to an end either by effluxion of time or determination by notice, it becomes a statutory tenancy so long as the tenant occupies the dwelling house as his residence.[217] On the statutory tenant's death, his or her spouse who resides in the dwelling house immediately before the death may become statutory tenant too.[218] Where there is no qualifying spouse, any person who was a member of the tenant's family and who was residing and had been residing with him in the dwelling house for two years immediately prior to the tenant's death may become statutory tenant.[219]

Once the protected tenant becomes a statutory tenant, the landlord cannot recover possession without the order of the court. Under s 98 of 1977 Act, an order for possession must not be made unless the court considers it reasonable to make such an order and either (a) the court is satisfied that suitable alternative accommodation is available for the tenant, or (b) that the landlord has established one of the cases for possession set out in Part I of Schedule 15. The court must direct itself to the question of reasonableness. However, if the landlord can establish one of the grounds in Part II of Schedule 15, the court has no discretion to refuse an order for possession.[220]

(a) Part I of Schedule 15

Case 1: Breach of obligation during the statutory tenancy

Case 2: Nuisance during the statutory tenancy

Case 3: Deterioration by waste or neglect during the statutory tenancy

Case 4: Deterioration of furniture by ill-treatment

Case 5: Tenant's notice to quit leading landlord to sell or let the house

Case 6: Assignment or subletting without landlord's consent

[There is no Case 7]

Case 8: Where the dwelling was let to an employee who has ceased to be an employee, and the dwelling is now required for landlord's new employee

---

213 Section 13 of the Rent Act 1977.

214 Sections 14–16 of the Rent Act 1977.

215 Section 24(3) of the Rent Act 1977.

216 Section 67 of the Rent Act 1977.

217 Section 2(1)(a) of the Rent Act 1977.

218 Section 2(1)(b) and Sched 1, para 2 of the Rent Act 1977.

219 Section 2(1)b) and Sched 1, para 2 of the Rent Act 1977.

220 Section 98(2) of the Rent Act 1977.

Case 9: Dwelling required for landlord's use

Case 10: Subletting of part at an excessive rent

(b) Part II of Schedule 15

Case 11: Where the landlord is an owner-occupier and has, before the tenancy starts, given written notice that possession might be recovered under Case 11. He may recover possession if the dwelling house is required as his residence or a residence of a member of his family or his successor in title, or where the mortgagee is entitled to vacant possession, or if the dwelling house is not suitable to the landlord's needs and he needs to get vacant possession in order to sell it and buy a more suitable dwelling house.

Case 12: Where the landlord intends to occupy the dwelling house as his retirement home and has served notice before the tenancy starts that possession may be recovered under Case 12.

Case 13: Where the dwelling house has been used as a holiday home prior to the commencement of the tenancy, and the tenancy does not exceed eight months and notice has been served before the tenancy starts that possession may be recovered under Case 13.

Case 14: Where the dwelling house has been let to student prior to the commencement of the tenancy, and the tenancy does not exceed 12 months and notice has been served before the tenancy starts that possession may be recovered under Case 14.

Case 15: Where the dwelling house is now required for as a residence of a minister of religion and notice that possession may be recovered under this case has been given.

Cases 16 to 18: Dwelling house once occupied by persons in agriculture and is so required provided notice has been given.

Case 19: In the case of protected shorthold tenancies,[221] when at the end of the shorthold tenancy no grant of a further tenancy has been made, or if there was such a grant it was to a person who immediately before the grant was in possession of the dwelling house as a protected or statutory tenant.

Case 20: lettings by servicemen

A statutory tenancy comes to an end when the statutory tenant ceases to reside there as his residence.[222] Where the dwelling house has been a matrimonial home, occupation by the spouse is sufficient.[223] But occupation by an ex-spouse is not.[224] Where the tenant is absent for sufficiently long with no intention to

---

221 A protected shorthold tenancy is a tenancy of not less than one year nor more than five years.

222 Section 2(1)(a), (3) of the Rent Act 1977.

223 *Brown v Draper* [1944] KB 309; *Hoggett v Hoggett* (1979) 39 P & CR 121; s 1(6) of the Matrimonial Homes Act 1983.

224 *Metropolitan Properties Ltd v Cronan* (1982) 44 P & CR 1.

return, security is lost.[225] If the tenant has two homes, he must use the dwelling house under the statutory tenancy as his main residence.[226]

A statutory tenant may surrender his statutory tenancy. He may also give notice, sufficient to terminate his previous protected tenancy, to quit.[227] But a minimum period of four weeks' notice is required,[228] and if no notice was required under the protected tenancy, for example, if it is a fixed term tenancy, then a minimum of three months' notice is needed.[229]

A subtenant who has a protected or statutory tenancy against his landlord may claim the protection of the Rent Act 1977 against the superior landlord on the determination of his own landlord's tenancy.[230]

Rent Act 1977: restricted contracts

The Rent Act 1977 has also provided protection to tenants and licensees who are excluded from s 1(1) of the Act in the form of a restricted contract. This contract does not give the tenant or licensee security of tenure, but regulates the landlord's right to take possession. It also subjects the tenancy or licence to rent control. Restricted contracts are gradually phased out by the Housing Act 1988. Section 36(1) of the 1988 Act prohibited the creation of new restricted contracts as from 15 January 1989. Furthermore, if the parties under an existing restricted contract agree to vary the terms (eg a new rent), this will be regarded as a new contract which cannot be a restricted contract.[231]

A restricted contract is a contract whereby one person grants to another person, before or pursuant to a contract made before 15 January 1989, in consideration of a rent which includes payment for the use of furniture or for services, the right to occupy a dwelling as a residence.[232] The rateable value of the dwelling under a restricted contract must not exceed the statutory limit.[233]

Section 19(5) of the Rent Act 1977 provides a list of contracts which are not restricted contracts. For example, a contract for the letting of any premises at a rent which includes payment for board is not a restricted contract if the value of the board forms a substantial part of the whole rent.[234] Section 19(7) further provides that a contract whereby a person is granted a right to occupy a dwelling house for a holiday cannot be a restricted contract.[235]

---

225 *Duke v Porter* [1986] 2 EGLR 101.

226 *Landford Property Co v Tureman* [1949] 1 KB 29, approved in *Hampstead Way Investments Ltd v Lewis-Weare* [1985] 1 All ER 564, HL.

227 Section 3(3) of the Rent Act 1977.

228 Section 5 of the Protection from Eviction Act 1977.

229 Section 3(3) of the Rent Act 1977.

230 Section 137 of the Rent Act 1977.

231 Section 36(2) of the Housing Act 1988.

232 Section 19 of the Rent Act 1977.

233 From 1 April 1973, £1500 in Greater London, £750 elsewhere; Before 1 April 1973, £400 in Greater London and £200 elsewhere: s 19(4) of the Rent Act 1977, Classes D and E.

234 Section 19(5)(c) of the Rent Act 1977.

235 Section 19(7) of the Rent Act 1977.

A tenancy, whereby the landlord resides in a separate part of the same building and the building is not a purpose-built block of flats, cannot be a protected tenancy,[236] but qualifies as a restricted contract.[237] If it is a flat, but the tenant occupies part of it where the landlord also resides, it is also a restricted contract.[238] Similarly, where under the contract the tenant has exclusive occupation of any accommodation, but shares other accommodation with the landlord, it is a restricted contract.[239]

Under a restricted contract, either landlord or tenant or licensee may at any time apply to the Rent Tribunal to register a reasonable rent for the dwelling house[240] Notice to quit in the case of a periodic restricted contract is regulated by ss 103–06A of the Rent Act 1977.

Housing Act 1980: protected shorthold tenancies

The scope of Rent Act 1977 has, even before 15 January 1989, been narrowed by the Housing Act 1980 by the introduction of protected shorthold tenancies. The key feature of protected shorthold tenancies is that there is no security of tenure. The landlord can recover possession under Case 19 of Schedule 15 to Rent Act 1977. However, notice of the intention to bring possession proceedings must be served three months before the shorthold tenancy ends, and there is a complex procedure for termination. The tenancies are still subject to the fair rent system.

A protected tenancy granted after 28 November 1980 for not less than a year nor more than five years and where landlord has no right to give notice to quit before it expires is a protected shorthold tenancy provided before the grant the tenant has been given notice that it is a protected shorthold tenancy.[241] This is replaced by assured shorthold tenancies under the Housing Act 1988 which will be discussed below.[242]

A protected shorthold tenancy cannot be assigned at all,[243] but it may be sublet although the subtenant cannot claim protection under s 137 of the Rent Act 1977.[244]

A protected shorthold tenant has an absolute right, which cannot be contracted out of, to give notice to quit.[245] One month's notice is needed if the lease is for two years or less, and three months' notice is needed if the lease is for more than two years.

236 Section 12 of the Rent Act 1977.
237 Section 20 of the Rent Act 1977.
238 Section 20 of the Rent Act 1977.
239 Section 21 of the Rent Act 1977.
240 Section 77 of the Rent Act 1977.
241 Section 52 of the Housing Act 1980.
242 Section 34(2) of the Housing Act 1988.
243 Section 54(2) of the Housing Act 1980.
244 Section 54(1) of the Housing Act 1980.
245 Section 53(1), (2) of the Housing Act 1980.

Housing Act 1988, Part I: assured tenancies

As mentioned, the Rent Act protected tenancies can no longer be created. This is now substituted by assured tenancies under Part I of the Housing Act 1988 which gives the tenant a curtailed version of protection. A tenancy granted on or after 15 January 1989 where, if the tenancy was granted or contracted for before 1 April 1990, the dwelling has a rateable value not exceeding £1,500 (in Greater London areas) or £750 (elsewhere), or if the tenancy was granted on or after 1 April 1990, the annual rent does not exceed £25,000, and the dwelling house is let as a separate dwelling, and the tenant occupies the dwelling house as his only or principle home, is an assured tenancy.[246] The requirement that a dwelling house must be let as a separate dwelling and that the tenant occupies the dwelling house as his only or principal home is rather similar to that of protected tenancy under the Rent Act 1977. A tenancy created after the Housing Act 1996 will take effct as an assured shorthold tenancy unless notice of an assured tenancy is given by the landlord.[246a]

The following tenancies, specified in Schedule 1 to the Housing Act 1988, cannot qualify as assured tenancies under the Act:

(a) Tenancies granted on or after 15 January 1989 pursuant to a contract made before that date, and tenancies granted to a previous protected or statutory tenant under the Rent Act 1977.

(b) Tenancies of dwelling houses with high rental or rateable value.

(c) Tenancies at a low rent. If the lease is for more than 21 years, it can be a long residential tenancy under the Local Government Housing Act 1989 (see above).

(d) Business tenancies (see Part II of the Landlord and Tenant Act 1954).

(e) Tenancies of licensed premises.

(f) Tenancies of agricultural land.

(g) Tenancies of agricultural holdings.

(h) Lettings to students by specified educational institutions.

(i) Holiday lettings.

(j) Tenancies granted by residential landlords.

(k) Crown tenancies.

(l) Tenancies by local authorities and other bodies.

An assured tenancy may be a periodic tenancy, or a fixed term tenancy. In the case of an assured periodic tenancy, the tenancy is continued by the Act despite the landlord's notice to quit. In the case of an assured fixed term tenancy, a statutory periodic tenancy arises when the tenancy comes to an end, and the tenant under that fixed term tenancy is not expressly granted another tenancy. In both cases, the landlord may only take possession by court order.[247] To obtain a court order the landlord must prove one or more grounds for possession.[248] The grounds for possession are specified in Schedule 2 to the 1988 Act, some of which are discretionary, others are mandatory. In addition, the

246 Section 1 of the Housing Act 1988.

246aSection 19A of the Housing Act 1988 as inserted by s 96(1) of the Housing Act 1996.

247 Section 5(1) of the Housing Act 1988.

248 Section 7(1) of the Housing Act 1988.

landlord must serve on the tenant a prescribed form notice under s 8 before any proceedings for possession.

There is generally no statutory rent control in the case of an assured tenancy. Both the landlord and the tenant are contractually bound by the rent agreed. They cannot apply to the rent assessment committee for the rent to be increased or reduced. Where a statutory assured periodic tenancy arises after the expiry of the initial assured fixed term tenancy, the rent payable will continue as before.[249] The landlord may, however, propose a rent increase. The tenant who disagrees with the landlord's proposed rent increase may refer his rent to the rent assessment committee.

The 1988 Act also provides a limited succession scheme under s 17. Where the assured periodic tenant dies and immediately before his death, his spouse occupied the dwelling house as her only or principal home, the tenancy vests in the spouse. Only a single succession is allowed for under the Act.

Housing Act 1988, Part I: assured shorthold tenancies

The Housing Act 1988 also introduced assured shorthold tenancies to replace protected shorthold tenancies. Section 20 of the Act defines assured tenancies as including assured shorthold tenancies. Thus, the provisions applicable to assured tenancies also apply to assured shorthold tenancies, save as modified by rules which are applicable specifically to assured shorthold tenancies. Therefore, when a fixed term assured shorthold tenancy comes to an end, a statutory periodic assured shorthold tenancy arises.

An assured shorthold tenancy must be granted for a minimum period of six months, but there is no maximum period.[250] Thus, while a six month fixed term tenancy can be an assured shorthold tenancy, an initial periodic tenancy cannot be an assured shorthold tenancy. This is because an initial minimum period of six months must be granted. A periodic tenancy granted or arising after the initial six month assured shorthold tenancy can, however, be an assured shorthold tenancy. The landlord should not be given a right to terminate the assured shorthold tenancy within the first six months.[251] If he is given such a right, the tenancy will be an assured tenancy. A statutory notice in the prescribed form that the tenancy is an assured shorthold tenancy must be given to the tenant before the tenancy is created.[252] Where such a notice is not given, the tenancy will presumably be an assured tenancy.

The general grounds for possession applicable to assured tenancies also apply to assured shorthold tenancies.[253] In addition, the landlord may take possession by a specific re-possession procedure.[254] Under this procedure, the court must grant a possession order if the landlord has given two months'

249 Section 5(3) of the Housing Act 1988.

250 Section 20(1)(a) of the Housing Act 1988. An assured shorthold tenancy does not now need to have a minimum fixed term of six months under the Housing Act 1996.

251 Section 21(1)(b) of the Housing Act 1988.

252 Section 20(2) of the Housing Act 1988. This is not necessary for tenancies created after the Housing Act 1996.

253 Section 21(1) of the Housing Act 1988.

254 Section 21(1) of the Housing Act 1988.

notice (which may expire on the contractual date of termination of the initial fixed term), and the assured shorthold tenancy has come to an end, and no further assured tenancy other than an assured shorthold tenancy, whether statutory or not, is in existence.[255]

The tenant under an assured shorthold tenancy may refer the rent to a rent assessment committee under s 22(1) during the initial fixed term. The rent assessment committee will assess the rent which the landlord may reasonably be expected to obtain. If the tenant's application is successful, he cannot refer the rent to the committee for a second time. If he does not refer the rent to the committee during the initial fixed term, once the initial fixed term has expired, he has no right to refer the rent under the new assured shorthold tenancy.[256]

Landlord and Tenant Act 1954, Part I: long residential tenancies

Rent Act style protection was also extended to long residential tenancies by the Landlord and Tenant Act 1954, Part I. Tenants of long residential tenancies are also given other rights in the form of enfranchisement or an extended lease by the Leasehold Reform Act 1967. Furthermore, long leaseholders of flats are now entitled collectively to buy out the freeholder and any superior leaseholders under the Leasehold Reform, Housing and Urban Development Act 1993. These will be discussed below.

A tenancy of a dwelling house for a term exceeding 21 years at a low rent granted before or pursuant to a contract made before 15 January 1989 is a long residential tenancy if it also satisfies the qualifying condition. The long lease must be for a term exceeding 21 years and not determinable by the landlord[257] before the end of the term. The tenancy must be one under which no rent is payable or the rent is less than two-thirds of the rateable value. If the tenancy is granted on or after 1 April 1990, it is granted at a low rent if the rent is not more than £1,000 a year for Greater London areas and not more than £250 a year elsewhere. The qualifying condition is that the tenancy would have been a protected tenancy under the Rent Act 1977 but for the low rent.[258]

At the expiry of fixed term, provided that the tenant still occupies the dwelling house as his residence, a continuation tenancy arises and continues until determined by the landlord or by the tenant. A continuation tenancy is not a new tenancy nor a statutory tenancy. It is an indefinite statutory extension of the contractual tenancy upon the same terms, and therefore at the same rent as before.[259] The tenant may determine the continuation tenancy simply by surrender with the landlord's consent,[260] or by giving to the landlord one month's written notice.[261] The landlord may terminate the continuation tenancy

255 Section 21(1) of the Housing Act 1988. But the notice cannot take effect earlier than six months after the commencement of the initial fixed term: s 21(5) of the Housing Act 1988 as inserted by s 99 of the Housing Act 1996.

256 Section 22(2)(b) of the Housing Act 1988, s 22(2)(b).

257 The tenant may, however, terminate the tenancy earlier.

258 Section 2(1) of the Landlord and Tenant Act 1954.

259 Section 3 of the Landlord and Tenant Act 1954.

260 Section 17 of the Landlord and Tenant Act 1954.

by giving not more than 12, but not less than six months' notice in the prescribed form and choose one of two ways to determine the continuation tenancy. He may either obtain possession by establishing one of the grounds in s 12 of the 1954 Act, or offer a statutory tenancy.

The grounds set out in s 12 are: (i) that the landlord (only local authority or certain type of public sector landlord) proposes to demolish or reconstruct the whole or a substantial part of the premises after the termination of the tenancy for the purposes of redevelopment;[262] (ii) those correspond to Cases 1–9 in Schedule 15 of the Rent Act 1977 (see above).

If the landlord chooses to offer a statutory tenancy, in his notice he must specify what premises are to constitute the dwelling house, the rent, the rental period and whether payable in advance or in arrears, payment of initial repairs, responsibility of repair during statutory tenancy and any other terms proposed. If the parties cannot agree on the terms (other than the amount of rent), the landlord may apply to the court for determination. Disagreement on the amount of rent is to be determined by the Rent Officer.

The statutory tenancy takes effect as a statutory tenancy under the Rent Act 1977 on the terms agreed by both parties or as determined by the court.[263] The tenant is protected as long as he remains in possession.

As from 15 January 1999, long tenancies granted before 15 January 1989 and still in existence on 15 January 1999 will not be governed by the Landlord and Tenant Act 1954. They will be governed by the Local Government and Housing Act 1989, s 186 and Schedule 10. The 1989 scheme is very similar to that of the Landlord and Tenant Act 1954 except the tenancy offered by the landlord following a statutory notice of termination will be an assured periodic tenancy under the Housing Act 1988 rather than a statutory tenancy under the Rent Act 1977.

The Local Government and Housing Act 1989, s 186 and Schedule 10 also applies to long residential tenancies at a low rent granted on or after 1 April 1990, which would have been assured tenancies under the Housing Act 1988 but for the low rent. Long tenancies granted on or after 15 January 1989 but before 1 April 1990 do not seem to be protected by either the Landlord and Tenant Act 1954 or the Local Government and Housing Act 1989.

As is the case under the 1954 Act, the tenant of a long lease governed by the 1989 Act is entitled to a continuation tenancy at the expiry of fixed term, provided that he still occupies the dwelling house as his residence. The landlord may terminate the continuation tenancy by giving not more than 12 but not less than six months' notice and choosing one of the two ways to determine the tenancy. He may either obtain possession by establishing one of the grounds in s 186, Sched 10, para 5(1), or offer an assured monthly periodic tenancy. It is the way in which the landlord may terminate the continuation tenancy which marks the difference between the 1954 and the 1989 schemes. The grounds set

261 Section 5 of the Landlord and Tenant Act 1954.

262 Sections 38 and 28 of the Leasehold Reform Act 1967.

263 Section 6(1) of the Landlord and Tenant Act 1954.

out in s 186 Sched 10, para 5(1) are: (i) the landlord (only public bodies to which s 28 of the Leasehold Reform Act 1967 applies) proposes to demolish or reconstruct the whole or a substantial part of the premises after the termination of the tenancy for the purposes of redevelopment; (ii) Grounds 6 and 9–15 in Sched 2 to the Housing Act 1988; (iii) premises required for landlord's residence.

If the landlord chooses to offer an assured periodic tenancy, in his notice he must specify the rent and that other terms are the same as the long tenancy. He may, however, propose new terms different from those in the long tenancy. The assured periodic tenancy takes effect in possession. Rent is payable in advance on a monthly basis. The rent and other terms are those proposed by the landlord unless the tenant proposes a different rent and terms, in which case the landlord may refer the rent and other terms to the rent assessment committee. If the landlord does not do so the rent and other terms shall be those proposed by the tenant.[264]

Rent (Agriculture) Act 1976: protected and assured tenancies of agricultural tied dwellings

Agricultural workers who occupied dwellings, sometimes known as 'tied cottages', provided for by their employers are given the status of 'protected occupiers' with similar Rent Act style protection.

A person is a 'protected occupier' if he is a 'qualifying worker' and has a 'relevant licence or tenancy' provided the dwelling is in 'qualifying ownership'.[265] A qualifying worker is a person who has worked full-time in agriculture for 91 out of the previous 104 weeks. A relevant licence or tenancy is an occupancy which would have been a protected tenancy under the Rent Acts but for the fact that it is a licence or a tenancy at a low rent. A dwelling is in qualifying ownership if the occupier is employed in agriculture and either his employer owns the dwelling or, where the dwelling is owned by a third person, has arranged for the dwelling to be occupied by his agricultural workers. On the death of the worker, there may be one succession to his occupancy by his spouse or a member of his family.[266]

On the expiration of the protected occupancy, the occupier who is in residence becomes a statutory tenant. This is so even if he is a mere licensee.[267] The employer may only repossess the dwelling on one or more of the grounds set out in ss 6, 7 and Sched 4. In addition, the employer may repossess, if vacant, possession of the dwelling for another agricultural workers is required in the interests of efficient agriculture, even if the employer cannot provide a suitable alternative accommodation.[268]

264 Section 186, Sched 10, para 10 of the Local Government and Housing Act 1989.

265 Sections 1, 2, Sched 3, Part I of the Rent (Agriculture) Act 1976.

266 Section 3 of the Rent (Agriculture) Act 1976.

267 Section 4 of the Rent (Agriculture) Act 1976.

268 Sections 27, 28 of the Rent (Agriculture) Act 1976.

Rent control under the Rent Acts also applies to protected agricultural occupancy.[269]

In line with the changes to the protected tenancies under the Rent Acts, no new protected agricultural occupancies can be created on or after 15 January 1989. They are replaced by assured agricultural occupancies.[270]

9 STATUTORY CONTROL ON PUBLIC SECTOR HOUSING

Housing Act 1985: secure tenancies

Since the Housing Act 1980, now consolidated in the Housing Act 1985, public sector tenants, who hold a secure tenancy of a dwelling house let as a separate dwelling, are also given similar protection from being evicted from their homes without good and sufficient cause as had been enjoyed by tenants in the private sector housing for many decades under the Rent Acts. To qualify as a secure tenancy,[271] the tenancy must be granted by certain public or quasi-public bodies, such as a local authority, a new town corporation, an urban development corporation etc,[272] and the tenant must occupy the dwelling house as his only or principal home.[273] A licence to occupy a dwelling house granted by the appropriate landlord may also qualify as a secure tenancy.[274] But a licence granted as a temporary expedient to a person who entered the dwelling house or any other land as a trespasser cannot qualify as a secure tenancy.[275]

A secure tenant enjoys security of tenure which can only be terminated by a court order.[276] On the expiry of a fixed term secure tenancy, a periodic tenancy arises automatically.[277] The court will not entertain proceedings for possession unless the landlord has served on the tenant a notice in prescribed form specifying the ground for possession.[278] An order for possession will only be made if one or more of the grounds specified in Schedule 2 to the Housing Act 1985 are established. The tenant's spouse, or other member of the tenant's family who has resided with the tenant throughout the period of 12 months ending with the tenant's death, is entitled to succeed to the secure tenancy on the death of the tenant.[279] A secure tenant is also given a statutory 'right to buy' which will be discussed below.

---

269 Section 13 of the Rent (Agriculture) Act 1976.

270 Sections 24, 25 of the Housing Act 1988.

271 Section 79(1) of the Housing Act 1985.

272 Section 80 of the Housing Act 1985.

273 Section 81 of the Housing Act 1985.

274 Section 79(3) of the Housing Act 1985.

275 Section 79(4) of the Housing Act 1985.

276 Section 82(1), (3) of the Housing Act 1985.

277 Section 86(1), (2) of the Housing Act 1985. *See London City Corpn v Brown* (1990) 60 P & CR 42.

278 Section 83(1), (2) of the Housing Act 1985. But the court now has discretion to dispense with notice if it appears 'just and equitable': s 83(1)(b) of the Housing Act 1985, as substituted by s 147(1) of the Housing Act 1996.

279 Sections 87, 113 of the Housing Act 1985.

10 COMMERCIAL LETTING

Landlord and Tenant Act 1954, Part II

Likewise, commercial tenants are also given certain statutory protection by Part II of the Landlord and Tenant Act 1954.[280] The Act applies to any tenant who occupies premises for the purposes of a business carried on by him.[281] Business' includes 'a trade, profession or employment and any activity carried on by a body of persons, whether corporate or unincorporate'.[282] Section 43 provides, however, a list of tenancy not covered by the Act.

A tenancy covered by Part II of the Landlord and Tenant Act 1954 'shall not come to an end unless terminated in accordance with the provisions of this Part of this Act.'[283] Under Part II of the Act, when the initial contractual tenancy expires, or where the landlord serves a notice to quit, or otherwise terminates the tenancy, a continuation tenancy arises. The continuation tenancy is on the same terms as the contractual tenancy. The landlord may only terminate the continuation tenancy by giving a notice under s 25 and establishing a ground for possession under s 30. If a notice has been served by the landlord, the tenant may state his unwillingness to give up possession and apply to the court for a new tenancy to be granted. If no notice has been served, the tenant may request by notice a new tenancy under s 26. In both cases, the landlord may only resist the new tenancy on one or more of the grounds in s 30.

Landlord and Tenant Act 1954

30. Opposition by landlord to application for a new tenancy

(1) The grounds on which a landlord may oppose an application under sub-s (1) of s 24 of this Act are such of the following grounds as may be stated in the landlord's notice under s 25 of this Act or, as the case may be, under sub-s (6) of s 26 thereof, that is to say:

(a) where under the current tenancy the tenant has any obligations as respects the repair and maintenance of the holding, that the tenant ought not to be granted a new tenancy in view of the state of repair of the holding, being a state resulting from the tenant's failure to comply with the said obligations;

(b) that the tenant ought not to be granted a new tenancy in view of his persistent delay in paying rent which has become due;

(c) that the tenant ought not to be granted a new tenancy in view of other substantial breaches by him of his obligations under the current tenancy, or for any other reason connected with the tenant's use or management of the holding;

---

280 For proposed reform see Landlord and Tenant: Business Tenancies: A Periodic Review of the Landlord and Tenant Act 1954 Part II, Law Com No 208, HC 224.

281 Section 23(1) of the Landlord and Tenant Act 1954.

282 Section 23(21) of the Landlord and Tenant Act 1954.

283 Section 24 of the Landlord and Tenant Act 1954.

(d) that the landlord has offered and is willing to provide or secure the provision of alternative accommodation for the tenant, that the terms on which the alternative accommodation is available are reasonable having regard to the terms of the current tenancy and to all other relevant circumstances, and that the accommodation and the time at which it will be available are suitable for the tenant's requirements (including the requirement to preserve goodwill) having regard to the nature and class of his business and to the situation and extent of, and facilities afforded by, the holding;

(e) where the current tenancy was created by the sub-letting of part only of the property comprised in a superior tenancy and the landlord is the owner of an interest in reversion expectant on the termination of that superior tenancy, that the aggregate of the rents reasonably obtainable on separate lettings of the holding and the remainder of that property would be substantially less than the rent reasonably obtainable on a letting of that property as a whole, that on the termination of the current tenancy the landlord requires possession of the holding for the purpose of letting or otherwise disposing of the said property as a whole, and that in view thereof the tenant ought not to be granted a new tenancy;

(f) that on the termination of the current tenancy the landlord intends to demolish or reconstruct the premises comprised in the holding or a substantial part of those premises or to carry out substantial work of construction on the holding or part thereof and that he could not reasonably do so without obtaining possession of the holding;

(g) subject as hereinafter provided, that on the termination of the current tenancy the landlord intends to occupy the holding for the purposes, or partly for the purposes, of a business to be carried on by him therein, or as his residence.

The court may order the grant of a new tenancy for a period up to 14 years.[284] If the landlord successfully resists the grant of a new tenancy on one or more of the last three grounds set out in s 30, the tenant is entitled to compensation for quitting the premises.[285] He may also be entitled to compensation for improvements effected in the premises which add to their letting value, provided that due notice prior to the improvement had been given to the landlord.[286]

The rent for the continuation tenancy will be the same as the initial contractual tenancy. The landlord may apply to the court, if he has given a s 25 notice or following a s 26 tenant's request, for the interim rent to be determined.[287] Where a new tenancy is ordered or granted, if the parties cannot agree on the rent payable, the court can fix a rent which can reasonably be expected in the open market by a willing lessor.[288]

284 Section 33 of the Landlord and Tenant Act 1954.

285 Section 37 of the Landlord and Tenant Act 1954, as amended by Sched 7 of the Local Government and Housing Act 1989.

286 Sections 1, 3 of the Landlord and Tenant Act 1927, as amended by Part III of the Landlord and Tenant Act 1954. See also Law Commission: Landlord and Tenant Law: Compensation for Tenants' Improvements, (1989) Law Com No 178; (1991) 11 *Legal Studies* 119 (Haley, M).

287 Section 24A(1) of the Landlord and Tenant Act 1954.

288 Section 34(1) of the Landlord and Tenant Act 1954. For new tenancies granted on or after 1 January 1996, in determining the rent, the court should also take into account the effect on rent of the operation of the provisions of the Landlord and Tenant (Covenants) Act 1995: see *ibid* s 30(1), Sched 1, para 3.

11 AGRICULTURAL HOLDINGS

Agricultural Holdings Act 1986: agricultural holdings

Protection as to compensation for improvements and termination of holdings without good cause were first given to agricultural holdings by the Agricultural Holdings (England) Act 1875 and the Agricultural Holdings Act 1923. Security of tenure and protection as to rent were also extended to agricultural holdings by the Agriculture Act 1947. These protections are today consolidated in the Agricultural Holdings Act 1986.

The Act applies to 'agricultural holdings'.

Agriculture Holding Act 1986

1. Principal definitions

(1) In this Act 'agricultural holding' means the aggregate of the land (whether agricultural land or not) comprised in a contract of tenancy which is a contract for an agricultural tenancy, not being a contract under which the land is let to the tenant during his continuance in any office, appointment or employment held under the landlord.

(2) For the purposes of this section, a contract of tenancy relating to any land is a contract for an agricultural tenancy if, having regard to:

(a) the terms of the tenancy;

(b) the actual or contemplated use of the land at the time of the conclusion of the contract and subsequently; and

(c) any other relevant circumstances,

the whole of the land comprised in the contract, subject to such exceptions only as do not substantially affect the character of the tenancy, is let for use as agricultural land.

(3) A change in user of the land concerned subsequent to the conclusion of a contract of tenancy which involves any breach of the terms of the tenancy shall be disregarded for the purpose of determining whether a contract which was not originally a contract for an agricultural tenancy has subsequently become one unless it is effected with the landlord's permission, consent or acquiescence.

(4) In this Act 'agricultural land' means:

(a) land used for agriculture which is so used for the purposes of a trade or business; and

(b) any other land which, by virtue of a designation under s 109(l) of the Agriculture Act 1947, is agricultural land within the meaning of that Act.

(5) In this Act 'contract of tenancy' means a letting of land, or agreement for letting land, for a term of years or from year to year; and for the purposes of this definition a letting of land, or an agreement for letting land, which, by virtue of sub-s (6) of s 149 of the Law of Property Act 1925, takes effect as such a letting of land or agreement for letting land as is mentioned in that subsection shall be deemed to be a letting of land or, as the case may be, an agreement for letting land, for a term of years.

2. Restriction on letting agricultural land for less than from year to year

(1) An agreement to which this section applies shall take effect, with the necessary modifications, as if it were an agreement for the letting of land for a tenancy from year to year unless the agreement was approved by the Minister before it was entered into.

(2) Subject to sub-s (3) below, this section applies to an agreement under which:

(a) any land is let to a person for use as agricultural land for an interest less than a tenancy from year to year; or

(b) a person is granted a licence to occupy land for use as agricultural land,

if the circumstances are such that if his interest were a tenancy from year to year he would in respect of that land be the tenant of an agricultural holding.

(3) This section does not apply to an agreement for the letting of land, or the granting of a licence to occupy land:

(a) made (whether or not it expressly so provides) in contemplation of the use of the land only for grazing or mowing (or both) during some specified period of the year; or

(b) by a person whose interest in the land is less than a tenancy from year to year and has not taken effect as such a tenancy by virtue of this section.

Where the land is used for agricultural and non-agricultural purposes, the Act applies to all or none. The test is whether the tenancy is in substance as a whole a tenancy of agricultural land.[289]

A tenancy for two years or more continues as a tenancy from year to year on its expiry, unless either party has given notice to quit not less than a year nor more than two years before the date of expiration.[290] A notice to quit is invalid if it purports to terminate the tenancy before the expiry of one year from the end of the then current tenancy.[291] Where a notice to quit has been served on the tenant, the tenant may serve a counter-notice on the landlord, which will, with eight exceptions,[292] render the landlord's notice to quit ineffective unless the Agricultural Land Tribunal consents to its taking effect on one of the grounds specified in s 27 of the Act.

Where one or more of the grounds are established, the tribunal must consent to the landlord's notice to quit unless it appears that 'a fair and reasonable landlord would not insist on possession'.[293]

When an agricultural tenancy is first granted, the parties are free to agree on the rent payable. However, the tenant may later submit the rent, not more than one in every three years, to the arbitration.[294]

---

289 *Monson v Bound* [1954] 1 WLR 1321.

290 Sections 3, 4 of the Agricultural Holdings Act 1986.

291 Section 25(1) of the Agricultural Holdings Act 1986.

292 Section 26, Sched 3 of the Agricultural Holdings Act 1986.

293 Section 27(1), (2) of the Agricultural Holdings Act 1986.

294 Sections 12, 84, Sched 2 of the Agricultural Holdings Act 1986.

A tenant who quits as a result of the landlord's notice is, in some cases, normally entitled to compensation from the landlord.[295] He may also be entitled to certain improvements which increase the value of the holding, or the value to an incoming tenant.[296]

12 TENANT'S STATUTORY 'RIGHT TO BUY'

Leasehold Reform Act 1967: leasehold enfranchisement of houses[297]

This Act gives a tenant under a long lease of a house, but not a flat, who occupies it as his residence, at a low rent, either the right to acquire the freehold or to obtain an extended lease for 50 years.[298] At the time the tenant gives notice of his intention to acquire the freehold or to have an extended lease, he must have been occupying the house as his residence for the last three years or for periods amounting to three years in the last 10 years.[299] While the right to give a notice, either to buy the freehold or to extend the lease, cannot be an interest in land,[300] it can be protected, after it is exercised by notice, as a C(iv) land charge in unregistered land, or a minor interest in registered land. It cannot be an overriding interest under s 70(1)(g) of the Land Registration Act 1925.[301]

The price for the freehold is to be the open market value of the house on the basis that they are subject to the tenancy.[302] Under the extended tenancy, only the rent is payable.[303] No price or premium can be charged. However, a higher rent may become payable on the expiry of 25 years of the extended term.[304] No right to terminate the lease before it expires can be reserved other than for breach of covenant.[305]

Landlord and Tenant Act 1987: rights of pre-emption

This Act gives the tenants of a block of flats the right of pre-emption short of a right to buy. This means that the landlord cannot dispose of his interest without

295 Sections 60, 61 of the Agricultural Holdings Act 1986.

296 Sections 64-66, Scheds 7–9 of the Agricultural Holdings Act 1986.

297 For an interesting case where the claim was rejected that Leasehold Reform Act 1967 was a violation of the European Convention on Human Rights, see *James v United Kingdom* (1986) 8 EHRR 123.

298 Sections 1–3, 8(1), 14(1) of the Leasehold Reform Act 1967. See also [1982] Conv 241 (letter to the editor by Boyes, Sutton and Perry). Section 106 of the Housing Act 1966 extends the right to enfranchisement to tenancies which fail only the low rent test.

299 Section 1(1)(b) of the Leasehold Reform Act 1967 as amended by s 141, Sched 21, para 1(1) of the Housing Act 1980.

300 *Uddin v Birmingham CC* (1990) 59 P & CR 341 at 345.

301 Section 5(5) of the Leasehold Reform Act 1967.

302 Section 9 of the Leasehold Reform Act 1967, as amended by s 66, Sched 15 of the Leasehold Reform, Housing and Urban Development Act 1995.

303 Section 15(2)(a) of the Leasehold Reform Act 1967.

304 Section 15(2)(b) of the Leasehold Reform Act 1967.

305 Section 15(5) of the Leasehold Reform Act 1967.

giving the qualifying tenants the right of first refusal. If the landlord intends to dispose of his interest, he must serve a notice to the qualifying tenants indicating the proposed sale price.[306] The notice is deemed statutorily to be an offer which may be accepted by the bare majority of the qualifying tenants.[307] If the offer is rejected, the landlord may sell during the next 12 months at a price not less than that originally offered to the qualifying tenants.[308]

Leasehold Reform, Housing and Urban Development Act 1993: collective leasehold enfranchisement[309]

As has been seen, Leasehold Reform Act 1967 has no application to long leasehold in a flat. Part I of the Leasehold Reform, Urban and Housing Development Act 1993 now deals with this problem. Qualifying tenants in a block of flats now enjoy a right of collective enfranchisement' at a statutorily determined price.[310] They are also entitled individually, on payment of a statutorily determined premium, to request for a new lease of 90 years at a peppercorn rent on the expiry of the existing lease.[311]

The Act only applies to premises which consist of a building containing two or more flats held by qualifying tenants.[312] The premises must be primarily substantially residential. Premises of which more than 10% of the internal floor area is designated for non-residential purpose, such as shops or other commercial premises, are not covered by the Act.[313] The Act does not apply to premises where there is a residential landlord and the premises do not contain more than four flats.[314] The qualifying tenants must collectively hold at least two-thirds of the flats in the building.[315]

Like the case under the Leasehold Reform Act 1967, qualifying tenants, under the 1993 Act, must hold a long lease at a low rent.[316] The qualifying tenants must have occupied their flats as their only or principal home either for the preceding 12 months or for periods totalling three years in the preceding 10 years.[317]

---

306 Section 1(1) of the Landlord and Tenant Act 1987.

307 Sections 5(2)(b), 5(6), 6(1)(b) of the Landlord and Tenant Act 1987. See now s 5 of the Landlord and Tenant Act, as substituted by Sched 6 of the Housing Act 1996.

308 Section 6(3) of the Landlord and Tenant Act 1987.

309 For an extremely useful guide to this Act, see Curran, T, *Buying Your Freehold or Extending Your Lease: The Flat Owner's Guide to Leasehold Enfranchisement*, 1993.

310 Section 1(1) of the Leasehold Reform, Housing and Urban Development Act 1993.

311 Sections 39(1), 56(1), Sched 13 of the Leasehold Reform, Housing and Urban Development Act 1993.

312 Section 3(1) of the Leasehold Reform, Housing and Urban Development Act 1993. The requirement that the freehold of the whole of the premises be owned by the same person is now deleted by s 107(1) of the Housing Act 1996.

313 Section 4(1) of the Leasehold Reform, Housing and Urban Development Act 1993.

314 Section 4(4) of the Leasehold Reform, Housing and Urban Development Act 1993.

315 Section 3(1)(c) of the Leasehold Reform, Housing and Urban Development Act 1993.

316 Section 5(1) of the Leasehold Reform, Housing and Urban Development Act 1993. For leases granted on or after 1 April 1990, the annual ground rent must not be more than £1,000 in London and £250 elsewhere: s 8(1)(c). Section 106 of the Housing Act 1996 extends the right to enfranchisement to tenancies which fail only the low rent test.

317 Section 6(1), (2) of the Leasehold Reform, Housing and Urban Development Act 1993.

It is for at least two-thirds of the qualifying tenants collectively to initiate a purchase by notice.[318]

Housing Act 1985: secure tenant's right to buy

Public sector qualifying secure tenants are also given a right to buy the home in which they live, since the Housing Act 1980, now consolidated in the Housing Act 1985. The secure tenant can buy the freehold only if the dwelling is a 'house' and his landlord owns the freehold.[319] If the dwelling is not a house but only a flat or if the landlord does not own the freehold, the secure tenant can only request for a long lease for a term of usually not less than 125 years at an annual rent not exceeding £10 with a statutorily determined market price minus a discount.[320]

Certain statutory conditions set out in s 138(1)[321] must be satisfied before the right to buy can be exercised. Once the statutory conditions are satisfied, the right to buy cannot be resisted by the landlord.[322] The secure tenant must also have been in occupation of the dwelling house for at least two years.[323]

The price for the freehold, or the long lease, is the price which such an interest would get on the open market, minus a discount which varies according to the length of the pre-existing secure tenancy. For a house, the discount ranges from 32% to a maximum of 60%, and for a flat from 44% to 70%.[324] In any case, the maximum discount allowed is £50,000.[325] If the tenant having exercised the right to buy to acquire the freehold, sold it or granted a long lease within three years of purchase, he is required to repay any discount, partly or wholly, which was made in his favour.[326]

The qualifying secure tenant in exercising his right to buy is also entitled to a mortgage finance advanced by the landlord authority under the 'rent to mortgage' scheme.[327] Under this scheme, the tenant can acquire the fee simple outright but must mortgage it to the landlord.[328] The periodic payments made by the tenant, fixed at a particular level, help him gradually to redeem the mortgage.

---

318 Section 13(1), (2) of the Leasehold Reform, Housing and Urban Development Act 1993.

319 Section 118(1)(a) of the Housing Act 1985.

320 Section 118(1)(b), Sched 6, Part III, paras 11, 12(1); ss 126, 127 of the Housing Act 1985.

321 As amended by Sched 22 of the Leasehold Reform, Housing and Urban Development Act 1993.

322 *Taylor v Newham LBC* [1993] 2 All ER 649 at 655e.

323 Section 119(1) of the Housing Act 1985. The period does not have to be continuous, or preceding immediately before the exercise of the right: Sched 4, paras 1, 2(a) of the Housing Act 1985.

324 Section 129(2) of the Housing Act 1985.

325 Section 131(2) of the Housing Act 1985; The Housing (Right to Buy) (Maximum Discount) Order 1989 (SI 1989/513).

326 Sections 155(1), (2), 159(1)(b) of the Housing Act 1985.

327 Section 143(1) of the Housing Act 1985, as substituted by s 108 of the Leasehold Reform, Housing and Urban Development Act 1993.

328 Housing Act 1985, as substituted by s 115 of the Leasehold Reform, Housing and Urban Development Act 1993.

Housing Act 1996: right to buy of tenant of registered social landlord

A tenant of a registered social landlord[1] also has the right to buy the dwelling of which he is a tenant if he is an assured tenant, and the dwelling was provided with public money and he satisfies other qualifying conditions.[2]

1 For bodies eligible for registration as social landlords see s 2 of the Housing Act 1996.

2 See s 16(1) of the Housing Act 1996.

CHAPTER 9

LEASEHOLD COVENANTS

1 INTRODUCTION

A covenant is a promise made in a deed. However, promises made in a valid agreement to create a legal lease under s 54(2) of the Law of Property Act 1925 are enforceable covenants even though no deed is used.[1] Covenants are different from conditions. A breach of condition automatically brings the term to an end. A breach of covenants does not end the term automatically and the landlord may not terminate the lease for breach of covenant in the absence of express provisions of forfeiture. Whether a term is a condition or a covenant depends on the intention of the parties. Generally, a term will be regarded as a covenant unless clear words are used to show that it is intended to be a condition.[2]

A lease contains various types of express and implied covenants relating to the rights and obligations of the landlord and tenant.

2 COVENANTS BY THE LANDLORD

Express covenants

These are covenants entered into expressly by the landlord. Most formal leases, for example, assured shorthold tenancies, business tenancies etc, contain detailed covenants relating to the landlord's rights and obligations such as, rights of access, obligations to repair,[3] to insure,[4] to allow the tenant quiet enjoyment etc. The lease may fail to contain covenants to deal with all eventualities. In the case of weekly and other periodic tenancies, the lease is often silent on many matters except the essential terms as to the parties, premises, rent and duration.

Implied covenants

Where the lease does not contain covenants relating to certain matters, these matters will be governed by implied covenants. But if the lease contains such an express covenant, 'there is no room for an implied covenant covering the same ground or any part of it'.[5]

---

1 *Boyer v Warbey* [1953] 1 QB 234.

2 *Doe d Henniker v Watt* (1828) 8 B & C 308.

3 In short leases, this obligation may be shared by the tenant. In longer leases, it is normal for the tenant to covenant to undertake all necessary repairs.

4 In some cases, the tenant may have to covenant to pay some, or all of the premium. In others, the tenant may have to undertake this obligation.

5 *Malzy v Eichholz* [1916] 2 KB 308 at 313.

(a) Covenant for quiet enjoyment

This does not mean that the landlord undertakes that the tenant will be free from the nuisance of noise. It means that the tenant will be free from disturbance by adverse rights over the land.[6]

(b) Not to derogate from his grant

This is an application of the general principle that a grantor must not derogate from his grant.[7] This means that the landlord must not do anything which will interfere with the purpose for which the tenancy was granted.[8] Most conduct in breach of the covenant for quiet enjoyment represents a derogation from the grant.[9]

(c) Covenants as to fitness and repair

The common law rule is that there is no implied covenant as to the state of fitness or repair of the subject matter of the lease.[10] This general principle is, however, subject to certain exceptions:

(i) Where a house is let furnished, the premises must be reasonably fit for human habitation at the start of the term.[11] This exception is, however, of very limited application. It does not apply to unfurnished premises,[12] and it only applies to a residential tenancy.

(ii) In some cases, where it is necessary to give effect to the business efficacy of the leasehold agreement, there may be an implied covenant that the landlord will exercise a duty of care to keep in reasonable repair and usability the common parts and facilities.[13] This is an implied contractual duty of care, and will only arise in order to give the lease business efficacy.

(iii) If a house is let at a low rent, there is a statutory implied covenant that it must be fit for human habitation at the commencement of the lease, and that it will be kept fit for human habitation, by the landlord, during the tenancy.[14] This is, however, of very limited importance today because it only applies if the rent does not exceed £80 a year in London and £52 elsewhere.[15]

(iv) Where a dwelling is let for less than seven years, there is an implied covenant by the landlord to keep the structure and exterior in repair and to keep in repair and working order the facilities for the supply of water, gas, electricity,

---

6 *Hudson v Cripps* [1896] 1 Ch 265 at 268.

7 *Palmer v Fletcher* (1663) 1 Lev 122. See (1964) 80 LQR 244 (Elliott, DW); (1965) 81 LQR 28 (Peel, MA).

8 *Harmer v Jumbil (Nigeria) Tin Areas Ltd* [1921] 1 Ch 200.

9 *Robinson v Kilvert* (1889) 41 Ch D 88 at 95.

10 *Gott v Gandy* (1853) 2 El & Bl 845 at 847; 118 ER 984, 985.

11 *Smith v Marrable* (1843) 11 M&W 5; 152 ER 693.

12 *Hart v Windsor* (1843) 12 M & W 68 at 87; 152 ER 1114 at 1122.

13 *Liverpool City Council v Irwin* [1977] AC 239, HL.

14 Section 8(1) of the Landlord and Tenant Act 1985.

15 Section 8(4) of the Landlord and Tenant Act 1985.

sanitation, space heating and heating of water.[16] Where the lease is granted on or after 15 January 1989, and the dwelling forms only part of a building, the implied covenant extends to any part of the building in which the landlord has an estate or interest.[17] Where a defect occurs in the demised premises themselves, the landlord is liable only when he has notice of the defect. No liability will arise unless and until the landlord is notified of the defect.[18] Thus, a landlord is not liable under s 11 of the Landlord and Tenant Act 1985 if the tenant suffers injury as a result of a latent and invisible defect.[19] Where the defect occurs in premises not comprised in the demised premises themselves, the landlord is in breach of his obligation to keep such premises in repair as soon as the defect occurs, not at the later time when he is informed of the defect and has failed to carry out the repair within reasonable time.[20]

(v) The landlord also owes a statutory duty of care to the tenant, and to other persons coming on to the property, to see that they will be safe from injury or damage to their property which may be caused by the defect in the property.[21]

If the landlord is under a duty to repair, it is implied that he can enter the premises to inspect and carry out necessary repairs at a reasonable hour.

3 COVENANTS BY THE TENANT

Express covenants

Matters agreed between the landlord and the tenant are normally covered by express covenants. Most common types of express covenant are covenants to pay rent and covenants either not to assign, sublet, or part with possession of the premises at all, or without the landlord's consent.

Where payments of rent have been agreed, the sum must be certain or capable of being rendered certain to be recoverable.[22] If the rent payable is based on as many hours' service as the landlord would require from time to time, it is not sufficiently certain.[23] A rent which is linked to the index of retail prices is regarded as sufficiently certain,[24] so is a sum representing 10% of the turnover of a business.[25] A new rent which can be ascertained in due course under a rent review clause is also certain.[26]

16 Sections 11–12 of the Landlord and Tenant Act 1985.

17 Section 11(1A) of the Landlord and Tenant Act 1985, as inserted by s 116(1) of the Housing Act 1988.

18 *O'Brien v Robinson* [1973] AC 912 at 926A, 930B.

19 *O'Brien v Robinson* [1973] AC 912 at 915G–26A.

20 *British Telecommunications plc v Sun Life Assurance Society plc* [1995] 4 All ER 44, CA.

21 Sections 1(1), 4 of the Defective Premises Act 1972.

22 *Walsh v Lonsdale* (1882) 21 Ch D 9.

23 *Barnes v Barratt* [1970] 2 QB 657.

24 *Blumental v Gallery Five Ltd* (1971) 220 Estates Gazette 483.

25 *Smith v Cardiff Corpn (No 2)* [1955] Ch 159.

26 *C H Bailey Ltd v Memorial Enterprises Ltd* [1974] 1 All ER 1003; *United Scientific Holdings Ltd v Burnley Borough Council* [1978] AC 904, HL.

If the tenant covenants not to assign or sublet or part with possession of the premises at all, the landlord may not be forced to give consent no matter how unreasonable the withholding of consent is. The landlord may, of course, on the other hand, waive the absolute prohibition. If the tenant covenants not to assign or sublet without the landlord's consent, then, under s 19(1)(a) of the Landlord and Tenant Act 1927, the landlord must not withhold consent unreasonably. The burden of proving unreasonable refusal is on the tenant. However, if the tenant applies in writing for the landlord's consent, the landlord has a statutory duty to make a decision within a reasonable time of the tenant's application.[27] In his reply, the landlord must either give consent or justify his refusal as being reasonable. This reverses the burden of proof onto the landlord. In the case of an assured tenancy, covenants not to assign without consent are implied by s 15 of the Housing Act 1988. But s 19 of the 1927 Act does not apply to an assured tenancy. So consent in those cases can be unreasonably withheld.

For new tenancies created on or after 1 January 1996, the tenancy agreement may specify the terms or conditions on which the landlord may grant or withhold consent to an assignment.

It should be noted that a lease granted or assigned in breach of an express covenant is still valid,[28] although if there is a forfeiture clause the landlord may re-enter. A covenant against assignment or subletting is construed against the landlord.[29] Thus, a covenant prohibiting assignment does not cover subletting. While, a covenant against assignment or subletting of 'any part' of the demised premises is breached if there is an assignment or subletting of the whole,[30] a covenant prohibiting assignment or subletting of the whole is not broken by an assignment or subletting of only a part.[31]

A lease also often contains express covenants to repair. In long leases, the tenant usually covenants to do all repairs. In short leases, it is more common for the landlord to assume responsibility expressly. The matter is, of course, open to negotiation, subject to the landlord's statutory liability to do repair in some cases discussed above.

Covenants to insure may also be made expressly by the tenant. Where there is such a covenant, there is a breach if the property is uninsured for any period however short and even if no damage occurs during that time.[32]

Implied covenants

In the absence of express agreement to the contrary in the lease, certain covenants are implied by law.

27 Section 1(3) of the Landlord and Tenant Act 1988.

28 *Parker v Jones* [1910] 2 KB 32.

29 *Montross Associated Investments SA v Moussaieff* [1992] 05 EG 160.

30 *Field v Barkworth* [1986] 1 WLR 137 at 139F–G, 140E–F.

31 *Wilson v Rosenthal* (1906) 22 TLR 233.

32 *Penniall v Harborne* (1848) 11 QB 368.

(a) Covenant to pay rent

This is implied in every lease.[33]

(b) Covenant to pay rates and taxes

Unless otherwise agreed, the tenant is generally liable to pay all rates and taxes except those for which the landlord is liable.

(c) Covenant not to commit waste

The tenant is under an implied obligation not to commit waste. In the case of a weekly, monthly and quarterly tenancy, the tenant is liable for voluntary waste but not permissive waste[34] and they must do the little jobs about the place which a reasonable tenant would do. In the case of a yearly tenancy, the position is the same except the tenant must also ensure that the premises are wind and water-tight,[35] but he is not liable for fair wear and tear.[36] A fixed term tenant is liable for voluntary and permissive waste.[37]

4 USUAL COVENANTS

When a grant is preceded by a contractual agreement, it is an implied term of the contract that the lease when granted will contain the 'usual covenants'.[38] The lease may be rectified if it fails to include usual covenants when granted. What is usual depends on the area in which the property stands. The list of usual covenant is never closed.[39] The following are always regarded as usual:

(a) The tenant will pay rent;

(b) The tenant will pay rates and taxes;

(c) The tenant will keep the premises in repair;

(d)If the landlord has covenanted to repair, he will be allowed reasonable access to view and repair the premises;

(e) The landlord will allow the tenant quiet enjoyment[40] and he will not derogate from his grant.

In addition to the above, unlike the position in a legal lease, the landlord has an implied right to re-enter should the tenant fail to pay his rent[41] and possibly for breach of other covenants.[42]

---

33 *Youngmin v Heath* [1974] 1 All ER 461.

34 *Mint v Good* [1951] 1 KB 517.

35 *Wedd v Porter* [1916] 2 KB 91.

36 *Warren v Keen* [1954] 1 QB 15.

37 *Yellowly v Gower* (1855) 11 Exch 274.

38 *Propert v Parker* (1832) 3 My & K 280 at 281; 40 ER 107. See [1992] Conv 18 (Crabb, L).

39 *Flexman v Corbett* [1930] 1 Ch 672 at 678.

40 *Budd-Scott v Daniell* [1902] 2 KB 351 at 355.

41 *Hodgkinson v Crowe* (1875) 10 Ch App 622 at 626.

42 *Chester v Buckingham Travel Ltd* [1981] 1 WLR 96 at 105E–F. See also (1981) 97 LQR 385 (Woodman, G); (1981) 131 NLJ 545 (Wilkinson, HW).

5 ENFORCEMENT OF COVENANTS IN A LEGAL LEASE – THE OLD RULES

```
L1 ————————— A1 ————————— A2
|
T1 ————————— T2 ————————— T3
                          |
                          ST
```

Fig 1

Privity of contract and privity of estate

A leasehold estate originates in contract. There is, thus, a contractual relationship between the immediate landlord (L1) and tenant (T1). There is what is often referred to as 'privity of contract' between L1 and T1. It defines the scope of the parties' contractual liability.

A leasehold estate which originates in contract also confers on the tenant an estate in land. There is, therefore, in addition to the relationship of 'privity of contract', a relationship of 'privity of estate' between L1 and T1. This defines the parties' liability under the tenancy, and where there are successive assignments of the tenancy or the reversion, it indicates the allocation of the tenancy.

Thus, as between L1 and T1, there is both 'privity of contract and 'privity of estate'. When the reversion is assigned to A1 (or A2), there is no privity of contract between A1 (or A2) and T1. But as A1 (or A2) is now put into L1's shoes and has become the landlord of T1, there is a privity of estate between them. L1 will, after the assignment of reversion to A1, cease to have privity of estate with T1. Likewise, when T1 assigns the tenancy to T2, T1 no longer holds the land, and ceases to have privity of estate with L1. T2 will have privity of estate with L1, because he is now the tenant. But there is no privity of contract between T2 and L1.

When land is sublet by T3 to ST, there is privity of estate between T3 and ST, because T3 is the landlord of ST insofar as the sublease is concerned. There is also privity of contract which defines T3 and ST's contractual liability. But as privity of estate describes the relationship of landlord and tenant, there is no privity of estate between ST and L1. This is because L1 is not the landlord of ST. L1 is the landlord of T3 with regard to the head lease between L1 and T3. Neither is there a privity of contract between L1 and ST, for they never make a contract between themselves.

Between original parties

For leases created before 1 January 1996, the covenanting parties (L1 and T1 in Fig 1) are liable under the doctrine of privity of contract even if they may have disposed of their interest in the property.

(a) Tenant's continuing liability

In the absence of contrary agreement with L1, T1 remains liable throughout the entire term of the tenancy irrespective of assignment.[43] Although L1 and T1 may agree that T1 should cease to be liable under the contract with the assignment of his term, this is not usually done in practice. The Law Commission points out that this is due to unequal bargaining power of landlords and tenants.[44] An express limitation of the tenant's continuing liability is almost unacceptable to the landlord. T1's continuing liability covers the covenants to pay rent,[45] payment of interest on unpaid rent by his assignee,[46] and any other covenants contained in the original lease.[47]

It used to be thought that T1 may even be made liable on the original covenants as varied by L1 and T2 or T3. This was so even if T1's liability was effectively increased by the subsequent variation of the original covenants,[48] or even if the variation was carried out by T2 or T3 without T1's consent or knowledge.[49] This was because, as Harman J put it in *Centrovincial Estates Plc v Bulk Storage Ltd*, each assignee was the owner of the whole estate and could deal with it so as to alter it or its term. The estate so altered then bound the original tenant, because the assignee had been put into the shoes of the original tenant and could do all such acts as the original tenant could have done.[50] Harman J had no sympathy for T1 because, in his view, T1 could have avoided this by subletting, on identical terms, the unexpired term minus two or three days, instead of assigning the whole of the term.[51]

However, Beldam LJ in *Friends' Provident Life Office v British Railways Board*[52] pointed out that Harman J was apparently wrong, that there was a distinction between the contractual liability of a lessee under his personal covenants and the liability of an assignee for the obligations of the covenants imprinted on the legal estate, and that the obligations accepted by a lessee in his contract with the

---

43 *Warnford Investments Ltd v Duckworth* [1979] Ch 127 at 138C. See also *W H Smith Ltd v Wyndham Investments Ltd* (1994) *The Times*, 27 May; *Hindcastle Ltd v Barbara Attenborough Associates Ltd* [1996] 1 All ER 737, HL (disclaimer of lease by liquidator of assignee company under s 178 of Insolvency Act 1986 does not terminate original tenant's continuing liability).

44 Law Commission, Landlord and Tenant: Privity of Contract and Estate; Duration of Liability of Parties to Leases, Working Paper No 95, March 1986, para 7.1(c); Law Commission, Landlord and Tenant: Privity of Contract and Estate (Law Com No 174, 29 November 1988), paras 2.17, 3.3, 3.17.

45 *Warnford Investments Ltd v Duckworth* [1979] Ch 127 at 138G–139A, 141H–142A.

46 Section 35A of the Supreme Court Act 1981; *Allied London Investments Ltd v Hambro Life Assurance Ltd* (1984) 269 *Estates Gazette* 41 at 42.

47 *Thames Manufacturing Co Ltd v Perrotts (Nichol & Peyton) Ltd* (1984) 271 *Estates Gazette* 284 at 286; *Weaver v Mogford* [1988] 31 *Estates Gazette* 49.

48 *Selous Street Properties Ltd v Oronel Fabrics Ltd* (1984) 270 *Estates Gazette* 643 at 650 (original tenant liable to pay increased rent fixed under a rent review negotiated by his assignee under a different basis). See (1984) 81 *Law Soc Gaz* 2214 (Reynolds, K).

49 *Centrovincial Estates plc v Bulk Storage Ltd* (1983) 46 P & CR 393 at 396.

50 *Centrovincial Estates plc v Bulk Storage Ltd* (1983) 46 P & CR 393 at 396.

51 *Centrovincial Estates plc v Bulk Storage Ltd* (1983) 46 P & CR 393 at 398.

52 [1996] 1 All ER 336.

lessor could not be varied or increased by a subsequent agreement made by the lessor with an assignee.

Friends' Provident Life Office v British Railway Board [1996] 1 All ER 336, CA

Beldam LJ: Apart from the passage in the judgment of Harman J in *Centrovincial Estates plc v Bulk Storage Ltd* (1983) 46 P & CR 393 at 396 referred to by the recorder in his judgment and the other cases based upon this *dictum*, there is no authority to support so radical a departure from the generally accepted view that it could not do so. The conventional view was put with great clarity by Nourse LJ in his judgment in *City of London Corp v Fell* [1993] 2 All ER 449 at 453, [1993] QB 589 at 603:

> A lease of land, because it originates in a contract, gives rise to obligations enforceable between the original landlord and the original tenant in contract. But because it also gives the tenant an estate in the land, assignable, like the reversion, to others, the obligations, so far as they touch and concern the land, assume a wider influence, becoming, as it were, imprinted on the term or the reversion as the case may be, enforceable between the owners thereof for the time being as conditions of the enjoyment of their respective estates. Thus landlord and tenant stand together in one or other of two distinct legal relationships. In the first it is said that there is privity of contract between them, in the second privity of estate. To what, in ordinary legal parlance, do we refer when we speak of a 'tenancy'? I think that we refer to a particular legal relationship between tenant and landlord under which land is held by the one of the other. A 'tenant', both by derivation and by usage, is someone who 'holds' land of another, for which purpose it is immaterial whether he does so by contract or by estate Although he may remain contractually liable to the landlord, an original tenant who has assigned the tenancy, equally with an assignee who has himself assigned, cannot properly be described as the tenant. He no longer holds the land. It is the assignee who now holds the land. It is he who has the tenancy. It follows that where an original tenant has assigned the tenancy before the end of the contractual J term the tenancy which s 24(1) [of the Landlord and Tenant Act 1954] provides shall not come to an end is, and can only be, the tenancy of the assignee. Since the contractual obligations of the original tenant form no part of the legal relationship between the landlord and the assignee, and since they are not independently continued by the subsection, they are in no way affected. If, as here, the original tenant has covenanted to pay rent only during the contractual term, the landlord cannot recover from him any rent payable in respect of a period after that date. Further elaboration of the principal question could only obscure the clarity of the answer. The defendants are entitled to succeed on this appeal.

This statement of law was indorsed as impeccable by Lord Templeman when the plaintiffs in that case appealed to the House of Lords. He added ([1993] 4 All ER 968 at 973-974, [1994] 1 AC 458 at 465):

> The common law did not release the original tenant from liability for breaches of covenant committed after an assignment because of the sacred character of covenant in English law. I understand that Scots law releases the original tenant once he has been replaced by a permitted or accepted assignee. This only means that the fortunate English landlord has two remedies after an assignment, namely his remedy against the assignee and his remedy against the original tenant. It does not follow that if the liability of the original tenant is released or otherwise disappears then the term granted by the lease will disappear or that

> the assignee will cease to be liable on the covenants. As between landlord and assignee the landlord cannot enforce a covenant against the assignee because the assignee does not covenant. The landlord enforces against the assignee the provisions of a covenant entered into by the original tenant, being provisions which touch and concern the land, because those provisions are annexed by the lease to the term demised by the lease. The assignee is not liable for a breach of covenant committed after the assignee has himself in turn assigned the lease because once he has assigned over he has ceased to be the owner of the term to which the covenants are annexed. Covenants are introduced on the creation of a lease but are not necessary to sustain a lease. Upon an assignment of a lease, the provisions of the covenants by the original tenant continue to attach to the term because those provisions touch and concern the land and not because there continues to exist an original tenant who has ceased to own any interest in the demised land but remains liable in contract to fulfil the promises he made under covenant.

These two judgments reassert with added emphasis the conventional distinction between the contractual liability of the lessee under his personal covenants and the liability of the assignee for the obligations of the covenants 'imprinted' on the legal estate. In principle therefore it is difficult to see how obligations accepted by the lessee in his contract with the lessor can be varied or increased by a subsequent agreement made by the lessor with the assignee. Relying on the judgments in *Baynton v Morgan* (1888) 22 QBD 74 for the general proposition that the assignee of a lease was empowered by the assignment to do anything that the original lessee could have done, Harman J in Centrovincial Estates appears to have concluded that the rights and obligations of the parties privy to the contract could be altered and made more onerous by agreement between the parties privy to the estate.

But the judges in *Baynton v Morgan* did not decide this. The question was not before them and it is clear from the judgments that if it had been the court would have been likely to decide the contrary. What the judges did decide was that the assignee of the lease had by the assignment been put into the position of lessee and in that character was authorised to vary the estate by surrender of part of the holding without such variation amounting to surrender and regrant of the term and thus without affecting the liability of the original lessee under a his covenants. Harman J was in my view correct in his assertion that an assignee s power to deal with a tenancy interest is as the owner of the whole estate who can deal with it so as to alter it or its terms, but in error in adding:

> The estate as so altered then binds the original tenant, because the assignee has been put into the shoes of the original tenant and can do all such acts as the original tenant could have done. (See *Centrovincial Estates plc v Bulk Storage Ltd* (1983) 46 P & CR 393 at 396.)

In stating that this proposition was supported by the judgments of Lord Esher MR, Fry and Lopes LJJ in *Baynton v Morgan*, it appears that Harman J was paraphrasing the following passage in Lord Esher MR's judgment (22 QBD 74 at 78):

> In this case I think that the terms of the lease, though altered without the knowledge of the lessee, were not altered without his authority, for I agree with the opinion expressed by AL Smith, J, in the court below, *viz*, that a lessee by assigning all his interest in the term to an assignee empowers the assignee, if he so desires, to surrender to the lessor all or any part of the demised premises. He gives to his assignee the powers which he might himself have exercised, and, as he himself might have surrendered part of the premises, he authorizes his assignee to do so.

Lord Esher MR was rejecting a submission that the liability of the original lessee was as surety or guarantor and that, the lessor and the assignee having altered the original contract without the consent or knowledge of the guarantor, he was released from further liability on the covenant.

The court firmly rejected the submission that the liability of the original lessee was as surety or guarantor so that the observations concerning the authority to surrender were not necessary for the decision in the case. But even if they had been, they went no further than to say that the assignee could surrender a part of the premises demised without affecting the original lessee's liability on his personal covenant.

Lord Esher MR's reference to the opinion expressed by AL Smith J is a reference to his judgment in the court below where he refers to the power of the assignee to agree with the lessor to a surrender of the whole or any part of the premises assigned and to the differing effects of surrender of part as opposed to the whole of the tenancy (see (1888) 21 QBD 101 at 102–103). His opinion is also reflected in the comment of Fry LJ in the course of argument on the appeal (22 QBD 74 at 76):

> The lessee by assigning all his interest to [the assignee], his executors, administrators and assigns, himself gave power to [the assignees] to surrender part of the premises. How, then, can such a surrender operate as suggested?

After rejecting the suggestion that the nature of the original lessee's contract was of suretyship or guarantee, Lord Esher MR said (at 78):

> What, then, is the nature of the promise? It is a covenant for the payment of what was the agreed rent at the time of the lease on the specified quarter days during the term. (My emphasis.)

When in *Baynton v Morgan* the lessee had agreed to surrender part of the premises the lessor had agreed that the rent should be reduced by apportioning a part to the surrendered portion. In the action the lessor had only claimed the appropriate proportion of rent. The court did not find it necessary to decide whether the lessor would have been entitled to claim the full rent but Lord Esher MR thought that if it could not be apportioned he would be so entitled and Fry LJ said (at 82):

> If it be true that the covenant is not apportionable, then I think that according to the authorities it must subsist in its entirety for the plain reason that the lessee has covenanted that he will pay this rent ...

If the court had thought that the lessee was bound by a subsequent alteration of the estate or of the obligations imprinted on the estate the court could not have considered this latter question or expressed the opinions it did.

Accordingly, I would reject the suggestion that the obligations of the lessee were varied by the deed of 20 January 1985 so as to make it liable for the increased rent of £35,000 payable quarterly in advance and for the excess rent. In my view, subject to the other arguments advanced by Mr Gaunt, the respondent remained liable on its covenant for the payment of £12,000 pa payable quarterly in arrear and for the insurance rent.

I would add that in my opinion the decisions in *Centrovincial Estates plc v Bulk Storage Ltd* (1983) 46 P & CR 393, *Selous Street Properties Ltd v Oronel Fabrics Ltd* (1984) 270 EG 643 and *GUS Property Management Ltd v Texas Home Care Ltd* (1993) 27 EG 130 could all have been reached on the ground that the original lessee's covenant contained a promise in each case to pay not only the original but also the reviewed rent but for the reasons indicated I do not think that they could be justified by Harman J's interpretation of the judgments in *Baynton v Morgan*.

In the event of breach of covenants by, say, T3, T1 cannot insist that L1 should first seek remedies against T3. 'Of course the expectation, commercially speaking,' said Harman J in *Allied London Investments Ltd v Hambro Life Assurance Ltd*, 'is that the assignee will pay, but the assignor does not by assignment get rid of one jot or tittle of his original liability'.[53] 'It has long been the law that the landlord may sue either the original lessee or the assignee, or both at the same time',[54] although, of course, L1 is not allowed to have double recovery for the same breach.[55] If T3 becomes insolvent, and T3's trustee in bankruptcy disclaims the lease, the disclaimer does not affect T1's continuing liability.[56] T1 is, however, not liable for rent unpaid by an assignee during a statutory extension of the assignee's term,[57] unless the terms of lease provide otherwise.[58]

In practice, L1's primary action for the enforcement of covenants is brought against the defaulting assignee, say, T3. However, as a result of mounting corporate insolvency, many landlords of commercial leases are having to have recourse against T1 for relief under the principles discussed above. T1 may in theory get indemnity from the defaulting assignee, T3 directly.[59] In *Moule v Garrett*,[60] the plaintiff assigned his lease to B, who in turn assigned to the defendants. The lease contained a covenant by the plaintiff and his assigns to repair. Both assignments contained covenants of indemnity. The defendants were in breach of the covenant to repair and the lessor recovered damages from the plaintiff instead. The plaintiff successfully recovered indemnity from the defendants.

Moule v Garrett (1872) LR 7 Ex 101

Cockburn CJ: The premises which are the subject of the lease being in the possession of the defendants as ultimate assignees, they were the parties whose duty it was to perform the covenants which were to be performed upon and in respect of those premises. It was their immediate duty to keep in repair, and by their default the lessee, though he had parted with the estate, became liable to make good to the lessor the conditions of the lease. The damage therefore arises through their default, and the general proposition applicable to such a case as the present, is that where one person is compelled to pay damages by the legal default of another, he is entitled to recover from the person by whose default the damage was occasioned the sum so paid. This doctrine, as applicable to cases like the present, is well stated by Mr Leake in his work on *Contracts*, p 41:

53 (1984) 270 Estates Gazette 948 at 950. See also *RPH Ltd v Mirror Group Newspaper and Mirror Group Holdings* (1992) 65 P & CR 252 (original tenant was liable for rent arrears of over £2 million).

54 *Norwich Union Life Insurance Society v Low Profile Fashions Ltd* (1992) 64 P & CR 187 at 192, *per* Beldam LJ.

55 *Brett v Cumberland* (1619) Cro Jac 521 at 523; 79 ER 446 at 447.

56 *Warnford Investments Ltd v Duckworth* [1979] Ch 127 at 138G–39A; *MEPC plc v Scottish Amicable Life Assurance Society* (1993) *The Times*, 6 April.

57 *City of London Corpn v Fell* [1993] 3 WLR 1164. See also (1994) CLJ 28 (Bridge, S).

58 *Herbert Duncan Ltd v Cluttons* [1993] 2 WLR 710 at 718E–G.

59 *Moule v Garrett* (1872) LR 7 Ex 101.

60 (1872) LR 7 Ex 101.

> Where the plaintiff has been compelled by law to pay, or, being compellable by law, has paid money which the defendant was ultimately liable to pay, so that the latter obtains the benefit of the payment by the discharge of his liability; under such circumstances the defendant is held indebted to the plaintiff in the amount.

... The lessee has been compelled to make good an omission to repair, which has arisen entirely from the default of the defendants, and the defendants are therefore liable to reimburse him.

T1 may also get indemnity from T2 under s 77 of the Law of Property Act 1925 as there is an implied covenant by an assignee to indemnify the assignor for breach of covenant.[61]

Law of Property Act 1925

77. Implied covenants in conveyance subject to rents

(1) In addition to the covenants implied under Part I of the Law of Property (Miscellaneous Provisions) Act 1994, there shall in the several cases in this section mentioned, be deemed to be included and implied, a covenant to the effect in this section stated, by and with such persons as are hereinafter mentioned, that is to say:

(c) In a conveyance for valuable consideration, other than a mortgage, of the entirety of the land comprised in a lease, for the residue of the term or interest created by the lease, a covenant by the assignee or joint and several covenants by the assignees (if more than one) in the terms set out in Part IX of the Second Schedule to this Act ...

Second Schedule

PART IX

COVENANT IN A CONVEYANCE FOR VALUABLE CONSIDERATION, OTHER THAN A MORTGAGE, OF THE ENTIRETY OF THE LAND COMPRISED IN A LEASE FOR THE RESIDUE OF THE TERM OR INTEREST CREATED BY THE LEASE

That the assignees, or the persons deriving title under them, will at all times, from the date of the conveyance or other date therein stated, duly pay all rent becoming due under the lease creating the term or interest for which the land is conveyed, and observe and perform all the covenants, agreements and conditions therein contained and thenceforth on the part of the lessees to be observed and performed:

And also will at all times, from the date aforesaid, save harmless and keep indemnified the conveying parties and their estates and effects, from and against all proceedings, costs, claims and expenses on account of any omission to pay the said rent or any breach of any of the said covenants, agreements and conditions.

Similar provision applies to registered land.[62]

61 Section 77(1)(c) of the LPA 1925 is repealed in relation to new tenancies granted on or after 1 January 1996: see s 30(2), Sched 2 of the Landlord and Tenant (Covenants) Act 1995.

62 Section 24(1)(b) of the LRA 1925. This section is now repealed in relation to new tenancies granted on or after 1 January 1996: see s 30(2), Sched 2 of the Landlord and Tenant (Covenants) Act 1995.

Land Registration Act 1925

24. Implied covenants on transfers of leaseholds

(1) On the transfer, otherwise than by way of underlease, of any leasehold interest in land under this Act, unless there be an entry on the register negativing such implication, there shall be implied:

(b) on the part of the transferee, a covenant with the transferor, that during the residue of the term the transferee and the persons deriving title under him will pay, perform, and observe the rent, covenants, and conditions by and in the registered lease reserved and contained, and on the part of the lessee to be paid, performed, and observed, and will keep the transferor and the persons deriving title under him indemnified against all actions, expenses, and claims on account of the non-payment of the said rent or any part thereof, or the breach of the said covenants or conditions, or any of them.

It should be noted, however, that where there are successive assignments of the lease to T2, T3, and T4, T1 can either sue his immediate assignee T2, or the defaulting T4 for indemnity. He cannot sue T3 unless T2 expressly assigns the benefit of the covenant of indemnity to him, and he cannot insist that T2 should assign the benefit of indemnity covenant to him.[63] Neither can he insist that T2 should enforce the covenant of indemnity against T3 so that T1 can in his turn recover indemnity from T2.[64]

The Law Commission regarded the tenant's continuing liability as intrinsically unfair. Changes have now been made to the rules as a result. For new tenancies, as will be seen, such continuing liability is now abolished. Although for existing leases, the original tenant remains liable, under s 17 of the Landlord and Tenant (Covenants) Act 1995, the landlord must, within six months of the charge becoming due, serve the original tenant a notice in the prescribed form of his intention to recover any fixed charge before he can recover such charge from the tenant. This provision is intended to protect the original tenant from unexpected claims. He remains liable despite having assigned his interest in the property. Where the tenant has to make payment pursuant to s 17, he is entitled to have an overriding lease granted to him in order that he can regain control over the situation and if necessary the property. By becoming the landlord of the defaulting tenant, he can pursue remedies directly against the defaulting tenant, or to take possession and make use of the property so that he can set off the return against his liability.

(b) Landlord's continuing liability

Likewise, the landlord remains liable under the contract for the covenants contained in the original lease, even if he has later assigned his reversion,[65] unless there is contractual agreement that his liability is limited to that which accrues when he owns the reversion.[66]

63 *RPH Ltd v Mirror Group Newspaper and Mirror Group Holdings* (1992) 65 P & CR 252.

64 *RPH Ltd v Mirror Group Newspaper and Mirror Group Holdings* (1992) 65 P & CR 252.

65 *Stuart v Joy* [1904] 1 KB 362 at 367.

66 *Bath v Bowles* (1905) 93 LT 801.

(c) Right to sue after assignment

As has been seen, the original landlord and tenant remain liable on the original covenants after assignment of their respective estates. However, L1 can only sue T1 for T3's default if L1 still retains his reversion. L1 cannot enforce the covenant if he has already disposed of his reversion.[67] In *Re King*,[68] Upjohn LJ said:

> The first question may be briefly stated in this way: Can a landlord, who has assigned his reversion to a lease, after the date of such assignment, sue the lessee in respect of breaches of covenant which occurred before the assignment? ...

His Lordship provided the answer in the passages cited below.

Re King [1963] Ch 459, CA

Upjohn LJ: [His Lordship read s 141(1) and (2) (see p 430 below) and continued.]

These sections re-enact in almost identical form s 10(1) of the Conveyancing Act, 1881 (as itself amended by s 2 of the Conveyancing Act, 1911), but splitting the words of that subsection into two subsections. For the purposes of this case, the only material differences between the Act of 1881 (as amended) and the Act of 1925 are, first, that by judicial decision it was held that s 10 only applied to leases in writing, whereas it is quite plain that s 141 applies to all leases, and, secondly, that s 10 applied only to leases made after the commencement of that Act, whereas s 141 applies to all leases whenever made.

I turn, then, to a consideration of the meaning of s 141 and construe the language used in its ordinary and natural meaning, which seems to me quite plain and clear. To illustrate this, consider the case of a lease containing a covenant to build a house according to certain detailed specifications before a certain day. Let me suppose that after that certain day the then lessor assigns the benefit of the reversion to an assignee, and at the time of the assignment the lessee has failed to perform the covenant to build. Who can sue the lessee for breach of covenant? It seems to me clear that the assignee alone can sue. Upon the assignment the benefit of every covenant on the lessee's part to be observed and performed is annexed and incident to and goes with the reversionary estate. The benefit of that covenant to build, therefore, passed; as it had been broken, the right to sue also passed as part of the benefit of the covenant and, incidentally, also the right to re-enter, if that has not been waived. I protest against the argument that because a right to sue is itself a chose in action it, therefore, has become severed from, and independent of, the parent covenant; on the contrary it remains part of it. The right to sue on breach is merely one of the bundle of rights that are contained in the concept 'benefit of every covenant' ... To return to my example. Suppose the right to sue for breach of that covenant did not pass, and that right remained in the assignor, then the assignee would take the lease without the benefit of that covenant and he could never enforce it. So he has not got the benefit of every covenant contained in the lease and the words of the section are not satisfied. That cannot be right. The obligation to build being (as I have assumed) clearly defined by detailed specifications in the lease, it seems to me quite plain that the assignee could bring an action for specific performance compelling the lessee to perform his covenant to build. That is one of the rights which passed to him

67 Section 141 of the LPA 1925; *Re King* [1963] Ch 459.

68 [1963] Ch 459.

when the benefit of that covenant passed. The assignor has by the operation of s 141 assigned his right to the benefit of the covenant and so has lost his remedy against the lessee. Of course, the assignor and assignee can always agree that the benefit of the covenant shall not pass, in which case the assignor can still sue, if necessary, in the name of the assignee.

Then suppose the lease contains a covenant to keep in repair which is broken at the date of the assignment, and that at all material times the premises were out of repair; that is, a continuing breach. It is an a *fortiori* case to the example I have just dealt with. Indeed, with all respect to the argument to the contrary, you cannot give any sensible meaning to the words of the section unless the entire benefit of a repairing covenant has passed, leaving the assignor without remedy against the lessee. Look at the absurd results if that were not so. The assignor of the reversion remains at liberty to sue the lessee for breaches down to the moment of the assignment. After assignment he sues and obtains judgment for certain damages. But then the premises are still out of repair and the breach continues. The assignee claims to re-enter or to sue because the premises are out of repair. What is the situation of the lessee? Either he has to pay damages twice or pay damages to the assignor and then reinstate the premises because otherwise the assignee will re-enter. This is impossible. Alternatively, the assignee's right to re-enter or to sue in respect of post-assignment breaches is in some way adversely affected by reason of the fact that the assignor has recovered a judgment for damages for pre-assignment breaches; therefore, the benefit of the covenant to keep in repair did not pass wholly to him even in respect of post-assignment breaches. That directly contradicts the words of the section.

On the other hand, it has been held in *City Properties v Greycroft Ltd* that T1 can sue L1 for A1's default, even if T1 has disposed of his leasehold interest.[69]

City Properties Ltd v Greycroft Ltd [1987] 1 WLR 1085

John Mowbray QC: The landlord bought a second floor flat (and, I think, the whole building) at 23, Belsize Crescent, London NW3, subject to a 99-year lease dated 16 July 1979 between Lansdowne Securities Ltd and Moonmoor Ltd. The tenant company acquired the lease on 11 August 1982, it says for £28,000. At that time the landlord was, as is now admitted, in serious breach of the lessor's structural repairing covenant in clause 5(3) of the lease.

The landlord's first defence is that, when the tenant assigned the lease, all its rights passed to the assignee, including any right to damages such as are claimed under the pre-existing specially endorsed writ, so the tenant has no cause of action left to support its claim. In my view that defence is not well founded. No authority was cited on the precise question whether a tenant who has assigned his lease can afterwards recover damages from the landlord for breaches of the landlord's covenants committed while the tenant held the lease. It is common ground, though, that a tenant (not the original lessee) who has assigned his lease again remains liable to the landlord for breaches of covenant which he committed while tenant: see Megarry and Wade, *The Law of Real Property*, 5th edn, 1984, p 750, para 5, Woodfall, *Landlord and Tenant*, 28th edn, 1978, vol 1, para 1–1095 and Halsbury's *Laws of England*, 4th edn, 1981, vol 27, para 395. Both this liability and the benefit of the landlord's covenants run with the lease at common law by privity of estate

69 [1987] 1 WLR 1085. But see Gray, at 865, fn 2.

under *Spencer's* case (1583) 5 Co Rep 16a: see Smith's *Leading Cases*, 13th edn, 1929, vol 1, p 51. There is a close analogy between the two. I take the view that, by this analogy, the landlord's liability to the tenant for existing breaches survives the assignment of the lease, in the same way as the tenant's liability to the landlord.

Mr Moss argued for the landlord here that the tenant's rights against the landlord did not survive the assignment of the lease, because on the assignment s 142(1) of the Law of Property Act 1925 made a statutory transfer of the tenant's rights to the assignee of the lease.

[His Lordship read s 142(1) (see below, p 429) and continued.]

Mr Moss argued that the middle part of s 142(1) carried out the transfer, that is the words 'and may be taken advantage of and enforced by the person in whom the term is from time to time vested by conveyance, devolution in law, or otherwise'. He pointed out that the Court of Appeal has held s 141(1) to make a statutory transfer of the whole benefit of a tenant's covenant to an assignee of the reversion: In *Re King, decd* [1963] Ch 459 and *London and County (A & D) Ltd v Wilfred Sportsman Ltd* [1971] Ch 764. He asked me to apply that principle by analogy to an assignment of the lease.

It is not possible to apply those decisions. They turned on words corresponding to the first part of s 142(1), 'shall ... be annexed and incident to and shall go with that reversionary estate ...'. The middle passage of s 142(1) is quite different. It does not say that the right to take advantage of the landlord's covenants is annexed or incident to the term, or 'shall go with' it, the graphic phrase specially relied on by Diplock LJ in *In Re King, decd* [1963] Ch 459 at 497. It is not possible to apply the Court of Appeal decisions to the middle passage. If the intention had been to effect a statutory transfer of the right to an assignee of the term, I should have expected words to have been used similar to those in s 141(1) and the beginning of s 142(1) itself. What is more, the middle passage of s 142(1) does not on its separate interpretation show any intention to restrict a tenant's proceedings to any particular period. The words 'from time to time' mean as occasion may require. If the intention had been to limit the tenant's right to recover damages to the time when he was tenant, I should have expected the subsections to say 'for the time being'.

Between persons other than original parties

To enforce covenants between persons other than the original parties, the claimant must show that he has the benefit of the covenants and that the defendant has the corresponding burden. Thus, if T1 wants to enforce the covenants made by L1 against A1 or A2, T1 being the original covenantee, has the benefit of the covenants, but he has to show that A1 or A2 has the corresponding burden. If T2 or T3 wants to enforce the covenants, made originally by L1 in favour of T1, against A1 or A2, T2 or T3 has to show that he has obtained the benefit of the covenants and that A1 or A2 has got the corresponding burden.

As will be seen, the rules relating to the effect of assignment on covenants can be complicated. This is worsened by the fact that slightly different rules apply to the covenants in a legal and an equitable lease. It is important to identify the covenant one is seeking to enforce, and address the question whether both the benefit and burden have run. What will be discussed here applies to covenants in a legal lease only. Rules on covenants in an equitable lease will be discussed separately later.

(a) Covenants by the original tenant (T1)

Suppose T1 covenants to keep the house in good repair, and T1 subsequently assigns the lease to T2 and L1 also assigns the reversion to A1. Whether A1 can enforce the covenant of repair depends on whether he has the benefit and whether T2 has the burden.

(i) Passing of benefit to landlord's assignee (assignment of reversion)

Section 141(1) of the Law of Property Act 1925 has reinforced the privity of estate by providing that the assignment of L1's reversion to A1 passes to A1 the benefit of all the covenants and conditions originally entered into by T1 in so far as these obligation have 'reference to the subject matter of the lease'.

Law of Property Act 1925

141. Rent and benefit of lessee's covenants to run with the reversion

(1) Rent reserved by a lease, and the benefit of every covenant or provision therein contained, having reference to the subject matter thereof, and on the lessee's part to be observed or performed, and every condition of re-entry and other condition therein contained, shall be annexed and incident to and shall go with the reversionary estate in the land, or in any part thereof, immediately expectant on the term granted by the lease, notwithstanding severance of that reversionary estate, and without prejudice to any liability affecting a covenantor or his estate.

(2) Any such rent, covenant or provision shall be capable of being recovered, received, enforced, and taken advantage of, by the person from time to time entitled, subject to the term, to the income of the whole or any part, as the case may require, of the land leased.

Thus, not all covenants made by T1 can benefit L1's assignee; only those which have reference to the subject matter of the lease or touch and concern the lease do. Privity of estate only converts private contractual rights between T1 and L1 which deserve such durability and which affect 'the landlord in his normal capacity as landlord or the tenant in his normal capacity as tenant'.[70] Rights which are substantially personal to L1 cannot therefore pass to A1 on the assignment of the reversion.

In *P & A Swift Investments v Combined English Stores Group plc*, a case concerning the running of benefit to the head tenant's assignee, Lord Oliver of Aylmerton again said:[71]

---

70 *Hua Chiao Commercial Bank Ltd v Chiaphua Industries Ltd* [1987] AC 99 at 107B.

71 [1989] AC 632 at 642.

> Formulations of definitive tests are always dangerous, but it seems to me that, without claiming to expound an exhaustive guide, the following provides a satisfactory working test for whether, in any given case, a covenant touches and concerns the land: (1) the covenant benefits only the reversioner for time being, and if separated from the reversion ceases to be of benefit to the covenantee; (2) the covenant affects the nature, quality, mode of user or value of the land of the reversioner; (3) the covenant is not expressed to be personal (that is to say neither being given only to a specific reversioner nor in respect of the obligations only of a specific tenant); (4) the fact that a covenant is to pay a sum of money will not prevent it from touching and concerning the land so long as the three foregoing conditions are satisfied and the covenant is connected with something to be done on, to or in relation to the land.

However, it has been pointed out that *P & A Swift Investments* is not strictly about s 141 because the defendant there was a surety for the sub-tenant's liability, and the plaintiff was the assignee of the headlease, and there was therefore no privity of contract or estate between them. Thus, the tests in *P & A Swift* is not applicable to s 141. To decide whether the covenant has 'reference to the subject matter of the lease' or 'touches and concerns' the land, it is necessary to ask whether it affects the mode of user of the land, and whether it is on its face personal.[72] For s 141 to operate, it is not necessary for the covenant to make any reference to the successors in title of the covenantor, and in any event s 78 of the Law of Property Act 1925 would supply such reference.[73]

Covenants which have been judicially accepted as having 'reference to the subject matter of the lease' are covenants by the tenant to pay rent,[74] to repair the premises,[75] to insure against fire,[76] to cultivate land in a particular way,[77] to contribute towards redecoration on quitting,[78] to use the premises as a private dwelling only,[79] not to assign without the landlord's consent.[80]

Covenants which are regarded as personal to the landlord are covenants by the tenant to pay an annual sum to a third party,[81] to pay rates in respect of other land,[82] to repair the tool of a smithy standing on the land,[83] not to employ a person living in other parishes to work in the demised land.[84]

---

72 *Caerns Motor Services Ltd v Texaco Ltd* [1995] 1 All ER 247.

73 *Caerns Motor Services Ltd v Texaco Ltd* [1995] 1 All ER 247.

74 *Perker v Webb* (1693) 3 Salk 5; 91 ER 656; *Kumar v Dunning* [1989] QB 193 at 200F–G; *P & A Swift Investments v Combined English Stores Group plc* [1989] AC 632 at 641F-G.

75 *Matures v Westwood* (1598) Cro Eliz 599, at 600; 78 ER 842; *Williams v Earle* (1868) LR 3 QB 739 at 751; *Kumar v Dunning* [1989] QB 193 at 200 F–G; *P & A Swift Investments v Combined English Stores Group plc* [1989] AC 632 at 641F–G.

76 *Vernon v Smith* (1821) 5 B & Ald 1 at 6; 106 ER 1094 at 1096.

77 *Chapman v Smith* [1907] 2 Ch 97 at 103.

78 *Boyer v Warbey* [1953] 1 QB 234; *Moss' Empires Ltd v Olympia (Liverpool) Ltd* [1939] AC 544.

79 *Wilkinson v Rogers* (1864) 2 De G J & S 62 at 67; 46 ER 298 at 300.

80 *Goldstein v Sanders* [1915] 1 Ch 549 at 556; *Cohen v Popular Restaurants Ltd* [1917] 1 KB 480 at 482.

81 *Mayho v Buckhurst* (1617) Cro Jac 438 at 439; 79 ER 374 at 375.

82 *Gower v Postmaster-General* (1887) 57 LT 527.

83 *William v Earle* (1868) LR 3 QB 739.

84 *Congleton Corpn v Pattison* (1808) 10 East 130.

It is perhaps convenient here to deal with the question of whether the benefit of a covenant, by a surety in favour of L1, to guarantee the due performance of T1's covenants can run to L1's assignee. In *P & A Swift Investments v Combined English Stores Group plc*,[85] the House of Lords held that if the surety's covenant is to guarantee the performance of T1's covenants which touch and concern the lease, the surety covenant 'must itself be a covenant which touches and concerns the land'.[86] Lord Templeman said:[87]

> A covenant by a surety that a tenant's covenant which touches and concerns the land shall be performed and observed must itself be a covenant which touches and concerns the land; the benefit of that surety's covenant will run with the reversion, and the covenant is therefore enforceable without express assignment. I agree. A surety for a tenant is a quasi tenant who volunteers to be a substitute or twelfth man for the tenant's team and is subject to the same rules and regulations as the player he replaces. A covenant which runs with the reversion against the tenant runs with the reversion against the surety.

This is later followed by the House of Lords in *Coronation Street Industrial Properties Ltd v Ingall Industries plc*.[88]

As already mentioned, once L1 assigns his reversion, he loses the right to sue on T1's covenants.[89] But he remains liable for his covenants after assignment.

(ii) Passing of burden to tenant's assignee (assignment of lease)

The assignee of T1 acquires the burden of all covenants in the legal lease which touch and concern the demised premises under the principle in *Spencer's* case.[90]

It may be mentioned first that the rule in *Spencer's* case does not apply to an equitable lease. In *Spencer's* case, Spencer and his wife leased land to a tenant who covenanted for himself, his executors and administrators that he, his executors and administrators, or assigns would build a brick wall on the land. The tenant assigned the lease to an assignee who in his turn assigned it to the defendant. The question was whether the defendant was liable on the covenant to build.

Spencer's case (1583) 5 Co Rep 16a

It was reported that after many arguments at the Bar, the case was excellently argued and debated by the Justices at the Bench: and in this case these points were unanimously resolved by Sir Christopher Wray, Chief Justice, Sir Thomas Gawdy, and the whole court.

---

85 [1989] AC 632.

86 [1989] AC 632, at 637H, 641G-H. See [1988] CLJ 180 (Harpum, C).

87 [1989] AC 632 at 637.

88 [1989] 1 WLR 304.

89 LPA 1925, s 141(1); *Re King* [1963] Ch 459.

90 (1583) 5 Co Rep 16a.

Three of the resolutions were:

1. When the covenant extends to a thing *in esse*, parcel of the demise, the thing to be done by force of the covenant is *quodammodo* annexed and appurtenant to the thing demised, and shall go with the land, and shall bind the assignee although he be not bound by express words: but when the covenant extends to a thing which is not in being at the time of the demise made, it cannot be appurtenant or annexed to the thing which hath no being: as if the lessee covenants to repair the houses demised to him during the term, that is parcel of the contract, and extends to the support of the thing demised, and therefore is *quodammodo* annexed appurtenant to houses, and shall bind the assignee although he be not bound expressly by the covenant: but in the case at Bar, the covenant concerns a thing which was not *in esse* at the time of the demise made, but to be newly built after, and therefore shall bind the covenantor, his executors, or administrators, and not the assignee, for the law will not annex the covenant to a thing which hath no being.
2. It was resolved that in this case, if the lessee had covenanted for him and his assigns, that they would make a new wall upon some part of the thing demised, that for as much as it is to be done upon the land demised, that it should bind the assignee; for although the covenant doth extend to a thing to be newly made, yet it is to be made upon the thing demised, and the assignee is to take the benefit of it, and therefore shall bind the assignee by express words. So on the other side, if a warranty be made to one, his heirs and assigns, by express words, the assignee shall take benefit of it, and shall have a *warrantia chartæ*. But although the covenant be for him and his assigns, yet if the thing to be done be merely collateral to the land, and doth not touch or concern the thing demised in any sort, there the assignee shall not be charged. As if the lessee covenants for him and his assigns to build a house upon the land of the lessor which is no parcel of the demise, or to pay any collateral sum to the lessor, or to a stranger, it shall not bind the assignee, because it is merely collateral, and in no manner touches or concerns the thing that was demised, or that is assigned over; and therefore in such case the assignee of the thing demised cannot be charged with it, no more than any other stranger.
4. It was resolved, that if a man makes a feoffment by this word *dedi*, which implies a warranty, the assignee of the feoffee shall not vouch ; but if a man makes a lease for years by this word *concessi* or *demisi*, which implies a covenant, if the assignee of the lessee be evicted, he shall have a writ of covenant; for the lessee and his assignee hath the yearly profits of the land which shall grow by his labour and industry for an annual rent, and therefore it is reasonable when he hath applied his labour, and employed his cost upon the land, and be evicted (whereby be loses all), that he shall take such benefit of the demise and grant, as the first lessee might, and the lessor hath no other prejudice than what his special contract with the first lessee hath bound him to.

However, the assignee of T1 is only liable for breaches which occur while he is in possession.[91] So T2 is not liable for breaches committed prior to the assignment of the lease to him,[92] nor is he liable for breaches committed by T3 after his assignment.[93]

91 *Johnsey Estates Ltd v Lewis and Manley (Engineering) Ltd* (1987) 54 P & CR 296 at 300.

92 *Grescot v Green* (1700) 1 Salk 199; 91 ER 179.

93 *Onslow v Corrie* (1817) 2 Madd 330 at 340; 56 ER 357 at 360.

However, in practice, before the landlord would consent to the assignment, T1's assignee may be required to covenant directly with the landlord to observe and perform all the original tenant's covenants. In such a case, the assignee will be liable also for all the covenants (which include those which do not touch and concern the land) for the remainder of the lease.[94]

(b) Covenants by the original landlord (L1)

Suppose L1 covenants to provide T1 with the services of a gardener, and T1 assigns the lease to T2, and L1 has assigned the reversion to A1. Whether T2 can call on A1 for the services of a gardener depends on whether he has the benefit of the covenant and whether A1 has the corresponding burden.

(i) Passing of benefit to tenant's assignees (assignment of lease)

The assignees of a tenant, T2 or T3, acquire the benefit of all covenants in the legal lease which touch and concern the demised premises.[95]

It should be noted that only the benefit of covenants which touch and concern the leasehold land can pass under *Spencer's* case.

(ii) Passing of burden to landlord's assignees (assignment of reversion)

Section 142(1) of the Law of Property Act 1925, reinforces privity of estate by providing that on assignment of the landlord's reversion, the burden of all the covenants and conditions originally entered into by L1 passes to the assignee insofar as these obligations have 'reference to the subject matter of the lease'.

Law of Property Act 1925

142. Obligation of lessor's covenants to run with reversion

(1) The obligation under a condition or of a covenant entered into by a lessor with reference to the subject matter of the lease shall, if and as far as the lessor has power to bind the reversionary estate immediately expectant on the term granted by the lease, be annexed and incident to and shall go with that reversionary estate, or the several parts thereof, notwithstanding severance of that reversionary estate, and may be taken advantage of and enforced by the person in whom the term is from time to time vested by conveyance, devolution in law, or otherwise; and, if and as far as the lessor has power to bind the person from time to time entitled to that reversionary estate, the obligation aforesaid may be taken advantage of and enforced against any person so entitled.

The requirement that the covenants must have 'reference to the subject matter of the lease' is the same as the requirement of 'touch and concern' the land in a lease under *Spencer's* case discussed later.[96]

94 *Estates Gazette v Benjamin Restaurants Ltd* [1995] 1 All ER 129.

95 *Spencer's* case (1583) 5 Co Rep 16a.

96 *Hua Chiao Commercial Bank Ltd v Chiaphua Industries Ltd* [1987] AC 99 at 106H–07A.

In *Hua Chiao Commercial Bank Ltd v Chiaphua Industries Ltd*, a case concerning the passing of burden to the landlord's assignee, Lord Oliver of Aylmerton said:[97]

> Their Lordships have been referred to and are content to adopt the following passage from Cheshire and Burn's *Modern Law of Real Property*, 13th edn, 1982, pp 430-31:
>
> > If the covenant has direct reference to the land, if it lays down something which is to be done or is not to be done upon the land, or, and perhaps this is the clearest way of describing the test, if it affects the landlord in his normal capacity as landlord or the tenant in his normal capacity as tenant, it may be said to touch and concern the land.
> >
> > Lord Russell CJ [in *Horsey Estate Ltd v Steiger* [1899] 2 QB 79 at 89] said: 'The true principle is that no covenant or condition which affects merely the person, and which does not affect the nature, quality, or value of the thing demised or the mode of using or enjoying the thing demised, runs with the land'; and Bayley J at an earlier date asserted the same principle [in *Congleton Corporation v Pattison* (1808) 10 East 130 at 1381]: 'In order to bind the assignee, the covenant must either affect the land itself during the term, such as those which regard the mode of occupation, or it must be such as *per se*, and not merely from collateral circumstances, affects the value of the land at the end of the term.'
> >
> > If a simple test is desired for ascertaining into which category a covenant falls, it is suggested that the proper inquiry should be whether the covenant affects either the landlord *qua* landlord or the tenant *qua* tenant. A covenant may very well have reference to the land, but, unless it is reasonably incidental to the relation of landlord and tenant, it cannot be said to touch and concern the land so as to be capable of running therewith or with the reversion.

It should be noted however that the assignee, A1 or A2 is only liable for breaches which take place while he is in possession of the reversion. He cannot be made liable for breaches committed by L1 prior to the assignment.[98]

Covenants which 'touch and concern' the lease include covenants by the landlord to renew the lease,[99] to supply water to the demised premises,[100] to allow the tenant quiet possession of the premises,[101] not to build on the adjoining land,[102] not to terminate a periodic tenancy during its first three years.[103]

Covenants which are personal and do not 'touch and concern' the lease include a covenant which gives the tenant an option to purchase the reversion at a stated price,[104] and covenants to pay for chattels which are not fixtures,[105]

---

97 [1987] AC 99 at 107.

98 *Pettiward Estates v Shephard* [1986] 6 CL 173; *Duncliffe v Caerfelin Properties Ltd* [1989] 2 EGLR 38 at 39M–40B. See also [1987] Conv 103 (Gorden, D); [1990] Conv 126 (Matin, JE).

99 *Richardson v Sydenham* (1703) 2 Vern 447; 23 ER 885.

100 *Jourdain v Wilson* (1821) 4 B & Ald 266 at 267; 106 ER 935.

101 *Celsteel Ltd v Alton House Holdings Ltd (No 2)* [1986] 1 WLR 666 at 672H.

102 *Ricketts v Enfield Churchwardens* [1909] 1 Ch 544 at 555.

103 *Breams Property Investment Co Ltd v Stroulger* [1948] 2 KB 1.

104 *Woodall v Clifton* [1905] 2 Ch 257 at 279.

105 *Gorton v Gregory* (1862) 3 B & S 90.

to pay the tenant £500 at the end of the lease if no new lease is granted,[106] and to allow the tenant to display advertising signs on other premises.[107] A covenant in restraint of trade is also personal.[108]

Position of sub-tenants

The rule in *Spencer's* case does not apply to sub-tenants (ST) because there is no privity of estate between a sub-tenant (ST) and the head landlord (L1, A2, or A3). The only occasion upon which a covenant can be enforced by the head landlord against a sub-tenant is where the covenant satisfies the rule in *Tulk v Moxhay*.[109] That is that the covenant must be negative and must 'touch and concern' the land. Furthermore, it will only bind the sub-tenant if he has notice of it.[110] In practice, the sub-tenant will inevitably have notice of the covenants in the head lease because these covenants are recited in identical terms in the sublease. Furthermore, the sub-tenant may have a contractual right to call for the superior title of the head lease,[111] and may therefore be fixed with constructive notice of the covenants contained therein.[112]

In the event of default of the covenants in the head lease by ST, although L1 cannot generally enforce the covenants against ST save where the rule in *Tulk v Moxhay* applies, L1 may, if he has reserved a right of re-entry, forfeit the head lease. This will have the effect of destroying any sublease created out of it,[113] and thereby enforcing the covenants indirectly.[114]

While the burden of positive covenants in the head lease cannot run to the sub-tenant, the benefit of the covenants in the head lease may, if desirable, be expressly assigned to him. This should be in writing and the person affected by the covenant should be notified.[115] Furthermore, it seems that the sub-tenant may obtain the benefit under s 78 of the Law of Property Act 1925.[116]

---

106 *Re Hunter's Lease* [1942] Ch 124.

107 *Re No 1, Albemarle Street* [1959] Ch 531.

108 *Thomas v Hayward* (1869) LR 4 Ex 311.

109 (1848) 2 Ph 774. (For the rules, see Chapter 14, pp 650–58); see *Hemingway Securities Ltd v Dunraven Ltd* (1996) 71 P & CR 30 at 33.

110 In unregistered land, leasehold covenants are not registrable as a Class D (ii) land charge (s 2(5) of the LCA 1972). Likewise, in registered land, leasehold covenants cannot be protected by an entry of notice on the register (s 50(1) of the LRA 1925), but are automatically binding on a transferee or sublessee (s 23(1)(a), (2), 24(1)(b) of the LRA 1925).

111 *Gosling v Woolf* [1893] 1 QB 39 at 40; (1893) 68 LT 89 at 90.

112 *Teape v Douse* (1905) 92 LT 319 at 320.

113 *Great Western Railway Co v Smith* (1876) 2 Ch D 235 at 253.

114 *Shiloh Spinners v Harding* [1973] AC 691.

115 Section 136(1) of the LPA 1925.

116 *Federated Homes Ltd v Mill Lodge Properties Ltd* [1980] 1 All ER 371. It does not matter that ST has not got the same estate as the head lease: *Smith and Snipes Hall Farm v River Douglas Catchment Board* [1949] 2 KB 500. Section 78 does not apply to new tenancies created on or after 1 January 1996; see s 30(4) of the Landlord and Tenant (Covenants) Act 1995.

Law of Property Act 1925

78. Benefit of covenants relating to land

(1) A covenant relating to any land of the covenantee shall be deemed to be made with the covenantee and his successors in title and the persons deriving title under him or them, and shall have effect as if such successors and other persons were expressed.

For the purposes of this subsection in connection with covenants restrictive of the user of land 'successors in title' shall be deemed to include the owners and occupiers for the time being of the land of the covenantee intended to be benefited.

(2) This section applies to covenants made after the commencement of this Act, but the repeal of section fifty-eight of the Conveyancing Act 1881 does not affect the operation of covenants to which that section applied.

So although there is no privity of contract or estate between L1 and ST, ST may enforce L1's covenants in the head lease against L1. When L1 assigns the reversion to A1, A1 will bear the burden under s 142(1) of the Law of Property Act 1925.

6 ENFORCEMENT OF COVENANTS IN AN EQUITABLE LEASE – THE OLD RULES

Hitherto, we have seen the rules relating to the enforcement of leasehold covenants in a legal lease. The rules relating to covenants in an equitable lease are largely similar to them, except that the rule in *Spencer's* case does not apply to an equitable lease.

Between original parties and their successors

As between the original parties, L1 and T1, as in a legal lease, their position is governed by privity of contract. The parties remain liable, as between themselves, for their respective covenants throughout the whole term.

Where L1 assigns his reversion, the benefit of the covenants by T1 in an equitable lease passes to A1 or A2 under s 141(1) of the Law of Property Act 1925. Section 141(1) applies equally to covenants in equitable leases.[117] However, when T1 assigns his lease, the burden of the covenants will not pass to T2 under *Spencer's* case.[118] Thus, while L1 or A1 may have the benefit of the covenants, he may be unable to enforce them against T1's assignee. On the other hand, L1 or A1 may enforce restrictive covenants under the rule in *Tulk v Moxhay* by injunction. Furthermore, they may forfeit the equitable lease if the equitable lease contains a forfeiture clause. The right to enforce restrictive covenants and the right of re-entry are both equitable. In unregistered land,

117 *Rye v Purcell* [1926] 1 KB 446 at 451; *Rickett v Green* [1910] 1 KB 253 at 259.

118 *Purchase v Lichfield Brewery Co* [1915] 1 KB 184 at 187. See also [1978] CLJ 98 (Smith, RJ).

they are not registrable[119] nor overreachable. They bind the whole world except the equity's darling. As T1 only has an equitable lease, his assignee, T2 or T3, also has an equitable lease only and cannot claim to be an equity's darling. In registered land, those covenants in an equitable lease would presumably bind the assignees.[120]

Where the covenants are originally made by L1, when he assigns the reversion to A1, the burden of the covenants, as is the case with legal lease, run to him under s 142(1) of the Law of Property Act 1925. Section 142(1) applies equally to equitable leases.[121] So T1 will be able to enforce the covenants in an equitable lease against A1, or indeed A2. If T1 assigns his lease to T2, as *Spencer's Case* does not apply to an equitable lease, T2 cannot obtain the benefit under this rule. It seems that he cannot obtain the benefit under s 78 of the Law of Property Act 1925 because a 'covenant' in an equitable lease, which is not by deed, is not technically a 'covenant'.[122]

The position of sub-tenant

Where the lease granted by L1 to T1 is equitable, ST's sublease, which is created out of T1's equitable head lease, must necessarily be equitable too. Can L1 or A1 enforce T1's covenant against ST? L1, of course, has the benefit of the covenants being the original covenantee. A1 will acquire the benefit under s 141(1) of the Law of Property Act 1925. L1 or A1 has to show that ST has the burden of T1's covenants. *Spencer's* case does not apply to transfer the burden for two reasons: (i) *Spencer's* case does not apply to an equitable lease, (ii) there is no privity of estate between L1 (or A1) and ST. However, the burden of restrictive covenants may run to ST under the rule in *Tulk v Moxhay*. As ST is an equitable sublessee, he cannot claim to be an equity's darling, and where equities are equal the first in time prevails. So ST will be bound by restrictive covenants which touch and concern the lease.

Can ST enforce covenants made by L1 against L1 or A1? ST does not get the benefit under the rule in *Spencer's* case because *Spencer's* case does not apply to an equitable lease and there is no privity of estate between L1 (or A1) and ST. ST is unlikely to get the benefit under s 78 of the Law of Property Act 1925. The benefit of the covenants may however be assigned expressly to ST.[123] L1 always bears the burden of his covenants even after assignment, while A1 has the burden under s 142(1) of the Law of Property Act 1925.

119 Restrictive covenants in a lease are not registrable as a land charge under s 2(5) of the LCA 1972. In *Shiloh Spinners Ltd v Harding* [1973] AC 691, it was held that an equitable right of re-entry was not a registrable land charge. See Chapter 6, pp 238–41.

120 Section 23(1)(a), (2) of the LRA 1925. They may well be overriding under s 70(1)(g) of the LRA 1925, as L1 or A1 is 'in receipt of the rents and profits thereof'.

121 *Weg Motors Ltd v Hales* [1962] Ch 49 at 73.

122 Section 78 clearly refers to a 'covenant': see p 433.

123 *Manchester Brewery v Coombs* [1901] 2 Ch 608.

7 ENFORCEMENT OF COVENANTS IN A LEGAL OR EQUITABLE LEASE – THE NEW RULES

The rules relating to the enforceability of leasehold covenants in a legal and equitable lease have now been changed as a result of the Law Commission's recommendations.[124] Enforcement of covenants in legal or equitable leases is now treated in the same way.[125] The new rules apply, however, only to a 'new tenancy', which is a tenancy granted on or after 1 January 1996[126] otherwise than in pursuance of (a) an agreement entered into before that date or (b) an order of a court made before that date, and to a landlord covenant or a tenant covenant contained in the tenancy, whether or not the covenant has reference to the subject matter of the tenancy, and whether the covenant is express, implied or imposed by law.[127] The new rules do not apply to an overriding lease which is granted in respect of a lease governed by the old rules.[128] But a lease which arises from a deemed surrender and a regrant occurring after the commencement of the Act will be treated as a new tenancy.[129] In relation to new tenancies, ss 78, 79, 141, and 142 of the Law of Property Act 1925 do not apply.[130]

Landlord and Tenant (Covenants) Act 1995

1. Tenancies to which the Act applies

(1) Sections 3–16 and 21 apply only to new tenancies.

(2) Sections 17–20 apply to both new and other tenancies.

(3) For the purposes of this section a tenancy is a new tenancy if it is granted on or after the date on which this Act comes into force otherwise than in pursuance of:

(a) an agreement entered into before that date, or

(b) an order of a court made before that date.

(4) Subsection (3) has effect subject to s 20(1) in the case of overriding leases granted under s 19.

(5) Without prejudice to the generality of sub-s (3), that subsection applies to the grant of a tenancy where by virtue of any variation of a tenancy there is a deemed surrender and regrant as it applies to any other grant of a tenancy.

---

124 See Law Commission, Landlord and Tenant: Privity of Contract and Estate (Law Com No 174, 29 November 1988); [1989] Conv 145 (Wilkinson, HW); (1991) 11 *Legal Studies* 47 (Thornton).

125 Section 28(1).

126 The date on which the 1995 Act came into force: Landlord and Tenant (Covenants) Act 1995 (Commencement) Order 1995 (SI 1995/2963).

127 Section 2(1) of the Landlord and Tenant (Covenants) Act 1995. For exceptions see s 2(2).

128 *Ibid*, s 1(4).

129 *Ibid*, s 1(5).

130 *Ibid*, s 30(4).

(6) Where a tenancy granted on or after the date on which this Act comes into force is so granted in pursuance of an option granted before that date, the tenancy shall be regarded for the purposes of sub-s (3) as granted in pursuance of an agreement entered into before that date (and accordingly is not a new tenancy), whether or not the option was exercised before that date.

(7) In sub-s (6) 'option' includes right of first refusal.

2 Covenants to which the Act applies

(1) This Act applies to a landlord covenant or a tenant covenant of a tenancy – (a) whether or not the covenant has reference to the subject matter of the tenancy, and (b) whether the covenant is express, implied or imposed by law, but does not apply to a covenant falling within sub-s (2).

Between original parties

The main effect of the 1995 Act is to release the original covenantors from their continuing liability after they have assigned their interest in the property.

(a) Covenant by the tenant

Under s 5 of the Act, if the tenant assigns the whole of the demised premises, he is released from the covenants he made (the tenant covenants) as from the assignment.[131] If he assigns part only of the demised premises, then he is released from the covenants in relation to that part of the demised premises.[132] However, the 1995 Act also provides that the landlord may require the tenant to enter into an 'authorised guarantee agreement' whereby the tenant guarantees the performance of the covenants by the assignee. This agreement will inevitably, in practice, be imposed on the tenant as quid pro quo for the landlord's giving consent to the assignment. The landlord can impose such an agreement where the lease contains a covenant that the assignment cannot be effected without his consent and that such consent will only be given subject to a condition that the tenant is to enter into an agreement guaranteeing the performance of covenants by the assignee.[133]

Landlord and Tenant (Covenants) Act 1995

5. Tenant released from covenants on assignment of tenancy

(1) This section applies where a tenant assigns premises demised to him under a tenancy.

(2) If the tenant assigns the whole of the premises demised to him, he:

(a) is released from the tenant covenants of the tenancy, and

(b) ceases to be entitled to the benefit of the landlord covenants of the tenancy, as from the assignment.

131 *Ibid*, s 5(2)(a).

132 *Ibid*, s 5(3)(a).

133 *Ibid*, s 16.

(3) If the tenant assigns part only of the premises demised to him, then as from the assignment he:

(a) is released from the tenant covenants of the tenancy, and

(b) ceases to be entitled to the benefit of the landlord covenants of the tenancy, only to the extent that those covenants fall to be complied with in relation to that part of the demised premises.

(4) This section applies as mentioned in sub-s (1) whether or not the tenant is tenant of the whole of the premises comprised in the tenancy.

(b) Covenant by the landlord

If the landlord assigns the reversion in the whole of the demised premises, his continuing liability in respect of the covenants he made (the landlord covenants) does not come to an end automatically. Instead, he may be released from such continuing liability if the tenant consents or if it is approved by the court.[134] The reason for keeping the landlord's continuing liability, subject to the landlord's successful application for release, is that tenants rarely, if ever, have a right to give or withhold consent to any assignment by the landlord, and would not be in a position to require continuing liability after an assignment of the reversion and to block an assignment if a condition for assignment was not agreed. Furthermore, landlords generally undertake far fewer obligations than tenants and may not be troubled by the prospect of continuing liability.[135] Thus, the landlord is given an option to apply for a release. If he assigns the reversion in part only of the demised premises, he may apply for a release from those covenants in relation to that part of those premises.[136]

Landlord and Tenant (Covenants) Act 1995

6 Landlord may be released from covenants on assignment of reversion

(1) This section applies where a landlord assigns the reversion in premises of which he is the landlord under a tenancy.

(2) If the landlord assigns the reversion in the whole of the premises of which he is the landlord:

(a) he may apply to be released from the landlord covenants of the tenancy in accordance with s 8; and

(b) if he is so released from all of those covenants, he ceases to be entitled to the benefit of the tenant covenants of the tenancy as from the assignment.

(3) If the landlord assigns the reversion in part only of the premises of which he is the landlord:

(a) he may apply to be so released from the landlord covenants of the tenancy to the extent that they fall to be complied with in relation to that part of those premises; and

134 For the procedure for seeking release see, *ibid*, s 8.

135 See para 4.16 of Law Com No 174.

136 Section 6(3)(a) of the Landlord and Tenant (Covenants) Act 1995.

(b) if he is, to that extent, so released from all of those covenants, then as from the assignment he ceases to be entitled to the benefit of the tenant covenants only to the extent that they fall to be complied with in relation to that part of those premises.

(4) This section applies as mentioned in sub-s (1) whether or not the landlord is landlord of the whole of the premises comprised in the tenancy.

(c) Right to sue after assignment

If the tenant assigns the whole of the demised premises, he also ceases to be entitled to the benefit of the landlord covenants as from the assignment.[137] If he assigns part only of the demised premises, he ceases to be entitled to the benefit of the landlord covenants in relation to that part of the demised premises.[138]

The same applies to the landlord if he is released from his covenants.[139]

Note that the landlord or tenant only loses the benefit of covenant as from the assignment. Thus, any accrued benefit or rights arising from an earlier breach of covenant will not be lost.[140]

(d) Excluded assignments

The release of landlord and tenant covenants do not occur in the case of excluded assignments. An excluded assignment is an assignment in breach of a covenant in the tenancy prohibiting assignment, or an assignment by operation of law, such as vesting of the lease or reversion in the deceased's personal representatives on death, or in the trustee in bankruptcy on bankruptcy.

Between persons other than original parties

Under the 1995 Act, the benefit and burden of all landlord covenants or the tenant covenants are annexed and incident to the whole and each and every part of the demised premises and of the reversion in them, and pass on the assignment of the whole or any part of the premises or of the reversion.[141] It is no longer necessary to ask whether the covenant touches and concerns the land or has reference to the subject matter of the land. However, these provisions do not apply to a covenant which is expressed to be personal to any person. Thus, a personal covenant remains unenforceable against the assignee of the covenantor.[142] Neither do they operate to make enforceable against any person any covenant which would otherwise be unenforceable against him for lack of registration under the Land Registration Act 1925 or the Land Charges Act 1972. Thus, an option to renew the lease or to purchase the reversion still requires registration before it can bind the assignee under the new provisions.

137 *Ibid*, s 5(2)(b).

138 *Ibid*, s 5(3)(b).

139 *Ibid*, s 6(2)(b), (3)(b).

140 *Ibid*, s 24(4).

141 *Ibid*, s 3(1).

142 *Ibid*, s 3(6).

The landlord's right of re-entry is likewise annexed to the reversion and passes to the assignee on assignment of the reversion.[143] The assignee is also entitled to enforce the right of re-entry for breaches that occur before the assignment.[144] A restrictive covenant is further binding on not only an assignee, but also any owner or occupier of the demised premises to which the covenant relates even though there is no express provision in the tenancy to that effect.[145] Thus a sub-tenant is bound by a restrictive covenant.

Landlord and Tenant (Covenants) Act 1995

3. Transmission of benefit and burden of covenants

(1) The benefit and burden of all landlord and tenant covenants of a tenancy:

(a) shall be annexed and incident to the whole, and to each and every part, of the premises demised by the tenancy and of the reversion in them, and

(b) shall in accordance with this section pass on an assignment of the whole or any part of those premises or of the reversion in them.

(2) Where the assignment is by the tenant under the tenancy, then as from the assignment the assignee:

(a) becomes bound by the tenant covenants of the tenancy except to the extent that:

(i) immediately before the assignment they did not bind the assignor, or

(ii) they fall to be complied with in relation to any demised premises not comprised in the assignment; and

(b) becomes entitled to the benefit of the landlord covenants of the tenancy except to the extent that they fall to be complied with in relation to any such premises.

(3) Where the assignment is by the landlord under the tenancy, then as from the assignment the assignee:

(a) becomes bound by the landlord covenants of the tenancy except to the extent that:

(i) immediately before the assignment they did not bind the assignor, or

(ii) they fall to be complied with in relation to any demised premises not comprised in the assignment; and

(b) becomes entitled to the benefit of the tenant covenants of the tenancy except to the extent that they fall to be complied with in relation to any such premises.

(4) In determining for the purposes of sub-s (2) or (3) whether any covenant bound the assignor immediately before the assignment, any waiver or release of the covenant which (in whatever terms) is expressed to be personal to the assignor shall be disregarded.

(5) Any landlord or tenant covenant of a tenancy which is restrictive of the user of land shall, as well as being capable of enforcement against an assignee, be capable of being enforced against any other person who is the owner or occupier of any demised

143 *Ibid*, s 4.

144 *Ibid*, s 23(3).

145 *Ibid*, s 3(5).

premises to which the covenant relates, even though there is no express provision in the tenancy to that effect.

(6) Nothing in this section shall operate:

(a) in the case of a covenant which (in whatever terms) is expressed to be personal to any person, to make the covenant enforceable by or (as the case may be) against any other person; or

(b) to make a covenant enforceable against any person if, apart from this section, it would not be enforceable against him by reason of its not having been registered under the Land Registration Act 1925 or the Land Charges Act 1972.

(7) To the extent that there remains in force any rule of law by virtue of which the burden of a covenant whose subject matter is not in existence at the time when it is made does not run with the land affected unless the covenantor covenants on behalf of himself and his assigns, that rule of law is hereby abolished in relation to tenancies.

4. Transmission of rights of re-entry

The benefit of a landlord's right of re-entry under a tenancy:

(a) shall be annexed and incident to the whole, and to each and every part, of the reversion in the premises demised by the tenancy, and

(b) shall pass on an assignment of the whole or any part of the reversion in those premises.

8 REMEDIES FOR BREACH OF COVENANTS

Damages and specific performance[146] or injunction are common contractual remedies available to both parties. In addition, however, there are special remedies available to the landlord or tenant.

Tenant's remedies against landlord

(a) Criminal liability for unlawful harassment

Under s 1(3A) of the Protection from Eviction Act 1977, it is a criminal offence for the landlord to perform acts which are likely to interfere with the tenant's peace or comfort, or to withdraw services reasonably required for occupation of the premises as a residence, with intention to cause the tenant to give up occupation or to refrain from exercising rights or to refrain from seeking any remedy in relation to the premises.

(b) Criminal liability for unlawful eviction

Under s 1(2) of the Protection from Eviction Act 1977, 'any person who unlawfully deprives a residential occupier of any premises of his occupation of

146 For example, *Co-operative Insurance Society Ltd v Argyll Stores (Holdings) Ltd* [1996] 3 All ER 934 (covenant to use premises as supermarket, damages inadequate, specific performance granted).

the premises, or any part thereof, or attempts to do so ... shall be guilty of an offence unless he proves that he believed, and had reasonable cause to believe, that the residential occupier had ceased to reside in the premises.'

(c) Civil remedies for unlawful harassment and eviction

Section 1 of the Protection from Eviction Act 1977 only imposes criminal liability on the landlord, and does not create any civil remedy for the tenant.[147] However, under s 27 of the Housing Act 1988, the tenant who is a victim of unlawful harassment or eviction can sue the landlord for damages.

(d) The tenant may also sue the landlord in nuisance, or trespass

Landlord's remedies against tenant

(a) Distress[148]

A landlord can enter the demised premises and take possession of the tenant's belongings up to the value of the unpaid rent. Distress may be levied only for rent arrears, and not other breach of covenant. It arises as soon as rent is in arrears.[149] The landlord cannot exercise the right to distrain against a sub-tenant[150] or licensee.[151] Distress is not available once a lease has been forfeited.[152] Neither is it available where the landlord has obtained a court judgment for the rent arrears.[153]

Distress cannot be levied between sunset and sunrise, nor on a Sunday.[154] The landlord may not obtain entry by breaking an outer door,[155] but inner doors may be broken down once entry without breaking down an outer door has been achieved.[156] Entry may be made through an open window,[157] but not through a window which is closed, even if it is unlocked.[158] Certain goods such as the tenant's clothing and tools of trade,[159] perishable foods,[160] tenant's

---

147 *McCall v Abelesz* [1976] QB 585, at 594C 597F

148 For an excellent account of the law of distress see Distress for Rent (Law Commission Working Paper No 97, May 1986), Chapter 2. See also (1990) 17 J Law and Society 363 (Loveland, I).

149 *Kerby v Harding* (1851) 6 Exch 234; 155 ER 527.

150 *Wade v Marsh* (1625) Lat 211; 82 ER 350.

151 *Hancock v Austin* (1863) 14 CB (NS) 634; 143 ER 593.

152 *Kirkland v Briancourt* (1890) 6 TLR 441.

153 *Chancellor v Webster* (1893) 9 TLR 568 at 569.

154 *Wreth v London & Westminster Loan and Discount Co* (1889) 5 TLR 521 at 522.

155 *Semayne's* case (1605) 5 Co Rep 91a at 92b; 77 ER 194 at 198.

156 *Browning v Dann* (1735) Bull NP 81.

157 *Long v Clarke* [1894] 1 QB 119 at 121.

158 *Nash v Lucas* (1867) LR 2 QB 590 at 594.

159 See s 4 of the Law of Distress Amendment Act 1888; s 89(1) of the County Courts Act 1984); at 2 of the Protection from Execution (Prescribed Value) Order 1980 (SI 1980/26).

160 *Morley v Pincombe* (1848) 2 Exch 101 at 102; 154 ER 423.

fixtures,[161] the property of lodgers,[162] and things in actual use[163] cannot be distrained. Distress may be made by the landlord in person or by a certificated bailiff. A leave of the court is needed for distress in the case of statutory tenancies.[164] After the seizure, the tenant must be given notice which states the reason for the distress and stipulates the place of sale.[165] The goods seized are held for five days and then sold if the rent remains unpaid.[166]

The tenant may set off any sum due to him, for example by way of a claim for damages for breach of covenant, against a claim by the landlord to levy distress.[167]

The law on distress is archaic and not always rational. In its Working Paper published in May 1986, the Law Commission said that the law of distress is 'riddled with inconsistencies, uncertainties, anomalies and archaisms', and reform is 'long overdue'.[168] It 'is a relic from the ancient laws of England which has no place in modern society',[169] and 'very little purpose would be served by collecting up the existing principles from the statutes and common law and restating them in modern terms in a codifying statute.'[170] In 1991, in its report, the Law Commission recommended that distress for rent should be abolished.[171]

(b) Forfeiture

This remedy is only available if the lease contains a forfeiture clause giving the landlord the right to re-enter, and the landlord must not have waived the breach, expressly or impliedly. In *Matthews v Smallwood*,[172] Parker LJ, having found that the lease contained a forfeiture clause, dealt with the question of waiver as follows.

Matthews v Smallwood [1910] 1 Ch 777

Parker J: The next question is whether that right of re-entry, which I have held accrued to the lessor in 1900, has been waived. I think that the law on the subject of waiver is reasonably clear. The right to re-enter is a legal right which, apart from release or abandonment or waiver, will exist, and can be exercised, at any time within the period fixed by the Statutes of Limitation; and if a defendant in an action of ejectment based upon that right of re-entry alleges a release or abandonment or waiver, logically

161 *Simpson v Hartopp* (1744) Willes 512, at 514; 125 ER 1295 at 1296.

162 Section 1 of the Law of Distress Amendment Act 1908.

163 *Simpson v Hartopp* (1744) Willes 512, at 516; 125 ER 1295 at 1297.

164 Section 147 of the Rent Act 1977.

165 Section 1 of the Distress for Rent Act 1689; s 9 of the Distress for Rent Act 1737.

166 Section 1 of the Distress for Rent Act 1689.

167 *Eller v Grovecrest Investments Ltd* [1994] 4 All ER 845.

168 Distress for Rent (Law Commission Working Paper No 97, May 1986), para 5.1(1).

169 Working Paper No 97, para 5.1(5).

170 Working Paper No 97, para 5.1(2).

171 Law Commission, Landlord and tenant: Distress for Rent (Law Com No 194, 4 February 1991), para 3.1. See also (1992) 45 CLP 81 (Clarke, A).

172 [1910] 1 Ch 777 at 786.

speaking the onus ought to lie on him to show the release or the abandonment or the waiver. Waiver of a right of re-entry can only occur where the lessor, with knowledge of the facts upon which his right to re-enter arises, does some unequivocal act recognising the continued existence of the lease. It is not enough that he should do the act which recognises, or appears to recognise, the continued existence of the lease, unless, at the time when the act is done, he has knowledge of the facts under which, or from which, his right of entry arose. Therefore, we get the principle that, though an act of waiver operates with regard to all known breaches, it does not operate with regard to breaches which were unknown to the lessor at the time when the act took place. It is also, I think, reasonably clear upon the cases that whether the act, coupled with the knowledge, constitutes a waiver is a question which the law decides, and therefore it is not open to a lessor who has knowledge of the breach to say 'I will treat the tenancy as existing, and I will receive the rent, or I will take advantage of my power as landlord to distrain; but I tell you that all I shall do will be without prejudice to my right to re-enter, which I intend to reserve.' That is a position which he is not entitled to take up. If, knowing of the breach, he does distrain, or does receive the rent, then by law he waives the breach, and nothing which he can say by way of protest against the law will avail him anything. Logically, therefore, a person who relies upon waiver ought to shew, first, an act unequivocally recognising the subsistence of the lease, and, secondly, knowledge of the circumstances from which the right of re-entry arises at the time when that act is performed.'

More recently, the law as stated in *Matthews v Smallwood* was restated by Aldous LJ in *Cornillie v Saha and Bradford & Bingley Building Society* (1996) 72 P & CR 147 thus: it is necessary to identify the alleged act of waiver and ask (i) whether the alleged act of waiver unequivocally recognises the subsistence of the prohibited act; (ii) whether the landlord has knowledge of the breach of covenant from which the right of re-entry arose at the time of the alleged act of waiver; and (iii) whether the act of recognition was communicated to the tenant. If the answer to all three questions are in the affirmative, the landlord's act constitutes a waiver.

A waiver is implied if, with actual or constructive knowledge of the breach, the landlord continues to act inconsistently with his right to forfeit, for example to demand or to accept any rent due after the breach.[173] Where the breach relates to non-payment of rent, demanding the rent does not constitute waiver. On the contrary, a formal demand is normally a pre-requisite to forfeiture proceedings. However, where there are more than one default in payment, for example, where the tenant is not paying rents which are due on 1 September and 1 December, while the demand of the December rent is not a waiver for the failure to pay that rent, it is a waiver for the failure to pay the September rent. This is because the demand of the December rent necessarily indicates acceptance of the continued existence of the lease on 1 December.[174]

Waiver of breach of a particular covenant cannot be deemed to extend to any other covenants, nor operate as a general waiver, unless the contrary

173 *David Blackstone Ltd v Burnetts (West End) Ltd* [1973] 1 WLR 1487 at 1498.

174 *Re a Debtor* (No 13A/10/95) [1996] 1 All ER 691.

appears.[175] Where the breach is of a continuing nature, the landlord may withdraw at any time his waiver and revitalise his right of forfeiture.[176]

A breach of covenants by the tenant does not terminate the lease automatically even if there is a forfeiture clause, but renders the lease voidable.[177] The landlord has to elect whether to waive the breach or to enforce the forfeiture clause.[178] Where the landlord has served a writ making an unequivocal election to forfeit a lease and the tenant has admitted the breach and the landlord's right to forfeit, the landlord will be precluded from claiming that as the notice is not valid the lease has not been forfeited after all.[179]

A right of re-entry is a proprietary interest in land. If it is 'exercisable over or in respect of a legal term of years absolute, or annexed, for any purpose, to a legal rentcharge', it is a legal interest.[180] If it is annexed to an equitable interest, it is itself equitable.[181]

Forfeiture for non-payment of rent

Where there is a right to forfeit the lease for breach of the covenant to pay rent, the landlord must first make a formal demand for rent unless the lease expressly excludes this requirement. Under s 210 of the Common Law Procedure Act 1852, no formal demand is required if at least half a year's rent is in arrears and goods present on the premises and available for distress are insufficient to cover the arrears due.

Common Law Procedure Act 1852

210. Proceedings in ejectment by landlord for non-payment of rent

In all cases between landlord and tenant, as often as it shall happen that one half year's rent shall be in arrears, and the landlord or lessor, to whom the same is due, hath right by law to re-enter for the non-payment thereof, such landlord or lessor shall and may, without any formal demand or re-entry, serve a writ in ejectment for the recovery of the demised premises ... which service ... shall stand in the place and stead of a demand and re-entry; and in case of judgment against the defendant for non-appearance, if it shall be made appear to the court where the said action is depending, by affidavit, or be proved upon the trial in case the defendant appears, that half a year's rent was due before the said writ was served, and that no sufficient distress was to be found on the demised premises, countervailing the arrears then due, and that the lessor had power to re-enter, then and in every such case the lessor shall recover judgment and execution, in the same manner as if the rent in arrears had been legally demanded, and a re-entry made; and in

175 Section 148(1), (2) of the LPA 1925.

176 *Doe d Ambler v Woodbridge* (1829) 9 B & C 376 at 377; 109 ER 140; *Greenwich LBC v Discreet Selling Estates Ltd* (1990) 61 P & CR 405 at 412.

177 *Bowser v Colby* (1841) 1 Hare 109 at 133; 66 ER 969 at 979.

178 *Billson v Residential Apartments Ltd* [1992] 1 AC 494 at 534D.

179 *G S Fashions Ltd v B & Q plc* [1995] 4 All ER 899.

180 Section 1(2)(e) of the LPA 1925.

181 Section 1(3) of the LPA 1925.

case the lessee or his assignee, or other person claiming or deriving under the said lease, shall permit and suffer judgment to be had and recovered on such trial in ejectment, and execution to be executed thereon, without paying the rent and arrears, together with full costs, and without proceeding for relief in equity within six months after such execution executed, then and in such case the said lessee, his assignee, and all other persons claiming and deriving under the said lease, shall be barred and foreclosed from all relief or remedy in law or equity, other than by bringing error for reversal of such judgment, in case the same shall be erroneous, and the said landlord or lessor shall from thenceforth hold the said demised premises discharged from such lease ... provided that nothing herein contained shall extend to bar the right of any mortgagee of such lease, or any part thereof, who shall not be in possession, so as such mortgagee shall and do, within six months after such judgment obtained and execution executed pay all rent in arrears, and all costs and damages sustained by such lessor or person entitled to the remainder or reversion as aforesaid, and perform all the covenants and agreements which, on the part and behalf of the first lessee, are and ought to be performed.

Where a formal demand for rent is required, once demanded, the landlord may then forfeit the lease by peaceful re-entry.[182] If the tenant refuses to give up possession voluntarily, proceedings for forfeiture are needed. Where the premises are let as a residence, the right can only be enforced with a court order.[183] As mentioned earlier, the landlord who obtains or seeks to obtain a re-entry without due legal process can also be guilty of a criminal offence for unlawful harassment or eviction.[184] Furthermore, the tenant may obtain damages in civil proceedings for unlawful harassment or eviction under s 27 of the Housing Act 1988.

In forfeiture proceedings, the court has an equitable jurisdiction to grant relief. Thus, if the tenant has paid all rents due and costs incurred by the landlord, the court may reinstate the lease.[185] The court's equitable jurisdiction to relief in respect of non-payment of rent is preserved by s 38(1) of the Supreme Court Act 1981.

Supreme Court Act 1981

38. Relief against forfeiture for non-payment of rent

(1) In any action in the High Court for the forfeiture of a lease for non-payment of rent, the court shall have power to grant relief against forfeiture in a summary manner, and may do so subject to the same terms and conditions as to the payment of rent, costs or otherwise as could have been imposed by it in such an action immediately before the commencement of this Act.

---

182 Modern authorities favour the view that although peaceable re-entry is lawful, it is undesirable, and the civilised method of determining the lease by forfeiture proceedings is preferable to the dubious and dangerous method of self-help re-entry: *Billson v Residential Apartments Ltd* [1992] 1 AC 494; *W G Clark (Properties) Ltd v Dupre Properties Ltd* [1992] Ch 297.

183 Section 2 of the Protection from Eviction Act 1977.

184 Section 1(2), (3) of the Protection from Eviction Act 197.

185 *Howard v Fanshawe* [1895] 2 Ch 581 at 592.

This jurisdiction is particularly useful where there has been a peaceable re-entry without court proceedings. Where possession proceedings are brought in the High Court for non-payment of rent, the tenant may stay the proceedings if he pays all rent arrears and costs before the date of judgment under s 212 of the Common Law Procedure Act 1852.[186]

Common Law Procedure Act 1852

212. Tenant paying all rent with costs, proceedings to cease

> If the tenant or his assignee do or shall, at any time before the trial in such ejectment, pay or tender to the lessor or landlord, his executors or administrators, or his or their attorney in that cause, or pay into the court where the same cause is depending, all the rent and arrears, together with the costs, then and in such case all further proceedings on the said ejectment shall cease and be discontinued; and if such lessee, his executors, administrators, or assigns, shall, upon such proceedings as aforesaid, be relieved in equity, he and they shall have, hold, and enjoy the demised lands, according to the lease thereof made, without any new lease.

Forfeiture for breach of other covenants

Forfeiture for breach of covenants other than that to pay rent is governed by s 146 of the Law of Property Act 1925.[187] Section 146 is mandatory and cannot be contracted out.[188] The landlord cannot re-enter, either by court order or by peaceable re-entry. He must first serve on the tenant a s 146 notice which specifies the breach, and requires that the breach be remedied if remediable,[189] and require the tenant to make compensation in money for the breach.[190] He must then allow reasonable time for the notice to be complied with before forfeiting the lease.[191] If the notice relates to a breach of the tenant's covenants to repair in a lease for a term of seven years or more, of which at least three years remain unexpired, it must provide information regarding the tenant's rights under the Leasehold Property (Repairs) Act 1938. Any notice which fails to comply with s 146 is void,[192] and any purported forfeiture in pursuance of it is likewise void.[193] The tenant may apply for relief under s 146(2) before the landlord re-enters but not after re-entry.

---

186 The power of the county court to grant relief is governed by s 138 of the County Court Act 1984.

187 Section 146 notice procedure does not apply to forfeiture for breach of a covenant to pay rent: s 146(11) of the LPA 1925.

188 Section 146(12) of the LPA 1925.

189 *Savva and Savva v Hussein* (1997) 73 P & CR 150.

190 Section 146(1) of the LPA 1925.

191 Section 146(1) of the LPA 1925.

192 *Expert Clothing Service & Sales Ltd v Hillgate House Ltd* [1986] Ch 340.

193 *Re Riggs, ex p Lovell* [1901] 2 KB 16 at 20.

When a head lease is forfeited the sublease is also destroyed.[194] But under s 146(4) a sub-tenant may apply for relief if the head lease is forfeited.[195] If relief is granted, he will become a tenant of the head landlord for the period of the sublease.[196] However, relief cannot be made under s 146(4) retrospectively from the date of forfeiture, but only from the date of the order.[197] The sub-tenant is unable to apply for relief until there is a forfeiture, and as there is often a delay between the forfeiture and the grant of relief, before relief is obtained, the sub-tenant becomes a trespasser and is liable to the head landlord for mesne profits. To avoid this, where the proceedings are based on non-payment of rent, the sub-tenant may apply for a relief under s 146(2) which allows relief to be made retrospectively from the date of forfeiture.[198] The definition of 'lessee' in s 146(5)(b) includes a sub-tenant who is a person deriving title under a lessee.[199]

Law of Property Act 1925

146. Restrictions on and relief against forfeiture of leases and underleases

(1) A right of re-entry or forfeiture under any proviso or stipulation in a lease for a breach of any covenant or condition in the lease shall not be enforceable, by action or otherwise, unless and until the lessor serves on the lessee a notice:

(a) specifying the particular breach complained of; and

(b) if the breach is capable of remedy, requiring the lessee to remedy the breach; and

(c) in any case, requiring the lessee to make compensation in money for the breach; and the lessee fails, within a reasonable time thereafter, to remedy the breach, if it is capable of remedy, and to make reasonable compensation in money, to the satisfaction of the lessor, for the breach.

(2) Where a lessor is proceeding, by action or otherwise, to enforce such a right of re-entry or forfeiture, the lessee may, in the lessor's action, if any, or in any action brought by himself, apply to the court for relief; and the court may grant or refuse relief, as the court, having regard to the proceedings and conduct of the parties under the foregoing provisions of this section, and to all the other circumstances, thinks fit; and in case of relief may grant it on such terms, if any, as to costs, expenses, damages, compensation, penalty, or otherwise, including the granting of an injunction to restrain any like breach in the future, as the court, in the circumstances of each case, thinks fit.

(4) Where a lessor is proceeding by action or otherwise to enforce a right of re-entry or forfeiture under any covenant, proviso, or stipulation in a lease, or for non-payment of

---

194 *Great Western Railway Co v Smith* (1876) 2 Ch D 235.

195 See also s 1 of the Law of Property (Amendment) Act 1929, which provides that nothing in s 146(8), (9) and (10) of the LPA 1925 shall affect the provision of s 146(4).

196 If the sublessee was a protected tenant of the head lessee, after the headlease is forfeited, the sublessee becomes a protected tenant of the landlord: *The Keepers and Governors of the Free Grammar School of John Lyon v Jordan* (1996) 72 P & CR 402.

197 *Cadogan v Dimovic* [1984] 2 All ER 168 at 172, 174, *per* Fox and Robert Goff LJJ respectively; *Escalus Properties v Dennis* [1995] 4 All ER 852 at 861d.

198 *Escalus Properties v Dennis* [1995] 4 All ER 852.

199 *Escalus Properties v Dennis* [1995] 4 All ER 852.

rent, the court may, on application by any person claiming as under-lessee any estate or interest in the property comprised in the lease or any part thereof, either in the lessor's action (if any) or in any action brought by such person for that purpose, make an order vesting, for the whole term of the lease or any less term, the property comprised in the lease or any part thereof in any person entitled as under-lessee to any estate or interest in such property upon such conditions as to execution of any deed or other document, payment of rent, costs, expenses, damages, compensation, giving security, or otherwise, as the court in the circumstances of each case may think fit, but in no case shall any such under-lessee be entitled to require a lease to be granted to him for any longer term than he had under his original sub-lease.

(5) For the purposes of this section :

(a) 'Lease' includes an original or derivative under-lease; also an agreement for a lease where the lessee has become entitled to have his lease granted; also a grant at a fee farm rent, or securing a rent by condition;

(b) 'Lessee' includes an original or derivative under-lessee, and the persons deriving title under a lessee; also a grantee under any such grant as aforesaid and the persons deriving title under him;

(c) 'Lessor' includes an original or derivative under-lessor, and the persons deriving title under a lessor; also a person making such grant as aforesaid and the persons deriving title under him;

(d) 'Under-lease' includes an agreement for an under-lease where the under-lessee has become entitled to have his under-lease granted;

(e) 'Under-lessee' includes any person deriving title under an under-lessee.

(8) This section does not extend:

(i) To a covenant or condition against assigning, underletting, parting with the possession, or disposing of the land leased where the breach occurred before the commencement of this Act; or

(ii) In the case of a mining lease, to a covenant or condition for allowing the lessor to have access to or inspect books, accounts, records, weighing machines or other things, or to enter or inspect the mine or the workings thereof.

(9) This section does not apply to a condition for forfeiture on the bankruptcy of the lessee or on taking in execution of the lessee's interest if contained in a lease of:

(a) Agricultural or pastoral land;

(b) Mines or minerals;

(c) A house used or intended to be used as a public-house or beershop;

(d) A house let as a dwelling house, with the use of any furniture, books, works of art, or other chattels not being in the nature of fixtures;

(e) Any property with respect to which the personal qualifications of the tenant are of importance for the preservation of the value or character of the property, or on the ground of neighbourhood to the lessor, or to any person holding under him.

(10) Where a condition of forfeiture on the bankruptcy of the lessee or on taking in execution of the lessee's interest is contained in any lease, other than a lease of any of the classes mentioned in the last subsection, then –

(a) if the lessee's interest is sold within one year from the bankruptcy or taking in execution, this section applies to the forfeiture condition aforesaid;

(b) if the lessee's interest is not sold before the expiration of that year, this section only applies to the forfeiture condition aforesaid during the first year from the date of the bankruptcy or taking in execution.

(11) This section does not, save as otherwise mentioned, affect the law relating to re-entry or forfeiture or relief in case of non-payment of rent.

(12) This section has effect notwithstanding any stipulation to the contrary.

Where the breach is remediable, the tenant must be given reasonable time to comply with the s 146 notice. If the tenant takes remedial action and pays reasonable compensation within that time, the landlord will be unable to forfeit the lease. But if no remedial action is taken and no compensation is made by the tenant, the landlord may forfeit the lease subject to the tenant's right to get relief against forfeiture.

If the breach is irremediable, the s 146 notice does not have to require the tenant to remedy the breach. It is sufficient if it specifies the breach and demands compensation. The landlord will then be able to forfeit after a reasonable interval, subject to the tenant's rights to relief against forfeiture.

It is, therefore, important to decide if a breach is remediable or irremediable. The test, as Slade LJ suggested in *Expert Clothing Service & Sales Ltd v Hillgate House Ltd,*[200] is whether the harm suffered by the landlord can be effectively remedied if the tenant were to comply with the notice requiring both remedy and compensation within a reasonable time. A breach is capable of being remedied if the landlord can be restored within a reasonable time to the position he would have been in if no breach had occurred.[201]

(a) Remediable breach

A breach of a positive covenant, whether continuing or 'once and for all', is normally capable of being remedied because it can be cured by belated performance.[202] This issue was fully dealt with by Slade LJ in *Expert Clothing Service & Sales Ltd v Hillgate House Ltd.*[203]

Expert Clothing Service & Sales Ltd v Hillgate House Ltd [1986] Ch 340, CA

Slade LJ: The first question which fell to be considered ... is whether those breaches are 'capable of remedy' within the meaning of s 146(1) of the Law of Property Act 1925. This

200 [1986] Ch 340 at 358C–D.

201 *Expert Clothing Service & Sales Ltd v Hillgate House Ltd* [1986] Ch 340 at 362E–F.

202 *Expert Clothing Service & Sales Ltd v Hillgate House Ltd* [1986] Ch 340 at 355B–C.

203 [1986] Ch 340.

is a question of crucial importance, for it is common ground that, if they are both capable of remedy in this sense, the s 146 notice, which asserted that they were irremediable and gave the first defendant no opportunity to remedy them, must have been a wholly invalid notice.

In a case where the breach is 'capable of remedy' within the meaning of the section, the principal object of the notice procedure provided for by s 146(1), as I read it, is to afford the lessee two opportunities before the lessor actually proceeds to enforce his right of re-entry, namely (1) the opportunity to remedy the breach within a reasonable time after service of the notice, and (2) the opportunity to apply to the court for relief from forfeiture. In a case where the breach is not 'capable of remedy', there is clearly no point in affording the first of these two opportunities; the object of the notice procedure is thus simply to give the lessee the opportunity to apply for relief.

Unfortunately, the authorities give only limited guidance as to what breaches are 'capable of remedy' within the meaning of the section. As Harman J pointed out in *Hoffmann v Fineberg* [1949] Ch 245 at 253:

> In one sense, no breach can ever be remedied, because there must always, *ex concessis*, be a time in which there has not been compliance with the covenant, but the section clearly involves the view that some breaches are remediable, and therefore it cannot mean that.

[His Lordship referred to *Rugby School (Governors) v Tannahill* [1934] 1 KB 695 and continued.]

In supporting the judge's conclusion that the breach relating to reconstruction of the premises was irremediable, Mr Collins, on behalf of the plaintiffs, has submitted to us three principal arguments. First, he pointed out that (as is common ground) the first defendant's failure to build by 28 September 1982 was a 'once and for all' breach of the relevant covenant, and not a continuing breach: see, for example, *Stephens v Junior Army and Navy Stores Ltd* [1914] 2 Ch 516 at 523, *per* Lord Cozens-Hardy MR. He submitted that the breach of a covenant such as this, which can only be broken once, is *ex hypothesi* in no case capable of remedy.

Some superficial support for this conclusion is perhaps to be found in the judgments in *Scala House & District Property Co Ltd v Forbes* [1974] QB 575, in which the Court of Appeal held that the breach of a covenant not to assign, underlet or part with possession was not a breach capable of remedy within the meaning of s 146(1) ...

It might well be regarded as anomalous if the once and for all breach of a negative covenant not to sublet were to be regarded as 'capable of remedy' within s 146, provided that the unlawful sub-tenancy was still current at the date of the s 146 notice, but (as Russell LJ considered) were not to be regarded as 'capable of remedy' if the unlawful sub-tenancy had been determined at that date. Russell LJ and James LJ who agreed with his reasoning (see particularly at p 591C–D), were clearly much influenced by this anomaly in reaching the conclusion that the breach of a covenant against underletting is never capable of remedy.

However, in the *Scala House* case [1974] QB 575 this court was addressing its mind solely to the once and for all breach of a negative covenant. No corresponding anomaly arises if the once and for all breach of a positive covenant is treated as capable of remedy. While the *Scala House* decision is, of course, authority binding on this court for the proposition that the breach of a negative covenant not to assign, underlet or part with possession is never 'capable of remedy,' it is not, in my judgment, authority for the proposition that the once and for all breach of a positive covenant is never capable of remedy.

Mr Neuberger, on behalf of the defendants, did not feel able to go so far as to support the view of MacKinnon J that the breach of a positive covenant is always capable of remedy. He accepted, for example, that the breach of a covenant to insure might be incapable of remedy at a time when the premises had already been burnt down. Another example might be the breach of a positive covenant which in the event would be only capable of being fully performed, if at all, after the expiration of the relevant term.

Nevertheless, I would, for my part, accept Mr Neuberger's submission that the breach of a positive covenant (whether it be a continuing breach or a once and for all breach) will ordinarily be capable of remedy. As Bristow J pointed out in the course of argument, the concept of capability of remedy for the purpose of s 146 must surely be directed to the question whether the harm that has been done to the landlord by the relevant breach is for practicable purposes capable of being retrieved. In the ordinary case, the breach of a promise to do something by a certain time can for practical purposes be remedied by the thing being done, even out of time. For these reasons, I reject the plaintiffs' argument that the breach of the covenant to reconstruct by 28 September 1982 was not capable of remedy merely because it was not a continuing breach.

[His Lordship rejected Mr Collin's second argument that the breach of the covenant to reconstruct was not capable of remedy because of the operation of the new rent review provisions in the lease.]

I therefore turn to the third, and far the most important point, relied on by Mr. Collins in support of the decision of the court below. His submissions in this context were to the following effect. The judgment of Maugham LJ in the *Rugby School* case [1935] 1 KB 87, 93 and other judicial *dicta* indicate that if a breach is to be 'capable of remedy' at all within the meaning of s 146, it must be capable of remedy within a 'reasonable time'. As was observed by Lord Herschell LC in *Hick v Raymond & Reid* [1893] AC 22, 29: 'there is of course no such thing as a reasonable time in the abstract. It must always depend upon circumstances'. In the present case, it was submitted, what was a reasonable time was a question of fact. In deciding that the breach of the covenant to reconstruct was not capable of remedy within a reasonable time, the judge expressed himself as 'having regard to the facts as I have found them'. ... in my opinion, in considering whether or not remedy within a reasonable time is possible, a crucial distinction (which I infer from the judgment did not feature prominently in argument before the judge) falls to be drawn between breaches of negative user covenants, such as those under consideration in the *Rugby School* and the *Esplanade Hotels* cases, and breaches of positive covenants. In the two last-mentioned cases, where the relevant breaches consisted of allowing premises to be used as a brothel, even full compliance with the covenant within a reasonable time and for a reasonable time would not have remedied the breach. As Maugham LJ pointed out in the *Rugby School* case, at p 94:

> '... merely ceasing for a reasonable time, perhaps a few weeks or a month, to use the premises for an immoral purpose would be no remedy for the breach of covenant which had been committed over a long period.'

On the facts of cases such as those, mere cesser by the tenant of the offending use within a reasonable period and for a reasonable period of time could not have remedied the breaches because it could not have removed the stigma which they had caused to attach to the premises. The harm had been irretrievably done. In such cases, as Harman J pointed out in *Hoffmann v Fineberg* [1949] Ch 245 at 257, mere cesser will not enable the tenant to '... make his record clean, as he could by complying, though out of time, with a failure to lay on the prescribed number of coats of paint'.

In contrast with breaches of negative user covenants, the breach of a positive covenant to do something (such as to decorate or build) can ordinarily, for practical purposes, be remedied by the thing being actually done if a reasonable time for its performance (running from the service of the s 146 notice) is duly allowed by the landlord following such service and the tenant duly does it within such time.

In the present case there is no question of the breach of the covenant to reconstruct having given rise to any 'stigma' against the lessors or the premises. Significantly, the lease in 1982 still had 20 years to run. Mr Collins has, I think, been able to suggest no convincing reasons why the plaintiffs would still have suffered irremediable damage if (i) the s 146 notice had required the lessee to remedy the breach and (ii) the lessors had then allowed a reasonable time to elapse sufficient to enable the lessee to comply with the relevant covenant, and (iii) the lessee had complied with the covenant in such reasonable time and had paid any appropriate monetary compensation. Though he has submitted that a requirement directed to the defendants to remedy the breach would have been purposeless, on the grounds that they had neither the financial means nor the will to do the necessary work, these are matters which, in my opinion, a landlord is not entitled to prejudge in drafting his notice. An important purpose of the s 146 procedure is to give even tenants who have hitherto lacked the will or the means to comply with their obligations one last chance to summon up that will or find the necessary means before the landlord re-enters. In considering what 'reasonable time' to allow the defendants, the plaintiffs, in serving their s 146 notice, would, in my opinion, have been entitled to take into account the fact that the defendants already had enjoyed 15 months in which to fulfil their contractual obligations to reconstruct and to subject the defendants to a correspondingly tight timetable running from the date of service of the notice, though, at the same time, always bearing in mind that the contractual obligation to reconstruct did not even arise until 29 June 1981, and that as at 8 October 1982 the defendants had been in actual breach of it for only some 10 days. However, I think they were not entitled to say, in effect: 'We are not going to allow you any time at all to remedy the breach, because you have had so long to do the work already.'

In my judgment, on the remediability issue, the ultimate question for the court was this: if the s 146 notice had required the lessee to remedy the breach and the lessors had then allowed a reasonable time to elapse to enable the lessee fully to comply with the relevant covenant, would such compliance, coupled with the payment of any appropriate monetary compensation, have effectively remedied the harm which the lessors had suffered or were likely to suffer from the breach? If, but only if, the answer to this question was 'No,' would the failure of the s 146 notice to require remedy of the breach have been justifiable. In *Rugby School (Governors) v Tannahill* [1935] 1 KB 87; *Egerton v Esplanade Hotels, London Ltd* [1947] 2 All ER 88 and *Hoffmann v Fineberg* [1949] Ch 245 the answer to this question plainly would have been 'No'. In the present case, however, for the reasons already stated, I think the answer to it must have been 'Yes'.

My conclusion, therefore, is that the breach of the covenant to reconstruct ... was 'capable of remedy.' In reaching this conclusion, I find it reassuring that no reported case has been brought to our attention in which the breach of a positive covenant has been held incapable of remedy, though I do not suggest that cases of this nature, albeit perhaps rarely, could not arise.

(b) Irremediable breach

Generally a 'once and for all' breach of negative covenant, such as a breach of covenant against assignment or subletting, is irremediable.[204]

Scala House and District Property Co Ltd v Forbes [1975] QB 575, CA

Russell LJ: ... the first question is whether a breach of covenant such as is involved in the present case is capable of remedy. If it is capable of remedy, and is remedied in reasonable time, the lessor is unable to prove that a condition precedent to his ability to seek to forfeit by action or otherwise has been fulfilled. Here at once is a problem. An unlawful subletting is a breach once and for all. The subterm has been created.

[His Lordship referred to *Jackson v Simons; Rugby School (Governors) v Tannahill* [1935] 1 KB 87; *Brothwick-Norton v Romney Warwick Estates Ltd* [1950] 1 All ER 798; *Hoffmann v Fineberg* [1949] Ch 245; *Egerton v Esplanade Hotels, London Ltd* [1947] 2 All ER 88; *Glass v Kencakes Ltd* [1966] 1 QB 611 and *Capital & Counties Property Co Ltd v Mills* [1966] EGD 96 and continued.]

In summary upon the cases we have therefore a number of cases of user of premises in breach of covenant in which the decision that the breach is not capable of remedy has gone upon the 'stigma' point, without considering whether a short answer might be – if the user had ceased before the s 146 notice – that it was *ex hypothesi* incapable of remedy, leaving the lessee only with the ability to seek relief from forfeiture and the writ unchallengeable as such. If a user in breach has ceased before the s 146 notice (quite apart from the stigma cases) then either it is incapable of remedy and after notice there is nothing in the way of a writ: or the cesser of use has somehow deprived the lessor of his ability to seek to forfeit though he has done nothing to waive the breach, a situation in law which I find extremely difficult to spell out of s 146. But whatever may be the position in user breach cases, which are of a continuing nature, there is no authority, other than that of *Capital & Counties Property Co Ltd v Mills*, to suggest that the creation of a subterm in breach of covenant is capable of remedy. I would make two particular comments on that decision, as reported. First: I find it difficult to see how a breach is said to be capable of remedy because the lessor can waive the breach, which would be involved in the suggestion that he could post hoc consent to the subletting. Second: I do not see how a breach by unlawful subletting can be said to be remedied by the lessee when he does nothing except wait for the subterm to come to an end by effluxion of time.

After this review of the cases, I come to the conclusion that breach by an unlawful subletting is not capable of remedy at all. In my judgment the introduction of such breaches into the relevant section for the first time by s 146 of the Act of 1925 operates only to confer a statutory ability to relieve the lessee from forfeiture on that ground. The subterm has been effectively created subject only to risks of forfeiture: it is a complete breach once for all: it is not in any sense a continuing breach. If the law were otherwise a lessee, when a sub-tenancy is current at the time of the s 146 notice, would have a chance of remedying the situation without having to apply for relief. But if the unlawful

204 *Scala House and District Property Co Ltd v Forbes* [1974] QB 575 at 588A–D.

subletting had determined before the notice, the lessee could only seek relief from forfeiture. The only escape from that wholly unsatisfactory difference would be to hold that in the second example by some analogy the lessor was disabled from issuing a writ for possession. But I can find nothing in the section to justify that limitation on the common law right of re-entry, bearing especially in mind that a lessor might discover a whole series of past expired unlawful sublettings which might well justify a refusal to grant relief in forfeiture proceedings.

I stress again that where there has been an unlawful subletting which has determined (and which has not been waived) there has been a breach which at common law entitles the lessor to re-enter: nothing can be done to remedy that breach: the expiry of the subterm has not annulled or remedied the breach: in such case the lessor plainly need not, in his s 146 notice, call upon the lessee to remedy the breach which is not capable of remedy, and is free to issue his writ for possession, the possibility of relief remaining. Can it possibly be that, while that is the situation in such case, it is otherwise if the lessee has failed to get rid of the subterm until after a notice served? Is the lessee then in a stronger position and the lessor in a weaker position? In my judgment not so. These problems and questions arise only if such a breach is capable of remedy, which in my judgment it is not. I consider that *Capital & Counties Property Co Ltd v Mills* [1966] EGD 96, if correctly reported, was wrongly decided. I should add that I find some support for any opinion in the comments of Fraser J in *Abrahams v Mac Fisheries Ltd* [1925] 2 KB 18 at 35, who expressed the view that the exceptions in s 14(6) of the Act of 1881 (as to, *inter alia*, subletting) were made to cover cases where the breach cannot be remedied specifically.

Where the breach is continuing, it is remediable if the harm caused to the landlord can be retrieved by the cesser of the prohibited activity. But if the 'stigma' which the tenant's activity in breach of covenant has caused to attach to the premises cannot be removed by a complete cesser of the prohibited activity, the breach is irremediable.[205] In *Rugby School (Governors) v Tannahill*,[206] the Governors of Rugby School let premises in London to tenants who assigned the lease to the defendant with the Governors' consent. The defendant used the premises as a brothel in breach of a covenant which prohibited use of the premises for illegal or immoral purposes. The lease contained a forfeiture clause for breach of covenant. The Governors served a s 146 notice which did not require the defendant to remedy the breach, nor require compensation in money. The question was (i) whether the breach was remediable, for if it was not, an omission to require it to be remedied would not invalidate the notice, and (ii) whether omission to require compensation in money invalidated the notice.

Rugby School (Governors) v Tannahill [1935] 1 KB 87, CA

Greer LJ: The first point is, whether this particular breach is capable of remedy. In my judgment MacKinnon J. was right in coming to the conclusion that it was not. I think perhaps he went further than was really necessary for the decision of this case in holding that a breach of any negative covenant – the doing of that which is forbidden – can never

205 *Rugby School (Governors) v Tannahill* [1935] 1 KB 87.

206 [1935] 1 KB 87.

be capable of remedy. It is unnecessary to decide the point on this appeal; but in some cases where the immediate ceasing of that which is complained of, together with an undertaking against any further breach, it might be said that the breach was capable of remedy. This particular breach, however – conducting the premises, or permitting them to be conducted, as a house of ill-fame – is one which in my judgment was not remedied by merely stopping this user. I cannot conceive how a breach of this kind can be remedied. The result of committing the breach would be known all over the neighbourhood and seriously affect the value of the premises. Even a money payment together with the cessation of the improper use of the house could not be a remedy. Taking the view as I do that this breach was incapable of remedy, it was unnecessary to require in the notice that the defendant should remedy the breach.

The further question is whether the absence of any statement in the notice requiring compensation in money in respect of the breach is fatal to the validity of the notice. As to that, the decision of the Court of Appeal in *Lock v Pearce* binds us to hold that the plaintiffs were under no obligation to require compensation in money. I can well understand that a body like the plaintiffs would be averse to touch money coming from a tenant in such circumstances. In any event, whatever might have been our view in the absence of authority, it is plain from the judgments in *Lock v Pearce* that the point is not open in this Court. Lindley LJ there used these words:

> Then, as regards the notices required by s 14, sub-s 1 [of the Conveyancing Act 1881], the statute requires notice to be given specifying the breach complained of, as the first thing, and, if the breach is capable of remedy, requiring the lessee to remedy it, and 'in any case requiring the lessee to make compensation in money for the breach'. Supposing the lessor does not want compensation, is the notice to be held bad because he does not ask for it? There is no sense in that. The meaning is to be found by looking a little further on. The subsection begins by saying that the right of re-entry or forfeiture shall not be enforceable unless proper notice is given and the lessee fails within a reasonable time afterwards to remedy the breach and to make reasonable compensation in money to the satisfaction of the lessor. The sense of that is that the lessor must tell the lessee what he wants done. The lessee is entitled to know what his landlord complains of, and, if his landlord is entitled to compensation, whether he wants compensation.

The Lord Justice there concluded his judgment in a paragraph of two sentences which are specially applicable to the present case; he said: 'On these grounds I am of opinion that this appeal fails. Upon the merits as well as upon the technicalities, all the points are against the appellants.' In the later case of *Civil Service Co-operative Society, Ltd v McGrigor's Trustee* [1923] 2 Ch 347, Russell J followed *Lock v Pearce* [1893] 2 Ch 271 as applicable to a case like this where the breach was incapable of remedy. The appeal must be dismissed.

The court's equitable jurisdiction to grant relief against forfeiture is not limited to breach of covenant to pay rent, but extends to breach of other covenants.[207] This jurisdiction is now confirmed in s 146(2) of the Law of Property Act 1925. The availability of this jurisdiction has recently been considered by the House of Lords at length in *Billson v Residential Apartments Ltd*.[208]

207 *Sanders v Pope* (1806) 12 Ves 282 at 289; 33 ER 108 at 110; *Billson v Residential Apartments Ltd* [1992] 1 AC 494 at 534G–H.

208 [1992] 1 AC 494.

Billson v Residential Apartments Ltd [1992] 1 AC 494, HL

Lord Templeman: By the writ in this action dated 19 July 1989 the landlords claim possession, damages for breach of covenant and damages for trespass. By their defence and counterclaim the tenants counterclaim for relief against forfeiture. By their reply the landlords claim that the court has no jurisdiction to grant the tenants relief from forfeiture. The trial judge, Mummery J (1990) 60 P & CR 392, and the Court of Appeal (Sir Nicholas Browne-Wilkinson VC, Parker and Nicholls LJJ) considered that they were constrained by authority to hold that the court had no jurisdiction to grant the tenants relief against forfeiture pursuant to s 146(2) because the tenants had not applied to the court for relief prior to the re-entry into possession by the landlords on 18 July 1989. The tenants now appeal.

By the common law, when a tenant commits a breach of covenant and the lease contains a proviso for forfeiture, the landlord at his option may either waive the breach or determine the lease. In order to exercise his option to determine the lease the landlord must either re-enter the premises in conformity with the proviso or must issue and serve a writ claiming possession. The bringing of an action to recover possession is equivalent to an entry for the forfeiture. Thus in *Jones v Carter* (1846) 15 M & W 718 at 726, Parke B said:

> the bringing of an ejectment for a forfeiture, and serving it on the lessee in possession, must be considered as the exercise of the lessor's option to determine the lease; and the option must be exercised once for all ... for after such an act, by which the lessor treats the lessee as a trespasser, the lessee would know that he was no longer to consider himself as holding under the lease, and bound to perform the covenants contained in it ...

This observation was cited and applied by Lord Denning MR in *Canas Property Co Ltd v K L Television Services Ltd* [1970] 2 QB 433 at 440.

Before the intervention of Parliament, if a landlord forfeited by entering into possession or by issuing and serving a writ for possession, equity could relieve the tenant against forfeiture but only in cases under the general principles of equity whereby a party may be relieved from the consequences of fraud, accident or mistake or in cases where the breach of covenant entitling the landlord to forfeit was a breach of the covenant for payment of rent.

Mr Reid, who appeared for the landlords, conceded that where equity claimed power to relieve against forfeiture, the tenant could apply for relief irrespective of the method by which the landlord had exercised his option to determine the lease. Relief could be granted whether the landlord had forfeited by entering into possession or had forfeited by issuing and serving a writ claiming possession.

In 1881, Parliament interfered to supplement equity and to enable any tenant to be relieved from forfeiture. The need for such intervention was and is manifest because otherwise a tenant who had paid a large premium for a 999-year lease at a low rent could lose his asset by a breach of covenant which was remediable or which caused the landlord no damage. The forfeiture of any lease, however short, may unjustly enrich the landlord at the expense of the tenant. In creating a power to relieve against forfeiture for breach of covenant, Parliament protected the landlord by conferring on the court a wide discretion to grant relief on terms or to refuse relief altogether. In practice, this discretion is exercised with the object of ensuring that the landlord is not substantially prejudiced or damaged by the revival of the lease.

Section 14(1) and (2) of the Conveyancing Act 1881 (44 & 45 Vict c 41) were provisions which conferred on the court power to relieve against forfeiture and those provisions were reproduced in s 146(1) and (2) of the Law of Property Act 1925 in identical terms. In referring to a s 146 notice I shall therefore mean and include a notice served under s 14(1) of the Act of 1881 and in referring to s 146(1) and (2) shall mean and include s 14(1) and (2) of the Act of 1881 where appropriate.

Section 146(1) prevents the landlord from enforcing a right of re-entry or forfeiture by action or otherwise so that the landlord cannot determine the lease by issuing and serving a writ or by re-entering the premises until the tenant has failed within a reasonable time to remedy the breach and make reasonable compensation. Section 146(2) enables the tenant to apply to the court for relief where the landlord 'is proceeding, by action or otherwise' to enforce his right of re-entry or forfeiture. If the landlord 'is proceeding' to determine the lease by issuing and serving a writ, the tenant may apply for relief after the writ has been served. If the landlord 'is proceeding' to determine the lease by re-entering into possession, the tenant may apply for relief after the landlord has re-entered.

Mr Reid submitted and referred to authority for the proposition that on the true construction of s 146(2) a tenant cannot apply for relief against forfeiture after the landlord has re-entered without obtaining a court order. Thereafter the landlord is no longer 'proceeding' to enforce his rights; he has succeeded in enforcing them. The proposition is in my opinion historically unsound because the effect of issuing and serving a writ is precisely the same as the effect of re-entry; in each case the lease is determined. The landlord is entitled to remain in possession if he has re-entered and he is entitled to possession if he has issued and served a writ because the lease no longer exists. In each case the tenant seeks relief because the lease has been forfeited, The proposition is also inconsistent with the language of s 146(2). The tenant may apply for relief where the landlord is 'proceeding, by action or otherwise' to enforce his rights. The tenant may apply for relief where the landlord is 'Proceeding' by action and also where the landlord is proceeding 'otherwise' than by action. This can only mean that the tenant may apply for relief where the landlord is proceeding to forfeit by re-entry after the expiry of a s 146 notice. If re-entry bars relief, the right of the tenant to apply for relief where the landlord is proceeding otherwise than by action is substantially inoperative and the words 'or otherwise' in s 146(2) have no application. In my opinion those words must have been included because Parliament intended that a tenant should be able to obtain relief against a landlord whether the landlord has asserted his rights by a writ or by re-entering. It is said that a tenant served with a s 146 notice could during and after the expiration of the notice apply for relief under s 146(2) but if he fails to do so he is at the mercy of the landlord who decides to re-enter and whose rights are therefore, it is said, quite unaffected by the provisions of s 146(2) designed to relieve tenants from the consequences of breach of covenant. In my opinion the ambiguous words 'is proceeding' can mean 'proceeds' and should not be construed so as to produce the result that a tenant served with a s 146 notice can only ensure that he will be able to apply for relief if he does so before he knows whether or not the landlord intends to proceed at all or whether, if the landlord decides to proceed, he will issue and serve a writ or will attempt to re-enter.

When a tenant receives a s 146 notice he will not know whether the landlord can be persuaded that there is no breach or persuaded to accept in due course that any breach has been remedied and that he has been offered adequate and satisfactory compensation or whether the landlord will seek to determine the lease by issuing and serving a writ or will seek to determine the lease by re-entering the premises. The tenant will not wish to institute proceedings seeking relief from forfeiture if those proceedings will be aggressive and hostile and may be premature and unnecessary. Parliament cannot have intended that if the landlord employs the civilised method of determining the lease by issuing and serving a writ, then the tenant will be entitled to apply for relief, but if the landlord employs the dubious and dangerous method of determining the lease by re-entering the premises, then the tenant will be debarred from applying for relief.

Mr Reid concedes that re-entry can only avail the landlord if the entry is lawful. Re-entry is unlawful where the premises are occupied by the tenant but not unlawful where the premises are occupied by the tenant's goods. If the argument of the landlords is correct, s 146 provides a method by which a landlord can sneak up on a shop at night, break into the shop, and install new locks so that the tenant loses his lease and can only press his nose against the shop window being unable to obtain the assistance of the court because he has become a trespasser entitled to no rights and to no relief. The farce in the present case when the landlords occupied the premises for four hours should not be allowed to defeat the statutory rights of the tenants.

The right conferred by s 146(2) on a tenant to apply for relief against forfeiture may without violence to the language, be construed as a right to apply 'where a lessor proceeds, by action or otherwise' to enforce a right of re-entry. So construed, s 146(2) enables the tenant to apply for relief whenever and however the landlord claims that the lease has been determined for breach of covenant. I have no doubt that this was the object and intention and is the effect of s 146.

In *Quilter v Mapleson* (1882) 9 QBD 672 a landlord forfeited a lease before the Act of 1881 came into force by issuing and serving a writ for possession. He recovered judgment, the tenant appealed and the Act of 1881 came into force before the appeal was heard. The Court of Appeal held that the Act was retrospective and granted relief to the tenant. Lindley LJ, at 676, decided that s 146(2) was applicable:

> The action was brought by the landlord on the ground of breaches committed before the Act, and he obtained judgment before the Act came into operation, but execution was stayed, so that he has never obtained possession. The original action then is not yet at an end ... So long as the tenant has not been turned out of possession he is within the terms of the enactment, for the lessor is proceeding to enforce his right of re-entry. The enactment then being in terms retrospective must be construed according to its terms as being retrospective.

The judgments of Sir George Jessel MR and Bowen LJ were to the like effect and it is now settled law that where a landlord forfeits a lease by issuing and serving a writ for possession the tenant may apply for relief before but not after the landlord has recovered judgment and re-entered. But although the court limited the time during which a tenant could apply for relief against forfeiture constituted by the issue and service of the writ, the court had no power and in my opinion did not intend to deprive a tenant of any right to apply for relief after a forfeiture constituted by re-entry without judgment. *Quilter v Mapleson* is authority for a case where the landlord forfeits by issue and service of a writ but is not authority for a case where the landlord forfeits by re-entry.

In *Rogers v Rice* [1892] 2 Ch 170, a landlord forfeited by the issue and service of a writ, recovered judgment and re-entered pursuant to the writ of possession then issued and was held to be no longer 'proceeding by action' within s 146(2). The tenant sought and was refused leave to set aside the verdict and the judgment. The tenant later issued an originating summons seeking relief from forfeiture under s 146(2). Lord Coleridge CJ said that a s 146 notice had been given and ignored, and continued, at pp 171–72:

> The action proceeded to judgment, the judgment was executed, so far as possession was concerned, and at the time when the present proceeding was commenced the lessor was in possession. The action then, so far as related to enforcing the right of re-entry, was at end, and it cannot be said that the landlord was 'proceeding' to enforce his right of re-entry. The case is clear on the terms of the Act, but I cannot omit to notice that the same view was taken by the judges of the Court of Appeal in *Quilter v Mapleson,* 9 QBD 672 at 677, where all three judges gave their opinion to this effect, though that was not the point on which their decision turned.

The decision can be supported on the grounds that no court could properly exercise its discretion to relieve against forfeiture after the landlord had issued and served a writ, recovered judgment in the action and entered into possession pursuant to that judgment. The decision can also be supported on the grounds set out in the speech of my noble and learned friend, Lord Oliver of Aylmerton. But the court had no power and in my opinion did not intend to deprive a tenant of any right to apply for relief after a forfeiture constituted by re-entry without judgment.

In *Pakwood Transport Ltd v 15, Beauchamp Place Ltd* (1977) 36 P & CR 112, the Court of Appeal rejected an argument by a landlord who had served a s 146 notice that the tenant could not apply for relief from forfeiture until proceedings for forfeiture had been instituted by the landlord. All three Lords Justices derived from *Quilter v Mapleson* (1882) 9 QBD 672 and *Rogers v Rice* [1892] 2 Ch 170 the proposition that, in the words of Orr LJ, (1977) 36 P & C R 112 at 117:

> ... a lessee could not apply for relief against re-entry or forfeiture after the landlord had obtained a judgment of the court entitling him to re-enter on a forfeiture; and it is claimed, and in my judgment rightly claimed, that the same principle must apply where the landlord has peaceably recovered possession. In other words, once he has either recovered possession or obtained an order for possession he can no longer be said to be 'proceeding by action or otherwise to enforce a right of re-entry or forfeiture.'

My Lords, I accept that it is now settled law that a tenant cannot apply for relief after the landlord has recovered judgment for possession and has re-entered in reliance on that judgment. But I do not accept that any court has deprived or is entitled to deprive a tenant of any right to apply for relief if the landlord proceeds to forfeit otherwise than by an action instituted for that purpose.

Orr LJ continued, at 117:

> On this basis the argument for the lessor appears to me to involve an absurdity, in that if the landlord has done no more than serve a s 146 notice, it is too early for the tenant to apply for relief; but if the landlord's next step is peaceably to recover possession, it is then too late for the tenant to apply. For my part, I am not prepared to accept an argument which leads to this absurdity, and I have no hesitation in holding that a landlord who serves a s 146 notice is at that stage 'proceeding to enforce a right of re-entry or forfeiture' in that the service of such a notice is a step which the law requires him to take in order to re-enter or forfeit.

My Lords, I accept the conclusion that a landlord who serves a notice under s 146(1) can be said, for the purposes of s 146(2) to be proceeding to enforce his rights under the lease. A tenant authorised by s 146(2) to apply to the court for relief against forfeiture if he fails to comply with a s 146 notice may make that application after service of the notice for the purpose of elucidating the issues raised by the notice, ascertaining the intentions of the landlord, and setting in train the machinery by which the dispute between the landlord and the tenant can be determined by negotiation or by the court. But the fact that the tenant may apply to the court for relief after service of the s 146 notice does not mean that if he does not do so he loses the right conferred on him by s 146(2) to apply for relief if and when the landlord proceeds, not by action but 'otherwise' by exercising a right of re-entry. No absurdity follows from a construction which allows the tenant to apply for relief before and after a landlord re-enters without first obtaining a court order.

In the words of Laskin JA in *In Re Rexdale Investments Ltd and Gibson* [1967] 1 OR 251 at 259 dealing with provisions in the Ontario legislation indistinguishable from s 146(2), the argument that a tenant cannot apply for relief after a landlord has determined the lease by re-entry:

> ... depends on a detached grammatical reading of the phrase 'is proceeding' ... which makes nonsense of the phrase 'or otherwise' (as covering physical re-entry) by making ineffective, in any practical sense, the provision for relief from forfeiture applicable to such re-entry. We do not construe statutes, especially when they are remedial ... to the point of self-contradiction. In my opinion, the phrase 'is proceeding' is more properly read in the sense of 'has proceeded,' and I am fortified in this view by the fact that the exercise of the power of termination is manifested effectively by the mere taking of proceedings as well as by physical re-entry. What [s 146(2)] means, therefore, is that when the landlord has terminated the lease by action or by actual re-entry without action, the tenant may seek relief from forfeiture in the pending action, if any, or, if none, by proceedings initiated by him. In the latter case, one would expect prompt reaction by the tenant ... The English cases relied on ... [*Rogers v Rice* [1892] 2 Ch 170; *Locke v Pearce* [1893] 2 Ch 271 and *Quilter v Mapleson* (1882) 9 QBD 672] are distinguishable, if need be ... by the fact ... that they relate to re-entry in pursuance of a judgment for possession.

These observations by a distinguished Canadian judge who subsequently became Chief Justice of the Supreme Court of Canada, support the views which I have formed concerning the construction of s 146 and the ambit and effect of the earlier decisions.

Mr Reid argued that your Lordships should not interfere with 19th century decisions and for my part I do not intend to do so on this occasion or to question the result of the decision of the Court of Appeal in *Pakwood Transport Ltd v 15, Beauchamp Place Ltd* (1977) 36 P & CR 112. But the authorities were never directed to the point now in issue and certainly never decided that issue.

It was suggested that Parliament in 1925 accepted the views expressed in the 19th century cases. I agree that Parliament accepted that a tenant cannot apply for relief under s 146(2) after the landlord has forfeited the lease by issuing and serving a writ for possession and in his action has recovered and enforced judgment. The 19th century cases were not directed to the problem which has now emerged.

We were informed that the researches of counsel had not disclosed any reported case in which a landlord has forfeited by re-entry and then successfully denied the right of the tenant to apply for relief.

The landlords or their advisers, perhaps incensed by the activities of the tenants in the present case, conceived and carried out a dawn raid which fortunately did not result in bloodshed. Since the decision of the Court of Appeal in the instant case there has been a proliferation of s 146 notices followed by pressure on tenants to surrender on terms favourable to the landlord. If this appeal were not allowed, the only safe advice for a tenant would be to issue proceedings for relief against forfeiture as soon as a s 146 notice is received at a time when the tenant cannot know whether relief will be necessary. A tenant ignorant of the development in the law pioneered by the landlords in the present case will be at the mercy of an aggressive landlord. The conclusions which I have reached will not entail these consequences and will not again involve Parliament in correcting judicial constructions of statute by further legislation.

The results of s 146 and the authorities are as follows. A tenant may apply for appropriate declarations and for relief from forfeiture under s 146(2) after the issue of a s 146 notice but he is not prejudiced if he does not do so. A tenant cannot apply for relief after a landlord has forfeited a lease by issuing and serving a writ, has recovered judgment and has entered into possession pursuant to that judgment. If the judgment is set aside or successfully appealed the tenant will be able to apply for relief in the landlord's action but the court in deciding whether to grant relief will take into account any consequences of the original order and repossession and the delay of the tenant. A tenant may apply for relief after a landlord has forfeited by re-entry without first obtaining a court order for that purpose but the court in deciding whether to grant relief will take into account all the circumstances, including delay, on the part of the tenant. Any past judicial observations which might suggest that a tenant is debarred from applying for relief after the landlord has re-entered without first obtaining a court order for that purpose are not to be so construed.

I would therefore allow the appeal and set aside the orders of the trial judge and the Court of Appeal.

9 DISCHARGE OF LEASEHOLD COVENANTS: ABANDONMENT

A covenant may be discharged through abandonment. If over a long course of usage, the tenant has acted inconsistently with the continuance of the covenant, the court can infer some legal proceeding which has put an end to the covenant in order to show that the usage has been and is now lawful, and not wrongful.[209] Thus, where the covenant required the lessee to erect one or more villa residences only, but parts of the leasehold land had been used to build high-rise multi-storey apartment blocks over a long period of time in breach of the covenant and the lessor was aware of the breach which was wholly inconsistent with the continued reliance on the covenant, the covenant was abandoned.[210]

209 *Hepworth v Pickles* [1900] 1 Ch 108 at 110, *per* Farwell J.

210 *AG of Hong Kong v Fairfax Ltd* [1997] 1 WLR 149, PC.

10 REFORM

At least three areas of leasehold covenants have been the subject matter of the Law Commission Reports. The first[211] relates to the landlord and tenant's continuing contractual liability and this has led to the passage of the Landlord and Tenant (Covenants) Act 1995, which has been discussed earlier. The second and the third relate to the current law on forfeiture and distress respectively.

Forfeiture

The Law Commission published a report in 1985 ('The First Report')[212] making recommendations for the simplification of the law of forfeiture. This report has not been acted upon by the legislature and the Law Commission has now published a second report[213] making proposals for the implementation of the recommendation in their First Report, with some modifications. The summary of the combined recommendations of the two reports are set out below.

Landlord and Tenant Law: Termination of Tenancies Bill (Law Com No 221, 1 February 1994)

Appendix B – Summary of Recommendations

This Appendix sets out the summary of recommendations relating to the landlords' termination order scheme contained in the First Report.[214] Where appropriate, we refer to the modifications proposed in the present Report to those recommendations ...

PART I GENERAL INTRODUCTION

(1) The law of forfeiture has become unnecessarily complicated, is no longer coherent and gives rise to injustices. The report recommends its replacement by a new system. [Para 1.3]

...

PART III DEFECTS IN THE PRESENT LAW AND AN OUTLINE OF OUR RECOMMENDATIONS

(2) Now that re-entry usually occurs constructively by the commencement of legal proceedings (actual re-entry being unlawful in many cases), and relief is usually available, it is anomalous that the tenancy should be ended in this way. In particular:

(a) The landlord's proceedings have to be framed as proceedings for possession when in reality they are proceedings designed to terminate the tenancy.

211 Law Commission, Landlord and Tenant: Privity of Contract and Estate (Law Com No 174, 29 November 1988); [1989] Conv 145 (Wilkinson, HW); (1991) 11 Legal Studies 47 (Thorton).

212 Law Commission, Codification of the Law of Landlord and Tenant: Forfeiture of Tenancies (Law Com No 142, 21 March 1985). See [1986] Conv 165 (Smith, PF); (1987) 84 LSG 1042 (Cherryman, J).

213 Landlord and Tenant Law: Termination of Tenancies Bill (Law Com No 221, 1 February 1994).

214 Report on Forfeiture of Tenancies (1985) Law Com No 142.

(b) During the period between the re-entry and the resolution of the legal proceedings, the position of the parties is unsatisfactory and equivocal. The doctrine of re-entry should be abolished and replaced by a scheme under which, apart from termination by agreement, court proceedings would always be necessary in principle to end a tenancy and the tenancy would continue in full force until the court ordered its termination. Such a scheme would have further advantages:

(1) It would serve to extend the principle of s 2 of the Protection from Eviction Act 1977.

(2) The landlord's primary right to end the tenancy would be merged with the tenant's (largely statutory) right to seek relief so as to produce a single principle: that the landlord has no right to terminate, but only a right to seek from the court a termination order which the court has a discretion to grant or to refuse.

(3) It would pave the way for reform of the law of waiver, which can take place only after the removal of the artificialities inherent in the doctrine of re-entry. [Paras 3.2–3.10]

(3) Under the present law there are two almost wholly distinct sets of rules for the granting of relief to a tenant: one for cases where he has failed to pay rent, and the other for cases where he has broken some other obligation. The scheme incorporates a uniform set of rules applicable to all cases. [Paras 3.11–3.13]

(4) Other defects exist in the present law – for example:

(a) The rule that a landlord cannot forfeit for breach of covenant unless there is a forfeiture clause serves only to add verbiage which should be unnecessary.

(b) The implied condition whereby a tenancy may be ended for denial of title is outdated.

(c) The law about relief against forfeiture has a number of detailed defects: and the parties' rights differ according as proceedings are taken in the High Court or a county court.

(d) The law about formal demand for rent is obsolete.

(e) The exceptional cases in which (under s 146(8)–(10) of the Law of Property Act 1925 the tenant is debarred from claiming relief are a source of potential unfairness and need not be reproduced.

(f) The general requirement (under s 146(1) of the Law of Property Act 1925) that preliminary notice be served on a tenant prior to forfeiture proceedings causes difficulties and uncertainties and need not be retained in its present form.

(g) Although a special notice regime should be retained for cases involving lack of repair, there is no justification for the two separate regimes which now exist (under s 147 of the Law of Property Act 1925, and the Leasehold Property Repairs Act 1938).

(h) The fact that a breach of covenant, once remedied, cannot be the subject of forfeiture proceedings, is unfair to the landlord, particularly since it may prevent the tenancy being ended for persistent breaches (for example, of the covenant to pay rent).

(i) Conversely, the doctrine of 'stigma', which leads to the almost automatic refusal of relief in particular classes of case, is unfair to the tenant.

(j) The rules about relief for sub-tenants and other derivative interest holders are in several ways inadequate.

(k) The court's present inability to grant relief to fewer than all of a number of joint tenants should be removed. [Paras 3.14-3.23]

DETAILS OF THE LANDLORDS' TERMINATION ORDER SCHEME PROPOSED TERMINATION ON THE APPLICATION OF THE LANDLORD

PART IV PRELIMINARY

(6) The scheme is based upon a system under which there would be no distinction between termination for non-payment of rent and termination for other reasons and under which the tenancy would continue in full force until the court made an order – a 'termination order' – determining the date on which it should end. [Para 4.1]

(7) It is not, however, inherent in the scheme that a full court hearing would take place in every case: a tenant who realised that his tenancy would inevitably be terminated could surrender it; and it would be possible for the landlord, under appropriate rules of court, to obtain summary judgment. [Paras 4.2 and 4.3]

(8) The scheme should apply to existing tenancies as well as future ones (subject only to the transitional provisions mentioned in paras (99)–(102) of this Summary). [Paras 4.4 and 4.5]

(9) To remove any possible doubt, it should be made clear that a tenancy cannot terminate, outside the scheme, through the doctrine of repudiatory breach. [Paras 4.6 and 4.7]

PART V GROUNDS FOR A TERMINATION ORDER: 'TERMINATION ORDER EVENTS'

(10) Grounds on which the landlord may base an application for a termination order may conveniently be called 'termination order events'. They should be of three kinds. [Para 5.1]

(a) Breaches of covenant

(11) All breaches of covenant by the tenant should be termination order events. We use the word 'covenant' in the wide sense, to include all the obligations owed by tenant to landlord, whether they are expressly undertaken or implied at common law or by statute. [Para 5.2]

(12) Although under the present law breaches of covenant are grounds for forfeiture only if they are expressly made so by the inclusion in the tenancy of a 'forfeiture clause', no such special provision should be necessary to make them termination order events. But:

(a) This should not apply to tenancies granted before the date on which the implementing legislation comes into force: in such tenancies a breach of covenant should be a termination order event only if covered by a forfeiture clause. [Paras 5.3–5.6]

(b) If a tenancy, though granted after that date, is granted in pursuance of a binding obligation in existence before that date, and the obligation was such that a forfeiture clause was not to be included (or was not to be included in relation to some of the tenant's covenants) then the obligation should be interpreted as requiring the inclusion of an express term excluding the termination order scheme in relation to the tenant's covenants (or some of them as the case may be). [Para 5.8]

(13) Where an obligation entered into before the date on which the implementing legislation comes into force was such that a forfeiture clause was to be included in a tenancy granted after that date, that requirement should be treated as fulfilled if the tenancy maintains silence on the point, so allowing breaches of covenant to be termination order events. [Para 5.9]

(b) Disguised breaches of covenant

(14) Termination order events should also include all events on the happening of which the tenancy (whether through the inclusion of a condition or limitation or for any other reason) is to cease (whether immediately or after a period) or the landlord is to have the right (whether or not on notice) to apply for a termination order, to forfeit the tenancy or to bring it to an end in any other way or to require its surrender or its assignment to a person nominated or to be nominated by him – [being events against which a landlord would be expected to protect himself (if he protected himself at all) through the imposition of a covenant upon the tenant and including (but without prejudice to the generality of the foregoing words) all events which consist in or result from any of the matters listed in para 5.18.] [Para 5.18, and see paras 5.10–5.17]

NOTE: In accordance with para 2.4 of the present Report, the draft Bill does not implement the part of the above recommendation in square brackets.

(c) Insolvency events

(15) Termination order events should also include all events on the happening of which the tenancy (whether through the inclusion of a condition, limitation or for any other reason) is to cease (whether immediately or after a period) or the landlord is to have the right (whether or not on notice) to apply for a termination order, to forfeit the tenancy or bring it to an end in any other way, or to require its surrender or its assignment to a person nominated or to be nominated by him - being events having to do with the actual or threatened bankruptcy or insolvency of the tenant or any surety and including (but without prejudice to the generality of the foregoing words): bankruptcy of, or the commission of any act of bankruptcy by, or the making of a receiving order against, a tenant or surety who is an individual; entering into liquidation, compulsory or voluntary, by any tenant or surety which is a company, or having a receiver appointed in respect of any of its assets; a tenant or surety entering into any arrangement or composition for the benefit of creditors; or a tenant suffering the tenancy to be taken in execution; or a tenant or surety suffering any distress or execution to be levied on goods. [Para 5.20; and see para 5.19]

Special considerations

(a) Non-payment of rent

(16) The law which now prescribes the circumstances in which a tenancy may be forfeited for non-payment of rent is unsatisfactory and is usually circumvented by the inclusion

in the tenancy of a 'dispensing term'. In future, non-payment of rent should become a termination order event without formal demand after 21 days (whether or not there is a dispensing term) – unless there is a dispensing term and it provides in this respect for a period different from 21 days, in which case the different period should apply. [Paras 5.21–5.26]

(17) The recommendation summarised in the preceding paragraph should apply whether the tenancy is granted before or after the coming into force of the implementing legislation. [Para 5.28]

(b) *Denial of title*

(18) In tenancies granted after the implementing legislation comes into force, there should no longer be an implied term to the effect that the tenant should not deny or disclaim the landlord's title; and any such term implied in a tenancy granted before that time should be ineffective. But this should not prevent the inclusion of, or render ineffective, any express term to similar effect. [Paras 5.32–5.35]

(c) *Severance of the tenancy*

(19) If parts of premises originally held as a whole under a single tenancy have been the subject of separate assignments to different people, a tenant of any one part should be at risk of termination proceedings in respect only of termination order events occurring in relation to that part. [Paras 5.36–5.38]

(d) *Should there be exceptions?*

(20) All events falling within the general definition of termination order events should attract the court's discretionary powers which correspond with its power to grant relief under the present law. The existing exceptions to the court's relief-giving powers under s 146(8)–(10) of the Law of Property Act 1925 should have no counterpart in the proposed scheme. [Paras 5.39–5.57]

PART VI WAIVER

(21) The law which now governs the circumstances in which a landlord is debarred by waiver from forfeiting a tenancy on a particular ground is unsatisfactory. A termination order event should be regarded as waived if, and only if, the landlord's conduct, after he has knowledge of the event, is such that it would lead a reasonable tenant to believe, and does in fact lead the actual tenant to believe, that he will not seek a termination order on the ground of that event. [Para 6.8]

(22) And if the event is a continuing breach of covenant, it should be a question of fact whether and how far the landlord has led the tenant reasonably to believe that he has waived it for the future as well as for the past. [Paras 6.8 and 6.9]

(23) It should be possible, according to analogous rules, for the landlord to grant a waiver which is conditional upon some action on the part of the tenant. [Para 6.10]

PART VII BREACHES SHOULD REMAIN GROUNDS FOR TERMINATION PROCEEDINGS EVEN THOUGH 'REMEDIED'

(24) A termination order event should generally remain available as a ground for a termination order despite the fact that its consequences may have been remedied. [Para 7.13; and see Part VII generally]

PART VIII STARTING PROCEEDINGS: TIME LIMITS AND NOTICES

(25) The landlord's right to start termination order proceedings on the ground of a termination order event should exist for only six months after he has actual knowledge of the facts constituting that event. If, however, the event is a continuing breach of covenant, and the breach continues after the landlord is first aware of it, the six month period should run from the date on which the breach was last continuing. (Extension of the six month period would be possible by use of the procedure mentioned in paras (29)–(32) of this Summary.) [Para 8.3; and see paras 8.1–8.19 generally]

Preliminary notice to the tenant

(a) No general requirement of notice

(26) There should be no general requirement such as now exists under s 146(1) of the Law of Property Act 1925, for the landlord to give notice to the tenant before starting termination proceedings. [Para 8.29; and see paras 8.21–8.32 generally]

(b) Compulsory notice procedure for repairs

(27) But in certain cases involving want of repair by the tenant, the giving of preliminary notice should be compulsory and, if the tenant served a counter-notice, the landlord should not be permitted to start termination proceedings unless he obtained the leave of the court. The full details of this new repairs regime are to be found in paras 8.33–8.60 of the Report and are not summarised here. The new regime is intended to supersede both the Leasehold Property (Repairs) Act 1938 and s 147 of the Law of Property Act 1925 and is based primarily on the former. [Paras 8.33–8.60]

(28) Since both the enactments mentioned in the preceding paragraph apply not only when the landlord wishes to forfeit but also when he claims damages for the breach of a repairing covenant, the new repairs regime should apply also to cases of claims to damages. [Paras 8.62–8.66]

(c) Optional notice procedure in other cases

(29) The landlord should have power in other cases, within the six months' time limit, to serve on the tenant a notice giving full particulars of the termination order event alleged and requiring specified remedial action. He should be entitled, but not bound, to specify a time for its completion. [The effect of such a notice would be to extend the time limit for starting legal proceedings: in general it should then end on a date six months after the service of the notice; but if the notice specified a time for the completion of the remedial action, the period should end on a date three months after the expiry of this time, if that date were later.] [Paras 8.67 and 8.68]

NOTE: The present Report modifies the part of the above recommendation in square brackets. The landlord's right to start proceedings would be suspended, and then revive, for a certain period. If the notice specified a period for the completion of the remedial action, the landlord's right would be suspended until the end of that period. If it did not specify such a period, his right to start proceedings would be suspended for six months after the service of the notice. After the end of the suspension period, the landlord would have three months during which he could start proceedings. This three months' time limit would not apply in the case of a breach of covenant which was still continuing when the period of suspension ended. [Para 2.15]

(30) A landlord's notice should be valid for this purpose if the remedial action which he specifies is within the range of action on which the court could suspend a remedial termination order (see para (44) of this Summary) and he has made a reasonable attempt to specify action which is appropriate to the situation. [Para 8.69]

(31) If the notice were served and complied with, the landlord should be debarred from obtaining a termination order of any kind on the strength of the event in question. But if compliance did not take place until after the landlord had properly begun termination proceedings, a termination order should be possible and the tenant might in any event be ordered to pay the costs. [Para 8.71]

(32) Incentives to use the optional notice procedure would be provided by the recommendations mentioned in paras (52) and (55) of this Summary. [Para 8.72]

(d) Notices: mode of service

(33) Having regard to the limited scope of this report, we propose no change in the law relating to the giving of notices, but recommend that the existing rules in s 196 of the Law of Property Act 1925, and s 18(2) of the Landlord and Tenant Act 1927, should apply. [Para 8.73–8.76]

NOTE: The present Report (para 2.26) modifies this recommendation in relation to abandoned premises: see note to recommendation (88) below.

PART IX THE COURT'S POWERS AT THE HEARING

Preliminary Matters

(a) The primary claim

(34) The landlord's main claim will simply be for 'a termination order'. [Para 9.2]

(b) Ancillary claims

(i) Costs incurred in relation to the termination order event

(35) If a termination order event has occurred, the tenant should be liable to repay any reasonable costs incurred by the landlord in ascertaining the existence and nature of the event and in deciding upon his course of action including the fees of a surveyor, valuer, legal adviser or other expert, and including such costs incurred in the preparation and service of a notice in those cases in which a notice is compulsory or voluntary (see paras (27)–(32) of this Summary). But if the tenant serves a counter-notice under the new repairs regime (see paras (27) and (28) of this Summary) then, notwithstanding any express term of the tenancy, the tenant's liability for such costs should not arise unless the landlord makes an application to proceed and, on such application, the court should have power to nullify or vary such liability. [Para 9.9; and see paras 9.4–9.10]

(ii) Rent

(36) Since the tenancy would not end until the date on which the court ordered that it should, rent would (subject only to the recommendation made in relation to 'respite' periods in para (4.1) of this Summary) remain payable until that date. In termination order proceedings the court should be bound at the landlord's request to order the tenant to pay rent. [Para 9.12(a)]

(37) If the tenant wrongfully retained possession for any period after the date on which the tenancy terminated, he would be liable to pay *mesne* profits during that period. But their amount should be taken to correspond with the amount of the rent unless fixed by the court at a higher figure on proof of value. [Para 9.12(b)]

(iii) Damages, injunction, etc

(38) If the court granted a remedial termination order (see paras (43) and (53) of this Summary) or refused a termination order altogether, it should have a power analogous to that in s 146(2) of the Law of Property Act 1925, enabling it to grant an injunction against the tenant, or order him to pay damages. [Paras 9.13 and 9.14]

(39) An absolute order, a remedial order and declining to make either order, may be combined with an ancillary order where appropriate.

The choices open to the court

(a) Absolute order

(40) An absolute order would reflect the court's view (arrived at in accordance with recommended criteria (see para (51) of this Summary)) that the tenancy should end without any further chances being offered to the tenant. [Para 9.15]

(41) An absolute order would have the effect of terminating the tenancy on a date specified in the order. In general, the date so specified should be the date on which the tenant is to give possession of the property let and the order should specifically require him to do so; but in setting the date the court should have full power to let him retain possession for a limited period after the hearing by way of respite. And during any such respite period the court should have power to vary the terms on which the tenant should be allowed to occupy the property and in particular to order that rent at a rate higher than the rent reserved should be payable. If, however, the tenant would be able to retain possession in any event under the Rent Act 1977, the Rent (Agriculture) Act 1976, the Housing Act 1980 [or the Housing Act 1988], then the date specified in the termination order for the ending of the tenancy should be the date on which the order is made. In this case, the order should not require the giving of possession and it should be made clear to the tenant that possession need not be given. [Paras 9.16–9.20]

(42) An absolute termination order could be combined with orders for the payment of costs incurred in reference to the termination order event (para (35) above), of rent (para (36)), or of damages for breach of covenant. [Para 9.20]

(b) Remedial order

(43) A remedial order would have the effect of ending the tenancy if, but only if, the tenant failed to take specified remedial action within a specified time. [Para 9.21]

(44) No exhaustive definition of remedial action is proposed, but it should specifically include:

(a) Making any payment to the landlord or any other person. This payment might be arrears of rent (para (36) of this Summary) or general costs (para (54)), or other payments due under the tenancy, or a payment of costs incurred in relation to the termination order event (para (35)) or of damages (para (38)). Although damages could not be recovered in respect of an event which was not a breach of covenant (eg breach of condition) the court should have power to suspend a remedial order upon the payment by the tenant of compensation in respect of such an event. (b) In the case of a termination order event which is a continuing breach of covenant, discontinuing the breach.

(c) In the case of any termination order event, taking action appropriate to rectify the consequences of the event.

(d) In the case of a termination order event which is an insolvency event (para (15) of this Summary), making an assignment of the tenancy which is permitted according to its terms.

(e) In the case of a termination order event which consists in the assignment or partial assignment of the tenancy, making a re-assignment to the former tenant.

(f) In the case of any termination order event, finding a satisfactory surety or replacement surety. [Para 9.23]

(45) The remedial order should specify a date on which the tenancy is to terminate if the remedial action has not been taken, and should automatically require the tenant to give possession on that date in those circumstances. Normally the date so fixed will be the date by which it is reasonable for the tenant to have completed the remedial action, but the court should have power to fix a later date if it wished the tenant to have a further period by way of respite. [Para 9.25]

(46) If, however, the tenant will enjoy statutory security of tenure after the termination of the contractual tenancy, the question of a period of respite does not arise; and in this case the order should not require the giving of possession but should make it clear, on the contrary, that possession need not be given. [Para 9.26]

(47) In all cases the court, having fixed the date, should have power, whether before or after it has passed, and provided only that possession has not actually been regained, to substitute a later date if circumstances were thought to justify a postponement. [Para 9.27]

NOTE: The present Report recommends that the legislation should make it clear that any application by a tenant for a later date to be substituted should be made before the current date for taking the remedial action has passed. It also recommends that the court should have power to substitute a new date for complying with the remedial order on a limited number of grounds. These grounds are external circumstances beyond the tenant's control, other than his financial circumstances, which were not previously taken into account by the court in fixing the date for compliance. [Paras 2.9–2.11]

(48) There should be no counterpart in the scheme of the present rule that the High Court has jurisdiction to grant relief, in a case involving non-payment of rent, at any time within six months after execution of the judgment. [Para 9.30]

(49) Even if a remedial order were not conditional on the payment of costs incurred in relation to the termination order event (para (35) of this Summary), or of rent (para (36)), or of damages etc (para (35)), it could be combined with an order for the payment of these sums. [Para 9.31]

(c) No order

(50) The court should also have power to refuse a termination order altogether. A decision to this effect would not preclude the making of an order for payment of any of the sums mentioned in the preceding paragraph. [Para 9.32]

Guidelines for the court's decision

(a) When the court should make an absolute order

(51) An absolute order should be made if, and only if:

(1) the court is satisfied, by reason of the serious character of any termination order events occurring during the tenure of the present tenant, or by reason of their frequency, or by a combination of both factors, that he is so unsatisfactory a tenant that he ought not in all the circumstances to remain tenant of the property; or

(2) the court is satisfied that an assignment of the tenancy has been made in order to forestall the making of an absolute order under Case (1) above, that there is a substantial risk of the continuance or recurrence of the state of affairs giving rise to a termination order event on which the proceedings are founded, and that the new tenant ought not in all the circumstances to remain a tenant of the property; or

(3) where a termination order event on which the proceedings are founded is a wrongful assignment, or is an insolvency event, the court is satisfied that no remedial action which it could order would be adequate and satisfactory to the landlord; or

(4) the court, though it would wish to make a remedial order, is not satisfied that the tenant is willing, and is likely to be able, to carry out the remedial action which would be required of him. [Paras 9.33–9.49]

(52) As to the Case (4) above, if the landlord has given the tenant time (whether by means of a preliminary notice or otherwise) to take full remedial action before the hearing, and the tenant has not done so, the court should take that fact into account in deciding whether he would be willing, and is likely to be able, to take the remedial action on which a remedial order would be suspended. [Para 9.50]

(b) When the court should make a remedial order or no order

(53) If the court does not make an absolute order, it should make a remedial one unless one of the following situations exists, in which case it should decline to make any termination order:

(a) Remedial action has already been taken.

(b) Remedial action is impossible or unnecessary.

(c) Remedial action ought not in all the circumstances to be required. [Para 9.51]

Distress

Law Commission, Landlord and Tenant: Distress for Rent (Law Com No 194, 4 February 1991)[215]

Part VI – Summary of Recommendations

6.2 We recommend that distress for rent should be abolished (Para 3.1).

6.3 Our recommendations relating to the application of the new legislation are:

(i) There should be no exception to the abolition of distress for rent for any type of landlord or tenancy (Para 3.28).

(ii) All forms of distress for rent should be abolished including rent payable under a rentcharge (Paras 4.2 and 4.3).

(iii) Distress in cases where the common law right to distrain for rent has been extended by agreement or statute should also be abolished (Para 4.4).

(iv) Once distress for rent has been abolished it should not be open to people to contract to adopt distress (Para 4.8).

(v) The Act implementing these recommendations should not come into force until six months after Royal Assent to allow landlords time to familiarise themselves with provisions and to consider changes in rent collection practices (para 4.10).

(vi) Where the process of distress for rent has begun at the date of commencement of the new legislation, the landlord should be permitted to continue it if goods have been removed from the premises or are subject to a walking possession agreement (Para 4.12).

(vii) The Bill should bind the Crown (Para 4.15).

6.5 We also recommend that a landlord claiming rent arrears should be able to claim any further arrears which accrued due between the date of commencement of the proceedings and the date of judgment. The court should be able to give judgment for the further arrears whether or not it gives judgment for the arrears due when the proceedings commenced. Implementation of this recommendation need not be delayed until the implementation of the recommendation to abolish distress for rent.

215 See also (1992) 45 CLP 81 (Clarke, A).

CHAPTER 10

LICENCES

1 INTRODUCTION

'By the laws of England, every invasion of land, be it ever so minute, is a trespass. No man can set his foot upon my ground without my licence.'[1] Thus, a licence is a purely personal permission given by the owner or occupier of land to a person to do something on that land which would otherwise be a trespass.[2] Examples of licences are a permission given to a boy to recover his ball from the garden, to play cricket on the licensor's land, to enter the licensor's land to carry felled timber away, to enjoy exclusive possession of a building for an indefinite period which would have been a lease if the period has been definite, rights of lodgers and guests in a hotel, exclusive right to supply refreshments in a theatre,[3] permission to view a race at Doncaster grandstand[4] or a film in a cinema.[5]

As we have seen, a licence is different from a lease[6] and, as will be seen, it is also different from an easement.[7] Unlike a lease or an easement, the traditional common law view is that a licence, being a defence to an action for trespass, does not create any proprietary interest. 'A dispensation or licence properly passeth no interest, nor alters or transfers property in any thing, but only makes an action lawful, which without it had been unlawful.'[8] It is not capable of binding a purchaser.[9] The purchaser can require the licensee to leave the land regardless of whether he takes the land for value or by way of gift, and whether he has notice of the licence or not. The licensee's only remedy, if any, is against the licensor.[10]

Furthermore, as has been seen, a licensee is not protected under s 1(1) of the Rent Act 1977.[11] He cannot grant a tenancy[12] or a sub-licence.[13] Neither can he sue in trespass or nuisance.[14]

---

1 *Entick v Carrington* (1765) 2 Wils KB 275 at 291; 95 ER 807 at 817, *per* Lord Camden CJ.

2 *Thomas v Sorrell* (1673) Vaugh 330 at 351.

3 *Frank Warr & Co Ltd v LCC* [1904] 1 KB 713.

4 *Wood v Leadbitter* (1845) 13 M & W 838.

5 *Hurst v Picture Theatres Ltd* [1915] 1 KB 1.

6 See Chapter 8.

7 See Chapter 15.

8 *Thomas v Sorrell* (1673) Vaugh 330 at 351; 124 ER 1098 at 1109.

9 *Clore v Theatrical Properties Ltd and Westby & Co Ltd* [1936] 3 All ER 4

10 *King v David Allen & Sons Billposting Ltd* [1916] 2 AC 54.

11 See Chapter 8, p 387.

12 He may create a tenancy by estoppel: *London Borough of Camden v Shortlife Community Housing* (1992) 90 LGR 358 at 381.

13 *Goldsack v Shore* [1950] 1 KB 708 at 714.

14 *Malone v Laskey* [1907] 2 KB 141 at 151 (nuisance); *Hill v Tupper* (1863) 2 H & C 121 at 127; 159 ER 51 at 53 (disturbance of exclusive right to put pleasure boats in a canal).

2 TYPES OF LICENCES

There are four types of licence: bare licences, contractual licences, licences coupled with an interest, and licences by proprietary estoppel. The last type is a recent creation of equity.

Bare licences

A bare licence is a simple permission granted otherwise than for valuable consideration. The licensee will not be a trespasser unless he goes beyond the geographical or temporal limit of the permission granted.[15] As Scutton LJ put it in *The Carlgarth*,[16] 'When you invite a person into your house to use the staircase, you do not invite him to slide down the banisters'. Likewise, if the licensee has entered land for a purpose other than that for which he is permitted or, having lawfully entered land, begins to pursue some unauthorised purpose, he becomes a trespasser.[17]

A bare licence may be granted expressly, as when a person is invited to a dinner or party, or impliedly. 'When a householder lives in a dwelling house to which there is a garden in front and does not lock the gate of the garden, it gives an implied licence to any member of the public who has lawful reason for doing so to proceed from the gate to the front door or back door, and to inquire whether he may be admitted and to conduct his lawful business.'[18] A licence may be implied in favour of all citizens, who 'reasonably think that they have' legitimate business, to knock on the door.[19] However, in the absence of clear permission from the occupier, or common law[20] or statutory power,[21] an implied licence 'ends with the knock on the door'.[22] 'The house of every one is to him as his castle and fortress'.[23]

A bare licence is revocable at will at any time without any prior notice,[24] even if it was granted by deed.[25] It is automatically revoked by the death of the licensor or a disposition of his land. Once revoked, the licensee has a reasonable time to pack up and leave the premises.[26]

15 *Hillen and Pettigrew v ICI (Alkali) Ltd* [1936] AC 65 at 69.

16 [1927] P 93 at 110.

17 *Savoy Hotel v BBC* (1983) 133 NLJ 105.

18 *Robson v Hallett* [1967] 2 QB 939, at 953–54.

19 *Lambert v Roberts* [1981] 2 All ER 15 at 19d.

20 *Sandon v Jervis* (1858) EB&E 935 at 940f; 120 ER 758 at 760; *McLorie v Oxford* [1982] QB 1290 at 1296B.

21 For example, ss 8(1), 17(1), 18(1) of the Police and Criminal Evidence Act 1984.

22 *Edwards v Attorney General* [1986] 2 NZLR 232 at 238.

23 *Semayne's* case (1604) 5 Co Rep 91a, at 91b; 77 ER 194 at 195.

24 *Lambert v Roberts* [1981] 2 All ER 15 at 19d.

25 *Wood v Leadbitter* (1845) 13 M & W 838 at 844f; 153 ER 351 at 354.

26 *Robson v Hallet* [1967] 2 QB 939 at 952G–53A.

Licences coupled with an interest

A licence may be granted together with the grant of an interest. For example, a person may be granted a right to hunt deer or cut trees with a licence to enter the land to take away the deer killed or the tree felled. Such a licence is often granted together with the grant of a profit *à prendre*. The interest must have been validly created. This type of licence cannot be revoked until the interest with which it was granted has come to an end.[27]

Contractual licences

A contractual licence is a licence granted for value, for example, a ticket for the cinema[28] or grandstand,[29] temporary parking in a commercial car park,[30] exclusive right to provide refreshments in a theatre.[31] As has been seen, a long term occupancy may also take the form of a licence instead of a tenancy. This is very common as a device by landowners to evade the Rent Acts protection.

The extent of the rights conferred by a contractual licence is largely governed by general contractual principles. Thus, the terms are often expressly agreed, but certain terms may be implied.[32]

A contractual licence is originally recoverable at the will of the licensor.[33]

Wood v Leadbitter (1845) 13 M & W 838

Alderson B: read the judgment of the Court: This was an action tried before my Brother Rolfe at the sittings after last Trinity Term. It was an action for an assault and false imprisonment. The plea (on which alone any question arose) was, that at the time of the alleged trespass the plaintiff was in a certain close of Lord Eglintoun, and the defendant, as the servant of Lord Eglintoun, and by his command, laid his hands upon the plaintiff in order to remove him from the said close, using no unnecessary violence. Replication, that, at the time of such removal, the plaintiff was in the said close by the leave and license of Lord Eglintoun. The leave and license was traversed by the defendant, and issue was joined on that traverse. On the trial it appeared that the place from which the plaintiff was removed by the defendant was the inclosure attached to and surrounding the great stand on the Doncaster race-course; that Lord Eglintoun was steward of the races there in the year 1843; that tickets were sold in the town of Doncaster at one guinea each, which were understood to entitle the holders to come into the stand, and the inclosure surrounding it, and to remain there every day during the races. These tickets were not signed by Lord Eglintoun, but it must be assumed that they were issued with

27 *Palmer v Fletcher* (1663) 1 Lev 122; *Muskett v Hill* (1839) 5 Bing NC 694.

28 *Winter Garden Theatre (London) Ltd v Millennium Productions Ltd* [1948] AC 173; *Hurst v Picture Theatres Ltd* [1915] 1 KB 1.

29 *Wood v Leadbitter* (1845) 13 M & W 838.

30 *Ashby v Tolhurst* [1937] 2 KB 242.

31 *Clore v Theatrical Properties Ltd and Westby & Co Ltd* [1936] 3 All ER 483.

32 *Smith v Nottinghamshire County Council* (1981) *The Times*, 13 November (implied term of quiet enjoyment); *Western Electric Ltd v Welsh Development Agency* [1983] QB 796 (implied term as to fitness of purpose envisaged by the licensee). See (1983) 34 NILQ 349 (Dawson, N); (1983) 80 Law Soc Gaz 2195 (Wilkinson, HW); [1983] Conv 319 (JEM).

33 *Wood v Leadbitter* (1845) 13 M & W 838.

his privity. It further appeared, that the plaintiff, having purchased one of these tickets, came to the stand during the races of the year 1843, and was there or in the inclosure while the races were going on, and while there, and during the races, the defendant, by the order of Lord Eglintoun, desired him to depart, and gave him notice that if he did not go away, force would be used to turn him out. It must be assumed that the plaintiff had in no respect misconducted himself, and that, if he had not been required to depart, his coming upon and remaining in the inclosure would have been an act justified by his purchase of the ticket. The plaintiff refused to go, and thereupon the defendant, by order of Lord Eglintoun, forced him out, without returning the guinea, using no unnecessary violence.

My Brother Rolfe, in directing the jury, told them, that, even assuming the ticket to have been sold to the plaintiff under the sanction of Lord Eglintoun, still it was lawful for Lord Eglintoun, without returning the guinea, and without assigning any reason for what he did, to order the plaintiff to quit the inclosure, and that, if the jury were satisfied that notice was given by Lord Eglintoun to the plaintiff, requiring him to quit the ground, and that, before he was forcibly removed by the defendant, a reasonable time had elapsed, during which he might conveniently have gone away, then the plaintiff was not, at the time of the removal, on the place in question by the leave and license of Lord Eglintoun. On this direction the jury found a verdict for the defendant. In last Michaelmas term, Mr Jervis obtained a rule *nisi* to set aside the verdict for misdirection, on the ground, that, under the circumstances, Lord Eglintoun must be taken to have given the plaintiff leave to come into and remain in the inclosure during the races; that such leave was not revocable, at all events without returning the guinea; and so that, at the time of the removal, the plaintiff was in the inclosure by the leave and license of Lord Eglintoun. Cause was shewn during last term, and the question was argued before my Brothers Parke and Rolfe and myself; and on account of the conflicting authorities cited in the argument, we took time to consider our judgment, which we are now prepared to deliver.

That no incorporeal inheritance affecting land can either be created or transferred otherwise than by deed, is a proposition so well established, that it would be mere pedantry to cite authorities in its support. All such inheritances are said emphatically to lie in grant, and not in livery, and to pass by mere delivering of the deed. In all the authorities and textbooks on the subject, a deed is always stated or assumed to be indispensably requisite.

And although the older authorities speak of incorporeal inheritances, yet there is no doubt but that the principle does not depend on the quality of interest granted or transferred, but on the nature of the subject-matter: a right of common, for instance, which is a profit *à prendre*, or a right of way, which is an easement, or right in nature of an easement, can no more be granted or conveyed for life or for years without a deed, than in fee simple. Now, in the present case, the right claimed by the plaintiff is a right, during a portion of each day, for a limited number of days, to pass into and through and to remain in a certain close belonging to Lord Eglintoun; to go and remain where if he went and remained, he would, but for the ticket, be a trespasser. This is a right affecting land at least as obviously and extensively as a right of way over the land – it is a right of way and something more: and if we had to decide this case on general principles only, and independently of authority, it would appear to us perfectly clear that no such right can be created otherwise than by deed. The plaintiff, however, in this case argues, that he is not driven to claim the right in question strictly as grantee. He contends, that, without any grant from Lord Eglintoun, he had license from him to be in the close in question at the time when he was turned out, and that such license was, under the circumstances, irrevocable. And for this he relies mainly on four cases, which he considers to be expressly in point for him, *viz Webb v Paternoster*, reported in five different books, namely, Palmer, 71; Roll, 143 and 152; Noy, 98; Popham, 151, and Godbolt, 282; *Wood v Lake* (Sayer, 3), *Tayler v Waters* (7 Taunt 374), and *Wood v Manley* 11 Ad & E 34; 3 Per & D 5 ...

Before, however, we proceed to this investigation, it may be convenient to consider the nature of a license, and what are its legal incidents. And, for this purpose, we cannot do better than refer to Lord C J Vaughan's elaborate judgment in the case of *Thomas v Sorrell*, as it appears in his Reports. The question there was as to the right of the Crown to dispense with certain statutes regulating the sale of wine, and to license the Vintners' Company to do certain acts notwithstanding those statutes.

In the course of his judgment the Chief Justice says (Vaughan, 351),

> A dispensation or license properly passeth no interest, nor alters or transfers property in anything, but only makes an action lawful, which without it had been unlawful. As a license to go beyond the seas, to hunt in a man's park, to come into his house, are only actions which, without license, had been unlawful. But a license to hunt in a man's park, and carry away the deer killed to his own use; to cut down a tree in a man's ground, and to carry it away the next day after to his own use, are licenses as to the acts of hunting and cutting down the tree, but as to the carrying away of the deer killed and tree cut down, they are grants. So, to license a man to eat my meat, or to fire the wood in my chimney to warm him by, as to the actions of eating, firing my wood, and warming him, they are licenses; but it is consequent necessarily to those actions that my property may be destroyed in the meat eaten, and in the wood burnt. So as in some cases, by consequent and not directly, and as its effect, a dispensation or license may destroy and alter property.

Now, attending to this passage, in conjunction with the title 'License' in Brooke's *Abridgment*, from which, and particularly from para 15, it appears that a license is in its nature revocable, we have before us the whole principle of the law on this subject. A mere license is revocable: but that which is called a license is often something more than a license; it often comprises or is connected with a grant, and then the party who has given it cannot in general revoke it, so as to defeat his grant, to which it was incident.

It may further be observed, that a license under seal (provided it be a mere license) is as revocable as a license by parol; and, on the other hand, a license by parol, coupled with a grant, is as irrevocable as a license by deed, provided only that the grant is of a nature capable of being made by parol. But where there is a license by parol, coupled with a parol grant, or pretended grant, of something which is incapable of being granted otherwise than by deed, there the license is a mere license; it is not an incident to a valid grant, and it is therefore revocable. Thus, a license by A to hunt in his park, whether given by deed or by parol, is revocable; it merely renders the act of hunting lawful, which, without the license, would have been unlawful. If the licence be, as put by Chief Justice Vaughan, a license not only to hunt, but also to take away the deer when killed to his own use, this is in truth a grant of the deer, with a license annexed to come on the land: and supposing the grant of the deer to be good, then the license would be irrevocable by the party who had given it; he would be estopped from defeating his own grant, or act in the nature of a grant. But suppose the case of a parol license to come on my lands, and there to make a watercourse, to flow on the land of the licensee. In such a case there is no valid grant of the watercourse, and the license remains a mere license, and therefore capable of being revoked. On the other hand, if such a license were granted by deed, then the question would be on the construction of the deed, whether it amounted to a grant of the watercourse; and if it did, then the license would be irrevocable ...

[His Lordships referred to the four cases relied on by the plaintiff mentioned above and continued.]

It appears, therefore, that the only authority necessarily supporting the present plaintiff in the proposition for which he is contending, is the case of *Tayler v Waters*, in which the real difficulty was not discussed, nor even stated. It was taken for granted, that, if the Statute of Frauds did not apply, a parol license was sufficient, and the necessity of an instrument under seal, by reason of the interest in question being a right in nature of an easement, was by some inadvertence kept entirely out of sight; and for these reasons, even if there had been no conflicting decisions, we should have thought that case to be a very unsafe guide in leading us to a decision, on an occasion where we were called on to lose sight of the ancient landmarks of the common law.

We are not, however, driven to say that we shall disregard that cue merely on principle. Giving it the full weight of judicial decision, it is met by several others, which we must entirely disregard, before we can adopt the argument of the plaintiff. In the cases of *Fentiman v Smith* (4 East, 107) and *Rex v Horndon-on-the-Hill* (4 M & S 562), which were before *Tayler v Waters*, Lord Ellenborough and the Court of King's bench expressly recognised the doctrine, that a license is no grant, and that it is in its nature necessarily revocable, and the further doctrine, that, in order to confer an incorporeal right, an instrument under seal is essential. And in the elaborate judgment of the Court of King's Bench, given by Bayley J, in *Hewlins v Shippam* (5 B & C 222), the necessity of a deed, for creating any incorporeal right affecting land, was expressly recognised, and formed the ground of the decision. It is true that the interest in question in that case was a freehold interest, and on that ground Bayley J, suggests that it might be distinguished from *Tayler v Waters*; but in an earlier part of that same judgment, he states, conformably to what is the clear law, that, in his opinion, the quantity of interest made no difference, and the distinction is evidently adverted to by him, not because he entertained the opinion that it really was of importance, but only in order to enable him to decide that case without, in terms, saying that he did not consider the case of *Tayler v Waters* to be law. The doctrine of *Hewlins v Shippam* has since been recognised and acted upon in *Bryan v Whistler* (8 B & C 288), *Cocker v Cowper* (I C M & R 418), and *Wallis v Harrison* (4 M & W 538), and it would be impossible for us to adopt the plaintiff's view of the law, without holding all those cases to have been ill decided. It was suggested that, in the present case, a distinction might exist, by reason of the plaintiff's having paid a valuable consideration for the privilege of going on the stand. But this fact makes no difference: whether it may give the plaintiff a right of action against those from whom he purchased the ticket, or those who authorised its being issued and sold to him, is a point not necessary to be discussed; any such action would be founded on a breach of contract, and would not be the result of his having acquired by the ticket a right of going upon the stand, in spite of the owner of the soil; and it is sufficient, on this point, to say, that in several of the cases we have cited (*Hewlins v Shippam*, for instance, and *Bryan v Whistler*), the alleged license had been granted for a valuable consideration, but that was not held to make any difference. We do not advert to the cases of *Winter v Brockwell* (8 East, 308) and *Liggins v*

Inge (7 Bing 682), or other cases ranging themselves in the same category, as they were decided on grounds inapplicable to the case now before us, and were, in fact, admitted not to bear upon it.

In conclusion, we have only to say, that, acting upon the doctrine relative to licenses, as we find it laid down by Brooke, by Mr Justice Dodderidge, and by CJ Vaughan, and sanctioned by *Hewlins v Shippam*, and the other modern cases proceeding on the same principle, we have come to the conclusion, that the direction given to the jury at the trial was correct, and that this rule must be discharged. Rule discharged.

However, as a result of the Supreme Court of Judicature Acts 1873 and 1875, the equitable remedy of an injunction or specific performance can be granted to prevent the breach of contract. Accordingly, a contractual licence for a specified period is not revocable until the contractual period has expired.[34]

Hounslow LBC v Twickenham Garden Developments [1971] Ch 233

Megarry J: There is, however, an alternative route to irrevocability, namely, by means of a contract. Let it be assumed that there is no 'interest' which can be coupled with a licence, but merely a contract. This, *per se*, may preclude revocation. In *Hurst v Picture Theatres Ltd* [1915] 1 KB 1 at 10, Buckley LJ put the point shortly:

> There is another way in which the matter may be put. If there be a licence with an agreement not to revoke the licence, that, if given for value, is an enforceable right. If the facts here are, as I think they are, that the licence was a licence to enter the building and see the spectacle from its commencement until its termination, then there was included in that contract a contract not to revoke the licence till the play had run to its termination. It was then a breach of contract to revoke the obligation not to revoke the licence, and for that the decision in *Kerrison v Smith* [1897] 2 QB 445 is an authority.

This point was developed further in the *Winter Garden* case in the Court of Appeal [1946] 1 All ER 678. In that case, there had been a grant of a licence to use a theatre for plays and so on in return for certain payments, with an option for the licensees to extend the licence, and this had been duly exercised. The licensors later purported to determine the licence, and there were cross claims for declarations as to the effectiveness of this revocation. The House of Lords reversed the decision of the Court of Appeal in favour of the licensees, the difference between the two decisions being essentially one of construction. The Court of Appeal held that the licensors had no power to revoke the licence, whereas the House of Lords held that they had that power. Nothing that I can see in the speeches in the House of Lords suggests that the Court of Appeal was wrong in the law which that court applied to an irrevocable licence. Indeed, Lord Uthwatt confessed that he found Lord Greene MR's propositions of law unanswerable: see [1948] AC 173 at 202.

Lord Greene MR, at 680, first disposed of any concept that a contractual licence was an entity distinct from the contract:

> Counsel for the respondents put in the forefront of his argument a proposition of this nature. There is a thing called a licence, which is something which, so to speak, has a separate existence, distinct from the contract which creates it; and there is a rule of law governing that particular thing which says that a licence is

34 *Hounslow LBC v Twickenham Garden Developments* [1971] Ch 233.

> determinable at will. That seems to me to be putting the matter on the wrong footing. A licence created by a contract is not an interest. It creates a contractual right to do certain things which otherwise would be a trespass. It seems to me that, in considering the nature of such a licence and the mutual rights and obligations which arise under it, the first thing to do is to construe the contract according to ordinary principles. There is the question whether or not the particular licence is revocable at all and, if so, whether by both parties or by only one. There is the question whether it is revocable immediately or only after the giving of some notice. Those are questions of construction of the contract. It seems to me quite inadmissible to say that the question whether a licence is revocable at all can be, so to speak, segregated and treated by itself, leaving only the other questions to be decided by reference to the true construction of the contract. As I understand the law, rightly or wrongly, the answers to all these questions must depend on the terms of the contract when properly construed in the light of any relevant and admissible circumstances.

Whereas in equity, at all events, a contract for a grant or conveyance may be regarded as bringing into being some estate or interest in the land, separate from the contract that creates it, a licence is no separate entity but merely one of the manifestations of the contract. I think that the speech of Lord Simon in the House of Lords is at least consistent with this view: see [1949] AC 173, 189 at 191.

Secondly, Lord Greene MR said, at p 684:

> The respondents have purported to determine the licence. If I have correctly construed the contract their doing so was a breach of contract. It may well be that, in the old days, that would only have given rise to a right to sue for damages. The licence would have stood revoked, but after the expiration of what was the appropriate period of grace the licensees would have been trespassers and could have been expelled, and their right would have been to sue for damages for breach of contract, as was said in *Kerrison v Smith* [1897] 2 QB 445. But the matter requires to be considered further, because the power of equity to grant an injunction to restrain a breach of contract is, of course, a power exercisable in any court. The general rule is that, before equity will grant such an injunction, there must be, on the construction of the contract, a negative clause express or implied. In the present case it seems to me that the grant of an option which, if I am right, is an irrevocable option, must imply a negative undertaking by the licensor not to revoke it. That being so, in my opinion such a contract could be enforced in equity by an injunction. Then the question would arise, at what time can equity interfere? If the licensor were threatening to revoke, equity, I apprehend, would grant an injunction to restrain him from carrying out that threat. But supposing he has in fact purported to revoke, is equity then to say: 'We are now powerless. We cannot stop you from doing anything to carry into effect your wrongful revocation'? I apprehend not. I apprehend equity would say: 'You have revoked and the licensee had no opportunity of stopping you doing so by an injunction; but what the court of equity can do is to prevent you from carrying that revocation into effect and restrain you from doing anything under it.' In the present case, nothing has been done. The appellants are still there. I can see no reason at all why, on general principles, equity should not interfere to restrain the licensors from acting upon the purported revocation, that revocation being, as I consider, a breach of contract. Looking at it in that rather simple way, one is not concerned with the difficulties which are suggested to arise from the decision of this court in *Hurst v Picture Theatres Ltd* [1915] 1 KB 1.

James Jones & Sons Ltd v Earl of Tankerville [1909] 2 Ch 440 does not appear to have been cited, but the views of Parker J at p 443 seem to have been similar.

Quite apart, then, from the question whether the contractor has a licence coupled with an interest, there is the question whether the contractor has a contractual licence which either expressly or by implication is subject to a negative obligation by the borough not to revoke it. If this is so, then, on the law laid down by the Court of Appeal, equity would interfere to prevent the borough from revoking the licence or, if it had been revoked, from acting on the revocation. *A fortiori*, equity would refuse to grant the borough an injunction to enforce the revocation.

But once the period expires, the licence terminates. Where no specified period has been agreed, the licence can be terminated on a reasonable notice.[35]

Winter Garden Theatre v Millennium Productions [1948] AC 173, HL

Viscount Simon: My Lords, the appeal relates to a licence under which the respondents were permitted to use the Winter Garden Theatre, Drury Lane, which is the property of the appellants, for the purpose of producing stage plays, concerts or ballets, in return for a weekly payment which at the time when the appellants sought to terminate the licence amounted to £300 per week. There was no express term in the licence providing that the appellants could revoke it and the principal question of the case is whether, as the respondents contend, and as the Court of Appeal decided, the respondents are entitled to continue their use of the theatre in perpetuity if they so desire, and continue the weekly payments, or whether, as the appellants contend, the licence is revocable by reasonable notice. It is to be noted that, although the expression 'rent' or 'rental' was used in the relevant documents, it is agreed between the parties (as is plainly the fact) that the respondents acquired no interest in land but were pure licensees for value, the consideration taking the form of a weekly payment. Such a licence is a contract, and this contract contains the express term that if the respondents, on proper notice, opt to continue the use of the theatre beyond the first 12 months, they may do so with the right of giving one month's notice of their intention of then terminating the licence. The licensors on the other hand are given by the documents no express right to terminate the licence at all: the question is, is such a right to be implied, and if so, on what terms?

The effect of a licence by A to permit B to enter upon A's land or to use his premises for some purpose is in effect an authority which prevents B from being regarded as a trespasser when he avails himself of the licence (*Thomas v Sorrell* (1674) Vaugh 330 at 351). Such a licence may fall into one of various classes. It may be a purely gratuitous licence in return for which A gets nothing at all, eg, a licence to B to walk across A's field. Such a gratuitous licence would plainly be revocable by notice given by A to B. Even in that case, however, notice of revocation conveyed to B when he was in the act of crossing A's field could not turn him into a trespasser until he was off the premises, but his future right of crossing would thereupon cease. There is another class of licences which may be called licences for value, in which B gives consideration for the permission he obtains from A, and this last class may be further sub-divided. In some cases the consideration may be given once for all, as for example by the payment of a capital sum or by conferring a single benefit at the beginning. The case of *Llanelly Ry & Dock Co v London and North Western Ry Co* (1875) LR 7 HL 550 to which I will refer later, is an example of

35 *Winter Garden Theatre v Millennium Productions* [1948] AC 173.

this. In other cases, the consideration may take the form of a periodic payment, as is the case in the appeal we are now considering. There is yet a third variant of a licence for value which constantly occurs, as in the sale of a ticket to enter premises and witness a particular event, such as a ticket for a seat at a particular performance at a theatre or for entering private ground to witness a day's sport. In this last class of case, the implication of the arrangement, however it may be classified in law, plainly is that the ticket entitles the purchaser to enter and, if he behaves himself, to remain on the premises until the end of the event which he has paid his money to witness. Such, for example, was the situation which gave rise to the decision of the Court of Appeal in *Hurst v Picture Theatres Ltd*. I regard this case as rightly decided, and repudiate the view that a licensor who is paid for granting his licensee to enter premises in order to view a particular event, can nevertheless, although the licensee is behaving properly, terminate the licence before the event is over, turn the licensee out, and leave him to an action for the return of the price of his ticket. The licence in such a case is granted under contractual conditions, one of which is that a well-behaved licensee shall not be treated as a trespasser until the event which he has paid to see is over, and until he has reasonable time thereafter to depart, and in *Hurst v Picture Theatres Ltd*, where these rights were disregarded and the plaintiff was forced to leave prematurely substantial damages for assault and false imprisonment rightly resulted.

[His Lordship referred to *Wood v Leadbitter* (1845) 13 M & W 838 and continued.]

... when the clauses of the present licence are carefully studied, the proper inference from the language used is that the licence was not perpetual but that the intention of the parties, to be inferred from the document, though not expressly stated, was that, upon the appellants' indicating their decision that the permission given by the licence would be withdrawn, the respondents were to have a reasonable time to withdraw after which they would become trespassers. There is, in my opinion, no reason at all for saying that the only alternative to a perpetual licence is an instant termination of the respondents' right without any period of notice at all.

However, where the licence constitutes a 'periodic licence' of a dwelling, at least four weeks' written notice in the prescribed form is required.[36] In addition, the licensor may only recover possession by a court order.[37]

Protection from Eviction Act 1977

3. Prohibition of eviction without due process of law

(1) Where any premises have been let as a dwelling under a tenancy which is neither a statutorily protected tenancy nor an excluded tenancy and:

(a) the tenancy (in this section referred to as the former tenancy) has come to an end; but

(b) the occupier continues to reside in the premises or part of them, it shall not be liable for the owner to enforce against the occupier, otherwise than by proceedings in the court, his right to recover possession of the premises.

---

36 Section 5(1A) of the Protection from Eviction Act 1977, as amended by s 32(2) of the Housing Act 1988.

37 Section 3(2A) and (2B) of the Protection from Eviction Act 1977, as amended by s 69(1) of the Housing Act 1980, and s 30(2) of the Housing Act 1988, respectively.

(2A) Subsections (1) and (2) above apply in relation to any restricted contract (within the meaning of the Rent Act 1977) which:

(a) creates a licence; and

(b) is entered into after the commencement of s 69 of the Housing Act 1980; as they apply in relation to a restricted contract which creates a tenancy.

(2B) Subsections (1) and (2) above apply in relation to any premises occupied as a dwelling under a licence, other than an excluded licence, as they apply in relation to premises let as a dwelling under a tenancy, and in those subsections the expressions 'let' and 'tenancy' shall be construed accordingly.

5. Validity of notices to quit

(lA) Subject to sub-s (1B) below, no notice by a licensor or a licensee to determine a periodic licence to occupy premises as a dwelling (whether the licence was granted before or after the passing of this Act) shall be valid unless:

(a) it is in writing and contains such information as may be prescribed; and

(b) it is given not less than four weeks before the date on which it is to take effect.

(1B) Nothing in sub-s (1) or sub-s (lA) above applies to:

(a) premises let on an excluded tenancy which is entered into on or after the date on which the Housing Act 1988 came into force unless it is entered into pursuant to a contract made before that date; or

(b) premises occupied under an excluded licence.

The court has always been reluctant to find that an informal family arrangement as to the enjoyment or occupation of property is governed by a contract, since the parties simply do not intend their arrangement to create any legal consequence.[38] In one extreme case, *Tanner v Tanner*,[39] where a young woman, with her children, had given up a Rent Act protected tenancy to move into a house owned by the man, when the woman was later thrown out of the house, the Court of Appeal held that she had a contractual licence to 'have accommodation in the house for herself and the children so long as they were of school age and the accommodation was reasonably required for her and the children'. In the circumstances, there was no express contract and the court simply implied a contract in favour of the woman.[40] This is extremely artificial and is unlikely to be followed today. Today, it seems that the court prefers to grant a licence on the wider and more flexible ground of proprietary estoppel.

38 *Balfour v Balfour* [1919] 2 KB 571.

39 [1975] 1 WLR 1346 at 1350E. See (1976) 92 LQR 168 (Barton, JL).

40 [1975] 1 WLR 1346 at 1350E–F.

Licences by estoppel

A licence by estoppel is a licence which arises by reason of the doctrine of proprietary estoppel.[41] Since *Taylors Fashions Ltd v Liverpool Victoria Trustees Co Ltd*,[42] it has been an established equitable principle that if a person has acted to his detriment in reliance on the belief or expectation that he owns or will acquire a right or interest in another person's land, and the landowner has either encouraged that belief or expectation or has acquiesced in his action, it is unconscionable for the landowner subsequently to deny a proper fulfilment of the person's belief or expectation. Once an estoppel is established, the court must look at the circumstances in each case to decide in what way the equity in favour of the person who has suffered detrimental reliance can be satisfied.[43] The way in which the equity is satisfied varies according to the length of the Chancellor's foot. In *Pascoe v Turner*,[44] where a woman had made improvement to the house in which she lived in the belief that she had been given the house, the court ordered that the house be conveyed to her gratuitously. The court has, however, frequently satisfied the equity by conferring a licence on the innocent party.[45] Thus, in *Inwards v Baker*,[46] the son, having acted on his father's suggestion to his detriment by building a bungalow on his father's land, partly at his own expense, believing that he could live there for life, was given a licence for life. In *Lim Teng Huan v Ang Swee Chuan*,[47] the defendant who built on the co-owned land, on an agreement with the plaintiff, was allowed to have the land conveyed outright to him subject to proper compensation to the plaintiff for giving up his half share. It should be noted that, in appropriate circumstances, the court may also impose a constructive trust on the legal owner granting the complainant a licence for life. Examples are *Binions v Evans*,[48] *Ungurian v Lesnoff*[49] and *Eves v Eves*[50] where the court imposed a constructive trust on the licensor for the licensee. The term of the licence so granted is a matter for the court in its absolute discretion in an attempt to satisfy the equity, but the licence so granted cannot be revoked at will.

It should perhaps be noted that theoretically a contractual licence and a licence by estoppel arise under slightly different situations. A contractual licence arises by reason of a validly created contract for valuable consideration. Thus, a contractual licence is more likely to arise in residential 'letting' to a

---

41 See Chapter 3.

42 [1982] QB 133.

43 *Plimmer v Wellington Corpn* [1884] 9 App Cas 699 at 713.

44 [1979] 1 WLR 431.

45 *Inwards v Baker* [1965] 1 All ER 446; *Re Sharpe* [1980] 1 All ER 198; *Greasley v Cooke* [1980] 3 All ER 710.

46 [1965] 1 All ER 446. See also *Matharu v Matharu* (1994) *The Times*, 13 May, CA; [1994] 2 FLR 597.

47 [1992] 1 WLR 113. See [1993] Conv 173 (Goo, SH).

48 [1972] Ch 359.

49 [1989] 3 WLR 840.

50 [1975] 1 WLR 1338.

stranger, or to a person where a legal relationship can be easily established, in circumstances where the licensee is not given exclusive possession. In most cases of informal family arrangement where no intention to create a legal relation can be found, the court has to rely on proprietary estoppel to give effect to the family arrangement. Where the licensee has acted to his detriment in reliance of certain beliefs, often created by the licensor's words or conduct, knowingly encouraged or acquiesced in by the licensor, the licensee may acquire a licence by estoppel. However, the same set of facts may give rise to a contractual licence or a licence by estoppel.

3 ENFORCEABILITY OF A LICENCE AGAINST THIRD PARTIES

Bare licences

A bare licence can be revoked by a successor in title of the licensor.

Licences coupled with an interest

A licence coupled with an interest can bind a successor in title of the licensor if he is bound by the interest to which the licence is coupled.

Contractual licences

A contractual licence does not bind the successor in title of the licensor because there is no privity of contract between them; the burden of the contractual licence cannot be transferred.[51] In *King v David Allen & Sons Billposting Ltd*, in a written agreement, Mr King granted the respondent (who was the plaintiff) company a licence to fix posters and advertisements to his cinema for a period of four years at a rent. Later Mr King leased the cinema to a company. The lease did not refer to the agreement. The company later refused the respondent the right to exercise its licence. The respondent brought an action against Mr King for damages.

King v David Allen & Sons Billposting Ltd [1916] 2 AC 54, HL

Lord Buckmaster LC: My Lords, it is impossible to approach the consideration of this case without feeling and expressing great regret for the unfortunate position in which the appellant, Mr King has found himself. He seems to me to have acted throughout the whole of these transactions with perfect straightforwardness and with a sincere and anxious desire to discharge the obligation which he undertook towards David Allen & Sons Ltd; but by circumstances which have passed beyond his control there has, in my view, been a breach of his obligation to the respondents, and for that breach he must be made responsible. The facts in the case are quite simple and free from controversy.

[His Lordship read the facts and continued.]

51 *King v David Allen & Sons Billposting Ltd* [1916] 2 AC 54; *Clore v Theatrical Properties Ltd and Westby & Co Ltd* [1936] 3 All ER 483.

The matter then is left in this way. There is a contract between the appellant and the respondents which creates nothing but a personal obligation. It is a licence given for good and valuable consideration and to endure for a certain time. But I fail to see – although I have done my best to follow the many authorities which the learned Solicitor-General has thought it right to place before our consideration – that there is any authority for saying that any such document creates rights other than those I have described. A case of *Wilson v Tavener* [1901] 1 Ch 578 was indeed referred to, but it really affords no assistance, for there the right conferred was to erect a hoarding upon the defendant's ground, while in the present case the sole right is to fix bills against a flank wall, and it is unreasonable to attempt to construct the relationship of landlord and tenant or grantor and grantee of an easement out of such a transaction, and I find it difficult to see how it can be reasonably urged that anything beyond personal rights was ever contemplated by the parties. Those rights have undoubtedly been taken away by the action on the part of the company, who have been enabled to prevent the respondents from exercising their rights owing to the lease granted by Mr King, and he is accordingly liable in damages, although it was certainly not with his will, and indeed against his own express desire, that the company has declined to honour his agreement.'

However, Denning LJ, in *Errington v Errington and Woods*,[52] held that the original contract could give rise to an equity which was enforceable, in unregistered land, against a third party according to the equitable doctrine of notice.[53] This was later followed by a differently constituted Court of Appeal in *Midland Bank Ltd v Farmpride Hatcheries Ltd*.[54]

Errington v Errington and Woods [1952] 1 KB 290, CA

Denning LJ: ... it seems to me that, although the couple had exclusive possession of the house, there was clearly no relationship of landlord and tenant. They were not tenants at will but licensees. They had a mere personal privilege to remain there, with no right to assign or sublet. They were, however, not bare licensees. They were licensees with a contractual right to remain. As such they have no right at law to remain, but only in equity, and equitable rights now prevail. I confess, however, that it has taken the courts some time to reach this position. At common law a licence was always revocable at will, notwithstanding a contract to the contrary: *Wood v Leadbitter* (1845) 13 M & W 838. The remedy for a breach of the contract was only in damages. That was the view generally held until a few years ago: see, for instance, what was said in *Booker v Palmer* [1942) 2 All ER 674 at 677. and *Thompson v Park* [1944] KB 408 at 410. The rule has, however, been altered owing to the interposition of equity.

Law and equity have been fused for nearly 80 years, and since 1948 it has been clear that, as a result of the fusion, a licensor will not be permitted to eject a licensee in breach of a contract to allow him to remain: see *Winter Garden Theatre, London v Millenium Productions Ltd, per* Lord Greene, and in the House of Lords *per* Lord Simon; nor in breach of a promise on which the licensee has acted, even though he gave no value for it:

52 [1952] 1 KB 290.

53 [1952] 1 KB 290 at 299; *National Provisional Bank Ltd v Hastings Car Mart Ltd* [1964] Ch 665 at 688.

54 (1980) 260 EG 493. But see *Patel v Patel* [1983] AC, unreported, where yet a different Court of Appeal held that the general rule was that a mere contractual licence did not confer any interest on the licensee in the land.

see *Foster v Robinson* where Sir Raymond Evershed MR said that as a result of the oral arrangement to let the man stay, he was entitled as licensee to occupy the premises without any payment of rent for the rest of his days. This infusion of equity means that contractual licenses now have a force and validity of their own and cannot be revoked in breach of the contract. Neither the licensor nor anyone who claims through him can disregard the contract except a purchaser for value without notice.

In the present case it is clear that the father expressly promised the couple that the property should belong to them as soon as the mortgage was paid, and impliedly promised that so long as they paid the instalments to the building society they should be allowed to remain in possession. They were not purchasers because they never bound themselves to pay the instalments, but nevertheless they were in a position analogous to purchasers. They have acted on the promise, and neither the father nor his widow, his successor in title, can eject them in disregard of it. The result is that in my opinion the appeal should be dismissed and no order for possession should be made.'

In registered land, Lord Denning suggested that the contractual licence might be overriding under s 70(1)(g) of the Land Registration Act 1925.[55] More recently, this issue came to be considered by the Court of Appeal in *Ashburn Anstalt v Arnold*[56] and *Canadian Imperial Bank of Commerce v Bello*.[57] In *Ashburn Anstalt v Arnold,* it was argued that a transferee of a registered title who contracted to take title 'subject to' the rights of a contractual licensee was bound by an overriding interest under s 70(1)(g) of the Land Registration Act 1925. The Court of Appeal rejected this argument. Fox LJ criticised *Errington v Errington and Woods*[58] as inconsistent with its earlier decisions and irreconcilable with the House of Lords decision in *King v David Allen & Sons Billposting Ltd*,[59] and that it was unsupported by authority and *per incuriam*.

Ashburn Anstalt v Arnold [1989] Ch 1, CA

Fox LJ: Down to this point we do not think that there is any serious doubt as to the law. A mere contractual licence to occupy land is not binding on a purchaser of the land even though he has notice of the licence.

We come now to a case which is of central importance on the present issue. That is *Errington v Errington and Woods* [1952] 1 KB 290. A father, wishing to provide a home for his son who had recently married, bought a house with the help of a building society mortgage. He paid a lump sum towards the purchase price, the remainder of which was provided by the building society's loan. The loan was repayable by instalments. He retained the conveyance in his own name and paid the rates, but he promised that if the son and daughter-in-law continued in occupation and duly paid all the instalments, he would then transfer the property to them. The father died and by his will left the house to his widow. Up to that time the son and his wife had lived in the house and paid the instalments. The son then separated from his wife and left the house. The

55 *National Provisional Bank Ltd v Hastings Car Mart Ltd* [1964] Ch 665 at 688.

56 [1989] Ch 1. See [1988] CLJ 353 (Oakley, AJ); [1988] Conv 201 (Thompson, MP); (1988) 51 MLR 226 (Hill, J); (1988) 104 LQR 175 (Sparkes, P).

57 (1992) 64 P & CR 48. See also *Nationwide Anglia Building Society v Ahmed and Balakrishnan* (1995) 70 P & CR 381 at 389.

58 [1952] 1 KB 290.

59 [1916] 2 AC 54.

daughter-in-law continued to pay the mortgage instalments. The widow then sought possession of the house from the daughter-in-law. The county court judge dismissed the action. He held that the daughter-in-law was a tenant at will and that the claim against her was statute-barred. That reasoning was rejected by the Court of Appeal, though the actual decision of the judge was upheld.

[His Lordship referred to the first two paragraphs of Denning LJ's judgment cited at 491 above and continued.]

It is not in doubt that the actual decision was correct. It could be justified on one of three grounds – (i) There was a contract to convey the house on completion of the payments giving rise to an equitable interest in the form of an estate contract which would be binding on the widow: see Megarry & Wade, *The Law of Real Property*, 5th edn, 1984, p 806. The widow was not a purchaser for value. (ii) The daughter-in-law had changed her position in reliance upon a representation binding on the widow as a privy of the representor: see Spencer Bower and Turner, *Estoppel by Representation*, 3rd edn, 1977, p 123. (iii) The payment of the instalments by the son or the daughter-in-law gave rise to direct proprietary interests by way of constructive trust, though it is true that, until *Gissing v Gissing* [1971] AC 886, the law relating to constructive trusts in this field was not much considered.

Accordingly, it does not appear to have been necessary, in order to produce a just result, to have accepted the broad principle stated, at 299, in the passage which we have quoted, that 'Neither the licensor nor anyone who claims through him can disregard the contract except a purchaser for value without notice.' That statement itself is not supported by any citation of authority, and indeed we do not think it could have been supported on the authorities. None of the cases prior to *Errington v Errington and Woods* to which we have referred, except *Thomas v Sorrell* (1674) Vaugh 330, is mentioned in the judgments and it does not appear that any was cited.

[His Lordship referred to *Winter Gardens Theatre (London) Ltd v Millennium Productions Ltd* [1948] AC 173; *National Provincial Bank Ltd v Hastings Car Mart Ltd* [1965] AC 1175; *In Re Solomon*, [1967] Ch 573. and continued.]

It is convenient to pause at this point because, although there are later cases in what may be regarded as this series, there is none in which a contractual licence is held to bind a third party in the absence of a finding that the third party took the land as a constructive trustee. It is therefore appropriate to review how the law stands, or ought to stand, in the absence of such a finding.

Young v Bristol Aeroplane Co Ltd [1944] KB 718 establishes the familiar rule that this court is bound to follow its own decisions save that (relevant to this case) it is entitled and bound to decide which of two conflicting decisions of its own it will follow, and it is bound to refuse to follow a decision of its own which, though not expressly overruled, cannot in its opinion stand with a decision of the House of Lords.

It must, we think, be very doubtful whether this court's decision in *Errington v Errington and Woods* [1952] 1 KB 290 is consistent with its earlier decisions in *Daly v Edwardes* (1900) 83 LT 548; *Frank Warr & Co v London County Council* [1904] 1 KB 713 and *Clore v Theatrical Properties Ltd* [1936] 3 All ER 483. That decision cannot be said to be in conflict with any later decision of the House of Lords, because the House expressly left the effect of a contractual licence open in the *Hastings Car Mart* case. But there must be very real doubts whether *Errington* (1901) can be reconciled with the earlier decisions of the House of Lords in *Edwardes v Barrington* (1901) 85 LT 650, and *King v David Allen and Sons (Billposting) Ltd* [1916] 2 AC 54. It would seem that we must follow those cases or choose between the two lines of authority. It is not, however, necessary to consider those alternative courses in detail, since in our judgment the House of Lords cases, whether or not as a matter of strict precedent they conclude this question, state the correct principle which we should follow.

Our reasons for reaching this conclusion are based upon essentially the same reasons as those given by Russell LJ in the *Hastings Car Mart Case* [1964] Ch 665 at 697 and by Professor Wade in the article, 'Licences and Third Parties' (1952) 68 LQR 337, to which Russell LJ refers. Before *Errington* the law appears to have been clear and well understood. It rested on an important and intelligible distinction between contractual obligations which gave rise to no estate or interest in the land and proprietary rights which, by definition, did. The far-reaching statement of principle in *Errington* was not supported by authority, not necessary for the decision of the case and per incuriam in the sense that it was made without reference to authorities which, if they would not have compelled, would surely have persuaded the court to adopt a different *ratio*. Of course, the law must be free to develop. But as a response to problems which had arisen, the *Errington* rule (without more) was neither practically necessary nor theoretically convincing. By contrast, the finding on appropriate facts of a constructive trust may well be regarded as a beneficial adaptation of old rules to new situations.

It should be noted, however, that the views expressed by Fox LJ were *obiter dicta* because, as have been seen,[60] the Court of Appeal in the end decided that the rights in issue were in fact rights of tenancy.

In *Canadian Imperial Bank of Commerce v Bello*,[61] the Court of Appeal was similarly of the view that not every personal contract could give rise to an interest in land.

Canadian Imperial Bank of Commerce v Bello (1992) 64 P & CR 48, CA

Dillon LJ: If the arrangement was a mere personal licence, then, in my judgment, it could not have amounted to an overriding interest. The relevant cases on that are gone through in detail in the judgment of another division of this court, Fox LJ, Neill LJ and Bingham LJ in *Ashburn Anstalt v Arnold*. Their conclusion on this point, after reviewing a number of authorities, including *Daly v Edwardes* (1900), *King v David Allen & Sons (Billposting) Ltd*, and *Clore v Theatrical Properties Ltd*, is that the earlier decisions prevail notwithstanding some views expressed by Lord Denning in *Errington v Errington and Woods*, and that in this court the principle to be followed is set out in the earlier cases. It is not every personal contract that gives an interest in land, even though the personal contract may give a right to use land. As for constructive trust, that again is dealt with in the judgment of this court in *Ashburn Anstalt v Arnold*.

With two fundamentally opposing views expressed by different Courts of Appeal at various times, an authoritative clarification by the House of Lords is now eagerly awaited.

60 See Chapter 8.

61 (1992) 64 P & CR 48 at 51.

Licences by estoppel

In *E R Ives Investment v High*,[62] Lord Denning expressed the view that a right arising in equity out of acquiescence or by estoppel was an equity which was capable of binding successor of the licensor in unregistered land under the old doctrine of notice. Admittedly, the right in issue in that case was an easement, but as a licence by estoppel is not a right which could ever have been created at law, following Lord Denning's view, it should bind a successor of the licensor with notice. Where the licensor's title is registered, there is yet no decision on the status of such a licence. Could it be overriding under s 70(1)(g)?

In the light of Fox LJ's criticisms of the view in *Errington v Errington and Woods*[63] that a contractual licence can be a proprietary binding on third party, the view expressed by Lord Denning in *E R Ives Investment v High*,[64] insofar as a licence by estoppel is concerned, must now be reconsidered. If a licence by estoppel is not regarded as a proprietary interest, it cannot be an overriding interest under s 70(1)(g).

4 THE FUTURE OF LICENCES

Although contractual licences, and possibly licences by estoppel, are not treated as proprietary interests, their very novelty as interests in land freely moulded to meet new situations, particularly in the area of informal family affairs, have not ceased to be attractive. They remain a useful devise for giving effect to transactions which are otherwise not sustainable on strict legal rules. Professor Gray explains that:[65]

> The ambivalence which surrounds the contractual licence is accounted for in part by the fact that it is above all a chameleonic device which has been adapted at different times and in wildly divergent contexts in order to fill various sorts of legal hiatus. (a) *Short-term functions* At one end of the spectrum the contractual licence provides the legal medium for relationships of an extremely short-term and intensely purposive character. The contractual licence frequently supplies a personal permission to be present on another's land for the purpose of business or entertainment ... (b) *Medium-term functions* The contractual licence is also quite capable of serving a number of medium-term objectives. The building contractor who works on a construction site enjoys a contractual licence to be present on another's land ... (c) *Long-term functions* At the other end of the spectrum the contractual licence has come, during the last 40 years, to play a rather different role from any mentioned so far. Although at times scarcely distinguishable from the parallel device of tenancy, the contractual licence has emerged as a common residential device peculiarly appropriate to modern social conditions. The contractual licence has acquired a wholly unaccustomed prominence as a "possible mode of land-holding – a mode which had certainly not been developed into anything like its current maturity in the 19th century.[66] The

62 [1967] 2 QB 379 at 395–96.

63 [1952] 1 KB 290.

64 [1967] 2 QB 379.

65 Gray, pp 902–03.

66 *Heslop v Burns* [1974] 1 WLR 1241 at 1252C–D, *per* Scarman LJ.

> contractual licence thus provides the legal explanation for the social reality of occupancy enjoyed by lodgers and by a wide range of family members living in informal and loosely organised 'family arrangements'.

As to the future of licences, Megarry and Wade suggest that:

> Licences have been going through a period of evolution like that which transformed restrictive covenants from mere contracts into interests in land after the decision in *Tulk v Moxhay* in 1848. A new chapter of the law of real property has been opening, in which licences have been held to be protected against revocation not only by the licensor but also by the licensor's successors in title. Subject to the possibility that the House of Lords might disavow these innovations,[67] licences must now be admitted into the family of interests in land capable of binding third parties. It is their very novelty as interests in land which makes them attractive, since having for so long laid outside the law of property they are free from some of the rules which govern leases, settlements, registration and other matters. Judges have been able to mould them freely to meet new situations, particularly in the area of family affairs where they wish to give efficacy to vague and informal transactions which would otherwise be legally futile.[68]

The views recently expressed by the Court of Appeal in *Ashburn Anstalt v Arnold*[69] and *Canadian Imperial Bank of Commerce v Bello*[70] seem, however, to favour the orthodox view. The future of licences as an interest in land thus remains uncertain. 'There are certain movements in the contemporary jurisprudence of property which make it not at all impossible that the contractual licence will one day be recognised as a species of property interest.'[71] It may indeed be asked why a contractual licence should not bind a third party who takes with notice? To say that because a contractual licence is not a 'property' and therefore cannot bind a third party is 'to turn the process on its head and to begin with a conclusion'.[72] 'Where an equitable interest is protected against third parties, the reality of the matter is not that it is protected in this way because it is 'property', but rather that it is 'property' precisely because – ultimately through the equitable intervention of the courts – it is indeed protected'.[73] Thus, the correct question to ask is surely whether a third party with notice of a licensee's contractual or estoppel right should nevertheless take free of it. Is it against the third party's conscience for him to claim his full legal right against the licensee? The same sort of question, as will be seen, was asked by Lord Cottenham LC in 1848 in *Tulk v Moxhay*,[74] in the context of covenants affecting freehold land. He said that the question is not whether the covenant was a proprietary interest and could therefore run with the land, 'but whether a

67 See *National Provincial Bank Ltd v Ainsworth* [1965] AC 1175 at 1239, *per* Upjohn, 1251, *per* Lord Wilberforce. These *dicta* are not hostile to new developments.

68 Megarry and Wade, at 798–99.

69 [1989] Ch 1.

70 (1992) 64 P & CR 48.

71 Gray, p 923 using contractual licences, treated indistinguishably from leases by s 79(3) of the Housing Act 1985 and s 2(2)(b) of the Agricultural Holdings Act 1986 as examples.

72 Gray, p 924.

73 Gray, p 924.

74 (1848) 2 Ph 774. See Chapter 14.

party shall be permitted to use the land in a manner inconsistent with the contract entered into by his vendor, and with notice of which he purchased'.[75]

5 LICENCES, PROPRIETARY ESTOPPEL AND CONSTRUCTIVE TRUST

In recent years, as Professor Pettit observed,[76] 'in a number of cases, mainly arising out of informal arrangements in a family setting, the court has taken the view that justice demanded that the plaintiff should have a remedy in circumstances where it was at least doubtful whether he was entitled to one under existing rules as previously understood.' The means by which the court sought to achieve a just result were the doctrines of proprietary estoppel and constructive trusts. As mentioned earlier, where a claim based on proprietary estoppel is established, the court has an absolute discretion to decide how to satisfy the equity. But the court quite often seeks to satisfy the equity by awarding the claimant a licence under the doctrine of proprietary estoppel.[77] In some cases, however, the court has been prepared to impose a constructive trust on the licensor.

Ashburn Anstalt v Arnold [1989] 1 Ch 1, CA

Fox LJ: The constructive trust principle, to which we now turn, has been long established and has proved to be highly flexible in practice. It covers a wide variety of cases from that of a trustee who makes a profit out of his trust or a stranger who knowingly deals with trust properties, to the many cases where the courts have held that a person who directly or indirectly contributes to the acquisition of a dwelling house purchased in the name of and conveyed to another has some beneficial interest in the property. The test, for the present purposes, is whether the owner of the property has so conducted himself that it would be inequitable to allow him to deny the claimant an interest in the property: see *Gissing v Gissing* [1971] AC 886 at 905, *per* Lord Diplock.

His Lordship referred to *Bannister v Bannister* [1948] 2 All ER 133; *In Re Schebsman, decd* [1944] Ch 83 and said that in *Binions v Evans* [1972] Ch 359, Lord Denning MR held that the plaintiffs took the property subject to a constructive trust for the defendant's benefit. In our view that is a legitimate application of the doctrine of constructive trusts. The estate would certainly have allowed the defendant to live in the house during her life in accordance with their agreement with her. They provided the plaintiffs with a copy of the agreement they made. The agreement for sale was subject to the agreement, and they accepted a lower purchase price in consequence. In the circumstances it was a proper inference that on the sale to the plaintiffs, the intention of the estate and the plaintiffs was that the plaintiffs should give effect to the tenancy agreement. If they had failed to do so, the estate would have been liable in damages to the defendant.

[His Lordship referred to *DHN Food Distributors Ltd v Tower Hamlets Borough Council* [1976] 1 WLR 852; *Re Sharpe* [1980] 1 WLR 219; *Lyus v Prowsa Developments Ltd* [1982] 1 WLR 1044 and continued.]

75 (1848) 2 Ph 774 at 777f, 41 ER 1143 at 1144.

76 Pettit, PH, *Equity and the Law of Trusts*, 7th edn, 1994, London: Butterworths, p 178.

77 For example, *Inwards v Baker* [1965] 1 All ER 446; *Re Sharpe* [1980] 1 All ER 198; *Greasley v Cooke* [1980] 3 All ER 710.

We come to the present case. It is said that when a person sells land and stipulates that the sale should be 'subject to' a contractual licence, the court will impose a constructive trust upon the purchaser to give effect to the licence: see *Binions v Evans* [1972] Ch 359 at 368, *per* Lord Denning MR. We do not feel able to accept that as a general proposition. We agree with the observations of Dillon J in *Lyus v Prowsa Developments Ltd* [1982] 1 WLR 1044 at 1051:

> By contrast, there are many cases in which land is expressly conveyed subject to possible incumbrances when there is no thought at all of conferring any fresh rights on third parties who may be entitled to the benefit of the incumbrances. The land is expressed to be sold subject to incumbrances to satisfy the vendor's duty to disclose all possible incumbrances known to him, and to protect the vendor against any possible claim by the purchaser ... So, for instance, land may be contracted to be sold and may be expressed to be conveyed subject to the restrictive covenants contained in a conveyance some 60 or 90 years old. No one would suggest that by accepting such a form of contract or conveyance a purchaser is assuming a new liability in favour of third parties to observe the covenants if there was for any reason before the contract or conveyance no one who could make out a title as against the purchaser to the benefit of the covenants.

The court will not impose a constructive trust unless it is satisfied that the conscience of the estate owner is affected. The mere fact that land is expressed to be conveyed 'subject to' a contract does not necessarily imply that the grantee is to be under an obligation, not otherwise existing, to give effect to the provisions of the contract. The fact that the conveyance is expressed to be subject to the contract may often, for the reasons indicated by Dillon J, be at least as consistent with an intention merely to protect the grantor against claims by the grantee as an intention to impose an obligation on the grantee. The words 'subject to' will, of course, impose notice. But notice is not enough to impose on somebody an obligation to give effect to a contract into which he did not enter. Thus, mere notice of a restrictive covenant is not enough to impose upon the estate owner an obligation or equity to give effect to it: *London County Council v Allen* [1914] 3 KB 642.

The material facts in the present case are as follows. (i) There is no finding that the plaintiff paid a lower price in consequence of the provision that the sale was subject to the 1973 agreement. (ii) The 1973 agreement was not contractually enforceable against Legal & General, which was not, therefore, exposed to the risk of any contractual claim for damages if the agreement was not complied with. The 1973 agreement was enforceable against Cavendish and it seems that in 1973 Cavendish was owned by Legal & General There is no finding as to the relationship between Cavendish and Legal & General in August 1985, when Legal & General sold to the plaintiff. And there is no evidence before the deputy judge as to the circumstances or the arrangements attending the transfer by Cavendish to Legal & General. (iii) Whilst the letter of 7 February 1985 is not precisely worded, it seems that Legal & General was itself prepared to give effect to the 1973 agreement.

In matters relating to the title to land, certainty is of prime importance. We do not think it desirable that constructive trusts of land should be imposed in reliance on inferences from slender materials. In our opinion the available evidence in the present case is insufficient. The deputy judge, while he did not have to decide the matter, was not disposed to infer a constructive trust, and we agree with him.

Where the claimant is given a licence for life under a constructive trust, the danger is that this can create a strict settlement under the Settled Land Act 1925.[78] On the other hand, a licence by estoppel, despite Lord Denning's suggestion in *E R Ives Investment v High*,[79] is only a personal interest and, when given for life, as in some cases, will not create a strict settlement.[80]

It is apparent that there is a substantial overlap and a close, but often difficult to differentiate, relationship between proprietary estoppel and constructive trust.[81] Browne-Wilkinson J found 'the present state of the law very confused and difficult to fit in with established equitable principles'.[82] However, bearing in mind the overriding consideration of equity, the doctrine of constructive trust or proprietary estoppel are means and not ends in themselves. The use of the doctrines depends on the facts of each case and how equity can be satisfied. Where a third party is involved whose conscience is affected by the claimant's right, it may be more appropriate to impose a constructive trust on the third party which is retrospective and the claimant be given an appropriate right as proprietary estoppel only takes effect from the date of the judgment.

78 For example, *Bannister v Bannister* [1948] 2 All ER 133; *Binions v Evans* [1972] 1 Ch 359; *Ungurian v Lesnoff* [1990] Ch 206.

79 [1967] 2 QB 379.

80 But see Russell LJ in *Dodsworth v Dodsworth* suggesting that licence for life under proprietary estoppel could create a strict settlement. Also Goff LJ in *Griffiths v Williams*.

81 See [1990] Conv 370 (D Hayton), [1993] 109 LQR 114 (Ferguson, P).

82 *Re Sharpe* [1980] 1 All ER 198 at 204d–e.

CHAPTER 11

STRICT SETTLEMENTS

As mentioned earlier,[1] land can be held on trust (express, resulting or constructive) for certain beneficiaries and when one looks at how the beneficial interests are enjoyed, and how these interests may affect subsequent transfer of the legal estate in the trust property from a conveyancer's point of view, the arrangements may be classified into three categories: strict settlements, trusts for sale and bare trusts. As from 1 January 1997,[2] under the Trusts of Land and Appointment of Trustees Act 1996 it is no longer possible to create strict settlements, save where they arise as sub-trusts created as resettlements of property already subject to a strict settlement,[3] and all existing trusts for sale are converted into the new form of trusts of land. However, as existing strict settlements will continue to exist and operate under the old law, it would still be necessary to know the old law for some time to come, consequently, treatment of the old law is retained in this chapter. Bare trusts and trusts for sale have been dealt with briefly earlier and trust of land will be discussed in Chapter 12.

1 INTRODUCTION

'Settlement' is a concept that describes the arrangement whereby land is held under a trust created by the settlor for various beneficiaries under the terms of the trust. It was to satisfy propertied class's aspirations in keeping their family wealth within the family that the concept of settlement evolved in the history of land law. The aspiration was to ensure that the family estates would remain in the family for many generations to come, but, at the same time, provision could be made from the income of the estate for the members of the family. This was made possible by the doctrine of estates which enabled the settlor to create a succession of different estates in the same plot of land, each having a limited interest, for example, 'to A for life, to B in tail and to C in fee simple'. Before 1926, those limited interests could exist at law.[4] No one had the entire legal estate and no one person alone could dispose of the entire legal estate. Such a gift would tie up the land at least until B became able to bar the entail on attaining his majority.[5] Even then he could create no more than a base fee[6] without the consent of A. However, if A and B collaborated, B could bar the entail and convert B's fee tail estate into a fee simple estate – the exact opposite to what the creator of the settlement (S) intended. But what often happened was

1 See Chapter 2.

2 Trusts of Land and Appointment of Trustees Act 1996 (Commencement) Order 1996 (SI 1996/2974).

3 Section 2 of the TLATA 1996.

4 But they were frequently left by the settlor on trust.

5 For barring the entail see Chapter 1, pp 5–7.

6 An estate which lasts for as long as the disentailing tenant and his lineal descendant are alive.

that A would in his turn feel obliged to preserve the land for the sake of yet more distant generations and would offer B some immediate benefit in the land in order to persuade B to resettle the land. By a process known as resettlement which was a simple procedure whereby A and B could collaborate and resettle the land upon A for life with remainder to B for life with remainder to B's eldest son (C) in tail, and the land could thus be tied up for another generation. Similarly, when B became entitled in possession after the death of A, B would persuade his eldest son C to effect a resettlement in favour of B for life with remainder to C for life with remainder to C's eldest son D in tail. The problem with this type of settlement was the self-perpetuating tendency of settlement and resettlement which gave rise to considerable disadvantages. First, so long as the settlement subsisted, the tenant for life in actual possession had no greater interest than a life estate. The fee simple estate became virtually inalienable. Secondly, the tenant for life was subject to restrictions imposed by the law of waste[7] which basically required him not to carry out activities which would do permanent damage to the freehold or inheritance of the land, or which would alter its nature or diminish its value. There was no effective way, for example, to exploit the mineral resources under the land and the life tenant had no real incentive to maintain and preserve the settled estate, because such expenditure would have to come out of his own purse. Over the years, attempts were made to remove the worst features of the strict settlement by granting the tenant for life express powers to deal with the land itself. Eventually, in the 19th century, Parliament intervened in a series of statutes designed to give the life tenant wide statutory powers in relation to the settled land.

The process of settling land mentioned above was often referred to as strict settlement. There was, however, another type of settlement which was of more recent origin, known as a trust for sale. This became widely used and it enabled the land owners to achieve two purposes: (i) to hold the estates for as long as the income was satisfactory but to sell and reinvest the proceeds when better bargains were available, and (ii) to keep the capital intact for later generations and to provide for the present members of their families.

Strict settlements and trusts for sale therefore represented two different ways of settling land.

2 STRICT SETTLEMENT UNDER THE SETTLED LAND ACT 1925

A strict settlement was governed by the Settled Land Act 1925. An arrangement was a strict settlement if the land was held in trust for certain limited beneficial owners. The Settled Land Act 1925 was later to add that if land was held for a minor beneficially, or where land was charged with a rentcharge, the land became settled.[8] However, strict settlements and trusts for sale were mutually exclusive and an arrangement was not a strict settlement if the land was held on

7 See Megarry and Wade, pp 95–102.

8 Section 1(1)(ii)(d), (v) of the SLA 1925.

trust for sale. An arrangement was a trust for sale if the trustees were imposed with a duty to sell the land and to hold the proceeds upon the trust as directed by the settlor. As the Law Commission put it:[9]

> The difference between the two systems lies principally in how the legal estate is held and who has the powers of management. Where successive interests are created under the Settled Land Act 1925, the tenant for life has a beneficial life interest. However, for the purposes of dealing with the land he also holds the legal estate.[10] He has wide powers of management. A purchaser will be able to acquire a legal fee simple absolute from the tenant for life free from the equitable interest created by the settlement provided that the purchaser pays the purchase money to at least two trustees or to a trust corporation. Where successive interests are created behind a trust for sale, the legal estate is held by the trustees, and generally it is they who have the powers of management. A purchaser will be able to acquire the legal estate free from the equitable interest from the trustees by paying the purchase money to the trustees.

Where there was a strict settlement, the person who had the right to enjoy the land currently was called the tenant for life. He was vested with the legal estate in the land. In registered land, he was the registered proprietor. He had a wide range of powers to deal with the land. There were also trustees of the settlement. This was a group of persons normally chosen by the settlor to safeguard the interests of the various beneficiaries under the settlement. They performed various statutory functions as a watch dog against abuse of the tenant for life's wide powers.

As will be seen, where land was held under a strict settlement it could only be disposed of in accordance with the cumbersome procedure laid down in the Settled Land Act 1925. With all the disadvantages a strict settlement entailed, a strict settlement was often not created intentionally. In some cases it was created unintentionally by an informal oral grant of a right to remain in the land for life.[11]

3 WHAT CONSTITUTED A STRICT SETTLEMENT?

Settled Land Act 1925

1. What constitutes a settlement?

(1) Any deed, will, agreement for a settlement or other agreement, Act of Parliament, or other instrument, or any number of instruments, whether made or passed before or after, or partly before and partly after, the commencement of this Act, under or by virtue of which instrument or instruments and land, after the commencement of this Act, stands for the time being:

---

9 See Law Commission's Working Paper (No 94, Trusts of Land), para 2.1, quoted at para 1.2 of the Law Commission's Report on Trusts of Land (Law Com No 181, 1989).

10 This is not so if he is an infant, or in some other way incapacitated, when there are complex provisions as to who should exercise the powers of the tenant for life (original footnote, renumbered for the purpose of this book).

11 For example, *Bannister v Bannister* [1948] 2 All ER 133; *Binions v Evans* [1972] Ch 359; *Ungurian v Lesnoff* [1990] Ch 206. See Law Commission's Working Paper (No 94, Trusts of Land) para 2.1, quoted at para 1.2 of the Law Commission's Report on Trusts of Land (Law Com No 181).

(i) limited in trust for any persons by way of succession; or

(ii) limited in trust for any person in possession:

(a) for an entailed interest whether or not capable of being barred or defeated;

(b) for an estate in fee simple or for a term of years absolute subject to an executory limitation, gift, or disposition over on failure of his issue or in any other event;

(c) for a base or determinable fee (other than a fee which is a fee simple absolute by virtue of s 7 of the Law of Property Act 1925) or any corresponding interest in leasehold land;

(d) being an infant, for an estate in fee simple or for a term of years absolute; or

(iii) limited in trust for any person for an estate in fee simple or for a term of years absolute contingently on the happening of any event; or

(iv) ...

(v) charged, whether voluntarily or in consideration of marriage or by way of family arrangement, and whether immediately or after an interval, with the payment of any rentcharge for the life of any person, or any less period, or of any capital, annual, or periodical sums for the portions, advancement, maintenance, or otherwise for the benefit of any persons, with or without any term of years for securing or raising the same;

creates or is for the purposes of this Act a settlement and is in this Act referred to as a settlement, or as the settlement, as the case requires.

Provided that, where land is the subject of a compound settlement, references in this Act to the settlement shall be construed as meaning such compound settlement, unless the context otherwise requires.

Strict settlements

As mentioned earlier, any new trusts of successive interests are now governed by the Trusts of Land and Appointment of Trustees Act 1996. However, existing strict settlements, ie strict settlements created before 1 January 1997 continue to exist and be governed by the Settled Land Act 1925. It is interesting to note that the Settled Land Act describes what is hitherto called a strict settlement a 'settlement'. As trusts for sale are also settlement in a general sense, settlements under the Settled Land Act 1925 are commonly referred to as strict settlements, a term which is used throughout the book.

Under s 1(1)(i) of the Settled Land Act 1925, where by any instrument (eg deed, will, etc) land was for the time being limited in trust for any persons by way of succession, there was a strict settlement. An example is a grant 'to A for life to B in tail, to C in fee simple'. Each one has a limited interest and is succeeded by another when his limited interest comes to an end until a person of full age is absolutely entitled to the whole of the land.

Under s 1(1)(ii)(a) where land was held on trust for any person in possession for an entailed interest, there was a strict settlement. As mentioned in Chapter 1, entailed interests were only equitable and must exist behind a trust. This trust was, under this subsection, a strict settlement, notwithstanding that the entailed interests were capable of being barred or defeated. An example is 'to A and the heirs of his body'. It is no longer possible to create an entailed interest under the Trusts of Land and Appointment of Trustees Act 1996. Any attempt to create an entail will take effect as a declaration of trust of the land for the person who would otherwise have had the entailed interest.[12]

Where land was held in fee simple on the condition that if a certain specified event occurred the fee simple would be divested or shifted to some other persons named in the grant, the fee simple, not being 'absolute' and being subject to a gift over (so not covered by s 7(1) of the Law of Property Act 1925 as amended), was equitable. The conditional fee could only exist behind a trust which was a strict settlement under sub-s (1)(ii)(b). An example is a grant 'to A in fee simple but to B when A qualifies as a solicitor'.

Similarly, where land was held in trust for a base or determinable fee (other than a fee which was a fee simple absolute by virtue of s 7 of the Law of Property Act 1925) or any corresponding interest in leasehold land, the trust upon which the land was held was a strict settlement under sub-s (1)(ii)(c). For example, 'to A in fee simple until he is admitted as a solicitor'. Another example is 'to A and the heirs of his body', but A then sells his entailed interest to C which produces only a base fee. Or 'to A for life, to B in tail' and B bars the entail without A's consent in favour of C who gets a base fee. As C only gets a base fee, he cannot get a greater interest than A himself has, and C acquires an interest which can be inherited by any of his own heirs, but which will last only for as long as the disentailing tenant (A) and his issue survive.

A trust covered by sub-s (1)(ii)(a), (b) and (c) was in fact covered by sub-s (1)(i) since in all these cases, there was an element of succession: the land was limited in trust for certain person by way of succession.

The Act also rendered the trust upon which land was held for the time being for an infant, for an estate in fee simple, or for a term of years absolute, a strict settlement. For example, 'to T in fee simple upon trust for A in fee simple', but A was under 18. The trust was a strict settlement under sub-s (1)(ii)(d). Similarly, in a grant 'to A in fee simple', but A was an infant, and being an infant A could not hold a legal estate,[13] so the legal estate would be held on trust which was a strict settlement for him under sub-s (1)(ii)(d). In these cases, the infant was unable to hold the legal estate and could not have any powers of the tenant for life under s 20(1) of the Settled Land Act 1925. The powers of the tenant for life were given, in the case of a settlement by will, to a personal representative where the settled land would already be vested in him under s 1(1) of the Administration of Estate Act 1925.[14] In the case of *inter vivos* settlement, the powers were given to the trustees of the settlement.[15] The legal estate was similarly vested in them. When A attained the age of 18, the strict settlement ceased to exist and a bare trust arose, and A could now request that the legal estate be transferred to him.[16] As from 1 January 1997 an attempt to

12 Schedule 1 para 5 of the TLATA 1996.

13 Section 1(6) of the LPA 1925.

14 Section 26(1)(b) of the SLA 1925.

15 Section 26(1)(b) of the SLA 1925.

16 Section 7(5) of the SLA 1925. This is in line with the rule in *Saunders v Vautier* (1841) 4 Beav 115.

dispose of land to a minor by will give rise to a declaration of trust of the land for the minor.[17]

Another type of trust classified as strict settlements under sub-s (1)(iii) was a trust upon which land was held for any person for an estate in fee simple or for a term of years absolute contingently on the happening of any event. This type of interest has been encountered[18] and is sometimes called a springing interest. The interest was not vested yet and might 'spring up' (be vested) in the future, when the specified condition was fulfilled.[19] An example is 'to trustees in trust for X in fee simple if his brother dies under the age of 21'. X's interest before his brother dies is contingent and future, and is no more than a chance of getting a fee simple. It could only exist as an equitable interest behind a trust which was a strict settlement. As from 1 January 1997, this type of arrangement will give rise to a trust of land.[20]

Where the land was for the time being charged, whether voluntarily or in consideration of marriage or by way of family arrangement, with the payment of any sums for the benefit of any persons, the land must be held under a strict settlement. Note that the land did not have to be held in trust. This enabled a settlor to give a legal estate in the land to one person but at the same time charged the land with the payment of sums of money for the maintenance of other persons.[21] The payment was made out of the income of the estate, which in general went to the tenant for life. Note that the payment must be made for the portions, advancement, maintenance or benefit of another person. If the land was subject to a rentcharge for the maintenance of a road, the land was not settled. Before 1926, land charged with the payment of a sum was not settled land and when the land was sold the practice was for the vendor to covenant to pay the rentcharge. After 1925, the land became settled and to dispose of the land, the Settled Land Act procedure must be followed. This was objected to by owners of land charged with a rentcharge. Section 1 of the Law of Property (Amendment) Act 1926 was passed to meet this situation. So, where land was settled under this subsection, on a subsequent transfer, the fee simple owner could either sell the land (i) free from the charges, by making use of the troublesome Settled Land Act procedure, eg appointment of trustees and execution of vesting deed, or payment into the court, or (ii) subject to the charges without using the Settled Land Act procedure, but with an indemnity by the vendor.[22] As from 1 January 1997, these arrangements will give rise to trusts of land.[23]

17 Schedule 1, para 1 of the TLATA 1996.

18 See Chapter 1, pp 17–18.

19 The interest must be vested, if at all, within the perpetuity period.

20 Section 1(6) of the TLATA 1996.

21 Rentcharges created in favour of the landowner's family thereby making the land settled under this subsection are not prohibited by the Rentcharges Act 1977.

22 Section 1 of the Law of Property (Amendment) Act 1926.

23 Schedule 1, para 3 of the TLATA 1996.

Limited in trust

As one would notice, in all the cases mentioned above, except where land was subject to a charge, the land must be 'limited in trust'. The words 'limited in trust' gave rise to some problems and produced some unintended results. In the majority of cases where land was intentionally settled by the settlor, the land was held under an express trust created by a trust instrument or by will. However, a strict settlement might be created unintentionally where the owner of a legal estate (S) informally granted a person (L) a right to remain in the land for life. Even if there was no express declaration that the land should be held on trust for L, the court might hold that the promise by S created a life interest and that S became a constructive trustee. As the land was now held on a constructive trust for L for a life interest, technically it was caught by sub-s (1)(i) and a strict settlement thereby arose. It was not necessary that the trust was expressly created, ie the land did not have to be expressly limited in trust. The courts were prepared to treat the land in such a case as settled land if there was no other way to protect the rights of the life resident.[24] This was essentially what happened in *Bannister v Bannister*[25] where an elderly lady conveyed her two freehold cottages to her brother-in-law who orally promised that she could remain in one of the cottages rent free for as long as she liked. The land was held settled because the brother-in-law was required to hold the cottage on a constructive trust for her for life.

Bannister v Bannister [1948] 2 All ER 133, CA

Scott LJ read the facts and continued: The plaintiff, having given the defendant notice to quit the downstairs front room of No 30, with which she refused to comply, commenced the present action, claiming by his particulars of claim dated 2 October 1947, possession of the room in question on the footing that the defendant had been occupying it as a tenant at will at no rent and that her tenancy at will had been duly determined by notice to quit. The defendant counterclaimed in the action for a declaration to the effect that the plaintiff held No 30 in trust for the defendant for life, with an alternative claim for specific performance which was not pursued, and ancillary claims for possession of No 30 other than the downstairs front room (which also was not pursued), and damages for trespass. In the result, the learned county court judge, by his order dated 19 September 1947, dismissed the plaintiff's claim with costs, and on the defendant's counterclaim awarded her £10 damages with costs and made a declaration to the effect claimed by her. In view of the learned county court judge's acceptance of the defendant's evidence he necessarily found as a fact that the oral agreement as a result of which the defendant conveyed Nos 30 and 31 to the plaintiff for £250 included an undertaking by the plaintiff to permit the defendant to stay in No 30 for as long as she liked rent free, and that, but for this undertaking, the defendant would not have sold the two cottages to the plaintiff at what, on the uncontradicted evidence of value, he rightly described as 'a bargain price'. He further found as a fact that there was no fraud in the case. On these findings of fact he held that on well-known equitable principles there was (as he put it) an implied or inferential trust, or, in other words, a constructive trust, of No 30 under which the plaintiff held that property in trust for the defendant for life.

24 See Law Commission's Working Paper on Trusts of Land (No 94), para 3.5.

25 [1948] 2 All ER 133.

The conclusion thus reached by the learned county court judge was attacked in this court on substantially the following three grounds: First, it was said that the oral undertaking found by the learned county court judge to have formed part of the agreement – namely, that the plaintiff would let the defendant stay in No 30 as long as she liked rent free – did not, as a matter of construction of the language used, amount to a promise that the defendant should retain a life interest in No 30, but amounted merely to a promise that the plaintiff would allow the defendant to remain in No 30 rent free as his tenant at will. Secondly, it was said that, even if the terms of the oral undertaking were such as to amount to a promise that the defendant should retain a life interest in No 30, a tenancy at will free of rent was, nevertheless, the greatest interest she could claim in view of the absence of writing and the provisions of ss 53 and 54 of the Law of Property Act 1925. Thirdly, it was said that a constructive trust in favour of the defendant (which the absence of writing admittedly would not defeat) could only be raised by findings to the effect that there was actual fraud on the part of the plaintiff and that the property was sold and conveyed to him on the faith of an express oral declaration of trust which it would be fraudulent of him to deny. It was, accordingly, submitted that the learned county court judge's conclusion that there was a constructive trust could not stand since it was negatived by his finding that there was no fraud in the case and by the absence of any evidence of anything amounting to an express oral declaration of trust.

In support of the first of these three objections reliance was placed on *Buck v Howarth*, in which a King's Bench Divisional Court held that the occupant of a house who had been told by a predecessor in title of the freeholder 'that he could live in the house until he died' (an oral and, it would seem, a purely voluntary promise) was given an uncertain interest in the premises and that the law would presume a tenancy at will, with the result that proceedings under the Small Tenements Recovery Act, 1838, could be taken. That was, obviously a very different case from the present one and we find ourselves unable to derive any assistance from it. The promise was a purely voluntary one, and any court would naturally have been slow to construe it as intended to confer a life interest, even if it was literally capable of that construction. Moreover, whatever the words may have meant, the case clearly fell within s 54 of the Law of Property Act 1925, under which interests in land created by parol have the force and effect of interests at will only. There was, of course, no question of a resulting trust as there might have been if the occupant of the house had been a former owner who had sold the freehold on the faith of a similar promise. In the present case the defendant did, on the facts found, sell and convey the property on the faith of the oral undertaking and would not otherwise have done so, and the undertaking must be assumed to have been regarded as reserving to her a benefit worth at least £150, or three-eights of the contemporary market value of the property without vacant possession. We, therefore, see no reason why the words of the undertaking should not be given the most favourable construction, from the defendant's point of view, of which they are properly capable. Similar words in deeds and wills have frequently been held to create a life interest determinable (apart from the special considerations introduced by the Settled Land Act 1925) on the beneficiary ceasing to occupy the premises: see eg *Re Carne's Settled Estates*, [1989] Ch 324 and *Re Boyer's Settled Estates*. In our view, that is the meaning which should, in the circumstances of the present case, be placed on the words of the oral undertaking found by the learned county court judge to have been given by the plaintiff. We are, accordingly, of opinion that the first objection fails, though the interest promised to the defendant by the plaintiff must, we think, be taken to have been a life interest determinable on her ceasing to occupy No 30 and not a life interest *simpliciter* as held by the learned county court judge.

As will be seen from what is said below, the second objection (based on want of writing) in effect stands or falls with the third, and it will, therefore, be convenient to deal with that next. It is, we think, clearly a mistake to suppose that the equitable principle on which a constructive trust is raised against a person who insists on the absolute character of a conveyance to himself for the purpose of defeating a beneficial interest, which, according to the true bargain, was to belong to another, is confined to cases in which the conveyance itself was fraudulently obtained. The fraud which brings the principle into play arises as soon as the absolute character of the conveyance is set up for the purpose of defeating the beneficial interest, and that is the fraud to cover which the Statute of Frauds or the corresponding provisions of the Law of Property Act 1925, cannot be called to aid in cases in which no written evidence of the real bargain is available. Nor is it, in our opinion, necessary that the bargain on which the absolute conveyance is made should include any express stipulation that the grantee is in so many words to hold as trustee. It is enough that the bargain should have included a stipulation under which some sufficiently defined beneficial interest in the property was to be taken by another. The above propositions are, we think, clearly borne out by the cases of which we were referred of *Booth v Turle*, *Chattock v Muller*, *Re Duke of Marlborough* (1878) 8 Ch D 177 and *Rochefoucauld v Boustead*. We see no distinction in principle between a case in which property is conveyed to a purchaser on terms that the entire beneficial interest in some part of it is to be retained by the vendor (as in *Booth v Turle* and a case, like the present, in which property is conveyed to a purchaser on terms that a limited beneficial interest in some part of it is to be retained by the vendor. We are, accordingly, of opinion that the third ground of objection to the learned county court judge's conclusion also fails. His finding that there was no fraud in the case cannot be taken as meaning that it was not fraudulent in the plaintiff to insist on the absolute character of the conveyance for the purpose of defeating the beneficial interest which he had agreed the defendant should retain. The conclusion that the plaintiff was fraudulent, in this sense, necessarily follows from the facts found, and, as indicated above, the fact that he may have been innocent of any fraudulent intent in taking the conveyance in absolute form is for this purpose immaterial. The failure of the third ground of objection necessarily also destroys the second objection based on want of writing and the provisions of ss 53 and 54 of the Law of Property Act 1925.

Some point was made of the payment by the plaintiff of the sched A tax and other outgoings in respect of both cottages as a circumstance inconsistent with the interest in No 30 to which the learned county court judge has held the defendant entitled. In our view, this circumstance was clearly a matter to be taken into account in determining whether the defendant's evidence as to the terms of her bargain with the plaintiff was to be accepted, and we have no reason to suppose that the learned county court judge did not take it into account. He held, nevertheless, that the defendant's version of the transaction was the true one, and we certainly cannot regard that finding of fact, turning as it did essentially on the credibility of the witnesses, as open to review on this ground. We think it is clear on the facts that there has been nothing amounting to a cesser or renunciation of occupation by the defendant so as to bring her determinable life interest in No 30 to an end. She has throughout been in per-sonal occupation either of the whole of No 30 or, latterly, of the downstairs front room. The learned county court judge has held that the plaintiff and his wife came to live in the other rooms by her permission, that is to say, as her licensees or tenants at will. Nor, in our view, can the plaintiff claim that the defendant's interest was affected by his letting the Freemans into occupation of these rooms after such permission was revoked. The learned county court judge has, indeed, held that since such revocation the plaintiff has been a mere trespasser.

In the result, we hold that the appeal fails and the order of the learned county court judge should be affirmed, but in the interests of accuracy we think his order should be varied by substituting a declaration to the effect that the plaintiff holds No 30 in trust during the life of the defendant to permit the defendant to occupy the same for so long as she may desire to do so and subject thereto in trust for the plaintiff. A trust in this form has the effect of making the beneficiary a tenant for life within the meaning of the Settled Land Act, 1925, and, consequently, there is a very little practical difference between such a trust and a trust for life *simpliciter*. The appeal will be dismissed with that variation in the form of the order. The plaintiff must pay the costs of the appeal.

The principle in *Bannister v Bannister* was followed in *Binions v Evans*,[26] where the purchaser of a cottage agreed to allow the widow of the vendor's employee to live in it for her life. Megaw and Stephenson LJJ conceded that it was difficult to see precisely how the Settled Land Act was applicable.[27] However, they felt bound by and were unable to distinguish the decision in *Bannister v Bannister*. As the purchaser clearly held the property on trust for the widow for life, she was a tenant for life of the settled land.

Binions v Evans [1972] Ch 359, CA

Lord Denning MR having read the facts continued: Those simple facts raise an interesting point of law. What was the nature of the defendant's interest in the cottage? Was it such as to avail her against purchasers who took with full notice of it? Did the plaintiffs take the house on trust to permit her to stay there?

1. *Tenancy at will*

Mr Pugh stressed the words 'as tenant at will'. Those words, he said, were used as a term of art. They have for centuries had a well-understood meaning in our law. It means determinable at the will of either party. Halsbury's *Laws of England*, 3rd edn, 1958, vol 23, p 505 states:

> ... although upon its creation it is expressed to be at the will of the landlord only or at the will of the tenant only, yet the law implies that it shall be at the will of the other party also; for every lease at will must in law be at the will of both parties.

Although the words 'tenants at will' are used in the agreement, the rest of it contains terms which are quite inconsistent with a tenancy at will as known to the law. Thus, the defendant is to be permitted to stay 'for the remainder of her life'. So the Tredegar Estate cannot turn her out at their will. Again, the defendant cannot herself determine the agreement except on four weeks' notice. That shows that she cannot determine it at will. These express terms prevail over the words 'tenancy at will'. It is a well-known maxim the '*modus et conventio vincunt legem*' which, when interpreted, means that the manner and agreement of the parties overrides the strict letter of the law.

In my opinion, therefore, this was not a tenancy at will.

26 [1972] Ch 359.

27 *Ibid*, at 370 and 372.

2. *Tenancy for life*

At the other extreme, it was suggested that the agreement created a tenancy for life in the defendant. At common law a tenancy for life was an estate of freehold. It could only be created by deed and not by parol: see *Doe d Warner v Browne* (1807) 8 East 165. But I need not pause upon this: 'because there can no longer be a tenancy for life at law, see s 1 of the Law of Property Act 1925'. Nowadays, if a lease is granted to a lessee for life, at a rent, it takes effect as a lease for 90 years, determinable, after the death of the lessee, by one month's notice: see s 149(6) of the Law of Property Act 1925. But, as this agreement was not at a rent, that section does not apply.

But it was suggested here that the defendant was a tenant for life under the Settled Land Act 1925, with some support from *Bannister v Bannister* [1948] 2 All ER 133. I cannot think this can be right. A tenant for life under that Act has power to sell the property, and to lease it (and to treat himself or herself as the owner of it): see ss 38 and 72 of the Settled Land Act 1925. No one would expect the defendant here to be able to sell the property or to lease it. It would be so entirely contrary to true intent of the parties that it cannot be right.

There is, I think, a short answer to this suggestion. The agreement of 15 March 1968, was not a settlement within s 1(1) of the Settled Land Act 1925. In order to be a settlement, the land would have, by this agreement, to be 'limited in trust for any persons by way of succession'. This land may be held on trust (that I will deal with hereafter): but it is not 'limited' in trust (which I take to be expressly limited): nor is it limited by way of succession (because there is no trace of a succession of one beneficiary after another). It would be, I think, quite out of place to call this agreement a 'settlement' of any kind.

In my opinion, therefore, the defendant was not a tenant for life.

3. *Any other tenancy*

Mr Webber suggested that, although the defendant might not have a tenancy for life, she might have a leasehold interest. He said it might be a 'hybrid' tenancy of some kind. I am afraid this will not do. In order to create a leasehold interest, it must be for a definite term of years. It must be expressed with certainty and specifically, or be capable of being ascertained with certainty at the time when the lease takes effect. That was settled by the decision of this court in *Lace v Chantler* [1944] KB 368, where a lease 'for the duration of the war' was held to be no lease. So also in *Buck v Howarth* [1947] 1 All ER 342, where a man, for no consideration, gave another permission to stay in a cottage until he died, it was held to be no lease but only a tenancy at will. Today it would be considered a bare licence, with no contractual right at all to stay there.

The defendant has not a tenancy at will, nor a tenancy for life. She has not a tenancy for years, nor a periodic tenancy. She has, therefore, no tenancy known to the law.

4. *An equitable interest*

Seeing that the defendant has no legal estate or interest in the land, the question is what right has she? At any rate, she has a contractual right to reside in the house for the remainder of her life or as long as she pleases to stay. I know that in the agreement it is described as a tenancy: but that does not matter. The question is: what is it in reality? To my mind it is a licence, and no tenancy. It is a privilege which is personal to her. On all the modern cases, which are legion, it ranks as a contractual licence, and not a tenancy: see *Shell-Mex and B P Ltd v Manchester Garages Ltd* [1971] 1 WLR 612.

What is the status of such a licence as this? There are a number of cases in the books in which a similar right has been given. They show that a right to occupy for life, arising by contract, gives to the occupier an equitable interest in the land: just as it does when it arises under a settlement: see *In Re Carne's Settled Estates* [1899] 1 Ch 324 and *In Re Boyer's Settled Estates* [1916] 2 Ch 404. The courts of equity will not allow the landlord to turn the occupier out in breach of the contract: see *Foster v Robinson* [1951] 1 KB 149 at 156; nor will they allow a purchaser to turn her out if he bought with knowledge of her right – *Errington v Errington and Woods* [1952] 1 KB 290 at 299.

It is instructive to go back to the cases before the Supreme Court Judicature Act 1873. They show that, if a landlord, by a memorandum in writing, let a house to someone, let us say to a widow, at a rent, for her life or as long as she pleased to stay, the courts of equity would not allow the landlord to turn her out in breach of his contract. If the landlord were to go to the courts of law and obtain an order in ejectment against her, as in *Doe d Warner v Browne*, 8 East 165, the courts of equity would grant an injunction to restrain the landlord from enforcing his rights at law, as in *Browne v Warner* (1808) 14 Ves 409. The courts of equity would give the agreement a construction, which Lord Eldon LC called an 'equitable construction', and construe it as if it were an agreement to execute a deed granting her a lease of the house for her life – *Browne v Warner* 14 Ves 156 at 158. They would order the landlord specifically to perform the contract, so construed, by executing such a deed. This court did so in *Zimbler v Abraham* [1903] 1 KB 577. This means that she had an equitable interest in the land. So much so that if a purchaser wished to buy her interest from her, he had to pay her its full value as such. Malins VC so held in *Re King's Leasehold Estates* (1873) LR 16 Eq 521 at 527, where he described it as an 'equitable interest'. It follows that, if the owner sold his reversion to another, who took with notice of the widow's interest, his successor could not turn her out any more than he could. She would have, I should have thought, at least as strong a case as the occupier in *Webb v Paternoster* (1619) Poph 151, which received the blessing of Lord Upjohn in *National Provincial Bank Ltd v Hastings Car Mart Ltd* [1965] AC 1175 at 1239.

Suppose, however, that the defendant did not have an equitable interest at the outset, nevertheless it is quite plain that she obtained one afterwards when the Tredegar Estate sold the cottage. They stipulated with the plaintiffs that they were to take the house 'subject to' the defendant's rights under the agreement. They supplied the plaintiffs with a copy of the contract: and the plaintiffs paid less because of her right to stay there. In these circumstances, this court will impose on the plaintiffs a constructive trust for her benefit: for the simple reason that it would be utterly inequitable for the plaintiffs to turn the defendant out contrary to the stipulation subject to which they took the premises. That seems to me clear from the important decision of *Bannister v Bannister* [1948] 2 All ER 133, which was applied by the judge, and which I gladly follow.

This imposing of a constructive trust is entirely in accord with the precepts of equity. As Cardozo J once put it: 'A constructive trust is the formula through which the conscience of equity finds expression' see *Beatty v Guggenheim Exploration Co* (1919) 225 NY 380 at 386: or, as Lord Diplock put it quite recently in *Gissing v Gissing* [1971] AC 886 at 905, a constructive trust is created 'whenever the trustee has so conducted himself that it would be inequitable to allow him to deny to the *cestui que* trust a beneficial interest in the land acquired'.

I know that there are some who have doubted whether a contractual licensee has any protection against a purchaser, even one who takes with full notice. We were referred in this connection to Professor Wade's article 'Licences and Third Parties' in (1952) 68 LQR 337, and to the judgment of Goff J in *In Re Solomon, A Bankrupt, ex p Trustee of the Property of the Bankrupt v Solomon* [1967] Ch 573. None of these doubts can prevail, however, when the situation gives rise to a constructive trust. Whenever the owner sells the land to a purchaser, and at the same time stipulates that he shall take it 'subject to' a contractual licence, I think it plain that a court of equity will impose on the purchaser a constructive trust in favour of the beneficiary. It is true that the stipulation (that the purchaser shall take it subject to the rights of the licensee) is a stipulation for the benefit of one who is not a party to the contract of sale; but, as Lord Upjohn said in *Beswick v Beswick* [1968] AC 58, 98, that is just the very case in which equity will 'come to the aid of the common law'. It does so by imposing a constructive trust on the purchaser. It would be utterly inequitable that the purchaser should be able to turn out the beneficiary. It is to be noticed that in the two cases which are said to give rise to difficulty *King v David Allen and Sons, Billposting Ltd* [1916] 2 AC 54 and *Clore v Theatrical Properties Ltd and Westby & Co Ltd* [1936] 3 All ER 483, there was no trace of a stipulation, express or implied, that the purchaser should take the property subject to the right of the contractual licensee. In the first case, if Mr King had protected himself by stipulating that the company should take the lease 'subject to the rights of David Allen', I cannot think that he would have been held liable in damages. In the second case the documents were exceedingly complicated, but if Mr Clore had acquired the theatre 'subject to the rights of the licensees', I cannot suppose that this court would have allowed him to disregard those rights.

In many of these cases the purchaser takes expressly 'subject to' the rights of the licensee. Obviously, the purchaser then holds the land on an imputed trust for the licensee. But, even if he does not take expressly 'subject to' the rights of the licensee, he may do so impliedly. At any rate when the licensee is in actual occupation of the land, so that the purchaser must know he is there, and of the rights which he has: see *Hodgson v Marks* [1971] Ch 892. Whenever the purchaser takes the land impliedly subject to the rights of the contractual licensee, a court of equity will impose a constructive trust for the beneficiary. So I still adhere to the proposition I stated in *Errington v Errington and Woods* [1952] 1 KB 290 at 299; and elaborated in *National Provincial Bank Ltd v Hastings Car Mart Ltd* [1964] Ch 665 at 686–89, namely, that, when the licensee is in actual occupation, neither the licensor nor anyone who claims through him can disregard the contract except a purchaser for value without notice.

5. *Conclusion*

In my opinion, the defendant, by virtue of the agreement, had an equitable interest in the cottage which the court would protect by granting an injunction against the landlords restraining them from turning her out. When the landlords sold the cottage to a purchaser 'subject to' her rights under the agreement, the purchaser took the cottage on a constructive trust to permit the defendant to reside there during her life, or as long as she might desire. The courts will not allow the purchaser to go back on that trust. I entirely agree with the judgment of Judge Bulger. I would dismiss this appeal.

Megaw LJ: What was the effect in law of that agreement, as between the trustees and the defendant? In my view, Judge Bulger was right in holding that the effect was the same as the effect of the agreement considered by this court in *Bannister v Bannister* [1948] 2 All ER 133. The court (Scott LJ, Asquith LJ and Jenkins J) held, at 137:

> ... the plaintiff holds No 30 in trust during the life of the defendant to permit the defendant to occupy the same for so long as she may desire to do so and subject

> thereto in trust for the plaintiff. A trust in this form has the effect of making the beneficiary a tenant for life within the meaning of the Settled Land Act 1925, and, consequently, there is a very little practical difference between such a trust and a trust for life *simpliciter*.

As was said by the court, at 136:

> Similar words in deeds and wills have frequently been held to create a life interest determinable (apart from the special considerations introduced by the Settled Land Act 1925) on the beneficiary ceasing to occupy the premises ...

I confess that I have had difficulty in seeing precisely how the Settled Land Act of 1925 was applicable. But the court in *Bannister v Bannister* [1948] 2 All ER 133 so held, and I am certainly content, and we are probably bound, to follow that authority. I see no relevant distinction. The fact that the transaction – the creation of the trust – was there effected orally, whereas here there is an agreement in writing, surely cannot be a ground for saying that the principle is not here applicable. The fact that there is here express provision for determination by the beneficiary cannot provide a relevant distinction. The defendant in *Bannister v Bannister* was free to give up occupation whenever she wished. The fact and nature of the obligations imposed upon the defendant by the agreement in the present case must tend in favour of, rather than adversely to, the creation of an interest in land, as compared with *Bannister's* case.

I realise that the application of the Settled Land Act 1925 may produce some odd consequences; but no odder than those which were inherent in the decision in *Bannister v Bannister*. I do not find anything in the possible, theoretical, consequences to lead me to the conclusion that *Bannister's* case should not be followed.

The plaintiffs took with express notice of the agreement which constitutes, or gives rise to, the trust. They cannot turn the defendant out of the house against her will; for that would be a breach of the trust which binds them.'

Stephenson LJ: Apart from authority, I would not have thought that such an interest could be understood to amount to a tenancy for life within the meaning of the Settled Land Act 1925, and I would have thought that the other terms of her tenancy (as I think it ought properly to be called) are inconsistent with a power to ask for the legal estate to be settled on her or to sell the cottage. But *Bannister v Bannister* is a clear decision of this court that such words as have been used in this agreement (excepting, I must concede, the words 'as tenant at will of them') create a life interest determinable (apart from the special considerations introduced by the Settled Land Act 1925) on the beneficiary ceasing to occupy the premises and the landlords hold the cottage on trust to permit her to occupy it 'during her life or as long as she lives', as Judge Bulger held, and subject thereto in trust for them.

To impose the statutory powers of a tenant for life on the elderly lady in *Bannister v Bannister* and the widow in *Binions v Evans* seemed contrary to the intention of the grantor. The grantor never intended to grant a life interest but merely a personal right of occupation. Therefore, it was not surprising that in *Binions v Evans*, Lord Denning was anxious to avoid the application of the Settled Land Act 1925. He agreed with the majority that the elderly lady could stay in the cottage for life, but did not think that she was a tenant for life under the Settled Land Act 1925. He said that she did not have a life interest but only had a personal contractual licence to reside in the cottage for life which was not an interest in land.[28] He added that the words 'limited in trust' meant expressly limited in trust.[29] As the purchaser held the property on a constructive trust which was not expressly limited, the Act did not apply. His view was, however, doubted by Goff LJ in *Griffiths v Williams*[30] and was not followed by Vinelott J in *Ungurian v Lesnoff*.[31]

In *Ungurian v Lesnoff*,[32] D gave up her flat and career in Poland to come and live in England with P. P promised that he would buy a house where they could live together. P later bought a house where he lived with D as man and wife with their children from previous relationships. The house was transferred into P's sole name. At the time of the acquisition, the house was in a poor state of repair, and D (and her sons) did a considerable amount of renovation work. Later, the relationship between them broke down and P sought to recover possession of the house. Vinelott J held that P held the house on constructive trust for himself and D because D had relied on a common understanding, that she should share the house with P, to her detriment. However, Vinelott J went on to say that D and P should be regarded as having successive rather than concurrent interests in the house. He said that a person who has a right to reside for his or her life has a life interest. Therefore, on the authorities of *Bannister* and *Binions*, the situation gave rise to a strict settlement. D was therefore able to call for the legal estate to be vested in her and could sell the property. She could either use the proceeds to buy another house or enjoy the income from it.[33] Vinelott J was not impressed by Lord Denning's view, and noted that it was not shared by Megaw and Stephenson LJJ. He said that both express trusts and trusts arising by operation of law came within the Settled Land Act 1925.

Ungurian v Lesnoff [1990] Ch 206

Vinelott J: Mrs Lesnoff claimed in her evidence that it was always understood between her and Mr Ungurian that he would buy her a house which would be her absolute property. It was in reliance on that promise that, like the defendant in *Maharaj v Jai Chand* [1986] AC 898, she gave up her flat in Wraclow which, while not transmissible to her family or capable of being sold, was for all practical purposes hers for life, and gave up her prospects of an academic career ... She acted on that promise or understanding and did everything he asked her to do. She entered into a marriage of convenience, brought her children here, and finally burnt her boats by giving up her flat in Poland and obtaining for herself and her children the right to reside permanently out of Poland. When the house was bought, he, in the presence of a solicitor or estate agent (she was not sure which) gave her a cheque made out ready for her to sign. Mr Pascoe on her behalf submitted that this was equivalent to a declaration of trust. Mr Pascoe relied also on Mrs Lesnoff's evidence as to the work done by her, which he submitted was only consistent with a belief that the house was her property.

28 [1972] Ch 359 at 367C.

29 *Ibid* at 366E–F.

30 [1977] 248 EG 947.

31 [1990] Ch 206 at 225C.

32 [1990] Ch 206. See (1991) 107 LQR 596 (J Hill).

33 [1990] Ch 206 at 226D.

[His Lordship went on to examine the evidence in detail.]

I have, therefore, come to the conclusion after anxious consideration that I cannot accept that Mr Ungurian promised, or that Mrs Lesnoff ever believed that he had promised, that if she burnt her boats and threw in her lot with him he would buy a house that would be her absolute property ...

I should, I think, make it clear that I found Mrs Lesnoff to be a woman of exceptional intelligence and of firm and forthright character. I do not think that she has deliberately invented evidence to mislead the court, but I do think that over the years she has come to impute an intention to Mr Ungurian which he did not have or express. I am satisfied that it was understood from Christmas 1968 onwards that, if Mrs Lesnoff threw in her lot with Mr Ungurian and made her home permanently abroad, he would provide her with the security of a home; something on which, amongst other things, she could rely if anything happened to him. Mrs Lesnoff was giving up a great deal, and moreover the two of them, with their experience of life behind the Iron Curtain, knew that the loss of her flat and the severance of her ties with Poland would be irrecoverable. The final step – the surrender of the flat in Wraclow – was not taken until after the house had been bought, but it was taken in reliance on the promise or understanding that Mrs Lesnoff would have the right to reside in the house in place of the flat. What I think has happened is that Mrs Lesnoff has come to read into a promise that Mr Ungurian would buy a house where they could live together with her and one or both of his children, and which would be a security on which she could rely if anything happened to him, a promise that the house would be hers absolutely. As I have pointed out, that is not how the claim was put when Mr Ungurian first sought to evict her from the house.

As to the conversation when the purchase was completed, I think it is probable that when Mrs Lesnoff and Mr Ungurian attended to complete the purchase, Mr Ungurian did say something to the effect that he was buying the house as a home for Mrs Lesnoff and the children, but I do not think it was intended or understood as a statement that the house was to be hers absolutely. Mrs Lesnoff at that time did not speak English fluently and was no doubt unfamiliar with the concept of private ownership of property. But she is an intelligent woman and must have known that the house was being conveyed to Mr Ungurian and not to her, and that he and not she would be in a position to dispose of it.

In summary, therefore, I am not satisfied that the house was bought by Mr Ungurian with the intention that it would belong to Mrs Lesnoff, either immediately or when she gave up her flat in Poland and obtained permission to live permanently abroad; but I am satisfied that it was bought with the common intention that Mrs Lesnoff would be entitled to live there with her children, sharing it with Mr Ungurian when he was in England, and with any of his children who were here for the purpose of being educated. I am satisfied that Mrs Lesnoff went through with this plan, initiated in Beirut and later elaborated, in the expectation that Mr Ungurian would provide her with a secure home and that she burnt her boats by giving up her flat in Wraclow in the belief that he had done so. The question is whether these facts, and the work subsequently done by Mrs Lesnoff, gives rise, either to a constructive trust under which Mrs Lesnoff became entitled to a beneficial interest in the house, or to a licence to reside, or to an estoppel preventing Mr Ungurian from denying her right to reside in the house.

Mr Pascoe submitted that these facts found the inference that there was a bargain or common intention that Mrs Lesnoff was to have a beneficial interest, and that the interest should be commensurate with the extent to which the value of the house was improved by her labours. I accept that Mrs Lesnoff and her sons did do a great deal of work to the house, though I think that in retrospect Mrs Lesnoff has probably come to exaggerate both the extent of the work she did, and in particular the skilled work. Mrs Lesnoff gave a graphic account of wielding a pickaxe. No doubt her solicitors had retailed to her the facts in *Eves v Eves* [1975] 1 WLR 1338 which they drew to the attention of Mr Ungurian's solicitors. In the course of her evidence this was reduced to a claim that she used a pickaxe to lever doorframes away from the brickwork where they needed to be replaced. I doubt whether Mrs Lesnoff used a tool as clumsy as a pickaxe at all, unless possibly she picked up one that had been left lying around by workmen and put it to some temporary, and possibly inappropriate, use. I am not persuaded that, as she claimed, she mastered the art of plastering walls. As I have said, I am satisfied that she and her sons did a substantial amount of work, but I think she did the work on the understanding that she had the right to reside in the house and because she wanted to make it more comfortable for her and Mr Ungurian, and for her growing sons. Mr Ungurian in particular wanted some privacy and the alterations to the ground floor were designed to that end.

In my judgment, the inference to be drawn from the circumstances in which the property was purchased and the subsequent conduct of the parties – the intention to be attributed to them – is that Mrs Lesnoff was to have the right to reside in the house during her life. It would be to that extent her house, and although the expectation was that Mr Ungurian would live there with her when he was in England, and that Paul, and possibly in due course his younger son also, would be accommodated there while they were being educated, that result would flow from the continued relationship between Mrs Lesnoff and Mr Ungurian and would be dependent on it. It must be borne in mind that Mr Ungurian was a man of considerable means with flats in Beirut, Amman and Switzerland. He was providing a house as a home for a woman much younger than himself who would be likely to survive him. I do not think that full effect would be given to this common intention by inferring no more than an irrevocable licence to occupy the house. I think the legal consequences which flow from the intention to be imputed to the parties was that Mr Ungurian held the house on trust to permit Mrs Lesnoff to reside in it during her life unless and until Mr Ungurian, with her consent, sold the property and bought another residence for her in substitution for it.

If that is the right conclusion, then the house became settled land within the Settled Land Act 1925 and Mrs Lesnoff is tenant for life and entitled to call for the execution of a vesting deed and for the appointment of trustees. Any understanding that Mr Ungurian was not to be entitled with her consent to sell the house and apply the proceeds, in whole or in part, towards the purchase of another house would be avoided by s 106 of the Settled Land Act 1925.

In *Bannister v Bannister* [1948] 2 All ER 133 an oral undertaking by the plaintiff that the defendant was to be allowed to live in a cottage rent free so long as she desired was held to create a determinable life interest constituting the defendant a tenant for life for the purposes of the Settled Land Act 1925. In *Binions v Evans* [1972] Ch 359 an agreement to permit the defendant to reside in and occupy a cottage as tenant at will, but with the right to determine the tenancy on notice, was similarly held by the Court of Appeal to give rise to a constructive trust to permit the defendant to reside in the house during her life or so long as she wished.

Lord Denning MR expressed the opinion that although the defendant had an equitable interest in the house which the court would protect by an injunction, she did not become a tenant for life under the Settled Land Act 1925. He said, at 366:

> But is was suggested here that the defendant was a tenant for life under the Settled Land Act 1925, with some support from *Bannister v Bannister.* I cannot think this can be right. A tenant for life under that Act has power to sell the property, and to lease it (and to treat himself or herself as the owner of it): see ss 38 and 72 of the Settled Land Act 1925. No one would expect the defendant here to be able to sell the property or to lease it. It would be so entirely contrary to the true intent of the parties that it cannot be right. There is, I think, a short answer to this suggestion. The agreement of 15 March 1968 was not a settlement within s 1(1) of the Settled Land Act 1925. In order to be a settlement, the land would have, by this agreement, to be 'limited in trust for any persons by way of succession'. This land may be held on trust (that I will deal with hereafter): but it is not 'limited' in trust (which I take to be expressly limited); nor is it limited by way of succession (because there is no trace of a succession of one beneficiary after another). It would be, I think, quite out of place to call this agreement a 'settlement' of any kind.

But that view was not, as I understand it, shared by Megaw LJ and Stephenson LJ.

[His Lordship referred to passages of the judgment of Megaw LJ and Stephenson cited above at 515–16 and continued.]

Although, of course, every judgment of Lord Denning is entitled to the greatest respect, I do not find the reasons he gives for the conclusion that the defendant in *Binions v Evans* [1972] Ch 359 was not a tenant for life persuasive. A person with a right to reside in an estate during his or her life, or for a period determinable on some earlier event, has a life or a determinable life interest as the case may be: see In *Re Boyer's Settled Estates* [1916] 2 Ch 404. The estate is necessarily limited in trust for persons by way of succession. That is so whether the trust is express or arises by operation of law. Of course, the power of sale given to a tenant for life by the Settled Land Act 1925 may override and defeat the intentions of the settlor or of the parties to a transaction which gives rise to a constructive trust or settlement. The 1925 legislation was designed to ensure that land was not taken out of commerce, and to that extent often defeats the intention of a settlor or testator who would prefer that land should remain in his family for as long as the law allows. Section 106 of the Settled Land Act 1925 is specifically aimed at avoiding any provision that would fetter a tenant for life from exercising, or would induce him not to exercise, his power of sale.

In my judgment, therefore, Mrs Lesnoff is entitled to a life interest in the house, and entitled to call on Mr Ungurian to execute a vesting deed in her favour, and, when the property is vested in her, will be entitled to sell it and to re-invest the proceeds in the purchase of another house or to enjoy the income from them.

More recently, in *Costello v Costello*[34] and *Dent v Dent,*[35] the same question arose for consideration whether an exclusive right to occupy property for life constitutes a strict settlement. In the former, the Court of Appeal followed Bannisters line of authorities referred to above. In the latter, a different answer was reached. Here, a father resettled part of his property on trust for his son

34 [1996] 1 FLR 805.

35 [1996] 1 All ER 659.

absolutely. Later, the father moved into the property with his new wife, M, and, in order to provide security to M, the son granted by deed rights of exclusive occupation of the property to his father for life or for such period as he might require and on his death to M on the same terms. After the father's death, M called for the property to be vested in her as tenant for life. David Young QC sitting as a deputy judge of the High Court, took a more pragmatic approach and held that the court would consider the context in which the right to occupy was granted or agreed to before determining whether it created a strict settlement, or some other property interest or form of licence. In the circumstances, the purpose of the grant was to formalise existing family arrangements and not to effect any restructuring of the estate. It created a personal obligation on the son, rather than conferred any interest on the father or M, and such permission to reside did not therefore lead to the conclusion that a settlement of land 'limited in trust' had been created.

The second point to note about*Ungurian v Lesnoff* is that Vinelott J failed to consider the apparent lack of documentation which creates a strict settlement. To constitute a strict settlement of a legal estate in land, there had to be a deed, will, agreement, or instrument etc under or by virtue of which land stood for the time being limited in the various circumstances which made it settled land. Where the interest arose under a contract or agreement, there was no difficulty, because that fell fairly and squarely within the words of s 1(1). But where what was set up was an equity arising from acting upon a representation, it was not obvious how that could be brought within the terms of s 1(1). Such a question was not considered by the courts in *Bannister* and *Binions* and Vinelott J did not explain how the state of affairs in *Ungurian v Lesnoff* fell within s 1(1). Goff LJ suggested that in such a case it might be the order of the court declaring the equity, which was an instrument which satisfied the definition of settlement under s 1(1) of the Act.[36]

Griffiths v Williams (1977) 248 EG 947, CA

Goff LJ: Where the interest arises under a contract or other agreement, of course, there is no difficulty, because that falls fairly and squarely within the words of sub-s (1) of s 1. But where what is set up is an equity arising from acting upon a representation, it is not obvious how that can be brought within the terms of s 1(1). There are two other cases in which this type of problem was considered by this court, namely, *Binions v Evans* [1972] Ch 359, [1972] 2 All ER 70, and *Bannister v Bannister* [1948] 2 All ER 133. In *Binions v Evans*, the Master of the Rolls thought that such an equity would not in any event create a settlement; but, with all respect, I think his reasoning leads to difficulties, because at 367, at 75 he reached the conclusion that it created an equitable interest, and once that is established then the ground on which he said (at 366, at 74) there was no settlement appears to me to be undermined. The other two Lord Justices who heard that case, Megaw LJ and Stephenson LJ, felt that they were bound by the earlier decision in *Bannister v Bannister* to hold that there was a settlement; but they did not direct themselves to any question under s 1; nor, I think, need they have done so, because in *Binions v Evans* and the earlier case of *Bannister v Bannister* there was actually an agreement. So that the difficulty which in my view arises, on the case of *Dodsworth v*

36 *Griffiths v Williams* (1977) 248 EG 947 at 950.

Dodsworth and upon the present case, of seeing whether there can be a settlement when you have an interest which appears to give you a tenancy for life but there does not obviously appear to be anything which is a 'settlement' within the Act, did not arise in those two earlier cases. If it were necessary, we would have to decide what is, I think, a serious problem – whether *Dodsworth v Dodsworth* is binding upon us or whether it was decided strictly *per incuriam* because the learned Lord Justices who heard it did not advert to s 1 of the Settled Land Act, and, if it be not binding upon us, whether in truth it be right, and if so, what is the answer to the conundrum posed by sub-s (1) of s 1. It may be that in such a case there is a settlement, and it is the order of the court declaring the equity, which is an 'instrument' and, therefore, the 'settlement' within the meaning of that subsection.

Some commentators have argued that perhaps the conveyance to the grantor was the document that created the settlement.[37]

The application of Settled Land Act 1925 to the informal grants mentioned above produced unintended results and could be extremely inconvenient. The land suddenly became settled and, as will be seen, any disposition must be carried out by the informal grantee, who had perhaps never expected to be given such an onerous task and the procedure of the Settled Land Act must be followed. This was one of the problems which prompted the recommendation of the Law Commission be that creation of strict settlements should no longer be possible.[38]

4 THE CREATION OF STRICT SETTLEMENTS

Strict settlement created *inter vivos*

As mentioned earlier, it is no longer possible to create a strict settlement. Prior to 1 January 1997, the settlor could choose to settle his land *inter vivos*. To do this, two documents in the form of a deed were required: a trust instrument and a vesting deed.[39]

Settled Land Act 1925

4. Authorised method of settling land *inter vivos*

(1) Every settlement of a legal estate in land *inter vivos* shall, save as in this Act otherwise provided, be effected by two deeds, namely, a vesting deed and a trust instrument and if effected in any other way shall not operate to transfer or create a legal estate.

37 (1991) LQR 596 at 599 (Hill, J).

38 See Law Commission's Working Paper (No 94), para 3.5, quoted at para 1.3 of the Law Commission's report on Trusts of Land (Law Com No 181); see also Law Com No 181, paras 4.2, 4.3.

39 The need of two documents has been thought to be unduly complex, particularly where several lands are acquired for the settlement after it has been created, there may be a considerable number of subsidiary vesting deeds: The Law Commission's Working Paper on Trusts of Land (No 94), para 3.15, quoted at para 1.3 of the Law Commission's report on Trusts of Land (Law Com No 181).

The idea was that a trust instrument would set out the details of beneficial entitlements which were often of a private nature. The trust instrument would therefore contain certain prescribed information:

Settled Land Act 1925

4. Authorised method of settling land *inter vivos*

(3) The trust instrument shall:

(a) declare the trusts affecting the settled land;

(b) appoint or constitute trustees of the settlement;

(c) contain the power, if any, to appoint new trustees of the settlement;

(d) set out, either expressly or by reference, any powers intended to be conferred by the settlement in extension of those conferred by this Act;

(e) bear any *ad valorem* stamp duty[40] which may be payable (whether by virtue of the vesting deed or otherwise) in respect of the settlement.

A sample of trust document is provided by the 1st Schedule, Form No 3 of the Settled Land Act 1925.

Form No 3

TRUST INSTRUMENT ON THE SETTLEMENT OF LAND

This trust Instrument is made [etc] between John H of [etc] (hereinafter called the Settlor) of the first part, Jane W of [etc] of the second part, and X of [etc], Y of [etc], and Z of [etc] (hereinafter called the trustees) of the third part.

Whereas by a deed (hereinafter called the Vesting Deed) bearing even date with but executed contemporaneously with these presents, and made between the same parties and in the same order as these presents, certain hereditaments situated at ... in the county of ... were vested in the Settlor Upon the trusts declared concerning the same by a trust instrument of even date therein referred to (meaning these presents).

Now in consideration of the intended marriage between the Settlor and Jane W, this Deed Witnesseth as follows:

1. The Settlor hereby agrees that he will hold the hereditaments and property comprised in the Vesting Deed In trust for himself until the solemnisation of the said marriage and thereafter Upon the trusts following, that is to say:

2. Upon trust for the Settlor during his life without impeachment of waste with remainder Upon trust if Jane W survives him that she shall receive out of the premises during the residue of her life a yearly jointure rentcharge of [etc] and subject thereto Upon trust for the trustees for a term of 800 years from the date of the death of the Settlor without impeachment of waste Upon the trusts hereinafter declared concerning the same. And subject to the said term and the trust thereof Upon trust for the first and other

40 As from 1 April 1993, payable at the rate of one per cent of the total value stated on the conveyance or transfer, unless the consideration does not exceed £60,000. If the property is given away for no consideration, no duty is payable.

sons of the said intended marriage successively according to seniority in tail male with remainder [etc] with an ultimate remainder in trust for the Settlor in fee simple.

[Here add the requisite trusts of the portions term, and any other proper provisions including the appointment of the trustees to be trustees of the settlement for the purposes of the Settled Land Act 1925, extension of Settled Land Act powers, and a power for the tenant for life for the time being of full age to appoint new trustees of the settlement.]

In witness [etc]

[NOTE – The Vesting Deed and the Trust Instrument can be executed as escrows till the marriage.]

A vesting deed, on the other hand, was a public document which was of principle concern to a purchaser. Under s 5(1) of the Settled Land Act, it must contain certain prescribed information:

Settled Land Act 1925

5. Contents of vesting deeds

(1) Every vesting deed for giving effect to a settlement or for conveying settled land to a tenant for life or statutory owner during the subsistence of the settlement (in this Act referred to as a 'principal vesting deed') shall contain the following statements and particulars, namely:

(a) A description, either specific or general, of the settled land;

(b) A statement that the settled land is vested in the person or persons to whom it is conveyed or in whom it is declared to be vested upon the trusts from time to time affecting the settled Land;

(c) The names of the persons who are the trustees of the settlement;

(d) Any additional or larger powers conferred by the trust instrument relating to the settled land which by virtue of this Act operate and are exercisable as if conferred by this Act on a tenant for life;

(e) The name of any person for the time being entitled under the trust instrument to appoint new trustees of the settlement.

A sample of vesting deed is provided by the 1st Schedule, Form No 2 of the Settled Land Act 1925.

Form No 2

VESTING DEED ON THE SETTLEMENT OF LAND

This Vesting Deed made [etc] between John H of [etc] of the first part, Jane W of [etc] of the second part, and X of [etc], Y of [etc], and Z of [etc] (hereinafter called the trustees) of the third part.

Witnesseth and it is hereby declared as follows::

1. In consideration of the intended marriage between John H and Jane W the said John H as Settlor hereby declares that

All that (setting out the parcels by reference to a schedule or otherwise) are vested in John H in fee simple (or in the case of leaseholds refer to the terms).

Upon the trusts declared concerning the same by a Trust Instrument bearing even date with but intended to be executed contemporaneously with these presents and made between the same parties and in the same order as these presents or upon such other trusts as the same ought to be held from time to time.

2. The trustees are the trustees of the settlement for the purposes of the Settled Land Act 1925.

3. The following additional or larger powers are conferred by the said trust instrument in relation to the settled land and by virtue of the Settled Land Act 1925, operate and are exercisable as if conferred by that Act on a tenant for life. [Here insert the additional powers.]

4. The power of appointing a new trustee or new trustees of the settlement is vested in the said [John H] during his life.

In witness [etc]

Where the settlor divested himself of all interests in the land, the vesting deed served as a conveyance, transferring the legal estate from the settlor to the tenant for life. Where the settlor was himself the tenant for life, no transfer of legal estate was needed, the vesting deed merely served as a declaration that he held the legal estate as a tenant for life under a settlement.[41]

Settled Land Act 1925

4. Authorised method of settling land *inter vivos*

(2) By the vesting deed the land shall be conveyed to the tenant for life or statutory owner (and if more than one as joint tenants) for the legal estate the subject of the intended settlement:

Provided that, where such legal estate is already vested in the tenant for life or statutory owner, it shall be sufficient, without any other conveyance, if the vesting deed declares that the land is vested in him for that estate.

Thus, a vesting deed was an important document of title and formed part of the evidence of title in unregistered conveyancing.

A settlement of a legal estate without a vesting instrument could not transfer a legal estate.[42] If it had not already been done, the tenant for life could require the trustees of the settlement to execute a vesting deed so as to transfer the legal estate to him.[43]

Settled Land Act 1925

9. Procedure in the case of settlements and of instruments deemed to be trust instruments

(2) As soon as practicable after a settlement, or an instrument which for the purposes of this Act is deemed to be a trust instrument, takes effect as such, the trustees of the

41 Section 4(2) of the SLA 1925.

42 Section 4(1) of the SLA 1925.

43 Section 9(2) of the SLA 1925.

> settlement may, and on the request of the tenant for life or statutory owner shall, execute a principal vesting deed, containing the proper statements and particulars, declaring that the legal estate in the settled land shall vest or is vested in the person or persons therein named, being the tenant for life or statutory owner, and including themselves if they are the statutory owners, and such deed shall, unless the legal estate is already so vested, operate to convey or vest the legal estate in the settled land to or in the person or persons aforesaid and, if more than one, as joint tenants.

Where the title to the land was registered, the same procedure followed except that a prescribed form of vesting transfer was used in place of vesting deed,[44] and more importantly, the legal estate would not vest in the tenant for life until he was registered as the new proprietor.[45] The tenant for life would be the registered owner and the beneficial interests of the settlement should be protected by an entry of a restriction or notice.[46] It was the duty of the proprietor to effect such an entry.[47] A restriction took the following form (Statutory Form 9).

Statutory Form 9

Restriction where Tenant for Life is registered as proprietor

No disposition under which capital money arises is to be registered unless the money is paid to ... (the trustees of the settlement ...), or into court.

Except under an order of the Registrar, no disposition is to be registered, unless authorised by the Settled Land Act 1925.

The two documents must be executed by the settlor at the same time. As will be seen, failure in this rendered the settlement imperfect.

Strict settlement by will

A settlor could choose to settle his land by will which would take effect on his death. Where land was settled by the will of a testator after 1925, the will was treated as the trust instrument.[48]

Settled Land Act 1925

6. Procedure in the case of settlements by will

Where a settlement is created by the will of an estate owner who dies after the commencement of this Act:

(a) the will is for the purposes of this Act a trust instrument; and

(b) the personal representatives of the testator shall hold the settled land on trust, if and when required so to do, to convey it to the person who, under the will, or by virtue of this Act, is the tenant for life or statutory owner, and, if more than one, as joint tenants.

---

44 Rule 99 of the LRR 1925.

45 Section 86(1) of the LRA 1925.

46 Sections 86(3), 49(1)(d) of the LRA 1925.

47 Rule 104(1) of the LRR 1925.

48 Section 6(a) of the SLA 1925.

On the testator's death, the legal estate vested immediately in the testator's personal representatives under s 1(1) of the Administration of Estates Act 1925. The personal representatives must, however, hold the estate on trust and were under a duty to transfer the legal estate to the tenant for life by a simple assent in writing (a vesting assent).[49] When the vesting assent was executed in the normal course of perfecting the settlement by will, a purchaser was not allowed to look at the will to see if the vesting assent contained the correct information. He had to assume that the land described and the persons named as tenant for life and trustees of settlement in the vesting assent were correct.[50]

Strict settlement created before 1926

A strict settlement could be created before 1926 by a single document (either trust instrument or will). That document was after 1925 treated as the trust instrument and a vesting deed should be executed by the trustees in favour of the tenant for life as soon as practicable.[51] The legal estate which was either vested in the trustees of the settlement or split up between a number of beneficiaries of various estates was now automatically vested in the tenant for life by the Law of Property Act 1925.[52] A subsequent vesting deed, therefore, did not convey the legal estate but provided documentary evidence of title. However, a purchaser was required to verify from the trust instrument which was created before 1926 that the settlement included the land described in the vesting deed and that the proper persons were named as tenant for life and trustees of the settlement.[53]

5 IMPROPERLY CONSTITUTED SETTLEMENT

As already mentioned, a strict settlement created after 1925 required two deeds. Where a strict settlement was declared by one document, it was treated as a trust instrument. No legal estate could be transferred from the settlor to the tenant for life until a vesting deed was executed.

Under s 13 of the Settled Land Act 1925, no disposition of a legal estate could be made until a vesting instrument had been executed. Until this had been done, any purported disposition of the land *inter vivos* by any person operated only as a contract for valuable consideration (registrable as an estate contract in unregistered land and to be protected as a minor interest in registered land) to carry out the transaction after the requisite vesting instrument had been executed.

---

49 Sections 6(b), 8(1) of the SLA 1925. A vesting assent is a document which transfers ownership of settled land from the personal representatives to the tenant for life. It must be signed by the personal representatives but need not be executed as a deed.

50 Section 110(2) of the SLA 1925. See Megarry and Wade, p 336.

51 2nd Schedule, para 1(1) of the SLA 1925.

52 1st Schedule, Part II of the LPA 1925I.

53 Section 110(2) of the SLA 1925.

Settled Land Act 1925

13. Dispositions not to take effect until vesting instrument is made

Where a tenant for life or statutory owner has become entitled to have a principal vesting deed or a vesting assent executed in his favour, then until a vesting instrument is executed or made pursuant to this Act in respect of the settled land, any purported disposition thereof *inter vivos* by any person, other than a personal representative (not being a disposition which he has power to make in right of his equitable interests or powers under a trust instrument), shall not take effect except in favour of a purchaser of a legal estate without notice of such tenant for life or statutory owner having become so entitled as aforesaid but, save as aforesaid, shall operate only as a contract for valuable consideration to carry out the transaction after the requisite vesting instrument has been executed or made, and a purchaser of a legal estate shall not be concerned with such disposition unless the contract is registered as a land charge.

Nothing in this section affects the creation or transfer of a legal estate by virtue of an order of the court or the Minister or other competent authority.

The purpose of s 13 was to ensure that tenant for life got a power vesting instrument which would form part of the evidence of title before he could exercise his powers under the Act. This was particularly important where the tenant for life was himself the settlor, because the legal estate was still with him and since he also had the title deeds of the land, he could suppress the trust instrument and attempt to dispose of the land in breach of trust. The effect of s 13 was to paralyse such an attempted transaction. Similarly, where the settlement was created before 1926 by one document and the legal estate was automatically vested in the tenant for life, s 13 of the Law of Property Act after 1925 paralysed any transaction carried out before a vesting deed was executed. However, s 13 only protected the beneficiaries under the settlement if the purchaser was aware of the need of the vesting deed. A purchaser of a legal estate without notice of the tenant for life having become entitled to a vesting instrument was not bound by s 13 and could take a good legal title whether a vesting deed had been executed or not.[54]

Other exceptions to s 13

(a) Section 13 itself provided an exception, that is, it did not apply where the disposition was made by a personal representative. This is in line with the rule that personal representatives should have power to deal freely with the land in the administration of the estate and to confer good title on a purchaser.

(b) It did not apply where the settlement had come to an end before the execution of a vesting instrument.[55] The settlement ended when one person became solely and absolutely entitled and the trusts of the trust instrument were otherwise exhausted. For example, where land was given to A in tail with remainder to B in fee simple, when property was passed to A in possession who

54 Section 13 of the SLA 1925, as amended by s 7 Schedule of the Law of Property (Amendment) Act 1926.

55 *Re Alefounders WT* [1927] 1 Ch 360.

then barred the entail in favour of C, C became absolutely entitled to the fee simple and a vesting deed was no longer needed. Once the barring of entail was done, the land ceased to be a settled land.

(c) As we have seen earlier, where a person of full age was beneficially entitled to land subject to family charges, the person could choose to dispose of the legal estate subject to the charges without a vesting deed.[56]

(d) Where the legal estate was created or transferred by virtue of an order of the court or the Minister or other competent authority, no vesting deed was required.[57]

Where the vesting deed was executed by the trustees of the settlement subsequently, just like a settlement made before 1926, any purchaser must investigate the trust instrument to make sure the deed contained the correct information.[58]

6 TENANTS FOR LIFE

Settled Land Act 1925

19. Who is tenant for life

(1) The person of full age who is for the time being beneficially entitled under a settlement to possession of settled land for his life is for the purposes of this Act the tenant for life of that land and the tenant for life under that settlement.

(2) If in any case there are two or more persons of full age so entitled as joint tenants, they together constitute the tenant for life for the purposes of this Act.

(3) If in any case there are two or more persons so entitled as joint tenants and they are not all of full age, such one or more of them as is or are for the time being of full age is or (if more than one) together constitute the tenant for life for the purposes of this Act, but this subsection does not affect the beneficial interests of such of them as are not for the time being of full age.

117. Definitions

(1) In this Act, unless the context otherwise requires, the following expressions have the meanings hereby assigned to them respectively, that is to say:

(xxviii) 'Tenant for life' includes a person (not being a statutory owner) who has the powers of a tenant for life under this Act, and also (where the context requires) one of two or more persons who together constitute the tenant for life, or have the powers of a tenant for life; and 'tenant in tail' includes a person entitled to an entailed interest in any property; and 'entailed interest' has the same meaning as in the Law of Property Act 1925.

56 Section 1 of the Law of Property (Amendment) Act 1926.

57 Section 13 of the SLA 1925, as added by s 6 of the Law of Property (Amendment) Act 1926.

58 Section 110(2) of the SLA 1925.

20. Other limited owners having powers of tenant for life

(1) Each of the following persons being of full age shall, when his estate or interest is in possession, have the powers of a tenant for life under this Act (namely):

(i) A tenant in tail, including a tenant in tail after possibility of issue extinct, and a tenant in tail who is by Act of Parliament restrained from barring or defeating his estate tail, and although the reversion is in the Crown, but not including such a tenant in tail where the land in respect whereof he is so restrained was purchased with money provided by Parliament in consideration of public services;

(ii) A person entitled to land for an estate in fee simple or for a term of years absolute with or subject to, in any of such cases, an executory limitation, gift, or disposition over on failure of his issue or in any other event;

(iii) A person entitled to a base or determinable fee, although the reversion or right of reverter is in the Crown, or to any corresponding interest in leasehold land;

(iv) A tenant for years determinable on life, not holding merely under a lease at a rent;

(v) A tenant for the life of another, not holding merely under a lease at a rent;

(vi) A tenant for his own or any other life, or for years determinable on life, whose estate is liable to cease in any event during that life, whether by expiration of the estate, or by conditional limitation, or otherwise, or to be defeated by an executory limitation, gift, or disposition over, or is subject to a trust for accumulation of income for any purpose;

(vii) A tenant by the courtesy;

(viii) A person entitled to the income of land under a trust or direction for payment thereof to him during his own or any other life, whether or not subject to expenses of management or to a trust for accumulation of income for any purpose, or until sale of the land, or until forfeiture, cesser or determination by any means of his interest therein, unless the land is subject to a trust of land;

(ix) A person beneficially entitled to land for an estate in fee simple or for a term of years absolute subject to any estates, interests, charges, or powers of charging, subsisting or capable of being exercised under a settlement;

(x) ...'

Section 19(1) of the Settled Land Act 1925 provided that 'the person of full age who is for the time being entitled under a settlement to possession of settled land for his life is for the purposes of this Act the tenant for life'. In addition, s 117(1)(xxviii) of the same Act defined 'tenant for life' as 'including a person (not being a statutory owner) who has the powers of a tenant for life'. Who were these persons? Section 20 of the Act conferred the statutory powers of a tenant for life to many other limited owners who were of full age and currently entitled to an estate or interest in possession.[59] The net result was that any person of full age beneficially entitled to the possession or the whole of the income from

59 This was thought to be unnecessarily complex: Law Commission's Working Paper (No 94), para 3.15, quoted at para 1.3 of the Law Commission's report on Trusts of Land (Law Com No 181).

the land was a tenant for life. But a person who was entitled to a future interest under s 1(1)(iii) of the Act could not be a tenant for life, because he was not entitled in possession.

Note that, as mentioned earlier, in some cases the powers of a tenant for life were vested in the statutory owners.[60] These persons were not tenants for life for the purpose of the Act although they were given the powers of tenant for life and the legal estate was vested in them.

To qualify as a tenant for life for the purposes of the Act, the person entitled in possession must be entitled to it under the settlement. So an assignee of a life interest was not a tenant for life under the Act as he held the life interest under the assignment.[61] In such a case, the assignor remained the tenant for life for the purposes of the Act though he had no more beneficial interest.

7 TRUSTEES OF THE SETTLEMENT

It should be apparent by now that it was very important to identify the trustees of the settlement, because they had important functions. It should be noted from the outset that the number of the trustees of the settlement must not be more than four.[62]

Who were the trustees of the settlement?

Settled Land Act 1925

30. Who are trustees for purposes of Act

(1) Subject to the provisions of this Act, the following persons are trustees of a settlement for the purposes of this Act, and are in this Act referred to as the 'trustees of the settlement' or 'trustees of a settlement', namely:

(i) the persons, if any, who are for th~ time being under the settlement trustees with power of sale of the settled land (subject or not to the consent of any person), or with power of consent to or approval of the exercise of such a power of sale, or if there are no such persons; then

(ii) the persons, if any, for the time being, who are by the settlement declared to be trustees thereof for the purposes of the Settled Land Acts 1882–90, or any of them, or this Act, or if there are no such persons; then

(iii) the persons, if any, who are for the time being under the settlement trustees with a power or duty to sell any other land comprised in the settlement and subject to the same limitations as the land to be sold or otherwise dealt with, or with power of consent to or approval of the exercise of such a power of sale, or, if there are no such persons; then

(iv) the persons, if any, who are for the time being under the settlement trustees with a future power or duty to sell the settled land, or with power of consent to or approval of

60 Sections 23(1) and 117(1)(xxvi) of the SLA 1925.

61 *Re Earl of Carnarvon's Chesterfield* [1927] 1 Ch 138.

62 Section 34 of the Trustee Act 1925.

the exercise of such a future power of sale, and whether the power or duty takes effect in all events or not, or, if there are no such persons; then

(v) the persons, if any, appointed by deed to be trustees of the settlement by all the persons who at the date of the deed were together able, by virtue of their beneficial interests or by the exercise of an equitable power, to dispose of the settled land in equity for the whole estate the subject of the settlement.

(3) Where a settlement is created by will, or a settlement has arisen by the effect of an intestacy, and apart from this subsection there would be no trustees for the purposes of this Act of such settlement, then the personal representatives of the deceased shall, until other trustees are appointed, be by virtue of this Act the trustees of the settlement, but where there is a sole personal representative, not being a trust corporation, it shall be obligatory on him to appoint an additional trustee to act with him for the purposes of this Act, and the provisions of the Trustee Act 1925, relating to the appointment of new trustees and the vesting of trust property shall apply accordingly.

Section 30(1) provided that the trustees of a settlement were, in a descending order of priority, as follows:

(i) Persons under the settlement with power of sale or power of consenting to or approving the exercise of such a power of sale. For example, a settlement to A for life, with remainder over, and X and Y were expressly given the power to sell the settled land. Under s 30(1) X and Y were the trustees in preference even to any other persons expressly named as the trustees for the purpose of the Settled Land Act 1925. The fact that under s 108(2) of the Settled Land Act 1925 this power of sale was in fact taken away from them and given to the tenant for life did not affect their status as trustees under this head.

(ii) Persons declared by a settlement to be trustees 'for the purposes of the Settled Land Act'. The words 'for the purpose of the SLA' must be added. This was the head under which trustees were commonly found and cases under head (i) above were rare.

(iii) Trustees with power of sale or of consenting to or approving a sale of any other land in the same settlement and upon the same trust. For example, if both Blackacre and Whiteacre were settled under the same settlement, and in that settlement X and Y were given a power of sale over Blackacre alone, under this head X and Y would also become trustees of the settlement of Whiteacre if none could be found for Whiteacre under the first two heads.

(iv) Persons with future power of sale under the settlement or under a future trust for sale, or with power of consenting to or approving the exercise of such a future power of sale. For example, if Greenacre was settled on A for life with remainder to X and Y on trust for sale. X and Y would be the trustees of the settlement under this head.

(v) Persons appointed by those able to dispose of the whole equitable interest in the settled land. For example, if land was settled for A for life, remainder to B in fee simple. A and B acting together could appoint trustees of the settlement under this head.

There was nothing in the Act to prevent the tenant for life from being one of the trustees. Where no Settled Land Act 1925 trustees could be found under the provisions mentioned above, the court had a power to appoint trustees of the settlement on the application of any person interested under the settlement.[63]

If a settlement arose under a will and there were no trustees, the personal representatives were trustees until others were appointed.[64]

Where a subsequent settlement referred to an earlier settlement, eg Blackacre was to be held on the limitations and subject to the powers and provisions of an earlier settlement under which Whiteacre was held, then unless trustees for the settlement of Blackacre were appointed separately for the purposes of the Settled Land Act under s 30(1)(ii) (see (ii) above) the trustees of the earlier settlement of Whiteacre became trustees of the later settlement of Blackacre which referred to it.[65]

8 WHO OWNED THE LEGAL ESTATE?

It was necessary to find out in a strict settlement who had the legal estate in the settled land, for it was he who was able to deal with the settled land. The Settled Land Act had deliberately chosen the tenant for life to vest the legal estate. The allocation of legal ownership was largely a matter of convenience because it was the tenant for life who had the most direct and immediate interest in the enjoyment of the trust property. He was, therefore, naturally the best person to be entrusted with the day-to-day management of the settled land. Thus, in a normal case where a strict settlement was created *inter vivos* by two deeds, the vesting deed would transfer the legal estate from the settlor to the tenant for life.[66] Where the settlement was created by will, the legal estate would pass to the settlor's ordinary personal representatives under the general law.[67] The personal representatives would then transfer the legal estate to the tenant for life by a vesting assent.[68]

It should be noted that where the settled land was registered, the tenant for life or the statutory owner was registered as the proprietor and the beneficial interest should be protected as a minor interest.

Land Registration Act 1925

86. Registration of settled land

(1) Settled land shall be registered in the name of the tenant for life or statutory owner.

---

63 Section 34 of the SLA 1925. The Law Commission thought that the present provisions for ascertaining who are the trustees of the settlement where none are appointed are complex: The Law Commission's Working Paper (No 94), para 3.15, quoted at para 1.3 of the Law Commission's report on Trusts of Land (Law Com No 181).

64 Section 30(3) of the SLA 1925.

65 Section 32(1) of the SLA 1925.

66 Section 4(2) of the SLA 1925.

67 Section 1(1) of the AEA 1925.

68 Sections 6(b), 8(1) of the SLA 1925.

(3) There shall also be entered on the register such restrictions as may be prescribed, or may be expedient, for the protection of the rights of the persons beneficially interested in the land, and such restrictions shall (subject to the provisions of this Act relating to releases by the trustees of a settlement and to transfers by a tenant for life whose estate has ceased in his lifetime) be binding on the proprietor during his life, but shall not restrain or otherwise affect a disposition by his personal representative.

49. Rules to provide for notices of other rights, interests and claims

(1) The provisions of the last foregoing section shall be extended by the rules so as to apply to the registration of notices of or of claims in respect of:

(a) The grant or reservation of any annuity or rentcharge in possession, either perpetual or for a term of years absolute:

...

(d) The right of any person interested in land subject to a trust of land or in land subject to a settlement to require that (unless a trust corporation is acting as trustee) there shall be at least two trustees of the trust or the settlement:

(2) A notice shall not be registered in respect of any estate, right, or interest which (independently of this Act) is capable of being overriden by the proprietor under a trust of land or the powers of the Settled Land Act 1925, or any other statute, or of a settlement, and of being protected by a restriction in the prescribed manner:

Provided that notice of such an estate right or interest may be lodged pending the appointment of trustees of land, or trustees of a settlement, and if so lodged, shall be cancelled if and when the appointment is made and the proper restriction (if any) is entered.

Where the tenant for life died and the land remained settled, for example, land was settled 'to A for life, to B in tail', the legal estate in the settled land vested automatically in his trustees of the settlement as the 'special personal representatives'.[69] The next person entitled under the settlement could require the special personal representative to vest the legal estate in him.[70] If the settlement had come to an end on the death of the tenant for life, for example, land was settled 'to A for life, to B in fee simple', then the legal estate would vest in his ordinary personal representative.[71] Similarly, the person who now became absolutely entitled to the beneficial interest could require the personal representatives to convey the legal estate to him.[72]

But in two cases the legal estate and the statutory powers of a tenant for life were vested in the 'statutory owner'.

---

69 Section 22(1) of the AEA 1925.

70 Section 7(1) of the SLA 1925.

71 In *Re Bright and Hayes' Contract* [1928] Ch 163 at 170.

72 Section 7(5) of the SLA 1925.

Tenant for life an infant

Settled Land Act 1925

26. Infants, how to be affected

(1) Where an infant is beneficially entitled in possession to land for an estate in fee simple or for a term of years absolute or would if of full age be a tenant for life of or have the powers of a tenant for life over settled land, then, during the minority of the infant:

(a) if the settled land is vested in a personal representative, the personal representative, until a principal vesting instrument has been executed pursuant to the provisions of this Act; and

(b) in every other case, the trustees of the settlement;

shall have, in reference to the settled land and capital money, all the powers conferred by this Act and the settlement on a tenant for life, and on the trustees of the settlement.

(2) If the settled land is vested in a personal representative, then, if and when during the minority the infant, if of full age, would have been entitled to have the legal estate in the settled land conveyed to or otherwise vested in him pursuant to the provisions of this Act, a principal vesting instrument shall, if the trustees of the settlement so require, be executed, at the cost of the trust estate, for vesting the legal estate in themselves, and in the meantime the personal representative shall, during the minority, give effect to the directions of the trustees of the settlement, and shall not be concerned with the propriety of any conveyance directed to be made by those trustees if the conveyance appears to be a proper conveyance under the powers conferred by this Act or by the settlement, and the capital money, if any, arising under the conveyance is paid to or by the direction of the trustees of the settlement or into court, but a purchaser dealing with the personal representative and paying the capital money, if any, to him shall not be concerned to see that the money is paid to trustees of the settlement or into court, or to inquire whether the personal representative is liable to give effect to any such directions, or whether any such directions have been given.

(4) This section does not apply where an infant is beneficially entitled in possession to land for an estate in fee simple or for a term of years absolute jointly with a person of full age (for which case provision is made in the Law of Property Act 1925), but it applies to two or more infants entitled as aforesaid jointly, until one of them attains full age.

(5) This section does not apply where an infant would, if of full age, constitute the tenant for life or have the powers of a tenant for life together with another person of full age, but it applies to two or more infants who would, if all of them were of full age, together constitute the tenant for life or have the powers of a tenant for life, until one of them attains full age.

Where the tenant for life was an infant, for example 'to A in fee simple' but A was an infant, the settled land continued to be vested in the personal representatives, if the settlement was created by will.[73] In this case, the statutory power

73 Section 26(1)(a) of the SLA 1925.

was given to the personal representative until the vesting instrument was executed, on the request of the trustees of the settlement to vest the legal estate and the statutory powers in themselves.[74] If the settlement was created *inter vivos*, the settled land would be vested in the trustees of the settlement.[75]

No tenant for life

There were cases where no one was entitled under the settlement as tenant for life. For example, where no one was entitled to the whole residue of income (eg where the trustees were directed to accumulate part of the income)[76] or where no one was entitled to the income at all (eg where trustees were given a power to distribute the income as they thought fit)[77] or where the trustees were directed to accumulate the income for a springing absolute interest. In these cases, the legal estate and the statutory powers of a tenant for life were in any person of full age upon whom the settlement expressly conferred the powers.[78] Where no one was given the powers expressly by the settlement, the trustees of the settlement were given the powers of a tenant for life.[79]

Settled Land Act 1925

23. Powers of trustees, etc when there is no tenant for life

(1) Where under a settlement there is no tenant for life nor, independently of this section, a person having by virtue of this Act the powers of a tenant for life then:

(a) any person of full age on whom such powers are by the settlement expressed to be conferred; and

(b) in any other case the trustees of the settlement;

shall have the powers of a tenant for life under this Act.

As has been seen, s 30 of the Settled Land Act provided a list, in a descending order, of persons who qualified as trustees of the settlement. Where no persons qualified as trustees of the settlement under s 30, if the settlement was created by will, the personal representatives would exercise the powers of trustees of the settlement.[80] If the settlement was not created by will, anyone who had an interest under the settlement could apply to the court for the appointment of trustees.[81]

---

74 Section 26(2) of the SLA 1925.

75 Section 26(1)(b) of the SLA 1925.

76 For example, *Re Jefferys (No 2)* [1939] Ch 205; *Re Frewen* [1926] Ch 580.

77 For example, *Re Atkinson* (1886) 31 Ch D 577; *Re Horne's SE* (1888) 39 Ch D 84; *Re Alston-Roberts-West's SE* [1928] WN 41.

78 Section 23(1)(a) of the SLA 1925. eg *Re Craven SE* [1926] Ch 985; *Re Norton* [1929] 1 Ch 84.

79 Section 23(1)(b) of the SLA 1925.

80 Section 30(3) of the SLA 1925.

81 Section 34 of the SLA 1925.

9 POWERS OF A TENANT FOR LIFE

The tenant for life had a life interest in the settled land. He could deal with his limited interest as he liked but these transactions would not bind his successors under the settlement. Any purchaser who wanted to gamble on the longevity of the tenant for life would only acquire an interest *pur autre vie*.[82]

On the other hand, the tenant for life also had the legal estate of the settlement vested in him. This was, as will be recalled, to remove the disincentive originally caused by the restrictions of a strict settlement to the life tenant in managing the settled land. The Settled Land Act 1925 gave him extensive powers[83] to sell or to exchange the settled land.[84] He could, therefore, sell the settled land despite the fact that the settlor's intention might have been to keep it in the family.[85] He had powers to lease,[86] to grant an option over,[87] or to mortgage the legal estate in the settled land.[88] However, he could only exercise these powers in the manner authorised by the Act. The court could however authorise the tenant for life to effect any transaction (not otherwise authorised by the Act or the settlement), affecting the settled land, which would be for the benefit of the settled land or all the beneficiaries under the settlement.[89]

Safeguard of the power

(a) Under s 16 of the Settled Land Act 1925 the tenant for life held the legal estate as a trustee for himself and the beneficiaries under the settlement. He had to exercise the powers in the interests of all other beneficiaries under the settlement.[90] Therefore, he could not sell the property at a price well below its value.[91] He could not make an investment which was undesirable even if it was

82 See Chapter 1.

83 The Law Commission thinks that it is appropriate to place these powers on the tenant for life. It therefore proposes that in the new trusts of land, it should be possible to delegate these powers which will be in the trustees of land to the beneficiaries in possession: see Law Commission, Transfer of Land: Trusts of Land, Law Com No 181, para 4.5.

84 Section 38 of the SLA 1925.

85 It is impossible for a remainderman to prevent the sale of the land, unless there is lack of good faith on the part of the tenant for life. This leaves the remainderman in a very weak position because the land may have already been sold before he becomes aware of the tenant for life's intention to sell (eg *England v Public Trustee* (1968) 112 SJ 70): see Law Commission's Working Paper (No 94, Trusts of Land), para 3.16 quoted at para 1.3 of the Law Commission's report on Trusts of Land (Law Com No 181).

86 Section 41 of the SLA 1925.

87 Section 51 of the SLA 1925.

88 Section 71 of the SLA 1925.

89 Section 64(1) of the SLA 1925; *Hambro v The Duke of Marlborough* (1994) *The Times* 25 March; [1994] 3 All ER 332.

90 Section 107 of the SLA 1925. The Law Commission has suggested that the current law does not provide an adequate safeguard against conflict of interest by the tenant for life and, in some cases, the remaindermen have no effective remedy: The Law Commission's Working Paper (No 94), para 3.16, quoted at para 1.3 of the Law Commission's report on Trusts of Land (Law Com No 181); see also Law Com No 181, para 4.4.

91 *Wheelwright v Walker (No 1)* (1883) 23 Ch D 752.

within his powers to do so.[92] He could not effect any transaction which would prejudice other beneficiaries.[93] The power must be exercised *bona fide* in the interest of the settlement and not for a collateral purpose. So if the interest of the tenant for life under the settlement would end on remarriage, she could not lease the property to her intended husband in order that she could continue to live in the house after the marriage, if it would be a mere device to evade the settlement.[94]

Middlemas v Stevens [1901] 1 Ch 574

Joyce J: I have no doubt in this case. A tenant for life in exercising any of the powers conferred by the Settled Land Acts must have regard to the interests of all parties entitled under the settlement. Here is a lady who is tenant for life during widowhood. Apart from any question as to her relationship to the gentleman who is the intended lessee, if I found a person, whose interest in the settled property would come to an end tomorrow, persisting in granting a lease which was objected to by all those entitled in remainder, I should regard the case with considerable suspicion. But this case goes beyond suspicion. It is clear from the correspondence that the real object of the lady in granting the lease is that she may herself continue in occupation of the premises. That, in my opinion, is not a *bona fide* exercise of her powers as a tenant for life. But it does not rest there, because it is admitted by the correspondence that she has no intention of granting the lease in the event of her not marrying the gentleman in question. I think the plaintiffs are entitled to an injunction restraining the defendant from granting the lease without their consent or the sanction of the court.

(b) Powers relating to sale, exchange, lease, mortgage or charge, or granting of an option could only be exercised after at least one month's notice had been given to the trustees of the settlement, and, if known, to the solicitor for the trustees.[95] Where the trustees of the settlement were statutory owners, this requirement was not needed.[96] Notice must be given to two trustees or more or a trust corporation.[97] So if there were no trustees, a tenant for life could not exercise these powers until trustees were appointed.[98] Trustees who were aware of the improper exercise of the powers could apply to the court for an injunction.[99] However, this safeguard was not satisfactory, because the trustees were under no obligation to do so.[100] The trustees for the settlement could, by writing, accept less than one month's notice, or waive it altogether.[101] Furthermore, in the case of a mortgage or charge, a general notice such as 'I

92 *Re Hunt's SE* [1905] 2 Ch 418.

93 *Hampden v Earl of Buckinghamshire* [1893] 2 Ch 531.

94 *Middlemas v Stevens* [1901] Ch 574.

95 Section 101(1) of the SLA 1925.

96 *Re Countess of Dudley's Contract* (1887) 35 Ch D 338.

97 Section 101(1) of the SLA 1925.

98 *Re Bentley* (1885) 54 LJ Ch 782.

99 Section 93 of the SLA 1925.

100 Sections 93 and 97 of the SLA 1925.

101 Section 101(4) of the SLA 1925.

intend to exercise any or all of my powers under the Settled Land Act 1925 from time to time' was enough.[102] Moreover, a person dealing in good faith with the tenant for life was not concerned to inquire whether notice had been given.[103]

(c) Where the settlement was created before 1926, the power to dispose of the principal mansion house could only be exercised with the consent of the trustees of the settlement or under a court order. Where the settlement was made after 1925, there was no requirement of consent under the Act but it could be expressly provided by the settlor.[104] The tenant for life's power to cut and sell timber was only exercisable with the consent of the trustees of the settlement or a court order.[105] The power to compromise claims was likewise subject to the consent of the trustees of the settlement.[106]

Powers of tenant for life were unfettered

Apart from the statutory requirement of consent, the tenant for life did not in general require consent before he exercised his powers. Statutory powers of the tenant for life were unfettered. Any attempt to forbid or prevent the exercise of such powers was void under s 106 of the Settled Land Act 1925.[107]

Section 106 made any attempt to forbid or prevent the exercise of the power of a tenant for life void. In *Re Ames*[108] a provision that the tenant for life should lose the right to monetary benefit if the land was sold was held void. This was because it attempted to prevent the exercise of the power of sale.

Section 106 could also render any indirect attempt to prevent the exercise of such powers void. A provision which said that the tenant for life would lose his interest in the property if he ceased to live in it could be held void. This was an indirect restriction on power of sale because once he sold the land, he ceased to live in it. The provision therefore discouraged the exercise of the power to sell or to let the property. So, in *Re Acklom*[109] it was held that if the tenant for life left the property in order to exercise the powers he would not lose his interest in the estate and the provision was void.

However, if the tenant for life left the property for some reason other than to exercise his statutory power (eg to have a holiday abroad), such a provision would be valid and he would lose his interest in the property.[110] This was because the provision would not be an attempt to fetter the exercise of the tenant for life's statutory powers.

---

102 Section 101(2) of the SLA 1925.

103 Section 101(5) of the SLA 1925.

104 Section 65 of the SLA 1925.

105 Section 66 of the SLA 1925.

106 Section 58 of the SLA 1925.

107 As a result, a strict settlement is not a particularly effective means of keeping land in the family, which frustrates the original purpose for which a strict settlement was designed: see Law Commission, Transfer of Land: Trusts of Land, Law Com No 181, para 4.3.

108 [1893] 2 Ch 479.

109 [1929] 1 Ch 195.

110 *Re Haynes* (1887) 37 Ch D 306.

Powers of tenant for life were not assignable

The powers were given to a tenant for life in his capacity as a trustee; he must exercise the powers for the benefit of the settlement. Section 104 of the Settled Land Act 1925 provided that the powers of a tenant for life were not assignable. He had to exercise these powers even after he had assigned his equitable interest.[111] The assignee would not be charged with the powers of the tenant for life. Furthermore, as already mentioned, the assignment of the tenant for life's equitable interest did not affect the legal ownership of the settled land which was still vested in him.

Where the tenant for life having disposed of his own equitable interest found himself uninterested in the management of the settled land, and unreasonably refused to exercise his statutory powers, any person interested in the settled land could apply to the court for an order authorising the trustees of the settlement to exercise the powers in the name and on behalf of the tenant for life, and the court could direct that any documents of title in the possession of the tenant for life be delivered to the trustees of the settlement.[112]

Power to sell and exchange

Power to sell and power to exchange could only be exercised if the best consideration in money could be reasonably obtained.[113] The tenant for life would execute the conveyance because he had the legal estate vested in him. The conveyance of the legal estate in the settled land only took effect if the capital money (the proceeds of sale) was paid to all the trustees of the settlement, who must be at least two in number (except where the trustee was a trust corporation), or into court. [114]

Power to lease

With regard to power to lease, the settled land could be leased for any period not exceeding 999 years for building or forestry, 100 years for mining, 50 years for any other purposes.[115] Leases of settled land must be made by deed[116] except where the lease was for not more than three years, in which case it could be made in a written agreement.[117]

A lease of the settled land must be granted for the best rent or a fine reasonably obtainable.[118] It must contain a covenant by the tenant to pay rent

---

111 *Re Earl of Carnarvon's Chesterfield SE* [1927] 1 Ch 138.

112 Section 24(1) of the SLA 1925.

113 Sections 39(1), 40(1) of the SLA 1925.

114 Section 18(1)(b), (c) of the SLA 1925.

115 Section 41 of the SLA 1925.

116 Section 42(1)(i) of the SLA 1925.

117 Section 42(5)(ii) of the SLA 1925. Compare with leases for three years or less of non-settled land under s 54(2) of the LPA which need not be created by deed or in writing: see s 2(5)(a) of the LP (MP) Act 1989.

118 Section 42(1)(ii) of the SLA 1925.

and a provision for re-entry if the rent remained unpaid for a period specified in the lease, not exceeding 30 days.[119] Where the term of the lease did not exceed three years, it must contain an agreement (instead of a covenant) by the lessee for payment of rent.[120] It must take effect in possession not more than 12 months after the date of creation.[121] If it took effect in reversion after an existing lease, the existing lease must have less than seven years to run.[122]

A lease at the best rent reasonably obtainable without a fine, for a term not more than 21 years, could be granted without notice to the trustees of the settlement of the intention to make the lease.[123]

Where rent was payable, it was paid entirely to the tenant for life whereas a fine was regarded as the capital money[124] and should be paid to the trustees who would invest it. Income arising from the investment was, however, payable to the tenant for life.

Where the requirements of the Act were not complied with, the lease was void as against the settlement,[125] but it could be effective in equity at the lessee's option as a contract for a lease, if the lessee was in possession and the lease was made in good faith.[126] This also applied to leases created before 1926 which did not comply with the Act.[127]

Furthermore, a purchaser (including a tenant) who dealt in good faith with the tenant for life was conclusively presumed to have given the best consideration reasonably obtainable and to have complied with the other requirements of the Act.[128] So in most cases, a tenant could rely on s 110(1) and did not have to rely on s 152 and s 154 of the Law of Property Act 1925 unless there was evidence to show that he had not given the best consideration reasonably obtainable.

Power to grant options

A tenant for life could, at any time, either with or without consideration, grant by writing an option to purchase or take a lease of the settled land, or any part thereof, or any easement, right, or privilege over the settled land.[129] But the price or rent for the purchase or lease etc must be fixed at the time of the grant of the option[130] and it must be the best reasonably obtainable.[131] Such options

119 Section 42(1)(iii) of the SLA 1925.

120 Section 42(5)(ii) of the SLA 1925.

121 Section 42(1)(i) of the SLA 1925.

122 Section 42(1)(i) of the SLA 1925.

123 Section 42(5) of the SLA 1925.

124 Section 42(4) of the SLA 1925.

125 Section 18 of the SLA 1925.

126 Section 152 of the LPA 1925.

127 Section 154 of the LPA 1925.

128 Section 110(1) of the SLA 1925.

129 Section 51(1) of the SLA 1925.

130 Section 51(1) of the SLA 1925.

131 Section 51(3) of the SLA 1925.

must be exercisable within an agreed number of years not exceeding 10 years.[132]

Power to mortgage

Legal estate in the settled land could only be mortgaged to provide money required to be raised under the settlement or to provide money reasonably required for certain specified purposes set out in s 71(1) of the Settled Land Act 1925.[133] These were mainly for improvements or costs of transactions authorised by the Act and discharging certain existing incumbrances or liabilities.

Other powers

The settlor could grant the tenant for life any extra powers not specifically covered by the Settled Land Act 1925.

10 EFFECT OF UNAUTHORISED TRANSACTIONS

Void if unauthorised by the Act

While the settlement continued, land could be dealt with only under the Settled Land Act. As we have seen, s 13 paralysed dealings in the settled land until a valid vesting instrument had been executed. Once the vesting instrument had been executed, and as long as the settlement continued, any disposition by the tenant for life or statutory owner was then governed by s 18 of the Act. Under s 18 any disposition unauthorised by the Act was void.

Settled Land Act 1925

18. Restrictions on dispositions of settled land where trustees have not been discharged

(1) Where land is the subject of a vesting instrument and the trustees of the settlement have not been discharged under this Act, then:

(a) any disposition by the tenant for life or statutory owner of the land, other than a disposition authorised by this Act or any other statute, or made in pursuance of any additional or larger powers mentioned in the vesting instrument, shall be void, except for the purpose of conveying or creating such equitable interests as he has power, in right of his equitable interests and powers under the trust instrument, to convey or create; and

(b) if any capital money is payable in respect of a transaction, a conveyance to a purchaser of the land shall only take effect under this Act if the capital money is paid to or by the direction of the trustees of the settlement or into court; and

(c) notwithstanding anything to the contrary in the vesting instrument, or the trust instrument, capital money shall not, except where the trustee is a trust corporation, be paid to or by the direction of fewer persons than two as trustees of the settlement.

132 Section 51(2) of the SLA 1925.

133 Section 71(1) of the SLA 1925.

In *Weston v Henshaw*,[134] where the father settled his land by will upon his son for life with remainder to a grandson, and the son mortgaged the land not for purposes authorised by the Act but for his own personal needs, it was held that the mortgage was void against the grandson and hence the mortgagee lost his security.

Protection to purchaser in good faith

Protections were, however, given by s 110(1) of the Settled Land Act 1925 to any purchasers who dealt in good faith with a tenant for life or statutory owner. Such purchasers were taken to have given the best consideration reasonably obtainable and to have complied with all the requirements of the Act.

Settled Land Act 1925

110. Protection of purchasers, etc

(1) On a sale, exchange, lease, mortgage, charge, or other disposition, a purchaser dealing in good faith with a tenant for life or statutory owner shall, as against all parties entitled under the settlement, be conclusively taken to have given the best price, consideration, or rent, as the case may require, that could reasonably be obtained by the tenant for life or statutory owner, and to have complied with all the requisitions of this Act.

The application of ss 18 and 110 had given rise to some difficulties.[135] In *Weston v Henshaw*[136] Danckwerts J took the view that s 110(1) only applied where the purchaser knew that he was dealing with a tenant for life, and since the mortgagee there thought he was dealing with an absolute owner, s 110(1) had no application. The result of this case was most odd because it was when the purchaser did not know that he was dealing with a tenant for life that the protection was most needed. This case was, however, decided without reference to *Mogridge v Clapp*,[137] where the Court of Appeal held that in a case concerning a lessee dealing in good faith in similar circumstances the remedy for the beneficiaries was to be against the tenant for life, not against the lessee, and the lease was valid. *Weston v Henshaw* had been criticised as contrary to common sense and against the general principle that a *bona fide* purchaser of a legal estate for value without notice of an equitable interest took free from it.[138]

On the other hand, in *Re Morgan's Lease*[139] where the tenant for life gave an option to renew a lease at a rent alleged by the remainderman to be inadequate and therefore in contravention of the Act, the question was whether the lessee could get the protection under s 110. The lessee did not seem to know that he was dealing with a tenant for life and following *Weston v Henshaw* would not

134 [1950] Ch 510.

135 See Law Commission's Working Paper (No 94, Trusts of Land), para 3.7; Law Commission, Transfer of land: Trusts of Land (Law Com No 181), para 1.3.

136 [1950] Ch 510.

137 [1892] 3 Ch 382.

138 (1991) 107 LQR 596 at 603 (Hill, J).

139 [1972] Ch 1.

have been protected by s 110. But Danckwerts J's view was doubted by Ungoed-Thomas J who held that the lessee was entitled to rely on s 110, whether or not he knew he was dealing with a tenant for life.

Re Morgan's Lease [1972] Ch 1

Ungoed-Thomas J: I come now to the third issue on the first question, whether s 110 of the Settled Land Act 1925 only applies if the purchaser knows that the other party to the transaction is a tenant for life. The landlords' submission was founded on *Weston v Henshaw* [1950] Ch 510.

[His Lordship referred to *Mogridge v Clapp* [1892] 3 Ch 382 and continued.]

Here Kay LJ, sitting in the Court of Appeal with Lindley LJ and Bowen LJ, seems to me to treat it as self-evident that a person dealing with a life tenant without knowing that he was a life tenant would be entitled to rely on s 110 of the Settled Land Act 1925; and, with the greatest respect for the decision in *Weston v Henshaw* [1950] Ch 510, that is the conclusion to which I would come independently of authority. There is, in the section, no express provision limiting its benefit to a purchaser who knows that the person with whom he is dealing is a tenant for life. On its face, it reads as free of limitation and as applicable to a person without such knowledge as to a person who has it. There is a limitation, namely, that the purchaser must act in good faith; but that limitation reads as applicable to a purchaser with such knowledge as without. So, despite the insertion of the limitation of good faith on the part of the purchaser, there is no insertion of the limitation for which the landlords contend. Thus, my conclusion is that s 110 applies whether or not the purchaser knows that the other party to the transaction is tenant for life.

Both *Weston v Hanshaw* and *Re Morgan's Lease* are cases of first instance, but the interpretation of Ungoed-Thomas J seemed to be more in line with common sense and was perhaps to be preferred.[140]

Another difficulty with the application of s 18 and s 110(1) was that while s 18 rendered all 'unauthorised transactions' void, the protection given by s 110 to the purchaser in good faith only applied to 'transactions under this Act'.[141]

Settled Land Act 1925

112. Exercise of powers; limitation of provisions, etc

(2) Where any provision in this Act refers to sale, purchase, exchange, mortgaging, charging, leasing, or other disposition or dealing, or to any power, consent, payment, receipt, deed, assurance, contract, expenses, act, or transaction, it shall (unless the contrary appears) be construed as extending only to sales, purchases, exchanges, mortgages, charges, leases, dispositions, dealings, powers, consents, payments, receipts, deeds, assurances, contracts, expenses, acts, and transactions under this Act.

---

140 Law Commission's Working Paper (No 94, Trusts of Land) commented that it was not clear whether s 110 offered any protection where the purchaser did not know that he was dealing with the tenant for life: para 3.7, quoted at para 1.3 of the Law Commission's Report on Trusts of Land (Law Com No 181).

141 Section 112(2) of the SLA 1925. Law Commission's Working Paper (No 94, Trusts of Land) stated that it was not clear whether s 18 or s 110 prevailed: para 3.7, quoted at para 1.3 of the Law Commission's Report on Trusts of Land (Law Com No 181).

It had been suggested that there was a difference between 'transactions under this Act' and those 'authorised by the Act'.[142] Some commentators suggested that the former were transactions essentially *intra vires* the Act whereas unauthorised transactions were transactions that violated some provision of the Act.[143] If such a distinction is drawn, any unauthorised transaction which was not under the Act (ie *ultra vires* the Act) would be void under s 18 and s 110 would not apply. An example of this might be a lease of residential premises granted by the tenant for life for a term exceeding 50 years (hence *ultra vires* or not under the Act) and the rent paid by the lessee was not the best reasonably obtainable (hence not authorised by the Act). In relation to transaction under the Act, for example, a lease for seven years (hence *intra vires* or under the Act) but not granted by deed (not authorised by the Act), a purchaser dealing in good faith with the tenant for life might get the protection of s 110.

11 OVERREACHING UNDER SETTLED LAND ACT

We have seen that in a strict settlement, the tenant for life was vested with the legal estate and was given wide powers to deal with the settled land, but that he could only deal with the settled land when a vesting instrument had been executed in his favour and that he must deal with the settled land in accordance with the Settled Land Act 1925. How were the interests of the successive beneficiaries protected as against a purchaser who bought the legal estate in the settled land from the tenant for life and *vice versa*?

Section 2(1)(i) of the Law of Property Act 1925 provides that:

> [a] conveyance to a purchaser of a legal estate in land shall overreach any equitable interest or power affecting that estate, whether or not he has notice thereof, if the conveyance is made under the powers conferred by the Settled Land Act 1925, or any additional powers conferred by a settlement, and the equitable interest or power is capable of being overreached thereby, and the statutory requirements respecting the payment of capital money arising under the settlement are complied with.

The requirements respecting the payment of capital money were laid down in s 18(1)(b) and (c), that is that the capital money must be paid to all the trustees of the settlement (not fewer than two) or a trust corporation, or into court. Once the legal estate in the settled land was conveyed to the purchaser by the tenant for life in the exercise of his powers under the Act, and the capital money was paid to the proper persons, all overreachable interests were overreached. The Act did not define 'overreachable interests'.

142 Megarry and Wade, p 342 and fn 56.

143 Gray, p 634.

Settled Land Act 1925

72. Completion of transactions by conveyance

(2) Such a deed, to the extent and in the manner to and in which it is expressed or intended to operate and can operate under this Act, is effectual to pass the land conveyed, or the easements, rights, privileges or other interests created, discharged from all the limitations, powers, and provisions of the settlement, and from all estates, interests, and charges subsisting or to arise thereunder, but subject to and with the exception of:

(i) all legal estates and charges by way of legal mortgage having priority to the settlement; and

(ii) all legal estates and charges by way of legal mortgage which have been conveyed or created for securing money actually raised at the date of the deed; and

(iii) all leases and grants at fee-farm rents or otherwise, and all grants of easements, rights of common, or other rights or privileges which:

(a) were before the date of the deed granted or made for value in money or money's worth, or agreed so to be, by the tenant for life or statutory owner, or by any of his predecessors in title, or any trustees for them, under the settlement, or under any statutory power, or are at that date otherwise binding on the successors in title of the tenant for life or statutory owner; and

(b) are at the date of the deed protected by registration under the Land Charges Act 1925, if capable of registration thereunder.

(3) Notwithstanding registration under the Land Charges Act 1925, of:

(a) an annuity within the meaning of Part II of that Act;

(b) a limited owner's charge or a general equitable charge within the meaning of that Act;

a disposition under this Act operates to overreach such annuity or charge which shall, according to its priority, take effect as if limited by the settlement.

Thus, it seemed that legal mortgage created prior to the settlement, legal mortgage created by the tenant for life under the settlement (provided that the mortgagee has actually paid the money to the trustees), leases, easements, and other rights granted by the tenant for life under the settlement, or otherwise binding on his successors in title and all equitable interests registrable under Land Charges Act 1972 which were duly registered were all not overreachable.[144] The purchaser took subject to these interests. However, an annuity, a limited owner's charge and a general equitable charge, even if it was already properly registered under Land Charges Act 1972, could be overreached whether they were created prior to, or under, the settlement.[145] Likewise, any equitable interests not covered by s 72(2)(i)–(iii) seemed to be capable of being overreached. Thus, on a sale by the tenant for life of the legal estate in the settled land, if the purchaser had paid the capital money in accordance with the Act, the equitable

144 Section 72(2) of the SLA 1925.

145 Section 72(3) of the SLA 1925.

interests of the successive beneficiaries would be overreached. The purchaser would take free of their beneficial interests, and their interests were now converted into the capital money which was now in the hands of the trustees of the settlement who would make proper investment. Incomes from the investment would be paid to the tenant for life in possession subject to apportionment and the capital would go to the remainderman in future.

12 END OF STRICT SETTLEMENTS

Settled Land Act 1925

3. Duration of settlements

Land which has been subject to a settlement which is a settlement for the purposes of this Act shall be deemed for the purposes of this Act to remain and be settled land, and the settlement shall be deemed to be subsisting settlement for the purposes of this Act so long as:

(a) any limitation, charge, or power of charging under the settlement subsists, or is capable of being exercised; or

(b) the person who, if of full age, would be entitled as beneficial owner to have that land vested in him for a legal estate is an infant.

This meant that a strict settlement came to an end when the fee simple was vested in a person of full age who was entitled to it in possession absolutely. After 1925, where the settled land had come to the hands of two or more persons concurrently as joint tenants, the land remained settled. But if they were entitled in possession concurrently as tenants in common whoever held the legal estate held it on a statutory trust which was an implied trust for sale. The land ceased to be settled and becomes subject to a trust for sale.[146] The trustees of the settlement could require the estate owner in whom the settled land was vested to convey the legal estate to them and they had to hold the land on statutory trust. Today, such a trust for sale would be converted into a trust of land.

When a settlement came to an end, the trustees must execute a deed of discharge declaring that they were discharged from their duties.[147] This was to ensure that a purchaser knew that it was safe to pay to the vendor, who could produce the deed of discharge to show that the land was no longer settled. There were, however, two situations in which no deed of discharge was required:

(a) When the person absolutely entitled was executed with a simple ordinary conveyance or assent which did not mention any settlement trustees.[148] Where the settlement ended on the death of a tenant for life, an ordinary assent was normally executed by the tenant for life's ordinary personal representative.[149]

146 Section 36 of the SLA 1925.

147 Section 17 of the SLA 1925.

148 Section 110(5) of the SLA 1925.

149 *In Re Bridgett and Hayes' Contract* [1928] Ch 163 at 170.

(b) Where the land ceased to be settled before a vesting deed was executed.[150] The settlor or his personal representatives would in this case execute an ordinary conveyance or assent to transfer the legal estate to the person currently entitled to the beneficial interest absolutely,[151] or where the land was now subject to a trust for sale to the trustees for sale.[152]

13 FUNCTIONS OF TRUSTEES OF THE SETTLEMENT

Trustees of the settlement were appointed to exercise a general supervision of the strict settlement for the benefit of the beneficiaries. They were there to ensure that the wide powers given to the tenant for life would not be abused to the detriment of those whose beneficial entitlements were deferred to a future date under the settlement. Thus trustees of the settlement had the following functions:

(a) To act as the statutory owners where there was no tenant for life or where the tenant for life was an infant and the property was not vested in the personal representative, or as special personal representatives[153] on the death of a tenant for life.

(b) To receive notice from the tenant for life of his intention to effect certain transactions under the Settled Land Act 1925 and to give consents to certain transactions by the tenant for life.

(c) To execute vesting deed where it was not provided when the trust instrument was executed, and to execute a document of discharge when the settlement came to an end.

(d) To receive the capital money and to make appropriate investment. The income from the investment would be paid to the tenant for life.

(e) To conduct the powers of the tenant for life where the tenant for life wished to purchase the land, or where he had unreasonably refused to exercise his statutory powers and a court order directed them to act.

14 REFORMS

The Law Commission in its report on Transfer of Land: Trusts of Land (Law Com No 181) concluded that strict settlements were unnecessarily complex, ill-suited to the conditions of modern property ownership, and liable to give rise to unforeseen conveyancing complications and should be replaced by an entirely new system applicable to all trusts of land, except existing strict settlements. The recommendations of the Law Commission have led to the enactment of the Trusts of Land and Appointment of Trustees Act 1996, which came into force on 1 January 1997. The new system is discussed in detail in the next chapter.

150 *Re Alefounder's Will Trusts* [1927] 1 Ch 360.

151 Section 7(2) of the SLA 1925.

152 Section 36 of the SLA 1925.

153 Section 22 of the AEA 1925.

CHAPTER 12

TRUSTS OF LAND

As mentioned earlier, prior to 1 January 1997, there were three types of trust: strict settlements, trusts for sale, and bare trusts. Strict settlements were trusts whereby the beneficial interests were held successively. Trusts for sale were more flexible and could cater for successive or concurrent beneficial ownership, while a bare trust was simply a trust where the sole beneficiary was of full age and the trustee had no duty to sell the land. From 1 January 1997, when the Trusts of Land and Appointment of Trustees Act 1996 came into force,[1] with the exception of existing strict settlements, all existing trusts, ie trusts for sale[2] and bare trusts, are now governed by the law relating to the new form of trust of land. In every new case in which land is held on trust, whether for successive or concurrent beneficial ownership, the trust will be governed by the 1996 Act and referred to by the Act as a 'trust of land'. The old law relating to trust for sale is therefore to a large extent redundant save where it is retained under the new Act.

Introduction

The 1996 Act introduces a new unitary system of holding land on trust which replaces the previous dual systems of trust for sale and the strict settlement as they no longer reflected the realities of modern property ownership.[3] In so far as successive beneficial ownership is concerned, the new trust of land is simpler than those it replaces and gives trustees more powers of delegation to achieve substantially the same results as a strict settlement without bringing into play the complex rules of the Settled Land Act 1925. As entailed interests could only be created behind a strict settlement which can no longer be newly created, new entails have to be prohibited. The Act also gives effects to the Law Commission's avowed policy goals in achieving greater parity between trusts of real and personal property by approximating the new rules to those relating to trusts of personalty. Thus, new entailed interests in personal property are also prohibited.[4]

As regards trusts for sale, which could be used for either successive or concurrent beneficial interests, if it is created expressly, it will be treated as a trust of land and the new rules will apply to such trust which basically give the trustees all the powers of an absolute owner,[5] including a power to postpone sale indefinitely.[6] It would appear therefore that the express duty to sell cannot

1 Trusts of Land and Appointment of Trustees Act 1996 (Commencement) Order 1996 (SI 1996/2974). This Act gives effect to the proposed reforms recommended by the Law Commission in its report on 'Transfer of Land: Trusts of Land' (Law Com No 181), preceded by its Working Paper (No 94, Trusts of Land).

2 See s 5, Sched 2, para 7 of the TLATA 1996.

3 See Law Com No 181, p iv.

4 Section 2, Sched 1, para 5 of the TLATA 1996.

5 Section 6(1) of the TLATA 1996.

6 *Ibid*, s 4(1).

now prevail over an implied power to postpone sale thereby abolishing the previous rule that the duty to sell prevails over the power to postpone sale 'unless all the trustees agree in exercising the power to postpone'.[7] Where there is a newly created trust for sale, the doctrine of conversion is abolished so that the land is not to be regarded as personal property.[8]

Where in the situation, there is no express trust for sale but previously an implied statutory trust would arise, there is now a trust of land instead. In this regard, the old provisions relating to how an implied trust for sale arises are retained to determine how a trust of land will arise impliedly. As there will be no implied trust for sale, the doctrine of conversion would simply not be relevant.

The Act retains the statutory mechanism for overreaching and removes the anomaly whereby the mechanism did not apply to bare trusts by abolishing bare trusts.[9]

Other important aspects of the new changes relate to the rights of the beneficiaries under a trust. The beneficiaries are given greater protection by being given a right to request the appointment or retirement of trustees, and to require the trustees to perform their function in a particular way, and by strengthening their rights to enjoy the physical occupation of the land rather than merely having an interest in the proceeds of sale.

1 MEANING OF TRUSTS OF LAND

The definition of 'trust of land' under the Act is all-embracing. First, it covers all trusts of property which consists of or includes land. Thus, where the trust consists also of personal property, it will still be governed by the new Act. Secondly, the definition refers to any trust however created (whether express, implied, resulting or constructive), including a trust for sale and a bare trust. Thus, however one looks at the trust, whether from the point of view of how it is created – whether expressly or impliedly by way of resulting or constructive trust, or from the point of view of a conveyancer – do the trustees have a duty to sell, the trust is now a trust of land. In other words, whether previously the trust is a trust for sale or a bare trust, the trustee is now a 'trustee of land'. This means that the trustee now has all the powers of an absolute owner which include the power to sell or to retain the land.[10] Thirdly, the definition also refers to trust created or arising before the commencement of the Act. Thus, all trusts created before the Act (whether it is a trust for sale or a bare trust) will now be governed by the new Act. The exceptions are existing settled land which continue to be governed by the Settled Land Act 1925, and land to which the Universities and College Estates Act 1925 applies.

7 *Re Mayo* [1943] 1 Ch 302.

8 Section 3(1) of the TLATA 1996.

9 See Law Commission, Transfer of Land: Overreaching: Beneficiaries in Occupation (Law Com No 188), 19 December 1989, para 3.10 (reproduced in the first edition of this work).

10 Section 6(1) of the TLATA 1996.

1. Meaning of 'trust of land'

(1) In this Act:

(a) 'trust of land' means (subject to sub-s (3)) any trust of property which consists of or includes land, and

(b) 'trustees of land' means trustees of a trust of land.

(2) The reference in sub-s (1)(a) to a trust:

(a) is to any description of trust (whether express, implied, resulting or constructive), including a trust for sale and a bare trust, and

(b) includes a trust created, or arising, before the commencement of this Act.

(3) The reference to land in sub-s (1)(a) does not include land which (despite s 2) is settled land or which is land to which the Universities and College Estates Act 1925 applies.

Section 1 therefore represents a crucial provision which implements the Law Commission's main proposal that the previous dual system of trusts for sale and strict settlements are to be replaced by a simple trust of land where the trustees have a power to sell and a power to retain the land. This applies to successive beneficial ownership as well as concurrent ones.

Successive interests

Prior to the commencement of the 1996 Act, successive interests could either be held under a strict settlement or a trust for sale. Now, newly created successive interests will exist behind a trust of land; the Settled Land Act 1925 will not apply to them.[11]

If a trust for sale is created expressly, under s 4(1) of the 1996 Act there will be an implied power, despite any contrary provision in the trust instrument, for the trustees to postpone sale even for an indefinite period. This is different from s 25 of the Law of Property Act 1925 (now repealed)[12] where the trustees' implied power to postpone sale was subject to any contrary intention in the trust instrument. In line with the Law Commission's proposals for a unitary system of trust where the trustees have a power to sell or to retain the land, any express duty to sell given to the trustees under a newly created trust cannot prevail over the implied power to postpone sale (although, admittedly, this is not made clear in the Act).

Existing trusts for sale are converted into trusts of land. However, existing strict settlements will continue until no land or heirlooms are subject to the settlement.[13] Settled land currently held on charitable, ecclesiastical or public trusts cease to be settled land and would now come under the new form of trust.[14]

---

11 However resettlement of an existing settlement will still be governed by the SLA: s 2(2) of the TLATA 1996.

12 Section 25(2) and Sched 4 of the TLATA 1996.

13 *Ibid*, s 2(4).

14 *Ibid*, s 2(5).

Trusts of Land and Appointment of Trustees Act 1996

2. Trusts in place of settlements

(1) No settlement created after the commencement of this Act is a settlement for the purposes of the Settled Land Act 1925; and no settlement shall be deemed to be made under that Act after that commencement.

(2) Subsection (1) does not apply to a settlement created on the occasion of an alteration in any interest in, or of a person becoming entitled under, a settlement which:

(a) is in existence at the commencement of this Act, or

(b) derives from a settlement within paragraph (a) or this paragraph.

(3) But a settlement created as mentioned in sub-s (2) is not a settlement for the purposes of the Settled Land Act 1925 if provision to the effect that it is not is made in the instrument, or any of the instruments, by which it is created.

(4) Where at any time after the commencement of this Act there is in the case of any settlement which is a settlement for the purposes of the Settled Land Act 1925 no relevant property which is, or is deemed to be, subject to the settlement, the settlement permanently ceases at that time to be a settlement for the purposes of that Act.

In this subsection 'relevant property' means land and personal chattels to which s 67(1) of the Settled Land Act 1925 (heirlooms) applies.

(5) No land held on charitable, ecclesiastical or public trusts shall be or be deemed to be settled land after the commencement of this Act, even if it was or was deemed to be settled land before that commencement.

Concurrent interests

It is common to find property held by beneficial owners concurrently. And trusts for sale were by far the most common form of trusts upon which co-owned property was held.[15] Almost every co-ownership in possession brought about a trust for sale,[16] normally expressly and quite frequently impliedly.[17] Express trusts for sale were often created by the transfer documents at the time when the property was acquired. As with trusts for sale for successive interests, an imperative direction to the trustees to sell the property and to hold the proceeds on trust for the beneficiaries absolutely must be made in the transfer documents and the trust instrument. An example is 'to X and Y upon trust to sell the land and hold the proceeds upon trust for A and B absolutely'.

15 See Law Commission's Working Paper (No 94, Trusts of Land), para 2.2, quoted at para 1.2 of the Law Commission's Report on Trusts of Land (Law Com No 181).

16 One exception was the case of joint tenancy for life with remainder to the survivor for life: s 19(2) of the SLA 1925. But if two or more persons were entitled in possession as tenants in common, the land ceased to be settled and a trust for sale arose: s 36(1)(2) of the SLA 1925.

17 The Law Commission suggested that trusts for sale were no longer suitable for the co-ownership of the social circumstances of today: The Law Commission's Working Paper (No 94), para 3.17, quoted at para 1.3 of the Law Commission's report of Trusts of Land (Law Com No 181); see also para 3.2 of the Law Commission's report No 181.

Trusts for sale were originally designed so that land could be held as an investment rather than for long-term occupation. Therefore, the trust imposed a duty on the trustees to sell the land. However, modern social conditions had changed as there were more owner-occupants,[18] most of which were occupied by joint owners. Thus, the imposition of a duty to sell was clearly inconsistent with the interests and intentions of the majority of those who acquired land as co-owners. In such cases the intention would rarely be that the land should be held pending a sale; it was much more probable that it would be retained primarily for occupation. While the courts recognised the 'use' value of the property and had sought to neutralise this artificiality by developing the 'collateral purpose' principle whereby if the purpose still subsisted, the court could, in the exercise of its discretion under s 30 of the Law of Property Act 1925 (now repealed), refuse to order a sale,[19] it was thought somewhat illogical that the courts should be required to develop and maintain a doctrine which took as its foundation the artificiality of the trust for sale.[20]

As a corollary of the duty to sell, and in accordance with the doctrine of conversion,[21] any interest held under a trust for sale was an interest in the proceeds of sale and not an interest in land as such. The courts had intervened to mitigate the artificiality of the position,[22] but their attitude on this issue had not been consistent.[23]

---

18 In 1914, 7% of houses were owner-occupied, the figure in 1938 being 43%. (Source: Housing Policy Technical Volume, Pt 1, (1977). Figures are for England and Wales only.) By 1984 the percentage had risen to 61%. (Source: Social Trends, (1986). Figures are for Great Britain as a whole.) See Law Com No 181, para 3.2; Working Paper No 94, para 3.17.

19 This discretion has been exercised very broadly indeed. In *Williams v Williams* [1976] Ch 278 at 285, Lord Denning MR suggested that '... [judges] nowadays have great regard to the fact that the house is bought as a home in which the family is to be brought up. It is not treated as property to be sold nor as an investment to be realised for cash'. Similarly, Ormrod LJ observed in *Re Evers' Trust* [1980] 1 WLR 1327 at 332, that '... [t]his approach to the exercise of discretion ... enables the court to deal with substance, that is reality, rather than form, that is, convenience of conveyancing ...'.

20 See Law Com No 181, para 3.3.

21 This doctrine is based on the maxim that 'equity looks on that as done which ought to be done'. As trustees had a duty to sell, equity 'anticipates' this sale and 'converts' the interests of the beneficiaries into interests in the proceeds of sale.

22 For example, in *Williams and Glyn's Bank Ltd v Boland* [1981] AC 487, Lord Wilberforce's observation that '... to describe the interests of spouses in a house jointly bought to be lived in as a matrimonial home as merely an interest in proceeds of sale, or rents and profits until sale, is just a little unreal ...'.

23 For example in *Irani Finance Ltd v Singh* [1971] Ch 59 at 80A, Cross LJ thought that 'the whole purpose of the trust for sale is to make sure, by shifting the equitable interests away from the land and into the proceeds of sale that a purchaser of the land takes free from the equitable interests. To hold these to be equitable interests in the land itself would be to frustrate this purpose.' And in *City of London Building Society v Flegg* [1987] 3 All ER 435 at 443g, j, Lord Oliver said that 'The whole philosophy of the Act ... is that a purchaser of the legal estate (which ... includes a mortgagee) should not be concerned with the beneficial interests ... which were shifted to the proceeds of sale ... Having thus established the trust for sale as the conveyancing machinery through which effect is given to the interests of owners in undivided shares, those interests are, by virtue of the equitable doctrine of conversion transferred to the proceeds of sale and the net rents and profits pending sale ...'. These statements contradict Lord Wilberforce's *dictum* in *Williams and Glyn's Bank Ltd v Boland* [1981] AC 487.

To solve these problems, as mentioned earlier, all existing trusts for sale are converted into trusts of land, all new express trusts for sale will be treated as trusts of land, and there will be no implied trusts for sale, instead there will be implied trusts of land. Under the new trust of land, the trustees no longer have a duty to sell. All trusts for sale which are expressly created will carry an implied power for the trustees to postpone sale.[24] And all land which previously would have been held under an implied trust for sale are now held under the trust of land where the trustees have a power to retain and a power to sell.[25] Furthermore, the doctrine of conversion is abolished.[26]

Trusts of Land and Appointment of Trustees Act 1996

3. Abolition of doctrine of conversion

(1) Where land is held by trustees subject to a trust for sale, the land is not to be regarded as personal property; and where personal property is subject to a trust for sale in order that the trustees may acquire land, the personal property is not to be regarded as land.

2 EXPRESS OR IMPLIED TRUSTS OF LAND

As mentioned earlier, an express trust for sale created after the 1996 Act will be treated as a trust of land under s 4. But where the trust does not impose a duty to sell on the trustee, or if the trust arises by way of implied, resulting or constructive trust, the trust will be treated as trusts of land. Under s 5, the statutory provisions which imposed a trust for sale of land in certain circumstances are amended so that in those circumstances there is instead a trust of the land (without a duty to sell).

Trusts of Land and Appointment of Trustees Act 1996

4. Express trusts for sale as trusts of land

(1) In the case of every trust for sale of land created by a disposition there is to be implied, despite any provision to the contrary made by the disposition, a power for the trustees to postpone sale of the land; and the trustees are not liable in any way for postponing sale of the land, in the exercise of their discretion, for an indefinite period.

(2) Subsection (1) applies to a trust whether it is created, or arises, before or after the commencement of this Act.

(3) Subsection (1) does not affect any liability incurred by trustees before that commencement.

5. Implied trusts for sale as trusts of land

(1) Schedule 2 has effect in relation to statutory provisions which impose a trust for sale of land in certain circumstances so that in those circumstances there is instead a trust of the land (without a duty to sell).

24 Section 4 of the TLATA 1996.

25 *Ibid*, s 5.

26 *Ibid*, s 3.

(2) Section 1 of the Settled Land Act 1925 does not apply to land held on any trust arising by virtue of that Schedule (so that any such land is subject to a trust of land).

Express trusts of land

This is a conveyance or transfer of land, to the trustees themselves expressed to be held on trust. In the case of acquisition by husband and wife, the husband and wife (H and W) may themselves be the trustees. In the case of land held by H and W as beneficial tenants in common, the declaration may also spell out their exact shares of beneficial entitlement, for example '... for themselves as to one third for W and two thirds for H as beneficial tenants in common'. The express declaration that the property is held on trust for H and W and the quantum of beneficial entitlement are normally conclusive even if one of the beneficial owners has provided all the purchase money.[27] The declaration of quantum of the beneficial interests is convenient and often desirable though not essential. Dillon LJ emphasised in *Walker v Hall*[28] that when the legal estate in a house was acquired by two persons in their joint names, solicitors should take steps to find out and declare what the beneficial interests were to be. Failure in this might render the solicitors liable for professional negligence. Sometimes there is a statement whereby H and W are trustees but there is no indication of the quantum of the beneficial entitlement. In this case, the presumption of resulting trust is that the beneficial interest goes to the person who provides the purchase money unless the presumption of advancement applies.[29] Where H has provided part of the purchase by cash, and W has contributed to the mortgage instalments, the land is held on trust for H and W on the proportions they each contributed.[30] Thus in *Walker v Hall*[31] it was held that the fact that the house could not be bought without W incurring liability as a co-mortgagor was a ground for inferring that she was intended to have some beneficial interest in it.

Implied trusts of land

Prior to the 1996 Act, a trust for sale for successive interests could not be implied; it had to be created expressly. After the 1996 Act, it is no longer possible to create a strict settlement. Thus, a trust for successive interest will be governed by the 1996 Act as trust of land.

In the case of concurrent interests, prior to the 1996 Act, a trust for sale was frequently imposed by statutes. As will be seen in Chapter 13, there are today

27 *Pettitt v Pettitt* [1970] AC 777. But see *City of London Building Society v Flegg* [1988] AC 54 where a house was conveyed to A and B expressly on trust for sale for themselves but about half of the purchase money was contributed by C and D, the House of Lords held that the house was held on trust for sale by A and B for A, B, C and D as a result of contribution from C and D.

28 [1984] 127 Sol Jo 550. See also *Cowcher v Cowcher* [1972] 1 WLR 425 at 442C; *Bernard v Josephs* [1982] Ch 391 at 403E.

29 *Pettitt v Pettitt* [1970] AC 777.

30 *Cowcher v Cowcher* [1972] 1 WLR 425.

31 [1984] 127 Sol Jo 550. See also *Grant v Edwards* [1986] 1 Ch 638.

basically two types of co-ownership: joint tenancy and tenancy in common. In the former each joint tenant owns the entire estate jointly with the other joint tenants, but he does not own any part of the estate by himself. He cannot leave his joint tenancy by will and when he dies the other joint tenants will succeed to his joint tenancy; the surviving joint tenants are said to have a 'right of survivorship'. In the case of a tenancy in common, each tenant has a distinct but undivided share in the estate. The tenant in common can pass his distinct share by will and other tenants in common have no right of survivorship. After 1925, the legal estate cannot be co-owned in tenancy in common.[32] It can only be held in joint tenancy. But the equitable interests behind a trust may still be owned in joint tenancy or tenancy in common. Co-ownership may therefore exist at law, or in equity or both at law and in equity.

Normally a co-owned property was held expressly on trust for sale. But if the co-owned property was merely declared expressly to be held on trust without any direction to sell the land, or where there was no express trust at all, but a constructive or resulting trust[33] was nevertheless imposed by implication of law, in a number of situations where there was either a co-ownership at law or in equity or both, the courts had held that there was a 'statutory trust' or 'trust for sale'. The imposition of a trust for sale in almost all cases of co-ownership was to give effect to the deliberate policy of the 1925 legislation of simplifying the conveyancing process and giving greater protection to a purchaser of a legal estate as well as the beneficiaries behind a trust of the legal estate. Bearing in mind this deliberate policy it was not surprising that in a number of situations of co-ownership, the judiciary had been 'straining the construction of too many of the provisions of the Property Legislation to be acceptable'[34] to find a trust for sale. These circumstances will today under the 1996 Act give rise to a trust of land instead of a trust for sale.

(a) Legal joint tenants

(i) 'To H and W'

Suppose the legal estate is conveyed 'to H and W' but no mention of the beneficial entitlements has been made, the legal estate is held by H and W as legal joint tenants because no legal tenancy in common can exist. Suppose there is no evidence as to the way in which the purchase has been financed or as to any agreement on the beneficial entitlement, the presumption at law is that H and W also own the beneficial interests as joint tenants and 'equity follows the law'.[35] The conveyance 'to H and W' does not expressly create a trust of land. However under s 36(1) of the Law of Property Act 1925, as amended, H and W are required to hold the legal estate (as legal joint tenants) in trust for themselves as beneficial joint tenants.

32 Sections 1(6), 34(1) of the LPA 1925.

33 For the circumstances in which resulting or constructive trusts could arise see Chapter 2.

34 (1944) 9 Conv (NS) 37 at 46.

35 *Campbell v Campbell* (1792) 4 Bro CC 15.

Law of Property Act 1925

Joint tenancies

36.–(1) Where a legal estate (not being settled land) is beneficially limited to or held in trust for any persons as joint tenants, the same shall be held in trust, in like manner as if the persons beneficially entitled were tenants in common, but not so as to sever their joint tenancy in equity.

Where, however, there is evidence that H and W have contributed in unequal share, equity presumes that they are beneficial tenants in common.[36] As before, the conveyance 'to H and W' does not expressly create a trust. Can an implied trust of land be imposed by statute? This situation is not clearly covered by s 36(1). But the court in *Re Buchanan-Wollaston's Conveyance*[37] has held, in the context of trust for sale, that there was a trust for sale and thought that it was the effect of ss 35 and 36 of the Law of Property Act 1925 without further explanation.

This interpretation does violence to s 36(1) because under the section to impose a trust for sale the legal estate should be *'beneficially* limited to or held in trust for any persons as *joint tenants'* but not as *tenants in common*. However, bearing in mind the policy of the 1996 Act which is to bring every co-ownership within a unitary system of trust of land, it is likely that the interpretation adopted in *Re Buchanan-Wollaston's Conveyance* will be followed.

(ii) 'To H and W' but the entire purchase money is paid by H (or W) alone.

As has been seen,[38] where the legal estate is not expressly held on trust, it is held on a resulting trust by H and W for H (or W) alone unless the presumption of advancement applies.[39] There may be a presumption of advancement in favour of W if H alone contributes to the purchase.[40] Where the presumption of advancement applies, the presumption is that the legal estate will be held on trust for H and W as beneficial joint tenants.[41] In such a case, as mentioned above, the trust is governed by the new Act. If the presumption of advancement does not apply or if W alone contributes to the purchase where there is unlikely to be a presumption of advancement in favour of H,[42] the legal estate will be held by H and W on trust for H or W alone as the sole beneficial owner. Again,

36 *Lake v Gibson* (1792) 1 Eq Ca Abr 290.

37 [1939] Ch 738 at 744, *per* Sir Wilfrid Green MR. See also *Goodman v Gallant* [1986] Fam 106 at 110C–D; *City of London Building Society v Flegg* [1988] AC 54 at 77G–H; *Re Hind* [1933] Ch 208 at 221; (1944) 9 Conv (NS) 37 at 45.

38 See Chapter 2.

39 *Dyer v Dyer* (1788) 2 Cox Eq Cas 92 at 93.

40 *Re Eykyn's Trusts* (1877) 6 Ch D 115 at 118. But see Lord Diplock's criticism in *Pettitt v Pettitt* [1970] AC 777 of the application of this presumption in modern society (at 824C).

41 See *Re Eykyn's Trusts* (1877) 6 Ch D 115 at 118, *per* Malins VC cited with approval in *Pettit v Pettit* by Lord Upjohn at 815 A–C.

42 *Mercier v Mercier* [1903] 2 Ch 98.

although the conveyance does not expressly create a trust, there is an implied trust and the trust is governed by the new provisions.[43]

(b) Attempted transfer of legal estate to any persons as tenants in common

Law of Property Act 1925

34. Effect of future dispositions to tenants in common

(1) An undivided share in land shall not be capable of being created except as provided by the Settled Land Act 1925 or as hereinafter mentioned.

(2) Where, after the commencement of this Act, land is expressed to be conveyed to any persons in undivided shares and those persons are of full age, the conveyance shall (notwithstanding anything to the contrary in this Act) operate as if the land had been expressed to be conveyed to the grantees, or, if there are more than four grantees, to the four first named in the conveyance, as joint tenants in trust for the persons interested in the land:

Provided that, where the conveyance is made by way of mortgage the land shall vest in the grantees or such four of them as aforesaid for a term of years absolute (as provided by this Act) as joint tenants subject to cesser on redemption in like manner as if the mortgage money had belonged to them on a joint account, but without prejudice to the beneficial interests in the mortgage money and interest.

(3A) In sub-ss (2) and (3) of this section references to the persons interested in the land include persons interested as trustees or personal representatives (as well as persons beneficially interested).

After 1925 a conveyance of a legal estate to any persons as tenants in common cannot create a tenancy in common at law. No legal estate can be held in undivided shares.[44] Today such a conveyance is given effect only in equity behind a trust under s 34(2) of the Law of Property Act 1925. This means that the legal estate is held on a trust by the trustees as joint tenants for themselves as beneficial tenants in common.

---

43 In this situation, although s 36(1) did not clearly cover this situation, prior to TLATA 1996, it was assumed in *Wilson v Wilson* [1969] 3 All ER 945 at 949C, *Young v Young* [1983] Court of Appeal Bound Transcript 466, *Mellowes v Collymore* (Unreported, Court of Appeal, 27 November 1981) (See also Law Commission, Transfer of land: Trusts of Land (Law Com No 181), para 3.1, fn 53) that there was nevertheless a trust for sale in this case without convincing statutory authority for such an assumption. Buckley J said that 'there is, in my judgment, no question but that the plaintiff and the defendant, as statutory trustees for sale under the provisions of the Law of Property Act 1925, hold the proceeds of sale and the rents and profits of the land until sale in trust for the defendant alone ...' (at 949C). Quite how the Court of Appeal in *Wilson v Wilson* came to the conclusion that there was a statutory trust for sale was not explained. But see MacKenzie, J-A and Phillips, M, *A Practical Approach to Land Law*, 4th edn, London: Blackstone Press, pp 229–30, and Megarry's Manual at 289 where it is suggested that there is no statutory trust for sale where there are several joint tenants of the legal estate holding as trustees for a sole beneficiary. This is now academic as it is clear that in such a situation today, there is a trust, and whatever trust it is, it is governed by the 1996 Act.

44 Section 1(6) of the LPA 1925.

If a legal estate is conveyed to more than four persons as tenants in common, the first four named in the conveyance become joint tenants of the legal estate on trust for all as beneficial tenants in common.[45]

(c) 'To H (or W)' but there is co-ownership in equity

Suppose H and W both contribute to the purchase of a legal estate but the legal estate is conveyed to H (or W) alone. As have been seen,[46] H will hold the legal estate on a resulting trust for H and W. If the legal estate is conveyed to W, she is likely to be required to hold it on a resulting trust for H and W.[47] Whether H and W hold as beneficial joint tenants or tenants in common depends on their contributions. In this situation, it used to be thought that an implied trust for sale would arise.[48] But today the trust is governed by the 1996 Act.

3 POWERS OF TRUSTEES OF LAND

Under s 6(1) of the 1996 Act, the trustees of land have all the powers of an absolute owner. This is based on the Law Commission's proposal. The Law Commission considered that trustees of land should be put in much the same position as an absolute owner because the circumstances of most trusts of land would be such that those persons to whom the legal label of 'trustee' was attached were quite likely to regard themselves as the 'owners' of the trust land. Even where this was not the case, the Law Commission thought that, it was desirable that the trustees should have the powers necessary to make efficient use of the land. These proposals were designed to reflect this state of affairs whilst maintaining the general equitable duties of trustees.[49] In recommending that trustees of land should have all the powers of an absolute owner, the aim was not simply to tack additional powers on to those which trustees for sale previously possess, so as to arrive at a more 'complete' inventory, but to make the scheme of powers as broadly based and as flexible as possible. Previously, powers of trustees for sale were expressed under s 28 of the Law of Property Act 1925 (which provided that trustees for sale had all the powers held by the tenant for life and the trustees of a strict settlement) as a rather clumsy, complex and fragmented set, and did not provide trustees for sale with a sufficiently extensive set of powers.

45 Section 34(2) of the LPA 1925 (as amended by TLATA 1996, s 5, Sched 2, para 3(2)).

46 See Chapter 2.

47 *Falconer v Falconer* [1970] 3 All ER 449, CA.

48 *Bull v Bull* 1955] 1 All ER 253; see (1955) 19 Conv 146 (Crane, FR). Denning LJ in the Court of Appeal, in two sentences, found that the land was held on trust for sale by the son. He said, 'I realise that since 1925 there has been no such thing as a legal tenancy in common (see s 1(6) of the Law of Property Act 1925). All tenancies in common now are equitable only and take effect behind a trust for sale (see s 36(4) of the Settled Land Act 1925)'. See also *Williams & Glyn's Bank Ltd v Boland* [1981] AC 487 at 503D *per* Lord Wilberforce and at 510G *per* Lord Scarman and *City of London Building Society v Flegg* [1988] AC 54 at 77H–78A where Lord Oliver also made reference to s 34(1) of the LPA 1925 and s 36(4) of the SLA 1925.

49 See Law Com (No 181) para 10.4.

Perhaps the most significant consequence of giving trustees the powers of an absolute owner is that, as the Law Commission pointed out, these trustees will now have a power either to sell or to retain the land. This also provides a foundation for restructuring the jurisdiction of the court under s 30 of the Law of Property Act 1925 (now repealed),[50] and facilitates the construction of a unitary trust in that (coupled with extended powers of delegation) it substantially retains the facility which was previously offered by the Settled Land Act 1925.[51]

Under s 6(3) the trustees of land have a power to apply proceeds of sale of trust land, or any part thereof, to the purchase of land, either for occupation by the beneficiaries, for investment or for any other reason. This reverses the restrictive approach previously taken by the court in *Re Power's Will Trusts*[52] that the trustees's express powers of investment could not be exercised to purchase land for occupation by beneficiaries, and Re Wakeman[53] that where all the trust land had been sold the trustees did not have power to purchase land. The power to purchase land extends to the purchase of freehold or leasehold legal estates. It is not restricted to property where the lease has more than sixty years left to run, as such a restriction is neither necessary nor desirable in today's economic climate, in which shorter leases may often be regarded as good and prudent investments and appropriate to the particular circumstances of the trust and the beneficiaries.[54] In the Law Commission's view, the fixing of a minimum period, of whatever length, could only be the result of an arbitrary decision and, bearing in mind that there are circumstances in which it is quite conceivable that even a freehold might represent an imprudent or inappropriate investment, it seems sensible to give trustees maximum flexibility, leaving general equitable rules to govern the use of such flexibility.[55]

Although the powers conferred by s 6 are very broad, their exercise will not be unfettered. In exercising these powers, trustees must have regard to the rights of the beneficiaries,[56] and must not contravene any other enactment or any rule of law and equity or any order made in pursuance thereof.[57] This, consequently, puts trusts of land on much the same footing as those of personalty.

The trustees are also given power to convey the land to the beneficiaries who are of full age and absolutely entitled to it, thereby discharging themselves from the trust.[58]

---

50 See s 25(2) and Schedule 4 of the TLATA 1996. For the power of the court now see s 14 of the 1996 Act.

51 See Law Com para 10.6.

52 [1947] Ch 572.

53 [1945] Ch 177. *Cf Re Wellstead's Will Trusts* [1949] Ch. 296.

54 Under s 73(1)(xi) of the SLA, capital money arising from the settlement may not be invested in leasehold land with less than 60 years to run.

55 Law Com, para 10.8.

56 Section 6(5) of the TLATA 1996.

57 *Ibid*, s 6(6).

58 *Ibid*, s 6(2).

The power of the trustees to partition land subject to a trust amongst consenting beneficiaries of full age and who are absolutely entitled to it is retained.[59]

Trusts of Land and Appointment of Trustees Act 1996

6. General powers of trustees

(1) For the purpose of exercising their functions as trustees, the trustees of land have in relation to the land subject to the trust all the powers of an absolute owner.

(2) Where in the case of any land subject to a trust of land each of the beneficiaries interested in the land is a person of full age and capacity who is absolutely entitled to the land, the powers conferred on the trustees by sub-s (1) include the power to convey the land to the beneficiaries even though they have not required the trustees to do so; and where land is conveyed by vlrtue of this subsection:

(a) the beneficiaries shall do whatever is necessary to secure that it vests in them, and

(b) if they fail to do so, the court may make an order requiring them to do so.

(3) The trustees of land have power to purchase a legal estate in any land in England or Wales.

(4) The power conferred by sub-s (3) may be exercised by trustees to purchase land:

(a) by way of investment,

(b) for occupation by any beneficiary, or

(c) for any other reason.

(5) In exercising the powers conferred by this section trustees shall have regard to the rights of the beneficiaries.

(6) The powers conferred by this section shall not be exercised in contravention of, or of any order made in pursuance of, any other enactment or any rule of law or equity.

(7) The reference in sub-s (6) to an order includes an order of any court or of the Charity Commissioners.

(8) Where any enactment other than this section confers on trustees authority to act subject to any restriction, limitation or condition, trustees of land may not exercise the powers conferred by this section to do any act which they are prevented from doing under the other enactment by reason of the restriction, limitation or condition.

7. Partition by trustees

(1) The trustees of land may, where beneficiaries of full age are absolutely entitled in undivided shares to land subject to the trust, partition the land, or any part of it, and provide (by way of mortgage or otherwise) for the payment of any equality money.

59 *Ibid*, s 7. This section re-enacts substantially the provision of s 28(3), (4) of the LPA 1925 which are now repealed by s 26(2) and Sched 4 of the 1996 Act.

(2) The trustees shall give effect to any such partition by conveying the partitioned land in severalty (whether or not subject to any legal mortgage created for raising equality money), either absolutely or in trust, in accordance with the rights of those beneficiaries.

(3) Before exercising their powers under sub-s (2) the trustees shall obtain the consent of each of those beneficiaries.

(4) Where a share in the land is affected by an incumbrance, the trustees may either give effect to it or provide for its discharge from the property allotted to that share as they think fit.

(5) If a share in the land is absolutely vested in a minor, sub-ss (1)–(4) apply as if he were of full age, except that the trustees may act on his behalf and retain land or other property representing his share in trust for him.

Exclusion and restriction of powers

The powers conferred on the trustees under ss 6 and 7 can be restricted by express limitation either by means of subjecting their exercise to the consent of some persons, or by an express limitation in the trust instrument, unless the trust falls within the category of charitable, ecclesiastical or public trusts.[60] These restrictions must not however affect the restrictions in other enactments.[61]

Trusts of Land and Appointment of Trustees Act 1996

8. Exclusion and restriction of powers

(1) Sections 6 and 7 do not apply in the case of a trust of land created by a disposition in so far as provision to the effect that they do not apply is made by the disposition.

(2) If the disposition creating such a trust makes provision requiring any consent to be obtained to the exercise of any power conferred by s 6 or 7, the power may not be exercised without that consent.

(3) Subsection (1) does not apply in the case of charitable, ecclesiastical or public trusts.

(4) Subsections (1) and (2) have effect subject to any enactment which prohibits or restricts the effect of provision of the description mentioned in them.

Delegation of power by trustees

The trustees of land may, by power of attorney, delegate their powers, including the power to sell, for any period or indefinitely,[62] to any beneficiary of full age and beneficially entitled to an interest in possession.[63] The limitation previously on the trustees for sale that they could not delegate their duty to

60 Section 8 of the TLATA 1996.

61 *Ibid*, s 8(4). For example, s 35(4) of the Pension Act 1995: see 570 HL Official Report (5th series) col 1532; 25 March 1996.

62 Section 9(5) of the TLATA 1996.

63 *Ibid*, s 9(1).

sell[64] is now removed. The trustees are liable for the act or default of the beneficiaries in the exercise of the powers delegated only if the trustees did not exercise reasonable care in deciding to delegate.[65] This reversed the previous position under s 29 of the Law of Property Act 1925 whereby trustees ceased to be liable to the other beneficiaries for the acts or defaults of the person to whom the powers had been delegated. This, however, does not fully give effect to the Law Commission's proposal which was for a strict liability.[66] The deviation from the Law Commission's recommendation will however encourage delegation and ensure that they observe the standard of a reasonably prudent person in deciding whether to delegate to a particular beneficiary.

Trusts of Land and Appointment of Trustees Act 1996

9. Delegation by trustees

(1) The trustees of land may, by power of attorney, delegate to any beneficiary or beneficiaries of full age and beneficially entitled to an interest in possession in land subject to the trust any of their functions as trustees which relate to the land.

(2) Where trustees purport to delegate to a person by a power of attorney under sub-s (1) functions relating to any land and another person in good faith deals with him in relation to the land, he shall be presumed in favour of that other person to have been a person to whom the functions could be delegated unless that other person has knowledge at the time of the transaction that he was not such a person.

And it shall be conclusively presumed in favour of any purchaser whose interest depends on the validity of that transaction that that other person dealt in good faith and did not have such knowledge if that other person makes a statutory declaration to that effect before or within three months after the completion of the purchase.

(3) A power of attorney under sub-s (1) shall be given by all the trustees jointly and (unless expressed to be irrevocable and to be given by way of security) may be revoked by any one or more of them; and such a power is revoked by the appointment as a trustee of a person other than those by whom it is given (though not by any of those persons dying or otherwise ceasing to be a trustee).

(4) Where a beneficiary to whom functions are delegated by a power of attorney under sub-s (1) ceases to be a person beneficially entitled to an interest in possession in land subject to the trust:

(a) if the functions are delegated to him alone, the power is revoked,

(b) if the functions are delegated to him and to other beneficiaries to be exercised by them jointly (but not separately), the power is revoked if each of the other beneficiaries ceases to be so entitled (but otherwise functions exercisable in accordance with the power are so exercisable by the remaining beneficiary or beneficiaries), and

64 Under s 25 of the Trustees Act 1925, as amended by s 9 of the Powers of Attorney Act 1971.

65 Section 9(8) of the TLATA 1996.

66 Law Com No 181, para 11.3.

(c) if the functions are delegated to him and to other beneficiaries to be exercised by them separately (or either separately or jointly), the power is revoked in so far as it relates to him.

(5) A delegation under sub-s (1) may be for any period or indefinite.

(6) A power of attorney under sub-s (1) cannot be an enduring power within the meaning of the Enduring Powers of Attorney Act 1985.

(7) Beneficiaries to whom functions have been delegated under sub-s (1) are, in relation to the exercise of the functions, in the same position as trustees (with the same duties and liabilities); but such beneficiaries shall not be regarded as trustees for any other purposes (including, in particular, the purposes of any enactment permitting the delegation of functions by trustees or imposing requirements relating to the payment of capital money).

(8) Where any function has been delegated to a beneficiary or beneficiaries under sub-s (1), the trustees are jointly and severally liable for any act or default of the beneficiary, or any of the beneficiaries, in the exercise of the function if, and only if, the trustees did not exercise reasonable care in deciding to delegate the function to the beneficiary or beneficiaries.

(9) Neither this section nor the repeal by this Act of s 29 of the Law of Property Act 1925 (which is superseded by this section) affects the operation after the commencement of this Act of any delegation effected before that commencement.

Consents and consultation

Although the trustees of land are now given all powers of an absolute owner, the settlor may place some restrictions on the exercise of those powers. He may require the trustees not to exercise their powers without the consents of certain beneficiaries. Where consents are required, the purchaser must ensure that consents have been obtained by the trustees. But if consents of more than two persons are required, the purchaser only has to be satisfied that any two of the named persons have consented.[67] Of course, the trustees should obtain all the requisite consents for their own protection.

If a beneficiary whose consent is required is a minor, the purchaser does not have to make sure that the minor's consent is obtained, but the trustees must obtain the consent of a parent with parental responsibility for the minor or his guardian.[68]

The trustees are required, so far as practicable, to consult the beneficiaries, and so far as consistent with the general interest of the trust, to give effect to the wishes of the majority by value.[69] This is the same as the requirement under s 26(3) of the Law of Property Act 1925 (now repealed) except, unlike s 26(3) which applied to an express trust for sale only if expressly included in the trust

67 *Ibid*, s 10(1). This subsection re-enacts s 26(1) of the LPA 1925 (now repealed by the s 26(2), Sched 4 of the 1996 Act 4). Section 10(1) does not apply to the exercise of a function by trustees of land held on charitable, ecclesiastical or public trusts.

68 Section 10(3) of the TLATA 1996.

69 *Ibid*, s 11(1).

instrument, this requirement applies to all trusts of land unless expressly excluded.[70]

The requirement of consultation is particularly important for the beneficiaries, who are not also the trustees or who have not been delegated the powers of the trustees, to keep themselves informed of any proposed action by the trustees, so that they may take any preventive measures.

The consultation requirement does not apply where the trust was created before the Act came into force unless the surviving settlor subsequently execute a deed to the effect that it is to apply.[71] Neither does it apply to a trust created or arising under a will made before the Act.[72]

Trusts of Land and Appointment of Trustees Act 1996

10. Consents

(1) If a disposition creating a trust of land requires the consent of more than two persons to the exercise by the trustees of any function relating to the land, the consent of any two of them to the exercise of the function is sufficient in favour of a purchaser.

(2) Subsection (1) does not apply to the exercise of a function by trustees of land held on charitable, ecclesiastical or public trusts.

(3) Where at any time a person whose consent is expressed by a disposition creating a trust of land to be required to the exercise by the trustees of any function relating to the land is not of full age:

(a) his consent is not, in favour of a purchaser, required to the exercise of the function, but

(b) the trustees shall obtain the consent of a parent who has parental responsibility for him (within the meaning of the Children Act 1989) or of a guardian of his.

11. Consultation with beneficiaries

(1) The trustees of land shall in the exercise of any function relating to land subject to the trust:

(a) so far as practicable, consult the beneficiaries of full age and beneficially entitled to an interest in possession in the land, and

(b) so far as consistent with the general interest of the trust, give effect to the wishes of those beneficiaries, or (in case of dispute) of the majority (according to the value of their combined interests).

(2) Subsection (1) does not apply:

(a) in relation to a trust created by a disposition in so far as provision that it does not apply is made by the disposition,

70 *Ibid*, s 11(2)(a).

71 *Ibid*, s 11(3).

72 *Ibid*, s 11(2)(b).

(b) in relation to a trust created or arising under a will made before the commencement of this Act, or

(c) in relation to the exercise of the power mentioned in s 6(2).

(3 Subsection (1) does not apply to a trust created before the commencement of this Act by a disposition, or a trust created after that commencement by reference to such a trust, unless provision to the effect that it is to apply is made by a deed executed:

(a) in a case in which the trust was created by one person and he is of full capacity, by that person, or

(b) in a case in which the trust was created by more than one person, by such of the persons who created the trust as are alive and of full capacity.

(4) A deed executed for the purposes of sub-s (3) is irrevocable.

4 POWER OF COURT

The court is now given, under s 14 of the 1996 Act, wider and more flexible powers to intervene in any dispute relating to the exercise by the trustees of any of their functions (including the requirements of consent and consultation) and in any matters relating to the nature or extent of a person's interest in the trust property.[73] A trustee or any person who has an interest in the trust property may apply to the court for an order.[74] Thus, where the trustees cannot agree unanimously in the exercise of their powers, for example, where all the trustees cannot reach a unanimous decision as to whether to sell the property or to retain it, they may apply to the court for an order under s 14. The powers of the court under s 14 can be exercised whether the application is made before or after the Act came into force.[75]

Trusts of Land and Appointment of Trustees Act 1996

14. Applications for order

(1) Any person who is a trustee of land or has an interest in property subject to a trust of land may make an application to the court for an order under this section.

(2) On an application for an order under this section the court may make any such order:

(a) relating to the exercise by the trustees of any of their functions (including an order relieving them of any obligation to obtain the consent of, or to consult. any person in connection with the exercise of any of their functions), or

(b) declaring the nature or extent of a person's interest in property subject to the trust as the court thinks fit.

(3) The court may not under this section make any order as to the appointment or removal of trustees.

73 *Ibid*, s 14(2).

74 *Ibid*, s 14(1).

75 *Ibid*, s 14(4).

(4) The powers conferred on the court by this section are exercisable on an application whether it is made before or after the commencement of this Act.

(a) Application by trustees or interested

In deciding what order to make, the court is now given, under s 15, a list of factors to be taken into account, including (a) the intentions of the settlor, (b) the purposes of the trust property, (c) the welfare of any minor who occupies or might reasonably be expected to occupy the trust property as his home, and (d) the interests of any secured creditor of any beneficiary. These are not intended to be exhaustive, and other relevant factors such as the wishes of any adult beneficiaries may be considered.

Section 15 essentially consolidates the approach previously taken by the court which was to look at all the circumstances of the case to see if it would be inequitable to order a sale.[76] The first two factors came from the doctrine of collateral purposes developed by the courts under s 30 of the Law of Property Act 1925, under which the court would not order sale if the original purpose for which the trust property was acquired could still be achieved,[77] but sale may be ordered if the purpose had come to an end.[78] The case law previously developed by the courts will no doubt be still relevant, in so far as it relates to defining the original intentions of the parties and the purpose of the trust, now that these are formally included in the list of factors to be considered by the court.

The third factor is not new either. Such a factor had always been taken into account by the court where there were dependent children living in the trust property with the co-owner who resisted sale.[79] The fourth factor is perhaps new in the context of an application made by a person other than the trustee in bankruptcy of any beneficiaries. Although such a factor was often a very influential factor in an application made by a trustee in bankruptcy, it rarely surfaced in an application made by other person.

In an application relating to the exercise of the trustees' power under s 13 to exclude or restrict the right of beneficiaries to occupy, the court should also take into account the circumstances and wishes of each of the beneficiaries who is entitled to occupy the trust property under s 12.[80]

In any other application, other than an application relating to the exercise of the trustees' power to convey the trust property to the beneficiaries under s 6(2), the court should also take into account the circumstances and wishes of any adult beneficiaries, or of a majority of them, who are entitled to an interest in possession.[81]

---

76 *Re Buchanan-Wollaston's Conveyance* [1939] Ch 738 at 747; *Jones v Challenger* [1961] 1 QB 176 at 183; *Jones v Jones* [1977] 1 WLR 438.

77 See eg *Jones v Jones* [1977] 1 WLR 438; *Stott v Ratcliffe* (1982) 126 Sol Jo 310; *Charlton v Lester* (1976) 238 EG 115; *Abbey National Plc v Moss* [1994] 1 FLR 307; *Harris v Harris* (1996) 72 P & CR 408 ('as a family home').

78 For example, *Jones v Challenger* [1961] 1 QB 176; *Bernard v Josephs* [1982] Ch 391.

79 For example, *Re Evers' Trust* [1980] 3 All ER 399.

80 Section 15(2) of the TLATA 1996.

81 *Ibid*, s 15(3).

Trusts of Land and Appointment of Trustees Act 1996

15. Matters relevant in determining applications

(1) The matters to which the court is to have regard in determining an application for an order under s 14 include:

(a) the intentions of the person or persons (if any) who created the trust,

(b) the purposes for which the property subject to the trust is held,

(c) the welfare of any minor who occupies or might reasonably be expected to occupy any land subject to the trust as his home, and

(d) the interests of any secured creditor of any beneficiary.

(2) In the case of an application relating to the exercise in relation to any land of the powers conferred on the trustees by s 13, the matters to which the court is to have regard also include the circumstances and wishes of each of the beneficiaries who is (or apart from any previous exercise by the trustees of those powers would be) entitled to occupy the land under s 12.

(3) In the case of any other application, other than one relating to the exercise of the power mentioned in s 6(2), the matters to which the court is to have regard also include the circumstances and wishes of any beneficiaries of full age and entitled to an interest in possession in property subject to the trust or (in case of dispute) of the majority (according to the value of their combined interests).

(4) This section does not apply to an application if s 335A of the Insolvency Act 1986 (which is inserted by Schedule 3 and relates to applications by a trustee of a bankrupt) applies to it.

(b) Application by trustee in bankruptcy

When a trustee is declared bankrupt, the legal estate in the trust property held by the bankrupt as a trustee is not affected by the bankruptcy; it stays with the bankrupt. But if the bankrupt also owns a beneficial interest in the trust property, all his beneficial interest in it vests automatically by operation of law in his trustee in bankruptcy.[82] The trustee in bankruptcy has a statutory duty to 'get in, realise and distribute' the bankrupt's beneficial interest behind the trust to satisfy the claims of creditors.[83] Where the bankrupt owns a beneficial joint tenancy, the vesting of the bankrupt's estate also operates as a severance so that the trustee in bankruptcy acquires the bankrupt's now distinct but undivided share.[84] Where other trustees resist sale of the trust property co-owned beneficially by the bankrupt, the trustee in bankruptcy ranks as a 'person interested'[85] and may therefore apply to the court under s 14 for an order for

82 Sections 283(1)(a), (3)(a), 306 of the Insolvency Act 1986.

83 Section 305(2) of the Insolvency Act 1986.

84 *Morgan v Marquis* (1853) 9 Exch 145.

85 *Re Solomon (a bankrupt)* [1967] Ch 573 at 586. This is a decision on the repealed s 30 of the LPA 1925, but should apply equally to s 14 of the 1996 Act.

sale. In exercising its discretion on such an application, a set of circumstances, rather different from those relevant to the disputes between the trustees of land, are to be taken into account by the court; the factors provided under s 15 will not apply.[86] Instead, s 335A of the Insolvency Act 1986 now provides that where an application is made by a trustee in bankruptcy under s 14, the interests of the bankrupt's creditors, and all the circumstances of the case other than the needs of the bankrupt, must be taken into account.[87] Where the trust property includes a dwelling house which is or has been the home of the bankrupt or the bankrupt's spouse or former spouse, then additional factors are to be taken into account: (i) the conduct of the spouse or former spouse, so far as contributing to the bankruptcy, (ii) the needs and financial resources of the spouse or former spouse, and (iii) the needs of any children.[88] This applies to an application made whether before or after the Act.[89]

Insolvency Act 1986

355A. Rights under trusts of land

(1) Any application by a trustee of a bankrupt's estate under s 14 of the Trusts of Land and Appointment of Trustees Act 1996 (powers of court in relation to trusts of land) for an order under that section for the sale of land shall be made to the court having jurisdiction in relation to the bankruptcy.

(2) On such an application the court shall make such order as it thinks just and reasonable having regard to:

(a) the interests of the bankrupt's creditors;

(b) where the application is made in respect of land which includes a dwelling house which is or has been the home of the bankrupt or the bankrupt's spouse or former spouse:

(i) the conduct of the spouse or former spouse, so far as contributing to the bankruptcy,

(ii) the needs and financial resources of the spouse or former spouse, and

(iii) the needs of any children; and

(c) all the circumstances of the case other than the needs of the bankrupt.

(3) Where such an application is made after the end of the period of one year beginning with the first vesting under Chapter IV of this Part of the bankrupt's estate in a trustee, the court shall assume, unless the circumstances of the case are exceptional, that the interests of the bankrupt's creditors outweigh all other considerations.

86 Section 15(4) of the TLATA 1996.

87 Section 335A(2)(a), (c) of the Insolvency Act 1986, (as added by s 25(1), Sched 3, para 23 of the TLATA 1996.

88 Section 335A(2)(b) of the Insolvency Act 1986. These factors are almost identical to the factors contained in s 336(4) of the 1986 Act which used to apply to an application by a trustee in bankruptcy under s 30 of the LPA 1925 for an order for the sale of land held on trust for sale.

89 Section 335A(4) of the Insolvency Act 1986 (as added by s 25(1), Sched 3, para 23 of the TLATA 1996.)

(4) The powers conferred on the court by this section are exercisable on an application whether it is made before or after the commencement of this section.

Where the application is made one year after the bankruptcy order, there is a presumption, unless the circumstances of the case are exceptional, that the interest of the bankrupt's creditors outweigh all other considerations.[90]

What then are exceptional circumstances? In a number of bankruptcy cases, with the exception of *Re Holliday*,[91] the court had been extremely slow in finding exceptional circumstances.[92] One example is the case of *Re Citro* (a bankrupt).[93] Here, although the matrimonial homes of the bankrupts were registered in the joint names of the bankrupts and their wives, s 336 of the Insolvency Act 1986 did not apply because it was not in force at the relevant time, but the court took into account similar factors.[94] In this case, two Citro brothers, Domenico and Carmine, ran a garage business as panel beaters and car sprayers. In 1985, they were declared bankrupt. They had half shares of the beneficial interests in their matrimonial homes. The trustee in bankruptcy of their joint and several estates sought to sell their homes under s 30 of the Law of Property Act 1925. Domenico was judicially separated from his wife, who lived in their house with their three children, the youngest of whom was 12. Carmine lived in his home with his wife. They also had three children, the youngest of whom was 10. Hoffmann J made an order for possession and sale, but postponed the order until the youngest child in each case became 16. The trustee in bankruptcy appealed. The Court of Appeal varied the order to the extent that possession and sale were now to be postponed for a period not exceeding six months, as there were no exceptional circumstances to justify postponing sale for a longer period.

Re Citro (a bankrupt) [1991] Ch 142, CA[95]

Nourse LJ: [His Lordship read s 30 of the Law of Property Act (now repealed) (similar to s 14 of the 1996 Act) and referred to *Jones v Challenger* [1961] 1 QB 176, [1960] 1 All ER 785; *Re Mayo* [1943] Ch 302, [1943] 2 All ER 440; *Re Buchanan-Wollaston's Conveyance* [1939] Ch 738, [1939] 2 All ER 302; *Re Solomon* [1967] Ch 573, [1966] 3 All ER 255; *Boydell v Gillespie* (1970) 216 EG 1505; *Re Hardy's Trust* (1970) *Times*, 23 October, *Re Turner* [1974] 1 WLR 1556, [1975] 1 All ER 5; *Re Densham* [1975] 1 WLR 1519, [1975] 3 All ER 726; *Re Bailey* [1977] 1 WLR 278, [1977] 2 All ER 26; *Re Holliday* [1981] Ch 405, [1980] 3 All ER 385; *Re Lowrie* [1981] 3 All ER 353; and continued:]

The broad effect of these authorities can be summarised as follows. Where a spouse who has a beneficial interest in the matrimonial home has become bankrupt under debts

---

90 Section 335A(3) of the Insolvency Act 1986.

91 [1981] Ch 405.

92 See eg *Re Densham (a bankrupt)* [1975] 1 WLR 1519; *Bird v Syme-Thomson* [1979] 1 WLR 440; *Re Lowrie (a bankrupt)* [1981] 3 All ER 353; *Re Bailey (a bankrupt)* [1977] 1 WLR 278; *Re Turner (a bankrupt)* [1974] 1 WLR 1556; *Re Citro (a bankrupt)* [1991] Ch 142; *Re Gorman (a bankrupt)* [1990] 1 WLR 616.

93 [1991] Ch 142.

94 [1991] Ch 142, at 146H, 147F.

95 See [1991] Conv 302 (Lawson, AMM); (1991) 107 LQR 177 (SM Cretney); [1991] CLJ 45 (Hall, JC).

which cannot be paid without the realisation of that interest, the voice of the creditors will usually prevail over the voice of the other spouse and a sale of the property ordered within a short period. The voice of the other spouse will only prevail in exceptional circumstances. No distinction is to be made between a case where the property is still being enjoyed as the matrimonial home and one where it is not.

What then are exceptional circumstances? As the cases show, it is not uncommon for a wife with young children to be faced with eviction in circumstances where the realisation of her beneficial interest will not produce enough to buy a comparable home in the same neighbourhood, or indeed elsewhere. And, if she has to move elsewhere, there may be problems over schooling and so forth. Such circumstances, while engendering a natural sympathy in all who hear of them, cannot be described as exceptional. They are the melancholy consequences of debt and improvidence with which every civilised society has been familiar. It was only in *Re Holliday* that they helped the wife's voice to prevail, and then only, as I believe, because of one special feature of that case. One of the reasons for the decision given by Sir David Cairns was that, it was highly unlikely that postponement of payment of the debts would cause any great hardship to any of the creditors, a matter of which Buckley LJ no doubt took account as well. Although the arithmetic was not fully spelled out in the judgments, the net value of the husband's half share of the beneficial interest in the matrimonial home was about £13,250, against which had to be set debts of about £6,500 or £7,500 as the sum required to obtain a full discharge. Statutory interest at 4 per cent on £6,500 for five years would have amounted to no more than £1,300 which, when added to the £7,500, would make a total of less than £9,000, well covered by the £13,250. Admittedly, it was detrimental to the creditors to be kept out of a commercial rate of interest and the use of the money during a further period of five years. But if the principal was safe, one can understand that that detriment was not treated as being decisive, even in inflationary times. It must indeed be exceptional for creditors in a bankruptcy to receive 100p. in the £ plus statutory interest in full and the passage of years before they do so does not make it less exceptional. On the other hand, without that special feature, I cannot myself see how the circumstances in *Re Holliday* could fairly have been treated as exceptional. I am confirmed in that view by the belief that it would be shared by Balcombe LJ, who in *Harman v Glencross* [1986] Fam 81, 95, [1986] 1 All ER 545, 556, said that the decision in *Re Holliday* was very much against the run of the recent authorities. I would not myself have regarded it as an exceptional circumstance that the husband had presented his own petition, even 'as a tactical move'. That was not something of the creditors' choosing and could not fairly have been held against them. I do not say that in other cases there might not be other exceptional circumstances. They must be identified if and when they arise ...

Did Hoffmann J correctly apply it to the facts which were before him? I respectfully think that he did not. First, for the reasons already stated, the personal circumstances of the two wives and their children, although distressing, are not by themselves exceptional. Secondly, I think that the judge erred in fashioning his orders by reference to those which might have been made in the Family Division in a case where bankruptcy had not supervened. That approach, which tends towards treating the home as a source of provision for the children, was effectively disapproved by the earlier and uncontroversial part of the decision of this court in *Re Holliday*. Thirdly, and perhaps most significantly, he did not ask himself the critical question whether a further postponement of payment of their debts would cause hardship to the creditors. It is only necessary to look at the substantial deficiencies referred to earlier in this judgment in order to see that it would. Since then a further 18 months' interest has accrued and the trustee has incurred the costs of these proceedings as well.

In all the circumstances, I think that these cases are clearly distinguishable from *Re Holliday* and ought to have been decided accordingly. Part at least of the reason why they were not was that the points with which we have been concerned were not as fully argued below as they have been here. In particular, a close examination of the figures in order to see whether a postponement would cause increasing hardship to the creditors was not undertaken. This is not to imply any criticism of counsel. It is a characteristic of our system that the higher court often seems partial towards thinking that the important point is the one which was not taken in the lower court ...

I would allow both appeals by deleting the provisos for postponement from Hoffmann J's orders and substituting short periods of suspension, the length of which can be discussed with counsel.

Bingham LJ: I have had the opportunity of reading in draft the judgment of Nourse LJ and I agree with it ...

The only case drawn to our attention in which the voice of the wife has been held to prevail over that of the trustee was in *re Holliday* [1981] Ch 405. If the judge was entitled to treat the present cases as fairly comparable with that case, then his exercise of discretion may not be disturbed. But Walton J in *In re Lowrie* [1981] 3 All ER 353, 356, observed of In *re Holliday* 'one can scarcely, I think, imagine a more exceptional set of facts' and one must examine the circumstances of that case to decide whether those of the present case are indeed fairly comparable.

Sir David Cairns listed the factors in *In re Holliday* which led him to conclude, at p 425, that the wife's voice should prevail. They were: (i) that it would be difficult if not impossible for the wife to secure another suitable home for the family in or near her then home; (ii) that it would be upsetting for the children's education if they had to move far away from their present schools, even if it were practicable, having regard to the wife's means, to find an alternative home at some more distant place; (iii) that it was highly unlikely that postponement of the payment of the debts would cause any great hardship to any of the creditors; (iv) that none of the creditors thought fit themselves to present a bankruptcy petition and it was quite impossible to know whether any one of them would have done so if the debtor had not himself done so. Although less explicitly stated, the same factors were no doubt in the mind of Buckley LJ.Whether these factors quite merit the description applied to them by Walton J in *In re Lowrie* may be debatable, but it is to be observed: (i) that in *In re Holliday*, unlike the present case, there might well have been no bankruptcy at all but for the debtor's action; (ii) that after the moratorium imposed by the court all the creditors could be paid in full with interest, albeit at the anachronistic statutory rate, which will not be the case here; (iii) that the sum available to the wife on sale was expected to be much smaller, even allowing for inflation, than would be available to either of these wives; (iv) that the children in that case were younger than those in these cases. Even so, the moratorium ordered by the Court of Appeal in *In re Holliday* was shorter than that ordered by Hoffmann J in the present case.

None of these matters was mentioned by Hoffmann J. As I read his judgment, he treated *In re Holliday* as entitling or obliging him simply to balance the interests of the creditors against those of the wife, the creditors' *prima facie* entitlement to their money being simply one element in the scales – and not a particularly weighty one at that. I would willingly adopt this approach if I felt free to do so. It is in my view conducive to justice in the broadest sense and it reflects the preference which the law increasingly gives to personal over property interests. I do not, however, think it reflects the principle which, as I conclude, clearly emerges from the cases, that the order sought by the trustee must be made unless there are, at least, compelling reasons, not found in the ordinary run of cases, for refusing it. I find it impossible to reach that conclusion on the present facts, which I would expect to be substantially repeated in many other cases of this kind.

As I have, I think, made clear, I regret this conclusion. But we must apply the law as we understand it, and where authority has indicated how a discretion should be exercised in the unexceptional case it is desirable that it should be followed, unless overruled, if arbitrariness is to be avoided. I do not think we are free to overrule the authority relevant to these appeals, and indeed it would be improper given the terms of s 336(5) of the Act of 1986.

I would allow the appeals and invite submissions on the length of the moratorium we should grant.

Sir George Waller: I regret to say that I do not agree with the conclusions of Nourse and Bingham L JJ and I will shortly and respectfully state my reasons. In these two cases the trustee in bankruptcy is appealing against the judgment of Hoffmann J that under s 30 of the Law of Property Act 1925 there should be an order for the sale of the two houses but that it should not be enforced in each case until the youngest child of the marriage reaches the age of 16, ie in one case five years and in the other case six years. It was submitted that there was no sufficient evidence of exceptional circumstances in either case to justify such an order. Although s 30 says the court 'may' make an order the authorities show that the court will make an order for sale unless the circumstances are exceptional. There are cases of joint ownership by husband and wife where parties have sought to persuade the court that the wife, or husband, will suffer hardship if a sale is ordered but in the absence of children the court has not been persuaded.

The principal Court of Appeal case to which we were referred was *In re Holliday* [1981] Ch 405, but before considering it I should just refer to three of the cases mentioned by Goff LJ and previously decided by him: *In re Solomon* [1967] Ch 573 and *In re Turner* [1974] 1 WLR 1556 where there was no mention of children, and *In re Densham* [1975] 1 WLR 278 where there was a son, but Sir Robert Megarry VC said in that case that the evidence of interference with education was very slight. In *Re Holliday* Goff LJ referred to the cases I have set out above in all of which he had made an order for sale and said that there would have to be 'some very special circumstances' to induce the court not to order a sale. He then said, at p 420:

> Nevertheless there is a discretion, and I would hear argument according to these principles on the question whose voice in the circumstances of this case ought to prevail, and in this connection it will be necessary to consider the schooling arrangements at present obtaining, and what could be done if the house were sold, but the evidence at present does not cover this very adequately.

Goff, LJ then set out the various inquiries about schooling which should be made. Both Buckley LJ and Sir David Cairns agreed with this judgment. Although he was fully aware of the position of the creditors and the fact that the debtor had presented his own petition, it is, I think, clear from Goff LJ's judgment that had it not been for the education of the children the court would not have given further consideration to the case.

After Goff LJ's death, when the facts were finally considered by Buckley LJ and Sir David Cairns, Buckley LJ set out fully the facts relating to the children's education. Then, after summarising the relative considerations of the creditors and the wife, he said, at p 424:

> Balancing the interest of the creditors and the interest of the wife, burdened, as I say, with the obligation to provide a home for the three children of the marriage, in my view the right attitude for the court to adopt is that the house should not at the present juncture be sold.

A decision was made in favour of the wife, Sir David Cairns emphasising that to do otherwise would be 'upsetting for the children's education' and Buckley LJ also mentioning the children's education while not finally deciding the case clearly thought that the education of the children was a matter to be taken into consideration, and Buckley LJ and Sir David Cairns postponed the sale for five years because 'the hardship for the wife and children would be much less or would have disappeared altogether by then.'

In *In re Lowrie* [1981] 3 All ER 353, the appeal against an order of postponement of 30 months was allowed but the two children were aged 3½ years and 18 months and Walton J did say in the course of his judgment that if their schooling had been involved, it might have been different.

In this case the judge set out the interests which had to be balanced, the creditors and the two wives and their children who were very much at the critical age for their education, in Mary Citro's case one son wanting to stay at school and to do 'A' levels and another son wanting to start at the same school. In Josephine Citro's case the eldest at school was 14. This can only have been mentioned because the sale of the house in each case would create educational difficulties. He set out fully in his judgment the situation of the families which fell clearly within the situation described in the judgments which I have quoted above. The circumstances relating to the two wives set out by the judge, the housing difficulty, education, difficulties of which were before him and his description of their position as being 'extremely unenviable' in different words describe exactly that which in *In re Holliday* was described as 'hardship' or 'very special circumstances'. That education was a fundamental element of the judge's order is clear from the order itself, namely the 16th birthday of the youngest child in each family.

The judge had to exercise his discretion and he followed the decision in *Re Holliday*. *In re Holliday* was a decision of the Court of Appeal which may possibly go further than earlier authorities, but it is a decision of this court and, although Goff LJ was not party to the final decision, he clearly had in mind in his judgment the possibility of such a decision. I have no difficulty in regarding the circumstances as very special; there has been no similar case with such problems. Although the judge's words may not have precisely followed the words of the judgments in *Re Holliday*, in my opinion he covered exactly the same points and I would dismiss the appeal in both cases.'

In *Re Holliday*,[96] a sale was postponed for five years until the two children of the marriage would be over 17. Here a husband and wife bought their matrimonial home which was conveyed to them on trust for sale as joint legal and beneficial owners. The husband left his wife for another woman, and the wife was now saddled with the burden of providing a proper home for her three children without any resources. The husband later petitioned voluntarily for a bankruptcy order but his outstanding liability was only in the region of £6,000.

96 [1980] 3 All ER 385.

Re Holliday (A Bankrupt) [1980] 3 All ER 385

Goff LJ: Where property is held on trust for sale and any person interested desires a sale but that is opposed, then the court has in all cases a discretion whether to order a sale or not, but the exercise of that discretion may be very much limited and controlled by the facts and circumstances of the case.

I shall first consider the position as it was before *Williams v Williams* [1976] Ch 278, [1977] 1 All ER 28, and then consider the impact of that case. Where the property in question is a matrimonial home, then the provision of a home for both parties is a secondary or collateral object of the trust for sale (see *per* Devlin LJ in *Jones v Challenger* [1961] 1 QB 176 at 181, [1960] 1 All ER 786 at 787) and the court will not ordinarily order a sale if the marriage be still subsisting and no question of bankruptcy has supervened.

Where, however, the marriage has come to an end by divorce or death of one of the parties or is dead in fact, though still subsisting at law, then apart from any question how far the secondary or collateral object can be said to be still subsisting if there are young or dependent children, though there remains a discretion it is one in which, as I see it, some very special circumstances need to be shown to induce the court not to order a sale: see *Jones v Challenger* and *Rawlings v Rawlings* [1964] P 398, [1964] 2 All ER 804.

[His Lordship also referred to *Burke v Burke* [1974] 1 WLR 1063 at 1067, [1974] 2 All ER 944 at 947 and continued:]

So the question is whether to adopt Salmon LJ's view expressed in *Rawlings v Rawlings* at 419, at 814, that the existence of young or dependent children prolongs the secondary or collateral purpose, or Buckley LJ's view expressed in *Burke v Burke* at 1067, 947, that the purpose is ended, but the existence of the children is a factor incidentally to be taken into account so far as they affect the equities in the matter as between the persons entitled to the beneficial interests in the property.

With all respect to both the Lords Justices concerned, I would prefer the view of Buckley LJ to that of Salmon LJ because, as Devlin LJ pointed out in *Jones v Challenger* at 184 at 789:

> The conversion of the property into a form in which both parties can enjoy their rights equally is the prime object of the trust; the preservation of the house as a home for one of them singly is not an object at all. If the true object of the trust is made paramount, as it should be, there is only one order that can be made ...

and in my view the preservation of the house as a home for the children can be no more an object than its preservation as a home for the spouse.

[His Lordship referred to *Williams v Williams* [1976] Ch 278 and continued:]

In my judgment, however, *Williams v Williams* itself is clearly distinguishable from the present and this case falls within *Jones v Challenger* because of the intervention of the trustee in bankruptcy...

The Family Division has no jurisdiction to make an order against him under s 24 [of the Matrimonial Causes Act 1973], because he is not a party to the marriage, and its power to make an order under s 23 [of the 1973 Act] against the debtor is at this stage much circumscribed by the fact that he is bankrupt ...

It seems to me, therefore, that we ought to decide the present case ourselves and not refer it back to the Family Division and that our discretion should be exercised in accordance with the law as established and as I have adumbrated it apart from *Williams v*

Williams [1976] Ch 278, [1977] 1 All ER 28; so, as it seems to me, we have to decide this case according to the principle of *Jones v Challenger* [1961] 1 QB 176 at 181, [1960] 1 All ER 785 at 787, as applied by me in the bankruptcy cases *Re Solomon* [1967] Ch 573, [1966] 3 All ER 255; *Re Turner* [1974] 1 WLR 1556, [1975] 1 All ER 5 and *Re Densham* [1975] 1 WLR 1519, [1975] 3 All ER 726. I laid down the relevant principle where there is a bankruptcy in *Re Turner* at 1558c at 7:

> In my judgment, the guiding principle in the exercise of the court's discretion is not whether the trustee or the wife is being reasonable but, in all the circumstances of the case, whose voice in equity ought to prevail ...

and I would apply that test to this case. So we have to decide having regard to all the circumstances, including the fact that there are young children and that the debtor was made bankrupt on his own petition, whose voice, that of the trustee seeking to realise the debtor's share for the benefit of his creditors or that of the wife seeking to preserve a home for herself and the children, ought in equity to prevail. In all those cases I held that the trustee must prevail as did the Divisional Court in *Re Bailey* [1977] 1 WLR 278; [1977] 2 All ER 26.

Nevertheless, there is a discretion, and I would hear argument according to these principles on the question whose voice in the circumstances of this case ought to prevail, and in this connection it will be necessary to consider the schooling arrangements at present obtaining, and what could be done if the house were sold, but the evidence at present does not cover this very adequately.

[While further evidence was obtained, Goff LJ died. The appeal was disposed of by Buckley LJ and Sir David Cairns.]

Sir David Cairns: I agree with Buckley LJ that in all the circumstances here the voice of the wife, on behalf of herself and the children, should prevail to the extent that the sale of the house should be deferred for a substantial period. I reach that view because I am satisfied that it would at present be very difficult, if not impossible, for the wife to secure another suitable home for the family in or near Thorpe Bay; because it would be upsetting for the children's education if they had to move far away from their present schools, even if it were practicable, having regard to the wife's means, to find an alternative home at some more distant place; because it is highly unlikely that postponement of the payment of the debts would cause any great hardship to any of the creditors; and because none of the creditors thought fit themselves to present a bankruptcy petition and it is quite impossible to know whether any one of them would have done so if the debtor had not himself presented such a petition.

Although there is apparently no previous reported case in which the interests of a debtor's family have been held to prevail over those of creditors in a bankruptcy, there have certainly been earlier cases in which family interests have been considered and set against those of the creditors: see *Re Turner* [1974] 1 WLR 1556, [1975] 1 All ER 5, where it was the wife's interest that was considered; and *Re Bailey* [1977] 1 WLR 278; [1977] 2 All ER 26, where it was the interests of a son of the family.

In the earlier cases the trustee has succeeded, because no sufficiently substantial case of hardship of dependents was established. That is where, in my judgment, this case differs from the earlier ones. It may well be, however, that the hardship for the wife and children would be much less, or would have disappeared altogether, in five years' time or possibly even earlier. I therefore agreed that it is appropriate that we should not at this stage defer sale for longer than five years or thereabouts, and that we should leave a loophole for earlier sale to be applied for if the circumstances change in such a way as to warrant it.

Furthermore, a bankrupt who is living with a person under the age of 18 at the time of bankruptcy has a 'right of occupation', that is if he is in occupation, not to be evicted or excluded except with the leave of the court, and if not already in occupation, a right with the leave of the court to enter into occupation.[97] The bankrupt's spouse on the other hand cannot acquire any statutory 'rights of occupation' in the bankrupt's estate under the Matrimonial Homes Act 1983 as between the date of bankruptcy petition and the date the bankrupt's estate is vested in a trustee in bankruptcy.[98] However, if the spouse has a right to occupy in the bankrupt's co-owned estate independently of the 1983 Act (for example if she has contributed to the initial purchase), or if she acquires the statutory rights of occupation before bankruptcy and has registered the rights as a charge,[99] such rights can only be terminated under s 336(4) of the Insolvency Act 1986 on the application by the trustee in bankruptcy under s 1 of the Matrimonial Home Act 1983.[100] A trustee in bankruptcy seeking to sell the bankrupt's estate must also apply for an order terminating the bankrupt and his spouse's rights of occupation to effect a sale with vacant possession.

Insolvency Act 1986

336. Rights of occupation etc of bankrupt's spouse

(1) Nothing occurring in the initial period of the bankruptcy (that is to say, the period beginning with the day of the presentation of the petition for the bankruptcy order and ending with the vesting of the bankrupt's estate in a trustee) is to be taken as having given rise to any rights of occupation under the Matrimonial Homes Act 1983 in relation to a dwelling house comprised in the bankrupt's estate.

(2) Where a spouse's rights of occupation under the Act of 1983 are a charge on the estate or interest of the other spouse, or of trustees for the other spouse, and the other spouse is adjudged bankrupt:

(a) the charge continues to subsist notwithstanding the bankruptcy and, subject to the provisions of that Act, binds the trustee of the bankrupt's estate and persons deriving title under that trustee, and

(b) any application for an order under s 1 of that Act shall be made to the court having jurisdiction in relation to the bankruptcy.

(4) On such an application as is mentioned in sub-s (2) or (3) the court shall make such order under s 1 of the Act of 1983 as it thinks just and reasonable having regard to:

(a) the interests of the bankrupt's creditors,

97 Section 337(1) and (2)(a) of the Insolvency Act 1986.

98 *Ibid*, s 336(1).

99 *Ibid*, s 336(2).

100 Where the bankrupt's spouse is also a trustee of land, she can of course have no statutory rights of occupation under the Matrimonial Home Act 1983 (see s 1(1), (11) of the 1983 Act).

(b) the conduct of the spouse or former spouse, so far as contributing to the bankruptcy,

(c) the needs and financial resources of the spouse or former spouse,

(d) all the circumstances of the case other than the needs of the bankrupt.

(5) Where such an application is made after the end of the period of one year beginning with the first vesting under Chapter IV of this Part of the bankrupt's estate in a trustee, the court shall assume, unless the circumstances of the case are exceptional, that the interests of the bankrupt's creditors outweigh all other considerations.

337. Rights of occupation of bankrupt

(1) This section applies where:

(a) a person who is entitled to occupy a dwelling house by virtue of a beneficial estate or interest is adjudged bankrupt, and

(b) any persons under the age of 18 with whom that person had at some time occupied that dwelling house had their home with that person at the time when the bankruptcy petition was presented and at the commencement of the bankruptcy.

(2) Whether or not the bankrupt's spouse (if any) has rights of occupation under the Matrimonial Homes Act 1983:

(a) the bankrupt has the following rights as against the trustee of his estate:

(i) if in occupation, a right not to be evicted or excluded from the dwelling house or any part of it, except with the leave of the court,

(ii) if not in occupation, a right with the leave of the court to enter into and occupy the dwelling house, and

(b) the bankrupt's rights are a charge, having the like priority as an equitable interest created immediately before the commencement of the bankruptcy, on so much of his estate or interest in the dwelling house as vests in the trustee.

(3) The Act of 1983 has effect, with the necessary modifications, as:

(a) the rights conferred by paragraph (a) of sub-s (2) were rights of occupation under that Act.

(b) any application for leave such as is mentioned in that paragraph were an application for an order under s 1 of that Act, and

(c) any charge under paragraph (b) of that subsection on the estate or interest of the trustee were a charge under that Act on the estate or interest of a spouse.

(4) Any application for leave such as is mentioned in sub-s (2)(a) or otherwise by virtue of this section for an order under s 1 of the Act of 1983 shall be made to the court having jurisdiction in relation to the bankruptcy.

(5) On such an application the court shall make such order under s 1 of the Act of 1983 as it thinks just and reasonable having regard to the interests of the creditors, to the bankrupt's financial resources, to the needs of the children and to all the circumstances of the case other than the needs of the bankrupt.

(6) Where such an application is made after the end of the period of one year beginning with the first vesting (under Chapter IV of this Part) of the bankrupt's estate in a trustee, the court shall assume, unless the circumstances of the case are exceptional, that the interests of the bankrupt's creditors outweigh all other considerations.

(c) Applications by mortgagee or chargee

Under the repealed s 30 where the applicant is a mortgagee or chargee and not a trustee in bankruptcy, it has been held that the principles in bankruptcy cases are equally applicable. In *Lloyds Bank plc v Byrne and Byrne*,[101] Parker LJ thought that the differences between the position of a trustee in bankruptcy and a chargee do not justify a difference in the approach to be taken. The same principles have also been extended to applicants who have obtained a charging order on the property.[102] It would appear that the same reasoning could apply to the new provisions.

5 PROTECTION OF PURCHASERS

As mentioned earlier, the trustees' powers may be subject to certain limitations, for example by requiring the consents of certain person or express limitation in the trust instrument. In line with the principle that a purchaser should not be required to examine a trust instrument to determine the validity of a conveyance, a purchaser is not affected by an express limitation of the trustees' powers unless they have notice of that limitation.[103] Clearly, it is in the interest of beneficiaries that there should be some means of ensuring that purchasers do have notice of such a restriction. Accordingly, the trustees are required to take reasonable steps to ensure that any restriction upon their powers is brought to the attention of prospective purchasers.[104] Again, a purchaser is not concerned to see that the trustees, in exercising their power, have had regard to the rights of the beneficiaries;[105] or have made the necessary consultation;[106] or where consent is required from each of the beneficiaries for partition,[107] that the trustees have obtained such consent.[108] Where the trustees have acted in breach of any enactment or rule of law or equity, or have exceeded any statutory restriction, limitation or condition, a purchaser who has no actual notice of the breach or contravention will not be affected by it.[109] These protections are however only given to a purchaser of unregistered land.[110] In registered land, the purchaser is only bound by interests which are protected by an entry on the

101 [1993] 1 FLR 369 at 372.

102 *Barclays Bank plc v Hendricks* [1996] 1 FLR 258.

103 Section 16(3)(b) of the TLATA 1996.

104 *Ibid*, s 16(3)(a).

105 As is required by *ibid* s 6(5).

106 As is required by *ibid* s 11(1).

107 As is required by *ibid* s 7(3).

108 *Ibid*, s 16(1).

109 *Ibid*, s 16(2).

110 *Ibid*, s 16(7).

register, and 'there shall also be entered on the register such restrictions as may be prescribed, or may be expedient, for the protection of the rights of the persons beneficially interested in the land'.[111]

In both registered and unregistered land, where the trustees have executed a deed of discharge after they have conveyed the trust property, under s 6(2) of the 1996 Act, to the beneficiaries entitled to it, a purchaser is entitled to assume that the land is no longer subject to the trust.[112]

Trusts of Land and Appointment of Trustees Act 1996

16. Protection of purchasers

(1) A purchaser of land which is or has been subject to a trust need not be concerned to see that any requirement imposed on the trustees by s 6(5), 7(3) or 11(1) has been complied with.

(2) Where:

(a) trustees of land who convey land which (immediately before it is conveyed) is subject to the trust contravene s 6(6) or (8), but

(b) the purchaser of the land from the trustees has no actual notice of the contravention, the contravention does not invalidate the conveyance.

(3) Where the powers of trustees of land are limited by virtue of s 8:

(a) the trustees shall take all reasonable steps to bring the limitation to the notice of any purchaser of the land from them, but

(b) the limitation does not invalidate any conveyance by the trustees to a purchaser who has no actual notice of the limitation.

(4) Where trustees of land convey land which (immediately before it is conveyed) is subject to the trust to persons believed by them to be beneficiaries absolutely entitled to the land under the trust and of full age and capacity:

(a) the trustees shall execute a deed declaring that they are discharged from the trust in relation to that land, and

(b) if they fail to do so, the court may make an order requiring them to do so.

(5) A purchaser of land to which a deed under sub-s (4) relates is entitled to assume that, as from the date of the deed, the land is not subject to the trust unless he has actual notice that the trustees were mistaken in their belief that the land was conveyed to beneficiaries absolutely entitled to the land under the trust and of full age and capacity.

(6) Subsections (2) and (3) do not apply to land held on charitable, ecclesiastical or public trusts.

111 Section 94(4) of the LRA 1925 as added by s 25(1), Sched 3, para 5(8) of the TLATA 1996.

112 Section 16(4), (5) of the TLATA 1996, and s 94(5) of the LRA 1925 (as added by s 25(1), Sched 3, para 5(8)) of the TLATA 1996.

6 OVERREACHING CONVEYANCE BY TRUSTEES OF LAND

The 1925 legislation aimed at providing greater protection to the purchaser of a legal estate held on trust for sale and the beneficiaries thereunder. This aim was achieved by a remarkably simple principle known as 'overreaching'.

In its classical form, where land was settled by the settlor to the trustees on trust for sale for certain beneficiaries, there often existed two documents: a conveyance or a vesting document vesting the legal estate in the trustees for sale, and a trust instrument.[113] The former showed that the trustees for sale have the legal estate and formed part of the evidence of title. The latter set out the trust, declaring the beneficial interests. The purchaser did not normally have to look at the trust instrument, and under the overreaching principle, he would be able to take the conveyance of the legal estate from the trustees for sale free of the beneficial interests stated in the trust instrument if he complied with the statutory requirement as to the payment of capital money.[114] In more modern cases where property was acquired by co-owners on trust for sale for themselves, there was often only one document: the deed of conveyance transferring the legal estate from the vendor to the co-owners and declaring the trust for sale.[115] This might or might not contain quantum of beneficial entitlements. This document also formed part of the document of title when the co-owners sold the legal estate subsequently. Under the doctrine of conversion, the beneficiaries' interests are in the proceeds of sale. A purchaser of a legal estate from the trustees did not have to be concerned with the trusts affecting the proceeds of sale of land as long as he paid the proceeds to all the trustees. He did not have to see that the proceeds of sale had been properly applied by the trustees for sale. He would automatically take the legal estate free of the beneficial entitlements if he had no notice of any irregularity. This process of 'overreaching' was later put on a statutory footing under s 2(1)(ii) of the Law of Property Act 1925, and under s 27(2) overreaching would take place if the proceeds are paid to at least two trustees for sale. The overreaching principle is now extended to trust of land, by an amendment to the previous s 2(1)(ii) of the Law of Property Act 1925.

Law of Property Act 1925

21. Conveyances overreaching certain equitable interests and powers

(1) A conveyance to a purchaser of a legal estate in land shall overreach any equitable interest or power affecting that estate, whether or not he has notice thereof, if:

---

113 What had long been the practice in the case of trusts for sale *inter vivos* was in fact later adopted by the 1925 legislation for creation of strict settlements after 1925. See (1927) 3 CLJ 62, 63 (Lightwood, JM); (1942) 8 CLJ 43, 44 (Bailey, SJ).

114 See the old s 27(1) of the LPA 1925 (before amendment by the TLATA 1996).

115 The express trust for sale will today be treated as a trust of land. Sometimes the deed of conveyance did not even declare the trust for sale, but before the TLATA 1996, an implied statutory trust for sale could nevertheless arise, and today, an implied trust of land will arise instead.

(ii) the conveyance is made by trustees of land and the equitable interest or power is at the date of the conveyance capable of being overreached by such trustees under the provisions of sub-s (2) of this section or independently of that section, and the requirements of s 27 of this Act respecting the payment of capital money arising on such a conveyance are complied with.

27. Purchaser not to be concerned with the trusts of the proceeds of sale which are to be paid to two or more trustees or to a trust corporation

(2) Notwithstanding anything to the contrary in the instrument (if any) creating a trust of land or in any trust affecting the net proceeds of sale of the land if it is sold, the proceeds of sale or other capital money shall not be paid to or applied by the direction of fewer than two persons as trustees, except where the trustee is a trust corporation, but this subsection does not affect the right of a sole personal representative as such to give valid receipts for, or direct the application of, proceeds of sale or other capital money, nor, except where capital money arises on the transaction, render it necessary to have more than one trustee.

Note that there is no provision for payment into courts. Once s 27(2) is satisfied, the purchaser can take an overreaching conveyance from the trustees of land free of the beneficial interests. Even purchaser with express notice of beneficial interests behind the trust may take free.[116]

The Law of Property Act however does not say what happens if s 27(2) is not complied with. The old doctrine of notice would seem to apply.[117] (This is different from a strict settlement where non-compliance of the statutory requirement renders the transfer of legal estate to purchaser void and the purchaser can only acquire the tenant for life's personal equitable interest and loses priority to the equitable interests under the settlement.)[118] So in unregistered land, a *bona fide* purchaser of a legal estate for value without notice of the beneficial interests will take the legal estate free of the beneficial interests.[119] The beneficiaries may be in occupation of the property. A purchaser is expected to make proper inquiries and inspection and if he fails to do so, he may be fixed with a constructive notice of the beneficial interests.[120] In registered land, the purchaser when registered as the proprietor will take subject to any minor interest appearing on the register and any overriding interest.[121] If there is an entry of restriction which normally contains the conditions that the proceeds must be paid to at least two trustees or a trust corporation, a purchaser who follows the conditions in the restriction will

116 *Cf City of London Building Society v Flegg* [1988] AC 54 at 83E–F, *per* Lord Oliver of Aylmerton. The Law Commission has recommended that the interest of a beneficiary who is in actual occupation should not be overreached unless he consents (Law Com No 188), para 5.3.

117 Megarry and Wade, pp 404–05.

118 Megarry and Wade, *ibid*. The Law Commission questioned whether it was necessary for the protection of a purchaser to vary in this way: see Law Commission's Working Paper (No 94, Trusts of Land), para 3.6, quoted at para 1.3 of the Law Commission's Report on Trusts of Land (Law Com No 181).

119 *Caunce v Caunce* [1969] 1 WLR 286.

120 See Chapters 1 and 13.

121 Section 20 of the LRA 1925.

overreach any equitable interests protected by the restriction. If the conditions are not followed, the purchaser will take subject to the beneficial interests. On the other hand, if there is no entry of restriction, when registered the purchaser will take free even if s 27 is not complied with unless the beneficiary is in actual occupation at the time the purchaser acquires the legal estate[122] and at the date of the purchaser's registration.[123] In the normal case where a purchaser buys land from trustees of land who are themselves the beneficiaries, after completion, the purchaser will have moved into possession of the land before he is registered as the new proprietor and no overriding interest will be claimed against him. But if one of the beneficiaries is not a trustee of land and the land is sold without his knowledge, if he is in actual occupation at the time the conveyance to the purchaser is executed, he may refuse to vacate possession and when the purchaser later registers himself, he will be bound by the beneficiary's overriding interest.

Suppose the purchaser buys the land from vendors who are trustees of land partly with the help of a mortgage and partly with financial contribution by his wife but the land is conveyed to the purchaser alone. Two trusts are involved here. In the first trust of land the original trustees, who are vendors, hold the land for their beneficiaries under the trust. In the second trust, the purchaser holds the land, when it is conveyed to him by the trustees on completion, on trust for himself and his wife. As mentioned above, if the purchaser has paid to two original trustees, he will be able to take the land free of the beneficiaries under the first trust. Questions may sometimes arise as to whether the mortgagee who finances the purchase is bound by the purchaser's wife's beneficial interest under the second trust. The mortgagee is a 'purchaser' for the purposes of the Law of Property Act 1925,[124] and the Land Registration Act 1925.[125] Where the mortgagee has paid the loan to two trustees (eg the purchaser and a new trustee appointed by him), he will take the mortgage free of any beneficial interest which will be overreached. If the mortgagee only pays to the purchaser alone, no overreaching will take place.

Two problems in relation to the old trust for sale need to be mentioned, as they are equally relevant to the new trust of land. First, it was thought that because no legal mortgage in land could be granted by a mortgagor until he had acquired the legal estate in it, and as soon as the legal estate was acquired by the purchaser, it was held on trust for sale for himself and his wife who contributed to the purchase, the mortgagee's interest only arose after the legal estate was acquired; there was a *scintillo temporis* between the purchase and the grant of the mortgage.[126] As such, the mortgagee would be bound by the wife's interest if he had notice of it, and in registered land, the mortgagee might be bound by the wife's overriding interest if the wife was in actual occupation at the time when

122 *Williams & Glyn's Bank Ltd v Boland* [1981] AC 487; *Abbey National Building Society v Cann* [1990] 1 All ER 1085.

123 Section 70(1)(g) of the LPA 1925; *Williams & Glyn's Bank v Boland* [1981] AC 487.

124 Section 205(1)(xxi) of the LPA 1925.

125 Section 3(xxi) of the LRA 1925.

126 *Church of England Building Society v Piskor* [1954] 2 All ER 85.

the mortgage was created and subsequently registered. This could happen when the purchaser and his wife were allowed to move into possession by the vendors after the completion. That however created great difficulties for the mortgagee as he was not able to enforce the security later against the wife or obtain vacant possession against her. Thus the House of Lords, in *Abbey National Building Society v Cann*[127] held that there was no *scintillo temporis* between the purchase and the grant of the mortgage if the purchase was partly or wholly financed by the mortgage. Thus the wife could not claim that her equitable interest was binding on the mortgagee. It would appear that this decision applies equally to a trust of land.

Secondly, in registered land, there was a conveyancing absurdity that if the wife for some reason moved into the house only after the mortgage had been granted but before it was registered, the mortgagee would still be bound by the wife's overriding interest even though he had no way of finding out the wife's actual occupation at the time the mortgage was granted. Such a conveyancing absurdity has now been removed by the House of Lords in *Abbey National Building Society v Cann*. It was held that the beneficiary's actual occupation must exist at the time of the completion of the grant of the mortgage and must continue right up until the mortgage was registered.

But if the purchaser (including a mortgagee) has paid to two trustees, the conveyance (the purchase or the grant of mortgage) will operate to overreach the beneficial interests and once they are overreached, even if the beneficial owners are in actual occupation at the date of the conveyance, their interests cannot be overriding under s 70 (1)(g) of the Land Registration Act 1925 when the purchaser registers his title later.[128]

Overreaching prior equitable interests

Under a trust of land, the purchaser has no power to take free of any legal estates binding on the trust and any prior equitable interests.[129] Some such prior equitable interests can only be overreached by an *ad hoc* trust of land. An *ad hoc* trust is a trust where the trustees are appointed or approved by the court or is a trust corporation.[130]

Law of Property Act 1925

2. Conveyances overreaching certain equitable interests and powers

(2) Where the legal estate affected is subject to a trust of land, then if at the date of a conveyance made after the commencement of this Act by the trustees, the trustees (whether original or substituted) are either:

(a) two or more individuals approved or appointed by the court or the successors in office of the individuals so approved or appointed; or

---

127 [1990] 1 All ER 1085.

128 *Cf City of London Building Society v Flegg* [1987] 3 All ER 435.

129 77 LJ News 57 (Lightwood, JM).

130 Section 2(2), (3) of the LPA 1925. See 61 *LJ News* 468 (Lightwood, JM); (1927) 3 CLJ 67 at 68 (Lightwood, JM).

(b) a trust corporation,

any equitable interest or power having priority to the trust shall, notwithstanding any stipulation to the contrary, be overreached by the conveyance, and shall, according to its priority, take effect as if created or arising by means of a primary trust affecting the proceeds of sale and the income of the land until sale.

(3) The following equitable interests and powers are excepted from the operation of sub-s (2) of this section, namely:

(i) Any equitable interest protected by a deposit of documents relating to the legal estate affected;

(ii) The benefit of any covenant or agreement restrictive of the user of land;

(iii) Any easement, liberty, or privilege over or affecting land and being merely an equitable interest (in this Act referred to as an 'equitable easement');

(iv) The benefit of any contract (in this Act referred to as an 'estate contract') to convey or create a legal estate, including a contract conferring either expressly or by statutory implication a valid option to purchase, a right of pre-emption, or any other like right;

(v) Any equitable interest protected by registration under the Land Charges Act 1925 other than:

(a) an annuity within the meaning of Part II of that Act;

(b) a limited owner's charge or a general equitable charge within the meaning of that Act.

Sale by a sole or sole surviving trustee for sale

The position of a purchaser in the case where there is only one trustee of land, or where there is only one surviving trustee will be considered in Chapter 13 together with co-ownership.

7 TRUSTEES LIMITED TO FOUR

Trustees of land and trustees of settlement are limited to four persons.[131] Where more than four persons are named as trustees, the four first named shall be the trustees, other persons named shall not be trustees unless appointed on the occurrence of a vacancy.[132]

Where the settlement or trust for sale was created before 1925 and there are still more than four trustees, no new trustees can be appointed until the number is reduced to less than four.[133]

131 Section 34(2)(b) of the Trustee Act 1925, as amended by s 25(1), Sched 3, para 3(9) of the TLATA 1996.

132 Section 34(2)(a) of the TA 1925.

133 Section 34(1) of the TA 1925.

8 NATURE OF A BENEFICIARY'S INTEREST[134]

Prior to the 1996 Act, where land was held on trust for sale, it was clear that after the sale, the beneficiaries' interests were in the proceeds of sale. But doubts were raised as to whether, before the sale, the beneficiaries had an interest in land or in the proceeds of sale. The answer to this question had become important as a result of certain provisions in the 1925 legislation which referred solely to 'interest in land'. It had always been understood that under the doctrine of conversion, as soon as a trust for sale was created, the beneficiaries' interests were in the proceeds of sale. This was because the trustees were under a duty to sell and equity regarded as done that which ought to be done. That which ought to be done was the selling of the land and so from the moment the trust was created, equity regarded the land as being sold so that notionally the land had been converted into money. So under the doctrine of conversion, the beneficiaries' interests were in the proceeds of sale not in the land even before sale. The doctrine of conversion did not apply to strict settlement because there was no duty to sell.

So following the doctrine of conversion, certain provisions which referred to interest in land could only apply to strict settlement but not trust for sale. For example, under the repealed s 40 of the Law of Property Act 1925, contract for the disposition of land or any interest in land was unenforceable unless the agreement or any memorandum was in writing signed by the party to be charged with. Following the doctrine of conversion, any contract for the sale of the beneficial interest under a trust for sale would not be caught by s 40. This was clearly not intended by Parliament. And the result was illogical. Why should the requirement of a contract be different depending on whether the beneficial interest existed behind a trust for sale or strict settlement? So in *Cooper v Critchley* [1955] Ch 431, the court held that a trust for sale beneficiary had an interest in land for the purpose of s 40. Under s 2 of the 1989 Act, a contract for the sale of an interest in land must be in writing, and s 2(6) specifically made it clear that interest in land meant any estate, interest or charge in or over land or in or over the proceeds of sale of land to solve the problem caused by the doctrine of conversion in this regard.[135]

But there was no consistent judicial view as to whether, before sale, the beneficiary's interest was in the proceeds of sale or in land. In *Irani Finance v Singh* [1971] Ch 59 at 80A, Cross LJ thought that the beneficiary's interest was in the proceeds so that a purchaser did not have to concern with it. Whereas in *Cooper v Critchley*, in order to avoid an illogical result the court held that the beneficiary had an interest in land. Similarly, in *Elias v Mitchell* [1972] 2 All ER 153; [1972] Ch 652, to enable the beneficiary to protect his interest as a minor interest, it was held that he had an interest in land for the purpose of s 54 of the Land Registration Act 1925 which allows any person interested in any land to lodge a caution.

134 See (1988) 104 LQR 367 (Gardner, S); [1990] CLJ 277 (Harpum, C).

135 Reference to 'or in or over the proceeds of sale of land' in the section has now been repealed as a result of the abolition of the doctrine of conversion under s 3 of the TLATA 1996: see *ibid* Sched 4.

Again, in *Williams & Glyn's Bank v Boland*, in order to give the beneficiary protection under s 70(1)(g) of the Land Registration Act 1925 which protects the beneficiary whose interest is subsisting in reference to land, Ormrod LJ at the Court of Appeal [1979] Ch 312, CA at 336 E–F and Lord Wilberforce in the House of Lords [1981] AC 487 at 507 F both said that the beneficiary under a trust for sale had an interest in land. But more recently, Lord Oliver in *City of London BS v Flegg* [1987] 3 All ER 435 at 443g, j had returned to the direction taken in *Irani v Singh*.

So there was no definite answer to the question whether before sale the beneficiary's interest had an interest in land or not. The court tended to look to realities and to reject the more pedantic applications of the doctrine of conversion where they did not operate in the interests of justice. As Cretney points out, the right approach was to ask for what purpose the land had been subjected to the trust (was it for the beneficiary's occupation or was it held on trust as an investment) and what was the policy of the legislation under which the question arose (was the legislation intended to apply to trust for sale).[136]

The Law Commission expressed concern about the problem caused by the doctrine of conversion and thought that the doctrine was wholly artificial[137] and should be abolished.[138] The doctrine of conversion is now duly abolished so that where the land is held by trustees on trust for sale (which is now treated as a trust of land), the land is not to be regarded as personal property.[139] Furthermore, under a trust of land, as the trustees have a power to sell and a power to retain, there is no room for the application of the doctrine. The beneficiary clearly has an interest in land.

9 BENEFICIARIES' RIGHT OF OCCUPATION

Prior to the 1996 Act, a tenant for life under a strict settlement clearly had a right to occupy. The position of a beneficiary under a trust for sale was less certain, though it was generally accepted that he also enjoyed such a right.[140] Now, under s 12 of the 1996 Act, a beneficiary who is beneficially entitled to an interest in possession in land held on trust is entitled by reason of his interest to occupy the land at any time provided that the occupation is within the purpose of the trust, or the land is held by the trustees so as to be available for occupation by the beneficiary.[141] The right of occupation is also subject to the condition that the land is either available or suitable for occupation by the beneficiary.[142]

136 (1971) 34 MLR 441 (Cretney, S).

137 The Law Commission's Working Paper (No 94), para 3.18, quoted at para 1.3 of the Law Commission's report on Trusts of Land (Law Com No 181); see also the Law Commission's report No 181, para 3.4.

138 Law Commission, Transfer of Land: Trusts of Land, Law Com No 181, paras 3.5, 3.6, 20.2.

139 Section 3(1) of the TLATA 1996.

140 See *Bull v Bull* [1955] 1 All ER 253, *Williams & Glyn's Bank Ltd v Boland* [1981] AC 487 at 507B–D, 510G, 511H; *City of London Building Society v Flegg* [1987] 2 WLR 1266 at 1281E.

141 Section 12(1)(a), (b) of the TLATA 1996.

142 *Ibid*, s 12(2).

In allowing a beneficiary into occupation, the trustees have a power to impose reasonable terms as to occupation rents, repairing obligations, and outgoings.[143] There is however, nothing in the Act which enables the trustees to exclude the beneficiary from occupying the land. Where there is more than one beneficiary with a right to occupy, the trustees can exclude or restrict the rights of any one or more (but not all) of them to occupy.[144] Such power to exclude or restrict must not, however, be exercised unreasonably.[145] A beneficiary who is already in occupation can only be replaced with his consent or the court's approval.[146] He may, however, be asked to make compensation or to forgo any benefit entitled in favour of those beneficiaries who are excluded or restricted from the occupation of the land.[147]

Trusts of Land and Appointment of Trustees Act 1996

12. The right to occupy

(1) A beneficiary who is beneficially entitled to an interest in possession in land subject to a trust of land is entitled by reason of his interest to occupy the land at any time if at that time:

(a) the purposes of the trust include making the land available for his occupation (or for the occupation of beneficiaries of a class of which he is a member or of beneficiaries in general), or

(b) the land is held by the trustees so as to be so available.

(2) Subsection (1) does not confer on a beneficiary a right to occupy land if it is either unavailable or unsuitable for occupation by him.

(3) This section is subject to s 13.

13. Exclusion and restriction of right to occupy

(1) Where two or more beneficiaries are (or apart from this subsection would be) entitled under s 12 to occupy land, the trustees of land may exclude or restrict the entitlement of any one or more (but not all) of them.

(2) Trustees may not under sub-s (1):

(a) unreasonably exclude any beneficiary's entitlement to occupy land, or (b) restrict any such entitlement to an unreasonable extent.

(3) The trustees of land may from time to time impose reasonable conditions on any beneficiary in relation to his occupation of land by reason of his entitlement under s 12.

(4) The matters to which trustees are to have regard in exercising the powers conferred by this section include:

143 *Ibid*, s 13(3), (5).

144 *Ibid*, s 13(1).

145 *Ibid*, s 13(2).

146 *Ibid*, s 13(7).

147 *Ibid*, s 13(6).

(a) the intentions of the person or persons (if any) who created the trust,

(b) the purposes for which the land is held, and

(c) the circumstances and wishes of each of the beneficiaries who is (or apart from any previous exercise by the trustees of those powers would be) entitled to occupy the land under s 12.

(5) The conditions which may be imposed on a beneficiary under sub-s (3) include, in particular, conditions requiring him:

(a) to pay any outgoings or expenses in respect of the land, or

(b) to assume any other obligation in relation to the land or to any activity which is or is proposed to be conducted there.

(6) Where the entitlement of any beneficiary to occupy land under s 12 has been excluded or restricted the conditions which may be imposed on any other beneficiary under sub-s (3) include, in particular, conditions requiring him to:

(a) make payments by way of compensation to the beneficiary whose entitlement has been excluded or restricted, or

(b) forgo any payment or other benefit to which he would otherwise be entitled under the trust so as to benefit that beneficiary.

(7) The powers conferred on trustees by this section may not be exercised:

(a) so as prevent any person who is in occupation of land (whether or not by reason of an entitlement under s 12) from continuing to occupy the land, or

(b) in a manner likely to result in any such person ceasing to occupy the land, unless he consents or the court has given approval.

(8) The matters to which the court is to have regard in determining whether to give approval under sub-s (7) include the matters mentioned in sub-s (4)(a)–(c).

CHAPTER 13

CO-OWNERSHIP

Co-ownership is ownership of land by two or more persons concurrently, for example, there is co-ownership if land is held by A and B in fee simple. As mentioned in Chapter 12, before the Trusts of Land and Appointment of Trustees Act 1996, almost all cases of co-ownership existed behind a trust for sale, except when there was a joint tenancy for life with remainder to the survivor for life where a strict settlement would arise.[1] Today, co-ownership will exist behind a trust of land. Thus co-ownership invariably involves a trust. Co-ownership may exist at law or in equity, or both at law and in equity. Those who co-own the legal estate are trustees of land (or where there is a strict settlement the tenants for life) and those who co-own the beneficial interests are the beneficiaries. The trustees of land and the beneficiaries may be the same persons.

The law of co-ownership has become increasingly important as a result of social changes in the way land is owned. The former social era in which limited interests in land were conferred on family members or married couples in a marriage settlement has long gone.[2] The modern social phenomenon is for land to be owned absolutely and concurrently. The 1925 legislation has introduced certain changes which affect the law of co-ownership and these should be dealt with first. In addition, the Trusts of Land and Appointment of Trustees Act 1996 has also introduced changes to the powers of the legal co-owners and the beneficiaries.

1 CHANGES INTRODUCED BY THE 1925 LEGISLATION

The object of the 1925 legislation was to simplify the transfer of legal estates and to make it easier for a purchaser to buy land. Provisions were made to subject all forms of co-ownership to the following changes:

Number of legal owners limited to four

The legal estate cannot be transferred to more than four persons.[3] This is essential to cut the number of persons required to join in the conveyance to a minimum in order to simplify the process.

Legal estate cannot be owned by co-owners as tenants in common[4]

This is extremely important in facilitating a speedy and simple conveyance. As already mentioned, where land is held by joint tenants, none of them can

1 Section 19(2) of the SLA 1925.

2 See Glendon, MA, *The New Family and the New Property*, 1981, Toronto: Butterworths.

3 Section 34(2) of the Trustee Act 1925; s 34(2) of the LPA 1925.

4 Sections 1(b) and 34(1) of the LPA 1925.

unilaterally leave their 'share' by will or intestacy. Where one of them dies, the others survive to his 'share' under the doctrine of survivorship. Therefore, the number of joint tenants can only get smaller. On the other hand, a tenant in common may leave his distinct albeit undivided share by will or under the rule of intestacy. Where this happens there may be more than one person to succeed to the deceased undivided share. Thus, the number of tenants in common can get bigger and bigger. As all the legal owners need to join in the conveyance of land, the more legal owners there are the more time consuming it is to get the signatures of all. Therefore, in order to simplify the conveyance of a legal estate, it was enacted under s 1(6) of the Law of Property Act 1925 that 'a legal estate is not capable of subsisting or of being created in an undivided share in land'. Today, any attempt to convey a legal estate to any persons as tenants in common shall take effect as legal joint tenants on trust for themselves as beneficial tenants in common.[5]

A legal joint tenancy cannot be severed after 1925[6]

As will be seen, a joint tenancy may be severed by the joint tenants during their lifetime. After severance, the joint tenancy becomes a tenancy in common. If the joint tenancy of a legal estate can be severed, the main object of simplifying the conveyancing process will be frustrated. It was, therefore, further enacted that a legal joint tenancy cannot be severed so that there is a legal joint tenancy at all times. It should be noted that this rule does not prevent one joint tenant from releasing his interest to the others in equity. Neither does it prevent one joint tenant from severing his equitable joint tenancy.

Implied trust on all co-ownership

Sections 1(6) and 36(2) were insufficient to simplify the process of investigating the title because if no express trust for sale had been created, the overreaching machinery in ss 2 and 27 of the Law of Property Act would not have applied. It was essential that overreaching machinery should be available so that the purchaser could rely solely on the legal title and overreach any beneficial interests behind the trust, and so that the beneficiaries would be protected in the form of proceeds of sale instead. This was achieved by imposing an implied statutory trust for sale on almost all forms of co-ownership. Today, a trust of land will arise in cases where a trust for sale would have arisen prior to the Trusts of Land and Appointment of Trustees Act 1996, and the overreaching principle is extended to a trust of land.

2 TYPES OF CO-OWNERSHIP

There are two types of co-ownership: joint tenancy and tenancy in common. 'Tenancy' simply means ownership and has nothing to do with leases, although there can be co-ownership of leasehold as well as of freehold.

5 Section 34(2) of the LPA 1925, as amended by s 5, Sched 2, para 3(2) of the TLATA 1996.

6 Section 36(2) of the LPA 1925.

Although co-owners must hold the co-owned land as joint tenants at law, they may own as joint tenants or tenants in common in equity. The distinction of ownership in equity is important because of the doctrine of survivorship.

In *Greenfield v Greenfield*[7] a dwelling house was bought by the defendant and A as beneficial joint tenants. The house was bought as a residence for themselves and their mother. Later the mother died. The defendant and his wife then occupied the ground floor and A and his wife, the plaintiff, occupied the first floor. No written notice of severance was given by either of them. Later, A died. A's wife brought an action seeking a declaration that she was entitled to half of the beneficial interest in the house. The defendant counterclaimed for possession. The question was 'Had the original joint tenancy between the defendant and A been severed'? If the answer was Yes, A would be able to pass his share to his wife on his death. If the answer was No, the right of survivorship would operate and the defendant would become the sole owner and would be entitled to possession. It was held that since there was no effective severance, the joint tenancy continued and was not affected by their separate occupation after their mother's death.

3 JOINT TENANCY

This is an undifferentiated kind of co-ownership in which all the co-owners own the entire estate.[8] Each one holds everything with the other co-owners but holds nothing individually.[9] Any reference to ownership in specific share, for example, 'to A as to one-third and to B as to two-thirds', negatives the existence of a joint tenancy.[10]

The characteristics of joint tenancy are (i) joint tenants enjoy as between themselves a right of survivorship (or *jus accrescendi*) and (ii) there exists the four unities.

Right of survivorship

As Blackstone put it most succinctly:

> ... when two or more persons are seised of a joint estate ... the entire tenancy upon the decease of any of them remains to the survivors, and at length to the last survivor; and he shall be entitled to the whole estate ... This is the natural and regular consequence of the union and entirety of their interest. The interest of two joint tenants is not only equal or similar, but also is one and the same. One has not originally a distinct moiety from the other; but, if by any subsequent act (as by alienation or forfeiture of either) the interest becomes separate and distinct, the joint tenancy instantly ceases. But, while it continues, each of two joint tenants has a concurrent interest in the whole; and therefore, on the death of his companion, the sole interest in the whole remains to the survivor.[11]

7 (1979) 38 P & CR 570.

8 *Hammersmith and Fulham LBC v Monk* [1992] 1 AC 478 at 492B.

9 *Re Rushton (A bankrupt)* [1972] Ch 197 at 203A; Challis at 367.

10 *Cowcher v Cowcher* [1972] 1 WLR 425 at 430H.

11 Bl Comm, Vol III at 183.

If land is held by A, B and C as joint tenants, in the eyes of the law A, B and C constitute an entity. On the death of A, the ownership of A's interest automatically remains in B and C. The entire interest in the land merely survives to B and C.[12] No new vesting deed is required. As a joint tenant does not individually have a share in the land, his interest cannot be disposed of by will or under the intestacy rule to Z (see Fig 1).[13]

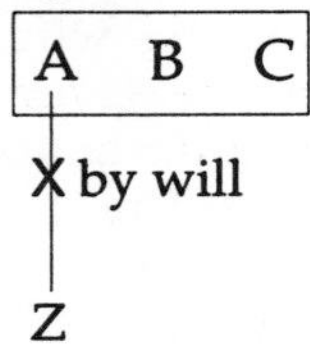

Fig 1

If two or more joint tenants died in circumstances rendering it uncertain which of them survived the other or others, the deaths are (subject to any order of the court) presumed to have occurred in order of seniority and accordingly the younger shall be deemed to have survived the elder.[14] In *Hickman v Peacey*, Viscount Simon LC said that while time was infinitely divisible, the section had no application if the relevant deaths were 'absolutely simultaneous'.[15] This view, however, ignores the virtual impossibility of two human beings ceasing to breathe at exactly the same moment of time.[16] A bare majority of the House of Lords held that s 184 applies unless it is possible to say for certain who died first.[17]

At common law, as a company or corporation could never die, there is no chance that the right of survivorship could operate and, therefore, it could not be a joint tenant.[18] But Parliament enacted in 1899 that a corporation should be able to acquire and hold any property in joint tenancy in the same manner as if it were an individual and if the corporation is ever dissolved, the jointly owned property devolves on the other joint tenant or tenants by right of survivorship.[19]

The joint tenant can, however, destroy the joint tenancy by severance *inter vivos* and turn his interest into a tenancy in common and dispose of it later. But he has to do it in his lifetime.

12 Litt, s 280; Co litt, at 181a.

13 Section 3(4) of the AEA 1925.

14 Section 184 of the LPA 1925. This rule is excluded in the case of husband and wife, where the intestate and his or her spouse die in circumstances rendering it uncertain who died first; the rule of intestacy applies (s 46(1) of the AEA 1925).

15 [1945] AC 304 at 314, 317.

16 See Cheshire and Burn, p 848.

17 See also *Re Bate* [1947] 2 All ER 418.

18 *Law Guarantee & Trust Society v Bank of England* (1890) 24 QBD 406 at 411; Bl Comm, 184.

19 Section 1 of the Bodies Corporate (Joint Tenancy) Act 1899.

Four unities

For any joint tenancy to exist the four unities must be present.[20] These are unities of possession, interest, titles and time. 'In other words, joint tenants have one and the same interest, accruing by one and the same conveyance, commencing at the one and the same time, and held by one and the same undivided possession'.[21]

(i) Unity of possession. This is common to all forms of co-ownership. Each co-owner is as much entitled to possession of any part of the land as the others.[22]

> joint tenants are said to be seised per my et per tout, by the half or moiety, and by all; that is, they each of them have the entire possession, as well of every parcel as of the whole. They have not, one of them a seisin of one half or moiety, and the other of the other moiety; neither can one be exclusively seised of one acre, and his companion of another; but each has an undivided moiety.[23]

He cannot point to any part of the land as his own to the exclusion of the others.[24] So, as a general rule, 'one joint tenant cannot have an action against another for trespass, in respect of his land; for each has an equal right to enter on any part of it',[25] unless the complainant has actually been ousted.[26] Nor can one co-owner in sole occupation be made to pay rent to another co-owner, unless the occupying co-owner has excluded or ousted the other from possession.[27]

(ii) Unity of interest.[28] The interest of each joint tenant must be the same in extent, nature, and duration, because in theory they hold but one estate.[29] This means that although in theory each has the whole of the land, the rents and profits thereof are to be divided equally between them. As Blackstone once wrote:[30]

> If two joint tenants let a verbal lease of their land, referring rent to be paid to one of them, it shall enure to both, in respect of the joint reversion.[31] If their lessee surrenders his lease to one of them, it shall also enure to both, because of the

20 *AG Securities v Vaughan* [1990] 1 AC 417 at 431H.

21 Bl Comm, Vol II at 180.

22 Litt 288; Bl Comm, Vol II at 182; *Wiseman v Simpson* [1988] 1 WLR 35 at 42E–G.

23 Bl Comm, 188.

24 *Meyer v Riddick* (1990) 60 P & CR 50 at 54.

25 Bl Comm, Vol II at 183, 194.

26 *M'Mahon v Burchell* (1846) 2 Ph 127; *Jones v Jones* [1977] 1 WLR 438 (this is a case of tenancy in common but the position is the same with joint tenancy, see Bl Comm, Vol II at 194).

27 *Murray v Hall* (1849) 7 CB 441; *Dennis v McDonald* [1981] 1 WLR 81 (tenancy in common); *Jones v Jones* [1977] 1 WLR 438; at 443B; see Alder (1978) 41 MLR 208 at 209. Gray suggests that there are numerous exceptions to this rule and that 'the *prima facie* position today may well be that rent should be paid' (at 477). However, these exception all involve 'some trauma in the personal or family relationship of the co-owners'.

28 See Megarry and Wade, p 420.

29 Megarry and Wade, p 420.

30 Bl Comm, 182.

31 Co Litt, 214.

> privity, or relation of their estate.[32] On the same reason, livery of seisin, made to one joint tenant, shall enure to both of them:[33] and the entry, or re-entry, of one joint tenant is as effectual in law as if it were the act of both.[34] In all actions also relating to their joint estate, one joint tenant cannot sue or be sued without joining the other.[35]

There can be no joint tenancy between those with interests of different nature or of different duration, eg between a freeholder and a tenant for years, an owner of a fee simple interest and an owner of a life interest.[36]

> One joint tenant cannot be entitled to one period of duration or quantity of interest in lands, and the other to a different; one cannot be tenant for life, and the other for years: one cannot be tenant in fee, and the other in tail.[37]

But if they hold the same interest for the time being, the fact that one joint tenant has a further and separate interest in the same property does not prevent them from being joint tenants for the time being, eg 'to A and B as joint tenants for lives, remainder to B in fee simple' would make A and B for the time being joint tenants for life notwithstanding B's remainder interest.[38]

'[O]ne joint tenant is not capable by himself to do any act, which may tend to defeat or injure the estate of the other ...'.[39] Any legal act such as a conveyance or lease[40] or surrender of a lease,[41] giving of a notice to quit[42] must be done by all joint tenants collectively, except in the case of the determination of periodic tenancies.[43] Notice to quit by one joint tenant is effective to terminate a periodic tenancy.[44] In *Hammersmith and Fulham LBC v Monk*,[45] Mr Monk and Mrs Powell had a weekly tenancy of a flat from the local authority. The tenancy was terminable by four weeks' notice. Later they fell out and Mr Powell left the flat. She consulted the local authority who agreed to rehouse her if she would give an appropriate notice to quit which she did without Mr

32 *Ibid*, 192.

33 *Ibid*, 49.

34 *Ibid*, 319, 364.

35 *Ibid*, 195.

36 *Kenworthy v Ward* (1853) 11 Hare 196 at 198, 199; Bl Comm, Vol II at 181.

37 Co Litt, 188; Bl Comm, 181.

38 *Wiscot's* case (1599) 2 Co Rep 60b.

39 Bl Comm, 183.

40 Bl Comm, 183.

41 *Leek and Moorlands Building Society v Clark* [1952] 2 QB 788.

42 *Newman v Keedwell* (1977) 35 P & CR 393.

43 *Doe d Aslin v Summersett* (1830) 1 B & Ad 135; *Parsons v Parsons* [1983] 1 WLR 1390 (notice by one joint landlord); *Leek and Moorland Building Society v Clark* [1952] 2 QB 788 at 793; *Greenwich LBC v McGrady* (1982) 46 R & CR 223; *Hammersmith and Fulham LBC v Monk* [1992] 1 AC 478 at 485D, 492G, HL (notice by one joint tenant).

44 It was suggested that to give such a notice without the others' consent might be a breach of trust: *Parsons v Parsons* [1983] 1 WLR 1390; *Hammersmith and Fulham LBC v Mink* [1992] 1 AC 478, at 493 (noted [1992] Conv 279 at 283 (Goulding, S).). But in *Crawley Borough Council v Ure* [1996] 1 All ER 724 (noted [1995] Conv 424 (Shorrock, K)) the Court of Appeal held that giving such a notice without consulting the others was not a breach of trust under s 26(3) of the LPA 1925. See also [1992] Conv 279 at 283 (Goulding, S).

45 [1992] 1 AC 478. See [1992] Conv 279 (Goulding, S).

Monk's knowledge or consent. The local authority notified him that the tenancy had been terminated and brought proceedings for possession. The House of Lords held that as a periodic tenancy is a tenancy from a period to a period so long as both parties (the landlord and the tenant) please, ie it continues only so long as it was the will of both parties that it should continue. Thus, applying this principle to the case of a yearly tenancy where either the lessor's or the lessee's interest is held jointly by two or more parties, logic dictates the conclusion that the will of all the joint parties is necessary to the continuance of the interest. So when one joint tenant gives a notice to quit, that is enough to discontinue the interest.

Hammersmith and Fulham LBC v Monk [1992] 1 AC 478, HL

Lord Bridge of Harwich: My Lords, the issue in this appeal is whether a periodic tenancy held by two or more tenants jointly can be brought to an end by a notice to quit by one of the joint tenants without the consent of the others. It arises for determination in the following circumstances.

[His Lordship read the facts and continued.]

In a previous decision of the Court of Appeal, *Greenwich London Borough Council v McGrady* (1982) 81 LGR 288, it was held that a notice to quit given by one of two joint tenants without the consent of the other was effective to determine the periodic tenancy to which it related. Much of the argument before the Court of Appeal in the present case was directed to the question whether the court was free to reach a conclusion at variance with *McGrady* on the grounds (1) that an earlier decision of the Court of Appeal, *Howson v Buxton* (1928) 97 LJKB 749, was, as the judge had held, binding authority to the opposite effect; or (2) that, in any event, the decision in *McGrady* was given *per incuriam*. The judgment of Slade LJ, with which Bingham LJ agreed, examined these issues very thoroughly and reached the conclusion that *Howson v Buxton* was not authority for the proposition sought to be derived from it and that *McGrady* was binding on the court. Nicholls LJ approached the issue more radically and held, both on principle and in reliance on a long line of authority prior to the decision in *McGrady*, that a joint periodic tenancy could be determined by a notice to quit given by one joint tenant.

Your Lordships are not technically bound by any previous decision and before examining the relevant authorities I think it helpful to consider whether the application of first principles suggests the answer to the question at issue. For a large part of this century there have been many categories of tenancy of property occupied for agricultural, residential and commercial purposes where the legislature has intervened to confer upon tenants extra-contractual periodic tenancy. It is primarily in relation to joint tenancies in these categories that the question whether or not notice to quit given by one of the joint tenants can determine the tenancy is of practical importance, particularly where, as in the instant case, the effect of the determination will be to deprive the other joint tenant of statutory protection. This may appear an untoward result and may consequently provoke a certain reluctance to hold that the law can permit one of two joint tenants unilaterally to deprive his co-tenant of 'rights' which both are equally entitled to enjoy. But the statutory consequences are in truth of no relevance to the question which your Lordships have to decide. That question is whether, at common law, a contractual periodic tenancy granted to two or more joint tenants is incapable of termination by a tenant's notice to quit unless it is served with the concurrence of all the joint tenants. That is the proposition which the appellant must establish in order to succeed.

As a matter of principle, I see no reason why this question should receive any different answer in the context of the contractual relationship of landlord and tenant than that which it would receive in any other contractual context. If A and B contract with C on terms which are to continue in operation for one year in the first place and thereafter from year to year unless determined by notice at the end of the first or any subsequent year, neither A nor B has bound himself contractually for longer than one year. To hold that A could not determine the contract at the end of any year without the concurrence of B and vice versa would presuppose that each had assumed a potentially irrevocable contractual obligation for the duration of their joint lives, which, whatever the nature of the contractual obligations undertaken, would be such an improbable intention to impute to the parties that nothing less than the clearest express contractual language would suffice to manifest it. Hence, in any ordinary agreement for an initial term which is to continue for successive terms unless determined by notice, the obvious inference is that the agreement is intended to continue beyond the initial term only if and so long as all parties to the agreement are willing that it should do so. In a common law situation, where parties are free to contract as they wish and are bound only so far as they have agreed to be bound, this leads to the only sensible result.

Thus the application of ordinary contractual principles leads me to expect that a periodic tenancy granted to two or more joint tenants must be terminable at common law by an appropriate notice to quit given by any one of them whether or not the others are prepared to concur. But I turn now to the authorities to see whether there is any principle of the English law of real property and peculiar to the contractual relationship of landlord and tenant which refutes that expectation or whether the authorities confirm it. A useful starting point is the following passage from *Blackstone's Commentaries*, Book II (1766) Ch 9, pp 145–47, which explains clearly how the law developed the concept of a yearly tenancy from the earlier concept of a tenancy at will which gave the tenant no security of tenure:

> The second species of estates not freehold are estates at will. An estate at will is where lands and tenements are let by one man to another, to have and to hold at the will of the lessor; and the tenant by force of this lease obtains possession. Such tenant hath no certain indefeasible estate, nothing that can be assigned by him to any other; for that the lessor may determine his will, and put him out whenever he pleases. But every estate at will is at the will of both parties, landlord and tenant, so that either of them may determine his will, and quit his connections with the other at his own pleasure. Yet this must be understood with some restriction. For, if the tenant at will sows his land, and the landlord before the corn is ripe, or before it is reaped, puts him out, yet the tenant shall have the emblements, and free ingress, egress, and regress, to cut and carry away the profits. And this for the same reason, upon which all the cases of emblements turn; *viz* the point of uncertainty: determine his will, and therefore could make no provision against it; and having sown the land, which is for the good of the public, upon a reasonable presumption, the law will not suffer him to be a loser by it. But it is otherwise, and upon reason equally good, where the tenant himself determines the will; for in this case the landlord shall have the profits of the land ...
>
> The law is however careful, that no sudden determination of the will by one party shall tend to the manifest and unforeseen prejudice of the other. This

> appears in the case of emblements before-mentioned; and, by a parity of reason, the lessee after the determination of the lessor's will, shall have reasonable ingress and egress to fetch away his goods and utensils. And, if rent be payable quarterly or half-yearly, and the lessee determines the will, the rent shall be paid to the end of the current quarter of half-year. And, upon the same principle, courts of law have of late years leant as much as possible against construing demises, where no certain term is mentioned, to be tenancies at will; but have rather held them to be tenancies *from year to year so long as both parties please,* especially where an annual rent is reserved: in which case they will not suffer either party to determine the tenancy even at the end of the year, without reasonable notice to the other.

I have added emphasis to the phrase 'from year to year so long as both parties please' because in its Latin version *'de anno in annum quamdiu ambabus partibus placuerit'* this same phrase is used repeatedly in a passage from *Bacon's Abridgment,* 7th edn, 1832, Vol IV, pp 838–39, which has always been treated as of the highest authority, as apt to describe the essential characteristics of a yearly tenancy.

Hence, from the earliest times a yearly tenancy has been an estate which continued only so long as it was the will of both parties that it should continue, albeit that either party could only signify his unwillingness that the tenancy should continue beyond the end of any year by giving the appropriate advance notice to that effect. Applying this principle to the case of a yearly tenancy where either the lessor's or the lessee's interest is held jointly by two or more parties, logic seems to me to dictate the conclusion that the will of all the joint parties is necessary to the continuance of the interest.

In *Doe d Aslin v Summersett* (1830) 1B & Ad 135, the freehold interest in land let on a yearly tenancy was vested jointly in four executors of a will to whom the land had been jointly devised. Three only of the executors gave notice to the tenant to quit. It was held by the Court of King's Bench that the notice was effective to determine the tenancy. Delivering the judgment, Lord Tenderden CJ said, at pp 140–41:

> Upon a joint demise by joint tenants upon a tenancy from year to year, the true character of the tenancy is this, not that the tenant holds of each the share of each so long as he and each shall please, but that he holds the whole or all so long as he and all shall please; and as soon as any one of the joint tenants gives a notice to quit, he effectually puts an end to that tenancy; the tenant has a right upon such a notice to give up the whole, and unless he comes to a new arrangement with the other joint tenants as to their shares, he is compellable so to do. The hardship upon the tenant, if he were not entitled to treat a notice from one as putting an end to the tenancy as to the whole is obvious; for however willing a man might be to be sole tenant of an estate, it is not very likely he should be willing to hold undivided shares of it; and if upon such a notice the tenant is entitled to treat it as putting an end to the tenancy as to the whole, the other joint tenants must have the same right. It cannot be optional on one side, and on one side only.

Now it was rightly pointed out in argument that part of the reasoning in this passage was dictated by considerations derived from the incidents of joint land tenure at law which were swept away by the reforming legislation of 1925. But this can in no way detract from the validity of the proposition emphasised in the judgment that the yearly tenant of a property let to him by joint freeholders 'holds the *whole* of *all* so long as he *and all* shall please'. This by itself is a sufficient and independent ground for the conclusion of the court that notice to quit by any one joint freeholder was effective to determine the tenancy. Precisely the same reasoning would apply to the operation of a notice to quit by one of two or more joint yearly tenants.

Summersett's case was followed in *Doe d Kindersley v Hughes* (1940) 7 M & W 139 and *Alford v Vickery* (1842) Car & M 280, both cases in which the validity of a notice to determine a yearly tenancy given to the tenant without the concurrence of one or more of the joint landlords was affirmed. It is interesting that throughout the 19th century there is no reported case in the books where the effect of a notice to quit given by one of two or more joint holders of the tenant's interest under a yearly or other periodic tenancy was ever called in question. I do not however find this surprising. The law was probably regarded as settled after *Summersett's* case, but, in any event, before the advent of statutory protection of tenants' rights of occupation, in the case of a notice to quit given by one of two or more joint periodic tenants the parties would in most cases have had little incentive to litigate. If the landlord was content that the other tenants should remain, there would have been nothing to litigate about. If the landlord wished to recover possession, he could do so by giving his own notice to quit.

[His Lordship then referred to the more recent cases of *Howson v Buxton*, 97 LJKB 749, *Leek and Moorlands Building Society v Clark* [1952] 2 QB 788, *Greenwich London Borough Council v McGrady* 81 LGR 288, *Smith v Grayton Estates Ltd* 1960 SC 349 and concluded that these cases supported the conclusion of the Court of Appeal.]

There are three principal strands in the argument advanced for the appellant. First, reliance is placed on the judgment in *Gandy v Jubber* (1865) 9 B & S 15, for the proposition that a tenancy from year to year, however long it continues, is a single term, not a series of separate lettings. The passage relied on reads, at18:

> There frequently is an actual demise from year to year so long as both parties please. The nature of this tenancy is discussed in 4 Bac Abr tit *Leases and Terms for Years*, 7th edn, pp 838, 839, being said to be the work of Gilbert CB. It seems clear that the learned author considered that the true nature of such a tenancy is that it is a lease for two years certain, and that every year after it is a springing interest arising upon the first contract and parcel of it, so that if the lessee occupies for a number of years, these years by computation from time past, make an entire lease for so many years, and that after the commencement of each new year it becomes an entire lease certain for the years past and also for the year so entered on, and that it is not a reletting at the commencement of the third and subsequent years. We think this is the true nature of a tenancy from year to year created by express words, and that there is not in contemplation of law a recommencing or reletting at the beginning of each year.

It must follow from this principle, Mr Reid submits, that the determination of a periodic tenancy by notice is in all respects analogous to the determination of a lease for a fixed term in the exercise of a break clause, which in the case of joint lessees clearly requires the concurrence of all. But reference to the passage from *Bacon's Abridgement*, 7th edn, vol IV, p 839, on which the reasoning is founded shows that this analogy is not valid. The relevant passage reads:

> A parol lease was made *de annon in annum, quamdiu ambabus partibus placuerit;* it was adjudged that this was but a lease for a year certain, and that every year after it was a springing interest, arising upon the first contract and parcel of it; so that if the lessee had occupied eight or ten years, or more, these years, by computation from the time past, made an entire lease for so many years; and if rent was in arrears for part of one of those years, and part of another, the lessor

> might distrain and avow as for so much rent arrear upon one entire lease, and need not avow as for several rents due upon several leases, accounting each year a new lease. It was also adjudged, that after the commencement of each new year, this was become an entire lease certain for the years past, and also for the year so entered upon; so that neither party could determine their wills till that year was run out, according to the opinion of the two judges in the last case. And this seems no way impeached by the statute of frauds and perjuries, which enacts, that no parol lease for above three years shall be accounted to have any other force or effect than of a lease only at will: for at first, this being a lease certain only for one year, and each accruing year after being a springing interest for that year, it is not a lease for any three years to come, though by a computation backwards, when five or six or more years are past, this may be said a parol lease for so many years; but with this the statute has nothing to do, but only looks forward to parol leases for above three years to come.

Thus, the fact that the law regards a tenancy from year to year which has continued for a number of years, considered retrospectively, as a single term in no way affects the principle that continuation beyond the end of each year depends on the will of the parties that it should continue or that, considered prospectively, the tenancy continues no further than the parties have already impliedly agreed upon by their omission to serve notice to quit.

The second submission for the appellant is that, whatever the law may have been before the enactment of the Law of Property Act 1925, the effect of that statute, whereby a legal estate in land vested in joint tenants is held on trust for sale for the parties beneficially entitled, coupled with the principle that trustees must act unanimously in dealing with trust property, is to reverse the decision in *Summersett's* case, 1 B & Ad 135 and to prevent one of two joint tenants deter-mining a periodic tenancy without the concurrence of the other. It is unnecessary to consider the position where the parties beneficially entitled are different from those who hold the legal interest. But where, as here, two joint tenants of a periodic tenancy hold both the legal and the beneficial interest, the existence of a trust for sale can make no difference to the principles applicable to the termi-nation of the tenancy. At any given moment the extent of the interest to which the trust relates extends no further than the end of the period of the tenancy which will next expire on a date for which it is still possible to give notice to quit. If before 1925 the implied consent of both joint tenants, signified by the omission to give notice to quit, was necessary to extent the tenancy from one period to the next, precisely the same applies since 1925 to the extension by the joint trustee beneficiaries of the periodic tenancy which is the subject of the trust.

Finally, it is said that all positive dealings with a joint tenancy require the concurrence of all joint tenants if they are to be effective. Thus, a single joint tenant cannot exercise a break clause in a lease, surrender the term or apply for relief from forfeiture. All these positive acts which joint tenants must concur in performing are said to afford analogies with the service of notice to determine a periodic tenancy which is likewise a positive act. But this is to confuse the form with the substance. The action of giving notice to determine a periodic tenancy is in form positive; but both on authority and on the principle so aptly summed up in the pithy Scottish phrase 'tacit relocation' the substance of the matter is that it is by his omission to give notice of termination that each party signified the necessary positive assent to the extension of the term for a further period.

For all these reasons I agree with the Court of Appeal that, unless the terms of the tenancy agreement otherwise provide, notice to quit given by one joint tenant without the concurrence of any other joint tenant is effective to determine a periodic tenancy.

An alternative ground advanced in support of the appeal relied on the particular terms of the tenancy agreement entered into by the appellant and Mrs Powell with the council as requiring notice to quit to be given by both joint tenants in order to determine the tenancy. I agree entirely with the reasons given by Slade and Nicholls LJJ, 89 LGR 357 at 373–74, 382, for rejecting this contention.

I would accordingly dismiss the appeal.

Lord Browne-Wilkinson: My Lords, there are two instinctive reactions to this case which lead to diametrically opposite conclusions. The first is that the flat in question was the joint home of the appellant and Mrs Powell: it therefore cannot be right that one of them unilaterally can join the landlords to put an end to the other's rights in the home. The second is that the appellant and Mrs Powell undertook joint liabilities as tenants for the purpose of providing themselves with a joint home and that, once the desire to live together has ended, it is impossible to require that the one who quits the home should continue indefinitely to be liable for the discharge of the obligations to the landlord under the tenancy agreement.

These two instinctive reactions are mirrored in the legal analysis of the position. In certain cases a contract between two persons can, by itself, give rise to rights and duties incapable of being founded in contract alone. The revulsion against Mrs Powell being able unilaterally to terminate the appellant's rights in his home is property based: the appellant's property rights in the home cannot be destroyed without his consent. The other reaction is contract based: Mrs Powell cannot be held to a tenancy contract which is dependant for its continuance on the will of the tenant.

The speech of my noble and learned friend, Lord Bridge of Harwich, traces the development of the periodic tenancy from a tenancy at will. He demonstrates that a periodic tenancy is founded on the continuing will of both landlord and tenant that the tenancy shall persist. Once either the landlord or the tenant indicates, by appropriate notice, that he no longer wishes to continue, the tenancy comes to an end. The problem is to determine who is 'the landlord' or 'the tenant' when there are joint lessors or joint lessees.

In property law, a transfer of land to two or more persons jointly operates so as to make them, *vis-à-vis* the outside world, one single owner. 'Although as between themselves joint tenants have separate rights, as against everyone else they are in the position of a single owner:' Megarry and Wade, *The Law of Real Property*, 5th edn, 1984, p 417. The law would have developed consistently with this principle if it had been held that where a periodic tenancy has been granted by or to a number of persons jointly, the relevant 'will' to continue the tenancy has to be the will of all the joint lessors or joint lessees who together constitute the owner of the reversion or the term as the case may be.

[His Lordship referred to *Grandy v Jubber* (1865) 9 B & S 15; *Doe d Whayman v Chaplin* (1810) 3 Taunt 120 and continued].

Despite this flirtation, the law was in my judgment determined in the opposite sense by *Doe d Aslin v Summersett* (1830) 1 B & Ad 135. The contractual, as opposed to the property, approach was adopted. Where there were joint lessors of a periodic tenancy, the continuing 'will' had to be the will of all the lessors individually, not the conjoint will of all the lessors collectively. This decision created an exception to the principles of the law of joint ownership: see Megarry and Wade, 5th edn, pp 421–22.

It was submitted that this House should overrule *Summersett's Case*. But, as my noble and learned friend, Lord Bridge of Harwich, has demonstrated, the decision was treated throughout the nineteenth century as laying down the law in relation to the rights of joint lessors. It is not suggested that the position of joint lessees can be different. Since 1925 the law as determined in *Summersett's* case has been applied to notices to quit given by one of several joint lessees. In my judgment no sufficient reason has been shown for changing the basic law which has been established for 160 years unless, as was suggested, the 1925 legislation has altered the position.

Before 1925 property belonging to two or more persons concurrently could be held by them in undivided or divided shares at law. The Law of Property Act 1925 changed this and requires that, even in the case of joint tenants, they hold the legal estate as joint tenants on trust for themselves as joint tenants in equity: s 36(1). It was suggested that the interposition of this statutory trust for sale has altered the position: since the appellant and Mrs Powell held the legal estate in the periodic tenancy as trustees and trustees must act unanimously, neither of them individually could give a valid notice to quit.

In my view this submission fails. The trust property in question was a periodic tenancy. As between the lessor and the lessees the nature of the contract of tenancy cannot have been altered by the fact that the lessees were trustees. The tenancy came to an end when one of the lessees gave notice to quit. It may be that, as between the lessees, the giving of the notice to quit was a breach of trust, theoretically giving rise to a claim by the appellant against Mrs Powell for breach of trust. Even this seems to me very dubious since the overreaching statutory trusts for sale imposed by the Law of Property Act 1925, do not normally alter the beneficial rights *inter se* of the concurrent owners: see *In Re Warren* [1932] 1 Ch 42 at 47, *per* Maugham J; and *Bull v Bull* [1955] 1 QB 234. But even if, contrary to my view, the giving of the notice to quit by Mrs Powell was a breach of trust by her, the notice to quit was not a nullity. It was effective as between the lessor and the lessees to terminate the tenancy. The fact that a trustee acts in breach of trust does not mean that he has no capacity to do the act he wrongly did. The breach of trust as between Mrs Powell and the appellant could not affect the lessors unless some case could be mounted that the lessors were parties to the breach, a case which Mr Reid, for the appellant, did not seek to advance. Therefore in my judgment the 1925 legislation does not affect this case.

For these reasons and those given by my noble and learned friend, Lord Bridge of Harwich, I too would dismiss this appeal.

Lord Brandon of Oakbrook, Lord Jauncey of Tullichettle, and Lord Ackner all concurred.

(iii) Unity of title. Each joint tenant must derive his title to the land from one and the same act or grant.[46] This requirement is normally satisfied by acquiring the joint tenancy by the same conveyance.

(iv) Unity of time. Each joint tenant must be vested with the interest at one and the same time as well as by one and the same title.[47]

46 Bl Comm, Vol II at 181.

47 Bl Comm, Vol II at 181.

> As in case of a present estate made to A and B; or a remainder in fee to A and B after a particular estate; in either case A and B are joint tenants of this present estate, or this vested remainder. But if, after a lease for life, the remainder be limited to the heirs of A and B; and during the continuance of the particular estate A dies, which vests the remainder of one moiety in his heir; and then B dies, whereby the other moiety becomes vested in the heir of B: now A's heir and B's heir are not joint tenants of this remainder, but tenants in common; for one moiety vested at one time, and the other moiety vested at another.[48]

4 TENANCY IN COMMON

In the case of a tenancy in common, each co-owner owns a distinct but yet undivided share.[49] The only unity required is unity of possession.[50] Where a property is owned by tenants in common, there is no right of survivorship.[51] So on the death of A, his distinct share may pass according to his will or intestacy to Z (see Fig 2).

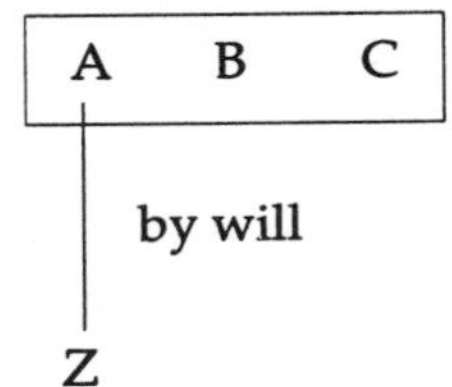

Fig 2

As with joint tenancy, each tenant in common is as much entitled to possession of the land as is the other.[52] If one actually turns the other out of possession, an action in trespass will lie against him.[53] Thus no tenant in common can demand compensation for the enjoyment by a co-owner unless the other has received more than comes to his just share or proportion.[54] He receives more than comes to his just share if the amount he receives and keeps is more than the proportion of his interest as such tenant.[55] In *Jones v Jones*,[56] Mr Jones asked his son Frederick Jones to give up his job in Kingston-upon-Thames and to move to live with him in Suffolk at Blunderston where Mr Jones bought a house for £4000. Frederick moved to the house and paid his father £1,000 but did not pay rent.

48 Co Litt, 188; Bl Comm, 181.

49 *Fisher v Wiggs* (1700) 12 Mod 296 at 302; Bl Comm, 191.

50 Bl Comm, Vol II at 191.

51 Bl Comm, Vol II at 194; Challis 368.

52 Bl Comm, Vol II at 194; *Wight v IRC* (1982) 264 *Estates Gazette* 935 at 936f.

53 Co Litt, 199; Bl Comm, Vol II at 194.

54 *Henderson v Eason* (1851) 17 QB 701 at 719; *Bull v Bull* [1955] 1 QB 234 at 237.

55 *Henderson v Eason* (1851) 17 QB 701.

56 [1977] 1 WLR 438.

When the father died, he left all his residuary estate to Frederick's stepmother. She tried to evict Frederick but the court held that Frederick had a 25% share in the house. The stepmother then sued for rent to be calculated on the basis of 75% of the market rental. The Court of Appeal rejected the claim on the ground that one tenant in common is not entitled to claim rent from another. Neither can a tenant in common bring an action in trespass against the other for exclusive use of the co-owned land[57] unless in the case of ouster.[58]

In *Dennis v McDonald*,[59] M and W, an unmarried couple, lived together with their children. The house was held by them as legal joint tenants on trust for sale (now it would be a trust of land) for themselves as beneficial tenants in common. M was violent to W. As a result W left the house taking the children with her. M remained in the house. Later W applied for an order for sale under s 30 of the Law of Property Act (repealed, see now s 14 of the Trusts of Land and Appointment of Trustees Act 1996) or, alternatively, for rent from M for his sole occupation. W was held entitled to the rent at half the fair rent for an unfurnished letting as she had been ousted and M had exclusive enjoyment of the property.

If the tenants in common are not in possession of the co-owned land, they are each entitled to the rents and profits from the land in strict proportion to the quantum of their shares.[60] If one is in possession but the other is not, as mentioned, the occupying tenant is not liable to pay rent unless in the case of ouster.[61] But if a stranger is in possession together with a tenant in common, the non-occupying tenant is entitled to share in the rents and profits received, if any, and the occupying tenant is liable to account for any income in excess of his own 'just share or proportion'.[62]

Where a tenant in common is left in sole occupation and uses his own labour and industry to produce income from the land, as long as the activities have not caused any long-term destruction of the land, he is entitled to keep the income.[63] However, if such activities have diminished the capital value of the property, he may be liable to account for income in excess of his 'just share or proportion'.[64]

---

57 *Jacobs v Seward* (1872) LR 5 HL 464 at 473.

58 Bl Comm, Vol II at 194; *Jacobs v Seward* (1872) LR 5 HL 464 at 472, 478.

59 [1981] 1 WLR 81. See [1982] Conv 305 (Martin, J); [1982] 98 LQR 519 (Webb, F).

60 *Henderson v Eason* (1851) 17 QB 701 at 719.

61 *Murray v Hall* (1849) 7 CB 441; *Dennis v McDonald* [1981] 1 WLR 810. It is not clear if the court has power under s 30 of the Law of Property Act 1925 to order one co-owner who enjoys sole occupation to pay an occupation rent to the other who is not in occupation. The Law Commission though that it is desirable that the court should have such power: Law Com Working Paper (No 94), para 3.20, quoted at para 1.3 of the Law Commission's report (Law Com No 181).

62 *Henderson v Eason* (1851) 17 QB 701 at 719.

63 *Henderson v Eason* (1851) 17 QB 701 at 720.

64 For example, *Jacobs v Seward* (1872) LR 5 HL 464.

Where a co-tenant spends money voluntarily on the repairs and improvements of the co-owned land, it seems that he is not entitled to call for contributions from other co-tenants[65] unless the repairs and improvements are done in pursuance of an agreement amongst themselves[66] or binding on them[67] or at their express or implied request.[68] If other cotenants do not make any contributions, the cotenant may recover his expenditure from the proceeds of sale when the co-owned land is eventually sold.[69] Where the cotenant is in sole occupation or is receiving rents and profits, this equity of recovering the expenditure is only available to him if he pays a fair share for his sole occupation or accounts for the rents and profits he has received.[70]

As already mentioned, this form of co-ownership can only exist in equity today.[71] Although today co-ownership of legal estate is necessarily a joint tenancy, the beneficial interests can still be held in equity as joint tenancy or as tenancy in common.

5 HOW TO DISTINGUISH JOINT TENANCY AND TENANCY IN COMMON

Joint tenancies and tenancies in common may be distinguished by the following steps:

The four unities

For there to be a joint tenancy, there must exist the four unities. If one of them is missing then it cannot be a joint tenancy.

Express intention

However, sometimes the 'four unities' is not a very helpful test because in practice today all co-owners normally acquire the same title at the same time. Thus, when four unities exist, you must see if there is an express intention to create a joint tenancy or tenancy in common. If there is one, that is conclusive.[72] Contradictory expressions such as 'jointly and severally' or 'as joint tenants in common in equal shares' were solved by the rule that the first word prevailed in a deed, but the last in a will.[73]

---

65 *Leigh v Dickeson* (1884–85) 15 QBD 60 at 65.

66 *Ibid*, at 64.

67 *Ibid*, at 66.

68 *Ibid*, at 64, 66.

69 *Ibid*, at 65, 67, 69.

70 *Pascoe v Swan* (1859) 27 Beav 508 at 509.

71 Section 1(6) of the LPA 1925.

72 *Barton v Morris* [1985] 1 WLR 1257.

73 Bl Comm, Vol II, 193; *Slingsby's* case (1587) 5 Co Rep 18b at 19a (deed); *Perkins v Baynton* (1781) 1 Bro CC 118 (will).

Presumption at law and words of severance

Where there is no such express intention, the presumption at law is in favour of a joint tenancy[74] unless words of severance are employed. Any words in the grant showing that the tenants were each to take a distinct share in the property would amount to words of severance and would thus create a tenancy in common.[75] Examples are 'to A and B in equal shares',[76] 'to be divided between them',[77] 'to them respectively'.[78]

Presumption in equity

Equity, however, prefers tenancy in common to the chance of 'all or nothing' on death which arises from joint tenancy.[79] There are special cases where joint tenants at law are compelled by equity to hold the legal estate upon trust for themselves as beneficial tenants in common, as follows:

(a) Purchase-money provided in unequal shares[80]

If the co-owners bought the co-owned land and provided the money in unequal shares, they were presumed to take beneficially as tenants in common in shares proportionate to their contributions.[81] This presumption may be rebutted if there is evidence that they intend to hold as beneficial joint tenants.[82] If, on the other hand, they provided the purchase money in equal shares, they were presumed to be beneficial joint tenants[83] unless there is evidence to show that although they provide the purchase money equally, they intend to take as beneficial tenants in common.[84] If the co-owned land was bought for a common purpose and the purpose later fails, equity presumes a beneficial tenancy in common even though the contributions were equal.[85]

(b) Loan on mortgage

> If two people join in lending money upon a mortgage, equity says, it could not be the intention, that the interest in that should survive. Though they take a joint security, each means to lend his own and take back his own.[86]

---

74 Bl Comm, Vol II at 193; *Campbell v Campbell* (1792) 4 Bro CC 15.

75 *Robertson v Fraser* (1871) 6 Ch App 696 at 699.

76 *Payne v Webb* (1874) LR 19 Eq 26.

77 *Peat v Chapman* (1750) 1 Ves Sen 542.

78 *Stephens v Hide* (1734) Cat Talb 27.

79 *Burgess v Rawnsley* [1975] Ch 429 at 438; *Gould v Kemp* (1834) 2 My & K 304 at 309; *R v Williams* (1735) Bunb 342 at 343.

80 See also *Springett v Defoe* [1992] 4 CL 24.

81 *Lake v Gibson* (1729) 1 Eq Ca Abr 290 at 291.

82 *Harris v Fergusson* (1848) 16 Sim 308; *Pink v Lawrence* (1977) 36 P & CR 98 ('joint tenants both at law and in equity').

83 *Gissing v Gissing* [1971] AC 886.

84 *Harrison v Barton* (1860) 1 J & H 287.

85 *Burgess v Rawnsley* [1975] Ch 429.

86 *Morley v Bird* (1798) 3 Ves 628 at 631, *per* Arden MR.

Thus, equity presumes that joint mortgagees are beneficial tenants in common, whether the money they advanced is equal or unequal.[87]

(c) Partnership assets

Partnership assets are presumed to be held by the partners as beneficial tenants in common.[88]

(d) Individual business purposes

As Lord Brightman said:[89]

> ... cases in which joint tenants at law will be presumed to hold as tenants in common in equity are ... not necessarily limited to the three categories above. There are other circumstances in which equity may infer that the beneficial interest is intended to be held by the grantees as tenants in common ... one such case is where the grantees hold the premises for their several individual business purposes.

In *Malayan Credit Ltd v Jack Chia MPH Ltd*,[90] two business tenants took a lease of some office space jointly for five years. But they paid rent and service charges in agreed proportions. The lease did not contain any words of severance and did not come within the three categories mentioned above. But it was held that they were beneficial tenants in common.

6 TRANSFER OF LEGAL ESTATE IN CO-OWNED LAND

As already mentioned, co-ownership may exist at law or in equity or both at law and in equity. Difficult issues can arise where the legal estate in the co-owned land is subsequently transferred. The changes introduced by the 1925 and the 1996 legislation ensure that the process of transferring land is simplified and that almost every co-ownership exists behind a trust of land so that the purchaser and the beneficiaries or the single beneficiary (ie the beneficial co-owners or single owner) are all protected. It is now necessary to examine the various situations of transfer in more detail.

Sale by all legal co-owners

Suppose the legal estate in the co-owned land is held by H and W, and both contributed to the purchase. As seen, the legal estate must necessarily be held on trust of land (by virtue of s 36(1) of the Law of Property Act 1925). They also own the beneficial interests either as joint tenants or as tenants in common depending on whether the contributions are equal.

As the land is held on trust, H and W have a power to sell with a power to postpone sale.[91] But, H and W *qua* trustees must also consult themselves as the

87 *Rigden v Vallier* (1751) 2 Ves Sen 252 at 258; *Petty v Styward* (1632) 1 Ch Rep 57.

88 *Jeffreys v Small* (1683) 1 Vern 217; *Lake v Craddock* (1732) 3 PW 158.

89 *Malayan Credit Ltd v Jack Chia MPH Ltd* [1986] AC 549 at 560.

90 [1986] AC 549.

91 Sections 6(1), 4(1) of the TLATA 1996.

beneficial co-owners and give effect to the wishes of the majority by value.[92] This means that if either H or W has a bigger share in the beneficial interest, he or she will be able to postpone the sale. Even if they have equal share in the beneficial interests, being a trustee H or W may refuse to join in the conveyance to effect the sale if he or she does not agree with the sale. However, the other may then apply to the court for an order under s 14 of the Trusts of Land and Appointment of Trustees Act 1996. If a third party, say, A also has a beneficial interest in the land but does not own the legal estate, if A's share is larger than those of H and W added together, A may in theory prevent a sale under s 11 of the 1996 Act but otherwise H and W will be free to make an ultimate decision.

When H and W do decide to sell the land, both will have to join in the conveyance. A purchaser is not concerned to see if s 11 has been observed.[93] It is vital for the purchaser to pay the purchase money, under s 27(2) of the Law of Property Act 1925, to all the legal co-owners, and in any event to at least two of them (in this case to H and W), in order to overreach the beneficial interests behind the trust. Thus, if A also owns a beneficial interest in the land sold, A's beneficial interest will now be shifted into the proceeds of sale which is now in the hands of H and W. A purchaser *prima facie* obtains a good title if s 27(2) is complied with.

The overreaching of beneficial interests takes effect notwithstanding occupation by a beneficiary (eg if A is in occupation) under the trust. In unregistered land, despite s 14 of the Law of Property Act 1925 which says that the interest of a person in possession or in actual occupation of land is not to be prejudicially affected by Part I of the Act (which includes s 2 and s 27), it has been held in *City of London Building Society v Flegg*[94] that the beneficial interests could be overreached under ss 2 and 27. Lords Templeman and Oliver said that to do otherwise would defeat the purpose of the legislation enacting the overreaching provisions.[95] In registered land, once the beneficial interest is overreached at the time of the transfer, there is nothing to be overriding under s 70(1)(g) of the Land Registration Act 1925 at the time when the purchaser is registered as the new proprietor.[96]

City of London Building Society v Flegg [1988] AC 54, HL

Lord Templeman: My Lords, the appellants, City of London Building Society, are the mortgagees under a charge by way of legal mortgage of registered land held at the date of the charge by two trustees on trust for sale and to stand possessed of the net proceeds of sale and rents and profits until sale on trust for four tenants in common including the respondents, Mr and Mrs Flegg. The legal charge was entered into by the trustees in breach of trust, although the appellants were unaware of this. The respondents, who were in actual occupation of the mortgaged land, claim that the appellants' legal charge is subject to the respondents' overriding interest. The Court of Appeal declined to order the respondents to deliver up possession of the land to the appellants; hence this appeal.

92 Section 11 of the TLATA 1996.

93 Section 11 of the TLATA 1996.

94 [1988] AC 54.

95 [1987] 3 All ER 435, at 440j, 446c.

96 *City of London Building Society v Flegg* [1988] AC 54.

By a conveyance dated 18 October 1977 the land appropriately named Bleak House was conveyed to Mr and Mrs Maxwell-Brown in fee simple on trust for sale and to stand possessed of the net proceeds of sale and rents and profits until sale on trust for the Maxwell-Browns as joint tenants. In fact, the purchase price paid by the Maxwell-Browns for Bleak House, amounting to £34,000, had been provided as to £18,000 or more by the respondents, who were the parents of Mrs Maxwell-Brown. In consequence and notwithstanding the express trusts set out in the conveyance, Bleak House was held by the Maxwell-Browns on trust for sale and to stand possessed of the net proceeds of sale and rents and profits until sale on trust for the Maxwell-Browns and the respondents as tenants in common in the proportions in which they had respectively contributed to the purchase price. The respondents were entitled to occupy Bleak House together with the Maxwell-Browns as tenants in common under the trust for sale and all four beneficiaries duly went into occupation.

By a legal charge by way of mortgage dated 12 January 1982 the Maxwell-Browns charged Bleak House to secure £37,500 advanced by the appellants to the Maxwell-Browns. The respondents knew nothing of the legal charge, which was granted by the Maxwell-Browns for their own purposes and in breach of trust. The appellants knew nothing of the respondents.

By s 27 of the Law of Property Act 1925 (as amended by the Law of Property (Amendment) Act 1926, Sched):

(1) A purchaser of a legal estate from trustees for sale shall not be concerned with the trusts affecting the proceeds of sale of land subject to a trust for sale ... or affecting the rents and profits of the land until sale ...

(2) Notwithstanding anything to the contrary in the instrument (if any) creating a trust for sale of land or in the settlement of the net proceeds, the proceeds of sale or other capital money shall not be paid to or applied by the direction of fewer than two persons as trustees for sale, except where the trustee is a trust corporation ...[97]

By s 205(1)(xxi) of the 1925 Act the expression 'purchaser' as used in ss 27 and 28 includes a chargee by way of legal mortgage, and the sum of £37,500 advanced by the appellants to the Maxwell-Browns was capital money within the meaning of s 27(2) and was duly paid to two persons as trustees for sale.

By s 28(1) of the Law of Property Act 1925 (now repealed), read in conjunction with s 71 of the Settled Land Act 1925, trustees for sale of land have powers to mortgage the land and –

> ... all capital money arising under the said powers shall, unless paid or applied for any purpose authorised by the Settled Land Act, 1925, be applicable in the same manner as if the money represented proceeds of sale arising under the trust for sale.

Section 17 of the Trustee Act 1925 provides:

> No purchaser or mortgagee, paying or advancing money on a sale or mortgage purporting to be made under any trust or power vested in trustees, shall be concerned to see that such money is wanted, or that no more than is wanted is raised, or otherwise as to the application thereof.

97 Section 27 is now amended by s 5, Sched 2, para 4(8) of the TLATA 1996.

Thus the appellants advancing money in good faith to two trustees for sale on the security of a charge by way of legal mortgage of Bleak House were not concerned with the trusts affecting the proceeds of sale of Bleak House or with the propriety of the trustees entering into the legal charge. As a result of the legal charge the interests of the beneficiaries in Bleak House pending sale were transferred to the equity of redemption vested in the Maxwell-Browns and to the sum of £37,500 received by the Maxwell-Browns from the appellants in consideration for the grant of the legal charge. The Maxwell-Browns did not account to the respondents for any part of the sum of £37,500 and defaulted in the performance of their obligations to the appellants under the legal charge. The appellants seek possession of Bleak House with a view to enforcing its security.

The respondents resist the claim of the appellants to possession of Bleak House and rely on s 14 of the Law of Property Act 1925. Sections 27 and 28 of that Act, which overreach the interests of the respondents under the trust for sale of Bleak House, are to be found in Part I of the Act. Section 14 provides:

> This Part of this Act shall not prejudicially affect the interest of any person in possession or in actual occupation of land to which he may be entitled in right of such possession or occupation.

The respondents were in actual occupation of Bleak House at the date of the legal charge. It is argued that their beneficial interests under the trust for sale were not overreached by the legal charge or that the respondents were entitled to remain in occupation after the legal charge and against the appellants despite the overreaching of their interests.

My Lords, the respondents were entitled to occupy Bleak House by virtue of their beneficial interests in Bleak House and its rents and profits pending the execution of the trust for sale. Their beneficial interests were overreached by the legal charge and were transferred to the equity of redemption held by the Maxwell-Browns and to the sum advanced by the appellants in consideration of the grant of the legal charge and received by the Maxwell-Browns. After the legal charge the respondents were only entitled to continue in occupation of Bleak House by virtue of their beneficial interests in the equity of redemption of Bleak House and that equity of redemption is subject to the right of the appellants as mortgagees to take possession. Sections 27 and 28 did not 'prejudicially' affect the interests of the respondents, who were, indeed, prejudiced but by the subsequent failure of the trustees for sale to account to their beneficiaries for capital money received by the trustees. A beneficiary who is entitled to share in the proceeds of sale of land held on trust for sale relies on the trustees. Section 26(3) of the Act (as amended)[98] requires trustees for sale to consult their beneficiaries and to give effect to the wishes of the majority of the beneficiaries 'but a purchaser shall not be concerned to see that the provisions of this subsection have been complied with'. If the argument for the respondents is correct, a purchaser from trustees for sale must ensure that a beneficiary in actual occupation is not only consulted but consents to the sale. Section 14 of the Law of Property Act 1925 is not apt to confer on a tenant in common of land held on trust for sale, who happens to be in occupation, rights which are different from and superior to the rights of tenants in common, who are not in occupation on the date when the interests of all tenants in common are overreached by a sale or mortgage by trustees for sale.

98 This section is now repealed by s 25(2), Sched 4 of the TLATA 1994. Now, see s 11(2) of TLATA 1996.

The Maxwell-Browns registered their title to Bleak House under the Land Registration Act 1925 with title absolute for a legal estate in fee simple in possession. They continued to hold Bleak House on trust for sale and to stand possessed of the net proceeds of sale and rents and profits until sale on trust for the Maxwell-Browns and the respondents as tenants in common. By s 74:

> ... neither the registrar nor any person dealing with a registered estate or charge shall be affected with notice of a trust express implied or constructive, and references to trusts shall, so far as possible, be excluded from the register.

By ss 2 and 18 proprietors of registered land may dispose of the land by transfer or by the creation of a legal estate including the grant of a legal charge by way of mortgages. Section 20(1) provides as follows:

> In the case of a freehold estate registered with an absolute title, a disposition of the registered land or of a legal estate therein, including a lease thereof, for valuable consideration shall, when registered, confer on the transferee or grantee an estate in fee simple or the term of years absolute or other legal estate expressed to be created in the land dealt with ... subject – (a) to the incumbrances and other entries, if any, appearing on the register ... and (b) unless the contrary is expressed on the register, to the overriding interests, if any, affecting the estate transferred or created, but free from all other estates and interests whatsoever ... and the disposition shall operate in like manner as if the registered transferor or grantor were (subject to any entry to the contrary in the register) entitled to the registered land in fee simple in possession for his own benefit.

Amongst the 'other estates and interests' which do not affect the legal estate transferred or created are 'minor interests' defined by s 3(xv) as:

> ... the interests not capable of being disposed of or created by registered dispositions and capable of being overridden (whether or not a purchaser has notice thereof) by the proprietors unless protected as provided by this Act, and all rights and interests which are not registered or protected on the register and are not overriding interests, and include – (a) in the case of land held on trust for sale, all interests and powers which are under the Law of Property Act, 1925, capable of being overridden by the trustees for sale, whether or not such interests and powers are so protected ... (now amended by s 5, Sched 2, para 5(2) of the TLATA 1996).

It follows that, when the legal charge in the present case is registered, the appellants will take free from all the interests of the beneficiaries interested under the trust for sale in the proceeds of sale and rents and profits until sale of Bleak House but subject to any overriding interest.

Section 70(1) of the Land Registration Act 1925 defines overriding interests, which include:

> (g) The rights of every person in actual occupation of the land or in receipt of the rents and profits thereof, save where enquiry is made of such person and the rights are not disclosed.

In my view, the object of s 70 was to reproduce for registered land the same limitations as s 14 of the Law of Property Act 1925 produced for land whether registered or unregistered. The respondents claim to be entitled to overriding interests because they were in actual occupation of Bleak House on the date of the legal charge. But the interests of the respondents cannot at one and the same time be overreached and overridden and at the same time be overriding interests. The appellants cannot at one and the same time take free from all the interests of the respondents yet at the same time be subject to some of those interests. The right of the respondents to be and remain in actual occupation of Bleak House ceased when the respondents' interests were overreached by the legal charge save in so far as their rights were transferred to the equity of redemption. As persons interested under the trust for sale the respondents had no right to possession as against the appellants and the fact that the respondents were in actual occupation at the date of the legal charge did not create a new right or transfer an old right so as to make the right enforceable against the appellants.

One of the main objects of the legislation of 1925 was to effect a compromise between, on the one hand, the interests of the public in securing that land held in trust is freely marketable and, on the other hand, the interests of the beneficiaries in preserving their rights under the trusts. By the Settled Land Act 1925 a tenant for life may convey the settled land discharged from all the trusts, powers and provisions of the settlement. By the Law of Property Act 1925 trustees for sale may convey land held on trust for sale discharged from the trusts affecting the proceeds of sale and rents and profits until sale. Under both forms of trust the protection and the only protection of the beneficiaries is that capital money must be paid to at least two trustees or a trust corporation. Section 14 of the Law of Property Act 1925 and s 70 of the Land Registration Act 1925 cannot have been intended to frustrate this compromise and to subject the purchaser to some beneficial interests but not others depending on the waywardness of actual occupation. The Court of Appeal took a different view, largely in reliance on the decision of this House in *Williams & Glyn's Bank Ltd v Boland* [1980] 2 All ER 408; [1981] AC 487. In that case, the sole proprietor of registered land held the land as sole trustee on trust for sale and to stand possessed of the net proceeds of sale and rents and profits until sale on trust for himself and his wife as tenants in common. This House held that the wife's beneficial interest coupled with actual possession by her constituted an overriding interest and that a mortgagee from the husband, despite the concluding words of s 20(1), took subject to the wife's overriding interest. But in that case the interest of the wife was not overreached or overridden because the mortgagee advanced capital moneys to a sole trustee. If the wife's interest had been overreached by the mortgagee advancing capital moneys to two trustees there would have been nothing to justify the wife in remaining in occupation as against the mortgagee. There must be a combination of an interest which justifies continuing occupation plus actual occupation to constitute an overriding interest. Actual occupation is not an interest in itself.

For these reasons, and for the reasons to be given by my noble and learned friend Lord Oliver, I would allow this appeal and restore the order of his Honour Judge Thomas, who ordered the respondents to deliver up Bleak House to the appellants.

Where s 27 is not complied with, in unregistered land as it is governed by the old doctrine of notice, such occupation may, however, provide evidence of the purchaser's constructive notice of the beneficial interests.[99] In registered land, the right of the beneficiary in actual occupation will be overriding when the purchaser's title is registered.[100]

99 *Kingsnorth Finance Co Ltd v Tizard* [1986] 1 WLR 783.

100 *Williams and Glyn's Bank v Boland* [1980] 2 All ER 408.

Williams and Glyn's Bank v Boland [1980] 2 All ER 408, HL

Lord Wilberforce: My Lords, these appeals, apart from one special point affecting only Mr Boland, raise for decision the same question: whether a husband or a wife (in each actual case a wife) who has a beneficial interest in the matrimonial home, by virtue of having contributed to its purchase price, but whose spouse is the legal and registered owner, has an 'overriding interest' binding on a mortgagee who claims possession of the matrimonial home under a mortgage granted by that spouse alone. Although this statement of the issue uses the words 'spouse', 'husband and wife', 'matrimonial home', the appeals do not, in my understanding, involve any question of matrimonial law, or of the rights of married women or of women as such. Exactly the same issue could arise if the roles of husband and wife were reversed, or if the persons interested in the house were not married to each other. The solution must be derived from a consideration in the light of current social conditions of the Land Registration Act 1925 and other property statutes.

The essential facts behind this legal formulation are as follows. Each wife contributed a substantial sum of her own money toward the purchase of the matrimonial home or to paying off a mortgage on it. This indisputably, made her an equitable tenant in common to the extent of her contribution. Each house being registered land was transferred into the sole name of the husband who became its registered proprietor. Later, each husband mortgaged the house by legal mortgage to the appellant bank, which made no inquiries of either wife. Default being made, the bank started proceedings, in the *Boland* case in the High Court and in the *Brown* case in the Dartford County Court, for possession, with a view to sale. In each case, the judge made an order for possession but his decision was reversed by the Court of Appeal ([1979] 2 All ER 697; [1979] Ch 312). So the question is whether the legal and registered mortgage takes effect against the matrimonial home, or whether the wife's beneficial interest has priority over it.

The legal framework within which the appeals are to be decided can be summarised as follows. Under the Land Registration Act 1925, legal estates in land are the only interests in respect of which a proprietor can be registered. Other interests take effect in equity as 'minor interests', which are overridden by a registered transfer. But the Act recognises also an intermediate, or hybrid, class of what are called 'overriding interests'; though these are not registered, legal dispositions take effect subject to them. The list of overriding interests is contained in s 70 and it includes such matters as easements, liabilities having their origin in tenure, land tax and tithe rentcharges, seigniorial and manorial rights, leases for terms not exceeding 21 years, and, finally, the relevant paragraph being s 70(1)(g):

> The rights of every person in actual occupation of the land or in receipt of the rents and profits thereof, save where enquiry is made of such person and the rights are not disclosed.

The first question is whether the wife is a 'person in actual occupation', and, if so, whether her right as a tenant in common in equity is a right protected by this provision. The other main legal element arises out of the Law of Property Act 1925. Since that Act, undivided shares in land can only take effect in equity, behind a trust for sale on which the legal owner is to hold the land. Dispositions of the land, including mortgages, may be made under this trust, and provided that there are at least two trustees, or a trust corporation, 'overreach' the trusts. This means that the 'purchaser' takes free from them, whether or not he has notice of them, and that the trusts are enforceable against the proceeds of sale: see s 2(2) of the Law of Property Act 1925, and s 2(3) which lists certain exceptions.

The second question is whether the wife's equitable interest under the trust for sale, if she is in occupation of the land, is capable of being an overriding interest, or whether, as is generally the rule as regards equitable interests, it can only take effect as a 'minor interest'. In the latter event a registered transferee, including a legal mortgagee, would take free from it.

The system of land registration, as it exists in England, which long antedates the Land Registration Act 1925, is designed to simplify and to cheapen conveyancing. It is intended to replace the often complicated and voluminous title deeds of property by a single land certificate, on the strength of which land can be dealt with. In place of the lengthy and often technical investigation of title to which a purchaser was committed, all he has to do is to consult the register; from any burden not entered on the register, with one exception, he takes free. Above all, the system is designed to free the purchaser from the hazards of notice, real or constructive, which, in the case of unregistered land, involved him in inquiries, often quite elaborate, failing which he might be bound by equities. The Law of Property Act 1925 contains provisions limiting the effect of the doctrine of notice, but it still remains a potential source of danger to purchasers. By contrast, the only provisions in the Land Registration Act 1925 with regard to notice are provisions which enable a purchaser to take the estate free from equitable interests or equities whether he has notice or not (see, for example, s 3(xv) sv 'minor interests'.) The only kind of notice recognised is by entry on the register.

The exception just mentioned consists of 'overriding interests' listed in s 70. As to these, all registered land is stated to be deemed to be subject to such of them as may be subsisting in reference to the land, unless the contrary is expressed on the register. The land is so subject regardless of notice actual or constructive. In my opinion, therefore, the law as to notice as it may affect purchasers of unregistered land, whether contained in decided cases or in a statute (eg s 3 of the Conveyancing Act 1882 and s 199 of the Law of Property Act 1925) has no application even by analogy to registered land. Whether a particular right is an overriding interest, and whether it affects a purchaser, is to be decided on the terms of s 70, and other relevant provisions of the Land Registration Act 1925, and on nothing else.

In relation to rights connected with occupation, it has been said that the purpose and effect of s 70(1)(g) of the Land Registration Act 1925 was to make applicable to registered land the same rule as previously had been held to apply to unregistered land (see *National Provincial Bank Ltd v Ainsworth*, [1964] 1 All ER 688 at 697; [1964] Ch 665 at 689 (*per* Lord Denning MR) and [1965] 2 All ER 472 at 501–02; [1965] AC 1175 at 1259 (in this House)).

I adhere to this, but I do not accept the argument which counsel for the appellant sought to draw from it. His submission was that, in applying s 70(1)(g), we should have regard to and limit the application of the paragraph in the light of the doctrine of notice. But this would run counter to the whole purpose of the Act. The purpose, in each system, is the same, namely, to safeguard the rights of persons in occupation, but the method used differs. In the case of unregistered land, the purchaser's obligation depends on what he has notice of, notice actual or constructive. In the case of registered land, it is the fact of occupation that matters. If there is actual occupation, and the occupier has rights, the purchaser takes subject to them. If not, he does not. No further element is material.

I now deal with the first question. Were the wives here in 'actual occupation'? These words are ordinary words of plain English, and should, in my opinion, be interpreted as such. Historically they appear to have emerged in the judgment of Lord Loughborough LC in *Taylor v Stibbert* (1794) 2 Ves 437 at 440; 30 ER 713 at 714 in a passage which repays quotation:

> ... whoever purchases an estate from the owner, knowing it to be in possession of tenants, is bound to inquire into the estates, those tenants have. It has been determined, that a purchaser being told, particular parts of the estate were in possession of a tenant, without any information as to his interest, and taking it for granted it was only from year to year, was bound by a lease, that tenant had, which was a surprise upon him. That was rightly determined; for it was sufficient to put the purchaser upon inquiry, that he was informed the estate was not in the actual possession of the person with whom he contracted; that he could not transfer the ownership and possession at the same time; that there were interests, as to the extent and terms of which it was his duty to inquire.

They were taken up in the judgment of the Privy Council in *Barnhart v Greenshields* (1853) 9 Moo PC 18, 14 ER 204. The purpose for which they were used, in that case, was evidently to distinguish the case of a person who was in some kind of legal possession, as by receipt of the rents and profits, from that of a person actually in occupation as tenant. Given occupation, ie presence on the land, I do not think that the word 'actual' was intended to introduce any additional qualification, certainly not to suggest that possession must be 'adverse': it merely emphasises that what is required is physical presence, not some entitlement in law. So, even if it were necessary to look behind these plain words into history, I would find no reason for denying them their plain meaning.

Then, were the wives in actual occupation? I ask: why not? There was physical presence, with all the rights that occupiers have, including the right to exclude all others except those having similar rights. The house was a matrimonial home, intended to be occupied, and in fact occupied, by both spouses, both of whom have an interest in it; it would require some special doctrine of law to avoid the result that each is in occupation. Three arguments were used for a contrary conclusion. First, it was said that if the vendor (I use this word to include a mortgagor) is in occupation, that is enough to prevent the application of the paragraph. This seems to be a proposition of general application, not limited to the case of husbands, and no doubt, if correct, would be very convenient for purchasers and intending mortgagees. But the presence of the vendor, with occupation, does not exclude the possibility of occupation of others. There are observations which suggest the contrary in the unregistered land case of *Caunce v Caunce* [1969] 1 All ER 722; [1969] 1 WLR 286, but I agree with the disapproval of these and with the assertion of the proposition I have just stated by Russell LJ in *Hodgson v Marks* [1971] 2 All ER 684 at 690; [1971] Ch 892 at 934–35. Then it was suggested that the wife's 'occupation' was nothing but the shadow of the husband's, a version I suppose of the doctrine of unity of husband and wife. This expression and the argument flowing from it was used by Templeman J in *Bird v Syme Thomson* [1978] 3 All ER 1027 at 1030; [1979] 1 WLR 440 at 444, a decision preceding and which he followed in the present case. The argument was also inherent in the judgment in *Caunce v Caunce* which influenced the decisions of Templeman J. It somewhat faded from the arguments in the present case and appears to me to be heavily obsolete.

The appellants' main and final position became in the end this: that, to come within the paragraph, the occupation in question must be apparently inconsistent with the title of the vendor. This, it was suggested, would exclude the wife of a husband-vendor because her apparent occupation would be satisfactorily accounted for by his. But, apart from the rewriting of the paragraph which this would involve, the suggestion is unacceptable. Consistency, or inconsistency, involves the absence, or presence, of an independent right to occupy, though I must observe that 'inconsistency' in this context is an inappropriate word. But how can either quality be predicated of a wife, simply qua wife? A wife may, and everyone knows this, have rights of her own; particularly, many wives have a share in a matrimonial home. How can it be said that the presence of a wife in the house, as occupier, is consistent or inconsistent with the husband's rights until one knows what rights she has? And if she has rights, why, just because she is a wife (or in the converse case, just because an occupier is the husband), should these rights be denied protection under the paragraph? If one looks beyond the case of husband and wife, the difficulty of all these arguments stands out if one considers the case of a man living with a mistress, or of a man and a woman (or for that matter two persons of the same sex) living in a house in separate or partially shared rooms. Are these cases of apparently consistent occupation, so that the rights of the other person (other than the vendor) can be disregarded? The only solution which is consistent with the Act (s 70(1)(g)) and with common sense is to read the paragraph for what it says. Occupation, existing as a fact, may protect rights if the person in occupation has rights. On this part of the case I have no difficulty in concluding that a spouse, living in a house, has an actual occupation capable of conferring protection, as an overriding interest, on rights of that spouse.

This brings me to the second question, which is whether such rights as a spouse has under a trust for sale are capable of recognition as overriding interests, a question to my mind of some difficulty. The argument against this is based on the structure of the Land Registration Act 1925 and on specific provisions in it.

As to structure, it is said that the Act recognises three things: (a) legal estates, (b) minor interests, which take effect in equity, and (c) overriding interests. These are mutually exclusive: an equitable interest, which is a minor interest, is incapable of being at the same time an overriding interest. The wife's interest, existing under, or behind, a trust for sale, is an equitable interest and nothing more. To give it the protection of an overriding interest would, moreover, contradict the principle according to which such an equitable interest can be overreached by an exercise of the trust for sale. As to the provisions of the Act, particular emphasis is placed on s 3(xv) which, in defining 'Minor interests', specifically includes in the case of land held on trust for sale 'all interests and powers which are under the Law of Property Act 1925, capable of being overridden by the trustees for sale' and excludes, expressly, overriding interests. (This subsection is now amended by s 5, Sched 2, para 5(2) of the TLATA 1996.) Reliance is also placed on s 86, which, dealing analogously, so it is said, with settled land, prescribes that successive or other interests created by or arising under a settlement take effect as minor interests and not otherwise, and on s 101, which, it is argued, recognises the exclusive character of minor interests, which in all cases can be overriden.

My Lords, I find this argument formidable. To reach a conclusion on it involves some further consideration of the nature of trusts for sale, in relation to undivided shares. The trusts on which, in this case, the land is to be held are defined (as 'statutory trusts') in s 35 of the Law of Property Act 1925 (now repealed), ie:

> ... upon trust to sell the same and to stand possessed of the net proceeds of sale, after payment of costs, and of the net rents and profits until sale after payment of rates, taxes, costs of insurance, repairs, and other outgoings, upon such trusts,

and subject to such powers and provisions, as may be requisite for giving effect to the rights of the persons ... interested in the land.

In addition to this specific disposition, the general provisions as to trusts for sale in ss 23–31,[101] where not inconsistent, appear to apply. The right of occupation of the land pending sale is not explicitly dealt with in these sections and the position as to it is obscure. Before the Act the position was that owners of undivided shares (which could exist at law) had concurrent rights of occupation. In *Bull v Bull* [1955] 1 All ER 253, [1955] 1 QB 234 it was held by the Court of Appeal, applying *Re Warren, Warren v Warren* [1932] 1 Ch 42; [1931] All ER Rep 702, that the conversion of these legal estates into equitable interests by the Law of Property Act 1925 should not affect the mutual rights of the owners. Denning LJ, in a judgment which I find most illuminating, there held, in a factual situation similar to that of the instant cases, that 'when there are two equitable tenants in common, then, until the place is sold, each of them is entitled concurrently with the other to the possession of the land and to the use and enjoyment of it in a proper manner' ([1955] 1 All ER 253 at 255, [1955] 1 QB 234 at 238). And he referred to s 14 of the Law of Property Act 1925 which provides that the Act 'shall not prejudicially affect the interest of any person in possession or in actual occupation of land to which he may be entitled in right of such possession or occupation'.

How then are these various rights to be fitted into the scheme of the Land Registration Act 1925? It is clear, at least, that the interests of the co-owners under the 'statutory trusts' are minor interests: this fits with the definition in s 3(xv). But I can see no reason why, if these interests, or that of any one of them, are or is protected by 'actual occupation they should remain merely as 'minor interests'. On the contrary, I see every reason why, in that event, they should acquire the status of overriding interests. And, moreover, I find it easy to accept that they satisfy the opening, and governing, words of s 70, namely, interests subsisting in reference to the land. As Lord Denning MR points out, to describe the interests of spouses in a house jointly bought to be lived in as a matrimonial home as merely an interest in the proceeds of sale, or rents and profits until sale, is just a little unreal; see also *Elias v Mitchell* [1972] 2 All ER 153, [1972] Ch 652 *per* Pennycuick VC, with whose analysis I agree, and contrast *Cedar Holdings Ltd v Green* [1979] 3 All ER 117, [1979] 3 WLR 31 (which I consider to have been wrongly decided).

There are decisions, in relation to other equitable interests than those of tenants in common, which confirm this line of argument. In *Bridges v Mees* [1957] 2 All ER 577, [1957] Ch 475 Harman J decided that a purchaser of land under a contract for sale, who had paid the price and so was entitled to the land in equity, could acquire an overriding interest by virtue of actual occupation, and a similar position was held by the Court of Appeal to arise in relation to a resulting trust (see *Hodgson v Marks* [1971] 2 All ER 684, [1971] Ch 892). These decisions (following the law as it undoubtedly existed before 1925: see *Barnhart v Greenshields* (1853) 9 Moo PCC 18 at 32, 14 ER 204 at 209, *Daniels v Davison* (1809) 16 Ves 249, 33 ER 978, *Allen v Anthony* (1816) 1 Mer 282 at 284, 35 ER 679, *per* Lord Eldon LC) provide an answer to the argument that there is a firm dividing line, or an unbridgeable gulf, between minor interests and overriding interests, and, on the contrary, confirm that the fact of occupation enables protection of the latter to extend to what without it would be the former. In my opinion, the wives' equitable interests,

101 Sections 23, 25, 26, 28–30, 31(3) are now repealed by s 25(2), Sched 4 of the TLATA 1996. Sections 24, 27, 31 of the LPA are now amended: see s 5 and Sched 2, paras 1, 4(7) and 4(8) of the TLATA 1996.

subsisting in reference to the land, were by the fact of occupation, made into overriding interests, and so protected by s 70(1)(g). I should add that it makes no difference to this that these same interests might also have been capable of protection by the registration of a caution (see *Bridges v Mees* [1957] 2 All ER 577 at 582; [1957] Ch 475 at 487 and s 59(6) of the Land Registration Act 1925).

There was finally an argument based on s 74 of the Land Registration Act 1925. Section 74 provides:

> Subject to the provisions of this Act as to settled land, neither the registrar nor any person dealing with a registered estate or charge shall be affected with notice of a trust express implied or constructive, and references to trusts shall, so far as possible, be excluded from the register.

The argument was that, if the overriding interest sought to be protected is, under the general law, only binding on a purchaser by virtue of notice, the section has the effect of denying the protection. It is obvious, and indeed conceded, that if this is right, *Hodgson v Marks* and *Bridges v Mees* must have been wrongly decided.

I am of opinion that this section has no such effect. Its purpose is to make clear, as I have already explained, that the doctrine of notice has no application to registered conveyancing, and accordingly to establish, as an administrative measure, that entries may not be made in the register which would only be appropriate if that doctrine were applicable. It cannot have the effect of cutting down the general application of s 70(1).

I would only add, in conclusion, on the appeal as it concerns the wives a brief observation on the conveyancing consequences of dismissing the appeal. These were alarming to Templeman J, and I can agree with him to the extent that whereas the object of a land registration system is to reduce the risks to purchasers from anything not on the register, to extend (if it be an extension) the area of risk so as to include possible interests of spouses, and indeed, in theory, of other members of the family or even outside it, may add to the burdens of purchasers, and involve them in inquiries which in some cases may be troublesome.

But conceded, as it must be, that the Act, following established practice, gives protection to occupation, the extension of the risk area follows necessarily from the extension, beyond the *paterfamilias*, of rights of ownership, itself following from the diffusion of property and earning capacity. What is involved is a departure from an easy-going practice of dispensing with inquiries as to occupation beyond that of the vendor and accepting the risks of doing so. To substitute for this a practice of more careful inquiry as to the fact of occupation, and, if necessary, as to the rights of occupiers, cannot, in my view of the matter, be considered as unacceptable except at the price of overlooking the widespread development of shared interests of ownership. In the light of s 70 of the Act, I cannot believe that Parliament intended this, though it may be true that in 1925 it did not foresee the full extent of this development.

Sale by surviving co-owner

Suppose H and W co-own the legal estate for themselves as beneficial co-owners. However, H dies later. As the legal estate must be owned by them as joint tenants, when H dies, the right of survivorship operates and, therefore, W becomes the sole surviving trustee. If the beneficial interests were held in joint tenancy, H's interest would have survived to W as well and W would become an absolute owner. The trust would have come to an end[102] and so would the co-ownership. Section 36(2) of the Law of Property Act[103] provides that 'Nothing in this Act affects the right of a survivor of joint tenants, who is solely and beneficially interested, to deal with his legal estate as if it were not held in trust.' W could decide what to do with the land.

However, H might have severed his beneficial joint tenancy before he died. If this is the case, when H dies his interest would pass to Z by will or intestacy. The sole surviving trustee for sale, W, is not solely entitled to the beneficial interest (see *Fig 3*).

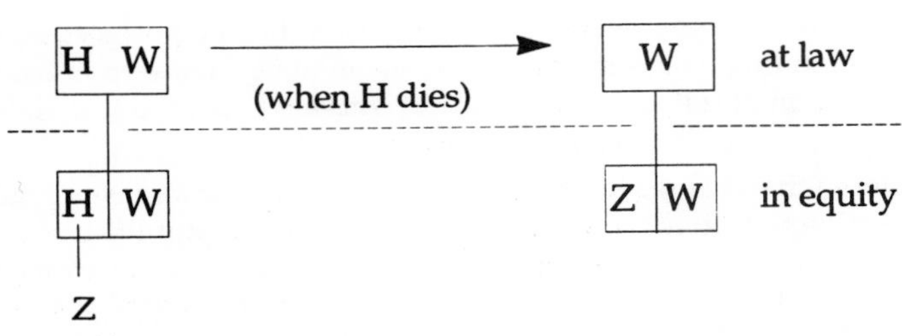

Fig 3

The possibility of H's severance before his death creates a problem because H's severance might be unknown to W and the purchaser. Both the purchaser and W might think that the right of survivorship operates when H dies. Although W is capable of conveying the legal estate which has now survived to her to the purchaser by her own conveyance, such a conveyance will not have any overreaching effect. Therefore, in order to overreach H's possible interest in the tenancy in common the tendency was to preserve the trust for sale by appointing a new trustee.

After 1925, the appointment of a new trustee is not absolutely necessary as a result of the Law of Property (Joint Tenants) Act 1964 which is extended to a trust of land.

Law of Property (Joint Tenants) Act 1964

1. Assumptions on sale of land by survivor of joint tenants

(1) For the purpose of s 36(2) of the Law of Property Act 1925, as amended by s 7 of and the Schedule to the Law of Property (Amendment) Act 1926, the survivor of two or more joint tenants shall in favour of a purchaser of the legal estate, be deemed to be solely and beneficially interested if the conveyance includes a statement that he is so interested.

102 *Re Cook, Beck v Grant* [1948] Ch 212.

103 As amended by s 7 of the Law of Property (Amendment) Act 1926, and s 5, Sched 2, para 4(3)(b) of the TLATA 1996.

Provided that the foregoing provisions of this subsection shall not apply if, at any time before the date of the conveyance by the survivor:

(a) a memorandum of severance (that is to say a note or memorandum signed by the join tenants or one of them and recording that the joint tenancy was severed in equity on a date therein specified) had been endorsed on or annexed to the conveyance by virtue of which the legal estate was vested in the joint tenants; or

(b) [a bankruptcy order] made against any of the joint tenants, or a petition for such an order, had been registered under the Land Charges Act 1925, being an order or petition of which the purchaser has notice, by virtue of the registration, on the date of the conveyance by the survivor.

(2) The foregoing provisions of this section shall apply with the necessary modifications in relation to a conveyance by the personal representatives of the survivor of joint tenants as they apply in relation to a conveyance by such a survivor.

2. Retrospective and transitional provisions

Section 1 of this Act shall be deemed to have come into force on 1 January 1926, and for the purposes of that section in its application to a conveyance executed before the passing of this Act a statement signed by the vendor or by his personal representatives that he was solely and beneficially interested shall be treated as if it had been included in the conveyance.

3. Exclusion of registered land

This Act shall not apply to any land the title of which has been registered under the provisions of the Land Registration Acts 1925 and 1936.

Section 1 of the Law of Property (Joint Tenants) Act 1964 provides that in favour of a purchaser of a legal estate a survivor of two or more joint tenants shall be *deemed* to be solely and beneficially interested if the conveyance includes a statement that he is so interested. If the survivor has himself died, his personal representative can include in the conveyance a statement that the deceased survivor was solely and beneficially entitled to the legal estate.[104] The Act is retrospective, being deemed to have come into operation on 1 January 1926.[105]

The Act, however, does not apply in three cases:

(i) If a memorandum of severance has been endorsed on or annexed to the original conveyance to the joint tenants. This tells the purchaser that the survivor is not solely and beneficially interested and reminds him of the need to have another trustee appointed.

(ii) If a bankruptcy petition or receiving order has been registered under s 5(1) of the Land Charges Act 1972 in the register of pending actions. A bankruptcy severs a joint tenancy,[106] and registration of a bankruptcy petition or receiving order[107] gives the world notice of the severance.

104 Section 1(2) of the Law of Property (Joint Tenants) Act 1964.

105 Section 2 of the Law of Property (Joint Tenants) Act 1964.

106 *Morgan v Marquis* (1853) 9 Exch 145.

107 An order made for the custody of a bankrupt's estate when the bankruptcy is established.

(iii) Where the title to the land is registered.[108] The power of a sole surviving trustee of registered land to pass a good title free of beneficial interests depends on the presence or absence of a restriction. If there is no entry of a restriction, a purchaser for value *prima facie* takes free from the beneficial interests even if the survivor is not solely and beneficially entitled[109] unless H's successor, Z is in actual occupation at the date of the conveyance to the purchaser which is then capable of enforcement as an overriding interest under s 70(1)(g).[110]

So any subsequent severance in equity of a joint tenancy will not prevent a purchaser from obtaining a good title from the sole surviving joint tenant, provided that he conveys as beneficial owner and no notice of severance is annexed to the conveyance. However, where it is clear from the title deed that there never was a beneficial joint tenancy, for example, where the deed of conveyance stated that the land was conveyed by the original vendor to 'H and W equally', on H's death, W cannot give an unencumbered title under s 1 of the 1964 Act because the conveyance discloses that H and W were tenants in common and W is not solely and beneficially entitled. When H dies, his share will pass to Z who is entitled under his will or intestacy. W will become the sole surviving trustee for herself and Z. When W sells the land, she can no doubt transfer the legal estate by her own conveyance. However, the conveyance will not overreach any beneficial interests which Z enjoys. The position will be similar to that of a sale by a sole trustee which will be dealt with below.

What if the title deed is silent as to H and W's beneficial entitlements? Can W rely on the Act? As we have seen, their beneficial entitlements depend on the presumption of equity. But the purchaser is in no position to find out the true position. It seems that the purchaser could assume that W is solely and beneficially entitled. This could, however, increase fraud at the expense of the beneficiaries. Although this is not what the Parliament envisaged, it appears to be the legal consequence in this situation.[111]

It is also uncertain whether a purchaser who has actual notice of the severance from other sources can safely rely on the Act where no memorandum is endorsed on the title deed. It seems that on the face of it, the Act even then protects the purchaser, although the court is sometimes unwilling to allow purchasers to take advantage of such provisions inequitably.[112] Professor Barnsley argued that the better view was that the Act gave no protection in these circumstances.[113] He said that the purpose of the Act was to remove a difficulty where no evidence of severance was forthcoming, and it could hardly be intended to operate when the purchaser knew the survivor was not solely and beneficially entitled. He added that the purchaser would also be bound if

108 Section 3 of the Law of Property (Joint Tenants) Act 1964.

109 Sections 20(1) and 59(6) of the LRA 1925.

110 *Williams & Glyn's Bank v Boland* [1980] 2 All ER 408; *Abbey National Building Society v Cann* [1990] 1 All ER 1085.

111 See Megarry and Wade, p 440; Barnsley, p 289.

112 See Megarry and Wade, p 441.

113 See Barnsley, p 289.

the beneficiary was in actual occupation, as that could give the purchaser constructive notice if he failed to make proper inquiries.[114]

Sale by a single legal owner as trustee

Suppose only H owns the legal estate, but both H and W contributed to the purchase. H holds the legal estate as a trustee for himself and W as in the case of *Bull v Bull*.[115] The co-ownership does not exist at law but in equity. Again H will be able to convey the legal estate by his conveyance. But the conveyance will have no overreaching effect. Is the purchaser bound by the beneficial interests behind the trust? In unregistered land it depends on the doctrine of notice. Where H's title contains express reference to a trust, that will give the purchaser notice of the beneficial interests. But there are many trusts the existence of which is unknown to the single trustee and the purchaser, for example, where the beneficial interest exists behind a resulting or constructive trust. In this case, if the purchaser has actual notice of the beneficial interests he will be bound by them unless he insists on the appointment of a new trustee to take advantage of overreaching machinery. It is more likely that he does not have actual notice. He will, however, be deemed to have constructive notice of the beneficial interests if he fails to make proper inquiries and inspection of the land.

The court adopted a very narrow view as to what constituted constructive notice in *Caunce v Caunce*[116] where a wife was living happily with a husband who solely owned the legal estate. Stamp J thought that such cohabitation was wholly consistent with the sole title offered by the husband to the purchaser (the bank in this case). The bank was perfectly entitled to assume that W was in occupation simply because she was married to the apparent owner. This applied to many other persons who were present in a family home such as the vendor's father, his uncle or aunt, any of whom might have contributed money towards the purchase of the property.[117]

Caunce v Caunce [1969] 1 WLR 286

Stamp J: The plaintiff and the first defendant to this action, now a bankrupt, are and were at all material times, husband and wife and they were living together.

[His Lordship then stated the facts and continued.]

Having held that the plaintiff has an equitable interest in the property, [the matrimonial home] the question I have to decide (and the only substantial question argued before me) is whether the third defendant, Lloyds Bank Ltd, which subsequently to the purchase advanced money on the security of the property, has priority over that equitable interest. By several mortgages, dated respectively 17 June 1964, 24 December 1964, and 22 February 1966, the husband charged the property by way of legal mortgage in favour of the Bank, to secure the respective sums of £500, £500 and £200 advanced to

114 *Ibid*, p 289.

115 [1955] 1 All ER 253 (a case of trust for sale).

116 [1969] 1 WLR 286 (a case of trust for sale).

117 [1969] 1 WLR 286 at 293G–H.

him, and other moneys therein mentioned. The plaintiff claims, and I find as a fact, that she was unaware of the creation of any of these three mortgages. Shortly after the receiving order the husband left the premises and he has not lived there, as I understand it, since then, and he left his wife living there without him. The bank, being in the same position as if it had obtained a legal estate (see s 87(1) of the Law of Property Act 1925) and there being no suggestion that the bank acted otherwise than *bona fide*, took the property free from the plaintiff's equitable interest unless it had constructive notice of the existence of that interest. The plaintiff seeks to fix the bank with notice of her interest on several grounds. It is urged – and this is really in the forefront of the plaintiff's argument –that today when so many matrimonial homes are purchased out of moneys provided in part by the wife, a purchaser – by which expression I include a mortgagee – who finds the matrimonial home vested in one of the spouses, more particularly in this case a husband, is put upon inquiry as to whether the other spouse has an equitable interest in the property, and it is urged that, if he does not inquire of the other spouse whether such an interest is claimed, he takes subject to the interest. As a bare proposition of law no authority has been cited for that proposition, and in view of the disinclination of the courts to extend the doctrine of constructive notice (see *Hunt v Luck* [1901] 1 Ch 45), I am not persuaded that it ought to be accepted. More particularly is this the case where, as was the fact here, the wife knew almost at the outset that the property was in the sole name of her husband, and had taken no step to assert her rights.

In coming to this conclusion I would guard myself from expressing any view whether it would make any difference if, at the time of the advance or purchase, the wife was in occupation of the property to the exclusion of the husband, a circumstance which, as was held by the majority of the Court of Appeal in *National Provincial Bank Ltd v Hastings Car Mart Ltd* [1964] Ch 665, put the lender upon inquiry as to whether the wife had what was then known as a 'deserted wife's equity'. Here the wife was living in the house with the husband at the time of each of the bank advances, and, in the absence of other facts, I could not hold that the mere fact that the house was the matrimonial home put the bank upon inquiry as to whether the wife had or had not an equitable interest in it. I shall say more about this later.

Then it is said that there were facts, known to the bank, which suggested that the wife in fact had an equitable interest in the property. The plaintiff was their customer. In April 1959 she had withdrawn £50 from her deposit account with the bank, the withdrawal taking the form of a cheque drawn by the bank in favour of Orange & Co, who were in fact the agents through whom the purchase of the property was negotiated. Then on about 26 October 1959, £289 13s 0d was drawn, on the plaintiff's account, in favour of Wright, Hassall & Co, solicitors, who were acting in connection with the purchase. Then, in June 1960, an additional sum was required by the builders for alterations to the specifications of the house which was to be built, and a sum of £139 10s was transferred by the plaintiff from her deposit account with the bank to a current business account, and a cheque for £139 10s was drawn on the business account in favour of A C Lloyd Ltd. There is no evidence that the bank knew at that time that Messrs Orange & Co were acting in relation to the purchase of the matrimonial home. There is no evidence that, at that time, the bank knew that Messrs Wright, Hassall & Co were acting in the purchase or, indeed, at that stage, that it had any actual knowledge of the purchase. Of course, a bank manager or a bank clerk may be sufficiently interested in the affairs of the bank's customers to examine the nature of the payments drawn on the customer's account and he may draw interferences from those payments regarded the activities of the customers. But in the absence of authority constraining me to hold otherwise, I cannot find that a bank has a duty to do so, or that when, five years later, the customer's husband asks for a loan on the security of the matrimonial home, the bank has a duty to the customer either to remember the details of the payments or the inferences to be drawn from them, or to examine the customer's account of five years earlier to see if there was ground for supposing that the customer provided the purchase price or any part of it. There is, however, here, a further fact which is sought to be added to what appears to me to be a somewhat flimsy structure. There is, in the possession of the bank, a note of an interview with the plaintiff, dated 7 November 1960. According to that note in the possession of the bank, the plaintiff called at the bank on that day 'to request a loan of £240 for purchase of furniture for new house at Radford Semele'. From that note it appears that the bank knew that the house had been bought, but one may peruse the note in vain to discover the slightest suggestion that the plaintiff had provided any part of the purchase money. The note is a fairly long one and I will not read it in detail, it being sufficient to say that there was a discussion about the security which the plaintiff could offer. She was at that time the owner of a small business which appears to have been doing reasonably well. It was a sweet-shop, I think, and there was a discussion between her and the official of the bank regarding the takings from that business, and what arrangements she could make to repay the amount borrowed for the purchase of the furniture. On behalf of the plaintiff, counsel is entitled to say that, as from that date, the bank knew that the house had been purchased, and had the manager or somebody then examined the plaintiff's account at the bank for the previous 12 months or so, he would or might have appreciated the probability that the plaintiff had put up part of the purchase price.

In fact, at a somewhat late stage of counsel's opening on behalf of the plaintiff, a further point was added and the case was put in a somewhat different alternative way. It is the fact that the husband had not proved to be always a very satisfactory customer from the point of view of the bank. There were record cards which, I think, must have been brought to the attention of the manager of the bank at the time of the first of the three legal charges, from which it appears that at the time of the purchase the husband was hard put to it to find a few pounds, and knowing that he was so low in funds the bank should – so the argument goes – have taken advantage of what appears to me to be the wholly fortuitous fact that the plaintiff wife's account was with the bank to refresh its memory by looking at that account to see if there was not ground for supposing that the plaintiff had in truth provided the money for the purchase. Had it done so and observed the withdrawals to which I have adverted, and particularly the payment of £289 to the solicitors and the fact that the plaintiff had a small business of her own and had raised money to buy the furniture for the new house, the source of the purchase-money of the house would have become tolerably clear. Ergo – so the argument runs – the bank is fixed with constructive notice of the plaintiff's equitable interest. How far, if the bank had made the inquiry which it is said it ought to have made, it would have been fixed with notice of the equitable interest is a matter which I need not decide, for, in my judgment, the bank never came under an obligation to make the inquiry. But I would, in passing, observe that it does not in the least follow that because £200 or £300 are found by a wife on the purchase of the matrimonial home that she has an equitable interest in it. It must be the commonest thing in the world for a wife to lend her husband a few hundred pounds in order that the house should be bought and for the loan to be repaid in a comparatively short time. As I have indicated, however, I cannot hold that the bank was bound to make any such inquiry as it has been urged it ought to have made. So to hold would, in my judgment, be to place upon a bank an intolerable burden and would stretch the doctrine of constructive notice to a point beyond its proper limits.

In this connection I would borrow two passages in the judgment of Farwell J in *Hunt v Luck* [1901] 1 Ch 45, to which I have already referred. The first is on 48 of the report, and runs as follows:

> This doctrine of constructive notice, imputing as it does knowledge which the person affected does not actually possess, is one which the courts of late years have been unwilling to extend. I am not referring to cases where a man wilfully shuts his eyes so as to avoid notice, but to cases like the present, where honest men are to be affected by knowledge which every one admits they did not in fact possess. So far as regards the merits of the case, even assuming both parties to the action to be equally innocent, the man who has been swindled by too great confidence in his own agent has surely less claim to the assistance of a court of equity than a purchaser for value who gets the legal estate, and pays his money without notice. Granted that the vendor has every reason to believe his agent an honest man, still, if he is mistaken and trusts a rogue, he, rather than the purchaser for value without notice who is misled by his having so trusted, ought to bear the burden.

And so it appears to me, as between a wife who has trusted her husband to have the property vested in his sole name, or who has not taken steps to get it vested in joint names, on the one hand and a mortgagee bank on the other.

The second passage of Farwell J's judgment is at 52 of the report, and runs as follows:

> Constructive notice is the knowledge which the courts impute to a person upon a presumption so strong of the existence of the knowledge that it cannot be allowed to be rebutted, either from his knowing something which ought to have put him to further inquiry or from his wilfully abstaining from inquiry, to avoid notice. How can I hold that the mortgagees here wilfully neglected to make some inquiry which is usual in cases of mortgages or sales of real estate in order to avoid acquiring some knowledge which they would thereby have obtained.

The last sentence of that passage appears to be applicable to the facts of the present case. Nor do I find the suggestion that a bank mortgagee should at its peril be bound to conduct an inquiry into the financial relations between husband and wife, before it can advance money on security of property vested in the husband, at all an attractive one, and in my view in this day and age husbands and wives ought to be able to bank at the same bank without having their accounts analysed by the bank in order to find out if one of them is deceiving the other.

The exercise which, it is submitted, ought to have been conducted in the present case would – so it seems to me – have been more appropriate to a police inquiry or that of a detective agency than to a bank manager who often no doubt arranges advances daily in the ordinary course of business. And one may ask the rhetorical question, At what point are such inquiries to end? Such inquiries perhaps lie within a small compass in the case of a country branch of a bank but would assume a most complicated and difficult character when embarked upon in a bank which carries many thousands of accounts. Is the bank, being uncertain how the borrower can have found the money, to search not only his wife's account but also, perhaps, his father's account? As Lord Upjohn pointed out in *National Provincial Bank Ltd v Hastings Car Mart Ltd* [1965] AC 1175 at 1233:

> It has been the policy of the law for over a hundred years to simplify and facilitate transactions in real property. It is of great importance that persons should be able freely and easily to raise money on the security of their property.

I can, perhaps, most conveniently summarise my judgment on this part of the case by referring to s 199 of the Law of Property Act 1925, and saying that at the times of the several advances to the husband an inquiry into the details of the plaintiff's bank account, with a view to ascertaining whether she had provided a part of the purchase price, was not an inquiry which ought reasonably to have been made within the meaning of sub-s (2) of that section.

I must now consider a further argument advanced on behalf of the plaintiff. It is contended that an inquiry ought to have been made on the property and that if such an inquiry had been made the plaintiff would have asserted her equitable interest, ergo – so the argument runs – the bank had constructive notice of that interest. Before going on to consider this contention it is, perhaps, convenient that I should remark by way of warning, that s 199 is a section designed not to extend but to limit the doctrine of constructive notice. The section does not operate so as to fix a purchaser with constructive notice prior to the coming into force of the Law of Property Act. The law, as I understand it, is this: if there be in possession or occupation of the property, contracted to be sold or mortgaged, a person other than the vendor, or, as in this case, other than the mortgagor, and the purchaser makes no inquiry of that person, he takes the property fixed with notice of that person's rights and interests, however that may be. (See the judgment in the Court of Appeal of Vaughan-Williams L J in *Hunt v Luck* [1902] 1 Ch 428 at 432.) Here it is said that the plaintiff was in possession or occupation. No inquiry was made of her and therefore the bank is fixed with notice of her equitable interest. In my judgment, it is here that the fallacy arises, for the plaintiff, unlike the deserted wife, was not in apparent occupation or possession. She was there, ostensibly because she was the wife, and her presence there was wholly consistent with the title offered by the husband to the bank.

A similar point was touched upon by Lord Wilberforce in *National Provincial Bank Ltd v Hastings Car Mart Ltd* [1965] A C 1175 at 1248, when he said:

> For to hold that the wife acquires on marriage a right valid against third parties to remain in the house where she lives with her husband would not only fly in the face of the reality of the marriage relationship which requires the spouses to live together, as they can agree, wherever circumstances may prescribe, but would create impossible difficulties for those dealing with the property of a married man. It would mean that the concurrence of the wife would be necessary for all dealings.

In my judgment, where the vendor or mortgagor is himself in possession and occupation of the property, the purchaser or the mortgagee is not affected with notice of the equitable interests of any other person who may be resident there, and whose presence is wholly consistent with the title offered. If you buy with vacant possession on completion and you know, or find out, that the vendor is himself in possession and occupation of the property, you are, in my judgment, by reason of your failure to make further inquiries on the premises, no more fixed with notice of the equitable interest of the vendor's wife who is living there with him than you would be affected with notice of the equitable interest of any other person who might also be resident on the premises, eg the vendor's father, his 'Uncle Harry' or his 'Aunt Matilda', any of whom, be it observed, might have contributed towards the purchase of the property. The reason is that the vendor being in possession, the presence of his wife or guest or lodger implies nothing to negative the title offered. It is otherwise if the vendor is not in occupation and you find another party whose presence demands an explanation and whose presence you ignore at your peril.

I would add this: Mr Nourse, in his very clear argument, has called attention to the fact that this is a conveyancing question, and I accept the point he makes that in such a matter the practice of conveyancers carries great weight. I have never heard it suggested, and no textbook or judicial utterance has been cited which suggests, that where one finds a vendor and his wife living together on the property a prudent solicitor acting for the purchaser ought to inquire of the wife whether she claims an interest in the house. Mr Nourse also points out, by reference to remarks made by Russell LJ in the Court of Appeal, in the case to which I have already referred in the House of Lords, *National Provincial Bank Ltd v Hastings Car Mart Ltd* [1964] Ch 665 at 700 and to the speeches of Lord Upjohn ([1965] AC 1229) and Lord Wilberforce ([1965] AC 1241) in that case, how unworkable and undesirable it would be if the law required such an inquiry – an inquiry, let me add, which would be as embarrassing to the inquirer as it would, in my view, be intolerable to the wife and the husband. Mr Nourse, I think, put it well when, in commenting on the whole of the plaintiff's case, he said it is not in the public interest that bank mortgagees should be snoopers and busybodies in relation to wholly normal transactions of mortgage. I must make it clear – because much reliance was placed, on behalf of the plaintiff, on what was said by the majority of the Court of Appeal in the *Ainsworth* case, *The National Provincial Bank Ltd v Hastings Car Mart Ltd* [1964] Ch 665, regarding the duty of a purchaser to make inquiries on the premises where the wife is living alone in the matrimonial home after her husband has left her – that about such a situation I say nothing whatsoever. Here the wife was living with her husband.

The restrictive application of the doctrine of constructive notice in *Caunce v Caunce* was disapproved of by the House of Lords in *Williams & Glyn's Bank Ltd v Boland*[118] and was relaxed in *Kingsnorth Finance Co Ltd v Tizard*.[119] In the latter case, the legal estate in the matrimonial home, known as Willowdown, was held by the husband on an implied trust for sale for himself and his wife (which would be an implied trust of land today). The wife slept in the house only when the husband was away. The husband secretly charged the legal title to a finance company and then disappeared to America. Before any charge was created, the mortgagee's agent made a pre-arranged visit on a Sunday afternoon for inspection and valuation. The husband fixed the time purposely to coincide with the wife's absence from the home, and all signs of her occupation had been temporarily removed by the husband. The agent discovered evidence of occupation by two teenage children but was told by the husband that their mother had left the home some time ago and lived elsewhere. The husband described himself as single in his loan application form. The High Court held that the fact that the husband had originally described himself as being 'single' and the presence of the children should have alerted the mortgagee to the need to make further inquiry as to the possible rights of a wife. Failure to make further enquiry as to the wife's possible beneficial interest fixed the mortgagee with constructive notice of it.

118 [1981] AC 487.

119 [1986] 1 WLR 783. See [1987] CLJ 28 (McHugh, PG); [1986] Conv 283 (Thompson, MP).

Kingsnorth v Tizard [1986] 1 WLR 783

Judge John Finlay QC having examined the facts in considerable detail continued: In *Williams & Glyn's Bank Ltd v Boland* [1981] AC 487, in each case the matrimonial home was registered land, the husband was the registered proprietor, the spouses lived together in the matrimonial home, and the wife had an equitable interest by reason of having contributed a substantial sum to the purchase price. The House of Lords held that in each case the wife was a 'person in actual occupation' within s 70(1)(g) of the Land Registration Act 1925 so that her interest was protected. Although there the land was registered and here it is not, the decision illuminates the manner in which the presence of a wife in the matrimonial home is to be regarded. Lord Wilberforce said, at 505–06:

> Then, were the wives in actual occupation? I ask: why not? There was physical presence, with all the rights that occupiers have, including the right to exclude all others except those having similar rights. The house was a matrimonial home, intended to be occupied, and in fact occupied by both spouses, both of whom have an interest in it: it would require some special doctrine of law to avoid the result that each is in occupation. Three arguments were used for a contrary conclusion. First, it was said that if the vendor (I use this word to include a mortgagor) is in occupation, that is enough to prevent the application of the paragraph. This seems to be a proposition of general application, not limited to the case of husbands, and no doubt, if correct, would be very convenient for purchasers and intending mortgagees. But the presence of the vendor, with occupation, does not exclude the possibility of occupation of others. There are observations which suggest the contrary in the unregistered land case of *Caunce v Caunce* [1969] 1 WLR 286 but I agree with the disapproval of these, and with the assertion of the proposition I have just stated by Russell LJ in *Hodgson v Marks* [1971] Ch 892 at 934. Then it was suggested that the wife's occupation was nothing but the shadow of the husband's – a version I suppose of the doctrine of unity of husband and wife. This expression and the argument flowing from it was used by Templeman J in *Bird v Syme-Thomson* [1979] 1 WLR 440 at 444, a decision preceding and which he followed in the present case. The argument was also inherent in the judgment in *Caunce v Caunce* [1969] 1 WLR 286 which influenced the decisions of Templeman J. It somewhat faded from the arguments in the present case and appears to me to be heavily obsolete. The appellant's main and final position became in the end this: that, to come within the paragraph, the occupation in question must be apparently inconsistent with the title of the vendor. This, it was suggested, would exclude the wife of a husband-vendor because her apparent occupation would be satisfactorily accounted for by his. But, apart from the rewriting of the paragraph which this would involve, the suggestion is unacceptable. Consistency, or inconsistency, involves the absence, or presence, of an independent right to occupy, though I must observe that 'inconsistency' in this context is an inappropriate word. But how can either quality be predicated of a wife, simple *qua* wife? A wife may, and everyone knows this, have rights of her own; particularly, many wives have a share in a matrimonial home. How can it be said that the presence of a wife in the house, as occupier, is consistent or inconsistent with the husband's rights until one knows what rights she has? And if she has rights, why, just because she is a wife (or in the converse case, just because an occupier is the husband, should these rights be denied protection under the paragraph? If one looks beyond the case of husband and wife, the difficulty of all these arguments stands out if one considers the case of a man living with a mistress, or of a man and a woman – or for that matter two persons of the same sex – living in a house in separate or

> partially shared rooms. Are these cases of apparently consistent occupation, so that the rights of the other person (other than the vendor) can be disregarded? The only solution which is consistent with the Act (section 70(1)(g)) and with common sense is to read the paragraph for what it says. Occupation, existing as a fact, may protect rights if the person in occupation has rights. On this part of the case I have no difficulty in concluding that a spouse, living in a house, has an actual occupation capable of conferring protection, as an overriding interest, upon rights of that spouse.

Mrs Tizard was, in my judgment, in occupation of Willowdown notwithstanding that Mr Tizard was living there also; and notwithstanding the fact that on numerous occasions she slept elsewhere. The 'physical presence' to which Lord Wilberforce refers does not connote continuous and uninterrupted presence; such a notion would be absurd. Nor, indeed, do I consider that the requisite 'presence' is negatived by regular and repeated absence. I find that Mrs Tizard was in Willowdown virtually every day for some part of the day; that her life and activities were based on her presence, interrupted though it was, in Willowdown; there she prepared herself for work; there she cared for her children; there she looked after the house and the concerns of herself and the children; she went in the morning and returned in the evening to discharge her duties as housewife and mother. It is clear that prior to the time, November 1983, when she ceased always to sleep in the house when her husband was there, she had been in occupation; and, in my judgment, she did not cease to be in occupation simply because she made that change in her habits, significant though the change was.

Willowdown, however, is not registered land. If it were, my findings that Mrs Tizard had equitable rights in the house and was at the material time in occupation would protect those rights against the mortgagee by reason of s 70(1)(g) of the Land Registration Act 1925. Do these two matters bring about the like result where the land is not registered?

[His Lordship then went on to examine the dealing before the mortgage was granted to see if the mortgagee had to make sufficient searches, inquiries and inspections.]

The plaintiffs received Mr Tizard's application in which he described himself as single; and received Mr Marshall's report in which there was mention of a son and daughter. The application mentioned two 'children and other dependents' who were stated to be both aged 15. The application had a space in which there fell to be inserted 'Age of spouse next birthday'. It was left blank. It also contained spaces for insertion of the spouse's name, and the name and address of the spouse's employers: and in these spaces there appeared 'N/A', not applicable. The application left in doubt whether the two 15-year-old dependents were children or others, but Mr Marshall's report made it clear that they were son and daughter of the applicant. Had Mr Marshall's report indicated that Mr Tizard was married, it seems to me to be clear that bearing in mind that the application stated over Mr Tizard's signature that he was single, the plaintiffs would have been put on notice that further investigation was required. Indeed, even if I am wrong in my view that Mr Marshall should have reported what Mr Tizard said about his wife, the reference to 'son and daughter' in the report should have alerted the plaintiffs to the need to make further inquiries. Primarily, the plaintiffs are to be taken to have been aware that Mr Tizard was married and had described himself as single; and in these circumstances their further inquiries should have led them to Mrs Tizard.

[His Lordship then referred to s 199(1) of the Law of Property Act 1925 and continued.]

'Purchaser' in that provision, includes a mortgagee: see s 205(1) of the Act.

Although a spouse's statutory rights of occupation under s 1 of the Matrimonial Homes Act 1983, and the statutory provisions replaced by that Act are capable of protection by registration as a Class F land charge, by virtue of the Land Charges Act 1972, the equitable interest of such a spouse in the matrimonial home is not capable of being so protected. The plaintiffs were prejudicially affected by the knowledge of their agent, Mr Marshall, that Mr Tizard, contrary to what he had said in his application, was married: see s 199(1)(ii)(b). That put them on notice that further inquiries were necessary; the inquiries which in these circumstances ought reasonably to have been made by the plaintiffs would, in my judgment, have been such as to have apprised them of the fact that Mrs Tizard claimed a beneficial interest in the property; and accordingly, they would have had notice of such equitable rights as she had and the mortgage in these circumstances takes effect subject to these rights: see s 199(1)(ii)(a).

I arrive at that conclusion without having considered the question: does the occupation of Mrs Tizard affect the mortgagees with notice of her rights, or are they only so affected if, as Mr Wigmore submits, they are aware of her occupation, that is, if they find her in occupation?

On the balance of probabilities, I find that the reason Mr Marshall did not find Mrs Tizard in the house was that Mr Tizard had arranged matters to achieve that result. He told Mrs Tizard that on a particular Sunday, and I find in that it was the Sunday that Mr Marshall did inspect, he was going to entertain friends to lunch and would she take the children out for the day. She did; and having regard to the manner in which I find that the signs of her occupation were temporarily eliminated by Mr Tizard, the reasonable inference is that he made this request so that Mr Marshall could inspect and find no evidence of Mrs Tizard's occupation.

In *Caunce v Caunce* [1969] 1 WLR 286, Stamp J held that where a wife who had an equitable interest in a property being mortgaged to the bank by her husband was resident with him in the property, that circumstance did not result in the bank taking the property fixed with notice of her rights because, finding her in occupation, the bank made no inquiry of her. Stamp J said, at 293:

> Here it is said that the plaintiff was in possession or occupation. No inquiry was made of her and therefore the bank is fixed with notice of her equitable interest. In my judgment, it is here that the fallacy arises, for the plaintiff, unlike the deserted wife, was not in apparent occupation or possession. She was there, ostensibly, because she was the wife, and her presence was wholly consistent with the title offered by the husband to the bank.

In *Williams & Glyn's Bank Ltd v Boland* [1981] AC 487 at 505, Lord Wilberforce said in the passage I have already read: 'But the presence of the vendor, with occupation, does not exclude the possibility of occupation of others.' He went on to say there were observations suggesting the contrary in *Caunce v Caunce* [1969] 1 WLR 286 but he agreed with the disapproval of those and with the assertion expressed by Russell LJ in *Hodgson v Marks* [1971] Ch 892 at 934. Russell LJ there stated:

> I would only add that I do not consider it necessary to this decision to pronounce on the decision in *Caunce v Caunce* [1969] 1 WLR 286. In that case, the occupation of the wife may have been rightly taken to be not her occupation but that of her

husband. In so far, however, as some phrases in the judgment might appear to lay down a general proposition that inquiry need not be made of any person on the premises if the proposed vendor himself appears to be in occupation, I would not accept them.

I have already stated my finding that the wife was in occupation. In the circumstances in which she was, I find that her occupation was not that of her husband. Guided by the high authority of the two passages I have just cited, Lord Wilberforce in *Williams & Glyn's Bank Ltd v Boland* [1981] AC 487, 505, and Russell LJ in *Hodgson v Marks* [1971] Ch 892 at 934, I conclude that had Mrs Tizard been found to be in occupation by the plaintiffs or their agent and so found in the context of what had been said by Mr Tizard to Mr Marshall and stated or implied in the forms he had signed, they, the plaintiffs, would clearly either have learned of her rights by inquiry of her or been fixed with notice of those rights had not inquiry of her been made.

In the light of my finding that Mr Marshall's information about Mr Tizard's wife is to be imputed to the plaintiffs and my conclusion that further inquiries should have been made by the plaintiffs because of that imputed knowledge, do I ask myself whether such an inspection as would have disclosed that Mrs Tizard was in the premises is one which ought reasonably to have been made by them, or is the proper question: can the plaintiffs show that no such inspection was reasonably necessary? The latter appears to me to be the proper way to put it. The plaintiffs did not make any further inquiries or inspections; had they done so it would have been open to them to contend that they had done all that was reasonably required and if they still had no knowledge of Mrs Tizard's rights or claims, that they were not fixed with notice of them. But in the absence of further inquiries or inspections, I do not think that it is open to the plaintiffs to say that if they had made a further inspection they would still not have found Mrs Tizard in occupation.

I would put it briefly thus. Mr Tizard appears to have been minded to conceal the true facts; he did not do so completely; the plaintiffs had, or are to be taken to have had, information which should have alerted them to the fact that the full facts were not in their possession and that they should make further inspections or inquiries; they did not do so; and in these circumstances I find that they are fixed with notice of the equitable interest of Mrs Tizard.

I return to the submissions made by Mr Romer and Mr Wigmore. Mr Romer's submission is that as Mrs Tizard was in fact in occupation, that circumstance itself fixed the plaintiffs with notice of such rights as she had; to the contrary is the submission made by Mr Wigmore that, in the case of unregistered land, it is only where the purchaser or mortgagee finds the claimant to an equitable interest in occupation that he has notice.

I accept Mr Wigmore's submission but subject to a significant qualification: if the purchaser or mortgagee carries out such inspections 'as ought reasonably to be made' and does not either find the claimant in occupation or find evidence of that occupation reasonably sufficient to give notice of the occupation, then I am not persuaded that the purchaser or mortgagee is in such circumstances (and in the absence, which is not the case here, of other circumstances) fixed with notice of the claimant's rights. One of the circumstances, however, is that such inspection is made 'as ought reasonably to be made' ...

How then is a purchaser or mortgagee to carry out such inspection 'as ought reasonably to have been made' for the purpose of determining whether the possession and occupation of the property accords with the title offered? What is such an inspection 'as ought reasonably to be made' must, I think, depend on all the circumstances. In the circumstances of the present case I am not satisfied that the pre-arranged inspection on a Sunday afternoon fell within the category of 'such inspections which ought reasonably to have been made,' the words in s 199 of the Law of Property Act 1925 which I have already read. The plaintiffs not having established that they made such an inspection, the conclusion that I have reached by another route is, in my view, fortified. It follows that the plaintiffs' claim for possession fails.

In registered land, the beneficial interest will be protected as a minor interest automatically by the Registrar by an entry of a restriction unless the trustees own the beneficial interest as joint tenants in equity.[120] The beneficiary who is in actual occupation at the time of the transfer to the purchaser would, however, be able to claim overriding interest under s 70(1)(g).[121]

7 DISPOSITION OF CO-OWNED EQUITABLE INTERESTS

Each beneficial co-owner can dispose of his equitable interest. Such a disposition of an equitable interest must be in writing signed by the disposing co-owner.[122] Such a disposition does not pass the legal estate to the purchaser; only legal co-owners can dispose of the legal estate. As will be seen, if the disposing co-owner is an equitable joint tenant, his disposition *inter vivos* will take effect as a severance of the joint tenancy turning it into an equitable tenancy in common. He cannot, of course, dispose of his joint tenancy by will unless he severs the joint tenancy before he dies.

Any agreement for the disposition of a beneficial interest made before 27 September 1989 must satisfy s 40 of the Law of Property Act 1925,[123] and from 27 September 1989, s 2 of the Law of Property (Miscellaneous Provisions) Act 1989.

8 LIMITATIONS ON THE CO-OWNERS' RIGHTS OF OCCUPATION

At common law before 1926 each co-owner had always enjoyed concurrent rights of occupation.[124] The rights of occupation of beneficial tenants in common were wholly unaffected by the fact that since 1925 a tenancy in common can exist only in equity. Therefore, it was held in *Bull v Bull*[125] that all beneficial tenants in common 'have the same right to enjoy the land as legal

120 Section 58(3) of the LRA 1925.

121 *Williams & Glyn's Bank Ltd v Boland* [1981] AC 487; *Abbey National Building Society v Cann* [1990] 1 All ER 1085.

122 Section 53(1)(c) of the LPA 1925.

123 *Cooper v Critchley* [1955] Ch 431.

124 *Henderson v Eason* (1851) 17 QB 701 at 720.

125 [1955] 1 All ER 253.

tenants used to have and that pending sale each tenant in common is concurrently entitled with the other to possession of the land and to the use and enjoyment of it in a proper manner'.[126] This has been confirmed by the House of Lords in *Williams and Glyn's Bank Ltd v Boland*[127] and *City of London Building Society v Flegg*.[128] Today, under s 12 of the Trusts of Land and Appointment of Trustees Act, the beneficiaries have rights of occupation subject to certain conditions.

As already seen, as every co-owner has a right of occupation, no one can turn another out of the property or interfere with the common enjoyment of the land. In the case of co-owned *matrimonial home*, this may be subject to some statutory interventions.

Section 1 of the Matrimonial Homes Act 1983

Where a non-owner spouse has a statutory 'rights of occupation' against an owner-spouse under s 1(1) and (11) of the Matrimonial Homes Act 1983,[129] s 1(2) and (3) of the Act empowers the court to give an order to exclude the owner-spouse from the property having regard to the conduct of the spouses in relation to each other and otherwise to their respective needs and financial resources, to the needs of any children and to all the circumstances of the case.

Matrimonial Homes Act 1983

1. Rights concerning matrimonial home where one spouse has no estate, etc

(2) So long as one spouse has rights of occupation, either of the spouses may apply to the court for an order:

(a) declaring, enforcing, restricting or terminating those rights; or

(b) prohibiting, suspending or restricting the exercise by either spouse of the right to occupy the dwelling house; or

(c) requiring either spouse to permit the exercise by the other of that right.

(3) On an application for an order under this section, the court may make such order as it thinks just and reasonable having regard to the conduct of the spouses in relation to each other and otherwise, to their respective needs and financial resources, to the needs of any children, and to all the circumstances of the case, and, without prejudice to the generality of the foregoing provision:

(a) may except part of the dwelling house from a spouse's right of occupation (and in particular a part used wholly or mainly for or in connection with the trade, business or profession of the other spouse);

(b) may order a spouse occupying the dwelling house or any part thereof by virtue of this section to make periodical payments to the other in respect of the occupation;

126 [1955] 1 QB 234 at 238.

127 [1981] AC 487 at 507B–D, 510G, 511H.

128 [1987] 2 WLR 1266 at 1281E

129 For s 1(1), (11) of the Matrimonial Homes Act 1983, see Chapter 6, p 235.

(c) may impose on either spouse obligations as to the repaid and maintenance of the dwelling house or the discharge of any liabilities in respect of the dwelling house.

Where both spouses are legal owners, s 9 of the 1983 Act gives either of them a similar right to suspend or restrict the other spouse's right to occupy the matrimonial home.

Matrimonial Homes Act 1983

9. **Rights concerning matrimonial home where both spouses have estate, etc**

(1) Where each of two spouses is entitled, by virtue of a legal estate vested in them jointly, to occupy a dwelling house in which they have or at any time have had a matrimonial home, either of them may apply to the court, with respect to the exercise during the subsistence of the marriage of the right to occupy the dwelling house, for an order prohibiting, suspending or restricting its exercise by the other or requiring the other to permit its exercise by the applicant.

(2) In relation to orders under this section, s 1(3) ... above shall apply as [it applies] in relation to orders under that section.

The Act applies only to married couples but either spouse may be entitled to the order against the other.

Section 1 of the Domestic Violence and Matrimonial Proceedings Act 1976

Section 1 of the Domestic Violence and Matrimonial Proceedings Act 1976 also empowers the court to make an order excluding the violent spouse from the matrimonial home. A spouse who has been forced to leave the property by the violence of his or her partner may obtain an order for re-entry to the premises together with an ouster injunction requiring the violent partner to leave.[130] This Act applies to married couples as well as unmarried cohabitees.[131]

9 SEVERANCE OF BENEFICIAL JOINT TENANCY

Severance is the process of separating off the share of a joint tenant, so that the concurrent ownership will continue but the right of survivorship will no longer apply. The parties will then hold separate shares as tenants in common.[132]

> Whenever or by whatever means the joint tenancy ceases or is severed, the right of survivorship or jus accrescendi instantly ceases with it. Yet, if one of three joint tenants aliens his share, the two remaining tenants still hold their parts by joint tenancy and survivorship. And if one of three joint tenants releases his share to one of his companions, though the joint tenancy is destroyed with regard to that

130 Section 1(1)(c), (d) of the Domestic Violence and Matrimonial Proceedings Act 1976.

131 *Ibid*, s 1(2).

132 *Harris v Goddard* [1983] 1 WLR 1203 at 1210E, *per* Dillon LJ.

part, yet the two remaining parts are still held in joint tenancy for they still preserves their original constituent unities.[133]

Severance has to take place during the joint tenant's lifetime. There can be no unilateral severance by will except in the case of severance by mutual will.

> [A] devise of one's share by will is no severance of the jointure; for no testament takes effect till after the death of the testator, and by such death the right of the survivor (which accrued at the original creation of the estate, and has therefore a priority to the other) is already vested.[134]

As mentioned, although no legal joint tenancy can be severed today[135] a beneficial joint tenancy can still be severed. The Law Commission has briefly considered three options for reform of severance,[136] and emphasised the need for reform.[137] The opportunity for legislative reform has not been taken up by the recent passage of the Trusts of Land and Appointment of Trustees Act 1996.

Mode of severance

Section 36(2) of the Law of Property Act 1925 provides that:

> No severance of a joint tenancy of a legal estate, so as to create a tenancy in common in land, shall be permissible, whether by operation of law or otherwise, but this subsection does not affect the right of a joint tenant to release his interest to the other joint tenants, or the right to sever a joint tenancy in an equitable interest whether or not the legal estate is vested in the joint tenants:
>
> Provided that, where a legal estate (not being settled land) is vested in joint tenants beneficially, and any tenant desires to sever the joint tenancy in equity, he shall give to the other joint tenants a notice in writing of such desire or do such other acts or things as would, in the case of personal estate, have been effectual to sever the tenancy in equity, and thereupon the land shall be held in trust on terms which would have been requisite for giving effect to the beneficial interests if there had been an actual severance.

(a) Williams v Hensman methods of severance

Prior to 1926, there were three categories of circumstances which could result in severance. These methods of severance have after 1925 been recognised by s 36(2) of the Law of Property Act which provides that severance can be affected in equity if a joint tenant does such other acts or things as would in the case of personal estate have been effectual to sever the tenancy in equity before 1926. The three methods identified by Page Wood VC in *Williams v Hensman*[138] are as follows:

> A joint tenancy may be severed in three ways: in the first place, an act of any one of the persons interested operating upon his own share may create a severance as

133 Bl Comm, 186.

134 Bl Comm, 185–6.

135 Section 36(2) of the LPA 1925.

136 Law Com Working Paper on Trust of Land (No 94, 1985), paras 16.11–16.14. For discussion of the three options see [1995] Conv 105 (Louise Tee).

137 Transfer of Land: Trusts of Law, Law Com No 181, 8 June 1989, para 1.3.

138 (1861) 1 John & H 546 at 557.

> to that share ... Secondly, a joint tenancy may be severed by mutual agreement. And, in the third place, there may be a severance by any course of dealing sufficient to intimate that the interests of all were mutually treated as constituting a tenancy in common. When the severance depends on an inference of this kind without any express act of severance, it will not suffice to rely on an intention, with respect to the particular share, declared only behind the backs of the other persons interested. You must find in this class of cases a course of dealing by which the shares of all the parties to the contest have been effected, as happened in the cases of *Wilson v Bell* (1843) 5 Ir Eq R 501 and *Jackson v Jackson* (1804) 9 Ves Jun 591.

(i) An act operating upon a joint tenant's share

A severance could be by an act of any one joint tenant operating upon his own share.[139] The act must have a final or irrevocable character which effectively estops the severing joint tenant from claiming the benefit of survivorship in the future.[140] Such an act normally takes the form of alienation of a joint tenant's share. An alienation would destroy the unity of title: 'for the grantee and the remaining joint tenant hold by different titles, (one derived from the original, the other from the subsequent grantor) though, till partition made, the unity of possession continues'.[141] The logical difficulty is that, by definition, a joint tenant does not own a 'share' in the joint tenancy of which he could dispose. Nevertheless, it has been regarded as an effective way of severing a joint tenancy.[142]

Where there is no outright transfer of 'share' but only a specifically enforceable contract to transfer, such a contract will operate in equity to transfer a joint tenant's share to the alienee under the doctrine of *Walsh v Lonsdale* and effectively sever the joint tenancy.[143]

Alienation may also be involuntary where the bankruptcy of one joint tenant will cause an immediate and involuntary assignment of the bankrupt's 'share' in favour of his trustee in bankruptcy.[144] Where the bankruptcy was governed by the Bankruptcy Act 1914, under the doctrine of relation back, the severance took effect, if the debtor was adjudicated bankrupt, restrospectively on the date of the first available act of bankruptcy. Thus, the act of bankruptcy operated to sever the joint tenancy with immediate effect.[145] This was so whether both joint tenants were still alive,[146] or whether the solvent joint tenant had died in the

139 *Ibid* at 557.

140 *Re Wilks* [1891] 3 Ch 59 at 61.

141 Bl Comm, 185.

142 Bl Comm, 185; *Bedson v Bedson* [1965] 2 QB 666 at 689D.

143 *Brown v Raindle* (1796) 3 Ves 256; *Goddard v Lewis* (1909) 101 LT 528; *Burgess v Rawnsley* [1975] Ch 429.

144 *Morgan v Marquis* (1853) 9 Exch 145.

145 *Re Dennis (A Bankrupt)* [1995] 2 FLR 387.

146 *Morgan v Marquis* (1853) 9 Exch 145.

interim,[147] or whether it was the debtor who had died.[148] Where, however, the bankruptcy takes place after the Insolvency Act 1986, the insolvency administration order does not take effect retrospectively so that if the debtor who is a joint tenant dies before the order is made, the right of survivorship will operate to pass his estate to the survivors.[149]

A mere declaration of intention to sever, whether communicated or not, is ineffective to cause a severance because a unilateral declaration is not operating upon his own share[150] unless the declaration is incorporated in a written notice under s 36(2) of the Law of Property Act, or it is made by deed,[151] or it is made in an application for a loan secured on co-owned property.[152] A litigation started by a joint tenant concerning a joint tenancy may also constitute an act operating upon the share of the litigated joint tenant.[153]

Where a joint tenant forges his co-tenant's signature to obtain a mortgage over the co-owned land, the forgery will operate to sever the joint tenancy.[154] Where the purchaser or mortgagee has colluded in the forgery, the beneficial joint tenancy will not be affected, the transaction being a nullity and a sham.[155]

(ii) Mutual agreement

The second method of severance referred to in *Williams v Hensman* is severance by 'mutual agreement' on the part of all the joint tenants. This form of severance is flexible. It need not take the form of a specifically enforceable contract.[156] Thus no evidence in writing of such an agreement was needed.[157] The agreement has the effect of severance even if it forms part of a consent order for ancillary relief which is yet to be approved by the court in divorce proceedings.[158]

It seems that this type of severance is not affected by s 2 of the Law of Property (Miscellaneous Provisions) Act 1989 because although an oral agreement is not a contract under s 2, it indicates a common intention to sever a joint tenancy. The significance of the agreement is 'not that it binds the parties; but that it serves as an indication of a common intention to sever'.[159]

---

147 *Smith v Stokes* (1801) 1 East 363, 102 ER 141.

148 *Re Palmer deceased (A Debtor)* [1994] 3 WLR 420.

149 *Re Palmer deceased (A Debtor)* [1994] 3 WLR 420.

150 *Davies v Davies* [1983] WAR 305 at 307.

151 *Re Sammon* (1979) 94 DLR (3d) 594 at 597ff; *Manton v Pavabelic* [1985] 2 NSWLR 361 at 369B–C.

152 *First National Securities v Hegerty* [1985] QB 850 at 854B, 862G–H.

153 *Re Draper's Conveyance* [1969] 1 Ch 486 at 492C.

154 *First National Securities v Hegerty* [1985] QB 850; *Ahmed v Kendrick and Ahmed* [1988] 2 FLR 22.

155 *Penn v Bristol and West Building Society* [1995] 2 FLR 938.

156 *Burgess v Rawnsley* [1975] Ch 429 at 444B–C.

157 *Wilson v Bell* (1843) 5 Ir Eq R 501 at 507.

158 *Hunter v Babbage* [1994] 2 FLR 806.

159 *Burgess v Rawnsley* [1975] Ch 429 at 444A, 446C; *Wilson v Bell* (1843) 5 Ir Eq R 501 at 507.

In *Burgess v Rawnsley*[160] an agreement made between the joint tenants for one to buy out the other's share was held sufficient to sever the joint tenancy even though the agreement was not in writing and was not specifically enforceable. The facts are interestingly summarised by Lord Denning in his judgment as follows:

> In 1966 there was a scripture rally in Trafalgar Square. A widower, Mr Honick, went to it. He was about 63. A widow, Mrs Rawnsley, the defendant, also went. She was about 60. He went up to her and introduced himself. He was not much to look at. 'He looked like a tramp,' she said. 'He had been picking up fag-ends.' They got on well enough, however, to exchange addresses. His was 36 Queen's Road, Waltham Cross, Hertfordshire. Hers was 74 Downton Avenue, Streatham Hill, London SW2. Next day he went to her house with a gift for her. It was a rose wrapped in a newspaper. Afterwards their friendship grew apace. She was sorry for him, she said. She smartened him up with better clothes. She had him to meals. She went to his house: he went to hers. They wrote to one another in terms of endearment. We were not shown the letters, but counsel described them as love letters.
>
> A few months later Mr Honick had the opportunity of buying the house where he lived at 36 Queen's Road, Waltham Cross. He had been the tenant of it for some years, but his wife had died and his married daughter had left; so that he was alone there. He talked it over with Mrs Rawnsley. He told her that the owner was willing to sell the house to him for £800. Mrs Rawnsley said she would go half shares: she would have the upper flat and he the lower flat.

In short, they bought the house as joint tenants, each providing half the purchase price. Later, their relation broke down. Mrs Rawnsley orally agreed to sell her share for £750 but later changed her mind. She demanded a higher price but Mr Honick died before negotiations could proceed further. The question was whether there had been a severance of the joint tenancy.

Burgess v Raunsley [1975] Ch 429, CA

Lord Denning MR: Was there a severance of the beneficial joint tenancy? The judge said:

> I hold that there has been a severance of the joint tenancy brought about by the conduct of the defendant in asking £750 for her share which was agreed to.

In making that statement the judge made a little slip. She did not ask £750. But it was a slip of no importance. The important finding is that there was an agreement that she would sell her share to him for £750. Almost immediately afterwards she went back upon it. Is that conduct sufficient to effect a severance?

Mr Levy submitted that it was not. He relied on the recent decision of Walton J in *Neilson-Jones v Fedden* [1975] Ch 222, given subsequently to the judgement of the judge here. Walton J held that no conduct is sufficient to sever a joint tenancy unless it is irrevocable. Mr Levy said that in the present case the agreement was not in writing. It could not be enforced by specific performance. It was revocable and was in fact revoked by Mrs Rawnsley when she went back on it. So there was, he submitted, no severance.

Walton J founded himself on the decision of Stirling J in *In Re Wilks Child v Bulmer* [1891] 3 Ch 59. He criticised *Hawkesley v May* [1956] 1 QB 304 and *In Re Draper's Conveyance* [1969] 1 Ch 486 and said that they were clearly contrary to the existing

160 [1975] Ch 429.

well-established law. He went back to *Coke upon Littleton*, 189a, 299b and to *Blackstone's Commentaries*. Those old writers were dealing with legal joint tenancies. *Blackstone* said, 8th edn, 1778, vol II, pp 180, 185:

> The properties of a joint estate are derived from its unity, which is fourfold; the unity of interest, the unity of title, the unity of time, and the unite of possession: ... an estate in joint tenancy may be severed and destroyed ... by destroying any of its constituent unities.

and he gives instances of how this may be done. Now that is all very well when you are considering how a legal joint tenancy can be severed. But it is of no application today when there can be no severance of a legal joint tenancy; and you are only considering how a beneficial joint tenancy can be severed. The thing to remember today is that equity leans against joint tenants and favours tenancies in common.

Nowadays everyone starts with the judgment of Sir William Page Wood VC in *Williams v Hensman* (1861) 1 John & Hem. 546, 557...

[His Lordship read Page Wood VC's statement cited at 720 above.]

In that passage, Page Wood VC distinguished between severance 'by mutual agreement' and severance by a 'course of dealing'. That shows that a 'course of dealing' need not amount to an agreement, expressed or implied, for severance. It is sufficient if there is a course of dealing in which one party makes clear to the other that he desires that their shares should no longer be held jointly but be held in common. I emphasise that it must be made clear to the other party. That is implicit in the sentence in which Page Wood VC says:

> ... it will not suffice to rely on an intention, with respect to the particular share, declared only behind the backs of the other persons interested.

Similarly, it is sufficient if both parties enter on a course of dealing which evinces an intention by both of them that their shares shall henceforth be held in common and not jointly. As appears from the two cases to which Page Wood VC referred of *Wilson v Bell*, 5 Ir Eq R 501 and *Jackson v Jackson*, 9 Ves Jun 591.

I come now to the question of notice. Suppose that one party gives a notice in writing to the other saying that he desires to sever the joint tenancy. Is that sufficient to effect a severance? I think it is. It was certainly the view of Sir Benjamin Cherry when he drafted s 36(2) of the Law of Property Act 1925 [now amended].

[His Lordship read s 36(2) of the Law of Property Act 1925 and continued.]

The word 'other' is most illuminating. It shows quite plainly that, in the case of personal estate one of the things which is effective in equity to sever a joint tenancy is 'a notice in writing' of a desire to sever. So also in regard to real estate.

Taking this view, I find myself in agreement with Havers J in *Hawkesley v May* [1956] 1 QB 304, 313–14, and of Plowman J in *In Re Draper's Conveyance* [1969] 1 Ch 486. I cannot agree with Walton J [1975] Ch 222 at 234–35, that those cases were wrongly decided. It would be absurd that there should be a difference between real estate and personal estate in this respect. Suppose real estate is held on a joint tenancy on a trust for sale and is sold and converted into personal property. Before sale, it is severable by notice in writing. It would be ridiculous if it could not be severed afterwards in like manner. I look upon s 36(2) as declaratory of the law as to severance by notice and not as a new provision confined to real estate. A joint tenancy in personal estate can be severed by notice just as a joint tenancy in real estate.

It remains to consider *Nielson-Jones v Fedden* [1975] Ch 222. In my view it was not correctly decided. The husband and wife entered upon a course of dealing sufficient to sever the joint tenancy. They entered into negotiations that the property should be sold. Each received £200 out of the deposit paid by the purchaser. That was sufficient. Furthermore there was disclosed in correspondence a declaration by the husband that he wished to sever the joint tenancy; and this was made clear by the wife. That too was sufficient.

I doubt whether in *In Re Wilks, Child v Bulmer* [1891] 3 Ch 59 can be supported. A young man who had just become 21 applied to the court to have one third of a joint fund paid out to him. He died just before the application was heard. Stirling J held that, if he had died just after, there would have been a severance: but, as he died just before, there was not. Ironically enough too, the delay was not on his side. It was the delay of the court. Nowadays, I think it should have been decided differently. The application was a clear declaration of his intention to sever. It was made clear to all concerned. There was enough to effect a severance.

It remains to apply these principles to the present case. I think there was evidence that Mr Honick and Mrs Rawnsley did come to an agreement that he would buy her share for £750. That agreement was not in writing and it was not specifically enforceable. Yet it was sufficient to effect a severance. Even if there was not any firm agreement but only a course of dealing, it clearly evinced an intention by both parties that the property should henceforth be held in common and not jointly.

On these grounds I would dismiss the appeal ...

Browne LJ: Mr Levy conceded, as is clearly right, that if there had been an enforceable agreement by Mrs Rawnsley to sell her share to Mr Honick, that would produce a severance of the joint tenancy; but he says that an oral agreement, unenforceable because of s 40 of the Law of Property Act 1925, is not enough. Section 40 merely makes a contract for the disposition of an interest in land unenforceable by action in the absence of writing. It does not make it void. But here the plaintiff is not seeking to enforce by action the agreement by Mrs Rawnsley to sell her share to Mr Honick. She relies upon it as effecting the severance in equity of the joint tenancy. An agreement to sever can be inferred from a course of dealing (see Lefroy B in *Wilson v Bell* (1843) 5 Ir Eq R 501 at 507 and Stirling J in *In Re Wilks, Child v Bulmer* [1891] 3 Ch 59) and there would in such a case *ex hypothesi* be no express agreement but only an inferred, tacit agreement, in respect of which there would seldom if ever be writing sufficient to satisfy s 40. It seems to me that the point is that the agreement establishes that the parties no longer intend the tenancy to operate as a joint tenancy and that automatically effects a severance. I think the reference in Megarry and Wade, *The Law of Real Property*, 3rd edn, 1966, pp 418, 419 to specifically enforceable contracts only applies where the suggestion is that the joint tenancy has been severed by an alienation by one joint tenant to a third party, and does not apply to severance by agreement between the joint tenants ...

The result is that I would uphold the county court judge's judgment on his second ground, namely, that the joint tenancy was severed by an agreement between Mrs Rawnsley and Mr Honick that she would sell her share to him for £750. In my view, her subsequent repudiation of that agreement makes no difference. I would dismiss the appeal on this ground.

I doubt whether there was enough evidence in this particular case as to a course of dealing to raise the question of the application of Page Wood VC's third category, 1 John

& Hem 546 at 557. I therefore prefer not to express any final opinion on these points. Lord Denning MR has dealt with them in his judgment and I have the advantage of knowing what Sir John Pennycuick is going to say about that aspect of the case ...

Sir John Pennycuick: I do not doubt myself that where one tenant negotiates with another for some rearrangement of interest, it may be possible to infer from the particular facts a common intention to sever even though the negotiations break down. Whether such an inference can be drawn must I think depend upon the particular facts. In the present case the negotiations between Mr Honick and Mrs Rawnsley, if they can be properly described as negotiations at all, fall, it seems to me, far short of warranting an inference. One could not ascribe to joint tenants an intention to sever merely because one offers to buy out the other for £X and then the other makes a counter-offer of £Y.

However, it seems that 'agreement in principle' which is subject to subsequent changes in the light of later developments will not be sufficient to effect a severance. In *Gore and Snell v Carpenter*,[161] Mr and Mrs Carpenter bought two houses as beneficial joint tenants. Later, relations broke down. Mr Carpenter proposed that one of the houses be transferred to his name and the other to hers. She agreed in principle but there were ancillary financial matters to be solved before a final agreement could be reached. Divorce proceedings were then started. Mr Carpenter took his own life. It was held that although the main points were agreed in principle, there was no mutual agreement so as to sever the joint tenancy because the parties each reserved their rights pending divorce proceedings.

Gore and Snell v Carpenter (1990) 60 P & CR 456

Judge Blackett-Ord: Mr and Mrs Carpenter were married in 1971. I think they were both teachers. In 1973 they bought 291 Sturry Road ('291') as their matrimonial home, with the help of a mortgage, and in 1975 they bought 8 Sundridge Close ('8'), also with a mortgage. They moved there and 291 was let and remained so until 1985. In 1974 Mr Carpenter met Mrs Snell and in 1976 they started an affair which, according to her evidence, continued up to his death. Gillian, the child of the marriage, was born in 1977. In 1978 it seems that Mrs Carpenter found out or suspected the affair. Mr Carpenter, whilst admitting friendship, denied that there was anything more. Although the marriage of Mr and Mrs Carpenter was not happy they decided to stay together for the time being for the sake of Gillian and I was told that Mr and Mrs Snell reached the same decision for the sake of their children. On 21 September 1985, the Carpenters' wedding anniversary, Mrs Carpenter's evidence was that she had a frightful row with her husband and she asked him to go, to leave the house, and he refused. But about a fortnight later he instructed his solicitor to draft a separation agreement, which is document 10 in the first bundle, and which provides in clause 3:

> The husband and wife hereby sever their joint tenancy of a property 8 Sundridge Road, Canterbury, Kent, so as to convert such tenancy into a tenancy in common in equal shares.

There is a conflict of evidence as to how this document came to be prepared. Mr Gore and, I think, also Mrs Snell said that they were told by Mr Carpenter that he had discussed its prospective terms with Mrs Carpenter and she had agreed them. And Mr

161 (1990) 60 P & CR 456.

Gore, in October, was being asked to give legal shape to an existing agreement between the parties. Mrs Carpenter flatly contradicts this and says that she was never consulted, but that her husband produced the document to her one day and told her that she had to sign it within a time limit, otherwise 'there would be trouble'. I accept her evidence on this point. I think that Mr Carpenter, as perhaps his subsequent history shows, was of an unstable nature. The conduct which she describes would seem to be in character and I believe what she says. The atmosphere in the home was clearly unhappy. In November, 1985, No 291 became vacant – the tenant left – and Mrs Carpenter took the opportunity of moving there with Gillian. It was on the other side, apparently, of Canterbury to No 8 and so provided a refuge some way from her husband.

Soon after this, proceedings in the magistrates' court in respect of the custody of Gillian came to a hearing and it was agreed by consent that there should be an order for joint custody. Mrs Carpenter said that she was anxious to press on and obtain a divorce, but Mr Carpenter would not agree. He was left alone in No 8. He made two or possibly three suicide attempts in the next few months and on 10 June 1986, Mrs Snell said that as a result of his pressure she moved into No 8 with him.

In July, 1986, Mr and Mrs Carpenter seem to have realised that divorce was the only course. There is in the file letter 29 from Mr Gore to Mrs Carpenter's solicitors:

> Dear Sirs, you act for Mrs Jean Carpenter and we have again been instructed by her husband, Mr David George Carpenter. We understand that our clients have recently been discussing the marriage and it has now been agreed by both of them that it has irretrievably broken down. Our client has instructed us to offer evidence of his adultery since 10th June, 1986, on a number of occasions with a person whom he does not wish to name. Your client could then divorce ours on an undefended basis, subject to the following terms of settlement being recorded in an order for ancillary relief. We understand that such terms have already been agreed between our respective clients.
>
> (1) Our client is to pay yours £4,000 and consent to the transfer of 291 Sturry Road into your client's sole name, after which she will be solely responsible for the mortgage.
>
> (2) Your client is to consent to the transfer of 8 Sundridge Road into our client's sole name, or as he shall direct and thereafter our client will be solely responsible for the mortgage on that property. We should mention that the mortgagees have consented to the proposed transfer and have indicated their agreement to increasing the existing mortgage so that our client can pay the above-mentioned £4,000.
>
> (3) Each party is to bear their own costs.
>
> (4) There has been an agreed order for joint custody of Gillian.
>
> We would be glad if you would kindly obtain your client's instructions and we await hearing from you.

There is a paragraph about the deeds, which I need not read:

> Finally we should mention that we understand the agreement between our respective clients is on the basis of a 'clean break' so that the eventual order for ancillary relief will include the usual clause that your client foregoes all claim for ancillary relief past present and future for herself, including claims in respect of capital property on our client's estate in the event of his death.
>
> Yours faithfully

A few days later on 29 July, Mr Carpenter made a will, leaving his whole estate to Mrs Snell and thereafter he provided evidence which could form the basis of Mrs Carpenter's divorce petition. In August he took steps to put No 8 on the market and he and Mrs Snell considered the purchase of another property.

By a letter of August 14 Mrs Carpenter's solicitors replied to Mr Gore's letter of 14 July:

> Dear Sirs, Carpenter and Carpenter. Thank you for your letters of 24 July, upon which we have now obtained our client's instructions.

(There was a second letter which was all about somebody being bitten by a dog and I can omit that.)

> With regard to the paragraphs which are numbered 1 to 4 in your letter [that is the one I read] we confirm our client's agreement to these in principle, though there are matters relating to the possibility of capital gains tax arising in respect of 291 Sturry Road, which will need to be settled before final agreement can be reached. Having spoken to your Mr Gore by telephone we understand that some of the urgency has gone from your client's position, which will enable ancillary matters to be settled during the course of the divorce proceedings. In the meantime, we look forward to receiving your client's confession statement in due course.

This rather slow reaction on the part of Mrs Carpenter was not satisfactory to her husband, who was seeking to raise a further mortgage not of £4,000 but of £6,000, and it seems that his reaction was to take No 8 off the market and stop looking for any other property. Mrs Carpenter was unhappy, she said, for various reasons: first, the question of capital gains mentioned in the letter; secondly she said that she wanted proper valuations of the properties, because No 291 was seriously out of repair. And, thirdly, she was concerned about the liability for tax on the rent which had been received for 291 whilst it was let and which she thought – rightly or wrongly I know not – had not been properly declared by her husband for tax purposes.

So, in my judgment, there was no agreement at that stage, although the parties were near it and the main points were agreed in principle.

Mr Brilliant, alleging an agreement, relies on letters 96 and 103 in the bundle, the first being from Mrs Carpenter's solicitors, Robinson & Allfree of 17 October saying:

> We confirm that we are now filing our client's petition on the basis of your client's confessions statement and there will be no application for costs. So far as the property transfers are concerned, we understand that our client will agree in principle to the transfers as suggested, on the basis that your client will be equally liable for any capital gains tax in relation to 291 Sturry Road. Bearing in mind that our client will be relying upon your client to comply with the agreement at some date in the future, we should appreciate your proposal as to how this should be effected to give our client adequate indemnity in the absence of a court order.

So there Messrs Robinson & Allfree are going half a step further. The liability for capital gains tax, if any, was agreed, but they were talking about an indemnity to protect Mrs Carpenter if the claim against Mr Carpenter became important. And letter 103 is a reply to that from Mr Gore:

> Thank you for your letter of the 17th. We formally confirm that should capital gains tax be payable on the sale of 291 Sturry Road by your client, our client fully accept his liability for one half thereof.

Then they go on to say that there should not be any capital gains tax liability. Then they say:

> So far as making provision now for any future liability is concerned, our client is not prepared to do this and indeed if he were to make such provision then it would be logical that your client should also make a similar provision. The effect of this would be to tie up quite substantial sums of money, to which neither of our clients would have access until such time, if any, that your client decides to sell the property. We should be glad to hear further from you in due course and to receive the divorce petition.

So there was still no concluded agreement and at this time Mr Gore was advising his client to serve severance notices in respect of the two properties which were held in joint tenancy so that the point at least would be cleared up and each party would be entitled to a half share. But Mr Carpenter refused to serve any such notices, because he thought it would be construed by his wife as a hostile act.

On 10 December 1986, the divorce papers were served. They are, I think, 126 and 127 in the bundle and are largely in a printed form. Under paragraph 4 of the relief sought Mrs Carpenter asks that 'she may be granted the following ancillary relief' and then there is just a list of various sorts of relief – order for maintenance pending suit; a periodical payments order; a secure periodical payments order; a lump sum order; a periodical payments order for the children, and so on – which might be ordered or agreed between the parties.

On 4 January 1987, Mr Carpenter took his own life. The question is what was the ownership of the properties after his death? Were they still held in joint tenancy, in which case, of course, Mrs Carpenter is the owner of them. Or, had there been some severance of the joint tenancy so that the parties were each entitled to each property in equal shares and the estate of Mr Carpenter would be entitled to half of each?

[His Lordship read s 36(2) of the Law of Property Act 1925 (now amended) and continued.]

That is considered to be a rather long-winded way of saying that a joint tenancy can now also be severed by a service of a written notice by one joint tenant on the other or others, expressing an intention to sever the tenancy in equity. And it has been pointed out that that has to be borne in mind when considering the cases decided on this subject prior to 1925.

Going through those possible methods of severance and trying to apply the facts to the present case, first there is the method of a joint tenant dealing with his own share and I think it is right that that means dealing with his own share to a third party as against releasing it to the other tenant in common. There is no suggestion that Mr Carpenter did deal with his share in that way. Any thoughts he may have had of doing it clearly came to nothing. Then there is mutual agreement between the parties. The correspondence does not, in my judgment, show any such mutual agreement. It is suggested that there was an agreement between Mr and Mrs Carpenter before he produced his draft separation agreement in 1985. But I have said that I believe Mrs Carpenter's evidence as to the events leading up to the production of that agreement. There was not, in my judgment, any mutual agreement. Afterwards, when the discussion ranged more over the proposal that each party should take one house and that there should be a financial settlement, again there was no agreement reached. They were very near it – it was an agreement in principle – but I think each party reserved their rights and when the divorce proceedings had come on, if they had come on, it would have been open to them to have argued for some other provision.

Then, was there a course of dealing? There were negotiations, as I have said, but negotiations are not the same thing as a course of dealing. A course of dealing is where over the years the parties have dealt with their interests in the property on the footing that they are interests in common and are not joint. As, for instance, in the case of *Wilson v Bell*, which was referred to by Vice Chancellor Page-Wood. But in the present case there were simply negotiations between the husband and the wife and again there was no finality and there was no mutuality. For severance to be effected by a course of dealing all the joint tenants must be concerned in such a course and in the present case there is no evidence that Mrs Carpenter was committing herself to accepting a tenancy in common prior to the property division which would have been made in the divorce proceedings. Amongst the recent authorities (I am not going to refer to all of them) is *Burgess v Rawnsley* and I was pressed with the dictum of Sir John Pennycuick.[162]

> I do not doubt myself that where one tenant negotiates with another for some rearrangement of interests, it may be possible to infer from the particular facts of a common intention to sever, even though the negotiations break down. Whether such an inference can be drawn must, I think, depend upon the particular facts.

In the present case there was, of course, such negotiation, but I cannot infer from it a common intention to sever, because I do not think that Mrs Carpenter was prepared to commit herself at that stage. As Sir John Pennycuick said:[163]

> 'An uncommunicated declaration by one party to the other, or indeed a mere verbal notice by one party to the other clearly cannot operate as a severance.'

I appreciate that as he also said in the next paragraph:

> 'The policy of the law as it stands today, having regard particularly to s 36(2) [now amended], is to facilitate severance at the instance of either party and I do not think the court should be over zealous in drawing a fine distinction from the pre-1925 authorities.'

It is, in my judgment, a question of intention and this applies also when it is a question of the fourth possible method of severance, namely the service of a notice under s 36(2) of the Law of Property Act. It is argued for the executors that the proposed separation agreement put forward by Mr Carpenter amounted to such a notice. It will be recalled that the paragraph I read expressly refers to severance, but that was only part of the deed and the deed was never accepted. It was put forward by Mr Carpenter, not in isolation but as part of the package of proposals, and was not intended in my judgment and therefore did not take effect as a notice under s 36(2). Later, as I have said, Mr Gore was advising Mr Carpenter to serve a notice or notices under the Act and Mr Carpenter refused to do so. I think that there is nothing in the correspondence which can fairly be called a notice of severance. The result is, in my judgment, that the joint tenancies were not severed and the properties, No 8 and No 291, do not form part of the estate of Mr Carpenter, but vest in Mrs Carpenter by survivorship.

An agreement to join in a sale or lease of the co-owned property to a third party or an agreement to split the income derived from a letting of the co-owned

162 [1975] Ch 429 at 447; 30 P & C R 221 at 34.

163 *Ibid* at 448; 235.

property is not enough because it does not exclude the possibility of survivorship in respect of the freehold reversion.[164] But an agreement that the proceeds of sale should be divided equally or unequally would effect a severance as survivorship is now excluded.[165]

(iii) Mutual course of dealings (mutual conduct)

Mutual course of dealings of the joint tenants which are sufficiently clear to indicate that their interests are mutually treated as constituting a tenancy in common can amount to an effective severance.

What amounts to sufficient mutual course of dealings for the purpose of severance? It is a question of construction depending on the facts of each case. Where the joint tenants have acted over a long period of time on the assumption that each owns a distinct share, this may be sufficient.[166]

Where the joint tenants concurrently execute mutual wills leaving their respective share to the survivor for life with remainder to some designated third party, the mutual wills would prevent the operation of right of survivorship and could amount to severance.[167]

A mere physical division of the co-owned property without partition or sale, for reasons of convenience only, would not be enough to amount to severance. In *Greenfield v Greenfield*[168] the mere fact that the two joint tenants occupied separate parts of the house was not sufficient to sever the joint tenancy.

Inconclusive negotiation between joint tenants concerning their respective shares which does not amount to severance under the head of mutual agreement was thought by Lord Denning in *Burgess v Rawnsley* as effective severance by mutual course of dealing.[169] The majority of the Court of Appeal, however, did not agree with him.[170]

In *Gore & Snell v Carpenter*,[171] it was accepted that it was possible to have a course of dealing even where negotiation had broken down.[172] However, on the facts, the judge found no evidence that Mrs Carpenter had committed herself to a tenancy in common prior to the property division in the divorce proceedings (see judgment cited above).

164 *Flannigan v Wotherspoon* [1953] 1 DLR 768 at 775.

165 *Ibid*, at 776.

166 *Wilson v Bell* (1843) 5 Ir Eq R 501 at 507; *Re Denny* (1947) 116 LJR 1029 at 1037; *Gore and Snell v Carpenter* (1990) 60 P & CR 456 at 462.

167 *Re Wilford's Estate* (1879) 11 Ch D 267 at 269.

168 (1979) 38 P & CR 570 at 578.

169 [1975] Ch 429 at 439C.

170 *Ibid*, at 444E, 447B.

171 (1990) P & CR 456.

172 *Ibid*, at 462.

Filing of divorce petition and discussions with solicitor on divorce proceedings and sale of matrimonial home are not sufficient course of conduct to indicate an intention to sever.[173]

(b) Statutory method

Apart from the *Williams v Hensman* modes of severance, s 36(2) of the Law of Property Act 1925 also provides a statutory method of severance. It allows a joint tenant to sever his joint tenancy by giving to the other joint tenants a 'notice in writing' of his 'desire' to sever the joint tenancy.

This type of severance is very convenient. No consent is required from other joint tenants.[174] Where the written notice is sent by post, it is enough if it has been duly posted in a registered letter to the other joint tenant[175] even if it is not received by them.[176]

The written notice need not be signed.[177] It may also take the form of a summons or a writ which starts a litigation concerning joint tenants' rights.[178] In *Gore & Snell v Carpenter* a clause severing the joint tenancy included in a separation agreement was held not sufficient to amount to an effective notice because it was not intended to be a notice of severance, but merely formed part of the proposals which were not accepted by Mrs Carpenter.[179] It was a mere proposal and was not a definite desire to sever.

Equitable joint tenants under a strict settlement cannot, however, use this statutory method to sever their joint tenancy. Section 36(2) expressly excludes its application in settled land.

There has been suggestion that only where the legal estate is owned by the same joint tenants at law and in equity can a joint tenant use s 36(2) to sever his joint tenancy (see Fig 4), but where there is an equitable joint tenant who does not own the legal estate then none of them can use s 36(2) (see Fig 5).[180]

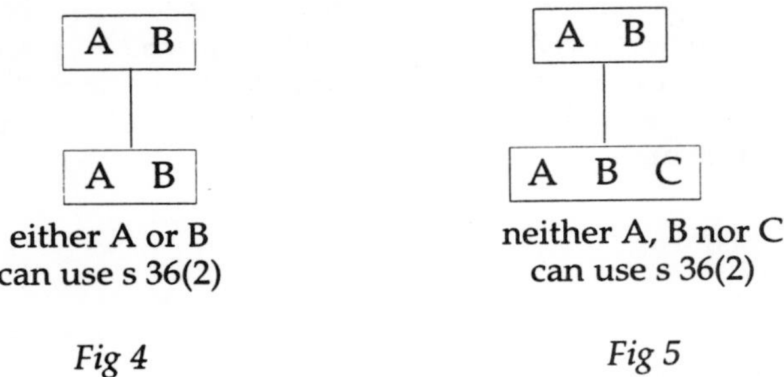

Fig 4

Fig 5

173 *McDowell v Hirschfield, Lipson & Rumney* [1992] 2 FLR 126, [1992] *The Times*, 13 February.
174 *Harris v Goddard* [1983] 1 WLR 1203 at 1209B.
175 Section 196 of the LPA 1925.
176 *Re 88 Berkeley Road* [1971] Ch 648 at 655C.
177 *Re Draper's Conveyance* [1969] 1 Ch 486 at 492A.
178 *Re Draper's Conveyance, supra* at 492C.
179 (1990) 60 P & CR 456 at 462.
180 [1976] CLJ 20 at 24 (Hayton, DJ).

Supporters for this view argue that this is because s 36(2) says 'where a legal estate (not being settled land) is vested in joint tenants beneficially, any tenant who desires to sever the joint tenancy in equity shall give to the other joint tenants a notice in writing of such desire'. Such a narrow view is clearly unsatisfactory. A wider view has been expressed by the Court of Appeal in *Burgess v Rawnsley*, that all beneficial joint tenants should be able to use the statutory method of severance.[181]

The written notice must express a desire to sever immediately and not a desire to sever at some time in the future.[182]

Before 1 January 1926, there was a type of co-ownership known as 'tenancy by entireties' which was restricted to ownership by husband and wife. It was essentially the same as joint tenancy except it could not be severed at all. This kind of co-ownership was converted on 1 January 1926 automatically into joint tenancies.[183] This type of joint tenancy can today be severed either by the *Williams v Hensman* methods or the statutory method of severance.[184]

10 DESTRUCTION OF CO-OWNERSHIP

Co-ownerships either in the form of joint tenancies or tenancies in common can be ended in two ways: by partition or by union in a sole tenant which has the effect of destroying the unity of possession.[185] Co-ownership is ended and each one has a separate ownership. This is different from severance of joint tenancy where after severance they will hold the property as tenants in common and remain co-owners.

Partition

Joint tenants and tenants in common can always make a voluntary partition of the land concerned by a unanimous agreement and their co-ownership comes to an end by each becoming sole tenant of the piece of land allotted to him. This must be done by deed under s 52(1) of the Law of Property Act 1925.

Where land is held on trust, the trustees of land may, where the beneficiaries of full age are absolutely entitled in undivided shares to land subject to the trust, partition the land with the consent of each of those beneficiaries.[186] If the trustees or any of the beneficiaries refuse to agree to a partition, any person interested may apply to the court under s 14 of the Trusts of Land and Appointment of Trustees Act 1996 for an order as the court thinks fit.

181 [1975] Ch 429 at 439G, 444F, 447G.

182 *Harris v Goddard* [1983] 1 WLR 1203 at 1209B.

183 Section 1, Part VI of the LPA 1925.

184 *Bedson v Bedson* [1965] 2 QB 666 at 689C, 690E.

185 Bl Comm, 185.

186 Section 7(1), (3) of the TLATA 1996.

Union in a sole tenant

Joint tenancies and tenancies in common may be destroyed by the entirety of the land becoming vested in a single beneficial owner. So, where one of two surviving joint tenants dies, the other becomes sole tenant and the co-ownership is at an end. Similarly, if one joint tenant or tenant in common buys out the interests of all his fellows, the co-ownership is at an end.

Co-ownership can also be destroyed by one joint tenant releasing[187] his interest to the other joint tenant.[188] Thus where A and B hold a property as joint tenants, A can destroy the co-ownership by releasing his interest to B and B will become the sole owner of the property.

Where A, B and C hold as joint tenants, A cannot sever the legal joint tenancy, but he can release his legal estate or equitable interest (or both) to B, so that B alone acquires A's one third share as a separate sole owner, meanwhile B remains a joint tenant with C as to the other two thirds (see Fig 6).[189]

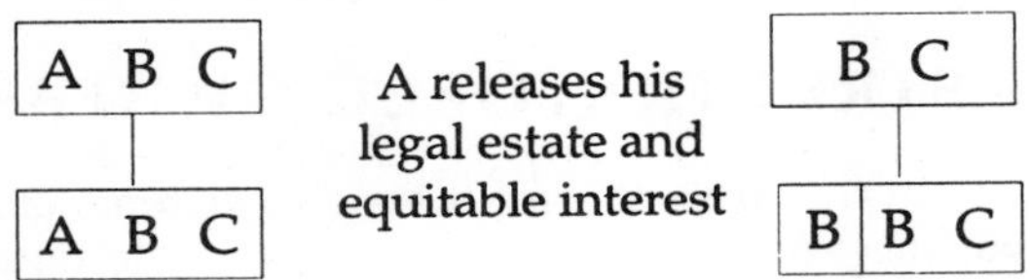

Fig 6

A tenant in common, on the other hand, cannot release his share to his fellows.[190]

Co-ownership in land is also extinguished when the land is sold to a purchaser who takes the land absolutely.

187 Discharging one's interest in favour of the others.

188 Section 36(2) of the LPA 1925.

189 Litt 304, 305.

190 Co Litt 193a, n 1.

CHAPTER 14

COVENANTS AFFECTING FREEHOLD LAND

When land is divided, the vendor who retains part of it and sells the other part may want to ensure that the part sold is not used in an undesirable way. Or, if a vendor owns two adjourning properties and sells one of them, he may want his new neighbour to use the property sold in a particular way or to restrain him from using the land in a particular manner. In a new housing estate, the developer may want to make sure that the estate will be maintained properly by all new owners so that the character of the area can be maintained and the market attraction can be enhanced. This form of private control of land use can be achieved by covenants in the transfer of freehold land. A covenant is an agreement made in a deed. The vendor or the developer may require the purchaser to covenant to do or not to do certain things in relation to a defined area of land. Similar covenants may be made in the transfer of leasehold land. However, this chapter deals with covenants relating to freehold land. Leasehold covenants have been dealt with in Chapter 9. The person who makes a covenant is called the covenantor. The person who receives the benefit of the covenant is the covenantee.

Covenant may be positive or negative. A positive covenant imposes on the covenantor an obligation to perform some specified act or activity in relation to a defined area of land, eg the covenantor shall maintain his neighbour's boundary fence in good repair. A negative covenant (or restrictive covenant) requires the covenantor not to use his land in a specified manner, eg not to carry on trade or business on the land.

It is the use of negative covenant which often achieves the purpose of preserving the condition of land. First, it curtails the potential scope of activities that may be carried out on the covenantor's land and secondly, as will be seen, only restrictive covenant may bind successors of the freehold servient land.

The law of freehold covenants enables a private agreement to be made between owners of neighbouring land as to the use of the land. It also ensures that the burdens and benefits of certain covenants thus created can be transmitted to third parties. Otherwise the control of land use would be destroyed on a transfer of the burdened land. However, if land is subject to vague and obscure covenants, it may become unmarketable, for no purchaser would want to buy land which is already subject to some ill-defined obligations. Thus, the law of freehold covenants has striven to maintain a balance between preserving the alienability of land and facilitating the private control of land use.

As a covenant is made for the benefit of certain land (called the benefited land), it is irrelevant whether the covenantor owns any estate in land. The covenant he makes may be enforceable against him even if he owns no estate in any burdened land.[1] In *Smith and Snipes Hall Farm Ltd v River Douglas Catchment*

1 *The Prior's* case (1368) YB 42 Edw III, pl 14, applied in *Smith and Snipes Hall Farm Ltd v River Douglas Catchment Board* [1949] 2 KB 500.

Board,[2] the defendant Board covenanted in 1938 with the freehold owners of the land to maintain the banks of a river in return for their contribution to the cost. In 1940, one of the owners of the benefited land sold the land with the benefit of the covenant to the first plaintiff, who leased it to the second defendant under a yearly tenancy. Later, due to the defendant's faulty work, the river banks broke and flooded the plaintiffs' land. They sued the defendant in tort and for breach of covenant. The Court of Appeal held that the defendant Board's positive covenant to repair and maintain the river banks was enforceable even though they did not own any estate in the land through which the river ran. However, the covenantee must hold some estate in the land to which the benefit of the covenant may accrue. If he does not own some estate in the land he can only sue for nominal damages when there is a breach of the covenant, because it is unlikely that he will suffer any real loss. Only the person who owns the benefited land will suffer loss.

Smith and Snipes Hall Farm Ltd v River Douglas Catchment Board [1949] 2 KB 500, CA

Tucker LJ: [Having found that the Catchment Board was in breach of the 1938 covenants continued.]

It remains to consider whether, in these circumstances, the plaintiffs, or either of them, can sue in respect of this breach. It is said for the defendants that the benefit of the covenant does not run with the land so as to bind a stranger who has not and never had an interest in the land to be benefited and there being no servient tenement to bear the burden.

With regard to the covenantor being a stranger the case of *The Prior* is referred to in *Spencer's* case,[3] in these words:

> In the case of a grandfather, father and two sons, the grandfather being seised of the manor of D, whereof a chapel was parcel: a prior, with the assent of his convent, by deed covenanted for him and his successors, with the grandfather and his heirs, that he and his convent would sing all the week in his chapel, parcel of the said manor, for the lords of the said manor and his servants, etc; the grandfather did enfeoff one of the manor in fee, who gave it to the younger son and his wife in tail; and it was adjudged that the tenants in tail, as terre-tenants (for the elder brother was heir), should have an action of covenant against the prior, for the covenant is to do a thing which is annexed to the chapel, which is within the manor, and so annexed to the manor, as it is there said.

The notes to *Spencer's* case state:

> When such a covenant (namely, covenants running with the land made with the owner of the land to which they relate) is made it seems to be of no consequence whether the covenantor be the person who conveyed the land to the covenantee or be a mere stranger.

In volume 4 of Bythewood and Jarman's *Conveyancing*, 4th edn, p 268, the following passage from the third report of the Real Property Commissioners is quoted with approval:

2 [1949] 2 KB 500. See (1949) 12 MLR 498 (Kiralfy, AKR).

3 (1368) 1 Sm L C 10th edn at 56, 73, 13th edn at 51, 65, 73.

> Expressions found in some books would lead to the opinion that, in considering this class of covenant with reference to the benefit of them, there is a distinction between those cases where the covenantor is a party by whom the estate is, or has been conveyed, and those in which he is a stranger to the estate. We think the authority of Lord Coke on this point (which is express (Co Litt 384b)) sufficient to warrant us in disregarding this distinction.

In *Rogers v Hosegood*,[4] Farwell J in a passage where he refers, amongst others, to *The Prior's* case – and I quote from Farwell J's judgment because, although this case went to the Court of Appeal, his judgment was approved, and the Court of Appeal had to deal with a rather different point – after stating what are the requirements in order that the covenant may run with the land, proceeds:

> It is not contended that the covenants in question in this case have not the first characteristic, but it is said that they fail in the second. I am of opinion that they possess both. Adopting the definition of Bayley J in *Congleton Corporation v Pattison*[5] the covenant must either affect the land as regards mode of occupation, or it must be such as *per se*, and not merely from collateral circumstances, affects the value of the land. It is to my mind obvious that the value of Sir J Millais's land is directly increased by the covenants in question. If authority is needed, I would refer to *Mann v Stephens*,[6] a case very similar to the present; *Vyvyan v Arthur*[7]; *The Prior's* case[8]; *Fleetwood v Hull*[9]; *White v Southend Hotel Co*[10] I see no difficulty in holding that the benefit of a covenant runs with the land of the covenantee, while the burden of the same covenant does not run with the land of the covenantor.

In this state of the authorities it seems clear, despite some dicta tending to the contrary view, that such a covenant if it runs with the land is binding on the covenantor though a mere stranger, and that this point will not avail the defendant board.

Denning LJ: Mr Nield also argued that there was no servient tenement. But that is only material when there is a question whether the burden of a covenant runs with the land. This is a question of the benefit running, and ever since *The Prior's* case it has been held that the covenantor is liable because of his covenant given to the owner of the dominant tenement and not because of his relationship to any servient tenement. In my opinion, therefore, the board are liable to the plaintiffs in damages for breach of covenant.

The enforcement of freehold covenant is reasonably straightforward if one first identifies the parties: who is seeking to enforce the covenant and against whom, and then asks, has the person seeking to enforce the covenant got the benefit of the covenant, and has the person against whom the covenant is enforced got the burden of the covenant? If the answers to the questions are in the affirmative, then the covenant is enforceable as between the parties.

---

4 [1900] 2 Ch 388 at 395.

5 (1808) 10 East 130 at 135.

6 (1846) 15 Sim 377.

7 (1823) 1 B & C 410; 25 R R 437.

8 (1368) 1 Sim LC 10th edn, 55, 13th edn, 51, 65, 73.

9 (1889) 23 QBD 35.

10 [1897] 1 Ch 767.

1 BETWEEN ORIGINAL COVENANTOR AND ORIGINAL COVENANTEE

As between the original covenantor and the original covenantee, the position is governed by the doctrine of privity of contract. It is a matter of contract. The covenantor imposes the burden on himself and confers an equivalent benefit on the covenantee. The covenant is enforceable by the covenantee against the covenantor as long as they are parties to the covenant. But it should be noted that only the person with whom the covenant is made can enforce the covenant. A person who has the benefit of the covenant but who is not a party to it cannot enforce it as he has no privity of contract. So, if A covenants with B for the benefit of C, C cannot enforce the covenant because the covenant is not made with him.

At common law only the person who was named as a party to the deed of covenant made *inter partes* could sue on the covenant.[11] Thus, if A covenants with B and C, both B and C can enforce the covenant, even if C was not present when the covenant was made. But if A covenants with B and the owner for the time being of the adjourning land, only B can enforce the covenant because only he is named as the covenantee.

This common law rule has been relaxed by s 56 of the Law of Property Act 1925.[12]

Law of Property Act 1925

56. Persons taking who are not parties and as to indentures

(1) A person may take an immediate or other interest in land or other property, or the benefit of any condition, right of entry, covenant or agreement over or respecting land, or other property, although he may not be named as a party to the conveyance or other instrument.

The effect of s 56 is not to abolish the doctrine of privity of contract in the context of covenant. So a third party remains unable to sue on the covenant made for his benefit. The covenant must purport to be made with him as covenantee. Thus, in *White v Bijou Mansions Ltd*[13] the plaintiff could not enforce a covenant which was not made with him even though he would benefit from it if it had been enforced.

White v Bijou Mansions Ltd [1938] Ch 351, CA

Sir Wilfrid Greene MR: ... whatever else s 56 may mean, it is, I think, confined to cases where the person seeking to take advantage of it is a person within the benefit of the covenant in question, if I may use that phrase. The mere fact that somebody comes along and says: 'It would be useful to me if I could enforce that covenant' does not make him a person entitled to enforce it under s 56. Before he can enforce it he must be a person who falls within the scope and benefit of the covenant according to the true construction of the document in question.'

11 *Lord Southampton v Brown* (1827) 6 B & C 718 at 719; 108 ER 615 at 616.

12 Replaces and extends s 5 of the Real Property Act 1845.

13 [1938] Ch 351.

Earlier in the High Court, Simonds J said:[14]

> Just as under s 5 of the Act of 1845 only that person could call it in aid who, although not a party, yet was a grantee or covenantee, so under s 56 of this Act only that person can call it in aid who, although not named as a party to the conveyance or other instrument, is yet a person to whom that conveyance or other instrument purports to grant some thing or with which some agreement or covenant is purported to be made.

The effect of s 56 is to remove the common law rule that only the person named as a covenantee can enforce the covenant. Thus, if A covenants with B and the owner for the time being of the adjourning land, such an unnamed owner would be able to enforce the covenant. It is sufficient that the claimant is designated as a covenantee under some clear generic description. He need not be named as such.[15]

Beswick v Beswick [1968] AC 58, HL

Lord Reid: The respondent's first answer is that the common law has been radically altered by s 56(1) of the Law of Property Act 1925, and that that section entitles her to sue in her personal capacity and recover the benefit provided for her in the agreement although she was not a party to it. Extensive alterations of the law were made at that time but it is necessary to examine with some care the way in which this was done. That Act was a consolidation Act and it is the invariable practice of Parliament to require from those who have prepared a consolidation Bill an assurance that it will make no substantial change in the law and to have that checked by a committee. On this assurance the Bill is then passed into law, no amendment being permissible. So, in order to pave the way for the consolidation Act of 1925, earlier Acts were passed in 1922 and 1924 in which were enacted all the substantial amendments which now appear in the Act of 1925 and these amendments were then incorporated in the Bill which became the Act of 1925. Those earlier Acts contain nothing corresponding to s 56 and it is therefore quite certain that those responsible for the preparation of this legislation must have believed and intended that s 56 would make no substantial change in the earlier law, and equally certain that Parliament passed s 56 in reliance on an assurance that it did make no substantial change.

In construing any Act of Parliament, we are seeking the intention of Parliament and it is quite true that we must deduce that intention from the words of the Act. If the words of the Act are only capable of one meaning, we must give them that meaning no matter how they got there. But if they are capable of having more than one meaning we are, in my view, well entitled to see how they got there ...

Section 56 was obviously intended to replace s 5 of the Real Property Act, 1845 (8 and 9 Vict c 106). That section provided:

> That, under an indenture, executed after 1 October 1845, an immediate estate or interest, in any tenements or hereditaments, and the benefit of a condition or covenant, respecting any tenements or hereditaments, may be taken, although the taker thereof be not named a party to the same indenture ...

[His Lordship read s 56 and continued.]

14 [1937] Ch 610 at 625.

15 *Beswick v Beswick* [1968] AC 58. See (1967) 30 MLR 687 (Treitel, GH).

If the matter stopped there it would not be difficult to hold that s 56 does not substantially extend or alter the provisions of s 5 of the Act of 1845. But more difficulty is introduced by the definition section of the Act of 1925 (s 205) which provides:

> (1) In this Act unless the context otherwise requires, the following expressions have the meanings hereby assigned to them respectively, that is to say: – (xx) 'Property' includes any thing in action, and any interest in real or personal property.

[His Lordship referred to Simonds J and Sir Wilfrid Greene MR's judgment cited at p 741 above and to *Re Miller's Agreement* [1947] Ch 615.]

I had thought from what Lord Simonds said in *White's* case that s 5 of the Act of 1845 did enable certain persons to take benefits which they could not have taken without it. if so, it must have given them rights which they did not have without it. And, if that is so, s 56 must now have the same effect ...

I can now return to consider the meaning and scope of s 56. It refers to any 'agreement over or respecting land or other property'. If 'land or other property' means the same thing as 'tenements or hereditaments' in the Act of 1845 then this section simply continues the law as it was before the Act of 1925 was passed, for I do not think that the other differences in phraseology can be regarded as making any substantial change. So any obscurities in s 56 are obscurities which originated in 1845. But if its scope is wider, then two points must be considered. The section refers to agreements 'over or respecting land or other property.' The land is something which existed before and independently of the agreement and the same must apply to the other property. So an agreement between A and B that A will use certain personal property for the benefit of X would be within the scope of the section, but an agreement that if A performs certain services for B, B will pay a sum to X would not be within the scope of the section. Such a capricious distinction would alone throw doubt on this interpretation.

Perhaps more important is the fact that the section does not say that a person may take the benefit of an agreement although he was not a party to it: it says that he may do so although he was not named as a party in the instrument which embodied the agreement. It is true that s 56 says 'although he may not be named'; but s 5 of the Act of 1845 says although he 'be not named a party'. Such a change of phraseology in a consolidation Act cannot involve a change of meaning. I do not profess to have a full understanding of the old English law regarding deeds. But it appears from what Lord Simonds said in *White's* case[16] and from what Vaisey J said in *Chelsea and Walham Green Building Society v Armstrong*[17] that being in fact a party to an agreement might not be enough; the person claiming a benefit had to be named a party in the indenture. I have read the explanation of the old law given by my noble and learned friend, Lord Upjohn. I would not venture to criticise it, but I do not think it necessary for me to consider it if it leads to the conclusion that s 56 taken by itself would not assist the present respondent.

In *Dyson v Forster*,[18] a covenant with the 'owners for the time being' of certain land was held to be annexed to the land then vested in the predecessor in title of the plaintiff. Thus, the benefit ran to the plaintiff even though his predecessor was not a party to the deed and was not named as a covenantee.

16 [1937] Ch 610.

17 [1951] Ch 853; [1951] 2 TLR 312; [1951] 2 All ER 250.

18 [1908] 1 KB 629 (a case under s 5 of the Real Property Act 1845).

However, those who are generically described as covenantees may only claim under s 56 if they are existing and identifiable individuals at the date of the covenant.[19] Thus, the covenantor cannot covenant with future purchasers under s 56. The future purchasers may benefit as assignees under the rules relating to passing of benefit but not under s 56. So, if A covenants with B and his successors in title, B's successor in title being a non-existing person at the time of the covenant cannot rely on s 56. As will be seen, he may, of course, claim the benefit through B.

Re Ecclesiastical Commissioners for England's Conveyance [1936] Ch 430

Luxmoore J: Having ascertained that restrictive covenants were imposed in respect of the West Heath House property and that the form of the covenants is such as to make the burden of them run with the land, it is necessary to consider whether they were imposed for the benefit of any and what other hereditaments. For it is well settled that, apart from any building scheme, restrictive covenants may be enforced if they are expressed in the original deed to be for the benefit of a particular parcel or particular parcels of land, either expressly mentioned or clearly identified in the deed containing the original covenants. It was argued on behalf of the applicants that the right to enforce such covenants is limited to the original covenantees and their successors in title the right in the case of the successors in title being limited to those whose land was the property of the original covenantees at the date when the covenants were imposed. It was also argued that the right to enforce the covenants did not extend to any owners of land who were neither express assignees of the benefit of the covenants, nor successors in title of the original covenantees in respect of land acquired by such successors from the Ecclesiastical Commissioners subsequent to the date of the deed by which the covenants were imposed. I think these arguments failed to give due consideration to the provisions of s 5 of the Real Property Act, 1845, as repealed and re-enacted by s 56 of the Law of Property Act, 1925. Section 5 of the Act of 1845 provides that under an indenture, executed after 1 October 1845, the benefit of a condition or covenant respecting any tenements or hereditaments may be taken, although the taker thereof be not named as a party to the indenture. In the case of *Forster v Elvet Colliery Co Ltd*,[20] it was held that the condition or covenant referred to in the section must, in order to be enforceable by a person not a party to the deed, be one the benefit of which runs with the land of the person seeking to enforce it. The actual decision was upheld in the House of Lords under the name *Dyson v Forster*,[21] but Lord Macnaghten expressed doubt whether the section ought to be so restricted. He refrained however from resolving the doubt, because he agreed with the view that the covenants in the particular case ran with the land and it was therefore unnecessary to do so.

The alteration which has been made in the verbiage of s 5 of the 1845 Act by s 56 of the 1925 Act, has not in my opinion affected the position so as to limit the right of a person not a party to the deed to enforce covenants affecting land to those which run with the land. The material words are as follows: 'A person may take ... the benefit of any condition ... covenant or agreement ... respecting land or other property, although he

19 *Re Ecclesiastical Commissioners for England's Conveyance* [1936] Ch 430.

20 [1908] 1 KB 629.

21 [1909] AC 98, 102.

may not be named as a party to the conveyance or other instrument.' It seems to me that the effect of these words is to enlarge the scope of the earlier words, for it extends the rights of a person not a party to a deed to covenants affecting every kind of property personal as well as real. So far as every species of personal property other than leasehold is concerned it is obvious that the covenants to be enforced cannot be restricted to those running with the property, for there are no such covenants. What it is necessary to consider is the true construction of the conveyance of 21 April 1887, in order to ascertain whether any persons, not parties thereto, are described therein as the covenantees, and whether such covenants are expressed to affect any and what hereditaments. To determine what is the true construction of that document it is necessary to consider the surrounding circumstances as they existed at the date when it was executed.

[His Lordship referred to the relevant surrounding circumstances including a detailed plan and continued.]

In the result, it is plain that at the date of the conveyance of West Heath House to Mr Gotto, the Ecclesiastical Commissioners had parted with all the rest of the land within the red verge line and had leased the land coloured green for a term of 999 years. They remained the owners of the freehold reversion in the green land and the freehold of the land coloured blue. They owned no land adjoining West Heath House.

2 BETWEEN ORIGINAL COVENANTOR AND SUCCESSOR OF ORIGINAL COVENANTEE – PASSING OF BENEFIT

As between the original covenantor and the successor of the original covenantee, the enforcement of the covenant depends on whether the benefit of the covenant has run with the land to the successor of the covenantee. The original covenantor still retains the burden and if the successor of the original covenantee has obtained the benefit, he is able to enforce it against the original covenantor.

Running of benefit at common law

The benefit of a covenant runs with the benefited land at common law if the following conditions are satisfied:[22]

(a) Covenant must 'touch and concern' the benefited land

This means that the covenant must be made *for the benefit of the land,* and not simply to benefit the covenantee personally. The covenantee and his successors in title must be able to benefit from the covenant. The test is essentially the same as that in *Spencer's* case[23] or the requirement of 'accommodation' in the law of easement.[24] The emphasis is on the land not the covenantees' personal benefit. It must be made to enhance the value of the land. It must either affect the way in

22 *P & A Swift Investments v Combined English Stores Group plc* [1989] AC 632 at 639H–40A, HL.

23 (1583) 5 Co Rep 16a; 77 ER 72.

24 *P & A Swift Investments v Combined English Stores Group plc* [1989] AC 632 at 640E–F.

which the land is occupied or affect its value as such.[25] In *Smith v River Douglas Catchment Board*,[26] the covenant by the defendant Catchment Board to keep river banks in repair was held to have touched and concerned the covenantee's land, which was flooded when repair was neglected, because 'it affects the value of the land *per se* and converts it from flooded meadows to land suitable for agriculture'.

(b) Original covenantee must have a legal estate in benefited land

No benefit can run at law where the original covenantee only has an equitable interest in his land.[27]

(c) Successor in title of original covenantee must have a legal estate in benefited land

Prior to 1926, it was thought that the successors in title must have the same legal estate as the original covenantee. So if the original covenantee was a fee simple owner, the benefit could only run with the land to a purchaser who owned the land in fee simple, but not to a lessee who only owned a term of years.[28] This rule is now affected by s 78 of the Law of Property Act 1925.

Law of Property Act 1925

78. Benefit of covenants relating to land

(1) A covenant relating to any land of the covenantee shall be deemed to be made with the covenantee and his successors in title and the persons deriving title under him or them, and shall have effect as if such successors and other persons were expressed.

For the purposes of this subsection in connection with covenants restrictive of the user of land 'successors in title' shall be deemed to include the owners and occupiers for the time being of the land of the covenantee intended to be benefited.

(2) This section applies to covenants made after the commencement of this Act, but the repeal of s 58 of the Conveyancing Act 1881 does not affect the operation of covenants to which that section applied.

In *Smith v River Douglas Catchment Board*,[29] it will be recalled, the original covenantee sold his land to the first plaintiff who, in his turn, leased the land to the second plaintiff. The Court of Appeal allowed an action for damages for breach of covenant brought by both the first (who was a fee simple owner) and the second plaintiffs (who only had a term of years). It was held that because the covenants were deemed to be made with the covenantee's successors in title,

25 *Mayor of Congleton v Pattison* (1808) 10 East 130 at 135; 103 ER 725 at 727; *Rogers v Hosegood* [1900] 2 Ch 388 at 395; *Smith and Snipes Hall Farm Ltd v River Douglas Catchment Board* [1949] 2 KB 500 at 506; *P & A Swift Investments v Combined English Stores Group plc* [1989] AC 632 at 640F.

26 [1949] 2 KB 500 at 506.

27 *Webb v Russell* (1789) 3 TR 393 at 402.

28 *Westhoughton UDC v Wigam* [1919] 1 Ch 159.

29 [1949] 2 KB 500.

s 78 allowed not only the original covenantee to enforce the covenants but also all his successors in title and all persons deriving title from such successors whether they held the same legal estate as the original covenantee or not.

(d) Benefit must have been intended to run with benefited land at the date of the covenant[30]

Prior to 1926 it was necessary for the covenantor to covenant with 'the covenantee, his successors in title, and those deriving title under him' or with 'the covenantee, his heirs and assigns' to show that the covenantor intended the benefit to run with the land. After 1925, such an intention is assumed by s 78 of the Law of Property Act 1925. 'The covenant is deemed to be made with the covenantee and his successors in title and the persons deriving title under him or them'.

In *Smith v River Douglas Catchment Board*, as has been seen, the plaintiffs, the successors of the original owners were allowed to sue on the covenant even though it was not made with them. Denning LJ held that the intention was deemed to exist by s 78. The Board was deemed to have covenanted with the covenantees and their successors in title.

Smith and Snipes Hall Farm Ltd v River Douglas Catchment Board [1949] 2 KB 500, CA

Denning LJ: It was always held, however, at common law that, in order that a successor in title should be entitled to sue, he must be of the same estate as the original owner. That alone was a sufficient interest to entitle him to enforce the contract. The covenant was supposed to be made for the benefit of the owner and his successors in title, and not for the benefit of anyone else. This limitation, however, was, as is pointed out in Smith's *Leading Cases*, capable of being 'productive of very serious and disagreeable consequences', and it has been removed by s 78 of the Law of Property Act 1925, which provides that a covenant relating to any land of the covenantee shall be deemed to be made with the covenantee and his successors in title, 'and the persons deriving title under him or them' and shall have effect as if such successors 'and other persons' were expressed.

The covenant of the catchment board in this case clearly relates to the land of the covenantees. It was a covenant to do work on the land for the benefit of the land. By the statute, therefore, it is to be deemed to be made, not only with the original owner, but also with the purchasers of the land and their tenants as if they were expressed. Now if they were expressed, it would be clear that the covenant was made for their benefit ; and they clearly have sufficient interest to entitle them to enforce it because they have suffered the damage.'

Where the above four conditions are satisfied the benefit of the original covenant run with the benefited land so the original covenantee's successors can sue on the covenant against the original covenantor. However, there may be situations where the conditions at common law are not satisfied, for example, the claimant

30 *Rogers v Hosegood* [1900] 2 Ch 388.

may not have a legal estate in the benefited land. He may be an equitable owner behind a trust.

Secondly, as mentioned above, if the original covenantee's successors in title had acquired the benefited land before 1926, but they did not acquire the same legal estate as that of the original covenantee, the benefit would not run at common law.[31] Neither would s 78 apply. Thirdly, as will be seen, where the burden runs in equity the claimant must also show that he has acquired the benefit in equity.[32]

Assignment of benefit at law

The benefit of a covenant may, however, be assigned at common law as a chose in action under s 136 of the Law of Property Act 1925. Such an assignment must, however, be made in writing,[33] and express notice of the assignment must be given to the covenantor. If the claimant has been assigned only part of the benefited land, the benefit of the covenant cannot be assigned at law because benefit cannot be assigned in pieces. It will have to be assigned as a whole or not at all.[34] As will be seen, equity, however, allows assignment in part.

Miles v Easter [1933] Ch 611, CA

Romer LJ: This is an appeal by the defendants from an order made by Bennett J on 29 July 1932, whereby it was declared that certain restrictive covenants affecting lands of the plaintiff at Shoreham and Lancing in the county of Sussex, and contained in two indentures dated respectively 23 October 1908, and 11 May 1909, are not enforceable by the defendants or either of them against the plaintiff.

The relevant facts, as to which there is no dispute, are fully stated in the judgment of the learned judge and need not be repeated here. The questions arising on the appeal depend upon the application to those facts of the law relating to restrictive covenants affecting land. That the plaintiff is bound by the covenants in question is not disputed, in view of the fact that he purchased his lands with notice of them. What is in dispute is the question whether the defendants are entitled to the benefit of such covenants. Now the defendants are not the original covenantees, and it therefore becomes necessary to ascertain what person other than the original covenantee is entitled to the benefit of a restrictive covenant affecting land. This question was put to himself by Hall VC in *Renals v Cowlishaw*,[35] and the answer was given in a judgment so well known that it is unnecessary to refer to it at length. It is a judgment that has received the approval both of this Court and of the House of Lords, and has always been regarded as a correct statement of the law upon the subject. Stated shortly it laid down this: that, apart from what are usually referred to as building scheme cases (and this is not a case of that sort), a purchaser from the original covenantee of land retained by him when he executed the conveyance containing the covenant will be entitled to the benefit of the covenant if the

31 *Westhoughton UDC v Wigam* [1919] 1 Ch 159.

32 *Miles v Easter* [1933] Ch 611.

33 Not by deed, because it is not a disposition of an interest in land, but a disposition of a chose in action.

34 *Re Union of London and Smith's Bank's Conveyance, Miles v Easter* [1933] Ch 611.

35 [1878] 9 Ch D 125.

conveyance shows that the covenant was intended to enure for the benefit of that particular land. It follows that, if what is being acquired by the purchaser was only part of the land shown by the conveyance as being intended to be benefited, it must also be shown that the benefit was intended to enure to each portion of that land. In such cases the benefit of the restrictive covenant will pass to the purchaser without being mentioned. It runs with the land. In all other cases, the purchaser will not acquire the benefit of the covenant unless that benefit be expressly assigned to him – or, to use the words of the Vice-Chancellor,[36] 'it must appear that the benefit of the covenant was part of the subject matter of the purchase'.

In *Renals v Cowlishaw*, the covenant was entered into with the covenantee, his heirs and assigns, and it appears to have been argued that the use of the word assigns showed an intention that the benefit of the covenant should run with the land. But, to use the language of Farwell J in *Rogers v Hosegood*:[37]

> ... there was nothing to shew what assigns were intended by the words of the covenant; there was no necessary implication that each assign of each parcel of the vendor's land, whether acquired before or after the date of the deed, was to have the benefit of the covenant; the inference, indeed, was to the contrary, and the Courts accordingly held that the covenant did not run, but must be expressly assigned in order to pass. Contrast this with the case of the ordinary covenants for title: these undoubtedly run with the land, and each purchaser of each portion of the land gets the benefit of the covenants so far as they relate to the land purchased by him. In both these cases the covenants are entered into with the heirs and assigns, but in the first case the word 'assign,' on the true construction of the deed, means 'assign of the covenant, 'in the latter 'assign of the land, to which is annexed the benefit of the covenant by virtue of the evidence of intention so to contract which is found in the deed and the surrounding circumstances.

In *Rogers v Hosegood*,[38] itself the benefit of the covenant was held to run with the land of the covenantees, for the covenant had been entered into with them, their heirs and assigns, with the express intent that the covenant would enure to the benefit of the covenantees, their heirs and assigns and others claiming under them to all or any of their lands adjoining or near to the premises then being conveyed to the covenantor. In *Renals v Cowlishaw*, the benefit of the covenant had never been expressly assigned by the covenantee. In neither of these cases, therefore, did it become necessary for the Court to inquire into the circumstances in which an express assignee of the benefit of a covenant that does not run with the land is entitled to enforce it. In the present case, however, it is necessary to do so, inasmuch as the defendants claim to be the express assignees of the benefit of the restrictive covenants contained in the deeds of 23 October 1908, and 11 May 1909.

Now it may be conceded that the benefit of a covenant entered into with the covenantee or his assigns is assignable. The use of the word 'assigns' indicates this: see Williams on *Personal Property*, 18th edn, p 33. But it by no means follows that the assignee of a restrictive covenant affecting land of the covenantor is entitled to enforce it against an assign of that land. For the burden of the covenant did not run with the land at law,

36 [1878] 9 Ch D 125 at 130.

37 [1900] 2 Ch 388 at 396.

38 [1900] 2 Ch 388.

and is only enforceable against a purchaser with notice by reason of the equitable doctrine that is usually referred to as the rule in *Tulk v Moxhay*.[39] It was open, therefore, to the Courts of Equity to prescribe the particular class of assignees of the covenant to whom they should concede the benefit of the rule. This they have done, and in doing so have included within the class persons to whom the benefit of the covenant could not have been assigned at law. For at law, the benefit could not be assigned in pieces. It would have to be assigned as a whole or not at all. And yet in equity the right to enforce the covenant can in certain circumstances be assigned by the covenantee from time to time to one person after another. Who then are the assignees of the covenant that are entitled to enforce it? The answer to this question is to be found in several authorities which it now becomes necessary to consider ...

It is plain, however, from these and other cases, and notably that of *Renals v Cowlishaw*, that if the restrictive covenant be taken not merely for some personal purpose or object of the vendor, but for the benefit of some other land of his in the sense that it would enable him to dispose of that land to greater advantage, the covenant, though not annexed to such land so as to run with any part of it, may be enforced against an assignee of the covenantor taking with notice, both by the covenantee and by persons to whom the benefit of such covenant has been assigned, subject however to certain conditions. In the first place, the 'other land' must be land that is capable of being benefited by the covenant – otherwise it would be impossible to infer that the object of the covenant was to enable the vendor to dispose of his land to greater advantage. In the next place, this land must be 'ascertainable' or 'certain', to use the words of Romer and Scrutton LJJ respectively. For, although the Court will readily infer the intention to benefit the other land of the vendor where the existence and situation of such land are indicated in the conveyance or have been otherwise shown with reasonable certainty, it is impossible to do so from vague references in the conveyance or in other documents laid before the Court as to the existence of other lands of the vendor, the extent and situation of which are undefined. In the third place, the covenant cannot be enforced by the covenantee against an assign of the purchaser after the covenantee has parted with the whole of his land.

As will be seen, today, benefit will normally run in equity by way of statutory annexation following the decision of *Federated Homes Ltd v Mill Lodge Properties Ltd*.[40] Thus, cases requiring express assignment may be far fewer in the future. However, if there is express provision to the effect that the covenant shall not take effect for the benefit of any owner or subsequent purchaser of any part of the estate unless the benefit is expressly assigned, it would still be necessary to show express assignment.[41]

Roake v Chadha [1983] 3 All ER 503

Judge Paul Baker QC: Counsel for the plaintiffs' method of applying it is simplicity itself. The Federated Homes case shows that s 78 brings about annexation, and that the operation of the section cannot be excluded by a contrary intention. As I have indicated, he supports this last point by reference to s 79, which is expressed to operate 'unless a

39 (1848) 2 Ph 774.

40 [1980] 1 All ER 371.

41 *Roake v Chadha* [1983] 3 All ER 503.

contrary intention is expressed', a qualification which, as we have already noticed, is absent from s 78. Counsel for the plaintiffs could not suggest any reason of policy why s 78 should be mandatory, unlike, for example, s 146 of the 1925 Act, which deals with restrictions on the right to forfeiture of leases and which, by an express provision, 'has effect notwithstanding any stipulation to the contrary'.

I am thus far from satisfied that s 78 has the mandatory operation which counsel for the plaintiffs claimed for it. But, even if one accepts that it is not subject to a contrary intention, I do not consider that it has the effect of annexing the benefit of the covenant in each and every case irrespective of the other express terms of the covenant. I notice that Brightman LJ did not go so far as that, for he said in the *Federated Homes* case:[42]

> I find the idea of the annexation of a covenant to the whole of the land but not to a part of it a difficult conception fully to grasp. I can understand that a covenantee may expressly or by necessary implication retain the benefit of a covenant wholly under his own control, so that the benefit will not pass unless the covenantee chooses to assign; but I would have thought, if the benefit of a covenant is, on a proper construction of a document, annexed to the land, *prima facie* it is annexed to every part thereof, unless the contrary clearly appears.

So at least in some circumstances Brightman LJ is considering that despite s 78 the benefit may be retained and not pass or be annexed to and run with land. In this connection, I was also referred by counsel for the defendants to Sir Lancelot Elphinstone's *Covenants Affecting Land* (1946) p 17, where the author says, with reference to this point (and I quote from a footnote on that page):

> ... but it is thought that, as a covenant must be construed as a whole, the court would give due effect to words excluding or modifying the operation of the section.

The true position as I see it is that, even where a covenant is deemed to be made with successors in title as s 78 requires, one still has to construe the covenant as a whole to see whether the benefit of the covenant is annexed. Where one finds, as in the *Federated Homes Case,* the covenant is not qualified in any way, annexation may be readily inferred; but, where, as in the present case, it is expressly provided that 'this covenant shall not enure for the benefit of any owner or subsequent purchaser of any part of the Vendor's Sudbury Court Estate at Wembley unless the benefit of this covenant shall be expressly assigned', one cannot just ignore these words. One may not be able to exclude the operation of the section in extending the range of covenantees, but one has to consider the covenant as a whole to determine its true effect. When one does that, then it seems to me that the answer is plain and in my judgment the benefit was not annexed. That is giving full weight to both the statute in force and also what is already there in a covenant.

Running of benefit in equity

Where the benefit does not run at common law to the successor of the original covenantee, equity may still enforce the benefit of certain covenants. In order for the benefit to run in equity, the covenant must touch and concern the land of the covenantee. This is the same as the rule at common law. It was, however, held

42 [1980] 1 All ER 371 at 381; [1980] 1 WLR 594 at 606.

in *Re Pinewood Estates*[43] that having established that the covenant touches and concerns land, the claimant must also show that he has acquired the benefit of the covenant in one of the three ways: by annexation, by assignment, or under a scheme of development.

(a) Annexation

Annexation is the process of fastening the benefit of a restrictive covenant on the covenantee's land so that it passes with any subsequent transfer of that land or any interest in it. Whether annexation has taken place depends on the intention of the original parties. Once an intention that the covenant should benefit the covenantee and his successors in title has been expressed, the benefit is annexed to the land and passes with it automatically on any subsequent transfer. Such an intention of annexation is often manifested in the express terms of the conveyance containing the covenant. Such an annexation is known as an express annexation. Where the conveyance has failed to manifest an express intention of annexation, the courts have, in recent years, been prepared to construe the conveyance in the light of the surrounding circumstances.[44] When so construed, if an intention of annexation can be implied, the benefit may still pass, for otherwise it would be 'not only an injustice but a departure from common sense'.[45] As will be seen, the courts have also held that annexation may take place automatically under s 78 of the Law of Property Act 1925.[46]

(i) Express annexation

The express intention that the benefit of the covenant should run with the benefited land must be manifested in the terms of the conveyance containing the covenant. It is often a matter of construction of the expression or language used in the deed of covenant. The covenantor must have intended that the covenant is made for the benefit of the benefited land, or for the benefit of the owner *qua* estate owner.[47] Thus, in *Rogers v Hosegood*,[48] the benefit was annexed where the parties expressed 'intent that the covenant may enure to the benefit of the vendors their successors and assigns and others claiming under them to all or any of their lands adjoining'.

Rogers v Hosegood [1900] 2 Ch 388, CA

Collins LJ: (read the judgment of the Court (Lord Alverstone MR, and Rigby and Collins LJJ)): This case raises questions of some difficulty, but we are of opinion that the decision of Farwell J is right and ought to be affirmed ...

43 [1957] 2 All ER 517, at 519. See [1957] CLJ 146 (Wade, HWR).

44 *J Sainsbury plc v Enfield LBC* [1989] 1 WLR 590 at 595H–96F; *Rogers v Hosegood* [1900] 2 Ch 388 at 408.

45 *Marten v Flight Refuelling Ltd* [1962] Ch 115 at 133.

46 *Federated Homes Ltd v Mill Lodge Properties Ltd* [1980] 1 All ER 371.

47 *Rogers v Hosegood* [1900] 2 Ch 388. See Preston, CHS and Newsom, GL, *Restrictive Covenants Affecting Freehold Land*, 7th edn, 1982, London: Sweet & Maxwell, p 20, paras 2–15.

48 [1900] 2 Ch 388 at 408.

The real and only difficulty arises on the question – whether the benefit of the covenants has passed to the assigns of Sir John Millais as owners of the plot purchased by him on 25 March 1873, there being no evidence that he knew of these covenants when he bought. Here, again, the difficulty is narrowed, because by express declaration on the face of the conveyances of 1869 the benefit of the two covenants in question was intended for all or any of the vendor's lands near to or adjoining the plot sold, and therefore for (among others) the plot of land acquired by Sir John Millais, and that they 'touched and concerned' that land within the meaning of those words so as to run with the land at law we do not doubt. Therefore, but for a technical difficulty which was not raised before Farwell J, we should agree with him that the benefit of the covenants in question was annexed to and passed to Sir John Millais by the conveyance of the land which he bought in 1873. A difficulty, however, in giving effect to this view arises from the fact that the covenants in question in the deeds of May and July 1869, were made with the mortgagors only, and therefore in contemplation of law were made with strangers to the land: *Webb v Russell*, to which, therefore, the benefit did not become annexed. That a court of equity, however, would not regard such an objection as defeating the intention of the parties to the covenant is clear; and, therefore, when the covenant was clearly made for the benefit of certain land with a person who in the contemplation of such a court was the true owner of it, it would be regarded as annexed to and running with that land, just as it would have been at law but for the technical difficulty.

[His Lordship referred to Jessel MR's observations in *London and South Western Ry Co v Gomm* (1882) 20 Ch D 562 at 583 and continued.]

These observations, which are just as applicable to the benefit reserved as to the burden imposed, shew that in equity, just as at law, the first point to be determined is whether the covenant or contract in its inception binds the land. If it does, it is then capable of passing with the land to subsequent assignees; if it does not, it is incapable of passing by mere assignment of the land. The benefit may be annexed to one plot and the burden to another, and when this has been once clearly done the benefit and the burden pass to the respective assignees, subject, in the case of the burden, to proof that the legal estate, if acquired, has been acquired with notice of the covenant.

[His Lordship referred to *Renals v Cowlishaw* (1878) 9 Ch D 125 at 130 and *Child v Douglas* (1854) Kay 560 at 571 and continued.]

These authorities establish the proposition that, when the benefit has been once clearly annexed to one piece of land, it passes by assignment of that land, and may be said to run with it, in contemplation as well of equity as of law, without proof of special bargain or representation on the assignment. In such a case, it runs, not because the conscience of either party is affected, but because the purchaser has bought something which inhered in or was annexed to the land bought. This is the reason why, in dealing with the burden, the purchaser's conscience is not affected by notice of covenants which were part of the original bargain on the first sale, but were merely personal and collateral, while it is affected by notice of those which touch and concern the land. The covenant must be one that is capable of running with the land before the question of the purchaser's conscience and the equity affecting it can come into discussion. When, as in *Renals v Cowlishaw*, there is no indication in the original conveyance, or in the circumstances attending it, that the burden of the restrictive covenant is imposed for the benefit of the land reserved, or any particular part of it, then it becomes necessary to examine the circumstances under which any part of the land reserved is sold, in order to see whether a benefit, not originally annexed to it, has become annexed to it on the sale, so that the purchaser is deemed to have bought it with the land, and this can hardly be the case when the purchaser did not know of the existence of the restrictive covenant. But when, as here, it has been once annexed to the land reserved, then it is not necessary to spell an intention out of surrounding facts, such as the existence of a building scheme, statements at auctions, and such like circumstances, and the presumption must be that it passes on a sale of that land, unless there is something to rebut it, and the purchaser's ignorance of the existence of the covenant does not defeat the presumption. We can find nothing in the conveyance to Sir John Millais in any degree inconsistent with the intention to pass to him the benefit already annexed to the land sold to him. We are of opinion, therefore, that Sir John Millais's assigns are entitled to enforce the restrictive covenant against the defendant, and that his appeal must be dismissed.

Covenant which was made with 'the vendors, their heirs and assigns' with no reference to the benefited land, although sufficient at common law, is not sufficient in equity to annex the benefit.[49] Equity requires a clear expression of annexation of benefit upon land, not on persons. In practice, the covenantor often covenants 'with the vendor for the benefit and protection of the vendor's land'.

Renals v Cowlishaw [1878] 9 Ch D 125

Hall VC: The law as to the burden of and the persons entitled to the benefit of covenants in conveyances in fee, was certainly not in a satisfactory state; but it is now well settled that the burden of a covenant entered into by a grantee in fee for himself, his heirs, and assigns, although not running with the land at law so as to give a legal remedy against the owner thereof for the time being, is binding upon the owner of it for the time being, in equity, having notice thereof. Who, then (other than the original covenantee), is entitled to the benefit of the covenant? From the cases of *Mann v Stephens*,[50] *Western v Macdermott*,[51] and *Coles v Sims*,[52] it may, I think, be considered as determined that any one who has acquired land, being one of several lots laid out for sale as building plots, where the court is satisfied that it was the intention that each one of the several purchasers should be bound by and should, as against the others, have the benefit of the covenants entered into by each of the purchasers, is entitled to the benefit of the covenant; and that this right, that is, the benefit of the covenant, enures to the assign of the first purchaser, in other words, runs with the land of such purchaser. This right exists not only where the several parties execute a mutual deed of covenant, but wherever a mutual contract can be sufficiently established. A purchaser may also be entitled to the benefit of a restrictive covenant entered into with his vendor by another or others where his vendor has contracted with him that he shall be the assign of it, that is, have the benefit of the covenant. And such covenant need not be express, but may be collected from the transaction of sale and purchase. In considering this, the expressed or otherwise apparent purpose or object of the covenant, in reference to its being intended to be

49 *Renals v Cowlishaw* (1878) 9 Ch D 125; see also *R v Westminster City Council* (1990) 59 P & CR 51 at 56, *per* Simon Brown J.

50 (1846) 15 Sim 377.

51 (1866) Law Rep 2 Ch 72.

52 (1854) Kay 56; 5 D M & G 1.

annexed to other property, or to its being only obtained to enable the covenantee more advantageously to deal with his property, is important to be attended to. Whether the purchaser is the purchaser of all the land retained by his vendor when the covenant was entered into, is also important. If he is not, it may be important to take into consideration whether his vendor has sold off part of the land so retained, and if he has done so, whether or not he has so sold subject to a similar covenant: whether the purchaser claiming the benefit of the covenant has entered into a similar covenant may not be so important.

The plaintiffs in this case, in their statement of claim, rest their case upon their being 'assigns' of the Mill Hill estate, and they say that as the vendors to Shaw were the owners of that estate when they sold to Shaw a parcel of land adjoining it, the restrictive covenants entered into by the purchaser of that parcel of land must be taken to have been entered into with them for the purpose of protecting the Mill Hill estate, which they retained; and, therefore, that the benefit of that restrictive covenant goes to the assign of that estate, irrespective of whether or not any representation that such a covenant had been entered into by a purchaser from the vendors was made to such assigns, and without any contract by the vendors that that purchaser should have the benefit of that covenant. The argument must, it would seem, go to this length, *viz*, that in such a case a purchaser becomes entitled to the covenant even although he did not know of the existence of the covenant, and that although the purchaser is not (as the purchasers in the present case were not) purchaser of all the property retained by the vendor upon the occasion of the conveyance containing the covenants. It appears to me that the three cases to which I have referred shew that this is not the law of this court; and that in order to enable a purchaser as an assign (such purchaser not being an assign of all that the vendor retained when he executed the conveyance containing the covenants, and that conveyance not shewing that the benefit of the covenant was intended to enure for the time being of each portion of the estate so retained or of the portion of the estate of which the plaintiff is assign) to claim the benefit of a restrictive covenant, this, at least, must appear, that the assign acquired his property with the benefit of the covenant, that is, it must appear that the benefit of the covenant was part of the subject matter of the purchase. Lord Justice Bramwell, in *Master v Hansard*,[53] said: 'I am satisfied that the restrictive covenant was not put in for the benefit of this particular property, but for the benefit of the lessors to enable them to make the most of the property which they retained.' In the present case, I think that the covenants were put in with a like object. If it had appeared in the conveyance to Bainbrigge that there were such restrictive covenants in conveyances already executed, and expressly or otherwise that Bainbrigge was to have the benefit of them, he and the plaintiffs, as claiming through him, would have been entitled to the benefit of them. But there being in the conveyance to Bainbrigge no reference to the existence of such covenants by recital of the conveyances containing them or otherwise, the plaintiffs cannot be treated as entitled to the benefit of them. This action must be dismissed with costs.

Secondly, the exact land to which the parties intend the benefit to annex must be ascertainable, eg for the benefit of 'the property known as the Bleak House', or for the benefit of 'No 1, Eastern Road'. If the description of the benefited land is not clear, eg 'the land adjourning the burdened land' then the claimant has to

53 (1876) 4 Ch D 718 at 724.

bring in extrinsic evidence to identify the particular benefited land the parties had in mind.[54]

Once an intention to annex can be shown and the land is sufficiently indicated, *prima facie* there is an express annexation.

Where a covenant is made for the benefit of the whole of the covenantee's land the annexation will only be effective if the whole of the land is capable of benefiting. Thus, in *Re Ballard's Conveyance*,[55] a restrictive covenant made for the benefit of an 'estate which was about 1,700 acres wide' could not run with the land when in fact only a small part of it could benefit from the covenant.

Re Ballard's Conveyance [1937] Ch 473

Clauson J: Is the covenant one which, in the circumstances of the case, comes within the category of a covenant the benefit of which is capable of running with the land for the benefit of which it was taken? A necessary qualification in order that the covenant may come within that category is that it concerns or touches the land with which it is to run: see *per* Farwell J in *Rogers v Hosegood*.[56] That land is an area of some 1,700 acres. It appears to me quite obvious that while a breach of the stipulations might possibly affect a portion of that area in the vicinity of the applicant's land, far the largest part of this area of 1,700 acres could not possibly be affected by any breach of any of the stipulations.

Counsel for the respondents asked for an adjournment in order to consider whether they would call evidence (as I was prepared to allow them to do) to prove that a breach of the stipulations or of some of them might affect the whole of this large area. However, ultimately no such evidence was called.

The result seems to me to be that I am bound to hold that, while the covenant may concern or touch some comparatively small portion of the land to which it has been sought to annex it, it fails to concern or touch far the largest part of the land. I asked in vain for any authority which would justify me in severing the covenant and treating it as annexed to or running with such part of the land as is touched by or concerned with it, though as regards the remainder of the land, namely, such part as is not touched by or concerned with the covenant, the covenant is not and cannot be annexed to it and accordingly does not and cannot run with it. Nor have I been able through my own researches to find anything in the books which seems to justify any such course. In *Rogers v Hosegood*, the benefit of the covenant was annexed to all or any of certain lands adjoining or near to the covenantor's land, and no such difficulty arose as faces me here; and there are many other reported cases in which, for similar reasons, no such difficulty arose. But the requirement that the covenant, in order that the benefit of it may run with certain lands, must concern or touch those lands, is categorically stated by Farwell J ... in terms which are unquestionably in accord with a long line of earlier authority.

This problem can be solved today by drafting the covenant for the benefit of the 'whole or any part or parts of the benefited land' or 'each and every part of the benefited land'. This practice was accepted by the Court of Appeal in *Marquess of Zetland v Driver*.[57]

54 *Wrotham Park Estate v Parkside Homes Ltd* [1974] 1 WLR 798.

55 [1937] Ch 473.

56 [1900] 2 Ch 388 at 395.

57 [1939] Ch 1.

Marquess of Zetland v Driver [1939] Ch 1

Farwell J: read the judgment of the Court of Appeal (Sir Wilfrid Greene MR, Luxmoore and Farwell JJ): [Having concluded that the covenant in question satisfied all the requirements, the Court of Appeal held that:]

> ... there does not appear to be any ground on which the appellant can properly be refused the relief which he seeks; but Bennett J took the opposite view and held that the benefit of the covenant had not passed to the appellant. In coming to that conclusion he founded himself upon a decision of Clauson J in *In Re Ballard's Conveyance*,[58] which he considered to be exactly in point and binding upon him. In our judgment the learned judge was wrong in thinking that Re Ballard's Conveyance was an authority in this case. It is not necessary for us, and we do not propose, to express any opinion as to that decision beyond saying that it is clearly distinguishable from the present case, if only on the ground that in that case the covenant was expressed to run with the whole estate, whereas in the present case no such difficulty arises because the covenant is expressed to be for the benefit of the whole or any part or parts of the unsold settled property.

But if the covenant is made for the benefit of the whole of the estate which is capable of benefiting, any purchaser of only a part of it would be able to enforce the covenant even if the benefit is not expressly annexed to each and every part of it. Brightman LJ in *Federated Homes Ltd v Mill Lodge Properties Ltd*[59] said that if the benefit of a covenant was annexed to the benefited land, *prima facie* it was annexed to every part thereof, unless a contrary intention appeared. Despite Brightman LJ's *dictum*, the practice has been to annex the benefit to each and every part of the benefited land.

The benefit, once annexed, runs automatically with the land, and each successor in title can enforce it even if he knows nothing of it at the time he acquired the land.[60]

(ii) Implied annexation

There may be circumstances where it is clear that the covenant has reference to a defined plot of land with reasonable certainty and there is evidence from the facts, despite the absence of express words of annexation, that the parties intended that the benefit should attach to that piece of land to which the covenant refers. It would be unjust and contrary to common sense if the benefit does not run. The court has therefore shown a willingness in appropriate cases to hold that implied annexation arises from the conveyance. A notable case is *Shropshire County Council v Edwards*.[61] In 1908, the plaintiff's predecessors in title covenanted that they and their successors and assigns would supply A, his heirs and assigns with water. This positive covenant made reference to the land. They also covenanted not to erect dwelling houses. This, however, made no reference

58 [1937] Ch 473.

59 [1980] 1 All ER 371.

60 *Rogers v Hosegood* [1900] 2 Ch 388 at 408. See also *R v Westminster City Council* (1990) 59 P & CR 51, *per* Simon Brown J at 57.

61 (1983) 46 P & CR 270.

to the land. The plaintiff had notice of the covenants. A's land later came to the hands of D1, D2, D3, and D4. The question was whether D1, D2, D3, and D4 could rely on the 1908 covenant relating to erection of dwelling houses. That depended on whether benefit ran. Because the burden could only run in equity here from the plaintiff's predecessors in title to the plaintiff, D1, D2, D3, and D4 had to show that the benefit had run in equity. Here, the question was whether they had acquired the benefit by one of the three ways. There was no assignment, no scheme of development. There was no statutory annexation because s 78 did not apply to covenant made before 1 January 1926. There was no express annexation because the covenant made no express reference to land. Looking at the 1908 conveyance as a whole, it was, however, clear that the covenants were made to provide the benefited land with water and to protect the land from the activities prohibited on that land in the future.

Rubin J, having reviewed the existing authorities came to the conclusion that although it was highly desirable that express words should have been used to annex the benefit, it was not necessary. He was prepared to hold that where, on the construction, the benefited land could be identified and the intention to benefit could be established, the benefit would be annexed.[62]

However, it should be noted that implied annexation can only be inferred from the conveyance containing the covenant. It cannot be inferred from the surrounding circumstances. The intention to annex the benefit must be shown in the conveyance itself.[63] In *J Sainsbury v Enfield LBC*,[64] W inherited a certain estate in 1882, and in April 1894, sold part of the land to the plaintiff's predecessors in title who covenanted not to use the land for building purposes or for trade or business. W also covenanted not to make roads or footways on a particular area of the land. W's other parts of the estate were subsequently sold at various times to various individuals who were defendants in this case. The plaintiffs acquired land from his predecessors and in 1985 contracted to sell it to J Sainsbury plc subject to a condition that the land was no longer bound by the 1894 restrictive covenants. J Sainsbury plc and the plaintiff applied together for a declaration that the 1894 covenants were no longer binding. The issue was whether the defendants had acquired the benefit of the covenants in equity. It was common ground that the covenants could, if enforced, benefit the defendants' land, and the land was sufficiently identified so that benefit could be annexed to it if they had intended annexation to take place.

There was no scheme of development nor was there any assignment of the benefit of the covenants. The 26 line covenants, as reported in the law report, without a simple punctuation mark except a full stop at the end, made no express reference to the land. There was, therefore, no express annexation. Was there any implied annexation? Morritt J, having reviewed the existing authorities, came to the conclusion that the intention to benefit the benefited land must be apparent from the conveyance. In the circumstances of the case, he could not infer an intention to annex the benefit to the benefited land. This was

62 (1983) 46 P & CR 270 at 277.

63 *J Sainsbury v Enfield LBC* [1989] 2 All ER 817.

64 [1989] 2 All ER 817.

because, while W's covenants made reference to the land, the purchasers' covenants did not. Morritt J, therefore, inferred that there was no intention to annex the benefit. He said that if annexation had been intended, it was remarkable that there was no reference to the land in the purchasers' covenants.

Morritt J's approach is different from that of Rubin J in *Shropshire County Council v Edwards*, where Rubin J allowed implied annexation even though the first covenant made reference to the land and the second did not.

In *J Sainsbury's* case, although under s 58 of the Conveyancing and Law of Property Act 1881, the covenants were deemed to have been made with the covenantee, his heirs and assigns, it was held that that was insufficient to amount to annexation.[65]

J Sainsbury plc v Enfield LBC [1989] 2 All ER 817

Morritt J: In *Federated Homes Ltd v Mill Lodge Properties Ltd*[66] the Court of Appeal decided that in the case of a covenant relating to land of the covenantee in the sense that it touched and concerned that land the effect of s 78 of the Law of Property Act 1925 was to cause the benefit of the covenant to run with that land and be annexed to it.

[His Lordship read s 78 and referred to Brightman LJ's judgment in *Federated Homes Ltd v Mill Lodge Properties Ltd* [1980] 1 All ER 371 at 379 cited at pp 766–69 below and continued.]

The defendant seeks to argue from this decision, and notwithstanding the reasoning expressed in it, that s 58 of the 1881 Act had the same effect. The same point was taken in *Shropshire CC v Edwards*[67] but was not decided.

In *Renals v Cowlishaw*[68] and *Reid v Bickerstaff*,[69] the covenants to which I have referred were entered into before s 58 of the 1881 Act came into force on 31 December 1881. Thus, this point was not of relevance in those cases. But in view of the date of the decision in *Renals v Cowlishaw* it would be very surprising if by enacting in s 58(1) of the 1881 Act that:

> A covenant ... shall be deemed to be made with the covenantee, his heirs and assigns, and shall have effect as if heirs and assigns were expressed.

Parliament intended to effect annexation when the Court of Appeal had already decided that such words if expressed did not suffice.

Between the 1881 Act and the 1925 Act the covenants in *Ives v Brown*[70] and *Miles v Easter*[71] were entered into. But s 58 of the 1881 Act was not referred to in either case.

In *Forster v Elvet Colliery Co Ltd*[72] the Court of Appeal did refer to s 58 of the 1881 Act. The case was not concerned with annexation of the benefit of covenants relating to freehold land. Cozens-Hardy MR said (at 635):

65 For a useful account of the decision in *J Sainsbury's* case see (1991) Conv 52 (Goulding, S).

66 [1980] 1 All ER 371, [1980] 1 WLR 594

67 (1982) 46 P & CR 270.

68 (1878) 9 Ch D 125, [1874–80] All ER Rep 359.

69 [1909] 2 Ch 305, [1908–10] All ER Rep 298.

70 [1919] 2 Ch 314.

71 [1933] Ch 611, [1933] All ER Rep 355.

72 [1908] 1 KB 629.

> The word 'lessee' is by the definition at the beginning of the lease to include also 'his executors, administrators and assigns, unless such construction be excluded by the sense or the context.' And by s 58 of the Conveyancing Act 1881, words of limitation are to be read into the covenant, assuming it to be a covenant 'relating to land.' Now, under the old law, it is settled that the owner of the surface, not being mentioned as a party to the deed, could not have sued on the covenant.

Fletcher Moulton LJ said (at 637–38):

> It is true that none of the plaintiffs in these actions were either owners or occupiers of any portion of these superjacent lands at the date of the lease. But the plaintiffs are successors in title of the then owners of portions of such lands by reason of being their assignees, and they urge that s 58, sub-s 1, of the Conveyancing and Law of Property Act 1881, applies to such a covenant as we have in this case, and that it must accordingly be deemed to have been made with the covenantee, his heirs and assigns. In other words, they say that, although the intention of the parties may have been to make a separate and direct covenant with each future owner, the fact that such a covenant would not be effectual does not prevent the present plaintiffs from claiming under the covenant made with their predecessors in title, 'who were owners of the lands at the date of the lease, and with whom, therefore, the lessee could and did effectually covenant'.

And Farwell LJ said (at 641):

> In the present case the lessors of the minerals and the owners of the surface are different persons. In my opinion, therefore, the owners for the time being mean, primarily at any rate, the owners at the date of the deed; and by s 58, sub-s 1, of the Conveyancing and Law of Property Act 1881, the covenant is made with them, their heirs and assigns. If any other owner not claiming as owner at that date, or as heir or assign of such owner, were to sue, the dictum of Sir George Jessel would apply to him. Some difficulty is created by the addition of the words 'occupier or occupiers'; this is used in contradistinction to owner, and the Conveyancing and Law of Property Act 1881, would therefore read into the covenant 'his or their executors, administrators or assigns' instead of heirs and assigns. Such a covenant could not run with the land, but I do not think that this can affect the right of the owners, as it has not been suggested that the covenants are with owners and occupiers jointly.

On the subsequent appeal to the House of Lords no reference was made to s 58 of the 1881 Act (*sub nom Dyson v Forster* [1909] AC 98, [1908–10] All ER Rep 212).

The Law of Property Act 1922 was an amendment Act. Section 96 provides so far as material:

> ... (2) Every covenant running with the land entered into before the commencement of this Act shall take effect subject to the provisions of this Act, and accordingly the benefit or burden of every such covenant shall, subject as aforesaid, vest in or bind the persons who by virtue of this Act succeed to the title of the covenantee or the covenantor, as the case may be.
>
> (3) The benefit of a covenant relating to land entered into after the commencement of this Act may be made to run with the land without the use of the words 'heirs' if the covenant is of such a nature that the benefit could have been made to run with the land before the commencement of this Act, and if an intention that the benefit shall pass to the successors in title of the covenantee appears from the deed containing the covenant.

(4) For the purposes of this section, a covenant runs with the land when the benefit or burden of it, whether at law or in equity, passes to the successors in title of the covenantee or the covenantor, as the case may be.

The section was, no doubt, passed to cater for the fact that succession rights had been altered. But it did not otherwise affect the operation of s 58 of the 1881 Act in relation to covenants entered into prior to the commencement of the 1922 Act.

The Law of Property (Amendment) Act 1924 was also, as its title indicates, an amending Act. Section 3 provided:

The amendments and provisions, for facilitating the consolidation of the stature law relating to conveyancing and property, contained in the Third Schedule to this Act, shall have effect.

And in Schedule 3, Pt I, para II, it is stated:

The following provision shall be inserted at the end of s 58 of the Conveyancing Act, 1881: For the purposes of this section in connexion with covenants restrictive of the user of land 'successors in title' shall be deemed to include the owners and occupiers for the time being of the land of the covenantee intended to be benefited.

That Act was to come into force on 1 January 1926 (see s 12(3)) but was in fact superseded by the Law of Property Act 1925, which came into force on the same day, and repealed s 3 of and Schedule 3 to the 1924 Act.

It may be that, as submitted, one purpose of para II of Pt I of Schedule 3 to the 1924 Act was to cater for the difficulty expressed by Farwell LJ in *Forster v Elvet Colliery Co Ltd* to which I have referred. But the overall effect of the amendments made by the 1922 and 1924 Acts was much wider than that. Thus, s 78 of the Law of Property Act 1925, which only applies to covenants entered into after 1 January 1926, was in radically different terms from s 58 of the 1881 Act, as Brightman LJ pointed out in *Federated Homes Ltd v Mill Lodge Properties Ltd*.[73] The principle of that case cannot be applied to s 58 of the 1881 Act. There are no words in s 58 capable by themselves of effecting annexation of the benefit of a covenant. All that section did was to deem the inclusion of words which both before and after the enactment of s 58 had, with the exception of *Mann v Stephens*,[74] been consistently held to be insufficient without more to effect annexation of the benefit of a covenant.

(iii) Statutory annexation

The problem of determining whether the language of a conveyance is sufficiently clear to show an intention to annex the benefit of a covenant has seemingly disappeared as regards covenants made after 1925 since the Court of Appeal's decision in *Federated Homes v Mill Lodge Properties Ltd*.[75] A statutory solution to the problem has been found in s 78 of the Law of Property Act 1925.

As we have seen, this section provides that a covenant relating to any land of the covenantee shall be deemed to be made with the covenantee, his

73 [1980] 1 All ER 371 at 379, [1980] 1 WLR 594 at 604.

74 (1846) 15 Sim 377; 60 ER 665.

75 [1980] 1 All ER 371.

successors in title, and those deriving title under him or them. The inclusion of the words 'successors in title' shows that the benefit is intended to pass to them and not merely personal to the covenantee.

In *Federated Homes v Mill Lodge Properties Ltd*,[76] there was a covenant by the defendant not to build more than 300 houses on his land. It was clear from the wording that the covenant was intended to benefit the 'adjourning or adjacent property retained' by the covenantee, although the terms of the covenant were not sufficiently expressed to annex the benefit to the covenantee's land according to the rule in *Rogers v Hosegood* (ie there were no express words of annexation). Later, the covenantee sold his land and, eventually, the plaintiff became the owner of the land. The benefit of the covenant was assigned in relation to one part of the land to the plaintiff. The problem was whether the plaintiff also acquired the benefit of the covenant in relation to other parts of the land. It was held by the Court of Appeal that the covenant touched and concerned the covenantee's land and, therefore, the benefit was annexed, under s 78, to the other part of the land. Brightman LJ said that if a covenant was deemed to be made with the covenantee and his successors in title or other persons deriving title under them, as was the case under s 78, then it could be enforced by the successors in title, as well as the covenantee, and other persons deriving title under them. And so it followed that the covenant ran with the land. Therefore, if s 78 is satisfied, ie there exists a covenant which touches and concerns the covenantee's land, the covenant runs automatically with the land for the benefit of the successors in title, and every person deriving title under them.

Brightman LJ rejected the narrow view that s 78 only saved the need of naming the covenantee's successors in title and that it only allowed annexation when, independently of the section, an annexation had already taken place but covenantee's successors in title had not been named.

Federated Homes v Mill Lodge Properties Ltd [1980] 1 All ER 371, CA

Brightman LJ: Counsel for the defendants submitted that there were three possible views about s 78. One view, which he described as 'the orthodox view' hitherto held, is that it is merely a statutory shorthand for reducing the length of legal documents. A second view, which was the one that counsel for the defendants was inclined to place in the forefront of his argument, is that the section only applies, or at any rate only achieves annexation, when the land intended to be benefited is signified in the document by express words or necessary implication as the intended beneficiary of the covenant. A third view is that the section applies if the covenant in fact touches and concerns the land of the covenantee, whether that be gleaned from the document itself or from evidence outside the document.

For myself, I reject the narrowest interpretation of s 78, the supposed orthodox view, which seems to me to fly in the face of the wording of the section. Before I express my reasons I will say that I do not find it necessary to choose between the second and third

76 [1980] 1 All ER 371. See (1980) 43 MLR 445 (Hayton, DJ); [1980] JPL 371 (Newsom, GH); (1980) 130 NLJ 531 (Bailey, T); [1980] Conv 216 (Sydenham, A). See also (1981) 97 LQR 32 (Newsom, GH); (1982) 98 LQR 202 (Newsom, GH); [1982] *Legal Studies* 53 (Hurst, DJ).

views because, in my opinion, this covenant relates to land of the covenantee on either interpretation of s 78 ...

The first point to notice about s 78(1) is that the wording is significantly different from the wording of its predecessor, s 58(1) of the Conveyancing and Law of Property Act 1881. The distinction is underlined by sub-s (2) of s 78, which applies sub-s (1) only to covenants made after the commencement of the Act. Section 58(1) of the earlier Act did not include the covenantee's successors in title or persons deriving title under him or them, nor the owners or occupiers for the time being of the land of the covenantee intended to be benefited. The section was confined, in relation to realty, to the covenantee, his heirs and assigns, words which suggest a more limited scope of operation than is found in s 78.

If, as the language of s 78 implies, a covenant relating to land which is restrictive of the user thereof is enforceable at the suit of (1) a successor in title of the covenantee, (2) a person deriving title under the covenantee or under his successors in title, and (3) the owner or occupier of the land intended to be benefited by the covenant, it must, in my view, follow that the covenant runs with the land, because *ex hypothesi* every successor in title to the land, every derivative proprietor of the land and every other owner and occupier has a right by statute to the covenant. In other words, if the condition precedent of s 78 is satisfied, that is to say, there exists a covenant which touches and concerns the land of the covenantee, that covenant runs with the land for the benefit of his successors in title, persons deriving title under him or them and other owners and occupiers.

This approach to s 78 has been advocated by distinguished textbook writers: see Dr Radcliffe in the *Law Quarterly Review*,[77] Professor Wade in the *Cambridge Law Journals*[78] under the apt cross-heading 'What is wrong with s 78?', and Megarry and Wade on the *Law of Real Property*.[79] Counsel pointed out to us that the fourth edition of Megarry and Wade's textbook indicates a change of mind on this topic since the third edition was published in 1966.

Although the section does not seem to have been extensively used in the course of argument in this type of case, the construction of s 78 which appeals to me appears to be consistent with at least two cases decided in this court. The first is *Smith v River Douglas Catchment Board*.[80] In that case, an agreement was made in April 1938 between certain landowners and the catchment board under which the catchment board undertook to make good the banks of a certain brook and to maintain the same, and the landowners undertook to contribute towards the cost. In 1940, the first plaintiff took a conveyance from one of the landowners of a part of the land together with an express assignment of the benefit of the agreement. In 1944, the second plaintiff took a tenancy of that land without any express assignment of the benefit of the agreement. In 1946, the brook burst its banks and the land owned by the first plaintiff and tenanted by the second plaintiff was inundated. The two important points are that the agreement was not expressed to be for the benefit of the landowner's successors in title; and there was no assignment of the benefit of the agreement in favour of the second plaintiff, the tenant. In reliance, as I understand the case, on s 78 of the Law of Property Act 1925, it was held that the second

77 (1941) 57 LQR 203.

78 [1972] CLJ 157.

79 4th edn, 1975, p 764.

80 [1949] 2 All ER 179; [1949] 2 KB 500.

plaintiff was entitled to sue the catchment board for damages for breach of the agreement. It seems to me that that conclusion can only have been reached on the basis that s 78 had the effect of causing the benefit of the agreement to run with the land so as to be capable of being sued on by the tenant.

The other case, *Williams v Unit Construction Co Ltd*,[81] was decided by this court in 1951. There a company had acquired a building estate and had underleased four plots to Cubbin for 999 years. The underlessors arranged for the defendant company to build houses on the four plots. The defendant company covenanted with Cubbin to keep the adjacent road in repair until adopted. Cubbin granted a weekly tenancy of one house to the plaintiff without any express assignment of the benefit of the covenant. The plaintiff was injured owing to the disrepair of the road. She was held entitled to recover damages from the defendant for breach of the covenant.

We were referred to observations in the speeches of Lord Upjohn and Lord Wilberforce in *Tophams Ltd v Earl of Sefton*[82] to the effect that s 79 of the Law of Property Act 1925 (relating to the burden of covenants) achieved no more than the introduction of statutory shorthand into the drafting covenants. Section 79, in my view, involves quite different considerations and I do not think that it provides a helpful analogy.

It was suggested by counsel for the defendants that if this covenant ought to be read as enuring for the benefit of the retained land, it should be read as enuring only for the benefit of the retained land as a whole and not for the benefit of every part of it; with the apparent result that there is no annexation of the benefit to a part of the retained land when any severance takes place. He referred us to a passage in *Re Union of London and Smith's Bank Ltd's Conveyance, Miles v Easter*,[83] which I do not think it is necessary for me to read.

The problem is alluded to in Megarry and Wade on the *Law of Real Property*:[84]

> ... in drafting restrictive covenants it is therefore desirable to annex them to the covenantee's land 'or any part or parts thereof'. An additional reason for using this form of words is that, if there is no indication to the contrary, the benefit may be held to be annexed only to the whole of the covenantee's land, so that it will not pass with portions of it disposed of separately. But even without such words the court may find that the covenant is intended to benefit any part of the retained land; and small indications may suffice, since the rule that presumes annexation to the whole only is arbitrary and inconvenient. in principle it conflicts with the rule for assignments, which allows a benefit annexed to the whole to be assigned with part, and it also conflicts with the corresponding rule for easements.

I find the idea of the annexation of a covenant to the whole of the land but not to a part of it a difficult conception fully to grasp. I can understand that a covenantee may expressly or by necessary implication retain the benefit of a covenant wholly under his own control, so that the benefit will not pass unless the covenantee chooses to assign; but I would have thought, if the benefit of a covenant is, on a proper construction of a document, annexed to the land, *prima facie* it is annexed to every part thereof, unless the

81 (1951) 19 Conv NS 262.

82 [1966] 1 All ER 1039 at 1048, 1053; [1967] 1 AC 50 at 73, 81.

83 [1933] Ch 611; [1933] All ER Rep 355.

84 4th edn, 1975, p 763.

contrary clearly appears. It is difficult to see how this court can have reached its decision in *Williams v Unit Construction Co Ltd* unless this is right. The covenant was, by inference, annexed to every part of the land and not merely to the whole, because it will be recalled that the plaintiff was a tenant of only one of the four houses which had the benefit of the covenant. There is also this observation by Romer LJ in *Drake v Gray* [1936] Ch 451. He was dealing with the enuring of the benefit of a restrictive covenant and he said:

> ... where ... you find, not 'the land coloured yellow', or 'the estate', or 'the field named so and so', or anything of that kind, but 'the lands retained by the vendor', it appears to me that there is a sufficient indication that the benefit of the covenant enures to every one of the lands retained by the vendor, and if a plaintiff in a subsequent action to enforce a covenant can say, 'I am the owner of a piece of land or a hereditament that belonged to the vendor at the time of the conveyance', he is entitled to enforce the covenant.

In the instant case, the judge in the course of his judgment appears to have dismissed the notion that any individual plotholder would be entitled, even by assignment, to have the benefit of the covenant that I have been considering. I express no view about that. I only say this, that I am not convinced that his conclusion on that point is correct. I say no more about it.

In the end, I come to the conclusion that s 78 of the Law of Property Act 1925 caused the benefit of the restrictive covenant in question to run with the red land and therefore to be annexed to it, with the result that the plaintiff company is able to enforce the covenant against Mill Lodge, not only in its capacity as owner of the green land, but also in its capacity as owner of the red land.

(iv) Criticism of Federated Homes

The decision has simplified the rules relating to passing of benefit in equity. But it has been criticised. First, it is said that if the decision is correct, then there will be no need for the devise of express assignment and express or implied annexation.[85] Secondly, the Law of Property Act 1925 is a consolidation Act, which does not normally change the law unless the words clearly constrain the court to do so.[86] If the words are capable of more than one construction, then the court should give effect to the construction which does not change the law. This is a strong argument for the narrow view. If Parliament intended to change the law, one would expect this to be expressed in unambiguous terms.[87] If Parliament intended s 78 to annex the benefit to the covenantee's land, why are words similar to those in s 76(6) (now repealed) and s 77(5) not used in s 78?

Thirdly, in *Federated Homes*, the defendant was the original covenantor. It was a case between the original covenantor and the successors in title of the original covenantee. The benefit could have run at common law, and there was

85 (1980) 43 MLR 445 at 447 (Hayton, DJ).

86 Preston, CHS and Newsom, GL, *Restrictive Covenants Affecting Freehold Land*, 7th edn, 1982, London: Sweet & Maxwell, p 18, paras 2–10, 2–11.

87 As in s 76(6) (now repealed) and s 77(5) of the LPA 1925 where it was enacted that the benefits of the covenants governed by s 76(6) (covenant for title) and s 77(5) (implied covenants in conveyances subject to rents) 'shall be annexed to, and shall go with, the estate or interest of the implied covenantee ...'.

no need for the court to consider the running of the benefit in equity. Therefore, any subsequent court may treat the dictum of Brightman LJ regarding statutory annexation under s 78 as merely *obiter dicta*. Preston and Newsom have submitted that if the House of Lords is given an opportunity to consider this issue, the Federated Homes decision will be overruled.[88]

Despite the criticism, *Federated Homes* has been applied in *Roake v Chadha*.[89]

Roake v Chadha [1983] 3 All ER 503

Judge Paul Baker QC: As to annexation, counsel for the plaintiffs conceded that the express terms of the covenant appeared to exclude annexation, and there was no suggestion that the case fell within the category known as building schemes. Counsel for the plaintiffs, however, in an interesting argument submitted that annexation had come about through the operation of s 78 of the 1925 Act, as interpreted in *Federated Homes Ltd v Mill Lodge Properties Ltd*,[90] a decision of the Court of Appeal. I can summarise his argument by the following four points. (1) The covenant was a covenant relating to the land of the covenantee. (2) Section 78(1) of the 1925 Act provides:

[His Lordship read s 78(1) of the Law of Property Act 1925.]

(3) In the *Federated Homes* case it was held that by virtue of that section the benefit of a covenant relating to land retained by the covenantee ran with that land and was annexed to it and to every part of it. (4) The provisions of s 78, unlike those of s 79 relating to the burden of the covenant, cannot be excluded by the expression of a contrary intention.

[His Lordship read s 79(1) and (2) and continued.]

Unlike s 78, which had a counterpart in s 58 of the Conveyancing Act 1881, s 79 was a new section in 1925. The important point to which attention is called is 'unless a contrary intention is expressed', and that appears in s 79. There is no corresponding expression in s 78. Those are the main points of the argument.

I have no difficulty in accepting that the covenant in the standard form of transfer which I have read is a covenant relating to the retained land of the covenantee, that is to say Wembley (C & W) Land Co Ltd, and that therefore s 78 comes into play. It is the third and fourth points which have given rise to the argument in this case. I must begin, therefore, by examining the *Federated Homes* case ...

Counsel for the defendants made a frontal attack on this use of s 78, which he reinforced by reference to an article by GH Newsom QC 'Universal Annexation?'[91] which is critical of the decision. The main lines of attack are: (1) the conclusion overlooks the legislative history of s 78 which it is said shows that it has a narrower purpose than is claimed and does not in itself bring about annexation; (2) this narrower purpose has been accepted in relation to the corresponding s 79 (relating to burden), which I have already read, by Lord Upjohn and Lord Wilberforce in *Tophams Ltd v Earl of Sefton*.[92] Further, it is said by way of argument *sub silentio* that in a number of cases, notably *Marquess of*

88 Preston, CHS and Newsom, GL, *Restrictive Covenants Affecting Freehold Land*, 7th edn 1982, London: Sweet & Maxwell, p 19, para 2–12.

89 [1983] 3 All ER 503.

90 [1980] 1 All ER 371; [1980] 1 WLR 594.

91 (1981) 97 LQR 32.

92 [1966] 1 All ER 1039 at 1048, 1053; [1967] 1 AC 50 at 73, 81.

Zetland v Driver[93] and *Re Jeffs's Transfer, Rogers v Astley (No 2)*,[94] the argument could have been used to good effect but was not deployed.

Now, all this is very interesting, and the views of Mr Newsom are entitled to very great respect seeing that until his recent retirement he was a practitioner of long experience who had made a special study of this branch of the law. He has written a valuable monograph on it. All the same, despite counsel for the defendants' blandishments, I am not going to succumb to the temptation of joining in any such discussion. Sitting here as a judge of the Chancery Division, I do not consider it to be my place either to criticise or to defend the decisions of the Court of Appeal. I conceive it my clear duty to accept the decision of the Court of Appeal as binding on me and apply it as best I can to the facts I find here.

(v) Limitations of s 78

As it stands, it appears that the decision suggests that the Court of Appeal will accept statutory annexation where it is clear that the covenant touches and concerns the covenantee's land. The statutory annexation will have effect on every part of the benefited land, as we have seen earlier. There is no need to rely on express or implied annexation. Neither is it necessary to have any express assignment of the benefit. However, since the decision is open to criticism, it would be safer to employ express words of annexation or express assignment when drafting covenants in order to show a clear intention for the running of the benefit.

Furthermore, there are limitations on s 78. The covenant must not exclude the operation of s 78 as to annexation. If a covenant expressly provides that it shall not take effect for the benefit of any owner or subsequent purchaser of any part of the estate unless the benefit is expressly assigned, then in the absence of express assignment, annexation does not take place.[95]

Secondly, s 78 only applies to covenants made after 1925. Its predecessor, s 58 of the Conveyancing and Law of Property Act 1881, was not capable of achieving statutory annexation.[96]

Thirdly, there are some cases in which the plaintiff would have to rely on the doctrine of scheme of development.[97] This is where the plaintiff obtained the title of a land from a common vendor within the area of a scheme before the defendant covenanted with the common vendor. Furthermore, the benefit of a covenant made under a scheme of development cannot be annexed to the plaintiff's land under s 78 because the plaintiff derived his title from the common vendor before the covenant was made. In such a case, he still has to rely on the doctrine of scheme of development which will be discussed later.

93 [1938] 2 All ER 158; [1939] Ch 1.

94 [1966] 1 All ER 937; [1966] 1 WLR 841.

95 *Roake v Chadha* [1983] 3 All ER 503.

96 *Sainsbury v Enfield* [1989] 1 WLR 590 at 601D–E; *Renals v Cowlishaw* (1878) 9 Ch D 125; *Federated Homes Ltd v Mill Lodge Properties Ltd* [1980] 1 WLR 594 at 604H–05A.

97 See Preston, CHS and Newsom, GL, *Restrictive Covenants Affecting Freehold Land*, 7th edn, 1982, London: Sweet & Maxwell, p 16, paras 2–5.

(vi) Annexation by s 62 LPA?

It is difficult to see how the benefit of covenant not already acquired by the successor of the original covenantee can be passed to him under s 62. This is because the right which is yet to be annexed cannot be said to be a right appertaining or reputed to appertain.[98]

Roake v Chadha [1983] 3 All ER 503

Judge Paul Baker QC: [Having considered the issue of annexation under s 78 of the Law of Property Act 1925 continued.]

> I must now turn to the alternative argument of the plaintiffs based on s 62 of the 1925 Act. This argument is directed to the conveyances or transfers conveying the alleged benefited land to the predecessors of the plaintiffs, and ultimately to the respective plaintiffs themselves. In each of these transfers, so I am prepared to assume, there is to be implied the general words of s 62:

> (1) A conveyance of land shall be deemed to include and shall by virtue of this Act operate to convey, with the land, all buildings, erections, fixtures, commons, hedges, ditches, fences. ways, waters, watercourses, liberties, privileges, easements, rights, and advantages whatsoever, appertaining or reputed to appertain to the land, or any part thereof, or, at the time of conveyance, demised, occupied, or enjoyed with or reputed or known as part or parcel of or appurtenant to the land or any part thereof ...

Then in sub-s (2) it deals with the conveyance of land having houses and buildings and various corresponding rights in relation to buildings. I do not think I need read that subsection.

The argument is that the benefit of the covenant contained in the original transfer to the predecessors of the defendants (that is to say William Lambert) was carried by the words 'rights, and advantages whatsoever, appertaining or reputed to appertain to the land, or any part thereof'.

It seems an argument on these lines was accepted by John Mills QC, the deputy judge who gave the decision at first instance in the *Federated Homes* case, but I have not seen it, and so cannot comment on it. The proposition now contended for is not a new one. In *Rogers v Hosegood* [1900] 2 Ch 388; [1900–03] All ER Rep 915, it was similarly put forward as an alternative argument to an argument based on annexation. In that case, however, it was decided that the benefit of the covenant was annexed so that the point on s 6 of the Conveyancing Act 1881, the forerunner of s 62 of the 1925 Act, did not have to be decided. Nevertheless, Farwell J, sitting in the Chancery Division, said ([1900] 2 Ch 388 at 398):

> It is not necessary for me to determine whether the benefit of the covenants would pass under the general words to which I have referred above, if such covenants did not run with the land. If they are not in fact annexed to the land, it may well be that the right to sue thereon cannot be said to belong, or be reputed to belong, thereto; but I express no final opinion on this point.

In the Court of Appeal, the point was canvassed in argument but not referred to in the judgment of the court, which was given by Collins LJ.

---

98 *Roake v Chadha* [1983] 3 All ER 503 at 506.

In the present case, the covenant in terms precludes the benefit passing unless it is expressly assigned. That being so, as it seems to me, it is not a right appertaining or reputed to appertain to land within the meaning of s 62 of the 1925 Act. On whether the benefit of a covenant not annexed can ever pass under s 62, I share the doubts of Farwell J. Counsel for the defendants suggested, and there may well be something in this, that the rights referred to in s 62 are confined to legal rights rather than equitable rights which the benefit of restrictive covenants is. But again I place it on construction. It cannot be described as a right appertaining or reputed to appertain to land when the terms of the covenant itself would seem to indicate the opposite.

(b) Assignment of benefit in equity

As we have seen, the claimant may acquire the benefit by express assignment at common law if the assignment satisfies the formal requirement of s 136 of the Law of Property Act 1925. If s 136 is not satisfied, as long as there is an agreement between the original covenantee and his successors in title for the assignment of the benefit, the assignment will take effect in equity provided that two conditions are also satisfied. First, the assignment must be contemporaneous with the transfer of the benefited land.[99] Equity only allows a transferee of the benefited land to enforce the covenant if the benefit has been assigned to him together with some or all of the land. Secondly, the covenant assigned must have been taken for the benefit of the land owned by the original covenantee at the date of the covenant. In *Newton Abbot Co-operative Society Ltd v Williamson and Traedgold Ltd*,[100] the original covenantee was an ironmonger. She sold a shop which she owned on the opposite side of the street to a purchaser. The purchaser covenanted not to trade as an ironmonger at the premises. The covenant did not provide which land was to benefit from the covenant. When the original covenantee died later, her successor, L, obtained the land and the benefit of the covenant in equity held by the deceased's executors as bare trustees. L purported to assign the benefit to a purchaser. It was held that from the circumstances it was clear that the covenant was taken for the protection of the shop in which the original covenantee carried out her ironmonger business. So the purchaser who bought her shop and had the benefit expressly assigned in equity to him could sue on the covenant.

Newton Abbot Co-operative Society Ltd v Williamson and Traedgold Ltd [1952] 1 Ch 286

Upjohn J: The sole issue before me is whether the plaintiffs are entitled to the benefit of the restrictive covenant, and, if so, whether they are entitled to enforce it against the defendants.

I will deal with the first point first. Mr Binney on behalf of the plaintiffs submitted first that the benefit of the restrictive covenant was annexed to Devonia so as to pass with the assignment of Devonia in equity without any express mention in that subsequent assignment; in other words, that the covenant runs with the land. Alternatively, he said that the plaintiffs are the express assigns of the benefit of the

99 *Miles v Easter* [1933] Ch 611.

100 [1952] 1 All ER 279. See (1952) 68 LQR 353 (Sir Lancelot Elphinstone).

covenant, and as such are entitled to enforce it. In this difficult branch of the law one thing in my judgment is clear, namely that in order to annex the benefit of a restrictive covenant to land, so that it runs with the land without express assignment on a subsequent assignment of the land, the land for the benefit of which it is taken must be clearly identified in the conveyance creating the covenant ...

Now, looking at the conveyance of 1923, I can find nothing whatever which identifies the land for the benefit of which the covenant is alleged to be taken. Mr Binney relies on the fact that Mrs Mardon is described as of Devonia, Fore Street, but that in my judgment is quite insufficient to annex the benefit of the covenant to those premises. There is no other mention whatever of Devonia in the conveyance.

In my judgment, therefore, the plaintiff fails on this point.

I turn then to his second submission, namely, that the plaintiffs are express assigns of the benefit of the restrictive covenant. Mr Bowles, on behalf of the defendants, contends that, even if it be assumed that his submission (with which I shall deal later) that the covenant was not taken for the benefit of Devonia, but of the business carried on thereat, is wrong, and the covenant was taken by Mrs Mardon for the benefit of Devonia to enable her to dispose of it to better advantage, yet there is here no complete chain of assignments vesting the benefit in the plaintiffs. He says that there was never any assignment of the benefit of the covenant by the executors of Mrs Mardon to Leonard Soper Mardon and therefore he was not in a position to assign the benefit of the covenant to the plaintiffs' predecessors in title. He relied on *Ives v Brown*[101] and *Lord Northbourne v Johnston & Son*.[102]

In my judgment, those authorities do not support his contention. The position as I see it was this: On the footing that the restrictive covenant was not annexed to the land so as to run with it, the benefit of the covenant is capable of passing by operation of law as well as by express assignment and formed part of Mrs Mardon's personal estate on her death: see *Ives v Brown*.

It was not suggested that there was any implied assent to the assignment of the benefit of the covenant to the residuary legatee, but in my judgment, when her estate was duly wound up and administered, and this case has been argued before me on the footing that that happened many years ago, the benefit of the covenant was held by the executors as bare trustees for the residuary legatee, Leonard Soper Mardon, who was himself one of the executors. He therefore became entitled to the benefit of this restrictive covenant in equity and, in my judgment, he was entitled to assign the benefit in equity on an assignment of Devonia. No doubt had the covenant been assigned to him by the executors, he could also have assigned it at law. That this is the position is, in my judgment, made clear by ... the judgment of Sargant J in *Lord Northbourne v Johnston & Son*[103] ...

The second main question was whether the defendants are liable to have the covenant enforced against them. This was Mr Bowles' main defence in this action and he says that the restrictive covenant was not taken for the benefit of Devonia, and he puts his case in this way: First, he says that in any event this was not taken for the benefit of

101 [1919] 2 Ch 314.

102 [1922] 2 Ch 209.

103 [1922] 2 Ch 309 at 317.

any land, but was a covenant with Mrs Mardon personally, solely for the benefit of her business. Secondly, he says that in order that an express assign of the benefit may sue an assignee of the burden of the covenant there must be some reference in the conveyance creating that covenant to the land for the benefit of which it was taken. It will be convenient to deal with the first point first.

Mr Bowles strongly urged that the covenant was taken solely to protect, the goodwill of the business carried on at Devonia, that it had no reference to the land itself, and that it was not taken for the benefit of that land; in brief, that it was a covenant in gross incapable of assignment. He urged that taking such a covenant would benefit the business in that an enhanced price could be obtained for the business, but no such enhanced price would be obtained for the land. He relied on the fact that the covenant did not mention the vendors' assigns and that it was a covenant against competition. Further, he pointed out that when Leonard Soper Mardon assigned to the Bovey Tracey Co-operative Society, the benefit of the covenant was assigned in the deed which assigned the business and not in the lease of Devonia ...

I do not accept this view of the transaction of 1923. In 1923, Mrs Mardon was carrying on the business of an ironmonger at Devonia. No doubt the covenant was taken for the benefit of that business and to prevent competition therewith, but I see no reason to think, and there is nothing in the conveyance of 1923 which leads me to believe, that that was the sole object of taking the covenant. Mrs Mardon may well have had it in mind that she might want ultimately to sell her land and the business and the benefit of the covenant in such manner as to annex the benefit of the covenant to Devonia for, by so doing, she would get an enhanced price for the totality of the assets which she was selling; a purchaser would surely pay more for a property which would enable him to sue in equity assigns of the defendants' premises taking with notice and to pass on that right, if he so desired, to his successors, than for a property which would only enable him to sue the original covenantor, for that is the result of the view urged on me by Mr Bowles.

Further, Mrs Mardon may well have thought that her own business might ultimately be closed down, or the goodwill thereof sold to someone who was going to carry it on some other premises. She would then be left with Devonia, and Devonia could be sold at an enhanced price to someone intending to carry on the business of an ironmonger, because, if, as part of the sale transaction, he obtained the benefit of the covenant, he could prevent competition from the defendants' premises opposite in that trade.

In my judgment, it was always open to Mrs Mardon, when she desired to dispose either of the land or the business, to assign the benefit of the covenant with the one or the other or both as she chose. By taking this covenant, she was thereby enabled to sell her premises, or her business, to better advantage as she thought fit ...

Accordingly, in my judgment, the defendants fail on this point.

Mr Bowles' second point was that, in order that the benefit of the covenant may be assignable, the land for which the benefit of the covenant is taken must in some way be referred to in the conveyance creating the covenant, and I was naturally pressed with the headnote in *Re Union of London and Smith's Bank Ltd's Conveyance*[104] which reads as follows:

---

104 [1933] Ch 611.

> Where on a sale otherwise than under a building scheme a restrictive covenant is taken, the benefit of which is not on the sale annexed to the land retained by the covenantee so as to run with it, an assign of the covenantee's retained land cannot enforce the covenant against an assign (taking with notice) of the covenantor unless he can show (i) that the covenant was taken for the benefit of ascertainable land of the covenantee capable of being benefited by the covenant, and (ii) that he (the covenantee's assign) is an express assign of the benefit of the covenant.

and with the following passage in the judgment of Bennett J:[105]

> In my judgment, in order that an express assignee of a covenant restricting the user of land may be able to enforce that covenant against the owner of the land burdened with the covenant, he must be able to satisfy the court of two things. The first is that it was a covenant entered into for the benefit or protection of land owned by the covenantee at the date of the covenant. Otherwise, it is a covenant in gross, and unenforceable except as between the parties to the covenant: see *Formby v Barker*.[106] Secondly, the assignee must be able to satisfy the court that the deed containing the covenant defines or contains something to define the property for the benefit of which the covenant was entered into: see James LJ in *Renals v Cowlishaw*.[107]

With all respect to the statement of the judge, I am unable to agree that where a person is suing as an assign of the benefit of the covenant there must necessarily be something in the deed containing the covenant to define the land for the benefit of which the covenant was entered into. In the first place, the passage in the judgment of James LJ in *Renals v Cowlishaw*, which I have already read, on which the judge relied, does not in my judgment support the statement of the law for which it was cited. In *Renals v Cowlishaw*, there was no express assignment of the benefit of the restrictive covenant (see the statement of fact in the report in the court below);[108] and when James LJ says that to enable an assign to take the benefit of restrictive covenants there must be something in the deed to define the property for the benefit of which they were entered into, he is, I think, dealing with the case where it is contended that the benefit of the covenant has been annexed to the land so as to run with the land. When he uses the word 'assign' he is using the word as meaning an assign of the land and not an assign of the benefit of the covenant. Secondly, the views expressed by Bennett J appear to me to be inconsistent with the views expressed in some of the earlier decisions. I do not propose to cite them, but I refer to the following observations on the law on this point, namely the observations of Collins LJ, delivering the judgment of the Court of Appeal in *Rogers v Hosegood*;[109] those of Vaughan Williams LJ in *Formby v Barker*; and to the observations of Cozens-Hardy MR in *Reid v Bickerstaff*;[110] and to the words of Buckley LJ in the same case. Finally, in *Re Union of London and Smith's Bank Ltd's Conveyance*,[111] Romer LJ, reading the judgment of the Court of Appeal, having considered the cases where the benefit of the covenant is annexed to land so as to run without express mention, says:

105 [1933] Ch 611 at 625.
106 [1903] 2 Ch 539.
107 (1879) 11 Ch D 866, CA.
108 (1878) 9 Ch D 125 at 127.
109 [1900] 2 Ch 388 at 407.
110 [1909] 2 Ch 305 at 319, 325.
111 [1933] Ch 611 at 628, 631.

In all other cases, the purchaser will not acquire the benefit of the covenant unless that benefit be expressly assigned to him or, to use the words of the Vice-Chancellor, 'it must appear that the benefit of the covenant was part of the subject matter of the purchase'.

[His Lordship referred to the last paragraph of Romer LJ's judgment cited at p 751 above and continued.]

In my judgment, therefore, the problem which I have to consider is this: First, when Mrs Mardon took the covenant in 1923, did she retain other lands capable of being benefited by the covenant? The answer is plainly yes. Secondly, was such land 'ascertainable' or 'certain' in this sense that the existence and situation of the land must be indicated in the conveyance or otherwise shown with reasonable certainty?

Apart from the fact that Mrs Mardon is described as of Devonia, there is nothing in the conveyance of 1923 to define the land for the benefit of which the restrictive covenant was taken, and I do not think that carries one very far; but, for the reason I have given, I am, in my judgment, entitled to look at the attendant circumstances to see if the land to be benefited is shown 'otherwise' with reasonable certainty. That is a question of fact and, on the admitted facts, bearing in mind the close juxtaposition of Devonia and the defendants' premises, in my view the only reasonable inference to draw from the circumstances at the time of the conveyance of 1923 was that Mrs Mardon took the covenant restrictive of the user of the defendants' premises for the benefit of her own business of ironmonger and of her property Devonia where at all material times she was carrying on that business, which last-mentioned fact must have been apparent to the purchasers in 1923.

I should perhaps mention that at the date of her death Mrs Mardon owned other property in Fore Street, but counsel on neither side founded any argument on that circumstance.

It follows, therefore, in my judgment, that Mrs Mardon could on any subsequent sale of her land Devonia, if she so chose, as part of the transaction of sale, assign the benefit of the covenant so as to enable the purchaser from her and his assignees of the land and covenant to enforce it against an owner of the defendants' premises taking with notice, and her legatee, Leonard Soper Mardon, was in no worse position. I do not regard the fact that he assigned the covenant in the deed containing the assignment of the business as affecting the matter. I say nothing as to the position when the plaintiffs' lease expires so that their estate in Devonia comes to an end, nor whether Leonard Soper Mardon, having apparently assigned away the entire benefit of the covenant, will then be in any position further to enforce it.

Mr Bowles took one further point. He submitted that a covenant restrictive of business could not be annexed to land, unless it was a covenant not to carry on a business so as to be a nuisance or annoyance to an adjoining occupier, but he cited no authority for that proposition and, in my judgment, it cannot be maintained: see *Nicoll v Fenning*.[112]

Accordingly, in my judgment, the plaintiffs are entitled to succeed in this action and to an injunction.

112 (1881) 19 Ch D 258.

Unlike assignment at law, equity allows the benefit to be assigned with any part or parts of the benefited land.[113] Assignment only gives the benefit to the immediate assignee and does not fasten the benefit on the benefited land for ever. So the benefit must be assigned afresh whenever there is a subsequent transfer of the benefited land. There must be a chain of assignment from the original covenantee to the current successor in title.[114]

(c) Scheme of development

This is a third way of acquiring benefit in equity. Where land is sold or let in lots according to a plan, it is crucial that the covenant, extracted from the purchaser of each lot for the benefit of the estate generally, is mutually enforceable by the purchasers *inter se*.

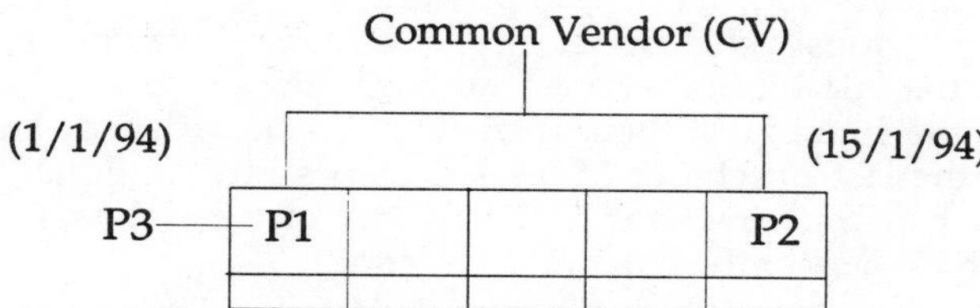

Suppose a covenant not to use the premises for business purposes is extracted by the common vendor from each purchaser (P1, P2 and P3, etc).

Fig 1

(i) How can P2 enforce the covenant against P1?

To make sure that P1 will comply with the covenant, it is important that P2 is able to enforce the P1–CV covenant because, when all the lots are sold, CV will disappear from the picture and even if CV can sue as an original covenantee, he will only get nominal damages. And, in any event, the CV may not want to sue as there is no incentive for him to do so. P1 may also have subsequently sold his property to other purchaser, P3, in which case the burden will only run, if at all, in equity. P2 must show that he gets the benefit in equity too. This can be achieved by requiring P1 to covenant for the benefit of the whole or any part of the land retained by CV. This will enable express annexation to take place.[115]

113 *Miles v Easter* [1933] Ch 611 at 630.

114 *Re Pinewood Estate* [1958] Ch 280. But see (1968) 84 LQR 22 at 31, 32 (PV Baker) where the author suggests that the assignment operates as a delayed annexation so that the benefit will thereafter run with the land without further assignment.

115 See Megarry and Wade, p 790.

(ii) How can P1 enforce the covenant against P2?

It is also important for P1 to be able to enforce the P2–CV covenant against P2. As P1 bought the lot before P2, the benefit of P2–CV covenant cannot be annexed. Neither can CV assign the benefit to P1 who is an earlier purchaser. To enable P1 to get the benefit, CV may ask P2 to covenant *with CV and the owners of the lots previously sold*, under s 56 of the Law of Property Act 1925.[116] But the effect of s 56 was not judicially pronounced until the case of *Dyson v Forster*,[117] by which time a set of rules relating to running of benefit under a scheme of development had been established.[118]

Also to enable P1's successor to sue on the P2–CV covenant, P2 must covenant with CV and owner of the lots previously sold *for the benefit of the lots*, so that P1's benefit can be annexed to his lots and pass to his successors. Again, as it was not fully understood that it was possible for P2 to covenant with the owners of the lots previously sold under s 56, this method was not used. Also, when the CV sold the last lot, he retained no land and so, as will be seen, an important rule for the running of the burden will not be satisfied. The burden will not run from the last purchaser to his successors in title. Equally, no one will get the benefit of the covenant made by the last purchaser unless he covenants also with owners of the lots previously sold.

It was the difficulty of ensuring that the purchaser, and his successors of each lot, complies with the covenants and the complexity of formal requirements, that equity developed a set of rules relating to schemes. Parker J in *Elliston v Reacher*[119] laid down strict requirements for the enforcement of covenants made within a scheme of development irrespective of the order in which the different lots were purchased by different individuals. In order to establish a scheme, four conditions had to be satisfied. (1) Both the plaintiff and the defendant must derive their titles from a common vendor. Thus, in *Re Pinewood Estate*,[120] a scheme was not upheld because there was no common vendor. The decision was made on a strict reading of *Elliston v Reacher*. (2) The common vendor must lay out, in advance of sales, the estate in defined lots now owned by the plaintiff and the defendant respectively. The common vendor must lay out his estate in lots, usually demonstrated by a lotted plan.[121] (3) The covenants extracted by a common vendor were intended for the benefit of all the lots within the scheme. This overlaps considerably with the fourth. (4) The

---

116 Where the covenants to be extracted from all the purchasers are identical, this problem may be solved by requiring CV, who still retained land now owned by P2, to covenant with P1 and his successors for the benefit of P1's land. When CV later sold land to P2, the covenant will bind P2 and indeed other purchasers of the lots. But in practice, often the covenants are not identical and the CV cannot pre-empt the subsequent covenants to be entered into by different purchasers.

117 [1908] 1 KB 629 (a case under s 5 of the Real Property Act 1845).

118 See Megarry and Wade, p 790, fn 33.

119 [1908] 2 Ch 374.

120 [1958] Ch 280.

121 In *Lawrence v South County Freeholds Ltd* [1939] Ch 656, absence of lotting was one of the reasons that failed the scheme.

plaintiff and the defendant bought their lots on the footing that the covenants were mutually enforceable by the owners of all the lots within the scheme. This is an important requirement for it is the mutuality that ensures that the owners of different lots have a common interest in maintaining the restrictions. The existence of a covenant in the conveyance to observe the restriction would obviously help to prove the existence of such understanding. Other evidence such as a lotted plan or common form of contract or conveyance can also be helpful. A further requirement was later added by the Court of Appeal in *Reid v Bickerstaff*[122] that the area covered by the scheme must be clearly defined.

Parker J's requirements were treated as if they were a legislative text. A strict adherence to the requirements made it very difficult to establish a scheme. In the period between 1908 and 1965, a scheme was only upheld in two reported cases.[123] As to the first requirement, as Preston and Newsom point out,[124] it is difficult to see in principle why two persons, who own two separate lands in severalty, should not agree to work together and sell the lands in lots under a common set of restrictive covenants. As regards the second requirement, no doubt the production of a lotted plan of the defined area is strong evidence in favour of a scheme, but why should it be a requirement? As long ago as in 1893 it was held in *Tucker v Vowles*[125] that it was not decisive.

The requirements set out in *Elliston v Reacher* have, since 1965, been relaxed. A wider equitable principle has been adopted, based on the reciprocity of obligation for the common interest of the community within the scheme: if there is a common intention and common interest in enforcing the covenants within a scheme, the court will give effect to the covenants. Thus, in *Re Dolphin's Conveyance*,[126] Stamp J thought that there is nothing in the wider principle of equity to require there to be a single common vendor. And in *Baxter v Four Oaks Properties Ltd*,[127] a scheme was upheld notwithstanding the absence of lotting. A similar decision was reached in *Re Dolphin's Conveyance*. So the present requirements are:

(i) The area affected by the scheme must be clearly defined.[128]

(ii) There must be a mutual intention to impose a scheme of mutually enforceable covenants in the interest of all the purchasers and their successors. It must be shown that each purchaser purchased on the footing that all would be mutually bound by, and mutually entitled to enforce, the covenants.

These two requirements have now been confirmed by the Privy Council in *Jamaica Mutual Life Assurance Society v Hillsborough Ltd*.[129]

---

122 [1909] 2 Ch 305, at 319 at 323.

123 *Bell v Norman* (1956) 7 P & CR 359; *Newman v Real Estate Debenture Corpn Ltd* [1940] 1 All ER 131.

124 Preston, CHL, and Newsom, GL, *Restrictive Covenants Affecting Freehold Land*, 7th edn, 1982, London: Sweet & Maxwell, p 58, paras 2–68.

125 [1893] 1 Ch 195.

126 [1970] Ch 654.

127 [1965] Ch 816.

128 *Reid v Bickerstaff* [1909] 2 Ch 305 at 319.

129 [1989] 1 WLR 1101 at 1106F–G, *per* Lord Jauncey of Tullichettle.

(d) Summary

Successors of the original covenantee may sue the original covenantor if he has acquired the benefit of the covenant. The benefit may run at common law if the covenant touches and concerns the land, both the covenantee and his successors have legal estate in the land, and the benefit is intended to run. For covenants made after 1925, intention that benefit should run is presumed by s 78. If benefit does not run at common law it may run in equity if it touches and concerns the land and the successor can show that he has obtained the benefit by annexation, assignment or scheme of development. For covenants made after 1925, s 78 allows annexation to take place automatically. In the case of covenants made within a scheme, rules relating to the running of benefit under a scheme of development are still applicable and have been simplified.

3 BETWEEN ORIGINAL COVENANTEE AND SUCCESSORS IN TITLE OF ORIGINAL COVENANTOR – PASSING OF BURDEN

Running of burden at common law

Where, after the covenants have been made between the original covenantor and the original covenantee, the original covenantor sells the burdened land to a purchaser, it is sometimes necessary to consider whether the original covenantee can enforce the covenants against the successors in title (the purchaser) of the original covenantor. At common law, it is a well established principle that the burden of a covenant relating to freehold estate cannot run with the land.[130] Thus, a covenant is not enforceable at common law against the successors in title of the original covenantor. As will be seen, equity, however, allows negative covenants to be enforced against the covenantor's successors in title who have notice of the covenants, provided the covenants touch and concern the covenantee's land which can be benefited by the covenant, and the burden of the covenant was intended to run with the covenantor's land.

These unnecessarily complicated and obscure rules have been much criticised[131] and have caused injustice in many cases. One recent example is the case of *Rhone v Stephens* (executrix).[132] Here, the freehold owner of an estate known as Walford House conveyed part of the estate known as Walford Cottage in 1960. Part of the roof of Walford House (the disputed roof) overhung a part of Walford cottage, and was conveyed to the owner of Walford Cottage. But the freehold owner of Walford House covenanted 'for himself and his

---

130 *Austerberry v Oldham Corpn* (1885) 29 Ch D 750; *Rhones v Stephens* [1994] 2 All ER 65, HL.

131 For defects in the law relating to positive covenants see *Report of the Committee on Positive Covenants Affecting Land* (1965) Cmnd 2719 (paras 2–7) and *Law Commission Report on Positive and Restrictive Covenants* 1984 (Law Com No 127, HC 201) paras 4.3–4.6. For defects in the law relating to restrictive covenants see *Law Commission Report on Restrictive Covenants* 1967 (Law Com No 11), paras 20–26, and Law Com No 127, paras 4.7–4.12.

132 [1994] 2 All ER 65.

successors in title ... to maintain to the reasonable satisfaction of the purchasers and their successors in title such part of the roof of Walford House ... as lies above the property conveyed in wind and watertight condition'. The house and cottage were later transferred to a Mrs Barnard and the plaintiffs. By 1984, severe leaks in the roof in question appeared. Mrs Barnard's attempt to repair the roof was inadequate, but she denied the plaintiffs access to do the work themselves. Mrs Barnard died after proceedings had been started. Nourse LJ held,[133] with sympathy, that the original covenant of repair, being positive in nature, could not bind the defendant, the original covenantor's successor in title at common law under the rule in *Austerberry v Oldham Corpn*.[134] As will be seen, neither could the plaintiffs enforce the positive covenant in equity.[135] The decision of the court of Appeal was subsequently affirmed by the House of Lords.

Rhone v Stephens [1994] 2 All ER 65, HL

Lord Templeman: For over 100 years it has been clear and accepted law that equity will enforce negative covenants against freehold land but has no power to enforce positive covenants against successors in title of the land. To enforce a positive covenant would be to enforce a personal obligation against a person who has not covenanted. To enforce negative covenants is only to treat the land as subject to a restriction.

Mr Munby, who argued the appeal persuasively on behalf of the plaintiffs, referred to an article by Professor Sir William Wade, 'Covenants – "a broad and reasonable view"' (1972) 31 CLJ 157, and other articles in which the present state of the law is subjected to severe criticism. In 1965, the Report of the Committee on Positive Covenants Affecting Land (Cmnd 2719), which was a report by a committee appointed by the Lord Chancellor and under the chairmanship of Lord Wilberforce, referred to difficulties caused by the decision in the *Austerberry* case and recommended legislation to provide that positive covenants which relate to the use of land and are intended to benefit specified other land should run with the land. In Transfer of Land: Appurtenant Rights (Law Commission Working Paper No 36, published on 5 July 1971) the present law on positive rights was described as being illogical, uncertain, incomplete and inflexible. The Law Commission Report Transfer of Land: The Law of Positive and Restrictive Covenants (Law Com No 127) laid before Parliament in 1984 made recommendations for the reform of the law relating to positive and restrictive obligations and submitted a draft Bill for that purpose. Nothing has been done.

In these circumstances your Lordships were invited to overrule the decision of the Court of Appeal in the *Austerberry* case. To do so would destroy the distinction between law and equity and to convert the rule of equity into a rule of notice. It is plain from the articles, reports and papers to which we were referred that judicial legislation to overrule the *Austerberry* case would create a number of difficulties, anomalies and uncertainties and affect the rights and liabilities of people who have for over 100 years bought and sold land in the knowledge, imparted at an elementary stage to every student of the law

133 *The Times*, 21 January; (1993) 137 Sol Jo LB 46. See (1993) Conv 234 (Goo, SH).

134 (1885) 29 Ch D 750.

135 *Haywood v Brunswick Permanent Benefit Building Society* (1881) 8 QBD 403: the rule in *Tulk v Moxhay* (1848) 2 Ph 774 does not apply to positive covenants.

of real property, that positive covenants affecting freehold land are not directly enforceable except against the original covenantor. Parliamentary legislation to deal with the decision in the *Austerberry* case would require careful consideration of the consequences. Moreover, experience with leasehold tenure where positive covenants are enforceable by virtue of privity of estate has demonstrated that social injustice can be caused by logic. Parliament was obliged to intervene to prevent tenants losing their homes and being saddled with the costs of restoring to their original glory buildings which had languished through wars and economic depression for exactly 99 years.

Mr Munby submitted that the decision in the *Austerberry* case had been reversed remarkably but unmarked by s 79 of the Law of Property Act 1925, which, so far as material, provides:

> (1) A covenant relating to any land of a covenantor or capable of being bound by him, shall, unless a contrary intention is expressed, be deemed to be made by the covenantor on behalf of himself his successors in title and the persons deriving title under him or them, and subject as aforesaid, shall have effect as if such successors and other persons were expressed ...

This provision has always been regarded as intended to remove conveyancing difficulties with regard to the form of covenants and to make it unnecessary to refer to successors in title. A similar provision relating to the benefit of covenants is to be found in s 78 of the 1925 Act. In *Smith v River Douglas Catchment Board* [1949] 2 All ER 179; [1949] 2 KB 500, followed in *Williams v Unit Construction Co Ltd* (1951) 19 Conv NS 262, it was held by the Court of Appeal that s 78 of the 1925 Act had the effect of making the benefit of positive covenants run with the land. Without casting any doubt on those long-standing decisions I do not consider that it follows that s 79 of the 1925 Act had the corresponding effect of making the burden of positive covenants run with the land. In *Jones v Price* [1965] 2 All ER 625 at 630; [1965] 2 QB 618 at 633' Willmer LJ repeated that: '... a covenant to perform positive acts ... is not one the burden of which runs with the land so as to bind the successors in title of the covenantor; see *Austerberry v Oldham Corpn*'.

In *Sefton v Tophams Ltd* [1966] 1 All ER 1039 at 1048, 1053; [1967] 1 AC 50 at 73, 81 Lord Upjohn and Lord Wilberforce stated that s 79 of the 1925 does not have the effect of causing covenants to run with the land. Finally, in *Federated Homes Ltd v Mill Lodge Properties Ltd* [1980] 1 All ER 371, at 380; [1980] 1 WLR 594 at 605–06, Brightman J referred to the authorities on s 78 of the 1925 Act and said:

> Section 79, in my view, involves quite different considerations and I do not think that it provides a helpful analogy.

... In the result I would dismiss the appeal ...'.

There are, however, several ways in which such a rule can be circumvented.

(a) The original covenantor remains liable by virtue of privity of contract even if he has sold his land to a subsequent purchaser. In practice, in order to protect himself the original covenantor usually asks the purchaser to make covenant of indemnity to indemnify him in the event of a breach of the covenant. If there is a breach, the original covenantee cannot sue the purchaser but may sue the original covenantor who will in turn sue on the covenant of indemnity against the purchaser. This will have the effect of imposing the burden of the covenant indirectly on the purchaser. The disadvantage is that as the chain grows it is likely that it may break. The original covenantor may have died or cannot be found or have become insolvent and not worth suing. Furthermore, the only remedy is damages, which may not be appropriate. Injunction or specific performance, which may be more appropriate, cannot be obtained.

(b) A long lease (which was originally granted for not less than 300 years and with more than 200 years to run) may be enlarged into a fee simple under s 153 of the Law of Property Act 1925.[136] It has been suggested that when a long lease is enlarged, under s 153(8) the fee simple will be subject to the same covenants contained originally in the lease. This is an untried and artificial device.

(c) Where a person covenants to take a burden, for example to contribute to the cost of maintaining a certain facility, in return for the benefit of using the facility, then he can only take the benefit if he fulfills his burden.[137] The burden of a freehold covenant may therefore pass indirectly to a successor in title of the covenantor under the doctrine of 'mutual benefit and burden'. Similarly, the covenantor's successor can only take the benefit if he bears the burden. The benefit and burden claimed, however, must not be too 'technical or minimal'.[138] In *Rhone v Stephens*,[139] the defendant did receive benefits from the plaintiffs in the form of an easement of eavesdrop for the passage of rain water from the roof of Walford House over the disputed roof and an easement of support for the roof of the House by the disputed roof. Nourse LJ thought,[140] however, that the easement of support was both technical and minimal and that of eavesdrop, if not technical, was certainly minimal.

(d) A right of entry may be reserved by the original covenantee against the original covenantor exercisable in the event of a breach.[141] Such a right of entry if duly created is a legal interest under s 1(2)(e) of the Law of Property Act 1925 exercisable against the original covenantor's successors in title. The right is, however, subject to the rule against perpetuities.

(e) When contribution to the maintenance of property is required, the covenantee may require the covenantor to grant him an estate rentcharge (a covenant to pay money or contribute to the maintenance of the property) often with a right of entry. An estate rentcharge is not prohibited by the Rentcharges Act 1977. If duly created, it is a legal interest. The right of entry for the breach of covenant is not subject to the rule against perpetuities.[142]

(f) One may also choose to lease the property, instead of selling it, with the covenants. The covenants in a lease can be enforced under the doctrine of privity of estate against the assignee of the covenantor. But where the covenantor sublet the property then there would be no privity of estate and the covenant may not be enforced.

---

136 See also s 8(3) of the Leasehold Reform Act 1967.

137 *Halsall v Brizell* [1957] Ch 169.

138 *Tito v Waddell (No 2)* [1977] Ch 106 at 305H.

139 [1994] 2 All ER 65.

140 *The Times*, 21 January 1993; (1993) 137 Sol Jo LB 46.

141 *Shiloh Spinners v Harding* [1973] AC 691.

142 Section 11(1) of the Perpetuities and Accumulations Act 1964.

(g) Section 79 provides that a covenant 'is deemed to be made by the covenantor on behalf of himself, his successors in title and the persons deriving title under him or them, and shall have effect as if such successors or other persons were expressed'. It has been said that '[i]t is one of the eternal mysteries of English land law that s 79(1) of the Law of Property Act 1925 seems never to have been invoked as a means of transmitting the burden of a positive covenant from one freeholder to another'.[143] Recently, in *Rhone v Stephens*,[144] Lord Templeman echoed the view expressed by Lords Upjohn and Wilberforce in *Tophams Ltd v Earl of Sefton*[145] that, in so far as positive covenants are concerned, s 79 achieved no more than the introduction of statutory shorthand into the drafting of them. If this section is given a wider construction similar to that given to s 78 in *Federated Homes*, the burden of positive covenant would run with the land.

Running of burden in equity

Equity took a different approach. In *Tulk v Moxhay*,[146] the plaintiff sold land in Leicester Square to the covenantor who covenanted on behalf of himself, his heirs and assigns to keep the land 'in an open state, uncovered with any buildings, in neat and ornamental order'. The covenantor subsequently sold the land to the defendant who had notice of the covenants. The defendant tried to build on the land and the plaintiff sought an injunction against him. Lord Cottenham said that the real issue was not whether the burden ran at law or in equity. The real issue was whether a party should be allowed to use land inconsistently with covenants of which he had notice. In order to prevent the defendant from acting unconscionably, the court should enforce the covenant against that person who bought the property with notice of it.

Tulk v Moxhay (1848) 2 Ph 774, 41 ER 1143

Lord Cottenham LC: (without calling upon the other side). That this court has jurisdiction to enforce a contract between the owner of land and his neighbour purchasing a part of it, that the latter shall either use or abstain from using the land purchased in a particular way, is what I never knew disputed. Here there is no question about the contract: the owner of certain houses in the square sells the land adjoining, with a covenant from the purchaser not to use it for any other purpose than as a square garden. And it is now contended, not that the vendee could violate that contract, but that he might sell the piece of land, and that the purchaser from him may violate it without this court having any power to interfere. If that were so, it would be impossible for an owner of land to sell part of it without incurring the risk of rendering what he retains worthless. It is said that, the covenant being one which does not run with the land, this court cannot enforce it; but the question is, not whether the covenant runs with the land, but whether a party shall be permitted to use the land in a manner inconsistent with the contract entered into by his vendor, and with notice of which he purchased. Of course, the price would be affected by the covenant, and nothing could be more inequitable than

143 Gray, p 1133, fn 17.

144 [1994] 2 All ER 65 at 72h–73a.

145 [1967] 1 AC 50 at 73 B–C, 82F.

146 (1848) 2 Ph 774.

that the original purchaser should be able to sell the property the next day for a greater price, in consideration of the assignee being allowed to escape from the liability which he had himself undertaken.

That the question does not depend upon whether the covenant runs with the land is evident from this, that if there was a mere agreement and no covenant, this court would enforce it against a party purchasing with notice of it; for if an equity is attached to the property by the owner, no one purchasing with notice of that equity can stand in a different situation from the party from whom he purchased. There are not only cases before the Vice Chancellor of England, in which he considered that doctrine as not in dispute; but looking at the ground on which Lord Eldon disposed of the case of *The Duke of Bedford v The Trustees of the British Museum*,[147] it is impossible to suppose that he entertained any doubt of it. In the case of *Mann v Stephens* before me, I never intended to make the injunction depend upon the result of the action: nor does the order imply it. The motion was, to discharge an order for the commitment of the defendant for an alleged breach of the injunction, and also to dissolve the injunction. I upheld the injunction, but discharged the order of commitment, on the ground that it was not clearly proved that any breach had been committed; but there being a doubt whether part of the premises on which the defendant was proceeding to build was locally situated within what was called the Dell, on which alone he had under the covenant a right to build at all, and the plaintiff insisting that it was not, I thought the pendency of the suit ought not to prejudice the plaintiff in his right to bring an action if he thought he had such right, and, therefore, I give him liberty to do so.

With respect to the observations of Lord Brougham in *Keppell v Bailey* (1834) 2 My & K 517, he never could have meant to lay down that this court would not enforce an equity attached to land by the owner, unless under such circumstances as would maintain an action at law. If that be the result of his observations, I can only say that I cannot coincide with it.

I think the cases cited before the Vice Chancellor and this decision of the Master of the Rolls perfectly right, and, therefore, that this motion must be refused, with costs.

The doctrine has a dramatic impact on both the law of contract and the law of property. It enlarges contractual rights into proprietary rights in land. In the early days of *Tulk v Moxhay*, positive covenants were enforced in equity.[148] Its application was subsequently modified and narrowed down to negative covenants in *Haywood v Brunswick Permanent Benefit Building Society*.[149]

Haywood v Brunswick Permanent Benefit Building Society (1881) 8 QBD 403, CA

Brett LJ: This appeal must be allowed. I am clearly of opinion, both on principle and on the authority of *Milnes v Branch*,[150] that this action could not be maintained at common law. *Milnes v Branch* must be understood, as it always has been understood, and as Lord

147 (1822) 2 My & K 552.

148 For example, *Morland v Cook* (1868) LR 6 Eq 252; *Cooke v Chilcott* (1876) 3 Ch D 694.

149 (1881) 8 QBD 403. For the view that the doctrine of *Tulk v Moxhay* is not limited to negative covenants see [1981] Conv 55 (Bell).

150 (1816) 5 M & S 411.

St Leonard's[151] understood it, and it will be seen, on a reference to his book, that he considers the effect of it to be that a covenant to build does not run with the rent in the hands of an assignee.

This being so, the question is reduced to an equitable one. Now the equitable doctrine was brought to a focus in *Tulk v Moxhay*, which is the leading case on this subject. It seems to me that that case decided that an assignee taking land subject to a certain class of covenants is bound by such covenants if he has notice of them, and that the class of covenants comprehended within the rule is that covenants restricting the mode of using the land only will be enforced. It may be also, but it is not necessary to decide here, that all covenants also which impose such a burden on the land as can be enforced against the land would be enforced. Be that as it may, a covenant to repair is not restrictive and could not be enforced against the land; therefore such a covenant is within neither rule. It is admitted that there has been no case in which any court has gone farther than this, and yet if the court would have been prepared to go farther, such a case would have arisen. The strongest argument to the contrary is, that the reason for no court having gone farther is that a mandatory injunction was not in former times grantable, whereas it is now; but I cannot help thinking, in spite of this, that if we enlarged the rule as it is contended, we should be making a new equity, which we cannot do.

I think also that *Cox v Bishop* shews that a Court of equity has refused to extend the rule of *Tulk v Moxhay* in the direction contended for, and that if we decided for the plaintiff we should have to overrule that case. But it is said that if we decide for the defendants we shall have to overrule *Cooke v Chilcott*. If that case was decided on the equitable doctrine of notice, I think we ought to overrule it. But I think there is much to shew that the ground of the decision was that Malins VC, was of the opinion – wrongly as it now turns out – that the covenant ran with the land, and the decision of the Court of Appeal appears to have proceeded on an admission.

Cotton LJ: I am of the same opinion on both points. I think that a mere covenant that land shall be improved does not run with the land within the rule in *Spencer's* case so as to give the plaintiff a right to sue at law. I also think that the plaintiff has no remedy in equity. Let us consider the examples in which a Court of Equity has enforced covenants affecting land. We find that they have been invariably enforced if they have been restrictive, and that with the exception of the covenants in *Cooke v Chilcott*, only restrictive covenants have been enforced. In *Tulk v Moxhay*, the earliest of the cases, Lord Cottenham says, 'That this court has jurisdiction to enforce a contract between the owner of land and his neighbour purchasing a part of it, that the latter shall either use or abstain from using it in a particular way, is what I never knew disputed.' In that case, the covenant was to use in a particular manner, from which was implied a covenant not to use in any other manner, and the plaintiff obtained an injunction restraining the defendant from using in any other manner, although the covenant was in terms affirmative. At p 778, Lord Cottenham says, 'If an equity is attached to property by the owner no one purchasing with notice of that equity can stand in a different situation from the party from whom he purchased.' This lays down the real principle that an equity attaches to the owner of the land. It is possible that the doctrine might be extended to cases where there is an equitable charge which might be enforced against the

151 Sug V & P, 14th edn, p 590.

land, but it is not necessary to decide that now; it is enough to say that with that sole exception the doctrine could not be farther extended. The covenant to repair can only be enforced by making the owner put his hand into his pocket, and there is nothing which would justify us in going that length. We are not bound here by *Cooke v Chilcott*,[152] and I do not think that the rule of *Tulk v Moxhay*[153] can be extended as Malins VC, there extended it. In *Morland v Cook*,[154] there are perhaps some expressions of Romilly MR, which favour the opposite contention, but the fact of there being a deed of partition in that case makes it distinguishable. That is the only case besides *Cooke v Chilcott* at all in favour of the plaintiff. *Cox v Bishop*[155] is distinctly the other way. There the covenants affected the owner, but not the land, and although the defendant was full equitable owner the Court refused an injunction. *Daniel v Stepney*,[156] where there was merely a grant of a rent to be distrained for on land adjoining the land demised, does not seem to me to be in point, and such observations of Bramwell, B, in *Aspden v Seddon*[157] as might possibly assist the plaintiff are extra judicial. There is therefore no ground for extending the equitable doctrine as we are asked to do.

Linsley LJ: I am of the same opinion. The practical question is, whether the defendants, being mortgagees in possession, are bound to repair under the circumstances of the case. It is said that the obligation to repair is imposed upon them because they took a conveyance of the land with notice of the covenant, and Stephen J, has thought himself bound by *Tulk v Moxhay*[158] and *Cooke v Chilcott*.[159]

Now I may first say that I do not think that the defendants could be hit by any process of circuity of action. As mortgagees they took the land subject to the rent-charge no doubt, so far as the liability to distress and re-entry were concerned. I do not think that either covenant runs with the land. Neither *Milnes v Branch*,[160] nor *Randall v Rigby*,[161] however, apply very closely. In *Milnes v Branch*, the plaintiff was not assignee in fee of the rent, having only a leasehold interest in that rent. In *Randall v Rigby*, the question was; whether debt or covenant was the proper form of action. There are *dicta* in the judgments, however, which favour the contention of the defendants in this case, and it is impossible not to see that the burden of the covenant does not run with the land. This is not a case of landlord and tenant: we must never lose sight of that distinction.

With regard to the question of notice, *Tulk v Moxhay* shews that a restrictive covenant will be enforced, and so do *Cox v Bishop*[162] and *Wilson v Hart*.[163] But I think that the result of these cases is that only such a covenant as can be complied with without expenditure of money will be enforced against the assignee on the ground of notice.

152 (1876) 3 Ch D 694.
153 (1848) 2 Ph 774.
154 (1868) Law Rep 6 Eq 252.
155 (1857) 26 LJ (Ch) 389.
156 (1874) Law Rep 9 Ex 185.
157 (1876) 1 Ex D 496.
158 (1848) 2 Ph 774.
159 (1876) 3 Ch D 694.
160 (1816) 5 M & S 411.
161 (1838) 4 M & W 130.
162 (1857) 8 De G M & G 815; 26 LJ (Ch) 389.
163 (1866) Law Rep 1 Ch App 463.

Especially does this appear from *Wilson v Hart*, where a covenant not to use a house as a beershop was enforced against a purchaser's tenant from year to year. It is absurd to suppose that such a tenant could have been compelled to perform a covenant to repair.

The principle of *Cooke v Chilcott* may or may not be applicable to this case, but the circumstances were wholly different. I should be sorry to overrule that case, and prefer to leave it to be reconsidered on some future occasion. It is enough to say that in the present case we have been asked to extend *Tulk v Moxhay* as it has never been extended before, and we decline to do so.

It is interesting to note that Nourse LJ, in *Rhone v Stephens*, conceded that it was difficult to see why the rule in *Tulk v Moxhay* should not apply to positive covenants particularly where each successor in title of the covenantor, by means of indemnity covenants, had notice of the covenant. His Lordship, however, felt bound by it.

Today, the original covenantee can only sue the successors in title of the original covenantor in equity if the following requirements are satisfied.

(i) The covenant must be negative in nature

As mentioned, only negative covenants are enforceable against the successors in title of the original covenantor.[164] The covenant has to be negative in substance not in form. A covenant can be enforced if it is negative in substance even if it is positive in form. So a covenant 'to use the property for residential purposes only' can be enforced because it is a covenant requiring the covenantor not to use the property for any other purposes. A covenant which is not negative in substance may not be enforced even if it is negative in form. So a covenant 'not to let the property fall into disrepair' is not enforceable because it is a positive covenant requiring the covenantor to carry out repair. It was suggested by Lindley LJ in *Haywood v Brunswick Permanent Benefit Building Society*[165] that the test was whether any expenditure of money was needed to comply with the covenant. Only such a covenant as can be complied with without expenditure of money will be enforced against a successor in title.

(ii) The covenant must touch and concern the covenantee's land

This is rather similar to the requirement of 'accommodation' in the law of easement.[166] The covenant must be made for the benefit of the benefited land.[167] At the date of the covenant the covenantee must have retained land which was benefited by the covenant.[168] It also follows that the benefited land must be sufficiently close to the burdened land so that the covenant imposed on

164 *Haywood v Brunswick Permanent Benefit Building Society* (1881) 8 QBD 403.

165 (1881) 8 QBD 403 at 410, and 409 *per* Cotton LJ.

166 See Chapter 15.

167 *Formby v Barker* [1903] 2 Ch 539 at 552; *Rogers v Hosegood* [1900] 2 Ch 388 at 395; *Re Ballard's Conveyance* [1937] Ch 473 at 480; *Marquess of Zetland v Driver* [1939] 1 Ch 1 at 8.

168 *London County Council v Allen* [1914] 3 KB 642.

the burdened land can benefit the benefited land. 'Land at Clapham would be too remote and unable to carry a right to enforce ... covenants in respect of ... land at Hampstead'.[169]

If the covenantee retains an interest in reversion, he would be able to enforce the covenant affecting the land. So a landlord (the covenantee), who has an interest in reversion, can sue the sub-tenant in equity on a restrictive covenant contained in the lease, even though there is no privity of contract or estate between them.[170] Similarly, a mortgagee has an interest in the mortgaged land in reversion, and can, therefore, enforce a restrictive covenant made in the mortgage.[171]

The rule that the covenantee must retain benefited land is modified in certain situations by statutes. For example, a covenant made with local authorities can be enforced by them even if they do not own any land which can benefit from the covenant.[172]

(iii) The burden of the covenant must have been intended to run with the covenantor's land

A covenant made prior to 1926 by the covenantor alone would not bind his successor in title.[173] In order to bind his successors, he had to make the covenant on behalf of himself, his heirs and assigns.[174] After 1925, the burden of a restrictive covenant is presumed, under s 79 of the Law of Property Act 1925, to be intended to run with the land of the covenantor unless a contrary intention appears.

Law of Property Act 1925

79. Burden of covenants relating to land

(1) A covenant relating to any land of a covenantor or capable of being bound by him, shall, unless a contrary intention is expressed, be deemed to be made by the covenantor on behalf of himself his successors in title and the persons deriving title under him or them, and, subject as aforesaid, shall have effect as if such successors and other persons were expressed.

This subsection extends to a covenant to do some act relating to the land, notwithstanding that the subject matter may not be in existence when the covenant is made.

(2) For the purposes of this section in connexion with covenants restrictive of the user of land 'successors in title' shall be deemed to include the owners and occupiers for the time being of such land.

---

169 *Kelly v Barrett* [1924] 2 Ch 379 at 404.

170 *Hall v Ewin* (1887) 37 Ch D 74.

171 *Regent Oil v J A Gregory Ltd* [1966] Ch 402 at 433A–B, F.

172 For a list of statutory exceptions see Maudsley and Burn, p 831, fn 11.

173 *Re Fawcett and Holmes' Contract* (1889) 42 Ch D 150.

174 See Megarry and Wade, p 776.

(3) This section applies only to covenants made after the commencement of this Act.

But if the covenant is worded so as to bind the covenantor alone, then s 79 is excluded.[175]

Re Royal Victoria Pavilion [1961] Ch 581

Pennycuick J: In order to answer the question raised by the summons it is necessary in the first place to determine the construction of clause 5 of the conveyance. By that clause Thanet Theatrical covenanted to procure that, during a term corresponding to the residue of its leasehold interest, the use of the Pavilion should be restricted as therein mentioned. The word 'procure' is defined in the *Oxford English Dictionary* (1909 edn), Vol VII, p 1419, as meaning 'obtain by care or effort', and can be more simply paraphrased as 'see to it'. The obligation undertaken by Thanet Theatrical is to see to it that a certain state of affairs prevails during the specified term. It seems to me that a covenant so expressed is naturally to be regarded as of a purely personal character. The tenant of property is in a position to ensure that during his tenancy the property is not to be used in a specified manner either by himself or by persons claiming under him, whether as licensees, underlessees or assignees, and the word 'procure' is appropriate to denote a personal obligation so to ensure. So here the covenant regarded purely as a personal covenant would have been perfectly sensible and workable had Thanet Theatrical remained in existence. On the other hand, it seems to me that a covenant so expressed is not naturally to be regarded as a covenant on behalf of the covenantor and his successors in title so as to run with the land. The causative verb 'procure' is not appropriate where successors in title are themselves to be bound. The covenantor under a covenant intended to run with the land would not sensibly be expressed as procuring his successors to abstain from doing whatever is covenanted not to be done.

The view that the covenant in clause 5 is intended to be of a purely personal character derives much support from the clauses which immediately precede and follow it. Clause 4, which as regards sub-paras (a) and (c) at any rate is plainly intended to run with the land, is introduced by the apt words 'The purchasers for themselves and their successors and assigns hereby covenant with the vendors.' Clause 6, which is plainly intended as a purely personal covenant, is introduced only by the words 'the vendors hereby covenant with the purchasers.' It would be strange draftsmanship to interpose between these two covenants a covenant intended to run with the land, and yet only introduced by the words 'the vendors hereby covenant with the purchasers'.

It is important in construing the covenant in clause 5 to bear in mind that the period covered by it is only 17 years. A restriction for so short a period can readily be achieved by a purely personal obligation, unlike a restriction in perpetuity which can only be fully effective if it runs with the land.

Mr Oliver for the defendant company points out that the covenant, though positive in form, may yet be negative in substance. This is so, and I imagine that here the covenant in clause 5 would be regarded as negative to this extent, that it imports an obligation on Thanet Theatrical itself not to do any of the prohibited acts, but I do not think that Thanet Theatrical's positive obligation to procure can, as regards persons claiming under it, be translated into a negative obligation on those parties if upon the natural construction of the covenant they are not bound by it at all.

---

175 *Re Royal Victoria Pavilion* [1961] Ch 581.

Mr Oliver further relies on s 79 of the Law of Property Act 1925.

[His Lordship read s 79 of the Law of Property Act 1925.]

So here it is contended that no contrary intention is expressed in the conveyance dated 7 July 1952, and that, therefore, the covenant in clause 5 must be deemed to be made by Thanet Theatrical on behalf of itself and its successors in title. If the words 'unless the contrary intention is expressed' in s 79 mean: unless the instrument contains express provision to the contrary, this contention would, I think, be unanswerable. But it seems to me the words 'unless a contrary intention is expressed' mean rather: unless an indication to the contrary is to be found in the instrument, and that such an indication may be sufficiently contained in the wording and context of the instrument even though the instrument contains no provision expressly excluding successors in title from its operation. It can hardly be the intention of the section that a covenant which, on its natural construction, is manifestly intended to be personal only, must be construed as running with the land merely because the contrary is not expressly provided.

Section 79 only applies to restrictive covenants and not positive covenants,[176] and only applies to restrictive covenants made after 1925.[177]

Where the conditions mentioned above are satisfied, the burden runs with the covenantor's land in equity. But because it runs in equity, it cannot be enforced against a *bona fide* purchaser for value of a legal estate without notice of the covenant,[178] or anyone who claims through such a person.[179] A restrictive covenant is enforceable against a squatter, because he is not a purchaser.[180]

The doctrine of notice applies to a restrictive covenant made before 1926. Restrictive covenants usually form part of the terms of a sale, or the root of title, thus giving notice to the purchaser. But a restrictive covenant made after 1925 relating to unregistered land is registrable as a Class D(ii) land charge.[181] It is for the covenantee or his successors in title to protect their benefit by the appropriate register prior to the transfer of title by the original covenantor. If it is not registered it is void against a subsequent purchaser for money or money's worth of a legal estate in land, even if the purchaser buys the land with notice of the covenant.[182] Covenants made between landlords and tenants are not affected by the Land Charges Act.[183]

In the case of registered land, it has to be protected as a minor interest by an entry of notice or caution in the Land Register.[184] In *Freer v Unwins Ltd*,[185] a covenant had been entered in the register of land charges while the land was

176 *Tophams Ltd v Earl of Sefton* [1967] 1 AC 50.

177 Section 79(3) of the LPA 1925.

178 *London & South Western Railways Co v Gomm* (1881–82) 20 Ch D 562.

179 *Wilkes v Spooner* [1911] 2 KB 473.

180 *Re Nisbet and Potts' Contract* [1906] 1 Ch 386.

181 Section 2(5)(ii) of the LCA 1972.

182 Section 4(6) of the LCA 1972; *Midland Bank Trust Co Ltd v Green* [1981] AC 513.

183 *Newman v Real Estate Debenture Corpn* [1940] 1 All ER 141.

184 Section 50(1) of the LRA 1925.

185 [1976] Ch 288.

unregistered. When the title was registered, the covenant was not entered in the charges register. The covenant was, therefore, not enforceable against the persons who purchased the land after their title was registered.

Where there is a scheme of development, it is not entirely clear if registration is required. It has been suggested that a scheme of development is outside the Land Charges Act 1972[186] because the scheme creates reciprocity of obligation between the purchasers and the common vendor cannot destroy the scheme, in whole or in part, by failing to register.[187] Others have, however, argued that the burden under a scheme has to be registered.[188] If the common vendor fails to register a covenant made by a purchaser of a lot making it unenforceable by a purchaser of another lot, it has been suggested that the purchaser who is free of the covenant is likewise unable to enforce a covenant by other purchasers within the scheme.[189] This is because the essence of a scheme is mutuality. 'Registration governs the running of the burden of the covenant, whereas the development scheme rules govern the running of the benefit.'[190] Such an issue has not, however, been judicially considered.

4 BETWEEN SUCCESSORS OF ORIGINAL COVENANTOR AND SUCCESSORS OF ORIGINAL COVENANTEE – RUNNING OF BOTH BURDEN AND BENEFIT

Where the burdened land and benefited land have respectively come to the hands of the successors in title of the original covenantors and covenantee, whether the successor of the original covenantee can enforce the covenant against the successor in title of the original covenantor depends on (i) whether the burden of the covenant has passed to the successors of the original covenantor *and* (ii) whether the benefit of the covenant has passed to the successors of the original covenantee. As the burden can only run in equity, equity requires the claimant to show that he has acquired the benefit in equity.[191] The rules relating to the running of burden and benefit in equity discussed above apply. In *J Sainsbury plc v Enfield LBC*,[192] as will be recalled, although the burden had passed to the covenantor's successors, the benefit did not pass to the claimant. The action therefore failed.

186 (1928) 78 LJ 39 (JML); (1933) 77 SJ 550; (1950) 20 Conv (NS) 370 (RG Rowley); Farrand, JT, *Contract and Conveyance* 2nd edn, pp 420–21; Barnsley, p 344.

187 Barnsley, pp 344–45.

188 Cheshire and Burn, p 599; Megarry and Wade, p 793; *Emmet on Title*, 19th edn (by Farrand, JT), 1986, Looseleaf, London: Longman, para 17.043.

189 See Preston, CHS, and Newsom, GL, *Restrictive Covenants Affecting Freehold Land*, 7th edn, 1982, London: Sweet & Maxwell, para 2–82.

190 Megarry and Wade, p 793.

191 *Miles v Easter* [1933] Ch 611.

192 [1989] 2 All ER 817.

5 DECLARATION AS TO THE ENFORCEABILITY OF RESTRICTIVE COVENANTS

Under s 84(2) of the Law of Property Act 1925, the courts have power, on the application of any person interested, to declare whether or not a freehold land is, or would be, affected by a restrictive covenant. If the land is so affected the court can declare the nature, extent and the enforceability of the restrictive covenant. This provision allows any one who wants to buy a property to find out whether some restrictive covenant is still operative or not. Such an application was made in *J Sainsbury plc v Enfield LBC*.[193]

Law of Property Act 1925

84. Power to discharge or modify restrictive covenants affecting land

(2) The court shall have power on the application of any person interested:

(a) to declare whether or not in any particular case any freehold land is, or would in any given event be, affected by a restriction imposed by any instrument; or

(b) to declare what, upon the true construction of any instrument purporting to impose a restriction, is the nature and extent of the restriction thereby imposed and whether the same is, or would in any given event be, enforceable and if so by whom.

Neither sub-ss (7) and (11) of this section nor, unless the contrary is expressed, any later enactment providing for this section not to apply to any restrictions shall affect the operation of this subsection or the operation for purposes of this subsection of any other provisions of this section.

6 REMEDIES FOR BREACH OF COVENANTS

If the plaintiff successfully claims the right to enforce a covenant against the defendant, the court may award damages if damages are adequate compensation.[194] Where the breach has not been carried out, the court is more likely to grant an injunction preventing breach. In some cases, where the breach of negative covenant has been carried out, the court may grant a mandatory injunction directing the performance of a positive act to remedy the breach, for example the demolition of the obstruction.[195] The court may also grant an order of specific performance in the case of a breach of positive covenant.

Where, however, a statutory body, such as a national health service trust, has been entrusted with statutory functions to be discharged in the public interest and has been given statutory power to acquire and hold land for the purpose of discharging that function, restrictive covenants affecting the land so

193 [1989] 2 All ER 817.

194 *Federated Homes Ltd v Mill Lodge Properties Ltd* [1980] 1 All ER 371 at 381h. See also *Jaggard v Sawyer* [1995] 1 WLR 269.

195 *Wakeham v Wood* (1982) 43 P & CR 40 (the defendant built, flagrantly in breach of covenant, obstructing the plaintiff's view of the sea. A mandatory injunction was granted requiring the demolition of the building).

acquired cannot be enforced by injunction or damages where the statute has provided for an exclusive remedy by way of statutory compensation.[196]

7 DISCHARGE AND MODIFICATION OF RESTRICTIVE COVENANT

Unity of ownership

If the benefited land and burdened land come into common ownership the covenant is permanently and automatically discharged.[197] The covenant will not revive when the two lands are subsequently separated again.

In the case of a scheme of development, when two plots come into common ownership the covenant is not discharged permanently. It would revive later when they are once again separated.[198]

Statutory modification or discharge

Some old 19th century restrictive covenants may become obsolete today. It will clearly be unsatisfactory if such covenants are to bind the burdened land indefinitely with no means of discharging or modifying them.

Section 84(1) of the Law of Property Act 1925 provides the Lands Tribunal with a discretionary power to modify or discharge a restrictive covenant on certain grounds with or without compensation.[199]

Law of Property Act 1925

84. Power to discharge or modify restrictive covenants affecting land

(1) The Lands Tribunal shall (without prejudice to any concurrent jurisdiction of the court) have power from time to time, on the application of any person interested in any freehold land affected by any restriction arising under covenant or otherwise as to the user thereof or the building thereon, by order wholly or partially to discharge or modify any such restriction on being satisfied:

(a) that by reason of changes in the character of the property or the neighbourhood or other circumstances of the case which the Lands Tribunal may deem material, the restriction ought to be deemed obsolete; or

(aa) that (in a case falling within sub-s (1A) below) the continued existence thereof would impede some reasonable user of the land for public or private purposes or, as the case may be, would unless modified so impede such user; or

196 *Brown v Heathlands Mental Health National Health Service Trust* [1996] 1 All ER 133.

197 *Re Tiltwood, Sussex* [1978] Ch 269.

198 *Texaco Antilles Ltd v Kernochan* [1973] AC 609.

199 Where there is a building scheme, there is a greater presumption that covenants will be upheld and so there is a greater onus of proof on the applicant to show that s 84 is satisfied: *Re Bromor Properties Ltd's Application* (1995) 70 P & CR 569.

(b) that the persons of full age and capacity for the time being or from time to time entitled to the benefit of the restriction, whether in respect of estates in fee simple or any lesser estates or interests in the property to which the benefit of the restriction is annexed, have agreed, either expressly or by implication, by their acts or omissions, to the same being discharged or modified; or

(c) that the proposed discharge or modification will not injure the persons entitled to the benefit of the restriction;

and an order discharging or modifying a restriction under this subsection may direct the applicant to pay to any person entitled to the benefit of the restriction such sum by way of consideration as the Tribunal may think it just to award under one, but not both, of the following heads, that is to say, either:

(i) a sum to make up for any loss or disadvantage suffered by that person in consequence of the discharge or modification; or

(ii) a sum to make up for any effect which the restriction had, at the time when it was imposed, in reducing the consideration then received for the land affected by it.

(1A) Subsection (1)(aa) above authorises the discharge or modification of a restriction by reference to its impeding some reasonable user of land in any case in which the Lands Tribunal is satisfied that the restriction, in impeding that user, either:

(a) does not secure to persons entitled to the benefit of it any practical benefits of substantial value or advantage to them; or

(b) is contrary to the public interest;

and that money will be an adequate compensation for the loss or disadvantage (if any) which any such person will suffer from the discharge or modification.

(1B) In determining whether a case is one falling within sub-s (1A) above, and in determining whether (in any such case or otherwise) a restriction ought to be discharged or modified, the Lands Tribunal shall take into account the development plan and any declared or ascertainable pattern for the grant or refusal of planning permissions in the relevant areas, as well as the period at which and context in which the restriction was created or imposed and any other material circumstances.

(1C) It is hereby declared that the power conferred by this section to modify a restriction includes power to add such further provisions restricting the user of or the building on the land affected as appear to the Lands Tribunal to be reasonable in view of the relaxation of the existing provisions, and as may be accepted by the applicant; and the Lands Tribunal may accordingly refuse to modify a restriction without some such addition.

There are four grounds on which one can apply for discharge or modification:

(i) The covenant is now obsolete by reason of changes in the character of the property or neighbourhood or other material circumstances (see, eg *Re Kennet Properties Ltd's Application* [1996] 2 EGLR 163). An example is a covenant prohibiting use of the premises as a takeaway would be deemed obsolete if the street in which the burdened land is situated is now full of takeaways and restaurants, because the covenant no longer provides any real protection to persons entitled to enforce it.

(ii) The restrictive covenant would impede some reasonable use of the land for public or private purposes, and either it no longer confers any practical benefit of substantial value,[200] or it is contrary to public interest,[201] and any loss can be adequately compensated in money. If the covenant can still confer a practical benefit, it will not be discharged or modified. The Lands Tribunal may refuse to discharge or modify a covenant if the benefit can be enjoyed by owners of other land nearby. Thus, in *Gilbert v Spoor*,[202] a covenant was not discharged or modified which preserved a beautiful landscape view, which could be seen from other land nearby, though not from the covenantee's land.

(iii) The persons entitled to the benefit of the restrictions have agreed, either expressly or by implication from their acts or omissions, to the discharge or modification.

(iv) The discharge or modification will not injure the person entitled to the benefit of the covenant.[203]

Common law discharge

A covenant may be discharged through abandonment where the covenantor has over a long period been acting inconsistently with the continuance of the covenant with the knowledge of the covenantee.[204]

8 RESTRICTIVE COVENANT, PLANNING AND COMPULSORY ACQUISITION

Modern legislations have taken over much of the role of controlling land use. There is a vast body of statute law and delegated legislation and reference to specialist books should be made.[205] It should, however, be noted that a landowner who wants to use his land in a particular way must ensure that his use will not be in breach of the private system of restrictive covenant and the public system of planning control. His use of land may be permitted by planning authorities. But the permission granted does not by itself authorise the breach of restrictive covenant.

However, if the landowner is a local authority, any use of land in accordance with planning permission is authorised by statute, even though this involves a breach of restrictive covenant. Compensation may, however, be payable.[206]

Where the land, bound by restrictive covenant, is acquired compulsorily by a public authority under statutory powers, and is used for the purposes

200 See, eg *Re Hydeshire Ltd's Application* (1994) 67 P & CR 93.

201 *Re Solarfilms (Sales) Ltd's Application* (1994) 67 P & CR 110.

202 [1983] Ch 27. See [1982] Conv 452 (Kenny, PH). See also *Re Sheehy's Application* (1992) JPL 78.

203 See, eg *Re Love's and Love's Application* (1994) 67 P & CR 101.

204 *Hepworth v Pickles* [1900] 1 Ch 108; *AG of Hong Kong v Fairfax Ltd* [1997] 1 WLR 149.

205 Heap, D, *An outline of Planning Law*, 10th edn, 1991, London: Sweet & Maxwell.

206 Section 127 of the Town and Country Planning Act 1971.

authorised by statute, no action will lie against the public authority for breach of restrictive covenant. Compensation may, again, be payable.[207]

9 REFORM

The rules relating to the running of benefit, for example, by annexation or scheme of development, are complicated. The rule relating to the running of burden are inconvenient and possibly unfair. The ways in which the rule in *Austerberry* can be circumvented are unsatisfactory. These have been the subject of much criticism by academics and the Law Commission.[208] The Law Commission Report, Transfer of Land: The Law of Positive and Restrictive Covenants 1984 (Law Com No 127), made the following proposals for reform:

(i) Creation of a new interest in land known as land obligation whether positive or negative.

(ii) Land obligations should run with both benefited and burdened land and enforceable as between current owners of the lands. Original covenantor will be free of the burden when he parts with the land.

(iii) There will be two types of land obligations: Neighbour obligations and development obligations. Neighbour obligations are obligations imposed on one piece of land for the benefit of the other. Development obligations are obligations imposed on one unit of land for the benefit of the other units within an area. This is similar to the current schemes of development.

(iv) To be legal, land obligations must be made by deed. They must be for a term equivalent to a fee simple absolute in possession or a term of years absolute, otherwise they will be equitable. Both legal and equitable obligations are registrable as a new Class C land charge in unregistered land and in registered land they are to be entered on the register of the titles of both benefited and burdened lands. They would not be overriding interests.

The government has agreed that, in conjunction with the commonhold proposals (see Chapter 17), the main recommendations will be implemented and the draft Land Obligation Bill will be substantially reproduced as Part II of the Law of Property Bill (which will implement the commonhold proposals).[209] If the proposals are implemented, the highly technical and complicated rules relating to the passing of burden and benefit of covenant will disappear.

More recently, the Law Commission has also recommended reform on the law relating to obsolete restrictive covenants and lost covenants.

---

207 *Kirby v Harrogate School Board* [1896] 1 Ch 437; *Marten v Flight Refuelling Ltd* [1962] Ch 115.

208 For defects in the law relating to positive covenants see Report of the Committee on Positive Covenants Affecting Land (1965) Cmnd 2719 (paras 2–7) and Law Commission Report on Positive and Restrictive Covenants 1984 (Law Com No 127, HC 201) paras 4.3–4.6. For defects in the law relating to restrictive covenants, see Law Commission Report on Restrictive Covenants 1967 (Law Com No 11), paras 20–26, and Law Com No 127, paras 4.7–4.12.

209 See Lord Chancellor's Consultation Paper on Commonhold (Cmnd 1345, November 1990) para 2.7; *Hansard*, HL Deb 1601, Friday 12 July 1991, The Lord Chancellor, Lord MacKay's speech.

Law Commission, Transfer of Land: Obsolete Restrictive Covenants, 16 July 1991, (Law Com No 201):

PART II – CONTINUING PROBLEMS: A SOLUTION[210]

Obsolete restrictive covenants

2.6 The case against permitting the continued existence of all old restrictive covenants rests on the view that they hamper conveyancing without offering compensating benefit. Those with experience of dealings in land know well that many properties are subject to extensive restrictive covenants and that after some years have passed since they were imposed some of them cease to have any real effect or serve any useful purpose.

2.7 Although for convenience we have entitled this Report Obsolete Restrictive Covenants, and we use the term 'obsolete' in our discussion, we do not propose to rely on it to define those covenants which should cease to have effect after 80 years. Rather, we suggest that the primary question should be whether, at the end of that period, it secures 'any practical benefits of substantial value or advantage' to the owners of the dominant tenement. This wording is capable of a wide interpretation.

2.8 Covenants which are obsolete in this sense do not usually cause any substantial impediment to disposing of the property affected, or even to developing it. Nevertheless, there are two good reasons for dispensing with them.

2.9 First, every time property which is subject to such covenants is acquired the prospective new owner or his professional adviser must consider and advise upon the covenants in detail. He may conclude that they are of no importance, but the need for that work adds time and expense to the conveyancing process and that need arises whether or not the title is registered. With covenants continuing indefinitely, that inconvenience recurs regularly in relation to the same covenants. Owner-occupied homes, eg are known to change hands on average a little more frequently than once every seven years.

2.10 Secondly, the process of the first registration of title to land – when the land is initially brought onto the register, so that title is no longer established merely by reference to title deeds – is impeded and unnecessarily made more expensive by the need for obsolete covenants to be noted or recorded on the register. If the covenants appear to be valid, the Registrar has no discretion to omit them. The objective of universal registration of title is now accepted as a major plank in modernising our system of dealing with property and it cannot be sensible that it should be impeded by the need to record obsolete covenants which, by definition, are often valueless.

2.11 The law offers well-established machinery for discharging or modifying obsolete restrictive covenants by application to the Lands Tribunal. This is regularly used, but experience shows that very many owners of properties burdened by obsolete covenants do not avail themselves of the facility. This may well be because they are reluctant to incur the cost of an application when there is little to be achieved: to have obsolete covenants cleared off their title will generally leave the value of their property unaltered. Some property owners who want to act in contravention of a covenant, which they believe to be spent, insure against the possibility of resulting

210 Original footnotes of the report are deleted.

claims. This is often cheaper and quicker than applying to the Lands Tribunal, but it leaves the covenants on the title. We previously recommended that the jurisdiction of the Lands Tribunal should be enlarged to cope with the problem of covenants which have outlasted their usefulness. Although this recommendation was implemented, more than 20 years' experience has shown that this was not enough to solve the problem.

Lost covenants

2.12 Another unsatisfactory feature of the present practice concerning restrictive covenants is that there are cases where it is know that a valid covenant, or one which must be assumed to be valid, exists but the terms of it have been lost. In the nature of things, this problem tends to arise in relation to older covenants rather than more recent ones. Not only does it affect unregistered titles, where a deed may physically have been lost or destroyed, but it will persist even after registration of title because the Registry cannot ignore evidence that the covenant is subsisting. The title to the property will be registered subject to the covenants of unknown content. The effect of that is thoroughly unsatisfactory: the owner of the land is subject to whatever obligations the covenants impose, even though he generally has no means of discovering their terms.

PART IV – SUMMARY OF RECOMMENDATIONS

4.1 The principal recommendations which we make in this report are:

(a) all restrictive covenants should lapse 80 years after their creation; and

(b) any covenant which is not then obsolete should be capable of being replaced by a land obligation to the like effect (para 3.1).

4.2 our detailed recommendations concerning the lapse of restrictive covenants may be summarised:

(a) the scheme should apply to all covenants restricting the use of freehold land (para 3.2), with the following exceptions:

(i) covenants between landlord and tenant, unless they will continue to have effect after the end of the lease term (para 3.9);

(ii) covenants imposed pursuant to statute which do not depend for their enforceability against successors in title on the person with the benefit being interested in an identifiable parcel of land (para 3.13);

(iii) covenants to which the Lands Tribunal's jurisdiction to modify or discharge restrictions does not apply (para 3.17);

(b) a restrictive covenant should lapse after 80 years (para 3.21), and for the purpose of calculating that period:

(i) the 80 years should start when the covenant was first imposed (whether or not the covenant was subsequently varied), which in the case of a new restriction ordered by the Lands Tribunal should be taken to be the date of creation of the covenant being modified (paras. 3.25, 3.27);

(ii) to provide an extension in transitional cases, the period should in no case expire before five years from the commencement date of the legislation (para 3.28);

(iii) if, when the period would otherwise have ended, a replacement application was pending and registered, the period should expire when the application was fully disposed of (para 3.29).

(c) the lapse of a restrictive covenant should take effect as a matter of law and without the parties taking action (para 3.30). Any register entry protecting the covenant should then be of no effect and should be cancelled on the application of anyone interested, or on the registrar's initiative (para 3.33).

4.3 Our detailed recommendations in relation to the replacement of lapsed covenants are, in summary:

(a) any application to modify or discharge a covenant which it is sought to replace should be consolidated with the replacement application (para 3.40);

(b) an applicant for replacement should have to establish:

(i) that there was a valid, subsisting covenant;

(ii) that an identified area of land was burdened with it;

(iii) that by reason of his interest in particular land he was entitled to enforce the covenant; and

(iv) that he enjoyed practical benefits of substantial value or advantage from the covenant (paras 3.41, 3.44);

(c) covenants imposed under a building scheme should be treated as if individually imposed (para 3.49);

(d) it should be possible for anyone interested in land intended to benefit from a restrictive covenant to apply to replace it (para 3.52);

(e) the respondents to an application should be the freeholder, and the owner of any lease or under-lease with more than 21 years to run at the date of the application, of any part of the land (para 3.54);

(f) a replacement application should only be made during the five years preceding the date on which the covenant would lapse (para 3.59);

(g) an application should be registrable as a pending land action (para 3.61);

(h) the Lands Tribunal should settle the form of the replacement land obligation (para 3.64);

(i) if a replacement application fails, the covenant should cease to have effect as soon as the application is finally disposed of (para 3.65);

(j) the applicant under a replacement application should be obliged to give notice of it to everyone else who enjoys the benefit of the covenant and they should have the right to be joined as parties (para 3.71);

(k) the Lands Tribunal should only have power to order a respondent to a replacement action to pay the applicant's costs where there are special reasons (para 3.74);

(l) the procedure of the Tribunal in dealing with replacement applications should be laid down by rules (para 3.75).

CHAPTER 15

EASEMENTS AND PROFITS[1]

Land can be used to achieve an infinitely unlimited range of purposes, social, residential, commercial, industrial, agricultural, etc. An efficient utilisation of land inevitably involves rights of access to, or exploitation of, the land. These rights primarily rest with the fee simple owners. A tenant may also be given these rights by his leasehold covenants. Others who wish to have access to or to exploit the land resources may be given such rights by the fee simple owners. These rights are sometimes called 'incorporeal hereditament'.[2] The most important rights are easements, profits *à prendre* and rights given by covenants in freehold[3] or leasehold land.[4] This chapter concerns, primarily, the law relating to easements but brief mention will be made on the law relating to profits.

An easement is essentially either a positive or negative right over another's land. It is a right to use another's land in a particular way or a right to prevent the owner of another land from using his own land in a particular way. The person who exercises the easement is a 'dominant owner' and the person whose land is used by the dominant owner is a 'servient owner'. A profit is a right to take the natural produce of another's land or any part of his soil.

1 NATURE OF EASEMENTS

It is difficult to define easements. However, they can be identified. A list of rights judicially recognised as easements can be found in the books.[5] These are proprietary rights which possess the characteristics identified in Cheshire's *Modern Real Property*, 7th edn, p 456, subsequently affirmed judicially in *Re Ellenborough Park*.[6] In that case, the vendors of Ellenborough Park and surrounding land sold the surrounding land to property developers who built on the land and sold the various plots to the purchasers with full enjoyment at all times in common with the other persons, of the pleasure ground (Ellenborough Park) but subject to the payment of a fair and just proportion of the costs, charges and expenses of keeping the ground in good order and

---

1 See Gray, Chapter 21; Megarry and Wade, pp 834–912; Maudsley & Burn, Chapter 10; Cheshire and Burn, Chapter 17; Megarry's *Manual*, Chapter 10 (Part 2); *Gale on Easements*, 15th edn, 1986, London: Sweet & Maxwell; Jackson, P, *The Law of Easements and Profits*, 1978, London: Butterworths; Sara, C, *Boundaries and Easements*, 1991, London: Sweet & Maxwell; (1964) 28 Conv (NS) 450 (Peel, MA).

2 Meaning interests in land which are heritable but have no physical existence. But see *Challis's Real Property*, 3rd edn (Sweet (ed)), 1911, pp 51 and 55; Jackson, P, *The Law of Easements and Profits*, 1978, London: Butterworths, p 23 pointing out that easements are not incorporeal hereditaments.

3 See Chapter 14.

4 See Chapter 9.

5 Cheshire and Burn, pp 524–26; Megarry and Wade, pp 838–42, 908-09; *Gale on Easements*, pp 36–38.

6 [1956] Ch 131.

condition. The plaintiff became the owner of the park and sought to prevent the purchasers of the plot from using the park. Evershed MR said:

The substantial question raised in this appeal is whether the respondent, or those whom he has been appointed to represent, being the owners of certain houses fronting upon, or, in some few cases, adjacent to, the garden or park known as Ellenborough Park in Weston-super-Mare, have any right known to the law, and now enforceable by them against the owners of the park, to the use and enjoyment of the park to the extent and in the manner later more precisely defined ...

The substantial question in this case, which we have briefly indicated, is one of considerable interest and importance ... if the house owners are now entitled to an enforceable right in respect of the use and enjoyment of Ellenborough Park, that right must have the character and quality of an easement as understood by, and known to, our law. It has, therefore, been necessary for us to consider carefully the qualities and characteristics of easements, and, for such purpose, to look back into the history of that category of incorporeal rights in the development of English real property law.

[His Lordship then referred to *Duncan v Louch* (1845) 6 QB 904, *Keith v Twentieth Century Club Ltd* (1904) 73 LJ Ch 545; 20 TLR 462; *International Tea Stores Co v Hobbs* [1903] 2 Ch 165 and *Attorney General v Antrobus* [1905] 2 Ch 188; 21 TLR 471 and concluded that they did not constitute a direct decision on the question now before the court.]

But, before we proceed to those matters of facts, it will be proper, as a foundation for all that follows in this judgment, to attempt a brief account of the emergence in the course of the history of our law, of the rights known to us as 'easements', and thereafter, so far as relevant for present purposes, to formulate what can now be taken to be the essential qualities of those rights. For the former purpose, we cannot do better than cite a considerable passage from the late Sir William Holdworth's *Historical Introduction to the Land Law* (Clarendon Press, 1927, p 265). The author states:

> Both the term 'easement' and the thing itself were known to the medieval common law. At the latter part of the 16th century it was described in Kitchin's book on courts, and defined in the later editions of the '*Termes de la Ley*'." After stating the definition and observing its obvious defects from the point of view of modern law, Sir William proceeds: 'But these defects in the definition are instructive, because they indicate that the law as to easements was as yet rudimentary.'
>
> It was still rudimentary when Blackstone wrote. In fact, right down to the beginning of the 19th century, there was but little authority on many parts of this subject. Gale, writing in 1839, said: 'The difficulties which arise from the abstruseness and refinements incident to the subject have been increased by comparatively small number of decided cases affording matter for defining any systematising this branch of law. Upon some points indeed there is no authority at all in English law.'
>
> The industrial revolution, which caused the growth of large towns and manufacturing industries, naturally brought into prominence such easements as ways, watercourses, light, and support; and so Gale's book became the starting-point of the modern law, which rests largely upon comparatively recent decisions.
>
> But, though the law of easements is comparatively modern. Some of its rules have ancient roots. There is a basis of Roman rules introduced into English law by Bracton, and acclimatised by Coke ... The law, as thus developed, sufficed for

> the needs of the country in the nineteenth century. But, as it was no longer sufficient for the new economic needs of the nineteenth century, an expansion and an elaboration of this branch of the law became necessary. It was expanded and elaborated partly on the basis of the old rules, which had been evolved by the working of the assize of nuisance, and its successor the action on the case; partly by the help of Bracton's *Roman Rules*; and partly, as Gale's book shows, by the help of the Roman rules taken from the *Digest*, which he frequently and continuously uses to illustrate and to supplement the existing rule of law.
>
> [His Lordship then went on to say that the passage from Sir William Holdsworth explained the appearance and the prominence of Roman *dicta* in the English law of easements, commonly called 'servitudes'. But he concluded that there has been no judicial authority for adopting the Roman view in English law that there is no right of *jus spatiandi*, that is the right to wander at will over another's land. The exact characteristics of the *jus spatiandi* mentioned by Roman lawyers has to be considered and its validity must depend on a consideration of the qualities attributed to all easements by the law relating to easements as it has now developed in England.]

For the purpose of the argument before us Mr Cross and Mr Goff were content to adopt, as correct, the four characteristics formulated in Cheshire's *Modern Real Property*, 7th edn, pp 456 *et seq*. They are (1) there must be a dominant and a servient tenement: (2) an easement must 'accommodate' the dominant tenement: (3) dominant and servient owners must be different persons, and (4) a right over land cannot amount to an easement, unless it is capable of forming the subject matter of a grant.

The four characteristics stated by Dr Cheshire correspond with the qualities discussed by Gale in his second chapter, ss 2, 5, 3, and 6 and 8 respectively ... .

The characteristics

(a) There must be a dominant and a servient tenement[7]

There must be a dominant land and a servient land. There must be a dominant land to which the right to use a servient land in a particular way is attached, and a servient land over which the right is exercised. An easement cannot exist in gross. It cannot exist independently of land.

London & Blenheim Estates Ltd v Ladbroke Retail Parks Ltd [1992] 1 WLR 1278

Judge Paul Baker QC: An easement cannot exist as an incorporeal hereditament unless and until there are both a dominant and a servient tenement in separate ownership. That never occurred in this case. Before the dominant tenement had been acquired as a dominant tenement the servient tenement had been disposed of. That, as it seems to me, is fatal to the creation of the easement ...

In this case the grant expressly stated that the dominant tenement was not identified until it had been acquired by the grantee and notice given. Extrinsic evidence would be needed to establish that the land so designated was capable of benefiting from the rights

7 *Ackroyd v Smith* (1850) 10 CB 164 at 187; *Alfred F Beckett Ltd v Lyons* [1967] Ch 449 at 483E *per* Winn LJ; *London & Blenheim Estates Ltd v Ladbroke Retail Parks Ltd* [1992] 1 WLR 1278.

granted, but that is not in issue here. Extrinsic evidence could not be admitted merely to identify potential as opposed to actual dominant tenements.

The question whether there can be a future easement is one which may arise after but not before the dominant and servient tenements have been identified as being in the separate ownership of the grantee and grantor respectively. In *Cable v Bryant* [1908] 1 Ch 259 an owner of a yard and a stable conveyed the stable to the plaintiff. The stable had a ventilator opening on to the yard. The yard was held under lease. The lessee subsequently acquired the freehold of the yard and erected a hoarding blocking the ventilator. In response to the plaintiff's action for infringement of the right to air over the yard it was objected that there could be no grant of easement in reversion. The case was resolved on the point that the defendant, the former lessee, as successor in title to the former lessor, could not derogate from the grant.

A more obvious case of a future easement would be where developments have to take place on the servient tenement before the easement can be enjoyed. Such a case is exemplified by *Dunn v Blackdown Properties Ltd* [1961] Ch 433, where a conveyance of land included a right to use the sewers and drains 'hereafter to pass under' a private road adjoining the land conveyed and which belonged to the vendor. It was held that such a grant was a grant of an easement to arise at a future date not limited to take effect within the perpetuity period and was therefore void. Since the Perpetuities and Accumulations Act 1964 it is seldom that grants to take effect in the future will fail on that ground, and even before the Act the rule could be complied with by careful drafting.

For myself, I would not see any impossibility in a grant to the owner of a dominant tenement to acquire an easement over the servient tenement at some future date. There are examples in this case: for that reason I read clause 1 of the schedule. But there must be at the date of the grant what are described as the essentials of an easement, albeit that the estate in the easement is a future estate or interest. In the old terminology, if it did not follow on some prior estate or interest, it would be a springing use. In other cases the estate might be purely reversionary, as where a freehold owner of land subject to a lease grants an easement to take effect on the falling in of the lease. However, that may be, in the case before me there was no dominant tenement at the date of the grant or at the date of the disposal of the potentially servient land. An estate or interest cannot subsist in a non-existent hereditament. That, in my judgment, as I said, is fatal to the plaintiffs' case.

The decision of Judge Paul Baker was affirmed by the Court of Appeal.[8] Peter Gibson LJ points out that the reasons for the rule lie in the policy against encumbering land with burdens of uncertain extent, and the reluctance of the law to recognise new forms of burden on property conferring more than contractual rights.[9] 'Incidents of a novel kind cannot be devised, and attached to property, at the fancy or caprice of any owner,'[10] and a right intended as an easement and attached to a servient tenement before the dominant tenement is identified would be an incident of a novel kind.[11]

8 See (1994) 67 P & CR 1.

9 *Ibid* at 6–7.

10 *Keppell v Bailey* (1834) 2 My & K 517 at 535, *per* Lord Brougham C.

11 *London & Blenheim Estates Ltd v Ladbroke Retail Parks Ltd* (1994) 67 P & CR 1 at 7.

The *London & Blenheim Estates* case was subsequently followed by the Court of Appeal in *Bell v Voice*[12] that there was no easement if the claimant had no interest in land capable of being a dominant land at the time of the grant. But if there is a dominant land and it is described with sufficient certainty, even if the grantee was not yet the owner of the dominant land at the time of the agreement to grant, the agreement is effective to confer an easement.

(b) The easement must 'accommodate' the dominant tenement

The right to use the servient land must be connected with the enjoyment or occupation of the dominant land. The use of the dominant land must be made more beneficial by the right. This resembles the requirement of 'touch and concern' the covenantee's land in the area of restrictive covenants. A pure personal advantage enjoyed by the owner of the dominant land is not enough. This involves an element of value judgment.

As will be recalled, in *Re Ellenborough Park*[13] a number of owners of residential property had been given a right of common enjoyment of a park which was enclosed by their houses. One of the questions was whether there was sufficient connection between the right granted and the enjoyment of the property. It was held that the right was an easement because the use of the park undoubtedly enhanced, and was connected with, the normal enjoyment of the houses adjoining it.

Re Ellenborough Park [1956] Ch 131, CA

Evershed MR: We pass, accordingly, to a consideration of the first of Dr Cheshire's conditions – that of the accommodation of the alleged dominant tenements by the rights as we have interpreted them. For it was one of the main submissions by Mr Cross on behalf of the appellant that the right of full enjoyment of the park, granted to the purchaser by the conveyance of 23 December 1864, was insufficiently connected with the enjoyment of the property conveyed, in that it did not subserve some use which was to be made of that property; and that such a right accordingly could not exist in law as an easement. In this part of his argument Mr Cross was invoking a principle which is, in our judgment, of unchallengeable authority, expounded, in somewhat varying language, in many judicial utterances, of which the judgments in *Ackroyd v Smith*[14] are, perhaps, most commonly cited. We think it unnecessary to review the authorities in which the principle has been applied; for the effect of the decisions is stated with accuracy in Dr Cheshire's *Modern Real Property*, 7th edn, at p 457. After pointing out that 'one of the fundamental principles concerning easements is that they must be not only appurtenant to a dominant tenement, but also connected with the normal enjoyment of the dominant tenement' and referring to certain citations in support of that proposition the author proceeded:

> We may expand the statement of the principle thus: a right enjoyed by one over the land of another does not possess the status of an easement unless it accommodates and serves the dominant tenement, and is reasonably necessary for the better enjoyment of that tenement, for it has no necessary connexion therewith, although it confers an advantage upon the owner and renders his

12 (1994) 68 P & CR 441.

13 [1956] Ch 131, CA.

14 (1850) 10 CB 164.

ownership of the land more valuable, it is not an easement at all, but a mere contractual right personal to and only enforceable between the two contracting parties.

In the course of the argument before us it was suggested that the principle thus formulated lacked completeness having regard to the judgment of Willes J in *Bailey v Stephens*[15] ...

In our judgment, Willes J, was merely emphasising that an easement must be appurtenant to an estate for the benefit of that estate and its owner and that it cannot at the same time lawfully be enjoyed by any other person. If, however, the judge was intimating that, if a right be of such a character that it can factually (as distinct from lawfully) be of benefit to persons other than the owner of the estate to whom the right is granted, it is incapable of legal recognition as an easement, the judge was enunciating a principle which, so far as we are aware, has no other authority to support it ...

In our judgment, accordingly, the statement of the law in Dr Cheshire's book, to which we have referred, is unaffected by the judgment of Willes J in *Bailey v Stephens*.

Can it be said, then, of the right of full enjoyment of the park in question, which was granted by the conveyance of 23 December 1864, and which, for reasons already given, was, in our view, intended to be annexed to the property conveyed to Mr Porter, that it accommodated and served that property? It is clear that the right did, in some degree, enhance the value of the property, and this consideration cannot be dismissed as wholly irrelevant. It is, of course, a point to be noted; but we agree with Mr Cross's submission that it is in no way decisive of the problem; it is not sufficient to show that the right increased the value of the property conveyed, unless it is also shown that it was connected with the normal enjoyment of that property. It appears to us that the question whether or not this connexion exists is primarily one in fact, and depends largely on the nature of the alleged dominant tenement and the nature of the right granted. As to the former, it was in the contemplation of the parties to the conveyance of 1864 that the property conveyed should be sued for residential and not commercial purposes ... As to the nature of the right granted, the conveyance of 1864 shows that the park was to be kept and maintained as a pleasure ground or ornamental garden, and that it was contemplated that it should at all times be kept in good order and condition and well stocked with plants and shrubs; and the vendors covenanted that they would not at any time thereafter erect or permit to be erected any dwelling house or other building (except a grotto, bower, summer-house, flower-stand, fountain, music-stand or other ornamental erection) within or on any part of the pleasure ground. On these facts Mr Cross submitted that the requisite connexion between the right to use the park and the normal enjoyment of the houses which were built around it or near it had not been established. He likened the position to a right granted to the purchaser of a house to use the Zoological Gardens free of charge or to attend Lord's Cricket Ground without payment. Such a right would undoubtedly, he said, increase the value of the property conveyed but could not run with it at last as an easement, because there was no sufficient nexus between the enjoyment of the right and the use of the house. It is probably true, we think, that in neither of Mr Cross's illustrations would the supposed right constitute an easement, for it would be wholly extraneous to, and independent of, the use of a house as a house, namely, as a place in which the householder and his family live and make

15 (1862) 12 CBNS 91.

their home; and it is for this reason that the analogy which Mr Cross sought to establish between his illustrations and the present case cannot, in our opinion, be supported. A much closer analogy, as it seems to us, is the case of a man selling the freehold of part of his house and granting to the purchaser, his heirs and assigns, the right, appurtenant to such part, to use the garden in common with the vendor and his assigns. In such a case, the test of connexion, or accommodation, would be amply satisfied; for just as the use of a garden undoubtedly enhances, and is connected with, the normal enjoyment of the house to which it belongs, so also would the right granted, in the case supposed, be closely connected with the use and enjoyment of the part of the premises sold. Such, we think, is in substance the position in the present case. The park became a communal garden for the benefit and enjoyment of those whose houses adjoined it or were in its close proximity. Its flower beds, lawns and walks were calculated to afford all the amenities which it is the purpose of the garden of a house to provide; and, apart from the fact that these amenities extended to a number of householders, instead of being confined to one (which on this aspect of the case is immaterial), we can see no difference in principle between Ellenborough Park and a garden in the ordinary signification of that word. It is the collective garden of the neighbouring houses, to whose use it was dedicated by the owners of the estate and as such amply satisfied, in our judgment, the requirement of connexion with the dominant tenements to which it is appurtenant. The result is not affected by the circumstance that the right to the park is in this case enjoyed by some few houses which are not immediately fronting on the park. The test for present purposes, no doubt, is that the park should constitute in a real and intelligible sense the garden (albeit the communal garden) of the houses to which its enjoyment is annexed. But we think that the test is satisfied as regards these few neighbouring, though not adjacent, houses. We think that the extension of the right of enjoyment to these few houses does not negative the presence of the necessary 'nexus' between the subject-matter enjoyed and the premises to which the enjoyment is expressed to belong.

[His Lordship said that he was referred to *Hill v Tupper* (1863) 2 H & C 121 by Mr Cross, but concluded that nothing in that case was contrary to the view which he had expressed.]

For the reasons which we have stated, we are unable to accept the contention that the right to the full enjoyment of Ellenborough Park fails in limine to qualify as a legal easement for want of the necessary connexion between its enjoyment and the use of the properties comprised in the conveyance of 1864, and in the other relevant conveyances.

Hill v Tupper[16] is the classic example of a right which was held to be a purely personal advantage. Here the owner of a canal leased land on the canal bank to the plaintiff. The plaintiff was given a 'sole and exclusive' right to put pleasure boats on the canal. The defendant put rival boats on the same canal. The plaintiff claimed that his right was an easement and had been interfered with by, and was enforceable against, the defendant. The court did not think that the plaintiff's right would make his occupation of the land more convenient, or would enhance his occupation of the land. It only benefited his business which he ran on his land. It was a mere licence which only bound the licensor. In *Re Ellenborough Park*, with reference to *Hill v Tupper*, Evershed MR said that 'it is clear that what the plaintiff was trying to do was to set up, under the guise of an easement, a monopoly which had no normal connection with the ordinary use

16 (1863) 2 H & C 121; 159 ER 51.

of his land, but which was merely an independent business enterprise. So far from the right claimed sub-serving or accommodating the land, the land was but a convenient incident to the exercise of the right'.[17]

But in *Moody v Steggles*[18] a right to hang a signboard on the adjoining house pointing towards a public house was held to be an easement even though here the right benefited the business on the dominant land.

Because there must be benefit conferred on the dominant land by the use of the servient land, the servient land must be sufficiently closely situated to give the dominant land a practical benefit.[19] The physical distance of the two plots of land must not be too big that no practical benefit could be said to have been conferred by the servient land on the dominant land. 'A right of way over land in Northumberland cannot accommodate land in Kent.'[20]

As Evershed MR pointed out in *Re Ellenborough Park*, there must be 'sufficient nexus between the enjoyment of the right and the use of [the dominant land]'.[21] The fact that the right enhances the market value of the dominant land is relevant but not conclusive. Thus, a right granted to a purchaser of a house to use the Zoological Gardens free of charge or to attend Lord's Cricket Ground without payment would undoubtedly increase the value of the property conveyed but could not run with it at law as an easement.

(c) The dominant and servient owners must be different persons

This means that the dominant and servient lands must be either owned or occupied by different persons. A tenant can acquire an easement over his landlord's land because although the dominant and servient lands are owned by the same persons, they are occupied by different persons.[22]

(d) The right must be capable of forming the subject-matter of a grant

This is because easements do not arise automatically. They must have been acquired legally by a grant or by prescription. There are several aspects of this rule.

(i) There must be a capable grantor and a capable grantee

No one who has no proprietary interest in the servient land is competent to grant an easement,[23] and no one can grant an easement for a period longer than his proprietary interest.[24] No one can claim that the right he has been granted is

17 [1956] Ch 131 at 175.

18 (1879) 12 Ch D 261.

19 *Bailey v Stephens* (1862) 12 CB (NS) 91.

20 *Bailey v Stephens* (1862) 12 CB (NS) 91 at 115, *per* Byles J.

21 [1956] Ch 131 at 174.

22 *Borman v Griffith* [1930] 1 Ch 493 at 499; *Beddington v Atlee* (1887) 35 Ch D 317 at 332; *Richardson v Graham* [1908] 1 KB 39.

23 *Quicke v Chapman* [1903] 1 Ch 659 at 668, 671.

24 *Booth v Alcock* (1873) 8 Ch App 663 at 666; *Lord Dynevor v Tennant* (1886) 32 Ch D 375, at 381; *Simmons v Dobson* [1991] 1 WLR 720 at 723C.

an easement if at the time of the supposed grant, the grantor is not legally capable of making the grant.[25] Thus, if it would be *ultra vires* a company's memorandum of association to grant a certain right, the right granted cannot acquire the status of an easement. Similarly, where the grantor has not a legal estate he cannot grant a legal easement. Such a grant may, however, take effect as an easement by estoppel as against the grantor,[26] and when the grantor subsequently acquires the legal title the estoppel is fed thereafter and perhaps also retrospectively.[27] It has been suggested that an easement may be granted by one of a number of joint owners of the servient land, provided that the incumbrance does not interfere with the rights of the other co-owners to possession and enjoyment of that land.[28]

Similarly, the grantee must be legally capable of receiving the grant.[29] The grantees must be a definite person or a definite body of persons. A right enjoyed by a vague and fluctuating body of persons, such as the local residence of the village, cannot amount to an easement. Such a right may amount to a local customary right.

(ii) The right itself must be sufficiently definite

It must not be 'too vague and uncertain'[30] or 'too vague and indefinite'.[31] An indefinite and unlimited right cannot be an easement.

Re Ellenborough Park [1956] Ch 131, CA

Evershed MR: ... whether it is inconsistent with the proprietorship or possession of the alleged servient owners, and whether it is a mere right of recreation without utility or benefit.

To the first of these questions the interpretation which we have given to the typical deed provides, in our judgment, the answer; for we have construed the right conferred as being both well defined and commonly understood. In these essential respects the right may be said to be distinct from the indefinite and unregulated privilege which, we think, would ordinarily be understood by the Latin term *'jus spatiandi'*, a privilege of wandering at will over all and every part of another's field or park, and which, though easily intelligible as the subject-matter of a personal licence, is something substantially different from the subject-matter of the grant in question, namely, the provision for a limited number of houses in a uniform crescent of one single large but private garden.

---

25 *Mulliner v Midland Railway Co* (1879) 11 Ch D 611 at 619.

26 *Rowbotham v Wilson* (1857) 8 E & B 123 at 145. The doctrine of estoppel does not, however, apply to an implied grant of easement: *Quicke v Chapman* [1903] 1 Ch 659 at 668, 670.

27 *Rajapakse v Fernando* [1920] AC 892 at 897; *Universal Permanent Building Society v Cooke* [1952] Ch 95 at 101.

28 Gray, p 1071 citing *Hedley v Roberts* [1977] VR 282 at 288f. Compare, however, *Paine & Co Ltd v St Neots Gas & Coke Co* [1939] 3 All ER 812 at 824A–D.

29 *National Guaranteed Manure Co Ltd v Donald* (1859) 4 H & N 8 at 17.

30 *Bryant v Lefever* (1879) 4 CPD 172.

31 *Harris v De Pinna* (1886) 33 Ch D 238 at 249.

Our interpretation of the deed also provides, we think, the answer to the second question; for the right conferred no more amounts to a joint occupation of the park with its owners, no more excludes the proprietorship or possession of the latter, than a right of way granted through a passage, or than the use by the public of the gardens of Lincoln's Inn Fields (to take one of our former examples) amount to joint occupation of that garden with the London County Council, or involve an inconsistency with the possession or proprietorship of the council as lessees. It is conceded that, in any event, the plaintiff owners of the park are entitled to cut the timber growing on the park and to retain its proceeds. We have said that in our judgment, under the deed, the flowers and shrubs grown in the garden are equally the park owners' property. We see nothing repugnant to a man's proprietorship or possession of a piece of land that he should decide to make it and maintain it as an ornamental garden, and should grant rights to a limited number of other persons to come into it for the enjoyment of its amenities.

[His Lordship was referred to *Copeland v Greenhalf* [1952] Ch 488 and Upjohn J's ratio quoted at p 825 below but concluded that it had no real relation to the present case. He then went on to consider the question whether the proposition that an easement had to be a right of utility and benefit and not 'one of mere recreation and amusement' was well founded.]

In any case, if the proposition be well-founded, we do not think that the right to use a garden of the character with which we are concerned in this case can be called one of mere recreation and amusement, as those words were used by Martin B. No doubt a garden is a pleasure – on high authority, it is the purest of pleasures – but, in our judgment, it is not a right having no quality either of utility or benefit as those words should be understood. The right here in suit is, for reasons already given, one appurtenant to the surrounding houses as such, and constitutes a beneficial attribute of residence in a house as ordinarily understood. Its use for the purposes, not only of exercise and rest but also for such domestic purposes as were suggested in argument – for example, for taking out small children in perambulators or otherwise – is not fairly to be described as one of mere recreation or amusement, and is clearly beneficial to the premises to which it is attached ... the right to the full enjoyment of Ellenborough Park, which was granted by the 1864 and other relevant conveyances, was, in substance, no more than a right to use the park as a garden in the way in which gardens are commonly used. In a sense, no doubt, such a right includes something of a *jus spatiandi*, inasmuch as it involves the principle of wandering at will round each part of the garden, except of course, such parts as comprise flower beds, or are laid out for some other purpose, which renders walking impossible or unsuitable. We doubt, nevertheless, whether the right to use and enjoy a garden in this manner can with accuracy be said to constitute a mere *jus spatiandi*. Wandering at large is of the essence of such a right and constitutes the main purpose for which it exists. A private garden, on the other hand, is an attribute of the ordinary enjoyment of the residence to which it is attached, and the right of wandering in it is but one method of enjoying it. On the assumption, however, that the right now in question does constitute a *jus spatiandi*, or that it is analogous thereto, it becomes necessary to consider whether the right, which is in question in these proceedings, is, for that reason, incapable of ranking in law as an easement.

[His Lordship referred to *dicta* of Farwell J in *International Tea Stores Co v Hobbs* [1903] 2 Ch 165 at 171 and *Attorney-General v Antrobus* [1905] 2 Ch 188 at 198, 199, 205 and concluded that Farwell J's view that a *jus spatiandi* was a right 'not known to our law' as *obiter* and not supported by authority.]

It will be noted that in both of these cases the judge said that a *jus spatiandi* is 'not known to our law' and the question arises as to what precisely he meant by using that phrase. He may have meant: (a) that it was unknown to our law, because it found no place in the Roman law of servitudes; (b) that it was repugnant to the ownership of land that other persons should have rights of user over the whole of it; (c) that the law will not recognise rights to use a servient tenement for the purposes of mere recreation and pleasure; or (d) that such rights are too vague and uncertain to be capable of definition. Which of these meanings the judge had in mind it is difficult to know; and indeed, he may have had some other meaning. If, however, one attributes to the phrase 'not known to the law' its ordinary signification, namely that it was a right which our law had refused to recognise, it is clear, we think, that he would at least have expressed himself in less general terms had his attention been drawn to *Duncan v Louch*.[32] That case was not, however, cited to him in either the *International Tea Stores* case[33] or in *Attorney-General v Antrobus*[34] for the sufficient reason that it was not relevant to any issue that was before the judge upon the questions which arose for decision. There is no doubt, in our judgment, but that *Attorney-General v Antrobus* was rightly decided; for no right can be granted (otherwise than by Statute) to the public at large to wander at will over an undefined open space, nor can the public acquire such a right by prescription. We doubt very much whether Farwell J had in mind, notwithstanding the apparent generality of his language, a so-called *jus spatiandi* granted as properly appurtenant to an estate; for the whole of his judgment was devoted to a consideration of public rights; and, although this cannot be said of his observations as to the gardens and park in the *International Tea Stores* case, the view which he there expressed was entirely obiter upon a point which was irrelevant to the case and had not been argued. Inasmuch, therefore, as this observation is unsupported by any principle or any authority that are binding upon us, and is in conflict with the decision in *Duncan v Louch*, we are unable to accept its accuracy as an exhaustive statement of the law and, in reference, at least, to a case such as that now before the court, it cannot, in our judgment, be regarded hereafter as authoritative.

Duncan v Louch, on the other hand, decided more than 100 years ago but not, as we have observed, quoted to Farwell J in either of the two cases which we have cited, is authoritative in favour of the recognition by our law as an easement of a right closely comparable to that now in question which, if it involves in some sense a *jus spatiandi*, is nevertheless properly annexed and appurtenant to a defined hereditament ... On the other hand, we agree with Danckwerts J in regarding *Duncan v Louch* as being a direct authority in the defendants' favour. It has never, so far as we are aware, been since questioned, and we think it should, in the present case, be followed.

For the reasons which we have stated, Danckwerts J came, in our judgment, to a right conclusion in this case and, accordingly, the appeal must be dismissed.

A right to a prospect or view was thought not to be an easement because it could not be defined.[35] Such a right can only be acquired by way of a restrictive covenant which prevents the owner of the neighbouring land from building on

32 (1845) 6 QB 904.

33 [1903] 2 Ch 165.

34 [1905] 2 Ch 188.

35 *William Aldred's* case (1610) 9 Co Rep 57b at 58b.

his land in such a way as to obstruct the view. Similarly, there is no easement of uninterrupted access of light or air which does not come through defined apertures in a building.[36] There is no easement of uninterrupted flow of air to one's chimney over the general surface of a neighbour's land.[37] Neither is there an easement of *jus spatiandi* (ie the right to wander at will over another's land).[38]

(iii) The right must be in the nature of an easement

This means that it must be within the categories of rights already recognised as easements or very similar in nature to such categories. Although the categories of easements are never closed, and must alter and expand with the changes that take place in the circumstances of mankind, as Lord St Leonards once observed in 1852,[39] the courts have been rather reluctant to admit new kinds of easement. This is particularly true with negative easement,[40] ie a right which is enjoyed without any action by the dominant owner (eg right to light).

In *Phipps v Pears*[41] D had demolished his adjoining house. As a result, the unpointed flank wall of P's house was exposed to the rigours of the weather. The rain found its way in and during the winter it froze and caused cracks in the wall. P sought damages on the ground that he had an easement of protection from the weather. The claim failed. The supposed right was entirely negative which would prevent the neighbour from pulling down his own house if successfully pleaded and, therefore, could not be recognised as an easement. Such a right could be more conveniently acquired by way of a restrictive covenant.[42]

Phipps v Pears [1965] 1 QB 76, CA

Lord Denning, MR: [The right to protection from the weather, the plaintiff said] was analogous to the right of support. It is settled law, of course, that a man who has his house next to another for many years, so that it is dependent on it for support, is entitled to have that support maintained. His neighbour is not entitled to pull down his house without providing substitute support in the form of buttresses or something of the kind, see *Dalton v Angus*.[43] Similarly, it was said, with a right to protection from the weather. If the man next door pulls down his own house and exposes his neighbour's wall naked to the weather whereby damage is done to him, he is, it is said, liable to damages.

---

36 *Harris v De Pinna* (1886) 33 Ch D 238 at 250, 262; *Lavet v Gas Light & Coke Co* [1919] 1 Ch 24 at 27. Whether there is an easement of uninterrupted flow of air through a definite aperture or channel over a neighbour's property was left open by the Court of Appeal in *Bryant v Lefever* (1879) 4 CPD 172. But the Court of Appeal in *Ough v King* [1967] 1 WLR 1547 at 1553A–C upheld an easement to light flowing through a defined aperture.

37 *Bryant v Lefever* (1879) 4 CPD 172 at 178, 180.

38 *Re Ellenborough Park* [1956] Ch 131 at 176.

39 *Dyce v Lady James Hay* (1852) 1 Macq 305 at 312.

40 *Phipps v Pears* [1965] 1 QB 76 at 82G–83A.

41 [1965] 1 QB 76. See [1964] CLJ 203 (K Scott); (1964) 80 LQR 318 (REM); (1964) 28 Conv (NS) 450 at 451 (Peel, MA).

42 [1965] 1 QB 76 at 83E–F.

43 (1881) 6 App Cas 740, HL.

The case, so put, raises the question whether there is a right known to the law to be protected – by your neighbour's house – from the weather. Is there an easement of protection?

There are two kinds of easements known to the law: positive easements, such as a right of way, which give the owner of land *a right himself to do something* on or to his neighbour's land: and negative easements, such as a right of light, which gives him *a right to stop his neighbour doing something* on his (the neighbour's) own land. The right of support does not fall neatly into either category. It seems in some way to partake of the nature of a positive easement rather than a negative easement. The one building, by its weight, exerts a thrust, not only downwards, but also sideways on to the adjoining building or the adjoining land, and is thus doing something to the neighbour's land, exerting a thrust on it, see *Dalton v Angus*,[44] *per* Lord Selborne LC.[45] But a right to protection from the weather (if it exists) is entirely negative. It is a right to stop your neighbour pulling down his own house. Seeing that it is a negative easement, it must be looked at with caution. Because the law has been very chary of creating any new negative easements.

Take this simple instance: Suppose you have a fine view from your home. You have enjoyed the view for many years. It adds greatly to the value of your house. But if your neighbour chooses to despoil it, by building up and blocking it, you have no redress. There is no such right known to the law as a right to a prospect or view, see *Bland v Moseley*[46] cited by Lord Coke in *Aldred's* case.[47] The only way in which you can keep the view from your house is to get your neighbour to make a covenant with you that he will not build so as to block your view. Such a covenant is binding on him by virtue of the contract. It is also binding in equity on anyone who buys the land from him with notice of the covenant. But it is not binding on a purchaser who has no notice of it, see *Leech v Schweder*.[48]

Take next this instance from the last century. A man built a windmill. The winds blew freely on the sails for 30 years working the mill. Then his neighbour built a schoolhouse only 25 yards away which cut off the winds. It was held that the miller had no remedy: for the right to wind and air, coming in an undefined channel, is not a right known to the law, see *Webb v Bird*.[49] The only way in which the miller could protect himself was by getting his neighbour to enter into a covenant.

The reason underlying these instances is that if such an easement were to be permitted, it would unduly restrict your neighbour in his enjoyment of his own land. It would hamper legitimate development, see *Dalton v Angus*[50] *per* Lord Blackburn.[51] Likewise here, if we were to stop a man pulling down his house, we would put a brake on desirable improvement. Every man is entitled to pull down his house if he likes. If it exposes your house to the weather, that is your misfortune. It is no wrong on his part.

44 (1881) 6 App Cas 740, HL.

45 (1881) 6 App Cas 793, HL.

46 (1587) cited in 9 Co Rep 58a.

47 (1610) 9 Co Rep 57b.

48 (1874) 9 Ch App 463.

49 (1861) 10 CBNS 268; (1862) 13 CBNS 841.

50 (1881) 6 App Cas 740.

51 (1881) 6 App Cas 824.

Likewise every man is entitled to cut down his trees if he likes, even if it leaves you without shelter from the wind or shade from the sun; see the decision of the Master of the Rolls in Ireland in *Cochrane v Verner*.[52] There is no such easement known to the law as an easement to be protected from the weather. The only way for an owner to protect himself is by getting a covenant from his neighbour that he will not pull down his house or cut down his trees. Such a covenant would be binding on him in contract: and it would be enforceable on any successor who took with notice of it. But it would not be binding on one who took without notice.

(iv) No exclusive or joint user can be an easement

No right can be recognised as an easement if it involves an element of exclusive possession or joint occupation of the supposedly servient land for a considerable period of time.

In *Copeland v Greenhalf*,[53] D had for 50 years used a narrow strip of land belonging to P for the purpose of storing vehicles awaiting and undergoing repair. He claimed that the right amounted to an easement by prescription. The claim was rejected because it was a claim to possession of the servient land, if necessary to the exclusion of the owner, for as long as he liked, which was wholly outside any normal idea of an easement.

Copeland v Greenhalf (1952) Ch 488

Upjohn J: I think that the right claimed goes wholly outside any normal idea of an easement, that is, the right of the owner or the occupier of a dominant tenement over a servient tenement. This claim (to which no closely related authority has been referred to me) really amounts to a claim to a joint user of the land by the defendant. Practically, the defendant is claiming the whole beneficial user of the strip of land on the south-east side of the track there; he can leave as many or as few lorries there as he likes for as long as he likes; he may enter on it by himself, his servants and agents to do repair work thereon. In my judgment, that is not a claim which can be established as an easement. It is virtually a claim to possession of the servient tenement, if necessary to the exclusion of the owner; or, at any rate, to a joint user, and no authority has been cited to me which would justify the conclusion that a right of this wide and undefined nature can be the proper subject-matter of an easement. It seems to me that to succeed, this claim must amount to a successful claim of possession by reason of long adverse possession. I say nothing, of course, as to the creation of such rights by deeds or by covenant; I am dealing solely with the question of a right arising by prescription.

In *Grigsby v Melville*,[54] a right of storage in a cellar was claimed to be an easement. The claim failed because, in the circumstances, it amounted to an exclusive right of user over the whole of the confined space in the servient land. Brightman J said that the issue was whether an easement of unlimited storage within a confined or defined space is capable of existing as a matter of law.

52 (1895) 29 ILT 571.

53 (1952) Ch 488.

54 [1973] 1 All ER 385.

Grigsby v Melville [1973] 1 All ER 385

Brightman J [having referred to Upjohn J's statement in *Copeland v Greenhalf* quoted above continued:] Counsel for the defendants countered by observing that *Copeland v Greenhalf*[55] was inconsistent with *Wright v Macadam*,[56] an earlier decision of the Court of Appeal in which it was held that the right of a tenant to store domestic coal in a shed on the landlord's land could exist as an easement for the benefit of the demised premises. I am not convinced that there is any real inconsistency between the two cases. The point of the decision in *Copeland v Greenhalf* was that the right asserted amounted in effect to a claim to the whole beneficial user of the servient tenement and for that reason could not exist as a mere easement. The precise facts in *Wright v Macadam* in this respect are not wholly clear from the report and it is a little difficult to know whether the tenant had exclusive use of the coal shed or of any defined portion of it. To some extent a problem of this sort may be one of degree.

In the case before me, it is, I think, clear that the defendants' claim to an easement would give, to all practical intents and purposes, an exclusive right of user over the whole of the confined space representing the servient tenement. I think I would be at liberty if necessary to follow *Copeland v Greenhalf*.

The test of non-exclusive possession is sometimes suppressed when the claim is meritorious. In *Wright v Macadam*,[57] the defendant let a top floor flat to the plaintiff. Throughout the plaintiff's seven years of occupation, the defendant had allowed him to store coal in the defendant's garden shed. The defendant later demanded payment for the use of the shed. It was held that the plaintiff had an easement to store coal in the garden shed even though it appeared that it was a right of exclusive user.

Whether a right involves exclusive possession or not is a matter of degree. So in *Miller v Emcer Products Ltd*[58] a right to use a lavatory on another's premises was held to be an easement, even though during the times when the dominant owner exercised the right (in the lavatory), there was an element of exclusive possession intermittently.

Miller v Emcer Products Ltd [1956] Ch 304, CA

Romer LJ: In my judgment the right had all the requisite characteristics of an easement. There is no doubt as to what were intended to be the dominant and servient tenements respectively, and the right was appurtenant to the former and calculated to enhance its beneficial use and enjoyment. It is true that during the times when the dominant owner exercised the right, the owner of the servient tenement would be excluded, but this in greater or less degree is a common feature of many easements (for example, rights of way) and does not amount to such an ouster of the servient owner's rights as was held by Upjohn J to be incompatible with a legal easement in *Copeland v Greenhalf*. No case precisely in point on this issue was brought to our attention, but the right to use a lavatory is not dissimilar, I think, to the right to use a neighbour's kitchen for washing, the validity of which as an easement was assumed without question in *Heywood v*

55 [1952] 1 All ER 809; [1952] Ch 488.

56 [1949] 2 KB 744.

57 [1949] 2 KB 744.

58 [1956] Ch 304; (1956) 72 LQR 172 (REM).

Mallalieu.[59] No objection can fairly be made based upon uncertainty, and it follows, in my judgment, that the right may properly be regarded as an easement which the lessors were professing to grant for a term of years; and such an easement would rank as an interest in or over land capable of being created at law by virtue of s 1(2) of the Law of Property Act 1925.

It seems that parking a car anywhere in a large area of neighbouring land does not amount to exclusive user, even though at the time of parking there is an element of exclusiveness.[60] If the right granted in relation to the area over which it is to be exercisable is such that it would leave the servient owner without any reasonable use of his land, whether for parking or anything else, it could not be an easement.[61] Parking at a defined area over a long period may amount to an exclusive possession.[62]

Finally, an easement cannot impose a positive burden on the servient owner. The courts will not accept an easement which requires expenditure by the servient owner.[63] Thus, it was held in *Regis Property Co Ltd v Redman*[64] that an undertaking to maintain a supply of hot water cannot be an easement because it imposes a positive obligation on the servient owner to secure the supply and perhaps to pay for the supply. Easement of fencing is an exception. In *Crow v Wood*,[65] a right to have the servient owner maintain a fence for the benefit of the dominant owner was held to be an easement even though it imposed expenses on the servient owner. There was no apparent reason for this exception save that it had long been a custom or practice for such a right to be adhered to.

Crow v Wood [1971] 1 QB 77, CA

Lord Denning MR: The question is, therefore, whether a right to have a fence or wall kept in repair is a right which is capable of being granted by law. I think it is because it is in the nature of an easement. It is not an easement strictly so called because it involves the servient owner in the expenditure of money. It was described by Gale [*Easements*, 11th edn, 1932, p 432] as a 'spurious kind of easement'. But it has been treated in practice by the courts as being an easement. Professor Glanville Williams on *Liability for Animals* (1939), says, at p 209: 'If we put aside these questions of theory and turn to the practice of the courts, there seems to be little doubt that fencing is an easement.' In *Jones v Price* [1965] 2 QB 618, 633, Willmer LJ said: 'It is clear that a right to require the owner of adjoining land to keep the boundary fence in repair is a right which the law will recognise as a quasi-easement.' Diplock LJ, at p 639, points out that it is a right of such a nature that it can be acquired by prescription which imports that it lies in grant, for prescription rests on a presumed grant.

It seems to me that it is now sufficiently established – or at any rate, if not established hitherto, we should now declare – that a right to have your neighbour keep up the fences

59 (1883) 25 ChD 357.

60 *Sweet & Maxwell Ltd v Michael-Michaels Advertising* [1965] CLY 2192.

61 *London & Blenheim Estates Ltd v Ladbroke Retail Parks Ltd* [1992] 1 WLR 127 at 1288 B–C.

62 See (1973) 37 Conv (NS) 60 (Hayton, DJ).

63 *Regis Property v Redman* [1956] 2 QB 612.

64 [1956] 2 QB 612.

65 [1971] 1 QB 77.

is a right in the nature of an easement which is capable of being granted by law so as to run with the land and to be binding on successors. It is a right which lies in grant and is of such a nature that it can pass under s 62 of the Law of Property Act 1925.

Comparison with similar rights[66]

So an easement is essentially a right attached to the dominant land, exercisable by the owner or occupier of the dominant land, to use the servient land owned or occupied by a different person in a particular way; or to prevent the owner or occupier of the servient land from using his land in a particular way. It is a proprietary interest which can benefit or bind third parties.

An easement is, however, different from a number of similar rights, such as profits *à prendre*, licences, restrictive covenants, public rights, natural rights, and local customary rights.

(a) Profits à prendre[67]

Easements are different from profits *à prendre* in that a profit allows the grantee to take part of the soil, minerals or natural produce of the servient land,[68] such as grass, crops, fruits, fish and wild animals.[69] An easement does not confer such a right. The owner of a profit is normally also granted a licence to enter into the servient land to take the profit. Such a licence cannot be revoked during the term of the profit.

Unlike an easement, a profit may exist 'in gross'.[70] This means that the owner of the profit does not have to own any adjoining land, ie there need not be a dominant land to which the profit is appurtenant. Of course, there is nothing to stop a profit from being appurtenant to a dominant land. Where a profit exists in gross, the owner can have unlimited profit from the servient land.[71] On the other hand, a profit appurtenant is limited to the needs of the dominant land. The law does not recognise unlimited profits appurtenant.[72]

Profits may be enjoyed by a particular person exclusively, called 'several' profits. They may be enjoyed in common with others including the servient owner, known as 'profits *à prendre* in common' or 'commons'. The Commons Registration Act 1965[73] requires that common land in England and Wales, its

66 See Jackson, P, *The Law of Easements and Profits*, 1978, London: Butterworths, pp 23–27; Gray, pp 1044–59.

67 See Jackson, P, *The Law of Easements and Profits*, 1978, London: Butterworths, Chapter 2.

68 *Alfred F Beckett Ltd v Lyons* [1967] Ch 449 at 482B.

69 *Finlay v Curteis* (1832) Hayes 496 at 499.

70 Bl Comm, Vol II, at 34; *Lord Chesterfield v Harris* [1908] 2 Ch 397 at 421; *Lovett v Fairclough* (1989) 61 P & CR 385 at 396.

71 *Staffordshire and Worcestershire Canal Navigation v Bradley* [1912] 1 Ch 91 at 103.

72 *Clayton v Corby* (1843) 5 QB 415 at 419; *Lord Chesterfield v Harris* [1908] 2 Ch 397.

73 This Act also applies to cattlegates or beastgates (ie a right to pasture a fixed number of beasts on the land of another for a part of the year only) and rights of sole or several vesture or herbage (ie the right not only to graze cattle, but also to take away the produce of the land) or of sole or several pasture, but does not include rights held for a term of years or from year to year. It also applies to waste land of a manor not subject to rights of common, and to town or village greens (s 22(1)).

owners, and claims to rights of common over such land, are all to be registered with the county council before August 1970.[74] If the land is not registered under the Act it ceases to be a common land. No right of common is exercisable unless it is registered under the Act or has been previously registered under the Land Registration Act 1925.[75] New commons may arise and must be registered. However, the land does not cease to be common land nor do the rights cease to be exercisable if they are not registered.

(b) Licences[76]

Easements are also different from licences. A licence is a mere permission. It is not generally regarded as a proprietary interest. A licence entitles the licensee exclusive occupation, but any exclusive right of use would be incompatible with easement.[77] The licensee can carry out any activity permitted by the owner. No formality for the creation of a licence is required. No dominant land is needed. The courts have sometimes looked to the express wording of the grant to see if a right is an easement or a licence. In *IDC Group v Clark*,[78] a grant of a 'licence' to use a door which led into another property as a fire escape was literally construed as a licence and not an easement.

(c) Restrictive covenants[79]

Easements are very similar to restrictive covenants in nature. A restrictive covenant restricts the servient owner's use of his land. A negative easement prevents the servient owner from using his own land in a manner which will destroy the dominant owner's easement. However, restrictive covenants only exist in equity and may not be acquired by prescription. Also, the subject matter of a restrictive covenant, unlike easements, is virtually unlimited.

(d) Public rights[80]

Public rights are rights that can be exercised by any member of the public. Some public rights may be similar to easements, for example, the public rights of way. They are, however, different from easements in that the members of the public who are entitled to exercise such rights do not have to own any land. Furthermore, public rights are not specifically granted by deed to the members of the public. Public rights of way are often the creation of statutes such as the Highways Act 1980, or at common law under the doctrine of 'dedication and acceptance' by uninterrupted long use by the public.[81] The fee simple owner

74 See Gadsden, *The Law of Commons* (1988); Clayden, *Our Common Land* (1985).

75 Commons Registration Act 1965, s 1(2); *Central Electricity Generating Board v Clwyd County Council* [1976] 1 WLR 151 (right of common extinguished for want of registration).

76 See Chapter 10.

77 *Copeland v Greenhalf* (1952) Ch 488.

78 [1992] *The Times*, 23 July, CA.

79 See Chapter 14.

80 See Tim Bonyhady, *The Law of Countryside: the Rights of the Public*, 1987, Abingdon: Professional; Riddall, JG and Trevelyan, J, *Rights of Way: A Guide to Law and Practice*, 2nd edn, 1992, London: Open Spaces Society: Ramblers' Association.

81 *Cubitt v Lady Caroline Maxse* (1873) LR 8 CP 704 at 715; *Turner v Walsh* (1881) 6 App Cas 626 at 639; *Folkstone Corpn v Brockman* [1914] AC 338 at 352, 362.

must have dedicated the highway to the public and the dedication must have been accepted.[82] The intention to dedicate may be inferred from the conduct of the fee simple owner. Where the fee simple owner has done some acts of interruption, such as a symbolic closure of the route for a day to deny the public access, no such intention can be inferred.[83] Under s 31(1) of the Highways Act 1980, there is a rebuttable presumption of dedication where the way has been 'actually enjoyed by the public as of right and without interruption for a full period of 20 years'.[84]

The public also has a common law right of navigation over navigable tidal waters,[85] and a statutory right of passage over non-tidal rivers and lakes.[86] There is also a public right of fishing in 'the sea of common right'[87] and in all tidal and salt waters.[88] These rights are similar to profits *à prendre*, but are different from them in that profits must be granted. There is, however, no public right of fishing in non-tidal rivers[89] or lakes.[90]

There may be a public right of recreational use over non-tidal waters by long use.[91] But otherwise, there is no general public right of recreation over hills or open countryside,[92] or shore or foreshore.[93]

(e) Natural rights

Easements are also different from natural rights such as the right to support for land.[94] These rights exist automatically and need not be granted.

A natural right of support confers on a landowner a right to see that his land will not subside as a result of the activities of the owner of the neighbouring land. This does not, however, give him a right of support for buildings on the

82 *R v Inhabitants of Tithing of East Mark* (1848) 11 QB 877 at 883–84; 116 ER 701, at 704.

83 *British Museum Trustees v Finnis* (1833) 5 C & P 460 at 465, 172 ER 1053 at 1056; *Poole v Huskinson* (1843) 11 M & W 827 at 830; 152 ER 1039 at 1041.

84 See *Gloucestershire CC v Farrow* [1985] 1 WLR 741; *Dyfed CC v Secretary of State for Wales* (1990) 59 P & CR 275.

85 *AG v Tomline* (1880) 14 Ch D 58.

86 Schedule 23 of the Water Resources Act 1991; s 22(6) of the Countryside Act 1968.

87 (1466) YB Mich 8 Edw IV, pl 30.

88 *Stephens v Snell* [1939] 3 All ER 622H; *Case of the Royal Fishery of the Banne* (1610) Dav 55; 80 ER 540 at 541.

89 Such a right belongs to the owner of the land through which the river runs: *Blundell v Catterall* (1821) 5 B & Ald 268 at 294; 106 ER 1190 at 1199.

90 *Johnstone v O'Neill* [1911] AC 552 at 568, 577, 592.

91 *R v Doncaster Metropolitan BC, ex p Braim* (1989) 57 P & CR 1 at 15; *Marshall v Ulleswater Steam Navigation Co* (1871) LR 7 QB 166 at 172; *Bloomfield v Johnston* (1868) IR 8 CL 68 at 87, 111; *Mickletthwait v Vincent* (1892) 67 LT 225 at 230; *Attorney-General (ex rel Yorkshire Derwent Trust Ltd) v Brotherton* [1992] 1 AC 425 at 434D. See also [1988] Conv 369 (Hill, J).

92 *Earl of Coventry v Willes* (1863) 9 LT 384 at 385; *Attorney-General v Antrobus* [1905] 2 Ch 188 at 208.

93 *Brinckman v Matley* [1904] 2 Ch 313 at 324; *Alfred F Beckett Ltd v Lyons* [1967] Ch 449 at 482E–F.

94 *Backhouse v Bonomi* (1861) 9 HL Cas 503 at 512; 11 ER 825, at 829.

land in the absence of an easement of support.[95] Neither does it give him a right to have land supported by subterranean water in neighbouring land.[96]

The landowner may also have a natural right to water which flows naturally in a defined channel through his land.[97] But there is no natural right to water which percolates underground in undefined channels[98] for such percolating water is 'a common reservoir or source in which nobody has any property, but of which everybody has, as far as he can, the right of appropriating the whole'.[99]

(f) Local customary rights

Easements differ from local customary rights in that the latter are enjoyed by the members of a local community[100] and are not appurtenant to any dominant land. Examples of local customary rights are the right of access to the local church,[101] sporting activities and pastimes on a piece of land,[102] the drying of fishing nets in a particular spot,[103] and the holding of annual fairs.[104]

2 RIGHTS OF WAY AND LIGHT

The main types of easement are rights of way, rights of light or rights to air or water in a defined channel, or rights to storage. There are other miscellaneous easements such as the right to hang washing over neighbour's land,[105] the right to hang a signboard on the adjourning house,[106] and the right to use a park by the residents of the houses surrounding it,[107] but not a right of recreation and amusement unconnected with the enjoyment of dominant land.

Two important easements: rights of way and rights of light are dealt with in more detail here.

95 *Dalton v Angus & Co* (1881) 6 App Cas 740 at 804; *Peyton v London Corpn* (1829) 9 B & C 725 at 753; 109 ER 269 at 273; *Ray v Fairway Motors (Barnstaple) Ltd* (1968) 20 P & CR 261 at 264; *Midland Bank plc v Bardgrove Property Services Ltd* [1991] 2 EGLR 283 at 286B.

96 *Stephens v Anglian Water Authority* (1988) 55 P & CR 348 at 351.

97 *Chasemore v Richards* (1859) 7 HL Cas 349 at 382; 11 ER 140 at 153; *Swindon Waterworks Co Ltd v Wilts and Berks Canal Navigation Co* (1875) LR 7 HL 697 at 704.

98 *Bradford Corpn v Pickles* [1895] AC 587 at 592, 595, 600.

99 *Ballard v Tomplinson* (1885) 29 Ch D 115 at 121.

100 *New Windsor Corpn v Mellor* [1975] Ch 380 at 391C–D; *Brocklebank v Thompson* [1903] 2 Ch 344 at 354.

101 *Brocklebank v Thompson* [1903] 2 Ch 344 at 355.

102 *New Windsor Corpn v Mellor* [1975] Ch 380 at 392H.

103 *Mercer v Denne* [1905] 2 Ch 538 at 577

104 *Wyld v Silver* [1963] Ch 243 at 256, 266.

105 *Drewell v Towler* (1832) 3 B & Ad 735 (the claim failed on procedural ground).

106 *Moody v Steggle* (1879) 12 Ch D 261.

107 *Re Ellenborough Park* [1956] Ch 131.

Rights of way

A right of way confers a right to pass and re-pass. It also confers certain ancillary rights necessary for the enjoyment of the right to pass and re-pass. Thus, the grantee may stop on the way for the purpose of loading and unloading,[108] repairing and developing or improving the way.[109] An easement may, however, be limited in various ways. It may be limited as to the intervals at which it may be used, for example, during daylight.[110] It may be limited as to the extent of use, such as a footway, horseway or motorway. It may be limited as to the purposes for which it may be used, for example, for agricultural purposes only.[111] Where the easement is granted, its extent and content depend on the proper construction of the grant. Where the easement is acquired through prescriptive user, its extent and content depend on the user proved. As Willes J put it in *Williams v James*:[112]

> The distinction between a grant and prescription is obvious. In the case of proving a right by prescription the user of the right is the only evidence. In the case of a grant the language of the instrument can be referred to, and it is of course for the court to construe the language; and in the absence of any clear indication of the intention of the parties, the maxim that a grant must be construed most strongly against the grantor must be applied.

(a) By grant

The grant of an easement is often construed in the light of the circumstances surrounding its execution. In *St Edmundsbury and Ipswich Diocesan Board of Finance v Clark (No 2)*, Sir John Pennycuick said, 'What is the proper approach upon the construction of a conveyance containing the reservation of a right of way? We feel no doubt that the proper approach is that upon which the court construes all documents; that is to say, one must construe the document according to the natural meaning of the words contained in the document as a whole, read in the light of surrounding circumstances.'[113] An apparently unlimited grant may, therefore, be limited to more restricted forms of user.

Cannon v Villars (1878) 8 Ch D 415, CA

Jessel MR: As I understand, the grant of a right of way *per se* and nothing else may be a right of footway, or it may be a general right of way, that is a right of way not only for people on foot but for people on horseback, for carts, carriages, and other vehicles. Which it is, is a question of construction of the grant, and that construction will of course depend on the circumstances surrounding, so to speak, the execution of the instrument. Now one of those circumstances, and a very material circumstance, is the nature of the locus in quo over which the right of way is granted. If we find a right of way granted over a metalled road with pavement on both sides existing at the time of the grant, the

108 *Bulstrode v Lambert* [1953] 1 WLR 1064 at 1071; *VT Engineering Ltd v Ricrad Barland & Co Ltd* (1968) 19 P & CR 890.

109 *Gerrard v Cooke* (1806) 2 Bos & Pul NR 109 at 115; *Mills v Silver* [1991] Ch 271 at 286H–87A.

110 *Collins v Slade* (1874) 23 WR 199.

111 *Reignolds v Edwards* (1741) Willes 282.

112 (1867) LR 2 CP 577 at 581.

113 [1975] 1 WLR 468 at 476. See also *White v Richards* (1994) 68 P&CR 105.

presumption would be that it was intended to be used for the purpose for which it was constructed, which is obviously the passage not only of foot passengers, but of horsemen and carts. Again, if we find the right of way granted along a piece of land capable of being used for the passage of carriages, and the grant is of a right of way to a place which is stated on the face of the grant to be intended to be used or to be actually used for a purpose which would necessarily or reasonably require the passing of carriages, there again it must be assumed that the grant of the right of way was intended to be effectual for the purpose for which the place was designed to be used, or was actually used.

Where you find a road constructed so as to be fit for carriages and of the requisite width, leading up to a dwelling house, and there is a grant of a right of way to that dwelling house, it would be a grant of a right of way for all reasonable purposes required for the dwelling house, and would include, therefore, the right to the user of carriages by the occupant of the dwelling house if he wanted to take the air, or the right to have a wagon drawn up to the door when the wagon was to bring coals for the use of the dwelling house. Again, if the road is not to a dwelling house but to a factory, or a place used for business purposes which would require heavy weights to be brought to it, or to a wool warehouse which would require bags or packages of wool to be brought to it, then a grant of right of way would include a right to use it for reasonable purposes, sufficient for the purposes of the business, which would include the right of bringing up carts and waggons at reasonable times for the purpose of the business. That again would afford an indication in favour of the extent of the grant. If, on the other hand, you find that the road in question over which the grant was made was paved only with flagstones, and that it was only four or five feet wide, over which a wagon or cart or carriage ordinarily constructed could not get, and that it was only a way used to a field or close, or something on which no erection was, there, I take it, you would say that the physical circumstances shewed that the right of way was a right for foot-passengers only. It might include a horse under some circumstances, but could not be intended for carts or carriages. Of course where you find restrictive words in the grant, that is to say, where it is only for the use of foot-passengers, stated in express terms, or for foot-passengers and horsemen, and so forth, there is nothing to argue. I take it that is the law. *Prima facie* the grant of a right of way is the grant of a right of way having regard to the nature of the road over which it is granted and the purpose for which it is intended to be used; and both those circumstances may be legitimately called in aid in determining whether it is a general right of way, or a right of way restricted to foot-passengers, or restricted to foot-passengers and horsemen or cattle, which is generally called a drift way, or a general right of way for carts, horses, carriages, and everything else.

A right of way is also construed with reference to the purpose for which is was granted reasonably contemplated by the parties at the date of the grant.[114] Where a right of way was granted for general purposes for the benefit of a house, when the house was converted into a hotel, the grantee could still exercise his right of way for the general purposes of the hotel.[115] A right with or without horses, carts and agricultural machines and implements to pass and repass over a strip of land within rectory grounds was held to include user by

114 *Hamble PC v Haggard* [1992] 1 WLR 122 at 136B.

115 *White v Grand Hotel Eastbourne Ltd* [1913] 1 Ch 113.

substantial traffic of lorries carrying sand when a sand and gravel pit was later opened in the land adjoining the rectory.[116]

In the absence of an express restriction, the form of the user is not cut down by the form of user employed in the past.[117] However, the servient owner may make an objection if the change in the form of user has imposed an excessive burden on the servient owner compared with the burden existing at the date of the grant. In *Jelbert v Davis*,[118] an agricultural land was conveyed to the plaintiff with 'a right of way at all times and for all purposes over the driveway retained by the vendor leading to the main road in common with all other persons having the like right'. The plaintiff subsequently obtained planning permission to use part of the land as a tourist and caravan site for up to 200 caravans and tents. The Court of Appeal held that the use of the driveway by caravans was not objectionable but the user by 200 caravans was excessive and could cause substantial interference with the use of the servient land by its owners.

Where the physical characteristics of the passage has been altered, in the absence of any express restrictions, a right of way for general purposes will include form of user previously not possible at the date of the grant. In *Keefe v Amor*,[119] a gap of 4 foot 6 inches wide allowed access from the strip of land over which a right of way was granted to the highway. Later the gap was widen to 7 foot 6 inches by the servient owner. The Court of Appeal held that the dominant owner was now entitled to a right of user by vehicles which was not possible when the original gap was smaller.

Similarly, when the dominant land was later altered, the right of way appurtenant to it may be unaffected. In *Graham v Philcox*,[120] ground floor and first floor flats were converted into a single dwelling house. The first floor flat had originally enjoyed a right of way over adjoining land. It was held that the change in the dominant land did not affect the right of way as it would not cause excessive user.

Graham v Philcox [1984] QB 747, CA

Purchas LJ: The only change that has now been made is that one dwelling unit is now housed where two dwelling units were previously housed. It does not follow of necessity that the *'de facto'* user of the right of way made by the members of the unit now occupying both parts of the coach house would be more than the user of that right to which the occupier personally and/or his servants, invitees and licensees would have been entitled as occupier of the dominant tenement confined to the first floor. Indeed, it is not difficult to conceive of circumstances in which it might be a good deal less. This change is entirely different from the dramatic structural changes, changes of use considered in the cases to which reference has already been made; and falls far more within the concept of the alteration to the dominant tenement which was held not to have prejudiced the right to use the coal shed in *Wright v Macadam* [1949] 2 KB 744, to

116 *Kain v Norfolk* [1949] Ch 163.

117 *Newcomen v Culson* (1877) 5 Ch D 133 at 138.

118 [1968] 1 WLR 589.

119 [1965] 1 QB 334, [1964] 2 All ER 517.

120 [1984] QB 747.

which May LJ has already referred and upon which Mr Reid relied in support of his submission that mere alteration to the extent of the dominant tenement was not effective to destroy an casement or right ... The right of way having been created by direct grant and its use continuing even though under statutory protection at the time of the conveyance, the use and enjoyment of that easement fell within the terms of s 62 of the Act and the judge was in error in holding that it did not. Nor, for the reasons I have already given, can I accept the submissions made by Mr Godfrey that by enlarging the physical dimensions or indeed altering the nature of the dominant tenement from two individual flats to one dwelling house has the easement, right or advantage been destroyed. The occupier of the dominant tenement, however, will be and will remain subject to the rules requiring that the character and extent of the burden imposed upon the servient tenement must not be enlarged. For want of a better definition, this burden must be said to be commensurate with the reasonable user of the means of access by the occupier, his servants, agents, invitees or licensees occupying a single dwelling unit. If by any change in the nature of his enjoyment of the dominant tenement the occupier thereof increases the burden upon the servient tenement beyond this, then he will be liable to the consequences of excessive user which may be imposed upon any person enjoying an easement, right or benefit of this kind.

(b) By prescription

Easements by prescription are proved by the user and their extent and content must, therefore, be limited to the kind of user prevailing over the period which gave rise to the prescriptive right.[121] Thus, although the prescriptive owner may repair the passage,[122] there is no right to improve it for this would increase significantly the burden on the servient land.[123] However, an increase in the user is not objectionable as long as there is no fundamental change in character or purpose of the original user.[124] In *British Railways Board v Glass*,[125] the British Railways Board's predecessors in title bought a strip of land for the construction of a railway line through a field owned by the defendant's predecessor in title but occupied by a tenant. The defendant's predecessor in title reserved a right of crossing the railway, including crossing for cattle, to and from one part of the land to the other part severed by the railway. Part of the field (known as the 'blue land') near the crossing had been used for many years prior to 1942 as a caravan site. By 1942 six caravans had been established on the site, but since then the numbers had grown, thereby increasing substantially the traffic of vehicles and people over the crossing. The plaintiffs brought proceedings to limit the user of the crossing. The questions were whether the right of way reserved covered the traffic of the caravanners, and whether the caravanners had acquired a right of crossing by prescription. The Court of Appeal (Lord Denning dissenting) held that the right of way reserved was general and not limited to agricultural purposes in the contemplation of the original parties to the conveyance. Secondly, a prescriptive right of crossing had been acquired by

121 *Ballard v Dyson* (1808) 1 Taunt 279 at 286; *Mills v Silver* [1991] Ch 271 at 287B–C.

122 *Mills v Silver* [1991] Ch 271 at 286F–G.

123 *Mills v Silver* [1991] Ch 271 at 287B–C.

124 *British Railways Board v Glass* [1965] Ch 538 at 562E–63A.

125 [1965] Ch 538. See (1965) 81 LQR 17 (REM).

the caravanners and the increase in number of caravanners since 1942 was not an excessive user.

British Railways Board v Glass [1965] 1 Ch 538, CA

Lord Denning dissenting: *The Prescriptive Right*. The defendant says that alternatively he obtained a right by prescription. The judge found that for 20 years before the action, from 1942–62, there had been six caravans on the site permanently, but that there had been 10 or 11 there at times from 1942–45 and thereafter, and increased to 28 or 29 immediately before the issue of the writ. It is clear that by prescription there is a right of way for six caravans. But is there a right for 28 or 29 caravans?

It is quite clear that, when you acquire a right of way by prescription, you are not entitled to change the character of your land so as substantially to increase or alter the burden upon the servient tenement. If you have a right of way for your pasture land, you cannot turn it into a manufactory and claim a right of way for the purposes of the factory. If you have a right of way by prescription for one house, you cannot build two more houses on the land and claim a right of way for the purposes of those houses also. I think this rule is not confined to the character of the property. It extends also to the intensity of the user. If you use your land for years as a caravan site for six caravans and thereby gain a prescriptive right over a level crossing, you are not thereby entitled to put 30 caravans on the site and claim a right for those 30. As Baggallay JA said in *Wimbledon and Putney Commons Conservators v Dixon*[126] 'You must neither increase the burden on the servient tenement nor substantially change the nature of the user.' This seems to me good sense. It would be very wrong that, because the plaintiffs have been so tolerant as to allow the occupants of six caravans to use the crossing, in consequence they are thereby to be saddled with the use of 30 caravans. Trains would be obstructed and delayed. Dangers would abound. After all, prescription is a presumed grant. No such grant for 30 caravans could ever be presumed from user for six.

On this part of the case, counsel for the defendant made a technical point. He said that the defendant had a prescriptive right to a 'caravan site' and so phrased it in his defence: and that in the reply the plaintiffs had admitted that the field had been used 'as a caravan site' since 1938. He says that, by this admission, the plaintiffs are debarred from saying that the defendant had a prescriptive right only for six caravans, and that the defendant has a right for as many caravans as the site will hold. I regard this as special pleading of the worst description. The facts and issues before the court are plain enough: and no one has been in the least misled by this verbal nicety. I would decide this case on the facts found, and I hold that the defendant had no prescriptive right to use the crossing for more than six caravans.

We were told that the local authority have taken steps to deal with this caravan site. They have exercised their statutory powers to see that it is gradually removed. All the caravans should be gone by 1966. That is satisfactory, in a way. But I do not see why the local authority should be forced to do this: or to pay compensation to the defendant. I think the plaintiffs are entitled to come to the court and ask for protection on their own account. I think they are entitled to restrain the defendant from putting this greatly increased burden on the crossing.

126 (1875) 1 Ch D 362, 374.

I would allow the appeal and grant a declaration and injunction as asked in the notice of appeal.

Harman LJ: It appeared from the evidence that before the last war there were three caravans and a tent dwelling permanently situated upon the 'blue land', and that this number increased after the war began, when the Admiralty moved some of its departments to Bath, to six permanent caravans and five more that came and went, and there was a further increase in the spring of 1942 after the first bombs fell on Bath, and that after the war there were further increases from time to time until shortly before the writ was issued the number of caravans had increased to 29 and it was of this burden that the plaintiffs not unnaturally complained. All the caravanners and those who visited them, and their suppliers, had no access to the blue land save over the level crossing.

This part of the case has become largely academic because the local planning authority has, by exercise of its statutory powers, ordered the gradual clearance of the site from caravans. At the date of the hearing in the court below the number had been reduced to 16 and will be reduced to none by the end of the year 1966 or thereabouts. Nevertheless, the judge considered the state of things when the writ was issued, and rightly so, and he came to the conclusion that the plaintiffs could not complain of the state of things as it then existed. He reached this conclusion upon the admissions appearing upon the face of the pleadings. The plaintiffs admitted that the 'blue land' was used 'as a caravan site,' that is to say, the whole of the 'blue land' and not merely such portions of it as had in fact been the standings of caravans. I understand that in fact there were no such permanent standings, but that caravans coming and going occupied any part of the field they chose. The prescriptive claim was not made in the right of individual caravans, which would have been a claim by individual caravanners, but by the defendant as the owner of the whole of the 'blue land' and on the footing that it constituted 'the caravan site'. It may be regrettable that this part of the case should turn on a point of pleading, as this to some extent was, but I do not think the judge could have come to this conclusion upon any other footing. The fact is that this expression 'caravan site' has only recently come into prominence, and it was not perhaps fully appreciated until the recent decision of this court in *Bliss v Smallburgh Rural District Council*[127] that it ought not to be used in a loose way. In that case a large area, which varied at various stages of the action from 70-odd acres to three or four, was claimed as being a 'caravan site', but the court came to the conclusion that there was no caravan site at all within the meaning of that phrase in the Caravan Sites and Control of Development Act, 1960, that the mere casual placing of caravans here and there on a large area did not constitute that area a 'caravan site.' So here, if the plaintiffs had not admitted that the 'blue land' constituted a 'caravan site,' the defendant might have been in great difficulty in defining the area of the site. He was relieved of that difficulty by the pleadings and his case was that, admitting the whole 'blue land' to be 'a caravan site', the mere increase from, say, 10–29 caravans did not constitute such an increase in the burden of the prescriptive right as was a legitimate subject of complaint by the plaintiffs. The leading case on this subject is *Williams v James*.[128] The headnote reads:

> The defendant being entitled by immemorial user to a right of way over the plaintiff's land from field N, used the way for the purpose of carting from field N

127 [1965] Ch 335; [1964] 3 WLR 88; [1964] 2 All ER 543, CA.

128 (1867) LR 2 CP 577.

> some hay stacked there, which had been grown partly there and partly on land adjoining. The jury found in effect that the defendant in so doing had used the way *bona fide*, and for the ordinary and reasonable use of field N as a field: Held, that the mere fact that some of the hay had not been grown on field N did not make the carrying of it over the plaintiff's land an excess in the user of the right of way.

Bovill CJ says this:[129]

> In all cases of this kind which depend upon user the right acquired must be measured by the extent of the enjoyment which is proved. When a right of way to a piece of land is proved, then that is, unless something appears to the contrary, a right of way for all purposes according to the ordinary and reasonable use to which that land might be applied at the time of the supposed grant. Such a right cannot be increased so as to affect the servient tenement by imposing upon it any additional burthen. It is also clear, according to the authorities, that where a person has a right of way over one piece of land to another piece of land, he can only use such right in order to reach the latter place. He cannot use it for the purpose of going elsewhere.

Willes J says this:[130]

> I agree with the argument of Mr Jelf that in cases like this, where a way has to be proved by user, you cannot extend the purposes for which the way may be used, or for which it might be reasonably inferred that parties would have intended it to be used. The land in this case was a field in the country, and apparently only used for rustic purposes. To be a legitimate user of the right of way, it must be used for the enjoyment of the nine acre field, and not colourably for other closes. I quite agree also with the argument that the right of way can only be used for the field in its ordinary use as a field. The use must be the reasonable use for the purposes of the land in the condition in which it was while the user took place.

Applying that to the present case, you must do what the judge did, namely base your conclusion on a consideration of what must have been the supposed contents of the lost grant on which the prescription rests. If this be supposed to be a grant of the right to use the 'blue land' as 'a caravan site', then it is clear that a mere increase in the numbers of the caravans using the site is not an excessive user of the right. A right to use a way for this purpose or that has never been to my knowledge limited to a right to use the way so many times a day or for such and such a number of vehicles so long as the dominant tenement does not change its identity. If there be a radical change in the character of the dominant tenement, then the prescriptive right will not extend to it in that condition. The obvious example is a change of a small dwelling house to a large hotel, but there has been no change of that character according to the facts found in this case. The caravan site never became a highly organised town of caravans with fixed standings and roads and all the paraphernalia attendant on such a place and in my opinion the judge was right in holding that there had been no such increase in the burden of the easement as to justify the plaintiffs in seeking as they did by injunction to restrict the user to three caravans or six or to prevent its use as what in the statement of claim is called 'a caravan camp or site'.

129 (1867) LR 2 CP 577 at 580.

130 (1867) LR 2 CPC 577 at 582.

I, accordingly, hold that the judge was right in both branches of the case and that the appeal should be dismissed.

In *Woodhouse Co Ltd v Kirkland (Derby) Ltd*,[131] there was an increase in the number of customers using a right of way acquired by prescription. Applying *British Railways Board v Glass*, Plowman J held that there was an important difference between an increase in user and a user of a different kind or for a different purpose, and that an increase in the number of customers using a right of way was a mere increase in user and not a user of a different kind or for a different purpose.

In *Giles v County Building Contractors (Hertford) Ltd*,[132] seven modern dwellings were built in the place of two houses by the defendant on the dominant land. The plaintiffs, who enjoyed a right of way with the defendant, failed in their action to restrain increased usage of the road by the defendant after the erection of seven dwellings on the dominant land. Brightman J, referring to Harman LJ in *British Railways Board v Glass*, said that:

> 'The important expressions, to my mind, are 'change of identity' and 'radical change in character'. In my view, the use of the convent site for the erection of seven modern dwelling units in place of the two existing houses, cannot properly be described as 'changing the identity' or 'radically changing the character' of the convent site. I think it is evolution rather than mutation.'

Rights of light[133]

English law does not recognise a right of unlimited free flow of light. It recognises, however, a right of light which comes through defined apertures.[134] These rights are commonly acquired by presumed grant at common law, by lost modern grant, or under s 3 of the Prescription Act 1832.[135] Express grants of easements of light are presumably very rare for uninterrupted rights to light can be easily secured by means of restrictive covenants preventing the owners of neighbouring land from building in such a manner so to obstruct light reaching the building on the dominant land.[136]

Where a right of light is established, the dominant owner is entitled to uninterrupted flow of sufficient light through his ancient windows for his comfortable enjoyment of the use of the building.[137] Where there is an interruption of light, the question is whether the amount of light remaining is sufficient for the comfortable enjoyment of his property by the dominant owner according to the ordinary notions of mankind.[138] Thus, a photographic studio

131 [1970] 1 WLR 1185.

132 (1971) 22 P & CR 978.

133 See Jackson, *The Law of Easements and Profits*, 1978, Chapter 9.

134 *Garris v De Pinna* (1886) 33 Ch D 238; *Lavet v Gas Light & Coke Co* [1919] 1 Ch 24; *Ough v King* [1967] 1 WLR 1547.

135 See pp 889–97 below.

136 See Chapter 14.

137 *Colls v Home and Colonial Stores Ltd* [1904] AC 179 at 187, 198, 204.

138 *Carr-Saunders v Dick McNeil Associations Ltd* [1986] 1 WLR 922 at 928E-F, *per* Millett J.

or a greenhouse may be entitled to an unusually large amount of light[139] while a church may only be entitled to the amount of light sufficient for the ordinary comfortable use of the people attending church.[140]

In *Colls v Home and Colonial Stores Ltd*,[141] the Home and Colonial Stores carried on their business in a building. They brought an action against Colls for building on the opposite side of the road, arguing that the building would obstruct their enjoyment of light. Joyce J refused an injunction and held that as a fact even after the erection of the building, the Home and Colonial stores would be 'well and sufficiently lighted for all ordinary purposes of occupancy as a place of business'. Joyce J's decision was reversed by the Court of Appeal but affirmed by the House of Lords.

Colls v Home and Colonial Stores Ltd [1904] AC 179, HL

Earl of Halsbury LC: The question may be very simply stated thus: after an enjoyment of light for twenty years, or if the question arose before the Act for such a period as would justify the presumption of a lost grant, would the owner of the tenement in respect of which such enjoyment had been possessed be entitled to all the light without any diminution whatsoever at the end of such a period?

My Lords, if that were the law it would be very far-reaching in its consequences, and the application of it to its strict logical conclusion would render it almost impossible for towns to grow, and would formidably restrict the rights of people to utilise their own land. Strictly applied, it would undoubtedly prevent many buildings which have hitherto been admitted to be too far removed from others to be actionable, but if the broad proposition which underlies the judgment of the Court of Appeal be true, it is not a question of 45 degrees, but any appreciable diminution of light which has been enjoyed (that is to say, has existed uninterruptedly for 20 years) constitutes a right of action, and gives a right to the proprietor of a tenement that has had this enjoyment to prevent his neighbour building on his own land.

My Lords, I do not think this is the law. The argument seems to me to rest upon a false analogy, as though the access to and enjoyment of light constituted a sort of proprietary right in the light itself. Light, like air, is the common property of all, or, to speak more accurately, it is the common right of all to enjoy it, but it is the exclusive property of none. If the same proposition against which I am protesting could be maintained in respect of air the progressive building of any town would be impossible ...

Lord Hardwicke, long ago in 1752 – *Fishmongers' Co v East India Co* (1752) 1 Dick 163 – dealing with this very question, the alleged obstruction to light, laid down what I believe to be law to-day. 'It is not sufficient,' he said, 'to say that it will alter the plaintiff's lights, for then no vacant piece of ground could be built on in the city, and here there will be 17 feet distance, and the law says it must be so near as to be a nuisance.'

... I am prepared to hold that the test given by Lord Hardwicke is the true one, and I do not think a better example could be found than the present case to shew to what extravagant results the other theory leads. The owner of a tenement on one side of a

139 *Allen v Greenwood* [1980] Ch 119 at 133C–D, 136G–H, 131B, 135A–B.

140 *Newham v Lawson* (1971) 22 P & CR 852 at 859.

141 [1904] AC 179, HL.

street 40 feet wide seeks to restrain his opposite neighbour from erecting a room which, when erected, will not then be of the same height as the house belonging to the complaining neighbour, and the only plausible ground on which the complaint rests is that on the ground floor he has a room not built in the ordinary way of rooms in an ordinary dwelling house, but built so that one long room goes through the whole width of the house to a back wall, a room which has no window at the back or sides, and which was, therefore, at the back of it, too dark for some purposes without the use of artificial light and even before the building on the other side of the street was erected.

I think that no tribunal ought to find as a fact that the building is a nuisance, and, altogether apart from the inappropriateness of the remedy by injunction, I am of opinion that the plaintiffs have no cause of action against the defendant.

Lord Davey: It has been thought that the 3rd section of the Prescription Act (2 & 3 Will 4, c 71) altered substantially the previously existing law as to ancient lights, and had the effect of conferring on the owner of the dominant tenement, by 20 years' enjoyment, an absolute and indefeasible right to the full amount of the light enjoyed during that period. And it must be admitted that the language of the section lends some plausibility to that opinion. It is, however, not consistent with the language of Lord Cranworth in *Clarke v Clark*, [1865] LR 1 Ch 16 and the point was expressly determined by James and Mellish LJJ in *Kelk v Pearson*, decided by them in the year 1871.

James LJ there says: 'I am of opinion that the statute has in no degree whatever altered the pre-existing law as to the nature and extent of this right. The nature and extent of the right before that statute was to have that amount of light through the windows of a house which was sufficient according to the ordinary notions of mankind, for the comfortable use and enjoyment of that house as a dwelling house, or for the beneficial use and occupation of the house if it were a warehouse, shop, or other place of business. That was the extent of the easement, a right to prevent your neighbour from building on his land so as to obstruct the access of sufficient light and air to such an extent as to render the house substantially less comfortable and convenient.' The statute, in fact, has only altered the conditions or length of user by which the right may be acquired, but not the nature of the right.

[His Lordship considered the arguments and authorities in great length and concluded.]

According to both principle and authority, I am of opinion that the owner or occupier of the dominant tenement is entitled to the uninterrupted access through his ancient windows of a quantity of light, the measure of which is what is required for the ordinary purposes of inhabitancy or business of the tenement according to the ordinary notions of mankind, and that the question for what purpose he has thought fit to use that light, or the mode in which he finds it convenient to arrange the internal structure of his tenement, does not affect the question. The actual user will neither increase nor diminish the right. The single question in these cases is still what it was in the days of Lord Hardwicke and Lord Eldon – whether the obstruction complained of is a nuisance.

In *Allen v Greenwood*,[142] a greenhouse had been in use for over 20 years by the plaintiffs. The defendants erected a fence on their adjoining property which left light sufficient for working in the greenhouse but insufficient for growing

142 [1980] Ch 119. See [1979] Conv 298 (Crane, FR); [1984] Conv 408 (Hudson, AH).

plants. An injunction was granted by the Court of Appeal against the defendants to restrain them from diminishing the quantity of light to the greenhouse.

Allen v Greenwood [1980] 1 Ch 119, CA

Goff LJ: The defendants argue on this as follows. (1) In *Colls' Case* [1904] AC 179 the House of Lords was seeking to limit, or restrict, the extent of the right to light, so as to prevent undue restrictions on the development or improvement of surrounding land or buildings, and the court should be very chary of any extension of the right. (2) Although the standards prescribed by the speeches in *Colls'* case are expressed in terms susceptible of a wider interpretation, in their context they must be taken as referring to illumination only. (3) In all cases, at least since *Colls*, the right to light has been tested or measured in terms of illumination only. They refer, for example, to Mr Waldram's calculations and the theory of the 'grumble point': see *Charles Semon & Co Ltd v Bradford Corporation* [1922] 2 Ch 737, 746–47, and to *Hortons' Estate Ltd v James Beattie Ltd* [1927] 1 Ch 75, where the question was whether the extent of the right to light should vary according to locality, and Russell J said, at p 78: 'The human eye requires as much light for comfortable reading and sewing in Darlington Street, Wolverhampton, as in Mayfair.' Mr Maddocks on the defendant's behalf, in his supporting argument, referred also to *Warren v Brown* [1900] 2 QB 722, 725, where the test was stated to be 'all ordinary purposes of inhabitancy or business', and to the test applied by the Court of Appeal in *Ough v King* [1967] 1 WLR 1547, ordinary notions of contemporary mankind. These, however, I think, are at best neutral and possibly tell the other way, since a greenhouse is perfectly normal and ordinary in private gardens. So far as the last case is concerned, however, Mr Maddocks relied upon the fact that this court approved of the county court judge having had a view, which again, he suggests, points to illumination as the test, though that I take leave to doubt.

(4) In no case since *Colls* [1904] AC 179 has the right to light been established, save on the basis of what is required for illumination. That is true, but in *Lazarus v Artistic Photographic Co* [1897] 2 Ch 214 Kekewich J expressly extended the right to light for photography, which is not simply illumination but extra light required to effect a chemical process. That case was wrongly decided, because he held that such a right could be acquired though the special light required for the purpose had been enjoyed for part only of the 20 years, but nevertheless it has, I think, some value as a negation of the defendants' argument. Moreover, in *Colls'* case itself [1904] AC 179, 203, Lord Davey instanced a photographic studio. True, he was there saying that one could not increase the burden on the servient tenement by changing over to such user within the 20 years, but at least he clearly envisaged a claim to light for such a purpose as a possibility.

(5) A distinction must be drawn between the heat and other properties of the sun and the light which emanates from it, and, the defendants say, having regard to the judge's findings, the only complaint that the plaintiffs can have is loss of heat or radiant properties, and they postulate the example of a swimming pool, part of which is fortuitously warmed by sunlight coming through a south window. They say, and I have no doubt rightly, that the owners could have no cause of action against one who, whilst leaving fully adequate light for the complete enjoyment of the swimming pool, so shaded the sun as to deprive it of this chance warmth. That, I think, is a very different case from the present. (6) In reality or in substance the injury here is not deprivation of light, but of heat or other energising properties of the sun and it is the plant life and not the human beings who are deprived.

I do not think this last point is in any case wholly accurate, as plants need light as well as heat, but it seems to me, with all respect to Blackett-Ord VC and to counsel, to lead to an absurd conclusion. It cannot, I think, be right to say that there is no nuisance because one can see to go in and out of a greenhouse and to pot plants which will not flourish, and to pick fruit which cannot properly be developed and ripened, still less because one can see to read a book.

The plaintiffs answer all this simply by submitting that they are entitled, by virtue of their prescriptive right to light, to all the benefits of the light, including the rays of the sun. Warmth, they say, is an inseparable product of daylight, and they stress the absurd conclusion which I have already mentioned, to which the contrary argument inevitably leads. This reply commends itself to me, and I adopt it.

So the overriding argument, in my judgment, does not prevail, and for the reasons I have already given the plaintiffs are right, both on their primary and their alternative case, and I would allow this appeal.

Subject to any observations of my brethren or of my counsel, I would grant an injunction on the following lines: restraining the defendants by themselves, their servants, contractors, workmen or otherwise from continuing to keep the caravan and fence in such a position on the defendants' property as to obstruct or diminish the access of light to the southerly and south-easterly walls and glass roof of the said greenhouse to such an extent as to cause a nuisance. Secondly, a mandatory order that the defendants do forthwith remove the said caravan and fence from such a position as so to obstruct or diminish the access of light to the said southerly and south-easterly glass walls and glass roof of the said greenhouse.

I desire, however, to add one important safeguarding proviso to this judgment. On other facts, particularly where one has solar heating (although that may not arise for some years) it may be possible and right to separate the heat, or some other property of the sun, from its light, and in such a case a different result might be reached. I leave that entirely open for decision when it arises. My judgment in this case is based upon the fact that this was a perfectly ordinary greenhouse, being used in a perfectly normal and ordinary manner, which user has, by the defendants' acts, been rendered substantially less beneficial than it was throughout the period of upwards of 20 years before action brought, and if necessary upon the fact that all this was known to the defendants and their predecessors for the whole of the relevant time.

A right of light is not deprived by the change in the use of the building to which the light comes through the window. In *Carr-Saunders v Dick McNeil Associates Ltd*,[143] the dominant owner had, during the prescription period, subdivided one large room into a number of smaller rooms, although the windows had remained unchanged. The dominant owner was entitled to damages for the obstruction to reasonable access to light to the reconstructed rooms.

Carr-Saunders v Dick McNeil Associates [1986] 1 WLR 922

Millett J: In my judgment, it is necessary to bear three principles in mind. First, s 3 of the Prescription Act 1832 provides:

> ... when the access and use of light to and for any dwelling house, workshop, or other building shall have been actually enjoyed therewith for the full period of 20

143 [1986] 1 WLR 922.

> years without interruption, the right thereto shall be deemed absolute and indefeasible ...

Accordingly, as Maugham J pointed out in *Price v Hilditch* [1930] 1 Ch 500, 508, the right acquired under s 3 of the Act of 1832 is an easement for the access of light to a building, not to a particular room within it; so that the extent of the right is not necessarily to be measured by the internal arrangements of the building.

Secondly, interference with the right constitutes the tort of nuisance. The question in every case, therefore, is whether there has been such a substantial interference with the use and enjoyment of his property by the dominant owner that it constitutes an actionable nuisance. This is, of course, qualified by the rule, now well established, that no actionable wrong is committed if the amount of light remaining is sufficient for the comfortable enjoyment of his property by the dominant owner according to the ordinary notions of mankind. Accordingly, the inquiry is directed not to the amount of light taken, but to the amount of light left. The wrong, however, consists in the disturbance of the dominant owner in the comfortable enjoyment, not of a particular room, but of his property.

Thirdly, the dominant owner's right of light is not measured by the particular use to which the dominant tenement has been put in the past: see *Price v Hilditch* [1930] 1 Ch 500. The extent of the dominant owner's right is neither increased nor diminished by the actual use to which the dominant owner has chosen to put his premises or any of the rooms in them: for he is entitled to such access light as will leave his premises adequately lit for all ordinary purposes for which they may reasonably be expected to be used. The court must, therefore, take account not only of the present use, but also of other potential uses to which the dominant owner may reasonably be expected to put the premises in the future: see *Moore v Hall* (1878) 3 QBD 178, where Cockburn CJ said, at p 182:

> The matter, in my opinion, to be considered is, whether there is any diminution of light for any purpose for which the dominant tenement may be reasonably considered available.

In my judgment, an alteration in the internal arrangement of the premises comes within the same principle. In *Colls v Home and Colonial Stores Ltd* [1904] AC 179, Lord Davey said, at p 202:

> The easement is for access of light to the building, and if the building retains its substantial identity, or if the ancient lights retain their substantial identity, it does not seem to me to depend on the use which is made of the chambers in it, or to be varied by any alternation which may be made in the internal structure of it.

And later on the same page:

> But while agreeing that a person does not lose his easement by any change in the internal structure of his building or the use to which it is put, and that regard may be had, not only to the present use, but also to any ordinary uses to which the tenement is adapted, I think it is quite another question whether he is entitled to be protected at the expense of his neighbour in the enjoyment of the light for some special or extraordinary purpose.

And, at p 204:

> According to both principle and authority, I am of opinion that the owner or occupier of the dominant tenement is entitled to the uninterrupted access through his ancient windows of a quantity of light, the measure of which is what is required for the ordinary purposes of inhabitancy or business of the tenement

according to the ordinary notions of mankind, and that the question for what purpose he has thought fit to use that light, or the mode in which he finds it convenient to arrange the internal structure of his tenement, does not affect the question.

In *Ough v King* [1967] 1 WLR 1547, it was pointed out that higher standards of light may now be demanded for comfort and it may well be that in today's economic conditions smaller as well as lighter rooms are now accepted.

In my judgment, therefore, even before the subdivision of the second floor it would have been necessary for the court to consider the effect of the defendants' building works, not only in the second floor as it was then used (that is to say, as a single open space) but on any other arrangement of that space which might reasonably be expected to be adopted in the future.

As essential question in the present case, therefore, is whether some subdivision (not necessarily the present subdivision) of the second floor is an ordinary and reasonable use to which that space may be put. I am satisfied that it is.

Mr Young took the view that any ordinary occupier would want to subdivide the second floor as it has been subdivided: first, because the present planning use is as medical consulting rooms; and secondly, because the area of Covent Garden in which the premises are situated tends to attract the smaller business occupier. Mr Anstey, by contrast, thought, the present use to be an extraordinary one: the subdivision, he thought, had resulted in tiny, poky rooms which no other user would want.

I do not propose to attempt to resolve that particular issue. Mr Anstey conceded that some subdivision of the second floor would be a natural and ordinary use of the space. He would not do it himself: but that, he conceded, was a matter of personal preference. He thought that an owner would be as likely to subdivide the space as not. Mr Anstey was specifically asked in cross-examination whether it was now possible to divide the area into two in such a way that both portions would be adequately lit, applying the 50–50 rule to each portion separately. This was, of course, easy before the defendants raised the height of 15, Short's Gardens; indeed, both the Red and Green rooms separately, as well as the whole of the rear portion comprising the corridor and the Red and Green rooms taken as a single whole, satisfied the 50–50 rule. Mr Anstey said that he was convinced that the division could be done, but that it would probably be necessary to reposition the staircase.

I am quite satisfied that it can no longer easily be done. There are only two natural ways in which the space can be divided into two. One is along the line of the corridor. This leaves the rear portion, adequately lit before the defendants' building works, now extremely dark and gloomy. The other is to divide the space by a line drawn at right angles to the corridor. Mr Young has calculated the result if the line is drawn in the most obvious place, at the point where the staircase ends, so that the total area is divided into two rectangles. His calculations show a substantial loss of daylight area in the larger of the two rectangles. He calculated that the proportion of the larger area enjoying at least one lumen of light at table level before the defendants' building works was 57% and after them is 43%, a reduction of 25%. Again, for the reasons I have already stated, these figures require a minor adjustment; but this does not affect the conclusion to be drawn from them.

In my judgment, therefore, the raising of the height of the defendants' premises has caused a substantial interference with the plaintiff's enjoyment of his property 2, Neal's Yard, since the space on the second floor can no longer comfortably be used for any purpose which requires the subdivision of that space. In my judgment, on the basis the plaintiff has established an actionable nuisance – not because the Red and Green rooms are no longer adequately lit (though they are not), but because the second floor can no longer (as it formerly could) conveniently be subdivided in such a way that the subdivided areas each receive an adequate amount of light.

3 ENFORCEABILITY OF EASEMENTS

An easement is a proprietary interest. Once created it annexes a burden to the servient land and an equivalent benefit to the dominant land. It is enforceable as between the original dominant and servient owners as a matter of contract. Where the dominant and servient lands have changed hands, it is enforceable between the new dominant and servient owners if *both* the benefit has passed to the new dominant owner *and* the burden to the new servient owner. The benefit of an easement, legal or equitable, passes with any subsequent *conveyance* by deed of the dominant land under s 62 of the Law of Property Act 1925. In practice, despite s 62, the seller often conveys the land expressly with any easement appertaining to the land to his successor.

Whether the successor of the servient owner is bound by the easement or not depends on whether the easement is legal or equitable and whether the servient land is registered or unregistered.

Registered land

The benefit of the easement may be entered on the 'property register' section of the dominant land but such an entry is not essential.[144] If the title of the servient land is registered, the burden of a legal easement should be registered by the dominant owner on the register of the servient owner's title in the 'charges register' section.[145] If it is so protected it binds the successors of the servient owner who are able to find out the burden from a full official search before the completion of sale.[146] If it is not registered, it only takes effect in equity.[147] It has to be protected as a minor interest by way of notice or caution. Certain equitable easements which are 'openly exercised and enjoyed' by the dominant owners at the date of the transfer of the servient land have also been regarded by Scott J in *Celsteel Ltd v Alton House Holdings Ltd*[148] as an overriding interest under s 70(1)(a) of the Land Registration Act 1925 in conjunction with r 258 of the Land Registration Rules.

144 LRR 1925, rr 3(2)(c), 252, 254, 257. The registration of a person as proprietor of land vests in him, together with the land, all rights, and appurtenances appertaining or reputed to appertain to the land ... including the appropriate rights and interests which would have passed under s 62 of the LPA 1925: r 25 of the LRR 1925.

145 LRR 1925, r 41.

146 Sections 20(1)(a), 23(1)(b) of the LRA 1925.

147 Sections 19(2), 22(2) of the LRA 1925; *Celsteel Ltd v Alton House Holdings Ltd* [1985] 1 WLR 204.

148 [1985] 1 WLR 204. See [1986] Conv 31 (Thompson, MP).

A newly created legal easement of an unregistered title is often set out on the register of title when the title is subsequently registered. If, for some reasons, it is not recorded on the register, it will be protected as an overriding interest under s 70(1)(a) of the Land Registration Act 1925.

Celsteel Ltd v Alton House Ltd [1985] 1 WLR 204

Scott J: Paragraph (a) of s 70(1) protects as overriding interests the following rights:

> Rights of common, drainage rights, customary rights (until extinguished), public rights, profits *à prendre*, rights of sheepwalk, rights of way, watercourses, rights of water, and other easements not being equitable easements required to be protected by notice on the register.

The rights over the rear driveway which the third plaintiff acquired by virtue of the facts pleaded in the paragraphs of the statement of claim which I have mentioned were certainly rights of way. If they were legal rights of way then the second defendants are bound by them. If they were only equitable rights of way then I must decide whether or not they are excepted from paragraph (a) by the phrase 'not being equitable easements required to be protected by notice on the register'.

The third plaintiff's entitlement to the easements comprised in the intended lease of garage 52 for the intended 120 year term is an *equitable* entitlement. It could only become a *legal* entitlement by the grant to him of the lease contracted to be granted and the registration of that lease at Her Majesty's Land Registry. But the meaning and scope of the provision 'equitable easements required to be protected by notice on the register' is somewhat obscure. In *E R Ives Investment Ltd v High* [1967] 2 QB 379 it was held by the Court of Appeal that easements acquired in equity by proprietary estoppel were not equitable easements for the purposes of s 10(1) Class D(iii) of the Land Charges Act 1925 (15 & 16 Geo 5, c 22). Lord Denning MR expressed the view that "equitable easements" referred simply to that limited class of rights which before the 1925 property legislation were capable of being conveyed or created at law but thereafter were capable of existing only in equity: see p 395. In *Poster v Slough Estates Ltd* [1969] 1 Ch 495 Cross J declined, at pp 506–07, to disagree with Lord Denning MR's view of the meaning of the expression and held that a right to re-enter premises after termination of a lease and to remove fixtures therefrom was not an 'equitable easement' for the purposes of the Land Charges Act 1925. These authorities might be thought to suggest by analogy that equitable easements in s 70(1)(a) should be given a similarly limited meaning. I am, however, reluctant to do that because in general the clear intention of the Land Registration Act 1925 is that equitable interests should be protected either by entry on the register or as overriding interests and, if equitable easements in general are not within the exception in paragraph (a), it would follow that they would rank as overriding interests and be binding upon registered proprietors of servient land even though such proprietors did not have and could not by any reasonable means have obtained any knowledge of them. That result could not possibly be supported. In my view, therefore, the *dicta* in the two cases are not applicable to the construction of 'equitable easements' in para (a) of s 70(1).

Mr Purle submitted that the exception expressed in s 70(1)(a) applied only to those equitable easements in respect of which a positive requirement that they be protected by notice on the register could be found in the Act. He submitted further that the Act contained no such requirement and that accordingly the expression covered nothing. It seems, however, from paragraph (c) of the proviso to s 19(2) of the Act that the draftsman assumed that easements would require to be protected either by registration as appurtenant to registered land or by entry of notice against the registered title of the servient land. I do not, therefore, feel able to accept these submissions.

In my opinion, the words 'required to be protected' in paragraph (a) should be read in the sense 'need to be protected.' The exception in the paragraph was, in my view, intended to cover all equitable easements other than such as by reason of some other statutory provision or applicable principle of law, could obtain protection otherwise than by notice on the register. The most obvious example would be equitable easements which qualified for protection under paragraph (g) as part of the rights of a person in actual occupation. In my view I must examine the easement claimed by the third plaintiff and consider whether there is any statutory provision or principle of law which entitles it to protection otherwise than by entry of notice on the register.

The matter stands in my opinion thus. At the time when Mobil acquired its registered leasehold title the third plaintiff's right to an easement of way for the benefit of garage 52 over a part of the property enjoyed under the leasehold title was an equitable and not a legal right. It was, in ordinary conveyancing language, an equitable easement. It was not protected by any entry on the register. On the other hand, it was at the relevant time openly exercised and enjoyed by the third plaintiff an appurtenant to garage 52. Section 144 of the Land Registration Act 1925 contains power for rules to be made for a number of specified purposes. The Land Registration Rules 1925 (SR & O 1925 No 1093) were accordingly made and r 258 provides:

> Rights, privileges, and appurtenances appertaining or reputed to appertain to land or demised, occupied, or enjoyed therewith or reputed or known as part or parcel of or appurtenant thereto, which adversely affect registered land, are overriding interests within s 70 of the Act, and shall not be deemed incumbrances for the purposes of the Act.

The third plaintiff's equitable right of way over the rear driveway was, in my view, at the time when Mobil acquired its registered leasehold title, a right enjoyed with land for the purposes of this rule. It was plainly a right which adversely affected registered land including the part of the rear driveway comprised in Mobil's lease. Rule 258 categorises such a right as an overriding interest. s 144(2) of the Act provides that 'Any rules made in pursuance of this section shall be of the same force as if enacted in this Act.' Accordingly, in my judgment, the third plaintiff's right ranks as an overriding interest, does not need to be protected by entry of notice on the register and is binding on Mobil.

Mr Davidson submitted that there was no power under s 144(1) for rules to add to the overriding interests specified in the various paragraphs of s 70(1). He submitted that r 258 was *ultra vires* and of no effect. I do not agree. Sub-paragraph (xxxi) of s 144(1) enables rules to be made:

> ... for regulating any matter to be prescribed or in respect of which rules are to or may be made under this Act and any other matter or thing, whether similar or not to those above mentioned, in respect of which it may be expedient to makes rules for the purpose of carrying this Act into execution.

This is a power in very wide terms. In my view, it is in terms wide enough to justify r 258 and I see no reason why it should be given a limited effect.

Accordingly, for these reasons, the third plaintiff's equitable right of way over the rear driveway enjoyed with garage 52 was and is, in my judgment, binding on Mobil.

Unregistered land

If the servient land is unregistered, the burden of a legal easement binds the whole world. If the easement is equitable and is created on or after 1 January 1926 then it is registrable as a Class D(iii) land charge.[149]

There are, however, certain equitable easements which are not registrable as land charges. In *E R Ives Investment Ltd v High*,[150] a certain Westgate, neighbour of the defendant, Mr High, erected a block of flats on his own land but their foundations encroached on Mr High's land by about a foot. They agreed that the foundations could remain but that Mr High should have a right of way for his car across Westgate's yard. This agreement was, however, never registered. The block of flats were later sold to the plaintiffs expressly subject to Mr High's right of way. The plaintiffs sued Mr High for trespass to the yard on the ground that he had no legal right of way and if it was an equitable easement it was void against them for want of registration. Lord Denning said that Mr High was entitled to a right of way in two ways.[151] (i) under the doctrine of mutual benefit and burden, and (ii) equity arising out of acquiescence. He then went on to consider if the plaintiffs were bound by Mr High's right and concluded that Class D(iii) only covered those equitable easements which prior to 1926 ranked as legal interest but by virtue of the Act became equitable. So an easement by estoppel or acquiescence is not registrable under Class D(iii) because it existed in equity even before 1926. Its enforcement depends on the doctrine of notice. It can be enforced against the successors of servient land if they have notice of its existence at the time of the transfer.

E R Ives Investment Ltd v High [1967] 2 QB 379, CA

Lord Denning MR: Now here is the point. The right of way was never registered as a land charge. The purchasers, the plaintiffs, say that it should have been registered under Class C(iv) as an estate contract, or under Class D(iii) as an equitable easement: and that, as it was not registered, it is void against them, the purchasers. Even though they had the most explicit notice of it, nevertheless they say that it is void against them. They claim to be entitled to prevent Mr High having any access to his garage across their yard: and thus render it useless to him. They have brought an action for an injunction to stop him crossing the yard at all.

One thing is quite clear. Apart from this point about the Land Charges Act, 1925, Mr High would have in equity a good right of way across the yard. This right arises in two ways:

1. *Mutual benefit and burden*

The right arises out of the agreement of 2 November 1949, and the subsequent action taken on it: on the principle that 'he who takes the benefit must accept the burden'. When adjoining owners of land make an agreement to secure continuing rights and benefits for each of them in or over the land of the other, neither of them can take the benefit of the agreement and throw over the burden of it. This applies not only to the

149 Section 2(5) of the LCA 1972.

150 [1967] 2 QB 379.

151 See [1967] 2 QB 379 at 394.

original parties, but also to their successors. The successor who takes the continuing benefit must take it subject to the continuing burden. This principle has been applied to neighbours who send their water into a common drainage system: see *Hopgood v Brown*;[152] and to purchasers of houses on a building estate who had the benefit of using the roads and were subject to the burden of contributing to the upkeep: see *Halsall v Brizell*.[153] The principle clearly applies in the present case. The owners of the block of flats have the benefit of having their foundations in Mr High's land. So long as they take that benefit, they must shoulder the burden. They must observe the condition on which the benefit was granted, namely, they must allow Mr High and his successors to have access over their yard: cf *May v Belleville*.[154] Conversely, so long as Mr High takes the benefit of the access, he must permit the block of flats to keep their foundations in his land.

2. *Equity arising out of acquiescence*

The right arises out of the expense incurred by Mr High in building his garage, as it is now, with access only over the yard: and the Wrights standing by and acquiescing in it, knowing that he believed he had a right of way over the yard. By so doing the Wrights created in Mr High's mind a reasonable expectation that his access over the yard would not be disturbed. That gives rise to an 'equity arising out of acquiescence.' It is available not only against the Wrights but also their successors in title. The court will not allow that expectation to be defeated when it would be inequitable so to do. It is for the court in each case to decide in what way the equity can be satisfied: see *Inwards v Baker*;[155] *Ward v Kirkland*[156] and the cases cited therein. In this case it could only be satisfied by allowing Mr High and his successors to have access over the yard so long as the block of flats has its foundations in his land.

The next question is this: was that right a land charge such as to need registration under the Land Charges Act, 1925? For if it was a land charge, it was never registered and would be void as against any purchaser: see s 13 of the Act. It would, therefore, be void against the plaintiffs, even though they took with the most express knowledge and notice of the right.

It was suggested that the agreement of 2 November 1949, was 'an estate contract' within Class C(iv). I do not think so. There was no contract by Mr Westgate to convey a legal estate of any kind.

It was suggested that the right was an 'equitable easement' within Class D(iii). This class is defined as 'any easement right or privilege over or affecting land created or arising after the commencement of this Act, and being merely an equitable interest'. Those words are almost identical with s 2(3)(iii) of the Law of Property Act 1925, and should be given the same meaning. They must be read in conjunction with ss 1(2)(a), 1(3) and 4(1) of the Law of Property Act 1925. It then appears that an "equitable easement" is a proprietary interest in land such as would before 1926 have been recognised as capable of being conveyed or created at law, but which since 1926 only takes effect as an

152 (1955) 1 WLR 213; [1955] 1 All ER 550 ,CA.

153 [1957] Ch 169; [1957] 2 WLR 123; [1957] 1 All ER 371.

154 [1905] 2 Ch 605.

155 [1965] 2 QB 29; [1965] 2 WLR 212; [1965] 1 All ER 446, CA.

156 [1966] 1 WLR 601; [1966] 1 All ER 609.

equitable interest. An instance of such a proprietary interest is a profit *à prendre* for life. It does not include a right to possession by a requisitioning authority: see *Lewisham Borough Council v Maloney*.[157] Nor does it include a right, liberty or privilege arising in equity by reason of 'mutual benefit and burden', or arising out of 'acquiescence', or by reason of a contractual licence: because none of those before 1926 were proprietary interests such as were capable of being conveyed or created at law. They only subsisted in equity. They do not need to be registered as land charges, so as to bind successors, but take effect in equity without registration: see an article by Mr CV Davidge on 'Equitable Easements' in (1937) 59 *Law Quarterly Review*, p 259 and by Professor HWR Wade in [1956] *Cambridge Law Journal*, pp 225–26.

The right of Mr High to cross this yard was not a right such as could ever have been created or conveyed at law. It subsisted only in equity. It therefore still subsists in equity without being registered. Any other view would enable the owners of the flats to perpetrate the grossest injustice. They could block up Mr High's access to the garage, whilst keeping their foundations in his land. This cannot be right.

I am confirmed in this construction of the statute when I remember that there are many houses adjoining one another which have drainage systems in common, with mutual benefits and burdens. The statute cannot have required all these to be registered as land charges.

I know that this greatly restricts the scope of Class D(iii) but this is not disturbing. A special committee has already suggested that Class D(iii) should be abolished altogether: see the report of the Committee on Land Charges (1956) Command Paper 9825, para 16.

If the equitable easement is created before 1 January 1926 then it is entirely governed by the doctrine of notice. Whether an easement is legal or equitable is, therefore, very important. It would be a legal easement if it is an interest equivalent to an estate in fee simple absolute in possession or a term of years absolute[158] and the easement must be created either by statute, by deed[159] or by prescription. If either of these two conditions are not satisfied the easement can only be equitable.

4 ACQUISITION OF EASEMENTS

Easements or profits may be acquired by statute, express grant or reservation, implied grant or reservation, and prescriptions. It some cases, an easement may arise by estoppel.[160]

157 [1948] 1 KB 50; 63 TLR 330; [1947] 2 All ER 36, CA.

158 Section 1(2)(a) of the LPA 1925.

159 Section 52 of the LPA 1925.

160 See Chapter 3. Examples are *Ward v Kirkland* [1967] Ch 194; *Crabb v Arun DC* [1976] Ch 179; *E R Ives Investment Ltd v High* [1967] 2 QB 379.

By statute

Modern examples of easement or profit created by statutes are those found in local Acts of Parliament. These are often given to public utility bodies which supply gas, electricity, water and sewerage.[161]

By express grant

Easements or profits are often granted expressly. An easement may be acquired by express words of grant which are normally incorporated in the conveyance of a legal estate to the owner of the dominant land. This is important and often done when the vendor is selling only part of his property. It is important to consider if any easement is to be granted to the buyer over the vendor's retained land and whether any easement is to be reserved to the vendor over the land being sold. Or it may be a separate grant without conveyance of a legal estate, as where a right of way is granted to the owner of a neighbouring land in return for a sum of money or maintenance of the passage.

In a grant, if the easement or profit is granted without words of limitation determining the duration of the easement or profit, it will confer on the grantee the most ample interest which the grantor is competent to confer unless a contrary intention appears.[162] This means that if the grantor has a fee simple the easement he granted will be an interest equivalent to a fee simple. This is so even if the easement is granted for the benefit of a leasehold estate.[163] But if the grantor only has a leasehold estate for 20 years he cannot grant an easement for more than what he has (ie 20 years). If the grantor does create an easement for more than 20 years there would be an easement by estoppel binding only on the grantor.

The grant of a legal easement or profit must be by deed.[164] If it is not created by deed, in the absence of statutory or prescriptive creation, the easement or profit will only be an equitable one if it is specifically enforceable, ie if it satisfies s 40 of the Law of Property Act 1925 or s 2 of the Law of Property (Miscellaneous Provisions) Act 1989.

By express reservation

Easements or profits may be reserved by a vendor. As mentioned above, when a vendor sells part of his land he may want to reserve an easement or profit over the land sold. Prior to 1926, such a reservation was commonly done by the

161 Windeyer J in the High Court of Australia said that 'The gas company has however no true easement; for there is no true dominant tenement unless it be said to be the gas works. However there is here an analogy to an easement as known to the common law; and if it be necessary to give some name to the right which the [company] enjoyed, it was what is nowadays very often called a "statutory easement".' Referring to Garner, JF (1956) 20 Conv (NS) 208 and *Gale on Easements*, 13th edn, 1959, London: Sweet & Maxwell, p 4(n): *Commissioner of Main Roads v North Shore Gas Co Ltd* (1967) 120 CLR 118 at 133.

162 See *Reid v Moreland Timber Co Pty Ltd* (1946) 73 CLR 1 at 13.

163 *Graham v Philcox* [1984] QB 747 at 761A–D.

164 See s 52 of the LPA 1925.

vendor reserving the right in the conveyance and requiring the purchaser to execute the conveyance. Such a conveyance then took effect as a conveyance of the land to the purchaser followed by a regrant of the easement or profit to the vendor.[165] After 1925, s 65(1) of the Law of Property Act 1925 allows a reservation to be done by the vendor's express words of reservation in the conveyance without any execution of the conveyance by the purchaser or any regrant by him. Express reservation is common today and is desirable as the courts are reluctant to imply a reservation.

Law of Property Act 1925

65. Reservation of legal estates

(1) A reservation of a legal estate shall operate at law without any execution of the conveyance by the grantee of the legal estate out of which the reservation is made, or any regrant by him, so as to create the legal estate reserved, and so as to vest the same in possession in the person (whether being the grantor or not) for whose benefit the reservation is made.

(2) A conveyance of a legal estate expressed to be made subject to another legal estate not in existence immediately before the date of the conveyance, shall operate as a reservation unless a contrary intention appears.

(3) This section applies only to reservations made after the commencement of this Act.

Where there is any ambiguity in the reservation, it has been held in *Johnstone v Holdway* that the reservation is construed in favour of the vendor (the dominant owner who reserves the easement or profit) against the purchaser.[166] This is because the general rule is that the grantor cannot derogate from his grant and so an express grant is construed strictly against the grantor in favour of the grantee.[167] In the case of an express reservation, as a result of the historical mode of reserving an easement by requiring the purchaser to execute the conveyance which took effect as a regrant, it is construed against the purchaser in favour of the vendor as if the easement had been granted by the purchaser.

In *Cordell v Second Clanfield Properties Ltd*[168] Megarry J took a different view and held that the document should be construed against the vendor (dominant owner). Here the plaintiff conveyed five parcels of land to the defendant company and retained a piece of land (the grey land) next to the land conveyed. The plaintiff reserved a right of way over roads constructed on the land conveyed. The defendant company constructed a road, called Clanfield Drive, on its land running roughly parallel with the nearest boundary of the grey land. The defendant company also erected some houses or bungalows between Clanfield Drive and the grey land leaving a plot of 57 or 58 feet in width undeveloped. Much later the defendant company built a bungalow on the previously undeveloped plot leaving a 12 foot access way to the plaintiff. The

165 *Durham & Sunderland Railway v Walker* (1842) 2 QB 940 at 967.

166 [1963] 1 QB 601. See (1963) 79 LQR 182 (REM).

167 *Bulstrode v Lambert* [1953] 1 WLR 1064 at 1067.

168 [1969] 2 Ch 9.

plaintiff brought this action for a declaration that he had a right of way of 28 feet wide over the plot to get to Clanfield Drive and an injunction ordering the defendant to pull down the part of the bungalow that interfered with his right of way. Megarry J refused the injunction. On the question of whether the defendant company is obliged to construct a road for the plaintiff or to permit the plaintiff to construct such a road for himself to connect the gray land to Clanfield Drive, Megarry J delivered the following judgment.

Cordell v Second Clanfield Properties Ltd [1969] 2 Ch 9

Megarry J: In this connection Mr Lyndon-Stanford raised an interesting question of law, to which Mr Evans for the defendant company replied in due course. It will be remembered that if on the conveyance of land it was desired to create anew in favour of the grantor some right such as an easement or profit which, unlike a rentcharge, did not issue out of the land granted, the reservation could formerly operate at law only if the grantee executed the instrument and so could be treated as the grantor of that right. The Conveyancing Act, 1881, s 62, in effect extended the Statute of Uses 1535, to such cases by providing that such reservations could instead be effected by a grant to uses, without execution by the grantee; by quoad the new right reserved the grantee was still treated as the grantor. The question is whether for the purposes of construing grants contra proferentem the purchaser should still be treated as the grantor of any easement reserved by the vendor, now that the law has been changed by the Law of Property Act 1925, s 65, in the manner to which I shall refer in a moment.

Mr Lyndon-Stanford contended that the reservation in the conveyance before me ought to be construed against the defendant company as being the purchaser, and thus the grantor of the easement reserved by the vendor. For his proposition that this was still the law, he cited *Bulstrode v Lambert* [1953] 1 WLR 1064, which concerned the reservation of an easement of way. There, Upjohn J said this, at p 1068:

> It is submitted by the defendant that the deed must be construed against the grantor, the plaintiff. I am not satisfied that this is correct. That rule, which applies to an exception from a conveyance, does not, I think, apply to a reservation which operates by way of regrant by the purchaser. The doctrine may well operate against the purchaser, but I need not say anything more about that.

It will be noticed how tentative that language is; and s 65 does not appear to have been mentioned.

Mr Lyndon-Stanford's contention may be further supported by a passage in *Mason v Clarke* [1954] 1 QB 460, a decision of the Court of Appeal which was reversed by the House of Lords [1955] AC 778 on a quite different point. In that case, in delivering the leading judgment, Denning LJ referred to words reserving sporting rights in a lease as operating not by way or reservation proper, but by way of regrant by the tenant, and then said [1954] 1 QB 460, 467:

> In former times there was a drawback in this view of the matter in that a reservation could not technically operate as a regrant unless the tenant executed the lease himself. This technical drawback was eliminated by s 65(1) of the Law of Property Act, 1925. So that a reservation now operates as a regrant without any execution by the tenant, but that section does not, I think, affect the substance of the obligations. In point of law the reservation still operates as a regrant by the tenant to the landlord and the rights of the parties must be ascertained on that footing.

Neither Romer LJ nor Somervell LJ mentioned the point.

It will be observed that in each of these cases it is said that a reservation 'operates by way of regrant,' or 'operates as a regrant.' The wording of s 65 (1) of the Law of Property Act 1925, is, however, that:

> A reservation of a legal estate shall operate at law without any execution of the conveyance by the grantee of the legal estate out of which the reservation is made, or any regrant by him, so as to create the legal estate reserved, and so as to vest the same in possession in the person (whether being the grantor or not) for whose benefit the reservation is made.

It thus appears that the reservation is made effective not only without any execution by the grantee but also 'without ... any regrant by him.' If what has disappeared is not merely the formality of execution by the grantee but also the whole basis of the doctrine whereby reservations of easements took effect as regrants, then it seems to me that the ancient law has suffered a statutory change. I find it somewhat difficult to reconcile the words of Denning LJ in relation to the subsection that 'a reservation now operates as a regrant' with the words of the subsection itself, that the 'reservation ... shall operate at law without ... any regrant'; these words, I observe, are not quoted in the judgment or in the report. If there is no regrant I do not see why a purchaser should be treated as the grantor of the easement in order that the grant may be construed against him as being the grantor.

It has long been the law that an exception, as distinct from a reservation, is to be construed against the vendor or grantor. A convenient authority is *Savill Brothers Ltd v Bethell* [1902] 2 Ch 523, where in delivering the judgment of the Court of Appeal Stirling LJ said, at p 537:

> It is a settled rule of construction that, where there is a grant and an exception out of it, the exception is to be taken as inserted for the benefit of the grantor, and is to be construed in favour of the grantee.

He then cited certain authorities. Now that the reservation of an easement, like an exception, no longer requires execution by the purchaser or grantee, and operates at law without any regrant, I do not see why the same rule should not apply to both, so that in any case of doubt each will be construed against the vendor or grantor and in favour of the purchaser or grantee. I see little merit in seeking to preserve in the twentieth century an ancient distinction based upon an outmoded technicality abolished over 40 years ago.

Accordingly, in my judgment I am entitled to differ from the views expressed in *Bulstrode v Lambert* [1953] 1 WLR 1064 and *Mason v Clarke* [1954] 1 QB 460. If in those cases the court had put a particular construction upon the words 'without ... any regrant by him' I should, of course, bow to authority. But as one judgment did not refer to the subsection and the other, although referring to it, made no mention of the particular words in question, I think that I must discharge my double duty of obedience to case law and to statute by giving effect to the statute. Accordingly, with great respect, I hold that in this case the reservation should be construed against the vendor, that is, against the plaintiff. So construed, it seems to me quite impossible to read it as imposing on the defendant company an obligation either to construct a road such as the plaintiff claims or to permit the plaintiff to do so. I may add that where a vendor wishes to retain for himself some right over the land that he has conveyed, a rule that requires him to ensure that the words inserted are ample enough to give him what he wants seems to me to be bottomed in practical common sense; and now the statute has put an end to the complications arising out of regrants of easements, I can see no intelligible ground for continuing to distinguish between exceptions and reservations in this respect. I do not think that the practice of conveyancing will suffer unduly if, after all these years, the Law of Property Act 1925, is held to have brought exceptions and reservations into line with each other in this way.

The rule in *Johnstone v Holdway* that a reservation should be construed against the purchaser was again doubted by Megarry J in *St Edmundsbury and Ipswich Diocesan Board of Finance v Clark (No 2)*.[169] When the case went on appeal, the Court of Appeal took a full review of the existing authorities and confirmed Megarry J's decision on a different ground but disagreed with him on the question of the construction of a conveyance containing a reservation.[170] It disapproved of *Cordell v Second Clanfield Properties Ltd* and followed *Johnstone v Holdway*.[171]

St Edmundsbury and Ipswich Diocesan Board of Finance v Clark (No 2) [1975] 1 WLR 468, CA

Sir John Pennycuick: Before reading Megarry J's conclusion, we will deal shortly with two matters of law which figured largely in his judgment and were fully argued before us. First, what is the proper approach upon the construction of a conveyance containing the reservation of a right of way? We feel no doubt that the proper approach is that upon which the court construes all documents; that is to say, one must construe the document according to the natural meaning of the words contained in the document as a whole, read in the light of surrounding circumstances ...

Second, is the maxim *'omnia praesumuntur contra proferentem'* applicable against the vendor or against the purchaser where there is a conveyance subject to the reservation of a new right of way? In view of the full discussion of this question by Megarry J, and of the fact that we do not agree with his conclusion, we think it right to deal fairly fully with it. But it is necessary to make clear that this presumption can only come into play if the court finds itself unable on the material before it to reach a sure conclusion on the construction of a reservation. The presumption is not itself a factor to be taken into account in reaching the conclusion. In the present case we have indeed reached a sure conclusion, and on this footing the presumption never comes into play, so that the view which we are about to express upon it is not necessary to the decision of the present case.

The point turns upon the true construction of s 65(1) of the Law of Property Act 1925, which enacts as follows:

> A reservation of a legal estate shall operate at law without any execution of the conveyance by the grantee of the legal estate out of which the reservation is made, or any regrant by him, so as to create the legal estate reserved, and so as to vest the same in possession in the person (whether being the grantor or not) for whose benefit the reservation is made.

Formerly the law was that on a conveyance with words merely reserving an easement, the easement was held to be created, provided that the purchaser executed the conveyance, without the necessity for words of regrant. The law treated the language of

169 [1973] 1 WLR 1572, Ch D.

170 [1975] 1 WLR 468.

171 [1963] 1 QB 601, CA.

reservation as having the same effect as would the language of regrant though there was not in terms a regrant, and in those circumstances regarded the purchaser as the *proferens* for present purposes. This was a relaxation of the strict requirements for the creation of an easement. (An easement could be created without execution by the purchaser of a conveyance by reference to the Statute of Uses, once s 62 of the Conveyancing Act 1881 removed the technical objection that that statute could not operate to create an easement. This method disappeared with the repeal of the Statute of Uses in the 1925 property legislation, and is not of direct relevance to the present problem: though it is part of the background to the abolition by s 65 of the Law of Property Act 1925 of the need for execution of the conveyance by the purchaser.)

Section 65 must be read in the light, therefore, of two aspects of the preceding law. First: that previously the law was sufficiently relaxed from its *prima facie* stringency to permit the language of mere reservation to have the effect of a regrant though it was not in truth a regrant by its language. Second: that for this purpose the purchaser must execute the conveyance if an easement was to be created; that is to say, although a regrant in terms was not required. Against that background, are the words in s 65 'without ... any regrant by' the purchaser to be regarded as altering the law so that the purchaser is no longer to be regarded as the relevant proferens? Or are they to be regarded as merely maintaining for the avoidance of doubt the situation that had been already reached by the development of the law, *viz* that mere words of reservation could be regarded as having the same effect as would the language of regrant though without there being in terms any purported regrant by the purchaser? We would, apart from authority, construe the words in the latter sense, so that the only relevant change in the law is the absence of the requirement that the purchaser should execute the conveyance. We read the section as if it were in effect saying that whereas an easement could be created by mere words of reservation without any words of regrant by the purchaser, provided that the purchaser executes the conveyance, hereafter the easement can be created by mere words of reservation without any words of regrant by the purchaser even if he does not execute the conveyance: it is not to be said that in the latter event the previous relaxation of the strict law has disappeared, so that the language of the conveyance must be more than the mere language of reservation. It will be observed that that view keeps in line, on the relevant point, a post-1925 conveyance executed by the purchaser, which is apparently not touched by s 65, and one which is executed by him.

The above is our view apart from authority. What then of authority? We start with the fact that Sir Benjamin Cherry, architect of the 1925 property legislation, made no reference to this suggested change of principle in the law in the first edition of Wolstenholme and Cherry's *Conveyancing Statutes* after the 1925 property legislation. Further, in more than one case since 1925, judges of high authority took it for granted that the old principle still prevails: see *Bulstrode v Lambert* [1953] 1 WLR 1064 *per* Upjohn J at p 1068; *Mason v Clarke* [1954] 1 QB 460, in the Court of Appeal, *per* Denning LJ at p 467 and in the House of Lords *per* Lord Simonds [1955] AC 778, 786. In these cases the contrary was not argued and the judicial statements are not of binding authority. But in *Johnstone v Holdway* [1963] 1 QB 601, in the Court of Appeal, Upjohn J, giving the judgment of the court, not only in terms re-stated the old principle but made it part of the *ratio decidendi* of his judgment. He said, at p 612:

> ... that the exception and reservation of the mines and minerals was to the vendor, that is the legal owner, but the exception and reservation of the right of way was to the company, the equitable owner. If the reservation of a right of way

> operated strictly as a reservation, then, as the company only had an equitable title, it would seem that only an equitable easement could have been reserved. But it is clear that an exception and reservation of a right of way in fact operates by way of regrant by the purchaser to his vendor and the question, therefore, is whether as a matter of construction the purchaser granted to the company a legal easement or an equitable easement.

The opposing view was expressed by Megarry J in *Cordell v Second Clanfield Properties Ltd* [1969] 2 Ch 9 (upon motion and without being referred to *Johnstone v Holdway* [1963] 1 QB 601) and in the present case (after a full review of the authorities, including *Johnstone v Holdway*). He distinguishes *Johnstone v Holdway* as a decision based on mistake and states his own conclusion in the following words, [1973] 1 WLR 1572 at 1591:

> The fair and natural meaning of s 65(1) seems to me to be that if a vendor reserves an easement, the reservation is to be effective at law without any actual or notional regrant by the purchaser, and so without the consequences that flow from any regrant. At common law, the rule that a reservation of an easement was to be construed against the purchaser depended solely upon the notional regrant. Apart from that, the words of reservation, being the words of the vendor, would be construed against the vendor in accordance with the general principle stated in Norton on *Deeds*, 2nd edn, 1928, just as an exception or a reservation of a rent would; it was the fiction of a regrant which made reservations of easements stand out of line with exceptions and reservations in the strict sense. With the statutory abolition of the fictitious regrant, reservations of easements fall into line with the broad and sensible approach that it is for him who wishes to retain something for himself to see that there is an adequate statement of what it is that he seeks to retain; and if after considering all the circumstances of the case there remains any real doubt as to the ambit of the right reserved, then that doubt should be resolved against the vendor. Accordingly, in this case I hold that the words 'subject also to a right of way over the land coloured red on the said plan to and from St Botolphs Church' in the 1945 conveyance should, if their meaning is not otherwise resolved, be construed against the church authorities and so in favour of Mr Clark.

We see much force in this reasoning. But we find it impossible to accept Megarry J's analysis of the decision in *Johnstone v Holdway*. We are not prepared to infer from the report that experienced and responsible counsel misrepresented the terms of s 65 to the court and that the judge based his decision on the terms of the section as so misrepresented. It follows that the decision in *Johnstone v Holdway* is binding upon this court and that we ought to follow it.

An express reservation can also be made in favour of a current or future owner or occupier of a specific dominant land. This is done by subjecting the legal estate to an easement in favour of the owner of a specific dominant land.[172] The owner of that specific dominant land can enforce the easement even though he is not actually referred to by name in the vendor's conveyance.[173]

172 Section 65(2) of the LPA 1925.

173 Section 56 of the LPA 1925; *Wiles v Banks* (1985) 50 P & CR 80.

Effect of s 62 of the Law of Property Act 1925

Law of Property Act 1925

62. General words implied in conveyances

(1) A conveyance of land shall be deemed to include and shall by virtue of this Act operate to convey, with the land, all buildings, erections, fixtures, commons, hedges, ditches, fences, ways, waters, watercourses, liberties, privileges, easements, rights, and advantages whatsoever, appertaining or reputed to appertain to the land, or any part thereof, or, at the time of conveyance, demised, occupied, or enjoyed with, or reputed or known as part or parcel of or appurtenant to the land or any part thereof.

(2) A conveyance of land, having houses or other buildings thereon, shall be deemed to include and shall by virtue of this Act operate to convey, with the land, houses, or other buildings, all outhouses, erections, fixtures, cellars, areas, courts, courtyards, cisterns, sewers, gutters, drains, ways, passages, lights, watercourses, liberties, privileges, easements, rights, and advantages whatsoever, appertaining or reputed to appertain to the land, houses, or other buildings conveyed, or any of them, or any part thereof, or, at the time of conveyance, demised, occupied, or enjoyed with, or reputed or known as part or parcel of or appurtenant to, the land, houses, or other buildings conveyed, or any of them, or any part thereof.

(4) This section applies only if and as far as a contrary intention is not expressed in the conveyance, and has effect subject to the terms of the conveyance and to the provisions therein contained.

(6) This section applies to conveyances made after the thirty-first day of December, eighteen hundred and eighty-one.

Once an easement, legal or equitable, is properly created, it passes to the successors of the dominant owners without the need to repeat the grant in the conveyance. This is the effect of s 62. It provides that a conveyance of land shall operate to convey with the land all liberties, privileges, easements, rights and advantages whatsoever, appertaining to the land, or at the time of the conveyance occupied or enjoyed with the land or any part thereof unless a contrary intention appears.

Section 62 was intended to be a word saving provision so that a grantee of a legal estate automatically acquires the benefit of an easement and right appurtenant to the land without having to insert numerous descriptive terms or general words about the easement in the conveyance.

However, the provision is so sweeping that it goes further and can create entirely new easements out of many quasi-easements, rights and privileges which have so far been enjoyed in respect of the land at the time of the conveyance. Rights which were not easements properly so called before the conveyance may be transferred into easements thereafter.[174] In *International Tea Stores Co v Hobbs*,[175] a landlord, the defendant, owned two plots of adjacent

174 *International Tea Stores v Hobbs* [1903] 2 Ch 165.

175 [1903] 2 Ch 165.

land in fee simple. He occupied one of them and leased the other to a tenant, the plaintiff company. The tenant was allowed, by permission which could be revoked at any time, to use a way across the land occupied by the landlord. Later, the landlord sold to the tenant the house leased to it and conveyed it by a deed which contained no reference to any right of way. It was held that the precarious right of way which the plaintiff enjoyed at the date of the deed passed to it by virtue of s 6(2) of the Conveyancing Act 1881 (the predecessor of s 62 of the Law of Property Act 1925).

International Tea Stores Co v Hobbs [1903] 2 Ch 165

Farwell J: (after stating the description of the land in the conveyance). Now, having got this conveyance of land with this description of boundaries, the Conveyancing Act, in the absence of any contrary intention expressed in the deed, provides that the conveyance shall be deemed to include, and shall by virtue of this Act operate to convey with the land (amongst other things), all ways, privileges, easements, rights, and advantages whatsoever appertaining or reputed to appertain to the land or any part thereof, or at the time of the conveyance demised, occupied, or enjoyed with or reputed or known as part or parcel of or appurtenant to the land or any part thereof. I am, therefore, thrown back on the inquiry whether it is or is not the fact that at the date of the conveyance the way in question was a way used and enjoyed with the property conveyed. If it was so in fact used and enjoyed, then it passed to the plaintiffs by the very words of the grant.

[Having stated the facts:]

Down to this point, therefore, I find that there was a way used in fact, and used for several years, by the plaintiffs before and at the date of the conveyance. But then Lord Coleridge (Counsel for the defendant) says that such use was wholly permissive. Cases such as the present necessarily arise where the defendant is the owner of the property which he has conveyed to the plaintiff in the action, and is also the owner of other property adjoining which he does not convey, over which the right in question is claimed. If the plaintiff has himself been owner in occupation of both properties, the point taken by Lord Coleridge cannot arise, but the question is one of the mere fact, was there a roadway which was in fact used for the convenience of the particular tenement? But in the case before me there is unity of title but not unity of possession, because the plaintiffs themselves were in possession as tenants of the adjoining tenement. The use of the road by them was not of right, because the lease did not give it to them. They must, therefore, have used the road either by licence or without licence. Unless I am prepared to say that in no case can a tenant obtain under the Conveyancing Act 1881, a right of way unless he has enjoyed it as of right, I must hold in this case that the fact of licence makes no difference. In all these cases the right of way must be either licensed or unlicensed. If it is unlicensed it would be at least as cogent an argument to say, 'True you went there, but it was precarious, because I could have sent a man to stop you or stopped you myself any day.' If it is by licence, it is precarious of course in the sense that the licence, being *ex hypothesi* revocable, might be revoked at any time; but if there be degrees of precariousness, the latter is less precarious than the former. But, in my opinion, precariousness has nothing to do with this sort of case, where a privilege which is by its nature known to the law – namely, a right of way – has been in fact enjoyed. Lord Coleridge's argument was founded upon a misconception of a judgment of mine in

Burrows v Lang,[176] where I was using the argument of precariousness to shew that the right which was desired to be enjoyed there was one which was unknown to the law – namely, to take water if and whenever the defendant chose to put water into a particular pond; such a right does not exist at law; but a right of way is well known to the law. The instance suggested by Lord Coleridge in his argument illustrates my meaning: he put the case of a man living in a house at his landlord's park gate, and having leave to use and using the drive as a means of access to church or town, and to use and using the gardens and park for his enjoyment, and asked, Would such a man on buying the house with the rights given by s 6 of the Conveyancing Act acquire a right of way over the drive, and a right to use the gardens and park? My answer is 'Yes' to the first, and 'No' to the second question, because the first is a right the existence of which is known to the law, and the latter, being a mere *jus spatiandi*, is not so known. The real truth is that you do not consider the question of title to use, but the question of fact of user; you have to inquire whether the way has in fact been used, not under what title has it been used, although you must of course take into consideration all the circumstances of the case, as appears from *Birmingham, Dudley & District Banking Co v Ross*[177] and *Godwin v Schweppes, Limited*.[178]

Further, with regard to this question of the materiality of the licence, I have the decision in *Kay v Oxley*[179] that the licence is immaterial. Blackburn J says:[180] 'I do not think it necessary to consider whether or not that parol licence, which was given by the defendant, to use the road, was revocable; or whether an action might not have been maintained for obstructing the tenant in doing that which he had a parol licence to do; or whether an action of trespass could have been brought against the tenant for using that road. I do not think it material to decide that. The licence was not in fact revoked.' He therefore, as I understand him, treats the only relevant question as being: Was the way in fact enjoyed at the date of the conveyance? If so, the fact that it was enjoyed under a licence which had not been revoked was immaterial. If it had been enjoyed without any licence at all for a number of years, although no prescriptive right had been or could have been acquired, still it was in fact enjoyed. It is in each case a question of fact to be determined on the circumstances of the case whether it has, or has not, been enjoyed within the meaning of the statute ...

In *Wright v Macadam*[181] a permission given by a landlord to his tenant to store coal in a garden shed became a legal easement of storage when the lease was renewed subsequently.

Wright v Macadam [1949] 2 KB 744, CA

Jenkins LJ: The question in the present case, therefore, is whether the right to use the coal shed was at the date of the letting of August 28, 1943, a liberty, privilege, easement, right or advantage appertaining or reputed to appertain, to the land, or any part thereof, or, at the time of the conveyance, demised, occupied or enjoyed with the land – that is

176 [1901] 2 Ch 502.

177 (1888) 38 Ch D 295.

178 [1902] 1 Ch 926 at 933.

179 LR 10 QB 360.

180 LR 10 QB 360 at 368.

181 [1949] 2 KB 744.

the flat – or any part thereof. It is enough for the plaintiffs' purposes if they can bring the right claimed within the widest part of the subsection – that is to say, if they can show that the right was at the time of the material letting demised, occupied or enjoyed with the flat or any part thereof.

The predecessor of s 62 of the Act of 1925, in the shape of s 6 of the Act of 1881 has been the subject of a good deal of judicial discussion, and I think the effect of the cases can be thus summarised. First, the section is not confined to rights which, as a matter of law, were so annexed or appurtenant to the property conveyed at the time of the conveyance as to make them actual legally enforceable rights. Thus, on the severance of a piece of land in common ownership, the quasi easements *de facto* enjoyed in respect of it by one part of the land over another will pass although, of course, as a matter of law, no man can have a right appendant or appurtenant to one part of his property exerciseable by him over the other part of his property. Secondly, the right, in order to pass, need not be one to which the owner or occupier for the time being of the land has had what may be described as a permanent title. A right enjoyed merely by permission is enough. The leading authority for that proposition is the case of *International Tea Stores Co v Hobbs*.[182]

[His Lordship said that that case had been followed or cited with approval in subsequent cases, in particular in *Lewis v Meredith*,[183] and *White v Williams* [1922] 1 KB 727 at 740.]

There is, therefore, ample authority for the proposition that a right in fact enjoyed with property will pass on a conveyance of the property by virtue of the grant to be read into it under s 62, even although down to the date of the conveyance the right was exercised by permission only, and therefore was in that sense precarious ...

For the purposes of s 62, it is only necessary that the right should be one capable of being granted at law, or, in other words, a right known to the law. If it is a right of that description it matters not, as the *International Tea Stores* case[184] shows, that it has been in fact enjoyed by permission only. The reason for that is clear, for, on the assumption that the right is included or imported into the parcels of the conveyance by virtue of s 62, the grant under the conveyance supplies what one may call the defect in title, and substitutes a new title based on the grant ...

I think those are all the cases to which I can usefully refer, and applying the principles deducible from them to the present case one finds, I think, this. First of all, on the evidence the coal shed was used by Mrs Wright by the permission of Mr Macadam, but *International Tea Stores Co v Hobbs* shows that that does not prevent s 62 from applying, because permissive as the right may have been it was in fact enjoyed.

Next, the right was, as I understand it, a right to use the coal shed in question for the purpose of storing such coal as might be required for the domestic purposes of the flat. In my judgment that is a right or easement which the law will clearly recognise, and it is a right or easement of a kind which could readily be included in a lease or conveyance by the insertion of appropriate words in the parcels. This, therefore, is not a case in which a title to a right unknown to the law is claimed by virtue of s 62. Nor is it a case in which it can be said to have been in the contemplation of the parties that the enjoyment

182 [1903] 2 Ch 165.

183 [1913] 1 Ch 571.

184 [1903] 2 Ch 165.

of the right should be purely temporary. No limit was set as to the time during which the coal shed could continue to be used. Mr Macadam simply gave his permission; that permission was acted on; and the use of the coalshed in fact went on down to 28 August 1943, and thereafter down to 1947. Therefore, applying to the facts of the present case the principles which seem to be deducible from the authorities, the conclusion to which I have come is that the right to use the coal shed was at the date of the letting of 28 August 1943, a right enjoyed with the top floor flat within the meaning of s 62 of the Law of Property Act 1925, with the result that (as no contrary intention was expressed in the document) the right in question must be regarded as having passed by virtue of that letting, just as it would have passed if it had been mentioned in express terms in cl 1, which sets out the subject-matter of the lease.

Tucker LJ and Singleton LJ agreed.

In *Goldberg v Edwards*[185] a permissive use of an alternative access became a legal easement on the grant of a lease.

Goldberg v Edwards [1950] 1 Ch 247, CA

Evershed MR: It was intended to be something which the plaintiffs should enjoy *qua* lessees during the term of the demise, though it should not be enjoyed by their servants, workmen or any other persons with their authority. Therefore, I think, to quote Jenkins LJ in the recent case of *Wright v Macadam*:[186]

> It is a right or easement of a kind which could be readily included in a lease or conveyance by the insertion of appropriate words in the parcels.

What those would be I will state later, because, in the view which I take, it is necessary to see that the injunction or declaration to which the plaintiffs may be entitled is properly formulated.

Wright v Macadam was decided after the Vice-Chancellor gave judgment in this case. That is of some importance, because he considered *Birmingham, Dudley & District Banking Co v Ross*,[187] and *International Tea Stores Co v Hobbs*.[188] He was of the opinion that *Birmingham, Dudley & District Banking Co v Ross* was nearer to the present case than *International Tea Stores Co v Hobbs*. But I think that it is the language of Farwell J in the latter case, expressly approved by the court in *Wright v Macadam*, which, on a proper analysis, is the more applicable here. On the hypothesis of fact which I am making, the privilege granted here was not temporary, like, for instance, a temporary right of light when it is obvious that buildings shortly to be erected will obscure it. The present privilege is in some ways indeed not dissimilar to that which in *Wright v Macadam* was held to be covered by s 62, namely, a privilege for the tenant to use a shed for storing her coal. I therefore think that, if the right which I have defined was one which was being enjoyed at the time of the conveyance, it is covered by s 62.

Cohen LJ and Asquith LJ agreed.

There are, however, some limitations to the operation of s 62. First, s 62 can only operate when those rights and privileges are capable of being an easement at

185 [1950] Ch 247.
186 [1949] 2 KB 744 at 752.
187 (1888) 38 Ch D 295.
188 [1903] 2 Ch 165.

law. In *Phipps v Pears*,[189] Lord Denning said that a right to protection from the weather is not a right known to the law and, therefore, cannot become an easement under s 62.

Phipps v Pears [1965] 1 QB 76, CA

Lord Denning MR: ... in order for s 62 to apply, the right or advantage must be one which is known to the law, in this sense, that it is capable of being granted at law so as to be binding on all successors in title, even those who take without notice, see *Wright v Macadam*. A fine view, or an expanse open to the winds, may be an 'advantage' to a house but it would not pass under s 62. Whereas a right to use a coal shed or to go along a passage would pass under s 62. The reason being that these last are rights known to the law, whereas the others are not. A right to protection from the weather is not a right known to the law. It does not therefore pass under s 62.

Secondly, the section does not operate unless there has been a 'conveyance' of land, a word which was statutorily defined as including 'a mortgage, charge, lease, assent, vesting declaration, vesting instrument, disclaimer, release and every other assurance of property or of an interest therein by any instrument, except a will'.[190] In *Borman v Griffith*,[191] an agreement for the grant of a lease was held not to be a conveyance. Here, on 10 October 1923, a lessor agreed to demise to the plaintiff a dwelling house, known as The Garden, which was situated in Wood Green Park. The agreement did not reserve any right of way to the plaintiff. But there was a drive way which ran through Wood Green Park, past the front door of The Gardens and then on to a dwelling house known as The Hall. The plaintiff constantly used the drive even though there was an untreated road at the back of The Garden. The lessor later leased The Hall to the defendant. The defendant obstructed the plaintiff in his use of the drive. The plaintiff claimed a right of way over the drive. The plaintiff had not obtained an easement under s 62 because he had not been using the passage prior to the agreement for the lease, and furthermore s 62 would not apply to an agreement which was not a conveyance.

Borman v Griffith [1930] 1 Ch 493

Maugham J: The date of the contract is a date before the coming into force of the Law of Property Act, 1925, and is a date at which the Conveyancing Act 1881, was still in force. The plaintiff relies on s 62, sub-ss 1 and 2, of the Law of Property Act 1925, under which certain general words are deemed to be included in a conveyance, and, in particular, the words 'ways ... reputed to appertain to the land, houses, etc' and 'reputed or known as part or parcel of or appurtenant to, the land, houses, etc': and he asserts that the way along the drive in the front of his house, and the branch drive leading directly to the back of his house, were ways enjoyed with the premises demised by the contract; and he points out that under sub-s 6, the section applies to conveyances executed after 31 December 1881, and that 'conveyance' is defined in s 205, sub-s 1(ii), to include 'a lease ... and every other assurance of property or of an interest therein by any instrument, except a will'.

---

189 [1965] 1 QB 76.

190 Section 205(1)(ii) of the LPA 1925.

191 [1930] 1 Ch 493.

If the contract of 10 October 1923, is an 'assurance of property or of an interest therein', a very curious result follows, for the definition of 'conveyance' in the Conveyancing Act, 1881, is limited to documents made by deed, and the contract in the present case is not by deed.[192] The result, therefore, of the argument put forward on behalf of the plaintiff would be that the plaintiff's rights may quite possibly have been enlarged, to the prejudice of the defendant and of the lessor; for this result, having regard to the fact that s 62 of the Law of Property Act 1925, is retrospective, will follow if it is to be held that the agreement of the present case is a 'conveyance' of land within the meaning of the definition in that Act.

On the whole, I think that it is not a 'conveyance', because it is not an 'assurance of property or of an interest therein'. It is true that, under the decision in *Walsh v Lonsdale*[193] it has been held that, where there is an agreement for a lease under which possession has been given, the tenant holds, for many purposes, as if a lease had actually been granted. 'He holds, therefore, under the same terms in equity as if a lease had been granted, it being a case in which both parties admit that relief is capable of being given by specific performance. That being so, he cannot complain of the exercise by the landlord of the same rights as the landlord would have had if a lease had been granted. On the other hand, he is protected in the same way as if a lease had been granted; he cannot be turned out by six months' notice as a tenant from year to year. He has a right to say: 'I have a lease in equity, and you can only re-enter if I have committed such a breach of covenant as would, if a lease had been granted, have entitled you to re-enter according to the terms of a proper proviso for re-entry.' That being so, it appears to me that, being a lessee in equity, he cannot complain of the exercise of the right of distress merely because the actual parchment has not been signed and sealed.' That is the well known judgment of Sir George Jessell MR, with which Cotton and Lindley LJJ agreed. But no Court has yet declared that an agreement for a lease for a term of more than three years is an 'assurance.' It has to be borne in mind that a lease for any term of more than three years must be by deed, and it is well known that, under s 3 of the Real Property Act, 1845, '... a lease, required by law to be in writing, of any tenements or hereditaments ... shall ... be void at law unless made by deed' (see now s 52 of the Law of Property Act 1925, and the repeal section.)

In my opinion, a contract for a lease exceeding a term of three years does not come within the meaning of the phrase 'assurance of property or of an interest therein' as that phrase is used in s 205, sub-s 1 (ii), of the Law of Property Act 1925: and accordingly I am unable to construe the agreement of 10 October 1923, as if the general words of s 62 of that Act were included in it.

[His Lordship, however, decided that the plaintiff enjoyed the right of way under the rule in *Wheeldon v Burrows*,[194] (see pp 884, 886 below).]

---

192 Section 2(v): '"Conveyance", unless a contrary intention appears, includes assignment, appointment, lease, settlement, and other assurance, and covenant to surrender, made by deed, on a sale, mortgage, demise, or settlement of any property, or on any other dealing with or for any property; and 'convey,' unless a contrary intention appears, has a meaning corresponding with that of conveyance.'

193 (1882) 21 Ch D 9 at 14.

194 (1878) 12 Ch D 31.

'Conveyance' may include a *written* lease taking effect in possession for a term not exceeding three years at the best rent without a fine under s 54(2) of the Law of Property Act 1925.

Wright v Macadam [1949] 2 KB 744, CA

Jenkins LJ: By virtue of the definition contained in s 205 sub-s 1, sub-para (ii), 'conveyance' includes a mortgage, charge, lease, assent, vesting declaration, and so on, and every other assurance of property or of an interest therein. It follows that the document of 28 August 1943, if it is a lease within the meaning of that definition, is a 'conveyance' for the purposes of s 62. It will be remembered that the letting was for a term of one year only. I think it follows from s 52, sub-s 2 (d) of the Law of Property Act 1925, read in conjunction with sub-s 2 of s 54, that this document, though expressed as an agreement, and though under hand only, is a 'lease' within the meaning of the definition. It will be remembered that s 52 provides by sub-s 1:

> All conveyances of land or of any interest therein are void for the purpose of conveying or creating a legal estate unless made by deed.

Subsection 2 provides:

> This section does not apply to (d): 'leases or tenancies or other assurances not required by law to be made in writing.'

Then s 54 lays down in sub-s 1 the general rule that interests in land created by parol shall have the force and effect of interests at will only, but sub-s 2, provides:

> 'Nothing in the foregoing provisions of this Part of this Act shall affect the creation by parol of leases taking effect in possession for a term not exceeding three years (whether or not the lessee is given power to extend the term) at the best rent which can be reasonably obtained without taking a fine.'

So that the document here in question was adequate for the purpose of passing to Mrs and Miss Wright the legal estate in the property for the term contemplated, and since the expiration of that term they have been holding over on the same terms. Accordingly, s 62 applies, inasmuch as the transaction under consideration is a 'conveyance' within the meaning of the section. It is, moreover, a conveyance of land, although it comprises only the upper floor of a house, inasmuch as the definition of 'land' in s 205, sub-s 1, sub-para (ix) provides that 'land' includes, amongst other things, 'buildings or parts of buildings'.

But the lease must be in writing and not merely oral because s 205 of the Law of Property Act 1925 requires there to be an instrument.[195]

Thirdly, the right must be enjoyed with the land at the time of the conveyance.[196] Section 62 will not transfer past rights or future rights which are not enjoyed at the time of the conveyance into easements.

---

195 *Cf Rye v Rye* [1962] AC 496. Lord MacDermot referring to s 205(1)(ii) said that 'the words "and every other assurance ... by any instrument" cannot be related solely to the word "release" and must be read as referring also to the earlier words, including "lease", so as to make of them a catalogue of instruments. In this context "instrument" must connote a document, and I therefore conclude that an oral tenancy will not be a "conveyance" ...' (p 508).

196 *Penn v Wilkins* (1974) 236 EG 203; *Nickerson v Barraclough* [1981] Ch 426.

Fourthly, it was held in *Long v Gowlett*[197] that if the right is enjoyed by a person who owns and occupies both the dominant and servient land prior to the conveyance, the right cannot be converted into an easement by a subsequent conveyance of the servient land to a different person. There must be a diversity of ownership or occupation of the two plots of land prior to the conveyance. So if A owns plot 1 and plot 2 and habitually walks across plot 2 from plot 1 to reach the highway, when he later conveys plot 1 to B, B cannot claim that the right of way over plot 2 enjoyed by A previously has been transferred by s 62 into an easement in his favour.[198] This is because where the lands are held under one ownership, whatever the owner does, he does as owner, and one cannot speak in any intelligible sense of rights or privileges enjoyed by the owner against himself.[199] Thus, when he conveys the land to B, there is no right that can be converted into an easement. As will be seen later, in such a case B will have to rely on the rule in *Wheeldon v Burrows*.[200]

Sovmots Investments Ltd v Secretary of State for the Environment [1979] AC 144, HL

Lord Wilberforce: The main argument before the inspector and in the courts below was that in this case and under the compulsory purchase order as made no specific power to require the creation of ancillary rights was necessary because these would pass to the acquiring authority under either, or both, of the first rule in *Wheeldon v Burrows* (1879) 12 Ch D 31 ('the rule') or of s 62 of the Law of Property Act 1925. Under the rule (I apologise for the reminder but the expression of the rule is important)

> on the grant by the owner of a tenement of part of that tenement as it is then used and enjoyed, there will pass to the grantee all those continuous and apparent easements (by which, of course, I mean quasi-easements), or, in other words, all those easements which are necessary to the reasonable enjoyment of the property granted, and *which have been and are at the time of the grant used* by the owners of the entirety for the benefit of the part granted (see *per* Thesiger LJ, at p 49, my emphasis).

Under s 62 a conveyance of land operates to convey with the land all ways, watercourses, liberties, privileges, easements, rights, and advantages whatsoever, appertaining or reputed to appertain to the land, or any part thereof, or, at the time of conveyance, demised, occupied or enjoyed with, or reputed or known as part or parcel or appurtenant to the land or any part thereof.

My Lords, there are very comprehensive expressions here, but it does not take much analysis to see that they have no relevance to the situation under consideration.

The rule is a rule of intention, based on the proposition that a man may not derogate from his grant. He cannot grant or agree to grant land and at the same time deny to his grantee what is at the time of the grant obviously necessary for its reasonable enjoyment.

197 [1923] 2 Ch 177.

198 For the controversy on the requirement of 'prior diversity of occupation' see (1977) 41 Conv (NS) 415, [1979] Conv 113 (Harpum, C); [1978] Conv 449, [1979] Conv 311 (Smith, P); Barnsley, p 491.

199 *Per* Lords Wilberforce and Edmund-Davies in *Sovmots Investments Ltd v Secretary of State for the Environment* [1979] AC 144 at 169B and 176C, following *Long v Gowlett* [1923] 2 Ch 177.

200 (1878) 12 Ch D 31.

To apply this to a case where a public authority is taking from an owner his land without his will is to stand the rule on its head: it means substituting for the intention of a reasonable voluntary grantor the unilateral, opposed, intention of the acquirer.

Moreover, and this point is relevant to a later argument, the words I have underlined show that for the rule to apply there must be actual, and apparent, use and enjoyment at the time of the grant. But no such use or enjoyment had, at Centre Point, taken place at all.

Equally, s 62 does not fit this case. The reason is that when land is under one ownership one cannot speak in any intelligible sense of rights, or privileges, or easements being exercised over one part for the benefit of another. Whatever the owner does, he does as owner and, until a separation occurs, of ownership or at least of occupation, the condition for the existence of rights, etc, does not exist: see *Bolton v Bolton* (1879) 11 Ch D 968, 970 *per* Fry J and *Long v Gowlett* [1923] 2 Ch 177 at 189, 198, in my opinion a correct decision.

A separation of ownership, in a case like the present, will arise on conveyance of one of the parts (eg the maisonettes), but this separation cannot be projected back to the stage of the compulsory purchase order so as, by anticipation to bring into existence rights not existing in fact.

Fifthly, under s 62(5) the right must have been granted by a capable grantor prior to the conveyance.[201] In *M R A Engineering v Trimster*,[202] the plaintiff, the owner of two adjoining plots of land, the green and the red land, used to get access to the red land by a track across the green land. This was because the red land was at the back of the green land and there was no access by road except a public footpath to it. The red land was later leased to a Mr Shaw with a right of way over the green land. In 1975, the plaintiff sold the green land to the defendant and granted them an option to purchase the red land when Mr Shaw's lease was terminated. In 1982, when Mr Shaw surrendered his lease, the defendant exercised their option to purchase the red land. The plaintiff argued that the red land should be valued on the basis that it enjoyed a right of way over the green land. The Court of Appeal held that as the plaintiff had transferred the green land in 1975 to the defendant, he ceased to have any power to grant any perpetual easement over it when he subsequently conveyed the red land to the defendant. Therefore no right of way over the green land could be transferred to the defendant under s 62.

MRA Engineering Ltd v Trimster Co Ltd (1988) 56 P & CR 1, CA

Dillon LJ: Mr Merrett, for the plaintiffs, says that the right of way which Mr Shaw had, had been enjoyed with the red land and therefore passed as an appurtenant to the red land under s 62(2) but was elevated into an easement in fee simple.

Of course, where an owner of land sells part of the land to a purchaser who has been in occupation of that part of the land before – for instance, as a tenant – and that person has had as appurtenant to his tenancy some right of way for the duration of the tenancy over land which the vendor is retaining, that right of way will pass by virtue of s 62 on

201 *MRA Engineering v Trimster* (1987) 56 P & CR 1 at 5, 7.

202 (1988) 56 P & CR 1.

the conveyance of the freehold of the land of which the purchaser was previously tenant, and it will pass, as the conveyance is in fee simple, as a right of way in fee simple appurtenant to the freehold. That is the ordinary mechanism of grant, and it can only apply where the owner of the land over which the right of way is thus impliedly granted has a sufficient estate to support making such a grant. Section 62 is concerned with what is granted and it cannot include something which at the time of the relevant conveyance the grantor had no power to grant.

In the present case, as there was no reservation in the conveyance of the green land in 1975, the plaintiffs, as vendors of the red land, had no power to grant to any third party any perpetual easement over the green land. The green land had, indeed, been conveyed to the defendants in 1975 subject to Mr Shaw's right of way, but that was appurtenant to his lease, which was surrendered before there was any exercise of the option. Therefore, it must follow, in my judgment, that there is no basis for saying that the plaintiffs could have granted, after the surrender of Mr Shaw's lease, any easement over the green land. Accordingly, no such easement could pass under s 62(2) on any conveyance of the red land in favour of anyone by the plaintiffs subsequent to the surrender of Mr Shaw's lease or, indeed, before that, because Mr Shaw's rights were his rights under the lease and not the rights of the plaintiffs as the reversioners.'

As the effect of s 62 is too sweeping, to prevent it from operating, one should either revoke the precarious rights before the conveyance or expressly exclude its operation in the conveyance. And in practice, it is important for the seller's solicitor to discuss with the seller whether a special condition should be included in the initial contract and the subsequent conveyance to exclude the operation of s 62.[203] The Standard Conditions of Sale 3.3.2 only exclude the buyer's right to light or air over the land retained by the seller. But otherwise it entitles both buyer and seller to have such easements as would have passed by the operation of law to a buyer. So where the Standard Conditions of Sale are used, the seller may want to modify the conditions to exclude rights that are not intended to be easements.

By implied grant

In some cases, where an easement is not expressly granted or reserved, it may still be acquired impliedly. It is an established principle that a grantor may not derogate from his grant.[204] 'A grantor having given a thing with one hand is not to take away the means of enjoying it with the other. And this principle will be carried out by a necessary implication of whatever fiction is required to support the origin of the right not to be interfered with by the grantor'.[205] There are three situations in which the law is prepared to imply an easement in favour of the grantee against the grantor:

203 See Storey, IR, *Conveyancing*, 4th edn, 1993, London: Butterworths, at 192–93; Barnsley, pp 165–67, 492.

204 *Aldridge v Wright* [1929] 2 KB 117 at 130.

205 *Birmingham, Dudley and District Banking Co v Ross* (1888) 38 Ch D 295 at 313, *per* Bowen LJ.

(a) Necessity

Where without the easement, the land would be inaccessible, the courts are willing to imply the grant of an easement on the ground of necessity.[206] Thus, in *Altmann v Boatman*[207] a right to use a staircase which was the sole access to the flat was implied by the court. The necessity must be one that exists at the date of the conveyance, and not one that merely arises after that date.[208] It is not sufficient to show that a particular access over the grantor's land is more convenient or reasonably necessary for the proper enjoyment of the claimant's dominant land. You have to show that without the easement, your land cannot be used at all.[209] In *M R A Engineering v Trimster*, as there was a public footpath to gain access on foot to the red land, no easement of necessity could be implied into the conveyance. The fact that there could be no access by car merely made the use of the red land difficult and inconvenient. The red land would not become inaccessible or useless.

M R A Engineering Ltd v Trimster Co Ltd (1988) 56 P & CR 1, CA

Dillon LJ: The alternative argument put for the plaintiffs on their respondent's notice is that there is to be implied on the execution of the conveyance to the defendants of the green land in 1975 the reservation of a way of necessity to the red land over the green land. It is of course well established that a way of necessity may arise by implied reservation as well as by implied grant. The law as to ways of necessity is in some respects archaic, and it may be that it is time that it was given closer consideration as against modern circumstances. As matters stand, however, there is a considerable difference between a way of necessity and a way which is implied to give effect to the presumed intention of the parties – see, for instance, so far as grant is concerned, the decision of Kay J in *Brown v Alabaster*. In the present case it is not practicable to explore any question of the presumed intention of the parties, nor has any attempt been made to do so in argument ...

In the textbooks, however, reference is made to a statement by Stirling LJ in *Union Lighterage Co v London Graving Dock Co*. In Gale on *Easements* it is said that Stirling LJ expressed the opinion that an easement of necessity is one without which the property retained cannot be used at all and not one merely necessary to the reasonable enjoyment of the property. In Gale it is said again with reference to *Union Lighterage Co*:

> ... speaking generally it does appear to be essential that the land is absolutely inaccessible or useless.

In Megarry and Wade's *Law of Real Property* there is the same citation from Stirling LJ:

> ... for the principle is that as easement of necessity is one 'without which the property retained cannot be used at all, and not one merely necessary to the reasonable enjoyment of that property.

As I have said, at the back of the red land and down one side of it there are public footpaths. It appears therefore that it is possible to obtain access to the red land and the

---

206 *Clark v Cogge* (1607) 2 Roll Abr 60, pl 17; 79 ER 149; (1981) 34 CLP 113 (Jackson, P); (1940) 56 LQR 93 (Stroud, DA).

207 (1963) 186 EG 109.

208 *Holmes v Goring* (1824) 2 Bing 76 at 84; *Corpn of London v Riggs* (1880) 13 Ch D 798 at 806.

209 *M R A Engineering Ltd v Trimster Co Ltd* (1988) 56 P & CR 1 at 6.

house on it by foot along the public footpaths. Mr Shaw certainly took a car in, although he garaged it on the green land, and a car could not go along the public footpath. As the judge said:

> ... nowadays one seems to think and it is very natural so to think, that everybody must have a car and the house must be approached by a car. It is certainly very inconvenient and could be very inconvenient to a very large extent.

This court could not differ from his conclusion of fact in view of the public footpaths that the property is usable in the ordinary sense of the word. It is not absolutely inaccessible or useless without the right of way claimed; merely difficult and inconvenient. In these circumstances, I would reject the only points taken in the respondent's notice and I would allow this appeal and discharge the order of the learned judge.

It seems, however, that easement of way of necessity only confers a right to pass and re-pass the servient land. There is no easement of necessity of light as the land is not useless without access to light.[210] Similarly, there is no easement of necessity in respect of drainage, sewerage and the supply of electricity.[211] These views are perhaps out of date today and are not consistent with modern conditions.[212]

Is easement of necessity based on public policy which requires that land should not be rendered unusable by being landlocked? Brightman LJ in *Nickerson v Barraclough*[213] thought that there was no such policy. He said that easement of necessity would only exist in association with a grant of land and depended on the intention of the parties and the implication from the circumstances. Therefore, if the grantor had expressly stated that no right of access was being granted, an easement of necessity could not be implied even if without the easement the land is landlocked. Such a view may seem harsh but it is understandable since an implied grant cannot override the express intention of the parties.

Nickerson v Barraclough [1981] 2 All ER 369, CA

Brightman LJ: In this court we have heard a great deal of argument about ways of necessity: what is their basis, how they can be acquired and whether they can be lost. With the utmost respect to Sir Robert Megarry VC, I have come to the conclusion that the doctrine of way of necessity is not founded on public policy at all but on an implication from the circumstances. I accept that there are reported cases, and textbooks, in which public policy is suggested as a possible foundation of the doctrine, but such a suggestion is not, in my opinion, correct. It is well established that a way of necessity is never found to exist except in association with a grant of land: see *Proctor v Hodgson* (1855) 10 Exch 824 where it was held that land acquired by escheat got no way of necessity; and *Wilkes v Greenway* (1890) 6 TLR 449 where land acquired by prescription got no way of necessity. If a way of necessity were based on public policy, I see no reason why land acquired by escheat or by prescription should be excluded. Furthermore, there would seem to be no particular reason to father the doctrine of way of necessity on public policy when

210 *Ray v Hazeldine* [1904] 2 Ch 17 at 20; [1989] Conv 355 at 356 (JEM).

211 *Union Lighterage Co v London Graving Dock Co* [1902] 2 Ch 557 at 573.

212 For a more modern approach see *Auerbach v Beck* (1985) 6 NSWLR 424 at 444D–45B.

213 [1981] 2 All ER 369.

implication is such an obvious and convenient candidate for paternity. There is an Australian case, *North Sydney Printing Pty Ltd v Sabemo Investments Corpn Pty Ltd* [1971] 2 NSWLR 150, where that conclusion was reached. Furthermore, I cannot accept that public policy can play any part at all in the construction of an instrument; in construing a document the court is endeavouring to ascertain the expressed intention of the parties. Public policy may require the court to frustrate that intention where the contract is against public policy, but in my view public policy cannot help the court to ascertain what that intention was. So I reach the view that a way of necessity is not founded on public policy, that considerations of public policy cannot influence the construction of the 1906 conveyance, and that this action is not concerned with a way of necessity strictly so called; nor, I think, did Sir Robert Megarry VC intend to suggest otherwise.

(b) Common intention

The second situation in which the court may imply an easement in favour of the grantee is when it is the common intention of the parties at the time of the conveyance that an easement should be granted.[214] This type of implied easement overlaps to a large extent with easement of necessity in that a common intention to grant an easement will normally be found in cases of necessity. This can be illustrated by the case of *Wong v Beaumont Property Trust Ltd*.[215] The defendant's predecessor in title had leased the basement of premises in Queen Street, Exeter to the plaintiff's predecessor in title for the express purpose of use as a restaurant. The plaintiff later bought the remainder of the lease intending to use the premises as a Chinese restaurant. He covenanted to comply with public health regulations which could only be fulfilled by installing a new ventilation system leading through the upstairs premises retained by the defendant. When the plaintiff wanted to construct a duct on the defendant's upstairs premises for the passage of air, the defendant refused him the permission. The Court of Appeal held that the plaintiff was entitled to an easement of necessity for the passage of air. Without the easement, the basement could not be used as a restaurant at all. It was also the common intention of the parties that the grantee should have all rights (including the easement) which were necessary for the use of the premises as a restaurant.

Wong v Beaumont Property Trust Ltd [1965] 1 QB 173, CA

Lord Denning MR: The plaintiff is the tenant of a Chinese restaurant in Exeter called the 'Chopstick'. It is situate underground below Nos 83 and 84, Queen Street, Exeter. He has a kitchen there where he cooks the food. It is so badly ventilated, however, that it is necessary to have an air duct so as to take the used air up to the roof. This duct will have to be fixed on to the back wall of the building which belongs to the landlords. The plaintiff asked the landlords for permission to erect the duct and to fix it on the back wall, but the landlords refused. The plaintiff now seeks a declaration that he is entitled to erect the duct and fix it on the wall without the landlords' consent. To do this, as it seems to me, he has got to show an easement of necessity ...

---

214 *Wong v Beaumont Property Trust Ltd* [1965] 1 QB 173, (1964) 80 LQR 322 (R E M); *Pwllbach Colliery Co Ltd v Woodman* [1915] AC 634 at 646; *Squarey v Harris-Smith* (1981) 42 P & CR 118 at 127; *Stafford v Lee* [1992] 45 LS Gaz R 27.

215 (1965) 1 QB 173.

He is not the original lessee, nor are the defendants the original lessors. Each is a successor in title. As between them, a right of this kind, if it exists at all, must be by way of an easement. In particular, an easement of necessity. The law on the matter was stated by Lord Parker of Waddington in *Pwllbach Colliery Co Ltd v Woodman*,[216] where he said,[217] omitting immaterial words:

> The law will readily imply the grant or reservation of such easements as may be necessary to give effect to the common intention of the parties to a grant of real property, with reference to the manner or purposes in and for which the land granted ... is to be used. But it is essential for this purpose that the parties should intend that the subject of the grant ... should be used in some definite and particular manner. It is not enough that the subject of the grant ... should be intended to be used in a manner which may or may not involve this definite and particular use.

That is the principle which underlies all easements of necessity. If you go back to Rolle's *Abridgment* you will find it stated in this way:[218]

> If I have a field inclosed by my own land on all sides, and I alien this close to another, he shall have a way to this close over my land, as incident to the grant; for otherwise he cannot have any benefit by the grant.

I would apply those principles here. Here was the grant of a lease to the lessee for the very purpose of carrying on a restaurant business. It was to be a popular restaurant, and it was to be developed and extended. There was a covenant not to cause any nuisance; and to control and eliminate all smells; and to comply with the Food Hygiene Regulations. That was 'a definite and particular manner' in which the business had to be conducted. It could not be carried on in that manner at all unless a ventilation system was installed by a duct of this kind. In these circumstances it seems to me that, if the business is to be carried on at all – if, in the words of Rolle's *Abridgment*,[219] the lessee is to 'have any benefit by the grant' at all – he must of necessity be able to put a ventilation duct up the wall. It may be that in Blackaby's time it would not have needed such a large duct as is now needed in the plaintiff's time. But nevertheless a duct of some kind would have had to be put up the wall. The plaintiff may need a bigger one. But that does not matter. A man who has a right to an easement can use it in any proper way, so long as he does not substantially increase the burden on the servient tenement. In this case a bigger duct will not substantially increase the burden.

There is one point in which this case goes further than the earlier cases which have been cited. It is this. It was not realised by the parties, at the time of the lease, that this duct would be necessary. But it was in fact necessary from the very beginning. That seems to me sufficient to bring the principle into play. In order to use this place as a restaurant, there must be implied an easement, by the necessity of the case, to carry a duct up this wall. The county court judge so held. He granted a declaration. I agree with him.

216 [1915] AC 634, 31 TLR 271, HL (E).

217 [1915] AC 634 at 646.

218 2 Rol Abr 60, pl 17, 18; 1 Saund (1871 edn) 570; see Gale on *Easements*, 13th edn, London: Sweet & Maxwell, p 98.

219 2 Rol Abr 60, pl 17, 18.

However, although this category covers easement of necessity, it goes further in that if it was the common intention that an easement should be granted, the grantee will be entitled to the easement even though the easement is not one without which the property cannot be used at all. An example is the case of *Cory v Davies*[220] where a row of terraced houses was built with a drive in front and an exit to the road at each end. One owner barred the exit at his end of the terrace requiring all traffic to go the other way. There was no express grant of an easement in favour of all the house owners over all parts of the drive, but the court found that the original parties had a common intention that the drive should be used at each end by all owners. An implied easement was therefore granted.

Cory v Davies [1923] 2 Ch 95

Lawrence J: The present case, in my opinion, falls within the second of the two classes of cases in which, according to Lord Parker's speech in *Pwllbach Colliery Co v Woodman*[221] easements may impliedly be created. Lord Parker there states that this class of cases does not depend upon the terms of the grant itself, but upon the circumstances under which the grant was made, and that the Court will readily imply the grant or reservation of such easements as may be necessary to give effect to the common intention of the parties to the grant with reference to the manner or purpose in and for which the land granted or some land retained by the grantor is to be used, pointing out, however, that it is an essential condition of the implied creation of such easements that the parties should intend that the subject of the grant or the land retained by the grantor should be used in some definite and particular manner and that it is not enough that the user intended by the parties might or might not involve that definite and particular use. The defendants, however, contend that the Court ought not to act on this principle, because in the circumstances of this case its application would involve the implication of a reservation in favour of the lessor, and that such an implication is contrary to the principle laid down in *Wheeldon v Burrows*.[222] That case, no doubt, lays down the general rule that, if a grantor intends to reserve any right over the tenement granted, it is his duty to reserve it expressly in the grant, and I think that there is great force in the argument that this general rule applies *a fortiori* where the grant, as in the present case, contains certain express reservation in favour of the grantor. It is evident, however, from the judgment in *Wheeldon v Burrows*, that there are exceptions to this general rule, and I am of opinion that the present case forms one of these exceptions. The three leases of 8 May 1857, were really parts of one transaction, by which the lessor was at the same moment disposing of the sites of all the three plots, that is to say, of the whole of the land over which the easements were to extend, and the easements were only required for the beneficial enjoyment by the lessees of the three plots. In fact the lessor in granting the three leases containing covenants to lay out the three plots in the form of a terrace was only giving effect to the arrangement made between the three lessees, and, therefore, this is not a case where the lessor or anybody deriving title under him by virtue of a subsequent grant is claiming the benefit of an implied reservation in favour of the lessor for his own benefit. In these circumstances the Court ought not, in my opinion, to let the general rule

220 (1923) 2 Ch 95.

221 [1915] AC 634, 646.

222 (1879) 12 Ch D 31.

stand in the way of holding that the appropriate grants and reservations, in order to carry out the common intention of the parties, ought to be implied, in spite of the fact that particular reservations in favour of the lessor are to be found in the leases. The argument based on the express reservations, in my opinion, loses much of its force owing to the fact that the leases, including of course the express reservations, are all in the common form adopted for the whole of the lessor's estate. It is perhaps not to be wondered at that the lessor did not sufficiently appreciate the advisability of adding to the common form of leases express provisions as to the drive and entrance gates, as his interest in those provisions was exceedingly remote and would only arise in the unlikely event of one or two of the leases terminating before the others or other of the leases. Nor perhaps is it to be wondered at that the lessees did not stipulate for the insertion of express grants and reservations, as it would hardly occur to them that, after the three plots had been laid out in the manner described, any one or two of them could have successfully contended that the drive and entrance gates were not constructed for the joint benefit of all three. For these reasons I am of opinion that neither the rule laid down by *Wheeldon v Burrows* nor the fact that the leases contain express reservations in favour of the lessor prevents the Court from implying the appropriate grants and reservations in order to give effect to the common intention of the parties to the leases.

(c) The rule in Wheeldon v Burrows

Apart from necessity and common intention, the court can also imply an easement under the rule in *Wheeldon v Burrows*.[223] Under the rule in *Wheeldon v Burrows*, when A transfers or agrees to transfer plot 1 to B but retains plot 2, the 'right' which was habitually exercised by A at the time when he owned plot 1, often called a quasi-easement, will pass to B.

When does the rule apply? Thesiger LJ in a celebrated *dictum* in *Wheeldon v Burrows* said that:

> ... on the grant by the owner of a tenement of part of that tenement as it is then used and enjoyed, there will pass to the grantee all those continuous and apparent easements (by which, I mean quasi-easements), or, in other words, all those easements which are necessary to the reasonable enjoyment of the property granted, and which have been and are at the time of the grant used by the owners of the entirety for the benefit of the part granted.[224]

It is clear that the rule only applies to those quasi-easements which are capable of being easements. Secondly, there must be a continuous and apparent quasi-easement. Continuous in this context means that the quasi-easement has been exercised passively, for example, a right to use drains or a right to light.[225] However, the court has also held that a right of way could pass under the rule in *Wheeldon v Burrows* even if it requires personal activity for its enjoyment.[226] Apparent means that it must be identifiable by a careful inspection of the premises,[227] such as a permanent mark on the land itself, or a worn track.[228]

223 (1879) 12 Ch D 31.

224 (1879) 12 Ch D 31 at 49.

225 Megarry and Wade, p 863.

226 *Borman v Griffith* [1930] 1 Ch 493 at 499.

227 *Pyer v Carter* (1857) 1 H & N 916 at 922; 156 ER 1472, at 1475.

228 *Hansford v Jago* [1921] 1 Ch 322 at 337; *Re St Clement's, Leigh-on-Sea* [1988] 1 WLR 720 at 729B–C.

Thesiger LJ also said that the quasi-easement must be necessary for the reasonable enjoyment of the property granted. Here necessity does not mean that the easement must be such that without it the property cannot be used at all.[229] It is sufficient if the easement is conducive to and would facilitate the reasonable enjoyment of the property. However, in *Wheeler v JJ Saunders Ltd*, where there were two entrances (the south entrance over the servient land, and the east entrance) to the dominant land, the majority of the Court of Appeal held that the south entrance was not necessary for the reasonable enjoyment of the dominant land because the east entrance would do just as well.[230] This view, then, suggests, rather unhelpfully, that the right must more than merely accommodate the dominant land but need not be an absolute necessity; it hovers, at an ill-defined point, somewhere between the two.[231]

It is not clear, however, whether the conditions of both 'continuous and apparent' and 'reasonable necessity' must be satisfied. Thesiger LJ used the word 'or'. Existing cases such as *Ward v Kirkland*[232] seem to suggest that both conditions must be met. But Oliver LJ in *Squarey v Harris-Smith*[233] commented that, 'the judge rejected the plaintiff's claim on the ground, *inter alia*, that the doctrine of *Wheeldon v Burrows* can only be prayed in aid where the easement claimed, in addition to being continuous and apparent, is necessary for the reasonable enjoyment of the dominant tenement. That is, in fact, a debatable proposition, for it is arguable that the continuity and apparency of and the necessity for the easement are alternative and not cumulative requirements'.

Fourthly, the quasi-easement must also have been enjoyed by the grantor right up to and until the date of the relevant grant.[234] In Thesiger LJ's words, the quasi-easements must 'have been and are at the time of the grant used by the owners of the entirety for the benefit of the part granted'.

In *Wheeldon v Burrows*, part of a land was conveyed to Wheeldon, and another part containing a workshop was later conveyed to Burrows. Three windows in the workshop received light from over Wheeldon's land. There was no express reservation of right by the original owner in the conveyance of the land to Wheeldon. The plaintiff, Wheeldon's widow and devisee, later erected

---

229 *Goldberg v Edwards* [1950] Ch 247 at 254; *Costagliola v English* (1969) 210 *Estates Gazette* 1425 at 1431; *Wheeler v JJ Saunders Ltd* [1995] 2 All ER 697 at 707j.

230 [1995] 2 All ER 697 at 702d, 712h *per* Staughton LJ and Sir John May respectively. Peter Gibson LJ differed on this point saying that 'I am not able to say that the judge erred when he found that the [south entrance] was necessary for the reasonable enjoyment of the property on the evidence before him' because he took the view that 'necessity' in this context did not have an ordinary meaning but a special meaning which meant simply that reasonable use of the property could not be had without the easement (at 708b).

231 See [1995] Conv 239 at 240 (Thompson, MP).

232 [1967] Ch 194 at 224D–25A. See also *Wheeler v JJ Saunders Ltd* [1995] 2 All ER 697 at 707, CA; *Millman v Ellis* (1996) 71 P & CR 158 at 162, CA; *Bayley v Great Western Railway Co* (1884) 26 Ch D 434 at 452; *Borman v Griffith* [1930] 1 Ch 493 at 499; *Horn v Hiscock* (1972) 223 *Estates Gazette* 1437 at 1441.

233 (1981) 42 P & CR 118 at 124 referring to Megarry and Wade, 4th edn, 1975, p 834. In *Simmons v Dobson* [1991] 1 WLR 720 at 722F, Fox LJ did not refer to the requirement of reasonable necessity at all.

234 *Re St Clement's, Leigh-on-Sea* [1988] 1 WLR 720 at 729B–C.

hoardings in a manner which excluded the light from the workshop. Burrows claimed that he had an easement of light and knocked down the hoardings. The plaintiff brought this action from trespass. It was held that Burrows had no right to knock down the hoardings because in the absence of express reservation of easement of light by the original owner, no such right passed to him from the owner.

Wheeldon v Burrows (1879) 12 Ch D 31, CA

Thesiger LJ: We have had a considerable number of cases cited to us, and out of them I think that two propositions may be stated as what I may call the general rules governing cases of this kind. The first of these rules is, that on the grant by the owner of a tenement of part of that tenement as it is then used and enjoyed, there will pass to the grantee all those continuous and apparent easements (by which, of course, I mean quasi easements), or, in other words, all those easements which are necessary to the reasonable enjoyment of the property granted, and which have been and are at the time of the grant used by the owners of the entirety for the benefit of the part granted. The second proposition is that, if the grantor intends to reserve any right over the tenement granted, it is his duty to reserve it expressly in the grant. Those are the general rules governing cases of this kind, but the second of those rules is subject to certain exceptions. One of those exceptions is the well-known exception which attaches to cases of what are called ways of necessity; and I do not dispute for a moment that there may be, and probably are, certain other exceptions, to which I shall refer before I close my observations upon this case.

Both of the general rules which I have mentioned are founded upon a maxim which is as well established by authority as it is consonant to reason and common sense, *viz*, that a grantor shall not derogate from his grant. It has been argued before us that there is no distinction between what has been called an implied grant and what is attempted to be established under the name of an implied reservation; and that such a distinction between the implied grant and the implied reservation is a mere modern invention and one which runs contrary, not only to the general practice upon which land has been bought and sold for a considerable time, but also to authorities which are said to be clear and distinct upon the matter. So far, however, from that distinction being one which was laid down for the first time by and which is to be attributed to Lord Westbury in *Suffield v Brown* (1864) 4 De GJ & Sm 185, it appears to me that it has existed almost as far back as we can trace the law upon the subject; and I think it right, as the case is one of considerable importance, not merely as regards the parties, but as regards vendors and purchasers of land generally, that I should go with some little particularity into what I may term the leading cases upon the subject.

... These cases in no way support the proposition for which the appellant in this case contends; but, on the contrary, support the propositions that in the case of a grant you may imply a grant of such continuous and apparent easements or such easements as are necessary to the reasonable enjoyment of the property conveyed, and have in fact been enjoyed during the unity of ownership, but that, with the exception which I have referred to of easements of necessity, you cannot imply a similar reservation in favour of the grantor of land.

Where the conditions in *Wheeldon v Burrows* are satisfied the rule applies even before the conveyance of the land to the grantee is carried out. It applies as soon as a contract for the conveyance is made.[235]

The rule also applies where A has sold plots 1 and 2 and conveyed the two plots at the same time to two different persons so that the quasi-easement previously enjoyed by A will now be enjoyed by the new dominant owner against the new servient owner.[236]

Again, if the seller does not want any quasi-easement he previously enjoyed to be given to the buyer as an easement, he has to exclude the rule in *Wheeldon v Burrows* in the contract for the sale of land. This is in fact a common practice.[237] It is important to note that the rule in *Wheeldon v Burrows* must be excluded in the contract. Otherwise, once the contracts are exchanged, the buyer is entitled to the easement and it cannot later be excluded by a provision in the deed of conveyance.

The rule in *Wheeldon v Burrows* contrasted with s 62

Both the rule in *Wheeldon v Burrows* and s 62 can convert a quasi-easement into an easement. But there are some differences between them:

(a) Wheeldon v Burrows

1. The quasi-easements are still enjoyed by the grantor prior to the conveyance or agreement to convey.

2. No diversity of occupation or ownership needed at the time the quasi-easements are enjoyed.

3. No conveyance needed. The quasi-easements pass under a will or an agreement.

4. The quasi-easements have to be continuous and apparent or reasonably necessary for the enjoyment of the dominant land.

(b) Section 62

1. The precarious rights are already enjoyed by the grantee or his predecessor prior to the conveyance.

2. There has to be a diversity of occupation or ownership at the time the precarious rights are enjoyed.

3. The precarious rights only become full easements on a conveyance.

4. The precarious rights do not have to be continuous and apparent, or reasonably necessary for the enjoyment of the dominant land as long as they are enjoyed at the time of the conveyance.

---

235 *Borman v Griffith* [1930] 1 Ch 493 at 499.

236 *Phillips v Low* [1892] 1 Ch 47.

237 Storey, IR, *Conveyancing*, 4th edn, 1993, London: Butterworths, pp 44–45, 192–93; Barnsley, p 166.

Implied reservation

As mentioned earlier, the seller can reserve an easement over the land sold expressly. If he fails to reserve his right expressly, the court may nevertheless allow the right to be impliedly reserved in certain circumstances. However, the court is less inclined to imply easements in favour of him because if he intends to retain a right over the land, he should reserve it expressly in the grant.[238] As a general rule there will be no implied reservation in his favour.[239] Therefore, it is not surprising that the seller cannot reserve an easement impliedly under the rule in *Wheeldon v Burrows*.[240]

The circumstances in which the court may allow an implied reservation of an easement are where an easement is a necessity or where it is the common intention of the parties that an easement should be reserved.

(a) Easement of necessity

Where A sells his land in such a way that the land he retains is landlocked and without a right of way across the land he has just sold, the land he retains will be inaccessible, then an easement of necessity may be impliedly reserved in favour of the grantor, A.[241]

It is not enough to show that the implied easement will facilitate reasonable or better enjoyment or would be more convenient for the vendor.[242]

In *M R A Engineering v Trimster*,[243] there was a public footpath which could be used to gain access to the retained land, therefore, no easement of necessity to cross over the land sold could be reserved in favour of the owner or occupier of the retained land.

(b) Intended easement

An easement may also be implied in favour of the grantor if it is necessary to give effect to their common intention.[244] For example, on the conveyance of one of the two adjacent buildings, easements of support by each other could be implied because it must have been the common intention of the parties that such a mutual support should be enjoyed by them.[245]

However, as the court is less willing to reserve easements in favour of the grantor, implied reservation on the grounds of necessity and common intention will only be allowed in rare cases where the easement is absolutely necessary for the use of the land or where the claimant can discharge a heavy burden of

---

238 *Broomfield v Williams* [1897] 1 Ch 602 at 616; *Wiles v Banks* (1985) 50 P & CR 80 at 83.

239 *Re Webb's Lease* [1951] Ch 808.

240 *Aldridge v Wright* [1929] 2 KB 117 at 124.

241 *Titchmarsh v Royston Water & Co Ltd* (1899) 81 LT 673 at 675; *Barry v Hasseldine* [1952] Ch 835 at 838.

242 *MRA Engineering Ltd v Trimster Co Ltd* (1988) 56 P & CR 1 at 6.

243 (1988) 56 P & CR 1.

244 *Pwllbach Colliery Co v Woodman* [1915] AC 634 at 646.

245 *Richard v Rose* (1853) 9 Exch 218 at 221: 156 ER 93 at 94.

proof that it was the common intention of the parties that an easement should be reserved.

Presumed grant[246]

An easement may be, and usually is, acquired by prescription, either at common law, or under the doctrine of lost modern grant, or the Prescription Act 1832. The idea is that where the dominant owner has used the servient land over a period of time, he should not be deprived of the benefit of the use merely because he cannot prove that such a right of user has been granted. He should acquire a legal easement by presumed grant and no evidence of a deed of grant is needed. Fry J once said in *Dalton v Angus*:[247]

> In my opinion, the whole law of prescription and the whole law which governs the presumption or inference of a grant or covenant rests upon acquiescence. The courts and the judges have had recourse to various expedients for quieting the possession of persons in the exercise of rights which have not been resisted by the persons against whom they are exercised; but in all cases it appears to me that acquiescence and nothing else is the principle upon which these expedients rest. It becomes then of the highest importance to consider of what ingredients acquiescence consists ... I cannot imagine any case of acquiescence in which there is not shewn to be in the servient owner: (1) a knowledge of the acts done; (2) a power in him to stop the acts or to sue in respect of them; and (3) an abstinence on his part from the exercise of such power.

The law of presumed grant or prescription is extremely complicated. Broadly speaking, the claimant must first satisfy three requirements:[248]

(i) The right to use the servient land must be enjoyed without force, secrecy or permission.[249]

(ii) The use must be in fee simple, ie the right must be enjoyed by a fee simple owner against an owner of fee simple servient land.[250]

(iii) The use must be continuous. This is a question of degree.[251]

The three requirements have recently come to be considered by the Court of Appeal in *Mills v Silver*.[252] Here, the defendants bought a derelict farm. The only access to the farm was along a track on the plaintiffs' adjoining land. A previous occupier of the farm had used the track but not frequently. No express grant or permission was ever given for the use, but the plaintiffs were aware of it. They had not prevented the use. The plaintiff now sought an injunction to

---

246 Jackson, P, *The Law of Easements and Profits*, 1978, London: Butterworths, Chapter 7; Gale on *Easements*, 14th edn, 1972, London: Sweet & Maxwell, Chapter 4.

247 (1881) 6 App Cas 740 at 773.

248 Where, however, the user is prohibited by statute, the right cannot be acquired by prescription: see *Hanning v Top Deck Travel Group Ltd* (1994) 68 P & CR 14.

249 *Gardner v Hodgson's Kingston Brewery Co Ltd* [1903] AC 229; *Tickle v Brown* (1836) 4 Ad & El 369.

250 *Bright v Walker* (1834) 1 Cr M & R 211, at 221; *Wheaton v Maple & Co* [1893] 3 Ch 48. This rule does not apply where the lessee of the dominant land has the right to enlarge his leasehold interest into a fee simple under s 153 of the LPA 1925: *Bosomworth v Faber* (1995) 69 P & CR 288.

251 *Dare v Heathcote* (1856) 25 LJ Ex 245.

252 [1991] Ch 271, CA.

restrain the defendants from using the track. The Court of Appeal held that there was a right of way under the doctrine of lost modern grant.

Mills v Silver [1991] Ch 271, CA

Parker LJ: [His Lordship considered the question of continuous user:] In *Sturges v Bridgman* (1879) 11 Ch D 852, 863, Thesiger LJ giving the judgment of the court said:

> ... the law governing the acquisition of easements by user stands thus: Consent or acquiescence of the owner of the servient tenement lies at the root of prescription, and of the fiction of a lost grant, and hence the acts or user, which go to the proof of either the one or the other, must be, in the language of the civil law, *nec vi, nec clam, nec precario*; for a man cannot, as a general rule, be said to consent to or acquiesce in the acquisition by his neighbour of an easement through an enjoyment of which he has no knowledge, actual or constructive, or which he contests and endeavours to interrupt, or which he temporarily licenses.

This passage is in my judgment of prime importance in the determination of the present appeal for it makes plain (i) that consent or acquiescence to the user asserted as giving rise to the easement is an essential ingredient of the acquisition of the easement and (ii) that it is the nature of the acts of user which has to be examined in order to see whether the easement is established.

Unless the acts of user are of the requisite character, consent or acquiescence is irrelevant. If they are then consent or acquiescence is essential.

In *Hollins v Verney* (1884) 13 QBD 304, 315, Lindley LJ giving the judgment of the court said:

> no actual user can be sufficient to satisfy the statute, unless during the whole of the statutory term ... the user is enough at any rate to carry to the mind of a reasonable person who is in possession of the servient tenement, the fact that a continuous right to enjoyment is being asserted, and ought to be resisted if such right is not recognised, and if resistance to it is intended.

This shows clearly that the crucial matter for consideration is whether for the necessary period the use is such as to bring home to the mind of a reasonable person that a continuous right of enjoyment is being asserted. If it is and the owner of the allegedly servient tenement knows or must be taken to know of it and does nothing about it the right is established. It is no answer for him to say, 'I "tolerated" it.' If he does nothing he will be taken to have recognised the right and not intended to resist it.

For the plaintiffs it was submitted that this apparently simple position had been altered or modified by later cases. I do not consider that it has. Certainly there are statements in speeches in the House of Lords and the judgments of this court in later cases which might appear to suggest that a claim will be defeated if there are two possible explanations of the situation or if it is not shown that the user is against the will of the owner or if the user has been 'tolerated.' Such statements, however, were in my judgment not statements of principle but statements relating to the particular facts of the cases under consideration.

I instance but one of such cases by way of example, namely *Gardner v Hodgson's Kingston Brewery Co Ltd* [1903] AC 229. In that case the owner of a house had for more than 40 years used a cart way from his stables through the yard of an adjoining inn. He paid 15s. a year to the owners of the yard but there was no conclusive evidence as to the origin of this payment. The owners of the yard contended that the payment was for rent or for a series of annual licences. The owner of the house contended that it was more probably a perpetual payment attached to some original grant of the alleged right of way. The observations in their Lordships speeches must therefore be considered in the light of these facts and contentions. The Earl of Halsbury LC said, at p 231:

> ... the right contemplated by the Act ... means a right to exercise the right claimed *against the will of the person* over whose property it is sought to be exercised. It does not and cannot mean an user enjoyed from time to time *at the will and pleasure of the owner* of the property over which the user is sought. (My emphasis.)

In my view when Lord Halsbury uses the words 'against the will of the person' he means no more than without the licence of the owner. He is doing so more than contrasting the position where there is a licence for consideration and where there is no such licence.

Lord Ashbourne said, at pp 232–33:

> In the absence of direct evidence, all that can be said is that the payment is consistent with inferences which have been drawn by both sides. The defendants insist that the most obvious and natural inference is that it was made for rent, or for a series of annual licences, given possibly by implication. The plaintiff, on the other hand, urges that it was more probably a perpetual payment attached to some original grant of the right of way. Rigby LJ has speculated with persuasive force on the probability of such a hypothesis. If I felt free to speculate on the possible and probable origin of this payment, I would be glad to draw the same inference. The onus of explanation is, however, I think on the plaintiff ... I do not say that the case is free from difficulty, but I am unable to arrive at the conclusion that the plaintiff has discharged the onus which lay upon her of satisfactorily explaining that the payment of 15s a year was consistent with her claim. I therefore think that the appeal should be dismissed.

He thus put the matter simply on onus of proof. To the like effect is Lord Davey, at p 238:

> To put the case most favourably for the appellant, the payment is of an ambiguous character, and capable of either explanation. But one explanation is inconsistent with an enjoyment as of right, while the other is not so, and it is for the appellant to make out that she and her predecessors in title have enjoyed 'as of right' and for that purpose to shew which is the true explanation of the annual payment, and this she has not done.

I come finally to the speech of Lord Lindley, at p 239:

> A title by prescription can be established by long peaceable open enjoyment only; but in order that it may be so established the enjoyment must be inconsistent with any other reasonable inference than that it has been as of right in the sense above explained. This, I think, is the proper inference to be drawn from the authorities discussed in the court below. If the enjoyment is equally consistent with two reasonable inferences, enjoyment as of right is not established; and this, I think, is the real truth in the present case. The enjoyment is equally open to explanation in one of two ways, namely, by a lost grant of a right of way in consideration and of a rent charge on the plaintiff's land of 15s a year, or by a succession of yearly licences not, perhaps, expressed every year, but implied and assumed and paid for.

In my judgment that passage is of no assistance to the plaintiffs. There being one of two possible explanations of the annual payment of 15s. one of which would and the other of which would not establish the easement claimed and the plaintiff being unable to prove which was the correct one, she simply failed to make out the case.

The statement made must be related to the facts and cannot be regarded as a statement of principle for if it were no one could as it seems to me ever establish an easement by prescription or by the fiction of lost modern grant.

On examination none of the other cases cited, in my judgment, detract from the principles so clearly stated in *Sturges v Bridgman* (1879), 11 Ch D 852 and *Hollins v Verney* (1884), 13 QBD 304. The true approach is to determine the character of the acts of user or enjoyment relied on. If they are sufficient to amount to an assertion of a continuous right, continue for the requisite period, are actually or presumptively known to the owner of the servient tenement and such owner does nothing that is sufficient, as May LJ said in *Goldsmith v Burrow Construction Ltd*, Court of Appeal (Civil Division) Transcript No 750 of 1987:

> I agree with Mr Mowbray's submission that it is not merely a question of the servient owner saying 'I could have locked the gate and therefore there was no permission'. The facts in this case is that he did lock the gate.

Every servient owner can always say, until it is too late: 'I could have stopped it.' That is not enough.

I add only this, that any statement that the enjoyment must be against the will of the servient owner cannot mean more than 'without objection by the servient owner'. If it did, a claimant would have to prove that the right was contested and thereby defeat his own claim.

In *Simmons v Dobson*[253] the owner of two adjoining freeholds retained one and leased the other. The lease was subsequently assigned to the plaintiff. The retained land was leased to the defendants. The plaintiff had used a passage-way along two sides of their land to reach the road from the rear of his garden. The defendants blocked the passageway. The plaintiff claimed a right of way under the doctrine of lost modern grant. The claim failed.

Simmons v Dobson [1991] 1 WLR 720, CA

Fox LJ: The plaintiff's case is put in two ways: first, on the basis of the rule in *Wheeldon v Burrows* (1879) 12 Ch D 31 and secondly on the basis of lost modern grant. The assistant recorder, who gave a very full judgment, decided in favour of the plaintiff on both bases.

Wheeldon v Burrows decided that on the grant of part of a tenement there pass to the grantee, as easements, all quasi-easements over the retained land which (a) were continuous and apparent and (b) had been and were at the time of the grant used by the grantor for the benefit of the part granted. Mr Vickers for the plaintiff accepts that there was no evidence before the assistant recorder which could justify her conclusion that a right of way was established under *Wheeldon v Burrows*. He does not, therefore, seek to sustain the holding.

I come then to the contention that the plaintiff succeeds on the basis of lost modern grant. That doctrine arises from the inadequacies of common law prescription. At common law, acquisition of a prescriptive right depended upon the claimant establishing (amongst other things) the requisite period of user. Thus, common law prescription was based upon a presumed grant. The grant would be presumed only where the appropriate user had continued from time immemorial. That was fixed as the

253 [1991] 1 WLR 720.

year 1189; that date originated in a mediaeval statute. It was usually impossible to satisfy that test. Accordingly, the courts held that if user "as of right" for 20 years or more was established, continued user since 1189 would be presumed. That was satisfactory as far as it went, but there were gaps. In particular the presumption of immemorial user could be rebutted by showing that, at some time since 1189, the right did not exist. For example, an easement of light could not be claimed in respect of a house built after 1189.

It was because of the unsatisfactory nature of common law prescription that the doctrine of lost modern grant was introduced. It was judge-made. The doctrine presumed from long usage that an easement had, in fact, been granted since 1189 but the grant had got lost. The form which the doctrine took was, initially, that juries were told that from user during living memory, or even during 20 years, they could presume a lost grant. After a time the jury were recommended to make that finding and finally they were directed to do so. Nobody believed that there ever was a grant. But it was a convenient and workable fiction. The doctrine was ultimately approved by the House of Lords in *Dalton v Henry Angus & Co* (1881) 6 App Cas 740.

Now in relation to common law prescription generally, user had to be by or on behalf of a fee simple owner against a fee simple owner. An easement can be granted expressly by a tenant for life or tenant for years so as to bind their respective limited interests, but such rights cannot be acquired by prescription: see *Wheaton v Maple & Co* [1893] 3 Ch 48 and *Kilgour v Gaddes* [1904] 1 KB 457. Thus, Lindley LJ in the former case said [1893] 3 Ch 48, 63:

> The whole theory of prescription at common law is against presuming any grant or covenant not to interrupt, by or with any one except an owner in fee. A right claimed by prescription must be claimed as appendant or appurtenant to land, and not as annexed to it for a term of years.

In *Kilgour v Gaddes* [1904] 1 KB 457 that was cited with approval by Collins MR, at p 465. Mathew LJ said, at p 467:

> I agree. In this case the fee simple of the supposed dominant and servient tenements belonged to the same person. It is clear that, under such circumstances, an easement like a right of way could not have been created by prescription at common law. Such an easement can only be acquired by prescription at common law where the dominant and servient tenements respectively belong to different owners in fee, the essential nature of such an easement being that it is a right acquired by the owner in fee of the dominant tenement against the owner in fee of the servient tenement. If authorities were necessary for that proposition, the case of *Wheaton v Maple & Co* [1893] 3 Ch 48 and 2 Wms. Saunders, 175(f), (i), would suffice.

In *Derry v Sanders* [1919] 1 KB 223, 237, Scrutton LJ said:

> It is established by decisions binding on this court that one tenant cannot acquire an easement of way by prescription against another tenant holding of the same landlord: *Kilgour v Gaddes*. This has the result that in parts of the country where lands are let for 99 or even 999 years, no right of way can be acquired between two tenements where they have the same owner in fee simple.

In *Cory v Davies* [1923] 2 Ch 95, 107–08, PO Lawrence J said:

> It is well settled that a lessee cannot acquire a right of way over the land of another lessee under the same lessor, either by prescription at common law or under the doctrine of a lost grant or by prescription under the Prescription Act 1832 ...

It is common ground that at all material times the fee simple of numbers 151 and 153 has been vested in the same person.

Against that background I take the view that, as a matter of authority, it is established that one tenant cannot acquire an easement by prescription at common law against another tenant holding under the same landlord. The position is, I think, the same in relation to s 2 of the Prescription Act 1832 (2 & 3 Will 4, c 71). The purpose of that section is to shorten the period required by common law prescription to 20 years prior to the bringing of the action. In *Dalton v Henry Angus & Co* (1881) 6 App Cas 740, 800, Lord Selborne LC said:

> The effect of [s 2], as I understand it, is to apply the law of prescription, properly so called, to an easement enjoyed as of right for 20 years, subject to all defences to which a claim by prescription would previously have been open, except that of showing a commencement within time of legal memory.

What we are concerned with here is neither common law prescription strictly so called nor a claim under the Prescription Act 1832 but a claim based on the lost modern grant doctrine. The question is whether the restrictive rule as to prescription by and against leaseholders applies to cases of lost modern grant.

In terms of practicalities, it is difficult to see if one were starting from scratch that there is serious objection to leaseholders prescribing against each other for the duration of their limited interests (but it has to be said that to introduce such a rule retrospectively now could affect what was hitherto bought and sold as clear titles). And, as Mr Vickers says, in a modern, urban situation it is hard to see why two householders on one side of the street should be able to prescribe for easements against each other's land because each holds in fee simple while on the other side of the street one leaseholder under the residue of a 999-year lease can for 20 years or more walk along a path at the back of his neighbour's garden (also held on a long lease) without acquiring any rights in respect thereof. That, however, is the way the law has gone in England. The point about long leaseholds held of the same landlord was recognised by Scrutton LJ in the passage in *Derry v Sanders* [1919] 1 KB 223, 237, to which I have referred, where he regarded the law as clear.

In *Wheaton v Maple & Co* [1893] 3 Ch 48, 63, Lindley LJ said:

> ... I am not aware of any authority for presuming, as a matter of law, a lost grant by a lessee for years in the case of ordinary easements, or a lost covenant by such a person not to interrupt in the case of light, and I am certainly not prepared to introduce another fiction to support a claim to a novel prescriptive right.

He then continued with the passage as to the theory of the common law prescription to which I have already referred.

The statements of Scrutton LJ and PO Lawrence J to which I have referred are wholly in line with Lindley LJ's view. Moreover, Collins MR in *Kilgour v Gaddes* [1904] 1 KB 457, 465 plainly agreed with Lindley LJ's exposition of the law in *Wheaton v Maple & Co* [1893] 3 Ch 48 and the tenor of the judgments of Romer and Mathew LJJ in *Kilgour v Gaddes* [1904] 1 KB 457 is that they agreed with it also.

While, therefore, there appears to be no case which directly decides that there can be no lost modern grant by or to a person who owns a lesser estate than the fee, the dicta are to the contrary and are very strong and of long standing. I take them to represent settled law. I should mention for completeness that the law in Ireland has gone the other way: *Flynn v Harte* [1913] 2 IR 322 and *Tallon v Ennis* [1937] IR 549.

As to any departure from that state of the law, there are, I think difficulties of principle. It is clear that common law prescription and prescription under the Act of 1832 are, as a matter of decision, not available by or to owners of less estates than the fee. Lost modern grant is merely a form of common law prescription. It is based upon a fiction which was designed to meet, and did meet, a particular problem. It would, I think, be anomalous to extend the fiction further by departure, in relation to lost modern grant, from the fundamental principle of common law prescription referred to by Lindley LJ.

I would allow the appeal.

McCowan LJ and Beldam LJ agreed.

Having established the three requirements, the claimant must show that he has acquired the right by one of the three methods of prescription:

(a) Common law

The right must have been enjoyed since 1189. But if the claimant can show that the right has been enjoyed for more than 20 years there is a presumption that the right has been enjoyed before 1189.[254] This presumption can be rebutted by showing that the user could not have been enjoyed at all before 1189, eg if you claim an easement of light coming through an aperture in your building under this head, proof that the building was built after 1189 would rebut the presumption.[255]

(b) Lost modern grant

Under this doctrine, if the claimant can show that he has enjoyed the right for 20 years, there is a presumption that a grant of easement has been made by deed after 1189 but that the deed has been misplaced or lost.[256] This presumption can be rebutted by showing that at some time during the 20 years of user, no person was capable of making the grant or receiving the grant.[257] The presumption, however, cannot be rebutted by evidence that no such grant was in fact made.[258]

However, it is not possible to claim a right of light under the doctrine of lost modern grant against owners of buildings in London because of the custom of London that a man may rebuild his house upon ancient foundations to what height he pleased even though ancient lights were stopped.[259]

(c) Prescription Act 1832

The purpose of the Act is to overcome the difficulties in acquiring easement at common law or under the doctrine of lost modern grant. The Act provides that if a right of common or profit *à prendre* has been enjoyed for 30 years before the

254 *Angus & Co v Dalton* (1877) 3 QBD 85 at 105; *Darling v Clue* (1864) 4 F & F 329 at 334.

255 *Duke of Norfolk v Arbuthnot* (1880) 5 CPD 390.

256 *Bryant v Foot* (1867) LR 2 QB 161 at 181; *Dalton v Angus & Co* (1881) 6 App Cas 740.

257 *Rochdale Canal Co v Radcliffe* (1852) 18 QB 287; *Oakley v Boston* [1976] QB 270.

258 *Tehidy Minerals Ltd v Norman* [1971] 2 QB 528 at 552.

259 *Plummer v Bentham* (1757) 1 Burr 248; *Perry v Eames* [1891] 1 Ch 658; *Bowring Services Ltd v Scottish Widows' Fund & Life Assurance Society* [1995] 1 EGLR 158.

action is brought, the claim to the right shall not be defeated merely by proving that the right was enjoyed after 1189 and if it has been enjoyed for 60 years, it shall be absolute unless enjoyed by written consent or agreement.[260] In the case of easements other than easements of light, the periods are 20 years and 40 years respectively.[261] In the case of a right of light, if it has been uninterruptedly enjoyed for 20 years, it shall be absolute unless enjoyed by written consent or agreement.[262]

The periods specified are periods *next before some suit or action* wherein the claim is brought into question.[263] This means that there must be an uninterrupted enjoyment for the period which immediately precedes and which terminates in an action.[264] For example, suppose a claimant can show that he has enjoyed a right of way over an adjoining land since 1924, but there is evidence that from 1952 to 1954 he had been the owner of the adjoining land. If the action in which the claim was made was brought in 1964, the claim under the Act would fail because he has only enjoyed uninterrupted use of the way for a period of 10 years immediately before the action. But if the action is brought in 1994, the claim will succeed because prior to the action there is an uninterrupted use of the way for a period of 40 years.

The period of enjoyment must be uninterrupted. Interruption means some act or obstruction which shows that the easement is disputed.[265] Section 4 of the 1832 Act provides that no act or obstruction is to be deemed an interruption for the purposes of the Act unless it has been submitted to or acquiesced in by the dominant owner for one year after he had notice of the interruption and of the person responsible therefor.

A notional obstruction of the right to light for a period exceeding 12 months which will defeat the claim under the 1832 Act can be made by registering an obstruction notice under s 3(2) of the Rights of Light Act 1959,[266] unless the claimant brings proceedings for obstruction before the end of the notice.

5 EXTINGUISHMENT OF EASEMENTS AND PROFITS

Easements may be extinguished in the following ways:

Statutory extinguishment

Easements may be extinguished by statute. Examples are ss 118 and 127 of the Town and Country Planning Act 1971, s 295 of the Housing Act 1985, s 19 of the

260 Section 1 of the Prescription Act 1832.

261 *Ibid*, s 2.

262 *Ibid*, s 3.

263 *Ibid*, s 4.

264 *Jones v Price* (1836) 3 Bing NC 52; *Parker v Mitchell* (1840) 11 Ad & El 788; *Hyman v Van den Bergh* [1908] 1 Ch 167.

265 *Carr v Foster* (1842) 3 QB 581.

266 For example, *Bowring Services Ltd v Scottish Widows' Fund & Life Assurance Society* [1995] 1 EGLR 158. For the background to the 1959 Act see Timothy Lloyd QC's judgment at 159G–60C.

New Towns Act 1981, etc where the certain acquiring authorities are able to extinguish all easements enjoyed over land acquired.

Unity of ownership and possession

Easements and profits are extinguished automatically if at any time the dominant and servient lands come into the ownership of the same person.[267] Where there is a mere unity of possession without unity of ownership, the easement is merely suspended and not destroyed.[268] Once the unity of possession is severed, the easement revives.

Release

An easement or profit may be released either expressly or impliedly.

(a) Express release

An express release must be by deed.[269] An easement or profit may, however, be released in equity by an informal agreement supported by consideration given by the servient owner or where it would be inequitable for the dominant owner to deny the extinguishment.[270]

(b) Implied release

An easement or profit may be extinguished by abandonment.[271] Non-user does not in itself amount to abandonment since 'it is one thing not to assert an intention to use a way, and another thing to assert an intention to abandon it'.[272] Neither could a short-lived cessation of user,[273] nor an agreed temporary suspension of a user[274] amount to abandonment. The dominant owner must express a clear intention 'never at any time thereafter to assert the right himself or to attempt to transmit it to anyone else'.[275]

The court has, in the past, been prepared to presume an intention to abandon where there is a discontinuation of user for 20 years without explanation for the non-user from the dominant owner.[276] However, the court now recognises that the dominant owner is not likely to abandon lightly such a valuable latent property which might be of considerable value in the future. Thus, it requires only very simple explanation for the non-user. In *Benn v*

---

267 *Tyrringham's* case (1584) 4 Co Rep 36b at 38a; 76 ER 973 at 980.

268 *Thomas v Thomas* (1835) 2 Cr M & R 34 at 40; 150 ER 15 at 17.

269 *Lovell v Smith* (1857) 3 CB (NS) 120 at 126; 140 ER 685 at 687.

270 *Davies v Marshall* (1861) 10 CB (NS) 697 at 710; 142 ER 627 at 633.

271 *Swan v Sinclair* [1924] 1 Ch 254 at 266.

272 *James v Stevenson* [1893] AC 162 at 168.

273 *Bulstrode v Lambert* [1953] 2 WLR 1064 at 1068.

274 *Payne v Sheddon* (1834) 1 Mood & R 382 at 383.

275 *Tehidy Minerals Ltd v Norman* [1971] 2 QB 528 at 553D; *Huckvale v Aegean Hotels Ltd* (1989) 58 P & CR 163 at 167, 171.

276 *Moore v Rawson* (1824) 3 B & C 332 at 339; 107 ER 756 at 759.

Hardinge,[277] the Court of Appeal refused to presume an intention to abandon a right of way even after a period of non-user of 175 years because the dominant owner was able to give a simple explanation that throughout this period the successive dominant owners had enjoyed an alternative means of access to their land.[278] Where the dominant owner has accepted a licence from the servient owner, the terms of which make it impossible for the easement and the licence to be exercised at the same time, the easement is impliedly abandoned.[279]

Unlike restrictive covenants,[280] there is no statutory provision for the discharge or modification of obsolete easements or profits. The courts have left the question open whether an easement can be discharged through change of circumstances.[281] In *Huckvale v Aegean Hotels Ltd*, the Court of Appeal did not rule out altogether the possibility of an easement being extinguished when it ceases to accommodate the dominant land.[282] Slade LJ, however, said that:

> In the absence of evidence of proof of abandonment, the court should be slow to hold that an easement has been extinguished by frustration, unless the evidence shows clearly that because of a change of circumstances since the date of the original grant there is no practical possibility of its ever again benefiting the dominant tenement in the matter contemplated by that grant.[283]

6 ACCESS TO NEIGHBOURING LAND ACT 1992[284]

At common law, without the neighbour's permission, a landowner has no right of access to a neighbouring land to carry out from there any necessary works on his own land.[285] This can be extremely inconvenient for a landowner who needs to enter the neighbouring land for repair. The Law of Commission's proposed changes to the law to overcome this problem were put into effect by the Access to Neighbouring Land Act 1992.[286] Under s 1 the court may make an 'access order' giving a landowner the right of access to adjoining or adjacent land to do works that are reasonably necessary for the preservation of his land if the works cannot be carried out (or would be substantially more difficult to be carried out) without entering the adjoining or adjacent land. The neighbouring owner will, where appropriate, receive compensation and, unless the applicant's property is residential land, be awarded fair and reasonable consideration reflecting the

---

277 (1992) *The Times*, 13 October.

278 See also *Gotobed v Pridmore* (1970) 115 Sol Jo 78; *Williams v Usherwood* (1983) 45 P & CR 235 at 256; *Snell & Prideaux Ltd v Dutton Mittors Ltd* [1995] 1 EGLR 259.

279 *Bosomworth v Faber* (1995) 69 P & CR 288.

280 Under s 84 of the LPA 1925. See Chapter 14, pp 800–02.

281 *Huckvale v Aegean Hotels Ltd* (1989) 58 P & CR 163, CA.

282 (1989) 58 P & CR 163 at 170, 172. See also [1990] Conv 292 (Kodilinye, G).

283 (1989) 58 P & CR 163 at 173.

284 Came into force on 31 January 1993 (SI 1992 No 3349); see [1992] Conv 225 (Wilkinson, HW).

285 *John Trenberth Ltd v National Westminster Bank Ltd* (1979) 39 P & CR 104 at 105.

286 Law Commission, *Rights of Access to Neighbouring Land* (Law Com No 151, Cmnd 9692, December 1985).

financial benefit to the applicant. The access order is for a short-term limited-purpose only. But it will bind successors in title to the adjoining or adjacent land if it is registered in the register of writs and orders affecting land under the Land Charges Act 1972[287] in unregistered land or protected by an entry of a notice or caution in registered land.[288]

7 REFORM

The law on easements and profits by prescription has been the subject of a Law Reform Committee's report entitled 'Acquisition of Easements and Profits by Prescription'[289] which recommended the abolition of the prescriptive acquisition of easements and profits. It also recommended a new system, should prescriptive acquisition of easements be retained. The proposals are summarised by the Law Reform Committee as follows.

Law Reform Committee, Fourteenth Report: Acquisition of Easements and Profits by Prescription (Cmnd 3100), October 1966

SUMMARY OF RECOMMENDATIONS

99. Our recommendations may be summarised as follows:

(1) In respect of both easements and profits *à prendre* prescription at common law and under the doctrine of a lost modern grant should be abolished (para 40).

(2) The Prescription Act 1832 should be repealed in its entirety (para 40).

(3) As regards profits, the Committee unanimously recommend (subject to the same transitional provisions as are recommended for easements) the discontinuance of all forms of prescription (para 98).

(4) As regards easements other than rights of support, eight members of the Committee recommend that no new system of prescription should be adopted (paras 32–36).

(5) Six members of the Committee recommend that for these easements a simplified and improved statutory system should be substituted for the existing forms of prescription (paras 37 and 38).

(6) If it were decided to substitute a new system, the following method should be adopted:

(i) The prescriptive period should be 12 years (para 41);

(ii) This period should be a period in gross, not one before action brought (paras 42 and 43);

(iii) Periods when servient land is occupied by an infant, a person of unsound mind, a married woman, or a tenant for life or for years should no longer be excluded from time counted for the purposes of prescription, nor should the time when an abated action was pending (para 44);

---

287 Section 6(1)(d) of the LCA 1972 as added by s 5(1) of the 1992 Act.

288 Section 49(1)(j) of the LRA 1925 as added by s 5(2) of the 1992 Act.

289 (1966), Cmnd 3100. See (1967) 30 MLR 189 (Wilkinson, HW).

(iv) Prescription should cease to be related to a presumed lost grant, but only rights capable of subsisting as easements should be capable of being acquired by prescription (para 45);

(v) A prescriptive easement should be capable of being acquired against the owner of a limited interest in the servient land so as to subsist as long as that servient owner's interest subsists (para 47);

(vi) Where the servient owner is a tenant for life or has the powers of a tenant for life of the servient land, an easement should be capable of being acquired against him by prescription to the full extent that he could grant one under the Settled Land Act 1925 (para 48);

(vii) Where a person is in occupation of the servient land in virtue of a beneficial interest under a trust for sale, his occupation should be regarded as that of the trustees (para 48);

(viii) The owner of a limited interest in the dominant tenement should continue, as at present, to be capable of obtaining a prescriptive title which will enure for the benefit of the freeholder (para 50);

(ix) A tenant should be able to prescribe against his own landlord and *vice versa* (para 51);

(x) No one for whom it would be *ultra vires* to acquire the easement by grant should be capable of acquiring such easement by prescription, but de facto enjoyment by such a person should be available to support a prescriptive claim by a successor in title (para 52);

(xi) Incapacity to make a grant on the part of a servient owner should not bar a prescriptive claim (para 53);

(xii) Enjoyment by force should not count in favour of the dominant owner (para 57);

(xiii) Enjoyment by the dominant owner must have been actually known to the servient owner or such that he ought reasonably to have known of it (para 58);

(xiv) Enjoyment must also have been of such a kind and frequency as, apart from consent or agreement, would only be justified by the existence of an easement (para 59);

(xv) It must also conduce to the beneficial enjoyment of ascertainable land of the dominant owner (para 60);

(xvi) Enjoyment by consent or agreement, whether written or oral, should not count, and the effect of consent or agreement should be assimilated to that of interruption. A consent or agreement which is indefinite as to its intended duration should operate only for, say, one year (paras 61–63);

(xvii) Notional interruption, on lines similar to those adopted in the Rights of Light Act 1959, should be made available in respect of all kinds of easements. This should be by registration against the dominant land in the local land charges register after notices given by registered post to the occupier of the dominant land and by advertisement (paras 64 to 69).

(xviii) Interruption, whether actual or notional, should endure for 12 months if it is to be effective in stopping time running (para 75);

(xix) If a workable statutory formula can be found, an easement acquired by prescription should be of the like character, extent and degree as the use enjoyed throughout the prescriptive period by the dominant owner (paras 76–79);

(xx) Where a dominant owner, having acquired an easement by prescription, thereafter for a sufficient period enjoys an easement of a more onerous character over the servient land, he should be prescriptively entitled to a new easement of the more burdensome character (para 80);

(xxi) Where a dominant owner, having acquired an easement by prescription, thereafter fails to make use of it to its full extent, this should not prejudice his right to the easement (para 80);

(xxii) Where a dominant owner, having acquired an easement by prescription, makes no use of it for a continuous period of 12 years, he should thereupon cease to be entitled to the easement (para 81).

(7) Whether prescription is abolished or a new system introduced, there should be a transitional period of 12 years at the end of which:

(a) recommendations (1) and (2) should take effect,

(b) any dominant enjoyment which had continued uninterrupted throughout the transitional period should confer a prescriptive title (paras 82 and 83).

(8) In relation to the support of buildings by land and the support of buildings by other buildings, a new code of rights and procedure should be introduced (paras 89 and 90).

(9) In relation to rights of support and other matters where a building is in the future subdivided into several units of ownership, a code of minimum obligations should be introduced in accordance with the recommendations of the Wilberforce Committee (para 93).

(10) In relation to existing buildings already subdivided into several units of ownership, the court or the Lands Tribunal should be empowered to make orders imposing rights of support, etc, on such conditions as to payment of compensation or otherwise as may be fair (para 94).

(11) As to rights of support, there should be a transitional period of 3 years during which servient owners against whom prescriptive easements of support are accruing might apply to the Lands Tribunal for an order for payment of compensation (para 95).

(12) Shelter of a building by an adjoining building, or of one part by another (lateral or superjacent) part of the same building, should be treated similarly to support (para 96).

(13) The Lands Tribunal should be empowered to discharge easements or substitute more convenient easements for existing easements on payment, where appropriate, of compensation (para 97).

CHAPTER 16

MORTGAGES

1 INTRODUCTION

Land, being immovable property and of a nature whereby it does not normally perish (although the character may change), it is often the best form of security for a loan. A landowner may grant an interest in his land as security (known as a mortgage) in favour of a person in return for a loan. The effect of a mortgage on land is to confer on the creditor a security for his loan so that if the debtor is in default of payment, the creditor is able to take the land, sell it and discharge the money owed. Such a creditor is a secured creditor and takes priority over unsecured creditors when the debtor is in liquidation or insolvency.

The facility of mortgage in modern time has played an important role in commercial activities and home ownership. Examples of institutions in the business of lending money on mortgage security are building societies, banks, finance companies and local authorities. There are various types of mortgage. The most common type of mortgage is perhaps the ordinary repayment mortgage. The capital is repayable over a specified term (usually 20 or 25 years). The monthly repayments during the early years of the mortgage term will comprise largely interest, but the relative proportions of interest and capital will alter during the course of the term until at the end of the term all of the capital and interest will have been paid off. The amount of monthly payment may vary from time to time as the interest rates change. There is the endowment mortgage where the entire capital is left outstanding during the mortgage term. The mortgagor only makes monthly payments of interest. However, the mortgagee will require the mortgagor to take a life assurance policy and assigns it to the mortgagee which will pay off the whole amount of the capital of the loan at the end of the mortgage term or in the event of the earlier death of the mortgagor. So the mortgagor must also pay for the premiums on the policy during the mortgage term. The third type of mortgage is the fixed-rate mortgage. This is similar to the ordinary repayment mortgage except with a fixed-rate mortgage the interest rate is guaranteed unchanged for an initial period (normally the first two or three years). This type of mortgage is increasingly common from banks and building societies. An ordinary repayment or a fixed-rate mortgage may also be combined with a mortgage protection policy. The mortgagor is still required to make monthly payments as usual and if he survives the mortgage term the policy will do nothing to the mortgage, but if he should die before the end of the mortgage term the policy will pay off the amount outstanding on the mortgage.

There is a technical distinction between a mortgage and a charge. A mortgage is a legal or equitable interest in land granted to the creditor as a security for the payment of a debt subject to the debtor's right of redemption.

The debtor is called the mortgagor and the creditor is called the mortgagee. Where a mortgage is granted by the mortgagee, the mortgagor has a legal or equitable interest in the mortgaged land conveyed to him.

A charge is different from a mortgage. In the case of a charge, the debtor (the charger) charges his land in favour of the creditor (the chargee) as security for the loan. Although a charge is, in itself, a legal or equitable interest in land, it does not convey a legal or equitable interest in the mortgaged land to the chargee. It only gives the chargee certain rights (eg rights of possession or sale). However, as the legal chargee has the same rights as the legal mortgagee, the distinction is not significant in practice.[1]

2 CREATION OF LEGAL MORTGAGES

Prior to 1926

A legal mortgage can only be granted over a legal estate or interest. Historically, a legal mortgage over a freehold land was created by a conveyance by the mortgagor of his fee simple estate to the mortgagee subject to a covenant for the mortgagee to reconvey the fee simple to the mortgagor when he redeemed the mortgage. To create a legal mortgage over a leasehold land, the mortgagor assigned the residue of his lease to the mortgagee subject to a proviso for the mortgagee to reassign the lease on repayment of the loan. So the mortgagee's security was the mortgagor's legal title in the land mortgaged. At common law, the mortgagor could not redeem the mortgage before or after the date fixed by the mortgage. He had to repay on the fixed day of redemption. If the mortgagor failed to redeem the mortgage by that date the mortgagee was entitled to retain the property for ever and the mortgagor remained liable for the debt.[2]

By the beginning of 17th century, equity began to intervene to redress this drastic consequence.[3] It allowed the mortgagor to redeem even after the fixed date has passed[4] but not before the fixed date[5] unless the date of redemption had been postponed to such an extent that it was unconscionable[6] or that the right became useless or if the mortgagee had sought payment, eg by taking possession.[7] However, if the mortgagor had not redeemed long after the due date, the mortgagee could apply to the court for a decree of foreclosure terminating the mortgagor's right of redemption.[8] But if the value of the

1 The Law Commission thought that the distinction is unnecessarily confusing and the two concepts should be amalgamated: Law Com No 204, paras 2.14–2.16.

2 *Kreglinger v New Patagonia Meat and Cold Storage Co Ltd* [1914] AC 25 at 35.

3 HEL, Vol v, 330–332.

4 *Salt v Marquess of Northampton* [1892] AC 1 at 18.

5 *Brown v Cole* (1845) 14 Sim 427; 60 ER 424.

6 *Knightsbridge Estate v Byrne* [1939] Ch 441.

7 *Bovill v Endle* [1896] 1 Ch 648; 65 LJ Ch 542.

8 *How v Vigures* (1628) 1 Ch Rep 32; HEL, Vol v, 331–32. When a mortgagee of land has been in possession of the mortgaged land for a period of 12 years, the mortgagor will lose the right to redeem: s 16 of the Limitations Act 1980.

property was more than the loan the court would order a sale of the property and the mortgagee would return the balance to the mortgagor after satisfying his debts.[9]

The mortgagor's right to redeem after the legal date of redemption is called the equitable right of redemption. It arises only when the legal date of redemption has passed.[10] This must not be confused with the mortgagor's equity of redemption, a term which is used to describe the sum total of the mortgagor's right of ownership subject to the mortgage, ie the legal right to redeem on the date of redemption and to have the land reconveyed to him on redemption plus the equitable right of redemption. The equity of redemption arises as soon as the mortgage is created.[11] It is an equitable interest in land which can be conveyed, devised, settled, leased or mortgaged, just like any other interest in land.[12] As the mortgagor only had an equity of redemption, any subsequent mortgage he granted must necessarily be equitable.

After 1925

Law of Property Act 1925

85. Mode of mortgaging freehold

(1) A mortgage of an estate in fee simple shall only be capable of being effected at law either by a demise for a term of years absolute, subject to a provision for cesser on redemption, or by a charge by deed expressed to be by way of legal mortgage:

Provided that a first mortgagee shall have the same right to the possession of documents as if his security included the fee simple.

(2) Any purported conveyance of an estate in fee simple by way of mortgage made after the commencement of this Act shall (to the extent of the estate of the mortgagor) operate as a demise of the land to the mortgagee for a term of years absolute, without impeachment for waste, but subject to cesser on redemption, in manner following, namely:-

(a) A first or only mortgagee shall take a term of three thousand years from the date of the mortgage:

(b) A second or subsequent mortgagee shall take a term (commencing from the date of the mortgage) one day longer than the term vested in the first or other mortgagee whose security ranks immediately before that of such second or subsequent mortgagee:

and, in this subsection, any such purported conveyance as aforesaid includes an absolute conveyance with a deed of defeasance and any other assurance which, but for this subsection, would operate in effect to vest the fee simple in a mortgagee subject to redemption.

9 Megarry and Wade, p 917.

10 *Brown v Cole* (1845) 14 Sim 427.

11 *Kreglinger v New Patagonia Meat & Cold Storage Co Ltd* [1914] AC 25 at 48.

12 *Casborne v Scarfe* (1738) 1 Atk 603 at 605.

(3) This section applies whether or not the land is registered under the Land Registration Act 1925, or the mortgage is expressed to be made by way of trust or otherwise.

86. Mode of mortgaging leaseholds

(1) A mortgage of a term of years absolute shall only be capable of being effected at law either by a subdemise for a term of years absolute, less by one day at least than the term vested in the mortgagor, and subject to a provision for cesser on redemption, or by a charge by deed expressed to be by way of legal mortgage; and where a licence to subdemise by way of mortgage is required, such licence shall not be unreasonably refused;

Provided that a first mortgagee shall have the same right to the possession of documents as if his security had been effected by assignment.

(2) Any purported assignment of a term of years absolute by way of mortgage made after the commencement of this Act shall (to the extent of the estate of the mortgagor) operate as a subdemise of the leasehold land to the mortgagee for a term of years absolute, but subject to cesser on redemption, in manner following, namely:

(a) The term to be taken by a first or only mortgagee shall be ten days less than the term expressed to be assigned;

(b) The term to be taken by a second or subsequent mortgagee shall be one day longer than the term vested in the first or other mortgagee whose security ranks immediately before that of the second or subsequent mortgagee, if the length of the last mentioned term permits, and in any case for a term less by one day at least than the term expressed to be assigned;

and, in this subsection, any such purported assignment as aforesaid includes an absolute assignment with a deed of defeasance and any other assurance which, but for this subsection, would operate in effect to vest the term of the mortgagor in a mortgagee subject to redemption.

(3) This section applies whether or not the land is registered under the Land Registration Act 1925, or the mortgage is made by way of sub-mortgage of a term of years absolute, or is expressed to be by way of trust for sale or otherwise.

87. Charges by way of legal mortgage

(1) Where a legal mortgage of land is created by a charge by deed expressed to be by way of legal mortgage, the mortgagee shall have the same protection, powers and remedies (including the right to take proceedings to obtain possession from the occupiers and the persons in receipt of rents and profits, or any of them) as if:

(a) where the mortgage is a mortgage of an estate in fee simple, a mortgage term for 3,000 years without impeachment of waste had been thereby created in favour of the mortgagee; and

(b) where the mortgage is a mortgage of a term of years absolute, a sub-term less by one day than the term vested in the mortgagor had been thereby created in favour of the mortgagee.

After 1925, there are two ways of creating a legal mortgage of freehold or leasehold land:

(a) Legal mortgage of freehold land

The old common law methods of creating a mortgage are abolished. It is impossible today to create a legal estate by the conveyance and reconveyance of the freehold. Any attempt to mortgage a freehold by the old common law method operates as a demise of the land to the mortgagee for a term of 3,000 years under s 85(2)(a) of the Law of Property Act 1925. Section 85(1) of the Law of Property Act 1925 provides that a legal mortgage of freehold land can only be created either by a demise (a grant of a lease) for a term of years absolute subject to a provision for cesser on redemption, or by a charge by deed expressed to be by way of legal mortgage.

(i) Legal mortgage by demise for a term of years absolute

This is, technically, a mortgage since it involves the grant of a substantial legal estate to the mortgagee. The mortgagor grants a long lease (usually a term of 3,000 years) to the mortgagee subject to the mortgagor's right of redemption. The legal date of redemption is normally six months after the grant. The mortgagor still holds the legal fee simple but the mortgagee has a legal estate – a term of years absolute which is binding on the mortgagor. This is not commonly used today.[13]

Legal mortgage[14]

THIS MORTGAGE is made the first day of January 1984 between A of etc. (hereinafter called the borrower) of the one part and B of etc (hereinafter called the lender) of the other part

WHEREAS:

(1) The borrower is seised in fee simple in possession free from encumbrances of the property hereby mortgaged

(2) The lender has agreed with the borrower to lend him the sum of £20,000 upon having the repayment thereof with interest thereon secured in the manner hereinafter appearing

NOW THIS DEED made in pursuance of the said agreement and in consideration of the sum of £20,000 now paid to the borrower by the lender (the receipt whereof the borrower hereby acknowledges)

WITNESSETH as follows::

1. The borrower hereby covenants with the lender to pay to the lender on the first day of July next the said sum of £20,000 with interest thereon from the date of this deed at the rate of £10% *per annum* and further if the said moneys shall not be so paid to pay to the lender interest at the rate aforesaid by equal half-yearly payments on the first day of January and first day of July in every year on the moneys for the time being remaining due on this security.

2. The borrower hereby demises unto the lender with [full/limited] title guarantee ALL THAT the property more particularly described in the Schedule

---

13 The Law Commission (Law Com No 204) thought that mortgage by demise is an inappropriate form as it creates an artificial relationship of landlord and tenant (para 2.18) and it is difficult to justify its continued existence given that it is no longer used in practice and has the same effect in law as the charge by way of legal mortgage (para 2.13).

14 Reproduced with kind permission from Megarry and Wade, pp 929–30.

hereto TO HOLD unto the lender for a term of 3,000 years from the date hereof without impeachment of waste subject to the proviso for cesser on redemption hereinafter contained PROVIDED ALWAYS that if the borrower shall on the first day of July next pay to the lender the sum of £20,000 with interest thereon in the meantime at the rate of £10% *per annum,* then and in such case the said term hereby granted shall absolutely cease and determine.

3. The borrower hereby covenants with the lender and it is hereby agreed and declared as follows:

[Here follow covenants by the mortgagor to repair, insure, etc. and any other terms agreed upon]

IN WITNESS, etc

Schedule

(ii) Legal mortgage by a charge by way of legal mortgage

This is the most commonly used method of creating a legal mortgage today. It is technically a charge but in substance it is the same as the mortgage by demise. The mortgagor simply executes a deed charging his land by way of legal mortgage with the repayment of the sums specified. Although the mortgagee is not granted a lease, and only obtains a charge, s 87(1) of the Law of Property Act 1925 gives him the same protection, powers and remedies (including the right to take proceedings to obtain possession) as if a lease of 3,000 years had been granted in his favour. So for most practical purposes, a charge is as good as a mortgage.

SCHEDULE 5

FORMS OF INSTRUMENTS

FORM No 1

CHARGE BY WAY OF LEGAL MORTGAGE

This Legal Charge is made [etc] between A of [etc] of the one part and B of [etc] of the other part.

[Recite the title of A to the freeholds or leaseholds in the Schedule and agreement for the loan by B.]

Now in consideration of the sum of .. .. .. pounds now paid by B to A (the receipt etc) this Deed witnesseth as follows:

1. A hereby covenants with B to pay [Add the requisite covenant to pay principal and interest).
2. A as Beneficial Owner hereby charges by way of legal mortgage All and Singular the property mentioned in the Schedule hereto with the payment to B of the principal money, interest, and other money hereby covenanted to be paid by A.
3. [Add covenant to insure buildings and any other provisions desired.]

In witness [etc] [Add Schedule].

NOTE – B will be in the same position as if a mortgage had been effected by a demise of freeholds or a subdemise of leaseholds.

(b) Legal mortgage of leasehold land

Just like a legal mortgage of freehold, under s 86(1) of the Law of Property Act 1925 a legal mortgage of leasehold land can only be created either by a subdemise for a term of years absolute, less by one day at least than the term vested in the mortgagor, subject to a provision for cesser on redemption, or by a charge by deed expressed to be by way of legal mortgage. Under s 86(2)(a) any attempt to use the old common law method of assignment of the lease operates as a subdemise of the leasehold land to the first or only mortgagee for a term equivalent to the term expressly assigned less by ten days, subject to cesser on redemption. If the purported assignment is made to a second or subsequent mortgagee, the term he takes should be one day longer than the term of the first or other mortgagee.

(i) Legal mortgage by subdemise

The mortgagor grants a sublease to the mortgagee which is less by one day at least than the term of the mortgagor's lease. If the mortgagor needs the original lessor's consent in granting a sublease by way of mortgage consent must not be unreasonably refused. This is again not very commonly used.

(ii) Legal mortgage by charge

Like freehold estate, a legal mortgage of leasehold estate may be created by a charge by deed expressed to be by way of legal mortgage. The chargee enjoys the same protection as if he has been given a sublease for a term less by one day than the mortgagor's term.[15] Here, since the mortgagor does not actually create a sublease, the grant of a charge will not amount to a breach of the covenant against subletting.[16]

As after 1925, the mortgagor retains the legal fee simple together with the equity of redemption, he can create many subsequent legal mortgages over the legal fee simple he retains. Any grant of a legal mortgage must, of course, be made by deed.[17]

Registered land

Where the title of the freehold or leasehold is registered, the following points must be noted:

(a) The registered proprietor of a registered land may, subject to any entry to the contrary on the register, mortgage, by deed or otherwise, the land or any part of it in any manner which would have been permissible if the land had been unregistered.[18] In addition to the ss 85 and 86 Law of Property Act 1925 methods of creating a legal mortgage, the proprietor of registered land may

15 Section 87(1)(b) of the LPA 1925.

16 *Gentle v Faulkner* [1900] 2 QB 267; *Matthews v Smallwood* [1910] 1 Ch 777.

17 Section 52(1) of the LPA 1925. 'Mortgage' comes within the definitionof 'conveyance': s 205(1)(ii) of the LPA 1925.

18 Section 106(1) of the LRA 1925.

simply charge the registered land with the repayment of loan.[19] Such a charge takes effect as a charge by way of legal mortgage[20] although it is not necessary to use the expression 'by way of legal mortgage'.[21] And this is the most common form of creating a mortgage over registered land. However a mortgage or charge is created, it is only completed by registration.[22] The registrar shall enter the name of the mortgagee or chargee and the particular of the charge in the Charges Register of the lender's title.[23] The land certificate is deposited at the registry, and a charge certificate is issued to the mortgagee or chargee. Once registered, the mortgagee or chargee takes the charge subject only to interest appearing on the register of the mortgagor's title and any overriding interest. The registered proprietor of a charge has the powers of the owner of a legal mortgage.[24]

(b) If the mortgage or charge is not registered, it takes effect only in equity and needs to be protected as a minor interest.[25] It can, however, become a registered charge by substantive registration as mentioned in (a) above.

(c) Where at the time of the mortgage or charge, the mortgagor or chargor was not the registered proprietor nor was he entitled to be registered as such, the mortgagee or chargee has a mortgage or charge by estoppel. Once the mortgagor acquires the legal estate later and is registered as the proprietor, the estoppel is fed, and the mortgagee or chargee is then entitled to register the mortgage or charge, and will rank in priority according to the order of registration.[26]

(d) Where an equitable mortgage or equitable charge is informally created, it must be protected as a minor interest.

(e) As will be seen, where there are two registered charges or more on the same land, subject to any contrary indication on the register, priority depends on the order in which they are entered on the register, and not according to the order in which they are created.[27]

3 THE CREATION OF EQUITABLE MORTGAGES

An equitable mortgage may be created in the following ways:

19 Section 25 of the LRA 1925.

20 Section 27(1) of the LRA 1925.

21 *Cityland and Property (Holdings) Ltd v Debrah* [1968] Ch 166 at 171D–E.

22 Section 106(2) of the LRA 1925.

23 Section 26 of the LRA 1925.

24 Section 34 of the LRA 1925.

25 Section 106(3) of the LRA 1925; *The Mortgage Corpn Ltd v Nationwide Credit Corpn Ltd, The Times*, 27 July 1992.

26 *First National Bank plc v Thompson* [1996] 1 All ER 140, CA.

27 Section 29 of the LRA 1925.

Informal mortgage of a legal interest

To create a legal mortgage under s 85 and s 86, a deed is needed under s 52 of the Law of Property Act 1925. If the mortgage is not by deed, equity will still enforce it if it is specifically enforceable as an agreement to create a legal mortgage under the doctrine of *Walsh v Lonsdale*.[28] Such a mortgage is an equitable mortgage. For there to be a specifically enforceable agreement, first, the agreement must satisfy the requirement of s 40 of the Law of Property Act 1925 (ie it must be evidenced in writing or supported by a sufficient act of part performance) if it was made before 27 September 1989. If the agreement is made on or after 27 September 1989, it must satisfy s 2 of the Law of Property (Miscellaneous Provision) Act 1989 (ie the agreement must itself be in writing and signed by both the mortgagor and the mortgagee incorporating all the terms expressly agreed by them).

Secondly, the money must have been advanced if the agreement is to be specifically enforceable.[29] This is because the remedy of damages at common law is regarded as adequate should there be a breach of contract.

Equitable mortgage of a legal estate by deposit of title deeds

Prior to 27 September 1989, a deposit of title deeds or land certificates by the mortgagor with the mortgagee was regarded as a sufficient act of part performance of an agreement to create a legal mortgage.[30] So an equitable mortgage could be created by an oral agreement coupled with a deposit of documents of title. Since 27 September 1989 as a result of s 2 of the 1989 Act which supersedes s 40 of the Law of Property Act 1925, an oral agreement together with the deposit of title deeds can no longer create an equitable mortgage.[31]

---

28 (1882) 21 Ch D 9.

29 *Sichel v Mosenthal* (1862) 30 Beav 371.

30 *Swiss Bank Corpn v Lloyds Bank Ltd* [1982] AC 584, at 594H–95A; *Russel v Russel* (1783) 1 Bro CC 269; *Thames Guaranty Ltd v Campbell* [1985] QB 210 at 218F; *Shaw v Foster* (1872) LR 5 HL 321. It has been suggested that a deposit of title creates an equitable charge but not an equitable mortgage because the part performance does not come from the mortgagee (see Treitel, GH, *The Law of Contract*, 7th edn, 1987, London: Sevens, pp 144–46. But there is no apparent reason why such a charge will not be void for not complying with s 53(1)(a) of the LPA 1925 (see Law Com, No 204, para 2.9, fn 26).

31 *United Bank of Kuwait plc v Sahib* [1996] 3 All ER 215, CA. See Law Com No 204, para 2.9; [1990] Conv 441 at 444 (Howell, J); [1991] Conv 12 (Adams, JE). But see Law Com No 204, fn 26; *Emmet on Title* (by Farrand, JT) 19th edn, 1986, Looseleaf London: Longman, para 25.116; Maudsley and Burn, p 717 suggesting that an oral mortgage by deposit of title deeds takes effect as an equitable charge and is therefore outside the scope of the 1989 Act. See also (1990) 106 LQR 396 at 400 (Hill, G); [1992] Conv 330 at 332 (Baughen, S). It has been held that an agreement to mortgage one's land for the debt of another person as a guarantee is not caught by s 40 of the LPA 1925 or s 2 of the LP (MP) Act 1989 but by s 4 of the Statute of Frauds 1677 which requires written evidence: *Deutsche Bank AG v Ibrahim* (1992) *Financial Times*, 15 January.

Mortgage of an equitable interest

To create a legal mortgage the subject matter of the security must be a legal interest. No legal mortgage can be created of an equitable interest. Any mortgage of an equitable interest, such as a life interest under a settlement or a beneficial interest behind a trust for sale, must be an equitable mortgage.

The method of creating such an equitable mortgage is the same as the old common law method of creating a legal mortgage. The mortgagor assigns the entire equitable interest he has to the creditor subject to a proviso for reassignment on redemption.[32] Such a disposition of an equitable interest in land is caught by s 53(1)(c) of the Law of Property Act 1925.[33] It must therefore be made in writing (not merely evidenced in writing) signed by the person disposing of the interest or by will. The mortgagee should protect himself by giving written notice of the equitable mortgage to the owner of the legal estate under s 137(1) of the Law of Property Act 1925 which incorporates the rule in *Dearle v Hall*.[34]

This type of mortgage may also be created accidentally as where the mortgagor purports to create a legal mortgage, but does not have the legal estate, or has no power to charge a legal estate. The purported legal mortgage takes effect as an equitable mortgage of the mortgagor's equitable interest.[35] It may also be created where one legal joint tenant purports to create a legal mortgage by forging the other legal owner's signature.[36]

Equitable charge

Where the charge of a legal estate is not made by deed, it may be equitable if it is made in writing signed by the charger.[37] An equitable charge may also be created over any equitable interest. It may also be created where one legal owner purports to charge the co-owned land by forgery.[38]

To create an equitable charge no specific words are needed. It is enough if an intention that the property is used as a security is expressed in writing.[39] Therefore, in *Matthews v Goodday*[40] a written contract by B charging his real estate to A with £500 was held to be an equitable charge.

---

32 *Thames Guaranty Ltd v Campbell* [1985] QB 210.

33 Section 2 of the 1989 Act requires an agreement to be signed by both parties whereas s 53 of the LPA 1925 requires the written disposition to be signed by one. There is no inconsistency here. Section 2 deals with an agreement for the disposition whereas s 53 deals with the disposition itself.

34 (1828) 3 Russ 1.

35 Section 63 of the LPA 1925, or equitable doctrine of part performance (*First National Securities Ltd v Hegerty* [1985] QB 850; *Thames Guaranty Ltd v Campbell* [1985] QB 210).

36 For example. *First National Securities Ltd v Hegerty* [1985] QB 850; *Ahmed v Kendrick* (1988) 56 P & CR 120.

37 Section 53(1)(a) of the LPA 1925.

38 For example, *First National Securities Ltd v Hegerty* [1985] QB 850; *Ahmed v Kendrick* (1988) 56 P & CR 120.

39 *National Provincial and Union Bank of England v Charnley* [1924] 1 KB 431.

40 (1861) 31 LJ Ch 282.

An equitable charge is technically different from an equitable mortgage, and they are different in effect. As will be seen, an equitable mortgagee of a legal estate is entitled to call for a legal mortgage, to foreclose, and to take possession, whereas an equitable chargee has no such rights. The distinction is not often observed in practice, and they are often confused. However, this confusion has not caused any significant problems in practice.[41]

The Law Commission took a full review of the law of land mortgages in its Working Paper[42] published in 1986 followed by a report in 1991.[43] It concluded that the proliferation of types of security interests in land no longer serves any useful purpose.[44] In its view, it is difficult to justify the continued existence of the mortgage by demise which is no longer used in practice and which has the same effect as a charge by way of legal mortgage.[45] As for equitable mortgage and charge of legal or equitable interest, it thought that whilst there are small differences in effect between these different types of equitable security, there is no apparent difference in function, and the differences in equitable mortgages or charges are of no practical significance.[46] The Law Commission's proposals for reform will be dealt with below.

4 FIXED AND FLOATING CHARGES[47]

A company frequently secures its borrowing by means of a mortgage on its assets. It may mortgage or charge a specific piece of land by the methods hitherto described. Such a charge is known as a 'fixed charge'. It may, however, create a 'floating charge' over all or some of its assets which may include land, its stock-in-trade, chattels, and book debts and its future property. A security thus given by a company is commonly known in company law and practice as a 'debenture'.[48] A 'debenture' is therefore a document which acknowledges a company's debt to the debenture holder and is generally secured by a fixed or a floating charge over the company's assets, and usually both.

Where a debenture is secured by a fixed charge, the effect is the same as an ordinary mortgage and affects the title to the property charged. So the company can only deal with the property subject to the charge. The nature of the charge will depend on the mode of creation and the interest charged, as discussed above. Where the debenture is secured by a floating charge, the company may deal with the property in the ordinary course of business before the charge crystallises or becomes fixed.[49] The charge crystallises when the debenture holder appoints a receiver on the occurrence of one of the events which under

41 See Law Com No 204, paras 2.15–2.16.

42 Land Mortgages, Working Paper No.99.

43 Law Com No 204, 13 November 1991.

44 Law Com No 204, para 2.13.

45 Law Com No 204, para 2.13.

46 Law Com No.204, para 2.13.

47 See Gower, LCB, *Principles of Modern Company Law*, 5th edn, 1992, London: Sweet & Maxwell, Chapter 16.

48 *Knightsbridge Estates Ltd v Byrne* [1940] AC 613, at 629.

49 *Re Florence Land Co* (1878) 10 Ch D 530, CA.

the debenture renders the charge enforceable, or if the company ceases to carry on business,[50] or goes into liquidation. It would also appear that a provision may be made in the debenture providing that the floating charge will crystallise on the occurrence of some specified events without the need for a further act by the chargee.[51]

Registration of company charges

A fixed charge created on unregistered land owned by a company may be registrable under the Land Charges Act 1972 in the same way as a mortgage granted by a private individual. A floating charge is registrable under s 2(4)(iii) of the Land Charges Act 1972 as a 'general equitable charge affecting land'. However, to save work at the Land Charges Registry, s 3(7) and (8) provides that registration of a floating charge with the company register is equivalent to registration under the Land Charges Act. A fixed charge created before 1 January 1970, or a floating charge created at any time may be registered at Companies House (the company register) under ss 395–98 of the Companies Act 1985 in place of registration under the Land Charges Act 1972, and takes effect as if the land charge had been registered under the 1972 Act.[52] But fixed charges created on or after 1 January 1970 must be registered under the 1972 Act. Thus, any purchaser of land owned by a company should search (in addition to searches at the Land Charges Registry) at Companies House to reveal any pre-1970 charges and the floating charges that may be affecting the land.

If the title to the land is registered, any fixed or floating charge must be registered under the Land Registration Act 1925.

In addition to any registration under the Land Charges Act 1972 or Land Registration Act 1925, the Companies Act 1985 contains detailed provisions which require a company to register certain charges at House Companies. It is impossible to even attempt to give a general summary of these provisions.[53] Suffice it to say that all company charges must be registered in the company's own register at its own registered office[54] and most charges have to be registered at Companies House with the Registrar of Companies.[55] The current law is governed by the old Part XII of the Companies Act 1985. A new Part XII of the Companies Act 1985 was enacted by Part IV of the Companies Act 1989 and is not yet in force. It seems unlikely that the new law will ever be implemented.

---

50 *Re Woodroffes (Musical Instruments) Ltd* [1985] 2 All ER 908.

51 *Re Brightlife Ltd* [1987] Ch 200; *Re Permanent Houses (Holdings) Ltd* [1988] BCLC 562. See also Gower, *Principles of Modern Company Law*, 5th edn, 1992, at 418.

52 Section 3(7), (8) of the LCA 1972.

53 For reference see Gower, *Principles of Modern Company Law*, 5th edn, 1992, pp 425–34; Charlesworth and Morse, *Company Law*, 14th edn, 1991, London: Sweet & Maxwell, pp 678–88; Farrar, JH, *Company Law*, 3rd edn, 1991, London: Butterworths, Chapter 19.

54 Section 411 of the Companies Act 1985.

55 New s 396 of the Companies Act 1985 as inserted by Part IV of the Companies Act 1989. See also the old s 396 of the Companies Act 1985.

The old Part XII of the Companies Act 1985

Section 396 provides a list of charges which are required to be registered with the Registrar at Companies House. These include a charge on land, wherever situated, or any interest in land.[56] The company is under a duty to submit the particulars of the charge and the charge instrument to the Registrar for registration within 21 days of its creation.[57] If a registrable charge is not registered, it is void as against the liquidator and creditors of the company.[58] An unregistered charge is, nevertheless, valid against the company. Registration constitutes notice to the world of the existence of the charge but not its content.[59]

5 PROTECTIONS AND RIGHTS OF MORTGAGORS

As Lord Henley LC once put it in *Vernon v Bethell*,[60] 'necessitous men are not, truly speaking, free men, but, to answer a present exigency, will submit to any terms that the crafty may impose upon them.' It is, therefore, not surprising that equity, as the guardian of conscience, has since the 17th century, intervened to prevent the exploitation of the mortgagor by the mortgagee.

Right of redemption

The mortgagor's equitable right of redemption is not affected by the 1925 legislation. Equity continues to allow redemption even though the legal date of redemption has passed.

As the right of redemption is regarded by equity as fundamentally important, equity insists that no 'clogs or fetters' can be imposed on the right. Any attempt to exclude the right will be regarded as void. Walker LJ in *Browne v Ryan* said:

> When a transaction appears, or has been declared to be a mortgage ... the mortgagor is entitled to get back his property as free as he gave it, on payment of principal, interest, and costs, and provisions inconsistent with that right cannot be enforced. The equitable rules, 'once a mortgage always a mortgage' and that the mortgagee cannot impose any 'clog or fetter on the equity of redemption' are merely concise statements of the same rule.

In *Samuel v Jarrah Timber and Wood Paving Corpn Ltd*[61] equity went so far as to hold that a term giving the mortgagee an option to purchase the mortgaged property outright within 12 months of the mortgage was void on the ground that it excluded the mortgagor's right of redemption even though on the facts it was a perfectly fair bargain. The option changed the nature of the transaction from mortgage to sale and it might be a result of unfair bargaining.

56 The old s 396(1)(d) of the Companies Act 1985, but not a charge for any rent or other periodical sum issuing out of land.

57 The old ss 398, 399 of the Companies Act 1985.

58 The old s 395 of the Companies Act 1985.

59 *Re Standard Rotary Machine Co Ltd* (1906) 95 LT 829.

60 (1762) 2 Eden 110 at 113, 28 ER 838 at 839.

61 [1904] AC 323.

Samuel v Jarrah Timber and Wood Paving Corpn Ltd [1904] AC 323, HL

Earl of Halsbury LC: (read by Lord Macnaghten): My Lords, I regret that the state of the authorities leaves me no alternative other than to affirm the judgment of Kekewich J and the Court of Appeal. A perfectly fair bargain made between two parties to it, each of whom was quite sensible of what they were doing, is not to be performed because at the same time a mortgage arrangement was made between them. If a day had intervened between the two parts of the arrangement, the part of the bargain which the appellant claims to be performed would have been perfectly good and capable of being enforced; but a line of authorities going back for more than a century has decided that such an arrangement as that which was here arrived at is contrary to a principle of equity, the sense or reason of which I am not able to appreciate, and very reluctantly I am compelled to acquiesce in the judgments appealed from.

Lord Macnaghten: In *Vernon v Bethell*, however, Northington LC (then Lord Henley) laid down the law broadly in the following terms: 'This Court, as a Court of conscience, is very jealous of persons taking securities for a loan and converting such securities into purchases. And therefore I take it to be an established rule that a mortgagee can never provide at the time of making the loan for any event or condition on which the equity of redemption shall be discharged and the conveyance absolute. And there is great reason and justice in this rule, for necessitous men are not, truly speaking, free men, but to answer a present exigency will submit to any terms that the crafty may impose upon them.'

This doctrine, described by Lord Henley as an established rule nearly 150 years ago, has never, as far as I can discover, been departed from since or questioned in any reported case. It is, I believe, universally accepted by text-writers of authority. Speaking for myself, I should not be sorry if your Lordships could see your way to modify it so as to prevent its being used as a means of evading a fair bargain come to between persons dealing at arms' length and negotiating on equal terms. The directors of a trading company in search of financial assistance are certainly in a very different position from that of an impecunious landowner in the toils of a crafty money-lender. At the same time I quite feel the difficulty of interfering with any rule that has prevailed so long, and I am not prepared to differ from the conclusion at which the Court of Appeal has arrived.'

Lord Lindley: Lord Hardwicke said in *Toomes v Conset*:[62] 'This Court will not suffer in a deed of mortgage any agreement in it to prevail that the estate become an absolute purchase in the mortgagee upon any event whatsoever.' But the doctrine is not confined to deeds creating legal mortgages. It applies to all mortgage transactions. The doctrine 'Once a mortgage always a mortgage' means that no contract between a mortgagor and a mortgagee made at the time of the mortgage and as part of the mortgage transaction, or, in other words, as one of the terms of the loan, can be valid if it prevents the mortgagor from getting back his property on paying off what is due on his security. Any bargain which has that effect is invalid, and is inconsistent with the transaction being a mortgage. This principle is fatal to the appellant's contention if the transaction under consideration is a mortgage transaction, as I am of opinion it clearly is.

---

62 (1745) 3 Atk 261.

The decision of the Court of Appeal in *Samuel* had earlier provoked strong words from Sir Frederick Pollock writing nearly a century ago.[63]

(1903) 19 LQR 359 (Pollock)

The doctrine of 'clogging' threatens to become an intolerable nuisance – an interference with the freedom of the subject. It was a useful enough doctrine in a primitive and more technical age when ignorant people were often entrapped into oppressive bargains, but today it is an anachronism and might with advantage be jettisoned. Instead the Courts have taken to emphasising the doctrine in all its original crudity. It was open to them a few years since to have moulded the doctrine to meet the changing conditions of modern life, and to have confined redress to cases where there was something oppressive or unconscionable in the bargain, to make this the test, as it was the origin, of the doctrine; but the Courts have preferred to adhere to technicality and an unprogressive judicial policy. The decision of the Court of Appeal in *Jarrah Timber and Wood Paving Corporation v Samuel* [1903] Ch 1, CA was inevitable after *Noakes & Co Ltd v Rice* [1902] AC 24; but see to what a conclusion it leads. A company with a board of directors composed of experienced men of business, advised by a competent solicitor, after it has invited a loan and settled considered terms is supposed to be the victim of some oppression at the hands of the mortgagee, because it has given the mortgagee an option of purchasing the mortgaged property at a certain price, and is permitted by the Court to repudiate its own bargain deliberately entered into in its own interests – surely a proceeding more unconscionable than anything involved in the so-called 'clogging', if there is any such thing as sanctity in contracts. Alas! for those cobwebs of technicality which lawyers are so fond of spinning, and which so often shut out the daylight of common sense.

On the other hand, the House of Lords was not entirely unaware of the iniquity that would arise from the use of the doctrine of 'clogging' by the mortgagor as a means of evading a fair bargain agreed between him and the mortgagee dealing at arms' length and negotiating on equal terms. Thus, in *Reeve v Lisle*,[64] an option to purchase which was granted to a mortgagee 10 days after the mortgage was made was held valid since it was a transaction separate from the original mortgage transaction.

Reeve v Lisle [1902] AC 461, HL

Earl of Halsbury LC: My Lords, it seems to me that the Court of Appeal has taken the right view upon the facts ...

The view of the Court of Appeal, who had all the facts before them is this, that the later transaction was entirely separate – that it was, in truth, a matter applicable to the contemplated partnership, and that the real position of the parties was this, that all the securities were already in their possession; that this further transaction altered the rate of interest, but that the real substance of the second transaction was the contemplated partnership. Under these circumstances it was a mere question of what inferences ought properly to be drawn from the nature of the instruments, and the object and purpose with which they were entered into, as well as what the documents contained in themselves. I come to the conclusion that what has been called here, and I think

63 (1903) 19 LQR 359.

64 [1902] AC 461.

accurately called, the question of fact between the parties, was rightly arrived at by the court of Appeal; and, if that is so, there is not and cannot be any question as to the law which ought to prevail in this case.'

Lord Macnaghten: My Lords, I am of the same opinion, and I take the same view of the facts that the Court of Appeal did. Notwithstanding the very able and ingenious argument addressed to us by Mr Warmington to prove that the purpose of this document was consolidation and rearrangement of the mortgages, in my opinion it was nothing of the kind. The respondents had the benefit of all these securities. There was merely a stipulation introduced at the request of the appellant, who was asking for time. Not being prepared to pay the money, he said, 'If you will give me five years, you shall have the whole of that time in which to determine whether to enter into the partnership or not.' When the respondents did make up their minds to enter into the partnership, the appellant turned round and said, 'Oh, but this transaction is entirely wrong; it strikes at the root of an equitable doctrine, and I am not bound by it.' I think on the facts as we have them before us he is bound by it, and must pay damages for having broken his agreement.

Generally, as mentioned earlier, equity does not allow redemption before the legal date of redemption. But any covenant made by the mortgagor not to redeem the mortgage before a certain date may be held void if it is oppressive and unconscionable. In *Knightsbridge Estate v Byrne*,[65] the mortgagor agreed to repay the loan over a period of 40 years. Later, when he wanted to redeem the mortgage earlier, the mortgagee objected. It was held that the mortgagor could not redeem before the period expired as he was bound by his covenant which was not unconscionable. The reason why it was not unconscionable was because it was a commercial agreement made by businessmen at arm's length and the mortgaged property was a fee simple. The postponement of redemption would not render the property valueless when redeemed. The decision was affirmed by the House of Lords, but no views were expressed on the reasoning of the Court of Appeal.

Knightsbridge Estates Trust Ltd v Byrne [1939] 1 Ch 441, CA

Sir Wilfrid Greene MR: We will deal first with the arguments originally presented on behalf of the respondents. The first argument was that the postponement of the contractual right to redeem for forty years was void in itself, in other words, that the making of such an agreement between mortgagor and mortgagee was prohibited by a rule of equity. It was not contended that a provision in a mortgage deed making the mortgage irredeemable for a period of years is necessarily void. The argument was that such a period must be a 'reasonable' one, and it was said that the period in the present case was an unreasonable one by reason merely of its length. This argument was not the one accepted by the learned judge.

Now an argument such as this requires the closest scrutiny, for, if it is correct, it means that an agreement made between two competent parties, acting under expert advice and presumably knowing their own business best, is one which the law forbids them to make upon the ground that it is not 'reasonable'. If we were satisfied that the rule of equity was what it is said to be, we should be bound to give effect to it. But in the

65 [1939] Ch 441.

absence of compelling authority we are not prepared to say that such an agreement cannot lawfully be made. A decision to that effect would, in our view, involve an unjustified interference with the freedom of business men to enter into agreements best suited to their interests and would impose upon them a test of 'reasonableness' laid down by the courts without reference to the business realities of the case.

It is important to remember what those realities were. The respondents are a private company and do not enjoy the facilities for raising money by a public issue possessed by public companies. They were the owners of a large and valuable block of property, and so far as we know they had no other assets. The property was subject to a mortgage at a high rate of interest and this mortgage was liable to be called in at any time. In these circumstances the respondents were, then the negotiations began, desirous of obtaining for themselves two advantages: (1) a reduction in the rate of interest, (2) the right to repay the mortgage moneys by instalments spread over a long period of years. The desirability of obtaining these terms from a business point of view is manifest, and it is not to be assumed that these respondents were actuated by anything but pure considerations of business in seeking to obtain them. The sum involved was a very large one, and the length of the period over which the instalments were spread is to be considered with reference to this fact. In the circumstances it was the most natural thing in the world that the respondents should address themselves to a body desirous of obtaining a long term investment for its money. The resulting agreement was a commercial agreement between two important corporations experienced in such matters, and has none of the features of an oppressive bargain where the borrower is at the mercy of an unscrupulous lender. In transactions of this kind it is notorious that there is competition among the large insurance companies and other bodies having large funds to invest, and we are not prepared to view the agreement made as anything but a proper business transaction.

But it is said not only that the period of postponement must be a reasonable one, but that in judging the 'reasonableness' of the period the considerations which we have mentioned cannot be regarded; that the Court is bound to judge 'reasonableness' by a consideration of the terms of the mortgage deed itself and without regard to extraneous matters. In the absence of clear authority we emphatically decline to consider a question of 'reasonableness' from a standpoint so unreal. To hold that the law is to tell business men what is reasonable in such circumstances and to refuse to take into account the business considerations involved, would bring the law into disrepute. Fortunately, we do not find ourselves forced to come to any such conclusion.

Mr Stamp, when pressed as to the matters which, upon the respondents' argument, the Court might legitimately consider, upon the question of reasonableness, made a curious concession. He said that the court might hold a longer period to be reasonable where the borrower was a body like the Corporation of the City of London with a long expectation of life than were the borrower was a private individual or a limited company which for this purpose (at any rate in the case of private companies) he treated as a mere body of individuals. This was because he said that the period of reasonableness must be judged by reference to the normal duration of human life – what age the borrower was to be assumed to be, and whether a longer period would be permissible for a borrower aged thirty than for a borrower aged 65 he preferred not to say. This was the extent of Mr Stamp's concession: the fact that it was made illustrates very pointedly what appears to us to be the inadmissibility of a principle by which the test of 'reasonableness' is to be so artificially circumscribed.

Assuming therefore, without in any way deciding, that the period during which the contractual right of redemption is postponed must be a 'reasonable' one (a question which we will now proceed to examine), we are of opinion that the respondents have failed to establish (and the burden is on them) that there is anything unreasonable in the mere extension of the period for 40 years in the circumstances of the present case.

But in our opinion the proposition that a postponement of the contractual right of redemption is only permissible for a 'reasonable' time is not well-founded. Such a postponement is not properly described as a clog on the equity of redemption, since it is concerned with the contractual right to redeem. It is indisputable that any provision which hampers redemption after the contractual date for redemption has passed will not be permitted. Further, it is undoubtedly true to say that a right of redemption is a necessary element in a mortgage transaction, and consequently that, where the contractual right of redemption is illusory, equity will grant relief by allowing redemption. This was the point in the case of *Fairclough v Swan Brewery*[66] decided in the Privy Council, where in a mortgage of a lease of 20 years the contractual right to redeem was postponed until six weeks before the expiration of the lease. The following passage from the judgment explains the reason for that decision:[67]

> The learned counsel on behalf of the respondents admitted, as he was bound to admit, that a mortgage cannot be made irredeemable. That is plainly forbidden. Is there any difference between forbidding redemption and permitting it, if the permission be a mere pretence? Here the provision for redemption is nugatory.

Moreover, equity may give relief against contractual terms in a mortgage transaction if they are oppressive or unconscionable, and in deciding whether or not a particular transaction falls within this category the length of time for which the contractual right to redeem is postponed may well be an important consideration. In the present case no question of this kind was or could have been raised.

But equity does not reform mortgage transactions because they are unreasonable. It is concerned to see two things – one that the essential requirements of a mortgage transaction are observed, and the other that oppressive or unconscionable terms are not enforced. Subject to this, it does not, in our opinion, interfere. The question therefore arises whether, in a case where the right of redemption is real and not illusory and there is nothing oppressive or unconscionable in the transaction, there is something in a postponement of the contractual right to redeem, such as we have in the present case, that is inconsistent with the essential requirements of a mortgage transaction? Apart from authority the answer to this question would, in our opinion, be clearly in the negative. Any other answer would place an unfortunate restriction on the liberty of contract of competent parties who are at arm's length – in the present case it would have operated to prevent the respondents obtaining financial terms which for obvious reasons they themselves considered to be most desirable. It would, moreover, lead to highly inequitable results. The remedy sought by the respondents and the only remedy which is said to be open to them is the establishment of a right to redeem at any time on the ground that the postponement of the contractual right to redeem is void. They do not and could not suggest that the contract as a contract is affected, and the result would accordingly be that whereas the respondents would have had from the first the right to

66 [1912] AC 565.

67 [1912] AC 565 at 570.

redeem at any time, the appellants would have had no right to require payment otherwise than by the specified instalments. Such an outcome to a bargain entered into by business people negotiating at arm's length would indeed be unfortunate, and we should require clear authority before coming to such a conclusion ...

We find ourselves unable to take the view that the court is entitled in such a case as the present to treat as unreasonable provisions in a mortgage deed entered into by two parties such as we have here with the assistance of competent advisers. For all the court can know, provisions which may appear to it to be disadvantageous to the mortgagor may have been regarded by him, and correctly regarded, as of no practical consequence from a business point of view.

In the present case during the negotiations for the loan the respondents asked for a term to be inserted enabling them to obtain the release from the security of such parts of the property as they might sell or let on long leases. They did not, however, insist on this and were willing to accept an assurance from the mortgagees upon the subject. We do not see how they can now turn round and say that the omission of such a term was unreasonable. In our opinion, if we are right in thinking that the postponement is by itself unobjectionable, it cannot be made objectionable by the presence in the mortgage deed of other provisions, unless the totality is sufficient to enable the court to say that the contract is so oppressive or unconscionable that it ought not to be enforced in a court of equity. If such other provisions are collateral advantages which are inadmissible upon the principles laid down by Lord Parker in the passage cited below, they will, of course, fall to be dealt with as such.

But if the postponement will render the right of redemption practically valueless then equity will allow a mortgagor to redeem prior to the fixed date even if he is not allowed to do so under the contract. In *Fairclough v Swan Brewery Co*,[68] a lease for 20 years was mortgaged. The mortgagor covenanted not to redeem until six weeks before the lease expired. It was held that the postponement was void.

Fairclough v Swan Brewery Co Ltd [1912] AC 565, PC

Lord Macnaghten: 'There is,' as Kindersley VC said in *Gossip v Wright*,[69] 'no doubt that the broad rule is this: that the Court will not allow the right of redemption in any way to be hampered or crippled in that which the parties intended to be a security either by any contemporaneous instrument with the deed in question, or by anything which this Court would regard as a simultaneous arrangement or part of the same transaction.' The rule in comparatively recent times was unsettled by certain decisions in the Court of Chancery in England which seem to have misled the learned judges in the Full Court. But it is now firmly established by the House of Lords that the old rule still prevails and that equity will not permit any device or contrivance being part of the mortgage transaction or contemporaneous with it to prevent or impede redemption. The learned counsel on behalf of the respondents admitted, as he was bound to admit, that a mortgage cannot be made irredeemable. That is plainly forbidden. Is there any difference between forbidding redemption and permitting it, if the permission be a mere pretence? Here the provision for redemption is nugatory. The incumbrance on the lease the subject of the mortgage

68 [1912] AC 565.

69 (1863) 32 LJ (Ch) 648 at 653.

according to the letter of the bargain falls to be discharged before the lease terminates, but at a time when it is on the very point of expiring, when redemption can be of no advantage to the mortgagor even if he should be so fortunate as to get his deeds back before the actual termination of the lease. For all practical purposes this mortgage is irredeemable. It was obviously meant to be irredeemable. It was made irredeemable in and by the mortgage itself.

Where the mortgage agreement is a regulated agreement under s 8(3) of the Consumer Credit Act 1974, the debtor has a right under s 94 of the Act, on giving notice to the creditor, to redeem prematurely at any time. A regulated agreement is a personal credit agreement by which a creditor provides a debtor with credit not exceeding £15,000 provided the agreement does not also fall within s 16 of the Act, which exempts credit agreements made with certain bodies, such as a local authority or a building society, from the scope of the Act.[70]

Consumer Credit Act 1974

8. Consumer credit agreements

(1) A personal credit agreement is an agreement between an individual ('the debtor') and any other person ('the creditor') by which the creditor provides the debtor with credit of any amount.

(2) A consumer credit agreement is a personal credit agreement by which the creditor provides the debtor with credit not exceeding £15,000.

(3) A consumer credit agreement is a regulated agreement within the meaning of this Act if it is not an agreement (an 'exempt agreement') specified in or under s 16.

16. Exempt agreements

(1) This Act does not regulate a consumer credit agreement where the creditor is a local authority ..., or a body specified, or of a description specified, in an order made by the Secretary of State, being:

(a) an insurance company,

(b) a friendly society,

(c) an Organisation of employers or Organisation of workers,

(d) a charity,

(e) a land improvement company,

(f) a body corporate named or specifically referred to in any Public general Act, or

(ff) a body corporate named or specifically referred to in an order made under s 156(4), 444(l) or 447(2)(a) of the Housing Act 1985,

(g) a building society, or

70 Section 8 of the Consumer Credit Act 1974.

(h) an authorised institution or wholly-owned subsidiary (within the meaning of the Companies Act 1985) of such an institution.

(2) Subsection (1) applies only where the agreement is:

(a) a debtor-creditor-supplier agreement financing:

(i) the purchase of land, or

(ii) the provision of dwellings on any land,

and secured by a land mortgage on that land, or

(b) a debtor-creditor agreement secured by any land mortgage; or

(c) a debtor-creditor-supplier agreement financing a transaction which is a linked transaction in relation to:

(i) an agreement falling within paragraph (a), or

(ii) an agreement falling within paragraph (b) financing:

(aa) the purchase of any land, or

(bb) the provision of dwellings on any land,

and secured by a land mortgage on the land referred to in paragraph (a) or, as the case may be, the land referred to in subparagraph (ii).

(6A) This Act does not regulate a consumer credit agreement where the creditor is a housing authority and the agreement is secured by a land mortgage of a dwelling.

(6B) In sub-s (6A) 'housing authority' means:

(a) as regards England and Wales, the Housing Corporation, Housing for Wales and an authority or body within s 80(1) of the Housing Act 1985 (the landlord condition for secure tenancies), other than a housing association or a housing trust which is a charity;

(7) Nothing in this section affects the application of ss 137–40 (extortionate credit bargains).

94. Right to complete payments ahead of time

(1) The debtor under a regulated consumer credit agreement is entitled at any time, by notice to the creditor and the payment to the creditor of all amounts payable by the debtor to him under the agreement (less any rebate allowable under s 95), to discharge the debtor's indebtedness under the agreement.

(2) A notice under sub-s (1) may embody the exercise by the debtor of any option to purchase goods conferred on him by the agreement, and deal with any other matter arising on, or in relation to, the termination of the agreement.

This equitable rule of no 'clogs or fetters' in mortgagor's equitable right of redemption, however, does not apply to a debenture.[71] A debenture can be made wholly or partly irredeemable.

71 Section 193 of the Companies Act 1985.

Companies Act 1985

193. Perpetual debentures

A condition contained in debentures, or in a deed for securing debentures, is not invalid by reason only that the debentures are thereby made irredeemable or redeemable only on the happening of a contingency (however remote), or on the expiration of a period (however long), any rule of equity to the contrary notwithstanding.

This applies to debentures whenever issued, and to deeds whenever executed.

Collateral advantages

Mortgagees may sometimes require mortgagors to confer other collateral advantages to the mortgagees. For example, breweries may require licensees of public houses to buy all their beer from them as a condition for loans. Similar arrangements can be made between petrol companies and garage owners. Such arrangements will be valid if they are not, as Lord Parker of Waddington declared, 'either (1) unfair and unconscionable, or (2) in the nature of a penalty clogging the equity of redemption, or (3) inconsistent with or repugnant to the contractual and equitable right to redeem'.[72] In *Kreglinger v New Patagonia Meat & Cold Storage Co Ltd*,[73] the mortgagor agreed that it would, for a period of five years, offer its sheep's skins to the mortgagee. Two years later the mortgage was duly redeemed, but the House of Lords held that the mortgagor was still liable to sell its sheep's skins to the mortgagee for the full period of five years. This was because the term was reasonable.

Kreglinger v New Patagonia Meat and Cold Storage Co Ltd [1914] AC 25, HL

Viscount Haldane LC: My Lords, the respondents have now, as they were entitled to do under the agreement, paid off the loan. They claim that such payment has put an end to the option of the appellants to buy the respondents' sheepskins. Under the terms of the agreement this option, as I have already stated, will, if it is valid, continue operative until 24 August 1915. What the respondents say is that the stipulation is one that restricts their freedom in conducting the undertaking or business which is the subject of the floating charge; that it was consequently of the nature of a clog on their right to redeem and invalid; and that, whether it clogged the right to redeem or was in the nature of a collateral advantage, it was not intended and could not be made to endure after redemption. The appellants, on the other hand, say that the stipulation in question was one of a kind usual in business, and that it was in the nature not of a clog but of a collateral bargain outside the actual loan, which they only agreed to make in order to obtain the option itself. They further say that even if the option could be regarded as within the doctrine of equity which forbids the clogging of the right to redeem, that doctrine does not in a case such as this extend to a floating charge ...

My Lords, before I refer to the decisions of this House which the courts below have considered to cover the case, I will state what I conceive to be the broad principles which must govern it.

72 *Kreglinger v New Patagonia Meat & Cold Storage Co Ltd* [1914] AC 25 at 56.

73 [1914] AC 25.

The reason for which a Court of Equity will set aside the legal title of a mortgagee and compel him to convey the land on being paid principal, interest, and costs is a very old one. It appears to owe its origin to the influence of the Church in the courts of the early Chancellors. As early as the Council of Lateran in 1179, we find, according to Matthew Paris (*Historia Major*, 1684 ed at pp 114–15), that famous assembly of ecclesiastics condemning usurers and laying down that when a creditor had been paid his debt he should restore his pledge.[74] It was therefore not surprising that the court of Chancery should at an early date have begun to exercise jurisdiction *in personam* over mortgagees. This jurisdiction was merely a special application of a more general power to relieve against penalties and to mould them into mere securities. The case of the common law mortgage of land was indeed a gross one. The land was conveyed to the creditor upon the condition that if the money he had advanced to the feoffor was repaid on a date and at a place named, the fee simple should revest in the latter, but that if the condition was not strictly and literally fulfilled he should lose the land for ever. What made the hardship on the debtor a glaring one was that the debt still remained unpaid and could be recovered from the feoffor notwithstanding that he had actually forfeited the land to his mortgagee. Equity, therefore, at an early date began to relieve against what was virtually a penalty by compelling the creditor to use his legal title as a mere security.

My Lords, this was the origin of the jurisdiction which we are now considering, and it is important to bear that origin in mind. For the end to accomplish which the jurisdiction has been evolved ought to govern and limit its exercise by equity judges. That end has always been to ascertain, by parol evidence if need be, the real nature and substance of the transaction, and if it turned out to be in truth one of mortgage simply, to place it on that footing. It was, in ordinary cases, only where there was conduct which the Court of Chancery regarded as unconscientious that it interfered with freedom of contract. The lending of money, on mortgage or otherwise, was looked on with suspicion, and the Court was on the alert to discover want of conscience in the terms imposed by lenders. But whatever else may have been the intention of those judges who laid the foundations of the modern doctrines with which we are concerned in this appeal, they certainly do not appear to have contemplated that their principle should develop consequences which would go far beyond the necessities of the case with which they were dealing and interfere with transactions which were not really of the nature of a mortgage, and which were free from objection on moral grounds. Moreover, the principle on which the Court of Chancery interfered with contracts of the class under consideration was not a rigid one. The equity judges looked, not at what was technically the form, but at what was really the substance of transactions, and confined the application of their rules to cases in which they thought that in its substance the transaction was oppressive. Thus in *Howard v Harris*[75] Lord Keeper North in 1683 set aside an agreement that a mortgage should be irredeemable after the death of the mortgagor and failure of the heirs of his body, on the ground that such a restriction on the right to redeem was void in equity. But he went on to intimate that if the money had been borrowed by the mortgagor from his brother, and the former had agreed that if he

74 Chron Maj ed Luard, 1874 (Rolls series) ii, 311: *'Si quis ab aliquo, commodata pecunia, possessiones in pignus acceperit, si deductis expensis sortem suam receperit ex fructibus possessionis'* – [the mortgagee is supposed to be in possession and pay himself out of the rents and profits] – *'pignus restituat debitori'*.

75 (1681) 1 Vern 33; 2 Ch Cas 147.

had no issue the land should become irredeemable, equity would not have interfered with what would really have been a family arrangement. The exception thus made to the rule, in cases where the transaction includes a family arrangement as well as a mortgage, has been recognised in later authorities.

The principle was thus in early days limited in its application to the accomplishment of the end which was held to justify interference of equity with freedom of contract. It did not go further. As established it was expressed in three ways. The most general of these was that if the transaction was once found to be a mortgage, it must be treated as always remaining a mortgage and nothing but a mortgage. That the substance of the transaction must be looked to in applying this doctrine and that it did not apply to cases which were only apparently or technically within it but were in reality something more than cases of mortgage, *Howard v Harris* and other authorities shew. It was only a different application of the paramount doctrine to lay it down in the form of a second rule that a mortgagee should not stipulate for a collateral advantage which would make his remuneration for the loan exceed a proper rate of interest. The Legislature during a long period placed restrictions on the rate of interest which could legally be exacted. But equity went beyond the limits of the statutes which limited the interest, and was ready to interfere with any usurious stipulation in a mortgage. In so doing it was influenced by the public policy of the time. That policy has now changed, and the Acts which limited the rate of interest have been repealed. The result is that a collateral advantage may now be stipulated for by the mortgagee provided that he has not acted unfairly or oppressively, and provided that the bargain does not conflict with the third form of the principle. This is that a mortgage (subject to the apparent exception in the case of family arrangements to which I have already alluded) cannot be made irredeemable, and that any stipulation which restricts or clogs the equity of redemption is void. It is obvious that the reason for the doctrine in this form is the same as that which gave rise to the other forms. It is simply an assertion in a different way of the principle that once a mortgage always a mortgage and nothing else.

My Lords, the rules I have stated have now been applied by Courts of Equity for nearly three centuries, and the books are full of illustrations of their application. But what I have pointed out shews that it is inconsistent with the objects for which they were established that these rules should crystallize into technical language so rigid that the letter can defeat the underlying spirit and purpose. Their application must correspond with the practical necessities of the time. The rule as to collateral advantages, for example, has been much modified by the repeal of the usury laws and by the recognition of modern varieties of commercial bargaining. In *Biggs v Hoddinott*[76] it was held that a brewer might stipulate in a mortgage made to him of an hotel that during the five years for which the loan was to continue the mortgagors would deal with him exclusively for malt liquor. In the 17th and 18th centuries a Court of Equity could hardly have so decided, and the judgment illustrates the elastic character of equity jurisdiction and the power of equity judges to mould the rules which they apply in accordance with the exigencies of the time. The decision proceeded on the ground that a mortgagee may stipulate for a collateral advantage at the time and as a term of the advance, provided, first, that no unfairness is shewn, and, secondly, that the right to redeem is not thereby clogged. It is no longer true that, as was said in *Jennings v Ward*,[77] 'a man shall not have

76 [1898] 2 Ch 307.

77 (1705) 2 Vern 520.

interest for his money and a collateral advantage besides for the loan of it.' Unless such a bargain in unconscionable it is now good. But none the less the other and wider principle remains unshaken, that it is the essence of a mortgage that in the eye of a Court of Equity it should be a mere security for money, and that no bargain can be validly made which will prevent the mortgagor from redeeming on payment of what is due, including principal, interest, and costs. He may stipulate that he will not pay off his debt, and so redeem the mortgage, for a fixed period. But whenever a right to redeem arises out of the doctrine of equity, he is precluded from fettering it. This principle has become an integral part of our system or jurisprudence and must be faithfully adhered to.

My Lords, the question in the present case is whether the right to redeem has been interfered with. And this must, for the reasons to which I have adverted in considering the history of the doctrine of equity, depend on the answer to a question which is primarily one of fact. What was the true character of the transaction? Did the appellants make a bargain such that the right to redeem was cut down, or did they simply stipulate for a collateral undertaking, outside and clear of the mortgage, which would give them an exclusive option of purchase of the sheepskins of the respondents? The question is in my opinion not whether the two contracts were made at the same moment and evidenced by the same instrument, but whether they were in substance a single and undivided contract or two distinct contracts. Putting aside for the moment considerations turning on the character of the floating charge, such an option no doubt affects the freedom of the respondents in carrying on their business even after the mortgage has been paid off. But so might other arrangements which would be plainly collateral, an agreement, for example, to take permanently into the firm a new partner as a condition of obtaining fresh capital in the form of a loan. The question is one not of form but of substance, and it can be answered in each case only by looking at all the circumstances, and not by mere reliance on some abstract principle, or upon the dicta which have fallen obiter from judges in other and different cases. Some, at least, of the authorities on the subject disclose an embarrassment which has, in my opinion, arisen from neglect to bear this in mind. In applying a principle the ambit and validity of which depend on confining it steadily to the end for which it was established, the analogies of previous instances where it has been applied are apt to be misleading. For each case forms a real precedent only in so far as it affirms a principle, the relevancy of which in other cases turns on the true character of the particular transaction, and to that extent on circumstances.

My Lords, if in the case before the House your Lordships arrive at the conclusion that the agreement for an option to purchase the respondents' sheepskins was not in substance a fetter on the exercise of their right to redeem, but was in the nature of a collateral bargain the entering into which was a preliminary and separable condition of the loan, the decided cases cease to present any great difficulty. In questions of this kind the binding force of previous decisions, unless the facts are indistinguishable, depends on whether they establish a principle. To follow previous authorities, so far as they lay down principles, is essential if the law is to be preserved from becoming unsettled and vague. In this respect the previous decisions of a court of co-ordinate jurisdiction are more binding in a system of jurisprudence such as ours than in systems where the paramount authority is that of a code. But when a previous case has not laid down any new principle but has merely decided that a particular set of facts illustrates an existing rule, there are few more fertile sources of fallacy than to search in it for what is simply resemblance in circumstances, and to erect a previous decision into a governing precedent merely on this account. To look for anything except the principle established or recognised by previous decisions is really to weaken and not to strengthen the importance of precedent. The consideration of cases which turn on particular facts may often be useful for edification, but it can rarely yield authoritative guidance. I desire to associate myself with what was said on this subject by Sir George Jessel in the case of *In Re Hallett's Estate*,[78] and I will add that the view of the true limits of the use of authority, which I agree with him in holding, is of especial importance where, as here, the principle to be applied arises in the elastic jurisdiction of a Court of Equity, and has been established simply as an instrument to give effect to well defined and governing purpose.

My Lords, it is not in my opinion necessary for your Lordships to form an opinion as to whether you would have given the same decisions as were recently given by this House in certain cases which were cited to us. These cases, which related to circumstances differing widely from those before us, have been disposed of finally, and we are not concerned with them excepting in so far as they may have thrown fresh light on questions of principle. What is vital in the appeal now under consideration is to classify accurately the transaction between the parties. What we have to do is to ascertain from scrutiny of the circumstances whether there has really been an attempt to effect a mortgage with a provision preventing redemption of what was pledged merely as security for payment of the amount of the debt and any charges besides that may legitimately be added. It is not, in my opinion, conclusive in favour of the appellants that the security assumed the form of a floating charge. A floating charge is not the less a pledge because of its floating character, and a contract which fetters the right to redeem on which equity insists as regards all contracts of loan and security ought on principle to be set aside as readily in the case of a floating security as in any other case. But it is material that such a floating charge, in the absence of bargain to the contrary effect, permits the assets to be dealt with freely by the mortgagor until the charge becomes enforceable. If it be said that the undertaking of the respondents which was charged extended to their entire business, including the right to dispose of the skins of which they might from time to time become possessed, the comment is that at least they were to be free, so long as the security remained a floating one, to make contracts in the ordinary course of business in regard to these skins. If there had been no mortgage such a contract as the one in question would have been an ordinary incident in such a business. We are considering the simple question of what is the effect on the right to redeem of having inserted into the formal instrument signed when the money was borrowed an ordinary commercial contract for the sale of skins extending over a period. It appears that it was the intention of the parties that the grant of the security should not affect the power to enter into such a contract, either with strangers or with the appellants, and if so I am unable to see how the equity of redemption is affected. No doubt it is the fact that on redemption the respondents will not get back their business as free from obligation as it was before the date of the security. But that may well be because outside the security and consistently with its terms there was a contemporaneous but collateral contract, contained in the same document as constituted the security, but in substance independent of it. If it was the intention of the parties, as I think it was, to enter into this contract as a condition of the respondents getting their advance, I know no reason either in morals or in equity which ought to prevent this intention from being left to have its

78 (1879) 13 Ch D 696.

effect. What was to be capable of redemption was an undertaking which was deliberately left to be freely changed in its details by ordinary business transactions with which the mortgage was not to interfere. Had the charge not been a floating one it might have been more difficult to give effect to this intention. To render it invalid the bargain must, when its substance is examined, turn out to have formed part of the terms of the mortgage and to have really cut down a true right of redemption. I think that the tendency of recent decisions has been to lay undue stress on the letter of the principle which limits the jurisdiction of equity in setting aside contracts. The origin and reason of the principle ought, as I have already said, to be kept steadily in view in applying it to fresh cases. There appears to me to have grown up a tendency to look to the letter rather than to the spirit of the doctrine. The true view is, I think, that judges ought in this kind or jurisdiction to proceed cautiously, and to bear in mind the real reasons which have led Courts of Equity to insist on the free right to redeem and the limits within which the purpose of the rule ought to confine its scope. I cannot but think that the validity of the bargain in such cases as *Bradley v Carritt*[79] and *Santley v Wilde*[80] might have been made free from serious question if the parties had chosen to seek what would have been substantially the same result in a different form. For form may be very important when the question is one of the construction of ambiguous words in which people have expressed their intentions. I will add that, if I am right in the view which I take of the authorities, there is no reason for thinking that they establish another rule suggested by the learned counsel for the respondents, that even a mere collateral advantage stipulated for in the same instrument as constitutes the mortgage cannot endure after redemption. The dicta on which he relied are really illustrations of the other principles to which I have referred ...

Lord Parker of Waddington: My Lords, the defendants in this case are appealing to the equitable jurisdiction of the Court for relief from a contract which they admit to be fair and reasonable and of which they have already enjoyed the full advantage. Their title to relief is based on some equity which they say is inherent in all transactions in the nature of a mortgage. They can state no intelligible principle underlying this alleged equity, but contend that your Lordships are bound by authority. That the court should be asked in the exercise of its equitable jurisdiction to assist in so inequitable a proceeding as the repudiation of a fair and reasonable bargain is somewhat startling, and makes it necessary to examine the point of view from which Courts of Equity have always regarded mortgage transactions. For this purpose I have referred to most, if not all, of the reported cases on the subject, and propose to state shortly the conclusions at which I have arrived ...

My Lords, after the most careful consideration of the authorities I think it is open to this House to hold, and I invite your Lordships to hold, that there is now no rule in equity which precludes a mortgagee, whether the mortgage be made upon the occasion of a loan or otherwise, from stipulating for any collateral advantage, provided such collateral advantage is not either (1) unfair and unconscionable, or (2) in the nature of a penalty clogging the equity of redemption, or (3) inconsistent with or repugnant to the contractual and equitable right to redeem.

---

79 [1903] AC 253.

80 [1899] 2 Ch 474.

In the present case it is clear from the evidence, if not from the agreement of 24 August 1910, itself, that the nature of the transaction was as follows: The defendant company wanted to borrow 10,000*l* and the plaintiffs desired to obtain an option of purchase over any sheepskins the defendants might have for sale during a period of five years. The plaintiffs agreed to lend the money in consideration of obtaining this option, and the defendant company agreed to give the option in consideration of obtaining the loan. The loan was to carry interest at 6% *per annum*, and was not to be called in by the plaintiffs for a specified period. The defendant company, however, might pay it off at any time. It was to be secured by a floating charge over the defendant company's undertaking. The option was to continue for five years, whether the loan was paid off or otherwise, and if the plaintiffs did not exercise their option as to any of the defendant company's skins, a commission on the sale of such skins was in certain events payable to the plaintiffs.

I doubt whether, even before the repeal of the usury laws, this perfectly fair and businesslike transaction would have been considered a mortgage within any equitable rule or maxim relating to mortgages. The only possible way of deciding whether a transaction is a portage within any such rule or maxim is by reference to the intention of the parties. It never was intended by the parties that if the defendant company exercised their right to pay off the loan they should get rid of the option. The option was not in the nature of a penalty, nor was it nor could it ever become inconsistent with or repugnant to any other part of the real bargain within any such rule or maxim. The same is true of the commission payable on the sale of skins as to which the option was not exercised. Under these circumstances it seems to me that the bargain must stand and that the plaintiffs are entitled to the relief they claim.

Other advantages to the mortgagee may be in the form of unreasonable restraints of trade. Such an agreement, preventing the mortgagor from competing with the mortgagee, or restricting the mortgagor's freedom in the way he carries on his trade or profession, may be void if it is not reasonably necessary to protect the mortgagee's interest.[81] A good example is the landmark decision of the House of Lords in *Esso Petroleum Co Ltd v Harper's Garage (Stourport) Ltd*.[82] The respondent company owned two garages. It entered into two separate agreements with the appellant Esso Petroleum Company in respect of each garage. Both agreements involved covenants by the respondent to buy its total requirements of motor fuel from the appellant in return for a reduced price, and to keep the garages open at all reasonable hours. The first agreement was to last for a period of four years and five months, whereas the second was for a period of 21 years. In addition, the second garage was also mortgaged to the appellant in return for a loan of £7,000 payable by instalments lasting for 21 years and not redeemable before the end of that period. It was held that the restriction on the first garage for four years and five months was not unreasonable but that the restriction on the second garage for 21 years was, and therefore void for restraint of trade.

81 See Furmston, MP, *Cheshire, Fifoot and Furmston's Law of Contract*, 12th edn, 1991, London: Butterworths, pp 397–417; Treitel, *The Law of Contract*, 8th edn, 1991, pp 401–24.

82 [1968] AC 269, HL. See (1969) 85 LQR 229 (Heydon, JD).

Esso Petroleum Co Ltd v Harper's Garage (Stourport) Ltd [1968] AC 269, HL

Lord Reid: If a contract is within the class of contracts in restraint of trade the law which applies to it is quite different from the law which applies to contracts generally. In general unless a contract is vitiated by duress, fraud or mistake its terms will be enforced though unreasonable or even harsh and unconscionable, but here a term in restraint of trade will not be enforced unless it is reasonable. And in the ordinary case the court will not remake a contract: unless in the special case where the contract is severable, it will not strike out one provision as unenforceable and enforce the rest. But here the party who has been paid for agreeing to the restraint may be unjustly enriched if the court holds the restraint to be too wide to be enforceable and is unable to adjust the consideration given by the other party.

It is much too late now to say that this rather anomalous doctrine of restraint of trade can be confined to the two classes of case to which it was originally applied. But the cases outside these two classes afford little guidance as to the circumstances in which it should be applied. In some it has been assumed that the doctrine applies and the controversy has been whether the restraint was reasonable. And in others where one might have expected the point to be taken it was not taken, perhaps because counsel thought that there was no chance of the court holding that the restraint was too wide to be reasonable ...

The main argument submitted for the appellant on this matter was that restraint of trade means a personal restraint and does not apply to a restraint on the use of a particular piece of land. Otherwise, it was said, every covenant running with the land which prevents its use for all or for some trading purposes would be a covenant in restraint of trade and therefore unenforceable unless it could be shown to be reasonable and for the protection of some legitimate interest. It was said that the present agreement only prevents the sale of petrol from other suppliers on the site of the Mustow Green Garage: It leaves the respondents free to trade anywhere else in any way they choose. But in many cases a trader trading at a particular place does not have the resources to enable him to begin trading elsewhere as well, and if he did he might find it difficult to find another suitable garage for sale or to get planning permission to open a new filling station on another site. As the whole doctrine of restraint of trade is based on public policy its application ought to depend less on legal niceties or theoretical possibilities than on the practical effect of a restraint in hampering that freedom which it is the policy of the law to protect.

It is true that it would be an innovation to hold that ordinary negative covenants preventing the use of a particular site for trading of all kinds or of a particular kind are within the scope of the doctrine of restraint of trade. I do not think they are. Restraint of trade appears to me to imply that a man contracts to give up some freedom which otherwise he would have had. A person buying or leasing land had no previous right to be there at all, let alone to trade there, and when he takes possession of that land subject to a negative restrictive covenant he gives up no right or freedom which he previously had. I think that the 'tied house' cases might be explained in this way, apart from *Biggs v Hodinott*,[83] where the owner of a freehouse had agreed to a tie in favour of a brewer who

83 [1898] 2 Ch 307; 14 TLR 504, CA.

had lent him money. Restraint of trade was not pleaded. If it had been, the restraint would probably have been held to be reasonable. But there is some difficulty if a restraint in a lease not merely prevents the person who takes possession of the land under the lease from doing certain things there, but also obliges him to act in a particular way. In the present case the respondents before they made this agreement were entitled to use this land in any lawful way they chose, and by making this agreement they agreed to restrict their right by giving up their right to sell there petrol not supplied by the appellants.

In my view this agreement is within the scope of the doctrine of restraint of trade as it had been developed in English law. Not only have the respondents agreed negatively not to sell other petrol but they have agreed positively to keep this garage open for the sale of the appellants' petrol at all reasonable hours throughout the period of the tie. It was argued that this was merely regulating the respondent's trading and rather promoting than restraining his trade. But regulating a person's existing trade may be a greater restraint that prohibiting him from engaging in a new trade. And a contract to take one's whole supply from one source may be much more hampering than a contract to sell one's whole output to one buyer. I would not attempt to define the dividing line between contract which are and contracts which are not in restraint of trade, but in my view this contract must be held to be in restraint of trade. So it is necessary to consider whether its provisions can be justified.

But before considering this question I must deal briefly with the other agreement tying the Corner Garage for 21 years. The rebate and other advantages to the respondents were similar to those in the Mustow Green agreement but in addition the appellants made a loan of £7,000 to the respondents to enable them to improve their garage and this loan was to be repaid over the 21 years of the tie. In security they took a mortgagee of this garage. The agreement provided that the loan should not be paid off earlier than at the dates stipulated. But the respondents now tender the unpaid balance of the loan and they say that the appellants have no interest to refuse to accept repayment now, except in order to maintain the tie for the full 21 years.

The appellants argue that the fact that there is a mortgage excludes any application of the doctrine of restraint of trade. But I agree with your Lordships in rejecting that argument. I am prepared to assume that, if the respondents had not offered to repay the loan so far as it is still outstanding, the appellants would have been entitled to retain the tie. But, as they have tendered repayment, I do not think that the existence of the loan and the mortgage puts the appellants in any stronger position to maintain the tie than they would have been in if the original agreements had permitted repayment at an earlier date. The appellants must show that in the circumstances when the agreement was made a tie for 21 years was justifiable ...

The Court of Appeal held that these ties were for unreasonably long periods. They thought that, if for any reason the respondents ceased to see the appellants' petrol, the appellants could have found other suitable outlets in the neighbourhood within two or three years. I do not think that that is the right test. In the first place there was no evidence about this and I do not think that it would be practicable to apply this test in practice. It might happen that when the respondents ceased to sell their petrol, the appellants would find such an alternative outlet in a very short time. But, looking to the fact that well over 90% of existing filling stations are tied and that there may be great difficulty in opening a new filling station, it might take a very long time to find an alternative. Any estimate of how long it might take to find suitable alternatives for the respondents' filling stations could be little better than guesswork.

I do not think that the appellants' interest can be regarded so narrowly. They are not so much concerned with any particular outlet as with maintaining a stable system of distribution throughout the country so as to enable their business to be run efficiently and economically. In my view there is sufficient material to justify a decision that ties of less than five years were insufficient, in the circumstances of the trade when these agreements were made, to afford adequate protection to the appellants' legitimate interests. And if that is so I cannot find anything in the details of the Mustow Green agreement which would indicate that it is unreasonable. It is true that if some of the provisions were operated by the appellants in a manner which would be commercially unreasonable they might put the respondents in difficulties. But I think that a court must have regard to the fact that the appellants must act in such a way that they will be able to obtain renewals of the great majority of their very numerous ties, some of which will come to an end almost every week. If in such circumstances a garage owner chooses to rely on the commercial probity and good sense of the producer, I do not think that a court should hold his agreement unreasonable because it is legally capable of some misuse. I would therefore allow the appeal as regards the Mustow Green agreement.

But the Corner Garage agreement involves much more difficulty. Taking first the legitimate interests of the appellants, a new argument was submitted to your Lordships that, apart from any question of security for their loan, it would be unfair to the appellants if the respondents, having used the appellants' money to build up their business, were entitled after a comparatively short time to be free to seek better terms from a competing producer. But there is no material on which I can assess the strength of this argument and I do not find myself in a position to determine whether it has any validity. A tie for 21 years stretches far beyond any period for which developments are reasonably foreseeable. Restrictions on the garage owner which might seem tolerable and reasonable in reasonably foreseeable conditions might come to have a very different effect in quite different conditions: the public interest comes in here more strongly. And, apart from a case where he gets a loan, a garage owner appears to get no greater advantage from a 20-year tie than he gets from a five-year tie. So I would think that there must at least be some clearly established advantage to the producing company – something to show that a shorter period would not be adequate – before so long a period could be justified. But in this case there is no evidence to prove anything of the kind. And the other material which I have thought it right to consider does not appear to me to assist the appellant here I would therefore dismiss the appeal as regards the Corner Garage agreement.

Extortionate credit agreement

Under s 137(1) of the Consumer Credit Act 1974, if the court finds a credit bargain extortionate, it may reopen the credit agreements so as to do justice between the parties. A credit bargain is extortionate if the payments to be made under it are 'grossly exorbitant' or if it 'otherwise grossly contravenes ordinary principles of fair dealing', taking into account the interest rates prevailing at the date of agreement, debtor's personal circumstances (such as age, experience, business capacity, state of health, and degree of financial pressure he had at the date of agreement), creditor's relationship to the debtor, the degree of risk accepted by the creditor and any other relevant considerations.[84] This section applies to all mortgages, provided that the mortgagor is an individual (including a partnership) and not a company. Nothing in s 16 of the Act affects the application of ss 137–40.[85]

Consumer Credit Act 1974

137. Extortionate credit bargains

(1) If the court finds a credit bargain extortionate it may reopen the credit agreement so as to do justice between the parties.

(2) In this section and ss 138–40:

(a) 'credit agreement' means any agreement between an individual (the 'debtor') and any other person (the 'creditor') by which the creditor provides the debtor with credit of any amount, and

(b) 'credit bargain':

(i) where no transaction other than the credit agreement is to be taken into account in computing the total charge for credit, means the credit agreement, or

(ii) where one or more other transactions are to be so taken into account, means the credit agreement and those other transactions, taken together.

138. When bargains are extortionate

(1) A credit bargain is extortionate if it:

(a) requires the debtor or a relative of his to make payments (whether unconditionally, or on certain contingencies) which are grossly exorbitant, or

(b) otherwise grossly contravenes ordinary principles of fair dealing.

(2) In determining whether a credit bargain is extortionate, regard shall be had to such evidence as is adduced concerning:

(a) interest rates prevailing at the time it was made,

(b) the factors mentioned in sub-ss (3)–(5), and

(c) any other relevant considerations.

(3) Factors applicable under sub-s (2) in relation to the debtor include:

(a) his age, experience, business capacity and state of health; and

(b) the degree to which, at the time of making the credit bargain, he was under financial pressure, and the nature of that pressure.

(4) Factors applicable under sub-s (2) in relation to the creditor include:

(a) the degree of risk accepted by him, having regard to the value of any security provided;

84 Section 138 of the Consumer Credit Act 1974.

85 Section 16(7) of the Consumer Credit Act 1974.

(b) his relationship to the debtor; and

(c) whether or not a colourable cash price was quoted for any goods or services included in the credit bargain.

(5) Factors applicable under sub-s (2) in relation to a linked transaction include the question how far the transaction was reasonably required for the protection of debtor or creditor, or was in the interest of the debtor.

139. Reopening of extortionate agreements

(1) A credit agreement may, if the court thinks just, be reopened on the ground that the credit bargain is extortionate:

(a) on an application for the purpose made by the debtor or any surety to the High Court, county court or sheriff court, or

(b) at the instance of the debtor or a surety in any proceedings to which the debtor and creditor are parties, being proceedings to enforce the agreement, any security relating to it or an linked transaction, or

(c) at the instance of the debtor or a surety in other proceedings in any court where the amount paid or payable under the credit agreement is relevant.

(2) In reopening the agreement, the court may, for the purpose of relieving the debtor or a surety from payment of any sum in excess of that fairly due and reasonable, by order:

(a) direct accounts to be taken, or (in Scotland) an accounting to be made, between any persons,

(b) set aside the whole or part of any obligation imposed on the debtor or surety by the credit bargain or any related agreement,

(c) require the creditor to repay the whole or part of any sum paid under the credit bargain or any related agreement by the debtor or a surety, whether paid to the creditor or any other person,

(d) direct the return to the surety of any property provided for the purposes of the security, or

(e) alter the terms of the credit agreement or any security instrument.

(3) An order may be made under sub-s (2) notwithstanding that its effect is to place a burden on the creditor in respect of an advantage unfairly enjoyed by another person who is a party to a linked transaction.

(4) An order under sub-s (2) shall not alter the effect of any judgment.

(5) In England and Wales, an application under sub-s (1)(a) shall be brought only in the county court in the case of:

(a) a regulated agreement, or

(b) an agreement (not being a regulated agreement) under which the creditor provides the debtor with fixed-sum credit not exceeding the county court limit or running-account credit on which the credit limit does not exceed the county court limit.

(5A) In the preceding subsection 'the county court limit' means the county court limit for the time being specified by an Order in Council under s 145 of the County Courts Act 1984 as the county court limit for the purposes of that subsection.

140. Interpretation of ss 137–139

Where the credit agreement is not a regulated agreement, expressions used in ss 137–39 which, apart from this section, apply only to regulated agreements, shall be construed as nearly as may be as if the credit agreement were a regulated agreement.

In *Woodstead Finance Ltd v Petrou*,[86] the Court of Appeal had to consider what could amount to an extortionate rate of interest.

Woodstead Finance Ltd v Petrou [1986] NLJ 188, CA

Sir Browne-Wilkinson: I must see what was the position as at the date in which the transaction was entered into. At that time both the husband and wife were jointly indebted to the Midland Bank in a sum exceeding £14,000. The bank has obtained an order for possession, within 28 days, of the matrimonial home where they and the wife's children by her first marriage all lived. There was a bankruptcy notice outstanding against the husband in relation to Customs and Excise matters. The husband's accountant had advised that the whole of his finances had to be reorganised by getting two forms of finance: first, long-term finance from the building society, and secondly, interim bridging finance to cover the period until the long-term finance had been available, such bridging finance being necessary to meet the pressing demands of, inter alia, the bank. The accountant had himself sought to find such short-term finance, but had failed to do so. There was no suggestion that the accountant was acting otherwise than in good faith in this matter.

It was in those circumstances that the plaintiffs, acting through the solicitor, offered the necessary short-term finance to meeting requirements of the husband's financial scheme. I confess that to my untutored eye the terms on which the plaintiff company offered such finance appear very harsh. But I have had to remind myself throughout this case that I must approach it on the basis of the evidence given before the judge as to the terms of that loan. The evidence ... was that, given the circumstances in which the loan was being sought and the husband's appalling record in relation to payments, an interest rate of 42% *per annum* was the normal or going rate which any reasonable moneylender would charge for a six months loan. There was absolutely no evidence led to contradict this ...

I emphasise that, so far as I am concerned, I am deciding this case only on the basis of the evidence actually given at the trial. Were there to have been evidence suggesting that the terms of the loan were unduly onerous, even having regard to their financial circumstances, my own views on this aspect of the case might well have been different ...

The only point argued on the appeal was an attempt to re-open the judge's finding that the terms of the loan were not extortionate. The claim that the rate of interest was extortionate, within the meaning of s 137 of the Consumer Credit Act 1974, requires the court, as s 138(2) makes clear, to have regard to 'such evidence as is adduced concerning' a number of different factors, including the prevailing interest rates, the age, experience, business capacity and state of health of the debtor, the financial pressure on the debtor

86 [1986] NLJ 188, (1986) *The Times*, 23 January.

and the degree of risk accepted by the creditor. It is clear that what we have to have regard to is the evidence adduced. As I have said, the evidence actually adduced at the trial all indicated that, given the circumstances and the payment record of the husband, the loan arrangement and the rate of interest was normal for a risk of this kind. Accordingly, it was impossible for the judge to hold that this was an extortionate credit bargain within the meaning of the Act. On this, as on the rest of the judgment, I think the judge was quite right. I would dismiss the appeal.

Mustill and Nourse LJJ concurred.

Judicial control of 'oppressive and unconscionable' terms

An important term is the rate of interest payable by the mortgagor. It is common for the rate of interest to be variable through out the loan period and this practice is now widely thought to be valid despite its inherent uncertainty.[87] Interest may also be linked to the Minimum Lending Rate (eg 2% above the MLR) or to the alteration in the rate of exchange between one currency and another.[88]

However, where the interest rate is so high that it is 'oppressive and unconscionable', the court has occasionally been prepared to exercise its inherent equitable power to intervene.[89] An example is *Cityland and Property (Holdings) Ltd v Dabrah*.[90] Here, a mortgage was granted to secure a loan. No interest was payable as such, but a premium was payable which represented an interest rate of 19% *per annum*. Goff J held that this was 'unfair and unconscionable' and that the plaintiff was only entitled to a reasonable rate of interest which was fixed at 7% *per annum*.[91] It is, however, not sufficient to show that the term is 'unreasonable'; it must be 'unfair and unconscionable'.[92] A term may be unfair and unconscionable if it is imposed in a morally reprehensible manner in a way which affects the mortgagee's conscience, for example, where advantage has been taken of a young, inexperienced or ignorant person to introduce a term which no sensible well-advised person or party would have accepted.[93]

Undue influence or misrepresentation

It is not uncommon for a mortgagor (eg a wife) to charge her property as a surety for a debtor (eg her husband) in favour of the mortgagee (eg the bank). This commonly occurs where the husband is in need of a loan for his business debts. When the business for which the loan is acquired fails, it has been

87 Wurtzburg and Mills, *Building Society Law*, 15th edn, 1989, para 6.22.

88 *Multiservice Bookbinding Ltd v Marden* [1979] Ch 84. See [1978] CLJ 211 (Oakley, AJ); (1978) 128 NLJ 1251 (Wilkinson, HW); [1978] Conv 318 (Crane, FR); (1979) 42 MLR 338 (Bishop, WD and Hindley, BV). See also [1978] Conv 346 (Wilkinson, HW).

89 The court may also intervene under the Moneylenders Act 1900–27.

90 [1968] Ch 166.

91 [1968] Ch 166 at 180D.

92 *Multiservice Bookbinding Ltd v Marden* [1979] Ch 84 at 110E.

93 [1979] Ch 84 at 110F.

common for a mortgagor to seek to set aside the mortgage. The most common ground upon which the mortgagor relies is the doctrine of undue influence or misrepresentation.[94]

(a) By the mortgagee

The mortgage may be set aside on the ground that the mortgage transaction has been entered into by him under undue influence or misrepresentation by the mortgagee. Where undue influence is alleged, the complainant has to prove undue influence as a fact. He must show 'some unfair and improper conduct, some coercion from outside, some overreaching, some form of cheating and generally, though not always, some personal advantage obtained by the guilty party'.[95] The leading case is *National Westminster Bank plc v Morgan*.[96] A husband and wife charged their co-owned matrimonial home in favour of the bank to secure a short-term loan. The bank manager visited the couple in their home with the mortgage documents. The wife said that she had no confidence in her husband's business but the bank manager misrepresented to her that the loan did not cover the husband's business. The wife later alleged that the bank manager had exercised undue influence in obtaining her signature. The bank manager's misrepresentation was not relied upon because by the time of the trial the husband's business debts had been paid off. The House of Lords held that there was no evidence of undue influence on the part of the bank manager.

National Westminster Bank plc v Morgan [1985] 1 AC 686, HL

Lord Scarman: As to the facts, I am far from being persuaded that the trial judge fell into error when he concluded that the relationship between the bank and Mrs Morgan never went beyond the normal business relationship of banker and customer. Both Lords Justices saw the relationship between the bank and Mrs Morgan as one of confidence in which she was relying on the bank manager's advice. Each recognised the personal honesty, integrity, and good faith of Mr Barrow. Each took the view that the confidentiality of the relationship was such as to impose upon him a 'fiduciary duty of care'. It was his duty, in their view, to ensure that Mrs Morgan had the opportunity to make an independent and informed decision: but he failed to give her any such opportunity. They, therefore, concluded that it was a case for the presumption of undue influence.

My Lords, I believe that the Lords Justices were led into a misinterpretation of the facts by their use, as is all too frequent in this branch of the law, of words and phrases such as 'confidence', 'confidentiality', 'fiduciary duty'. There are plenty of confidential relationships which do not give rise to the presumption of undue influence (a notable example is that of husband and wife, *Bank of Montreal v Stuart* [1911] AC 120); and there are plenty of non-confidential relationships in which one person relies upon the advice of another, eg many contracts for the sale of goods. Nor am I persuaded that the charge,

94 *National Westminster Bank plc v Morgan* [1985] AC 686 (there was misrepresentation but not pleaded in the trial, no undue influence, security upheld); *Cornish v Midland Bank plc* [1985] 3 All ER 513 (no undue influence from the bank, but set aside on ground of misrepresentation).

95 *Allcard v Skinner* (1887) 36 Ch D 145 at 181, *per* Lindley LJ.

96 [1985] AC 686.

limited as it was by Mr Barrow's declaration to securing the loan to pay off the Abbey National debt and interest during the bridging period, was disadvantageous to Mrs Morgan. It meant for her the rescue of her home upon the terms sought by her – a short-term loan at a commercial rate of interest. The Court of Appeal has not, therefore, persuaded me that the judge's understanding of the facts was incorrect.

But, further, the view of the law expressed by the Court of Appeal was, as I shall endeavour to show, mistaken. Dunn LJ, while accepting that in all the reported cases to which the court was referred the transactions were disadvantageous to the person influenced, took the view that in cases where public policy requires the court to apply the presumption of undue influence there is no need to prove a disadvantageous transaction. Slade LJ also clearly held that it was not necessary to prove a disadvantageous transaction where the relationship of influence was proved to exist ...

Like Dunn LJ, I know of no reported authority where the transaction set aside was not to the manifest disadvantage of the person influenced. It would not always be a gift: it can be a 'hard and inequitable' agreement (*Ormes v Beadel* (1860) 2 Gif 166, 174); or a transaction 'immoderate and irrational' (*Bank of Montreal v Stuart* [1911] AC 120, 137) or 'unconscionable' in that it was a sale at an undervalue (*Poosathurai v Kannappa Chettiar* (1919) LR 47 IA 1, 3–4). Whatever the legal character of the transaction, the authorities show that it must constitute a disadvantage sufficiently serious to require evidence to rebut the presumption that in the circumstances of the relationship between the parties it was procured by the exercise of undue influence. In my judgment, therefore, the Court of Appeal erred in law in holding that the presumption of undue influence can arise from the evidence of the relationship of the parties without also evidence that the transaction itself was wrongful in that it constituted an advantage taken of the person subjected to the influence which, failing proof to the contrary, was explicable only on the basis that undue influence had been exercised to procure it ...

The wrongfulness of the transaction must, therefore, be shown: it must be one in which an unfair advantage has been taken of another. The doctrine is not limited to transactions of gift. A commercial relationship can become a relationship in which one party assumes a role of dominating influence over the other. In *Poosathurai's* case (1919) LR 47 IA 1 the Board recognised that a sale at an undervalue could be a transaction which a court could set aside as unconscionable if it was shown or could be presumed to have been procured by the exercise of undue influence. Similarly a relationship of banker and customer may become one in which the banker acquires a dominating influence. If he does and a manifestly disadvantageous transaction is proved, there would then be room for the court to presume that it resulted from the exercise of undue influence.

This brings me to *Lloyds Bank Ltd v Bundy* [1975] QB 326. It was, as one would expect, conceded by counsel for the respondent that the relationship between banker and customer is not one which ordinarily gives rise to a presumption of undue influence: and that in the ordinary course of banking business a banker can explain the nature of the proposed transaction without laying himself open to a charge of undue influence. This proposition has never been in doubt, though some, it would appear, have thought that the Court of Appeal held otherwise in *Lloyds Bank Ltd v Bundy*. If any such view has gained currency, let it be destroyed now once and for all time: see Lord Denning MR, at p 336F, Cairns LJ, at p 340D, and Sir Eric Sachs, at pp 341H–42A. Your Lordships are, of course, not concerned with the interpretation put upon the facts in that case by the Court of Appeal: the present case is not a rehearing of that case. The question which the House does have to answer is: did the court in *Lloyds Bank Ltd v Bundy* accurately state the law?

Lord Denning MR believed that the doctrine of undue influence could be subsumed under a general principle that English courts will grant relief where there has been 'inequality of bargaining power' (p 339). He deliberately avoided reference to the will of one party being dominated or overcome by another. The majority of the court did not follow him; they based their decision on the orthodox view of the doctrine as expounded in *Allcard v Skinner*, 36 Ch D 145. The opinion of the Master of the Rolls, therefore, was not the ground of the court's decision, which was to be found in the view of the majority, for whom Sir Eric Sachs delivered the leading judgment.

Nor has counsel for the respondent sought to rely on Lord Denning MR's general principle: and, in my view, he was right not to do so. The doctrine of undue influence has been sufficiently developed not to need the support of a principle which by its formulation in the language of the law of contract is not appropriate to cover transactions of gift where there is no bargain. The fact of an unequal bargain will, of course, be a relevant feature in some cases of undue influence. But it can never become an appropriate basis of principle of an equitable doctrine which is concerned with transactions 'not to be reasonably accounted for on the ground of friendship, relationship, charity, or other ordinary motives on which ordinary men act' (Lindley LJ in *Allcard v Skinner*, at p 185). And even in the field of contract I question whether there is any need in the modern law to erect a general principle of relief against inequality of bargaining power. Parliament has undertaken the task – and it is essentially a legislative task – of enacting such restrictions upon freedom of contract as are in its judgment necessary to relieve against the mischief: for example, the hire-purchase and consumer protection legislation, of which the Supply of Goods (Implied Terms) Act 1973, Consumer Credit Act 1974, Consumer Safety Act 1978, Supply of Goods and Services Act 1982 and Insurance Companies Act 1982 are examples. I doubt whether the courts should assume the burden of formulating further restrictions ...

For these reasons, I would allow the appeal. In doing so, I would wish to give a warning. There is no precisely defined law setting limits to the equitable jurisdiction of a court to relieve against undue influence. This is the world of doctrine, not of neat and tidy rules. The courts of equity have developed a body of learning enabling relief to be granted where the law has to treat the transaction as unimpeachable unless it can be held to have been procured by undue influence. It is the unimpeachability at law of a disadvantageous transaction which is the starting-point from which the court advances to consider whether the transaction is the product merely of one's own folly or of the undue influence exercised by another. A court in the exercise of this equitable jurisdiction is a court of conscience. Definition is a poor instrument when used to determine whether a transaction is or is not unconscionable: this is a question which depends upon the particular facts of the case.

Once undue influence is established, it is not necessary to show that the transaction was also manifestly disadvantageous to the mortgagor.[97]

CIBC Mortgages plc v Pitt [1993] 4 All ER 433, HL

Lord Browne-Wilkinson: In the present case the Court of Appeal, as they were bound to, applied the law laid down in *National Westminster Bank plc v Morgan* [1985] 1 All ER 821,

97 *CIBC Mortgages plc v Pitt* [1993] 4 All ER 433, HL overruling *Bank of Credit and Commerce International SA v Aboody* [1990] QB 923.

[1985] AC 686 as interpreted by the Court of Appeal in *Bank of Credit and Commerce International SA v Aboody* (1988) [1992] 4 All ER 955, [1990] 1 QB 923: a claim to set aside a transaction on the grounds of undue influence whether presumed (Morgan) or actual (Aboody) cannot succeed unless the claimant proves that the impugned transaction was manifestly disadvantageous to him. Before your Lordships, Mrs Pitt submitted that the Court of Appeal in Aboody erred in extending the need to show manifest disadvantage in cases of actual, as opposed to presumed, undue influence. Adopting the classification used in O'Brien's case, it is argued that although Morgan's case decides that the claimant must show that the impugned transaction was disadvantageous to him in order to raise the presumption of undue influence within class 2A or 2B, there is no such requirement where it is proved affirmatively that the claimant's agreement to the transaction was actually obtained by undue influence within class 1.

In *Morgan* it was alleged that Mrs Morgan had been induced to grant security to the bank by the undue influence of one of the bank's managers. Mrs Morgan did not allege actual undue influence within class 1, but relied exclusively on a presumption of undue influence within class 2. it was held that the bank manager had never in fact assumed such a role as to raise any presumption of undue influence. However, in addition, it was held that Mrs Morgan could not succeed because she had not demonstrated that the transaction was manifestly disadvantageous to her. Lord Scarman (who delivered the leading speech) rejected a submission that the presumption of undue influence was based on any public policy requirements. In reliance on the judgment of Lindley LJ in *Allcard v Skinner* (1887) 36 Ch D 145, [1886–90] All ER Rep 90 and the decision of the Privy Council in *Poosathurai v Kannappa Chettiar* (1919) LR 47 Ind App 1, he laid down the following proposition ([1985] 1 All ER 821 at 827, [1985] AC 686 at 704):

> Whatever the legal character of the transaction, the authorities show that it must constitute a disadvantage sufficiently serious to require evidence to rebut the presumption that in the circumstances of the relationship between the parties it was procured by the exercise of undue influence. In my judgment, therefore, the Court of Appeal erred in law in holding that the presumption of undue influence can arise from the evidence of the relationship of the parties without also evidence that the transaction itself was wrongful in that it constituted an advantage taken of the person subjected to the influence which, failing proof to the contrary, was explicable only on the basis that undue influence had been exercised to procure it.

In *BCCI v Aboody* [1992] 4 All ER 955, [1990] 1 QB 923 the claimant had established that actual undue influence within class I had been exercised to induce her to enter into the impugned transaction. That transaction was not manifestly disadvantageous to her. The Court of Appeal, following a number of *dicta* in the Court of Appeal and a first instance decision subsequent to *National Westminster Bank plc v Morgan* [1985] 1 All ER 821, [1985] AC 686, held that the decision in *Morgan* applied as much to cases of class 1, actual undue influence, as to class 2, presumed undue influence. They placed reliance on certain passages in Lord Scarman's speech in *Morgan* which indicated a view that the demonstration of a manifest disadvantage was essential even in a class 1 case. The Court of Appeal were initially impressed by a submission that, if manifest disadvantage had to be shown in all cases, an old lady who had been unduly influenced by her solicitor to sell him her family house but had been paid the full market price for it, would be unable to recover. However, they were satisfied that in such a case the old lady would have a remedy under what they regarded as a wholly separate doctrine of equity, *viz* the right to set aside transactions obtained in abuse of confidence.

My Lords, I am unable to agree with the Court of Appeal decision in *BCCI v Aboody*. I have no doubt that the decision in *Morgan* does not extend to cases of actual undue influence. Despite two references in Lord Scarman's speech to cases of actual undue influence, as I read his speech he was primarily concerned to establish that disadvantage had to be shown, not as a constituent element of the cause of action for undue influence, but in order to raise a presumption of undue influence within class 2. That was the only subject matter before the House of Lords in *Morgan* and the passage I have already cited was directed solely to that point. With the exception of a passing reference to *Ormes v Beadel* (1860) 2 Giff 166, 66 ER 70 all the cases referred to by Lord Scarman were cases of presumed undue influence. In the circumstances, I do not think that this House can have been intending to lay down any general principle applicable to all claims of undue influence, whether actual or presumed.

Whatever the merits of requiring a complainant to show manifest disadvantage in order to raise a class 2 presumption of undue influence, in my judgment there is no logic in imposing such a requirement where actual undue influence has been exercised and proved. Actual undue influence is a species of fraud. Like any other victim of fraud, a person who has been induced by undue influence to carry out a transaction which he did not freely and knowingly enter into is entitled to have that transaction set aside as of right. No case decided before *Morgan* was cited (nor am I aware of any) in which a transaction proved to have been obtained by actual undue influence has been upheld nor is there any case in which a court has even considered whether the transaction was, or was not, advantageous. A man guilty of fraud is no more entitled to argue that the transaction was beneficial to the person defrauded than is a man who has procured a transaction by misrepresentation. The effect of the wrongdoer's conduct is to prevent the wronged party from bringing a free will and properly informed mind to bear on the proposed transaction which accordingly must be set aside in equity as a matter of justice.

I therefore hold that a claimant who proves actual undue influence is not under the further burden of proving that the transaction induced by undue influence was manifestly disadvantageous: he is entitled as of right to have it set aside.

(b) By the debtor

The mortgagor may also seek to set aside the mortgage transaction against the mortgagee on the ground that there has been undue influence or misrepresentation by the debtor, rather than the mortgagee. To succeed, the mortgagor must establish that there is undue influence[98] or misrepresentation by the debtor, and that either the debtor has acted as the mortgagee's agent,[99] or the mortgagee has notice, actual or constructive, of the undue influence or misrepresentation.[100] Leaving it all to the debtor to procure the mortgagor to agree to enter into a security transaction is not sufficient to justify an inference

98 Where a wife provides security for her husband's debts, or vice versa, there is no presumption of undue influence: *Howes v Bishop* [1909] 2 KB 390; *Bank of Montreal v Stuart* [1911] AC 121.

99 *Turnbull v Duval* [1902] AC 429; *Kings North Trust Ltd v Bell* [1986] 1 WLR 119; *Barclays Bank plc v O'Brien* [1992] 4 All ER 983 at 1009f, 1010g, CA, [1993] 4 All ER 417 at 425a, 427d, HL.

100 *Barclays Bank plc v O'Brien* [1993] 4 All ER 417; *Bank of Credit and Commerce International SA v Aboody* [1992] 4 All ER 955 at 979, *per* Slade LJ.

that the debtor was appointed as the mortgagee's agent.[101] Under the doctrine of notice, the mortgagor will have constructive notice of the debtor's undue influence or misrepresentation if the transaction is on the face of it not to the financial advantage of the mortgagor and there is a substantial risk that the debtor has used undue influence or misrepresentation to induce the mortgagor to enter into the transaction. The mortgagor may avoid the transaction if the mortgagee fails to warn the mortgagor of the risk he is running by standing as surety and to advise him to take independent advice.[102]

In *Barclays Bank plc v O'Brien*,[103] it will be recalled, Mrs O'Brien signed a legal charge over the co-owned family home as a security for her husband's business debts to the bank. The bank did not explain the contents of the mortgage documents to her when they were signed and did not advise her to obtain independent legal advice. Neither did she read the documents before signing them. She subsequently sought to set aside the transaction on the ground that she signed the documents under undue influence and misrepresentation by her husband. The Court of Appeal found that the influence by Mr O'Brien on his wife was not undue, but he had misrepresented the effect of the mortgage to her. The bank was aware of the fact that the couple were married, that Mr O'Brien was likely to have some influence on her and that she was likely to place reliance on him. But the bank had, nevertheless, failed to take reasonable steps to ensure that she had an adequate comprehension of the effect of the charge. As the bank had left it to Mr O'Brien to explain the transaction to her, it had to take the consequence of Mr O'Brien's conduct. As Mr O'Brien misrepresented to her that the charge was limited to £60,000, the bank could only enforce the security against Mrs O'Brien to that extent. The Bank appealed to the House of Lords. The claim based on undue influence was not pursued by Mrs O'Brien. The House of Lords, applying the doctrine of notice and dismissing the appeal, held that as the bank knew that Mr and Mrs O'Brien were married and that Mrs O'Brien acted as a surety for her husband's business debts with no direct pecuniary interest, the bank should have taken reasonable steps to explain the nature of the transaction to her and recommended her to take independent legal advice. As the bank failed to take such steps, and the security was obtained as a result of Mr O'Brien's misrepresentation, the bank had constructive notice of Mrs O'Brien's equity to set aside the transaction and is therefore bound by it.

In *Barclays Bank plc v O'Brien*, Lord Browne-Wilkinson thought that the same rule should apply to other unmarried persons. A mortgagee should likewise be put on notice in similar circumstances where there is an emotional relationship between unmarried cohabitees, whether heterosexual or homosexual.[104]

---

101 *Barclays Bank plc v O'Brien* [1992] 4 All ER 983 at 1009f, 1010g, CA; [1993] 4 All ER 417 at 425a, 427d, HL.

102 *Barclays Bank plc v O'Brien* [1993] 4 All ER 417 at 428j–429b, 429f–g, 430g, HL; see also *Goode Durrant Administration v Biddulph* [1994] 2 FLR 551; *Midland Bank plc v Greene* [1994] 2 FLR 827; *Dunbar Bank plc v Nadeem* [1997] 1 FLR 318.

103 [1993] 4 All ER 417, HL. See (1994) 57 MLR 467 (Fehlberg, B); (1994) LQR 167 (Lehane, JRF); [1994] Conv 140 (Thompson, MP); [1994] Fam Law 78 (Cretney, S); [1995] *Oxford Journal of Legal Studies* 119 (Goo, SH).

104 *Barclays Bank plc v O'Brien* [1993] 4 All ER 417 at 431d–g, HL.

Notice of any undue influence etc by the debtor (eg knowledge of the true purpose of the loan which raises the possibility of undue influence etc by the debtor on the mortgagor) which is acquired by the lender's solicitor can also be imputed to the lender. Where, however, the solicitor is acting for both the mortgagor and the lender in the same transaction, knowledge of some fact about the transaction which it is his duty not to disclose to the lender without the mortgagor's consent cannot be imputed to the lender.[105] This is because in such a case, the solicitor cannot disclose the fact to the lender without the mortgagor's consent. Yet it is at the same time his duty to inform the lender of it. There is therefore a conflict of interest and the proper course for the solicitor to take would be to notify the lender that he can no longer act for the lender. It follows, therefore, that such knowledge acquired by the solicitor cannot be imputed to the lender.

What are the necessary steps required to be taken by the lender? Lord Browne-Wilkinson said that in order to avoid being fixed with constructive notice, where the lender only knows that the wife is to stand as surety for her husband's debts, the lender should insist that she attends a private meeting (in the absence of the husband) with a representative of the lender at which she is told of the extent of her liability as surety, warned of the risk she is running and asked to take independent legal advice.[106] In exceptional cases, where the lender knows further facts which make the presence of undue influence not only possible but probable, the lender should insist that the wife is separately advised.[107] Whilst Lord Browne-Wilkinson's guidance is to operate prospectively, it has been used as the yardstick to measure the propriety of past transanctions. Thus, in *Midland Bank plc v Massey*,[108] the Court of Appeal held that it was sufficient for the bank to require the surety to seek independent advice.

Once the mortgagee has advised the mortgagor to take independent advice, the mortgagee is entitled to assume that the solicitor consulted by the mortgagor has provided honest and proper advice and the mortgagee is not under any duty to inquire into what has transpired at the interview between the mortgagor and the solicitor.[109] If the surety is independently advised by a solicitor who does not act for the lender, the lender is entitled to assume that the solicitor has properly discharged his professional duty to the surety.[110] So long as the lender has required the surety to sign a form of declaration in the presence of a solicitor, whose honesty and competence the lender was entitled to rely and who also signed the form certifying that prior to the execution of the charge its nature and effect had been explained to the surety, the lender has

105 *Halifax Mortgage Services Ltd v Stepsky* [1995] 4 All ER 656.

106 *Barclays Bank plc v O'Brien* [1993] 4 All ER 417 at 430g.

107 *Ibid* at 430b, 431b.

108 [1994] 2 FLR 342.

109 *Massey v Midland Bank plc* [1995] 1 All ER 929, CA; *Banco Exterior International v Mann* [1995] 1 All ER 936, CA.

110 *Midland Bank plc v Serter* [1995] 1 FLR 1034.

discharged its duty to take reasonable steps.[111] This is so even if the solicitor acting for the surety was in fact instructed by the lender.[112]

It should however be noted that it is not the lender's business to ask itself why the surety was willing to stand surety for the borrower's indebtedness but merely to ensure that the surety knew what she was doing and wanted to do it having received independent legal advice about the nature and effect of the transaction.[113] Partial or incomplete explanation would not suffice. In *Credit Lyonnais Bank Nederland NV v Burch*,[114] the defendant who was a junior employee at a modest wage provided security for an increased overdraft for the employer company from £250,000 to £270,000 by giving a second charge over her flat and an unlimited all moneys guarantee. The mortgage document was signed in the presence of P the company's main shareholder and alter ego at the office of the bank's solicitors. The defendant was not informed either by P or the bank of the company's indebtedness to the bank and the extent of the overdraft facility being granted. But the bank's solicitor informed the defendant that the guarantee was unlimited both in time and amount and advised her to seek independent legal advice before signing the transaction but she did not do so. It was held that it was not sufficient for the bank's solicitors to tell her the nature of the guarantee since without being informed of the amount of the company's indebtedness to the bank or the extent of the overdraft facility being granted she was not in a position to assess the significance of the guarantee being unlimited.

What is interesting is that the court there suggested that it was not enough for the employee to be advised to take independent legal advice; it was at the least necessary that she should receive such advice.[115] Millett LJ went even further to suggest that:

> it is not sufficient that she should have received independent advice unless she has acted on that advice. If this were not so, the same influence that produced her desire to enter into the transaction would cause her to disregard any advice not to do so. [The cases] also show that the solicitor must not be content to satisfy himself that his client understands the transaction and wishes to carry it out. His duty is to satisfy himself that the transaction is one which his client could sensibly enter into if free from improper influence; and if he is not so satisfied to advise her not to enter into it, and to refuse to act further for her if she persists. He must advise his client that she is under no obligation to enter into the transaction at all and, if she still wishes to do so, that she is not necessarily bound to accept the terms of any document which has been put before her but (where this is appropriate) that he should ascertain on her behalf whether less onerous terms might be obtained.[116]

Thus, if the lender is aware of the likelihood of undue influence, it must also have known that no competent solicitor could have advised the surety to enter

111 *Banco Exterior International v Mann* [1995] 1 FLR 602; *Bank of Baroda v Rayarel* [1995] 2 FLR 376.

112 *Barclays Bank plc v Thomson* [1997] 1 FLR 156.

113 *Banco Exterior International SA v Thomas* [1997] 1 All ER 46.

114 [1997] 1 All ER 144.

115 *Ibid* at 152a–b.

116 *Ibid* at 156f–j.

into such transaction. Millett LJ's view seems to require a higher standard of prudence than that suggested by Lord Browne-Wilkinson.

In *O'Brien*, the husband was joint owner with his wife of the mortgaged property. He was a party to the mortgage transaction which could be set aside by Mrs O'Brien. However, if the husband had not been a party to the mortgage, conceptually there would be no mortgage transaction between him and Mrs O'Brien which could be set aside by the latter, and the mortgage between the bank and Mrs O'Brien would be an independent transaction unaffected by the husband's wrongful act. This question arose in *Banco Exterior International SA v Thomas*.[117] Sir Richard Scott VC was not troubled by it and said that '[no] sensible system of jurisprudence could justify a difference in result that depended on whether the debtor (the husband) happened to be a party to the transaction between the surety (the wife) and the lender (the bank). In such a case, if the lender had constructive (or actual) notice of the misrepresentation or undue influence by the borrower that had led the surety to contract with the bank, the surety would surely be able to set aside the contract'.[118]

Where undue influence etc can be established the transaction can be set aside in its entirety and the court has no discretion to allow rescission on terms, since normally the mortgagor would not have entered into the mortgage if he had known its true nature,[119] unless the surety has obtained some benefit from the transaction, in which case, the surety must make restitution to the lender for the benefit acquired.[120]

Where, however, the loan is advanced for the joint use of the mortgagor and the debtor (as distinct from the sole use of the debtor), then as it is ostensibly a routine transaction, there is nothing to put the mortgagee on notice. The mortgagee does not have to warn the mortgagor of the risk he is running as a surety and to advise him to obtain independent advice.[121] In *CIBC Mortgages plc v Pitt*,[122] Mr Pitt needed money to buy shares on the stock market. He persuaded his wife to charge their legally co-owned home in favour of CIBC Mortgages plc. The loan was stated to be for the proposed purchase of a holiday home. Mrs Pitt did not read the documents she signed. When Mr Pitt later failed to keep up with the mortgage payments, the lender sought possession. Mrs Pitt claimed that the mortgage was not enforceable against her because of her husband's undue influence. The House of Lords refused to set aside the mortgage transaction because the loan was stated to be for the proposed purchase of a holiday home for the benefit of both the debtor and the mortgagor. The bank was not put on notice of the debtor's undue influence over the mortgagor.

117 [1997] 1 All ER 46.

118 *Ibid* at 54a–d. Roch LJ reserved his view on this question for another case (at 57b).

119 *Barclays Bank plc v O'Brien* [1993] 4 All ER 417 at 432f; *Allied Irish Bank plc v Byrne* [1995] 2 FLR 325 at 354F; *TSB Bank plc v Camfield* [1995] 1 FLR 751 at 758F, 760B; *Castle Phillips Finance v Piddington* [1995] 1 FLR 783 at 789H; *Bank Melli Iran v Samadi-Rad* [1995] 2 FLR 367.

120 *Dunbar Bank plc v Nadeem* [1997] 1 FLR 318; *Midland Bank plc v Greene* [1994] 2 FLR 827.

121 *CIBC Mortgages plc v Pitt* [1993] 4 All ER 433, HL.

122 [1993] 4 All ER 433, HL.

CIBC Mortgages plc v Pitt [1993] 4 All ER 433, HL

Lord Browne-Wilkinson: Even though, in my view, Mrs Pitt is entitled to set aside the transaction as against Mr Pitt, she has to establish that in some way the plaintiff is affected by the wrongdoing of Mr Pitt so as to be entitled to set aside the legal charge as against the plaintiff.

The Court of Appeal in the present case treated themselves as bound by the Court of Appeal decision in *Barclays Bank plc v O'Brien* [1992] 4 All ER 983, [1993] QB 109. They were unwilling to distinguish *O'Brien* on the ground that the instant case is one of a loan to the husband and wife jointly whereas *O'Brien* was a surety case. However, pre-echoing our decision in *O'Brien*, they distinguished it on the grounds of notice. Peter Gibson LJ said:

> We are concerned with the application of equitable principles. I start with the fact that equity does not presume undue influence in transactions between husband and wife. Further, *bona fide* purchasers for value without notice are recognised in equity as having a good defence to equitable claims. On principle, therefore, a creditor who is not on notice of any actual or likely undue influence in a transaction involving a husband and wife ought not to be affected by the exercise of undue influence by the husband. Of course if the creditor leaves it to the husband to procure the wife's participation in the transaction or otherwise makes the husband the creditor's agent, whether in a strict or some looser sense, then the creditor is affected by the acts of the agent and notice of undue influence by the husband can be imputed to the creditor. By reason of the *O'Brien* case, I must accept that in a case where a wife provides security for a husband's debts, the creditor, unless it takes steps to ensure that the wife understands the transaction and that her consent was true and informed, may be affected by any undue influence exerted by the husband to procure the wife's actions, even if the creditor has no knowledge of the undue influence; but that is explicable on the basis that such a transaction, favouring a husband at the expense of his wife, on its face puts the creditor on notice of the possibility of undue influence by the husband. By parity of reasoning, if there is a secured loan to a husband and wife but the creditor is aware that the purposes of the loan are to pay the husband's debts or otherwise for his (as distinct from their joint) purposes, the creditor, without taking precautionary steps, may be affected by the husband's misconduct. On that footing, on the facts of the present case it is in my judgment clear that the plaintiff had no actual knowledge of the acts of Mr Pitt relied on by Mrs Pitt as constituting undue influence. Nor was there anything to put the plaintiff on notice that this was other than a routine transaction for the benefit of both Mr and Mrs Pitt. It was, so far as the plaintiff was aware, partly a remortgaging transaction, and partly the raising of money to purchase other property for the joint benefit of Mr and Mrs Pitt and the cheque was made payable to them jointly. True it is that there was a greatly increased borrowing on their house, but the valuation showed that there would be a substantial equity in the house after the borrowing. In my judgment therefore the innocent plaintiff is not affected by the undue influence exercised by Mr Pitt over Mrs Pitt and accordingly on this ground Mrs Pitt's defence to these proceedings fails.

I agree with this conclusion and, save to the extent that it recognises as good law the reasoning of the Court of Appeal in *O'Brien*, with the analysis of Peter Gibson LJ. Applying the decision of this House in *O'Brien*, Mrs Pitt has established actual undue influence by Mr Pitt. The plaintiff will not however be affected by such undue influence unless Mr Pitt was, in a real sense, acting as agent of the plaintiff in procuring Mrs Pitt's agreement or the plaintiff had actual or constructive notice of the undue influence. The judge has correctly held that Mr Pitt was not acting as agent for the plaintiff. The plaintiff had no actual notice of the undue influence. What, then, was known to the plaintiff that could put it on inquiry so as to fix it with constructive notice?

So far as the plaintiff was aware, the transaction consisted of a joint loan to the husband and wife to finance the discharge of an existing mortgage on 26 Alexander Avenue and, as to the balance, to be applied in buying a holiday home. The loan was advanced to both husband and wife jointly. There was nothing to indicate to the plaintiff that this was anything other than a normal advance to a husband and wife for their joint benefit.

Mr Price QC for Mrs Pitt argued that the invalidating tendency which reflects the risk of there being class 2B undue influence was, in itself, sufficient to put the plaintiff on inquiry. I reject this submission without hesitation. It accords neither with justice nor with practical common sense. If third parties were to be fixed with constructive notice of undue influence in relation to every transaction between husband and wife, such transactions would become almost impossible. On every purchase of a home in joint names, the building society or bank financing the purchase would have to insist on meeting the wife separately from her husband, advise her as to the nature of the transaction and recommend her to take legal advice separate from that of her husband. If that were not done, the financial institution would have to run the risk of a subsequent attempt by the wife to avoid her liabilities under the mortgage on the grounds of undue influence or misrepresentation. To establish the law in that sense would not benefit the average married couple and would discourage financial institutions from making the advance.

What distinguishes the case of the joint advance from the surety case is that, in the latter, there is not only the possibility of undue influence having been exercised but also the increased risk of it having in fact been exercised because, at least on its face, the guarantee by a wife of her husband's debts is not for her financial benefit. It is the combination of these two factors that puts the creditor on inquiry.

For these reasons I agree with the Court of Appeal on this issue and would dismiss the appeal.

Disposition

The right of redemption was, until 1925 legislation, an equitable interest in the mortgaged property which could be sold, bought or mortgaged. The purchaser from the mortgagor of the mortgaged property was simply put into the shoe of the mortgagor so he only had an equitable interest which was subject to the legal mortgage.

After 1925, the mortgagor retains his legal estate with an equitable right of redemption. So, in theory, he can deal with the mortgaged property in any way consistent with the rights of the mortgagee. He may sell the legal estate in the mortgaged property or grant a second legal mortgage on it. But the practical problem he has is that in almost all cases his title deeds will have been retained by the mortgagee or his land certificate retained by the Land Registry. Without title deeds or land certificate, he is unable to show his title before the completion of sale. Any purchaser will then know that the property has been mortgaged and would require the vendor to discharge the mortgage. As regards the creation of a second mortgage, in unregistered system, a first legal mortgage, despite being a legal interest, only binds the whole world if the mortgagee has the title deeds. If he does not have the title deeds, he must register his legal mortgage as a *puisne* mortgage.[123] Where the title deeds are deposited with the first mortgagee, the mortgagor will be unable to produce them thereby alerting to the second mortgagee the possibility of the existence of a first mortgage. Where the first mortgagee has not got the title deeds, provided he has registered his mortgage, the second mortgagee will have notice of it on an official search of the land charges registration. Of course, priority in registered system depends on the order of registration or entry, but without land certificate a second legal mortgage cannot be registered. So, in practice, the second mortgagee is often able to find out if there exists a first mortgage and can decide whether the land offered is a sufficient security for the proposed loan. Having said that, some mortgagors do manage to sell or grant a second mortgage either by fraud or by the first mortgage's returning the documents of title. Priority in these cases will be discussed below.

Possession

As a matter of strict law, as will be seen, it is the mortgagee who has the right to be in possession because he is granted a term of years absolute.[124] But, normally, the mortgage deed itself will contain a covenant that the mortgagee will not take possession so long as the mortgagor performs his obligation under the mortgage. Where a mortgagor is left in possession he has the right to sue, as against third parties other than the mortgagee to protect his possession, eg to prevent trespass, nuisance, damage to property or breach of restrictive covenant.[125]

Where the mortgage is regulated by the Consumer Credit Act 1974, the right of possession is enforceable only on an order of the court.[126] The mortgagee is likewise only entitled to recover possession of the land from the mortgagor on an order of the court.[127]

Leasing

(a) Leases granted after the mortgage is granted

Because the mortgagor retains a legal estate in the mortgaged property, he may grant a lease even after the mortgage is created. But, in theory, any lease granted will only take effect in reversion because he has just granted a legal lease in possession to the mortgagee. To overcome this, s 99 of the Law of Property Act 1925, however, gives a mortgagor who is in possession a statutory

---

123 Section 2(4)(i) of the LCA 1972, s 2(4)(i). See Chapter 6, pp 221, 223.

124 *Fourmaids Ltd v Dudley Marshall Ltd* [1957] Ch 317.

125 Section 88 of the LPA 1925.

126 Section 126 of the Consumer Credit Act 1974.

127 Section 92(2) of the Consumer Credit Act 1974.

power to grant from time to time any lease of the mortgaged land for a term authorised by s 99(3).[128] Such a lease will be binding on both the mortgagor and the mortgagee and will take effect in possession unless s 99 is excluded by the mortgage deed or otherwise in writing.[129]

If the power to grant a lease under s 99 is excluded and the mortgagor nevertheless grants an unauthorised lease then the lease is void as against the mortgagee and his successors in title.[130] But the lease will still be valid as a tenancy by estoppel against the mortgagor. The mortgagee can treat the lessee as a trespasser and exercise his right to take possession.[131] If the mortgagee does not treat him as a trespasser but does some acts which confirm such a letting eg by receiving the rent from the lessee, he is taken to have impliedly consented to it and hence a lease is created as between the mortgagee and the lessee.[132] The mortgagee's consent will not be implied from the mortgagee's mere knowledge of the lease.[133]

The practice of Building Societies and Banks is to exclude the mortgagor's power of leasing and to prohibit borrower from leasing without their written consent. Where the mortgagor let the property in breach of the covenant prohibiting letting without mortgagee's consent, the mortgagee who had no knowledge of the lease can still claim possession even if the tenant has now become a protected[134] statutory tenant by virtue of the Rent Act 1977.[135]

In *Britannia Building Society v Earl*,[136] the first defendant, the mortgagor, in breach of a covenant prohibiting letting of the mortgaged property without the plaintiff building society's consent, let the property for a period of nine months to the second defendants, who had no knowledge of the mortgage. They became statutory tenants by virtue of the Rent Act 1977 when the lease expired. The mortgagor was later in default of mortgage payment and the building society sought possession. The second defendants claimed to be entitled to possession under s 98 of the Rent Act 1977, or alternatively to adjournment of the proceedings under s 36 of the Administration of Justice Act 1970 because they are prepared to make mortgage payments for the mortgagor. The second defendants' claims failed.

---

128 After 1925 a mortgagor can grant a lease for any term not exceeding 50 years for agricultural purposes or occupation, 999 years for building purposes: s 99(3). Any lease granted must comply with the statutory conditions set out in s 99, eg the lease must reserve the best rent reasonably obtainable.

129 Section 99(1)(13) of the LPA 1925.

130 *Rust v Goodale* [1957] Ch 33.

131 See [1991] JSWL 220 (DG Barnsley); Law Com No 204 (1991), para 6.19.

132 *Stroud Building Society v Delamont* [1960] 1 WLR 431.

133 *Taylor v Ellis* [1960] Ch 358.

134 *Dudley and District Benefit Building Society v Emerson* [1949] 2 All ER 252.

135 *Britannia Building Society v Earl* [1990] 1 WLR 422.

136 [1990] 1 WLR 422.

Britannia Building Society v Earl [1990] 1 WLR 422, CA

McCowan LJ: ... it is said that by reason of being statutory and not contractual tenants a possession order can only be made against the second defendants under the provisions of s 98 of the Rent Act 1977, irrespective of whether proceedings are brought by the landlords or by the mortgagees as holders of the title paramount.

[His Lordship read ss 1, 2(a) and 98 of the Rent Act 1977 and referred to various authorities.]

Mr Keith, for the second defendants, argues that a statutory tenant enjoys no more than a personal right, a status of irremovability good against the whole world. The lack of a legal estate, he says, is demonstrated in a number of ways. For example, a statutory tenant has no interest in land capable of assignment or testamentary disposition; a statutory tenancy cannot pass to the tenant's trustee in bankruptcy; and the ordinary law as to joint tenancy is not applied in its full strictness to a statutory tenancy: see *Lloyd v Saddler* [1978] QB 774. However, Mr Keith conceded that what his argument entailed, looking at the facts of the present case, was that in the course of the nine months of the contractual tenancy – at which time the second defendants were protected tenants under s 1 of the Rent Act 1977 – they would have had no right to possession as against the plaintiffs. But, on his argument once the nine months were up and the second defendants became statutory tenants, the plaintiffs could no longer recover possession from them. I am bound to say I find this quite illogical.

Mr Keith spoke of s 98 of the Rent Act 1977 (to which I have already referred) as providing a complete code for recovery of possession of dwelling houses. It is to be noted, however, that this section equates 'protected' and 'statutory' tenancies so far as security of tenure is concerned. Yet he is asking this court to make a profound distinction between them as against mortgagees in the circumstances here obtaining.

Mr Keith further placed reliance on views expressed in an article by Peter Smith of the Faculty of Law, Manchester University, entitled 'Statutory Tenants and Mortgagees' (1977) 41 *The Conveyancer* 200, which support the views which he is submitting. On the first page of that article I read this passage.

> The result may be harsh on mortgagees. For their rights to possession may well depend on the presence of a notice to quit given by a landlord, who had no power to grant the lease, to a tenant who holds under a lease which was not binding on him (the mortgagee). A court may be reluctant to find such a result. The opposite conclusion is however no less harsh on a tenant who has regularly paid his rent, only to be told he is a squatter and a trespasser.

However, the remark that rejection of the opinion there expressed would be harsh on a statutory tenant who has regularly paid his rent would equally apply to a protected tenant who has regularly paid his rent. (Incidentally, Mr Neuberger points out that in the same volume of *The Conveyancer* is an article by another, Jill Martin, who argues a view contrary to that of Mr Smith.)

Our attention was drawn by Mr Neuberger to *dicta* of Templeman LJ in *Quennell v Maltby* [1979] 1 WLR 318 at 323:

> The lease to the statutory tenant was made by the landlord after the date of the mortgage without the consent of the bank and was therefore in breach of the landlord's covenant contained in the mortgage. That lease was binding on the landlord but void against the bank. On expiry of the lease the tenant became a statutory tenant as against the landlord but not as against the bank.

Mr Neuberger concedes that the point was not argued there, but nonetheless it is very persuasive authority and I respectfully follow it. I am, therefore, quite unpersuaded by Mr Keith's first point.

It seems to me that, having regard to the characteristics of a statutory tenant, a statutory tenant has not got an estate or interest in the land ...

Mr Neuberger submits that s 39(1), the definition section, only applies to assignment of the property and does not include tenants. He says that if he is wrong about that and it does include tenants, it does not include statutory tenants who do not derive title at all. I would accept those submissions. But Mr Neuberger has a further point if those are wrong. He says that the very existence of the tenancy in this case is a breach of an obligation arising under the mortgage. The only ground for seeking possession here against the mortgagor was the arrears, but unknown to the mortgagee there was another perfectly good ground, namely, the breach of the covenant against leasing, of which breach the mortgagees were unaware.

This leads him to his third point. He submits that the power can only be exercised under s 36(1) if the breach can be remedied. The present default, he says, cannot be remedied save by the departure of the tenant. Mr Keith seeks to counter this by submitting that the words in s 36(1) 'any other obligation' should be construed as obligations 'affecting the mortgagee's security.' For my part, I see no justification for construing the phrase 'any other obligation' as if those words were added. 'Any other obligation,' in my judgment, means what it says. Consequently, in my judgment, Mr Keith's second point fails.

I would therefore dismiss the appeal.

In *Britannia Building Society v Earl*,[137] as in *Dudley and District Benefit Building Society v Emerson*,[138] the title to the property appeared to be unregistered and the mortgagee had a paramount title to the mortgaged property. In the case of registered land, the mortgagee will only get a paramount title on registration of the mortgage. Thus, if the prohibited lease is granted after the mortgage is created but before it is registered, and the lease is for a term less than 21 years, the lease being an overriding interest under s 70(1)(k) of the Land Registration Act 1925 will take priority over the unregistered mortgage.[139] Where the lease is for more than 21 years, then unless it is registered substantially before the mortgage is registered, the mortgage will have priority both being unregistered minor interests.[140]

(b) Tenancies by estoppel

Suppose the mortgaged property is purchased with the help of the mortgage, and suppose the mortgagor purports to grant a lease of the mortgaged property before the mortgage is created which enables him to purchase the property. Here, although the purchaser-mortgagor has not acquired the legal estate in the

137 [1990] 1 WLR 422.

138 [1949] 2 All ER 252.

139 *Barclays Bank plc v Zaroovabli* [1997] 2 All ER 19.

140 *Cf Barclays Bank Ltd v Taylor* [1974] Ch 137.

mortgaged property and is therefore incapable of granting a legal lease of it, he is estopped from denying the lessee's title.[141] The lease between the lessee and the purchaser-mortgagor is a tenancy by estoppel. When the purchaser-mortgagor acquires the legal estate in the property subsequently, by reason of the mortgage, the tenancy is fed and becomes a full legal tenancy. In theory, the mortgagor cannot grant a mortgage of a legal estate before he acquires the legal estate. So the conveyance of the legal estate necessarily precedes the grant of the mortgage. Thus, there is a *scintilla temporis* or a fragment of time between the acquisition by the mortgagor of the legal estate and the grant of the mortgage in favour of the mortgagee. It used to be thought that such a legal estate was free of the mortgage which funded the purchase in that split second. And in that split second the tenancy by estoppel was fed by the legal estate which was free of the mortgage and being a legal tenancy it then bound the mortgagee.[142]

A classic example of the *scintilla temporis* theory is the case of *Church of England Building Society v Piskor*.[143] Here the mortgagor was allowed possession of land before the completion of his purchase. He then purported to grant periodic tenancies to two tenants who moved in before the completion. The mortgagor subsequently completed the purchase with the loan from the mortgagee. The mortgagee later sought possession when the mortgagor was in default of payments. The Court of Appeal held that the tenant had priority over the mortgagee. This was because the tenants' tenancies by estoppel were fed by the acquisition of the legal estate by the mortgagor which took place before the grant of the mortgage.[144]

However, as will be seen later, the House of Lords has now, in *Abbey National Building Society v Cann*,[145] conclusively rejected the idea of *scintilla temporis* where the purchase of the property and the mortgage which wholly or partly funded the purchase were simultaneous. There is no *scintilla temporis* in which the purchaser-mortgagor could get a legal estate free of the mortgage and feed the tenancy by estoppel. The purchaser obtains no more than an equity of redemption (ie a legal estate with a right of redemption subject to the mortgagee's interest) and when the equity of redemption feeds the tenancy by estoppel, the tenancy is also subject to the mortgagee's interest. To this extent the *Piskor's* case is overruled. Thus a tenancy by estoppel does not bind the mortgagee.

Where an unauthorised lease is granted after the first mortgage is created but the first mortgage is later discharged by a second mortgage terms, the question sometimes arises whether there is a *scintilla temporis* between the discharge of the first mortgage and the creation of the second mortgage when the lease can become lawful and bind the second mortgagee. The Court of

141 *Cuthberston v Irving* (1859) 4 H & N 742; *Industrial Properties (Barton Hill) Ltd v Associated Electrical Industries Ltd* [1977] QB 580.

142 *Church of England Building Society v Piskor* [1954] Ch 553.

143 [1954] Ch 553.

144 [1954] Ch 553 at 561, 564.

145 [1990] 1 All ER 1085. See (1990) 106 LQR 32, 545 (Smith, RJ); [1990] CLJ 397 (Oakley, AJ); (1990) 87 LSG 19–24, 34–19 (Beaumont, M); [1991] Conv 116 (Baughen, S); [1991] Conv 155 (Evans, PT).

Appeal in *Walthamstow Building Society v Davies*[146] took the view that where in reality there was only one advance and the second mortgage was created merely to vary the terms of the first mortgage there was no *scintilla temporis* between the discharge of the first mortgage and the creation of the second. Similarly, in *Equity and Law Home Loan Ltd v Prestidge*[147] the Court of Appeal held that where the first mortgage is discharged by a second mortgage there is no *scintilla temporis* between the discharge of the first and the creation of the second mortgage.

6 RIGHTS OF LEGAL MORTGAGEES AND CHARGEES

Possession of documents of title

As against any prior legal or equitable interests, the mortgagee, like any ordinary purchaser, will make proper investigation of title, inspection of property and searches before the mortgage is created. But, as will be seen, to make sure that he has priority over any subsequent purchaser or mortgagee (in case the mortgagor grants more than one mortgage) it is crucial for the mortgagee to retain the title deeds. Prior to 1926, the mortgagee had a right to hold the title deeds, because the legal estate was conveyed to him. Today, although mortgagees are not conveyed the entire legal estate in the mortgaged property, a first mortgagee is given a statutory right to possession of the documents of title.[148] A legal chargee is also given the same right.[149] Where the title of the mortgaged property is registered, the land certificate will be retained in the Land Registry[150] and the mortgagee or chargee will be issued with a charge certificate.

The possession of title documents also helps the mortgagee later should the power of sale become exercisable.

Insurance at mortgagor's expense

To ensure that the value of the mortgaged property will not diminish in case it is damaged, the mortgagee is entitled to insure the property at the mortgagor's expense.[151]

Action on covenant to repay

The mortgagee can always sue for the money due on the covenant to repay as soon as the date fixed for repayment has arrived.[152] Any action for the arrears

146 (1990) 60 P & CR 99, CA.

147 [1992] 1 All ER 909. See (1993) 44 NILQ 51 (Goo, SH); [1992] Conv 206 (Thompson, MP); (1992) LQR 108/371 (Smith, RJ).

148 Sections 85(1) and 86(1) of the LPA 1925.

149 Section 87 of the LPA 1925.

150 Section 65 of the LRA 1925.

151 Section 101(1)(ii) of the LPA 1925.

152 *Bolton v Buckenham* [1891] 1 QB 278.

of interest must be brought within six years after it is due.[153] An action for the mortgage principal is statute-barred after 12 years from the date of accrual of the right to receive it.[154] But these actions may not be a practical remedy in the short term since the reason why the mortgagor has fallen behind with repayment is usually because of financial difficulties. There are, therefore, other remedies available for him to enforce his security, as follows.

Possession

Mortgage possession actions, including residential and non-residential mortgages, are common occurrences and are on an upward trend.[155] To recover unpaid interest the mortgagee may simply exercise his right to take possession so that he can let the property and receive rent and profit to satisfy the arrears. To recover the capital or such sum which is outstanding he may exercise his power of sale. Vacant possession is necessary for a good sale price.

As a legal mortgage gives the mortgagee a legal estate in possession he is entitled, subject to any agreement to the contrary, to take possession of the mortgaged property as soon as the mortgage is created, even if the mortgagor is not guilty of default.[156] The mortgagee 'may go into possession before the ink is dry on the mortgage'.[157] A legal chargee has a similar right under s 87(1) of the Law of Property Act 1925.

Four-Maids Ltd v Dudley Marshall (Pty) Ltd [1957] 1 Ch 317

Harman J: This is an originating summons for possession. The plaintiffs, being proprietors of a legal charge on the register, have under s 34(1) of the Land Registration Act 1925, all the powers and rights of a legal mortgagee. This subject is one which is constantly being agitated in this court. I have had my attention called to some observations I made on it recently in *Hughes v Waite*,[158] and even more recently in *Alliance Perpetual Building Society v Belrum Investments Ltd*,[159] which came before me on an application to commit the editor of the *Daily Mail* for comments on a mortgagee's action for possession of a sort exactly similar to the present. The comments and, indeed, the arguments of counsel for the newspaper showed an entire misapprehension of what an originating summons for possession is about. They all assumed that it involved some kind of default on the part of the mortgagor, but I said there, and I repeat now, that the right of the mortgagee to possession in the absence of some contract has nothing to do with default on the part of the mortgagor. The mortgagee may go into possession before

153 Section 20(5) of the Limitation Act 1980.

154 Section 20(1) of the Limitation Act 1980.

155 Records show that possession actions increased from 27,105 in 1980 to 64,301 in 1985, to 72,655 in 1988 and 91,418 in 1989: see Judicial Statistics Annual Report 1989, Cm 1154, table 4.6 (referred to in Law Com No 204, para 2.4, fn 3). See also Central Statistical Office, Social Trends 23 (1993, edn London), at 121 (chart 8.19) which shows that the figures of repossession are 8,400 in 1983 and 75,500 in 1991.

156 *Fourmaids Ltd v Dudley Marshall (Properties) Ltd* [1975] Ch 317.

157 *Ibid*, at 320.

158 [1957] 1 WLR 713; [1957] 1 All ER 603.

159 [1957] 1 WLR 720; [1957] 1 All ER 635.

the ink is dry on the mortgage unless there is something in the contract, express or by implication, whereby he has contracted himself out of that right. He has the right because he has a legal term of years in the property or its statutory equivalent. If there is an attornment clause, he must give notice. If there is a provision that, so long as certain payments are made, he will not go into possession, then he has contracted himself out of his rights. Apart from that, possession is a matter of course ... it has become a very fashionable form of relief because, owing to the conditions now prevailing, if it is desired to realise a security by sale, vacant possession is almost essential. Where, therefore, the mortgagor is in occupation, a summons for possession is taken out, and no other relief is sought, and where the mortgagee is in a position to exercise his power of sale, that is all the help he requires from the court ...

The mortgagor said here that his default was of a very small order. So it was. If this were a case where there was discretion in the matter, I should feel that it was a hard case. But the mortgagor has entered into a contract with the mortgagee, and the mortgagee asks for his rights under the contract, and this court, in my judgment, has no power to refuse him those rights.

The mortgagee's immediate right to possession may, however, be excluded by the mortgage terms which expressly or impliedly reserve such a right to the mortgagor.[160] It is common for the mortgagor to be given the right to be in possession until default. The term also implies that the mortgagee will not take possession if the mortgagor is not in default.[161] Such a term may also be implied in a mortgage which is repayable by instalments.[162] However, where it was necessary in the circumstances for the mortgagee to take possession to preserve his security, the fact that a mortgage was an instalment mortgage would not be conclusive for the court to imply an exclusion of the mortgagee's right to possession.[163]

Western Bank Ltd v Schindler [1977] 1 Ch 1, CA

Buckley LJ: The judge then considered the mortgagees' right to possession in these circumstances. It was common ground before him, as it has been in this court, that a legal mortgagee, which the plaintiffs are, has a right to possession at any time, irrespective of default on the mortgagor's part, unless the parties have agreed otherwise: see *Four-Maids Ltd v Dudley Marshall (Properties) Ltd* [1957] Ch 317. Before Goulding J the argument turned on the effect of s 36 of the Administration of Justice Act 1970. It was not suggested below that the parties had restricted the mortgagees' right to possession by any contractual term. The judge concluded that the section applied and in the exercise of his discretion he declined to assist the mortgagor except to the very limited extent indicated by the order. In this court Mr Lightman has taken a new point, *viz* that a term should be implied in the mortgage that the mortgagees should not be entitled to possession except on a default under the mortgage by the mortgagor. He points out that taking possession has been said to amount to a demand for payment (*Bovill v Endle* [1896] 1 Ch 648, 651)

160 *Doe d Roylance v Lightfoot* (1841) 8 M & W 553 at 546; 151 ER 1158 at 1163.

161 *Birmingham Citizens Permanent Building Society v Caunt* [1962] Ch 883.

162 *Esso Petroleum Co Ltd v Alstonbridge Properties Ltd* [1975] 1 WLR 1474 at 1484B.

163 *Western Bank Ltd v Schindler* [1977] Ch 1. See (1977) 40 MLR 356 (Harpum, C).

and that to permit this would conflict with the term of the mortgage providing for payment on 4 January 1983. Moreover, Mr Lightman contends that, since Clause 4(A) of the mortgage stipulates that the statutory powers of sale and of appointing a receiver shall only be exercisable in the events there stated, which include failure to make payment in full on the date for the payment, the right to take possession, which he says is a lesser remedy, must by implication be similarly restricted.

Mr Bromley for the mortgagees has objected to this new point being taken. He says on the authority of *Prenn v Simmonds* [1971] 1 WLR 1381, that the mortgage must be construed in the light of the factual background known to the parties at the time of its execution and of its genesis and purpose objectively viewed, aspects to which, he says, the evidence has not been fully directed or deployed. We have, however, heard able arguments on the new point and I am prepared to treat it as open to the mortgagor, whether it is strictly so or not. In my judgment, there is no ground in this case for implying the suggested term. A legal mortgagee's right to possession is a common law right which is an incident of his estate in the land. It should not, in my opinion, be lightly treated as abrogated or restricted. Although it is perhaps most commonly exercised as a preliminary step to an exercise of the mortgagee's power of sale, so that the sale may be made with vacant possession, this is not its only value to the mortgagee. The mortgagee may wish to protect his security: see *Ex parte Wickens* [1898] 1 QB 543 at 547, 549. If, for instance, the mortgagor were to vacate the property, the mortgagee might wish to take possession to protect the place from vandalism. He might wish to take possession for the purpose of carrying out repairs or to prevent waste. Where the contractual date for repayment is so unusually long delayed as it was in this case, a power of this nature to protect his security might well be regarded as of particular value to the mortgagee.

Mr Lightman has argued that a term excluding the right of a mortgagee to enter into possession should normally be implied if and for so long as the terms of the mortgage preclude the mortgagee from making immediate demand for payment or otherwise immediately enforcing his security. He drew our attention to *Esso Petroleum Co Ltd v Alstonbridge Properties Ltd* [1975] 1 WLR 1474, and in particular to what Walton J said at pp 1483 and 1484. The judge there said that he accepted that the court would be ready to find such an implied term in an instalment mortgage, but that there must be something in the mortgage upon which to hang such a conclusion other than the mere fact that it is an instalment mortgage. In other words, he accepted that the fact that the mortgage was an instalment mortgage might make the inference easier to draw but would not in itself be a sufficient ground. With this I am disposed to agree. In my judgment, the proposition in the wide form in which Mr Lightman propounds it cannot be accepted. The conventional form of mortgage invariably fixed a contractual redemption date at some time in the future – very often six months after the date of the mortgage. An instalment mortgage *ex hypothesi* postpones payment of the instalments to dates after the date of the mortgage. If Mr Lightman were right in his submission, in none of these cases could the mortgagee be entitled to demand possession immediately after the execution of the mortgage, and yet by common consent that is his right at law, graphically described by Harman J in *Four-Maids Ltd v Dudley Marshall (Properties) Ltd* [1957] Ch 317 as a right to go into possession before the ink is dry on the mortgage.

Taking possession may be tantamount to demanding payment in the context of the question whether the mortgagee can thereafter insist on notice to redeem, which was the question in *Bovill v Endle* [1896] 1 Ch 648. It would be an obvious inequity if the mortgagor could be turned out without an immediate right to resist this or to recover possession by redemption. By way of contrast, for reasons already indicated, a right to possession does not seem to me to be inconsistent with a postponed redemption date, particularly when that date is long postponed; and I see no equitable grounds for thinking that such a right would bear unfairly on the mortgagor if, as in this case, possession cannot be used as a mere stepping stone to a sale with vacant possession unless and until some event has occurred which makes the power of sale available to the mortgagee. Until such event occurs, the right to possession can only be exercised to protect the security, not as a means of enforcing it. As soon as his power of sale becomes available to him, the mortgagee should certainly be free to exercise his right to possession unless he has most clearly bound himself not to do so. In the present case the availability of the power of sale does not depend only upon some default under the mortgage. It could arise upon any one of a number of contingencies outside the mortgagor's control which could happen at any time before the contractual date for redemption ...

When the mortgagee is bound by a lease granted by the mortgagor, he cannot take vacant possession but he can still take possession in the sense that he can receive rents and profits under the lease.[164]

A mortgagee's right to possession is, however, subject to certain restraints:

(a) Consumer Credit Act 1974

Where the mortgage agreement is a regulated agreement under the Consumer Credit Act 1974, the debtor can only enforce the security by reason of any breach of the regulated agreement after he has served a notice under s 87 of the Consumer Credit Act 1974. Furthermore, a land mortgage securing a regulated agreement is enforceable on an order of the court only.[165] Thus, a mortgagee cannot exercise his right of possession and of sale without such an order.[166]

(b) Administration of Justice Act 1970

Where the mortgaged property is or includes a dwelling house, the court has a discretion under s 36 of the Administration of Justice Act 1970 to regulate the recovery of possession by the mortgagee where there appears to be a realistic possibility that the mortgagor may remedy his default or pay *any sums due under the mortgage* within a reasonable period of time. Among other things the court may postpone the delivery of possession.

Administration of Justice Act 1970

36. Additional powers of court in action by mortgagee for possession of dwelling house

(1) Where the mortgagee under a mortgage of land which consists of or includes a dwelling house brings an action in which he claims possession of the mortgaged property, not being an action for foreclosure in which a claim for possession of the mortgaged property is also made, the court may exercise any of the powers conferred

164 *Moss v Gallimore* (1779) 1 Doug KB 279 at 283; 99 ER 182 at 184; s 205(1)(xix) of the LPA 1925.

165 Section 126 of the Consumer Credit Act 1974.

166 But if he sells without an order, he can pass a good title to the purchaser: s 177(2) of the Consumer Credit Act 1974.

on it by sub-s (2) below if it appears to the court that in the event of its exercising the power the mortgagor is likely to be able within a reasonable period to pay any sums due under the mortgage or to remedy a default consisting of a breach of any other obligation arising under or by virtue of the mortgage.

(2) The court:

(a) may adjourn the proceedings, or

(b) on giving judgment, or making an order, for delivery of possession of the mortgaged property, or at any time before the execution of such judgment or order, may:

(i) stay or suspend execution of the judgment or order, or

(ii) postpone the date for delivery of possession,

for such period or periods as the court thinks reasonable.

(3) Any such adjournment, stay, suspension or postponement as is referred to in sub-s (2) above may be made subject to such conditions with regard to payment by the mortgagor of any sum secured by the mortgage or the remedying of any default as the court thinks fit.

(4) The court may from time to time vary or revoke any condition imposed by virtue of this section.

(5) This section shall have effect in relation to such an action as is referred to in sub-s (1) above begun before the date on which this section comes into force unless in that action judgment has been given, or an order made, for delivery of possession of the mortgaged property and that judgment or order was executed before that date.

(6) In the application of this section to Northern Ireland, 'the court' means a judge of the High Court in Northern Ireland, and in sub-s (1) the words from 'not being' to 'made' shall be omitted.

The words 'any sums due under the mortgage' created uncertainty. In *Halifax Building Society v Clark*[167] the mortgage instalments in arrears only amounted to £100, but on the husband's default the entire capital debt of over £1,400 became 'due' in accordance with the terms of the mortgage. The deserted wife had no realistic prospect of raising this larger sum within a reasonable period. It was, therefore, held that the precondition of s 36 was not satisfied.

As a result, s 8(1) of the Administration of Justice Act 1973 was passed to define the words 'any sums due' as 'such amounts as the mortgagor would have expected to be required to pay' if the mortgage had not contained a clause rendering the entire mortgage monies payable.

Section 8(2), however, provides that the court should not exercise its power under s 36 unless it is satisfied that the mortgagor or the applicant can pay not only the sum due (as defined by s 8(1)) but also any further amounts which will be due.

167 [1973] Ch 307. See (1973) 89 LQR 171 (Baker, PV); (1973) 36 MLR 550 (Jackson, P); (1973) 37 Conv (NS) 213 (Crane, FR).

Administration of Justice Act 1973

8. Extension of powers of court in action by mortgagee of dwelling house

(1) Where by a mortgage of land which consists of or includes a dwelling house, or by any agreement between the mortgagee under such a mortgage and the mortgagor, the mortgagor is entitled or is to be permitted to pay the principal sum secured by instalments or otherwise to defer payment of it in whole or in part, but provision is also made for earlier payment in the event of any default by the mortgagor or of a demand by the mortgagee or otherwise, then for purposes of s 36 of the Administration of Justice Act 1970 (under which a court has power to delay giving a mortgagee possession of the mortgaged property so as to allow the mortgagor a reasonable time to pay any sums due under the mortgage) a court may treat as due under the mortgage on account of the principal sum secured and of interest on it only such amounts as the mortgagor would have expected to be required to pay if there had been no such provision for earlier payment.

(2) A court shall not exercise by virtue of sub-s (1) above the powers conferred by s 36 of the Administration of Justice Act 1970 unless it appears to the court not only that the mortgagor is likely to be able within a reasonable period to pay any amounts regarded (in accordance with sub-s (1) above) as due on account of the principal sum secured, together with the interest on those amounts, but also that he is likely to be able by the end of that period to pay any further amounts that he would have expected to be required to pay by then on account of that sum and of interest on it if there had been no such provision as is referred to in sub-s (1) above for earlier payment.

In exercising the power under s 36 the court will have to balance the interest of the mortgagor who wants to remain in occupation and the interest of the mortgagee who wants to realise his security. The size of the arrears and other relevant circumstances must be considered by the court.

In *First National Bank v Syed*,[168] where the total sum accrued was about £10,000 and there was little prospect that the mortgagors could meet the interest let alone the arrears, the court refused to exercise its discretion under s 36.

In assessing what is a 'reasonable period' for the purposes of s 36 of the 1970 Act and s 8 of the 1973 Act, the court must take into account, *inter alia*, the whole of the remaining part of the original term of the mortgage. The following considerations have been suggested by Evans LJ in *Cheltenham and Gloucester Building Society v Norgan*:[169]

> (a) How much can the borrower reasonably afford to pay, both now and in the future? (b) If the borrower has a temporary difficulty in meeting his obligations, how long is the difficulty likely to last? (c) What was the reason for the arrears which have accumulated? (d) How much remains of the original term? (e) What are relevant contractual terms, and what type of mortgage is it, ie when is the principal due to be repaid? (f) Is it a case where the court should exercise its power to disregard accelerated payment provisions (s 8 of the 1973 Act)? (g) Is it reasonable to expect the lender, in the circumstances of the particular case, to

168 [1991] 2 All ER 250.

169 [1996] 1 All ER 449 at 463.

recoup the arrears of interest (1) over the whole of the original term, or (2) within a shorter period, or even (3) within a longer period, ie by extending the repayment period? Is it reasonable to expect the lender to capitalise the interest, or not? (h) Are there any reasons affecting the security which should influence the length of the period for payment?

What is a 'reasonable period' is therefore a question for the court in each case.[170] Where there are clear evidence that the completion of the sale of a property, perhaps by piecemeal disposal, can take place in six or nine months or even a year the court may conclude that the mortgagor is likely to be able within a reasonable period to pay any sums due under the mortgage.[171]

Only the mortgagor or any person deriving title under the original mortgagor can prevent recovery under s 36.[172] A spouse is, however, given a statutory power under s 1(5) of the Matrimonial Homes Act 1983 to continue payment on the mortgage if the spouse mortgagor defaults. And s 8(2) of the Matrimonial Homes Act 1983 gives the spouse who has a right to tender mortgage payments a statutory right to apply to the court to be joined as a party in any proceeding brought by a mortgagee for possession provided that he or she can satisfy the pre-conditions of s 36 of the Administration of Justice Act 1970.[173] This enables a spouse to stop the mortgagee from taking possession. Sometimes a spouse does not know that his or her partner is in default of mortgage payment and, therefore, will not be able to take advantage of s 1(5) and s 8(2) of the Matrimonial Homes Act 1983. At common law a mortgagee does not have to inform the mortgagor's spouse of his or her partner's default.[174] Under s 8(3) of the Matrimonial Homes Act 1983, if the spouse is entitled to have a right of occupation and has protected the right as a Class F land charge or by an entry of notice, the mortgagee is statutorily obliged to serve a notice of his possession proceedings on the spouse. Section 8(3) is somewhat unsatisfactory because its operation depends on whether the spouse's right of occupation has been protected and often a spouse is not aware of his or her statutory right of occupation and does not know that the right has to be protected by a registration or an entry of notice.

Matrimonial Homes Act 1983

1. Rights concerning matrimonial home where one spouse has no estate, etc

(5) Where a spouse is entitled under this section to occupy a dwelling house or any part thereof, any payment or tender made or other thing done by that spouse in or towards satisfaction of any liability of the other spouse in respect of rent, rates, mortgage payments or other outgoings affecting the dwelling house shall, whether or not it is made or done in pursuance of an order under this section, be as good as if made or done by the other spouse.

---

170 *National and Provincial Building Society v Lloyd* [1996] 1 All ER 630 at 638b. See also *Bristol & West Building Society v Ellis and Ellis* (1997) 73 P & CR 158.

171 *National and Provincial Building Society v Lloyd* [1996] 1 All ER 630.

172 Section 39 of the Administration of Justice Act 1970.

173 Section 8(2)(b) of the Matrimonial Homes Act 1983.

174 *Hastings and Thanet Building Society v Goddard* [1970] 1 WLR 1544. See (1971) 35 Conv (NS) 48 (Crane, FR).

8. Dwelling house subject to mortgage

(2) Where a mortgagee of land which consists of or includes a dwelling house brings an action in any court for the enforcement of his security, a spouse who is not a party to the action and who is enabled by s 1(5) ... above to meet the mortgagor's liabilities under the mortgage, on applying to the court at any time before the action is finally disposed of in that court, shall be entitled to be made a party to the action if the court-

(a) does not see special reason against it, and

(b) is satisfied that the applicant may be expected to make such payments or do such things in or towards satisfaction of the mortgagor's liabilities or obligations as might affect the outcome of the proceedings or that the expectation of it should be considered under s 36 of the Administration of Justice Act 1970.

(3) Where a mortgagee of land which consists or substantially consists of a dwelling house brings an action for the enforcement of his security, and at the relevant time there is:

(a) in the case of unregistered land, a land charge of Class F registered against the person who is the estate owner at the relevant time or any person who, where the estate owner is a trustee, preceded him as trustee during the subsistence of the mortgage, or

(b) in the case of registered land, a subsisting registration of a notice under s 2(8) above or a notice or caution under s 2(7) of the Act of 1967,

notice of the action shall be served by the mortgagee on the person on whose behalf the land charge is registered or the notice or caution entered, if that person is not a party to the action.

Statutory tenants under the Rent Act 1977 are precluded from applying for an adjournment of the possession proceedings under s 36, even though they are willing and likely to be able, within a reasonable period, to pay any sums due under the mortgage, because they do not derive title from the original mortgagor[175] They derive their statutory tenancy from the Act.

The court has no jurisdiction under s 36 to postpone possession proceedings indefinitely,[176] or stay or suspend the execution of the order for possession after it had been executed unless (i) the order was itself set aside; (ii) the warrant had been obtained by fraud; or (iii) there had been an abuse of process or oppression in its execution.[177] It also seems that where the mortgagee seeks possession not on the ground that mortgage moneys have become due, s 36 has no application.[178]

175 *Britannia Building Society v Earl* [1990] 1 WLR 422 at 430A.

176 *Royal Trust Co of Canada v Markham* [1975] 1 WLR 1416; *National Westminster Bank plc v Skelton* (Note) [1993] 1 WLR 72 at 81A.

177 *Hammersmith and Fulham London Borough Council v Hill* [1994] 2 EGLR 51; *National & Provincial Building Society v Ahmed* [1995] 2 EGLR 127 at 129C.

178 *Habib Bank Ltd v Tailor* [1982] 1 WLR 1218. See [1983] Conv 80 (Kenny, PH); (1983) 133 NLJ 247 (Wilkinson, HW). See, however, *Western Bank Ltd v Schindler* [1977] Ch 1 where Buckley LJ (at 13D–E) and Scarman LJ (at 19F) both thought that s 36 should be applicable whether or not there was default, for otherwise an innocent mortgagor would be in a less advantageous position than a defaulting mortgagor.

Where the proceeds of sale were likely to discharge the mortgage debt, the court has power under s 36 to suspend a warrant for possession of mortgaged property so that the mortgagor can apply for sale under s 91 of the Law of Property Act 1925, but not where the mortgage debt would not be fully discharged, in the absence of other funds being available to the mortgagor to make up the shortfall.[179]

Where a possession order has been made but suspended on terms, the court has power to vary the terms or to allow the possession order to be enforced if the circumstances have changed.[180]

The court may also postpone possession order if '[the mortgagors] are in a far better position to sell it than the [mortgagee] would be'.[181] In *Target Home Loans Ltd v Clothier*[182] Nolan LJ thought that the prospect of an early sale would be greatly enhanced by leaving the mortgagor in possession since an occupied house 'is far more likely to look attractive and to command a buyer than one which has been repossessed by a mortgage company'.

Target Home Loans Ltd v Clothier [1994] 1 All ER 439, CA

Nolan LJ: But the fact remains that during the last two years he has failed to meet his mortgage commitments. On the evidence there is no way in which he is going to meet them except by the sale of this house. That leads directly to the question: is there a prospect of an early sale? If so, is it better in the interests of all concerned for that to be effected by him and his wife or by the mortgage company? If the view is that the prospects of an early sale for the mortgagees as well as for Mr Clothier are best served by deferring an order for possession, then it seems to me that that is a solid reason for making such an order but the deferment should be short.

I would for my part propose an order granting possession in three months' time. If in that time Mr and Mrs Clothier have not succeeded in discharging the whole of their indebtedness to the plaintiffs, they will lose possession. It would be open to them if they were unable to meet that deadline to come back to the court. I can only express the firm view in the light of the history of this matter and from what we have heard today that there should be no further deferment and if Mr and Mrs Clothier are unable to find a buyer and to pay off their debts within three months, then without doubt the time will have come for the mortgage company to be given possession. But I would propose an order for possession in three months for those reasons.

But if the presence of the mortgagor pending sale would depress the sale price, or if the mortgagor would not co-operate in the sale of the property, then possession would not be deferred.[183]

179 *Cheltenham and Gloucester plc v Krausz* [1997] 1 All ER 21.

180 *Abbey National Mortgages plc v Bernard* (1996) 71 P & CR 257.

181 *Target Homes Loans Ltd v Clothier* [1994] 1 All ER 439.

182 [1994] 1 All ER 439.

183 *Cheltenham and Gloucester Building Society plc v Booker* [1997] 1 FLR 311.

(c) Mortgagor's right of set-off?

It seems that the mortgagee's right to possession will not be affected by the mortgagor's counterclaim or cross-claim of unliquidated damages by way of equitable right of set-off even if such a claim is admitted and the amount of set-off may exceed the mortgage debt.[184] This issue has more recently been considered by the Court of Appeal in *National Westminster Bank plc v Skelton (Note)*[185] and *Ashley Guarantee plc v Zacaria.*[186]

National Westminster Bank plc v Skelton and another (Note) [1993] 1 WLR 72, CA

Slade LJ: ... the mortgage does not itself restrict the bank's right to take immediate possession of the property as legal mortgagee, the defendants have to submit and do submit that these rights have been abrogated by virtue of the events alleged in the disputed paragraphs of their pleading. One formidable obstacle in the way of such submission is the line of authority which clearly establishes the principle that the existence of a cross-claim, even if it exceeds the amount of a mortgage debt, will not by itself defeat a right to possession enjoyed by a legal chargee. I refer in particular to the decision of Nourse J in *Mobil Oil Co Ltd v Rawlinson* (1982) 43 P & CR 221, *Barclays Bank Plc v Tennet,* 6 June 1984 and the decision of Mervyn Davies J in *Citibank Trust Ltd v Ayivor* [1987] 1 WLR 1157.

The principle in my view has much to commend it, since it could lead to abuse if a mortgagee were to be kept out of his undoubted *prima facie* right to possession by allegations of some connected cross-claim which might prove wholly without foundation: see and compare the observations of Russell LJ in *Samuel Keller (Holdings) Ltd v Martins Bank Ltd* [1971] 1 WLR 43, 51D. I will refer to the principle established by this line of cases as 'the *Mobil Oil* principle'. Mr Brock, however, has submitted that the principle is not applicable to the present case essentially on two alternative grounds. First, he submitted, that it is not applicable in a case where the cross-claims are not mere cross-claims but claims which would give the mortgagors rights by way of an equitable set-off.

I say nothing about the case where a mortgagor establishes that he has a claim to a quantified sum by way of equitable set-off. Possibly such a claim might have the effect of actually discharging the mortgage debt. In my judgment, however, the *Mobil Oil* principle is applicable both where the cross-claim is a mere counterclaim and where it is a cross-claim for unliquidated damages which, if established, would give rise to a right by way of equitable set-off. In none of the decisions mentioned has any distinction been drawn between the two. In *Mobil Oil Co Ltd v Rawlinson* (1982) 32 P & CR 221 Nourse J referred in terms to the possibility of a counterclaim or set-off. Though there was no claim for possession in the *Samuel Keller* case [1971] 1 WLR 43, the court did not find it necessary to advert explicitly to the possibility that the claim to damages on the relevant counterclaim might give rise to a claim by equitable set-off, as opposed to a bare cross-claim. Russell LJ said, at p 50:

---

184 *Mobil Oil Co Ltd v Rawlinson* (1982) 43 P & CR 221; *Samuel Keller (Holdings) Ltd v Martins Bank Ltd* [1971] 1 WLR 43.

185 [1993] 1 WLR 72.

186 [1993] 1 WLR 62.

> It was argued that if the outcome of the Birmingham action was that damages were awarded on the counterclaim exceeding the amount due under the mortgage debt it would prove that the mortgagee would not have been justified in obtaining the money from the bank and treating it as their own to meet their mortgage debt. It was submitted that by reason of the counterclaim the mortgage debt no longer existed, but that, to my mind, is plainly not so and I so hold.

I cannot accept the submission that the *Mobil Oil* principle is not applicable where the mortgagor has a claim to unliquidated damages by way of equitable set-off, and in my judgment it makes no difference that such a claim may in the event prove to exceed the amount of the mortgage debt.

The other ground upon which Mr Brock submitted that the *Mobil Oil* principle is not applicable was that special considerations apply where the mortgage is merely one by way of guarantee intended to afford security for the debts of a third party. In this context he relied strongly on a passage in Halsbury's *Laws of England*, 4th edn, vol 20 (1978), p 102, para 190, which was not referred to by the judge and states the rights of creditor and surety in these terms:

> On being sued by the creditor for payment of the debt guaranteed, a surety may avail himself of any right to set off or counterclaim which the principal debtor possesses against the creditor, and any division of the High Court can give effect to it or to any equitable defence raised.

Correspondingly, Mr Brock submitted, in the present case, on being sued by the creditor bank for possession the defendant sureties are entitled to avail themselves of the assumed right of set-off which the company in liquidation possesses against the bank.

Rowlatt on *The Law of Principal and Surety*, 4th edn, 1982, at p 103, contains a statement similar to that cited from Halsbury's *Laws of England*, In the following terms:

> Where the principal is entitled to a set-off against the creditor's demand arising out of the same transaction as the debt guaranteed, and in fact reducing that debt, the surety is entitled to plead it in an action by the creditor against the surety alone.

Mr Mann challenged the correctness of both these statements of law, and in support of this submission referred us to the judgment of Isaacs J in the Supreme Court of New South Wales in *Cellulose Product Pty Ltd v Truda* (1970) 92 WN(SNW) 561. In that case Isaacs J subjected the passage in Halsbury's *Laws of England* and an equivalent passage in Rowlatt on the *Law of Principal and Surety*, 3rd edn (1936), p 137 to very searching criticism. His conclusion was that the cases cited in the notes to Halsbury's *Laws of England*, did not bear out the statement in the text. He expressed his ultimate conclusion as follows, at p 588.

> This review of the cases lends no support to the submission that a surety when sued is entitled to set up in equity or at law as an equitable plea any cross action for unliquidated damages which the debtor may have against the creditor in respect of the transaction, the performance of which the guarantor had entered upon his guarantee; that is, in the absence of the debtor being before the court in the proceedings so as to be bound by verdict and judgments. This of course does not mean that the guarantor is without remedy; when he is sued he has a right immediately to join the debtor as a third party and claim complete indemnity from him. The debtor has then a right to join the plaintiff as a fourth party, claiming damages for breach of warranty and so obtain indemnity either in whole or in part. All the actions would be heard together, the rights of all

> persons determined and appropriate set-offs made after verdict, and if there be any surplus of damages over and above that which is required to meet the guarantee, the debtor will have recovered from the creditor who, in the result, will get no more than that to which he was justly entitled.

The decision in the *Cellulose* case was followed by Australian courts in two subsequent decisions, namely *Covino v Bandag Manufacturing Pty Ltd* [1983] 1 NSWLR 237 and *Indrisie v General Credits Ltd* [1958] VR 251.

The reasoning of Isaacs J in the *Cellulose* case is, with respect to him, impressive, but for my part I would not think it right, on this striking out application, to decide that there is any general rule that a guarantor cannot avail himself of the remedies which otherwise may be open to the principal debtor as against the creditor or, if there is such a general rule, that it necessarily applies in the present case. First, Isaacs J himself expressly recognised, at p 585, that exceptions to his general rule might arise in cases such as the present where a debtor is insolvent so that, instead of having a full right of exoneration by the principal debtor, the surety can only prove in the liquidation of the principal debtor for a dividend. Secondly, the Court of Appeal in *Hyundai Shipbuilding & Heavy Industries Co Ltd v Pournaras* [1978] 2 Lloyd's Rep 502 expressly accepted the correctness of the passage in Halsbury's *Laws of England*, 4th edn, vol 20, para 190, though regarding it as inapplicable on the particular facts of that case because of the form of guarantee which had been employed.

However, even accepting for present purposes the correctness of the general principle stated in Halsbury's *Laws of England*, that statement is expressed to apply in cases where the surety is being sued by the creditor for payment. We have been referred to no decisions establishing that it applies in cases in which a mortgagor surety is being sued by a mortgagee creditor for possession of the mortgage premises, and I am not satisfied that it necessarily does apply. Secondly, and I regard this as the conclusive point in the present case, any rights which a surety would ordinarily enjoy at common law against the creditor by virtue of the principle stated in Halsbury's *Laws of England* would in any event be capable of being excluded by agreement between himself and the creditor. The decisions in *Hyundai Shipbuilding & Heavy Industries Co Ltd v Pournaras* [1978] 2 Lloyd's Rep 502 itself shows that this is so.

In the present case Clause 11 of the mortgage, so far as material, provided:

> as between the mortgagor and the bank this mortgage is to be deemed to be a primary security and the mortgaged property is to be deemed to stand charged with the moneys or liabilities hereby secured as if they were primarily due from the mortgagor.

In my judgment, as Mr Mann submitted, this provision makes it clear that in any dispute between the bank and the mortgagors, their obligation as mortgagors, including their obligations to deliver up possession when called upon to do so, are to be no less extensive than they would be if the debts in question were due from them as primary debtors rather than as mere guarantors. In particular this provision, in my view, makes it clear that in any dispute between the bank and the mortgagors it is not to be open to the mortgagors to rely upon any right of cross-claim or set-off to which the principal debtor, the company, may be entitled as against the creditor bank.

Ashley Guarantee Plc v Zacaria [1993] 1 WLR 62, CA

Nourse LJ: In *National Westminster Bank Plc v Skelton (Note)*, Post, p 72, this court decided that the mortgagor cannot usually resist a legal mortgagee's action for possession by claiming an equitable set-off for an unliquidated sum exceeding the amount of the mortgage arrears. Now we have to decide whether any distinction is to be made where the mortgagor is not the principal debtor of the mortgagee but only a guarantor ...

It is noted that Slade LJ expressed no view as to the effect of a cross-claim for a liquidated sum giving rise to a right of equitable set-off. That is no question for decision here. However, Mr Warwick, who appears for the defendants and to whose conscientious argument the court is indebted, accepts that *National Westminster Bank Plc v Skelton (Note)* is authority, binding on this court, for the view that the *Mobil Oil* principle applies where the mortgagor's cross-claim is one for unliquidated damages which, if established, would give him a right of equitable set-off. He maintains that that decision can be distinguished on a ground which can best be understood by starting with a further reference to that case, in which counsel for the mortgagors had gone on to submit that the *Mobil Oil* principle was not in any event applicable because special considerations applied where the mortgage was merely one by way of guarantee intended to afford security for the debts of a third party ...

I can see no distinction in principle between a case where the mortgagor is the principal debtor of the mortgagee and one where he is only a guarantor. In each case the mortgagee has, as an incident of his estate in the land, a right to possession of the mortgaged property. In each case the cross-claims cannot be unilaterally appropriated in discharge of the mortgage debt. The fact that in the latter case the mortgagor is not primarily liable for payment of the debt is immaterial. When he comes to be made liable his position *vis-à-vis* the appropriation of the cross-claims is at best no different from, and certainly cannot be better than, that of a mortgagor who is the primary debtor ...

(d) Equitable restriction

Lord Denning in *Quennell v Maltby*[187] once suggested that 'in modern times equity can step in so as to prevent a mortgagee, or a transferee from him, from getting possession of a house contrary to the justice of the case.' Here H mortgaged his property to a bank. Later, he created an unauthorised lease in favour of Ts. H wanted to sell his property with vacant possession on the open market, but Ts refused to leave and claimed that they were statutory tenants under the Rent Act. H asked the bank to get rid of Ts. The bank refused. H then asked his wife W to pay off the bank. She did so and the bank was bound to transfer the property to W. W now became the new mortgagee and brought an action for vacant possession as mortgagee. The Court of Appeal was not willing to allow this evasive device to be used to circumvent the protection given by the Rent Act. W's action for possession was not brought to enforce the security but to evade the Rent Act which H could not have done himself.

Although the result of the case was just, Lord Denning's judgment is contrary to the traditional view that apart from contractual agreement to the contrary a mortgagee has an absolute right to possession from the moment the mortgage is created.

187 [1979] 1 WLR 318 at 322G–H. See [1979] CLJ 257 (Pearce, RA).

The courts, however, do have an inherent equitable jurisdiction to postpone or stay possession proceedings. This jurisdiction is often exercised by the Masters of the Chancery Division.[188] However, this can only provide a temporary form of relief, giving 'the mortgagor a limited opportunity to find means to pay off the mortgagee or otherwise satisfy him if there was a reasonable prospect of either of those events occurring'.[189]

(e) Liability to account

Where the mortgagee does exercise his right to take possession, he is subject to very stringent control.[190] He must account for rents and profits he received to the mortgagor.[191] The income received must be used solely to reduce the interest or capital due under the mortgage.[192] He is also liable to pay additional rent that he would have received if he had managed the property with due diligence.[193]

Palk v Mortgage Service Funding Plc [1993] 2 WLR 415, CA

Sir Donald Nicholls VC: If he takes possession he might prefer to do nothing and bide his time, waiting indefinitely for an improvement in the market, with the property empty meanwhile. That he cannot do. He is accountable for his actual receipts from the property. He is also accountable to the mortgagor for what he would have received but for his default. So he must take reasonable care to maximise his return from the property. He must also take reasonable care of the property.

White v City of London Brewery Co (1889) 42 Ch D 237, CA

Cotton LJ: A mortgagee in possession must account for the rents which, but for his wilful default, he would have received. The Plaintiff says that if he fails as to the brewers' profits yet he ought to have a larger sum in respect of the rents which the mortgagees would, but for their wilful default, have received. The learned Judge has allowed in addition of £20 a year from the 19 of August 1874, down to the date of the sale, in addition to the rent obtained by the mortgagees ...

At the time the brewers took possession, the trade in the neighbourhood was in a bad state. We know that when trade is in a bad state workmen have not money to spend in beer, so the custom would fall off, and when a public-house has got into a low state there is a difficulty in re-establishing its business. This house at the time when the brewers took possession could not be let, because nobody could carry it on without a loss, as the brewers found by experience. As soon after as they could let it at all, they let it to Moulton, who found a rent of £40 too high, and was allowed to remain at a rent of £30. On the evidence before us, there is nothing which satisfies my mind that they could

188 See RSC Ord 88, r 7.

189 *Birmingham Citizens Permanent Building Society v Caunt* [1962] Ch 883 at 891. See (1962) 78 LQR 171 (REM).

190 *Robertson v Norris* (1859) 1 Giff 428 at 436; 65 ER 986 at 989.

191 *Lord Trimleston v Hamill* (1810) 1 Ball & B 377 at 385. See (1979) 129 NLJ 334 (Markson, HE).

192 *Comyns v Comyns* (1871) 5 IR Eq 583.

193 *Palk v Mortgage Services Funding plc* [1993] 2 WLR 415 at 420H–421A; *White v City of London Brewery Co* (1889) 42 Ch D 237.

by any possibility have obtained a larger rent than that, during the tenancy of Mr Moulton. Then I think the learned Judge was right in saying, when there was a change in the tenancy, that there was no ground for charging the brewers with more than the £60 rent which they received from Hake during the first year of his occupation; but after that time, when he had established himself, the learned judge thought that something more ought to be allowed. The evidence on that question is of a somewhat doubtful character, but I think the plaintiff has not established that more should be given him than what the learned Judge has allowed, *viz* £20 a year, which comes altogether, as the Master of the Rolls has said, to £100.

As a result of the stringent duty imposed on the mortgagee it is very rare for him to take possession unless, and until, the mortgagor is in default and the mortgagee wants to sell the property to recover the capital. If the mortgagee only wants to recover interests from the income derived from the mortgaged property it would be better for him to appoint a receiver.

Appointment of receiver[194]

To recover interest arrears, the mortgagee may appoint a receiver to manage the property in order to produce an income to repay the debt. The mortgagee has a statutory power, under s 101(1)(iii) of the Law of Property Act 1925, to appoint in writing such person as he thinks fit to manage the mortgaged property or to receive income of it. This power, however, only arises and becomes exercisable in exactly the same way as the statutory power of sale, ie the mortgage must be made by deed and have become due and must not contain expression of contrary intention which would prevent the mortgagee from exercising his power of appointment.[195] In addition, the mortgagee must show that either the mortgagor has been in default for three months following the service upon him of a notice requiring payment of the mortgage money, *or* some interest under the mortgage has remained unpaid for two months after becoming due, *or* there has been a breach of some other mortgage terms.

This power is useful when the mortgagee does not want to get possession or to sell the property. The receiver will collect all the income derived from mortgaged property to satisfy the mortgage payment and his own commission. He will account to the mortgagor for any surplus.[196]

The receiver is statutorily deemed to be the agent of the mortgagor.[197] Therefore, unless the mortgage deed otherwise provides, the mortgagee is not liable for any negligent act of the receiver.

Power of sale

In the case of serious default by the mortgagor, the commonly used remedy is the exercise of the mortgagee's power of sale. It is almost inevitable for the

194 See *Shanli v Johnson Matthay* [1991] BCLC 36.

195 Section 109(1) of the LPA 1925, s 109(1).

196 Section 109(8) of the LPA 1925, s 109(8).

197 Section 109(2) of the LPA 1925, s 109(2).

mortgagee to take vacant possession, which is an essential condition of a good sale price, before he exercises his power of sale. As we have seen, a mortgagee is generally entitled to take possession, subject to various statutory interventions. And if he has priority over any other legal or equitable interest, he can get vacant possession and may then exercise his power of sale.

It must be noted that the exercise of power of sale does not depend on the mortgagee's ability to get vacant possession. The mortgagee may still exercise his power of sale even if he cannot get vacant possession so long as the statutory conditions in ss 101 and 103 are satisfied. The mortgagee must first show that the power of sale has arisen. He must then show that it is now exercisable. The conditions upon which the power of sale arises and becomes exercisable can, however, be varied or excluded by the mortgage terms. It is common for the mortgagee to exclude s 103 altogether by express mortgage term.[198]

When does the power of sale arise? Under s 101 of the Law of Property Act 1925 the mortgagee's power of sale arises if all three conditions are satisfied: (1) the mortgage must be made by deed; (2) the mortgage must have become due; (3) the mortgage itself must not contain expression of contrary intention which would prevent the mortgagee from exercising his power of sale.

Once the power has arisen then it becomes exercisable if any one of the conditions shown in s 103 is satisfied. The conditions in s 103 are: (1) the mortgagor has been in default for three months following the service upon him of a notice requiring payment of the mortgage money; (2) some interest under the mortgage has remained unpaid for two months after becoming due; (3) there has been a breach of some mortgage term 'other than and besides a covenant for the payment of mortgage money or interest thereon'.

The mortgagee has no power to sell until the statutory power has arisen and become exercisable.[199] If he purports to sell before the power arises, the conveyance will not pass the mortgagor's legal estate to the purchaser.[200] The purchaser will only acquire the rights that the mortgagee enjoys in his capacity as a mortgagee.

If the mortgagee purports to sell the property after the power has arisen but before it is exercisable, the purchaser will acquire a title which is statutorily declared to be unimpeachable.[201] But the mortgagee will be liable in damages in an action brought by the mortgagor.[202] However, if the purchaser had actual

---

198 See, for example, National Westminster Bank's standard mortgage terms.

199 Where the mortgagee has no power of sale, he may apply to the court for an order for sale under s 91(2) of the LPA 1925. Even if the mortgagee has power of sale, in exceptional circumstances, he can apply for such order, for example where the prospects of the mortgagor successfully impeaching the sale were utterly remote, the mortgagor's conduct justified the mortgagee's apprehension that the mortgagor would not hesitate to threaten proceeding against the purchaser if that would spoil the sale, and the mortgagee's fear of losing the sale unless an order was obtained was not unreasonable: *Arab Bank plc v Merchantile Holdings Ltd* [1994] 2 All ER 74.

200 See Megarry and Wade, p 937.

201 Section 104(2) of the LPA 1925.

202 Section 104(2) of the LPA 1925.

notice that the power of sale was not exercisable or that there was some impropriety in the sale, he cannot claim the protection under s 104(2) because he cannot use the statute as an instrument of fraud.[203] Constructive notice of irregularities may not be enough although in *Bailey v Barnes*,[204] Stirling J warned that the purchaser must not 'wilfully shut his eyes and abstain from making inquiries which might have led to a knowledge of impropriety or irregularities'.

It is interesting to note that Nicholls VC observed in *Palk v Mortgage Services Funding plc* that in exercising his power of sale the mortgagee is 'not entitled to conduct himself in a way which *unfairly prejudices* the mortgagor'.[205] A mortgagee is entitled to enforce the security to satisfy his claim, and to give first, but not exclusive, consideration to his own interest.[206] The interest of the mortgagor should not be thereby unfairly prejudiced.

It seems that the mortgagee must act in good faith. He must not deal 'wilfully and recklessly ... with the property in such a manner that the interests of the mortgagor are sacrificed'.[207] In addition, he also owes a duty of care to the mortgagor.[208] He must 'act in a prudent and business-like manner, with a view to obtain as large a price as may fairly and reasonably, with due diligence and attention, be under the circumstances obtainable'.[209] He must 'take reasonable precautions to obtain the true market value of the mortgaged property at the date on which he decides to sell it'.[210]

Once the power is exercisable the mortgagee can sell the property whenever he likes.[211] Despite Lord Denning's view in *Standard Chartered Bank v Walker*,[212] that it is at least arguable that in choosing the time he must exercise a

---

203 *Lord Waring v London and Manchester Assurance* [1935] Ch 310 at 318; *Bailey v Barnes* [1894] 1 Ch 25 at 30.

204 [1894] 1 Ch 25 at 30.

205 *Palk v Mortgage Services Funding plc* [1993] 2 WLR 415 at 420H.

206 *Palk v Mortgage Services Funding plc* [1993] 2 WLR 415 at 420G; *Palmer v Barclays Bank Ltd* (1972) 23 P & CR 30 at 35.

207 *Kennedy v De Trafford* [1897] AC 180 at 185.

208 *Cuckmere Brick Co Ltd v Mutual Finance Ltd* [1971] Ch 949. The duty of care is imposed by law but may be excluded by express statement. Whether it has been excluded depends on the construction of the wording of the exclusion in the context in which the phrase appears: *Bishop v Bonham* [1988] 1 WLR 742. (Here the agreement allows the mortgagee to sell the mortgaged shares in such manner, upon such terms and for such consideration as he may think fit and he would not be liable for any loss 'howsoever arising in connection with the sale'. It was held that on its true construction he could only do as he thought fit within the limits of the duty of care imposed by law. The court interpreted the words 'howsoever arising' as being confined to sales authorised by the general law where there had been no negligence in the sale.)

209 *Matthie v Edwards* (1846) 2 Coll 465 at 480; 63 ER 817 at 824. Building Societies are under a statutory duty to take 'reasonable care to ensure' that the price obtained is 'the best price that can reasonably be obtained': s 13(7), Schedule 4, para 1(1)(a), (2) of the Building Societies Act 1986.

210 *Cuckmere Brick Co Ltd v Mutual Finance Ltd* [1971] Ch 949 at 968H–69A; *Palk v Mortgage Services Funding plc* [1993] 2 WLR 415 at 421A.

211 *Cuckmere Brick Co Ltd v Mutual Finance Ltd* [1971] Ch 949 at 965G.

212 [1982] 1 WLR 1410 at 1415G.

reasonable degree of care, the Privy Council has recently held in *China and South Sea Bank Ltd v Tan Soon Gin* that the mortgagee can 'decide in his own interest if and when he should sell'[213] and in *Downsview Nominees v First City Corpn*[214] that the mortgagee owes no general duty of care but only a duty of good faith. However, where a delay in the sale would cause the mortgagor to suffer financially, in the absence of clear evidence of an upward surge in the property market, the court may order a sale on the request of the mortgagor or of any person interested either in the mortgage money or in the right of redemption.[215]

The mortgagee cannot sell the property either to himself alone, unless the sale is directed by the court[216] or to himself and others, or his solicitor,[217] his own trustees, or his agent.[218] A sale by a person to himself 'is no sale at all' even if the sale price is the full value of the property.[219] A sale by the mortgagee to a less closely associated person such as a business acquaintance or a company in which he is himself a shareholder is not necessarily ineffective. But the court will scrutinise it carefully and will intervene if it appears from the surrounding circumstances that the sale is not *bona fide*. In *Tse Kwong Lam v Wong Chit Sen*,[220] the mortgagee sold the property by public auction. The mortgagee's wife was the only bidder. She acted on behalf of a family company of which both she and the mortgagee were directors and shareholders. The property was sold at the reserve price fixed by the mortgagee which was clearly known to her. The purchase was financed by the mortgagee himself. The Privy Council held that the mortgagee had failed to show that he had taken reasonable steps to obtain the best price reasonably obtainable and the sale was not properly conducted. However, the transaction was not set aside because the prosecution of the case had been delayed and he who seeks equity must not delay.

In *Cuckmere Brick Co Ltd v Mutual Finance Ltd*,[221] the mortgagee, having been informed of the granting of a planning permission relating to the mortgaged property, failed to make adequate reference in the auction advertisement to the full extent of the permission. As a result the sale was undervalued. The Court of Appeal held that the mortgagee was liable in damages for breach of the duty of care.

213 [1990] 1 AC 536 at 545D. See also *Palk v Mortgage Services Funding plc* [1993] 2 WLR 415 at 425E–F.

214 [1993] 2 WLR 86.

215 LPA 1925, s 91(2); *Palk v Mortgage Services Funding plc* [1993] 2 WLR 415.

216 *Palk v Mortgage Sevices Funding plc* [1993] 2 WLR 415 at 423C.

217 *Martinson v Clowes* (1882) 21 Ch D 857 at 860.

218 *Downes v Grazebrook* (1817) 3 Mer 200 at 209; 36 ER 77 at 80.

219 *Farrar v Farrar* (1888) 40 Ch D 395.

220 [1983] 1 WLR 1349. See [1984] Conv 143 (Jackson, P).

221 [1971] Ch 949. See (1971) 87 LQR 303.

The mortgagee must act like a prudent vendor who is selling his own property, so, for example, he may have to seek expert advice as to the method of sale,[222] or to take reasonable steps to ascertain the value of the property.[223] Although he does not have to hold a sale by auction, if he chooses to do so a reserve price should be fixed with expert advice and the bidder should not be informed of the price.[224]

Tse Kwong Lam v Wong Chit Sen [1983] 1 WLR 1349, PC

Lord Templeman: In the view of this Board on authority and on principle there is no hard and fast rule that a mortgagee may not sell to a company in which he is interested. The mortgagee and the company seeking to uphold the transaction must show that the sale was in good faith and that the mortgagee took reasonable precautions to obtain the best price reasonably obtainable at the time. The mortgagee is not however bound to postpone the sale in the hope of obtaining a better price or to adopt a piecemeal method of sale which could only be carried out over a substantial period or at some risk of loss. This view of the matter is consistent with the decision of the House of Lords in *York Buildings Co v Mackenzie* (1795) 3 Paton 378 ...

In the present case in which the mortgagee held a large beneficial interest in the shares of the purchasing company, was a director of the company, and was entirely responsible for financing the company, the other shareholders being his wife and children, the sale must be closely examined and a heavy onus lies on the mortgagee to show that in all respects he acted fairly to the borrower and used his best endeavours to obtain the best price reasonably obtainable for the mortgaged property.

[His Lordship referred to various authorities and continued.]

In the result their Lordships consider that in the present case the company was not debarred from purchasing the mortgaged property but, in view of the close relationship between the company and the mortgagee and in view in particular of the conflict of duty and interest to which the mortgagee was subject, the sale to the company for $1.2m can only be supported if the mortgagee proves that he took reasonable precautions to obtain the best price reasonably obtainable at the time of sale.

On behalf of the mortgagee it was submitted that all reasonable steps were taken when the mortgagee, with adequate advertisement, sold the property at a properly conducted auction to the highest bidder. The submission assumes that such an auction must produce the best price reasonably obtainable or, as Salmon LJ [in *Cuckmere Brick Co Ltd v Mutual Finance Ltd* [1971] Ch 949] expressed the test, the true market value. But the price obtained at any particular auction may be less than the price obtainable by private treaty and may depend on the steps taken to encourage bidders to attend. An auction which only produces one bid is not necessarily an indication that the true market value has been achieved.

In the present case, the mortgagee threatened on 28 February 1966, to sell the property if certain arrears of interest were not paid; it was then obvious that the borrower was in difficulties. On 28 April, the mortgagee called in the principal and gave

222 *Tse Kwong Lam v Wong Chit Sen* [1983] 1 WLR 1349 at 1357H, 1359G.

223 *Tse Kwong Lam v Wong Chit Sen* [1983] 1 WLR 1349 at 1357H–58A.

224 *Tse Kwong Lam v Wong Chit Sen* [1983] 1 WLR 1349 at 1357H, 1358C.

notice of his intention to sell the property if the principal and interest, which the mortgagee alleged to amount to $1.6m were not paid by 29 May 1966. The mortgagee had ample opportunity to consult and instruct estate agents. The property could have been offered for sale by auction or by private treaty or by announcing that the property would be sold by public auction if not previously sold by private treaty. The property could have been sold as a whole or in units. The mortgagee might have been advised that, as happened, a sale by auction might not produce any independent bidders; that the number of potential purchasers able and willing in 1966 to pay over $1m for this building was limited; that, to obtain a purchaser by private treaty or to obtain sufficient interest to justify an auction, it would be necessary for the estate agents to approach their clients and other persons known to be interested in property purchase, investment and speculation and to provide them with full information about the construction of the building, the terms upon which parts had already been sold, the provisions for sharing expenses and maintenance, the existing condition of the building, its advantages and prospects. The auctioneers to be employed in selling the property by auction, if this was necessary or desirable, could have been instructed to seek out potential purchasers and bidders and to arouse interest in the property. The mortgagee was advised by his solicitor's managing clerk that a sale by auction was 'fairer' but the mortgagee does not appear to have considered the possibility that a higher price could be obtained by a sale by private treaty to an independent third party at a price recommended by an estate agent as being the best obtainable after the agent had had an opportunity to explore the market. Moreover the mortgagee does not appear to have taken any step to secure any interest in the auction. The mortgagee instructed auctioneers who prepared particulars and conditions of sale which were dated 9 June. On the same day the sale was advertised in three newspapers. There is no evidence that the advertisement did more than give notice of the bare fact of the auction coupled with a minimum description of the property. The particulars and conditions of sale contained only the legal requirements. There was no evidence that anyone requested a copy of the particulars and conditions or asked to inspect the property. The conditions of sale disclosed that there was a reserve price, that the vendor reserved the right to bid, that 20% of the purchase price was payable after the auction and that the balance was payable one month thereafter, time being of the essence. A reader of the first advertisement had just 15 days in which to make detailed inquiries and investigations and to organise his finances so that he was prepared to engage in competitive bidding possibly with a vendor and with a borrower who knew all about the property and might be puffing the sale. There was no evidence that anyone took the elementary precautions which a purchaser of a building for a sum in excess of $1m would expect to take before venturing to bid at an auction.

The mortgagee could have consulted estate agents about the method of sale and about the method of securing the best price. At the very least he could have consulted an estate agent about the level of the reserve price. The auctioneer was not informed of the reserve price until immediately before the auction and in evidence he very properly declined to comment on the reserve because he had not valued the property. This confirms the impression that the auctioneers were not instructed to do more than put the property under the hammer, a procedure which may be appropriate to the sale of second-hand furniture but is not necessarily conducive to the attainment of the best price for freehold or leasehold property. It was not of course in the interests of the company that enthusiasm for the sale should be stimulated or that the reserve should be settled by anyone other than the mortgagee. The reserve of $1.2m was fixed by the mortgagee and was the price at which he advised and intended that the company should purchase. The mortgagee was a property investor and speculator. The company was his family company and he held shares in and financed the company. The mortgagee would not have advised the company to bid $1.2m for the property unless he thought that was an advantageous price for the company to pay.

The company, unlike an independent bidder, knew all about the property through the mortgagee and knew the amount of the reserve in advance. The company and the mortgagee did not have to arrange finance. The company bought the property for $1.2m provided by the mortgagee, who received back that sum in reduction of his mortgage debt. The sale transferred from the borrower to the mortgagee's family company at a price advised by the mortgagee the chance of making a profit which the mortgagee could not acquire for himself. The borrower was exposed to an action for $200,000 being the difference between $1.2m, the price paid by the company and $1.4m the amount of the mortgage debt. That left the mortgagee with a hold over the borrower which he exercised when the borrower complained about the sale. If, as appeared probable, the borrower could not pay $200,000 the mortgagee would suffer a loss which he could have prevented by advising the company to bid $1.4m for the property. No doubt the mortgagee did what was best for himself and the company.

The only indication that $1.2m represented the market value of the property was the fact that no one at the auction bid more than $1.2m. But the fact that no one bid more than $1.2m at this auction does not necessarily mean that the property could not have been sold for more than $1.2m if the mortgagee had consulted estate agents about the method of sale and the amount of the reserve and had instructed them to try to interest the investing public in the property. There was no competitive bidding and the company purchased the property at a price fixed by the mortgagee. There is no sufficient evidence that this particular auction produced the true market value ...

At the trial and on this appeal the mortgagee adopted the attitude that a mortgagee exercising his power of sale is entitled to secure the mortgaged property for a company in which he is interested at a price advised by the mortgagee provided that the property is properly advertised and sold by auction. A decision to this effect would expose borrowers to greater perils than those to which they are now subject as a result of decisions which enable a mortgagee to choose the date of the exercise of his power. A mortgagee who wishes to secure the mortgaged property for a company in which he is interested ought to show that he protected the interests of the borrower by taking expert advice as to the method of sale, as to the steps which ought reasonably to be taken to make the sale a success and as to the amount of the reserve. There was no difficulty in obtaining such advice orally and in writing and no good reason why a mortgagee, concerned to act fairly towards his borrower, should fail or neglect to obtain or act upon such advice in all respects as if the mortgagee were desirous of realising the best price reasonably obtainable at the date of the sale for property belonging to the mortgagee himself.

Where a mortgagee fails to satisfy the court that he took all reasonable steps to obtain the best price reasonably obtainable and that his company bought at the best price, the court will, as a general rule, set aside the sale and restore to the borrower the equity of redemption of which he has been unjustly deprived. But the borrower will be left to his remedy in damages against the mortgagee for the failure of the mortgagee to secure the best price if it will be inequitable as between the borrower and the purchaser for the sale to be set aside. In the present case it is submitted on behalf of the mortgagee and the company that the borrower is debarred by the terms of his mortgage from any remedy save damages. Alternatively the mortgagee and the company submit that the delay on the part of the borrower in pursuing his counterclaim has rendered it unjust for the building to be restored to the borrower ...

The borrower has however been guilty of inexcusable delay in prosecuting his counterclaim ...

The borrower contends that these delays have not been prejudicial to the mortgagee, who will receive principal and interest. But the borrower also seeks an account from the mortgagee on the basis of wilful default. Moreover either the mortgagee or the company must have been put to expense in maintenance and repairs of the building and may have laid out moneys on other matters which could have been better employed elsewhere. The borrower by his delay achieved a favourable position; if the property decreased in value he could either abandon his action or seek damages in setting aside the sale. If the property increased in value he could persist with his claim to set aside the sale. In the circumstances the Board consider that the borrower is not[225] entitled to the alternative remedy of damages. That was the view taken by the trial judge.

The measure of damages must be the difference between the best price reasonably obtainable on 24 June 1966, and the price of $1.2m paid by the company.

Cuckmere Brick Co v Mutual Finance Ltd [197] 1 Ch 949, CA

Salmon LJ: I will now turn to the law. It is well settled that a mortgagee is not a trustee of the power of sale for the mortgagor. Once the power has accrued, the mortgagee is entitled to exercise it for his own purposes whenever he chooses to do so. It matters not that the moment may be unpropitious and that by waiting a higher price could be obtained. He has the right to realise his security by turning it into money when he likes. Nor, in my view, is there anything to prevent a mortgagee from accepting the best bid he can get at an auction, even though the auction is badly attended and the bidding exceptionally low. Providing none of those adverse factors is due to any fault of the mortgagee, he can do as he likes. If the mortgagee's interests, as he sees them, conflict with those of the mortgagor, the mortgagee can give preference to his own interests, which of course he could not do were he a trustee of the power of sale for the mortgagor ...

It is impossible to pretend that the state of the authorities on this branch of the law is entirely satisfactory. There are some dicta which suggest that unless a mortgagee acts in bad faith he is safe. His only obligation to the mortgagor is not to cheat him. There are other dicta which suggest that in addition to the duty of acting in good faith, the mortgagee is under a duty to take reasonable care to obtain whatever is the true market value of the mortgaged property at the moment he chooses to sell it: compare, for example, *Kennedy v de Trafford* [1896] 1 Ch 762; [1897] AC 180 with *Tomlin v Luce* (1889) 43 Ch D 191, 194.

The proposition that the mortgagee owes both duties, in my judgment, represents the true view of the law. Approaching the matter first of all on principle, it is to be observed that if the sale yields a surplus over the amount owed under the mortgage, the mortgagee holds this surplus in trust for the mortgagor. If the sale shows a deficiency,

225 The word 'not' should be omitted as in [1983] 3 All ER 54 at 64.

the mortgagor has to make it good out of his own pocket. The mortgagor is vitally affected by the result of the sale but its preparation and conduct is left entirely in the hands of the mortgagee. The proximity between them could scarcely be closer. Surely they are 'neighbours'. Given that the power of sale is for the benefit of the mortgagee and that he is entitled to choose the moment to sell which suits him, it would be strange indeed if he were under no legal obligation to take reasonable care to obtain what I call the true market value at the date of the sale ...

Cross LJ: I shall first deal with the law applicable to this case. A mortgagee exercising a power of sale is in an ambiguous position. He is not a trustee of the power for the mortgagor for it was given him for his own benefit to enable him to obtain repayment of his loan. On the other hand, he is not in the position of an absolute owner selling his own property but must undoubtedly pay some regard to the interests of the mortgagor when he comes to exercise the power.

Some points are clear. On the one hand, the mortgagee, when the power has arisen, can sell when he likes, even though the market is likely to improve if he holds his hand and the result of an immediate sale may be that instead of yielding a surplus for the mortgagor the purchase price is only sufficient to discharge the mortgage debt and the interest owing on it. On the other hand, the sale must be a genuine sale by the mortgagee to an independent purchaser at a price honestly arrived at.

Suppose, however, that the mortgagee acts in good faith but that through the negligence either of the mortgagee himself or of an agent employed by him a smaller purchase price is obtained than would otherwise have been the case? ...

There is no doubt that a mortgagee who takes possession of the security with a view to selling it has to account to the mortgagor for any loss occurring through his negligence or the negligence of his agent in dealing with the property between the date of his taking possession of it and the date of the sale, including, as in the *McHugh* case [1913] AC 299, steps taken to bring the property to the place of sale. It seems quite illogical that the mortgagee's duty should suddenly change when one comes to the sale itself and that at that stage if only he acts in good faith he is under no liability, however negligent he or his agent may be.

Standard Chartered Bank v Walker [1982] 1 WLR 1410, CA

Lord Denning MR: We have had much discussion on the law. So far as mortgages are concerned the law is set out in *Cuckmere Brick Co Ltd v Mutual Finance Ltd* [1971] Ch 949. If a mortgagee enters into possession and realises a mortgaged property, it is his duty to use reasonable care to obtain the best possible price which the circumstances of the case permit. He owes this duty not only to himself, to clear off as much of the debt as he can, but also to the mortgagor so as to reduce the balance owing as much as possible, and also to the guarantor so that he is made liable for as little as possible on the guarantee. This duty is only a particular application of the general duty of care to your neighbour which was stated by Lord Atkin in *Donoghue v Stevenson* [1932] AC 562 and applied in many cases since: see *Dorset Yacht Co Ltd v Home Office* [1970] AC 1004 and *Anns v Merton London Borough Council* [1978] AC 728. The mortgagor and the guarantor are clearly in very close 'proximity' to those who conduct the sale. The duty of care is owing to them – if not to the general body of creditors of the mortgagor. There are several *dicta* to the effect that the mortgagee can choose his own time for the sale, but I do not think this means that he can sell at the worst possible time. It is at least arguable that, in choosing the time, he must exercise a reasonable degree of care.

The duty of care is owed to the mortgagor.[226] It was held recently by the Court of Appeal in *Parker-Tweedale v Dunbar Bank plc*[227] that such a duty of care is not owed to a beneficiary of the mortgaged property of which the mortgagor was the trustee, even if the mortgagee has notice of the beneficiary's interest. Similarly, the mortgagee does not owe a duty of care to a guarantor (who contracts to pay if the mortgagor does not pay) for the decline in value of the mortgaged property, unless the mortgagee is personally responsible for the decline.[228]

Parker-Tweedale v Dunbar Bank Plc (1990) 60 P & CR 83, CA

Nourse LJ: It was settled by the decision of this court in *Cuckmere Brick Co Ltd v Mutual Finance Ltd* that a mortgagee, although he may exercise his power of sale at any time of his own choice, owes the mortgagor a duty to take reasonable care to obtain a proper price for the mortgaged property at that time. But there is no support, either in the authorities or on principle, for the proposition that where the mortgagor is a trustee, even a bare trustee, of the mortgaged property, a like duty is owed to a beneficiary under the trust of whose interest the mortgagee has notice.

In seeking to support that proposition the plaintiff relied on the decision of this court in *Jarrett v Barclays Bank Ltd*. For reasons which were stated by Peter Gibson J and need not be repeated here, that case does not assist him. He also relied on the following passage in the judgment of Salmon LJ in *Cuckmere Brick Co Ltd v Mutual Finance Ltd*:[229]

> Approaching the matter first of all on principle, it is to be observed that if the sale yields a surplus over the amount owed under the mortgage, the mortgagee holds this surplus in trust for the mortgagor. If the sale shows a deficiency, the mortgagor has to make it good out of his own pocket. The mortgagor is vitally affected by the result of the sale but its preparation and conduct is left entirely in the hands of the mortgagee. The proximity between them could scarcely be closer. Surely they are 'neighbours'. Given that the power of sale is for the benefit of the mortgagee and that he is entitled to choose the moment to sell which suits him, it would be strange indeed if he were under no legal obligation to take reasonable care to obtain what I call the true market value at the date of the sale.

This reference to 'neighbours' has enabled the plaintiff to argue that the duty is owed to all those who are within the neighbourhood principle; ie to adapt the words of Lord Atkin, to all persons who are so closely and directly affected by the sale that the mortgagee ought reasonably to have them in contemplation as being so affected when he is directing his mind to the sale. Further support for the application of the neighbourhood principle in this context can be gained from the judgment of Lord Denning MR in *Standard Chartered Bank Ltd v Walker* where it was held that the duty to take reasonable care to obtain a proper price was owed to a surety for the mortgage debt as well as to the mortgagor himself.

---

226 *Standard Chartered Bank v Walker* [1982] 1 WLR 1410 at 1415E–G.

227 (1990) 60 P & CR 83 at 90–92.

228 *China and South Sea Bank Ltd v Tan Soon Gin (alias George Tan)* [1990] 1 AC 536; [1989] 3 All ER 839, PC.

229 [1971] Ch 949 at 966; 22 P & CR 624 at 636.

In my respectful opinion it is both unnecessary and confusing for the duties owed by a mortgagee to the mortgagor and the surety, if there is one, to be expressed in terms of the tort of negligence. The authorities which were considered in the careful judgments of this court in *Cuckmere Brick Co Ltd v Mutual Finance Ltd* demonstrate that the duty owed by the mortgagee to the mortgagor was recognised by equity as arising out of the particular relationship between them. Thus Salmon LJ himself said:[230]

> It would seem, therefore, that many years before the modern development of the law of negligence, the courts of equity had laid down a doctrine in relation to mortgages which is entirely consonant with the general principles later evolved by the common law.

The duty owed to the surety arises in the same way. In *The China and South Sea Bank Ltd v Tan*, Lord Templeman, in delivering the judgment of the Privy Council, having pointed out that the surety in that case admitted that the moneys secured by the guarantee were due, continued:[231]

> But the surety claims that the creditor owed the surety a duty to exercise the power of sale conferred by the mortgage and in that case the liability of the surety under the guarantee would either have been eliminated or very much reduced. The Court of Appeal [in Hong Kong] sought to find such a duty in the tort of negligence but the tort of negligence has not yet subsumed all torts and does not supplant the principles of equity or contradict contractual promises ... Equity intervenes to protect a surety.

Once it is recognised that the duty owed by the mortgagee to the mortgagor arises out of the particular relationship between them, it is readily apparent that there is no warrant for extending its scope so as to include a beneficiary or beneficiaries under a trust of which the mortgagor is the trustee. The correctness of that view was fully established in the clear and compelling argument of Mr Lloyd, who drew particular attention to the rights and duties of the trustee to protect the trust property against dissipation or depreciation in value and the impracticabilities and potential rights of double recovery inherent in giving the beneficiary an additional right to sue the mortgagee, a right which is in any event unnecessary.

The only exception for which Mr Lloyd allowed was the special case where the trustee has unreasonably refused to sue on behalf of the trust or has committed some other breach of his duties to the beneficiaries, eg by consenting to an improvident sale, which disables or disqualifies him from acting on behalf of the trust. In such a case the beneficiary is permitted to sue on behalf of the trust. This exception is established by a series of authorities, some of which were recently considered by the Privy Council in *Hayim v Citibank NA*. In delivering the judgment of their Lordships, Lord Templeman said:[232]

> These authorities demonstrate that a beneficiary has no cause of action against a third party save in special circumstances which embrace a failure, excusable or inexcusable, by the trustees in the performance of the duty owed by the trustees to the beneficiary to protect the trust estate or to protect the interests of the beneficiary in the trust estate.

230 [1971] Ch 949 at p 967; 22 P & CR 624 at 637.

231 [1990] AC 536 at 543–44.

232 [1987] AC 730 at 748.

It is important to emphasise that when a beneficiary sues under the exception he does so in right of the trust and in the room of the trustee. He does not enforce a right reciprocal to some duty owed directly to him by the third party.

China and South Sea Bank Ltd v Tan Soon Gin [1990] 1 AC 536, PC

Lord Templeman: In May 1982 the appellant creditor, China and South Sea Bank Ltd, advanced $HK30m to the debtor, Carrian Holdings Ltd. By deed of guarantee dated 18 May 1982 the respondent surety, George Tan, undertook to repay the principal sum advanced to the debtor and the monthly interest thereon ... By a mortgage dated 19 May 1982 and a deposit of securities, Filomena Ltd mortgaged shares in Carrian Investments Ltd to secure the principal sum and interest advanced by the creditor to the debtor. The mortgage contained the usual power of sale.

By deed of variation dated 18 August 1982 it was agreed by and between Filomena Ltd, the surety, the debtor, and the creditor that the principal sum and interest payable by the debtor, guaranteed by the surety and secured by the mortgage should become payable on 18 November 1982. By a letter dated 31 October 1983 the creditor demanded from the surety payment of the principal sum of $HK30m and interest of $3,496,438.34 accrued at 28 October 1983 and unpaid and any interest arising after 28 October 1983.

By a writ and indorsed statement of claim dated 9 November 1983 and an Ord 14 summons dated 9 April 1984 the creditor sought summary judgment against the surety for the principal and interest secured by the guarantee. Master Hansen gave judgment in favour of the creditor and his decision was upheld by Rhind J but reversed by an order of the Court of Appeal of Hong Kong (Cons VP, Barker and Power JJA) granting the surety unconditional leave to defend. The creditor now appeals with leave to the Board.

The surety claims that he is not liable to pay anything to the creditor by reason of the following allegations which he offers to prove at trial. (1) The shares mortgaged by Filomena were worth $HK60m on 19 May 1982, the date of the mortgage. (2) The shares were worth not less than $HK30m on 18 November 1982 when the principal sum became due. (3) The shares had admittedly become worthless. (4) The creditor knew or ought to have known of the declining value of the shares and should have sold them before they became worthless.

The surety does not and cannot impugn the validity of the provisions of the guarantee and admits that the moneys claimed by the creditor are due in accordance with the express terms of the guarantee. But the surety claims that the creditor owed the surety a duty to exercise the power of sale conferred by the mortgage and in that case the liability of the surety under the guarantee would either have been eliminated or very much reduced. The Court of Appeal sought to find such a duty in the tort of negligence but the tort of negligence has not yet subsumed all torts and does not supplant the principles of equity or contradict contractual promises or complement the remedy of judicial review or supplementary statutory rights.

Equity intervenes to protect a surety. In *Watts v Shuttleworth* (1860) 5 H & N 235, 157 ER 1171 the creditor had covenanted to insure mortgaged goods and failed to insure. A surety was released. Pollock CB said (5H & N 235 at 247–48; 157 ER 1171 at 1176):

> The substantial question in the case is, whether the omission to insure discharges the defendant, the surety. The rule upon the subject seems to be that if the person guaranteed does any act injurious to the surety, or inconsistent with his rights, or if he omits to do any act which his duty enjoins him to do, and the omission

> proves injurious to the surety, the latter will be discharged ... the rights of a surety depend rather on principles of equity than upon the actual contract ...

In *Walruff v Jay* (1872) LR 7 QB 756 the creditor failed to register a mortgage as a bill of sale and failed to take possession of the mortgaged chattels which were then seized by the trustee in bankruptcy of the mortgagor. A surety for the debt owed by the bankrupt to the creditor and secured by the mortgage was discharged to the value of the mortgaged chattels. Cockburn CJ said (at 762–63):

> Cases have been cited and authorities have been referred to in Story's Equity Jurisprudence, which abundantly establish that which is a common and well-known proposition, that where a debt is secured by a surety, it is the business of the creditor, where he has security available for the payment and satisfaction of the debt, to do whatever is necessary to make the security properly available. He is bound, if the surety voluntarily proposes to pay the debt, to make over to the surety what securities he holds in respect of that debt, so that, being satisfied himself, he shall enable the surety to realise the securities and recoup himself the amount of the debt which he has had to pay. That is now a well-known proposition. Here, by registering the bill of sale, and by afterwards availing themselves of the power which they possessed to take possession, the plaintiffs might have secured the payment of the debt to themselves, or by protecting the securities and holding them in their hands they could have made them over to the surety when the surety was willing, or was called on, to pay; but by omitting to do what was necessary in order to place themselves in that position, and by allowing bankruptcy to supervene so as to enable the trustee under the bankruptcy to take possession of those goods adversely, it is clear that they have placed the surety in a position very detrimental and prejudicial to the surety; and for that the surety ought to have, according to the general doctrine, a remedy.

Hannen J approved the following rule (at 764):

> As a surety, on a payment of the debt, is entitled to all the securities of the creditor, whether he is aware of their existence or not, even though they were given after the contract of suretyship, if the creditor who has had, or ought to have had, them in his full possession or power, loses them or permits them to get into the possession of the debt or does not make them effectual by giving proper notice, the surety to the extent of such security will be discharged. A surety, moreover, will be released if the creditor, by reason of what he has done, cannot, on payment by the surety, give him the securities in exactly the same condition as they formerly stood in his hands.

Quain J (at 765) approved the rule that:

> ... if through any neglect on the part of the creditor, a security to the benefit of which a surety is entitled is lost, or is not properly perfected, the surety is discharged.

In the present case the security was neither surrendered nor lost nor imperfect nor altered in condition by reason of what was done by the creditor. The creditor had three sources of repayment. The creditor could sue the debtor, sell the mortgage securities or sue the surety. All these remedies could be exercised at any time or times simultaneously or contemporaneously or successively or not at all. If the creditor chose to sue the surety and not pursue any other remedy, the creditor on being paid in full was bound to assign the mortgage securities to the surety. If the creditor chose to exercise his power of sale over the mortgage security he must sell for the current market value but the creditor must decide in his own interest if and when he should sell. The creditor does not become a trustee of the mortgaged securities and the power of sale for the surety unless and until the creditor is paid in full and the surety, having paid the whole of the debt is entitled to a transfer of the mortgaged securities to procure recovery of the whole or part of the sum he has paid to the creditor.

The creditor is not obliged to do anything. If the creditor does nothing and the debtor declines into bankruptcy the mortgaged securities become valueless and if the surety decamps abroad the creditor loses his money. If disaster strikes the debtor and the mortgaged securities but the surety remains capable of repaying the debt then the creditor loses nothing. The surety contracts to pay if the debtor does not pay and the surety is bound by his contract. If the surety, perhaps less indolent or less well protected than the creditor, is worried that the mortgaged securities may decline in value then the surety may request the creditor to sell and if the creditor remains idle then the surety may bustle about, pay off the debt, take over the benefit of the securities and sell them. No creditor could carry on the business of lending if he could become liable to a mortgagee and to a surety or to either of them for a decline in value of mortgaged property, unless the creditor was personally responsible for the decline. Applying the rule as specified by Pollock CB in *Watts v Shuttleworth* (1860) H & N 235 at 247–48; 157 ER 1171 at 1176, it appears to their Lordships that in the present case the creditor did no act injurious to the surety, did no act inconsistent with the rights of the surety and the creditor did not omit any act which his duty enjoined him to do. The creditor was not under a duty to exercise his power of sale over the mortgaged securities at any particular time or at all.

Their Lordships will humbly advise Her Majesty that this appeal should be allowed, the order of the Court of Appeal set aside and the order made by Rhind J restored. The respondent must pay the appellant's costs in the Court of Appeal and before their Lordships' Board.

Appeal allowed

The mortgagor's remedy for improper exercise of power of sale depends on the type of irregularities involved. In the case of breach of duty of care, s 104(2) of the Law of Property Act 1925 provides that the mortgagor can claim damages against the mortgagee for the loss suffered. Where there is a breach of duty of good faith, the sale can be set aside and the mortgagor can recover his equity of redemption.[233] However, rescission would only be allowed if it would not be inequitable to do so. In *Tse Kwong Lam* rescission was not allowed because it would be inequitable having regard to the mortgagor's inexcusable delay in prosecuting his claim. Here only damages were granted.

Law of Property Act 1925

104. Conveyance on sale

(2) Where a conveyance is made in exercise of the power of sale conferred by this Act, or any enactment replaced by this Act, the title of the purchaser shall not be impeachable on the ground:

(a) that no case had arisen to authorise the sale; or

233 *Tse Kwong Lam v Wong Chit Sen* [1983] 1 WLR 1349 at 1359H–60A.

(b) that due notice was not given; or

(c) where the mortgage is made after the commencement of this Act, that leave of the court, when so required, was not obtained; or

(d) whether the mortgage was made before or after such commencement, that the power was otherwise improperly or irregularly exercised;

and a purchaser is not, either before or on conveyance, concerned to see or inquire whether a case has arisen to authorise the sale, or due notice has been given, or the power is otherwise properly and regularly exercised; but any person damnified by an unauthorised, or improper, or irregular exercise of the power shall have his remedy in damages against the person exercising the power.

Where the mortgaged property is properly sold the mortgagee is statutorily rendered trustee of the proceeds of sale under s 105 of the Law of Property Act 1925. He must use the proceeds firstly to pay all costs, charges and expenses properly incurred by him in connection with the sale and secondly to discharge the mortgage and interest due under it and thirdly to pay the residue to the mortgagor.

Where a mortgagee sells under his statutory or express power of sale the conveyance will vest the mortgagor's full legal estate in the purchaser, subject only to any legal interests which have priority over the mortgagee.[234] The conveyance will also overreach prior equitable interests which are capable of being overreached.[235] The exercise of the power of sale will disable the mortgagor from redeeming the mortgage. The power is considered exercised as soon as the mortgagee contracts to sell and the mortgagor cannot frustrate the contract and redeem the mortgage by a belated payment.[236]

Suppose the mortgagor contracts to sell his legal estate to P1 before the mortgagee sells the mortgaged property to P2. Suppose the mortgagor – P1's estate contract is properly registered as a Class C(iv) land charge. The mortgagee can still pass a good title to P2 and it will not be affected by the mortgagor – P1's estate contract even if the estate contract is properly registered.[237] This is because while the mortgage remained unredeemed, P1 only has an equity of redemption which can be destroyed when the power of sale is exercised. In registered land, on completion of the mortgagee's sale by registration his charge and all incumbrances and entries inferior thereto shall be cancelled.[238]

234 Sections 88(1), 89(1) of the LPA 1925.

235 Section 2(1)(iii) of the LPA 1925.

236 *Lord Waring v London & Manchester Assurance Co Ltd* [1935] 1 Ch 310; *Property and Bloodstock Ltd v Emerton* [1968] Ch 94.; *National & Provincial Building Society v Ahmed* [1995] 2 EGLR 127.

237 *Duke v Robson* [1973] 1 WLR 267, CA.

238 Section 34(4) of the LRA 1925.

Foreclosure

To recover the capital, the mortgagee may apply for a decree of foreclosure. This is a drastic action which a mortgagee can seek to realise his security. Its effect is to vest the mortgagor's entire legal estate in the mortgagee.[239] This remedy is today rarely sought let alone granted. '[F]oreclosure actions are almost unheard of today and have been so for many years'.[240] As a result, the Law Commission has proposed the abolition of foreclosure.[241]

An application for foreclosure must be made to the court.[242] The action must be brought within 12 years after the date when the mortgage moneys become due.[243] The court will, when satisfied, only grant a *foreclosure nisi* in the first instance allowing the mortgagor a period (normally six months) to repay the mortgage money. If no such payment is forthcoming, an order for *foreclosure absolute* will then be granted. However, during the interim period (between the order nisi and the order absolute) the mortgagor can apply under s 91(2) of the Law of Property Act 1925 for an order directing a sale of the property.

Even after an order is granted, in appropriate circumstances the court may re-open the order on the mortgagor's application and allow redemption.[244] However, it is unlikely that the court will do this if a third party has bought the property some time previously without notice of the circumstances which might influence the court to interfere.[245]

Consolidation

The mortgagee may also reserve his right to consolidate a number of mortgages vested in him and may not allow the mortgagor to redeem one without the other. This principle which is based on the equitable maxim 'he who comes to equity must do equity' operates to protect the mortgagee. Suppose the mortgagor mortgaged both Whiteacre and Blackacre each worth £40,000 to the mortgagee for two loans, £30,000 each. If the value of Whiteacre later increased to £90,000, but the value of Blackacre diminished to £20,000, it would be unfair to allow the mortgagor to redeem Whiteacre leaving Blackacre unredeemed. Thus, equity allows the mortgagee to insist that the mortgagor redeems both Whiteacre and Blackacre or not at all.

However, a mortgagee must satisfy the following conditions before equity would allow him to consolidate:

239 Section 88(2) of the LPA 1925.

240 *Palk v Mortgage Services Funding plc* [1993] 2 WLR 415 at 419E.

241 Law Com No 204 (1991), para 7.27.

242 *Ness v O'Neil* [1916] 1 KB 706 at 709.

243 Section 15(1) of the Limitation Act 1980.

244 *Campbell v Holyland* (1877) 7 Ch D 166.

245 *Campbell v Holyland* (1877) 7 Ch D 166.

(a) Right to consolidate must be reserved

Prior to 1882, a mortgagee had an automatic right to consolidate provided that the other conditions discussed below were satisfied. After 1881, such a right must be reserved unless at least one of the mortgages allows consolidation.[246] This is today re-enacted under s 93(1) of the law of Property Act 1925.

Law of Property Act 1925

93. Restriction on consolidation of mortgages

(1) A mortgagor seeking to redeem any one mortgage is entitled to do so without paying any money due under any separate mortgage made by him, or by any person through whom he claims, solely on property other than that comprised in the mortgage which he seeks to redeem.

This subsection applies only if and as far as a contrary intention is not expressed in the mortgage deeds or one of them.

(2) This section does not apply where all the mortgages were made before the first day of January, eighteen hundred and eighty-two.

(3) Save as aforesaid, nothing in this Act, in reference to mortgages, affects any right of consolidation or renders inoperative a stipulation in relation to any mortgage made before or after the commencement of this Act reserving a right to consolidate.

Thus, unless the two mortgagees were created before 1882, or at least one of them allows consolidation, no such right would exist. However, as s 93 only applies if there is no contrary intention expressed in the mortgage deed, in practice, it is common for a mortgage deed to exclude s 93, thereby permitting consolidation.

(b) Dates for redemption passed

The legal dates for redemption must have passed.[247] This is because a right of consolidation is equitable and cannot affect the mortgagor's legal right of redemption.

(c) Same mortgagor

Both mortgages must have been made by the same mortgagor.[248] Thus if A mortgages Whiteacre to C, and B, as trustee for A, mortgages Blackacre to C, C cannot later consolidate mortgages on Whiteacre and Blackacre, even if the legal estate in Blackacre has later come into A's hands. Similarly, if X mortgages Whiteacre, and X and Y jointly mortgage Blackacre, the mortgagee cannot consolidate the mortgages.[249]

---

246 Section 17(2) of the Conveyancing Act 1881, replaced by s 93(1) of the LPA 1925.

247 *Cummins v Fletcher* (1880) 14 Ch D 699.

248 *Sharp v Rickards* [1909] 1 Ch 109.

249 *Thorneycroft v Crockett* (1848) 2 HLC 239.

It is, however, not necessary to show that the two mortgages were made to the same mortgagee as long as they are now in the hands of one mortgagee.[250] Thus, if X mortgages Whiteacre to A and Blackacre to B, if B later acquires A's mortgage he may consolidate the two mortgages. Similarly, if:

X mortgages Whiteacre to A,

X mortgages Blackacre to B,

A and B transfer their mortgages to D,

X cannot redeem Whiteacre leaving Blackacre unredeemed.

This principle applies to more complicated cases such as,

X mortgages 1 and 2 to A

X mortgages 3 to B

X mortgages 4, 5 and 6 to C

X transfers his equities of redemption on 1, 2, 3, 4, 5 and 6 to Y

A, B and C transfer all their mortgages to D

Here D has become the ultimate mortgagee and Y the ultimate mortgagor. D can require Y to redeem all the properties or none.

This principle also applies even if at the time of consolidation, the equities of redemption have come into the hands of different mortgagors:

A mortgages 1, 2 and 3 to B

A transfers the equity of redemption on 1 to C

Here A remains the mortgagor for properties 2 and 3, but C is now the mortgagor for property 1. B remains the mortgagee. C cannot redeem property 1 without also redeeming properties 2 and 3.[251]

In the words of Lord Davey in *Pledge v White*:[252]

> Consolidation is allowed only if, at the date when redemption is sought, all the mortgages, having originally been made by one mortgagor, are vested in one mortgagee and all the equities are vested in one person, or if, after these two things have once happened, the equities of redemption have become separated.

However, the transferee of an equity of redemption would not be subject to consolidation in respect of mortgages created after the transfer to him. Neither is he subject to consolidation in respect of mortgages which, though created before the transfer to him, became vested in one mortgagee afterwards.[253] Thus, if:

X mortgages 1 and 2 to A

X mortgages 3 to B

X mortgages 4, 5 and 6 to C

X transfers his equities of redemption on 1 and 2, to Y and 3, 4, 5 and 6 to Z

A, B and C transfer all their mortgages to D

250 *Pledge v White* [1896] AC 187.

251 *Pledge v White* [1896] AC 187, at 198.

252 [1896] AC 187 at 198.

253 *Harter v Colman* (1882) 10 Ch D 630.

Here there can be no consolidation because at no one moment has there been a same mortgagor and a same mortgagee. D cannot require either Y or Z to redeem all the properties or none.

7 REMEDIES AVAILABLE TO EQUITABLE MORTGAGEE

Taking possession

It seems that an equitable mortgagee has no right to take possession in the absence of a court order.[254]

Foreclosure

An equitable mortgagee may apply for a foreclosure, although the court may simply order a sale instead.[255] The order will require the mortgagor to convey the entire legal estate in the mortgaged land to the mortgagee free from any right of redemption.

Power of sale

The statutory power of sale under s 101(1) of the Law of Property Act 1925 can only be exercised if the equitable mortgage is made by deed, eg mortgage of an equitable interest made by deed. But such power only covers the sale of the mortgaged equitable interest and not the legal estate.[256] So a power of attorney to sell the legal estate is required.[257] But most of the equitable mortgages are not made by deed. Such mortgagees have no automatic right to sell under s 101. But they may apply to the court under s 91(2) of the Law of Property Act. The court may grant an order for sale or an order to vest the legal estate in the mortgagee so that he can acquire the right to sell under s 101 subsequently.

To appoint a receiver

Again, statutory power to appoint a receiver is only available if the mortgage is made by deed.[258] Where the mortgage is not made by deed the mortgagee may apply to the court for such an order under s 37 of the Supreme Court Act 1981.

8 REMEDIES AVAILABLE TO EQUITABLE CHARGEE

Powers of sale under s 101(1) of the Law of Property Act 1925 would arise if the charge was by deed but otherwise the primary remedies are to apply to the court

254 *Barclays Bank Ltd v Bird* [1954] Ch 274 at 280; *Ladup Ltd v Williams & Glyn's Bank plc* [1985] 1 WLR 851 at 855B; *Ashley Guarantee plc v Zacaria* [1993] WLR 62 at 69H. See Megarry and Wade pp 951–52 suggesting that an equitable mortgagee has a right of possession. See also (1954) 70 LQR 161 (REM); (1955) 71 LQR 204 (HWRW).

255 *James v James* (1873) LR 16 Eq 153 at 154.

256 *Re Hodson & Howes' Contract* (1887) 35 Ch D 668.

257 But see *Re White Rose Cottage* [1965] Ch 940 at 951.

258 Section 101(1)(iii) of the LPA 1925.

for an order for sale[259] or for the appointment of a receiver.[260] The chargee cannot foreclose[261] or take possession[262] because he has no legal estate or equitable interest in the mortgaged land vested in him.

9 PRIORITIES

The issue of priorities can arise in two situations: (i) where the mortgaged property is also subject to prior or subsequent incumbrances (other than a mortgage); (ii) where the mortgaged property is subject to two mortgages. The rules of priority governing the two situations are essentially the general rules about the relationship of legal and equitable interests which have been considered in Chapters 6 and 7 with the exception that where there are two competing mortgages, both unprotected by title deeds, confusion can sometimes arise under s 97 of the Law of Property Act 1925. Some consideration will also be given to priority between company charges.

Priority

(a) Against interests created prior to the mortgage

(i) Unregistered system

Where the title of the mortgaged property is unregistered, any prior legal estate or interest will bind the mortgagee.

Insofar as equitable interests are concerned, any prior registrable equitable interests will bind the mortgagee if duly registered.[263] Equitable interests registrable under Class B or C (other than estate contracts), if unregistered, are void against a mortgagee for valuable consideration. Thus a prior equitable charge registrable under Class C(iii) is void, if unregistered, against a subsequent mortgagee for value[264] Equitable interests registrable under Class D and estate contracts, if unregistered, are void against a mortgagee of a legal estate for money or money's worth.[265] Thus, an agreement to create a legal mortgage, if unregistered, loses priority to a mortgagee who takes a legal estate.[266] If the mortgagee only takes an equitable interest, then a prior unregistered Class D land charge or estate contract takes priority because where equities are equal the first in time prevails.[267]

---

259 Under s 91(2) of the LPA 1925.

260 *Tennant v Trenchard* (1869) 4 Ch App 537; *Re Owen* [1894] 3 Ch 220.

261 *Tennant v Trenchard* (1869) 4 Ch App 537 at 542; *Re Lloyd* [1903] 1 Ch 385 at 404.

262 *Garfitt v Allen* (1887) 37 Ch D 48 at 50.

263 Section 199(1)(i) of the LPA 1925.

264 Section 4(5) of the LCA 1972. But see s 97 of the LPA 1925.

265 Section 4(6) of the LCA 1972.

266 Section 4(6) of the LCA 1972. But see s 97 of the LPA 1925.

267 *McCarthy & Stone Ltd v Julian S Hodge & Co Ltd* [1971] 1 WLR 1547.

Beneficial interests behind a settlement can be overreached provided the mortgagee pays the loan to all the trustees of the settlement.[268] If the mortgagee did not pay to all the trustees of the settlement or a trust corporation or into court, the mortgage is void unless he deals in good faith with the tenant for life.[269] Where the mortgaged property is held on trust of land, if the mortgagee did not pay to two trustees or a trust corporation, priority depends on old doctrine of notice.[270] It is essential for the mortgagee to inspect the property and to make proper enquiry of the beneficiary as to his interest in the property. In *Hodgson v Marks*, Russell LJ said that 'it is plain that [the mortgagee] made no inquiries on the spot save as to repairs; it relied on [the first defendant], who lied to it, and I waste no tears on it'.[271]

Where the mortgaged property was held on trust for sale, the court had tried to water down the effect of non-compliance with the requirement of payment of capital money to trustees for sale by no less than two methods. These considerations would appear to be relevant to a trust of land. First, where the mortgage and the acquisition of the mortgaged property were contemporaneous, a beneficial owner who knew that the mortgage was being granted to enable the property to be bought would be taken to have agreed to defer his priority to the mortgagee.[272]

Bristol and West Building Society v Henning [1985] 2 All ER 606, CA

Browne-Wilkinson LJ: Therefore, in order to determine what, on the assumption made, is the nature of Mrs Henning's right in the Devon house, it is necessary first to determine from the parties' actions what were their express or imputed intentions as to her beneficial interest. Once that is identified as the relevant question, in my judgment the answer becomes obvious. Mr and Mrs Henning did not contemporaneously express any intention as to the beneficial interests in the property. Therefore such intention if it exists has to be imputed to them from their actions. Mrs Henning knew of and supported the proposal to raise the purchase price of the Devon house on mortgage. In those circumstances, it is in my judgment impossible to impute to them any common intention other than that she authorised Mr Henning to raise the money by mortgage to the society. In more technical terms, it was the common intention that Mr Henning as trustee should have power to grant the mortgage to the society. Such power to mortgage must have extended to granting to the society a mortgage having priority to any beneficial interests in the property. I would not impute to the parties an intention to mislead the society by purporting to offer the unencumbered fee simple of the property as security when in fact there was to be an equitable interest which would take priority to the society. Indeed in evidence Mrs Henning said: 'I would have realised that the building society was expecting to be able to rely on the full value of the house as security for the loan, but I

268 Sections 2(1)(ii), 27 of the LPA 1925; *City of London Building Society v Flegg* [1988] AC 54; ss 2(1)(i), 18, 72 of the LPA 1925; *Re Morgan's Lease* [1972] Ch 1; compare *Weston v Henshaw* [1950] Ch 510.

269 Sections 18, 110 of the SLA 1925; *Re Morgan's Lease* [1972] Ch 1; compare *Weston v Henshaw* [1950] Ch 510.

270 See *Kingsnorth Finance Co Ltd v Tizard* [1986] 1 WLR 783.

271 [1971] Ch 892, at 932B.

272 *Abbey National Building Society v Cann* [1990] 1 All ER 1085 at 1101f–g; *Bristol and West Building Society v Henning* [1985] 2 All ER 606, followed in *Paddington Building Society v Mendelsohn* (1985) 50 P & CR 244.

never really thought about it; if somebody had explained it to me as you have now I would have appreciated it.' This evidence shows that, although she had no actual relevant intention at the time, it would be wrong to impute to the parties any intention other than that the society was to have a charge in priority to the parties' beneficial interests. Counsel for Mrs Henning sought to avoid this conclusion by pointing out that such an intention left Mrs Henning at the mercy of Mr Henning and failed to provide the security which the house was designed to give her and her children. He pointed out that Mr Henning could at any time cease to pay the mortgage instalments and the society would then be able to take possession from Mrs Henning. That is true. But the fact that the arrangements made did not, because of the rights of a third party, provide full security cannot alter the only intention it is possible to impute to the parties. There was no way in which the Devon house could have been bought at all without the assistance of the mortgage to the society and the mortgage to the society could not be properly granted without giving the society a charge over the whole legal and equitable interest. Since the nature of Mrs Henning's interest has to be found in the imputed intention of the parties and the imputed intention of the parties must have been that her interest was to be subject to that of the society, it is impossible for Mrs Henning to establish that she is entitled to some form of equitable interest which gives her rights in priority to the rights of the society. I would therefore hold that, even on the assumption that Mrs Henning has some equitable interest or right in the Devon house, such interest or right is subject to the society's charge and provides no defence to the society's claim for possession.

Similarly, where the first mortgage was discharged by money raised in a second mortgage, the beneficial owner who knew that the first mortgage was obtained to finance the purchase of the mortgaged property was held to have also postponed her beneficial interest to the second mortgagee for the amount of the first mortgage and on no less favourable term than the first.[273]

Equity and Law Home Loans Ltd v Prestidge [1992] 1 All ER 909, CA

Mustill LJ: It seems to me that these facts, and the order now under appeal, require consideration of the following four questions. (1) What, if any, beneficial interest did the appellant acquire as a result of the transaction leading up to the mortgage and purchase? (2) What was the status of this interest *vis-à-vis* the charge in favour of Britannia created by the mortgage for £30,000? (3) What would the status of this interest have been if the new mortgage in favour of Equity and Law had been for no more than £30,000 plus any interest unpaid on the old mortgage? (4) What difference does it make that the new mortgage secured a larger amount?

In the event we have not been called upon to decide the first of these questions. In the light of the evidence, read against the background of *Grant v Edwards* [1986] 2 All ER 426, [1986] Ch 638, the plaintiffs have not sought to argue, and could not have hoped to argue with success, that the appellant had no beneficial interest at all ...

The second question is also the subject of no contest ...

The third question requires the application of the reasoning in *Bristol and West Building Society v Henning* [1985] 2 All ER 606; [1985] 1 WLR 778 to a new set of facts.

273 *Equity & Law Home Loans Ltd v Prestidge* [1992] 1 All ER 909. See (1993) 44 NILQ 51 (Goo, SH).

[His Lordship referred to Browne-Wilkinson LJ's judgment quoted at pp 1002–03 above ([1985] 2 All ER 606 at 609–10) and continued:]

So it seems to me that one must ask this question: what intention must one impute to the parties as regards the position which would exist if the mortgage which had been obtained in order to enable the purchase of the house, and which the parties intended to have priority over Mrs Brown's beneficial interest, should be replaced by another mortgage on no less favourable terms?

In my judgment, this question need only to be posed for it to be answered in favour of the new mortgages. Any other answer would be absurd, for it would mean that, if Mr Prestidge had in good faith and without the knowledge of the appellant transferred the mortgage to another society in order (say) to obtain a more favourable rate of interest, Mrs Brown would suddenly receive a windfall in the shape of the removal of the encumbrance which she had intended should be created in consequence of a transaction which could not do her any harm and of which she was entirely ignorant.

If this answer is correct, it disposes of two objections to the judgment of the learned recorder which were canvassed in argument. First, it is said that the appellant's interest could not be encumbered by a mortgage of which she was unaware, especially in circumstances where there was ample on the documents to put the society on notice of that interest. Well, this would have been right if the mortgage to Equity and Law had been the first and only transaction. But it was not. The new mortgage was made against the background of a consent by the appellant to the creation of an encumbrance so that the transaction could proceed. This imputed consent must, in common sense, apply to the creation of a new encumbrance in replacement of the old, whether the appellant knew about it or not, provided that it did not change her position for the worse.

The second objection receives the same answer. It presupposes that there was a *scintilla temporis* between the discharge of the first mortgage and the attachment of the second when the property was entirely unencumbered and the appellant's interest therein was also unencumbered. It could be said that this interest could not effectively be re-encumbered by a transaction of which she was unaware. I doubt whether this argument is even technically correct, for it may very well be that if the position in law were closely examined (which very sensibly it was not in the argument before us) it would be found that the transactions were simultaneous. But, apart from this, to give effect to such a technicality would go against the grain of the broad equity expounded in *Henning's Case*. If it was just to enforce the first mortgage, it must inevitably be just to enforce the second by virtue of an imputed consent which applied to the creation of both.

This leaves the fourth question: what is the position where the replacement mortgage creates a greater encumbrance than before? If Equity and Law had sought to argue that they could enforce their charge in full the judgment in *Henning's* case would have provided a conclusive answer, for no intention to prefer a mortgage in any amount greater than £30,000 plus interest could properly be imputed to the appellant. But the judge has not made any order to this effect, nor have Equity and Law sought by cross-appeal to obtain one. The issue is therefore not whether the new mortgage has made the appellant's position worse, but whether, as she contends, it has made it very much better. This would be a strange result if it were so, and I do not think that it is so. I repeat that the purchase could not have taken place at all without some encumbrance, and in my view it is a natural development of *Henning's* case to hold that in justice to both parties the original or substituted encumbrance should rank ahead of the beneficial interest as far as, but no further than, the consent which is to be imputed to the appellant. I therefore conclude that the judge's order was right.

Finally, I must add two comments on an argument advanced by Mr Brown based on the failure by the respondents to follow up the clear hints in the documents that someone besides Mr Prestidge might have an interest in the house. In the form deployed by Mr Brown, this was a complaint that if Equity and Law had been more alert and had made more inquiries the appellant would have realised that Mr Prestidge was up to no good and that she was being left with a property encumbered by a mortgage whose instalments she could not pay. In such circumstances she would, so it is said, have prevailed on the Department of Social Security to keep up the instalments, something which they now will not do because the unpaid sums have in the interval become so greatly increased. Thus, she is being made homeless through a combination of Mr Prestidge's dishonesty and Equity and Law's incompetence and, she might well add, some serious mistakes by her first solicitors. I am by no means convinced that this will be the practical result of upholding the judgment, for it may happen that a result can be negotiated which will keep the appellant and her family in the house, while recognising the full mutual rights of the parties. I certainly hope so. But in any event I am quite unable to see how Equity and Law could be regarded as owing towards her any duty of care which could alter the consequences of her initial imputed consent to the encumbering of the property.

This leads to the second observation. After the conclusion of the argument I had begun to wonder whether the combination of Equity and Law's means of knowledge with the fact that the appellant's interest was in the nature of an equity might mean that they could not claim to be *bona fide* purchasers without notice whose title defeated the equity. This point was not raised on the argument of the appeal, and we have not sought to open it up by further argument because on reflection it appears unsound. The rights of the mortgagees are preferred, not because they override the equity, but because the appellant's beneficial interest was of a very special kind, which from the outset had carved out of it by anticipation a recognition of the rights of the mortgagees whose finance was intended to bring the purchase into being. In my view once this is recognised the problem disappears.

I would therefore dismiss the appeal. The appellant has been cruelly deceived, and has suffered grievous hardship, but this is not something to be laid to the account of Equity and Law.

SH Goo (1993) NILQ 51

Mustill LJ's approval of the extension of the *Henning* principle was in effect based on Browne-Wilkinson LJ's statement in *Henning*[274] interpreting *Gissing v Gissing*[275] as deciding that, in the absence of express agreement or express trust, a right to a beneficial interest under a constructive trust could be established by proving an express or *imputed intention* that a party other than the legal owner should have a beneficial interest in the property. In *Gissing v Gissing*, however, Lord Diplock had declared that that was not the law.[276] Furthermore, Mustill LJ's approach seems inconsistent with that adopted by the

274 [1985] 1 WLR 778 at 782.

275 [1971] AC 886.

276 *Ibid*, at 904.

courts when asked to determine the acquisition of beneficial interests between beneficial co-owners. In *Lloyds Bank plc v Rosset*[277] Lord Bridge stated that the courts are not willing to impute an intention 'where there is no evidence to support a finding of an agreement or arrangement to share, however reasonable it might have been for the parties to reach such an arrangement if they had applied their minds to the question'.[278] It appears that Lord Bridge's approach is to be preferred. It is not only consistent with Lord Diplock's dicta in *Gissing v Gissing*, but also more realistic. Had the beneficial owners applied their minds to the question of how the beneficial interest in the property was to be held at the time when the original mortgage was to be substituted by the new mortgage, they might well have decided not to go ahead with the substitution. It is extremely artificial to impute an intention to the parties which they might not have had if they had considered the matter.

Although, on the facts, it is difficult to see why Mrs Brown should receive a windfall because a subsequent mortgage has been substituted for the original, it is equally difficult to see why the plaintiff's position should be improved by Mr Prestidge's use of the money in discharging the original mortgage. Had Mr Prestidge used the money for other purposes, leaving the original mortgage outstanding, the plaintiff in order to succeed in its claim would have had to show that it was a *bona fide* purchaser of a legal estate for value without notice of Mrs Brown's equitable interest. This means that it would have had to make sufficient inquiries as to the beneficial ownership and inspection of the house.[279] Although the plaintiff was satisfied from Mr Prestidge's replies that Mrs Brown was a non-owner occupant, it had not enquired of Mrs Brown as to her beneficial entitlements[280] and it knew that Mrs Brown had not executed a deed of consent. In those circumstances the plaintiff's claim would clearly have collapsed, as the plaintiff would then have had constructive notice of Mrs Brown's beneficial interests.

It seems that the decision in *Prestidge* did not prejudice Mrs Brown's position in that the original mortgage was replaced by a new mortgage on no less favourable terms. However, the legal reasoning behind it is somewhat dubious, and there are potential problems of a practical nature. Since mortgage terms can vary, when is a new mortgage made on 'no less favourable terms'? Is a mortgage for a sum equivalent to the original mortgage and at a similar rate of interest, but to be paid back within a longer period of time, made on 'no less favourable terms'? Suppose the new mortgage is for a sum equivalent to the original mortgage, but at a higher rate of interest than the original mortgage. To what extent is the appellant's beneficial interest encumbered by the new mortgage? Although it seems clear from Mustill LJ's approach that the appellant should not be liable on less favourable terms – that is, she should not be liable for more than the interest accumulated under the original mortgage – the decision in *Prestidge* fails to take into account the fact that the appellant is now subject to a higher danger of default as the rate of interest increases. The decision appears to be yet another attempt by the court to water down the impact of *Williams and Glyn's Bank Ltd v Boland*.[281]

277 [1991] 1 AC 107.

278 *Ibid*, at 132–33.

279 Section 199(1)(ii) of the LPA 1925.

280 See *Kingsnorth Finance Co Ltd v Tizard* [1986] 1 WLR 783.

281 [1981] AC 487.

The extension of the *Henning* principle is also perhaps unnecessary in the light of the House of Lords' decision in *Abbey National Building Society v Cann*.[282] In *Prestidge*, the appellant argued that there was a *scintilla temporis* between the discharge of the original mortgage and the creation of the new mortgage, during which the appellant's interest was entirely unencumbered and could bind the plaintiff. Mustill LJ did not agree with this argument: the discharge of the original mortgage and the creation of the new one were simultaneous.[283] As Mrs Brown was bound by the original mortgage, she was also bound by the new one which discharged the original. This is consistent with the decision in *Cann*, where it was held that there was no *scintilla temporis* between the transfer and a simultaneous mortgage providing the purchase money; a purchaser whose purchase was funded either wholly or partly by a mortgage only acquires an equity of redemption (a fee simple encumbered by the mortgage). On this basis, Mrs Brown's knowledge of the original mortgage was irrelevant; Mr Prestidge could only acquire an equity of redemption. Similarly, when the original mortgage was substituted by the new one, Mrs Brown's knowledge of the substitution was irrelevant; Mr Prestidge could only acquire an equity of redemption in the new mortgage.

If the House of Lords in *Cann* is correct in abolishing the doctrine of *scintilla temporis*, then the decision should be, and indeed has been, applied in *Prestidge*. When so applied, Mrs Brown should, like Mrs Cann, be liable to a sum larger than was necessary to finance the purchase or to substitute the original mortgage which financed the purchase. Had this been the case, it would have been grossly unfair to Mrs Brown, who was wholly unaware of the substitution. Mrs Brown was, however, not held liable for a sum larger than that of the original mortgage. This shows an inconsistency in the practical outcome for the beneficial owner in *Prestidge* and *Cann*, which may be difficult to justify. It could be argued that in *Cann* Lord Oliver found that Mrs Cann permitted her son to raise money on the security of the property *without any limitation*,[284] whereas in *Prestidge*, in contrast, Mrs Brown only consented to the amount of the first mortgage, and thus her equity of redemption in any subsequent mortgage which replaced the original must have been limited to the same amount. However, where there is no *scintilla temporis* between the transfer of the property and the creation of a mortgage which finances the purchase (or between the discharge of the original mortgage and the creation of the new mortgage which discharges the original), the equitable owners are bound by the amount of the mortgage whether they have knowledge of it or not. Their consents, therefore, do not seem to be relevant.

Prestidge is thus a good example of potential problems caused by the House of Lords' decision in *Cann* that the *scintilla temporis* doctrine is incorrect.

It also appears that it was unnecessary for the House of Lords in *Cann* to have overruled *Church of England Building Society v Piskor*.[285] Mrs Cann's failure to protect her equitable interest by entering a restriction meant that she could not have priority over the mortgagee.[286] Neither could she claim an overriding interest; even if the doctrine of *scintilla temporis* had not been overruled, her equitable interest would have arisen in the

282 [1990] 1 All ER 1085.
283 [1992] 1 All ER 909 at 915.
284 [1990] 1 All ER 1085 at 1101.
285 [1954] 2 All ER 85.
286 Section 20 of the LRA 1925.

scintilla of time between the transfer taking effect and the legal charge taking effect, and would not have overridden the legal charge at the date of the registration of the legal charge because she did not have actual occupation at the date of completion of the legal charge.

The result in *Prestidge* might have been achieved had the doctrine of subrogation applied. If so, the plaintiff would have been able to assert the priority of the building society over Mrs Brown. However, subrogation does not occur automatically. In *Orakpo v Manson Investments Ltd*,[287] Lord Diplock was of the opinion that the mere fact that money lent had been expended upon discharging a secured liability of the borrower did not give rise to any implication of subrogation unless the contract under which the money was borrowed provided that the money was to be applied for this purpose.[288] It is not clear on the facts of *Prestidge* whether the plaintiff was aware of the existence of the original mortgage and, if so, whether it had required the original mortgage to be paid off. As the new mortgage to the plaintiff was said to be for the improvement of Mr Prestidge's house, it may be fair to assume that the plaintiff had not required Mr Prestidge to use the new mortgage to redeem the original mortgage and so the doctrine of subrogation would not apply.

It is interesting to note, however, that a second lender who has not required its advance to be used to discharge an earlier mortgage, but whose advance is in fact so used, can still get priority following the decision in *Cann*. As mentioned above, there is no *scintilla temporis* between the discharge of the earlier mortgage and the creation of the plaintiff's advance. Thus, *Cann* appears to do violence to the long established doctrine of subrogation and is inconsistent with Lord Diplock's dictum in *Orakpo*.

If the doctrine of *scintilla temporis* had not been abolished, a beneficial interest behind a trust would have taken priority over a subsequent equitable mortgage (whether original or subsequent) because where equities are equal the first in time prevails. Where the mortgage is legal, then whether it has priority over the beneficial owner or not would have depended on whether the beneficial interest had been overreached, and if not overreached, whether the mortgagee had notice of the beneficial ownership. Such a beneficial interest could have been overreached if the mortgagee had paid the advance to two trustees.[289] As Mr Prestidge held the property on a bare trust for Mrs Brown, such a course was impossible in *Prestidge* unless the plaintiff insisted on the appointment of a new trustee. As Mrs Brown's beneficial interest had not been overreached, it should have bound the plaintiff who had constructive notice of it. This was because the plaintiff had not enquired of Mrs Brown as to her beneficial entitlement in the house, despite knowing that she was living in it and that she had not executed a deed of consent. Thus, to get priority the plaintiff would have to take a legal mortgage, which it did, and make proper inquiries. Had beneficial interests been discovered, it should not have advanced the money unless and until the deed of consent had been obtained. Where practicable, it should also have insisted on paying the loan to at least two trustees to take advantage of the overreaching machinery. In the case of registered land, the mortgagee could also have taken advantage of the overreaching machinery.[290] If the beneficial interest had not

287 [1978] AC 95.

288 *Ibid*, at 105.

289 Sections 2(1)(ii) and 27 of the LPA 1925.

290 See *City of London Building Society v Flegg* [1988] AC 54.

been overreached, it would only have bound the mortgagee if either it had been protected by the entry of a restriction or the beneficial owner had enjoyed an overriding interest by virtue of s 70(1)(g) of the Land Registration Act 1925.[291] Had the title in *Prestidge* been registered, Mrs Brown's beneficial interest would not have been protected as a minor interest, but her actual occupation at the date of completion of the new mortgage coupled with her beneficial interest would have amounted to an overriding interest binding on the new mortgagee.

If the doctrine of *scintilla temporis* had not been abolished, Mrs Brown would, therefore, have won the case whether the title was registered or unregistered. This was because her presence in the premises would have given rise to constructive notice of her beneficial interest in unregistered land, or enabled her to enjoy an overriding interest by virtue of her actual occupation in the case of registered land, under s 70(1)(g) of the 1925 Act. The beneficial owner's presence in the premises is always a very good indication of the existence of an undisclosed beneficial interest. It should, of course, be of a kind sufficiently clear to be discoverable upon proper inspection and inquiries. The doctrine of *scintilla temporis* emphasises the importance of a legal interest and the need to get a deed of consent from the beneficial owners. It also makes it necessary, in practice, for a legal mortgagee to make proper inspection and inquiries. This seems to be a better solution. It seems wrong in principle to allow the lender in *Prestidge* to be protected by a security which has been obtained without the clear consent of the true owner, Mrs Brown, when it could have either taken advantage of the overreaching machinery or obtained Mrs Brown's consent before it made the advance. The lender could also have requested Mr Prestidge to discharge the original mortgage with its advance. None of these clearly established principles had apparently been followed by the plaintiff, an institutional mortgagee with sufficient resources to obtain proper legal advice. On the facts, if the court had held that the plaintiff had constructive notice of Mrs Brown's beneficial interest and was bound by it, Mrs Brown would have received a windfall. But the plaintiff does not seem to deserve to win because it had not taken advantage of the legal safeguards available to it and so was the author of its own misfortune.

The result in *Prestidge* seems inevitable. As the House of Lords has abolished the doctrine of *scintilla temporis*, it is impossible to hold that the plaintiff is fixed with constructive notice of, and bound by, Mrs Brown's beneficial interest. On the other hand, to apply the principle of *Cann* would unfairly postpone Mrs Brown's interest to a mortgage for a sum larger than that of the original mortgage. Thus, it seems desirable to extend further the principle in *Bristol and West Building Society v Henning* despite the criticisms mentioned above. As it appears that Mr Prestidge was not required to use the advance to discharge the original mortgage, the doctrine of subrogation is inapplicable.

As at present, with the abolition of the doctrine of *scintilla temporis*, mortgagees have obtained an undue advantage in priority disputes with borrowers. As long as the money they advance partly or wholly finances the purchase of a property or discharges an original mortgage which financed the purchase of the property, they take priority over the beneficial owners. A legal or equitable mortgagee in those circumstances will be able to get priority over the beneficial owners even if the latter are unaware of the mortgage. It also appears that it is no longer necessary for mortgagees to make proper inspection and inquiries in respect of beneficial ownership. This can encourage the legal

291 Section 20 of the LRA 1925.

owner/cohabitee to obtain financial contributions from the cohabitee and a mortgage from a building society to finance a purchase and to abscond, subsequently leaving the cohabitee at the mercy of the building society. It also creates the anomalous results in *Cann* and *Prestidge* with regard to the level of liability they each held, which can only be reconciled by holding that they each had a different level of equity of redemption. This in turn depends on the consent to be imputed based on the somewhat dubious extension of the *Henning* principle. Should we not return to the basic principles of land law? Where the title is unregistered, a purchaser of a legal estate for value with notice (actual or constructive) of a not overreached equitable interest is bound by it. In registered land, the matter is governed by s 20 of the Land Registration Act 1925. Instead of artificially imputing to the parties an intention they might not have had had they considered the matter, or abolishing the doctrine of *scintilla temporis*, these basic principles are capable of providing a satisfactory solution to the problem.

Secondly, where the purchase of the mortgaged property was wholly or partly funded by the mortgage the legal owner of the mortgaged property owned nothing more than an 'equity of redemption'. And the beneficial owners likewise could not own more than an 'equity of redemption'. There was no *scintilla temporis* between the completion of the purchase and the creation of the mortgage. This meant that such mortgagee would always have priority over the legal as well as the equitable owners.[292] In *Abbey National Building Society v Cann*,[293] it will be recalled, Mrs Cann claimed that her beneficial interest took priority over the charge because, *inter alia*, it was created before the charge. The claim was rejected by the House of Lords.

Abbey National Building Society v Cann [1991] 1 AC 56, HL

Lord Oliver of Aylmerton: It is argued, however, that because the creation of a charge on property in favour of the society necessarily posits that the charger has acquired an interest out of which the charge can be created, there must notionally be a point of time at which the estate vested in him free from the charge and in which the estoppel affecting him could be 'fed' by the acquisition of the legal estate so as to become binding on and take priority over the interest of the chargee. This is a puzzling problem on which it is not easy to reconcile the authorities.

The appellants rely on the decision of the Court of Appeal in *Church of England Building Society v Piskor* [1954] 2 All ER 85, [1954] Ch 553, a case concerned with unregistered conveyancing. The sequence of events in that case was that an agreement to purchase leasehold property was entered into in September 1946, the purchaser being let into possession in the following month on part payment of the price. He proceeded to grant a number of weekly tenancies under which the tenants took possession in November. At that stage the contract remained uncompleted and the tenancies were, therefore, necessarily equitable only. On 25 November 1946 completion took place and the property was assigned to the purchaser, being simultaneously charged by him in favour of the building society whose moneys had enabled the purchase to be completed. The charge contained the usual provision against leasing by the charger. Default having

292 *Abbey National Building Society v Cann* [1990] 1 All ER 1085 at 1098b–1100j, 1108c–d (a case of registered land, but the same principle applies to unregistered land).

293 [1990] 1 All ER 1085.

been made in payment of principal and interest, the society sought possession against the tenants, who argued that they had acquired tenancies by estoppel which was 'fed' by the acquisition of the legal estate, thus converting their tenancies into legal tenancies binding on the society. The argument of the society was that the conveyance and the charge were in reality one single transaction with the result that the legal estate vested in the purchaser was, from the outset, subject to the society's charge and so could not be available to feed the estoppel free from it. This argument was rejected by the Court of Appeal. It was held that, despite the fact that the two documents were executed contemporaneously, the transaction necessarily involved conveyancing steps which, in contemplation of law, must be regarded as taking place in a defined order, so that there was a *scintilla temporis* between the purchaser's acquisition of the legal estate and the creation of the society's charge during which the estoppel could be fed. Reliance was also placed on a recital in the charge that the legal estate was 'now vested in the mortgagors' which precluded the society from denying that the estate had not already vested at the time when the charge was granted. This was, however, only a subsidiary ground for the decision which rested squarely on the acquisition of the estate out of which the charge was granted as an essential preliminary to the charge.

On the other side of the line are *Re Connolly Bros Ltd (No 2), Wood v The Company* [1912] 2 Ch 25 and *Security Trust Co v Royal Bank of Canada* [1976] 1 All ER 381, [1976] AC 503. In the former, a company had granted debentures creating a first and floating charge on all the property present and future of the company and prohibiting the creation of any charges ranking in priority to or *pari passu* with the debentures. Subsequently, the company, being desirous of acquiring further freehold property, approached a Mrs O'Reilly, who agreed to advance the price but on terms that the loan be secured by a charge on the property. The company then agreed to buy the property. The contract was completed on 31 March 1904 and Mrs O'Reilly was present at completion. She drew a cheque in favour of the company, which was paid into its account, and, at the same time, it drew a cheque for the balance of the price in favour of the vendor, the same solicitor acting for all parties. The conveyance was executed but was retained, together with the other title deeds, by the solicitor on the vendor's behalf, and a few days later the company executed a memorandum of deposit in her favour. Warrington J held that her charge had priority over the charge created by the debentures and his decision was upheld by the Court of Appeal, Cozens-Hardy MR remarking (at 31):

> ... we should be shutting our eves to the real transaction if we were to hold that the unencumbered fee simple in the property was ever in the company so that it became subject to the charge of the debenture-holders.

The reasoning, both of the Master of the Rolls and of Buckley LJ, seems to have been that, since Mrs O'Reilly had a contractual right to the security at the time when she advanced the money, she necessarily had priority over the debentures. But that is, of course, always the case when a lender advances money on the understanding that he will get a security.

Re Connolly Bros was cited in *Piskor's* case but was distinguished by Evershed MR on the ground that it involved a question of equitable priorities. So it did but I respectfully question whether this can be a valid ground of distinction. The debentures in *Re Connolly Bros* were duly registered and Mrs O'Reilly clearly had constructive notice of their terms. The question was whether there was ever property on which those terms could operate and the fact that both the charge in the debentures and Mrs O'Reilly's charge under her contract and the memorandum of deposit were equitable only was entirely immaterial.

The question in issue was whether the company's legal estate, without the existence of which her charge could never have taken effect, existed at any point of time free from her charge so that the prior interest of the debenture holders could attach. No other analysis of the decision is possible save that the court considered the transaction consisting of the conveyance, the advance and the memorandum of deposit as a single transaction.

The more recent decision of the Privy Council in *Security Trust Co v Royal Bank of Canada* [1976] 1 All ER 381, [1976] AC 503 is equally capable of analysis only on the 'single transaction' basis. The facts were complicated, but reduced to their simplest terms involved a contract for the purchase by a company of certain real estate on terms that a certain proportion of the price should be paid by a fixed date and that the balance should be secured by mortgage to the vendor. A conveyance and mortgage were executed and were held in escrow pending payment of the agreed proportion of the price. Default was made in payment by the fixed date but there was no rescission. The purchaser then created a debenture, creating a fixed charge on its existing property and a floating charge on future property. Under that debenture a receiver was appointed. Whether the sale agreement was then still on foot is open to doubt but the date for completion was extended in January 1971 by agreement with the receiver to 30 April of that year. On 30 April the contract was completed. The question which arose in the subsequent liquidation of the purchaser was whether the charge in the debenture took priority over the vendor's mortgage. In delivering the judgment of the Board, Lord Cross contrasted *Piskor's Case* and *Re Connolly Bros*, observing ([1976] 1 All ER 381 at 392, [1976] AC 503 at 519–20):

> But the basic difference between the two lines of cases is that in cases such as *Re Connolly Bros Ltd (No 2)* and this case the charge under the debenture only bites on property which is already fettered by the agreement to give the other charge, whereas on the facts of the *Piskor* case the tenancy was created out of an interest which was then unfettered by any such agreement.

Again, I respectfully question whether this, although it records accurately what the Court of Appeal held in *Piskor's* case, really affords a valid ground for distinction. However one looks at it, the interests of the tenant in that case had to be legal interests in order to gain any priority and they could only be so by separating the conveyance and the charge and treating them as separate transactions. Although Romer LJ, in the course of his judgment, touched on the question of what the position would have been had there been evidence of some prior agreement to create the charge, this was never fully considered and the court never grasped the nettle that the transaction necessarily involved an enforceable agreement for the grant of a charge at the stage when the money was advanced in order to enable the conveyance to take place.

These three authorities were carefully reviewed by Mustill LJ in the course of his judgment in *Lloyds Bank plc v Rosset* [1988] 3 All ER 915 at 934–37, [1989] Ch 350 at 388–93. He concluded that it was difficult to see how they could live together. I agree. I do not, for my part, consider that they can be reconciled. In neither *Re Connolly Bros* nor the *Security Trust Co* case could the charge which was given priority have been created unless and until the legal estate had been obtained by the charger. In both cases the chargee had notice of the existence of the charge which failed to achieve priority. Both necessarily rest therefore on the proposition that, at least where there is a prior agreement to grant the charge on the legal estate when obtained, the transactions of acquiring the legal estate and granting the charge are, in law as in reality, one indivisible transaction. It may be possible to justify the actual decision in *Piskor's* case on the subsidiary ground there advanced of an estoppel by deed, but I do not, for myself, see how it is possible to uphold the principal ground for the decision except by rejecting the ratio of *Re Connolly Bros* and the *Security Trust Co* case.

One is therefore presented with a stark choice between them. Of course, as a matter of legal theory, a person cannot charge a legal estate that he does not have, so that there is an attractive legal logic in the ratio in *Piskor's* case. Nevertheless, I cannot help feeling that it flies in the face of reality. The reality is that, in the vast majority of cases, the acquisition of the legal estate and the charge are not only precisely simultaneous but indissolubly bound together. The acquisition of the legal estate is entirely dependent on the provision of funds which will have been provided before the conveyance can take effect and which are provided only against an agreement that the estate will be charged to secure them. Indeed, in many, if not most, cases of building society mortgages there will have been, as there was in this case, a formal offer of acceptance of an advance which will ripen into a specifically enforceable agreement immediately the funds are advanced, which will normally be a day or more before completion. In many, if not most, cases the charge itself will have been executed before the execution, let alone the exchange, of the conveyance or transfer of the property. This is given particular point in the case of registered land where the vesting of the estate is made to depend on registration, for it may well be that the transfer and the charge will be lodged for registration on different days so that the charge, when registered, may actually take effect from a date prior in time to the date from which the registration of the transfer takes effect (see s 27(3) of the 1925 Act and the Land Registration Rules 1925, SR & 0 1925/1093, r 83(2)). Indeed, under r 81 of the 1925 rules, the registrar is entitled to register the charge even before registration of the transfer to the charger if he is satisfied that both are entitled to be registered. The reality is that the purchaser of land who relies on a building society or bank loan for the completion of his purchase never in fact acquires anything but an equity of redemption, for the land is, from the very inception, charged with the amount of the loan without which it could never have been transferred at all and it was never intended that it should be otherwise. The *scintilla temporis* is no more than a legal artifice and, for my part, I would adopt the reasoning of the Court of Appeal in *Re Connolly Bros Ltd (No 2)* [1912] 2 Ch 25 and of Harman J in *Coventry Permanent Economic Building Society v Jones* [1951] 1 All ER got and hold that *Piskor's* case was wrongly decided. It follows, in my judgment, that Mrs Cann can derive no assistance from this line of argument.

However, where the mortgagor forged his co-owner's signature to grant a mortgage, the transaction would be totally ineffective to create a legal mortgage.[294] The co-owner incurred no liability to the mortgagee under the instrument because she did not execute the instrument. The mortgagee could not claim to have overreached the co-owner's interest because there had been no true dealing with two trustees for sale. The instrument only created a valid equitable mortgage or charge on the mortgagor's beneficial interest which could be enforced by obtaining a charging order under the Charging Order Act 1979.[295] So the innocent beneficial owner would not be affected by the charge.

294 *First National Securities v Hegerty* [1984] 3 All ER 641, CA.

295 Since the mortgagee does not have a legal or equitable mortgage, he cannot exercise his power of sale under s 101 of the LPA 1925. He may, however, apply to the court under s 30 of the LPA 1925 for a sale of the property.

First National Securities v Hegerty [1985] 1 QB 850, CA

Sir Denys Buckley: It is common ground that the only matter which was before the judge for decision was whether the charging order nisi should or should not be made absolute. The judge, however, (rightly, in my opinion) took into consideration the possible effect upon the husband's interest in 24, Mill Road of the two forged documents. He expressed the view that, if the husband and the wife were up to then equitable as well as legal joint owners of the house, the forged legal charge (or it might, I think, have been the forged application for a loan, but it does not matter which) was a sufficient act of alienation of the husband's interest to sever the beneficial joint tenancy and to create a valid equitable charge upon the husband's joint tenancy and to create a valid equitable charge upon the husband's beneficial interest in favour of the plaintiffs. It must follow that it was the judge's view, though he did not expressly say so, that if the husband and the wife were then already equitable tenants in common of the beneficial interest in the house, the husband's share became equitably charged; and that if the husband was alone beneficially interested, his equitable interest under the statutory trust for sale would likewise have become equitably charged. In no circumstances can the house itself have become charged, nor can any interest of the wife under the statutory trusts have been affected. The judge also took into consideration the fact that the plaintiffs could not in any event sell the house, except with the concurrence of the wife, without obtaining an order for sale under s 30 of the Law of Property Act 1925 [repealed, see now s 14 of the Trusts of Land and Appointment of Trustees Act 1996], at which stage all competing equities would be carefully weighed by the court, but the court has no power under that section to vary beneficial interests ...

Whether a prior non-overreachable and unregistrable interest, such as an equitable easement by estoppel, has priority over the mortgagee also depends on the old doctrine of notice.[296]

Where, however, the prior competing interest is a legal mortgage, the same rule that a legal interest binds the whole world applies except the legal mortgage must also be protected by the title deeds to bind the whole world. If the legal mortgage is not protected by title deeds, it must be registered as a puisne mortgage under Class C(i). If it is not so registered, it is void against a mortgagee for valuable consideration.[297] However, if the subsequent mortgage is also unprotected by title deeds, the position is complicated by s 97 of the Law of Property Act 1925 which provides that priority depends on the date of registration. Take the following example.

1/1/93, A is granted a mortgage registrable as C(i) or C(iii) land charge

2/1/93, B is granted a mortgage registrable as C(i) or C(iii) land charge

3/1/93, A registers his land charge

4/1/93, B registers his land charge

According to s 97 priority depends on date of registration, so A takes priority over B. But according to s 4(5) of the Land Charges Act 1972, A's mortgage will be void for non registration against B whether B's mortgage is legal or equitable (purchaser of land or any interest in land).

296 *E R Investment Ltd v High* [1967] 2 QB 379.

297 Section 4(5) of the LCA 1972. But see s 97 of the LPA 1925.

There is, therefore, a clear conflict between s 97 of the Law of Property Act 1925 and s 4(5) of the Land Charges Act 1972. There is an argument that because s 97 deals specifically with priority of mortgages, s 97 prevails and s 4 of the Land Charges Act is only drawn into the picture because s 17 of the Act defines 'purchaser' as including a mortgagee. On the other hand, the view is more convincing that s 4 prevails because it is difficult to see how, if the first mortgage is void under s 4(5), as against the second, the subsequent registration of the first can give priority to something which has no existence as regards the second.[298] 'One of the main objects of registration is to enable a mortgagee to discover the state of the mortgagor's title, but if he is to be displaced by a registration effected after it has been certified to him by the Registrar that no prior charge stands in his way, the object will certainly be frustrated.'[299] Furthermore, s 4 of the Land Charges Act 1972 being a later enactment than s 97 of the Law of Property Act 1925, the latter is impliedly overruled by the former insofar as there is any inconsistency between them.

Where the prior mortgage is equitable, if it is protected by title deeds, it binds the whole world except equity's darling. The fact that the owner of the mortgaged property is unable to produce title deeds for the inspection by the subsequent mortgagee will alert the latter to the possibility of the existence of an earlier mortgage. Thus, the subsequent mortgagee will not normally be able to claim that he is equity's darling and will lose priority to the prior equitable mortgagee, unless the subsequent mortgagee has asked for the production of title deeds and is met with reasonable explanation for non-production.[300] If the prior equitable mortgage is not protected by title deeds, it must be registered as a C(iii) land charge. Non-registration renders it void as against the subsequent mortgagee. Again confusion may be caused by s 97 of the Law of Property Act 1925 in some cases.

(ii) Registered system

Where the title is registered, then all prior legal or equitable interests must be properly registered or entered on the register at the time when the legal mortgage is registered. If they are not registered or protected, when the mortgage is registered, the mortgagee takes subject only to any entry on the register and any overriding interest.[301] If the mortgage is itself not registered, it is a minor interest. The priority is governed by the rule that where equities are equal the first in time prevails.[302]

Thus, prior to the creation of a mortgage, the mortgagee wants to make proper investigation of title and inspection of property to find out if there are any incumbrances (including overriding interests) which may have priority

298 See Megarry and Wade, p 1000.

299 Cheshire and Burn, p 722.

300 See *Oliver v Hinton* [1899] 2 Ch 264, deeds related also to other property, not good excuse; *Hewitt v Loosemore* (1851) 9 Hare 449, not free to produce deeds now but would do so later, good excuse; *Agra Bank v Barry* (1874) LR 7 HL 135, deeds were in Ireland, where land was situated, good excuse.

301 Sections 26(3) and 9, 10, 11 and 12 of the LRA 1925.

302 *Barclays Bank Ltd v Taylor* [1973] Ch 63.

over his mortgage. The mortgagee is often more concerned with the interests of undisclosed beneficial owners because they can potentially render the property valueless as a security. Where any beneficial interests are discovered the mortgagee may either insist on paying to two trustees (where the mortgaged property is held on trust of land) or all the trustees of the settlement (where mortgaged property is settled land) to overreach the beneficial interests, or he may require the beneficial owners to execute a deed of consent to postpone their interests to that of the mortgagee's.

As with unregistered land, where the acquisition of registered land is contemporaneous with the grant of the mortgage with the knowledge of a beneficial owner, the beneficial owner is taken to have deferred his interest to that of the mortgagee.[303] Any substituted mortgagee will also have priority over the beneficial owner.[304] In any event, the beneficial owner only has an equity of redemption, so that the mortgagee has priority.[305]

(b) Against interests created after the mortgage

The key is that the mortgagee must protect his interest by appropriate means. The position can be summarised as follows:

(i) Unregistered system

This depends on whether the mortgaged property is legal or equitable.

1. Where the property mortgaged is legal

Whether the mortgage is legal (eg by deed) or equitable (eg not by deed), the mortgagee must protect his interest by the possession of title deeds. If the mortgagee has the title deeds and the mortgage is legal any subsequent purchaser (including a second mortgagee) will be bound by it. If the mortgage is equitable, it will depend on whether the subsequent purchaser is a *bona fide* purchaser for value without notice.[306] The fact that the mortgagor is unable to produce title deeds will perhaps give the purchaser (or the second mortgagee) a constructive notice of the earlier equitable mortgage. But if the subsequent purchaser has asked for title deeds but has been given reasonable excuse for non-production, the subsequent purchaser being owner of a legal estate, will take priority. What is a reasonable excuse depends on the facts.[307]

But if the mortgagee does not have the title deeds, then he has to protect his interest by registration. A legal mortgage unprotected by title deeds is to be registered under Class C(i) as a *puisne* mortgage.[308] Failure in this renders the

---

303 *Bristol and West Building Society v Henning* [1985] 2 All ER 606, followed in *Paddington Building Society v Mendelsohn* (1985) 50 P & CR 244.

304 *Equity & Law Home Loans Ltd v Prestidge* [1992] 1 All ER 909. See (1993) 44 NILQ 51 (Goo, SH).

305 *Abbey National Building Society v Cann* [1990] 1 All ER 1085.

306 Megarry and Wade suggest that a protected equitable mortgage may be registrable as an estate contract, but point out that this interpretation would weaken the protection given by the 1925 legislation to equitable mortgagees (at 998).

307 See *Oliver v Hinton* [1899] 2 Ch 264, deeds related also to other property, not good excuse; *Hewitt v Loosemore* (1851) 9 Hare 449, not free to produce deeds now but would do so later, good excuse; *Agra Bank v Barry* (1874) LR 7 HL 135, deeds were in Ireland, where land was situated, good excuse.

308 Section 2(4)(i) of the LCA 1972.

mortgage void against a purchaser (including a second mortgagee) of land or any interest in land.[309] An unprotected equitable mortgage is to be protected as an equitable charge under Class C(iii).[310] An unprotected equitable mortgage will lose priority to any subsequent purchaser for valuable consideration.[311] Note that where the subsequent competing interest is a second mortgage, and both mortgages are unprotected by title deeds, as mentioned earlier, s 97 of the Law of Property Act 1925 may alter priority if it prevails over s 4(5) of the Land Charges Act 1972.

2. Where the property mortgaged is equitable

Where the interest mortgaged is equitable, priority between successive equitable mortgages is governed by the rule in *Dearle v Hall*[312] which is incorporated into s 137 of the Law of Property Act 1925. Under this rule, the mortgagee must give written notice of the equitable mortgage to the trustees of the strict settlement or trustees of land, so priority depends on the order in which notices have been received by the trustees.

(ii) Registered system

Again, priority depends on whether the property mortgaged is legal or equitable.

1. Where property mortgaged is legal

A mortgage of a legal estate by deed should be registered as a registered charge. A legal mortgage is created when registered.[313] Priority of registered charges is therefore governed by the order of entry in the register unless it otherwise provides.[314] If the mortgage is not so registered, it should be protected as a minor interest to take priority over any subsequent registered interests. If the subsequent competing interest is a minor interest, then the unregistered legal mortgage will have priority because where equities are equal the first in time prevails.[315]

If it is not created by deed or if it is created by deposit of land certificate pursuant to a written agreement, it can only be an equitable mortgage and must be protected as a minor interest. Otherwise it would not bind a transferee or grantee of a legal estate for valuable consideration whether or not he has notice of it.[316] But if the subsequent competing interest is also a minor interest, the first in time prevails.[317]

309 Section 4(5) of the LCA 1972.

310 See Megarry and Wade, p 997. But see Emmet on *Title* (by Farrand, JT), 19th edn, 1986, Looseleaf London: Longman, who prefers the view that it is a Class C(iv) land charge (at 25.117).

311 Section 4(5) of the LCA 1972.

312 (1828) 3 Russ 1.

313 Section 26(1) of the LRA 1925; *Schwab v McCarthy* [1975] 31 P & CR 196.

314 Section 29 of the LRA 1925.

315 Section 102 of the LRA 1925.

316 Section 20(1) of the LRA 1925.

317 *Barclays Bank Ltd v Taylor* [1973] Ch 63.

2. Where the property mortgaged is equitable

Where the competing interests are equitable, priority used to be governed by the order of entry in the Minor Interests Index at the Land Registry. This Index has been abolished and priority is now governed by the rule in *Dearle v Hall*.[318] So priority depends on the order in which notices are given to the legal owners.

Tacking of further advances

A mortgagee may make further advances after an initial mortgage to the mortgagor on the security of the same property. He may 'tack' his further advances to his original mortgage thereby obtaining priority over any intervening mortgages. This has the effect of increasing the loan of the original mortgage and diminishing the security of the intervening mortgagee.

In unregistered land, under s 94(1) of the Law of Property Act 1925, a prior mortgagee has a statutory right to tack his further advances if the intervening mortgagee agrees, or if he makes the further advances without notice of the intervening mortgage. Where the intervening mortgage is registrable (for example it is not protected by title deeds), then registration will give notice. If it is protected by title deeds and so not registrable, the old doctrine of notice applies. If the prior mortgage was expressed to be security for further advances without imposing an obligation on the mortgagee to make further advances, the mortgagee may not tack the further advances if he has actual notice of the intervening mortgage. He is not deemed to have notice merely because the intervening mortgage has been registered.[319] Thus, it is essential for the intervening mortgagee to give actual notice of his mortgagee to the prior mortgagee.

Where, however, the original mortgagee imposes an obligation on the mortgagee to make further advances, then not even actual notice of the intervening mortgage can prevent the tacking of further advances.[320]

In registered land, where the prior mortgagee is under an obligation, noted on the register, to make further advances, the mortgagee can tack any further advances.[321] Where the prior mortgagee is not under an obligation to make further advances, but the registered charge is made for securing any further advances, the prior mortgagee may tack further advances until he is given notice by the Registrar of his intention to make an entry which would prejudicially affect the priority of any further advances.[322]

Priority of company charges

A company charge may be registrable under the Land Charges Act 1972 or Land Registration Act 1925. In addition, it is also registrable under Companies

318 Section 5 of the LRA 1986.

319 Section 94(2) of the LPA 1925.

320 Section 94(1)(c) of the LPA 1925.

321 Section 30(3) of the LRA 1925.

322 Section 30(1) of the LRA 1925.

Act 1985. Priority between an earlier fixed mortgage, created since 1 January 1970 of land owned by the company and a subsequent purchaser of the land is governed by the general property law discussed above. Where the fixed mortgage was created before 1 January 1970 and registered at Company House, it will bind the subsequent purchaser. Similarly, any floating charge registered at Companies House will bind a subsequent purchaser unless the sale is in the course of business.

Where the question arises as between two competing mortgages or charges, it is necessary to consider the provisions of the Companies Act 1985.

Under the old provisions

As an unregistered charge is void as against the liquidator and creditors of the company,[323] an unregistered earlier fixed charge is void as against a subsequent fixed charge. But if an earlier fixed charge is duly registered within 21 days, it takes priority over a subsequent fixed charge. Likewise, an earlier unregistered floating charge is void against a subsequent floating charge. But if the earlier floating charge is registered, it takes priority over a subsequent floating charge.

But priority between a prior registered floating charge and a subsequent fixed charge is more complicated. Under s 464 of the 1985 Act, an instrument creating a floating charge may contain provision prohibiting the creation of any subsequent fixed or floating charge having priority over, or ranking *pari passu* with, the earlier floating charge. It may also contain provisions regulating the order of priority as between the earlier floating and subsequent fixed or floating charge.[324] If the floating charge provides that the company is not to create any mortgage or charge having priority over or ranking *pari passu* with the floating charge, any subsequent fixed mortgagee or chargee may still have priority over the floating charge if the later fixed chargee has no notice of this provision. Registration of the floating charge at Companies House under the provision mentioned above is constructive notice of the charge, but not constructive notice of a provision of the charge prohibiting creation of subsequent charges with priority.[325] But if the subsequent fixed chargee has notice of the restriction, the earlier floating charge will have priority.

Where no provision is made in the instrument creating the floating charge to regulate the order of priority, then under s 464(3) and (4), a fixed charge created before a floating charge crystallises has priority over the floating charge.

---

323 Section 395 of the old Companies Act 1985.

324 This does not affect the priority of a fixed charge arising by operation of law which has priority over the floating charge (s 464(2) of the Companies Act 1985). Neither does it affect the priority of preferential debts over a floating charge (ss 40, 175, 386 and Sched 6 of the Insolvency Act 1986; s 196 of the Companies Act 1985).

325 *Re Standard Rotary Machine Co Ltd* (1906) 95 LT 829.

10 DISCHARGE OF MORTGAGES

A mortgage is discharged when it is redeemed by the mortgagor. A receipt indorsed on or annexed to the mortgage deed, signed by the mortgagee and stating the name of the person paying the money, will take effect as a valid discharge.[326] The receipt may take the following form.

SCHEDULE 3

FORMS OF TRANSFER AND DISCHARGE OF MORTGAGES

FORM NO 2

FORM OF RECEIPT ON DISCHARGE OF A MORTGAGE

I, A.B., of [etc] hereby acknowledge that I have this .. .. day of .. .. .. 19 .. , received the sum of £ .. .. representing the [aggregate] [balance remaining owing in respect of the] principal money secured by the within [above] written [annexed] mortgage [and by a further charge dated, etc or otherwise as required] together with all interest and costs, the payment having been made by CD of [etc] and EF of [etc]

As witness, etc

NOTE – If the persons paying are not entitled to the equity of redemption state that they are paying the money out of a fund applicable to the discharge of the mortgage.

The mortgagor may, however, request for a reassignment, surrender, release or transfer executed instead, particularly where only part of the mortgage is redeemed.[327]

A registered charge is discharged on redemption by delivering the charge certificate with a prescribed form (Form 53) to the Land Registry.[328] The charge is then deleted from the register.

11 REFORM

In August 1986, the Law Commission published a Working Paper[329] in which it examined the defects in the present law of mortgages of interests in land. In November 1991, a report was published[330] in which a fundamental reform of the existing law was proposed. The Law Commission was of the opinion that the law of land mortgages is unnecessarily complicated and has reached a state of artificiality and complexity that is now difficult to defend.[331]

326 Section 115(1) of the LPA 1925. For discharge of building society mortgages see Sched 4, para 2 of the Building Societies Act 1986.

327 Section 115(4) of the LPA 1925.

328 Rule 151 of the LRR 1925.

329 Land Mortgages, Working Paper No 99.

330 Law Commission, Transfer of Land: Land Mortgages (Law Com No 204, 13 November 1991).

331 Law Commission, Transfer of Land: Land Mortgages, (Law Com No 204), para 2.1. For criticism of the present law see (1961) 24 MLR 123, at 131 (Grove, GA); (1978) 94 LQR 571 (Jackson, P).

The Law Commission recommends that all existing methods of consensually mortgaging or charging any legal or equitable estate or interest in land should be replaced by the formal and informal land mortgages. The Law Commission also thinks that it is necessary to create a class of 'protected mortgages' covering all mortgages (whether formal or informal) of property which include a dwelling house except those where either (a) the mortgagor is a body corporate, or (b) enforcement of the mortgage would not affect the occupation of the dwelling house or (c) the dwelling house is occupied under a service tenancy.

Law Commission, Transfer of Land: Land Mortgages (Law Com No 204), 13 November 1991

Summary of Recommendations

The new mortgages

10.2 All existing methods of consensually mortgaging or charging interests in land should be abolished and replaced by new forms of mortgage (the formal land mortgage and the informal land mortgage) the attributes of which would be expressly defined by statute, and which would be the only permissible methods of mortgaging any interest in land, whether legal or equitable. (Paras 2.20–2.30.)

10.3 In principle, the rights, powers, duties and obligations of mortgagor and mortgagee under a land mortgage should be such as are appropriate for making the mortgaged property security for the performance of the mortgagor's obligations. (Paras 3.2 and 6.1 to 6.3.)

Variable and overriding provisions

10.4 The statutory provisions defining the rights, powers, duties and obligations of the parties to a land mortgage should be categorised as either 'variable' or 'overriding'. Variable provisions should be variable or excludable, either directly by an express term of the mortgage or indirectly by necessary implication from any express term. Overriding provisions should apply notwithstanding any provision to the contrary contained in the mortgage or in any other instrument. Any provision of a mortgage or any other instrument should be void to the extent that it (i) purports to impose a liability which has the effect of allowing the mortgagee to escape or mitigate the consequences of an overriding provision, or to be reimbursed the consequences of complying with it or (ii) has the effect of preventing or discouraging the mortgagor or any other person from enforcing or taking advantage of an overriding provision. (Para 3.3.)

Requirement of good faith

10.5 The rights, remedies and powers of a mortgagee under a land mortgage should be expressly stated to be exercisable only in good faith and for the purposes of protecting or enforcing the security. This should apply to all the mortgagee's rights, remedies and powers, whether derived from statute, contract, or elsewhere. (Para 3.4.)

Creation of formal land mortgage

10.6 A formal land mortgage should not be valid unless made by deed, whether the property mortgaged is a legal estate or an equitable interest. No particular form of words should be necessary in order for it to be a valid formal land mortgage, provided the words used demonstrate an intention to make the mortgaged property security for performance of the mortgagor's obligations. As an additional requirement where the mortgagor's title to all or part of the mortgaged property is registered at H.M. Land Registry, the mortgage should not qualify as a formal land mortgage unless it is substantively registered against that title. (Paras 3.5–3.8.)

Informal land mortgage

10.7 Informal mortgages should be recognised, to the extent that any purported consensual security over any interest in land that does not constitute a formal land mortgage but would, in the present law, give rise to an equitable mortgage or charge, should take effect as an informal land mortgage, provided the formal requirements for the creation of an informal land mortgage (para 10.9 below) are satisfied. (Paras 3.6, 3.9, and 3.10.)

10.8 A mortgagee under an informal land mortgage should have no right to enforce the security, nor to take any other action in relation to the mortgaged property, but should have a right to have the mortgage perfected by having a formal land mortgage granted to it. In the case of a protected mortgage (para 10.16 below) the mortgagee should not be allowed to have the mortgage perfected without a court order; in all other cases a mortgagee who was able to procure perfection of the mortgage without recourse to the court (for example, by use of a power of attorney) should be entitled to do so. (Paras 3.11 to 3.13 and 5.12.)

10.9 An informal land mortgage should not be valid unless it is made by deed or it satisfies requirements equivalent to those set out in s 2 of the Law of Property (Miscellaneous Provisions) Act 1989, that is unless it is in writing signed by or on behalf of the parties to it and incorporating (either directly, or indirectly by reference to another document) all the terms expressly agreed between the parties. (Paras 3.14 to 3.17.)

All other consensual securities void

10.10 Any purported security interest that does not constitute a formal land mortgage or an informal land mortgage should be void (in the sense that, whilst the purported mortgagor remains personally liable to pay the debt or discharge the liabilities incurred, the purported mortgagee acquires no interest in the property and no right of recourse to it). This should not apply to non-consensual charges (that is, equitable charges arising by operation of law, statutory charges and liens): these are not affected by our recommendations. (Para 2.6.)

Protection and priority

10.11 Where the mortgagor's title to the mortgaged property is registered at H.M. Land Registry, a formal land mortgage of that property should be substantively registrable. Unless and until registered it should take effect as an informal land mortgage. Once registered, it would constitute a registered charge for the purposes of the Land Registration Acts 1925–88. As such, its priority would depend on the date of its registration. (Paras 3.18 to 3.19; Schedule 1, paras 9–15.)

10.12 An informal land mortgage of a legal estate in registered land should be protectable by notice where the informal land mortgage is acknowledged by the registered proprietor. Otherwise, it should be protectable by caution. Protection by notice of deposit and notice of intended deposit should be abolished. The priority of informal land mortgages protected by notice or caution should, for the present, continue to be governed by the rules applicable to the priority of minor interests in the present law. (Paras 3.20 and 3.21.)

10.13 Formal and informal land mortgages of commercial equitable interests in registered land should be protectable by entry of notice or caution, but for the present, protection and priority of trust equitable interests should continue to be governed by the rule in *Dearle v Hall*. (Paras 3.22–3.29.)

10.14 In unregistered land all formal land mortgages of a legal estate or a commercial equitable interest should be registrable as Class C(i) land charges, and all informal land mortgages of a legal estate or a commercial equitable interest should be registrable as Class C(iii) land charges. Formal and informal mortgages of trust equitable interests should continue to be governed by the rule in *Dearle v Hall*. (Paras 3.30–3.33.)

10.15 Section 4(5) of the Land Charges Act 1972 should be amended to remove the possibility of insoluble priority circles arising where there are successive mortgages of the same property. (Para 3.34.)

Protected mortgages

10.16 There should be a class of protected mortgage consisting of all formal and informal land mortgages of any interest in land which includes a dwelling house except those where either (a) the mortgagor is a body corporate, or (b) enforcement of the mortgage would not affect the occupation of the dwelling house or (c) the dwelling house is occupied under a service tenancy. (Part IV.)

Standardisation

10.17 The front page of a protected mortgage should be in a form to be prescribed by regulations. The document should set out all the statutorily implied overriding and variable mortgage provisions (as varied, in the case of variable provisions) and also comply with regulations to be made about form and content of protected mortgages. In a protected mortgage the mortgagee should be under a duty to provide copies of the mortgage to those undertaking an obligation under it, in circumstances to be specified by regulations. (Paras 5.1–5.11.)

Rights and duties during the security

Documents of title

10.19 It should be a variable provision of a first formal land mortgage that the mortgagee is entitled to possession of the mortgagor's documents of title (including, if title is registered, the mortgagor's land certificate). Whenever a mortgagee has a statutory or contractual right to the mortgagor's documents of title, the mortgagee should also have an overriding duty to keep them safely, and the mortgagor should have overriding rights of inspection and production and to take copies. (Paras 6.4–6.8.)

Possession

10.23 During the security, the mortgagor should remain entitled to possession. The mortgagee should be entitled to take possession only in specified circumstances for the purposes of protecting or enforcing the security. (Para 6.16.)

Leasing

10.24 It should be an overriding implied term of all formal land mortgages that when in possession the mortgagor is entitled to grant such leases of the property as it thinks fit, without having to obtain the mortgagee's consent. However, no lease granted by the mortgagor will be binding on the mortgagee unless granted with the mortgagee's written consent. (Paras 6.17 to 6.21.)

10.25 It should also be an overriding implied term that the mortgagee when in possession, and a receiver appointed by the mortgagee, is entitled to grant leases, but only with the mortgagor's consent, or if required by statute, or if it is reasonably necessary to do so to protect or enforce the security. As an additional requirement in the case of protected mortgages, neither the mortgagee nor a receiver should be entitled to grant a lease of any part of a dwelling house comprised in the mortgaged property without leave of the court. (Para 7.47.)

Transfer

10.26 There should be no restrictions on the right of a mortgagee to transfer or otherwise deal with the mortgage, if the mortgage is not a protected mortgage. In the case of protected mortgages, if legislation is thought appropriate, it should provide that it is an overriding implied term of a protected mortgage that the mortgagee is not entitled to transfer the mortgage without having first obtained the written consent of the mortgagor, consent not to be unreasonably withheld. Regulations should prescribe the procedure to be followed by the mortgagee in applying for the mortgagor's consent, and the information to be supplied to the mortgagor. A transfer made without consent should be liable to be set aside by the court, or a ceiling on the rate of interest payable under the mortgage imposed. (Paras 6.22–6.30.)

10.27 The mortgagor's interest in the mortgaged property should remain freely alienable, subject to any express restriction contained in the mortgage. (Para 6.31.)

Interest rates

10.28 In all protected mortgages, a provision that purports to increase the rate of interest payable on default should be void. In all other mortgages, such a provision should be challengeable only under the general law relating to penalties or under the new general statutory jurisdiction to set aside or vary mortgage terms described in Part VIII of this Report. (Paras 6.33 and 6.34.)

10.29 In the case of all mortgages, the court should have jurisdiction to vary interest rates under the new general statutory jurisdiction described in Part VIII of this Report if the mortgage has become challengeable as a result of a variation of or failure to vary the rate of interest payable, even if under the mortgage the mortgagee is fully entitled to vary or not vary interest rates as it chooses. (Para 6.36.)

10.30 In the case of protected mortgages, the court should also be entitled to alter the interest rate payable, if satisfied by the mortgagor that the mortgagee has unreasonably varied or failed to vary the interest rate payable under the mortgage. In order to assess whether a variation or failure to vary is unreasonable, the court should be required to have particular regard to whether the difference between the rate complained of and the current market rate charged for loans made in equivalent circumstances is substantially greater than the difference between the rate originally charged and the then market rate. The Office of Fair Trading should have power to exempt specified lenders from these provisions. (Paras 6.35–6.41.)

Redemption

10.31 The equitable right to redeem the property free from the mortgage after the contractual redemption date by paying and discharging all obligations under it should apply to formal and informal mortgages as it applies to all other mortgages and charges. (Para 6.42.)

10.32 In protected mortgages, any term of the mortgage which postpones the mortgagor's right to redeem should be void, unless the property includes non-residential premises. If it includes non-residential property, or the mortgage is not protected, then a postponement of the right to redeem should be challengeable only under the new general statutory jurisdiction described in Part VIII of this Report. (Para 6.43(a).)

10.33 In protected mortgages any term of the mortgage which requires the mortgagor to give notice of intention to redeem, or requires payment of interest in *lieu* of notice, should be void. (Para 6.43(b).)

10.34 Mortgagors under a protected mortgage whose repayments are calculated on the basis of the loan remaining outstanding for a specified period should be entitled to the appropriate rebate on earlier repayment. (Para 6.43(c).)

Consolidation

10.35 In relation to all land mortgages the right to consolidate should be abolished. (Para 6.44.)

Discharge

10.36 A land mortgage should be discharged by the mortgagor discharging all his obligations under it: no document should be necessary in order to complete the discharge. A standard form discharge should be provided by regulations to be made: use of the standard form should not be mandatory, but if the standard form is used it should operate as a good receipt for the money due under the mortgage, and a purchaser should be entitled to rely on it as sufficient evidence of discharge. (Para 6.45.)

Enforcement of the security

Sale

10.37 It should be a variable implied term of all formal land mortgages that the mortgagee has power to sell the mortgagor's interest in the mortgaged property, free from the mortgagee's own mortgage and from subsequent mortgages and other interests to which the mortgage has priority, but subject to all prior mortgages and interests taking priority over the mortgage. The power should not be exercisable unless a specified 'enforceable event' has occurred and is still operative. This restriction on the exercise of the power of sale should be overriding and should also apply to the statutory power of sale as varied or replaced by any contractual provisions. (Paras 7.5–7.10.)

10.38 If the mortgage is a protected mortgage, the mortgagee should not be entitled to exercise the power of sale without leave of the court. (Paras 7.14–7.15.)

10.39 In addition in the case of protected mortgages, before exercising the power of sale the mortgagee should first have served on the mortgagor an enforcement notice in prescribed form specifying the enforceable event on which the mortgagee relies and the action (if any) to be taken by the mortgagor to remedy any default. The enforcement notice should also explain the consequences of default and how to obtain help and advice. Once the mortgagor has taken the action required by the notice, or the enforceable event is no longer operative for some other reason, the power of sale should not be exercisable. (Paras 7.11–7.13.)

10.40 If the mortgagee exercises the power of sale after having been notified that the mortgagor has contracted to sell to someone else, the mortgagee should be liable to indemnify the mortgagor for any sum the mortgagor becomes liable to pay to a third party by reason of being unable to complete his sale contract. This should not apply if the mortgagee contracted to sell before receiving notice of the mortgagor's sale contract, or if it was reasonable for the mortgagee to sell, either because the mortgagor's contract was for sale at a price insufficient to pay off the mortgagee in full, and the mortgagee was able to sell at a higher price than the mortgagor's price, or because the mortgagor's sale was not completed within a reasonable time, or because of some other reason. (Paras 7.16–7.19.)

10.41 A purchaser from a mortgagee purporting to sell in exercise of the power of sale should get a good title, provided there is a valid formal land mortgage and the purchaser is in good faith, unless the purchaser has notice that the power of sale is not exercisable or that the exercise is improper for some other reason. Notice should include constructive notice. (Paras 7.20–7.21.)

10.42 A mortgagee under a formal land mortgage should be entitled to exercise the power of sale by selling the property to itself, provided leave of the court is first obtained. The court should not grant leave unless satisfied that sale to the mortgagee is the most advantageous method of realising the security. (Paras 7.22 –7.27.)

10.43 A mortgagee and a receiver appointed under a formal land mortgage should have an overriding duty (owed to the mortgagor, to any guarantors of the mortgagor, and to any subsequent mortgagees) to take reasonable care to ensure that on a sale the price is the best price that can reasonably be obtained. (Para 7.23.)

10.44 After paying off prior encumbrances, the mortgagee should hold the proceeds of sale on trust to be applied first in payment of the costs of sale, secondly in payment of everything due under the mortgage, and thirdly to be paid to the person next entitled (that is the subsequent encumbrancers or, if none, the mortgagor). (Para 7.25.)

Foreclosure

10.45 The remedy of foreclosure should be abolished. (Paras 7.26 and 7.27.)

Possession

10.46 In all formal land mortgages there should be an implied overriding provision that the mortgagee is entitled to take possession of the mortgaged property when it is reasonably necessary to do so to enable the property to be sold pursuant to the mortgagee's power of sale. Once in possession the mortgagee should be under an overriding duty to sell as quickly as is consonant with the duty to take reasonable care to ensure that on sale the price is the best price that can reasonably be obtained. (Paras 7.28 –7.30.)

10.47 In protected mortgages the mortgagee should not be entitled to possession without serving an enforcement notice and obtaining a court order. The court making an order for possession should have discretion to order that interest payable under the mortgage should cease to accrue twelve weeks (or such other period as the court thinks fit) after the execution of the order for possession. Similar provisions should apply if the mortgagor leaves voluntarily in response to a demand for possession from the mortgagee. In both cases the mortgagee should be free to apply to the court for an extension of time at any stage. The Secretary of State should have power by order to vary the period of twelve weeks. (Paras 7.31–7.35.)

10.48 In formal land mortgages which are not protected, the mortgagee should also have a right to take possession of the property when it is reasonably necessary to do so in order to preserve its value. Once in possession, the mortgagee should be entitled to remain there only for so long as is reasonable, given that the purpose of being there is to preserve the value of the property. (Para 7.36(a) and (b).)

10.49 A mortgagee under a protected mortgage should have no right to take possession of the property for the purpose of preserving its value unless the property includes non-residential property. If non-residential property is included the mortgagee should be entitled to apply to the court for possession for this purpose: the court should be entitled to make an order affecting the non-residential part only on the same grounds as if it were a non-protected mortgage, but should not be entitled to make an order affecting the residential part unless satisfied that it would not otherwise be possible to preserve the value of the property. The court making an order for possession for this purpose should have the same discretion to order that interest should cease to accrue as if possession was for sale, and the same should apply if the mortgagor leaves voluntarily in response to a demand for possession from the mortgagee. (Para 7.36 (c), (d) and (e).)

10.50 A mortgagee who is in possession, for whatever purpose, should have a duty to repair (para 10.22 above) and a liability to account. The liability to account should not apply during a period when interest has ceased to accrue. (Paras 6.14 and 7.37–7.38.)

Appointment of a receiver

10.51 It should be a variable implied term of a formal land mortgage that the mortgagee should have power to appoint a receiver of the income of the property who should be the agent of the mortgagor. (Paras 7.39–7.41.)

10.52 The power should be exercisable only in circumstances in which the power of sale would be exercisable. In deciding whether to grant leave for the appointment of a receiver under a protected mortgage, the court should consider the effect the appointment would have on the occupation of any dwelling house on the mortgaged property: if the effect would be to disturb that occupation, leave should be refused unless the court is satisfied that either (i) the object of the appointment is to enable the mortgagee to sell or (ii) the security cannot be protected properly by any other means. All provisions relating to the exercise of the power to appoint should be overriding. (Para 7.42.)

10.53 Provisions defining the powers of a receiver should be variable, but not so as either to exclude or restrict the liability of the receiver to the mortgagor, or to confer on the receiver any powers that a mortgagee could not have. (Para 7.43 to 7.45.)

10.54 No-one should be entitled to act as a receiver under a formal land mortgage unless satisfying requirements as to qualifications and suitability to be laid down by regulation. (Para 7.46.)

Jurisdiction of the court on enforcement

10.55 In the case of a formal land mortgage which is not protected, if a mortgagee applies to the court for an order to enforce or protect the security, the court should have no specific powers to delay or withhold the remedy requested once the mortgagee has established that the right to take the appropriate action is available and has become exercisable. (Paras 7.48 and 7.49.)

10.56 On an application by a mortgagee to protect or enforce a protected mortgage, or for payment of sums due under a protected mortgage, the court should have powers equivalent to those currently applicable to residential mortgages by virtue of Part IV of the Administration of Justice Act 1970 and the Consumer Credit Act 1974. In addition, it should have power to order the mortgagee to accept re-scheduled payments in some circumstances, and it should be allowed to consider whether any of the terms of the mortgage ought to be set aside or varied. It should not have power to refuse or delay an enforcement order on the ground that a tenant of the mortgagor whose tenancy is not binding on the mortgagee has offered to pay all sums due under the mortgage, nor should it have power to order that the mortgagor's interest should be transferred to such a tenant. (Paras 7.48–7.59.)

Jurisdiction to set aside or vary terms of the mortgage

10.57 There should be a new statutory jurisdiction for the court to set aside or vary terms of a land mortgage. The new jurisdiction should be in addition to the court's general law powers to set aside terms or bargains on grounds such as fraud, mistake, rectification, estoppel, undue influence, or restraint of trade. The equitable jurisdiction to set aside a term of a land mortgage which constitutes a clog or fetter on the equity of redemption should be abolished in so far as it relates to land mortgages, and the extortionate credit bargain provisions of the Consumer Credit Act 1974 should be amended so that they no longer apply to credit bargains secured by a land mortgage. (Paras 8.1–8.4 and 8.8.)

10.58 Under the new jurisdiction the court should have power to set aside or vary any term of a mortgage with a view to doing justice between the parties if (a) principles of fair dealing were contravened when the mortgage was granted, or (b) the effect of the terms of the mortgage is that the mortgagee now has rights substantially greater than or different from those necessary to make the property adequate security for the liabilities secured by the mortgage, or (c) the mortgage requires payments to be made which are exorbitant, or (d) the mortgage includes a postponement of the right to redeem. (Paras 8.4 and 8.5.)

10.59 In deciding whether to exercise its powers on grounds (b) or (d) the court should discount the fact that the terms were freely negotiated between the parties, but in such circumstances should have a discretion to order the mortgagor to compensate the mortgagee. Otherwise, the powers the court should have under the new jurisdiction, and the factors it ought to take into account should be analogous to those now contained in the extortionate credit bargain provisions of the Consumer Credit Act 1974. (Paras 8.6–8.8.)

Miscellaneous matters

Tacking of further advances

10.60 Section 94 of the Law of Property Act 1925 should be amended to make it clear (a) that registration of a later mortgage under the Companies Act 1989 does not constitute notice of it to an earlier mortgagee seeking to tack advances made after the creation of the later mortgage, and (b) that a mortgagee who is under an obligation to make further advances remains entitled to rely on s 94 despite any default by the mortgagor releasing the mortgagee from the obligation. (Paras 9.3 –9.4.)

10.61 It should be made clear in s 30 of the Land Registration Act 1925 that where it is noted on the register that a charge contains an obligation to make further advances, subsequent charges that are unregistered, as well as those that are registered, will take subject to any such further advances made. (Para 9.5.)

Land mortgages and the Consumer Credit Act 1974

10.62 The Consumer Credit Act 1974 should continue to apply to land mortgages in so far as it regulates the carrying on of mortgage lending business, but no longer apply in so far as it regulates the form and content of mortgages and their enforcement. (Para 9.6.)

CHAPTER 17

LAND AND PROPERTY

1 INTRODUCTION

Property

'Property' may be divided into real and personal property. The classification is historical as Megarry and Wade explain:[1]

> In early law, property was deemed 'real' if the courts would restore to a dispossessed owner the thing itself, the 'res', and not merely give compensation for the loss. Thus if X forcibly evicted Y from his freehold land, Y could bring a 'real' action whereby he could obtain an order from the court that X should return the land to him. But if X took Y's sword or glove from him, he could bring only a personal action which gave X the choice of either returning the article or paying the value thereof. Consequently a distinction was made between real property (or 'realty'), which could be specifically recovered, and personal property (or 'personalty'), which was not thus recoverable. Nature has provided one division of property, namely into immovables (ie land) and movables; the English division into real and personal property is similar with one important exception. In general, all interests in land are real property, with the exception of leaseholds (or 'terms of years'), which are classified as personalty.
>
> This peculiar exception was first of all due to the fact that leases were foreign to the feudal system of landholding by tenure, under which, in its earliest form, the social and economic status of every member of society was fixed. Originally leases were rather regarded as personal business arrangements under which one party allowed the other the use of his land in return for a rent. They were, in other words, personal contracts, operating in personam between the parties and not creating or transferring any rights *in rem*, ie rights in the land itself which could affect feudal status. Leases helped to supply a useful form of investment for a society which knew nothing of stocks and shares. Money might be employed in buying land and letting it out on lease in order to obtain an income from the capital, or in buying a lease for a lump sum which would be recovered with interest out of the produce of the land. These were commercial transactions, more in the sphere of money than of land, as land-owning was then understood. Once leaseholds were classed with personal property it was discovered that the position was not without its advantages. Not only were leases then immune from feudal burdens and the intricate legal procedure required for freeholds: they could be bequeathed by will in times when wills of other land were still not allowed. Thus the illogical position continued until it became too well settled to alter.
>
> Leaseholds are still, therefore, personalty in law. But having now for so long been recognised as interests in land and not merely contractual rights, they have been classed under the paradoxical heading of 'chattels real'. The first word indicates their personal nature (cattle were the most important chattels in early days, hence the name), the second shows their connection with land.

1 Megarry and Wade, pp 10–11.

Land

'Land', on the other hand, as universally defined in the 1925 legislation, include real property, but not personal property other than leases.[2]

Law of Property Act 1925

205. General definitions

(1) In this Act unless the context otherwise requires, the following expressions have the meaning hereby assigned to them respectively, that is to say:-

(ix) 'Land' includes land of any tenure, and mines and minerals, whether or not held apart from the surface, buildings or parts of buildings (whether the division is horizontal, vertical or made in any other way) and other corporeal hereditaments; also a manor, an advowson, and a rent and other incorporeal hereditaments, and an easement, right, 'privilege, or benefit in, over, or derived from land; and 'mines and minerals' include any strata or seam of minerals or substances in or under any land, and powers of working and getting the same; and 'manor' includes a lordship, and reputed manor or lordship; and 'hereditament' means any real property which on an intestacy occurring before the commencement of this Act might have devolved upon an heir.

(a) Of any tenure

This means that freehold tenures and leasehold tenures are regarded as land. Thus, although leaseholds are personalty, they are nevertheless 'land' for the purposes of the 1925 legislation.

(b) Corporeal hereditaments

This means the physical land itself and other physical objects attached to and form part of the physical land. This includes buildings constructed on the land, fixtures attached to the land, plants growing on it, minerals, and a limited extent of airspace.

(c) Incorporeal hereditaments

These are rights over land which have no physical existence and exist 'only in contemplation'.[3] Examples are rentcharges, easements and profits.

Thus in Megarry and Wade's classification, land may be classified as follows:[4]

2 See s 205(1)(ix) of the LPA 1925, s 3(viii) of the LRA 1925, s 117(1)(ix) of the SLA 1925, s 68(1)(6) of the Trustee Act 1925, s 17(1) of the LCA 1972.

3 Bl Comm, Vol II, at 17.

4 Megarry and Wade, p 11.

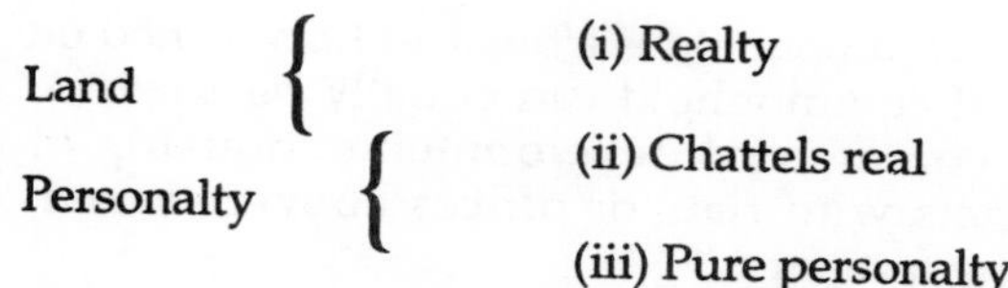

It should be noted that 'property', personal or real, may be used to mean the thing itself, for example, the car, or the house. So is the word 'land'. But to lawyers, as we have seen throughout this book, 'property' and 'land' are used to mean the 'rights' over the thing itself, for example, the rights over one's car or one's house, or the title to one's land.

As English lawyers do not talk in terms of ownership of the thing itself, but ownership of the rights to the thing, it is not surprising that ownership of 'property' or 'land' is a relative concept. That is, in a dispute over a thing, English courts are only interested to know who, as between the parties in court, has the better rights over (or title to) the thing. They are not concerned to find out who is the actual owner of the thing. As Murphy and Roberts explain:[5]

> If you pick up a jewel in the street, and someone takes it from you and will not give it back, you can take him to court and recover its full value, even though it is obvious that a third person has a better title to the jewel than either of you. The person who took the jewel from you cannot defeat your claim by pointing to the defects in your title. He must pay you the full value of the thing, not some lesser sum reflecting your 'merely' possessory title. Your earlier possession suffices. The 'true owner' asserts his rights in exactly the same way ...

It should also be noted that, as Murphy and Roberts's example shows, possession is the evidence of ownership of the rights over property or land. The earlier possession of a claimant enables him to succeed against a person who has later possession.

2 PROPOSALS FOR A NEW FORM OF REAL PROPERTY OR LAND: COMMONHOLD

The Law Commission has made proposals for the introduction of a new form of property: a third type of tenure known as commonhold.[6] This will be classified as a 'real property' and will presumably be included in the definition of 'land'. It is 'a freehold development of two or more 'units' which share services and facilities and so require a system for communal management, and for the ownership of any common parts'.[7] 'A commonhold must consist of at least two units because the concept of shared services and facilities is of the essence of the commonhold system.'[8]

5 Murphy, WT and Roberts, S, *Understanding Property Law*, 2nd impression, 1989, London: Fontana, p 42.

6 See The Aldridge Working Group (set up by the Law Commission in response to the Lord Chancellor's request) on Freehold Flats and Freehold Ownership of Other Interdependent Buildings, Cmnd 179, July 1987; Lord Chancellor's Department, 'Commonhold – A Consultation Paper' (Cmnd 1345, November 1990) and the draft Law of Property Bill. See also [1986] Conv 361 (Aldridge, TM); [1991] Conv 70, [1991] Conv 170 (Wilkinson, HW).

7 Lord Chancellor's Consultation Paper, para 3.1.

8 *Ibid*, para 3.1.

Although an obvious example of a commonhold is a block of flats owned on a long-leasehold basis, the system of commonhold can equally be used for non-residential purposes such as commercial developments, housing or industrial estates, shopping precincts with flats or offices above, or even agricultural buildings and surrounding farmland.[9]

As we have seen, two problems with the existing system of land ownership are, first, it is difficult for the owner of freehold property to enforce a positive covenant due to the rule in *Austerberry v Oldham Corpn* which has been reaffirmed by the House of Lords in *Rhones v Stephens*.[10] This problem is particularly acute in the case of a block of flats where the enforcement of positive covenants such as a covenant to repair or to pay service charges for the maintenance is crucial. In many cases this difficulty has been avoided by the owner by granting leases of each separate flat or 'unit' within the block. In this way the positive covenants can be enforced as between the owner and the leaseholder under the rules for the running of leasehold covenants.[11] This device has, however, brought about a second problem. Many leases were granted for 99 years and as the lease gets shorter, it becomes a less attractive security for a mortgagee. Thus these units become unsaleable. It is to overcome these problems that the commonhold scheme was proposed. Under this system, each 'unit holder' will own exclusively the freehold estate in the unit. An incorporated management association will be set up to own the common parts of the grounds and building. Each unit holder will be a member of the management association. The association will provide maintenance for the common parts and services within the scheme. Each unit holder will pay a service charge to the association. The detailed obligations of the individual unit owners would be set out in 'Commonhold Regulations' which would be a standard form laid down by statutory instrument. These Commonhold Regulations would deal with such matters as the enjoyment of common services and facilities, the obligation of the unit owner to maintain his unit, rights of access of the commonhold association to inspect and for the association or other unit owners to enter and carry out work in an emergency, and any restrictions on the use to which the unit may be put.[12] The benefit and burden of these rights and obligations will be enforceable within the scheme.

Following the Lord Chancellor's Department's consultation paper in 1990,[13] the Government has announced its proposals for the introduction of commonhold,[14] and promised to introduce commonhold legislation as soon as parliamentary time allows.[15] It remains to be seen whether this significant innovation in English law of real property will find its way to the statute book.

9 *Ibid*, para 3.2.

10 See Chapter 14, pp 783–86.

11 See Chapter 9, pp 417–35.

12 Lord Chancellor's Consultation Paper, para 3.18.

13 Cmnd 1345.

14 *Hansard*, HL Deb Vol 530, 1601, Friday 12 July 1991.

15 *Hansard*, HL Deb Vol 543, 1332, Tuesday 16 March 1993; *Hansard*, HC Deb Vol 236, 326w (27 January 1994), 528w (31 January 1994).

INDEX